WILEY PLUS

www.**wiley**plus.com

Wiley is committed to making your entire *WileyPLUS* experience productive & enjoyable by providing the help, resources, and personal support you & your students need, when you need it. It's all here: www.wileyplus.com

TECHNICAL SUPPORT:

- ⊕ A fully searchable knowledge base of FAQs and help documentation, available 24/7
- ⊕ Live chat with a trained member of our support staff during business hours
- ⊕ A form to fill out and submit online to ask any question and get a quick response
- ⊕ **Instructor-only** phone line during business hours: 1.877.586.0192

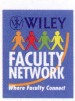

FACULTY-LED TRAINING THROUGH THE WILEY FACULTY NETWORK:
Register online: www.wherefacultyconnect.com
Connect with your colleagues in a complimentary virtual seminar, with a personal mentor in your field, or at a live workshop to share best practices for teaching with technology.

1ST DAY OF CLASS...AND BEYOND!
Resources You & Your Students Need to Get Started & Use *WileyPLUS* from the first day forward.

1st DAY OF CLASS ...AND BEYOND!

- ⊕ 2-Minute Tutorials on how to set up & maintain your *WileyPLUS* course
- ⊕ User guides, links to technical support & training options
- ⊕ *WileyPLUS for Dummies*: Instructors' quick reference guide to using *WileyPLUS*
- ⊕ Student tutorials & instruction on how to register, buy, and use *WileyPLUS*

YOUR *WileyPLUS* ACCOUNT MANAGER:
Your personal *WileyPLUS* connection for any assistance you need!

WILEY PLUS QuickStart

SET UP YOUR *WileyPLUS* COURSE IN MINUTES!
Selected *WileyPLUS* courses with QuickStart contain pre-loaded assignments & presentations created by subject matter experts who are also experienced *WileyPLUS* users.

Interested? See and try WileyPLUS *in action!*
Details and Demo: *www.wileyplus.com*

7th Edition

Information Technology for Management

Improving Performance in the Digital Economy

7th Edition

Information Technology for Management

Improving Performance in the Digital Economy

EFRAIM TURBAN, University of Hawaii at Manoa

LINDA VOLONINO, Canisius College

with contributions by:

CAROL POLLARD, Appalachian State University

JANICE C. SIPIOR, Villanova University

DOROTHY LEIDNER, Baylor University

LINDA LAI, Macau Polytechnic University of China

CHRISTY CHEUNG, Hong Kong Baptist University

DEBORRAH CRISTOBAL, University of Santo Tomas, Philippines

WILEY John Wiley & Sons, Inc.

VICE PRESIDENT AND EXECUTIVE PUBLISHER	Donald Fowley
ACQUISITIONS EDITOR	Beth Lang Golub
ASSOCIATE EDITOR	Jen Devine
EDITORIAL ASSISTANT	Mike Berlin
PRODUCTION SERVICES MANAGER	Dorothy Sinclair
PRODUCTION EDITOR	Janet Foxman
EXECUTIVE MARKETING MANAGER	Christopher Ruel
CREATIVE DIRECTOR	Harry Nolan
TEXT/COVER DESIGNER	Madelyn Lesure
SENIOR PHOTO EDITOR	Lisa Gee
SENIOR ILLUSTRATION EDITOR	Anna Melhorn
MEDIA EDITOR	Lauren Sapira
PRODUCTION SERVICES	Suzanne Ingrao/Ingrao Associates
COVER IMAGE	© Comstock/Punchstock

This book was set in 10/12 Times Roman by Preparé and printed and bound by Courier/Kendallville. The cover was printed by Courier/Kendallville.

This book is printed on acid-free paper. ∞

To order books or for customer service, please call 1-800-CALL WILEY (225-5945).

ISBN 978-0-470-28748-4 (Main Book)
ISBN 978-0-470-41828-4 (Binder-Ready Version)

Printed in the United States of America

10 9 8 7 6 5 4 3 2 1

BRIEF CONTENTS

*Can be accessed online at www.wiley.com/college/turban

CONTENTS

x Contents

*Part VI, the Technology Guides, and the Tutorials can be accessed online at www.wiley.com/college/turban.

The Web Revolution

We have been witnessing the most influential technological revolution in the modern era—the Web revolution. The access and connectivity provided by the Web keep transforming the way that we work, shop, vote, invest, study, play, interact, and conduct our lives. The Web-driven transformation is much faster than occurred during the Industrial Revolution, and with more far-reaching impacts. For example, two years ago when we last revised this book, social networks were a novelty, and Apple had not yet introduced the iPhone. Today more than 500 million people participate in social networking—an instrument used in commerce, politics, healthcare, finance, travel, and entertainment—with over 50 million participating in mobile social networking from their cell phones or 3G iPhones. From your experience, you know that these developments are *only* the tip of the iceberg.

Managing Information Technology. Driving the Web revolution are information technologies (IT) and mobile computing devices that are advancing exponentially. Companies such as Google, Facebook, Second Life, Apple, and Yahoo continuously introduce innovations into corporate and government operations as well as into most aspects of our lives. Capabilities of computers, mobile devices, and ITs are making it more crucial and more difficult to keep up with developments that are influencing every area of business.

Information Technology for Management, 7th Edition, addresses the basic tactical and strategic principles of management information systems (MIS) in light of these new developments. One strategic development, for example, is an enterprise's ability to lease or buy IT services that deliver business applications over the Internet—similar to the way companies buy electricity. This utility, or *on-demand*, computing is helping companies to better meet their performance and business objectives while reducing hardware and software expenses. Other strategic changes include green computing, active data warehousing, real-time data alerts, search engine marketing, and the commercialization of social networking. These Web-revolution issues as well as the management of key ITs to improve performance are discussed throughout this textbook. You will learn the role of numerous ITs in private, public, and government enterprises.

Transforming Enterprises to the Digital Economy

This book is based on the premise that the major role of IT is to provide enterprises with *strategic advantage by facilitating problem solving, increasing productivity and quality, increasing speed, improving customer service, enhancing communication and collaboration*, and *enabling business process restructuring*. By taking a practical, managerial-oriented approach, the book demonstrates that IT is being provided by information systems departments, vendors, service providers, supply chain partners, and end users. Intelligently managing information resources, technologies, and communication networks is a—or even *the*—critical success factor in enterprise operations, and essential to their survival.

We emphasize the *innovative* uses of IT throughout the enterprise while also recognizing the importance of the technology, system development, and functional transaction processing systems. The rapidly increased use of the Web, the Internet, intranets, extranets, e-business and e-commerce, social computing, and mobile computing changes how business is done in almost all enterprises. This fact is reflected in our book: Every chapter and major topic point to the role of the Web in facilitating competitiveness, effectiveness, profitability, compliance, and ethics. Of special importance are the second-generation e-commerce applications—mobile commerce, c-commerce, e-learning, and e-government. Also, the integration of enterprise resource planning (ERP), customer relationship management (CRM), and knowledge management with e-commerce is vitally important. The role of social network services such as MySpace, Facebook, and YouTube is highlighted, especially in our new chapter on the topic (Chapter 8). There is a resurgence of intelligent systems and automated decision systems, both for facilitating homeland security as well as for increasing productivity and competitive advantage (Chapter 12). The critical role of IT in compliance and security management is described throughout the book because of their significant costs. Between 2006 and 2008, consumers had lost an estimated $8.5 billion to viruses, spyware, and phishing attacks.

Features of this Text

In developing the 7th Edition of *Information Technology for Management*, we have crafted a book to serve the current and future needs of managers. This book reflects our vision of where IT and information systems (IS) are going and the direction of IS education in business and e-business programs. This vision is represented by the following features that we have integrated throughout the book.

- *Social Computing.* The commercialization of social computing receives major attention. We cover the new phenomenon in many chapters in addition to Chapter 8.

- *Managerial Orientation.* Most IS textbooks identify themselves as either technology or socio-behavioral oriented. While we recognize the importance of both, our emphasis is on *managerial* orientation. To implement this orientation, we assembled all major technological topics in six Technology Guides, located on the book's Web site. Furthermore, we attempted not to duplicate detailed presentations of behavioral sciences topics, such as dealing with resistance to change or motivating employees. Instead, we concentrate on managerial decision making, cost-benefit justification, return on investment (ROI), supply chain management, business process management, restructuring, and CRM as they relate to IT.

- *Global Perspective and a Totally Revised Chapter on Global Information Systems.* Global competition, collaboration, partnerships, and trading is rapidly increasing. We've updated and expanded the chapter that focuses on global information systems (Chapter 10). International examples are highlighted with a special globe icon, a Global Index appears at the back of the book, and the book's Web site includes international cases.

- *Agile and Responsive Enterprise.* The rapid and large fluctuations in the business environment require businesses to be able to respond promptly and properly to changes—often in real-time. IT facilitates agility and flexibility. Furthermore, building or upgrading ISs must be done quickly by digital and agile enterprises.

- *The On-Demand Revolution.* Demand-driven operations and on-demand enterprises refer to the changes brought on by e-business in which manufacturing starts only after an order (standard or customized) is received. Build-to-order manufacturing cannot be done economically without IT—primarily RFID devices, ERP, and collaborative technologies.

- *Focus on Security.* Computer and IT security issues are critical at the personal, enterprise, national, and global levels. Data breaches and spyware software are common, mobile phone viruses have been found, and consumers have a 1 in 6 chance of being victimized by cybercrime. The security risks of virtualization, social networks, and Web 2.0 had become so severe that the 2008 annual Black Hat conference was dedicated to those issues. We show how information security (infosec) needs to be implemented to counter targeted attacks against enterprise data repositories, theft of intellectual property, identity theft, cyber-terrorism, and foreign and domestic threats to homeland security. Security and business continuity are now in Chapter 5.

- *Digital Economy Focus.* This book recognizes that enterprises transform their business processes and practices, collaboration and Web-based systems, and e-strategy business models to succeed in the digital economy. Furthermore, they need to plan the transformation processes, which are dependent on IT and enabled by it.

- *Functional Relevance.* Frequently, non–IS major students wonder why they must learn technical details. In this text, the relevance of IT to the major functional areas is an important theme. We show, through the use of icons, the relevance of topics to accounting, finance, marketing, production/operations management, human resource management, and government. In addition, our examples cover service industries, government, small businesses, as well as the international settings.

- *E-Business, E-Commerce, and the Use of the Web.* We strongly believe that e-business, e-commerce, Internet, intranets, and extranet portals are changing the world of business. Not only is an entire chapter (Chapter 6) dedicated to e-business, but we also demonstrate the significance of e-business in every chapter and major topic. In this edition, we also have expanded coverage of m-commerce applications.

- *Real-World Orientation.* Extensive, vivid examples from large corporations, small businesses, government, and non-profit agencies make concepts come alive by showing students the capabilities of IT, its cost and justification, and the innovative ways actual enterprises are using IT in their operations.

- *Failures and Lessons Learned.* We acknowledge the fact that many systems fail. Many chapters include discussions or examples of failures, the contributing factors, and the lessons learned from them. For example, Chapter 10 cites some ERP failures, and Chapter 17 discusses economic aspects of failures and runaway projects.

- *Solid Theoretical Backing.* Throughout the book, we present the theoretical foundation necessary for understanding IT, ranging from Moore's law to Porter's competitiveness models, including his latest e-strategy adaptation.

- *Up-to-Date Information.* The book presents the most current IT topics, as evidenced by the many new cases and examples throughout the book, and by 2007 and 2008 citations. Every topic in the book has been researched to find the most up-to-date information and features.

- *Economic Justification.* IT is mature enough to stand the difficult test of economic justification. It is our position that IT investments must be scrutinized like any other investment despite the difficulties of measuring technology benefits. In addition to discussion throughout the text, we devote an entire chapter (Chapter 17, IT Economics) to this subject. We emphasize enterprisewide, interorganizational, and global systems. We also present technologies that support this integration, including Web Services and XML.

- *Ethics.* The importance of ethics is growing rapidly in the digital economy. Topics relating to ethics are introduced in every chapter, and are highlighted by icons in the margin. A primer on ethics is provided in Online Tutorial #3. This resource poses 14 ethics scenarios and asks students to think about responses to these situations.

What's New in this Edition?

In preparing the new 7th Edition we made the following large-scale changes:

- **IT-Business Performance Management Model.** In Chapter 1, we developed a model that illustrates the support IT provides to business performance management. This model is cyclical, starting with corporate mission and ending with performance improvement (see Figure IT 7eU). IT is shown in the center of the major corporate activities of setting objectives, measuring performance, assessing performance, and improving it. The model is shown at the start of each chapter with highlighting of the areas discussed in the chapters and relevant to the activities.

- **Social Computing.** Social computing has become a major phenomenon since 2006 with its tools of blogging, wikis, mashups, and so forth changing the way business is done, especially collaboration. Chapter 8 is fully dedicated to the topic and it is new in this edition.

- **Business Process Management and IT implementation.** This is also a new chapter. We discuss key issues that are driving IT decisions in companies today.

- **Tutorials.** We created six online tutorials. These can be used by students who lack certain backgrounds or are interested in more depth.

- **End Part Cases.** Larger case studies of major corporations are provided at the end of each of the five parts of the book. Each case is related to the topics covered in the preceding chapters. Cases cover the following companies: Cisco Systems, Federal Express, Google, Wal-Mart, and Toyota—all world-class IT users.

- **Videos.** These are a new and fitting addition. Numerous valuable online demos are provided by ven-

dors, research centers, social networks, and consulting companies. These videos add reality to the learning experience. We have incorporated video resources into student assignments for each chapter. Additional video suggestions are in the Instructor Manual.

- **Green IT.** We examine the greening of computing and the supply chain, that is, how companies are practicing green procurement, manufacturing, distribution, service, and recycling in environmentally responsible ways. We emphasize how enterprises that invest in green hardware find that the energy savings, extended product lifecycle, positive public image, and other benefits exceed the additional costs of that hardware.

- **Consolidation of Topics.** We consolidated all decision support systems (DSS)-related topics in one chapter, centered around business intelligence. We also consolidated all major enterprise systems in one chapter. We preserved important topics in online tutorials.

- **Change of Authors.** We added a major co-author to the book, professor Linda Volonino. Linda is known for developing and teaching cutting-edge IT and telecommunications courses to provide students with critical thinking abilities, predictive and analytic skills, an understanding of intended and unintended consequences, and ethical and socially responsible decision making. Linda also provides seminars to senior and middle-level executives on IT-related issues. She is a senior editor of *Information Systems Management* and an associate editor of the *Business Intelligence Journal*.

- **Innovative and Futuristic System.** Starting with Chapter 2, we emphasize special innovative as well as futuristic systems.

- **Book Case Study.** A large and comprehensive case study of a global company that deals with many of the book's topics is available online.

- **Hands-On Experiences.** In this edition, we introduce a large number of hands-on exercises in the chapters. These include quantitative analysis using spreadsheets to calculate cost-benefits, creation of collaborative online groups who conduct comparisons of Web sites, viewing Web seminars and answering questions about the topics covered, viewing demos and summarizing lessons learned, and much more. Major additions are problem-solving cases.

- **Problem-Solving Activity.** At the end of every chapter, we provide a problem-solving activity. Students are given a business- or IT-related problem that requires them to apply their critical thinking and analysis skills, and often to do so by developing a decision support system using spreadsheet software.

- **Other Changes and Updates**
  - Chapter 1 has refocused on agility, green IT, social networking, and on-demand and real-time strategy.

- Networks—communication, collaboration, and search—are discussed in greater detail and business context. More technical foundations are provided in the tutorials.
- Chapters have been revised to introduce new research, current examples and case studies, exercises, and updated reference materials.
- We have streamlined and smoothed the logical flow throughout the text, eliminating duplications, reducing chapter lengths, as well as the number of topics covered in some cases.

Organization of the Book

The book is divided into five major parts, composed of 17 regular chapters (two of which are online) supplemented by six online tutorials and six Technology Guides. Parts and chapters break down as follows:

Part I: IT in the Organization. Part I gives an overview of IT in the enterprise. Chapter 1 introduces the drivers of the use of IT in the digital economy and gives an overview of ISs and IT trends. Chapter 2 presents the foundations of ISs and their strategic use. Special attention is given to cutting-edge topics.

Part II: IT Infrastructure. This part introduces two major building blocks of IT: data and networks. Other building blocks are covered in the online Technology Guides. We cover basic infrastructures, business applications, infosec, business continuity, and fraud prevention. We examine the current topic of master data management, which improves data sharing across multiple locations through synchronization, that is, integrating data accumulated from a variety of sources.

Part III: The Web Revolution. The three chapters in Part III introduce the Web-based technologies and applications starting with the topics of e-business and e-commerce (Chapter 6), mobile and wireless computing in Chapter 7, and social networking and the Web 2.0 environment in Chapter 8.

Part IV: Organizational Applications. Part IV begins with IT applications in transaction processing, functional applications, and integration of functional systems. Other topics covered are supply chain management, Web-based enterprise systems, CRM, and knowledge management (Chapter 9). We cover inter-organizational, large scale, and global systems in Chapter 10.

Part V: Decision Making and Strategy. Part V explores the implementation, evaluation, construction, and maintenance of ISs that give greater visibility into all corners of the enterprise. ITs that support enterprise performance—namely, business intelligence, decision support systems, data visualization tools, and data mining—are discussed in Chapter 12. We cover how IT can support the strategic direction of the enterprise, how to optimize IT investments, and achieve long-term cost savings (Chapter 13). We cover the management of IT projects, processes, and the organizational changes that result from IT implementations, and the increases in ROI that result when projects, processes, and people are managed correctly (Chapter 14). Lastly, we describe IT impacts on individuals and enterprises, and the ways enterprises are operating greener businesses, eco-friendly data centers, and Enterprise Web 2.0 applications (Chapter 15).

Online Chapters: Implementing and Managing IT. In the two chapters available online at the book's Web site, we explore acquiring and developing business applications and infrastructure (Chapter 16) and the economics of IT (Chapter 17).

The five **Technology Guides**, which are online, cover hardware, software, databases, telecommunications, the essentials of the Internet, and an introduction to systems analysis and design. They contain condensed, up-to-date presentations of all of the material necessary for the understanding of these technologies. They can be used as a self-study refresher or for class presentation. There are glossaries in the Tech Guides, questions for review and discussion, and case studies. All are available on our Web site (*wiley.com/college/turban*).

Pedagogical Features

We developed a number of pedagogical features to aid student learning and tie together the themes of the book.

- *Chapter Outline.* The chapter outline provides a quick indication of the major topics covered in the chapter.
- *Learning Objectives.* Learning objectives listed at the beginning of each chapter help students focus their efforts and alert them to the important concepts that will be discussed.
- *Opening Cases.* Each chapter opens with a *real-world* example that illustrates the use of information technology in modern enterprises. These cases have been carefully chosen to demonstrate the relevance, for business students, of the topics introduced in the chapter. They are presented in a standard format (problem or opportunity, IT solution, and results) that helps model a way to think about business problems. The opening case is followed by a brief section called "Lessons Learned from This Case" that ties the key points of the opening case to the topics of the chapter.
- *"IT at Work" Boxes.* The IT at Work boxes spotlight some real-world innovations and new technologies that companies are using to solve organizational dilemmas or create new business opportunities. Each box concludes with "for further exploration" questions and issues. Some of these boxes are online.
- *"A Closer Look" Boxes.* These boxes contain detailed, in-depth discussions of specific concepts or

procedures, often using real-world examples. Some boxes enhance the in-text discussion by offering an alternative approach to information technology. Some of these boxes are included in the online materials.

- *Highlighted Icons.* Icons appear throughout the text to relate the topics covered within each chapter to some major themes of the book. The icons alert students to the related functional areas, to IT failures, and to global and ethical issues. Icons also indicate where related enrichment resources can be found on the book's companion Web site. The following list summarizes these icons. (They also are summarized for students in a marginal annotation in Chapter 1.)

 Ethics-related topic

 Global enterprises and issues

 Lessons to be learned from IT failures

 Accounting example

 Finance example

 Government example

 Human resources management example

 Marketing example

 Production/operations management example

 Service-company example (for example, health services, educational services, and other non-manufacturing examples)

 Material at the book's Web site: *wiley/com/college.turban*

- **Section Review Questions.** Each section of each chapter ends with detailed questions for review.
- *Online Chapter Resources.* Each chapter is supported by many online files divided into two categories: *Online Briefs* that supplement topics, and *Online Minicases.* These files are cited in the text, as they include in-depth discussions, technically oriented materials, examples, cases, and illustrations. The Online Chapter Resources can be accessed by going to the Student Website at *www.wiley.com/college/turban,* then clicking on Online Chapter Resources.
- *Managerial Issues.* The final text section of every chapter explores some of the special concerns managers face as they adapt to an increasingly technological environment. The issues highlighted in this section can serve as a springboard for class discussion and challenge business students to consider some of the actions they might take if placed in similar circumstances.
- *Glossary of Key Terms.* The key terms and concepts are typeset in boldface blue when first introduced in a chapter, and are defined at the end of the book.
- *Chapter Highlights.* Important concepts covered in the chapter are listed at the end of the chapter and are linked by number to the learning objectives introduced at the beginning of each chapter, to reinforce the important ideas discussed.
- *Virtual Company Assignment.* The Virtual Company Assignment centers around the ongoing situation at a simulated company, The Wireless Café. Students are "hired" by the restaurant as consultants, and in each chapter are given assignments that require them to use the information presented in the chapter to develop solutions and produce deliverables to present to the owners of The Wireless Café. These assignments get the student into active, hands-on learning to complement the conceptual coverage of the text. The assignments are found on the Student Resources site at *www.wiley.com/college/turban.*
- *End-of-Chapter Questions and Exercises.* Different types of questions measure student comprehension and students' ability to apply knowledge. *Questions for Review* ask students to summarize the concepts introduced. Discussion Questions are intended to promote class discussion and develop critical thinking skills.
- *Exercises and Projects.* Exercises are challenging assignments that require the students to apply what they have learned in each chapter to a situation. This includes many hands-on exercises as described earlier, including the use of search engines and the Web.
- *Group Assignments.* Comprehensive group assignments, including Internet research, oral presentations to the class, and debates, are available in each chapter.
- *Internet Exercises.* Close to 200 hands-on exercises send the students to interesting Web sites to explore

those sites; find resources; investigate an application; compare, analyze, and summarize information; or learn about the state of the art of a topic.

- *Minicases.* A real-world minicase is found at the end of each chapter that outlines IT problems and opportunities encountered by enterprises. Discussion questions and assignments are included. A number of additional minicases are also available online at the book's Web site.
- *Problem-Solving Activity.* These are open-ended (unresolved) problem-solving scenarios at the end of all chapters. Students are actively involved in the solution. Students need to do research or develop DSSs to arrive at viable solutions.

Supplementary Materials

An extensive package of instructional materials is available to support this 7th edition.

- *Instructor's Manual.* The Instructor's Manual presents objectives from the text with additional information to make them more appropriate and useful for the instructor. The manual also includes practical applications of concepts, case study elaboration, answers to end-of-chapter questions, questions for review, questions for discussion, and Internet exercises.
- *Test Bank.* The test bank contains over 1,000 questions and problems (about 70 per chapter) consisting of multiple-choice, short answer, fill-ins, and critical thinking/essay questions.
- *Computerized Test Bank.* This electronic version of the test bank allows instructors to customize tests and quizzes for their students.
- *PowerPoint Presentation.* A series of slides designed around the content of the text incorporates key points from the text and illustrations where appropriate.
- *Video Series.* A collection of video clips provides students and instructors with dynamic international business examples directly related to the concepts introduced in the text. The video clips illustrate the ways in which computer information systems are utilized in various companies and industries.
- *Business Extra Select.* (*www.wiley.com/college/bxs*). Business Extra Select enables you to add copyright-cleared articles, cases, and readings from such leading business resources as *INSEAD, Ivey and Harvard Business School Cases, Fortune, The Economist, The Wall Street Journal*, and more. You can create your own custom CoursePack, combining these resources along with content from Wiley's Business Textbooks, your own content such as lecture notes, and any other third-party content. Or you can use a ready-made CoursePack for Turban's *IT for Management*, 7th Edition.

- *Textbook Web Site.* (*wiley.com/college/turban*). The book's Web site greatly extends the content and themes of the text to provide extensive support for instructors and students. Organized by chapter, it includes Chapter Resources: tables, figures, cases, questions, exercises, and downloadable media-enhanced PowerPoint slides; Media Resource Library which includes links to websites and videos which can be used in class to engage student and provides discussion questions to be used in class after viewing each resource; self-testing material for students; working students' experiences with using IT; and links to many of the companies discussed in the text and to the Virtual Company Web site.
- *WileyPlus.* WileyPlus is a powerful online tool that provides instructors and students with an integrated suite of teaching and learning resources, including an online version of the text, in one easy-to-use website. To learn more about WileyPlus, and view a demo, please visit *www.wileyplus.com*.

    WileyPlus enables instructors to assign automatically graded practice questions from the Test Bank; track your students progress in an instructor's gradebook; access all teaching and learning resources, including an online text, and student and instructor resarces, in one easy to use website; and create class presentations using Wiley-provided resources, with the ability to customize and add your own materials.

Acknowledgments

Several individuals helped us with the creation of the 7th Edition: Janice C. Sipior (Villanova University), Carol Pollard (Appalachian State University), Dorothy Leidner (Baylor University), Linda Lai (Macau Polytechnic University of China), Christy Cheung (Hong Kong Baptist University), and Deborrah Cristobal (University of Santo Tomas, Philippines). Thanks to all for their valuable contributions.

Faculty feedback was essential to the development of the book. Many individuals participated in focus groups and/or acted as reviewers. Several others created portions of chapters or cases, especially international cases, some of which are in the text and others on the Web site.

Thanks, too, to the following reviewers: Lawrence Andrew, Western Illinois University; Bay Arinze, Drexel University; Benli Asilani, University of Tennessee Chattanooga; Mary Astone, Troy State University; Cynthia Barnes, Lamar University; Andy Borchers, Kettering University; Sonny Butler, Georgia Southern University; Jason Chen, Gonzaga University; Roland Eichelberger, Baylor University; Jerry Flatto, University of Indianapolis; Marvin Golland, Polytechnic University of Brooklyn; Vipul Gupta, St. Joseph's University; Jeet Gupta, University of Alabama, Huntsville; David Harmann, University of Central Oklahoma; Shohreh Hashemi, University of

Houston, Downtown; Richard Herschel, Saint Joseph's University; Phil Houle, Drake University; Jonathan Jelen, Mercy College; Tim Jenkins, ITT Institute of Technology, San Bernadino; Gerald Karush, Southern New Hampshire University; Joseph Kasten, Dowling College; Stephen Klein, Ramapo College; Kapil Ladha, Drexel University; Albert Lederer, University of Kentucky; Chang-Yang Lin, Eastern Kentucky University; Liping Liu, The University of Akron; Steve Loy, Eastern Kentucky University; Dana Kristin McCann, Central Michigan University; Roberto Mejias, Purdue University; Luvai Motiwalla, University of Massachusetts, Lowell; Sean Neely, City University Bellevue; Luis Rabelo, University of Central Florida; W. Raghupathi, Fordham University; Mahesh Raisinghani, University of Dallas; Tom Schambach, Illinois State University; Werner Schenk, University of Rochester; Sheryl Schoenacher, SUNY Farmingdale; Richard Segall, Arkansas State University; Victor Smolensky, San Diego State University; Bruce White, Quinnipiac University; Geoffrey Willis, University of Central Oklahoma; and Marie Wright, Western Connecticut State University.

Please see *wiley.com/college/turban* for a list of acknowledgments for past editions of this book.

Many individuals helped us with the administrative work. Several individuals helped with typing, figure drawing, and more. Among those are Kathy Sherman and Daphne Turban. Thanks to Rose Twardowski for help in graphic design. Hugh Watson of the University of Georgia, the Information Systems Advisor to Wiley, guided us through various stages of the project.

We would like to thank the dedicated staff of John Wiley & Sons: Chris Ruel, Jen Devine, Mike Berlin, and Trish McFadden. We also appreciate the outside production management services of Suzanne Ingrao. A special thank you to Jen Devine and Beth Lang Golub, whose considerable energy, time, expertise, and devotion have contributed significantly to the success of this project. Thanks to Bob Weiss for reviews and edits that improved readability. Last, but not least, is the help provided by Judy Lang, who has been with this book since its inception, helping with research, finding cases, and, most importantly, trouble shooting.

Finally, we recognize the various enterprises that provided us with material and permissions to use it.

Efraim Turban
Linda Volonino

DR. EFRAIM TURBAN

Dr. Efraim Turban obtained his M.B.A. and Ph.D. degrees from the University of California, Berkeley. His industry experience includes eight years as an industrial engineer, three of which were spent at General Electric Transformers Plant in Oakland, California. He also has extensive consulting experience to small and large corporations as well as to governments. In his over thirty years of teaching, Professor Turban has served as Chaired Professor at Eastern Illinois University, and as Visiting Professor at City University of Hong Kong, Nanyang Technological University in Singapore, National Sun Yat-Sen University in Taiwan, and University of Science and Technology in Hong Kong. He has also taught at UCLA, USC, Simon Fraser University, Lehigh University, California State University, Long Beach, and Florida International University.

Dr. Turban was a co-recipient of the 1984/85 National Management Science Award (Artificial Intelligence in Management). In 1997, he received the Distinguished Faculty Scholarly and Creative Achievement Award at California State University, Long Beach.

Dr. Turban has published over 110 articles in leading journals, including the following: *Management Science, MIS Quarterly, Operations Research, Journal of MIS, Communications of the ACM, International Journal of Electronic Commerce, Information Systems Frontiers, Decision Support Systems, International Journal of Information Management, Heuristics, Expert Systems with Applications, International Journal of Applied Expert Systems, Computers and Operations Research, Computers and Industrial Engineering, IEEE Transactions on Engineering Management, Omega, International Journal of Electronic Commerce, Organizational Computing and Electronic Commerce, Electronic Markets, and Journal of Investing, Accounting, Management and Information Systems.* He has also published 23 books, including best sellers such as *Neural Networks: Applications in Investment and Financial Services*, 2nd edition (Richard D. Irwin, 1996); *Decision Support Systems and Business Intelligence*, 8th edition (Prentice Hall, 2007*)*; *Expert Systems and Applied Artificial Intelligence* (MacMillan Publishing Co., 1992), *Electronic Commerce: A Managerial Approach*, 5th edition (Prentice Hall, 2008), *Introduction to Information Technology*, 4th edition (Wiley, 2007), and *Introduction to Electronic Commerce*, 2nd edition (Prentice Hall, 2009). His newest book is *Business Intelligence* (Prentice Hall, 2008).

Professor Turban is a Visiting Scholar with the Pacific Institute for Management Information Systems, College of Business, University of Hawaii at Manoa. His major research interests include electronic commerce, strategy, and implementation.

DR. LINDA VOLONINO

Dr. Linda Volonino obtained her M.B.A. and Ph.D. degrees from the State University of New York at Buffalo. She is a Senior Editor of *Information Systems Management*, and Associate Editor of *Business Intelligence Journal.* She holds professional certifications as a Certified Information Systems Security Professional (CISSP) and Associate Certified Fraud Examiner (ACFE). She is a consultant for Receivable Management Services, a Dun & Bradstreet strategic partner, providing on-site seminars for senior and financial managers at large U.S. corporations. Dr. Volonino is a member of local and national organizations, including the Teradata University Network (TUN), Information Systems Audit and Control Association (ISACA), Information Systems Security Association (ISSA), the FBI's Infragard, and the Academy of Computing Machinery (ACM).

Professor Volonino developed and directed the Master of Science degree program in Telecommunications Management at Canisius College, Buffalo, NY, and has served as department chair for six years. She has taught as a visiting professor at the University of Southern California (in their overseas program in Germany), the University of Hawaii at Manoa, University of Virginia, City University of Hong Kong, University of Lyon (France), University of Hamburg (Germany), Federal University (Brazil), and Etisalat Academy (Dubai).

Dr. Volonino has coauthored five IT-related books, and has published numerous articles in IT and legal journals, including the *Journal of Data Warehousing, Journal of Management Information Systems, Erie County Bar Bulletin, Ohio Bar Bulletin, Communications of the Association for Information Systems,* and *Information Systems Management.* She has presented over a hundred seminars and workshops on cutting-edge IT topics.

Chapter 1

IT Supports Organizational Performance in Turbulent Business Environments

Learning Objectives

After studying this chapter, you will be able to:

❶ Describe characteristics of the digital economy and digital enterprises.

❷ Define information systems, computer-based information systems, and information technology.

❸ Explain the relationships between performance, environmental pressures, organizational responses, and information technology.

❹ Identify major pressures in the business environment and describe major organizational responses to them.

❺ Describe adaptive enterprises and why they are IT-dependent.

❻ Explain the function and impacts of social computing and social networking.

❼ Understand the importance of learning about information technology.

Integrating *IT*

 ACC   **FIN**   **MKT**   **OM**   **HRM**   **IS**

IT-PERFORMANCE MODEL

The focus of this chapter is on the environmental business pressures that are impacting organizational performance, and on the role of information technology (IT) as support for organizational activities that counter the environmental pressures. (*Information technology* refers to the collection of computing systems in an organization; see Section 1.2). IT also helps promote innovations and helps organizations to be leaders in exploiting the opportunities created by the changing environment to improve their performance and competitive edge.

The business performance management cycle and IT model.

TOYOTA SCION'S INNOVATIVE ADVERTISING STRATEGIES

The Problem

Increasing global competition is changing the environment facing most companies today. The automotive industry is a global multibillion dollar business where competition is very intense. Both General Motors (GM) and Toyota are competing to be the world's No.1 car manufacturer. At stake is not only how many cars can be sold, but also how much profit can be made.

Toyota is becoming the No. 1 car manufacturer and is aggressively competing with GM, Honda, and other car manufacturers. Toyota has been known for decades for its manufacturing innovations. Now it's taken an innovative lead on the Web. Here we look at one of its newest brands, the Scion, geared toward Generation Y (Gen Y), which includes those born between1980 and 1994. As of 2009, Gen Y and Gen X (the generation before Gen Y) combined are expected to account for at least 40 percent of vehicle sales.

The Solution

Toyota is using segmented advertising as its major media-based strategy for Scion. The company also uses search engine marketing, mass advertising, and one-to-one targeted marketing, all of which are aimed at increasing brand recognition.

- According to a ClickZ report, Toyota uses Scion display ads that reach urban audiences via sites such as *blastro.com* and *hiphopdx.com* (Rodgers, 2007). It also works in tandem with them on efforts deeply woven into content as a way to make it attractive to respective site readership. Those range from photo galleries to social networking profile pages offering interactive features.

- In August 2007, Toyota launched *Club Scion*, a three-story virtual nightclub with dance floors, music, and hot tubs in a virtual world site. Each level reflects a different Scion model, including xA hatchback, xB SUV, xD subcompact, and tC sports coupe.

- Scion maintains a presence in other large virtual worlds, including *secondlife.com*, *whyville.com*, and *gaia.com*. Toyota tracks virtual return on investment (ROI) through online chatter. Each virtual world lends itself to a different marketing strategy. In Whyville, where users tend to fall between ages 8 and 15, the company launched a virtual driver's education. Since *there.com* is populated by older teens, Toyota made sure to create a more provocative social environment.

- Using live chats is another smart strategy. Toyota made effective use of the Internet by using live chat to attract the 18- to 24-year-old audience. The campaign includes the use of *microapplication ads* that allow consumers to stencil designs over the picture of the Scion.

Source: Courtesy of Toyota Motor Sales, U.S.A, Inc.

To capitalize on wireless technology, in 2004 Toyota launched a mobile *advergame* (game to advertise a product), called "Scion Road Trip." Players earn virtual miles when they send e-cards to friends and get back responses. The campaign lasted for several months.

- For the 2008 xB SUV, Toyota created a special Web site *want2bsquare.com*. Visitors to the site can earn points by playing games, watching videos, and e-mailing others about the site. The site features eight *microsites*, including user community features; each has a unique theme and its own design. There are microsites that focus on music, resemble a Monty Python set, feature a haunted house, and include a town square and an urban zoo.

- Toyota targets children as a means to influence their parents. In April 2007, Toyota began placing its Scion on *whyville.net*, an online interactive community populated almost entirely by 8- to 15-year-olds. Toyota hopes Whyvillians will do two things: influence the users' parents' car purchases and persuade the users to buy Toyotas themselves when they grow up. The power of younger consumers has grown stronger in recent years. According to *MediaBuyerPlanner.com* (2006), a study by Packaged Facts showed that 39 percent of parents of 10- and 11-year-olds say their children have a significant impact on brand purchases.

- Finally, like several other automakers, Toyota is creating its own broadband channel. These channels are a way to move from push to pull marketing where the consumer decides what materials to view and when. A content-rich, broadband-friendly site is an always-on marketing channel to which people will return.

- Toyota created its own social network called Scion Speak where Scion lovers can socialize, communicate, and play. Scion owners can choose from hundreds of symbols and create customized logos for their cars. They can then download the logos and make window decals, or have them painted onto their cars.

The Results

According to *MarketingVox.com* (2007a), Scion has 80 percent brand recognition. As of April 2007, Scion was the No. 1 brick-and-mortar e-tailer among consumers 35 and younger. Scion had not even made it into the top 25 sites in 2006; so the amazing jump to the No. 1 ranking was due to the interactive and community-oriented nature of the Scion online experiences.

The Scion Web site is highly personalized. Sophisticated customization tools allow people to build their own virtual cars on the site. This online information is then integrated off-line—a local dealership locates the desired or similar vehicle for each virtual car builder and contacts the builder for a test drive. Other digital frills such as a social network for Scion car buyers and a Web site that plays music and lists concert information create superb brand experiences. Let's look at some of the specific advertising activities.

- The brand's Scion City in Second Life generated 10,000 blog posts between April and June 2007 and is the third most recognized brand in Second Life awareness.

- The on-site chat feature gets hundreds of conversations per week. Prior to the chat, users are asked a few questions, one of which is where they live. Interestingly, Toyota found that many of the chatters reside in areas where Scion is not even available, providing valuable information for dealer expansion plans.

- *The New York Times* reported that visitors to the site had used the word "Scion" in online chats more than 78,000 times; hundreds of virtual Scions were purchased using "clams," the currency of Whyville; and the community meeting place "Club Scion was visited 33,741 times.

- Short messaging service (SMS, or text message) is being used to alert players of their accrued virtual miles and weekly contest events.

Sources: Compiled from *scion.com* (accessed April 2008), Bosman (2006), *MediaBuyerPlanner.com* (2006), *MarketingVox.com* (2007a, 2007b, and 2007c), and Rodgers (2007).

This digital revolution has been responsible for changing business and consumer trends. Even traditional manufacturers such as car builders are embracing information technology (IT) not only to support their production processes (as they've done since the 1950s), but also to expand their activities to sales and advertising. In this case, we illustrate how Toyota is using cutting-edge Web tools known as Web 2.0, which include social networks and virtual worlds, to advertise its newer cars. Toyota has experimented broadly with new interactive technologies. Such IT-supported innovations can provide strategic advantage in our global hypercompetitive world. IT support is a necessity for any organization to excel or survive, and to manage the intense business environmental pressures on organizations.

This brief "Lessons Learned"section ties the key points of the opening case to the topics that will be covered in the chapter.

1.1 Doing Business in the Digital Economy

GLOBAL

The opening case introduced us to an enterprise that does extensive Web-based advertising and is on its way to becoming a digital enterprise. Similarly, thousands of organizations are moving to become more digital. What a digital enterprise is, and how it operates in the digital economy and society, is the subject of this section.

THE DIGITAL ENTERPRISE

Various icons are used throughout the book to identify a particular perspective or functional area related to the nearby example. This icon, for example, indicates an international perspective. Refer to the preface for a listing of all of the icons.

The term **digital enterprise** refers to an organization that uses computers and information systems (ISs) to perform or support its activities. A digital enterprise (organization) can be characterized in various ways. The digital enterprise uses IT to accomplish one or more of three basic objectives:

1. Reach and engage customers more effectively, as in Toyota's Scion case
2. Boost employee productivity
3. Improve operating efficiency

It also uses converged communication and computing technology to improve business processes and performance. One example is Thomson Corp. (*thomson.com*)—a publishing company that CEO Harrington transformed from a traditional $8 billion publishing business to an information services provider and specialty publisher for professionals. In five years, Thomson's revenue increased over 20 percent and profit increased by more than 65 percent (Harrington, 2006). Even Hollywood and Disney are making the transition from conventional to digital moviemaking including filming, production, storage, and distribution (Brandon, 2008).

WHAT IS THE DIGITAL ECONOMY?

The **digital economy** refers to an economy based on digital technologies and whose members are better informed and able to communicate because of IT. We use the term digital economy to emphasize the convergence of computing and telecommunications via the Internet—and the resulting flow of information that's stimulating e-commerce, online transactions, and organizational changes. In this economy, wired and wireless networking and communication infrastructures provide the platform over which people and organizations devise strategies, interact, communicate, collaborate, and search for information. Consider this: US online population is estimated to be over 200 million in 2008 (eMarketer, January 2008). And each Internet visitor may be a buyer. Thus, the entire economy is becoming more and more digital.

The digital economy is flooded with digital products and services. Representative examples include the following:

1. Information and entertainment products that are digitized:
   - Paper-based documents
   - Graphics (photographs, postcards, calendars, maps, posters, x-rays)
   - Audios (music recordings, speeches, lectures, industrial voice)

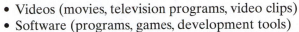

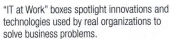

- Videos (movies, television programs, video clips)
- Software (programs, games, development tools)

2. Symbols, tokens, and concepts:
- Tickets and reservations: airlines, hotels, concerts, sports events, transportation
- Financial instruments: checks, electronic currencies, credit cards, securities, letters of credit

3. Processes and services:
- Government services: forms, benefits, welfare payments, licenses
- Electronic messaging: letters, faxes, telephone calls
- Business-value-creation processes and transactions
- Auctions, bidding, bartering
- Remote education, telemedicine, other interactive services
- Interactive entertainment, social networks, virtual communities

The major characteristics of the digital economy are listed in Table 1.1.

Opportunities for Entrepreneurs. The digital economy provides unique opportunities for entrepreneurs of all ages to startup online companies and apply innovative business models. These startup companies sell not only products (including music and movies), but also an entire array of online services—online dating, banking, insurance, employment, auctions, travel, and healthcare advice. Also provided are support services ranging from computer security to electronic payments. Business owners and managers saw an opportunity to do business without physical storefronts or borders. Some companies, notably Google, made their founders billionaires. An interesting example is the case of entrepreneurs Kim, Lindsey, and Mak, and their jetpens.com business, described in *IT at Work 1.1*. Don Kogen's Thaigem.com business is described in Online Minicase 1.1.

TABLE 1.1	Major IT Characteristics in the Digital Economy
Area	**Description**
Globalization	Global communication and collaboration and global electronic marketplaces are necessary to find global customers, suppliers, and partners.
Digital systems	From TV to telephones and instrumentation, analog systems are being converted to digital ones.
Speed	A move to real-time transactions, thanks to digitized documents, products, and services. Many business processes are expedited by 90 percent or more.
Information overload, search, and retrieval	Although the amount of information generated is accelerating, intelligent search tools can help users find what they need.
Markets	Markets are moving online. Physical marketplaces are being replaced or supplemented by electronic markets; new markets are being created, increasing competition and market efficiency.
Digitization	Music, books, pictures, movies, software, and more are digitized for fast and inexpensive distribution.
Business models and processes	New and improved business models and processes provide opportunities to new companies and industries. Cyberintermediation and no intermediation are on the rise.
Innovations	Digital and Internet-based innovations continue at a rapid pace. More patents are being granted than ever before.
Obsolescence	The fast pace of innovations creates a high rate of obsolescence.
Opportunities	Opportunities abound in almost all aspects of life and business.
Fraud	Criminals employ a slew of innovative schemes on the Internet. Cybercons are everywhere.
Wars	Conventional wars are changing to cyberwars.
Organizations	Many companies are attempting to move to a full or at least partial digital status.

IT at Work 1.1

How College Students Become Entrepreneurs

Stanford University students Lily Kim, Shu Lindsey, and Adrian Mak use computers and the Internet extensively. They also do extensive writing (on paper) and especially liked using ultra-thin pens with tips half the width of the average ballpoint. They learned about these pens when they were in Japan. Since these pens were not available in stores, they purchased them online directly from Japan. When they showed them to their friends (an example of the power of social marketing), they found there was a great interest in such pens in the United States.

Sensing opportunity in 2004, they decided to use their $9,000 savings to open a business, called Jetpens.com (*jetpens.com*), selling pens they imported from Japan. Soon after, they opened an online storefront, and began advertising their products via e-mail to students. When demand grew, they searched the Internet and found artists to design their own pens and arranged for their manufacture in Japan. Their product line included character collection pens, such as the popular *Hello Kitty*. To keep costs low, they used free software (from osCommerce) to build and run the store. They also use a small advertising budget for Google ads. By using smart keywords, they rank at the top of search engines when you search for "Japanese pens" (try a Google search to verify). This is called *site optimization* (e.g., see Turban et al., 2008).

To meet the demand, they originally kept an inventory of pens in their bedrooms, but now they rent space.

In 2007, the owners expanded the product line by adding interesting office supplies, including a best-selling eraser with 28 corners, which increased sales volume to over 10,000 items per month. Other best sellers include a pen with a tip fine enough to write on a grain of rice (*signobit*), erasable jet ink pens, a *popcorn* pen that has ink that puffs-up on the page, *BeGreen* environmentally friendly pens, and much more. To find friends and customers, they use Facebook and have a blog on their own site.

By keeping a tight cap on operating expenses and using Internet advertising successfully, the young entrepreneurs are also able to do what many others failed to do—generate profit within two years and grow by hundreds of percentages every year.

Sources: Compiled from Blakely (2007) and *jetpens.com* (accessed April 2008).

For Further Exploration: Go to *jetpens.com* and examine their catalog. What impresses you the most? What role does IT play on the site? Do you think that a business such as this can succeed as an independent physical store? Why or why not?

ELECTRONIC COMMERCE AND NETWORKED COMPUTING

Two major features of a digital enterprise are *e-commerce* and *networked computing*. **Electronic commerce** (also, e-commerce or EC) is the process of buying, selling, transferring, or exchanging products, services, or information via the Internet or other networks. For example, Siemens AG (*siemens.com*) was an established old-economy company that saw the need to transform itself into a digital enterprise. Its use of Web-based systems to support buying, selling, collaboration, and customer service exemplifies EC.

The underlying infrastructure for digital organizations and EC is **networked computing,** which enables computers and other electronic devices to be connected via telecommunication networks. Such connections give users access to remote information. Users may be connected to the public network—the *Internet*, to private value-added networks (VANs), or to the Internet's counterpart within organizations, called an *intranet*. Companies link their intranets to those of their business partners over networks to create what are called *extranets*. These connections are done via wireline systems, and since 2000, increasingly via *wireless systems* (see Minicase at the end of this chapter). Figure 1.1 illustrates how networks connect companies internally and externally.

NEW *VS.* OLD EXAMPLES

Changes brought by the digital economy have become so common that you may not even notice them. We tend not to notice what is all around us. Computer-based information systems of all kinds are the tools or weapons that have enhanced business[1] competitiveness or created strategic advantage. Let's look at a few examples that illustrate differences between doing business in the new economy (see Group Assignment #2) and doing so in the old one.

[1]Note that here and throughout the book, we use the term business to refer not only to for-profit organizations, but also to not-for-profit public organizations and government agencies that need to be run like businesses.

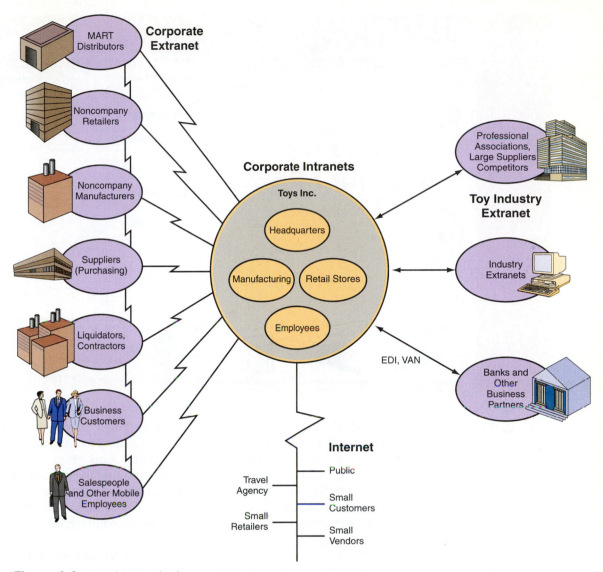

Figure 1.1 Digital networked enterprise.

Example#1: Buying or Renting a Movie Online. The cost of going to a movie is per person, you must travel to the theater, and you can go only at scheduled show times. In contrast, when you rent or buy a movie, many can view for the same cost, at any time, and in the convenience of your home.

Old Economy. You go to a retail store, browse the selections, hopefully find what you want, pay for it, and take the movie home. Movies need to be returned, of course, usually within a few days. Some stores are open 24 hours; others are not. In some areas you can buy or rent from self-serve kiosks, but the selection is minimal. Even in a specialized store, such as Blockbuster, you will not find more than 10,000 different titles in one location, with multiple copies available for only some titles. Note: Blockbuster is now offering an additional online marketing channel.

New Economy. Netflix (*netflix.com*) rents out DVDs from a selection of over 60,000 titles. Ordering is done online. Rental is done by mail, and Netflix pays all shipping costs. A monthly subscription fee allows you to rent as many movies as you want each month (up to three at a time). You can also view Netflix movies on your computer, including a wireless one. And soon you will be able to view them on your cell phone. This rental model increased demand and motivated the company to create a recommendation intelligent agent called *Cinematch* that recommends movies to each

individual based on his or her personality. For a general recommendation, visit *movies.yahoo.com*, and for further details, see the Netflix case in Chapter 6.

Even more convenient is downloading films from Netflix, Movielink, or CinemaNow to your computer. Although currently the selection is very limited, the movie can be yours forever, and you can stream a copy to a TV. You pay more for this convenience than you pay for rentals. You can also download TV episodes for $1.99 each using iTunes, for which there are no commercials.

Example #2: Paying for Goods: The Checkout Experience. It can take more time to check out than to shop, which can be a really frustrating experience.

Old Economy. In the old economy, you take your items to a cashier, who swipes (sometimes twice or more) the *barcode* of each item over a "reader." The reader captures data on the price and the description of each item and automatically enters those data into the database. You receive an itemized printout of your purchases, the total price, and the change if you paid in cash.

New Economy. In the new economy, you take your items to a self-service kiosk (e.g., visit the nearest Home Depot store; some supermarkets offer the service, too), where you swipe the barcode of each item over a reader. After you have swiped all of your items, the kiosk gives you directions about how to pay (cash, credit card, or debit card). You still may have to wait if there are lines to get to the self-service kiosk; often, some shoppers need help to learn the technology. But, your checkout time could be much faster, and the company's labor costs are lower.

In the upcoming generation of checkout technology, items will have *radio frequency identification* (RFID) tags (see Chapter 2) either attached to or embedded in them. After you have finished shopping, you will simply walk your cart with all of its items through a device similar to an airport security scanner. This device will "read" the wireless signals from each and all items at once. An electronic payment system will generate an itemized account of all of your items, calculate the total price, contact your bank, and debit your debit card or credit card (after recognizing your face or fingerprint), all in a few seconds. You will not wait in line at all. For more on accelerating checkouts, see Schuman (2007).

FIN   IS   SVR

Example #3: The Power of E-Commerce. The power of e-commerce is demonstrated in the following examples:

• Using his blog site (*oneredpaperclip.blogspot.com*), Kyle MacDonald of Canada was able to trade a red paper clip into a three-bedroom house. He started by advertising in the barter section of *craigslist.org* (see Chapter 8) that he wanted something bigger or better for an exchange of his one red paper clip. In the first iteration, he received a fish-shaped pen, and he posted similar requests on Craigslist again and again. Following many iterations and publicity on TV, he finally, after one year, received a house.

• Camera-equipped cell phones are used in Finland as health and fitness advisors. A supermarket shopper using the technology can snap an image of the bar code on a packet of food. The phone forwards the code number to a central computer, which sends back information on the item's ingredients and nutritional value. The computer also calculates how much exercise the shopper will have to do to burn off the calories based on the shopper's height, weight, age, and other factors.

• Several banks in Japan issue smart cards that can be used only by their owners. When using the cards, the palm vein of the owner's hand is compared with a pre-stored template of the vein stored on the smart card. When the owner inserts the card into the ATM or a vendor's card reader that is equipped with the system, it dispenses the person's money. The police are alerted if anyone other than the card's owner tries to use it.

• During the 2008 Olympics in Beijing, over 12 million tickets were equipped with RFID. Over 1,000 gates leading to all events were equipped with RFID readers. The major purpose was to eliminate counterfeiting. The technology had tremendous success and it will be implemented in the 2010 World Expo in Shanghai, where 70 million tickets will be equipped with RFID. The RFID may include additional functions such as paying for parking and for use in the concession stands. RFIDs were also attached to one shoe of the Marathon runners to track them and record their times at specific distances.

We can see the advantage of the new way of doing business over the old one in terms of at least one of the following: cost, quality, speed, convenience, strategic competitive advantage, and customer service. What is amazing is the *magnitude* of this advantage. In the past, business improvements were in the magnitude of 10 to 25 percent. Today, improvements can be hundreds or even thousands of times faster or cheaper. The new economy brings not only digitization, but also the opportunity to use new business models, illustrated in the examples above and, in the case of Jetspens.com, selling and buying on the Internet.

BUSINESS MODELS IN THE DIGITAL ECONOMY

A **business model** is a method of doing business by which a company can generate revenue to sustain itself. The model spells out how the company creates or adds value in terms of the goods or services the company produces in the course of its operations. Some models are very simple. For example, Nokia makes and sells cell phones and generates profit from these sales. On the other hand, a TV station provides free broadcasting. Its survival depends on a complex model involving factors such as advertisers and content providers. Internet portals, such as Yahoo!, also use a similar complex business model. Further details of business models and examples of new business models brought about by the digital revolution are listed in *A Closer Look 1.1*. Further discussion of these models will be found throughout the book (especially in Chapter 6), and at *digitalenterprise.org*.

According to McKay and Marshall (2004), a comprehensive business model is composed of the following six elements:

1. A description of all *products* and *services* the business will offer

2. A description of the *business process* required to make and deliver the products and services

A Closer Look 1.1

Four Representative Business Models of the Digital Age

MKT

Four popular e-commerce models are listed here.

Tendering via Reverse Auctions. If you are a big buyer, private or public, you are probably using a *tendering* (bidding) system to make your major purchases. In what is called a *request for quote* (RFQ), the buyer indicates a desire to receive bids on a particular item, and interested sellers bid on the job. The lowest bid wins (if price is the only consideration), hence the name *reverse auction.* Now tendering can be done online, saving time and money.

Affiliate Marketing. *Affiliate marketing* is an arrangement in which marketing partners (the host site) place a banner ad for a retailer (the advertiser), such as Amazon.com, on their Web site. Every time a customer clicks on the banner, moves to the advertiser's Web site, and makes a purchase there, the advertiser pays a commission of 3 to 15 percent to the host site. In this way, businesses can turn the hot sites into their *virtual commissioned sales force.* Pioneered by *CDNow,* the concept is now employed by thousands of retailers and direct sellers. In a variation of this model, the advertiser pays for any click made by a potential customer even if a purchase is not made (of course, the commission is much lower).

Product and Service Customization. With **customization**, a product or service is created according to the buyer's specifications. Customization is not a new model, but what *is* new is the ability to quickly configure customized products online for consumers at costs not much higher than noncustomized counter-

parts. Dell is a good example of a company that customizes PCs for its customers.

Many companies are following Dell's lead: The automobile industry is customizing its products and expects to save billions of dollars in inventory reduction alone every year by producing made-to-order cars. Mattel's *My Design* lets fashion-doll fans custom-build a friend for Barbie at Mattel's Web site; the doll's image is displayed on the screen before the person places an order. Nike allows customers to customize shoes, which can be delivered in a week. See the process in Figure 1.2. *Lego.com* allows customers to configure several of their toys. Finally, De Beers allows customers to design their own engagement rings.

Configuring the details of the customized products, including the final design, ordering, and paying for the products, is done online. Also known as *build-to-order,* customization can be done on a large scale, in which case it is called *mass customization.* For a discussion, see Chapter 2 and Tutorial #1.

E-Marketplaces and Exchanges. Electronic marketplaces have existed in isolated applications for decades. Examples are the stock exchanges, some of which have been fully computerized since the 1980s. Since the late 1990s, thousands of electronic marketplaces of different varieties have sprung up. E-marketplaces introduce operating efficiencies to trading, and if well organized and managed, they can provide benefits to both buyers and sellers. Chapter 6 will explore e-marketplaces and exchanges in more detail.

---

3. A description of the *customers* to be served and the company's relationships with these customers, including what constitutes value from the perspective of the customers (*customers' value proposition*)

4. A list of the *resources* required and the identification of which ones are available, which will be developed in-house, and which will need to be acquired

5. A description of the organization's *supply chain,* including *suppliers* and other *business partners*

6. A description of the revenues expected (*revenue model*), anticipated costs, sources of financing, and estimated profitability (*financial viability*)

Models also include a *value proposition,* which is an analysis of the benefits of using the specific model (tangible and intangible), including the customers' value proposition. *A Closer Look 1.1* shows specific examples.

Review Questions

1. Define digital enterprise.
2. Define and describe digital economy.
3. Define electronic commerce.
4. Define networked computing.
5. Define a business model.

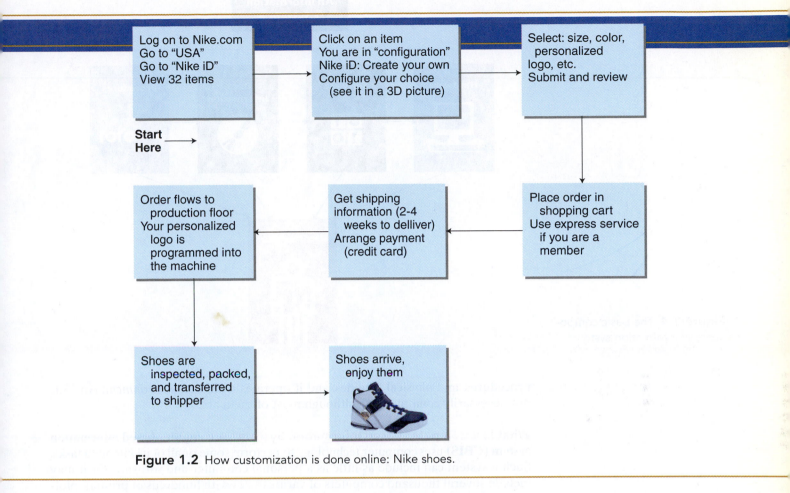

Figure 1.2 How customization is done online: Nike shoes.

1.2 Information Systems and Information Technology

This book deals with IT and its major component—information systems that are computer-based. Their definitions follow.

WHAT IS AN INFORMATION SYSTEM?

An **information system (IS)** collects, processes, stores, analyzes, and disseminates information for a specific purpose. Like any other system, an IS includes *inputs* (data, instructions) and *outputs* (reports, calculations). It *processes* the inputs by using technology such as PCs and produces outputs that are sent to users or to other systems via electronic networks. A *feedback* mechanism that controls the operation may be included (see Figure 1.3). Like any other system, an IS also includes people,

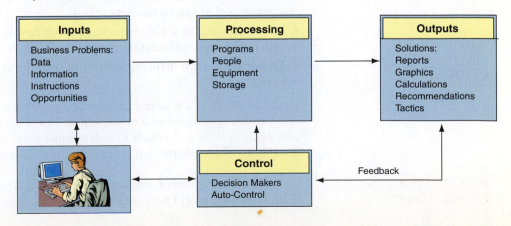

Figure 1.3 A schematic view of an information system.

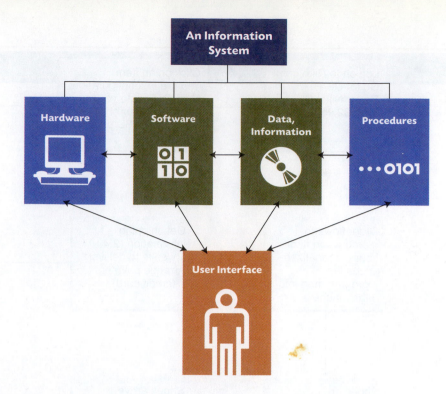

Figure 1.4 The basic components of information systems.

procedures, and physical facilities, and it operates within an *environment*. An IS is not necessarily computerized, although most of them are.

What Is a Computer-Based Information System? A **computer-based information system (CBIS)** uses computer technology to perform some or all of its intended tasks. Such a system can include as little as a personal computer and software. Or it may include several thousand computers of various sizes with hundreds of printers, plotters, and other devices, as well as communication networks (wireline and wireless) and databases. In most cases, an IS also includes people. The basic components of ISs are listed next and shown in Figure 1.4. Note that not every system includes all of these components.

- *Hardware* is a set of devices such as processor, monitor, keyboard, and printer. Together, they accept data and information, process them, and display them (TG 1).
- *Software* is a set of programs that instruct the hardware to process data (TG 2).
- *Data* is an essential part processed by the system and, if needed, stored in a *database* is a collection of related files, tables, relations, and so on, that stores data and the associations among them (TG 3).
- A *network* is a connecting system that permits the sharing of resources by different computers. It can be wireless (TG 4).
- *Procedures* are the set of instructions about how to combine the above components in order to process information and generate the desired output (TG 2, 6).
- *People* are those individuals who work with the system, interface with it, or use its output.

In addition, all ISs have a *purpose* and possibly a *social context*. A typical purpose is to provide a solution to a business problem. The social context of the system consists of the values and beliefs that determine what is admissible and possible within the culture of the people and groups involved. ISs also provide social environments.

WHAT IS INFORMATION TECHNOLOGY?

Broadly, the collection of computing systems used by an organization is termed **information technology (IT);** its use, strategy, and management are the focus of this book.

TABLE 1.2	Major Capabilities of Information Systems

Perform high-speed, high-volume, numerical computations.

- Provide for fast, accurate, reliable, and inexpensive communication within and between organizations, any time, any place.
- Store huge amounts of information in easy-to-access, small spaces.
- Allow quick and inexpensive access to vast amounts of information worldwide at any time.
- Enable collaboration anywhere, any time.
- Increase the effectiveness and efficiency of people working individually as well as in groups in one place or in several locations.
- Vividly present information that challenges the human mind.
- Facilitate work in hazardous environments.
- Automate both semiautomatic business processes and manually done tasks.
- Facilitate interpretation of vast amounts of data and voice.
- Facilitate global trade.
- Enable automation of routine decision making and facilitate complex decision making.
- Utilize wireless options, thus supporting unique applications anywhere.
- Accomplish all of the above much less expensively than when done manually.

IT has become the major facilitator of business activities in the world today. IT is also a catalyst of fundamental changes in the strategic structure, operations, and management of organizations due to the capabilities shown in Table 1.2. These capabilities support the following six business objectives:

- Improving productivity
- Reducing costs
- Improving decision making
- Facilitating collaboration
- Enhancing customer relationships
- Developing new strategic applications

IT, in its narrow definition, refers to the technological side of an information system. It includes the hardware, software, data and database, networks, and other electronic devices. It can be viewed as a subsystem of an information system. Sometimes, though, the term information technology is also used interchangeably with *information system*. In this book, we use the term *IT* in its broadest sense—to describe an organization's collection of information systems, their users, and the management that oversees them. The purpose of this book is to acquaint you with all aspects of information systems/information technology.

Review Questions

1. Define an information system.
2. Describe a computer-based information system.
3. Define information technology.

1.3 Business Performance Management, Business Pressures, Organizational Responses, and IT Support

Organizations have missions and goals that they attempt to achieve by performing certain activities. However, organizations do not operate in isolation. They are part of an environment that includes economic, legal, and other factors. For example, they are usually part of an industry and are subject to government regulations. In many cases, organizations are influenced by what is going on in their relevant environment.

BUSINESS PERFORMANCE MANAGEMENT AND ORGANIZATIONAL ENVIRONMENT

Most people, sports teams, and organizations are trying to improve their *performance*. Improving performance can be a challenge: a requirement for survival, or the key to improved life, profitability, or reputation.

Business Performance Management. Organizations have to manage their performance. This usually is done in a four-step cyclical process.

Step 1. Decide on desired performance levels. Namely, *what does the company want to achieve*? Such targets are decided upon and expressed as goals and objectives, based on the organization mission. Also, specific metrics should be set for desirable and measurable performance topics so that the company can evaluate its success.

Step 2. Determine how to attain the performance levels. The issue is *how to get there*? This is done by the corporate strategies and specific short-, medium-, and long-term plans.

Step 3. Periodically assess where the organization stands with respect to its goals, objectives, and measures. The issue here is to find *how are we doing*? This is accomplished by monitoring performance and comparing it to the values set in Step 1.

Step 4. Adjust performance and/or goals. If performance is too low, i.e., there is a negative gap between where we want to be and where we are, corrective actions need to be taken (*how do we close the gap*)? If it is very high, the goals for the next period are elevated.

The four steps in their totality are called **business performance management (BPM).** See Chapter 12 for details.

The execution of these steps is a cyclical process as shown in Figure 1.5. Note that IT can support all steps and that the process is surrounded by the business environment.

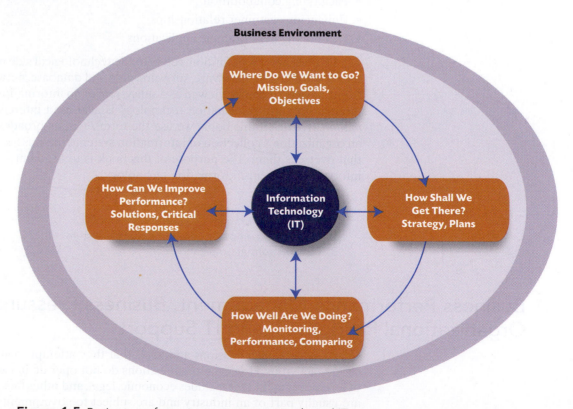

Figure 1.5 Business performance management cycle and IT.

Impact of the Business Environment. Unfortunately, frequently your performance level (monitored in Step 3) depends not only on what you do, but also on what others are doing and the forces of nature. We refer to such events, in totality, as the *business environment*. Such an environment may create significant pressures that impact performance in an uncontrollable, undesirable, or unpredictable way. The environment is shown as the outer ring in Figure 1.5.

Companies need to respond frequently and quickly to both the *threats* and the *opportunities* resulting from changes in their business environment. With the pace of the change and degree of uncertainty in competitive environments accelerating, organizations are under increasing pressures to produce more, using fewer resources.

In order to succeed in this dynamic world, companies must not only take traditional actions, such as lowering costs (see Porter models in Tutorial #2), but also undertake innovative activities, such as changing organization structure or business processes, or devise a competitive strategy. We refer to these reactions as **critical response activities.** A response can be a reaction to an existing or expected pressure or an activity that *exploits an opportunity* created by changing conditions. This is essentially done in Steps 2 and 4 of the process. Most response activities can be greatly facilitated by IT.

In the remainder of this section, we examine in more detail two components of our model—the business environmental pressures and organizational responses.

BUSINESS ENVIRONMENTAL PRESSURES

The business environment consists of a variety of factors—societal, legal, political, technological, and economical. Figure 1.6 presents a schematic view of major pressures that interrelate and affect each other. For more detailed information on these pressures, see Online Brief 1.1.

Impact of the Business Environment Factors. The business environment factors presented in Figure 1.6 can impact the performance of individuals, departments, and

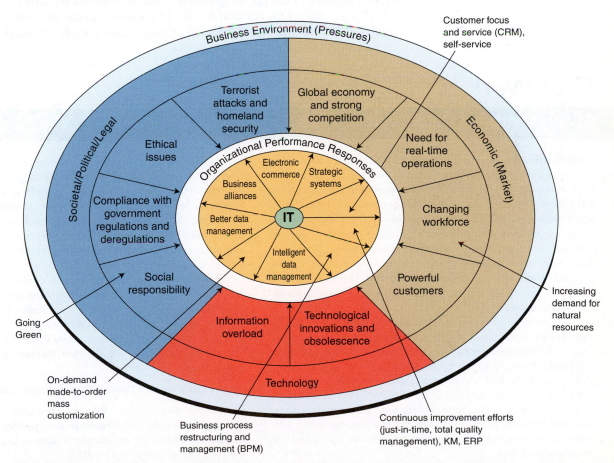

Figure 1.6 Business pressures, organizational performance and responses, and IT support.

entire organizations. Some create constraints that limit the flexibility required for an agile organization. Others cost a great deal of money or create a considerable headache, such as the Sarbanes-Oxley Act (SOX) (see Chapter 15), especially during the first years after they are instituted.

In addition to compliance with SOX, companies need IT to be able to comply with other legal requirements, such as the USA PATRIOT Act, Gramm-Leach Bliley (GLB) Act, Environmental Protection Agency (EPA) requirements, and Heath Information Portability and Accountability Act (HIPAA).

Note that pressures may come from *business partners*. For example, Wal-Mart Stores, Inc., mandated that their top suppliers adopt the RFID technology (see the case at the end of Part IV). Similar requirements are imposed by other large buyers, including federal and state governments.

Green IT. With an increased awareness about the damage to the physical environment and ecosystem, organizations and individuals are looking at potential improvements and savings that can be made in the IT industry. These efforts are known as **Green IT.** For example, energy use in *data centers* (a data center is a facility used to house computer systems and associated components, such as storage, telecommunications; see Chapter 3) is a major concern to corporations (see *IT at Work 1.2*). Green IT is a growing movement that will be a permanent fixture in the IT world from now on. Many IT organizations, however, are just starting to understand the influence that their IT purchase decisions have on data center power, cooling, and space consumption, all of which affect a company's green status.

Data center servers are known to be both power-hungry and heat-generating. PC monitors consume about 80 to 100 billion kilowatt hours of electricity every year in the United States. Both Intel and AMD are producing new chips aimed at reducing this amount of energy usage. Notice that PCs should be turned off when not in use. PCs generate CO_2 (carbon dioxide) that damages the atmosphere. Finally, discarded PCs and other computer equipment causes waste disposal problems. An

IT at Work 1.2

Saving Energy at Data Centers: Wells Fargo and Monsanto Inc.

Wells Fargo is a large financial institution that offers a wide range of services including consumer and corporate banking, insurance, investments, and mortgages. Its revenue in 2007 exceeded $50 billion. The company is data-dependent and known for its eco-friendliness. In 2007, with the increase in energy costs, the company decided to go "green" in its two new data centers. Data centers must ensure security and availability of their services, and when they are planned from scratch, they can be energy efficient with low power consumption. The two new facilities have over 8,000 servers that consume considerable power and generate heat.

Several energy-saving features were introduced, including water-based economizers that regulate energy usage and cool the physical environment, computer-controlled central fan system for cooling the floors, direct air to cool specific hot spaces, and semiconductor chips that automatically shut off power until it is needed. With increasing volumes of data, Wells Fargo constantly expands and renovates its data centers, taking environmental concerns into consideration. The company experimented with a solar system for making hot water, with motion-detector lights, and with variable-speed fans.

Monsanto Inc., a large global provider of agriculture products with 2007 revenues of $10 billion, is building an energy-efficient data center that supports analysis of its worldwide operations. Two factors driving investment in the new center were the 50 percent annual growth in data usage and high cooling costs for the old data center. The new energy-efficient center houses 900 servers and uses air for cooling rather than water. Another feature is the exterior glass shield that deflects 90 percent of the sun's heat.

Both companies have their data centers certified by the Leadership in Energy and Environmental Design (LEED) of the U.S. Green Building Council. In the United States, data centers consume about 20 to 30 billion KWH per year, and the number of servers is growing at 50 percent every three years. In both Wells Fargo and Monsanto, virtualization technologies increase the speed of data processing.

Sources: Compiled from Duvall (2007a) and Watson (2007).

For Further Exploration: Why are companies willing to spend money to be eco-friendly? How can energy-efficient data centers be justified? What are organizations such as LEED doing (check the Web site at *usgbc.org/leed*)?

important issue is how to recycle old equipment and whose responsibility (the manufacturers?, the users?) it is to take care of the problem. **Green software** refers to software products that help companies save energy or comply with EPA requirements.

Political and economic activities add to environmental complexity and turbulence. Organizations must be ready to take responsive actions and identify opportunities. How organizations respond to business pressures is described next.

ORGANIZATIONAL RESPONSES

Organizations can respond in many different ways. For example, Intel developed an innovative product and rushed it to the marketplace by using collaboration technologies. It also improved its customer service during its chip war with AMD Corp. (Whelan, 2006). We assembled a list of organizational responses and summarized them in Table 1.3. For more detail on these responses, see Online Brief 1.2. Others are described in various chapters of the book. In evaluating organizational responses, one must pay attention to ethical issues.

TABLE 1.3	Innovative Organizations' Responses to Pressures and Opportunities
Response/Action	**Description**
Develop strategic systems	Employ unique systems that provide strategic advantage (e.g., new features, low prices, super service) (Chapters 9–14).
Introduce customer-focused systems, CRM, and customer loyalty programs	Make the customer happy—a first priority (Chapters 6, 7).
Improve decision making and forecasting	Use analytical methods to optimize operations, reduce cost, expedite decision making, support collaboration, automate routine decisions (Chapter 12).
Restructure business processes and organization structure	Restructure business processes to make them more efficient/effective. Use business process management methodology (Chapter 14) and business process reengineering (Chapter 14).
Use self-service approach	Have your customers, employees, or business partners use self-service whenever possible (e.g., tracking status, changing an address, or managing your inventory) (Chapters 6, 7).
Continuously improve quality	Sustain competitive edge by improving quality (Chapters 9–12, 14).
Use mass customization	Fulfill customized orders (like Dell Computer does; see Chapter 6) using efficient procedures and processes. Compete in price with standard products.
Employ on-demand manufacturing/service and superb supply chain management	Meet the demands of your customers for standard or customized products/services efficiently and effectively (Chapters 9–12).
Promote business alliances and partner relationship management	Create business alliances, even with your competitors, to reduce risks and costs. Collaborate effectively; provide benefits to your partners (Chapters 4, 6–11).
Innovate and be creative— necessary as part of the culture. Promote R&D	Encourage innovation and creativity via rewards and collaboration. Encourage learning (Chapters 4, 8, 15).
Use e-commerce and digital systems	Automate business processes, procedures, and routine operations. Use new business models and electronic markets (Chapters 6, 7).
Share information and knowledge, manage knowledge	Encourage information and knowledge creation, storage, and reuse (Chapters 3, 8, 12).
Go global—but do it carefully	Buy and/or sell globally, find business partners globally, and outsource offshore. Do it all with proper risk analysis (Chapter 11 and Online Chapter 17).
Use leading-edge and emerging technologies, including digital ones	Keep yourself up on all technological developments, conduct competitive analysis, plan properly, and conduct cost/benefit/risk analyses (Chapter 1 and Online Chapter 17).
Use enterprise and integrated systems	Integrating systems of internal information applications together with partners' systems facilitate collaboration, reduce costs and errors, and provide competitive advantage (Chapters 10, 11, 16).
Go Green	Save energy and the environment (Chapter 1).
Reduce cycle time	Increase speed via automation, collaboration, and innovation (Chapters 6, 7, 9, 14).

IT use may raise ethical issues ranging from employee e-mail monitoring to invasion of privacy of millions of customers whose data are stored in private and public databases. On the book's Web site, you will find an ethics tutorial (Tutorial #3) that will help you develop and strengthen your understanding of ethical issues related to business and to IT management. The tutorial consists of two parts: (1) a general framework of ethics in business and society, and (2) an *Ethics Primer* that poses various ethical situations and asks you to think about responses to these situations. In addition to the materials there, specific ethical issues are discussed in all chapters of the book and are highlighted by an icon in the margin.

ETHICS

Ethical Issues. Ethical issues create pressures or constraints on business operations. **Ethics** relates to standards of right and wrong, and *information ethics* relates to standards of right and wrong in information management practices. Ethical issues have the power to damage the image of an organization and the morale of employees. Ethics is a difficult area because ethical issues are not cut-and-dried. What is considered ethical by one person may seem unethical to another. Likewise, what is considered ethical in one country may be unethical in others.

Two of the major organizational responses, as well as a major step in business performance management, are IT strategy and IT support of enterprise strategy.

Review Questions

Define *business performance management* and show its cycle.

1. Describe the impact of the business environment and list some of its components.
2. What is Green IT and why has it become important?
3. List some environmental issues of data centers.
4. Describe organizational responses.
5. Define *ethics*.

1.4 Strategy for Competitive Advantage and IT Support

For many organizations, especially for-profit ones, a strategy is necessary for survival, and it provides a competitive edge.

WHAT IS A STRATEGY?

As you recall from Step 2 in our business performance management (BPM) model (Figure 1.5), a **strategy** is the component that defines how to attain our mission, goals, and objectives. It specifies the necessary plans, budgets, and resources. Strategy addresses fundamental issues such as the company's position in its industry, its available resources and options, and future directions. A strategy addresses questions such as:

- What is the long-term direction of our organization?
- What is the overall plan for deploying our organization's resources?
- What trade-offs are necessary? What resources will it need to share?
- What is our unique positioning vis-à-vis competitors?
- How do we achieve sustainable competitive advantage over rivals in order to ensure lasting profitability?

A major component of strategy is the various methodologies and tools that can be used to execute the various steps in its process (see Tutorial #2). Two of the most well-known methodologies were developed by Porter. Their essentials are presented next.

PORTER'S COMPETITIVE FORCES MODEL AND STRATEGIES

Porter's **competitive forces model** has been used to develop strategies for companies to increase their competitive edge. It also demonstrates how IT can enhance competitiveness.

The model recognizes five major forces that could endanger a company's position *in a given industry*. Other forces, such as those cited in this chapter, including the impact of government, affect all companies in the industry, and therefore may have less impact on the relative success of a company within its industry. Although the details of the model differ from one industry to another, its general structure is

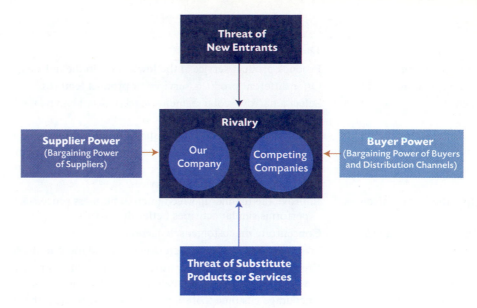

Figure 1.7 Porter's competitive forces model.

universal. The five major forces in an industry that affect the degree of competition and ultimately the degree of profitability are:

1. Threat of entry of new competitors
2. Bargaining power of suppliers
3. Bargaining power of customers or buyers
4. Threat of substitute products or services
5. Rivalry among existing firms in the industry

The strength of each force is determined by the industry's structure. Existing companies in an industry need to protect themselves against the forces; alternatively, they can use the forces to improve their position or to challenge the leaders in the industry. The relationships are shown in Figure 1.7. The definitions and details are provided in Tutorial #2.

While implementing Porter's model, companies can identify the forces that influence competitive advantage in their marketplace and then develop a *strategy*. Porter (1985) proposed three such strategies—cost leadership, differentiation, and niche strategies.

In Table 1.4, we list first Porter's three classical strategies, plus nine other general strategies, for dealing with competitive advantage. Each of these strategies can be enhanced by IT, as will be shown throughout the book and in Tutorial #2. Forthcoming chapters will show: (1) how different ITs impact the five forces, and (2) how IT facilitates the 12 strategies. Porter strategies were supplemented by others. Some are italics presented in Tutorial #2. For an interesting example see the *Blue Ocean Strategy* (en.wikipedia.org/wiki/blue_ocean_strategy).

PORTER'S VALUE CHAIN MODEL

According to Porter's **value chain model** (Porter, 1985), the activities conducted in any manufacturing organization can be divided into two parts: *primary activities* and *support activities*.

Primary activities are those business activities through which a company produces goods, thus creating value for which customers are willing to pay. Primary activities involve the purchase of materials, the processing of materials into products, and delivery of products to customers. Typically, there are five primary activities:

1. Inbound logistics (incoming raw materials and other inputs)
2. Operations (manufacturing and testing)

TABLE 1.4	Strategies for Competitive Advantage
Strategy	**Description**
Cost leadership	Produce product/service at the lowest cost in the industry.
Differentiation	Offer different products, services, or product features.
Niche	Select a narrow-scope segment (*market niche*) and be the best in quality, speed, or cost in that segment.
Growth	Increase market share, acquire more customers, or sell more types of products.
Alliance	Work with business partners in partnerships, alliances, joint ventures, or virtual companies.
Innovation	Introduce new products/services; put new features in existing products/services; develop new ways to produce products/services.
Operational effectiveness	Improve the manner in which internal business processes are executed so that the firm performs similar activities better than rivals.
Customer orientation	Concentrate on customer satisfaction.
Time	Treat time as a resource, then manage it and use it to the firm's advantage.
Entry barriers	Create barriers to entry. By introducing innovative products or using IT to provide exceptional service, companies can create entry barriers to discourage new entrants.
Customer or supplier lock-in	Encourage customers or suppliers to stay with you rather than going to competitors. Reduce customers' bargaining power by locking them in.
Increase switching costs	Discourage customers or suppliers from going to competitors for economic reasons.

3. Outbound logistics (packaging, storage, and distribution)

4. Marketing and sales (to buyers)

5. Services

The primary activities usually take place in a sequence from 1 to 5. As work progresses, value is added to the product in each activity. To be more specific, the incoming materials (1) are processed (in receiving, storage, etc.) in activities called *inbound logistics*. Next, the materials are used in *operations* (2), where significant value is added by the process of turning raw materials into products. Products need to be prepared for delivery (packaging, storing, and shipping) in the *outbound logistics* activities (3). Then *marketing and sales* (4) attempt to sell the products to customers, increasing product value by creating demand for the company's products. The value of a sold item is much larger than that of an unsold one. Finally, *after-sales service* (5), such as warranty service or upgrade notification, is performed for the customer, further adding value. The goal of these value-adding activities is to make a profit for the company.

Primary activities are supported by the following **support activities:**

1. The firm's infrastructure (accounting, finance, management)

2. Human resources management

3. Technology development (R&D)

4. Procurement (purchasing)

Each support activity can be applied to any or all of the primary activities, and the support activities may also support each other, as shown in Figure 1.8.

Innovation and adaptability are critical success factors (CSFs) related to Porter's models. CSFs are those things that must go right for a company to achieve its mission. CSFs must be measurable, such as the increase in the number of customers. An example of innovative strategy is provided in *IT at Work 1.3*.

ADAPTIVE AND INNOVATIVE ORGANIZATIONS (ENTERPRISES)

Charles Darwin, the renowned scientist, said, "It's not the strongest of species that survives, nor the most intelligent; but the one most responsive to change." What is true in nature is true today in organizations that operate in a rapidly changing environment, which we described in Section 1.3. The digital revolution and rapid environmental changes bring myriad opportunities, as well as risks. Bill Gates is aware

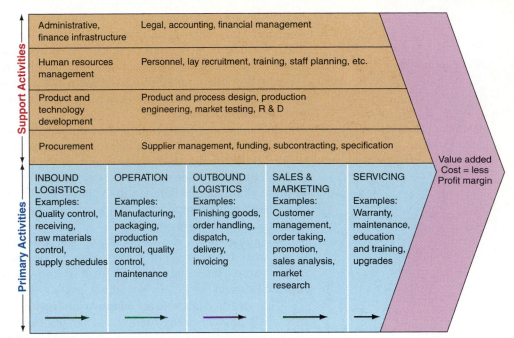

		Administrative, finance infrastructure	Legal, accounting, financial management				Value added Cost = less Profit margin

Support Activities

- Administrative, finance infrastructure — Legal, accounting, financial management
- Human resources management — Personnel, lay recruitment, training, staff planning, etc.
- Product and technology development — Product and process design, production engineering, market testing, R & D
- Procurement — Supplier management, funding, subcontracting, specification

Primary Activities

INBOUND LOGISTICS	OPERATION	OUTBOUND LOGISTICS	SALES & MARKETING	SERVICING
Examples: Quality control, receiving, raw materials control, supply schedules	Examples: Manufacturing, packaging, production control, quality control, maintenance	Examples: Finishing goods, order handling, dispatch, delivery, invoicing	Examples: Customer management, order taking, promotion, sales analysis, market research	Examples: Warranty, maintenance, education and training, upgrades

Value added
Cost = less
Profit margin

Figure 1.8 The firm's value chain. The arrows illustrate the flow of goods and services (the internal part of the supply chain). *(Source: Drawn by E. Turban.)*

IT at Work 1.3

How IT Enabled the Boston Red Sox to Win the World Series

One of the best U.S. baseball teams is the Boston Red Sox, who won the World Series in 2004 and 2007. Important to their success, the team developed a sophisticated recruitment and layoff strategy that is heavily supported by IT. Obviously, baseball success depends on players and their working together as a team. Winning is, in part, the result of finding players with the talents you need before competing teams. It's also necessary to determine exactly how long to keep each player.

Extensive, detailed data are available on both individual players and specific games. Players' performance can be measured down to every swing, step, or throw taken. Baselines are easy to establish on every facet of an athlete such as height, weight, medical condition, arm strength, hitting discipline, and mental errors. If a statistic is not available, one is created through ratings. The Red Sox even require players in their farm system to keep a log of their every at-bat.

As seen in Figure 1.5, it is necessary to develop a strategy to attain the goal of winning games. The sports data need to be analyzed to see if actual performance of each player generated more than the average (and desired) number of wins. This determines whether or not to pay $10 to $20 million per year to a star pitcher or other player, as well as when to retire a player. Furthermore, some teams can afford to pay more for players, and acquire the best players. However, IT can provide strategic advantage for all teams. The tool used is called **business intelligence (BI)**, which is a technology for collecting and organizing vast amounts of data so they will be easily accessible for analysis by managers and ana-

lysts. BI helps identify the winning characteristics of "human capital" before the competition finds them. BI does analysis with *sabermetrics*.

Sabermetrics is the mathematical analysis of player batting and pitching performances. Baseball is a sport already brimming with statistics, yet sabermetrics—the term derived from the acronym SABR, which stands for the Society for American Baseball Research, a community of baseball enthusiasts—is a departure from traditional player metrics, such as runs batted in and batting averages.

Sabermetricians have come up with measures that accurately reflect a player's value toward achieving a win, such as "runs created." This statistic counts the number of times a batter gets on base, be it by walk or hit, and factors in an added value for the power of a hit, be it a single or a home run. The purpose is to determine what the batter does at the plate to create an opportunity for his team to score a run.

Sabermetrics can help teams more accurately find minor league prospects who will succeed in the big leagues. Similarly, sabermetricians claim they can use the analysis to determine which major league players deserve a $10 million paycheck and which "stars" can be dumped.

Sources: Compiled from Duvall (2004) and Duvall (2007b).

For Further Exploration: Can management strategy be executed without IT? Why is it difficult for competitors to copy this strategy? Is this a sustainable strategic advantage?

of this. Microsoft is continually developing new Internet and IT products and services. Yet Gates recognizes that Microsoft is always two years away from failure—that somewhere out there is an unknown competitor who could render Microsoft's business model obsolete (Heller, 2006). Competition is not only among products or services, but also among business models, customer service, and supply chains.

The concept of value chain has been supplemented by the concepts of *value system* and *value network*.

A firm's value chain is part of a larger stream of activities, which Porter calls a value system. A **value system** includes the suppliers that provide the inputs necessary to the firm and their value chains. Once the firm creates products, they pass through the value chain of distributors, all the way to the buyers (customers). All parts of these chains are included in the value system. Gaining and sustaining a competitive advantage, and supporting that advantage by means of IT, this requires an understanding of entire value system.

A *value network* is a complex set of social and technical resources. Value networks work together via relationships to create social goods (public goods) or economic value. This value takes the form of knowledge and other intangibles and/or financial value. (For details see en.wikipedia.org/wiki/value_network.)

This section deals with an **adaptive enterprise** (or organization) that can respond in a timely manner to environmental changes. This section is divided into three parts: the process of becoming adaptive, an example of real-time systems, and IT failures.

Process of Becoming an Adaptive Organization.
Organizations must become *adaptive* or *agile* to deal properly and quickly with problems and opportunities. To become adaptive, an organization should:

- **Recognize environmental and organizational changes as quickly as they occur, or even before they occur.** Predictive analytical software, business intelligence software, and competitive intelligence software have proven to be extremely helpful. Systems such as Cisco's *virtual close* keep companies informed in near real time. Early detection is critical.

- **Deal with changes properly and correctly.** For example, optimization software (Chapter 12) enables companies to determine prices of products in real time. *What-if* analysis enables companies to evaluate possible courses of action and analyze risks in minutes.

- **Not wait for competitors to introduce change.** Do it first, if at all possible (*first-mover* strategy).

- **Have a scalable and appropriate IT architecture.** Scalability can be done by using emerging technologies such as *service-as-an-architecture*. To be agile it is necessary to have a flexible IT architecture (*mitsloan.mit.edu/cisr*). This includes enterprise systems, standardization, an innovation culture, and the use of **open-source software.** An open-source software is one for which the source code (how the software was actually written is available for anyone free of charge; see TG 2 and en.wikipedia.org/wiki/Open_source for details).

- **Develop an innovation culture.** Organizations need an innovative culture and enterprise-level thinkers who understand how to exploit IT tools.

- **Follow activities listed in Table 1.3 (p. XX).**

An example of an appropriate IT infrastructure is that of HP Development Company.

HP MODEL OF BUILDING ADAPTIVE ENTERPRISE

Hewlett-Packard Development Company *hp.com*, a major IT company, envisioned being an adaptive enterprise that helps other organizations become adaptive. To be adaptive, IT must be synchronized with **business processes.** Business processes are a collection of activities performed to accomplish a clearly defined goal(s), with starting and ending points. Today, organizations need IT solutions that improve business processes, increase business agility and performance, and improve competitive advantage. They cannot afford any "blindspots" — not knowing what's going on as it's going on. For more details, see Online Brief 1.3.

REAL-TIME, ON-DEMAND IT SUPPORT

Eliminating blindspots requires *real-time systems*. A **real-time system** is an IS that provides fast enough access to information or data so that an appropriate decision can be made, usually before data or situation changes (operational deadlines from event to system response). Fast enough may mean less than a second if you are buying a stock, or before a business opens in the morning when you determine a price. It can be a day or two in other situations. In Online Minicase 1.2, we provide an example of a digital hospital. When a patient is admitted to the hospital, the patient's medical records must be readily accessible. The longer the wait, the higher the risk to the patient. The real-time enterprise is a necessity since the basis of competition is often time or speed. Web-based systems (such as tracking stocks online) provide us with these capabilities. Some examples are the following:

- Salespeople can check to see whether a product is in inventory by looking directly into the inventory system.
- Suppliers can ensure adequate supplies by looking directly into the forecasting and inventory systems.
- An online order payment by credit card is checked for the balance and the amount of the purchase is debited all in one second. This way authorization is given "fast enough" for both a seller and a buyer.

OM   SVR

Example of Real-time IT Support. HyperActive Technologies (*hyperactivetechnologies.com*) has developed a system by which cameras mounted on the roof of a fast food restaurant track vehicles pulling into the parking lot or drive-through. Other cameras track the progress of customers moving through the ordering queue. Using predictive analysis, the system predicts what customers might order. In addition, a database includes historical car-ordering data, such as 20 percent of cars entering the lot will usually order at least one cheeseburger at lunch time. Based on the camera's input and the database, the system predicts what customers will order 1.5 to 5 minutes before they actually order. Cooks are better informed, minimizing customers' waiting time and the cost of overheated food without flavor. The real-time enterprise is also referred to as *on-demand enterprise*. Such an enterprise must be able to fulfill orders as soon as they are needed.

Innovation and Creativity. Organizational responses are usually taken in reaction to change in the business environment or to competitors' actions. Sometimes such response may be too late. Therefore, organizations can play a proactive role and make significant changes in their industry before anyone else. A first mover strategy is risky, but can be very rewarding if successful.

Examples

Successful first-movers

eBay	eBay was a first mover into the online auction market. Listening to customers and constantly adding new features and services has kept eBay on top.
Blogger	*Blogger.com* (a Google company) was the first Web site to provide Weblog (blog) hosting services to blog authors; it is still the dominant provider.
Apple Computer	Being first with Windows Desktop, mouse, hard floppy disk, floppyless laptops, and wireless technology has given Apple a frontier-pushing reputation that keeps it in the personal computer operating system market, while others (e.g., IBM's OS/2) have floundered in the face of the Microsoft Windows juggernaut.

Companies that had first-mover advantage, but lost the marketplace battle to late movers

Chemdex	The original B2B digital exchange closed down when revenue growth slowed, and the owners decided to change to a different business model.
Netscape	The world's first Internet browser company saw its dominance of the browser market diminish as Microsoft bundled Internet Explorer into the Windows operating system.

INFORMATION SYSTEMS FAILURES

Use of this icon indicates a description of an IT failure, and discussion of the lessons that can be learned from it.

So far, we have introduced you to several success stories. You may wonder, though, is IT always successful? Absolutely not. There are many failures. We will show you some of these (marked with a "lessons from failures" icon) in this book or on our Web site. We can learn from failures as much as we can learn from successes, as illustrated in *A Closer Look 1.2* below.

Examples of more recent failures are the following:

• February 24, 2008, about two-thirds of the world was unable to see YouTube for several hours. This happened when the Pakistan Telecommunication Authority decided to block offensive content in their own country. Their ISP, together with Hong Kong PCCW telecommunication, incorrectly programmed a block video on YouTube that reached around the world instead (Claburn, 2008).

A Closer Look 1.2

Failures at Nike and AT&T

In certain retail stores, fans of Nike's Air Terra Humara 2 running shoe hit the jackpot. Once selling for over $100 US, they were selling for less than $50 in fall 2001. The cheaper shoes were the aftermath of the breakdown in Nike's supply chain, a breakdown attributed to a software problem.

Nike had installed a $400 million supply chain system in early 2001. The system was supposed to forecast sales demand, and plan supplies of raw materials and finished products accordingly. However, the newly deployed demand and supply planning application apparently overestimated the demand for certain shoes in some locations and underestimated demand in others. As a result, some raw materials were over-purchased, while inventory levels of other materials were insufficient. Some shoes were over-manufactured, while the most-demanded ones were under-manufactured. To speed the right shoes to market, Nike had to spend around $5 a pair in air freight cost, compared to the usual cost of 75 cents by ocean shipping. In all, Nike attributed some $100 million in lost sales in the third quarter of 2001 alone to this problem.

What went wrong? The system was developed with software from i2, a major supply chain management software producer. However, Nike insisted on modifying the i2 standard software, customizing it to its needs. Specifically, Nike wanted a forecast by style, by color, and by size in order to make thousands of forecasts very rapidly to respond quickly to changing market conditions and

consumer preferences. To meet Nike's needs, it was necessary to customize the standard software, and to do so quickly because Nike wanted the system fast. The reprogramming was apparently done *too* fast. The software had bugs like most new software. Software testing is a critical, time-consuming task. Customizing standard software requires a step-by-step process (see Technology Guide 5). It should be done only when an off-the-shelf product is not available, and it must be planned extensively.

Nike fixed the problem after spending an undisclosed amount of time and money in 2002. Nike is not the only major corporation that suffered an IT failure. Hundreds of documented cases exist; the giant AT&T is an example.

A customer relationship system at AT&T Wireless, which was upgraded in 2003 to improve customer care, crashed during the upgrade. As a result, customer service representatives could not set up or access new accounts. The system breakdowns, which continued through February 2004, swamped other AT&T systems and gridlocked the customer service phone system. Thousands of furious customers moved to competitors, costing AT&T Wireless an estimated $100 million in lost revenue, and hastened its sale to Cingular for only $15/share—about half the value AT&T Wireless' shares were when it went public in April 2000.

Sources: Compiled from Sterlicchi and Wales (2001), from *nike.com* press releases (2002, 2003), and Koch (2004).

- In June 2007, computer failure caused major flight delays and cancellations along the enter U. S. eastern seaboard.
- In October 2007, the city of Mesa, Arizona, suffered from a major hardware glitch that erased many municipal documents and hindered access to e-mail.
- In August 2007, 200 million users of Skype were unable to talk due to a software glitch that took down its network.
- Outdated computer programs at the IRS failed to catch an estimated $200 million fraudulent requests for tax refunds in 2006.
- On August 26, 2008 the FAL Flight-Plan System, which is 20 years old, crashed, effecting most of the major airports in the US for 90 minutes. The crash resulted from a single corrupt file—most likely a virus—that had entered the system and somehow torpedoed it into uselessness.

Review Questions

1. Describe business strategy.
2. Explain the Porter models and relate them to business strategy.
3. Describe adaptive and agile organizations.
4. Describe real-time business and information systems.
5. Describe failure of IT systems.

1.5 Social Computing and Networking and Virtual Worlds

In recent years, we witnessed the emergence of social computing and wireless computing. Both are described next.

SOCIAL COMPUTING

Social computing is a general term for computing that is concerned with the intersection of social behavior and ISs. Social computing has to do with supporting any social behavior in or through ISs. Blogs, mashups, instant messaging, social network services, wikis, social bookmarking, and other *social software* and marketplaces are types of social computing.

While traditional computing systems concentrate on supporting organizational activities and business processes, and zero in on cost reduction and increase of speed, social computing concentrates on improving collaboration and interaction among people. It is a shift from the traditional top-down management and communication to bottom-up strategy where individuals in communities with their activities become a major organizational power. In social computing and commerce, people can collaborate online, get advice from one another and from trusted experts, and find goods and services they really like.

Example. Advances in social computing are affecting travel decisions and arrangements. Travelers share information and warn others of bad experiences, particularly at *tripadvisor.com*.

The premise of social computing is to make socially produced information (e.g; user-driven content) available to others. This information may be provided directly, as when systems show the number of users who have rated a review as helpful or not (e.g., at *amazon.com*). Or the information may be provided after being filtered and aggregated, as is done when systems recommend a product based on what else people with similar purchase histories have purchased (e.g., at *amazon.com* and *netflix.com*). Or the information may be provided indirectly, as is the case with Google's page rank algorithms, which order search results based on the number of pages that (recursively) point to them. In all of these cases, information that is produced by individuals is used to support the system.

A **social network** is a Web site where people create their own space, or home page, on which they write blogs and wikis, and post pictures, videos, or music; share ideas; and link to other Web locations they find interesting. Social networkers chat using instant messaging and tag the content they post with their own keywords, which makes their content searchable. In effect, they create *online communities* of people with similar interests. **Social network services (SNSs),** such as MySpace, allow people to build their home pages for free, and provide basic communication and other support tools to conduct different activities in the social network. These activities are referred to as *social networking.* Social networks are people-oriented. For example, 15-year-old Filipino singer Pempengco thought her music career was doomed when she lost a local singing competition in 2006. But YouTube gave her the "cyber break" of a lifetime when a clip of her singing Jennifer Holliday's "And I'm Telling You I Am Not Going" caught the attention of TV host Ellen DeGeneres and Grammy award-winning producer David Foster. But, as we will see in Chapter 8, corporations are starting to have an interest in this EC feature (e.g., see *linkedin.com*, a network that connects businesses by industry, functions, geography, and areas of interest).

Major examples of SNSs are the following:

- Facebook.com—facilitates socialization by students
- Flickr.com—user shared photos
- Classmates.com—focuses on school, college, and military groups
- Friendster.com—provides a platform to find friends and make contacts
- YouTube.com and Metcafe.com—users can upload and view videoclips
- YUB.com—A social network for discount shoppers
- Cyworld.rate.com—Asia's largest social network
- Habbohotel.com—Entertaining country-specific sites for kids and adults
- MySpace.com—The most visited social network (see *IT at Work 1.4*)

Enterprise Social Networks. *Enterprise social networks* are networks whose primary objective is to facilitate business. Two major types exist: Private and Public. *Private networks* are owned and operated by one company such as CocaCola or Sony. They can be internal (serving employees, like in Wells Fargo Bank) or external, serving customers and other business partners. *Public networks* are owned and operated by an independent company. A prime example is LinkedIt, which has had close to 30 million members by fall 2008.

Another example is Craigslists.org, the super site for classified ads that offers many social-oriented features (see Chapter 8). Yet, its major objective is to help people find accommodations, barter items, or conduct other business-oriented activities.

Carnival Cruise Lines sponsors a social networking site (*carnivalconnections.com*) to attract cruise fans. Visitors can use the site to exchange opinions, organize groups for trips, and much more. It cost the company $300,000 to set up the site, but Carnival anticipates that the cost will be covered by increased business. For detailed discussion on what companies can do on enterprise social networks, see Rutledge (2008).

A special class of social networking is the virtual world. A **virtual world** is a *computer-based simulated environment* intended for its *users* to inhabit, and virtual spaces interact via avatars. These *avatars* are usually depicted as textual, two-dimensional, or *three-dimensional graphical* representations, although other forms are possible. Some, but not all, virtual worlds allow for multiple users. According to *en.wikipedia.org/wiki/Virtual_world*, the *computer-simulated* world presents perceptual stimuli to the user, who in turn can manipulate elements of the modeled world and thus experiences *telepresence* to a certain degree. The model world may simulate situations and rules based on the real world or some fantasy world. Examples of rules are *gravity, topography, locomotion, real-time actions,* and *communication.* Communication between users has ranged from text, graphical icons, visual gesture, sound, and so forth.

Until 2007, virtual worlds were seen most of the time as 3D games including massively multiplayer online games. But recently they have become a new way for people

IT at Work 1.4

MySpace: The World's Most Popular Social Networking Web Site

MySpace is an interactive social network of user-submitted blogs, profiles, groups, photos, MP3s, videos, instant messaging, and an internal e-mail system. It has become an increasingly influential part of contemporary pop culture. The site claims to have over 115 million members (the world's third most popular English-language Web site) and draws 1.5 million new members each week.

Contents of a MySpace Profile. Each member's profile contains two "blurbs": "About Me" and "Who I'd Like to Meet." Profiles also can contain optional sections about personal features, such as marital status, physical appearance, and income. Profiles can be customized and also contain a blog with standard fields for content, emotion, and media. MySpace also supports uploading images and videos.

Users can choose a certain number of friends to be displayed on their profiles in the "Top Friends" area. In 2006, MySpace allowed up to 24 friends to be displayed. The "Comments" area allows the user's friends to leave comments. MySpace users can delete comments or require all comments to be approved before posting. The site gives users some flexibility to modify their user pages, or "MySpace editors" are available to help.

MySpace Celebrities and Artists. MySpace has led to the emergence of MySpace celebrities, popular individuals who have attracted hundreds of thousands of "friends," leading to coverage in other media. Some of these individuals have remained only Internet celebrities; others have been able to jump to television, magazines, and radio.

MySpace is also used by some independent musicians and filmmakers who upload songs and short films on their profiles. These songs and films can also be embedded in other profiles, adding to MySpace's appeal.

Major Issues Surrounding MySpace. The following are several major issues surrounding MySpace use.

Restricting Access Many schools and public libraries in the United States and the United Kingdom have begun to restrict access to MySpace because it has become "such a haven for student gossip and malicious comments" and because MySpace was consuming up to 40 percent of the daily *Internet bandwidth*, impeding delivery of Web-based courses. Regular administrative functions may also be slowed down, making the normal running of universities difficult.

Potential Damage to Students The *Chicago Tribune's* RedEye printed an article concerning MySpace and an individual's search for employment. The author argued that young college graduates compromise their chances of starting careers because of the content they post on their accounts. An employer may not hire a highly qualified candidate because the candidate maintains an account that suggests overly exuberant behavior.

Security and Safety. MySpace allows registering users to be as young as 14. Profiles of users with ages set to 14 to 15 years are automatically private. Users whose ages are set at 16 or over do have the option to restrict their profiles, as well as the option of merely allowing certain personal data to be restricted to people other than those on their "friends list." The full profiles of users under age 18 are restricted to direct MySpace friends only. Safety for children from sex offenders and others is of great concern. For example, a 2007 widely publicized case involved a teenage girl who committed suicide after she received extremely negative feedback from a "boy, " which was actually sent by the mother of the victim's former friend.

Globalization and Competition In 2006, News Corporation took MySpace to China, where it is spreading rapidly (in Chinese, of course). In Korea, a competitor, Cyworld (see Chapter 8), launched a U.S. version in 2006.

Other Issues. Other issues affecting MySpace are musicians' rights and the user agreement, social and cultural issues, and legal issues.

Revenue Model and Competition When News Corporation purchased MySpace in July 2005 for $580 million, many questioned the wisdom of paying so much for a site with no income and questionable advertisement revenue sources. However, in August 2006, Google paid MySpace $900 million for allowing Google to place its search and advertising on MySpace pages. This is helpful to MySpace, too, because now its users do not have to leave the site to conduct a Google search. MySpace also collects money from advertisers which do not use the Google system.

Major Capabilities

- Instant messenger (MySpace IM)
- Groups that can be easily created
- MySpace TV for video sharing
- MySpace Mobile is a service for accessing MySpace with mobile devices
- MySpace News is the display of news from RSS feeds submitted by users
- MySpace classifieds are for person-to-person advertising
- Others include: MySpace Books, MySpace Horoscopes, MySpace Jobs, and MySpace Movies

MySpace's major competitors in 2008 were Xanga, Bebo, Reunion, Friendster, and Facebook. See Chapter 8 for details.

Sources: Compiled from Hupfer et al. (2007), Sellers (2006), and *en.wikipedia.org/wiki/MySpace* (accessed April 2008).

For Further Exploration: Why does MySpace attract so many visitors? What are the benefits to MySpace and Google from their collaboration, and why is the company faced with so many implementation issues?

to socialize and even do business. An example is Second Life (*secondlife.com*), which is described in Chapter 8. There.com focuses more on social networking activities such as chatting, creating avatars, interacting playing, and meeting people. According to Rutledge (2008) there will be more than 20 million members in virtual worlds by 2010.

Business Activities and Value in Virtual Worlds. As businesses no longer only compete in the real world, they also compete in *virtual worlds*. Many companies and organizations now incorporate virtual worlds as a new form of advertising and sales (see the Scion Opening Case). An example of this would be Apple creating a virtual store within "Second Life." This allows the users to browse the latest and innovative products. You cannot actually purchase a product, but having these *virtual stores* is a way of accessing a different clientele and customer demographic. The use of advertising within virtual worlds is a relatively new idea. In the past, companies would use an advertising agency to promote their products. Using a virtual world, companies can reduce cost and time constraints by keeping this "in-house" (see *A Closer Look 1.3*).

Using virtual worlds gives companies the opportunity to gauge customer reaction and receive feedback about new products or services. This can be crucial as it will give the companies an insight as to what the market and customers want from new products, which can give them a competitive edge.

Social computing is an implementation of Web 2.0 technologies. A discussion of these technologies (such as blogs and wikis) is provided in Chapter 2. The strategic integration of Web 2.0 technologies into enterprises' intranet, extranet, and business processes results in what we call **Enterprise 2.0.** Enterprise 2.0 includes activities in enterprise social networking and virtual worlds, and it is growing exponentially.

Review Questions

1. Define social computing and list its types.
2. List some characteristics of social computing.
3. Define social networks services (SNSs).
4. What is an enterprise social network?
5. Define virtual worlds and list their characteristics.

A Closer Look 1.3

How Businesses Can Use Second Life

Example 1: Collaboration More than 2,000 IBM employees sign up as members of Second Life, using the site to share ideas and work on projects. IBM holds an "alumni block party" in Second Life, allowing current and former employees from around the globe to get together in virtual meetings. IBM purchases islands for use as meeting places and technology showcases, and for experiments in virtual reality business. IBM sets up a Circuit City store and a Sears appliance store (see attached photo) as virtual commerce demonstration projects.

Example 2: Market Research and Product/Service Design Starwood Hotels constructed a prototype of the new Aloft brand hotels before they appear in the real world in 2008. The company purchases two islands: Aloft, for the hotel prototype, and Argali, where visitors can view the development project. Working from a preliminary architectural sketch, the designers begin roughing out the layout, furnishings, and textures of the hotel, which are then refined in response to feedback from the brick-and-mortar architects and from Second Life visitors who were invited to critique design and layout. Developers begin remodeling the hotel in response to feedback from Second Life residents.

Source: Linden Research/Sipa Press/NewsCom.

1.6 Why Should You Learn About Information Technology?

In this part of the chapter, we describe some specific benefits you can derive from studying IT.

BENEFITS FROM STUDYING IT

A major role of IT is being an enabler and *facilitator* of organizational activities, processes, and change for increased performance and competitiveness. That role will become more important as time passes. Therefore, it is necessary that every manager and professional staff member learn about IT not only in his or her specialized field, but also in the entire organization and in interorganizational settings as well.

Obviously, you will be more effective in your chosen career if you understand how successful information systems are built, used, and managed. You also will be more effective if you know how to recognize and avoid unsuccessful systems and failures. Also, in many ways, having a comfort level with information technology will enable you, off the job and in your private life, to take advantage of new IT products and systems as they are developed. (Wouldn't you rather be the one explaining to friends how some new product works, than the one asking about it?) Finally, you should learn about IT because being knowledgeable about IT can also increase employment opportunities. Even though computerization eliminates some jobs, it also creates many more (Wolff, 2005, and Chabrow, 2006).

The demand for traditional staff—such as programmers, systems analysts, and designers—is substantial. In addition, many well-paid opportunities are appearing in emerging areas such as the Internet and e-commerce, m-commerce, network security, Web 2.0 and social networking, object-oriented programming, telecommunications, multimedia design, and document management. (See Online Brief 1.4 at the book's Web site for a more detailed listing of jobs in e-commerce.)

According to a study by the U.S. Bureau of Labor Statistics, four of the top ten fastest-growing occupations projected through 2016 fall within IT- or computer-related fields. These top four occupations are (Luftman, 2008) the following:

1. Network systems and data communications analysts
2. Computer applications software engineers
3. Computer systems analysts
4. Network and computer systems administrators

Dannen (2008) predicted that the IT job growth rate would double between 2008 and 2010.

At about $65,000 per year (and growing 4 to 5 percent yearly), workers in the software and information services industries were the highest-paid U.S. wage earners in 2008, about twice that of the average worker in the private sector. Furthermore, earnings of IT employees were growing twice as fast as those in the entire private sector. Thus, salaries for IT employees are generally high. For IT managers' salaries, see Murphy (2007). Furthermore, during the 2008 economic slowdown IT jobs hit record highs.

To exploit the high-paying opportunities in IT, a college degree in any of the following fields, or combination of them, is advisable: computer science, computer information systems (CIS), management information systems (MIS), e-commerce, and e-business. Within the last few years, many universities have started e-commerce or e-business degrees (e.g., see *is.cityu.edu.hk* and *cgu.edu*). Many schools offer graduate degrees with specialization in information technology.

Majoring in an IT-related field can be very rewarding. For example, students graduating with baccalaureate degrees in MIS usually earn the highest starting salaries of all undergraduate business majors (more than $48,000 per year). MBAs with experience in Web technologies and e-commerce are getting starting salaries of over $100,000/year, plus bonuses. Many students prefer a double major, one of which is MIS. Similarly, MBAs with an undergraduate degree in computer science have little difficulty getting well-paying jobs, even during recessionary times. Many MBA students select IS as a major, a second major, or an area of specialization. In addition, nondegree programs are also available on hundreds of topics. Top Chief Information Officers (CIOs) make $1 to 10 million annually (Nash, 2007). For details about careers in IT, see *unixl.com* and also "Career resources" and "Technology careers" at *wageweb.com* and Chabrow (2006).

Finally, another benefit from studying IT is that it may contribute to future organizational leadership. In the past, most CEOs came from the areas of finance and marketing. Lately, however, we see a trend to appoint CEOs who have strong IT knowledge and who have emerged from the technology area.

Review Questions

1. Why is IT a major enabler of business performance and success?
2. Explain why it is beneficial to study IT today?
3. Why might it be easier to find jobs in a functional area if you know more about IT?

1.7 Plan of the Book

A major objective of this book is to demonstrate how IT in general and Web systems in particular support different organizational activities. In addition, we will illustrate the role that networked computing plays in our society today and will play tomorrow. Furthermore, we describe how information systems should be developed, maintained, and managed.

The book is divided into seven parts. Figure 1.9 shows how the chapters are positioned in each part and how the parts are connected. Notice that in the center of the figure are the six Technology Guides. These guides can be found on the book's Web site (*wiley.com/college/turban*).

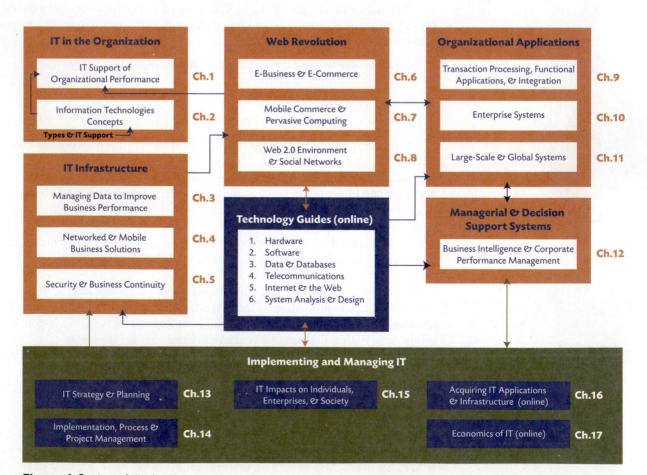

Figure 1.9 Plan of the book.

1.8 Managerial Issues

At the end of every chapter, you will find a list of some of the special concerns managers face as they adapt technology to their organization's needs.

1. Recognizing opportunities for using IT and Web-based systems for strategic advantage. These opportunities are highlighted and discussed in most chapters of the book, but especially in Chapters 6–14.

2. Who will build, operate, and maintain the information systems? This is a critical issue because management wants to minimize the cost of IT while maximizing its benefits. Some alternatives are to *outsource* portions, or even all, of the IT activities, and to divide the remaining work between the IS department and the end users. Details are provided in Chapters 13 through 16 and in Technology Guide 5.

3. How much IT? This is a critical issue related to IT planning. IT does not come free, but *not* having it may be much costlier. Chapters 12 and 13 deal with this issue.

4. What social networking activities should be pursued? The main decision to be made is whether to deploy a social networking application inside the organization or to use a public network such as Facebook (see Chapter 8).

5. How important is IT? In some cases, IT is the only approach that can help organizations. As time passes, the *comparative advantage* of IT increases.

GLOBAL

6. Globalization. Global competition will have an impact on many companies. However, globalization opens many opportunities, ranging from selling and buying products and services online in foreign markets, to conducting joint ventures or investing in them. IT supports communications, collaboration, and discovery of information regarding all of the above (Chapter 11).

ETHICS

7. Ethics and social issues. The implementation of IT involves many ethical and social issues that are constantly changing due to new developments in technologies and environments. These topics should be examined any time an IT project is undertaken.

8. Transforming the organization to the digital economy. The transformation can be done on several fronts. Management should study the opportunities, consider alternatives, and prioritize them. Large companies may consider proprietary services from companies such as HP.

How *IT* Benefits You

Now that you have a sense of how this book is structured and organized, we'll conclude the chapter by discussing how and why IT is relevant to students with various business-related majors. As you review this section, keep in mind that technology is playing an increasingly vital role in every department and business process of modern organizations.

Accounting Major

Data and information are the lifeblood of accounting. Therefore, many students double major in accounting/information systems. For those that do not, it is critical to keep up with new IT developments. Both groups, however, need to know the IT needs of the other functional areas. The Internet has vastly increased the number of transactions (especially global) in which modern businesses engage. Transactions such as billing customers, preparing payrolls, and purchasing and paying for materials provide data that the accounting department must record and track. These transactions, particularly with customers and suppliers, now usually take place online. Finally, security of information systems and their auditing are extremely important.

Finance Major

The modern financial world turns on speed, volume, and accuracy of information flow. Information systems and networks make these things possible. You invest in stocks and get a confirmation in less than a second. Finance departments use information systems such as business intelligence to monitor world financial markets and to provide quantitative analyses (e.g., for cash flow projections and budgetary control). They use computerized analysis to support financial decision making (e.g., portfolio management). Financial managers use data mining software to analyze information in data warehouses. Finally, large-scale enterprise information systems (e.g., enterprise resource planning packages) tightly integrate finance with all other functional areas.

Human Resources Management Major

Information systems provide valuable support for human resources (HR) management. For example, personnel record keeping has greatly improved in terms of speed, convenience, and accuracy as a result of technology. Further, disseminating HR information throughout the company via intranets enables employees to receive consistent information and handle much of their personal business (e.g., configuring their benefits) without help from HR personnel. The Internet revolutionized recruiting (e.g., online and in social networks) and training, moving them online; better selection can be made as well as personnel development.

IS Major

The Information Systems Department (ISD) directly supports all other functional areas in an organization. The overall objective of IS personnel is to help users increase performance and solve business problems using IT. The IS function is rapidly changing its role from computer programming to that of a major strategic player.

While some IS employees still write computer programs, they also act as analysts, interfacing between business users on one hand and the programmers or vendors on the other.

Marketing Major

Marketing now uses customer databases, decision support systems, sales force automation, business intelligence, and data mining software to better perform its functions. The Internet has created an entirely new global trading environment and extensive Internet marketing. It also has dramatically increased the amount of information available to buyers and sellers, who can now compare prices quickly and thoroughly. As a result, shoppers' buying habits and strategies are changing. In turn, marketing managers must work harder to acquire and retain the well-informed customers. To accomplish this goal they now use customer relationship management software and special online promotions. The Internet helps here, because it provides for much closer contact between the customer and the supplier, as well as one-to-one seller/buyer relationship. Of special interest are the new advertising approaches in social network services.

Operations Management Major

Organizations are competing on price, quality, time (speed), and customer service—all of which are concerns of productions and operations management. Every process in a company's operations that adds value to a product or service (e.g., purchasing inventory, quality control, receiving raw materials, and shipping products) can be enhanced by the use of Web-based information systems. Production is changing from mass production to on-demand mass customization. Further, information systems have enabled the OM function to link the organization to other organizations along the firm's supply chain. Performance in manufacturing can be significantly increased with IT support.

Key Terms

Chapter Highlights

(Numbers Refer to Learning Objectives)

❶ The world is moving to a digital economy, which can be viewed as a major economic, societal, and organizational revolution. This revolution automates business processes by using the Internet, intranets, VANs, and extranets to connect organizations and people.

❶ The digital economy is characterized by extensive use of information technology in general and the Internet in particular. These drive new business models that dramatically reduce cost and increase quality, customer service, and speed.

❶ Companies are trying to transform themselves to e-businesses by converting their information systems to Web-based and by automating as many business processes as possible.

❷ An information system collects, processes, stores, and disseminates information for a specific purpose. A computer-based information system uses computers to perform some or all of these activities.

❷ Information technology refers to the network of all information systems in an organization.

❸ Business performance management (BPM) is a cyclical process that begins with mission statement, goals, and targets, and then the strategy and plans of how to attain the targets. After measuring actual performance, one needs to compare it to the target. Finally, if a negative gap exists, corrective actions should be taken.

❸ Many market, technology, and societal pressures surround the modern organization, which is responding with critical response activities supported by information technology.

❸ An accelerated rate of technological change, complexity, and turbulence and a move toward a global economy today characterize the business environment. In addition, the competition faced by businesses is ever increasing.

❸ Organizational responses include strategic information systems, continuous improvements, business process restructuring, electronic commerce, and business alliances. IT plays a major role in all of these.

❹ To succeed or even survive, organizations must be able to adapt to quick and frequent changes. IT enables organizations to become adaptive.

❹ IT is a major enabler of strategic systems. It can support organizational strategy or act as a direct strategic weapon.

❺ Social computing is a major shift in computing and provides organizations with the most innovative opportunities for advertising, marketing, and collaboration.

❻ Learning about IT is essential because the role of IT is rapidly increasing in the support of organizations. We are getting more dependent on IT as time passes. Also, more IT-related jobs with high salaries are available.

Virtual Company Assignment

Starting Your Internship at The Wireless Café

Go to The Wireless Café's link on the Student Web Site. There you will find a description of your internship at this restaurant, as well some assignments that will help you learn more about how IT solutions could help the restaurant improve its business.

Instructions for accessing The Wireless Café on the Student Web Site:

1. Go to *wiley.com/college/turban*.
2. Select Turban/Volonino's *Information Technology for Management*, 7th Edition.
3. Click on Student Resources site, in the toolbar on the left.
4. Click on the link for Virtual Company Web site.
5. Click on Wireless Café.

Questions for Discussion

1. Discuss the motivation for becoming an e-business.
2. Review the examples of the new versus the old economy cases. In what way did IT make the difference?
3. Explain why IT is a business pressure and also an enabler of response activities that counter business pressures.
4. Why are there more opportunities for entrepreneurs in the digital economy?
5. It is said that networked computing and the Web change the way we live, work, and study. Why?
6. Explain the sequence of events in the business performance management model (Figure 1.5).
7. Why is the Internet said to be the creator of new business models?
8. Discuss why some information systems fail.

9. Relate the real-time enterprise to the adaptive enterprise.
10. Enter *scion.com* and check into "Little Deviant." Check the content of two chapters and explain your experience with the advergame.
11. Is the strategy to target children really worthwhile? Find additional research on this topic (see Scion opening case).
12. Examine Scion's presence in two different virtual worlds. Summarize your experience from an advertising point of view.
13. Explain why business process management is a cyclical process.
14. Describe the commerce activities in social networking.

Exercises and Projects

1. Review the examples of IT applications in Section 1.1, and identify the business pressures in each example. Also identify the business models used.

2. The market for optical copiers is shrinking rapidly. It is expected that by 2012 as much as 90 percent of all duplicated documents will be done on computer printers. Can a company such as Xerox Corporation survive?
   a. Read about the problems and solutions of Xerox in 2000–2008 at *fortune.com*, *findarticles.com*, and *google.com*.
   b. Identify all of the business pressures on Xerox.
   c. Find some of Xerox's response strategies (see *xerox.com*, *yahoo.com*, and *google.com*).

   d. Identify the role of IT as a contributor to the business technology pressures (e.g., obsolescence).
   e. Identify the role of IT as a facilitator of the critical response activities.

3. The group's mission is to explore the role of IT in support of agility and innovation. Check what the Advanced Practices Council (APC) of the Society for Information Management (SIM) is doing in this area. Also check MIT Center for Information Systems Research (*mitsloan.mit.edu/cisr*) and other sources. Prepare a report.

Group Assignments and Projects

1. Create an online group for studying IT or a part of it you are interested in. Each member of the group must have a Yahoo e-mail account (free). Go to Yahoo: Groups (*groups.yahoo.com*) and at the bottom see a section titled "Create your own Group."
   Step 1: Click on "Start a Group Now."
   Step 2: Select a category that best describes your group (use the Search Group Categories, or use Browse Group Categories tool). You *must* find a category.
   Step 3: Describe the purposes of the group and give it a name.
   Step 4: Set up an e-mail address for sending messages to all group members.
   Step 5: Each member must join the group (select a "profile"); click on "Join this Group."
   Step 6: Go to Word Verification Section; follow instructions.
   Step 7: Finish by clicking "Continue."
   Step 8: Select a group moderator. Conduct a discussion online of at least two topics of the group's interest.
   Step 9: Arrange for messages from the members to reach the moderator at least once a week.
   Step 10: Find a similar group (use Yahoo's "find a group" and make a connection). Write a report for your instructor.

2. Enter *teradatastudentnetwork.com* (ask your instructor for a password). Find the Web Seminar "Turning Active Enterprise Intelligence into Competitive Advantage," by Imhoff, Hawkings, and Lee (2006). Identify the business environment pressures and real-time responses. Finally, identify how business intelligence strategies (Chapters 2 and 12) can support the organizations described. Prepare a report.

3. Review the *Wall Street Journal, Fortune, Business Week,* and local newspapers of the last three months to find stories about the use of Web-based technologies in organizations. Each group will prepare a report describing five applications. The reports should emphasize the role of the Web and its benefit to the organizations. Cover issues discussed in this chapter, such as productivity, quality, cycle time, and globalization. One of the groups should concentrate on m-commerce and another on electronic marketplaces. Present and discuss your work.

4. Identify Web-related new business models in the areas of the group's interests. Identify radical changes in the operation of the functional areas (accounting, finance, marketing, etc.), and tell the others about them.

5. Enter Facebook, MySpace, and Second Life. Find out ten different commercial activities conducted by corporations (e.g., advertise, sell, recruit, collaborate). Be specific.

Internet Exercises

1. Enter the Web site of UPS (*ups.com*).
   a. Find out what information is available to customers before they send a package.
   b. Find out about the "package tracking" system; be specific.
   c. Compute the cost of delivering a $10'' \times 20'' \times 15''$ box, weighing 40 pounds, from your hometown to Long Beach, California. Compare the fastest delivery against the least cost.
   d. Prepare a spreadsheet for two different types of calculations available on the site. Enter data and solve for two different calculators. Use Excel.

2. Enter *digitalenterprise.org*. Prepare a report regarding the latest EC models and developments in the digital age.

3. Visit some Web sites that offer employment opportunities in IT (such as *execunet.com* and *monster.com*). Compare the IT salaries to salaries offered to accountants. For other information on IT salaries, check *Computerworld's* annual salary survey and *unixl.com*.

4. Prepare a short report on the role of information technology in government. Start with *whitehouse.gov/omb/ego, e-government.govt.nz,* and

worldbank.org/egov. Find e-government plans in Hong Kong and in Singapore (*igov.gov.sg*; check action plan).

5. Enter *h71028.www7.hp.com/enterprise/cache/483789-0-0-0-121.html* and find out what IT solutions are offered to enable the adaptive enterprise. Write a summary.

6. Enter *x-home.com* and find information about the easy life of the future.

7. Enter *tellme.com* and *bevocal.com*. Observe the demos. Write a report on the benefits of such technologies.

8. Enter *dell.com* and configure the computer of your dreams. (You do not have to buy it.) What are the advantages of such configuration? Any disadvantages?

Minicase

IS   SVR

Dartmouth College Goes Wireless

Dartmouth College, one of the oldest in the United States (founded in 1769), was one of the first to embrace the wireless revolution. Operating and maintaining a campus-wide information system with wires is very difficult, since there are 161 buildings with more than 1,000 rooms on campus. In 2000, the college introduced a campus-wide wireless network that includes more than 500 Wi-Fi (wireless fidelity; see Chapter 4) systems. By the end of 2002, the entire campus became a fully wireless, always-connected community—a microcosm that provides a peek at what neighborhood and organizational life may look like for the general population in just a few years.

To transform a wired campus to a wireless one requires lots of money. A computer science professor who initiated the idea at Dartmouth in 1999 decided to solicit the help of alumni working at Cisco Systems. These alumni arranged for a donation of the initial system, and Cisco then provided more equipment at a discount. (Cisco and other companies now make similar donations to many colleges and universities, writing off the difference between the retail and the discount prices for an income tax benefit.)

As a pioneer in campus-wide wireless, Dartmouth has made many innovative usages of the system, some of which are the following:

- Students are continuously developing new applications for the Wi-Fi. For example, one student has applied for a patent on a personal-security device that pinpoints the location of campus emergency services to one's mobile device.

- Students no longer have to remember campus phone numbers, as their mobile devices have all the numbers and can be accessed any time from anywhere on campus.

- Students primarily use laptop computers on the network. However, an increasing number of Internet-enabled PDAs and cell phones are used as well.

- An extensive messaging system is used by the students, who send SMSs to each other. Messages reach the recipients in a split second, any time, anywhere, as long as they are sent and received within the network's coverage area. This is in addition to text messages provided by the regular cell phone provider.

- Usage of the Wi-Fi system is not confined just to messages. Students can submit their class work by using the network, as well as by watching streaming video and listening to Internet radio.

- An analysis of wireless traffic on campus showed how the new network is changing and shaping campus behavior patterns. For example, students log on in short bursts, about 16 minutes at a time, probably checking their messages. They tend to plant themselves in a few favorite spots (dorms, TV room, student center, and on a shaded bench on the green) where they use their computers, and they rarely connect beyond those places.

- Some students have invented special complex wireless games that they play online.

- One student has written a code that calculates how far away a networked PDA user is from his or her next appointment, and then automatically adjusts the PDA's reminder alarm schedule accordingly.

- Professors are using wireless-based teaching methods. For example, students can evaluate material presented in class and can vote online on a multiple-choice questionnaire relating to the presented material. Tabulated results are shown in seconds, promoting discussions. According to faculty, the system "makes students want to give answers," thus significantly increasing participation.

- Faculty and students have developed a special voice-over-IP application for PDAs and iPAQs that uses live two-way voice-over-IP chat.

Driven by the need for centralized wireless management, privacy protection, and high level of security options, Dartmouth selected Aruba Networks for a massive infrastructure upgrade that would adapt to the changing wireless environment. The Wi-Fi network is built to support voice, cable TV, and data along other wireless services by Aruba's wireless technology. With voice, video, and data running over its Wi-Fi, Dartmouth improves its ability to quickly supply multi-media services to students and faculty at any time in any place while reducing capital and operational costs from physical cabling changes that must be made.

Sources: Compiled from McHugh (2002), Hafner (2003), *Internet Ad Sales* (2005), and *dartmouth.edu* (April 2008).

Questions

1. In what ways is the Wi-Fi technology changing the life of Dartmouth students? Relate your answer to the concept of the digital society.

2. Some say that the wireless system will become part of the background of everybody's life—that the mobile devices are just an afterthought. Explain.

3. Is the system contributing to improved learning, or just adding entertainment that may reduce the time available for studying? Debate your point of view with students who hold different opinions.

4. What are the major benefits of the wireless system over the previous wireline one? Do you think wireline systems will disappear from campuses one day? (Do some research on the topic.)

5. Relate this case to the book's performance management model.

Problem-Solving Activity

Saving the Family Business

Healthbeau (fictitious name) is a family-owned business in Middletown, a small town of 20,000 people. Founded in 1983, the business provides health food, nature-based beauty products, and nature-based medicines. It grew rapidly in the 1990s when people became more nature-oriented and health conscious. Both revenue and profits were growing and the company added space and opened another store in town.

However, things changed since 2001. First, the local supermarkets started to offer organic produce at lower prices. Second, the local drug store began offering herb-based and other nature-based vitamins and medicine also at lower prices. As a result, both sales and profits declined. In 2005, the company started to lose customers at an accelerated rate, especially the young customers. A quick investigation revealed that customers were buying competing products over the Internet in the convenience of their homes and at lower prices. The company had its first loss in 2005. The losses widened in 2006 when sales declined further, forcing the closure of the second store. By 2008 the trend had become clear: it was getting worse and worse.

You are the youngest child in the family and have just started taking a course on IT for management. The family has asked for your help. You just finished reading Chapter 1 and you understand that the problem stems from the environ-

mental pressures including Internet marketing. Can you help your family?

Here is what we suggest you do:

1. Identify the business pressures that caused the problem.

2. Solicit suggestions from your family and friends as to possible responses.

3. Open a home page at *facebook.com* (it is free) and ask for help. Describe what is going on in the business and *request* suggestions from your new friends about what to do.

4. Check how similar small businesses use Facebook, MySpace, and YouTube to improve their operations in similar situations.

5. Go to *linkedin.com* and see if you can solicit any ideas on what to do.

6. Use *google.com* to find sources on small businesses and surf their Web sites for any clues on possible solutions.

7. Prepare a report titled "Saving Healthbeau" in which you recommend what your family should do and what part IT should play in supporting your suggestions. Estimate the cost of providing your solution and state the assumptions you made in your estimates. Send a copy to your professor.

Online Resources

More resources and study tools are located on the Student Web site and on WileyPLUS. You'll find additional chapter materials and useful Web links. In addition, self-quizzes that provide individualized feedback are available for each chapter.

Online Briefs for Chapter 1 are available at wiley.com/college/turban:

1.1 Environmental Business Pressures

1.2 Typical Organizational Responses to Environmental Pressures

1.3 The HP Model of Building Adaptive Enterprise

1.4 Jobs in Electronic Commerce

Online Minicases for Chapter 1 are available at wiley.com/college/turban:

1.1 Diamonds Forever—Online

1.2 A Digital Hospital Increases Performance and Saves Lives

References

Blakely, L., "Making Their Point," *Business 2.0*, April 23, 2007.

Bosman, J., "Hey, Kid, You Want to Buy a Toyota Scion?" *The New York Times*, June 14, 2006. *nytimes.com/2006/06/14/business/media/14adco.html?_r=2&oref=slogin&oref=slogin* (accessed April 2008).

Brandon, J., "Disney Fast-Forwards into the Digital Age" *Baseline Magazine*, July 2008.

Chabrow, E., "The Management Boom," *InformationWeek*, October 2, 2006.

Claburn, T., "Pakistan Blocks YouTube, Puts Blinders on the World," *InformationWeek*, February 25, 2008. *informationweek.com/news/internet/showArticle.jhtml;jsessionid=DWXUMKL2WZQQSQSNDLOSKHSCJUNN2JVN?articleID=206900017&_requested=308045* (accessed April 2008).

Dannen, C., "What Are the Top Jobs of 2008?" *MSNBC*, February 22, 2008. *msnbc.msn.com/id/23037164* (accessed April 2008).

Dartmouth.edu (accessed April 2008).

Duvall, M., "Boston Red Sox: Backstop Your Business," *Baseline*, May 14, 2004.

Duvall, M., "Monsanto Grows Green," *Baseline*, November 29, 2007a.

Duvall, M., "Playing By the Numbers: Baseball and BI," *Baseline*, October 29, 2007b.

Hafner, K., "A New Kind of Revolution in the Dorms of Dartmouth," *The New York Times*, September 23, 2003.

Harrington, R., "The Transformer" (e-mail interview with *Baseline*'s editor-in-chief, J. McCormic), *Baseline*, April 2006.

Heller, R., "SWOT: Assess the Strengths and Weaknesses of Your Business, as Well as the Opportunities and Threats, with SWOT Analysis," *Thinking Managers*, July 8, 2006. *thinkingmanagers.com/management/strengths-weaknesses.php* (accessed April 2008).

Hupfer, R., et al., *MySpace for Dummies*, Hoboken, NJ: Wiley Publishing, Inc., 2007.

Internet Ad Sales, "Dartmouth College Chooses Aruba Networks for Deployment of Nation's Largest University Wi-Fi System," February 28, 2005. *internetadsales.com/modules/news/article.php?storyid=4809* (accessed April 2008).

Jetpens.com (accessed April 2008).

Koch, C., "Nike Rebounds," *CIO.com*, December 7, 2004. *cio.com.au/index.php/id;1800426724;fp;4;fpid;19* (accessed April 2008).

Luftman, J., "Yes, the Tech Talent Shortage Is Real," *InformationWeek*, January 12, 2008.

MarketingVox.com, "Automakers Look to Create Own Broadband Channels," July 10, 2007a. *marketingvox.com/archives/2007/07/10/automakers-look-to-create-own-broadband-channels* (accessed April 2008).

MarketingVox.com, "Scion Joins Fourth - Yes, Fourth - Virtual World," August 16, 2007b. *marketingvox.com/scion-joins-fourth-yes-fourth-virtual-world-032282* (accessed April 2008).

MarketingVox.com, "Scion's Online Strategy Favors Niche Over Reach," July 5, 2007c. *marketingvox.com/scions-online-strategy-favors-niche-over-reach-031136* (accessed April 2008).

McHugh, J., "Unplugged U.," *Wired*, October 2002.

McKay, J., and P. Marshall, *Strategic Management of E-Business*, Milton Old, Australia: John Wiley & Sons, 2004.

MediaBuyerPlanner.com, "Toyota Targets Kids, Hopes to Influence Parents," June 14, 2006. *mediabuyerplanner.com/2006/06/14/toyota_targets_kids_hopes_to* (accessed April 2008).

Murphy, C., "The Six-Figure Club," *InformationWeek*, April 30, 2007.

Nash, K. S., "When the CIO Earns $9M," *CIO Insight*, July 17, 2007. *cioinsight.com/c/a/Past-News/When-The-CIO-Earns-9M-%5B2%5D* (accessed April 2008).

Nike.com Press releases 2002, 2003 Not online any more.

Porter, M. E., "Strategy and the Internet," *Harvard Business Review*, March 2001.

Rodgers, Z., "Scion Goes Urban, Eschewing Big Reach Buys," *Clickz.com*, July 3, 2007, *clickz.com/showPage.html?page=3626318* (accessed April 2008).

Rutledge P.A., *Profiting from Social Networking*, Upper Saddle River, NJ: FT Press, 2008.

Schuman, E., "Five Innovations Changing Retail," *Baseline*, December 2007.

Scion.com (accessed April 2008).

Sellers, P., "MySpace Cowboys," *Fortune*, September 4, 2006.

Sterlicchi, J., and E. Wales, "Custom Chaos: How Nike Just Did It Wrong," *Business Online* (*BolWeb.com*), June 2001.

Turban, E., et al., *Electronic Commerce: A Managerial Perspective*, 4th ed., Upper Saddle River, NJ: Prentice–Hall, 2008.

Watson, B., "Cool Cash," *Baseline*, October 29, 2007.

Whelan, D., "Only the Paranoid Resurge," *Forbes*, April 10, 2006.

Wolff, E. N., "The Growth of Information Workers in the U.S. Economy," *Communications of the ACM*, October 2005.

Learning Objectives

After studying this chapter, you will be able to:

❶ Define information systems and describe various types of information systems and categorize specific systems you observe.

❷ Relate and contrast transaction processing and functional information systems.

❸ Identify the major enterprise internal support systems and relate them to managerial functions.

❹ Analyze the support IT provides to people in different roles in the organization.

❺ Describe the support IT provides to business processes and the supply chain.

❻ Explain information infrastructure and different types of information architectures.

❼ Distinguish the major types of Web-based information systems and understand their functionalities.

❽ Describe emerging information technologies.

❾ Analyze innovative and futuristic IT systems and applications.

Integrating *IT*

 ACC   **FIN**   **MKT**   **OM**   **HRM**   **IS**

IT-PERFORMANCE MODEL

In this chapter we focus on the essentials of IT systems and on the support they provide to people so the performance and productivity of enterprises, managers, and data workers can be improved.

The business performance management cycle and IT model.

MARY KAY'S IT SYSTEMS

Founded in 1962, Mary Kay (*marykay.com*) has about 1.8 million consultants (independent sales force people) selling its cosmetics and fragrances in 34 countries. In 2006, the company had about $2.3 billion in wholesale sales.

Because the company has based its reputation on personal contacts in door-to-door visits and home gatherings, it may seem that computerized systems would be the last way the company would benefit. Actually, the opposite is true. Currently, more than 95 percent of Mary Kay's independent sales force people place orders via the Internet, a major change that has occurred since 2003.

The Problem/Opportunity

The cosmetics market is very competitive, but it is growing rapidly, especially in developing countries. Mary Kay's business model enables rapid growth into new markets. By the early 2000s it became clear that the then existing information system, a combination of home-grown and packaged applications installed over time, no longer met the users' needs. Also, the consultants faced an increasing demand for Internet use as more and more customers started to shop online. With a long and global supply chain (which offered more products to customers worldwide) and the need to manage almost 2 million consultants, it was clear that a major overhaul of the information systems was needed. The company, over the years, had cobbled together different systems to handle such tasks as incident handling, asset management, and change management. But the systems did not communicate with each other, making a comprehensive picture of the company's IT infrastructure nearly impossible. Finally, it became clear that the emergence of social computing might provide a golden opportunity for Internet marketing by the company.

The IT Solutions

The IT department is split into three divisions: e-commerce, supply chain (Tutorial #1), and back office support (for order fulfillment, accounting, and finance). For the makeover, the company focused on e-commerce because of the contact with sales consultants.

The first major IT project was the introduction of a technology called *business service management*. **Business service management (BSM)** is the concept of how to connect IT departments to the ultimate customer. In Mary Kay it became a way to connect with the consultants. To this end, a study of the business processes and the workflow (Chapter 14) was conducted. This study identified three core areas that have a significant impact on the business: downtime associated with incident and problem management, changes to the IT application systems and other infrastructure components, and the management of the IT assets.

Then goals and objectives were set based on the industry best practices. As you recall from Figure 1.5 in Chapter 1, once we know "where we want to be," it is necessary to determine how to get there and to find out "where we actually are," and see how big the gap is. Then we must use a strategy and planning to close the gap. This is exactly what was done with the help of BSM (from Maryville Technologies). The solution included an electronic service desk that ensures consultants in 30 countries are served in a standardized way. Then a global electronic ordering system called Atlas, between the consultants and the company warehouses, was introduced. A data repository that dynamically maintains a logical model of the IT environment allows Mary Kay IT staff to access a consolidated view of the entire IT environment.

Use of Social Computing. Mary Kay and its consultants are making extensive use of social computing. Representative examples are the following:

- The company posts job opening announcements on several sites including MySpace Jobs (*jobs.myspace.com*).
- Movies and videotapes about the company and its products are available on YouTube (*youtube.com*) and on *movies.go.com*.
- Several blogs are available both for and against the company (e.g., *marykayandrews.com/blog*). The company tries to counter the negative comments.
- Auctions and fixed price items are available for sale on eBay.

- For the millions of shoppers, Mary Kay provides a consultant locator on the Internet (*marykay.com/locator*).

Extensive hardware and software infrastructure supports all of the above, including a wireless remote management system at the 760,000-square-foot corporate headquarters (in Dallas, TX), an extensive wide area network (WAN, see Chapter 4), and a large data center. Some of the information systems are used enterprisewide (e.g., service desk, ticketing system for events, and service requests). Others are functional (e.g., accounting, finance, marketing, and inventory control). The company uses an intranet for its internal communications as well as hundreds of applications corporatewide. Finally, productivity software is available for the consultants' personal use from MSM Technologies (*msmtech.com*).

In addition to providing better IT support to consultants, the IT produced other benefits such as greater efficiency, reduced costs and downtime, and improved service. For example, IT staff members now have a shared language and can view, on a single screen, information that previously required 10 separate reports. The new technology also enabled the reduction in the number of computer servers, which saved money—not only in terms of hardware and maintenance, but also in terms of administrative burdens and data center space. In terms of human resources, it allowed the company to handle its rapid growth without a substantial increase in staffing. The changes also allowed IT personnel to focus on strategic tasks. Mary Kay found that its engineers and technical people now have time to spend on innovative engineering options.

Sources: Compiled from Rubin (2007), *Channel Insider* (2007), *LGC Wireless* (2008), Dubie (2006), and *marykay.com* (accessed April 2008).

Lessons Learned from This Case

This case demonstrates the need for computerized support and the variety of systems and networks employed by Mary Kay and its independent consultants. You will notice that systems are available for different types of users (employees, consultants, customers) and for different purposes (sales, finance, collaboration, advertising, social networking, and more). The systems range from small (supporting one person) to enterprise and global systems used for communication and controls. These types of systems and the support they provide are the major topics of this chapter, which also presents the basic concepts of information systems and their components as well as innovative and futuristic information systems.

2.1 Information Systems: Concepts and Definitions

In Chapter 1 we defined an **information system (IS)** as one that collects, processes, stores, analyzes, and disseminates data and information for a specific purpose. The composition of information systems is usually the same: each contains hardware, software, data, procedures, networks, and people. Key elements of a simple desktop information system are shown in the nearby photo.

Another possible component of an information system is one or more smaller information systems. Information systems that contain smaller systems are typical of large companies. For example, FedEx's corporate information system contains hundreds of smaller information systems (see the case at the end of Part I), which are referred to as "applications." An **application program** is a computer program designed to support a specific task or a business process (such as execute the payroll) or, in some cases, to support another application program.

Source: istockphoto.com

There are dozens of applications in each functional area. For instance, in managing human resources, it is possible to find one application for screening job applicants and another for monitoring employee turnover. Some of the applications might be completely independent of each other, whereas others are interrelated. The collection of application programs in a single department is usually considered a *departmental information system,* even though it is made up of many applications. For example, the collection of application programs in the human resources area is called the *human resources information system (HRIS).*

Information systems are usually connected by means of *electronic networks.* The connecting networks can be *wireline* and/or *wireless.* Information systems can connect an entire organization, or even multiple organizations.

Before we focus on the details of IT and its management, it is necessary to describe the major concepts of information systems and organize the IT systems in some logical manner. That is the major purpose of this chapter.

DATA, INFORMATION, AND KNOWLEDGE

Information systems are built to attain several goals. One of the primary goals is to economically process data into information or knowledge. Let us define these concepts:

Data items refer to an elementary description of things, events, activities, and transactions that are recorded, classified, and stored, but not organized to convey any specific meaning. Data items can be numeric, alphanumeric, figures, sounds, or images. A student grade in a class is a data item, and so is the number of hours an employee worked in a certain week. A **database** consists of stored data items organized for retrieval.

Information is data that has been organized so that they have meaning and value to the recipient. For example, a student's grade point average is information about the student's overall performance. The recipient interprets the meaning and draws conclusions and implications from the information. A video posted at YouTube.com can be considered information. Data items typically are processed into information by means of an application. Such processing represents a more specific use and a higher added value than simple retrieval and summarization from a database. The application might be a Web-based inventory management system, a university online registration system, or an Internet-based buying and selling system.

Finally, **knowledge** consists of data and/or information that have been organized and processed to convey understanding, experience, accumulated learning, and expertise as they apply to a current problem or activity. For example, the GPA of a student applying to a graduate school can provide an admissions officer with the knowledge of how good the student is only when it is compared with the GPAs of other students and schools. Knowledge can be expressed in all types of data and information. For example, there are many videos from which to learn. Data that are processed to extract critical implications and to reflect past experiences and expertise provide the recipient with *organizational knowledge,* which has a very high potential value.

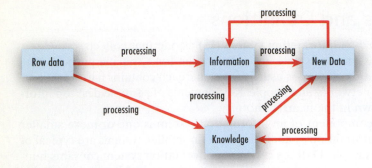

Figure 2.1 The relationship among data, information, and knowledge.

Knowledge is an important enterprise resource and needs to be managed (see Chapter 10 for more on how this is accomplished).

Data, information, and knowledge can be *inputs* to an information system, and they can also be *outputs*. For example, data about employees, their wages, and time worked are processed as inputs in order to produce an organization's payroll information (output). The payroll information itself can later be used as an input to another system that prepares a budget or advises management on salary scales or recruiting strategy.

The relationship between data, information, and knowledge is illustrated in Figure 2.1.

As can be seen in the figure, raw data is processed to information and/or to knowledge. Information can be processed to knowledge, but it may generate data as well.

INFORMATION SYSTEMS CONFIGURATIONS

Information systems are made of components that can be assembled in many different configurations, resulting in a variety of information systems and applications, much as construction materials can be assembled to build different types and shapes of homes. The size and cost of a home depend on the purpose of the building, the availability of money, and constraints such as ecological, environmental, and legal requirements. Just as there are many different types of houses, so there are many different types of information systems. We classify houses as single-family homes, apartments (or flats), townhouses, and cottages. Similarly, it is useful to classify information systems into groups that share similar characteristics. Such a classification may help in identifying systems, analyzing them, planning new systems, planning integration of systems, and making decisions such as the possible outsourcing of systems. This classification can be done in several alternative ways, as shown next.

Review Questions

1. Define *information system*.
2. What is an *application program*?
3. Define *data*, *information*, and *knowledge*.
4. What types of information systems are used at Mary Kay?

2.2 Classification and Types of Information Systems

Information systems are classified in this section by organizational levels and by the type of support provided. This classification shows the diversity of systems as well. The classification can be used as a guide for the content of this book.

CLASSIFICATION BY ORGANIZATIONAL LEVELS

Organizations are made up of components such as divisions, departments, and work units, organized in hierarchical levels. For example, most organizations have functional departments, such as marketing and accounting, which report to plant management, which in turn reports to a division head. The divisions report to the corporate headquarters. Although some organizations have restructured themselves in innovative ways, such as those based on cross-functional teams (i.e., a team composed of members from two or more departments), today the vast majority of organizations still have a traditional hierarchical structure. Thus, we can find information systems built according to this hierarchy. Such systems can stand alone, but usually they are interconnected.

The organizational levels that are supported by information systems are shown in Figure 2.2 as a triangle. The following are the specific levels recognized (from bottom up).

Personal and Productivity Systems. These are small systems that are built to support many individuals. Known as **personal information management (PIM),** such a

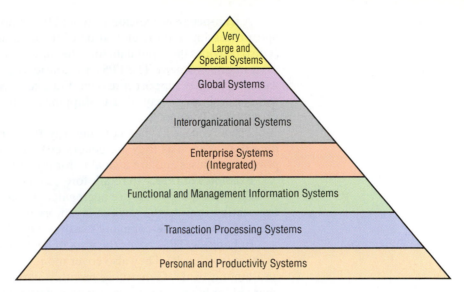

Figure 2.2 Levels of information systems.

system intends to support the activities we, as individuals, perform to ease our work or life, through the acquisition, organization, maintenance, retrieval, and sharing of information. An example of such systems are the systems that support the consultants at Mary Kay. A popular PIM tool is the personal digital assistant (PDA), with functions such as calendars, calculators, schedulers, and computer memory. End-user decision support systems built with Excel is another example. Such systems are designed to increase our productivity and satisfaction. Such systems are abundant in organizations, are inexpensive, and have fairly standard capabilities.

Transaction Processing Systems. Any organization that performs periodic financial, accounting, and other routine business activities faces repetitive information processing tasks. For example, employees are paid at regular intervals, customers place purchase orders and are billed, and expenses are monitored and compared to the budget. Table 2.1 presents a list of representative routine, repetitive business transactions in a manufacturing organization. The information system that supports such processes is called the *transaction processing system*.

TABLE 2.1	Routine Business Transactions in a Manufacturing Company
Payroll and personnel	Employee time cards
	Employee pay and deductions
	Payroll checks
	Fringe benefits
Purchasing	Purchase orders
	Deliveries
	Payments (accounts payable)
Finance and accounting	Financial statements
	Tax records
	Expense accounts
Sales	Sales records
	Invoices and billings
	Accounts receivable
	Sales returns
	Shipping
Production	Production reports
	Quality control reports
Inventory management	Material usage
	Inventory levels

A **transaction processing system (TPS)** supports the monitoring, collection, storage, processing, and dissemination of the organization's basic business transactions. It also provides the input data for other information systems. Sometimes several TPSs exist in one company. The TPSs are considered critical to the success of any organization since they support core operations, such as purchasing of materials, billing customers, preparing a payroll, and shipping goods to customers. The details of TPSs are provided in Chapter 9.

The TPS collects data continuously, frequently on a daily basis, or even in *real time* (i.e., as soon as they are generated). Most of these data are stored in the corporate databases and are available for processing.

Examples of TPSs. In retail stores, data flow from point-of-sale (POS) terminals to a database where they are aggregated. When a sale is completed, an information transaction reduces the level of inventory on hand, and the collected revenue from the sale increases the company's cash position.

In banking, TPSs cover the area of deposits and withdrawals (which are similar to inventory levels). They also cover money transfers between accounts in the bank and among banks. Generating monthly statements for customers and setting fees charged for bank services are also typical transaction-processing activities for a bank.

Functional and Management Information Systems. The transaction-processing systems cover the core activities of an organization. The *functional areas,* however, cover many other activities; some of these are repetitive, while others are only occasional. For example, the human resources department hires, advises, and trains people. Each of these tasks can be divided into subtasks. Training may involve selecting topics to teach, selecting people to participate in the training, scheduling classes, finding teachers, and preparing class materials. These tasks and subtasks are frequently supported by information systems specifically designed to support functional activities.

The primary functional information systems are organized around the traditional departments in a company. These are *accounting, finance, production/operations, marketing and sales,* and *human resources management.* The information systems department serves these primary departments (see Figure 2.3). Functional information systems are put in place to ensure that business strategies come to fruition in an efficient manner. Typically, a functional system provides periodic reports about such topics as operational efficiency, effectiveness, and productivity by extracting information from databases and processing it according to the needs of the user.

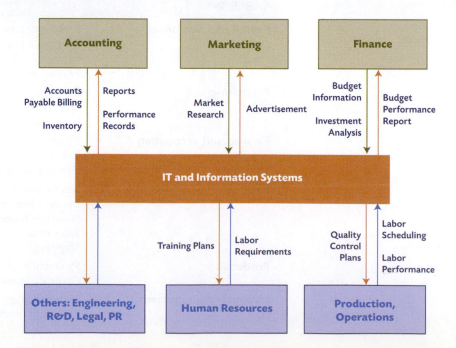

Figure 2.3 Functional information systems.

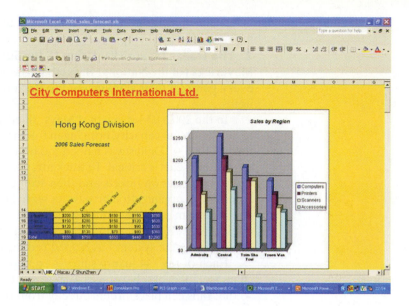

Figure 2.4 Sales forecast by region, generated by marketing MIS.

Functional information systems are of two types: those that support managers, and those that support other employees in the functional areas (e.g., analysts, schedulers, staff). The systems that support managers are referred to as **management information systems (MISs).** MISs support functional managers by providing them with periodic reports that include summaries, comparisons, and other statistics. Examples are weekly sales volume and comparison of actual expenses to the budget.

Note that the term MIS is also used to describe the study of information systems in business. In many universities the name of the department that teaches the subject of IT was (and sometimes still is) the MIS Department. Also, in many organizations the title of the information systems department was (and sometimes still is) the Department of MIS.

Management information systems are also used for planning, monitoring, and control. For example, a sales forecast by region is shown in Figure 2.4. Such a report can help the marketing manager make better decisions regarding advertising and pricing of products. Another example is that of a human resources information system (HRIS), which provides a manager with a daily report of the percentage of people who were on vacation or called in sick, as compared to forecasted figures.

Functional information systems that support analysts and other departmental employees can be fairly complex, depending on the type of employees supported.

Examples of Functional/Enterprise Systems. The following examples show the support IT provides to the five major functional areas. Some of the examples cover two functional areas. In each example, we explain the IT support to critical performance and response activities described in Chapter 1.

1. Computerized Analysis Helps Texas Collect $400 Million Additional Taxes. Tax gaps exist between taxes owed and the amount collected in many public entities. The State of Texas is no exception. To overcome the problems, tax collectors perform *audits*, which are time consuming and expensive to conduct manually. Also, many audits are unproductive—resulting in little or no tax recovery. In order to make better decisions on whom to audit (and thus increase the percentage of productive audits), the State of Texas uses *predictive analytics* (described later in the Chapter).

Millions of records are stored in the State data warehouse (a special repository for data; see Chapter 3). Using data mining—based software (for sophisticated analysis, see Chapter 12) from *spss.com*, the agency can cross-match millions of records identifying promising leads. Specifically, the system helps identify thousands of businesses that were operating in the State without complying with the tax obligations. Also, it helps field auditors in adopting better audit target selections. Once the employees gained confidence in the program, they started to use it extensively, saving over $150 million a year. (*Sources:* Compiled from Gates, 2005, and Staff, 2005.)

Beginning here, and continuing throughout the book, icons positioned in the margins will call out the functional areas to which our real-world examples apply. In addition, we will point to IT applications in government and in other public services such as healthcare and education by using icons. Finally, you've already seen that other icons will identify global examples—IT used by non-U.S.-based companies or by any company with significant business outside the country of its headquarters. For a key that identifies the icons, see the note in the Preface.

Critical response activities supported: analyzing large amounts of data, decision making, improved employee productivity, and increased revenue.

2. The Dallas Mavericks: Using IT for Successful Play and Business. The Dallas Mavericks (of the National Basketball Association, NBA) expect to fill every seat at every game in their stadium, and to maximize sales from concessions and souvenir items.

In the 2002–03 season, the "Mavs" filled the 19,200-seat American Airlines Center to 103.7 percent capacity, bringing in folding chairs to handle the overflow demand for tickets. In 2003 Dallas was named the best NBA city by *The Sporting News*.

Filling seats is critical. To track attendance, the Mavs became the first NBA team to put barcodes on tickets and then scan them, in part to find out if group sales and community organization giveaways were putting bodies in seats or just wasting tickets. The team's business managers have found other uses for the attendance information as well. By enabling improved attendance forecasting for particular games, for example, the system has helped reduce beverage inventories by 50 percent.

Each of the 144 luxury suites is equipped with a PC that handles orders for merchandise, food, and beverages. Wireless access from all seats in the arena is available so that fans can place orders directly from their seats. All 840 cash registers at concessions stands, restaurants, stores, and bars use a sophisticated point-of-sale system. In the big retail store on the ground floor, salespeople using handheld computing devices ring up credit-card purchases when lines get too long. The system allows the Mavs to process credit-card transactions in less than 3 seconds, because there is an always-on Internet connection to the processing facility. During a game, managers can see which concession stands are busy and which ones can be closed early to cut labor costs.

Technology also supports the Mavs on the court. The team has 10 assistant coaches, and each has a laptop computer and a handheld computing device. Game films can be streamed over the Web for coaches to view on the road or at home. A digital content management system developed in-house matches game footage with the precise, to-the-minute statistics provided for every play of every game by the NBA. The searchable database allows coaches to analyze the effectiveness of particular plays and combinations of players in different game situations. In 2006, the team was one of the NBA leaders.

In 2002, the Mavs started using handheld computers to track the performance of each referee in every one of their games. The coaches can look at patterns and trends—for example, to see which referee favors a given team or which one calls more three-second violations—and they can tell the team's players. Another program logs different offensive and defensive schemes used against the Mavs. This system will let coaches make real-time adjustments using statistics from previous games. (*Source*: Compiled from Cone, 2003a and 2003b.)

Critical response activities supported: decision making, increased sales, improved customer service, improved inventory management, and better utilization of capacity.

3. Army Trains Soldiers with Virtual Worlds. The U.S. Army enlists video games and virtual worlds to teach soldiers interpersonal skills and cultural awareness for combat environments such as Iraq and Afghanistan. The technology supports computerized exercises that can sharpen physical reflexes and shooting skills. It prepares soldiers for a war and with the desire to win. The new systems (see Gonsalves, 2008) train for difficult communication situations abroad. For example, negotiation skills are heavily dependent on culture. Soldiers learn how to think and communicate under pressure and stress. The system is a multiplayer simulation game (up to 64 players on the networked computer system over an intranet). Players direct their avatars through the realistic war zone cyberspace. Participants serve as either role players or evaluators with tasks and experiences that vary according to role. Instructors can create or modify scenarios, monitor training, and jump in to change the direction of the game at any time. The interactions practiced in the game help soldiers deal with local customs, build trust with natives in foreign war zones, and equip and train locals to aid U.S. military efforts. All training is done faster than manual training, learners are happier, and the cost of training is lower. Similar games have been developed by the military for other purposes. Industry also uses games to simulate critical response activities such as increasing efficiency, expediting training, reducing cost, and improving learner satisfaction.

4. Mobile Banking at Handelsbanken of Sweden. Handelsbanken of Sweden is the largest bank in Scandinavia, where more than 80 percent of the population over 15 years old carries mobile phones. Operating in a very competitive banking environment, the bank is trying to meet customers' expectations of using their mobile phones to organize their personal and working lives while on the move. Mobile banking services, including stock trading, was an opportunity for the bank to gain a competitive edge, and so the bank became the world's first to have mobile banking applications.

An interactive service allows customers to access up-to-the-minute banking information, including the latest stock market and interest rate data, whenever and wherever they like. Handelsbanken's e-banking has become so popular that it is used by tens of thousands of customers. It opens up critical business and personal information to safe and easy access from mobile devices. Both the bank's financial advisors and its customers can access general and personalized stock market and account information, transfer money, request loans, buy and sell stocks and bonds, and pay bills. This move into mobile banking is a key first step in a strategy to exploit the potential of e-business, while also extending the bank's brand reach. (*Sources*: Compiled from IBM's case study: Handelsbanken at *www-3.ibm.com/e-business/doc/content/casestudy/35433.html* (no longer available online), and from press releases at *handelsbanken.com(2008)*.)

Critical response activities supported: improved customer service, innovative strategic marketing methods, and competitive advantage.

Enterprise Information Systems. While functional systems support isolated activities within a single department, enterprise systems support business processes that are performed by two or more departments. For example, evaluating a request for a loan is a business process, and so is purchasing a part, or conducting an advertising campaign. The activities in the process are frequently done in sequence, but some can be conducted simultaneously.

Figure 2.5 illustrates examples of four processes that cross not only departmental boundaries, but also organizational boundaries, such as extending activities to

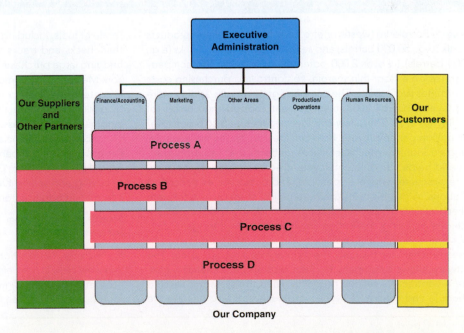

Figure 2.5 Business processes across and beyond the enterprise.

suppliers and/or customers. Process A describes a typical TPS, crossing three functional areas. Process B describes procurement, and as such it is extended to a supplier. Process C involves customer service, reaching customers. Finally, Process D involves order taking (from customers) and fulfilling it after obtaining some materials from a supplier.

An example of a system that provides support to both functional departments and business processes is provided in *IT at Work 2.1*.

Enterprise systems follow such processes, and they usually integrate tasks done in different departments. One of the most popular enterprise applications is *enterprise resources planning (ERP),* which enables companies to plan and manage the resources of an entire enterprise. Other popular enterprise systems are customer relationship management (CRM), knowledge management (KM), and business intelligence (BI) (see Chapters 10 and 12).

Interorganizational Systems. Some information systems connect two or more organizations. They are referred to as *interorganizational information systems* (IOSs).

Most common IOSs are systems that connect sellers and buyers. There one can order electronically, bill electronically from suppliers, and pay electronically. Since such transactions are fairly standard, they can be supported by standardized computer languages in electronic data interchanges (EDIs) (see Tutorial 6). Figure 2.6 shows IOSs connecting three organizations. The IOSs are connected with some internal systems, such as the functional systems shown for Corporate A, or to enterprise systems shown for Company B. Basically, IOSs enable computers to process large amounts of information that flows between organizations. In addition, they enable computers to "talk" with other computers in different organizations.

Global Information Systems. IOSs that connect companies located in two or more countries are referred to as **global information systems.** Many e-commerce systems are now global. If you have customers from other countries who buy from you online, you may need the support of a global system. The same is true if your supplies are overseas. For details see Chapter 11.

IT at Work **2.1**

Generating $62 Million per Employee at Western Petroleum

Western Petroleum (*westernpetro.com*) buys petroleum products in bulk (e.g., 50,000 barrels) and sells them in smaller chunks (e.g., 5,000 barrels) to over 2,000 potential customers. The company operates on a razor-thin margin, so controlling purchasing costs determines profitability. The company grew rapidly, adding more employees, but by 2003, management capped the number of employees at 58. These few employees generate $3.6 billion (over $62 million per employee). How can they do it? The answer is: by using an industry-specific software platform that facilitates trading and helps schedule employees. The basic idea was to automate processes wherever possible, and outsource all noncritical functions. A key piece of the automation strategy is a software called PetroMan (see *sisugrp.com*). The industry-specific software includes a trading application (buying and selling triggers), contract management, risk management, accounting program, and pipeline scheduler. Basically, it is an integrated hybrid system. The software allows a company to place bids and automatically capture a contract for refined products. Then the system is used to schedule and confirm deliveries in pipelines. It also handles the resale of fuels, including electronic invoicing and a credit module that checks and tracks a customer's credit risk. This is done by hedging large purchasing contracts by selling futures on the New York Mercantile (Commodities) Exchange. This way the company is protected against a large drop in oil prices. The software is plugged directly into the primary commodity exchanges, thus automating the process.

Accounting/financial information flows automatically from PetroMan to the company's financial application, a package called Global Financials (from Global Software). Thus, the entire process of buying and selling fuels and moving the accounting/financial information is fully automated.

Sources: Compiled from Duvall (2005) and from *westernpetro.com* (accessed April 2008).

For Further Exploration: What processes are being automated and why? How is risk being evaluated? It is probable that all major competitors use the same software. So, do you see any advantage for the company to use it too? Why?

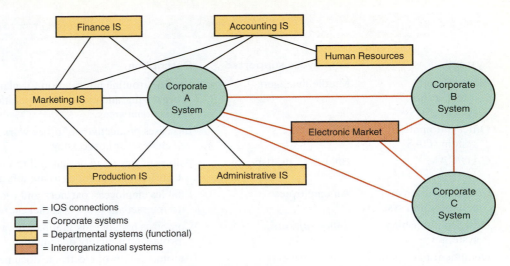

Figure 2.6 Departmental, enterprise, and interorganizational information systems.

Very Large and Special Systems. Some systems are very large, and they are often global in nature. Such systems include many subsystems of the previous levels. Some information systems are designed for only one industry, such as an airline reservation system. Universities using administrative information systems as well as academic information systems in a multicampus system is another example. Some cities (e.g., in China) have citywide systems and regional or national healthcare systems that can be very large and complex

Example: National Health Care System in Denmark. In Denmark all 5.3 million Danish residents and 150,000 healthcare professionals have access to the "Danish National e-Health Portal" (*sundhed.dk*). It provides both general and detailed personal information, including medical records. It facilitates communication among doctors and between doctors and patients, increases collaboration among healthcare professionals, boosts efficiency in the delivery system, and significantly improves the quality of care. It enables quick communication with all healthcare providers, government agencies, pharmacies, healthcare professionals, and any other participants in the healthcare system. The system is delivered over the Internet and its technology includes complicated hardware and software from IBM and other vendors. For details see Pratt (2007).

In the next section, we will describe the classification of information systems by the type of support they provide.

CLASSIFICATION BY THE TYPE OF SUPPORT PROVIDED

Another way to classify information systems is according to the type of support they provide, regardless of the functional area. For example, an information system can support office workers in almost any functional area. Likewise, managers working from various geographical locations can be supported by a computerized collaboration system. The main types of support systems are listed and described in Table 2.2 together with the types of employees they support. The evolution of these systems and a brief description of each is provided in Online Brief 2.1.

The two types of systems that attracted the most attention in 2008 were collaboration systems (Chapter 4) and business intelligence systems (*A Closer Look 2.1* and Chapter 12).

HOW DO DIFFERENT INFORMATION SYSTEMS RELATE TO EACH OTHER?

The relationship among the different types of support systems can be described as follows: Each support system has sufficiently unique characteristics so that it can be classified as a special entity. Moreover, there is information flow among these entities and systems. For example, an MIS extracts information from a TPS, and BI

TABLE 2.2	Main Types of IT Support Systems		
System	**Employees supported**	**Description**	**Detailed description in:**
Management information system (MIS)	Middle managers	Provides routine information for planning, organizing, and controlling operations in functional areas	Chapter 9
Office automation system (OAS)	Office workers	Increases productivity of office workers; includes word processing	Chapters 4, 9
CAD/CAM	Engineers, draftspeople	Allows engineers to design and test prototypes; transfers specifications to manufacturing facilities	Chapter 9
Communication and collaboration systems	All employees	Enables employees, partners, and customers to interact and work together more efficiently	Chapters 4, 8
Desktop publishing system	Office workers	Combines text, photos, graphics to produce professional-quality documents	Chapter 3
Document management system (DMS)	Office workers	Automates flow of electronic documents	Chapter 3
Decision support system (DSS)	Decision makers, managers	Combines models and data to solve semistructured problems with extensive user involvement	Chapter 12
Group support system, groupware	People working in groups	Supports working processes of groups of people (including those in different locations)	Chapters 4, 12
Expert system (ES)	Knowledge workers, nonexperts	Provides stored knowledge of experts to nonexperts; provides decision recommendations based on built-in expertise	Chapter 12
Knowledge management system (KM)	Managers, knowledge workers	Supports the gathering, organizing, and use of an organization's knowledge	Chapters 10
Data and text mining	Knowledge workers, professionals	Enables learning from historical cases, even with vague or incomplete information	Chapters 3, 12
Business intelligence	Decision makers, managers, knowledge workers	Gathers and uses large amounts of data for analysis by business analytics and intelligent systems	Chapters 3, 12
Mobile computing systems	Mobile employees	Support employees who work with customers or business partners outside the physical boundaries of the organization	Chapter 7
Automated decision support (ADS)	Frontline employees, middle managers	Supports customer care employees and salespeople who need to make quick, real-time decisions involving small dollar amounts	Chapter 12

A Closer Look 2.1

Business Intelligence for Competitive Advantage

Definition. **Business intelligence (BI)** is an umbrella term that combines software architectures, databases, analytical tools, applications, graphical displays, and decision-making methodologies. It means different things to different people. BI's major objective is to enable timely and even interactive access to data, and to give business managers and analysts the ability to conduct appropriate analysis. By analyzing historical and current data, situations, and performances, decision makers obtain valuable insights that enable them to make more informed and better decisions.

The Architecture of BI. A BI system has four major components: a *data warehouse* (or large database) with its source data; *business analytics*, a collection of tools for manipulating, mining, and analyzing the data in the data warehouse; *business performance management (BPM)* for monitoring and analyzing performance; and a *user interface and display* (e.g., a dashboard). The relationship among these components is illustrated in Chapter 12 and Turban et al. (2008).

A major component in BI and in business performance management is the dashboard. A **dashboard** is a visual presentation

(continued on next page)

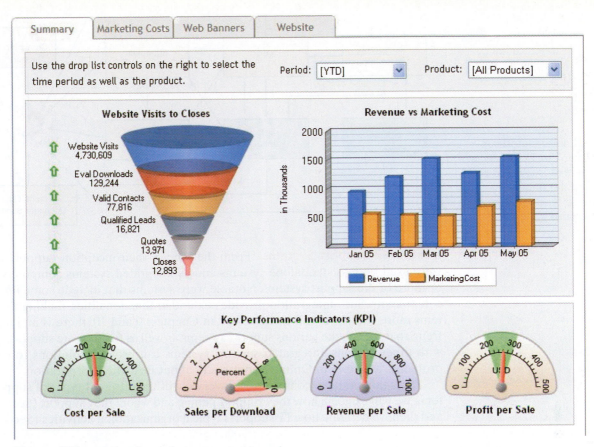

Figure 2.7 Sample of a performance dashboard.
Source: Dundas Software, demos1.dundas.com/DundasGauge/MarketingDashboard/Summary.aspx.

of critical data (e.g., results of a report or analysis) for users including executives. It allows users to see "hot spots" at a glance, such as deviations from targets, exceptional performance, or Web analytics summaries. An example is provided in Figure 2.7, which displays a number of key performance indicators (KPI) and critical data for a software company. From the dashboard, it is easy to see, for instance, that the KPIs are all good (i.e., they are all in the green), that for all stages of the pipeline the revenues are trending upward (i.e., they are all green arrows pointing upward), and that the growth in revenues is outpacing the increase in marketing costs. This particular dashboard enables end users to see whether there are any differences by time period or product (the dropdowns on the upper right) and to further analyze marketing costs. One major analytical tool in BI is *data mining*. **Data mining** is a computerized process for conducting searches in large amounts of data and information in an attempt to discover unknown valuable relationships in the data (e.g., among variables). Data mining helps in making predictions and improving decision making.

Examples of how data mining works: Two examples of useful applications that show how data mining can support organizations follow:

Example 1. The National Australia Bank uses data mining to aid its predictive marketing. The tools are used to extract and analyze data stored in the bank's Oracle database. Specific applications focus on assessing how competitors' initiatives are affecting the bank's bottom line. Data mining tools are used to generate market analysis models from historical data. The bank considers BI to be crucial to maintaining an edge in the increasingly competitive financial services marketplace.

Example 2. The FAI Insurance Group uses data mining to reassess the relationship between historical risk from insurance policies and the pricing structure used by its underwriters. The data analysis capabilities allow FAI to better serve its customers by more accurately assessing the insurance risk associated with a customer request.

$
FIN

receives information from data warehouses and MIS (see Figure 2.8). In many cases, two or more support systems can be integrated to form a hybrid system, as is the case in business intelligence or CRM. Finally, as the technologies change, the interrelationships and coordination among the different types of systems continue to evolve.

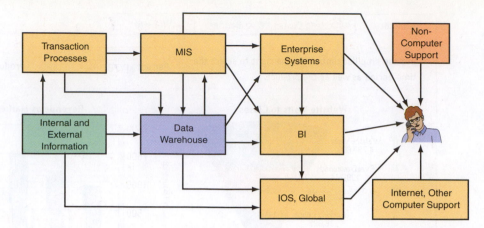

Figure 2.8 Interrelated support systems. The TPS collects information that is used to build the MIS and the data warehouse. These feed the BI and other enterprise systems.

Integrated Support Systems. From the time of their inception, support systems were used both as standalone systems and as integrated systems composed of two or more of the support systems. Notable were systems that include some intelligent components. Such integration provides extended functionalities, making these systems more useful. As will be discussed in Chapters 9 and 10, there is an increasing trend to integrate the various support systems as well as to integrate support systems with other systems. Integrated support systems can provide solutions to complex problems, as shown in Online Minicase 2.1 about Best Buy Corporation.

Now that we have completed an overview of the different types of support systems, we will examine how they support people and whom they support (Section 2.3), and then we describe how IT supports typical organizational activities (Section 2.4).

Review Questions

1. Define *TPS* and provide an example.
2. What is a *functional information system*?
3. Define an *enterprise information system*; list the major types.
4. Describe a *global information system*.
5. List five types of IT support systems.

2.3 How IT Supports People

In this section we describe how IT supports people in the organization. First, we describe the major classes of work that managers and knowledge workers do and look at an example of what problems they may face, and then we look at the major categories of workers and what IT tools support them.

OPERATIONAL, MANAGERIAL, AND STRATEGIC ACTIVITIES

It is customary to classify organizational activities into the following three levels: operational, managerial, and strategic. In this section we take a closer look at each one.

Operational Activities. *Operational activities* deal with the day-to-day operations of an organization, such as assigning employees to tasks and recording the number of hours they work, or placing a purchase order. Operational activities are short-term in nature. The information systems that support them are mainly TPSs, MISs, functional automated decision support systems (ADSs), groupware, and office automation. Mobile employees outside the organization are supported by mobile devices. Operational systems are used mostly by supervisors (first-line managers), operators, clerical employees, field employees, customer service employees, and the like.

Managerial Activities. *Managerial activities*, also called tactical activities or decisions, deal in general with middle-management activities such as short-term planning,

TABLE 2.3	Support Provided by MISs and BI for Managerial Activities
Task	**MIS support**
Statistical summaries	Summaries of new data (e.g., daily production by item, monthly electricity usage)
Exception reports	Comparison of actual performances to standards (or target). Highlight only deviations from a threshold (e.g., above or below 5%)
Periodic reports	Generated at predetermined intervals
Ad-hoc reports	Generated as needed, on demand. These can be routine reports or special ones
Comparative analysis and early detection of problems	Comparison of performance to metrics or standards. Includes analysis such as trends and early detection of changes
Projections, forecasting	Projection of future sales, cash flows, market share, trend analysis, etc.
Automation of routine decisions	Standard modeling techniques applied to routine decisions such as when and how much to order or how to schedule work
Connection and collaboration	Internal and external Web-based messaging systems, e-mail, voice mail, and groupware (see Chapter 4)

organizing, and control. Computerized managerial systems are frequently *equated with MISs* that are designed to summarize data and prepare reports. Middle managers also can get quick answers to queries from such systems as the need for answers arises, using BI reporting and query capabilities.

Managerial information systems are broader in scope than operational information systems, but like operational systems, they use mainly internal sources of data. They provide the major, representative types of support shown in Table 2.3.

Strategic Activities. As described in Chapter 1, *strategic activities* deal with situations that may significantly change the manner in which business is done (hopefully for the better). For example, merger and acquisition decisions are clearly strategic. Strategic decisions that involve IT could be, depending on if and how much to outsource activities. Strategic decisions are made by top management and require elaborate research as well as extensive internal and external communication and collaboration. IT support systems that may be useful are BI, business analytics , collaboration tools (e.g., Lotus Notes from IBM), and intelligent systems.

WHO PERFORMS WHAT ACTIVITIES IN ORGANIZATIONS, AND HOW ARE THEY SUPPORTED BY IT?

So far in this section, we have looked at operational, managerial, and strategic activities, and at how IT supports them. Here, we take a different look at these activities by looking at the people who typically perform them in an organization. The relationships between the people supported in all functional areas and the decision types are shown in Figure 2.9. The triangular shape of the figure also illustrates the number of employees involved in the various types of activities and the decisions relating to those activities.

Executives and Managers. At the top of the triangle are the executives. They are few in number and responsible for the strategic decisions. Their major support today is derived from business intelligence (BI) and business performance management systems (Chapter 1).

Middle managers make tactical decisions, and are supported mainly by functional information systems and MIS in the areas where they work. Lately, they have started to enjoy the support of BI and intelligent systems available over intranets. For more details on the benefits to managerial decision making, see Online Brief 2.2. These

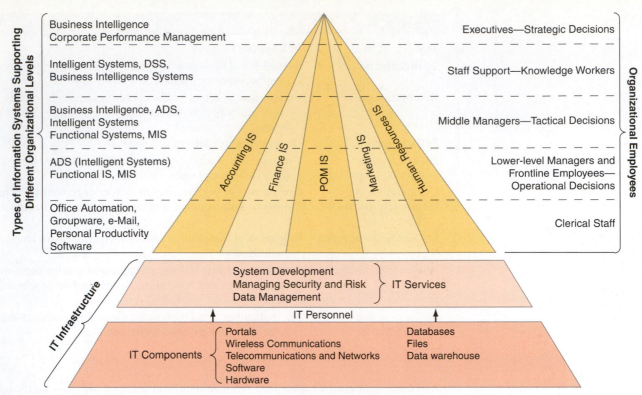

Figure 2.9 The information systems' support of people in organizations.

benefits can be seen in the many examples throughout the book as well as in the problem-solving exercise at the end of this chapter.

Knowledge Workers, Clerical Staff, and Data Workers. As you can see in Figure 2.8, a level of *staff support* is introduced between top and middle management. These are professional people, such as financial and marketing analysts. They act as advisors and assistants to both top and middle management. Many of these professional workers are classified as **knowledge workers,** people who create information and knowledge as part of their work and integrate it into the business. Knowledge workers are engineers, financial and marketing analysts, production planners, lawyers, and accountants, to mention just a few. They are responsible for finding or developing new knowledge for the organization and integrating it with existing knowledge. Therefore they must keep abreast of all developments and events related to their profession. In many developed countries, 60 to 80 percent of all workers are knowledge workers.

Information systems that support knowledge workers range from Internet and intranet search engines (which help knowledge workers find information) and automated decision support systems (which provide advice and information interpretation) to Web-based computer-aided design (which shapes and speeds a product design process) and sophisticated data management systems (which help increase productivity and quality of work). Knowledge workers also contribute to the creation of organizational knowledge that is supported by *knowledge management*.

Another large class of employees is *clerical workers,* who support managers at all levels. Among clerical workers, those who use, manipulate, or disseminate information are referred to as **data workers.** These include, for example, bookkeepers, secretaries who work with word processors, electronic file clerks, and insurance claim processors. Data workers are supported by office automation and communication systems including document management, workflow, e-mail, and coordination software.

Infrastructure for the Support Systems. All of the systems in the support triangle (Figure 2.8) are built on *IT infrastructure*. Consequently, all of the employees who are supported work with infrastructure technologies such as the Internet, intranets, corporate portals, security systems, and corporate databases. Therefore, the IT infrastructure is shown as the *foundation* of the triangle; it is described in more detail in Section 2.5.

WHY DO PEOPLE NEED IT SUPPORT?

Today it is very difficult to find business people who do not use computers. As will be seen in the remaining chapters, IT is helping find and analyze information, evaluate decision alternatives, communicate and collaborate with employees and business partners, and much more. All this is done rapidly and inexpensively from anywhere at any time. The specific help that is needed and the specific IT support depend on many factors ranging from the managerial level and industry to the country where business is done, and the size of the organization as well as the type of situation and the decisions involved.

Example. In 2008, the financial services industry—including giant banks—went into crisis. Some of the problems stemmed from improper loan-giving decisions. In Figure 2.10, we illustrate representative questions and decisions made by people in this industry. They relate mainly to performance management, customer relationships, and risk management. The answers to the questions presented in the figure require the use of IT tools (mostly tools for BI and collaboration).

Review Questions

1. Define operational, managerial, and strategic activities.
2. List the levels of employees (e.g., executives) in an organization.
3. What is the role of IT infrastructure? (Hint: see Figure 2.8.)
4. Describe knowledge workers and data workers.

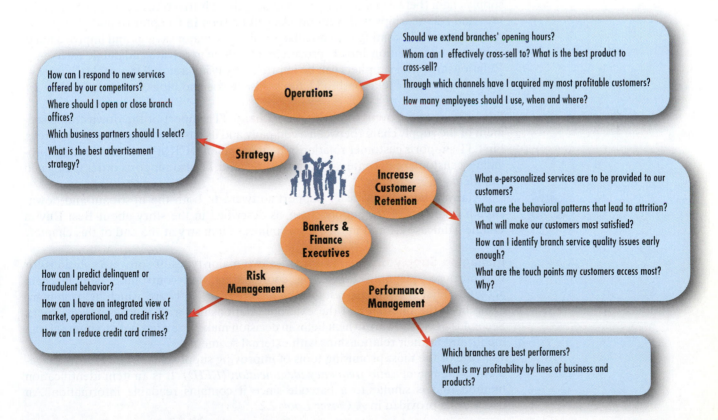

Figure 2.10 Representative questions in the financial services industry.

2.4 How IT Supports Supply Chains and Business Processes

So far, we have described support to different types of employees at different organizational levels. There are also special systems designed to support business processes along the *supply chain*. They also support activities related to internal organizational processes. These systems also support people doing work jointly with colleagues in other organizations such as those who work with suppliers. To understand IT support in such cases, it is worthwhile to review the essentials of organizations working with their business partners, especially along the supply chains. This is done in Tutorial #1. A detailed presentation on the relationship of supply chain and IT is provided in Chapters 10 and 11.

IT SUPPORT OF SUPPLY CHAINS

Supply chains can be complex and difficult to manage due to the need to coordinate several business partners, several internal corporate departments, numerous business processes, and possibly many customers (see Tutorial #1). Managing medium-to-large supply chains manually can be very difficult. IT support of supply chains can be divided according to the three segments of the supply chain. These segments are: inside a company (internal), with suppliers (upstream), and with customers (downstream).

Support of the Internal Supply Chain. Some of the IT support of the internal supply chain was described in the previous two sections. It involves the TPS and other corporatewide (enterprisewide) information systems, and it covers all of the functional information systems. Special software called supply chain management (SCM) software is available to support segments of the chain. For example, in manufacturing, there is software for production scheduling and inventory management.

Support of the Upstream Supply Chain. The major IT support of the upstream supply chain (between a company and its suppliers) is to improve procurement activities and relationships with vendors. As will be seen in Chapters 6 and 10, using e-procurement is becoming very popular, resulting in major savings and improvements in buyer–seller relationships. E-procurement is done in private and public exchanges. Relationships with suppliers can be improved by using a supplier portal (Chapter 4) and other supplier relationship IT tools. Also, wikis and blogs can be helpful.

Support of the Downstream Supply Chain. IT support of the downstream segment of the supply chain (between a company and its customers) is done in two areas. First, IT supports customer relationship management (CRM) activities, such as providing a customer call center (Chapter 10). Second, IT also supports order taking and shipments to customers.

Many vendors provide IT support software to both the upstream and downstream segments of the supply chain, as described in the story about Best Buy in Online Minicase 2.1 and in the Airbus minicase industry at the end of this chapter.

Managing Supply Chains. IT provides two major types of software solutions for this purpose—planning, organizing, coordinating, and controlling—supply chain activities. First is *enterprise resource planning (ERP)* software, which helps in managing both the internal and the external relationships with the business partners. Second is *SCM* software, which helps in decision making related both to internal segments and to their relationships with external segments.

One of the most promising tools of improving supply chains and their management is the use of *radio frequency identification (RFID)*. It is an item identification method that is similar to a barcode since it contains readable information. An overview is provided in *A Closer Look 2.2*.

A Closer Look **2.2**

What is a Radio Frequency Identification (RFID) System?

Radio frequency identification (RFID) is a technology that uses electronic tags (chips) instead of bar codes to identify objects or items. The tags can be attached to or embedded in objects, animals, or humans. RFID readers use radio waves to interact with the tags. The radio waves enable the unique identification of the objects, transmission of data, and/or storage of information about the object (or to locate the item). The major benefits of RFID are the following:

- Quick tracking of where items are (their location) in real time
- Finding extensive information about the items
- Enabling quick inventory taking of items

In contrast with a *barcode*, the information can be read from a much greater distance (30 feet or 10 meters) and no line-of-sight is required. Also, much more information can be stored on the RFID tag and it is more durable. The technology is in extensive use in transportation, hospitals, libraries, and the like (see *en.wikipedia.org/wiki/Rfid*). Its most promising use is in enterprise supply chain management to improve the efficiency of inventory tracking.

RFID implementation is slow due to privacy and security concerns, especially when it involves consumers (see Chapter 7). On the other hand, an increasing number of companies use the technology internally, frequently in combination with other IT systems, as is done by Nokia.

RFID at Nokia. Security guards employed at Nokia carry a mobile phone handset with an attached RFID tag. RFID tags are also installed at various points around the facility. At the start of a shift, guards use the phone to read their RFID-enabled name badges. Then, security guards do their rounds, operating the handsets to read the various tags as they pass by them. Details of the phone number and RFID tag just read are transmitted over the cell phone network. Supervisors are thus given accurate information as to when a particular guard started and finished a shift, whether the guard patrolled all of the required locations, and where the guard was at a particular point in time. In addition, supervisors can use the text and phone function to ask guards to recheck an area, vary their route, and the like.

For RFID implementation at Airbus Industries, see the minicase at the end of this chapter.

Finally, the concepts of build-to-order production and e-commerce have put a new spin on supply chain management; for providing what customers really want and for interactive elaboration, see Tutorial #1.

IT SUPPORT OF OTHER SYSTEMS

So far we have described IT support to internal parts of organizations and to different types of employees. We also described the support provided to business partners along the supply chain. But IT supports other types of systems. Here are a few examples.

Industry-Specific Systems. These are systems that are designed to serve an industry such as banking, retail, transportation, oil, utilities, or universities. The systems can be specific for one or two applications, or they can be suites that cover multiple needs. An example of the petroleum industry was provided in *IT at Work 2.1* (page 48). Many software vendors specialize in industry-specific systems. One example is JDA Systems (*jdasystems.com*), which caters to the retail industry.

Supporting E-Commerce Business Models. The use of e-commerce implies using business models such as e-auctions, exchanges, e-procurement, or the use of electronic meetings. A large number of software vendors are developing IT software support for such business models.

Supporting Online Search. When you ask Google to search some information for you, its search engines may check millions of files and documents to provide you the answers. Searching the entire Internet or even the files of one company (called desktop search) and to do it in seconds, requires the support of IT hardware (e.g., Google uses over 600,000 servers), analytical programs (e.g., search algorithms), and other IT tools. Searching photos, videos, and audio can be even more complex, and it can not be done efficiently without IT support.

Supporting Social Networking. Social Network Services (SNSs) such as Facebook and MySpace have multimillions of members and a very large number of daily visitors. To accommodate such traffic, they need an extensive network of services, security protection, many servers, and a large number of software-based applications. Furthermore, to maintain the interest of their members, SNSs need to provide the capability of creating new applications. The support of IT to SNSs is described in Chapter 8 and online Chapter 16.

Review Questions

1. Describe how IT supports the three segments of the supply chain.
2. What is RFID? What are its major benefits?
3. How does IT support non-supply-chain-related activities?
4. How does IT support EC and social networks?
5. How does IT support online search?

2.5 Information Systems Infrastructure, Architecture, and Emerging Computing Environments

The support provided by IT requires information architecture and infrastructure. In addition, emerging technologies provide for improved effectiveness and efficiency.

INFRASTRUCTURE

An **information infrastructure** consists of the physical facilities, services, and management that supports all shared computing resources in an organization. There are five major components of the infrastructure: (1) computer hardware, (2) software, (3) networks and communication facilities (including the Internet and intranets), (4) databases and data workers, and (5) information management personnel. Infrastructures include these resources as well as their integration, operation, documentation, maintenance, and management. The architecture of FedExNet, for example, is described in the Federal Express case at the end of Part I. If you go there and examine the attached figure and introduce specific names instead of general ones (e.g., instead of "Merchant PC," say "Dell server"), you will get a picture of the system's infrastructure. Infrastructures are further discussed in online Chapter 16, and in Weill and Vitale (2001). IT infrastructure is derived from the IT architecture.

THE IT ARCHITECTURE

Information technology architecture is a high-level map or plan of the information assets in an organization, including the physical design of the building that holds the hardware.* On the Web, IT architecture includes the content and organization of the site and the interface to support browsing and search capabilities. The IT architecture of an e-business (a travel agency) is shown in Technology Guide 5. IT architecture is a guide for current operations and a blueprint for future directions. It assures managers that the organization's IT structure will meet its strategic business needs. (See the *Journal of Information Architecture* for examples, tutorials, news, products, etc.) Technology Guides are located at the book's Web site.

Creating the IT architecture is a cyclical process, which is driven by the business architecture. This process is described in Technology Guide 5. It is based on **business architecture,** which describes organizational plans, visions, objectives, and problems, and the information required to support them. The potential users of IT must play a critical role in the creation of business architecture, in order to ensure that business architectures are properly linked and meet the organization's long-term needs.

*Information technology architecture needs to be distinguished from *computer architecture* (see technology Guide 1). For example, the architecture for a computer may involve several processors, or it may have special features to increase speed, such as reduced instruction set computing (RISC). Our interest here is in information architecture only.

Once the business architecture is finished, the system developer can start a five-step process of building the IT architecture. The details and definitions of those steps are provided by Koontz (2000) and are shown in Technology Guide 5.

WEB-BASED SYSTEMS

Technically, the term **Web-based systems** refers to those applications or services that are resident on a server that is accessible using a Web browser and is therefore accessible from anywhere in the world via the Web.

Web-Based E-Commerce Systems. Most e-commerce applications run on the Internet, intranet, and extranets, using Web-based features. Therefore, Web-based systems are the engines of e-commerce. They enable business transactions to be conducted seamlessly 24 hours a day, seven days a week. A central property of the Web and e-commerce is that you can instantly reach millions of people, anywhere, any time. The major components of Web-based EC are electronic storefronts and malls (Chapter 6), electronic markets (Chapter 6), and mobile commerce (Chapter 7).

Electronic Markets. Web-accessed electronic markets are rapidly emerging as a vehicle for conducting e-commerce. An **electronic market** is a network of interactions and relationships over which information, products, services, and payments are exchanged. Electronic markets can reside in one company, where there is either one seller and many buyers, or one buyer and many sellers. These are referred to as *private marketplaces*. Alternatively, electronic markets can have many buyers and many sellers. Then they are known as *public marketplaces* or *exchanges*.

Web 2.0 Environments. The term **Web 2.0** was coined by O'Reilly Media in 2004 to refer to what is considered a revolution in the computer industry caused by the move to the Internet and the Web as a platform, and in an attempt to understand the rules for success on that new platform. It is a supposed second generation of Internet-based services that let people collaborate and share information online in perceived new ways—such as social networking sites, wikis, and blogs. O'Reilly Media, in collaboration with MediaLive International, used the phrase as a title for a series of conferences. Since then, it has become a popular, if ill-defined and often criticized, buzzword in the technical and marketing communities.

O'Reilly (2005) provides the following examples to illustrate the differences between Web 2.0 and the previous generation, referred to as Web 1.0.

Web 1.0		Web 2.0
DoubleClick	$\longrightarrow$	Google AdSense
Ofoto	$\longrightarrow$	Flickr
Akamai	$\longrightarrow$	BitTorrent
Mp3.com	$\longrightarrow$	Napster
Britannica Online	$\longrightarrow$	Wikipedia
Personal Web sites	$\longrightarrow$	Blogging
Evite	$\longrightarrow$	Upcoming.org
Domain name speculation	$\longrightarrow$	Search engine optimization
Page views	$\longrightarrow$	Cost per click
Screen scraping	$\longrightarrow$	Web services
Publishing	$\longrightarrow$	Participation
Content management systems	$\longrightarrow$	Wikis
Directories (taxonomy)	$\longrightarrow$	Tagging ("folksonomy")
Stickiness	$\longrightarrow$	Syndications

The major characteristics of Web 2.0 are described in Chapter 8 and at *en.wikipedia.org/wiki/Web_2.0.*

EMERGING COMPUTING ENVIRONMENTS

As the demand for faster and more powerful computers increases, and as the number and variety of applications increases, the need for more capable computing environments increases, too. The following major emerging computing environments are briefly introduced here.

Service-Oriented Architecture (SOA). Many companies are constrained by their current IT architectures and infrastructures, which don't support the level of *flexibility* needed in rapidly changing business environments. Furthermore, many enterprises have a great deal of intellectual capital and other resources tied up in older, legacy systems. Much of the IT expertise today is focused on these older systems rather than on newer Web-based technologies. An attempted emerging solution is SOA.

Concepts and Benefits of SOA. **Service-oriented architecture (SOA)** is an architectural concept that defines the use of services to support a variety of business needs. The basic idea of SOA is to *reuse* and *reconnect* existing IT assets (called services) rather than more time-consuming and costly development of new systems.

In a service-oriented environment, organizations make resources available to participants via a network (the Internet or an intranet), as independent services.

Many experts agree that adoption of SOA can lead to significant benefits. The major benefits are the following:

- Reduced integration cost
- Improved business/IT alignment
- Extension and leveraging of existing IT investments
- Faster time to assemble new applications
- Lower IT maintenance cost

For additional information on SOA, see Chapter 13, Online Chapter 16 *en.wikipedia.org/wiki/Service-oriented_architecture*, and *service-architecture.com*.

Most SOAs are accessed and implemented in a standardized way using Web Services (see *en.wikipedia.org/wiki/Web_Services*). Also see the *SOA Web Services journal*.

Web Services. **Web Services** are software systems designed to support machine—to—machine interactions over a network. They are self-contained, self-describing business and consumer modular applications, that users can select and combine through almost any device, ranging from personal computers to mobile phones. By using *a set of shared protocols and standards*, these applications permit disparate systems to "talk" with one another—that is, to share data and services—without requiring human beings to translate the conversation. The result promises to be real-time links among the online processes of different systems and companies. These links could foster new interactions among businesses, and create a more user-friendly Web for consumers. Web Services provide for inexpensive and rapid solutions for application development and integration, access to information, and application development. For further details, see en.wikipedia.org/wiki/web_services and online Chapter 16.

Software-as-a-Service and Utility Computing. An increasingly popular enterprise model in which computing resources are made available to the user when the resources are needed is the **Software-as-a-Service (SaaS)** model. Whether referred to as *SaaS, on-demand computing, utility computing,* or *hosted services,* the idea is basically the same: instead of buying and installing expensive packaged enterprise applications, users can access applications over a network, with an Internet browser being the only absolute necessity. Thus, usually there is no hardware and software to buy since the applications are used over the Internet and paid for through a fixed subscription fee, or payable per an actual usage fee.

The SaaS model was developed to overcome the common challenge to an enterprise of being able to meet fluctuating demands on IT resources efficiently, which is a requirement of the adaptive enterprise. Because an enterprise's demand on computing resources can vary drastically from one time to another, maintaining sufficient resources to meet peak requirements can be costly. Conversely, if the enterprise cuts costs by maintaining only minimal computing resources, there will not be sufficient resources to meet peak requirements. Jainschigg (2008), reports that IT leaders confirmed that SaaS delivers robust applications—typically at a lower cost. Major complementation problems are data security and difficulty in integration. For details, see *en.wikipedia.org/wiki/software_as_a_service*.

A simple analogy is the use of an electrical appliance. The user does not directly negotiate with the electricity company to use power for a specific appliance. There are standards and controls, but they are broad enough that an electrical appliance can be plugged into the service without the user's notifying the electrical utility. On its side, the electrical utility company takes care of the complexity of power generation, including matching capacity to demand, and it can change which generators and circuits deliver the power—all without coordinating these events with the millions of users who rely on the service. This is why the concept is frequently referred to as *utility computing*.

The Utility Computing Concept. **Utility computing** is computing that is as available, reliable, and secure as electricity. The vision behind utility computing is to have computing resources available on demand from providers around the globe—always on and highly available, secure, efficiently metered, priced on a pay-as-you-use basis, dynamically scaled, self-healing, and easy to manage. In such a setting, enterprises would plug in, turn on the computer, and (it is hoped) save lots of money.

If (or when) it becomes successful, utility computing will change the way software is sold, delivered, and used in the world. Some experts believe that all software will become a service and be sold as a utility one day. Preparing for this day, IBM is moving aggressively into the application software providers (ASPs) area (see Chapter 13). The ASPs will operate the supply channels of utility computing that provide software applications on demand.

Example. The Mobil Travel Guide rates over 25,000 restaurants and hotels in the United States and publishes travel guides for various regions. To accommodate the ever-increasing traffic of Web servers that are looking for the ratings, the company is using IBM's applicable services. With this service, the company not only solved all capacity problems but also increased security—all at a 30 percent cost reduction, compared to having its own servers (Greenemeier, 2003).

For more on the subject, see *en.wikipedia.org/wiki/utility_computing*, *utility_computing.itworld.com*, *utilitycomputing.com*, and *oracle.com/ondemand*.

Grid Computing. Conventional networks, including the Internet, are designed to provide communication among devices. The same networks can be used to support the concept of **grid computing,** in which the unused processing capabilities of all computers in a given network can be utilized to create powerful computing capabilities. Grid computing coordinates the use of a large number of servers and storage, acting as one computer by sharing and coalescing the computing power (see *en.wikipedia.org/wiki/Grid_Computing*). Thus problems of spikes in demand are solved without the cost of maintaining reserve capacity (see *oracle.com/grid*).

Examples. A well-known grid-computing project is the SETI (Search for Extraterrestrial Intelligence) @Home project. In this project, PC users worldwide donate unused processor cycle times to help the search for signs of extraterrestrial life by analyzing signals coming from outer space. The project relies on individual volunteers to allow the project to harness the unused processing power of the users' computers. This method saves the project both money and resources.

A major commercial application of grid computing in the consumer market is Sony's attempt to link online thousands of Sony video-game consoles. For details, see Lohr (2003). Investment banks are embracing grid computing rapidly (Shread, 2006). An example of real-world use is provided in *IT at Work 2.2*.

IT at Work 2.2

Grid Computing at J.P. Morgan

J.P. Morgan Chase Investment Bank (*jpmorgan.com*) provides investment banking and commercial banking products and services. It also advises on corporate strategy and structure, risk management, and raising of capital. J.P. Morgan Chase, the largest financial institution in the United States, employs 11,000 IT professionals.

The company faced a problem of ever-increasing demand for computing resources. There were 2,000 PCs that run on 50 mid-size servers. Some were overutilized, whereas others were underutilized, creating staffing inefficiencies and poor service to the company's securities traders. The PCs were designed to help traders assess and manage financial exposures, such as interest rates, equities, foreign exchange, and credit derivatives.

In 2003, the company began use of grid computing, at a cost of $4.5 million. The system saved $1 million in computing costs in 2003 and $5 million in 2004. The savings come from lower costs for hardware (need for fewer servers), reduced development and operation costs, and a more effective system management. For example, when an isolated server fails, the system can still provide the real-time information required by the traders.

The system also provides scalability: new applications are now being built in 10 weeks instead of 20. Also, any increase in new business volume is handled quickly and efficiently. The system was considered the world's largest-known grid computing commercial application in 2004.

The introduction of grid computing was an impressive project because of the huge mind shift away from the old system. It was necessary to make an organizational shift, overcoming skepticism from internal users who for years had run applications on their own dedicated servers. It was necessary to take away the perceived flexibility that the business units thought they needed, and there was a lot of resistance to the change. A major success factor was the emphasis on problem solving rather than on pushing a new technology.

Other banks and financial institutions are experimenting with or are already using grid computing. For other applications, see *egenera.com* and Shread (2006).

Sources: Compiled from Hamblen (2004), and *jpmorgan.com* (accessed May 2008).

For Further Exploration: Why is grid computing so popular with investment banking? Is this a functional, enterprise, or global system?

Cloud Computing. An emerging topic that incorporates "SaaS", utility computing, grid computing, and Web 2.0 concepts is *cloud computing,* according to en.wikipedia.org/wiki/cloud_computing.

Cloud computing is Internet ('Cloud')-based development and use of computer technology ('Computing'). The cloud is a metaphor for the Internet and is an abstraction for the complex infrastructure it conceals. It is a style of computing where IT-related capabilities are provided as a service, allowing users to access technology-enabled services from the Internet without knowledge of, expertise with, or control over the technology infrastructure that support them. The "cloud" consists of thousands of computers and servers, all linked and accessible to you via the Internet.

According to the IEEE Computer Society cloud computing "is a paradigm in which information is permanently stored in servers on the Internet and cached temporarily on clients that include desktops, entertainment centers, table computers, notebooks, wall computers, handhelds, etc."

Cloud computing is a general concept where the common theme is reliance on the Internet for satisfying the computing needs of the users. For example, Google Apps provides common business applications online that are accessed from a web browser, while the software and data are stored on the servers.

According to Miller (2008), cloud computing will change computing as we know it. No longer are you tied to using expensive programs stored on your computer. No longer will you be able to only access your data from one computer. No longer will you be doing business only from your work computer or playing only from your personal computer.

With cloud computing, everything you do is now web-based instead of being desktop-based; you can access all your programs and documents from any computer that's connected to the Internet. Whether you want to share with your family, coordinate volunteers for a community organization, or manage a multi-faceted project in a large organization, cloud computing can help you do it more easily than ever before.

Mobile and Pervasive Computing. Mobile computing is a computing paradigm designed for mobile employees and others who wish to have a real-time connection from anywhere between a mobile device and other computing environments. An example is provided in Online Minicase 2.2 about Maybelline. Much of mobile computing is done on a wireless infrastructure (see Chapter 4). **Mobile commerce** or **m-commerce** (see Chapter 7) is commerce (buying and selling of goods and services) in a *wireless environment,* such as through wireless devices like cellular telephones and PDAs. Also called "next-generation e-commerce," m-commerce enables users to access the Internet without needing to find a place to plug in. So-called *smart phones* offer Internet access, fax, e-mail, and phone capabilities all in one, paving the way for m-commerce to be accepted by an increasingly mobile workforce as well as millions of consumers (see *IT at Work 2.3,* below).

An emerging mobile technology is pervasive computing.

Pervasive Computing. With **pervasive computing** we envision a situation in which computation becomes part of the environment. Computation is embedded in *things,* not in computers. The use of pervasive computing not only improves efficiency in work and living tasks, but also enriches the quality of life through art, design, and entertainment (see Chapter 7). Relentless progress in semiconductor technology, low-power design, and wireless technology will make embedded computation less and less obtrusive. An example is provided in Online Minicase 2.3 that describes an application in the healthcare field.

Open Source. Implementing SOA and Web Services requires a set of standards for the flow of information among the participants. These are related to the concept of *open source* (see Chapter 13 and *en.wikipedia.org/wiki/Open_Source*). Open source enables easy flow of information and integration in different computing systems. Open source is entering the mainstream of IT and it is growing very rapidly.

Virtualization. *Virtualization* or *virtualization computing* is a new concept that has several meanings in information technology and therefore several definitions. The major type of virtualization is *hardware virtualization* (usually referred to just as *virtualization*). In general, virtualization separates business applications and data from hardware resources. This allows companies to pool hardware resources—rather than

IT at Work 2.3

Wireless Pepsi Increases Productivity

Pepsi Bottling Group (PBG), the largest manufacturer, seller, and distributor of Pepsi-Cola, has a mountainous job stocking and maintaining their Pepsi vending machines—including a huge amount of paperwork and frustrating searches for parts and equipment necessary to fix the machines. Any time a machine is out of stock or not functioning, the company loses revenue and profits. There are tens of thousands of machines to service.

In 2002, the company began to equip its service technicians with handheld devices, hooked into a wireless wide-area network (WWAN). A mobile database application allows wireless communications around the United States in real time. The database includes the repair parts inventory that is available on each service truck, so dispatchers know where and who to send for maintenance at any given moment. It also has a back-office system that maintains the overall inventory. In the near future, the company will also be able to locate the whereabouts of each truck in real

time, using global positioning systems (GPSs). The aim is to make scheduling and dispatching more effective.

In the summer of 2002, only about 700 technicians used the wireless system, but already the company was saving $7 million per year. Each technician has been able to handle one more service call each day than previously. PBG provided the wireless capability to about 300 more technicians in 20 more locations in late 2002, and to most corporate technicians by 2006.

Sources: Compiled from Rhey (2002) and from *pepsi.com* (accessed April 2008).

For Further Exploration: What are the capabilities of the handheld devices? Relate the handheld devices to the mobile database. The case deals with the maintenance issue. In what ways, if any, can wireless help with stocking issues? How is Pepsi's competitive advantage increased?

to dedicate servers to applications—and assign those resources to applications as needed.

The major types of virtualization are the following:

- *Storage virtualization* is the pooling of physical storage from multiple network storage devices into what appears to be a single storage device that is managed from a central console.

- *Network virtualization* combines the available resources in a network by splitting the network load into manageable parts, each of which can be assigned (or reassigned) to a particular server on the network.

- *Hardware virtualization* is the use of software to emulate hardware or a total computer environment other than the one the software is actually running in. It allows a piece of hardware to run multiple operating system images at once. This kind of software is sometimes known as a *virtual machine*.

Virtualization can increase the flexibility of IT assets, allowing companies to consolidate IT infrastructure, reduce maintenance and administration costs, and prepare for strategic IT initiatives such as grid computing, utility computing, and service-oriented architecture.

Virtualization helps to bring new products and services to the market quicker, and also enables business continuity (Chapter 5) in the event of a system failure. Finally, it enables sharing computing resources with other organizations. For more information, see *virtualization.info*, *roughtype.com*, *Contingency Planning and Management* (2008), *and en.wikipedia.org/wiki/virtualization*.

Commercial Efforts in New Computing Environments. Several software companies currently are developing major products in the emerging computer environments. Many will incorporate utility computing, pervasive computing, and Web Services sometime in the future. Microsoft launched a major research effort, known as *Microsoft.Net* (*microsoft.com/net*). IBM is developing its WebSphere platform (*ibm.com/software/websphere*). Sun Microsystems is building a new system architecture in its N1 Project and Oracle is developing several projects all related to the above technologies.

Whether an organization uses mainframe-based legacy systems or cutting-edge Web-based ones, its information resources are extremely important organizational assets that need to be protected and managed. This topic is presented in Chapter 14 and Online Chapter 16.

Review Questions

1. Define information infrastructure and information architecture.
2. Describe Web-based systems and Web-based EC systems.
3. What is the Web 2.0 environment?
4. Describe SOA and its benefits.
5. Describe software-as-a-service and its benefits. Why is it referred to as utility computing?
6. Define open source.
7. Describe virtualization.

2.6 Innovative and Futuristic Information Systems

There are a large number of information systems that have been developed for special purposes and to help solve complex problems ranging from traffic jams to pollution control to healthcare delivery. Also, some futuristic systems are in their conceptual design providing innovative solutions. A few representative examples are included in this chapter. First, let's look at a hypothetical scenario.

First, imagine this scenario: It's a Monday morning in the year 2012. Executive Joanne Smith gets into her car, and her voice activates a wireless telecommunications-access workstation. She requests that all open and pending voice and mail messages, as well as her schedule for the day, be transmitted to her car. The office workstation consolidates these items from home and office databases. The message-ordering "knowbot" (knowledge robot), which is an enhanced e-mail messaging system, delivers the accumulated messages (in the order she prefers) to the voice and data wireless device in Joanne's car. By the time Joanne gets to the office, she has heard the necessary messages, sent some replies, revised her day's schedule, and completed a to-do list for the week, all of which have been filed in her virtual database by her personal organizer knowbot. She has also accessed the Internet by voice and checked traffic conditions, stock prices, and top news stories.

The virtual organizer and the company intranet have made Joanne's use of IT much easier. No longer does she have to be concerned about the physical location of data. She is working on a large proposal for the Acme Corporation today; although segments of the Acme file physically exist on several databases, she can access the data from her *wireless workstation* wherever she happens to be. To help manage this information resource, Joanne uses an *information visualizer* that enables her to create and manage dynamic relationships among data collections. This information visualizer has extended the graphical user interface to a three-dimensional graphic structure.

Joanne could do even more work if her car were able to drive itself and if it were able to find an empty parking space on its own. Although this kind of car is still in an experimental stage, it will probably be in commercial use before 2015, due to developments in pervasive computing.

It may be possible for parts of this year 2012 scenario to become a reality even sooner, owing to important trends in information technology. The future can be predicted by existing trends. Representative trends fall into two categories: general and networked computing. Others are described in the Technology Guides on the book's Web site. A description of some of the trends is provided in Online Brief 2.3.

Some of the most innovative information systems are those that are aimed at reducing traffic congestion and air pollution, eliminating accidents, providing aid to travelers, and more. In this section, we illustrate some of these systems. Several systems are illustrated in Chapter 7 (e.g., car navigation, NextBus information, crash notification, and smart cars). Our presentation begins with a true story (see *A Closer Look 2.3*).

Predictive analysis tools help determine the probable future outcome for an event or the likelihood of a situation occurring. They also identify relationships and patterns. A complete description is provided in Chapter 12. An example of how predictive analysis can help you avoid traffic jams is provided in Online Minicase 2.4.

Predictive analysis uses sophisticated algorithms designed to sift through a data warehouse and identify patterns of behavior that suggest, for example, which offers your customers might respond to in the future, or which customers you might be in danger of losing. For instance, when sifting through a bank's data warehouse, predictive analysis might recognize that customers who cancel an automatic bill payment or automatic deposit often move to another bank within a certain period of time.

An interesting application of predictive analysis is described next.

Innovative Health Care Wireless Predictive System. A remote medical monitoring system can help with early diagnosis of heart failures. A person stands regularly on a special bathroom weight scale that can transmit, wirelessly, data to a clinician's screen. A computer analyzes the weight change and triggers an alarm for a suspected anomaly that predicts a possible trouble. The medical technician then

A Closer Look 2.3

How Useful Traffic Lights Can Be

In the good old days (and even today in many countries), traffic flow at intersections was aided by traffic officers. In what people called progress, traffic lights were installed at the intersections (green, yellow, and red). Lights changed at constant intervals, but were they really useful?

In 1993 one of the authors of this book visited a university in Taiwan. A city tour with a student was organized. It was 10:00 a.m., and the tour entered the city center. Very soon it became clear that many times drivers did not stop at red lights. The author asked the student, "Why do you not stop at the red lights?" The answer was, "Because they are not useful." "Why is this so?" asked the author. And the answer was, "If there is no cross traffic, why should I stop? It is a waste of time, money (cost of gasoline), and it increases pollution, and I don't know how long I will have to wait for the green light." "So why do you have lights here?" asked the

author. And the answer was: "During the day, these are for warning, during the night, they are for decoration."

Fifteen years later the author visited the same university and was taken on a city tour. This time it was different. Many lights at intersections were intelligent, as shown in the attached figure. An approaching car or a pedestrian can see how many seconds it has to wait (red), or cross (green). The cameras on the top can see how many cars are waiting (or approaching) in each direction and, using *automated decision system* business rules (Chapter 12), calculate the time needed for the lights to change. So if there are no cars in the cross direction, traffic flows, and if there is only one car, the time given is very short.

The student driver stopped at all of the red lights this time. Similar systems have been installed all over the world in an attempt to save gasoline and reduce pollution.

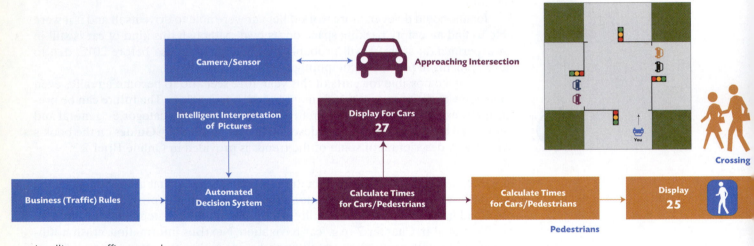

Intelligent traffic control system.

calls the person to discuss medication, need to see a doctor, etc. The system keeps patients healthier and cuts health costs.

Similar remote monitoring devices are used to treat children with asthma, adults with mental disorders, patients with diabetes, and more. Some systems allow for real-time audio and video consultation with a physician. A unique system sells an electronic pill box that records whether, and when, patients take their medicine. Interested? Try Health Buddy and visit eWeel.com's Health Care Center for the latest news, views, and analysis of technology's impact on healthcare.

THE NRI MODEL

One of the most difficult tasks that enterprise managers need to address is to figure out how IT will look in the future. Bouton (2008) provides a futuristic view of the 10 IS technologies that will force changes in industry models, business processes, vendor types, products, services, and user models. Several of these are described here; others are presented in Chapter 8.

An interesting look into the near future is provided by the Nomura Research Institute (NRI) in Japan and is shown in Figure 2.11. The figure shows that sensors will collect vast amounts of information from the Internet and other networks.

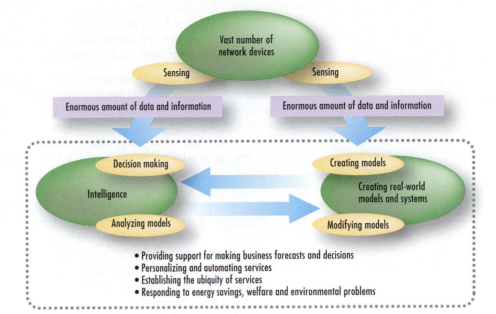

Figure 2.11 Features of information systems in 2010.
Source: Nakamoto, H. and M. Komeicji, "IT Roadmap toward 2010," Nomura Research Institute, March 1, 2006, Figure 5, p. 7. nri.co.jp/english/opinion/papers/2006/pdf/np2006102.pdf.

Intelligent systems will then process the information in complex models through several iterations of improvements. This will provide the best organizational strategy for responses to environmental pressures, as described in Chapter 1. Also, the systems will utilize wireless and automated services.

Risks and Failures of Introducing IT Systems. *Example.* Britain's National Health Information System. What is probably the world's biggest IT disaster on record occurred in England when an IT project budgeted for $12 billion cost over $24 billion, and probably much more once it is completed. The 10-year project that started in 2003 is supposed to digitize England's entire healthcare system and be able to deliver electronic lifelong records for over 55 million people in England. Doctors can order prescriptions online, patients can schedule appointments and procedures, and much more. Because of government delays, the project's biggest contractor (Accenture, $3.75 billion) walked away. Delays in the work of one vendor caused delays in the work of other vendors. By October 2006, only 6 of the 24 systems were completed. Vendors that were supposed to be paid only when their projects were complete lost millions of dollars. The project cost overrun continues to increase. The estimates regarding data collection and availability were incorrect as was the preliminary system analysis and design. The coordination among vendors, healthcare providers, government agencies, and so forth became too complex. (McCartney, 2006)

Methods for dealing with such risks and avoiding failures are presented throughout this book.

Review Questions

1. Describe an intelligent traffic control system.
2. How can an intelligent system help you avoid a traffic jam?
3. What are the essential elements of the NRI model?

2.7 Managerial Issues

A modern organization possesses many information resources. In addition to the infrastructures, numerous applications exist, and new ones are continuously being developed. Applications have enormous strategic value. Firms rely on them so heavily that, in some cases, when they are not working even for a short time, an organization cannot function. Furthermore, the acquisition, operation, security, and maintenance of these systems may cost a considerable amount of money. The resources are scattered throughout the organization, and some of them change frequently. Therefore, it may be rather difficult to manage IS resources. It is essential to manage these information systems properly.

1. **The transition to a digital enterprise.** Converting an organization to a networked-computing-based digital enterprise may be a complicated process. The digital enterprise requires a client/server architecture, an intranet, an Internet connection, and e-commerce policy and strategy, all in the face of many unknowns and risks. However, in many organizations, this potentially painful conversion may be the only way to succeed or even to survive. When to do it, how to do it, what will be the role of the enabling information technologies, and what will be the impacts of such a conversion are major issues for organizations to consider.

The transition process may involve a move from the legacy systems to a Web-based client/server enterprisewide architecture. While the general trend is toward Web-based client/servers, there have been several unsuccessful transformations and many unresolved issues regarding the implementation of these systems. The introduction of intranets seems to be much easier than that of other client/server applications. Yet, moving to any new architecture requires new infrastructure and a decision about what to do with the legacy systems, which may have a considerable impact on people, quality of work, and budget. A major aspect is the introduction of wireless infrastructure. These important issues are discussed in detail in Chapters 13 through 15 and in Technology Guide 5.

It should be noted that many companies need high-speed computing of high-volume data. Here the client/server concept may not be effective. In such cases, management should consider transformation of the legacy systems to new types of mainframes that use innovations for making the systems smaller and cheaper. Other options such as grid computing are available.

2. **How to deal with the outsourcing and utility computing trends.** As opportunities for outsourcing are becoming cheaper, available, and viable, the concept becomes more attractive. In the not-so-distant future, we will see outsourcing in the form of software-as-a-service. How much to outsource is a major managerial issue (see Chapters 13 and 14). Another issue is the offshore outsourcing to countries such as India and China.

3. **Ethical issues.** Introducing computerized support, especially support systems that involve significant change, may create ethical problems. For example, older employees may resist training or changes in their work habits. Fear of losing jobs or reduction of their importance may be important topics in IT adoption (Chapter 14). Relationships with supply chain partners may involve ethical issues, such as requiring the use of RFID. See Tutorial #4 on ethics.

4. **The risk of introducing new technologies.** New technologies introduce changes and do not guarantee success. We discuss how to deal with change management in Chapter 14 and risk management in Chapter 13.

5. **The importance of supply chain management.** In this chapter we stressed the support needed for supply chain management. Managing supply chains can be difficult, especially if global suppliers and/or customers are involved. The questions involved include which software (vendor) to use from the many available, how to gain the cooperation of the business partners along the supply chain, and how to secure the supply chain information support systems.

6. **The importance of business intelligence.** During the last few years business intelligence (BI) has become one of the top three most important IT support tools. The reason is that the increased availability of capable tools and the opportunity to lease rather than buy them through utility computing provides an extremely effective and efficient analytical tool for management. The problems are to determine: (1) if you really need the tool, (2) which product and vendor should you use, (3) how to integrate the tool with your existing system, and (4) how to utilize the tool in the most appropriate way?

How *IT* Benefits You

Accounting Major

Accountants must understand the types of information systems that exist in organizations and the way they support users to better design and audit systems. Furthermore, they must understand how TPSs work since most TPSs are accounting-related information flows. Finally, the accountants must be familiar with various compliance requirements and the flow of data and information to comply with the requirements.

Finance Major

Financial analysts and managers are often involved in cost/benefit and justification of IT applications and, therefore, they must understand the various configurations of information systems, the options available, and the ways systems support users in other departments. Financial issues are critical both in assessing information systems (Chapter 13 and Online Chapter 17) and in managing the health of organizations. Finally, understanding emerging systems and their capabilities and benefits will help finance people to better review the budgets requested from users for their acquisition and operations.

Human Resources Management Major

Information systems are designed to support people in various job positions and functional areas. Understanding how this is done can help HRM people in assessing human performance and in improving recruiting, promotions, and training programs. Furthermore, some of the emerging technologies provide the HRM function with opportunities to improve its own performance. Thus, it is important to know the various available systems and their capabilities.

IS Major

The Information Systems Department (ISD) is a support service to other departments and an extremely important and strategically growing field. The ISD must understand the use of IT by end users and the interdependency among systems. Furthermore, the ISD may be involved in IT training as well as problem resolution in the functional areas. The IS people must understand all of the options to acquire and build both traditional and emerging types of systems. Finally, IS people are responsible for shared information resources and their protection, and appropriate use in the functional areas.

Marketing Major

Understanding the internal flow of information in organizations is vital for improving order fulfillment and status tracking so marketing and salespeople can be responsive to customer inquiries. Furthermore, knowledge of emerging systems and future needs of existing and prospective customers allows the marketing department to improve its own operations. Several enterprise systems are crucial for marketing (e.g., CRM, ERP), so knowledge about their architecture can be very useful.

Operations Management Major

Changing production/operations to on-demand, real time, and mass customization requires changes in the supporting information systems. Therefore, knowledge about types of systems available and the support they render is critical. Furthermore, POM interact with partners along the supply chain, so collaborative systems and their operations must be understood.

Key Terms

Chapter Highlights

1 Information systems collect, process, store, analyze, and disseminate data and information for a specific purpose. They do it primarily in application programs.

1 Information systems can be organized according to organizational hierarchy (e.g., departmental, enterprisewide, and interorganizational) or by the nature of the supported task (e.g., operational, managerial, and strategic).

2 The transaction processing system (TPS) covers the core repetitive organizational transactions such as purchasing, billing, or payroll.

2 The data collected in a TPS are used to build other support systems, especially MIS and BI.

2 The major functional information systems in an organization are accounting, finance, manufacturing (operations), human resources, and marketing.

2 3 The term *management information system (MIS)* refers to the department that manages information systems in organizations. The acronym MIS is also used more generally to describe the field of IT as well as systems that support routine tasks of middle-level managers.

3 The main IT support systems are TPS, MIS, office automation systems, decision support systems, business intelligence systems, group support systems (groupware), knowledge management systems, enterprise information systems, expert systems, and artificial neural networks.

3 Managerial activities and decisions can be classified as operational, managerial (tactical), and strategic. Each can be supported by some IT tools.

4 Three of the major IT-supported managerial activities are (1) improving supply chain operations, (2) integrating departmental systems with ERP, and (3) introducing a variety of customer relationship management (CRM) activities. IT is a major enabler of all of these.

5 Information architecture provides the conceptual foundation for building the information infrastructure and specific applications. IT maps the information requirements as they relate to information resources.

6 The information infrastructure refers to the shared information resources (such as corporate networks, databases) and their linkages, operation, maintenance, and management. These support an array of applications.

6 IT supports individual business processes in all functional areas (with MIS applications). It also supports activities along the supply chain such as procurement, relationship with suppliers, supply chain management, customer relationship management, and order fulfillment.

6 Information architecture is the high-level map of the IT assets. It is based on business architecture. It appears in several varieties, such as Web-based architecture, client-server, and service-oriented architecture.

7 Web-based systems refer to those applications or services that reside on a server that is accessible using a Web browser and that work with Internet protocols. Examples are e-procurement, corporate portals, electronic markets and exchanges, and mobile commerce.

8 There is a trend for renting application software as needed rather than buying it. This way, there is no need to build systems or own software. This approach, called software-as-a-service (*utility computing*), is similar to buying water or electricity when needed.

8 The major emerging technologies include software-as-a-service (see next highlight), utility computing, grid computing, mobile and pervasive computing, Web Services, open source, and virtualization.

9 Innovative information systems include an integrated system with powerful computing tools, an intelligent component, sensor(s), and powerful visualization.

Virtual Company Assignment

Information Architecture at The Wireless Café

Go to The Wireless Café's link on the Student Web Site. There you will be asked to study the restaurant's existing information technologies and document its information architecture.

Instructions for accessing The Wireless Café on the Student Web Site:

1. Go to *wiley.com/college/turban*.
2. Select Turban/Leidner/McLean/Wetherbe's *Information Technology for Management*, Sixth Edition.
3. Click on Student Resources site, in the toolbar on the left.
4. Click on the link for Virtual Company Web Site.
5. Click on Wireless Café.

Questions for Discussion

1. Discuss the logic of building information systems in accordance with the organizational hierarchical structure.

2. Distinguish between interorganizational information systems (IOS) and electronic markets.

3. Relate an MIS to a functional information system.
4. Explain how operational, managerial, and strategic activities are related to various IT support systems.
5. Relate an enterprise information system to business processes.
6. Web-based applications such as e-commerce and e-government exemplify the platform shift from legacy systems to Web-based computing. Discuss the advantages of a Web-based computing environment.
7. Is the Internet an infrastructure, architecture, or application program? Why? If none of the above, then what is it?
8. Discuss why SOA is considered to be a major key to business agility.
9. Some speculate that utility computing will be the dominating option of the future. Do you agree? Discuss why or why not.
10. Compare and contrast grid computing and utility computing.
11. Discuss the relationship between SOA and on-demand computing.
12. RFID is considered superior to bar codes. Discuss why this is so.
13. Discuss the benefits of predictive analysis.
14. Compare and contrast information architecture and infrastructure.

Exercises and Projects

1. Classify each of the following systems as one (or more) of the IT support systems and design a business performance management for each:

   a. A student registration system in a university
   b. A system that advises farmers about which fertilizers to use
   c. A hospital patient-admission system
   d. A system that provides a marketing manager with demand reports regarding the sales volume of specific products
   e. A robotic system that paints cars in a factory

2. Enter *teradatastudentnetwork.com* (ask your instructor for the password) and find the Webcase on "BI Approaches in Healthcare, Financial Services, Retail, and Government" (2006). Explain the IT support. What challenges are common across the industries? Write a report.

3. Review the following systems in this chapter and *identify* the support provided by IT and globalization issues:
   - J.P. Morgan (*IT at Work 2.2*)
   - Best Buy online (see Online Minicase 2.1)
   - Mary Kay (see Opening Case)
   - Pepsi (*IT at Work 2.3*)

Group Assignments and Projects

1. Observe a checkout counter in a supermarket that uses a scanner. Find some material that describes how the scanned code is translated into the price that the customers pay.

   a. Identify the following components of the system: inputs, processes, and outputs.
   b. What kind of a system is the scanner (TPS, DSS, BI, ES, etc.)? Why did you classify it as you did?
   c. Having the information electronically in the system may provide opportunities for additional managerial uses of that information. Identify such uses.
   d. Checkout systems are now being replaced by self-service checkout kiosks and scanners. Compare the two.

2. Explore the relationship of IT and innovation. The group explores sites that deal with innovation such as *ideablog.com*. Explore the innovations they sponsored within the last 12 months and identify those which are related to IT. Explore *google.com* for similar sites. Prepare a report.

Internet Exercises

1. Enter the site of Federal Express (*fedex.com*) and find the current information systems used by the company or offered to FedEx's customers. Explain how the systems' innovations contribute to the success of FedEx.

2. Enter the Web site of Hershey Foods (*hersheys.com*). Examine the information about the company and its products and markets. Explain how an intranet can help such a company compete in the global market.

3. Investigate the status of utility computing by visiting *utilitycomputing.com/forum, aspnews.com* (discussion forum), *google.com, ibm.com, oracle.com,* and *cio.com*. Prepare a report that will highlight the progress today and the current inhibitors.

4. Enter *argus-acia.com* and learn about new developments in the field of information architecture. Also, view the tutorials at *webmonkey.com* on this topic. Summarize major new trends.

5. Enter *oracle.com, sap.com,* and *wikipedia.org* and identify material related to supply chain and corporatewide systems as it relates to IT. Prepare a report.

6. Enter *oracle.com* and read about grid computing. View the demo. Write a summary on business applications of grid computing.

7. Experience customizations by designing your own shoes at *nike.com*, your car at *jaguar.com*, your CD at *saregama.com*, and your business at *iprint.com*. Summarize your experiences.

Minicase

Airbus Improves Productivity with RFID

Because it is in constant competition with Boeing, the European aircraft manufacturer Airbus is looking for every opportunity to increase productivity, reduce costs, and make its production process more efficient. One of its latest efforts is to use RFID technology in both manufacturing and maintenance of its airplanes. The basic idea is to use RFID to track parts and tools, which are scattered over a large area. Airbus had major delays in completing its A380, the two-decker, 525-seat airplane scheduled for completion in 2007 and 2008.

Airbus hopes that RFID will become "as everyday as bar coding." The company experimented with the technology for three years before signing a multimillion dollar deal with vendors to implement the technololgy. It also created a value cabin visibility and RFID unit to implement the biggest private sector RFID deal ever.

Airbus has implemented process-improvement projects involving RFID to track parts inside warehouses, as they move from one region to another, and as they are built into aircraft, as well as to track how and where tools are used for manufacturing and maintenance. The new RFID software infrastructure lets Airbus employees and systems exchange information collected by RFID readers. The infracfructure also integrates RFID data with business systems such as Airbus' core ERP system.

The software also manages data from bar codes, which remain an important part of Airbus' supply chain. RFID tags can hold more information and require a line-of-sight reader, but they typically cost more than $1 per tag. So Airbus uses them only on rolling cages, pallets, cases, and high-cost parts.

Airbus expects RFID to augment ongoing supply chain process improvements, saving money by reducing time spent searching for parts, reducing inventory, and improving productivity.

Airbus is assessing a few pilot projects with suppliers tagging parts before shipping them, and the new software makes it possible to extend parts tracking from the supplier side to Airbus. Boeing, which has its own extensive RFID tests, said its first 787 Dreamliner would be delivered in the third quarter of 2009, instead of the first, due to supplier delays, unanticipated rework, and longer testing. Airlines that ordered the plane are pressing for compensation for the delays.

To close its RFID deal, Airbus had to navigate a still highly fragmented RFID industry. There have been hundreds of vendors; each tells you a different story, with different architectures and different payoffs. To sort it out, Airbus assigned a 25-person team of IT, business, and process analysts for about two years to develop a company-side RFID approach. Airbus is employing RFID across two main categories: non-flyable and flyable.

- *Non-flyable* consists of ground-based processes, such as supply chain, transportation, logistics, manufacturing, and assembly-related applications.
- *Flyable* refers to all in-service processes, including operational, maintenance, and payload-tracking applications.

Sources: Compiled from Hayes-Weier (2008) and *RFID Journal News* (2007).

Questions

1. What are the drivers of the RFID project?
2. What information technologies are cited here and are related to the implementation?
3. What categories of people will be supported by the RFID?
4. What managerial levels and tasks will be supported by the RFID?
5. What are the performance management implications? (Relate to the book's model).

Problem-Solving Activity

Handling the High Cost of Gasoline

The price of gasoline is surging and most probably will continue to escalate in the foreseeable future until new sources of energy will be able to catch up with the globally increasing demand for energy. Individuals, corporations, and government are involved in solving this issue. It is very likely that you are, too. What can you do? This assignment will help you deal with the problem.

Exercises

1. Use a calculator to determine the overall consumption cost. (You can find such calculators at *fuelcost-calculator.com* and *gaspricesmapquest.com*.)

- Calculate the cost of driving a Honda Accord from your home to Las Vegas and back.
- How can such a tool help you determine your route?
2. Enter *feuleconomy.gov*.
- How can such a tool help you decide what car to buy?
3. If you live in a large metropolitan area, you know that gas prices can vary. How can you find the cheapest gas?
- *Automotive.com* provides a free application (called a widget), a real-time, continually updated tool that monitors gas prices. (Check *automotive.com/widgets/gasprices/index.html*.) Explain the benefit of its use.
- You can use your cell phone as well. Try *getmobio.com/learn/cheapgas*. Explain how it can help you save on gas.

4. Explore mass transit options. You may be surprised how much you can save each month. Do not forget to include the cost of parking and amortization when you assess the savings. Try *google.com/transit*. Write a short report.

5. Find stations with alternative fuels. Alternative fuels such as E85 (contains 85 percent ethanol) or compressed natural gas can be helpful. Try *altfuelprices.com*.
  • How useful is this tool?

6. Also try *gasbuddy.com* and *gaspricewatch.com*. Conduct a search for additional ways to save on gas.

7. You have just been promoted to a fleet manager in a food company that uses 250 cars of different sizes. Prepare a report to top management on how to save on gas if the price is at $4, $5, $6, and $7 per gallon. A spreadsheet will help support your report (use the what-if option in Excel).

Online Resources

More resources and study tools are located on the Student Web Site and on WileyPLUS. You'll find additional chapter materials and useful Web links. In addition, self-quizzes that provide individualized feedback are available for each chapter.

Online Briefs for Chapter 2 are available at wiley.com/college/turban:

2.1 The Evolution of Support Systems

2.2 Why We Use Computerized Decision Support

2.3 Trends in IT

Online Minicases for Chapter 2 are available at wiley.com/college/turban:

2.1 Best Buy Improves Its Supply Chain

2.2 Mobile Computing Supports Field Employees at Maybelline

2.3 Elite Care Supported by Intelligent Systems

2.4 Predictive Analysis Can Help You Avoid Traffic Jams

References

Bouton, C., "The Future of IS Technologies That Will Force Change (The 10 Most Disruptive Technologies)," *eWeek*, April 19, 2008.

Channel Insider, "Mary Kay Gets IT Makeover," April 25, 2007, *channelinsider.com/c/a/News/Mary-Kay-Gets-IT-Makeover* (accessed April 2008).

Cone, E., "Customer Management," *eWeek*, October 2003a, *findarticles.com/p/articles/mi_zdewk/is_200310/ai_ziff109716* (no longer available online).

Cone, E., "Dallas Mavericks: Small Companies, Big Returns," *Baseline Magazine*, October 1, 2003b, *baselinemag.com/article2/0,1540,1313703,00.asp* (accessed May 2008).

Contingency Planning and Management, "Study: Companies Using Virtualization to Support Business Continuity, Disaster Recovery to Increase," February 19, 2008, *contingencyplanning.com/articles/58671* (accessed April 2008).

Dubie, D., "Mary Kay Makes Over Its WAN," *Network World*, June 1, 2006. *networkworld.com/newsletters/accel/2006/0529netop2.htm* (accessed April 2008).

Duvall, M., "Supercharged," *Baseline*, October, 2005.

Gates, L., "State of Texas Recovers $400 Million through Predictive Analytics," *ADTmag.com*, May 26, 2005, *adtmag.com/article.asp?id=11214* (accessed May 2008).

Gonsalves, C., "Halo 3 Meets Second Life," *Baseline*, February 2008.

Greenemeier, L., "IBM Expands On-Demand Services," *Information Week*, September 30, 2003.

Jainschigg, J., "SaaS Serving Up," *Baseline Magazine*, July 2008.

Hamblen, M., "J.P. Morgan Harnesses Power with Grid Computing System," *ComputerWorld*, March 15, 2004.

"Handelsbanken," IBM Case Study, *www-3.ibm.com/e-business/doc/content/casestudy/35433.html* (no longer available online).

Handelsbanken.com (accessed May 2008).

Hayes-Weier, M., "Airbus' Sky-High Stakes on RFID," *InformationWeek*, April 18, 2008.

Koontz, C., "Develop a Solid Architecture," *e-Business Advisor*, January 2000.

LGC Wireless, "Case Study: Mary Kay Puts a New Face on Wireless," 2008, *lgcwireless.com/downloads/Case_Study_Mary_Kay.pdf* (accessed April 2008).

Lohr, S., "Sony to Supercharge Online Gaming," *International Herald Tribune*, February 28, 2003.

MaryKay.com (accessed April 2008).

McCartney, L., "$12.6 Billion Cost Overrun," *Baseline*, December 2006.

Miller M., *Cloud Computing: Web-Based Applications that Change the Way You Work and Collaborate Online*, Indianapolis, IN.: Que Pub., 2008.

O'Reilly, T. "What Is Web 2.0?" *OReillynet.com*, September 30, 2005, *oreilly.net/pub/a/oreilly/tim/news/2005/09/30/what-is-web-20.html* (accessed May 2008).

Pepsi.com (accessed April 2008).

Pratt , M. K., "Portal Panacea," *Computerworld*, November 19, 2007.

RFID Journal, "Airbus to Present Case Study at RFID Journal Live! Europe 2007," *RFIDJournal.com*, September 5, 2007, *rfidjournal.com/article/articleview/3596/1/1/definitions_off* (accessed May 2008).

Rhey, E., "Pepsi Refreshes, Wirelessly," *PC*, September 17, 2002, pp. 4-5.

Rubin, C., "More than Skin Deep," *Communication News*, March 2007.

Shread, P., "Banking on Grids," *Gridcomputingplant.com*, April 25, 2006, *gridcomputingplanet.com/news/article.php/3601451* (accessed May 2008).

Staff, "SPSS Predictive Analytics Helps Texas Recover $400 Million in Unpaid Taxes," *B-eye-network.com*, May 16, 2005, *b-eye-network.com/view/868* (accessed May 2008).

Turban, E., et al., *Business Intelligence: A Managerial Approach*. Upper Saddle River, NJ: Prentice-Hall, 2008.

Weill, P., and M. R. Vitale, *Place to Space: Migrating to eBusiness Models*. Boston: Harvard Business Press, 2001.

WesternPetro.com (accessed April 2008).

Building an E-Business at Fedex Corporation

FedEx Corporation was founded in 1973 by entrepreneur Fred Smith. Today, with a fully integrated physical and virtual infrastructure, FedEx's business model supports 24–48-hour package delivery to anywhere in the world. FedEx operates one of the world's busiest data-processing centers, handling over 100 million information requests per day from more than 3,000 databases and more than 500,000 archive files. It operates one of the largest real-time, online client/server networks in the world. The core competencies of FedEx are now in express transportation and in e-solutions.

The Problem/Opportunity

Initially, FedEx grew out of pressures from mounting inflation and global competition. These pressures gave rise to greater demands on businesses to expedite deliveries at a low cost and to improve customer services. FedEx didn't have a business problem per se but, rather, has endeavored to stay ahead of the competition by looking ahead at every stage for opportunities to meet customers' needs for fast, reliable, and affordable overnight deliveries. Lately, the Internet has provided an inexpensive and accessible platform upon which FedEx has seen further opportunities to expand its business scope, both geographically and in terms of service offerings. For example, FedEx created an e-fulfillment system. Orders placed by customers to merchants are both managed and fulfilled by FedEx. FedEx is attempting to attain two of its major goals simultaneously: 100 percent customer service and 0 percent downtime.

The IT Solution/Project

A prime software application used by FedEx is e-Shipping Tools, a Web-based shipping application that allows customers to check the status of shipments through the company's Web page. FedEx is also providing integrated solutions to address the entire selling and supply chain needs of its customers. Its e-Commerce Solutions provide a full suite of services that allow businesses to integrate FedEx's transportation and information systems seamlessly into their own operations. These solutions have taken FedEx well beyond a shipping company.

FedEx markets several e-commerce hardware/software solutions: FedEx PowerShipMC (a multicarrier hardware/software system), FedEx Ship Manager Server (a hardware/software system providing high-speed transactions and superior reliability, allowing an average of eight transactions per second), FedEx ShipAPI™ (an Internet-based application that allows customization, eliminating redundant programming), and FedEx Net-Return® (a Web-based item-return management system). This infrastructure is now known as FedEx Direct Link. It enables business-to-business electronic commerce through combinations of global virtual private network (VPN) connectivity, Internet connectivity, leased-line connectivity, and VAN (value-added network) connectivity.

The figure on page 75 provides an example of one of FedEx's e-commerce solutions: ❶ Merchants place their catalogs online, and ❷ FedEx customers browse the catalog deciding what to buy. When a customer places a purchase order online, it is sent to a FedEx Web server ❸. Information about the order and the customer is then sent to the merchant's PC, and ❹ a message is sent to the customer to confirm receipt of the order. After the order is received and acknowledged, the FedEx Web server sends a message to the merchant's bank to obtain credit approval ❺. At the same time, the order is sent via electronic data interchange (EDI) to a FedEx mainframe ❻ that activates the *warehouse management system* ❼. The order is processed (goods are picked and packed), the warehouse inventory system is updated, and the shipping process is activated. Information regarding the processing of the order is accessible at the three remote electronic data centers (EDCs) located in the United States, the Europe/Mediterranean (EMEA) region, and the Asia Pacific (APAC) region. During the entire process, the customer, the merchant, and FedEx employees can track at any time the status of the order and its fulfillment via the Web.

The Results

The e-commerce-based FedEx business model creates value for customers in a number of ways: It facilitates better communication and collaboration between the various parties along the selling and supply chains. It promotes efficiency gains by reducing costs and speeding up the order cycle. It encourages customers not only to use FedEx as a shipper but also to outsource to FedEx all their logistics activities. It also provides FedEx a competitive edge and increased revenue and profits. Thus, FedEx has changed from an old-economy shipping company to an e-business logistics enterprise. In 2006, FedEx was delivering over 6 million packages a day in over 220 countries. It is considered the second most admired company in the United States and fourth in the world.

Sources: Based on Conley et al. (2000), Colvin (2006), and updated with information from *fedex.com* (accessed April 2008).

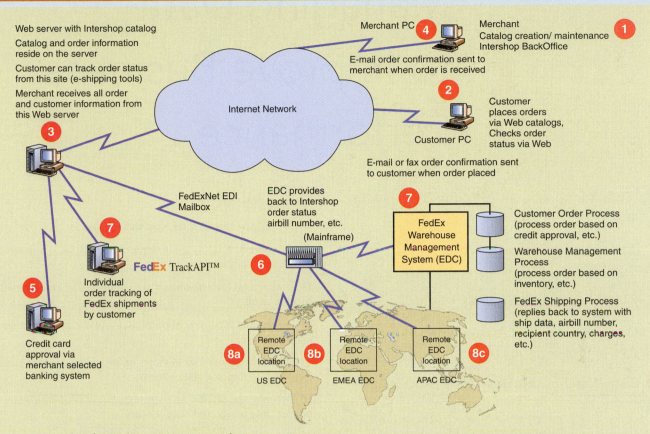

An example of a FedEx e-commerce solution.

Source: Based on a SIM 2000 award-winning paper written by William L. Conley, Ali F. Farhoomand, and Pauline S.P. Ng, at simnet.org/library/doc/2ndpalce.doc, no longer available online. Courtesy of William Conley.

References

Colvin, G., "The FedEx Edge," *Fortune*, April 3, 2006.

Conley, W. L., A. F. Farhoomand, and P. S. P. Ng, "Building an E-Business at FedEx Corporation," *Society for Information Management Annual Awards Paper Competition*, 2000, simnet.org/library/doc/2ndplace.doc (no longer available online).

Fedex.com (accessed April 2008).

Questions

1. Identify the networks cited in this case.
2. How does IT improve the performance of Fedex? (Relate to the book's performance management model).
3. In what ways are personalization and customization provided?
4. What are the benefits to the customers?

Chapter 3

Managing Data to Improve Business Performance

Learning Objectives

After studying this chapter, you will be able to:

❶ Describe how data and document management impact profits and performance.

❷ Understand how managers are supported or constrained by data quality.

❸ Discuss the functions of databases and database management systems.

❹ Understand how logical views of data provide customized support and improve data security.

❺ Describe the tactical and strategic benefits of data warehouses, data marts, and data centers.

❻ Describe transaction and analytic processing systems.

❼ Explain how enterprise content management and electronic records management reduce cost, support business operations, and help companies meet their regulatory and legal requirements.

Integrating IT

 ACC   **FIN**   **MKT**   **OM**   **HRM**   **IS**

IT-PERFORMANCE MODEL

In this chapter, we focus on the role of data, data management, business records, and data infrastructure. **Data infrastructure** refers to the fundamental structure of an information system, which determines how it functions and how flexible it is to meet future data requirements. We explain how effective data management improves the performance and productivity of enterprises, managers, and data workers. Real-time access to data that can be quickly analyzed and used to anticipate needs of customers, suppliers, or business partners are key prerequisites to business performance.

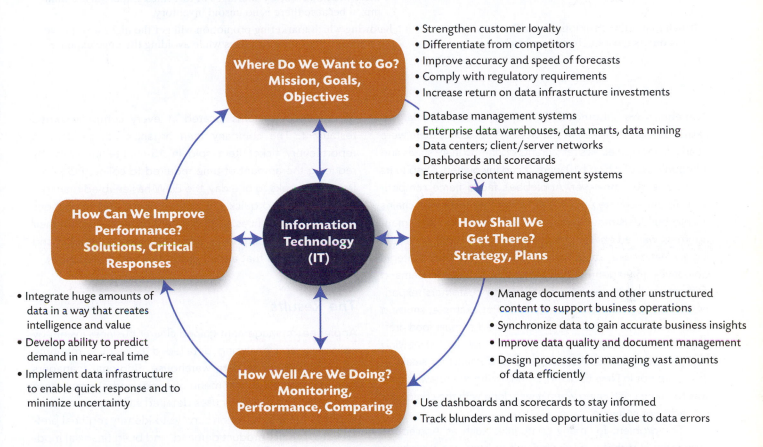

• Strengthen customer loyalty
• Differentiate from competitors
• Improve accuracy and speed of forecasts
• Comply with regulatory requirements
• Increase return on data infrastructure investments

• Database management systems
• Enterprise data warehouses, data marts, data mining
• Data centers; client/server networks
• Dashboards and scorecards
• Enterprise content management systems

Where Do We Want to Go? Mission, Goals, Objectives

How Can We Improve Performance? Solutions, Critical Responses

Information Technology (IT)

How Shall We Get There? Strategy, Plans

How Well Are We Doing? Monitoring, Performance, Comparing

• Integrate huge amounts of data in a way that creates intelligence and value
• Develop ability to predict demand in near-real time
• Implement data infrastructure to enable quick response and to minimize uncertainty

• Manage documents and other unstructured content to support business operations
• Synchronize data to gain accurate business insights
• Improve data quality and document management
• Design processes for managing vast amounts of data efficiently

• Use dashboards and scorecards to stay informed
• Track blunders and missed opportunities due to data errors

The business performance management cycle and IT model.

APPLEBEE'S INTERNATIONAL LEARNS AND EARNS FROM ITS DATA

The Problem

Over the past decades, businesses have invested heavily in IT infrastructures (e.g., ISs) to capture, store, analyze, and communicate data. However, the creation of ISs to manage and process data and the deployment of communication networks by themselves does not generate value, as measured by an increase in *profitability*. Viewed from the basic profitability or net income model (profit = revenues − expenses), profit increases when employees learn from and use the data to increase revenues, reduce expenses, or both. In this *learn and earn model*, managers learn—that is, gain insights—from their data to predict what actions will lead to the greatest increase in **net earnings.** Net earnings is also referred to as net income or the *bottom line*. The pursuit of earnings is the primary reason companies exist. Reducing uncertainty can improve the bottom line, as the examples in Table 3.1 show.

Applebee's International, Inc. (*applebees.com*), headquartered in Kansas, had faced these and other common business uncertainties and questions, but the company lacked the data infrastructure to answer them. Applebee's International develops, franchises, and operates restaurants under the

TABLE 3.1 How Data Can Reduce Uncertainty and Improve Accuracy and Performance

Business uncertainty	Business impact and value
What will be monthly demand for Product X over each of the next three months?	Knowing demand for Product X means knowing how much to order. Sales quantity and sales revenues are maximized because there are no inventory shortages or lost sales. Expenses are minimized because there is no unsold inventory.
Which marketing promotions for Product Y are customers most likely respond to?	Knowing which marketing promotion will get the highest response rate maximizes sales revenues while avoiding the huge expense of a useless promotion.

Applebee's Neighborhood Grill & Bar brand, the largest casual dining enterprise in the world. As of 2008, there were nearly 2,000 Applebee's restaurants operating in 49 states and 17 countries, of which 510 were company owned. Despite its impressive size, however, Applebee's faced fierce competition. To differentiate Applebee's from other restaurant chains and to build customer loyalty (defined as *return visits*), management wanted guests to experience a good time while having a great meal at attractive prices. To achieve their strategic objectives, management had to be able to forecast demand accurately and to become familiar with customers' experiences and regional food preferences. For example, knowing which new items to add to the menu based on past food preferences helps motivate return visits. However, identifying regional preferences, such as a strong demand for steaks in Texas but not in New England, by analyzing the relevant data was too time consuming when it was done with the company's spreadsheet software.

The problem for many companies such as Applebee's International is that it is very difficult to bring together huge quantities of data located in different databases in a way that creates value. Without efficient processes for managing vast amounts of customer data and turning these data into usable knowledge, companies can miss critical opportunities to find insights hidden in the data.

The Solution

Applebee's International implemented an **enterprise data warehouse (EDW)** from Teradata (*teradata.com*) with data analysis capabilities that helped management acquire an accurate understanding of sales, demand, and costs. An EDW is a data repository whose data are analyzed and used throughout the organization to improve responsiveness and ultimately net earnings. Each day, Applebee's collects data concerning the previous day's sales from hundreds of point-of-sale (POS) systems located at every company-owned restaurant. The company then organizes these data to report every ticket item sold in 15-minute intervals. By reducing the amount of time required to collect POS data from two weeks to one day, the EDW has enabled management to respond quickly to guests' needs and to changes in guests' preferences. With greater knowledge about their customers, the company is better equipped to market and provide services that attract customers and build loyalty.

The Results

Applebee's management gained clearer business insight by collecting and analyzing detailed data in near real-time using an enterprise data warehouse. Regional managers can now select the best menu offerings and operate more efficiently. The company uses detailed sales data and data from customer satisfaction surveys to identify regional preferences, predict product demand, and build financial models that indicate which products are strong performers on the menu and which are not. By linking customer satisfaction ratings to specific menu items, Applebee's can determine which items are doing well, which ones taste good, and which food arrangements on the plates look most appetizing.

With detailed, near real-time data, Applebee's International improved their customers' experience, satisfaction, and loyalty—and increased the company's earnings. For the third quarter of 2007, total system-wide sales increased by 3.9 percent over the prior year, and Applebee's opened 16 new restaurants.

Sources: Compiled from *Applebees.com* (2008), Business Wire (2007), and Teradata (2004).

Lessons Learned from This Case

This case illustrates the importance of timely and detailed data collection, data analysis, and execution based on insights from that data. It demonstrates that it is necessary to collect vast amounts of data, organize and store them properly in one place, analyze them, and then use the results of the analysis to make better marketing and strategic decisions. Companies seldom fail for lack of talent or strategic vision. Rather, they fail because of poor execution.

The case also illustrates data stages, as shown in Figure 3.1. First, data are collected, processed, and stored in a data warehouse. They are then processed by analytical tools such as data mining and decision modeling. Knowledge acquired from this data analysis directs promotional and other deci-

sions. Finally, by continuously collecting and analyzing fresh data, management can receive feedback regarding the success of management strategies.

In this chapter, we explain how businesses manage data, files, and documents in order to improve their performance. We examine the current topic of master data management, which improves data sharing across multiple locations through synchronization, that is, integrating data accumulated from a variety of sources. We also discuss fact-based, data-driven business processes to learn what factors improve business performance. We conclude by considering the regulatory and legal requirements for managing electronic records that all types of organizations currently face.

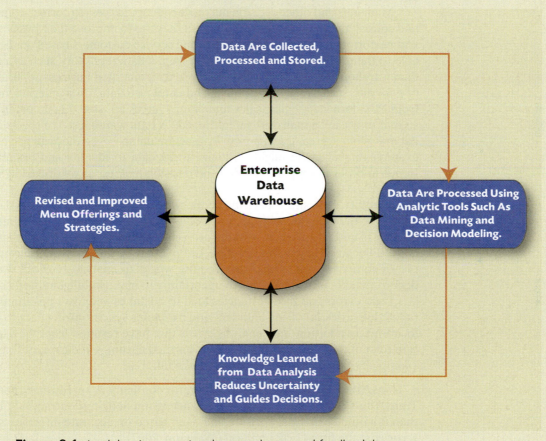

Figure 3.1 Applebee's enterprise data warehouse and feedback loop.

3.1 Data, Master Data, and Document Management

Data management is one of the most difficult challenges facing today's organizations. Modern companies create and stockpile vast quantities of data through some type of storage method. Data management helps companies improve productivity by insuring that people can find what they need without having to conduct a long and difficult search.

THE IMPORTANCE OF DATA MANAGEMENT

Why does data management matter? And, how much does it matter? These are crucial questions because data management determines the productivity of managers and employees. The goal of data management is to provide the infrastructure and tools to transform raw data into usable corporate information of the highest quality. Data are an organization's informational assets. Just as you study how to manage financial assets (i.e., identify, control, protect, analyze, and invest capital) to maximize their value in accounting and finance courses, here you learn how to manage informational assets. You will notice that the underlying concepts for managing financial and nonfinancial assets are similar. The basic rule is that, to maximize earnings, companies invest in data management technologies that increase

- The opportunity to earn revenues (e.g., customer relationship management, or CRM)
- The ability to cut expenses (e.g., inventory management)

When organizations analyze data, they need to consider all relevant expenses, including the expected costs of lost customers and earnings, penalties for noncompliance with regulations, and legal fines and losses stemming from the failure to protect confidential data from identity thieves. They calculate these costs by multiplying the probability of an event by the cost of the loss.

Managers and other decision makers need rapid access to correct, comprehensive, and consistent data across the enterprise if they are to improve their business processes and performance. They make decisions and service customers based on the data available to them. They rely on data retrieved from a data repository, such as a **database** or **data warehouse.** Databases store enterprise data that their business applications create or generate, such as sales, accounting, and employee data. Data entering the databases from POS terminals, online sales, and other sources are stored in an organized format so that they can be managed and retrieved. A data warehouse is a specialized type of database that aggregates data from transaction databases so they can be analyzed. For example, management might scrutinize these data to identify and examine business trends in order to support planning and decision making, as we discuss in Section 3.3.

UNCERTAINTY: A CONSTRAINT ON MANAGERS

The viability of business decisions depends on access to high-quality data, and the quality of the data depends on effective approaches to data management. Too often managers and information workers are actually constrained by data that cannot be trusted because they are incomplete, out of context, outdated, inaccurate, inaccessible, or so overwhelming that they require weeks to analyze. In those situations, the decision maker is facing too much uncertainty to make intelligent business decisions.

Data errors and inconsistencies lead to mistakes and lost opportunities, such as failed deliveries, invoicing blunders, and problems synchronizing data from multiple locations. In addition, data analysis errors that have resulted from the use of inaccurate formulas or untested models have harmed earnings and careers. Here are three examples of damages due to data analysis failures:

- TransAlta is a Canadian power generator company. A spreadsheet mistake led to TransAlta's buying more U.S. power transmission hedging contracts at higher prices than it would have if the decision had been based on accurate information. The data error cost the firm US$24 million (Wailgum, 2007).
- In the retail sector, the cost of errors due to unreliable and incorrect data alone is estimated to be as high as $40 billion annually (Snow, 2008).
- In the healthcare industry, one of the largest industries in the United States, data errors not only increase healthcare costs by billions of dollars, but also cost thousands of lives, as discussed in *A Closer Look 3.1.*

The design of data infrastructures to provide employees with complete, timely, accurate, accessible, understandable, and relevant data is what data management is about. Data management decisions require tough tradeoffs among many complex factors, especially in recessionary times when cost-cutting is a powerful force. Cost-cutting efforts should not make it more difficult to generate revenues, but that is what

A Closer Look 3.1

Data Errors Cost Billions of Dollars and Put Lives at Risk

Every day, administrators in the healthcare system and throughout the healthcare supply chain waste 24 to 30 percent of their time correcting data errors. Each incorrect transaction costs $60 to $80 to correct. In addition, about 60 percent of all invoices among supply chain partners have errors, and each invoice error costs $40 to $400 to reconcile. Altogether, errors and conflicting data increase supply costs by 3 to 5 percent. In other words, each year billions of dollars are wasted in the healthcare supply chain because of supply chain *data disconnects*, which refer to one organization's IS not understanding data from another's IS. Unless the healthcare system developed a data synchronization tool to prevent data disconnects, any attempts to streamline supply chain costs by implementing new technologies, such as radio frequency identification (RFID) to automatically collect data, would be sabotaged by *dirty data* before they were even implemented. RFID is data transmission using radio waves. Dirty data—that is, poor-quality data—lack integrity and cannot be trusted. New regulatory requirements, such as the Florida Pedigree Act, mandate that important information accompany each drug throughout the supply chain. Using RFID, healthcare companies can capture required information such as drug name, dosage, container size, number of containers, lot/control numbers, etc.

As one example of the problems created by the lack of data consistency, customers of the Defense Supply Center Philadelphia (DSCP), a healthcare facility operated by the Department of Defense (DoD), were receiving the wrong healthcare items, the wrong quantity of items, or an inferior item at a higher price. Numerous errors occurred whenever a supplier and DSCP (or any other DoD healthcare facility) referred to the same item (e.g., a surgical instrument) with different names or item numbers. These problems were due in large part to inaccurate or difficult-to-manage data.

For three years, efforts were made to synchronize DoD's medical/surgical data with data used by medical industry manufacturers and distributors. First, the healthcare industry had to develop a set of universal data standards or codes that uniquely identified each item. Those codes would enable organizations to accurately share data electronically because everyone would refer to each specific item the same way. The tool used for synchronization, called *data sync*, provided data consistency from cataloging through purchasing and billing. Results from this effort will improve DSCP's operating profit margin and free personnel to care for patients rather than spend their time searching through disparate product data. Other potential improvements and benefits of the data synch efforts are the following:

- Accurate and consistent item information enabling easier and faster *product sourcing*. Product sourcing simply means finding products to buy
- Matching of files to ensure lowest contracted price for purchases for quicker, automatic new item entry. If the lowest contracted prices cannot be matched and verified automatically, then it must be done manually
- Significantly reduced unauthorized purchasing and unnecessary inventories
- Leveraging purchasing power to get lower prices because purchase volumes were now apparent
- Greater patient safety
- Improved operating efficiency and fewer invoice errors

Sources: Compiled from Barlow (2007), Chisholm (2008), and Levine (2007).

For Further Exploration: How do dirty data create waste? Why is data synchronization across an enterprise a challenging problem?

---

happens in the business and healthcare sectors. In recessionary times, the payoff from having accomplished effective IT strategy and planning (the topic of Chapter 13) becomes very evident. We focus now on data management and infrastructure.

DATA MANAGEMENT

Data management is a structured approach for capturing, storing, processing, integrating, distributing, securing, and archiving data effectively throughout their life cycle, as shown in Figure 3.2. The life cycle identifies the way data travel through an

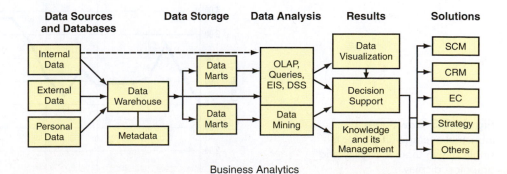

Figure 3.2 Data life cycle.

organization, from their capture or creation to their use in supporting data-driven solutions, such as supply chain management (SCM), customer relationship management (CRM), and electronic commerce (EC). SCM, CRM, and EC are enterprise applications that require current and readily accessible data to function properly. One of the foundational structures of a business solution is the data warehouse. We discuss managing data and applying them to solving business problems throughout this chapter.

Three general data principles illustrate the importance of the data life cycle perspective and guide IT investment decisions.

1. Principle of diminishing data value. Viewing data in terms of a life cycle focuses attention on how the value of data diminishes as the data age. The more recent the data, the more valuable they are. This is a simple, yet powerful, principle. Most organizations cannot operate at peak performance with blind spots (lack of data availability) of 30 days or longer.

2. Principle of 90/90 data use. Being able to act on real-time or near real-time operational data can have significant advantages. According to the 90/90 data-use principle, a majority of stored data, as high as 90 percent, is seldom accessed after 90 days (except for auditing purposes). Put another way, data lose much of their value after three months. Recall that Applebee's managers had access to detailed data on restaurant sales by the next day, when it was most valuable to their planning process. Given the perishable nature of food, getting sales data many weeks later could result in lost sales both from being unresponsive to customers' likes and dislikes and from higher food costs due to waste.

3. Principle of data in context. The capability to capture, process, format, and distribute data in near real-time or faster requires a huge investment in data management infrastructure to link remote POS systems to data storage, data analysis systems, and reporting applications. The investment can be justified on the principle that data must be integrated, processed, analyzed, and formatted into "actionable information." End users need to see data in a meaningful format and context if the data are to guide their decisions and plans.

Data Visualization. To format data into meaningful contexts for users, businesses employ **data visualization** and decision support tools (see Figure 3.2). Data or information visualization, as the name suggests, refers to presenting data in ways that are faster and easier for users to understand. To better understand this process, examine the two data displays in Figure 3.3. The tabular and graphical displays both depict one-day changes in the Dow Jones Industrial Average (DJIA). The table provides more precise data, whereas the graph takes much less time and effort to understand. Data presentation and visualization tools offer both display options.

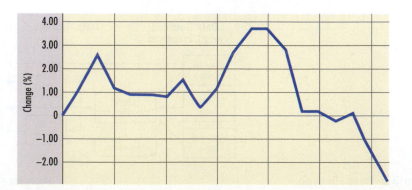

Last:	**11,893.690** Net Change:	**−146.700**% Change: **−1.22**%	
Open	12,039.090	52-Week High	14,198.100
High	12,094.210	52-Week Low	11,634.820
Low	11,819.690	Volume	07,579.268

Figure 3.3 Dow Jones industrial average (DJIA) for a single day in tabular display and graphical display.

A Closer Look 3.2

Finding Million-Dollar Donors in Three Minutes

The development department at Dartmouth University faced a common data problem. Their database stored millions of rows of alumnae data, but the only reports available to them were those created by the IT department. Unfortunately, these reports did not contain the types of information that development needed. Specifically, the data could not answer the basic questions that were critical to the success of the $1.3 billion capital campaign:

- Which alumnae had the greatest donation potential?
- Which alumni segments are most likely to donate, and in what ways?
- Which prospects are not donating to their potential?

In order for the managers to explore and navigate on their own and collect data that mattered to their campaign, the university invested in visual discovery software tools produced by Advizor Solutions (*advizorsolutions.com*). The development department used these tools to create a set of **dashboards,** which

they made available over the Web. Dashboards are visual displays similar to the dashboard on an automobile. (For examples, see *advizorsolutions.com/vizgallery.htm.*) Once the dashboards were created, the development managers were able to answer the questions listed above, without help from the IT department, by using data visualization and predictive analytics tools. Managers now get answers within three minutes that used to take three weeks because of bottlenecks in the IT department. Most importantly, better-targeted prospect messages and trips have been critical to achieving the goal of the capital campaign.

Sources: Compiled from Advizor Solutions (*advizorsolutions.com*) and Teradata (2005).

For Further Exploration: Why were managers missing opportunities to obtain donations from prospective donors? How did end-user data visualization tools improve the managers' ability to perform their jobs?

Data visualization tools and technology are becoming more popular and widely used as they become less expensive and easier to manipulate. As one example, Dartmouth University's development department, which is responsible for fundraising, realized that their efforts to target alumnae for contributions to its capital campaign were not as effective as they could be. To reduce missed opportunities, they invested in data visualization tools that they were able to use themselves. As described in *A Closer Look 3.2,* these tools enabled the development department to overcome data limitations. That is, they knew where and when to invest their time to maximize return on that time. The value of the data visualization tools can be measured by Dartmouth's hugely successful capital campaign.

DATA MANAGEMENT: PROBLEMS AND CHALLENGES

Corporate data are assets. Managing the quality and usability of those assets is vital to productivity and profitability. Remember that dirty data result in poor business decisions, poor customer service, inadequate product design, and other wasteful situations.

In *A Closer Look 3.1* you learned of the problems and costs associated with non-standardized, unsynchronized data among organizations in the healthcare supply chain. Similar data management problems can occur *within* an organization. One widespread problem is that people do not get data in the format they need to do their jobs. Therefore, even if the data are accurate, timely, and clean, they still might not be usable. According to the market intelligence firm IDC (*idc.com*), organizations with at least 1,000 knowledge workers (such as data-handling workers) lose $5.7 million annually in time wasted by employees reformatting data as they move among applications. Just as workers waste time tracking down and correcting invoicing and ordering errors among healthcare suppliers, they also spend significant amounts of time getting data into usable formats. In Chapter 4 you'll learn how businesses resolve these data deficiencies using information or **enterprise portals,** which are a set of software applications that consolidate, manage, analyze, and transmit data to users through a standardized Web-based interface.

Managing, searching for, and retrieving data located throughout the enterprise is a major challenge, for various reasons:

- The volume of data increases exponentially with time. New data are added constantly and rapidly. Business records must be kept for a long time for auditing or legal reasons, even though the organization itself may no longer access them. Only a small percentage of an organization's data is relevant for any specific application or time, and those relevant data must be identified and found in order to be useful.

• External data that need to be considered in making organizational decisions are constantly increasing in volume.

• Data are scattered throughout organizations and are collected and created by many individuals using different methods and devices. Data are frequently stored in multiple servers and locations and also in different computing systems, databases, formats, and human and computer languages.

• Data security, quality, and integrity are critical, yet easily jeopardized. In addition, legal requirements relating to data differ among countries, and they change frequently.

• Data are being created and used offline without going through quality control checks; hence, the validity of the data is questionable.

• Data throughout an organization may be redundant and out-of-date, creating a huge maintenance problem for data managers.

To deal with these difficulties, organizations invest in data management solutions. Historically, data management has been geared to supporting transaction processing by organizing the data in one location. This approach supports more secure and efficient high-volume processing. Because the amount of data being created and stored on end-user computers is increasing so dramatically, however, it is inefficient or even impossible for queries and other ad hoc applications to use traditional data management methods. Therefore, organizations have implemented relational databases, in which data are organized into rows and columns, to support end-user computing and decision making. We examine data organization more closely in Section 3.3.

With the prevalence of **client/server networks** (also called client/server computing) and Web technologies, numerous distinct databases are created and spread throughout the organization, creating problems in managing those data so that it's consistent in each location. Client/server networks consist of user PCs, called *clients*, linked to high-performance computers, called *servers*, that provide software, data, or computing services over a network. (Recall that Applebee's International invested in a data warehouse to collect and analyze data relating to sales, demand, and costs.) As businesses become more complex and their volumes of enterprise data explode, they increasingly are turning to *master data management* as a way to intelligently consolidate and manage these data.

MASTER DATA MANAGEMENT

Master data management (MDM) is a process whereby companies integrate data from various sources or enterprise applications to provide a *more unified view* of the data. Although vendors may claim that their MDM solution creates "a single version of the truth," this claim is probably not true. In reality MDM cannot create a single unified version of the data because constructing a completely unified view of all master data is simply not possible. Realistically, MDM consolidates data from various data sources into a **master reference file,** which then feeds data back to the applications, thereby creating accurate and consistent data across the enterprise. In *A Closer Look 3.2,* participants in the healthcare supply chain were essentially developing a master reference file to obtain a more unified version of the data. A master data reference file is based on data entities. A **data entity** is anything real or abstract about which a company wants to collect and store data. Common data entities in business include customer, vendor, product, and employee.

Master Data Entities. Master data entities are the main entities of a company, such as customers, products, suppliers, employees, and assets. Each organizational department has distinct master data needs. Marketing, for example, is concerned with product pricing, brand, and product packaging, whereas production is concerned with product costs and schedules. A customer master reference file can feed data to all enterprise systems that have a customer relationship component, thereby providing a unified picture of the customers. Similarly, a product master reference file can feed data to all of the production systems within the enterprise. Three benefits of a unified view of customers are the following:

- Better, more accurate customer data to support marketing, sales, support, and service initiatives
- Better responsiveness to ensure that all employees who deal with customers have up-to-date, reliable information on the customers
- Better revenue management and more responsive business decisions

An MDM includes tools for cleaning and auditing the master data elements as well as tools for integrating and synchronizing data to make the data more accessible. MDM offers a solution for managers who are frustrated with how fragmented and dispersed their data sources are. According to Ventana Research (*ventanaresearch. com*), 4 percent of the 515 respondents to their survey said their organizations had implemented MDM, and 31 percent reported that their organizations had projects currently under way (Stodder, 2007).

TRANSFORMING DATA INTO KNOWLEDGE

Our discussion thus far has focused primarily on ways in which businesses accumulate and integrate data. Businesses do not run on raw data, however. They run on data that have been processed into information and knowledge, which managers apply to business problems and opportunities. As real-world examples throughout this chapter illustrate, knowledge learned from data fuels business solutions. Everything from innovative product designs to brilliant competitive moves relies on timely knowledge. However, because of the difficulties inherent in managing data, deriving knowledge from collected data is a complicated process.

Organizations transform data into knowledge in several ways. In general, this process resembles the one illustrated in Figure 3.2. The desired data are extracted from databases and preprocessed to fit the format of a data warehouse or a **data mart,** into which they are loaded. A data mart is a small data warehouse designed for a strategic business unit (SBU) or a single department. This series of processes is referred to as **ETL,** which stands for **e**xtract, **t**ransform, and **l**oad. Figure 3.4 shows

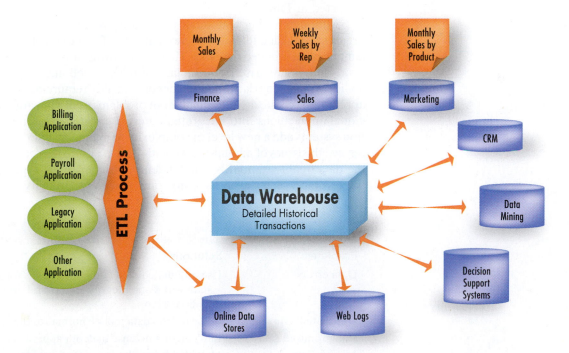

Figure 3.4 Model of an enterprise data warehouse. (*Source: From Syncsort, synchsort.com. Used with permission.*)

the data transformation model of Syncsort Inc., which develops, markets, and services high-performance software for data management and data protection. ETL processes move data from multiple sources, reformat and cleanse them, and load them into another data warehouse or data mart for analysis, or onto another operational system to support a business process.

Users then access the data warehouse or data mart and take a copy of the data needed for analysis. They scrutinize this material using data analysis and data mining tools. Data mining tools are specialized software used to analyze data to find patterns, or correlation, or trends, or other meaningful relationships. Data mining, which may also be called data discovery, is the process of analyzing data from different perspectives and summarizing it into information that can be used to increase revenue, decrease costs, or both. Data mining software allows users to analyze data from various dimensions or angles, categorize it, and find correlations or patterns among fields in the data warehouse. These activities ultimately generate valuable information and knowledge. Both the data (at various times during the process) and the knowledge (derived at the end of the process) may need to be circulated and presented to users via visualization tools.

DATA QUALITY AND INTEGRITY

Data collection is a highly complex process that can create problems concerning the quality of the data that are being collected. Therefore, regardless of how the data are collected, they need to be validated so users know they can trust them. Classic expressions that sum up the situation are "garbage in, garbage out" (GIGO) and the potentially riskier "garbage in, gospel out." In the latter case, poor-quality data are trusted and used as the basis for planning. You have encountered data safeguards, such as integrity checks, to help improve data quality when you fill in an online form. For example, the form will not accept an e-mail address that is not formatted correctly.

Data quality is a measure of the data's usefulness as well as the quality of the decisions based on the data. It has the following five dimensions: *accuracy, accessibility, relevance, timeliness,* and *completeness*. As we have discussed, data frequently are inaccurate, incomplete, or ambiguous, particularly when they are stored in large, centralized databases. Examples of common data problems and possible solutions are listed in Table 3.2.

Although having high-quality data are essential for business success, numerous organizational and technical issues make it difficult to reach this objective. One problematic issue is data ownership. That is, who owns or is responsible for the data? Data ownership issues arise from the lack of policies defining responsibility and accountability in managing data. Inconsistent data quality requirements of various stand-alone applications create an additional set of problems as organizations try to combine individual applications into integrated enterprise systems. Interorganizational information systems add a new level of complexity to managing data quality. Companies must resolve the issues of administrative authority to ensure that each partner complies with the data quality standards. The tendency to delegate data quality responsibilities to the technical teams, who have no control over data quality, as opposed to business

TABLE 3.2	**Data Problems and Solutions**
Problems	**Solutions**
Data errors	Use automated data entry, Web forms for individuals entering data with data integrity checks and drop-down menus and radio buttons.
Duplicated data	Redesign the data model; normalize the relational database.
Compromised data	Implement a defense in depth approach to data security.
Missing data	Make fields mandatory on data entry forms.

A Closer Look 3.3

National Security Depends on Intelligence and Data Mining

Individuals and groups driven by ideological or political motives or the intent to do harm use the Internet to plan and coordinate their activities, as was the case for the September 11, 2001, attacks. Terrorists use various tactics and technologies to carry out their destructive plans—hacking, spamming, phishing, identity theft, and Web site propaganda and recruitment. Computers seized in Afghanistan reportedly revealed that al Qaeda was collecting intelligence on targets and sending encrypted messages via the Internet.

National security depends on timely intelligence efforts to detect these activities as early as possible. Intelligence agencies, such as the FBI (*fbi.gov*) and CIA (*cia.gov*) in the United States and MI6 (*intelligence.gov.uk/agencies/mi6.asp*) and Defense Intelligence Staff (DIS) (*intelligence.gov.uk/agencies/dis.asp*) in the United Kingdom, mine enormous amounts of data to monitor potential threats to national security. Some data collection might infringe on citizens' privacy rights. The DIS, for example, conducts intelligence analysis from both overt and covert sources.

Data mining for intelligence purposes combines statistical models, powerful processors, and artificial intelligence (AI) to find and retrieve valuable information. There are two types of data mining systems: *subject-based systems* that retrieve data to follow a lead, and *pattern-based systems* that look for suspicious behaviors.

An example of a subject-based technique is *link analysis*, which uses data to make connections among seemingly unconnected people or events. Link analysis software identifies suspicious activities, such as a spike in the number of e-mail exchanges between two parties (one of whom is a suspect), checks written by different people to the same third party, or airline tickets bought to the same destination on the same departing date. Intelligence personnel then follow these "links" to uncover other people with whom a suspect is interacting.

Experts consider intelligence efforts such as these to be crucial to global security. Some military experts believe that war between major nations is becoming obsolete and that our future defense will rely far more on intelligence officers with databases than on tanks and artillery. A key lesson of September 11 is that America's intelligence agencies must work together and share information to act as a single, unified intelligence enterprise to detect risks.

Sources: Compiled from *Whitehouse.gov* (2004), Volonino et al. (2007), and Worthen (2006).

For Further Exploration: How does data mining provide intelligence to decision makers? What are the two types of data mining systems, and how do they provide value to defense organizations?

---

users who do have such control, is another common pitfall that stands in the way of accumulating high-quality data (Loshin, 2004).

DATA PRIVACY AND ETHICAL USE

Businesses that collect data about employees, customers, or anyone else have the duty to protect these data. Data should be accessible only to authorized people. Securing data from unauthorized access and from abuse by authorized parties is expensive and difficult. To motivate companies to invest in data security, the government has imposed enormous fines and penalties for data breaches, as you will see in Chapter 5.

Furthermore, providing information required by the government or regulators adds to the expense of data management. An example is the situation of homeland security described in *A Closer Look 3.3*.

DOCUMENT MANAGEMENT

All companies create **business records**, which are documents that record business dealings such as contracts, research and development, accounting source documents, memos, customer/client communications, and meeting minutes. **Document management** is the automated control of imaged and electronic documents, page images, spreadsheets, voice and e-mail messages, word processing documents, and other documents through their life cycle within an organization, from initial creation to final archiving or destruction.

Document management systems (DMS) consist of hardware and software that manage and archive electronic documents and also convert paper documents into e-documents and then index and store them according to company policy. For example, companies may be required by law to retain financial documents for at least seven years, whereas e-mail messages about whereas marketing promotions would be retained for a year and then discarded. DMS have query and search capabilities so they can be identified and accessed like data in a database. These systems range from those designed to support a small workgroup to full-featured, Web-enabled enterprise-wide systems. DMS may be part of a newer integrated system called enterprise content management (ECM), which is discussed in Section 3.5.

Departments or companies whose employees spend most of the day filing or retrieving documents or warehouse paper records can reduce costs significantly with DMS. These systems minimize the inefficiencies and frustration associated with managing paper documents and paper workflows. Significantly, however, they do not create a *paperless office* as had been predicted. Offices still use a lot of paper.

A DMS can help a business to become more efficient and productive by

- Enabling the company to access and use the content contained in the documents
- Cutting labor costs by automating business processes
- Reducing the time and effort required to locate information the business needs to support decision making
- Improving the security of the content, thereby reducing the risk of intellectual property theft
- Minimizing the costs associated with printing, storage, and searching for content

The major document management tools are workflow software, authoring tools, scanners, and databases. When workflows are digital, productivity increases, costs decrease, compliance obligations are easier to verify, and **green computing** becomes possible. Green computing is an initiative to conserve our valuable natural resources by reducing the effects of our computer usage on the environment. We cover green computing in Chapter 15. Businesses also use a DMS for disaster recovery and business continuity, security, knowledge sharing and collaboration, and remote and controlled access to documents. Because DMS have multilayered access capabilities, employees can access and change only the documents they are authorized to handle. Visit *altimate.ca/flash/viewer.html* to see how files can be opened directly within the Web browser without the file's native application installed locally on the user's computer. When companies select a DMS, they ask the following questions:

1. Is the software available in a form that makes sense to your organization, whether you need the DMS installed on your network or will purchase the Software as a Service (SaaS, covered in Chapter 13)?

2. Is the software easy to use and accessible from Web browsers, office applications and e-mail applications, and Windows Explorer? (If not, people won't use it.)

3. Does the software have lightweight, modern Web and graphical user interfaces that effectively support remote users via an intranet, a virtual private network (VPN, discussed in Chapter 4), and the Internet? (A VPN allows a worker to connect to a company's network remotely through the Internet. VPN is less expensive than having workers connect using a modem or dedicated line).

A Closer Look 3.4 describes how several companies currently use DMS.

Review Questions

1. What is the goal of data management?
2. What constraints do managers face when they cannot trust data?
3. Why is it difficult to manage, search, and retrieve data located throughout the enterprise?
4. How can data visualization tools and technology improve decision making?
5. What is master data management?
6. What are three benefits of document management systems?

A Closer Look 3.4

How Companies Use Document Management Systems

We have seen that companies use document management systems to manage data and documents. Below are some examples of how real-life companies utilize DMS.

The Surgery Center of Baltimore stores all medical records electronically, providing instant patient information to doctors and nurses anywhere and at any time. The system also routes charts to the billing department, who can then scan and e-mail any relevant information to insurance providers and patients. The DMS helps maintain the required audit trail, including providing records when they are needed for legal purposes. How valuable has the DMS been to the center? Since it was implemented, business processes have been expedited by more than 50 percent, the costs of these processes have been significantly reduced, and the morale of office employees in the center has improved noticeably (see *laserfiche.com/newsroom/baltimore.html*).

American Express (AMEX) uses TELEform, a DMS developed by Alchemy and Cardiff Software, to collect and process more than 1 million customer satisfaction surveys every year. The data are collected in templates that consist of more than 600 different survey forms in 12 languages and 11 countries. AMEX integrated TELEform with AMEX's legacy (older) system, which enables it to distribute processed results to many managers. Because the survey forms are now so readily accessible, AMEX has been able to reduce the number of staff who process these forms from 17 to 1, thereby saving the company more than $500,000 each year (see *cardiff.com/customers/index.html*).

In Toronto, Canada, the Department of Works and Emergency Services uses a Web-based document-retrieval solution. This DMS gives the department's employees immediate access to drawings and documents related to roads, buildings, utility lines, and other structures. The department has installed laptop computers loaded with maps, drawings, and historical repair data in each vehicle. Quick access to these documents enables emergency crews to solve problems and, more importantly, to save lives (see *laserfiche.com/newsroom/torontoworks.html*).

The University of Cincinnati provides authorized access to the personnel files of 12,000 active employees and tens of thousands of retirees. The university receives more than 75,000 queries about personnel records every year and then must search more than 3 million records to answer these queries. Using a microfilm system to find answers took days. The solution was a DMS that digitized all paper and microfilm documents, without help from the IT department, making them available via the Internet and the university's intranet. An authorized employee can now use a browser and access a document in seconds (see *captaris.com/alchemy*).

Finally, the European Court of Human Rights has implemented a Web-based knowledge portal and document and case management systems that support more than 700 internal users and millions of external users worldwide. The DMS has streamlined case processing, which in turn has made internal operations more efficient and has significantly improved the court's services to the public. The Human Rights Documents project has had a significant return on investment (see *opentext.com/customers/globalstar/awards/2007/winners-na-2007.html*).

For Further Exploration: What types of waste can DMS reduce? How? What is the value of providing access to documents via the Internet or a corporate intranet?

3.2 File Management Systems

The previous section discussed how businesses use computer systems, particularly DMS, to manipulate data much more efficiently and productively. In this section we explain how these systems actually work.

A computer system essentially organizes data into a hierarchy that begins with bits and proceeds to bytes, fields, records, files, and databases (see Figure 3.5). A *bit* represents the smallest unit of data a computer can process, which is either a 0 or a 1. A group of eight bits, called a *byte*, represents a single character, which can be a letter, a number, or a symbol. Characters that are combined to form a word, a group of words, or a complete number constitute a *field*. A key characteristic of a field is that all of the entries are related in some way. For example, a field titled "Cust_Name" might include the names of a company's customers. It would *not*, however, contain addresses or telephone numbers.

Just as related characters can be combined into a field, related fields—such as vendor name, address, and account data—can constitute a *record*. Moving up the hierarchy, a collection of related records is called a *file* or *data file*. For example, the records of all noncommercial customers who have a mortgage loan at a financial institution would constitute a data file. Finally, as we saw in our discussion of data management, a logical group of related files would constitute a database. All customer loan files, such as mortgages and auto, personal and home equity loans, could be grouped to create a noncommercial loan database.

Level 3 Customer Data Tables

Product Preferences Table

Field Name	Type	Length
Product SKU *	Number	12
Product name	Text	20
Product type	Text	12
Product characteristics	Number	30
Customer ID **	Number	8

Shop Locations Table

Field Name	Type	Length
Store number *	Number	8
Store neighborhood	Text	20
Store sales	Currency	8
Store customers	Number	5
Product SKU **	Number	12

Customer Contact Table

Field Name	Type	Length
Customer ID *	Number	8
Customer name	Text	20
Customer address	Text	30
Customer phone	Number	12

* Primary Key ** Foreign Key

Product Sales Table

Field Name	Type	Length
Product SKU *	Number	12
Product name	Text	20
Product price	Currency	8
Product cost	Currency	8
Customer ID **	Number	8

Figure 3.5 Example of primary and foreign keys.

Another way of thinking about database components is that a record describes an *entity*. Each characteristic describing an entity is called an **attribute.** (An attribute corresponds to a field on a record.) Examples of attributes are customer name, invoice number, and order date.

Each record in a database needs an attribute (field) to uniquely identify it so that the record can be retrieved, updated, and sorted. This unique identifier field is called the **primary key.** Primary keys are typically numeric because they are easier to create. For example, the primary key of a product record would be the product ID. To find a group of records based on some common value (locating all products manufactured in Mexico) requires the use of secondary keys. **Secondary keys** are nonunique fields that have some identifying information (e.g., country of manufacture). **Foreign keys** are keys whose purpose is to link two or more tables together. Figure 3.6 illustrates primary and foreign keys.

ACCESSING RECORDS FROM COMPUTER FILES

Records can be arranged in several ways on a storage medium. The arrangement determines how individual records can be accessed and how long it takes to access them. In **sequential file organization,** which is the way files are organized on tape, data records must be retrieved in the same physical sequence in which they are stored. The operation is like a tape recorder. In **direct file organization,** or **random file organization,** records can be accessed directly regardless of their location on the storage medium. The operation is like a DVD drive. Magnetic tape uses sequential file organization, whereas magnetic disks use direct file organization.

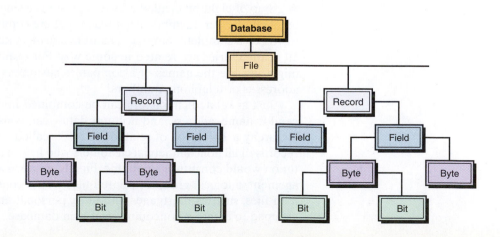

Figure 3.6 Hierarchy of data for a computer-based file.

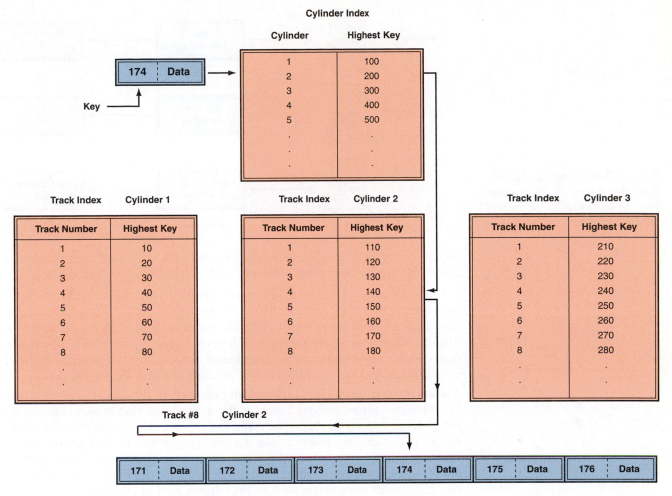

Figure 3.7 Indexed sequential access method.

The **indexed sequential access method (ISAM)** uses an index of key fields to locate individual records (see Figure 3.7). An *index* to a file lists the key field of each record and where that record is physically located on the storage media. Records are stored on disks in their key sequence. To locate a specific record, the system looks at the index (called track index) to locate the general location (identified by the cylinder and track numbers) containing the record. It then points to the beginning of that track and reads the records sequentially until it finds the correct record.

The **direct file access method** uses the key field to locate the physical address of a record. This process uses a mathematical formula called a *transform algorithm* to translate the key field directly into the record's storage location on disk. The algorithm performs a mathematical calculation on the record key, and the result of that calculation is the record's address. The direct access method is most appropriate when individual records must be located directly and rapidly for immediate processing, when a few records in the file need to be retrieved at one time, and when the required records are not in any particular order.

LIMITATIONS OF THE DATA FILE ENVIRONMENT

When organizations began using computers to automate processes, they started with one application at a time, usually accounting, billing, or payroll. Each application was designed to be a stand-alone system that worked independently of other applications. For example, for each pay period, the payroll application would use its own employee and wage data to calculate and process the payroll. No other application would use those data without some manual intervention because, as just stated, the applications functioned independently of one another. This data file approach led to redundancy,

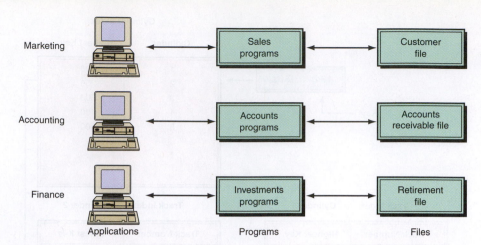

Figure 3.8 Computer-based files of this type cause problems such as redundancy, inconsistency, and data isolation.

inconsistency, data isolation, and other problems. We examine these problems below, and we illustrate them using a university file environment in Figure 3.8.

- **Data redundancy.** Because different programmers create different data-manipulating applications over long periods of time, the same data could be duplicated in several files. In the loan example, each data file contains records about customers' loans. Significantly, many of these customers will be represented in other data files. This redundancy wastes physical storage media, makes it difficult to obtain a comprehensive view of customers, and increases the costs of entering and maintaining the data.

- **Data inconsistency.** Data inconsistency means that the actual data values are not synchronized across various copies of the data. Recall that unsynched data caused the problems faced by Applebee's and Dartmouth's development office discussed earlier in this chapter. For example, if a financial institution has customers with several loans, and for each loan there is a file containing customer fields (e.g., name, address, email, and telephone number), then a change to a customer's address in only one file creates inconsistencies with the address field in other files.

- **Data isolation.** File organization creates silos of data that make it extremely difficult to access data from different applications. For example, a manager who wants to know which products customers are buying and which customers owe more than $1,000 would probably not be able to obtain the answer from a data file system. To get the results, he would have to filter and integrate the data manually from multiple files.

- **Data security.** Securing data is difficult in the file environment because new applications are added to the system on an ad hoc basis. As the number of applications increases, so does the number of people who can access the data.

- **Lack of data integrity.** In a file environment, it's harder to enforce **data integrity** rules, which include preventing data input errors. For example, a Social Security field should not allow alphabetic characters. It is difficult to enforce data integrity constraints across multiple data files.

- **Data concurrency.** At the exact time that one application is updating a record, another application may be accessing that record. In that situation, the second application does not get the most current data. To prevent a concurrency problem, applications and data need to be independent of one another. In the file environment, however, applications and their data are dependent on one another.

Data management problems arising from the file environment approach led to the development of databases and database management systems (DBMS).

Review Questions

1. What are three limitations of the file management approach?
2. Why does each record in a database need a unique identifier (primary key)?
3. How do the data access methods of sequential file organization and direct file access methods differ?

3.3 Databases and Database Management Systems

Data flow into companies continuously and from many sources: clickstream data from Web and e-commerce applications, detailed data from POS terminals, and filtered data from CRM, supply chain, and enterprise resource planning applications. Databases are the optimal way to store and access organizational data. In this section we examine databases and programs that provide access to them, known as database management systems (DBMSs).

DATABASES

Database management programs can provide access to all of the data, alleviating many of the problems associated with data file environments. Therefore, data redundancy, data isolation, and data inconsistency are minimized, and data can be shared among users of the data. In addition, security and data integrity are easier to control, and applications are independent of the data they process. There are two basic types of databases: centralized and distributed.

Centralized Databases. A *centralized database* stores all related files in one physical location (see Figure 3.9). For decades the main database platform consisted of centralized database files on large, mainframe computers, primarily because of the

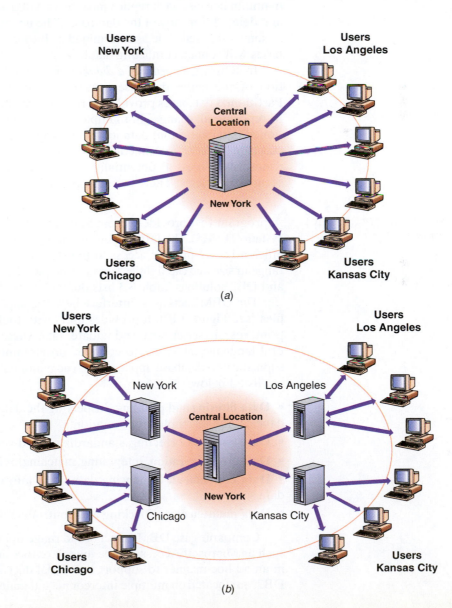

(a)

(b)

Figure 3.9 (a) Centralized database. (b) Distributed database with complete or partial copies of the central database in more than one location.

enormous capital and operating costs associated with the alternative systems. Centralized databases offer many benefits to organizations. Files can generally be made more consistent with one another when they are physically kept in one location because file changes can be made in a supervised and orderly fashion. Also, files are not accessible except via the centralized host computer, where they can be protected more easily from unauthorized access or modification.

At the same time, however, centralized databases, like all centralized systems, are vulnerable to a single point of failure. That is, when the centralized database computer fails to function properly, all users are affected. Additionally, when users are widely dispersed and must perform data manipulations from great distances, they often experience transmission delays.

Distributed Databases. A *distributed database* has complete copies of a database, or portions of a database (see Figure 3.9). There are two types of distributed databases: replicated and partitioned.

A *replicated database* stores complete copies (replicas) of the entire database in multiple locations. This arrangement provides a backup in case of a failure or problems with the centralized database. It also improves the response time because it is local (closer) to users. On the negative side, it is much more expensive to set up and maintain because each replica must be updated as records are added to, modified in, and deleted from any of the databases. The updates may be done at the end of a day or some other schedule as determined by business needs. Otherwise, the various databases will contain conflicting data.

In contrast, a *partitioned database* is divided up so that each location has a portion of the entire database—usually the portion that meets users' local needs. Partitioned databases provide the response speed of localized files without the need to replicate all changes in multiple locations. One significant advantage of a partitioned database is that data in the files can be entered more quickly and kept more accurate by the users immediately responsible for the data. One disadvantage is that widespread access to potentially sensitive company data can significantly increase security problems. There are examples of such security problems in Chapter 5.

DATABASE MANAGEMENT SYSTEMS

A program that provides access to databases is known as a **database management system (DBMS).** The DBMS permits an organization to centralize data, manage them efficiently, and provide access to the stored data by application programs. DBMSs range in size and capabilities from the simple Microsoft Access to full-featured Oracle and DB2 solutions. Table 3.3 lists the major capabilities and advantages of DBMSs.

The DBMS acts as an interface between application programs and physical data files (see Figure 3.10). It provides users with tools to add, delete, maintain, display, print, search, select, sort, and update data. These tools range from easy-to-use natural language interfaces to complex programming languages used for developing sophisticated database applications. The major data functions performed by a DBMS are listed below.

- **Data filtering and profiling.** Inspecting the data for errors, inconsistencies, redundancies, and incomplete information.
- **Data quality.** Correcting, standardizing, and verifying the integrity of the data.
- **Data synchronization.** Integrating, matching, or linking data from disparate sources.
- **Data enrichment.** Enhancing data using information from internal and external data sources.
- **Data maintenance.** Checking and controlling data integrity over time.

Companies use DBMSs in a broad range of information systems. Some DBMSs, such as Microsoft Access, can be loaded onto a single user's computer and accessed in an ad hoc manner to support individual decision making. Others, such as IBM's DB2, are located on multiple interconnected mainframe computers to support large-

TABLE 3.3	**Advantages and Capabilities of a DBMS**

- **Permanence.** Attributes are permanently stored on a hard drive or other fast, reliable medium until explicitly removed or changed.

- **Querying.** Querying is the process of requesting attribute information from various perspectives. Example: "How many 2-door cars in Texas are green?"

- **Concurrency.** Many people may attempt to change or read the same attributes at the same time. Without rules for sharing changes, the attributes may become inconsistent or misleading. For example, if you change the color attribute of car 7 to be "blue" at the very same time somebody is changing it to "red," results are unpredictable. DBMSs provide various tools and techniques to deal with such issues. "Transactions" and "locking" are two common techniques for concurrency management.

- **Backup and replication.** Backup copies need to be made in case of equipment failure. A periodic copy may be created for a remote organization that cannot readily access the original. DBMSs usually provide utilities for backups and duplicate copies.

- **Rule enforcement.** Applying rules to attributes to keep them clean and trustworthy. For example, a rule can state that each car can have only one engine associated with it (identified by engine number). If somebody tries to associate a second engine, the DBMS stops it and displays an error message. However, with new hybrid gas-electric cars, such rules may need to be relaxed. Rules can be added and removed as needed without significant redesign.

- **Security.** Limits on who can see or change attributes are necessary.

- **Computation.** Rather than have each computer application perform calculations, the DBMS performs them.

- **Change and access logging.** The DBMS creates a record and audit trail of who accessed what attributes, what was changed, and when it was changed.

- **Automated optimization.** If there are frequent usage patterns or requests, many DBMSs can adjust to improve the response time.

scale transaction processing systems, such as order entry and inventory control systems. DBMSs such as Oracle 11g are interconnected throughout an organization's local area networks (LANs), giving individual departments access to corporate data. LANs are private networks owned and managed by the organization, and are discussed in detail in Chapter 4.

A DBMS enables many different users to share data and process resources. How can a single, unified database meet the differing requirements of so many users? For example, how can a single database be structured so that sales personnel can view customer, inventory, and production maintenance data while the human resources department maintains restricted access to private personnel data?

The answer is that a DBMS provides two views of the data: a physical view and a logical view. The physical view deals with the actual, physical arrangement and

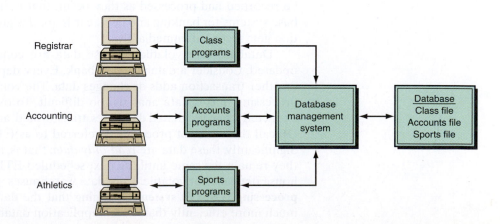

Figure 3.10 Database management system provides access to all data in the database.

location of data in the direct access storage devices (DASDs). Database specialists use the physical view to configure storage and processing resources.

Users, however, need to see data differently from how they are stored, and they do not want to know all of the technical details of physical storage. After all, a business user is primarily interested in using the information, not in how it is stored. The logical view, or user's view, of data is meaningful to the user. What is important is that a DBMS provides endless logical views of the data. This feature allows users to see data from a business-related perspective rather than from a technical viewpoint. Clearly, users must adapt to the technical requirements of database information systems to some degree, but the logical views allow the system to adapt to the business needs of the users. The way in which you see data (the logical view or user's view) can vary; the storage of data (physical view) is fixed.

Review Questions

1. What is a database? A database management system (DBMS)?
2. What are three data functions of a DBMS?
3. What is the difference between the physical view of and the logical view of data?

3.4 Data Warehouses, Data Marts, and Data Centers

It's not necessarily the biggest companies that are the most successful, but the smartest ones. Being a smart company means having on-demand access to relevant data, understanding them (usually with the help of data visualization tools), and using what you learn from them to increase productivity and/or profitability. Having complete information is critical to this process. Data warehouses enable managers and knowledge workers to leverage data (use data for advantage) from across the enterprise, thereby helping them make the smartest decisions.

Recall from our discussion of data management that a data warehouse is a repository (a type of database) in which data are organized so that they can be readily analyzed using methods such as data mining, decision support, querying, and other applications. Examples of uses of a data warehouse are revenue management, customer-relationship management, fraud detection, and payroll-management applications. To better understand data warehouses, it helps to compare them to databases.

COMPARING DATABASES WITH DATA WAREHOUSES

Data warehouses and regular databases both consist of data tables (files), primary and other keys, and query capabilities. The main difference is that databases are designed and optimized *to store* data, whereas data warehouses are designed and optimized *to respond* to analysis questions that are critical for a business.

Databases are **online transaction processing (OLTP) systems** in which every transaction has to be recorded quickly. Consider, for example, financial transactions, such as withdrawals from a bank ATM or a debit account. These transactions must be recorded and processed as they occur, that is, in real-time. Consequently, database systems for banking and debit cards are designed to ensure that every transaction gets recorded immediately.

Databases are volatile because data are constantly being added, edited, or updated. Consider a database of a bank. Every deposit, withdrawal, loan payment, or other transaction adds or changes data. The volatility caused by the transaction processing makes data analysis too difficult. To overcome this problem, data are extracted from designated databases, transformed, and loaded into a data warehouse. (Recall this series of processes is referred to as ETL, as discussed in Section 3.1.) Significantly, these data are *read-only data*; that is, they cannot be updated. Rather, they remain the same until the next scheduled ETL. Unlike databases, then, warehouse data are not volatile. Thus, data warehouses are designed as **online analytical processing (OLAP) systems,** meaning that the data can be queried and analyzed much more efficiently than OLTP application databases.

TREND TOWARD MORE REAL-TIME SUPPORT FROM A DATA WAREHOUSE

The modern business world is experiencing a growing trend toward real-time data warehousing and analytics. In the past, data warehouses primarily supported strategic applications, which did not require instant response time, direct customer interaction, or integration with operational systems. Today, businesses increasingly use information in the moment to support real-time customer interaction. Companies with an active data warehouse will be able to interact appropriately with a customer to provide superior customer service, which in turn will enhance the companies' revenues (Zeehandelaar and Lawrence, 2005).

Companies, such as the credit card company Capital One, track each customer's profitability and use that score to determine the level of customer service. For example, when a customer calls Capital One, that customer is asked to enter the credit card number, which is linked to a profitability score. Low-profit customers get a voice response unit only; high-profit customers get a live person—a customer service representative (CSR).

Consider, for example, the case of Charles, who is calling the customer service center because of frequent dropped cell calls. Through the call center application (attached to the active data warehouse), the CSR accesses not only the complete history of Charles's calls to the company but also a full view of all the services to which he subscribes—DSL, Internet, and cellular—along with his customer profitability score, which lets the CSR know how profitable (valuable) he is to the company. Intelligent and selective customer service is possible because all service lines and calls to customer service are stored in the active data warehouse. The CSR uses the data and company information to determine the best action or offer to resolve this issue to Charles's satisfaction. Additionally, the CSR will have the insight to cross-sell or up-sell additional services based on the details in Charles' profile and company interaction information. In this example, the active data warehouse provided a view of the customer that indicated what intervention to take based on the customer's profitability to the company. Because Charles subscribes to the company's high–profit-margin services, the company wants to minimize the risk of losing him as a customer.

THE NEED FOR DATA WAREHOUSING

Many organizations built data warehouses because they were frustrated with inconsistent decision support data, or they needed to improve reporting applications or better understand the business. Viewed from this perspective, data warehouses are infrastructure investments that companies make to support current and future decision making.

The most successful companies are those that can respond quickly and flexibly to market changes and opportunities, and the key to this response is to use data and information effectively and efficiently, as illustrated in the Applebee's case. Companies perform this task not only via transaction processing but also through analytical processing, in which company employees—frequently end users—analyze the accumulated data. Analytical processing, also referred to as business intelligence (BI), includes data mining, decision support systems (DSSs), enterprise systems, Web applications, querying, and other end-user activities.

BENEFITS OF A DATA WAREHOUSE

According to Teradata Corp., the benefits of a data warehouse are both business- and IT-related. From the business perspective, companies can make better decisions because they have access to better information. From an IT perspective, DWs deliver information more effectively and efficiently. Several areas of an organization that benefit from a DW are (*teradata.com, 2006*) the following:

- **Marketing and sales.** Use a DW for product introductions, product information access, marketing program effectiveness, and product line profitability. Use the data to maximize per customer profitability.
- **Pricing and contracts.** Use the data to calculate costs accurately to optimize pricing of a contract. Without accurate cost data, prices may be below or too near to cost or prices may be uncompetitive because they are too high.
- **Forecasting.** The DW assists in the timely visibility of end customer demand.

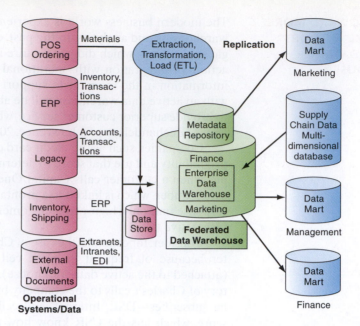

Figure 3.11 Data warehouse framework and views.

- **Sales performance.** Use the data to determine sales profitability and productivity for all territories and regions; can obtain and analyze results by geography, product, sales group, or individual.
- **Financial.** Use daily, weekly, or monthly results for improved financial management.

Figure 3.11 diagrams the process of building and using a data warehouse. The organization's data are stored in operational systems (left side of the figure). Not all data are necessarily transferred to the data warehouse. Frequently only a summary of the data is transferred. The data that are transferred are organized within the warehouse in a form that is easy for end users to access and locate. The data are also standardized. Then, the data are organized by subject, such as by functional area, vendor, or product.

Characteristics of a Data Warehouse. All types of data warehousing share nine major characteristics. We list them below.

1. Organization. Data are organized by subject (e.g., by customer, vendor, product, price level, and region) and contain information relevant for decision support only.

2. Consistency. Data in different databases may be encoded differently. For example, gender data may be encoded 0 and 1 in one operational system, and "m" and "f" in another. In the warehouse they will be coded in a consistent manner.

3. Time variant. The data are kept for many years so they can be used for identifying trends, forecasting, and making comparisons over time.

4. Nonvolatile. Once the data are entered into the warehouse, they are not updated.

5. Relational. Typically the data warehouse uses a relational structure.

6. Client/server. The data warehouse uses the client/server architecture mainly to provide the end user an easy access to its data.

7. Web-based. Today's data warehouses are designed to provide an efficient computing environment for Web-based applications.

8. Integration. Data from various sources are integrated. Web Services are used to support integration.

9. Real-time. Although most applications of data warehousing are not in real-time, it is possible to arrange for real-time capabilities.

For an example of how Sprint decreased customer churn (turnover) from its data warehouse, see Online Brief 3.1.

BUILDING A DATA WAREHOUSE

Building and implementing a data warehouse can present problems. Because a warehouse is very large and expensive to build, it's important to understand the key success factors in implementing one. Specifically, a company that is considering building a data warehouse first needs to address a series of basic questions:

- Does top management support the data warehouse?
- Do users support the data warehouse?
- Do users want access to a broad range of data? If they do, which is preferable: a single repository or a set of standalone data marts?
- Do users want data access and analysis tools?
- Do users understand how to use the data warehouse to solve business problems?
- Does the unit have one or more power users who can understand data warehouse technologies?

Architecture and Tools. There are several basic architectures for data warehousing. Two common ones are two-tier and three-tier architectures. In three-tier architecture, data from the warehouse are processed twice and deposited in an additional *multidimensional database,* in which they can be organized for easy multidimensional analysis and presentation or replicated in data marts.

There are two main reasons for creating a data warehouse as a separate data store. First, the performance of a separate data store is better because it is not competing (or waiting) for processing time. Second, modeling a database that can be used for both operational and analytical purposes can be difficult. Figure 3.12 represents an EDW developed by Teradata Corp. This centralized approach reduces the amount of data the technical team has to transfer, thereby simplifying data management and

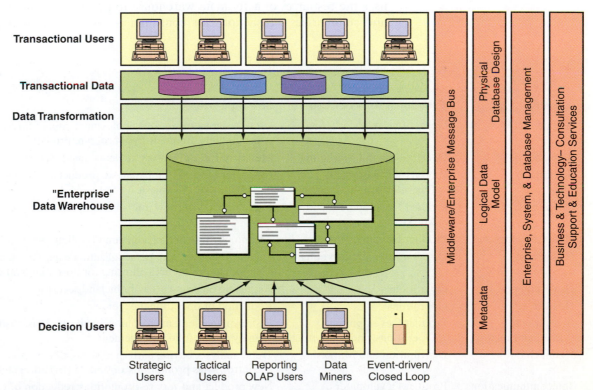

Figure 3.12 Teradata Corp.'s enterprises data warehouse. (*Source: Teradata Corporation [teradata.com], with permission.*)

administration. Users are also provided with access to all of the data in the data warehouse instead of being limited to individual data marts.

Putting the Warehouse on the Intranet. Data warehouse content can be delivered to decision makers throughout the enterprise via an intranet. Users can view, query, and analyze the data and produce reports using Web browsers. This is an extremely economical and effective method of delivering data.

Suitability. Data warehousing is most appropriate for organizations that have some of the following characteristics:

- End users need to access large amounts of data.
- The operational data are stored in different systems.
- The organization employs an information-based approach to management.
- The organization serves a large, diverse customer base (such as in a utility company or a bank; for example, AT&T's 26-terabyte data warehouse is used for marketing analysis by 3,000 employees).
- The same data are represented differently in different systems.
- Data are stored in highly technical formats that are difficult to decipher.
- Extensive end-user computing is performed (many end users performing many activities).

Table 3.4 summarizes some of the successful applications of data warehouses. Hundreds of other successful applications have been reported (e.g., see client success stories and case studies at Web sites of vendors such as Hyperion Inc., Business Objects, Cognos Corp., Information Builders, NCR Corp., Oracle, Computer Associates, and Software A&G). For further discussion of this topic, visit the Data Warehouse Institute (*tdwi.org*).

Many organizations, buoyed by the success of their data warehouse efforts, are taking data warehouse public. One example is Wells Fargo. Its development effort uses the resources of a Teradata warehouse to provide an online tool that collects and summarizes transactions for consumers—credit card, debit card, online bill

TABLE 3.4	Strategic Uses of Data Warehousing	
Industry	**Functional Areas of Use**	**Strategic Use**
Airline	Operations and Marketing	Crew assignment, aircraft deployment, mix of fares, analysis of route profitability, frequent-flyer program promotions
Apparel	Distribution and Marketing	Merchandising, inventory replenishment
Banking	Product Development, Operations, and Marketing	Customer service, trend analysis, product and service promotions, reduction of IS expenses
Credit card	Product Development and Marketing	Customer service, new information service for a fee, fraud detection
Defense contracts	Product Development	Technology transfer, production of military applications
E-Business	Distribution and Marketing	Data warehouses with personalization capabilities, marketing/ shopping preferences allowing for up-selling and cross-selling
Government	Operations	Reporting on crime areas, homeland security
Healthcare	Operations	Reduction of operational expenses
Investment and insurance	Product Development, Operations, and Marketing	Risk management, market movements analysis, customer tendencies analysis, portfolio management
Retail chain	Distribution and Marketing	Trend analysis, buying pattern analysis, pricing policy, inventory control, sales promotions, optimal distribution channel decisions
Telecommunications	Product Development, Operations, and Marketing	New product and service promotions, reduction of IS budget, profitability analysis

payments, checking account—and generates an analysis of online banking sessions. Consumers are better able to understand their spending patterns, and they have reported a higher level of customer satisfaction.

Another company that continues to grow its enterprise using a public data warehouse is Travelocity. Part of the company's success lies in its innovative use of its EDW for marketing and CRM.

DATA MARTS, OPERATIONAL DATA STORES, AND MULTIDIMENSIONAL DATABASES

Organizations frequently implement data marts, operational data stores, and multidimensional databases either as supplements or substitutes for data warehouses. In this section we take a closer look at these systems, beginning with data marts.

Data Marts. The high costs of data warehouses can make them too expensive for a company to implement. As an alternative, many firms create a lower-cost, scaled-down version of a data warehouse called a data mart. Data marts are designed for a strategic business unit (SBU) or a single department.

In addition to lower costs (less than $100,000 versus $1 million or more for data warehouses), data marts require significantly shorter lead times for implementation, often less than 90 days. In addition, because they allow for local rather than central control, they confer power on the using group. They also contain less information than the data warehouse. Thus, they respond more quickly, and they are easier to understand and navigate. Finally, they allow a business unit to build its own decision support systems without relying on a centralized IS department.

Operational Data Stores. An **operational data store** is a database for transaction processing systems that uses data warehouse concepts to provide clean data. It brings the concepts and benefits of the data warehouse to the operational portions of the business at a lower cost. Thus, it can be viewed as being situated between the operational data (in legacy systems) and the data warehouse. An operational data store is used for short-term decisions involving mission-critical applications rather than for the medium- and long-term decisions associated with the regular data warehouse. These decisions require access to much more current information. For example, a bank needs to know about all the accounts for a customer who is calling on the phone.

Multidimensional Databases: From Tables to Data Cubes. A data warehouse can be based on a multidimensional model, called a **multidimensional database,** that views data in the form of a data cube. For example, a data cube may let you view a specific variable, or piece of information, such as *product sales*, in three dimensions (3D). Think of a dimension as a unit of measure. A product's 3D data cube could show three measures: item name, quantity sold, and geographical region. For an illustration of a 3D data cube, see Online Brief 3.2.

System Failures. Unfortunately, despite their potential benefits, implementations of large information systems often fail. Examples and reasons for failures are summarized in Table 3.5. Suggestions on how to avoid data warehouse failure are provided at *datawarehouse.com,* at *bitpipe.com,* and at *teradatauniversitynetwork.com.*

CONSOLIDATING DATA MARTS INTO AN ENTERPRISE DATA WAREHOUSE

To minimize the investment or risk of failure of a large information system, companies may start with data marts, and then later want to consolidate them into an enterprisewide data warehouse.

Consolidating data marts into a DW helps drive better business decisions as well as save money. Two other business benefits are compliance and going green.

- **Compliance.** Storing integrated data in an EDW makes it easier for the company to control which people can access and use sensitive financial data. In addition, an EDW can help a company meet regulatory compliance requirements by providing increased accuracy in reporting financial results, data security, encryption of sensitive data, and disaster recovery planning.

TABLE 3.5	Reasons Data Warehouses Fail

Data warehousing design:

- Unrealistic expectations
- Inappropriate architecture
- Vendors overselling capabilities
- Insufficient logical design
- Lack of development expertise
- Unclear business objectives
- Lack of effective project sponsorship

Data warehousing implementation:

- Poor user training
- Failure to align data warehouses and data marts
- Lack of attention to cultural issues
- Corporate policies not updated

Data warehousing operation:

- Poor upkeep of technology
- Failure to upgrade modules
- Lack of integration
- Poor data quality
- Inappropriate format of information

• **Going green.** Maintaining separate data marts impacts the environment. Consolidating power-hungry servers, which are often underutilized, reduces both electricity consumption and the amount of heat produced, which in turn reduces the amount of energy required for cooling the equipment.

DATA CENTERS

Data center is the name given to the newer facilities containing mission-critical ISs and components that deliver data and IT services to the enterprise. Data centers integrate networks, computer systems, and storage devices. Data centers need to insure the availability of power and provide physical and data security. The newest data centers are huge and include temperature and fire controls, physical and digital security, redundant power supplies such as uninterruptible power sources (UPS), and redundant data communications connections. For example, in 2008, Christus Health Medical Center in Texas built a $23 million data center to house its patient insurance records, CT scans, and other data and documents. The size of the data center is 48,000 square feet, which was over ten times the size of the hospital's former 4,000-square-foot data center. Demands for imaging data were growing quickly as more types of health reports and records get digitized, stored, and archived for decades.

Many companies are building or reconfiguring their data centers to save money. Some cannot afford the electricity and cooling costs. Others need more computing, storage, or network capacity to handle new applications or to cope with acquisitions. Still others need to improve their disaster recovery capabilities. Creating—or reducing the cost of—a disaster recovery site is often part of a data center upgrade plan. Disaster recovery is discussed in Chapter 5.

Next-generation data centers will be more efficient in lowering operating expenses and energy consumption. They will have greater availability (*uptime*) to meet business needs and will be easier to manage. A networking company, Cisco (*cisco.com*), offers several podcasts and video demos of data centers.

1. What is the main difference in the designs of databases and data warehouses?
2. Compare databases and data warehouses in terms of data volatility and decision support.
3. What is an advantage of an active data warehouse?
4. What are the data functions performed by a data warehouse?
5. How can a data warehouse support a company's compliance requirements and going green initiatives?
6. Why are data centers important to performance?

3.5 Enterprise Content Management

Enterprise content management (ECM) has become an important data management technology, particularly for large and medium-sized organizations. ECM includes electronic document management, Web content management, digital asset management, and electronic records management (ERM). ERM infrastructures help reduce costs, easily share content across the enterprise, minimize risk, automate expensive time-intensive and manual processes, and consolidate multiple Web sites onto a single platform.

Four key forces are driving organizations to adopt a strategic, enterprise-level approach to planning and deploying content systems:

• Compounding growth of content generated by organizations

• The need to integrate that content within business processes

• The need to support increasing sophistication for business user content access and interaction

• The need to maintain governance and control over content to ensure regulatory compliance and preparedness for legal discovery

Modern businesses generate volumes of documents, messages, and memos that, by their nature, contain unstructured content (data or information). Therefore, the contents of e-mail and instant messages, spreadsheets, faxes, reports, case notes, Web pages, voice mails, contracts, and presentations cannot be put into a database. However, many of these materials are business records (as discussed in Section 3.1) that need to be retained. As materials are not needed for current operations or decisions, they are archived—moved into longer-term storage. Because these materials constitute business records, they must be retained and made available when requested by auditors, investigators, the SEC, the IRS, or other authorities. To be retrievable, the records must be organized and indexed like structured data in a database.

Records are different from documents in that they cannot be modified or deleted except in controlled circumstances. In contrast, documents generally are subject to revision. Figure 3.13 shows the differences between documents and records as well as the relationship between document management and records management.

ELECTRONIC RECORDS AND DOCUMENT MANAGEMENT

In Section 3.1 you learned that document management systems organize and store e-mail, instant messages, and other types of unstructured content. In this section, we examine the related topic of ERM.

Simply creating backups of records is not a form of ERM, because the content is not organized so that it can be accurately and easily retrieved. ERM requires the involvement of not only key players in recordkeeping, such as records managers or record librarians, but also IT personnel and administrators under a shared responsibility to establish ERM policies. Those policies include schedules for retaining and destroying records, which must comply with state and federal regulations.

The requirement to manage records—regardless of whether they are paper or electronic—is not new. What is new is the volume of electronic records that must be reviewed to determine whether they should be retained or destroyed. Properly

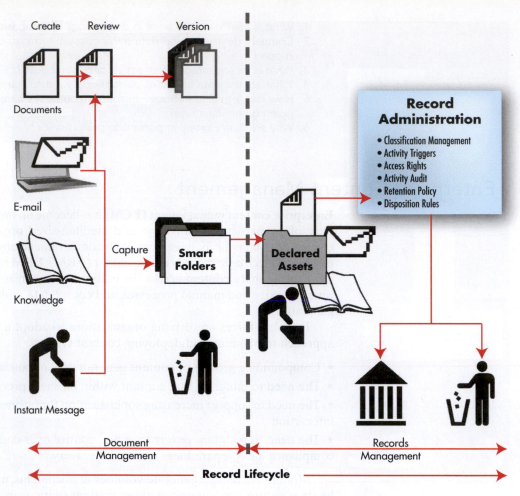

Figure 3.13 Electronic records management from creation to retention or destruction.

managed, electronic records are strategic assets. Improperly managed or destroyed, they are liabilities.

THE BUSINESS VALUE OF ELECTRONIC RECORDS MANAGEMENT

Companies need to be prepared to respond to an audit, federal investigation, lawsuit, or any other legal action against it. Types of lawsuits against companies include patent violations, product safety negligence, theft of intellectual property, breach of contract, wrongful termination, harassment, discrimination, and many more.

Nearly 90 percent of U.S. corporations become engaged in lawsuits; and at any one time, the average $1 billion company in the United States faces 147 lawsuits (Kish, 2006). Each lawsuit will involve discovery, or the request for information (almost always involves the request for e-mail and other electronic communications). **Discovery** is the process of gathering information in preparation for trial, legal or regulatory investigation, or administrative action as required by law. When electronic information is involved, the process is called electronic discovery, or e-discovery. When a company receives an e-discovery request, the company must produce what is requested—or face charges of obstructing justice or being in contempt of court.

Several cases where a company incurred huge costs for not responding to e-discovery are the following:

- Failure to save e-mails resulted in a $2.75 million fine for Phillip Morris.
- Failure to respond to e-discovery requests cost Bank of America $10 million in fines.
- Failure to produce backup tapes and deleted e-mails resulted in a $29.3 million jury verdict against USB Warburg in what became a landmark case, *Zubulake v. UBS Warburg*.

ECM AND ERM GROWTH

At the 2008 EMC World Conference in Las Vegas, 9,000 attendees heard about the future of EMC for content management, virtualization, and Web 2.0 storage—indicating the importance of these technologies. Stored data is expected to reach 2 trillion gigabytes by the year 2011. Keeping corporate data safe will be an incredible challenge, as you will read in Chapter 5.

While unlike any other aspect of business, planning and managing electronic documents and records is an element of every business process. This situation has increased both the number of ECM and ERM vendors and the capabilities they provide. Vendors sell suites of products, including document management, collaboration, portals, and business intelligence.

Numerous major IT companies have become ECM and ERM vendors. ECM vendors include IBM (*ibm.com*), Oracle (*oracle.com*), and EMC (*emc.com*).

Major ERM vendors include Hummingbird (*hummingbird.com*), Iron Mountain (*ironmountain.com*), Oracle (oracle.com), and AccuTrac (*accutrac.com*). Visit *ironmountain.com/services/tours/records.asp* or *ironmountain.com/services/tours/dms.asp* to view videos of electronic records management and a records management center.

Review Questions

1. Define ECM.
2. What is the difference between a document and a record?
3. Why is ERM important to an organization?
4. Define discovery and e-discovery.
5. How does creating backups of electronic records differ from ERM?

3.6 Managerial Issues

1. **Reducing uncertainty.** Performance and profitability improve when managers can reduce uncertainty by learning or gaining insights from their data. Reducing uncertainty requires a data infrastructure that can capture, process, and report information in near real-time.

2. **Cost-benefit issues and justification.** Some of the data management solutions discussed in this chapter are very expensive and therefore are justifiable only in large corporations. Smaller organizations can make the solutions cost effective if they leverage (make use of) existing databases rather than create new ones. However, they must undertake a careful cost-benefit analysis before making any commitment to new technologies.

3. **Where to store data physically.** Should data be distributed close to their users? This arrangement could speed up data entry and updating, but it could also generate replication and security risks. Alternatively, should data be centralized for easier control, security, and disaster recovery? This alternative offers fewer communications and single-point-of-failure risks.

4. **Legal issues.** Failure to manage electronic records exposes companies to fines or sanctions from the courts or regulatory agencies such as the SEC and the IRS.

5. **Internal or external?** Should a firm invest in internally collecting, storing, maintaining, and purging its databases of information? Or, should it subscribe to external databases, where providers are responsible for data management and data access controls?

6. **Disaster recovery.** Can an organization's business processes, which have become dependent on databases and data warehouses, recover and sustain operations after an information systems disaster? (See Chapter 5.) How can a data warehouse be protected? At what cost?

7. **Data security and ethics.** Are the company's customer and other competitive data safe from snooping and sabotage? Are confidential data, such as

personnel details, safe from improper or illegal access and alteration? A related question is, Who owns such personal data?

8. **Privacy.** Data mining may violate state, federal, or foreign privacy laws. Storing data in a warehouse and conducting data mining may result in the invasion of individual privacy. What will companies do to protect individuals? What can individuals do to protect their privacy?

9. **The legacy data problem.** One very real issue, often known as the legacy data acquisition problem, is what to do with the mass of information already stored in a variety of systems and formats. Data in older, perhaps obsolete, databases still need to be available to newer database management systems. Many of the legacy application programs used to access the older data cannot be converted into new computing environments without considerable expense. Basically, there are three approaches to solving this problem. One is to create a database front end that can act as a translator from the old system to the new. The second is to integrate the older applications into the new system so that data can be seamlessly accessed in the original format.

10. **Data delivery.** Moving data around an enterprise efficiently is often a major problem. The inability to communicate effectively and efficiently among different groups situated in different geographical locations is a serious roadblock to implementing distributed applications properly, especially given the mobility of today's workers and the many remote sites where they can be located. Mobile and wireless computing are addressing some of these difficulties.

How *IT* Benefits You

For the Accounting Major
IT budgets have become one of the larger line item expenses at many companies, and IT successes as well as mistakes can have a direct impact on a firm's bottom line. Transaction data are crucial for financial statements, cost control, inventory control, accounts payable, and accounts receivable. Determining financial performance with accurate transaction data can be very costly to organizations, as we have seen in the past decade. In accounting, data must be reliable and accurate.

For the Finance Major
Financial systems rely on database management systems for their successful operation. Financial analysts use historical data residing in data warehouses to create forecasts and analytical reports for investors.

For the Human Resources Management Major
Human resources managers use database management systems to manage employee data (e.g., health benefits, retirement, and insurance).

For the IS Major
Managing information systems means managing data. Data administrators manage all aspects of the process whereby data are entered into the system and accessed from the system.

For the Marketing Major
Web-based systems allow companies to personalize direct marketing approaches that in turn attract new customers and build customer loyalty.

For the Production/Operations Management Major
By employing data related to inventory, production, distribution, logistics, and shipping, managers can make better decisions faster.

Key Terms

Chapter Highlights

(Numbers Refer to Learning Objectives)

❶ Data are the foundation of any information system and need to be managed throughout their useful life cycle, which converts data to useful information, knowledge, and a basis for decision support. Viewed from the basic profitability or net income model (profit = revenues − expenses), profit increases when employees learn from and use the data to increase revenues, reduce expenses, or both.

❷ Managers and information workers may be constrained by data that cannot be trusted because they are incomplete, out of context, outdated, inaccurate, inaccessible, or so overwhelming that they require too much time to analyze.

❷ Data errors and inconsistencies lead to mistakes and lost opportunities, such as failed deliveries, invoicing blunders, and problems in synchronizing data from multiple locations.

❷ Many factors that impact the quality of data must be recognized and controlled.

❸ Programs that manage data and provide access to the database are called database management systems (DBMSs).

❸ Data and documents are managed electronically. They are digitized, stored, and used in electronic management systems.

❸ The benefits of using a DBMS include improved strategic use of corporate data, reduced complexity of the data environment, reduced data redundancy and enhanced data integrity, improved security, reduced data maintenance costs, and better access to data.

❹ The logical view, or user's view, of data is meaningful to the user. Restricting access to data based on the users' job responsibilities increases data security.

❹ The logical model is a detailed view of the data in which high-level entities are broken down into manageable data entities (e.g., customer data into product preferences, customer contact, shop locations, and product sales).

❺ Data warehouses and data marts support the demanding data need of decision makers. Relevant data are indexed and organized for easy access by end users.

❻ Online analytical processing (OLAP) creates meaningful and actionable views of data.

❼ Electronic document management, the automated control of documents, is a key to greater efficiency in handling documents in order to gain an edge on the competition.

❼ How an organization manages its electronic records can directly affect its ability to compete intelligently, to comply with laws and regulations, to respond to litigation, and to recover from disaster. Regulatory requirements such as Sarbanes-Oxley, privacy requirements, and anti-fraud legislation have made managing information both a business priority and a legal obligation.

Virtual Company Assignment

WILEY PLUS

Data Management at The Wireless Café

Go to The Wireless Café's link on the Student Web Site. There you will be asked to think about how to better manage the various types of data that the restaurant uses in its activities.

Instructions for accessing The Wireless Café on the Student Web Site:

1. Go to *wiley.com/college/turban*.
2. Select Turban/Volonino's *Information Technology for Management,* Seventh Edition.
3. Click on Student Resources site, in the toolbar on the left.
4. Click on the link for Virtual Company Web site.
5. Click on Wireless Café.

Questions for Discussion

1. How would reducing uncertainty lead to an improvement in net earnings? Use the *net income model* in your answer.
2. Explain how having detailed real-time or near real-time data can improve productivity and decision quality.
3. Why does data management matter? Why are data an organizational asset?
4. List three types of waste or damages that data errors can cause.
5. Explain the *principle of 90/90 data use*.
6. How does data visualization improve decision making?
7. Discuss the major drivers and benefits of data warehousing.
8. Why is master data management (MDM) important in companies with multiple data sources?
9. A data mart can substitute for a data warehouse or supplement it. Compare and discuss these options.
10. What ethical duties does the collection of data about customers impose on companies?
11. How are organizations using their data warehouses to improve consumer satisfaction and the company's profitability?
12. Relate document management to imaging systems.
13. Discuss the factors that make document management so valuable. What capabilities are particularly valuable?
14. Distinguish between operational databases, data warehouses, and data marts.
15. Discuss the interaction between real-time data and profitability in the Applebee's case.

Exercises and Projects

1. Read *A Closer Look 3.1* "Data Errors Cost Billions of Dollars and Put Lives at Risk." Answer the further exploration questions. Then visit the SAS Web site at *sas.com* and search for their data synchronization or data integration solution. List the key benefits of the SAS solution.
2. Interview a manager or other knowledge worker in a company you work for or to which you have access. Find the data problems they have encountered and the measures they have taken to solve them.
3. Read *A Closer Look 3.2* "Finding Million-Dollar Donors in Three Minutes." Answer the further exploration questions. Then visit the Business Objects Web site at *businessobjects.com* and search for "Xcelsius 2008 Demos and Sample Downloads." Click on one of the images of a dashboard or model to launch an interactive demo. Use the simulated controls in the demo to see *Xcelsius 2008 in action* (*or visit businessobjects. com/product/catalog/xcelsius/demos.asp*). Identify the model or dashboard whose interactive demo you viewed. Explain the benefits to decision makers of that dashboard or model.
4. Visit Analysis Factory at *analysisfactory.com*. Click to view the *Interactive Business Solution Dashboards*. Select one type of dashboard and explain its value or features.
5. Read *A Closer Look 3.3* "National Security Depends on Intelligence and Data Mining." Answer the further exploration questions. Visit Oracle at *oracle.com* and do a search for Oracle Data Mining (ODM). Identify three functionalities of ODM.
6. At *teradatastudentnetwork.com*, read and answer the questions to the case: "Harrah's High Payoff from Customer Information." Relate results from Harrah's to how other casinos use their customer data.
7. Go to *Teradata Magazine*, Volume 6, Number 2, and read "The Big Payoff." Then go to *teradatastudentnetwork.com*, and read the case study "Harrah's High Payoff from Customer Information." What kind of payoff are they having from this investment in data warehousing?
8. At *teradatastudentnetwork.com*, read and answer the questions of the assignment entitled "Data Warehouse Failures." Choose one case and discuss the failure and the potential remedy.

Group Assignments and Projects

1. Prepare a report on the topic of "data management and the intranet." Specifically, pay attention to the role of the data warehouse, the use of browsers for query, and data mining. Each group will visit one or two vendors' sites, read the white papers, and examine products (Oracle, Red Bricks, Brio, Siemens Mixdorf IS, NCR, SAS, and Information Advantage). Also, visit the Web site of the Data Warehouse Institute (*tdwi.org*).
2. Using data mining, it is possible not only to capture information that has been buried in distant court-

houses but also to manipulate and cross-index it. This ability can benefit law enforcement but invade privacy. In 1996, Lexis-Nexis, the online information service, was accused of permitting access to sensitive information on individuals. The company argued that the firm was targeted unfairly, because it provided only basic residential data for lawyers and law enforcement personnel. Should Lexis-Nexis be prohibited from allowing access to such information? Debate the issue.

3. Ocean Spray Cranberries, Inc., is a large cooperative of fruit growers and processors. Ocean Spray needed data to determine the effectiveness of its promotions and its advertising and to respond strategically to its competitors' promotions. The company also wanted to identify trends in consumer preferences for new products and to pinpoint marketing factors that might be causing changes in the selling levels of certain brands and markets.

Ocean Spray buys marketing data from InfoScan (*us.infores.com*), a company that collects data using barcode scanners in a sample of 2,500 stores nationwide and from A.C. Nielsen. The data for each product include sales volume, market share, distribution, price information, and information about promotions (sales, advertisements).

The amount of data provided to Ocean Spray on a daily basis is overwhelming (about 100 to 1,000 times more data items than Ocean Spray used to collect on its own). All of the data are deposited in the corporate marketing data mart. To analyze this vast amount of data, the company developed a decision support system (DSS). To give end users easy access to the data, the company uses a data-mining process called CoverStory, which summarizes information in accordance with user preferences. CoverStory interprets data processed by the DSS, identifies trends, discovers cause-and-effect relationships, presents hundreds of displays, and provides any information required by the decision makers. This system alerts managers to key problems and opportunities.

    a. Find information about Ocean Spray by entering Ocean Spray's Web site (*oceanspray.com*).

    b. Ocean Spray has said that it cannot run the business without the system. Why?

    c. What data from the data mart are used by the DSS?

    d. Enter *scanmar.nl* and click the Marketing Dashboard. How does the dashboard provide marketing and sales intelligence?

Internet Exercises

1. Conduct a survey on document management tools and applications.

2. Access the Web sites of one or two of the major data management vendors, such as Oracle, IBM, and Sybase, and trace the capabilities of their latest BI products.

3. Access the Web sites of one or two of the major data warehouse vendors, such as NCR or SAS; find how their products are related to the Web.

4. Access the Web site of the GartnerGroup (*gartnergroup.com*). Examine some of their research notes pertaining to marketing databases, data warehousing, and data management. Prepare a report regarding the state of the art.

5. Explore a Web site for multimedia database applications. Review some of the demonstrations, and prepare a concluding report.

6. Enter *microsoft.com/solutions/BI/customer/biwithinreach_demo.asp* and see how BI is supported by Microsoft's tools. Write a report.

7. Enter *teradatauniversitynetwork.com*. Prepare a summary on resources available there. Is it valuable to a student? To practicing managers?

8. Enter *www-306.ibm.com/*. Find services related to dynamic warehouse and explain what it does.

Minicase

Pushing Corporate Data to Employees' Facebook Pages

IS   SVR

The ever-advancing computing environments of the workplace and the Web are merging. Enterprises are implementing newer and better models for delivering corporate data. One example is WorkLight™ (*myworklight.com*), a server-side software product that offers secure, personalized Web 2.0 computing environments to enterprises. WorkLight specializes in transferring corporate data to consumer Web-based applications.

WorkLight, a New Category of Server-Based Software

WorkLight is a new category of server-based software product that lets enterprise information workers and consumers increase productivity by defining their own enterprise application experience. With WorkLight, workers can receive corporate application data in a timely and secure fashion via RSS feeds or secure AJAX widgets. WorkLight simplifies difficult tasks such as acquiring data from enterprise applications, enforcing access control, and conforming to corporate security policies.

WorkLight enables employees to broadcast proprietary information about themselves and their specialties to one another over their Facebook (*facebook.com*) homepages. David Lavenda, VP of marketing and product strategy for WorkLight, explains that the tool, called WorkBook, has been designed so that sensitive corporate data aren't visible to Facebook members outside the organization and don't ever reside on Facebook's servers.

Applying the Web Experience to the Enterprise

For 20-something employees, there is a huge gap between their home Web experience and the interfaces they're tied into at work. Most enterprises have lagged far behind the Web 2.0 revolution. With the *Enterprise 2.0* software solution, companies can leverage RSS feeds and AJAX to deliver corporate data. Employees log on to see sales leads, relevant news headlines, stock prices—everything they might see at home, but with a business-focused spin. "The more we talked to companies, it became clear that collaboration and social networking is really important to them," Lavenda commented.

Statistically speaking, Facebook's 55 million users indicate that it is the right tool to use. Using social networking sites in the workplace has become popular. In fact, a survey conducted by Nucleus Research found that 40 percent of the workforce accessed one or more social networking sites regularly. Like social networking, Web 2.0 technologies have become a part of both an employee's work life and personal life.

WorkLight has made its name by taking data from old proprietary customer relationship management (CRM) and enterprise resource planning (ERP) systems and pushing them to popular online portals such as iGoogle pages. Because customers use a WorkLight server that sits behind a firewall, the information does not pass through Google's servers.

WorkBook allows employees to share information about projects and personal expertise over Facebook and then build networks based on that knowledge. When the staffers log on to Facebook, they don't immediately have access to the corporate data. Rather, they first must type in a corporate user name and password. Allowing people who are geographically remote but performing similar jobs to communicate with one another over Facebook is valuable to the enterprise.

Sources: Compiled from Lynch (2007) and *Myworklight.com* (2008).

Questions for Minicase

1. In your opinion, is Workbook a document management system?
2. What are the benefits of WorkLight and WorkBook for large enterprises with distributed workforces?
3. What are the benefits of WorkLight and WorkBook for small or medium enterprises?
4. Visit the company's site at *myworklight.com*, and view the demo for WorkBook. How does WorkBook provide secure enterprise social networking?
5. Visit the company's site at *myworklight.com*, and review the Product FAQs. Is WorkLight secure enough to deliver sensitive data? Why or why not?
6. After viewing the demo, explain why you would or would not want this capability in your workplace.
7. Visit Xerox at *xerox.com*, and review their document management solutions. Compare Workbook's document management system to that of Xerox. Which DMS would you prefer to use? Explain why.

Problem-Solving Activity

Calculating the Impact of Poor Document Management on the Bottom Line

Spring Street Company (SSC, *a fictitious company*) faced rising costs not only from sky-high energy prices, but also from what it considered "hidden costs" associated with its paper-intensive processes. The employees jokingly predicted that if the windows in the offices blew open on a very windy day, there would be total chaos as the papers started flying. The financial implications were that, if such a disaster occurred, the business would grind to a halt.

The company's accountant, Sam Spring, decided to calculate the costs of their paper-driven processes to identify their impact on the bottom line. He recognized that several employees spent most of their day filing or retrieving documents. In addition, there were the monthly costs to warehouse old paper records. Sam observed and measured the activities related to the handling of printed reports and paper files. His average estimates are as follows:

- It takes an employee five minutes to walk to the records room, locate a file, act on it, re-file it, and return to his desk.
- Employees need to locate a file, act on it, and so on five times per day.
- There are 12 full-time employees who perform these functions.
- Once per day a document gets "lost" (destroyed, misplaced, or covered with massive coffee stains) and must be re-created. The total cost of replacing each lost document is $220.
- Warehousing costs as of the present time for the current volume of stored documents are $75 per month.

Sam would prefer a system that lets employees find and work with business documents without leaving their desks. He's most concerned about the human resources and accounting departments. These personnel are traditional heavy users of paper files and would greatly benefit from a modern document management system. At the same time, however, Sam is also risk averse. He would rather invest in solutions that would reduce the risk of higher costs in the future. He recognizes that the U.S. PATRIOT Act's requirements that organizations provide immediate government access to records apply to SSC. He has read that manufacturing and government organizations rely on efficient document management to meet these broader regulatory imperatives. Finally, Sam wants to implement a disaster recovery system.

Your Mission

Prepare a report that provides Sam with the data and information he needs to select and implement a cost-effective alternative to the company's costly paper-intensive approach to managing documents. You will need to conduct research to provide data to prepare this report. Your report should include the following information:

1. Explain the similarities and differences between document imaging systems and document management systems (DMS). List the benefits and the basic hardware and software requirements for each system. Put this information into a table to help Sam readily understand the comparison.

2. Discuss why a DMS transforms the way a business operates. How should SSC prepare for a DMS if they decide to implement one?

3. Collect estimates for the costs of buying or implementing a DMS at SSC.

4. Using the data collected by Sam, create a spreadsheet that calculates the costs of handling paper at SSC based on hourly rates per employee of $16, $22, and $28. Add the cost of lost documents to this. Then, add the costs of warehousing the paper, which increases by 10% every month due to increases in volume. Present the results showing both monthly totals and a yearly total. Prepare graphs as visualization tools so that Sam can easily perceive the projected growth in warehousing costs over the next three years.

5. Identify at least one additional cost factor (other than better security) that might be reduced or eliminated with the DMS.

6. How can DMS also serve as a disaster recovery system in case of fire, flood, or break-in?

7. Submit your recommendation for a DMS solution. Identify two vendors in your recommendation.

Online Resources

More resources and study tools are located on the Student Web Site and on WileyPlus. You'll find additional chapter materials and useful Web links. In addition, self-quizzes that provide individualized feedback are available for each chapter.

Online Brief for Chapter 3 is available at wiley.com/college/turban:

3.1 Using a Data Warehouse to Manage Customer Churn at Sprint

3.2 A Multidimensional Database

Online Minicases for Chapter 3 are available at wiley.com/college/turban:

3.1 Finding Diamonds by Data Mining at Harrah's Entertainment, Inc.

3.2 Data Integration at the U.S. Department of Homeland Security

References

Barlow, R. D., "Sync or Swim: Who Should Blink First and Why?" *Healthcare Purchasing News*, April 2007, *hpnonline.com/inside/2007-04/0704-DataSynch1.html* (accessed June 2008).

Business Wire, "Applebee's International Reports Third Quarter 2007 Results," October 29, 2007.

Chisholm, P., "Synchronizing the Supply Chain," Military Medical Technology, 12(2), March 7, 2008, *military-medical-technology.com/article.cfm?DocID=1218* (accessed June 2008).

Kish, L., "Most U.S. Companies Engaged in Lawsuits." E-Discovery Advisor, May 2006.

Levine, L., "In Sync: Getting the Supply Chain Act Together," Healthcare Purchasing News, April 2007. *hpnonline.com/inside/2007-04/0704-DataSynch2.html* (accessed June 2008).

Loshin, D., "Issues and Opportunities in Data Quality Management Coordination," *DM Review*, April 2004.

Lynch, C. G., "Tool Pushes Corporate Data to Employee Facebook Pages," *CIO.com*. December 20, 2007, *cio.com/article/167101/Tool_Pushes_Corporate_Data_to_Employee_Facebook_Pages* (accessed June 2008).

Snow, C., "Embrace the Role and Value of Master Data Management," *Manufacturing Business Technology*, 26(2), February 2008.

Stodder, D., "Microsoft Buys its Way into MDM," Ventana Research, June 19, 2007, *ventanaresearch.com/research/article.aspx?id=2268* (accessed June 2008).

Teradata, Applebee's International," *Teradata.com*, 2004, *teradata.com/t/page/87786* (accessed June 2008).

Volonino, L., R. Anzaldua, and J. Godwin, *Computer Forensics: Principles and Practice,* Chapter 10. Upper Saddle River. NJ: Prentice-Hall, 2007.

Wailgum, T., "Eight of the Worst Spreadsheet Blunders," *CIO.com*, August 17, 2007, *cio.com/article/131500/Eight_of_the_Worst_Spreadsheet_Blunders* (accessed March 2008).

Whitehouse.gov, 2008 (accessed June 2008).

Worthen, B., "IT versus Terror," *CIO*, August 1, 2006.

Zeehandelaar, R., and P. Lawrence, "Getting Support from the Active Data Warehouse," *Teradata Magazine*, September 2005, *teradata.com/t/page/138739/index.html* (accessed June 2008).

Chapter 4

Networks and Collaboration as Business Solutions

Networked Devices and Collaboration Portal Tackle Super Bowl Logistics

4.1 Enterprise Networks, Connectivity, and Trends

4.2 Network Management and Collaboration Technology

4.3 Wireless, Enterprise Mobility, and IP Telephony

4.4 Discovery, Search, and Customized Delivery

4.5 Collaboration and Web-Based Meetings

4.6 Social, Legal, and Ethical Issues

4.7 Managerial Issues

Minicase: *Wikis, Blogs, and Chats Support Collaboration at DrKW*

Problem-Solving Activity: *Comparing the Costs of Using Web Meetings and Collaboration*

Online Minicases:
4.1 Safeway Collaborates in Designing Stores
4.2 Network Computing at National Semiconductor Corporation

Online Brief:
4.1 Closer Look: Fila's Collaboration Software Reduces Time-to-Market

Learning Objectives

After studying this chapter, you will be able to:

❶ Describe networks, network standards, and compatibility issues.

❷ Describe the impacts of collaboration on business performance.

❸ Explain fixed, wireless, and mobile network infrastructures.

❹ Understand the influence of search engines and enterprise search.

❺ Identify ways to customize search and delivery to increase productivity.

❻ Describe the fundamental principles and capabilities of group work technologies.

❼ Evaluate the managerial, social, and ethical issues related to the use of network computing, messaging, and collaboration.

Integrating *IT*

 ACC
 FIN
 MKT
 OM
 HRM
 IS

IT-PERFORMANCE MODEL

The success of every aspect of the enterprise depends on *connectivity*—being connected via networks and networked devices. Networks and collaboration systems enable distributed business operations, Internet transactions with customers and suppliers, and wireless connections with employees. A lot is riding on wired and wireless networks, network management, and bandwidth-intensive services. Radio frequency (RF) transmission technology for wireless local area networks has been well standardized for several years. This 802.11 specification, dubbed Wi-Fi, together with laptops and devices embedded with Wi-Fi chips are driving the business environment into hyper-connectivity. Pressures to deliver secure service to customers and business partners at reduced costs, to be environmentally responsible, and to support the 24/7 data needs of mobile and remote workers have increased demands on corporate networks. This chapter focuses on network infrastructures and networked devices that are supporting and transforming communication, collaboration, and commerce.

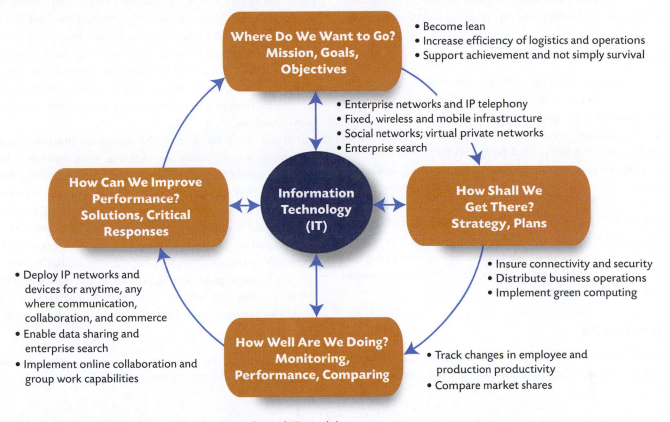

The business performance management cycle and IT model.

NETWORKED DEVICES AND A COLLABORATION PORTAL TACKLE SUPER BOWL LOGISTICS

The National Football League (NFL, (*nfl.com*) designated Florida's Jacksonville Sheriff's office (JSO) as the lead agency for coordinating and securing local operations for Super Bowl XXXIX. Security at the Super Bowls after 2001 was subject to the authority of the U.S. federal government. The federal government mandated that JSO be capable of *in-synch* (synchronized) communication and real-time collaboration with federal and national security agencies for terrorism prevention and intervention. To see the video case study, go to *convergencecom.com/downloads/Superbowl-medium.wmv*.

The Problem

Providing logistic support for a Super Bowl is a challenge of scope and scale. JSO had to manage 150,000 spirited fans, provide security at 6,000 events, and coordinate 53 separate agencies at the local, county, state, and federal levels. Those agencies included the Jacksonville Fire and Rescue Department, Florida Highway Patrol, FBI, Federal Emergency Management Agency (FEMA), Secret Service, and Department of Homeland Security (DHS). JSO also had to provide an undisrupted Super Bowl experience for the teams, fans, two former presidents, and megastar Sir Paul McCartney. Movements of the New England Patriots and Philadelphia Eagles had to be monitored by mobile units. That required collaboration of over 4,000 personnel to plan, build, and execute land, sea, and air activities. Business continuity and incident response plans had to be coordinated at 35 venues for 10 days leading up to and including the game.

The Solution

The Information Systems Management (ISM) department implemented a real-time Web-based communication and collaboration portal, called e-Sponder, from Convergence Communications (*convergencecom.com*). More than 1,900 laptop users were connected to the portal.

E-Sponder is accessed through a browser and runs on the Microsoft Office platform. Users learned the system quickly because of its familiar Office interface. E-Sponder uses Microsoft's SharePoint Portal Server for online collaboration. As soon as information is entered into the system, it is instantly available for anyone else. Since users viewed everything that was going on, there was less need to coordinate personnel using radio communication.

The Results

Previously, command staff sat around a table, each listening to radio communications from their ground personnel. Not only did this system create noisy distractions, but it only provided individuals with pieces of information. There was no way to communicate to everyone present the entire picture of what was happening as it was happening, which is something we now take for granted.

The incident command team, including Secret Service and fire and police chiefs, watched events unfold on a wall-sized screen display. Around the room, representatives from 25 agencies sat at computers running e-Sponder. Down the hall in the dispatch room, dispatchers and 911 operators sat at similar terminals. These personnel formed the front line to the command center, listening to radio calls from many police units and undercover agents stationed in various locations around campus and along President Bush's motorcade routes. As information came in, dispatchers entered it into the portal, which updated the screen display in the command center in real time.

When a fire broke out in a house on the president's motorcade route, within seconds the news came into the dispatch center and was recorded on an *unplanned incident* form that showed up on all 25 desktops in the command center. As dispatchers continued to receive news from on-site supervisors managing ground personnel, it was relayed onto that screen so commanders could make decisions based on what was happening at that moment. Fire trucks were given a police escort to the house and the fire was contained, without having to re-route the president. The networked and collaboration operations were a success.

Sources: Compiled from *Convergencecom.com* (2006), Careless (2006), and *e-sponder.com* (accessed May 2008).

Lessons Learned from This Case

Super Bowl's collaboration portal created a real-time view of "what was going on as it was going on" that made informed decisions possible. This transparency, or *real-time awareness*, is critical to the outcome of operations, logistics, and many other enterprise transactions.

By integrating collaboration tools, networks, wireless devices, and instant communication such as text messaging, companies can replace inefficient paper-based processes, improve the capture and archiving of information for knowledge retention, and reduce paper-handling personnel. Networks, collaboration, wireless standards, and mobile computing infrastructures are discussed in this chapter. We also examine new enterprise tools and trends, including enterprise search, customized delivery, and the battle of the search engines for control of the enterprise desktop.

4.1 Enterprise Networks, Connectivity, and Trends

Companies rely on the capability of their private networks, connectivity to partners' networks, and the Internet for data, voice, and video communications to conduct business. Network and collaboration strategies have a major impact on competitive outcomes through their ability to improve employee and production productivity. Productivity can be measured as the amount of output (e.g., quantity produced) relative to the amount of input (e.g., number of labor hours). In turn, productivity improvements influence market share through their impact on costs, prices, and the quality of products or services offered. The use of advanced communications technologies can greatly improve business performance and employee productivity, as discussed in this chapter.

NETWORKED DEVICES

Networked devices are devices that communicate with a network. Network devices and technologies—including laptops, PDAs, cell and smartphones, wikis, intranets, extranets, GPSs, POS (point of sale) terminals, and RFID (radio frequency identification)—allow information to be rapidly collected, processed, shared, and acted upon. New feature-rich wireless devices make collaboration easier and more productive. Consider these developments in networked devices and developments that point toward a more integrated, always-connected business environment and lifestyle:

- Within 30 hours of its release in June 2007, Apple sold 270,000 iPhones. iPhones combine a mobile phone, iPod media player, and Web accessibility running on AT&T's wireless network. By October 2008, sales of iPhones had reached 10 million units. They had cost $399 on average and required a pricey 2-year AT&T contract. Despite their high costs, strong sales growth is expected through 2012 with the new iPhone 2.0 that runs on the faster 3G (third generation) wireless Internet service. New software features, such as support for third-party applications, will also attract users. 3G is mobile phone service with data rates of at least 144 Kbps (kilobits per second) while in motion, and 2 Mbps (megabits per second) from a fixed location.

- Americans bought about 4.2 million smartphones in the third quarter of 2007 (3Q07), which amounts to 11 percent of the 38 million phones sold. That's roughly a 180 percent increase over 3Q06 sales of 1.5 million smartphones (Frommer, 2007).

- Executives who have experienced the benefits of professional productivity through wireless Internet devices, such as the BlackBerry or Treo, running over high-speed networks are influencing departments to adopt those devices. A touch-screen BlackBerry was released at the end of 2008 to compete with the popular iPhone. Vendors are adding business-friendly software to their handhelds to make them more attractive and cost-justifiable to managers and road warriors.

- Social networking via mobile phones is shrinking the world to the size of a small screen. Twitter (*twitter.com*), Pownce (*pownce.com*), Jaiku (*jaiku.com*; owned by Google), and Dodgeball (*dodgeball.com*) are popular **micro-blogging** sites with mobile social networking applications. Micro-blogging is the sending of messages up to 140 characters. Twitter, for example, is a free service that lets people keep in touch with others by sending tweets (text posts) to the Twitter Web site using the web, phone, or IM. Tweets are delivered immediately to those signed up to receive them via the same methods. With more than three billion mobile handsets in use in the world (one for every two people on the planet) and mobile networking technologies connecting them to one another, a powerful force for changes in business and collaboration as well as politics and societies has emerged (Warner, 2008). News media, universities, public safety, and other organizations are using this technology to deliver information to a wide audience very quickly. In Los Angeles, the fire department used Twitter to keep residents informed of the devastating wildfires in October 2007.

TABLE 4.1 Growth Toward High-Capacity Networks

Network standard	Generation	Data transfer rates (Capacity)	Used by	Upgrades
GSM (Global System for Mobile Communications)	2G	9.6 Kbps	Cingular, T-Mobile, most European carriers	Upgrades include GPRS, EDGE, UMTS, HSDPA.
CDMA (Code Division Multiple Access)	2.5G	307 Kbps	Verizon, Sprint	Upgrades include 1xRTT, EV-DO, EV-DV.
EDGE (Enhanced Data for Global Evolution)	3G	474 Kbps	Cingular, T-Mobile	
EV-DO (Evolution Data Only)	3G	2.4 Mbps	Verizon, Sprint	Third upgrade to CDMA.
EV-DV (Evolution Data and Voice)	3G	3.1 Mbps	Not in the U.S.	Most advanced CDMA upgrade.
HSDPA (High Speed Data Packet Access)	3.5G	10 Mbps (6–7 Mbps is more realistic)	Cingular	Most advanced GSM upgrade.

			Features and advantages	
WiBro (Wireless broadband)	4G	50 Mbps	Provides *handover functionality* and, therefore, ubiquitous connection. 4G networks will integrate wired and wireless networks to enable seamless service anytime, anywhere. Developed and launched in South Korea.	
WiMax (IEEE 802.16e) (Worldwide Interoperability for Microwave Access)	4G	70 Mbps	Enables delivery of the *last mile* (from network to user) wireless broadband access, as an alternative to cable and DSL. The technology has a technical lead over the competition.	
UMTS LTE (Long-Term Evolution)	4G	277 Mbps	This standard is developed by the Third Generation Partnership Project (3GPP), the same standards body already responsible for the GSM, GPRS, UMTS, and HSDPA standards.	

Figure 4.1 Example of an HSDPA handset.
(Source: GUSTAU NACARINO/Reuters/Landov.)

• Mobile handsets equipped with high-speed data transfer technology (e.g., HSDPA) were introduced in 2006. **HSDPA (high-speed downlink** (or data) **packet access)** allows for data speeds up to 10 Mbps, as shown in Table 4.1. In January 2007, Cingular launched Motorola's V3xx, the first 3G phone for Cingular capable of running on 3.6 Mbps HSDPA. The V3xx is tri-band GSM/EDGE/HSDPA, meaning that it can run on any of those three networks, as listed in Table 4.1. Employees and customers will have broadband-ready handsets capable of sending and receiving all types of media at very high speeds using HSDPA mobile handsets, an example of which is shown in Figure 4.1. By the end of 2008, 40 million people owned these powerful handsets. With telecommunication technology improving rapidly, data transfer rates have increased from Kbps to Mbps. The 4G (fourth generation) mobile network standards, such as WiMax, WiBro, and UMTS LTE, enable faster data transfer rates (see Table 4.1). Even though individual networks, ranging from 2G to 3G, started separately with their own purposes, soon they will be converted to the 4G network. What is significant about 4G networks is that they do not have a circuit-switched subsystem, as do current 2G and 3G networks. Instead, 4G is based purely on the Internet Protocol (IP).

• Advances in GPS positioning and short-range wireless technologies, such as Bluetooth and Wi-Fi, can provide unprecedented intelligence. They could, for example, revolutionize traffic and road safety. Intelligent transport systems being developed by car manufacturers allow cars to communicate with each other and send alerts about sudden braking. In the event of a collision, the car's system could automatically call emergency services. The technology could also apply the brakes automatically if it was determined that two cars were getting too close to each other.

• Sensors integrated with Bluetooth technology may soon alert emergency services when someone has a heart attack. Sensors implanted into people at risk of heart or diabetic attack would allow doctors to monitor them remotely. If the *in-body network* recorded the person had collapsed, it would send an alert to a hospital (Sherwin, 2008).

Advancements in networks, devices, and wireless sensor networks (e.g., RFID) are changing enterprise information infrastructures and business environments dramatically. The preceding examples and network standards illustrate the declining need for a physical computer, as other devices provide access to data, people, or services at *anytime, anywhere* in the world, on high-capacity networks using IP technology. Slow wireless speeds relative to wireline speeds had been a constraint. Development of 4G networks and advanced handsets operating on multiple network standards offer universal connectivity.

IP-based network technology (called *IP network,* for short) forms the backbone that is driving the merger of voice, data, video, and radio waves by digitizing content into packets. Packets can be sent via any digital network. This convergence is happening on a global scale and is changing the way in which people, devices, and applications communicate. As shown in Table 4.1, improved network performance, which is measured by its data transfer capacity, provides fantastic opportunities for mobile commerce, collaboration, supply chain management, remote work, and other productivity gains.

Many of the examples of improved competitive advantage or profits that you read about in Chapters 1 through 3 illustrate the importance of timely data and communications to keep informed or collaborate. In the next section, we discuss network and collaboration technologies and how they can improve performance.

Review Questions

1. How can networked devices improve collaboration and personal productivity?
2. What is micro-blogging and how is it done?
3. What advantages do Twitter and other micro-blogging Web sites offer over traditional forms of communication?
4. Why are handsets displacing computers?
5. What are the unique characteristics or features of 4G network standards compared to 2G and 3G?

4.2 Network Management and Collaboration Technology

Computer networks are the circulatory system of information, communication, or collaboration systems. Networks provide the means to communicate and deliver/receive information from the growing number of devices used to run an enterprise. Effective communication is the key to success in everything from business partnerships to personal and professional relationships. Most professional communication relies heavily on technology—cell phone, e-mail, and texting.

With few exceptions, when the network goes down or access is blocked, so does the ability to operate or function. Imagine a "network blackout" in which you could not access the Internet, e-mail, voice-mail, software, and data files. At most companies, employees would have nothing to do without network connectivity. Obvious damages when a company cannot operate or fulfill its promises due to technical problems include lost sales and productivity, financial consequences from not being able to send and receive payments, and inability to process payroll and inventory.

MODEL OF THE NETWORK, COLLABORATION, AND PERFORMANCE RELATIONSHIP

In the 21st century's fast-paced global business environment, performance depends on the capabilities and qualities of networks and collaboration technologies. Figure 4.2 presents a model of key network and collaboration factors that influence profitability, sales growth, and ability to innovate.

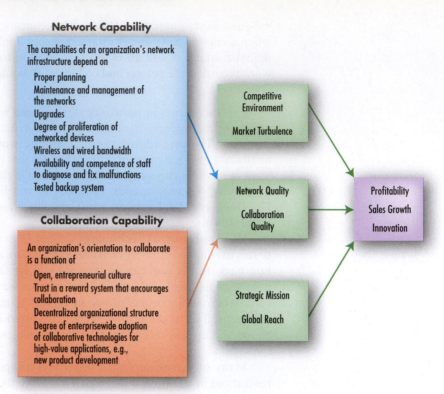

Figure 4.2 Model of network, collaboration, and performance relationship.

As the model in Figure 4.2 illustrates, an enterprise's network capability depends on proper planning, maintenance, management, upgrades, and bandwidth of the network to insure that it has sufficient capacity and connectivity to link people, locations, and data. It also requires that those who need to access the network are equipped with the devices making it possible to do so. As a comparison, a highway system needs to be planned carefully to support peak traffic demands, monitored for compliance with driving rules, cleaned and maintained regularly, and expanded (upgraded) when it no longer meet the needs of those who rely on it.

When problems inevitably occur (e.g., a network crash or car crash), trained staff are needed to restore the network promptly or to switch to a backup system to minimize disruption during the restoration. *A Closer Look 4.1* illustrates the importance of these factors and the consequences of bad planning and testing.

The network architecture is certainly critical because it provides the infrastructure for collaborative work within the company and with external partners and customers, regardless of their location. Often overlooked is the fact that the capability and willingness to collaborate depends on a corporate culture that people trust and that gives them the information, tools, and authority to plan and make decisions. When knowledge workers have such authority, the organization has a decentralized (also called *flatter*) organizational structure. A decentralized organization is more responsive to opportunities and problems than a centralized organization where top-level managers, who are typically less involved in day-to-day operations, make decisions.

Quality of the network and collaboration depend on how effectively network and collaboration capabilities, respectively, are put to use: for example, to monitor operations, manage relationships with customers and suppliers, or conduct mobile or e-commerce. Together with external forces and strategic plans, network and collaboration quality influence performance.

The purpose of this model is to illustrate that network infrastructure alone does not improve business performance. Rather, it is how network capabilities combine

A Closer Look 4.1

U.S. Customs' Network Crash at LAX Strands Passengers

Los Angeles Airport (LAX) is the fifth busiest U.S. airport. In August 2007, more than 20,000 international travelers were stranded at LAX for up to eleven hours because the U.S. Customs and Border Protection (CBP) Agency could not process passengers due to a network crash. A network crash brings immigration to a halt. The crash and long outage was blamed on the cumulative effect of poor network planning, insufficient disaster preparation, a malfunctioning router and network interface card (NIC), mistakes in diagnosing the cause of the outage, and the lack of staff available to repair the network.

Immediate Causes of the Crash and Crisis. The outage started with a malfunctioning NIC on a single workstation on the CBP's local area network (LAN). Instead of simply failing, the NIC began sending packets through the network causing a "data storm" that crashed the LAN. Later, a switch on the network crashed also, compounding the problem. Misdiagnosing the problem and blaming it on routers provided to Sprint wasted about six hours. Sprint tested the lines remotely, then sent a Sprint technician on site to run more tests, and finally concluded after six hours that the routers were fine, and that it was a LAN issue.

Policy Remained in Force, but Not a Backup System. Because of a zero-tolerance policy, all travelers must be processed and screened through national law enforcement databases located in Washington, D.C. There was a backup system consisting of a local copy of the database in case of a loss of connectivity to Washington. But the backup system ran on the same LAN and there was no backup system for a LAN failure.

Human or Machine Error? Human errors were a bigger part of the outage than technological ones. Michael Krigsman, the CEO of Brookline, a Massachusetts-based software and consulting company, wrote on his blog (*blogs.zdnet.com*) that the cause was a breakdown common in low-cost equipment and gross incompetence. Some experts were baffled that a single NIC could have caused so much trouble. However, a single NIC can take down an older network such as the CBP's, but not updated ones. Furthermore, if a network is not well managed, it increases the number of hours offline to identify and fix the problem. Newer networks are a lot more intelligent and able to self-diagnose.

CBP's Response to Avoid Another Crash. The CBP recognized the need to improve its IT staff, equipment, and infrastructure. They planned to improve diagnostic capabilities at both the human and technological levels to prevent such a head-scratching incident from happening again. They also will get the right technology and staff in place at LAX and other ports.

Sources: Compiled from Krigsman (2007) and Poeter (2007).

For Further Exploration: How would you rate the network quality of the CBP's system? Use the network capabilities in Figure 4.2 to support your answer. What were the technical and management factors that contributed to the failure of the backup system?

---

with collaboration technologies to support employees and cross-functional work, connect remote locations, service customers, and coordinate with supply chain partners.

CONVERGENCE AND INTEROPERABILITY OF INFORMATION SERVICES

Various information services—data, documents, voice, and video—have functioned independently of each other. Traditionally, they were transmitted using different protocols (standards) and carried on either packet-switched or circuit-switched networks as shown in Table 4.2. Multiple networks were needed because of the lack of **interoperability** or connectivity between devices. Interoperability refers to the ability to provide services to and accept services from other systems or devices. Lack of interoperability limited access to information and computing and communications resources—and increased costs. Technical details on interoperability and networking protocols are in Technology Guide 4.

Internet Protocol Suite and IP/TCP Architecture. The **Internet protocol suite** is the standard used with almost any network service. The Internet protocol suite consists of the **Internet Protocol (IP)** and **Transport Control Protocol (TCP),** or TCP/IP. TCP/IP refers to the whole protocol family.

Not surprisingly, IP is the single most popular network protocol in the world, and it provides the architecture that made convergence possible. In preparation for transmission, data and documents are converted (digitized) into packets based on the Internet Protocol and sent via *packet-switched* computer networks or local area networks, called LANs. LANs connect network devices over a relatively short distance. LANs are capable of transmitting data at very fast rates, but operate in a limited area, such as an office

TABLE 4.2   Networks, Protocols, and Transfer Methods of Information Services

Information service	Network	Format	Protocol	Transfer method
Data and documents	Packet	Converted to packets based on Internet Protocol (IP).	TCP (Transmission Control Protocol)	Each packet can take a different route to the destination, where the packets are recompiled. If a packet does not arrive (gets dropped), the entire transmission is resent. For non-real-time data, documents, or email, TCP provides for error correction, packet sequencing, and retransmission to assure correct transmission.
Voice	Circuit	Sent as analog signals between the telephone and the telco's central office (called *local loop*). Traffic between telephone offices is digital.		Whether analog or digital, each call creates a circuit that reserves a channel between two parties for the entire session. The entire message follows the same path in order.
Video streams	Packet	Compressed and converted to IP packets.	UDP (User Datagram Protocol)	No checking for missing packets. Malformed packets are simply dropped (i.e., discarded).
Voice over IP, or IP telephony	Packet	Voice communication is digitized into data packets.	Typically UDP, though sometimes TCP	TCP/IP's error-checking approach to connection management is inappropriate for voice, which takes place in real-time between sender and receiver. Requesting retransmission because of dropped packets or other errors would cause breaks in playback, or require the buffering of large amounts of data, which would delay and ruin the conversation.

building, campus, or home. They provide shared access to printers and file servers, and connect to larger networks, such as wide area networks (WANs) or the Internet. WANs cover a much larger geographic area, such as a state, province, or country.

A comparison of the basic network protocols is presented in Table 4.2. Packets of data are transmitted using TCP. TCP does error checking to provides reliable delivery. If any packets are dropped along the way and never arrive at the destination, TCP will request that the packets be re-sent. For data and document delivery, error checking is necessary to insure that all content has been delivered. Since the error checking process can cause delivery delays, TCP is not well suited for digital voice or video transmissions. For those transmissions, a dropped packet would be insignificant.

Voice that is sent as analog signals, or audio sound waves, is sent over circuits on *circuit-switched* telephone networks. Video streams are compressed and sent as IP packets using the **User Datagram Protocol (UDP).** This suite of protocols is referred to as the UDP/IP model. UDP does not check for errors, and as a result, it has less of overhead and is faster than connection-oriented protocols such as TCP. With UDP, the quality of the transmission (lack of errors) is sacrificed for speed. Compared to TCP, UDP sends packets much faster, but less reliably.

Voice over IP (VoIP), or **IP telephony,** involves an analog-to-digital conversion. With VoIP, voice and data transmissions travel over telephone wires, but the content is sent as data packets. VoIP is discussed in Section 4.3.

Benefits of the Internet Protocol. Primary benefits of an IP-based network strategy are the cost savings and better operations from using one converged network instead of several smaller networks dedicated to specific purposes, such as data, voice, and video. Packets can be transmitted over high-speed networks that are wireline, wireless, or a combination of both. High-speed networks are commonly called **broadband,** which is short for *broad bandwidth*. Another benefit of network convergence is enabling new applications, as discussed in Section 4.1.

Benefits of Converged Networks. Until networking technology had advanced to enable almost all information services to be transmitted as packets, convergence of these services was not possible. A **converged network** is a powerful architecture that enables enterprisewide integration of voice, data, video, and other information services. Improved collaboration along the entire supply chain—partners, suppliers, and customers—is possible. With a single converged network, companies can improve their business-to-business (B2B), business-to-customer (B2C), and mobile commerce (m-commerce) processes. When all information services are handled the same way over a high-speed packet network using either wireline or wireless, the technical barriers to collaborative work are eliminated. Then it is no longer difficult or prohibitively expensive to use multimedia applications because the network would not restrict the kinds of devices that can connect to it.

Benefits of Session Initiation Protocol (SIP). The human factor is critical to use, too. Users need easy, intuitive access to the network from any device, anywhere, any time seamlessly. The protocol and industry standard for doing this is **Session Initiation Protocol (SIP).** SIP standardizes the signaling of calls or communications between different types of devices/end-points from different vendors, such as IP phones, instant messaging (IM) clients, **softphones** (computers that function as a telephone via VoIP), smartphones, and so on. A benefit of SIP is that multiple users can join an online meeting with simultaneous voice and data interaction and be talking, sharing a spreadsheet or slide presentation, or browsing Web sites together regardless of the users' locations. These innovations can revolutionize the management of inventory, global supply chains, and offshore operations—as well as group decision making, order fulfillment, and database marketing (topics covered throughout the book).

Impacts on the Enterprise. Having fewer networks to maintain and support can decrease networking costs significantly. The costs of integrating applications and bandwidth are lower because traffic is consolidated over one network. Converged networks can save travel costs associated with intra- and interorganizational meetings. Despite advances in converged networks and SIP, there are still barriers to full integration until 4G networks become widespread.

BARRIERS TO FULL INTEGRATION OF INFORMATION SERVICES

Data utilization is quickly increasing on laptops, smartphones, and other handhelds. In addition, newer mobile devices and mobile consumer electronics devices will further drive up data traffic on mobile wireless networks. Demand for wireless networks, and a willingness to pay for those services, are encouraging investments in 4G wireless networks and convergence.

Market projections indicate that in 2011, approximately 200 million notebooks will ship annually. Ericsson anticipates that 50 percent of those notebooks will feature a built-in HSPA mobile broadband module. An advantage of HSPA (High Speed Packet Access) is that the technology is a natural extension of existing WCDMA/GSM networks, or about 85 percent of the world's existing wireless networks. Therefore, it has the potential to be readily available to a large number of wireless users, creating a mass market for mobile broadband. HSPA is the world's most widely deployed mobile broadband technology, with more than 185 commercially deployed networks available around the world, serving more than 1 billion subscribers as of mid-2008. By 2010, 71 percent of mobile broadband connections are projected to be HSPA-based.

Users will increasingly have the option to take their broadband connections with them, delivering on the promise of full-service broadband, which is anytime, anywhere access from the screen or device of choice. While worldwide growth in wireline and wireless telecommunications (telecom) is forecasted to remain steady, the growth rate of wireless is eight times greater than the growth rate of wireline. The availability of high-speed wireless bandwidth, 4G networks, and the mobile services it can support has increased demand for wireless services. Wireline usage will still be widely used because VoIP will lessen the migration to wireless. VoIP had been primarily for residential use because, until now, it was too unreliable for business use.

Developing software for wireless devices had been challenging because there was no widely accepted standard for wireless devices. Therefore, software applications had to be customized for each type of device with which the application communicates. To keep down the cost of wireless services, software engineers have had to develop code that optimizes resource usage. Supporting different displays can force painstaking changes to multiple software modules and applications. Different CPUs, operating systems, storage media, and mobile platform environments create time-consuming porting and testing issues. Yet, despite these many challenges, development timelines are shrinking and wireless service operators and consumers demand a reliable device with a high-quality user experience.

THE INTERNET AND WWW

Many people believe that the Web is synonymous with the Internet, but that is not the case. The Internet functions as the *transport mechanism*, and the **Web** (**WWW**) is an *application* that runs on the Internet, as does e-mail, IM, and VoIP. The Web is a system with universally accepted standards or protocols for storing, retrieving, formatting, and displaying information via client/server architecture. The usual protocol is http, which stands for hyper-text transport protocol. The Web handles all types of digital information, including text, video, graphics, and sound.

Internet Application Categories.   The Internet supports applications in the following categories:

- **Discovery.** Discovery involves browsing, finding, and retrieving information. It can involve querying, downloading, and processing information from databases. Software agents to contend with the vast information on the Internet and intranets can automate discovery. Discovery methods and issues are described in Section 4.4.
- **Communication.** Developments in Internet-based and wireless communication such as podcasting, RSS, and micro-blogging are transforming business communications, marketing channels, and supply chain management—to name a few.
- **Collaboration.** As you have read, online collaboration between individuals, groups, and organizations is common. Numerous tools and technologies are available, ranging from online meetings with screen sharing to videoconferencing and group support systems. Collaboration software products, called groupware and workflow, can be used on the Internet or other networks.

THE NETWORK COMPUTING INFRASTRUCTURE: INTRANETS AND EXTRANETS

In addition to the Internet and Web, there are a few other major infrastructures of network computing: value-added networks (VANs) (see Technology Guide 4), intranets, and extranets.

Intranets.   As discussed in Chapter 2, an **intranet** is a network designed to serve the internal informational needs of a company, using Internet tools. It provides easy and inexpensive browsing and search capabilities. Using screen sharing and other groupware tools, intranets can be used to facilitate group work. Companies deliver policies, pay stub information for direct deposits, benefits, training materials, and news to their employers via their intranets. For extensive information about intranets, see *intranetjournal.com*.

Like most ITs, intranets have the power to change organizational structures, cultures, and procedures. Intranets can be implemented using different types of LAN technologies including wireless LANs.

Extranets. An **extranet** is a private, company-owned network that uses IP technology to securely share part of a business's information or operations with suppliers, vendors, partners, customers, or other businesses. Extranets can use **virtual private networks (VPNs).** VPNs are created using specialized software and hardware to encrypt/send/decrypt transmissions over the Internet. Using specialized software to encrypt and decrypt transmissions, a VPN creates, in effect, a private encrypted tunnel within the Internet or other public network, as shown in Figure 4.3. A VPN connects remote sites or users together privately. Instead of using a dedicated, physical connection such as a leased line, a VPN uses "virtual" connections routed through the Internet from the company's private network to the remote site or employee.

Basically, an extranet is a network that connects two or more companies so they can securely share information. In some cases, an extranet is an extension of the company's intranet that is designed to connect to a customer or trading partner for B2B commerce. In other cases, an extranet is a restricted portal that, for example, gives account customers instant access to their account details. In this way, customers can manage their own accounts quickly and easily. United Rentals, the largest equipment rental company in the United States., has more than 750 rental locations throughout North America, with a diverse customer base of construction and industrial companies, utilities, municipalities, and homeowners. United Rentals' extranet portal at *URdata.UR.com* makes it convenient for account customers worldwide to request equipment, manage rental equipment by project, view invoices, calculate job costs, and so on—and at lower

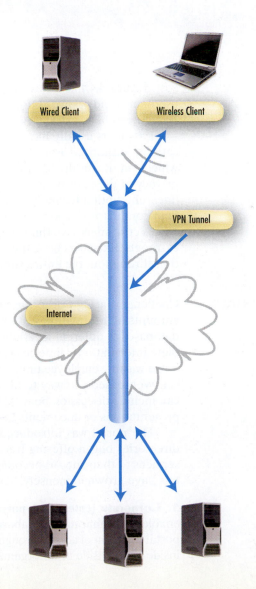

Figure 4.3 Virtual private network (VPN).

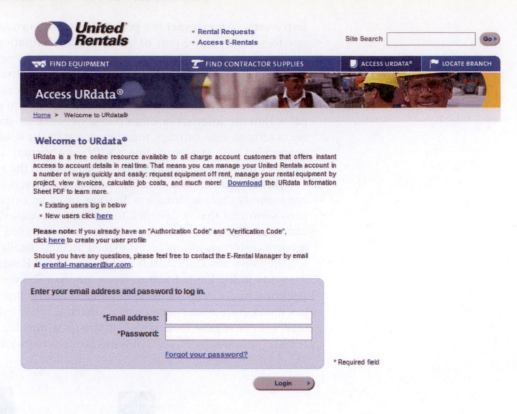

Figure 4.4 United Rentals' extranet portal.

cost. Figure 4.4 illustrates the familiar Internet-interface of an extranet, the use of usernames and passwords for access control and authentication, and self-help features. For a demo of an extranet, visit *ur.com/files/course/urdata/glimpse/*.

Extranets usually have a central server that stores data, documents, and applications. Authorized users can remotely access them from any Internet-enabled device, which can drastically reduce storage space on individual hard drives. To protect the privacy of the information being transmitted, extranets need secure communication lines, encryption technologies, and access and authentication control. The National Semiconductor Corporation (NSC) case study in Online Minicase 4.2 explains how NSC's customers save time and effort in design by using design support available via extranets. Extranets have the potential for significant improvements in communication throughout the entire supply chain.

INFORMATION PORTALS

Challenges facing workers are information overload and information scatter—huge amounts of information scattered across numerous documents, e-mail messages, and databases at different locations and systems. Accessing relevant, accurate, and complete information is time consuming and requires access to multiple systems. To minimize wasting employee time, companies use portals. A **portal** (or information portal) is a Web-based gateway to files, information, and knowledge on a network. Portals can include discussion boards, document sharing, and workspaces. Users can upload presentations or documents to share with peers.

The portal was introduced in 1997 when several Internet search engines and directories began offering free e-mail accounts, stock quotes, news, and other Web services to their sites to become jumping-off points for Web surfers. Since then, portals have grown immensely. Several types of portals are described below.

1. Corporate (enterprise) portals are private gateways to corporate Web sites that enable communication, collaboration, and access to company information. A corporate portal is a point of access through a Web browser to critical business information located inside and outside of an organization. Companies deploy portals to support strategic business initiatives and use them as a tactical tool for managing enterprise applications. To see a demo on corporate portals, visit *weboffice.com/EN/Demo/*.

2. Commercial portals such as About (*about.com*), Google Web directory (*google.com/dirhp*), and Yahoo! (*dir.yahoo.com*) are gateways to general information on the Internet.

3. Publishing portals are intended for communities with specific interests. These portals involve relatively little customization of content, but they provide extensive online search in a specific area and some interactive capabilities. Examples are *techweb.com* and *zdnet.com*.

4. Vertical portals, also called **vortals,** target specific markets. Vortals usually offer industry news, event calendars, links to related sites, and lists of vendors and businesses that offer products and services. Examples are Pharmaceutical Online (*pharmaceuticalonline.com*) and Bakery Online (*bakeryonline.com*).

Integration of Portals. WebSphere Portal from IBM allows companies to create multiple portals as one unit. It enables a single company to use three different portals—a portal for business partners (B2B), a portal for employees (B2E), and a portal for customers (B2C).

IT at Work 4.1 describes how Kaiser Permanente used a Google tool for its corporate portal. A portal's value depends on the design and users' knowledge of search techniques. It is estimated that Internet searchers are successful at finding what they seek only 50 percent of the time or less. Not surprisingly, the same problem applies to intranets. Consequently, companies incur the costs of time wasted searching for information that could not be found and then re-creating it—and costs arising from not being able to use existing information at the time it was needed.

Review Questions

1. How might a company's business performance be affected by its network's capabilities?
2. What is the difference between IP and UDP?
3. What are the benefits of an IP-based network strategy?
4. What is a virtual private network (VPN)?
5. What is the difference between an extranet and an intranet?

IT at Work 4.1

Kaiser Permanente Uses Google to Build a Portal

Kaiser Permanente (*kaiserpermanente.org*), America's largest nonprofit health maintenance organization (HMO), has 8.6 million members. Kaiser Permanente had changed the economics of healthcare by focusing on preventive care to keep patients healthy, rather than just treating their illnesses. With the amount of medical knowledge doubling about every 7 years, keeping up-to-date with that knowledge is essential to the HMO's mission.

When Kaiser Permanente developed a clinical knowledge corporate portal for its 50,000 doctors, nurses, and other caregivers, search was a part of the plan. The Permanente Knowledge Connection, available from anywhere in the Kaiser WAN, gives medical staff access to diagnostic information, best practices, publications, educational material, and other clinical resources. Putting the right information quickly and easily into healthcare providers' hands is essential to the clinical portal's success. Kaiser

selected the Google Search Appliance, which enabled the indexing of 150,000 documents across the Kaiser network. Clinicians search the site for research and urgent care from exam rooms to emergency rooms. Doctors and nurses use the search engine to help reach diagnoses and specify treatments, check side effects of medications, and consult clinical research studies and other medical publications. Google's spellchecking capability is especially useful in the medical profession: Doctors' handwriting can be problematic, and pharmaceutical product names are difficult.

Sources: Compiled from Kaiser (*ckp.kp.org/newsroom/national*, 2008), *Google.com* (2005).

For Further Exploration: Why did Kaiser Permanente need Google's Search Appliance? What benefits did Kaiser gain from implementing Google's Search Appliance?

4.3 Wireless, Enterprise Mobility, and IP Telephony

Enterprise mobility is an area of great interest. Enterprises are moving away from unsystematic adoption of mobile devices and infrastructure to a strategic build-out of mobile capabilities. As the technologies that make up the mobile infrastructure evolve, identifying strategic technologies and avoiding wasted investments is difficult. But the cost and competitive pressures to do so continue to intensity.

Factors contributing to a consolidated and enterprisewide approach to mobility include the following:

- New wireless technologies and standards, primarily the arrival of the 802.11n standard
- High-speed wireless networks
- Ultra-mobile devices
- More robust operating systems and applications
- Increased competitive pressure as others start adopting mobile technology
- Overall increased speed of business
- Operational inefficiencies from wasted use of human operators

See Online Brief 4.1 for an example of how Internet-based collaboration tools improved supply chain management at Fila.

MOBILE AND WIRELESS INFRASTRUCTURE

Mobile multimedia technologies make it possible for businesses to reinvent the traditional workplace from an office-based activity to a virtual one. Employees can collaborate closely in real time with other employees, customers, or partners regardless of anyone's location.

Mobile or wireless infrastructure consists of the integration of technology, software, support, security measures, and devices for the management and delivery of wireless communications. Major software products needed for mobile computing are presented in Table 4.3.

TABLE 4.3	Software for Mobile Computing
Software	**Description**
Microbrowser	A browser with limited bandwidth and memory requirements. Provides wireless access to the Internet.
Operating system (OS) for mobile client	An OS for mobile devices.
Bluetooth (named for a Viking king)	Chip technology for short-range communication among wireless devices. Uses digital two-way radio frequency (RF). It is an almost universal standard for wireless personal area network (WPAN) for data and voice. See *bluetooth.com*.
User interface	Application logic for handheld devices. It is often controlled by the microbrowser.
Legacy application software	Residing on the mainframe, it is a major source of data to wireless systems.
Application middleware	Provides connection among applications, databases, and Web-based servers.
Wireless middleware	Links wireless networks to application servers.
Wireless application protocol (WAP)	A set of communication protocols that enables wireless devices to "talk" to a server on a mobile network, so users can access the Internet. Specially designed for small screen. A competing standard is the J2ME platform that offers better security and graphics (see *wapforum.org*).
Wireless markup language (WML)	An XML-based scripting language for creating content for wireless systems.
Voice XML	An extension of XML designed to accommodate voice.

1. **Radio-equipped access point connected to the internet (or via a router). It generates and receives radio waves (up to 400 feet).**
2. **Several client devices, equipped with PC cards, generate and receive radio waves.**
3. **Router is connected to the internet via a cable or DSL modem, or is connected via a satellite.**

Figure 4.5 How Wi-Fi works.

WI-FI NETWORKING STANDARDS

Wi-Fi is a technology that allows computers to share a network or internet connection wirelessly without the need to connect to a commercial network. Wi-Fi networks beam large chunks of data over short distances using part of the radio spectrum, or they can extend over larger areas, such as municipal Wi-Fi networks. Municipal networks are not common because of huge expenses. The city of Philadelphia debated whether to go forward with its plans to install a wireless network, which would cost the 135-square-mile city $10 million to install, or about $75,000 per square mile. The cost for running the network the first two years would be $5 million.

Wi-Fi networks usually consist of a router, which transmits the signal, and one or more adapters, which receive the signal and are usually attached to computers. See Figure 4.5 for an illustration of how Wi-Fi works. More powerful transmitters, which cover a wider area, are known as base stations. See the Wi-Fi Alliance at *wi-fi.org*. Wi-Fi networking standards are:

• **802.11b.** This standard shares spectrum with 2.4 GHz cordless phones, microwave ovens, and many Bluetooth products. Data are transferred at up to 11 megabits per second (Mbps) per channel, at distances up to 300 feet.

• **802.11a.** This standard runs on 12 channels in the 5 GHz spectrum in North America, which reduces interference issues. Data are transferred about 5 times faster than 802.11b, improving the quality of streaming media. It has extra bandwidth for large files. Since the 802.11a and b standards are not interoperable, data sent from an 802.11b network cannot be accessed by 802.11a networks.

- **802.11g.** This standard runs on three channels in 2.4 GHz spectrum, but at the speed of 802.11a. It is compatible with the 802.11b standard.

- **802.11n.** This standard improves upon the previous 802.11 standards by adding multiple-input multiple-output (MIMO) and many other newer features. Frequency will be 2.4 GHz or 5GHz with a data rate of about 22 Mbps, but perhaps as high as 100 Mbps. Users will notice two things about this new and improved wireless technology: significantly greater speed and range.

WIRELESS WIDE AREA NETWORKS (WWANs)

There are three general types of mobile networks: wide area networks (WANs), WiMax (Worldwide Interoperability for Microwave Access), and local area networks (LANs). WANs for mobile computing are known as **WWANs (wireless wide area networks).** The breadth of coverage of a WWAN depends on the transmission media and the wireless generation, which directly affects the availability of services. Key components of mobile and wireless infrastructures are wireless local area networks, WiMax, and VoIP.

WLAN (Wireless Local Area Network). A WLAN is a type of local area network that uses high-frequency radio waves rather than wires to communicate between computers or devices such as printers, which are referred to as nodes on the network. A WLAN typically extends an existing wired LAN. WLANs are built by attaching a wireless access point (AP) to the edge of the wired network.

WiMax. The WiMax Forum (*wimaxforum.org*) describes **WiMax** as "a standards-based technology enabling the delivery of last mile wireless broadband access as an alternative to cable and DSL." WiMax is essentially an 802.16-based broadband wireless metropolitan area network (MAN) access standard that can deliver voice and data services at distances of up to 30 miles, without the expense of cable or the distance limitations of DSL. WiMax does not require a clear line of sight to function. Figure 4.6 illustrates the components of a WiMax communication network.

Mobile WiMax enables 3 Mbps network access for mobile users because it facilitates real-time applications such as VoIP. Mobile Wimax 802.16e will amass 80 million mobile subscribers globally by 2013, according to Juniper Research (Kamath, 2007).

WiMax technology got a boost at the end of 2007 when the International Telecommunications Union approved the wireless data transmission system as a 3G standard. This allows operators to provide WiMax in spectrums allocated for 3G phone networks. Making WiMax available in portable devices is the goal for companies such as Intel. The technology already is being deployed in developing countries in the Middle East, Asia, and Africa that have unreliable or no fixed-line broadband networks.

VoIP. VoIP or Internet telephony is rapidly replacing conventional telephony. As of 2005, U.S. companies bought more new IP phone connections than conventional phone lines for the first time. Demand for VoIP connections is high because businesses can create their own customized voice communication to give them a competitive edge. The competitive advantage of VoIP stems from its use as a unifying platform for business applications that require flexible or intelligent voice communications. As several innovative firms have proven, flexibility allows companies to set up and conduct business in ways that could not have been done before because they were technically or economically infeasible.

In general, telephony service via VoIP costs less than equivalent service from traditional telecommunications companies. Figure 4.7 illustrates the common components of a VoIP network.

With non-IP phones, calls originate from a hardware device (e.g., phone on your desk), travel as analog signals along a dedicated circuit-switched telephone network, and then arrive at the destination hardware devices at specific locations (phones on

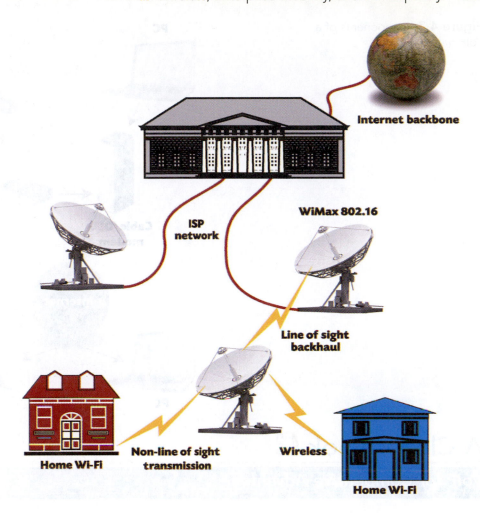

Figure 4.6 WiMax network.

the recipients' desks). In contrast, with VoIP calls, calls originate from a VoIP phone or PC, are digitized, and then sent via a packet-switched network such as a WAN or the Internet. Calls are tied neither to physical locations nor to specific devices. Since VoIP uses common IP standards, it can talk to any device that uses IP.

As shown in Figure 4.7, making VoIP calls is simple. Callers can use an ordinary telephone connected to a VoIP adapter (converter) box, which plugs into an Internet connection. Or callers can use an IP phone that looks like a traditional telephone, but connects directly to the Internet instead of a phone jack. A third option is to use softphone software on a PC or PDA with a headset. With VoIP service, a businessperson could take a VoIP adapter to Europe or Asia, plug it into a broadband connection at a hotel, and seamlessly receive calls at the home office phone number. With a VoIP softphone, the adapter is not needed.

Considerable cost savings are possible by using a single network to carry voice and data, especially when companies have underutilized network capacity. VoIP is used by companies to eliminate call charges between offices by using their data network to carry interoffice calls. VoIP is attractive for international calls because it eliminates international long-distance fees. VoIP is not just a new technology for making cheaper calls. It is fundamentally changing how companies use voice communications. What makes VoIP powerful is the turning of voice into digital data packets, which can be stored, copied, combined with other data, and distributed to other devices that connect to the Internet. All of the functionality of a corporate phone can be provided to anyone, anywhere there is broadband access. VoIP can be used to achieve business objectives and competitive advantage as explained in *A Closer Look 4.2.*

Figure 4.7 Components of a VoIP network.

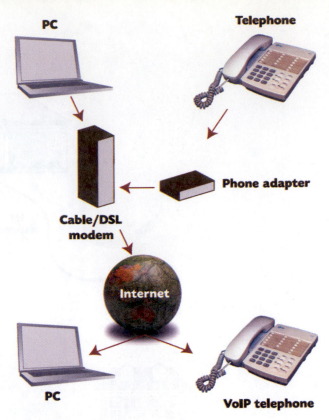

A Closer Look 4.2

VoIP for Competitive Advantage

With a VoIP infrastructure, the phone system is an environment for developing and managing communications. VoIP will be able to support new communications functions that do not yet exist. Just as the first generation of static corporate Web sites evolved into multimedia, interactive, business-enhancing uses of the Internet, VoIP will serve as a platform for more strategic converged voice-and-data communications. VoIP's potential as a strategic tool comes from three types of capability: virtualization, customization, and intelligence.

Virtualization. Virtualization makes it easy for users to operate in a seamless and consistent fashion across a geographically diverse network environment. A virtual version of one's phone can exist anywhere at any time without the time and expense of setting up a traditional phone system. This gives teleworkers, customer service representatives, and mobile workers access to communication and information systems to perform their jobs from anywhere. The government of Marin County, California, uses VoIP to give its employees and officials location-independent access to resources. Using an IP system that integrates voice recognition, voice synthesis, and e-mail, they can listen to and compose e-mails by phone, check and schedule appointments, create task lists, and launch calls from a contact list as well as customize preferences for notification based on priority level or sender.

Customization. Voice applications can be deployed that reinforce branding, enhance customer service, and improve internal communications. Developer Steve Wynn installed VoIP as part of a competitive strategy to address changing demand and differen-

tiate service at his Las Vegas Wynn hotel and casino. In the early 2000s, the primary revenue source for Las Vegas resorts shifted from gambling to guest services such as entertainment, dining, and recreation. Using VoIP phones in every room, guests can call the concierge to arrange dinner reservations while browsing menus and pictures of dining rooms on the phone's color display.

Intelligence. Business processes are dependent on communication for coordination. Recall the Super Bowl case at the beginning of the chapter. With VoIP, communication can be precisely targeted according to business rules to define who needs to be contacted, when, and how. Avaya Labs, the research arm of a VoIP vendor, has a demo of how VoIP can enhance supply chain management (SCM). A simulated supply chain disruption automatically launched a multicompany VoIP conference call. The VoIP system reached participants through whatever device they were closest to and then automatically linked their computers to IM, streaming video, and a secure Web site with key documents. VoIP platforms have the intelligence to know whom to contact and how, because they are linked into corporate directories, databases, and SCM applications. In a real application, at Rhode Island Hospital, nurses wear small wireless clip-on badges made by Vocera (*vocera.com*). Instead of having to leave a patient's bedside for help or information, a nurse just pushes a button on the badge. The system uses speech recognition, connected to the hospital's directory system, to route the request to the right person or to broadcast it to team members.

Sources: Compiled from Resende (2005), Werbach (2005), and *vocera.com* (accessed June 2008).

IT at Work 4.2

IS   MKT   OM

Thrifty Car Rental Uses IP Telephony to Increase Operational Efficiency and Customer Service

Thrifty Car Rental operates more than 1,200 locations in 64 countries, including in-terminal rentals at 86 U.S. airports, off-terminal rental services at 57 additional airports, and at all major airports in Canada. More than 30 percent of Thrifty's callers were rate shoppers. Agents were bogged down providing pricing information that could easily be retrieved from an automated self-help system or Web site. The company wanted more profitable use of their agents and to reduce the operational dependencies they had on human talent for each and every customer interaction.

Online reservation requests at *thrifty.com* were growing rapidly. While the company's Web site had strong transactional capabilities, it lacked the same high-quality customer service Thrifty provided in its brick and mortar and telephone-based world. The company wanted to improve its Web-based customer service functionality and differentiate from other car rental providers in its market.

To enable Thrifty to keep pace with the industry, its new customer contact solution blended human help with automated, self-help services across all channels of interaction, including phone, Web, chat, or e-mail. To integrate these channels and provide intelligent contact management, Thrifty invested in Cisco IP Communications, which is an enterprise solution of IP telephony, unified communications or messaging, and customer contact. Their IP-based customer contact solutions resulted in substantial cost savings. **Unified messaging (UM)** is the concept of bringing together all messaging media such as e-mail, voice, mobile text, SMS, and fax into a combined communications medium. Minimally, UM can involve a unified mailbox with alert service. Or it can give users the ability to retrieve and send voice, fax, and e-mail messages from a single interface, such as handhelds or PCs.

For Web collaboration, Thrifty deployed Cisco's Intelligent Contact Management (ICM), an intelligent, multi-channel routing system that is used to interact with customers via phone, Web, and e-mail and is integrated with an automatic call distributor (ACD), private branch exchange (PBX), interactive voice response (IVR), database, and desktop applications. Thrifty also installed Web Collaboration Option, a Web-centric visual collaboration tool. This tool enables customers to interact with agents over the Web, while conducting a voice conversation or text chat, E-Mail Manager Option for managing high volumes of customer inquiries submitted to company mailboxes or Web site, and Computer Telephony Integration (CTI) Option for desktop call control, CTI screen pops, and CRM integration.

Thrifty receives four million calls per year that had required 150 agents in its two customer contact locations during regular seasons and 180 during the peak summer season. With the IP-telephony customer contact solution, between 35 and 40 fewer agents are required. Employee turnover has dropped to 20 percent from a high of 40 percent since installing the Cisco solution.

Sources: Compiled from Thrifty (*thrifty.com*) and Cisco Systems (*cisco.com*; accessed June 2008).

For Further Exploration: Why did Thrifty Car Rental need IP telephony? What benefits did Thrifty gain from implementing Cisco's unified communications and Web collaboration option?

IP telephony is evolving beyond basic telephony upgrades as enterprises look for increased flexibility and mobile solutions for their workers and business processes. Voice and data networks play a critical role at companies by supporting key business activities like order entry, shipping, payroll, and finance. As companies expand and extend their operations, it becomes more and more costly to operate and manage two separate networks. A converged network that combines voice and data traffic on the same IP infrastructure could reduce administrative costs, while providing an easier path for growth and new applications. *IT at Work 4.2* explains the value of convergence and IP telephony at Thrifty Car Rental.

WHAT IS A MOBILE ENTERPRISE?

A **mobile enterprise** is one that has the ability to connect and control suppliers, partners, employees, products, and customers from any location. Companies are extending the mobile work style to unprecedented numbers of employees. Mobile technologies such as WLANs, sensor or RFID networks, and handhelds expand the reach and control of companies. According to research firm Gartner, even when IT spending is tightly controlled, revenue from WLANs increased 21 percent from 2006 to 2007 and wireless spending overall will increase from 10 to 14 percent yearly from 2008 through 2012 (Martin, 2008).

IT at Work 4.3

Mobile Developments

At the *2008 Mobile World Congress (mobileworldcongress.com)* in Barcelona, mobile industry leaders across the world debated the future of wireless services and technology and how best to serve the world's 2.5 billion mobile phone users. The World Congress provides a *Mobile Planet Press Preview*, which is a documentary showcasing the global reach and impact of mobile phones. It was recorded in March 2008 and made available at *web20.telecomtv.com/pages/?id=96a0e6f6-cca6-4ae3-a4d6-c4c9ffd86d86*. Global Mobile Awards 2008 winners and those highly recommended include the following:

- Mobile social networking service: *myGamma.com*, by BuzzCity, is a mobile internet community where people worldwide exchange ideas. Using mobiles, members interact via their personal profiles, blogs, discussion groups, and many other community features.

- Mobile handset: The 3 Skypephone mobile is a small handset with Skype functionality built in, the first of its kind in the world. Skype contacts and calls are completely integrated into the address book, adding presence awareness to the consumer's phonebook. The 3 Skypephone's Internet browser brings powerful applications to the mobile world using a mixture of IP and 3G voice technology.

- Use of Mobile for Economic Development: Grameenphone CellBazaar is a virtual marketplace accessible via mobile phone or PC to nearly 17 million people in Bangladesh. In developing countries, limited communications hinder

commerce. Using CellBazaar (*www.cellbazaar.com*), buyers and sellers trade basic goods from their mobiles, bringing the benefits of information exchange and one-to-many trading to a previously unwired rural population. While common telephony establishes one-to-one communication, CellBazaar links many-to-many using the same mobile infrastructures.

- Mobile Enterprise Product or Service: Microsoft Windows Mobile 6 makes it easier for businesses to go mobile by increased integration with existing Microsoft technology, new mobile security features, and added functionality to help employees collaborate while on the go.

- Billing and Customer Care Solution: mChek on Airtel offers instantaneous anytime anywhere mobile bill payments from any mobile phone or web page (see example on *mchek.com*). Customers register credit cards, debit cards, or bank accounts and link them to their mobile phone with a user-created 6-digit PIN. Users can pay bills by sending a simple SMS and entering their PIN. This was the first service of its kind.

Sources: Compiled from *mobileworldcongress.com* and *globalmobileawards.com/winners.shtml* (accessed June 2008).

For Further Exploration: What collaborative efforts are possible with these mobile networking advancements? How might business processes change as a result of increased mobile capabilities?

Thirty-two percent of enterprise respondents to *Forrester's Enterprise Network and Telecommunications Survey* of North America and Europe in 2007 cited "mobile and wireless strategy and policies" as a priority (Forrester, 2007). An additional 15 percent stated that enterprise mobility is a critical priority for their business.

WHY ENTERPRISE MOBILITY MATTERS

All enterprises face many technology investments and application decisions as they move toward a goal of ubiquitous mobility. In today's interactive world, many employees do not spend most of their time at their desks. To be productive, employees have to be mobile to effectively engage customers, solve problems, and collaborate with partners and other employees. *IT at Work 4.3* describes several of the latest developments in mobile technologies and services.

At least once per month, a company announces new integrative technologies that will make wireless the default and wireline the exception. For example, in mid-2008, 3Com Corporation announced a new wireless, SIP-based IP phone that gives enterprise users greater mobility by delivering VoIP communications on a WLAN (802.11b/g) infrastructure. Their wireless phone enables workers to roam a building or office park and stay connected with customers, partners, and co-workers while utilizing VoIP, wireless email, and data applications. For current developments and announcements in enterprise mobility network solutions, see Cisco (cisco.com) and Motorola's (*motorola.com*) Web sites.

Review Questions

1. What factors are contributing to a consolidated and enterprisewide approach to mobility?
2. What is IP telephony?
3. What is a mobile enterprise?
4. What major vendors are helping drive the mobile enterprise?

4.4 Discovery, Search, and Customized Delivery

Trying to describe information on the Internet is like trying to describe the universe — *it's everything.* The sheer endlessness of the information available through the Internet, which seems like its major strength, is also its greatest weakness. As you have read and experienced, often it is too hard to find the right data or answers. The amounts of information at your disposal are too vast.

Since you are familiar with the Internet and Web searches, this section will focus on business solutions being made possible by new technologies and innovative ideas. Topics include advanced search tools and Internet technologies that deliver customized information to users, often as soon as it becomes available, such as robust search engines, intelligent software agents, podcasting, XML, and RSS. Of course, many tools fit into more than one category. For example, wikis are cross-functional services — that continue to expand in scope. A wiki can be a software program, discovery tool, collaboration site, and social network.

SEARCH ENGINES, DIRECTORIES, AND ENTERPRISE SEARCH

Search engines, directories, enterprise search engines, and wikis help bring order to the chaotic Internet universe. Recent enhancements to improve search results are outlined next.

Search Engines, Directories, and Intelligent Agents. **Search engines** are Web sites designed to help people find information stored on other sites. They index billions of pages, and respond to many millions of queries per day. There are differences in the ways various search engines work, but they all perform three basic tasks:

1. They search the Internet based on key words.

2. They keep an index (database) of the words they find, and where they find them.

3. They allow users to search for words or combinations of words found in that index.

The generic term *search engine* describes intelligent agents or crawler-based search engines and human-powered directories. The types of search engines are the following:

1. Intelligent agents or crawler-based. Search engines can be powered by intelligent agents, which are also called software agents, robots, or bots. Intelligent agents are computer programs that carry out a set of routine computer tasks. Crawler-based search engines, such as Google and Yahoo!, create their listings automatically. They crawl or spider the web taking various factors into consideration, but the algorithm the search engine uses to rank results is confidential. One rule in a ranking algorithm involves the location and frequency of keywords on a Web page.

2. Human-powered. This type of search engine, such as the Open Directory, depends on humans for its listings. Individuals submit a short description to the directory for a Web site, or editors write one for sites they review. Only information that is submitted is put into the index. As the name implies, a directory organizes topics into categories. Popular directories are *Yahoo.com* and *google.com/dirhp*.

3. Hybrids. Both types of results typically are presented. A hybrid search engine may be biased in favor of one type of listings over another. MSN Search, for example, is more likely to present human-powered listings. However, it does also present crawler-based results provided by Inktomi, especially for obscure queries.

Ask, Google, del.icio.us, flikr, and other search engines compete fiercely for Web visitors, although Google is by far the most popular search engine. *IT at Work 4.4* describes market share changes and new features among browsers and search engines to attract business customers by better serving their business needs.

Enterprise Search Technology. **Enterprise search** offers the potential of cutting much of the complexity accumulated in applications and intranet sites throughout an organization. An example of enterprise search architecture is shown in Figure 4.8. These engines can crawl through various types of content—external Web sites, network shares and local file servers, Microsoft Exchange and Lotus Notes folders, and databases. Tools are available to help users create queries and do custom searches. Content is indexed for faster results. Enterprise search takes advantage of available metadata and provides access control, simple and advanced search, and browser-based administration. They also can support HTML, PDF, and the usual office file formats, and European, Arabic, and Asian languages.

Google. Google made a big move on the corporate market with two hardware search appliances that index content on a corporate network. *Google Search Appliance* (*google.com/enterprise*) is aimed at large businesses. It has a range of tools for searching corporate databases and enterprise resource planning systems. *Google Mini Search Appliance* (*google.com/mini*) is aimed at small businesses that want to index content. With the Google Mini, employees can securely search across intranets, file servers, and business applications.

BLOGS AND BLOGGING

Blogs are barely a decade old as a publishing medium and are already part of the mainstream media. Blogs started out as Internet journaling and personal publishing tools, but enterprises now use these systems to replace e-mail and support collaborative work. Blogs are simple to build due to user-friendly programs from *wordpress.com*,

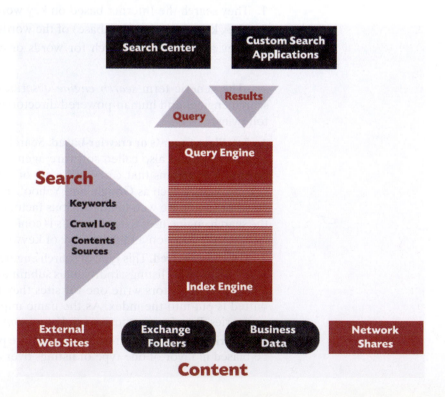

Figure 4.8 Enterprise search architecture.

blogger.com, *blogspot.com*, and others. Bloggers who create and maintain blogs are handed a fresh space on their Web site to write in each day. They can easily edit, add entries, and broadcast whatever they want by simply clicking the send key. For a dictionary of blog terms, see *samizdata.net*.

Blog servers require far fewer dedicated resources than an enterprise intranet. Using blog platforms can free up IT hardware and support resources for other uses to lower support costs and license fees for systems that may no longer serve the needs of users.

IT at Work 4.4

Browsers Compete for Business through Sharing and Collaboration Applications

Major Web browsers compete fiercely to become the focal point for handling business transactions and running programs over the Internet rather than simply displaying Web sites. Changes in market shares of browsers from 2007 to 2008 and their rankings, listed in Table 4.4, show that Google Desktop increased its share the most, with an increase of 1.5 percent.

TABLE 4.4	Market Shares of Browsers in 2007 and 2008				
	2008		**2007**		
Browser	**Market share**	**Ranking**	**Market share**	**Ranking**	
Internet Explorer (IE)	65.5%	1	66.7%	1	
Firefox	15.0%	2	16.1%	2	
Netscape	10.6%	3	10.2%	3	
Google Desktop	3.3%	4	1.8%	6	
Mozilla	2.2%	5	1.5%	5	
Opera	.98%	6	2.0%	7	
Safari	.95%	7	.80%	4	

To capture market share, business applications are being migrated (shifted) online. Major Internet companies such as Google, Yahoo!, and Microsoft are devoting tremendous resources to developing these Web applications. In March 2008, Microsoft announced that the *Office Live Workspace* beta (*office.microsoft.com*) was publicly available for everyone to access. The site, a free Web-based extension of Microsoft Office, lets users access their documents online and share their work with others. Some say that the service's launch is a direct response to Google's entry into the Web office space with their Google Docs online service (*docs.google.com*). Both Google Docs and Office Live Workspace are free services, but each has a unique set of features for sharing and collaboration. Both offer address book integration for finding recipients' email addresses, but a comparison of their sharing and collaboration features indicates that Google Docs offers better sharing and collaboration support.

Sharing. Google Docs allows for sharing of a file or files by checking the checkbox next to them and clicking *share* from the menu. Those who are invited to share can be invited as *Collaborators* or *Viewers*. Documents and presentations can be shared with 200 combined viewers, but spreadsheets have no limit.

Office Live Workspace allows users to share documents or workspaces with others and mark them as *editors* or *viewers*. There is the option to allow "everyone to view this without signing in," and to "send me a copy of the sharing invitation." Files or workspaces can be shared with up to 100 others.

Collaboration. In Google Docs, collaborators can work together on files in real time. Ten people may edit and/or view a document or presentation at any given time. Fifty people can edit a spreadsheet at the same time.

Office Live Workspace allows for collaboration, but it is not real-time, online collaboration. If one user is editing a file, another will be informed the file is "checked out." When they finish editing and save their changes, the document is checked back in for other users to access.

Sources: Compiled from Web sites of Google, Microsoft, and Yahoo! (accessed June 2008).

For Further Exploration: Why might Google Desktop be stealing market share away from other browsers? What sharing features offered by Office Live Workspace and Google Desktop are valuable to business workers? What collaboration features offered by Office Live Workspace and Google Desktop are valuable to business workers?

Blogs have become one of the fastest growing enterprise solutions as businesses recognize that the ability to easily find information contained within enterprise blogs is critical to improving worker productivity. The combination of enterprise blogging technology with searching capabilities helps organizations improve the quality and efficiency of collaboration internally and externally.

WIKIS

Wikis are a user-driven response to the shortcomings of search engines. Technically, a wiki is server software that allows users to freely create and edit Web page content. This is possible because wikis support hyperlinks and have simple text syntax for creating new pages and crosslinks between internal pages. Wiki Web pages are created through the collaboration efforts of numerous contributors. The relevance of these efforts—the wiki—is often better than that of algorithmically ranked lists of search results. These collaborations fill the gaps left by conventional search tools. A single page in a wiki is referred to as a "wiki page," whereas the entire body of pages, which are usually highly interconnected via hyperlinks, is "the wiki"—in effect, a very simple, easy-to-use database.

Commercial Aspects of Wikis and Their Derivatives. Wikis being a relatively new technology, it is difficult to assess their commercial potential. However, research firm Gartner Group predicts that wikis will become mainstream collaboration tools in at least 50 percent of companies by 2009 (reported by *WikiThat.com* 2005). In addition to collaboration, wikis can replace e-mail, since using wikis is an open source, spam-free communication tool.

Angel.com, a subsidiary of MicroStrategy Inc., develops integrated voice response (IVR) and call center automation software (as used by Thrifty Car Rental). The company uses wikis as a central communications tool for its sales teams. They use a wiki to log daily lead counts, post partnership information, and read documents posted by product management and marketing. The wiki is used to publish position papers, marketing material, messaging, and scripts for customer inquiries. It is shared with customers and helps the team cope with a 14-hour time difference with an Australian client.

PODCASTING

Podcasting is a way to distribute or receive audio and, more recently, video files called **pods** or **podcasts** over the Internet. The term *pod* came about from Apple's iPod digital player, although an iPod is not needed to hear or view a podcast. Pods can be downloaded or streamed from a Web site. Authors called **podcasters** create a pod by making a file such as an MP3 audio file available on the Internet. This can be done by posting the file on a Web server or **BitTorrent tracker,** which is a server used in the communication between peers using the BitTorrent protocol. BitTorrent is used to transfer extremely large files, such as full-length movies. For a directory of podcasts, see *ipodder.org,* and *podcast.net* or *podcastdirectory.com.*

Many content providers offer podcast feeds at no cost. These feeds deliver audio broadcasts to a computer, which can be listened to using iTunes; or they can be loaded onto an MP3 player or iPod. To automate notice and delivery of new content, iTunes uses RSS to auto-download new podcasts as they become available.

RSS

RSS refers to various standards of Web feed formats, usually Really Simple Syndication. RSSs automate the delivery of Internet content. They are an easy way to receive newly released information customized to a person's interests and needs. Web feeds provided through RSS offer headlines, summaries, and links from sites in an XML file that can be viewed using software called a *reader* (newsreader) or *aggregator* that brings the information directly to a computer or iPod.

RSS readers are software that monitors blogs or sites for new content. With RSS and a newsreader, whenever there is new content, it is delivered and shows up automatically on the newsreader. RSS feeds dramatically cut down on the time it takes to search for information online and you can then go back for greater detail after finding out first what is available. See Figure 4.9 for an example of how an RSS can be searched and RSS feeds located.

Mainstream media such as National Public Radio (NPR) are using RSS. News organizations are setting up their own RSS feeds as are operators of traditional informational Web sites and government agencies. Companies are using RSS feeds to get their messages out to anyone who wants them—a key goal of marketing. RSS technology could be a valuable marketing tool and is becoming a greater part of firms' overall marketing mix. RSS technology is simple, and RSS content is easily produced by the conversion of existing content. Content can be sent using a subscription plan, replacing the current e-mail delivery process.

All of these tools and technologies help deal with Internet information overload. They can minimize time and effort wasted looking for information that exists, but cannot be found or accessed. Clearly, the future is in highly customized information that gets pulled through podcasts, videos on demand, RSS feeds, mobile devices, blogs, interactive wizards, and other yet-unknown vehicles for experiencing services in ways and at times of users' choosing.

XML AND XBRL

Another helpful format for locating and sharing information is **eXtensible Markup Language (XML).** XML is a meta-language for describing markup languages for documents containing structured information. XML-based systems facilitate data sharing across different systems and particularly systems connected via the Internet. Actually, RSS is a form of XML. RSS files must conform to the XML 1.0 specification (see *w3.org/TR/REC-xml*), as published on the World Wide Web Consortium (W3C) Web site.

The **eXtensible Business Reporting Language (XBRL)** is a version of XML for capturing financial information throughout a business's information processes. XBRL

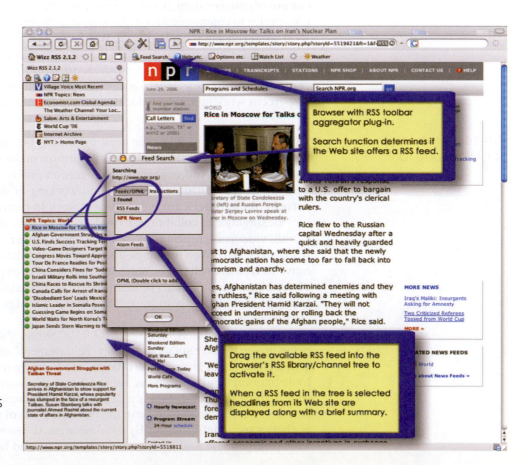

Figure 4.9 National Public Radio's (NPR) Web site with RSS toolbar aggregator and search function. *(Courtesy of NPR. Used with permission.)*

makes it possible to format reports that need to be distributed to shareholders, SOX regulators, banks, and other parties. The goal of XBRL is to make the analysis and exchange of corporate information more reliable (trustworthy) and easier to facilitate. The use of XBRL for business reporting is seen as a source of fundamental change in the business information supply chain. XBRL has the potential to affect interorganizational electronic business interactions by considerably enhancing information and communication flows and increasing the creation and sharing of knowledge among organizations. XBRL is also discussed in Chapter 9.

Review Questions

1. How do search engines function? What are the three types of search engines?
2. What is enterprise search and what does it offer enterprises?
3. What are blogs and how can they reduce IT hardware costs?
4. What are wikis and what are they capable of replacing? Why?
5. What is podcasting? Why is it popular?
6. How does RSS customize delivery of content to users?
7. How do XML and XBRL support locating and sharing information?

4.5 Collaboration and Web-based Meetings

Collaboration is a key driver of overall performance in companies worldwide, according to the study "Meetings Around the World: The Impact of Collaboration on Business Performance," conducted by Frost and Sullivan and sponsored by Verizon Business and Microsoft Corp (Frost and Sullivan, 2006). The impact of collaboration on performance was twice as significant as a company's aggressiveness in pursuing new market opportunities (its strategic orientation) and five times as significant as the external market environment. The study also showed that while there is a global culture of collaboration, there are regional differences in how people in various countries prefer to communicate. Of all of the collaboration technologies that were studied, Web conferencing (also known as Web-based meetings) was used more extensively in high-performing companies than in low-performing ones. These results make sense when viewed with estimates from *NetworkWorld* (*networkworld.com*) that 90 percent of employees work away from their company's headquarters and 40 percent work at a remote location, away from their supervisors.

MESSAGING AND COLLABORATION

Several factors are driving the need for messaging and collaboration. People need to work together and share documents. Groups make most of the complex decisions in organizations. And organizational decision making is difficult when team members are geographically spread out and working in different time zones. Nearly 87 percent of employees around the world work in remote offices.

Messaging and collaboration tools include older communications media such as e-mail, videoconferencing, fax, and IM—and newer media such as blogs, podcasts, RSS, wikis, VoIP, Web meetings, and torrents (for sharing very large files). As media move to IP, there will not be much left that is not converged onto data networks. One of the biggest components of many Web 2.0 sites and technologies is collaboration. Much of Web 2.0 is about harnessing the knowledge and work of many people to create value.

The results of the *April 2006 "CIO Role" Survey* showed that IT investments were being driven by their ability to support "achievement" and not simply "survival" (Alter, 2006). CIOs (chief information officers) are focusing more on new infrastructure and tools than on new applications. Table 4.5 presents some of the survey results. Survey results show that companies are deploying technologies (architecture, infrastructure, and data quality tools) to achieve the business goals of improving processes and making better use of information. By a wide margin, the most deployed IT (over 47%) was *team collaboration tools* to improve productivity and help users work with data.

TABLE 4.5	Technologies Considered Most Likely to Provide Business Value			
Networking, mobile, and collaboration technology	**Deployed**	**Testing or piloting**	**Evaluating**	*Total*
Smart cards	18%	14%	29%	*61%*
3G wide-area services	13%	12%	28%	*53%*
Location-based services and GPS	13%	10%	24%	*47%*
RFID/wireless sensors	11%	11%	31%	*53%*
WiMax	9%	14%	34%	*57%*
Team collaboration tools	47%	27%	17%	*91%*
Web mapping	27%	23%	24%	*84%*
RSS	18%	15%	30%	*63%*
Podcasts	14%	14%	23%	*51%*
Social networks	14%	12%	23%	*49%*
Wikis	13%	14%	26%	*53%*

Source: Alter (2006).

VIRTUAL COLLABORATION

Leading businesses are moving quickly to realize the benefits of e-collaboration. For example, the real estate franchiser RE/MAX uses an e-collaboration platform to improve communications and collaboration among its nationwide network of independently owned real estate franchises, sales associates, and suppliers. Similarly, Marriott International, the world's largest hospitality company, started with an online brochure and then developed a collaborative e-commerce system that links corporations, franchisees, partners, and suppliers, as well as customers, around the world.

There are many examples of e-collaboration. Here we present some additional representative ones.

Information Sharing Between Retailers and Their Suppliers: P&G and Wal-Mart. One of the most publicized examples of information sharing is between Procter & Gamble (P&G) and Wal-Mart. Wal-Mart provides P&G access to sales information on every item Wal-Mart buys from P&G. The information is collected by P&G on a daily basis from every Wal-Mart store, and P&G uses the information to manage the inventory replenishment for Wal-Mart.

Retailer—Supplier Collaboration: Asda Corporation. Supermarket chain Asda (*asda.com*) has begun rolling out Web-based electronic data interchange (EDI) technology to 650 suppliers. Web-EDI technology is based on the AS2 standard, an internationally accepted HTTP-based protocol used to send real-time data in multiple formats securely over the Internet. It promises to improve the efficiency and speed of traditional EDI communications, which route data over third-party value-added networks (VANs).

Lower Transportation and Inventory Costs and Reduced Stockouts: Unilever. Unilever's 30 contract carriers deliver 250,000 truckloads of shipments annually. Unilever's Web-based database, the Transportation Business Center (TBC), provides these carriers with site specification requirements when they pick up a shipment at a manufacturing or distribution center or when they deliver goods to retailers. TBC gives carriers all of the vital information they need: contact names and phone numbers, operating hours, the number of dock doors at a location, the height of the dock doors, how to make an appointment to deliver or pick up shipments, pallet configuration, and other special requirements. All mission-critical information that Unilever's carriers need to make pickups, shipments, and deliveries is now available electronically 24/7.

Reduction of Product Development Time: Caterpillar, Inc. Caterpillar, Inc. (*caterpillar.com*) is a multinational heavy-machinery manufacturer. In the traditional mode of operation, cycle time along the supply chain was long because the process involved paper-document transfers among managers, salespeople, and technical staff. To solve the problem, Caterpillar connected its engineering and manufacturing divisions with its active suppliers, distributors, overseas factories, and customers, through an extranet-based global collaboration system. By means of the collaboration system, a request for a customized tractor component, for example, can be transmitted from a customer to a Caterpillar dealer and on to designers and suppliers, all in a very short time. Customers also can use the extranet to retrieve and modify detailed order information while the vehicle is still on the assembly line.

Next we will discuss group decision processes and ways to improve them. Then developments in messaging and collaboration technologies are covered.

THE NATURE OF GROUP WORK

Managers and staff continuously make decisions: They design and manufacture products, develop policies and strategies, prepare financial statements, determine how to meet compliance mandates, design software, and so on. By design or default, group processes emerge with varying degrees of functionality.

Group Decision Processes. When people work in groups, they perform **group work,** which simply refers to work done together by two or more people. While the definition is simple, the process can be quite complex depending on the task, human factors, and available decision support. Some characteristics of group work are listed below:

- Group members may be located in different places or work at different times.
- Group members may work for the same or for different organizations.
- A group can be at a single managerial level or span several levels.
- There can be synergy (process and task gains) or conflict in group work.
- There can be gains and/or losses in productivity from group work.
- Some of the needed data, information, or knowledge may be located in many sources, several of which are external to the organization.
- The expertise of non-team members may be needed.
- Groups perform many tasks; however, groups of managers and analysts concentrate frequently on decision making.

Despite the long history and benefits of collaborative work, groups are not always successful. A key reason is that collaborative work processes can be characterized not only by benefits but also by dysfunctions, as listed in Tables 4. 6 and 4.7 (from Turban, 2006).

TABLE 4.6	**Benefits of Working in Groups (Process Gains)**

- It provides learning. Groups are better than individuals at understanding problems.
- People readily take ownership and responsibility of problems and their solutions.
- Group members have their egos embedded in the decision, and so they will be committed to the solution.
- Groups are better than individuals at catching errors.
- A group has more information (knowledge) than any one member. Groups can leverage this knowledge to create new knowledge. More creative alternatives for problem solving can be generated, and better solutions can be derived (e.g., through stimulation).
- A group may produce synergy during problem solving. The effectiveness or quality of group work can be greater than the sum of what is produced by independent individuals.
- Working in a group may stimulate the creativity of the participants and process.
- A group may have better and more precise communication working together.

TABLE 4.7	Dysfunctions of the Group Process (Process Losses)

- Social pressures of conformity that may result in groupthink (people begin to think alike and do not tolerate new ideas—yielding to conformance pressure)
- Time-consuming, serial process (only one member can speak at a time)
- Lack of coordination of the meeting and poor meeting planning
- Inappropriate influences (domination of time, topic, opinion by one or few individuals; fear of contributing because of the possibility of flaming; and so on)
- Tendency of group members to either dominate the agenda or free-ride by relying on others to do most of the work
- Some members may be afraid to speak up
- Tendency to produce compromised solutions of poor quality
- Nonproductive time (socializing, preparing, waiting for latecomers—air-time fragmentation)
- Tendency to repeat what was already said because of failure to remember or process
- High cost of meeting from travel, participation, etc

Improving Meeting Processes and Small Group Dynamics. Meetings are the most universal—and universally disliked—part of business life. More and more companies are team-based (e.g., project management teams) in which most work gets done in meetings. Meetings can be more effective if one understands what can go wrong and intelligently manages decision processes and group dynamics to avoid problems. For example, newly formed groups whose members do not know each other have much different dynamics than groups with an established history and routine, and need more socialization time before they become productive. Researchers have developed methods for improving the processes of group work, namely, increase the benefits of meetings and minimize the detriments. Some of these methods are known as group dynamics. The challenges of group work processes are more intense for virtual teams, as described in *IT at Work 4.5*. **Virtual teams** are groups of people who work interdependently with shared purpose across space, time, and organization boundaries using technology to communicate and collaborate.

Vendors' Collaborative Products. Numerous vendors offer collaborative technologies. Here are several vendors and their products:

- IBM's collaborative platform software based on UC2 (unified communications and collaboration) solution for businesses is Lotus Sametime (*306.ibm.com/software/lotus/products/sametime/standard*). Lotus Sametime Standard software offers integrated, enterprise instant messaging, VoIP, video chats, and Web conferencing capabilities with the security features required for business use. Lotus Sametime Standard software can help organizations:
  - Resolve problems and questions through clear, high-quality communications
  - Access global teams in real time
  - Communicate quickly with anybody where regulation permits and with policy controls in place
  - Work with others as if they are in the same room
  - Offer access to expertise and knowledge throughout the organization

- WebEx (*webex.com*) provides on-demand web meetings and collaborative business applications. By combining the ease of audio conferencing with the interactivity of video conferencing directly from the desktop, WebEx creates a truly personalized interactive experience.

• Microsoft Office Groove 2007 (*office.microsoft.com/en-us/groove/HA101672641033.aspx*) is a collaboration software program that helps teams work together dynamically and effectively, even if team members work for different organizations, work remotely, or work offline. Working in Groove workspaces saves time, increases productivity, and strengthens the quality of team deliverables.

• Oracle Collaboration Suite 10g (*oracle.com/technology/products/cs/index.html*) is a component of the Oracle Fusion Middleware products. It is the first product to leverage a relational database to securely, reliably, and cost-effectively simplify business communications and consolidate information by reducing hardware, software, and administration costs.

The key features for supporting group work, and which are typically bundled with vendors' product lines, are described next.

IT at Work 4.5

Virtual Teams at Sabre, Inc.

SVR **GLOBAL**

Sabre, Inc., is one of the leading firms providing travel reservation services worldwide. Sabre, Inc., employs over 6,000 people in 45 countries and generates over $2 billion in annual revenues. Sixty thousand travel agents in 114 countries rely on Sabre to make travel arrangements for their clients. The total volume of reservations processed by the system each year exceeds 400 million, which represents 40 percent of all travel reservations worldwide. Consumers may be familiar with Travelocity.com, which is Sabre's business-to-consumer (B2C) travel site; corporate travel agents would recognize Get-There—the world's leading supplier of business-to-business online travel reservation systems operated by Sabre.

With employees working in headquarters and field offices scattered around the globe, Sabre made a decision to use *virtual teams* to improve customer focus, enhance productivity, and grow market share and profitability. The company discovered that cross-functional teams were better suited for the marketplace demands than the single-function teams it had used in the past. A typical virtual team at Sabre includes representatives from several areas of the company: account executives sell reservation systems, technicians install and service the systems, trainers teach travel agents how to use the systems, account management specialists handle billing and collections, and customer service representatives respond to miscellaneous inquiries.

Following the introduction of virtual teams, Sabre encountered several challenges related to managing and working in the teams. One of the primary challenges was building trust among team members. Managers and employees soon recognized that building trust requires a high level of responsiveness to electronic communications from other team members, dependable performance, and a proactive approach to completing team tasks. The second challenge involved generating synergy in virtual teams—making the team greater than the sum of its parts. To resolve this challenge, Sabre offered team-building activities, as well as extensive classroom and computer-based training that preceded the launch of new virtual teams. A third challenge was that team members had to cope with the feeling of isolation and detachment that characterizes virtual teamwork. The company discovered that cer-

tain employees preferred independent work and operated well without much social interaction. Thus, Sabre conducted interviews with potential team members to determine their suitability for virtual teamwork. Furthermore, the company's teams are only partially virtual—the relationships may occasionally involve face-to-face interactions during certain meetings and teambuilding exercises. In addition, employees have the option to work either from home or from an office where they can interact with other employees, who may or may not be their teammates.

The fourth challenge involved balancing technical and interpersonal skills among team members. Sabre was surprised to find that despite the infrequent face-to-face communications, interpersonal abilities were extremely valuable and important to virtual teams. As a result, the company made a change in its hiring and team-member selection practices, to shift the emphasis from technical to interpersonal skills.

A fifth major challenge was related to employee evaluation and performance measurement. Over time, the company implemented a system of team-level and individual metrics that were intended to measure objective, quantifiable contributions of each team member and the performance of the virtual team as a whole. Nevertheless, the company admits that striking the right balance between the measures of individual contributions and group performance continues to be difficult.

The results of creating virtual teams at Sabre have been quite positive. Most managers and employees of the company agree that the shift from functional face-to-face teams to cross-functional virtual teams improved customer service. Customers' ratings support these assertions.

Sources: Compiled from Kirkman et al. (2002) and *sabre-holdings.com* (accessed 2006).

For Further Exploration: Are the challenges faced by virtual teams at Sabre unique to this company, or are they common throughout the business world? What additional challenges with virtual teams might Sabre encounter in the future? If you were an employee at Sabre, would you prefer to work in a physical face-to-face environment or in a virtual team?

Real-Time Collaboration. Collaborative IM, online meetings (also called Web conferencing), and presence are becoming critical components of communication and collaboration strategies.

Collaborative Instant Messaging. As companies become comfortable with telecommuting and at-home workers, it is IM, more so than e-mail, that ties their staffs together and supports distributed project teams. There are several reasons for the growth in corporate IM use. Workers are more mobile and harder to track down. The next generation of IM is not just about text chats, but offers integration with voice and video. IM's real-time features and the ability to track someone down no matter where he or she is located have proven attractive to customers, partners, and suppliers who need a guaranteed method of communication.

4.6 Social, Legal, and Ethical Issues

Management needs to consider ethical and social issues, such as quality of working life. Workers will experience both positive and negative impacts from being linked to a 24/7 workplace environment, working in computer-contrived virtual teams, and being connected to handhelds whose impact on health can be damaging. A 2008 study by Solutions Research Group found that always being connected is a borderline obsession for many people. According to the study, 68 percent of Americans may suffer from disconnect anxiety—feelings of disorientation and nervousness when deprived of Internet or wireless access for a period of time. The study also found that 63 percent of BlackBerry users admitted to having sent a message from the bathroom. Technology addiction has gone so far that U.S. psychiatrists are considering adding this "compulsive-impulsive" disorder to the next release of the DSM (Diagnostic and Statistical Manual of Mental Disorders) in 2011. Approximately 25 percent people stayed connected with work while on vacation in summer 2008, which was about double what it had been in 2006, according to a CareerBuilder.com survey (Perelman, 2008).

Consider that there other social developments and their implications:

• **Debate over DWY** (Driving While Yakking). Several studies show cell phones are a leading cause of car crashes. Yet driving while talking or DWY is not illegal. It is estimated that cell phone-distracted drivers are four times more likely to be in a car wreck. Laws have been passed to discourage drivers from cell phone use when they should be paying attention to safety. The hands-free July 2008 Californian law is not expected to solve problems of car accidents due to cell phone distractions based on New York City's lack of improvement after having had "hands free" for several years. At any given moment, more than 10 million U.S. drivers are talking on handheld cell phones, according to the National Highway Traffic Safety Administration (*NHTSA.dot.gov*). Why is this a problem? Cell phones are a known distraction, and the NHTSA has determined that driver inattention is a primary or contributing factor in as many as 25 percent of all police-reported traffic accidents. This doesn't include the thousands of accidents that *are not* reported to the authorities.

• **Health risks.** The Food and Drug Administration recommends minimizing potential risk by using hands-free devices and keeping cell-phone talk to a minimum. A few studies have indicated that using a cell phone for an hour each day over a 10-year period can increase the risk of developing a rare brain tumor and that those tumors are more likely to be on the side of the head used to talk on the phone. More research is needed in this area.

• **RF emissions and SAR.** The Federal Communications Commission (FCC) requires manufacturers to report the relative amount of RF (radio frequency) absorbed into the head by any given cell phone. This number is known as the SAR, or specific absorption rate. Visit *fcc.gov/oet/rfsafety/sar.html* to find out how to check a phone's SAR.

• **Virtualization of trust.** Meeting face-to-face is the fastest way to build trust and relationships among team members. For globally distributed teams this is very expensive due to travel costs. Once a working trust-based relationship among people has been established by meeting face-to-face, collaborating over long distance becomes much more efficient. When teams work only in a virtual world, potential problems that can result are social isolation, frustration over not being able to resolve problems, and disruptive meeting times because of time zone differences. Trust can be built even if a global team cannot get together physically. But this process takes far more time than an initial face-to-face meeting, as team members have to let their work literally speak for themselves (Gloor et al, 2004).

The importance of understanding ethical issues has been recognized by the Association to Advance Collegiate Schools of Business (AACSB International, *aacsb.edu*). For business majors, the AACSB International has defined Assurance of Learning Requirements for ethics at both the undergraduate and graduate levels. In *Standard 15: Management of Curricula* (AACSB Accreditation Standards, 2006), AACSB identifies general knowledge and skill learning experiences that include "ethical understanding and reasoning abilities" at the undergraduate level. At the graduate level, *Standard 15* requires learning experiences in management-specific knowledge and skill areas to include "ethical and legal responsibilities in organizations and society" (AACSB International Ethics Education Resource Center, 2006). Ethical issues are discussed after the social impacts of social networks are examined.

SOCIAL NETWORKS AND WIKIS

Social networks, or social networking services, are Web sites that allow anyone to build a homepage for free. People can list personal information, communicate with others, upload files, communicate via IM, or blog. Social networks can contain links to user-generated content. Although blogs and wikis are influential social tools, social software also includes IM, RSS, Internet forums, and social network services such as MySpace and Bebo.

Social Networks. Social networks are redefining the way people communicate. MySpace is a social network that started as a site for fans of independent rock music in Los Angeles. MySpace was bought by Rupert Murdoch for $580 million in 2005. By the end of 2006, MySpace (*myspace.com*) had over 106 million users—and was estimated to be the world's fourth most popular English-language Web site. Competition in the social networking arena is fierce. Bebo (*bebo.com*), which is a backronym for "Blog early, blog often," attracts a majority of U.K. visitors and had over 22 million registered members by March 2006 (Wikipedia, *2008*). Bebo was acquired by AOL in March 2008 for $850 million. In October 2007, Bebo launched a mobile service, which allows users to receive text alerts and update their profiles via their mobile phones. Buzznet, Facebook, Xanga, TagWorld, and Friendsorenemies are competitors. These social networks can exert immeasurable influence on politics, public opinion, and attitudes toward work and recreation.

MySpace (or any other social network) addiction affects many users who are driven to MySpace several dozen times a day. Addicts neglect other important things in life by checking and posting bulletins every hour. Such addictions are depriving users of sleep, making them late for work because they couldn't stop refreshing their pages. They may keep MySpace open in another window while at work, interfering with their jobs and in-person forms of interaction.

LIFE OUT OF CONTROL

The technologies covered in this chapter blur work, social, and personal time. IT keeps people connected with no real off-switch. Tools that are meant to improve the productivity and quality of life in general can also intrude on personal time. Managers need to be aware of the huge potential for abuse by expecting 24/7 response from workers. See *IT at Work 4.6* for a look at life in a connected world.

4.7 Managerial Issues

1. **Organizational impacts.** Technology-mediated communications are having various organizational impacts. The primary business benefit of networks and mobile communications is keeping workers connected at lower costs. Mobile and collaboration technologies need to be in place to ensure that employees can be productive.

2. **Future of technology support.** From a technology perspective, the second half of this decade will be seen as a period in which technology moved to support collaborative work. Whereas the computer industry had focused on providing computing for the individual (PC + laptop + notebook + PDA), the emphasis is now firmly on connectivity, communication, and collaboration through convergence.

3. **Extending organizational boundaries.** Extranets connect businesses to their customers and supply chain partners. As high-bandwidth wireless networks become widespread, collaborative networking solutions are available for companies of any size.

4. **Virtual work and teams.** Mobile multimedia technologies make it possible for businesses to reinvent the traditional workplace from an office-based activity to a virtual one. Employees can collaborate closely in real time with other employees, customers, or partners regardless of anyone's location.

5. **Single view of the truth.** Information silos are the bane of most organizations as they try to integrate and share data to get a clearer understanding of customers, products, and other objects of interest. Regulatory compliance, performance management, and collaborative business relationships demand a single view of relevant information.

6. **Social and ethical issues.** Social networks are redefining the way people communicate. Tools that are meant to improve the productivity and quality of life in general can also intrude on the personal lives of managers and employees.

IT at Work 4.6

Internet 2007—Life in the Connected World

Changes brought about by the Internet are as profound as previous historic milestones such as the Renaissance or Industrial Revolution. Every person can be a creative artist and freely distribute work to millions—characteristics of both the Renaissance and Industrial Revolution. Google's existence is a testament to the power of the individual in the connected age—a better research tool than major corporations had in the 1990s. Other empowering tools such as VoIP and wikis enable anyone to call or share files for free.

Communication technologies—writing, printing, cable, telephone, radio, and TV—have always played a central role in human history. The marginal cost of collecting, storing, accessing, and transmitting information is approaching zero. Over 1 billion people have Internet access, and over 1.5 billion use mobile phones. The potential for the spread of wireless access to the Internet is enormous.

Major companies face small but powerful challenges and competitors that are undermining traditional business models. Consumers and employees can counteract marketing strategies by posting harsh criticisms in blogs. EBay shops can underprice. Intranets, extranets, and social networks are diminishing perimeters between companies and individuals' lives—and making them more transparent. People check Internet resources for ratings and prices before they buy books, vacations, cars, and so on. Amazingly, in places such as Tanzania, political activists worked on a new constitution using a wiki. Communication and collaboration tools can collectively create a compelling force whose impacts are not yet known.

Businesses have to learn to cope with a world that is far more competitive, dynamic, and connected.

Sources: Compiled from Kirkpatrick (2006) and Wolf (2006).

For Further Exploration: How has the use of communication tools impacted your ability to get your work done? How has it impacted your personal life? Has IT been liberating or overwhelming? What ethical issues does this raise for managers?

How *IT* Benefits You

For the Accounting Major

Accounting information systems are dependent on networks. Payment functions such as accounts payable and receivable are done over networks. To meet regulatory compliance requirements, accountants need to compile data from various remote databases, consolidate financial statements, and distribute financial performance reports to shareholders and regulators on a quarterly and annual basis. Significant cost savings result when financial statements are distributed via networks instead of conventional paper methods. Federal agencies, such as the SEC, require that reports be submitted electronically.

For the Finance Major

Financial systems rely on speed and accuracy. Investment and quantitative analyses demand real-time data delivered via computing networks. Transactional and operational data may reside in countries without a reliable wireline communications infrastructure—making wireless networks a necessity. Financial analysts rely on networks for the delivery of real-time data. Financial planning and budgeting meetings can be held via Web conferencing or collaboration portals instead of in-person.

For the Human Resources Management Major

Intranets can be used as efficient HR portals. Intranets more cheaply and reliably distribute government forms, policies, handbooks, and other materials to employees. HR portals can be used to keep employees informed of the status of performance evaluations, vacations, medical plans, and so on. These self-help capabilities reduce costs and better support employees' information needs. Training employees in local or remote locations can be done via streamed video to PCs or handheld devices.

For the IS Major

Business operations are fully dependent on the capabilities of their information networks—wireline and wireless. Networks and collaboration tools are strategic assets. Senior executives look to the ISD for help in managing those assets. Other departments look to the ISD to help them meet their communication and collaboration requirements. Information systems professionals must keep up to date with rapid changes in wireless protocols that enable convergence of various technologies.

For the Marketing Major

Wireless networks, podcasts, RSS, wikis, social networks, and streaming technologies provide new ways to reach customers—anywhere and any time. Customer relationship management and customer retention programs can be improved through creative uses of these technologies. Marketers will need to design and develop programs for delivery to portable devices over various types of network protocols. Voice applications can be deployed that reinforce branding, enhance customer service, and improve internal communications.

For the Production/Operations Management Major

The performance, efficiency, and cost of a company's supply chain operations—inventory purchasing, receiving, quality control, production, and shipping—are fully dependent on communication networks. Production managers can be kept informed in real time of potential disruptions in logistics and are able to take action directly from handheld devices that connect them to databases and suppliers. By integrating collaboration tools, mobile computing networks, wireless devices, and instant communication such as text messaging, production and operations departments can replace inefficient paper-based processes and reduce required personnel for operations and administration.

Key Terms

Chapter Highlights

❶ In preparation for transmission, data and documents are converted into digital packets based on the Internet Protocol (IP) and sent via computer (i.e., packet-switched) networks or LANs.

❶ Data, voice, and video networks are converging into a single network based on packet technology, such as IP and VoIP.

❷ Real-time awareness, provided by Web-based collaboration solutions can significantly improve the outcome of complex operations involving numerous remote or mobile workers.

❷ Convergence eliminates the need for separate networks. When all information services are handled the same way by one high-speed packet network, the technical barriers to collaborative work are eliminated. Multimedia applications become possible because the network does not restrict the kinds of computing devices that could be used.

❷ Broadband wireless computing allows users to collaborate via the Internet at any time, share files, or perform other group work functions that previously required a PC and wireline infrastructure.

❸ The major drivers of mobile computing are large numbers of users of mobile devices, especially cell phones; widespread use of cell phones throughout the world; new vendor products; declining prices; increasing bandwidth; and the explosion of collaboration tools.

❸ Intranets distribute frequently needed employee handbooks, government forms, policies, and other materials to employees over the company network.

❸ An extranet connects the company with its customers or trading partners for B2B commerce and real-time supply chain management. Extranets give account customers instant access to their account details.

❸ Wireless technology can give a company a competitive advantage through increased productivity, better customer care, and more timely communication and information exchange.

❸ VoIP can be customized as a strategic tool because of its virtualization, customization, and intelligence capabilities. Location-based advertising and advertising via SMSs on a very large scale is expected.

❸ Mobile portals provide multimedia broadcasts and other content (e.g., news and sports) to billions.

❹ Search engines, directories, enterprise search engines, and wikis help bring order to the chaotic Internet universe.

❺ Many B2B and B2C applications in the service and retail industries can be conducted with wireless devices. SMS and IM provide employees with relatively low-cost connectivity.

❺ Messaging and collaboration tools include older media such as e-mail, videoconferencing, fax, and IM—and new media such as podcasts, RSS newsfeeds, wikis, VoIP, Web meetings, and torrents (for sharing very large files). As media move to IP, there will not be much left that is not converged onto data networks.

❻ Managers and staff continuously make decisions: They design and manufacture products, develop policies and strategies, prepare financial statements, determine how to meet compliance mandates, design software, and so on.

❻ Collaboration and communication technologies covered in this chapter blur work, social, and personal time. IT keeps people connected with no real off-switch. Tools that are meant to improve the productivity and quality of life in general can also intrude on personal time. Managers need to be aware of the huge potential for abuse by expecting 24/7 response from workers.

Virtual Company Assignment

WILEY **PLUS**

Network Computing at The Wireless Café

Go to The Wireless Café's link on the Student Web Site. There you will find a description of some communications problems the restaurant is having as a result of its 24/7 operations. You will be asked to identify ways network computing can facilitate better staff communications.

Instructions for accessing The Wireless Café on the Student Web Site:

1. Go to *wiley.com/college/turban*.
2. Select Turban/Volonino's *Information Technology for Management*, Seventh Edition.
3. Click on Student Resources site, in the toolbar on the left.
4. Click on the link for Virtual Company Web site.
5. Click on Wireless Café.

Questions for Discussion

1. Why will 4G wireless networks bring about significant changes in connectivity?
2. There is growing demand for video to handheld devices. Explain at least three factors enabling or driving this demand.
3. Why attend class if you can view or listen to the podcast?
4. Discuss some of the potential applications of collaborative technologies in the service sector and manufacturing sector.
5. Discuss some of the potential applications of wireless technologies in the financial sector.
6. Discuss the components of a mobile communication network.
7. Explain the role of protocols in mobile computing and their limitations.

8. Discuss the impact of wireless computing on emergency response services.
9. Describe the ways in which WiMax is affecting the use of cellular phones for m-commerce.
10. Which of the current mobile computing limitations do you think will be minimized within five years? Which ones will not?
11. It is said that Wi-Fi is winning a battle against 3G. In what sense is this true? In what sense is this false?
12. Discuss the ethical issues of social networks and any-time-anywhere accessibility.
13. What health and quality of life issues are associated with social networks and a 24/7 connected life style?

Exercises and Projects

1. CALEA is the Communications Assistance for Law Enforcement Act, a federal requirement to allow law enforcement agencies to conduct electronic surveillance of phone calls or other communications. What dilemmas are caused by the convergence of voice, video, and data and the requirements of CALEA?
2. Compare the various features of broadband wireless networks (e.g., 3G, Wi-Fi, and WiMax). Visit at least three broadband wireless network vendors.
   a. Prepare a list of capabilities of each network.
   b. Prepare a list of actual applications that each network can support.
   c. Comment on the value of such applications to users. How can the benefits be assessed?

3. Compare the advanced features of three search engines.
   a. Prepare a table listing five advanced features of each search engine.
   b. Perform a search for "VoIP vendors" on each of those search engines.
   c. Compare the results.
   d. In your opinion, which search engine provided the best results. Why?
4. Read *IT at Work 4.1* about how Kaiser Permanente used a Google tool for its corporate portal, and answer the discussion questions.
5. Read *IT at Work 4.2* on Thrifty Car Rental Uses IP Telephony to Increase Operational Efficiency and Customer Service, and answer the discussion questions.

Group Assignments and Projects

1. Visit *wordpress.com*. Read how to create a blog. Each team will design and develop content from this course for a blog. Then create a blog and make it available online.
2. Each team should examine a major vendor of mobile devices (Nokia, Kyocera, Motorola, Palm, BlackBerry, etc.). Each team will research the capabilities and prices of the devices offered by each company and then make a class presentation, the objective of which is to convince the rest of the class why one should buy that company's products.
3. Each team should explore the commercial applications of mobile communication in one of the following areas: financial services, including banking, stocks, and insur-

ance; marketing and advertising; manufacturing; travel and transportation; human resources management; public services; or healthcare. Each team will present a report to the class based on its findings.
4. Each team will investigate an online (Web) meeting software suite, such as GoToMeeting and Lotus Sametime. Download the free trial version and/or video demonstration. The teams will investigate the features and business purposes of the software, and then present a report to the class based on their findings.
5. Each team will investigate a standards-setting organization and report on its procedures and progress in developing wireless standards. Start with the following: *atis.org, etsi.org,* and *tiaonline.org.*

Internet Exercises

1. Enter *e-sponder.com* and describe its Collaboration Portal.

2. View the flash demo of the IBM Information Server Blade at *ftp://ftp.software.ibm.com/software/data/integration/demos/blade/demo.swf*, and describe the benefits of the information server to the company, employees, and the environment.

3. Enter Twitter (*twitter.com*). Describe the features of their micro-blogging platform.

4. Learn about Lotus Sametime Standard by visiting *www-306.ibm.com/software/lotus/products/sametime/standard/*. Click onto *View the Screenshots*, or enter *www306.ibm.com/software/lotus/products/sametime/standard/screenshots.html*. Prepare a report of the software's capabilities that support real-time collaboration.

5. Enter *mobileworldcongress.com* and *web20.telecomtv.com/*. List three mobile communication-related issues of current interest.

6. Search and research the status of 3G and 4G networks and devices. Prepare a report on the status of 3G and 4G based on your findings.

7. Explore *nokia.com*. Prepare a summary of the types of mobile services and applications Nokia currently supports and plans to support in the future.

8. Enter *kyocera-wireless.com*. Take the smart tour and view the demos. What is a smartphone? What are its capabilities? How does it differ from a regular cell phone?

9. Enter *mobile.commerce.net* and find information about car navigation systems. Write a report.

10. Enter *ibm.com*. Search for *wireless e-business*. Research the resulting stories to determine the types of wireless capabilities and applications IBM's software and hardware support. Describe some of the ways these applications have helped specific businesses and industries.

11. Using a search engine, try to determine whether there are any commercial Wi-Fi hotspots in your area. Enter *wardriving.com*. Based on information provided at this site, what sorts of equipment and procedures could you use to locate hotspots in your area?

12. Enter *mapinfo.com* and look for the location-based services demos. Try all the demos. Find all of the wireless services. Summarize your findings.

13. Enter *packetvideo.com* and *microsoft.com/mobile/pocketpc*. Examine their demos and products and list their capabilities.

14. Enter Dodgeball (*dodgeball.com*) and watch the video that shows how to micro-blog.

15. Enter *onstar.com*. What types of *fleet* services does OnStar provide? Are these any different from the services OnStar provides to individual car owners?

16. Enter *autoidcenter.org*. Read about the Internet of Things. What is it? What types of technologies are needed to support it? Why is it important?

17. Enter *fcc.gov/oet/rfsafety/sar.html* to find out how to check a phone's SAR.

18. Enter *attwireless.com/mlife* and prepare a list of the services available there.

19. Enter *wirelesscar.com*. Examine all the services provided and relate them to telemetry.

20. Enter the site of a wireless e-mail provider (BlackBerry, T-mobile, Handspring); collect information about the capabilities of the products and compare them.

Minicase

Wikis, Blogs, and Chats Support Collaboration at DrKW

Dresdner Kleinwort Wasserstein (DrKW) is the international investment banking arm of Dresdner Bank. Headquartered in London and Frankfurt, DrKW provides capital market and advisory services employing 6,000 people worldwide—in New York, Paris, Luxembourg, Tokyo, Singapore, and Hong Kong.

Because their employees are culturally diverse and geographically distributed, DrKW wanted them to have a full set of collaboration tools—not only e-mail and telephones. Blogs, wikis, instant messaging, chat, and audio/videoconferencing let workers select and switch communication modes, depending on which is appropriate at the time. DrKW installed a primitive open source wiki in 1997. The company reviewed Socialtext products in March 2004 and ran a small pilot on the hosted service in July 2004. Based on the pilot, DrKW decided to upgrade to Socialtext Enterprise, which was installed in the third quarter of 2004.

DrKW chose Socialtext because it needed strong authentication, permissions, information sharing, and communication among the various company silos. DrKW is highly regulated, requiring that their communications be recorded, archived, searchable, and retrievable for auditors or other investigators. Those communications are business records, which must be retained according to financial regulations such as the Sarbanes-Oxley Act of 2002.

Usage and Benefits

The Information Strategy team was the first group to use Socialtext on a hosted service, followed by IT Security. The teams use it as a communications tool, collective discussion tool, and storehouse for documents and information. The User-Centered Design (UCD) team uses external-facing applications. The wiki allows team members to upload information easily, which encourages collaboration and increases transparency, which is not possible with e-mail messages. UCD also uses the wiki to explain what its function is and why it's important to the entire DrKW community.

The wiki tracks project development so that the team and management know the status of projects and progress, who is doing what, the status of each project, and what actions should follow.

The Equity Delta1 equity financing team is one of the largest users of the wiki. This unit deals with loans, equity swaps, and so on. The wiki eliminates the burden of mountains of e-mails, shows the development of business plans, and stores commonly used information. The team creates an open forum where anyone can post views, comments, and questions on given subjects; publish and share whitepapers and bulletins; coordinate sales and marketing activities; and organize important team tasks.

One of the most enthusiastic user groups is Digital Markets, the division responsible for developing, deploying, and operating DrKW's online products and services. Digital Markets combines front office, support, and IT specialists in one unit. It has a wide cross section of users who must all be brought together on the same page.

The E-Capital London Team develops back-end applications for the Digital Markets business line and supports a number of legacy systems. They share and develop new system specifications and product overviews, and help with documentation. The wiki provides an instantly editable collaboration platform that simplifies the publication process. The

version history function is useful for product specs where it is important to retain a complete audit trail.

Users keep others informed by posting timely notes such as "this is what we're thinking about now." The limitation is that the wiki only works when everyone supports and is comfortable in such an open environment. Wikis fail in organizations where people are frightened to talk and publish. It works in DrKW, especially in Digital Markets where people willingly say "look, here it is." Their openness stimulates good debate and allows them to generate great ideas.

Sources: Compiled from *SocialText.com/node/80* (2008) and *BusinessWeek Online* (2005).

Questions for Minicase

1. What are the capabilities of the wiki that are not available in regular e-mail?

2. Why would so many tools—blogs, wikis, instant messaging, chat, and audio/videoconferencing—be needed?

3. How does the wiki increase employee productivity? What types of waste does it reduce?

4. Do a search of the Internet to determine whether content sent via instant messages or posted on wikis are business records that must be preserved. Report what you learned.

5. What are some social, cultural, and ethical issues involved in the use of wikis for business collaboration?

Problem-Solving Activity

Comparing the Costs of Using Web Meetings and Collaboration

DUMBO Company (*a fictitious company*) needed to reduce travel costs and productivity losses. Web conferencing would be used internally for collaboration and externally for sales demonstrations to customers in geographically dispersed areas. The company's CFO, Chris Bridges, decided to invest in one of the large vendors' Web meeting software, either a pay-per-use basis or per-user licensing plan based on the number of seats or participants. Chris has estimated that Web conferencing cost estimates should be based on:

- approximately three meetings per week (about 360 days) or 1,000 meetings per year
- an average of 8 participants per meeting
- each meeting lasting about one hour, which takes into consideration the need to get the meeting set up at least 15 minutes in advance and 45-minute meetings
- 300 unique participants, consisting of 100 employees and 200 customers

Chris wants you to research and develop a spreadsheet comparing the pay-per-use basis *vs* buying seats (licenses) for Microsoft's LiveMeeting and Cisco's WebEx. Precise cost comparisons are difficult because there are so many variables, but a basic cost analysis between LiveMeeting and WebEx is feasible. Using a spreadsheet:

1. Calculate the total minutes per year for Web conferencing at DUMBO.

2. Research LiveMeeting and WebEx to find the costs for a pay-per-use basis or the cost to buy the software.

3. Prepare cost comparisons of the vendors' licensing options and pay-per-usage.

4. Identify other criteria that should be taken into account when making such a decision (for example, vendor support or the ability to integrate with Outlook).

5. Make a recommendation to Chris.

Online Resources

More resources and study tools are located on the Student Web Site and on WileyPLUS. You'll find additional chapter materials and useful Web links. In addition, self-quizzes that provide individualized feedback are available for each chapter.

Online Brief for Chapter 4 is available at wiley.com/college/turban:
4.1 Fila's Collaboration Software Reduces Time-to-Market

Online Minicases for Chapter 4 are available at wiley.com/college/turban:
4.1 Safeway Collaborates in Designing Stores
4.2 Network Computing at National Semiconductor Corporation

References

AACSB Accreditation Standards, Management of Curricula, *aacsb.edu/eerc/std-15.asp* (accessed June 2008).

AACSB International, Ethics Education Resource Center, Accreditation Standards, *aacsb.edu/resource_centers/EthicsEdu/standards.asp* (accessed June 2008).

Alter, A. E., "Emerging Computing and Software Technologies," *CIO Insight*, May 4, 2006, *cioinsight.com/article2/0,1540,1957596,00.asp* (accessed July 3, 2006).

Careless, J., "Convergence Communications E-SPONDER," *Law and Order*, March 2006, *hendonpub.com/publications/lawandorder/otherarticles.asp?ID=545* (accessed June 2008).

Cisco.com (accessed May 2008).

"Ericsson and Dell Connect on HSPA in Next-Generation Laptops," *FoxBusiness*, May 13, 2008, *foxbusiness.com/story/markets/industries/telecom/ericsson-dell-connect-hspa-generation-laptops/-1211758065* (accessed June 2008).

E-Sponder Case Study, "Embracing Technology at Super Bowl XXXIX," *Convergence Communications*, March 1, 2005, *convergencecom.com/casestudy_techatsuperbowl.shtml* (accessed June 2008).

Esponder.com (Accessed June 2008).

Forrester, Business Data Services, *Enterprise Network and Telecommunications Survey*, Q1 2007.

Frommer, D., "Smartphone Sales Soar, iPhone Grabs 27% of Market," *Silicon Alley Insider*, November 20, 2007, *alleyinsider.com/2007/11/smartphone-sales-soar-iphone-grabs-27-percent-of-market.html* (accessed June 2008).

Frost and Sullivan, "Meetings Around the World: The Impact of Collaboration on Business Performance," 2006, *newscenter.verizon.com/kit/collaboration/MAW_WP.pdf* (accessed June 2008).

Globalmobileawards.com/winners.shtml (accessed June 2008).

Gloor, P., C. Heckman, and F. Makedon, "Ethical Issues in Collaborative Innovation Networks," 2004, *ccs.mit.edu/pgloor%20papers/COIN4Ethicomp.pdf* (accessed June 2008).

Google.com (accessed June 2008).

Kamath, J-P., Mobile WiMax Set to Grow," *Computer Weekly*, Dec. 2007, *computerweekly.com/Articles/2007/12/12/228564/mobile-wimax-set-to-grow.htm* (accessed June 2008).

Kirkman, B., et al., "Five Challenges to Virtual Team Success: Lessons from Sabre, Inc.," *Academy of Management Executive*, 16(3), August 2002.

Kirkpatrick, D., "Life in a Connected World," *Fortune*, July 10, 2006.

Krigsman, M., LAX IT Failure: Leaps of Faith Don't Work," *ZDNet*, August 15, 2007, *blogs.zdnet.com/projectfailures/?p=346* (accessed June 2008).

Martin, R., Motorola Aims for All-Wireless Enterprise," *InformationWeek*, March 17, 2008, *informationweek.com/news/mobility/convergence/showArticle.jhtml?articleID=206904190* (accessed June 2008).

Microsoft.com (accessed June 2008).

Perelman, D., "Has the Disconnected Vacation Become Extinct?" *eWeek.com*, May 5, 2008, *eweek.com/c/a/Careers/Has-the-Disconnected-Vacation-Become-Extinct/?kc=EWKNLCSM060308FEA* (accessed June 2008).

Poeter, D., "NIC Card Soup Gives LAX a Tummy-Ache," *ChannelWeb*, August 17, 2007, *crn.com/networking/201801022* (accessed June 2008).

Resende, P., "R.I. Hospital Keeps Nurses Connected with Wi-Fi Badges," *Journal of New England Technology*, February 12, 2005, *vocera.com/downloads/Vocera_20Communications.pdf* (accessed June 2008).

Sabre, Inc., *sabre-holdings.com* (accessed June 2008).

Sherwin, A., New Wi-Fi Devices Warn Doctors of Heart Attacks," *Times Online*, May 7, 2008, *technology.timesonline.co.uk/tol/news/tech_and_web/article3883082.ece* (accessed June 2008).

SocialText, "Dresdner Kleinwort Wasserstein (DrKW)," *Customer Success Story at SocialText.com*, 2004, *socialtext.com/customers/customerdrkw* (accessed June 2008).

Turban, E., et al., *Electronic Commerce*, 4th ed. Upper Saddle River, NJ: Prentice-Hall, 2006.

Vocera.com (accessed June 2008).

Warner, B., "It's Not All Just Geek Talk and Texts—Phones Are First with the News," *Times Online*, May 9, 2008, *technology.timesonline.co.uk/tol/news/tech_and_web/article3896667.ece* (accessed June 2008).

Werbach, K., "Using VoIP to Compete," *Harvard Business Review*, September 2005.

Wolf, M., "The World Must Get to Grips with Seismic Economic Shifts," *Financial Times*, February 1, 2006.

Yahoo.com (accessed June 2008).

Chapter 5

Securing the Enterprise and Business Continuity

Learning Objectives

After studying this chapter, you will be able to:

❶ Recognize the business and financial value of information security.

❷ Recognize IS vulnerabilities, threats, attack methods, and cybercrime symptoms.

❸ Describe the factors that contribute to risk exposure and the methods to mitigate them.

❹ Explain key methods of defending information systems, networks, and wireless devices.

❺ Describe internal control and fraud and the related legislation.

❻ Understand business continuity and disaster recovery planning methods.

❼ Discuss the role of IT in defending critical infrastructures.

Integrating *IT*

 ACC
 FIN
 MKT
 OM
 HRM
 IS

IT-PERFORMANCE MODEL

Losses and disruptions due to IT security breaches can seriously harm or destroy a company both financially and operationally. As the effectiveness of the technology and tactics used by cybercriminals—people who commit crimes using the Internet—increases, so do the costs of staying ahead of deliberate attacks, viruses and other malware infections, and unintentional errors. Managers have a fiduciary responsibility to protect confidential data that they collect and store. Yet, according to research published by Computer Economics (*computereconomics.com*), many companies of all sizes fail to invest in basic security management best practices, such as IT security training for their employees or the auditing of computers to ensure that unauthorized programs or content are not present. To comply with federal, state, and foreign laws, companies must invest in IT security to protect their data, other assets, the ability to operate, and net income.

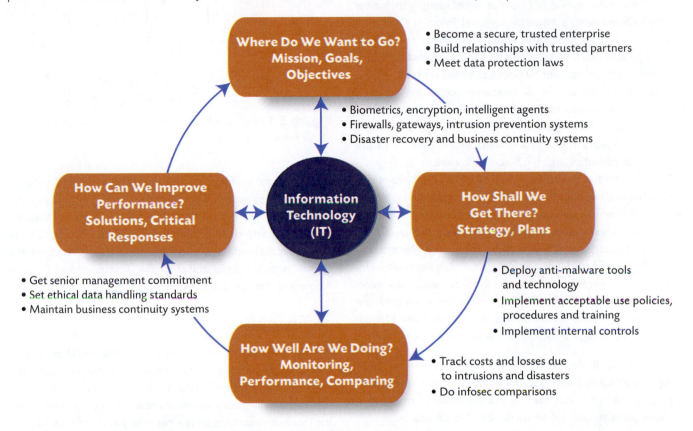

The business performance management cycle and IT model.

$55 MILLION DATA BREACH AT CHOICEPOINT

ETHICS   ACC   FIN   HRM   IS   OM   GOV

ChoicePoint is a leading data broker and credentialing service. It maintains 19 billion public records on more than 220 million U.S. citizens. The company buys personal data, including names, Social Security numbers, birthdates, employment data, and credit histories, and then sells the data to businesses and government agencies. Marketing, human resources, accounting, and finance departments rely on ChoicePoint's data for customer leads, background checks, and verification. Roughly, 70 percent of ChoicePoint's revenue is generated by selling consumer records for insurance claim verifications and workplace background screenings.

ChoicePoint was exposing the data to risk by ignoring its policy to verify that potential customers were legitimate before selling data. Disaster was foreseeable. In early 2000, without doing an adequate background check, ChoicePoint provided the hackers with customer accounts, which they used to illegally access databases and steal confidential data. By May 2008, that security lapse had cost the company over $55 million in fines, compensation to potential victims of identity theft, lawsuit settlements, and legal fees. Then in June 2008, the company also paid $10 million to settle a class action lawsuit.

Disclosing the Problem Publicly

On February 15, 2005, ChoicePoint reported that personal and financial data of 145,000 individuals had been "compromised." All of the individuals were at risk of identity theft after Olatunji Oluwatosin, a Nigerian national living in California, had pretended to represent several legitimate businesses. Ironically, Oluwatosin's credentials had not been verified, which enabled him to set up over 50 bogus business accounts. Those accounts gave him access to databases containing personal financial data. Oluwatosin was arrested in February 2005, pleaded guilty to conspiracy and grand theft, and was sentenced to 10 years in prison and fined $6.5 million. The state and federal penalties facing ChoicePoint were much larger.

Privacy and antifraud laws required that ChoicePoint disclose what had happened. California's privacy breach legislation requires that residents be informed when personal information has been compromised. Outraged Attorneys General in 44 states demanded that the company notify every affected U.S. citizen. At the federal level, ChoicePoint was charged with multiple counts of negligence for failing to follow *reasonable* information security practices. In 2005, the company was hit with the largest fine in Federal Trade Commission (FTC) history—$15 million. The FTC charged ChoicePoint with violating:

- The Fair Credit Reporting Act (FCRA) for furnishing credit reports to subscribers who did not have a permissible purpose to obtain them, and by not maintaining reasonable procedures to verify their subscribers' identities
- The FTC Act for false and misleading statements about privacy policies on its Web site

On March 4, 2005, in what was a first for a publicly held company, ChoicePoint filed an 8-K report with the SEC warning shareholders that revenue would be adversely affected by the data breach. In January 2006, with the public announcement of the extent of the fines, ChoicePoint's stock price plunged, as shown in Figure 5.1.

The Solution

When a company violates SEC, federal, or state laws, the solution to their problem is going to be dictated to them. The solution to ChoicePoint's risk exposure was mandated by the FTC. The company had to implement new procedures to ensure that it provides consumer reports only to legitimate

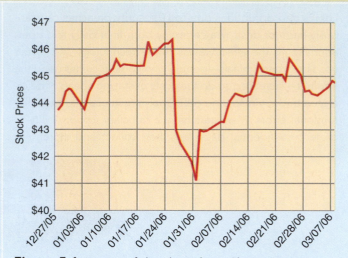

Figure 5.1 Impact of data breach on ChoicePoint's stock price.

businesses for lawful purposes. In addition, the FTC ordered ChoicePoint to establish and maintain a comprehensive information security program and to obtain audits by an independent third-party security professional biyearly until 2026. To reassure stakeholders, ChoicePoint hired Carol DiBattiste, the former deputy administrator of the Transportation Security Administration, as chief privacy officer (CPO).

The Results

ChoicePoint reformed its business practices and data security measures, which were too lax relative to its risk exposure. The company had to stop putting risky business practices that focused on short-term revenues ahead of long-term profitability. This business decision is a necessary and ethical trade-off.

ChoicePoint's data breach brought businesses' security policies to national attention. It signaled the need for improved corporate governance (see *corpgov.net*). Although there is no generally accepted definition, **corporate governance** refers to the rules and processes ensuring that the enterprise adheres to accepted ethical standards, best practices, and laws. Companies that collect sensitive consumer information have a responsibility to keep it secure. Together with high-profile frauds and malware, data breaches have triggered an increase in laws and government involvement to hold companies and their management accountable for lapses in governance. Yet, since ChoicePoint's record-setting data breach, many other infosec incidents and data thefts have occurred.

Sources: Compiled from *ftc.gov*, *Gross* (2005), Kaplan (2008), Mimoso (2006), and Scalet (2005).

Lessons Learned from This Case

Every enterprise has information assets that criminals worldwide attempt to steal. IT security risks are business risks. **IT security** refers to the protection of information, communication networks, and traditional and e-commerce operations to assure their confidentiality, integrity, availability, and authorized use. The purpose is to defend against operational risk and disruptions, outraged customers, and financial loss and liability. **Operational risk** is the risk of any loss resulting from inadequate or failed internal processes, people, systems, or external events. IT security is so integral to business objectives that it cannot be treated as a stand-alone function. Failures have a direct impact on business performance, customers, business partners, and stakeholders.

In this chapter we begin with an overview of enterprisewide security issues. We discuss technologies, such as firewalls and malware, internal controls, information assurance, and the COBIT framework. We introduce a risk exposure model for identifying what to protect and how much to invest in that protection. We describe major threats and types of fraud—and how they have increased the incidence of spam, bots, and phishing. Note, we use the term information security (or *infosec*, for short) to refer broadly to the security of data, networks, applications, communications, and everything digital needed for the enterprise to function.

5.1 Data and Enterprise Security Incidents

Until 2002, infosec was mostly a technical issue assigned to the IT department. Incidents were handled on a case-by-case "cleanup" basis rather than by taking a pre-emptive approach to protect ahead of the threats. Infosec was viewed as a *cost*—rather than as a *resource* for preventing business disruptions and satisfying governance responsibilities. The cost-based view turned out to be dangerously inadequate at securing the enterprise against dishonest insiders and the global reach of cybercrimes, malware, spyware, and fraud. Cleanup costs after a single incident are already into the tens or hundreds of millions of dollars. For up-to-date information and blogs on spyware, see SpywareGuide, a public reference site, at *spywareguide.com*.

INFOSEC THREATS AND INCIDENTS

Threats to infosec range from high-tech exploits to gain access to a company's networks and databases to non-tech tactics to steal laptops and whatever is available. Because infosec terms, such as threats and exploits, have precise meanings, the key terms and their meanings are listed in Table 5.1.

Controlling physical and remote access to proprietary systems and information continues to present IT security challenges. A vast majority of data breaches involve some sort of insider error or action, either intentional or unintentional. (These threats are discussed in Section 5.2.) Threats from employees, referred to as **internal threats,** are a major hurdle largely due to the huge number of ways available to an employee to carry out malicious activity. The following internal incidents could have been prevented if stringent infosec policies and defenses had been enforced. They also point out that victims of breaches are often third parties, such as customers, patients, social network users, credit card companies, and shareholders.

- In May 2006, the theft of a laptop during a home burglary of a Veterans Affairs employee cost taxpayers $100 million to remedy. See *IT at Work 5.1* for a description of the Department of Veterans Affairs data theft.
- In January 2007, TJX Companies disclosed that data from 100 million credit and debit cards had been stolen by hackers starting in July 2005. TJX's data heist was the largest breach ever to date, based on the number of records involved. Following the disclosure, banks said that tens of millions of dollars of fraudulent charges were made on the cards. The Massachusetts Bankers Association sued TJX for negligence. The FTC filed a complaint alleging TJX did not have the proper security measures in place

TABLE 5.1	IT Security Terms
Term	**Definition**
Threat	Something or someone that may result in harm to an asset
Vulnerability	Weakness that threatens the confidentiality, integrity, or availability of an asset
Risk	Probability of a threat exploiting a vulnerability
CIA triad (confidentiality, integrity, availability)	The three main principles of IT security
Risk management	Process of identifying, assessing, and reducing risk to an acceptable level
Exposure	The estimated cost, loss, or damage that can result if a threat exploits a vulnerability
Exploit	A tool or technique that takes advantage of a vulnerability
Access control	Security feature designed to restrict who has access to a network, IS, or data. Access to resources on a computer is restricted using a logical or physical control designed to protect against unauthorized entry or use
Countermeasure	Safeguard implemented to mitigate (lessen) risk
Audit	The process of generating, recording, and reviewing a chronological record of system events to ascertain their accuracy
Encryption	Transforming data into scrambled code to protect it from being understood by unauthorized users
Plaintext or clear-text	Readable text
Ciphertext	Encrypted text
Authentication	Method (usually based on username and password) by which an IS validates or verifies that a user is really who he or she claims to be
Malware	Malicious software, such as a virus, worm, or Trojan horse
Biometrics	Methods to identify a person based on a biological feature, such as a fingerprint
Perimeter security	Security measures to ensure that only authorized users gain access to the network
Endpoint security	Security measures to protect the *end points*, such as desktops and laptops, in the enterprise
Firewall	A method (hardware or software) of guarding a private network from a public network (Internet) by analyzing data packets entering or exiting it
Packet	A unit of data for transmission over a network with a *header* containing the source and destination of the packet
IP address (Internet Protocol address)	An address that uniquely identifies a specific computer or other device on a network
Public key infrastructure (PKI)	A system to identify and authenticate the sender or receiver of an Internet message or transaction
Intrusion detection system (IDS)	A defense tool used to monitor network traffic (packets) and provide alerts when there is suspicious traffic, or to quarantine suspicious traffic
Router	Device that transfers (routes) packets between two or more networks
Fault tolerance	The ability of an IS to continue to operate when a failure occurs, but usually for a limited time or at a reduced level
Backup	A duplicate copy of data or programs kept in a secured location
Spoofing	An attack carried out using a trick, disguise, deceit, or by falsifying data
Denial of service (DOS) or Distributed denial of service (DDOS)	An attack in which a system is bombarded with so many requests (for service or access) that it crashes or cannot respond
Zombie	An infected computer that is controlled remotely via the Internet by an unauthorized user, such as a spammer, fraudster, or hacker
Spyware	Stealth software that gathers information about a user or a user's online activity
Botnet (Bot network)	A network of hijacked computers that are controlled remotely—typically to launch spam or spyware. Also called software robots. Bot networks are linked to a range of malicious activity, including identity theft and spam.

IT at Work 5.1

$100 Million Data Breach at the U.S. Department of Veterans Affairs GOV IS

One of the largest single thefts of personal data occurred on May 3, 2006, when a laptop and external hard drive belonging to the U.S. Department of Veterans Affairs (VA) were stolen during a home burglary. The VA reported that data on 26.5 million veterans and spouses was stored in plaintext (not encrypted) on the laptop stolen from the home of a senior-level IT specialist. He had taken the laptop and data from the office to do after-hours work. The data included veterans' names, birthdates, and Social Security numbers. VA Secretary Jim Nicholson testified before Congress that it would cost at least $10 million to inform veterans of the security breach.

VA Ignored Risks and Failed to Enforce Security Policy. The VA's policy required all personnel to encrypt sensitive data, and it prohibited them from removing VA data from their offices. Employees either had not been informed of the policy, however, or they realized it was not being enforced. In fact, the IT specialist, who had access to sensitive information, admitted he had been taking data home since 2003.

After the Security Breach. To mitigate the VA's risks, Nicholson promised:

- To have all VA employees take cybersecurity and privacy training courses

- To increase background checks of employees with access to sensitive information
- To review data access controls to minimize employees' access to sensitive data

Despite the enormous cost of the VA's data breach, it may not scare companies into more rigorous security policy monitoring and training. Rick LeVine, a senior manager in Accenture's global security practice (a consulting company; *accenture.com*), predicted that "It's going to take several high-profile incidents at Fortune 500 companies to cause people to say, 'Oh, my God, one guy's cell phone can lose us a billion dollars'" (Spangler, 2006).

Sources: Condensed from Spangler (2006), and several articles from the *Washington Post* and *InformationWeek*, May–June 2006.

For Further Exploration: Could such a massive security breach happen at any company? Why or why not? Do you agree with LeVine's prediction? What prediction would you make?

to prevent unauthorized access to the sensitive, personal customer information. The total cost of the data breach was an estimated $197 million. To compare this cost to TJX's financials, see *finance.google.com/finance?fstype=ia&q=NYSE:TJX*.

- Three medical data breaches occurred in May 2008. Unauthorized peer-to-peer (P2P) file-sharing led to a data breach at Walter Reed Army Medical Center that exposed the personal data of 1,000 patients. Patients at Staten Island University Hospital in New York were told that a computer with their medical records was stolen. Information on patients of the University of California San Francisco Medical Center was accidentally made accessible on the Internet.

- In February 2008, security company Symantec (*symantec.com*) warned of a critical flaw in the ActiveX control of image uploaders, which had been distributed to Facebook and MySpace users. Hackers could exploit the flaw to install malicious code on users' computers and take control of them. As a result, the Canadian legal professionals filed charges accusing Facebook of 22 privacy violations. Facebook is coming under increased attack by spammers and phishers, according to the company's security chief.

- In June 2008, Microsoft warned Windows XP and Vista users who had installed Safari on their machines that they were at risk from a blended attack and malicious code.

- In January 2008, T. Rowe Price began notifying 35,000 clients that their names and Social Security numbers might have been compromised. The breach stemmed from the December 2007 theft of computers from the offices of a third-party services provider, which was preparing tax forms on behalf of T. Rowe Price.

- Names, e-mail and home addresses, and phone numbers of an estimated 1.6 million job seekers were accessed from *Monster.com's* résumé database in August 2007. Though widely described as a hacking, the data were actually accessed by attackers using legitimate usernames and passwords, possibly stolen from professional recruiters or human resources personnel who were using *Monster.com* to look for job candidates.

- In November 2007, the United Kingdom's tax agency disclosed that it had lost unencrypted disks containing personal data, bank details, and national ID numbers on 25 million juvenile benefits claimants. The disks disappeared in transit to the U.K. National

Audit Office. Analyst firm Gartner Inc. estimated that the closure of compromised accounts and establishment of new ones cost British banks about $500 million.

As the preceding examples illustrate, infosec breaches harm profitability and customer relations. Since January 2005, the Privacy Rights Clearinghouse has identified more than 215 million records belonging to U.S. residents that have been compromised due to a security breach. Plus, a 2007 study conducted by the Ponemon Institute determined that the total average cost for exposed data grew to $197 per compromised record, an 8 percent increase since 2006 and 43 percent increase since 2005.

INCREASING VULNERABILITY

Information resources are distributed throughout the organization and beyond because Internet and wireless technologies extend and connect organizational boundaries. The **time-to-exploitation** of today's most sophisticated spyware and mobile viruses has shrunk from months to days. Time-to-exploitation is the elapsed time between when a vulnerability is discovered and when it is exploited. IT staff have ever-shorter timeframes to find and fix flaws before being compromised by an attack.

New vulnerabilities are continuously being found in operating systems, applications, and wired and wireless networks. Microsoft, for example, releases **service packs** (see *support.microsoft.com/sp*) to update and patch vulnerabilities in its operating systems, including Vista, and other software products, including Office 2007. Left undetected or unprotected, vulnerabilities provide an open door for IT attacks—and business disruptions and their financial consequences. Despite even the best defenses, infosec incidents can still occur. For an example, read how UBS PaineWebber's business operations were shut down by malicious code planted by an employee in Online Minicase 5.1.

With data resources available on demand 24/7, companies benefit from the opportunities for productivity improvement and data sharing with customers, suppliers, and business partners in their supply chain. IT on demand is an operational and competitive necessity for global companies, but the vulnerabilities it creates require strong IT governance as described in *A Closer Look 5.1*.

GOVERNMENT REGULATION

Data must be protected against existing and future attack schemes, and defenses must satisfy ever-stricter government and international regulations. SOX, Gramm-Leach-Bliley Act (GLB), Federal Information Security Management Act (FISMA), and

A Closer Look 5.1

IT Governance Best Practices

ACC   FIN   HRM   IS   OM   ETHICS

Five IT governance requirements to maximize value and security of information assets are:

1. Align IT strategy with the business strategy.
2. Disseminate strategy, goals, and policies down into the enterprise.
3. Measure and monitor IT's performance.
4. Provide organizational structures that facilitate the implementation of strategy, goals, and policies.
5. Insist that an IT control framework be adopted, implemented, and enforced.

Addressing these issues is at the core of IT governance. To help organizations successfully meet business challenges and regulatory requirements, the IT Governance Institute (*itgi.org*) publishes *Control Objectives for Information and Related Technology* (COBIT). See *isaca.org* to download a copy of COBIT. COBIT 4.1, issued in July 2007, is an internationally applicable and accepted IT governance and control framework for aligning IT with business objectives,

delivering value, and managing associated risks. It provides a reference for management, users, and IS audit, control, and security practitioners. According to a 2008 PricewaterhouseCoopers survey, most IT executives are aware of best-practices frameworks like COBIT, but very few have enough IT staff to actually implement them.

One Sarbanes-Oxley Act (SOX) mandate is providing evidence that financial applications and supporting systems are secured so financial reports can be trusted. This requires that IT security managers work with business representatives to do a risk assessment to identify which systems depend on technical controls rather than on business process controls. All IT projects should have the same objectives, which are based on:

- The higher principle of economic use of resources (effectiveness and efficiency)
- The principle of legality (meets legal requirements)
- Accounting standards regulations, which are integrity, availability, and reliability

USA Patriot Act in the United States; Japan's Personal Information Protection Act; Canada's Personal Information Protection and Electronic Document Act (PIPEDA); Australia's Federal Privacy Act; the United Kingdom's Data Protection Act; and Basel II (global financial services) all mandate the protection of personal data. The director of the FTC's bureau of consumer protection warned that the agency would bring enforcement action against small businesses lacking adequate policies and procedures to protect consumer data.

INDUSTRY STANDARDS

Industry groups imposed their own standards to protect their customers and their members' brand images and revenues. One example is the **Payment Card Industry Data Security Standard (PCI DSS)** created by Visa, MasterCard, American Express, and Discover.

PCI is required for all members, merchants, or service providers that store, process, or transmit cardholder data. In June 2008, Section 6.6 of the PCI DSS went into full effect. In short, this section of PCI DSS requires merchants and card payment providers to make certain their Web applications are secure. If done correctly, it could actually help curb the number of Web-related security breaches. PCI DSS Section 6.6 mandates that retailers ensure that Web-facing applications are protected against known attacks by applying either of the following two methods:

1. Have all custom application code reviewed for vulnerabilities by an application security firm.

2. Install an application layer firewall in front of Web-facing applications. Each application will have its own firewall to protect against intrusions and malware.

The purpose of the PCI DSS is to improve customers' trust in e-commerce, especially when it comes to online payments, and to increase the Web security of online merchants. To motivate following these standards, the penalties for noncompliance are severe. The card brands can fine the retailer, and increase transaction fees for each credit or debit card transaction. A finding of noncompliance can be the basis for lawsuits.

CompTIA INFOSEC SURVEY

In its 2008 information security survey, the Computing Technology Industry Association (CompTIA, *comptia.org*), a nonprofit trade group, reported how companies in the United States, United Kingdom, Canada, and China are attempting to improve their infosec standards. Key findings are the following:

- Nearly 66 percent of U.S. firms, 50 percent of U.K. and Chinese firms, and 40 percent of Canadian firms have implemented written IT security policies.
- The percentage of IT budget that companies dedicate to security is growing year after year. In the United States, companies spent 12 percent of their 2007 IT budget for security purposes, up from 7 percent in 2005. The bulk of the budget was used to buy security-related technologies.
- About 33 percent of U.S. firms require that IT staff be certified in network and data security; in China, 78 percent of firms require IT security certification.

INFORMATION SYSTEMS BREAKDOWNS BEYOND COMPANY CONTROL

Some types of incidents are beyond a company's control. Uncertain events that can cause IS breakdowns, such as in the following incidents, require disaster recovery and business continuity plans (which are covered in Section 5.6):

Incident 1. Cybercriminals had launched an attack to extort money from StormPay, an online payment processing company. The attack shut down both of StormPay's data centers and its business for two days, causing financial loss and upsetting 3 million customers.

Incident 2. Lower Manhattan (see Figure 5.2) is the most communications-intensive real estate in the world. Many companies lacked off-site-based business continuity plans and permanently lost critical data about their employees, customers, and operations in the aftermath of the September 11 attacks. Mission-critical systems and

Figure 5.2 Lower Manhattan, the most communications-intensive real estate in the world. *(Photo courtesy of Verizon Communications. Used with permission.)*

Figure 5.3 Verizon's Central Office (CO) at 140 West St. harpooned by steel girders. *(Photo courtesy of Verizon Communications. Used with permission.)*

LEADING FACTORS IN INFOSEC INCIDENTS: MISTAKES, MALFUNCTIONS, MISUNDERSTANDINGS, AND MOTIVATION

networks were brought down. They also lost network and phone connectivity when 7 World Trade Center (WTC) collapsed and Verizon's central office (CO)—which was located at 140 West Street, directly across from the WTC—suffered massive structural damage. This CO, which was one of the largest and most complex telecommunications facilities in the world, was harpooned by huge steel girders, as shown in Figure 5.3. In all, 300,000 telephone lines and 3.6 million high-capacity data circuits served by that CO were put out of service.

These incidents illustrate the diversity of infosec problems, and the substantial damage that can be done to organizations anywhere in the world as a result.

Criminals use the Internet and private networks to hijack large numbers of PCs to spy on users, spam them, shake down businesses, and steal identities. But why are they so successful? The Information Security Forum (*securityforum.org*), a self-help organization that includes many Fortune 100 companies, compiled a list of the top information problems and discovered that nine of the top ten incidents were the result of three key factors:

- Mistakes (human error)
- Malfunctioning systems
- Misunderstanding the effects of adding incompatible software to an existing system

Unfortunately, these factors can often overcome the IT security technologies that companies and individuals use to protect their information. (We discuss security later in the chapter.) A fourth factor identified by the Security Forum is motivation, as described in *A Closer Look 5.2*.

As you have read throughout this book, business success depends on fast and easy access to accurate information—and keeping it protected. For e-commerce to survive, with its potential number and scope of customers, companies must invest in complex and expensive information management, identity management, and security management systems. IT security and internal control of this magnitude require an enterprisewide model, which is discussed next.

IT SECURITY AND INTERNAL CONTROL MODEL

Successful implementation of any IT project depends on the commitment and involvement of executive management, also referred to as the "tone at the top." The same is true of IT security. When senior management shows its commitment to IT security, it becomes important to others, too. It makes users aware that insecure practices and mistakes will not be tolerated. Therefore, an IT security and internal control model begins with senior management commitment and support, as shown in Figure 5.4. The

Figure 5.4 Enterprisewide information security and internal control model.

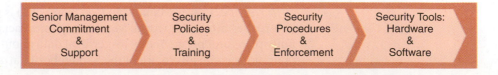

| Senior Management Commitment & Support | Security Policies & Training | Security Procedures & Enforcement | Security Tools: Hardware & Software |

A Closer Look 5.2

Money Laundering, Organized Crime, and Terrorist Financing

According to the U.S. Department of State (*state.gov*), transnational organized crime groups have long relied on money laundering to fund their operations. This practice poses international and national security threats because it corrupts government and corporate officials and sometimes entire legal systems. It undermines free enterprise by crowding out the private sector, and it threatens the financial stability of countries and the international free flow of capital.

Like money laundering, terrorist financing represents an exploitable vulnerability. In money laundering, transnational organized crime groups deliberately distance themselves from the actual crime, but they are never far from the eventual revenue stream. By contrast, funds used to finance terrorist operations are very difficult to track. Despite this obscurity, by adapting methods used to combat money laundering, such as financial analysis and investigations, authorities can significantly disrupt the financial networks of terrorists and build a paper trail and base of evidence to identify and locate leaders of terrorist organizations and cells.

International organized crime syndicates, al-Qaida groups, and other cybercriminals steal hundreds of billions of dollars every year. Cybercrime is safer and easier than selling drugs, dealing in black market diamonds, or robbing banks. Online gambling offers easy fronts for international money-laundering operations.

Sources: Compiled from the U.S. Department of State (2008), Altman (2006), and Wolfe (2006).

---

model views infosec as a combination of people, processes, and technology. We examine the four steps in this model below. For detailed practices and guidelines for insuring Internet security, see *Online Brief 5.1 Managing Internet Security*.

Step 1: Senior Management Commitment and Support. Senior managers' influence is needed to implement and maintain security, ethical standards, privacy practices, and internal control. The Committee of Sponsoring Organizations of the Treadway Commission (COSO) (*coso.org/key.htm*) defines **internal control** as a *process* designed to provide *reasonable* assurance of effective operations and reliable financial reporting. Internal control will be discussed in detail in Section 5.6.

Step 2: Security Policies and Training. The next step in building an effective IT security program is to develop security policies and provide training to ensure that everyone is aware of and understands them. The greater the understanding of how security affects production levels, customer and supplier relationships, revenue streams, and management's liability, the more security will be incorporated into business projects and proposals.

Most critical is an **acceptable use policy (AUP)** that informs users of their responsibilities. An AUP is needed for two reasons: (1) to prevent misuse of information and computer resources, and (2) to reduce exposure to fines, sanctions, and legal liability. To be effective, the AUP needs to define users' responsibilities, acceptable and unacceptable actions, and consequences of noncompliance. E-mail, Internet, and computer AUPs should be thought of as an extension of other corporate policies, such as those that address physical safety, equal opportunity, harassment, and discrimination. Survey results in *A Closer Look 5.3* illustrate the importance of AUP training and consent, particularly because of increased use of handheld devices.

The key findings from the CompTIA Research Survey released in April 2008 are the following:

• Infosec is seen as a key risk among firms, with 80% of US respondents indicating that it is considered top priority by management. Nearly two-thirds of US firms, more than half of UK and Chinese firms, and two-fifths of Canadian firms have implemented written IT security policies.

• The most widespread threats in the United States stem from spyware, the lack of user awareness, and virus and worm attacks. Canadian organizations indicate riskier browser-based attacks and wireless networking security. Chinese organizations indicate significant threats from spyware, viruses, worms, and browser-based attacks.

• The percentage of their IT budget that companies dedicate to security is growing. In the United States, companies allocated 12% of their IT budget in 2007 for security purposes—up from only 7% in 2005.

A Closer Look 5.3

Mobile Workers and Handheld Devices

CompTIA commissions major research projects on infosec and the workforce. Their 2007 study indentified new threats coming from remote and mobile worker, and the unique set of security challenges that these workers pose to organizations. A majority of the organizations surveyed said handheld devices and wireless networks for data access and transfer have increased security risks.

The increasing pervasiveness of remote access to confidential data and applications by mobile employees and wireless networks creates vulnerabilities. Each remote connection or access point is another potential security vulnerability that must be secured. The survey also revealed a change in priorities from pro-

tecting sensitive data from attack by outsiders to addressing internal threats. Nearly 80 percent cited the human factor as the root cause for information security failures. That result is not surprising given that only 32 percent of companies that allow data access by remote or mobile employees have implemented security awareness training programs for these employees.

Sources: Compiled from Venator (2007) and Westervelt (2007).

For Further Exploration: What are some reasons why employees do not follow internal security policies and procedures? How can they be motivated to diligently follow AUPs and security procedures?

Companies spend substantial amounts on prevention because security breaches can be costly if they occur. In the past year, US firms shelled out an average of over $200,000 as a result of security breaches, a third of which was attributed to the loss of employee productivity. Moreover, in the last year in the US, Canada and UK, IT staff members spent over 10% of their time dealing with security breaches, and in China, almost 20% of their time.

Step 3: Security Procedures and Enforcement. If users' activities are not monitored for compliance, the AUP is useless. Therefore, the next step is to implement monitoring procedures, training, and enforcement of the AUP. Businesses cannot afford the infinite cost of perfect security, so they calculate the proper level of protection. The calculation is based on the digital assets' risk exposure. The risk exposure model for digital assets is comprised of the five factors shown in Table 5.2.

Another risk assessment method is the **business impact analysis (BIA).** BIA is an exercise that determines the impact of losing the support or availability of a resource. For example, for most people, the loss of a cell phone or car would have a greater impact than the loss of a digital camera. BIA helps identify the minimum resources needed to recover, and prioritizes the recovery of processes and supporting systems. A BIA needs to be updated as new threats to IT emerge. After the risk

FIN   **HRM**   **MKT**

TABLE 5.2	Risk Exposure Model for Digital Assets
Factor	**Cost and operational considerations**
1. Asset's value to the company	What are the costs of replacement, recovery, or restoration? What is the recoverability time?
2. Attractiveness of the asset to a criminal	What is the asset's value (on a scale of low to high) to identity thieves, industrial spies, terrorists, or fraudsters?
3. Legal liability attached to the asset's loss or theft	What are the potential legal costs, fines, and restitution expenses?
4. Operational, marketing, and financial consequences	What are the costs of business disruption, delivery delays, lost customers, negative media attention, inability to process payments or payroll, or a drop in stock prices?
5. Likelihood of a successful attack against the asset	Given existing and emerging threats, what is the probability the asset will be stolen or compromised?

exposure of digital assets has been estimated, then informed decisions about investments in infosec can be made.

Step 4: Security Tools: Hardware and Software. The last step in the model is implementation of software and hardware needed to support the policy and enforce secure practices. Keep in mind that security is an ongoing process and not a problem that can be solved with hardware or software tools. Hardware and software security defenses cannot protect against irresponsible business practices. For more information on the reasons for a multilayered security approach, read *Online Brief 5.2 Spyware: A Financial Assault Weapon*. We cover basic security hardware and software later in the chapter.

Review Questions

1. Why are cleanup costs after a single data breach or infosec incident in tens of millions of dollars?
2. Who are the potential victims of an organization's data breach?
3. What is time-to-exploitation? What is the trend in the length of such a time?
4. What is a service pack?
5. What are two causes of the top information problems at organizations?
6. What is an acceptable use policy (AUP)? Why do companies need an AUP?

5.2 IS Vulnerabilities and Threats

One of the biggest mistakes managers make is underestimating vulnerabilities and threats. Most workers use their PCs and laptops for both work and leisure, and in an era of multitasking, they often do both at the same time. Yet off-time or off-site use of personal computers remains risky because, despite years of policies designed to control them, employees continue to engage in dangerous surfing and communication habits that can make them a weak link in an organization's otherwise solid security efforts. These threats can be classified as *unintentional* or *intentional*.

UNINTENTIONAL THREATS

Unintentional threats fall into three major categories: human errors, environmental hazards, and computer system failures.

• **Human errors** play a role in many computer problems, as you have read. Errors can occur in the design of the hardware or information system. They can also occur in the programming, testing, data collection, data entry, authorization, and instructions. Not changing default passwords on a firewall creates a security hole. Human errors contribute to the majority of internal control and infosec problems.

• **Environmental hazards** include earthquakes, severe storms (e.g., hurricanes, blizzards, or sand), floods, power failures or strong fluctuations, fires (the most common hazard), defective air conditioning, explosions, radioactive fallout, and water-cooling-system failures. In addition to the primary damage, computer resources can be damaged by side effects, such as smoke and water. Such hazards may disrupt normal computer operations and result in long waiting periods and exorbitant costs while computer programs and data files are recreated.

• **Computer systems failures** can occur as the result of poor manufacturing, defective materials, and outdated or poorly maintained networks (recall the network crash at LAX in Chapter 4). Unintentional malfunctions can also happen for other reasons, ranging from lack of experience to inadequate testing.

INTENTIONAL THREATS

Examples of intentional threats include: theft of data; inappropriate use of data (e.g., manipulating inputs); theft of mainframe computer time; theft of equipment and/or programs; deliberate manipulation in handling, entering, processing, transferring, or programming data; labor strikes, riots, or sabotage; malicious damage to computer resources; destruction from viruses and similar attacks; and miscellaneous computer abuses and Internet fraud. See *Online Brief 5.3 VoIP Security Alert: Hackers Attack for Cash* for an example. The scope of intentional threats can be against an entire country or economy. Defenses against the possibility of *cyberattacks* by some countries against others are identified in *A Closer Look 5.4*.

Intentional crimes carried out on the Internet are called cybercrimes (also discussed later). **Hacker** is the term often used to describe someone who gains unauthorized access to a computer system. *Black-hat hackers*, also referred to as crackers, are criminals. A **cracker** is a *malicious hacker,* who may represent a serious problem for a corporation.

Hackers and crackers may involve unsuspecting insiders in their crimes. In a strategy called **social engineering,** criminals or corporate spies trick insiders into giving them information or access that they should not have. Social engineering is a collection of tactics used to manipulate people into performing actions or divulging confidential information. Notorious hacker Kevin Mitnick, who served time in jail for hacking, used social engineering as his primary method to gain access to computer networks. In most cases, the criminal never comes face-to-face with the victim, but communicates via the phone or e-mail.

Not all hackers are malicious, however. *White-hat hackers* perform ethical hacking, such as performing penetrating tests on their clients' systems or searching the Internet to find the weak points so they can be fixed. White-hat hacking by Finjan, an information security vendor, for example, led to the discovery of a **crime server** in Malaysia in April 2008, as described in *A Closer Look 5.5*. A crime server is a server used to store stolen data for use in committing crimes. Finjan discovered the crime server while running its real-time code inspection technology to diagnose customers' Web traffic.

METHODS OF ATTACK ON COMPUTING FACILITIES

There are many methods of attack, and new ones appear regularly. In this section, we look at some of these methods. Two basic approaches are used in deliberate attacks on computer systems: data tampering and programming attack.

Data tampering is a common means of attack that is overshadowed by other types of attacks. It refers to an attack when someone enters false, fabricated, or fraudulent data into a computer, or changes or deletes existing data. Data tampering is extremely serious because it may not be detected. This is the method often used by insiders and fraudsters.

Programming attacks are popular with computer criminals who use programming techniques to modify other computer programs. For these types of crimes, programming skill and knowledge of the targeted systems are needed. Examples are

A Closer Look 5.4

Global IT Security Efforts

Most countries are updating laws and regulations to protect networked information.

- In May 2006, Transport and Communication Minister Christopher Mushowe announced the government of Zimbabwe would pass legislation to curb cybercrime in the country in view of its increasing threat to world economies.

- Zhang Changsheng, Vice President of China Netcom, stated that China Netcom would play an active role in a series of countermeasures, including regulation on SMS and mobile services,

registration of mobile phone users' legal names, cleaning up Internet domain names, and elimination of spam.

- In 2006, the U.S. Department of Homeland Security (DHS) launched *Cyber Storm*, the first wide-scale government-led IT security exercise to examine response, coordination, and recovery mechanisms in simulated cyberattacks against critical infrastructures. One of the exercise scenarios simulated a breach against a utility company's computer systems, causing numerous disruptions to the power grid. The exercise was done to show the interconnectivity between computer and physical infrastructures.

A Closer Look 5.5

1.4 Gigabytes of Stolen Data and E-Mail Found on Crime Server

In April 2008, Finjan Software researchers found compromised data from patients, bank customers, business e-mail messages, and Outlook accounts on a Malaysia-based server, which has since been shut down. Data included usernames, passwords, account numbers, social security and credit card numbers, patient data, business-related e-mail communications, and captured Outlook accounts containing e-mails. The stolen data were all less than one month old, and consisted of 5,388 unique log files from around the world. The server had been running for three weeks before it was found. Data were stolen from victims in the United States, Germany, France, India, England, Spain, Canada, Italy, the Netherlands, and Turkey. More than 5,000 customer records from 40 international financial institutions were stolen.

Dubbed a *crime server,* it held more than 1.4 gigabytes of business and personal data stolen from computers infected with Trojan horses. While gathering data, it was also a *command and control server* for the malware (also called crimeware) that ran on the infected PCs. The command and control applications enabled the hacker to manage the actions and performance of the crimeware, giving him control over the uses of the crimeware and its victims. Since the crime server's stolen data were left without any access restrictions or encryption, the data were freely available for anyone on the Web.

This was not an isolated situation. Two other crime servers holding similar information were found and turned over to law enforcement for investigation.

Sources: Compiled from Higgins (2008) and McGlasson (2008).

---

viruses, worms, and Trojan horses, which are types of malicious code, called **malware.** Programming attacks appear under many names, as shown in *Online Brief 5.3.* Several of the methods were designed for Web-based systems. Malware can be used to launch **denial of service (DoS) attacks.** A DoS attack occurs when a server or Web site receives a flood of traffic—much more traffic or requests for service than it can handle, causing it to crash.

Malware. Malware is any unwanted software that exploits flaws in other software to gain illicit access. In 2007, malware fundamentally changed as criminals used the Internet as the primary attack vector for infecting computers. As more companies defended their e-mail **gateways** against intruders with stronger security mechanisms, cybercriminals shifted their efforts to planting malware on insecure Web sites, waiting for visitors, and then infecting them. A gateway is a network access point that acts as an entrance to other networks.

In the past, virus writers were typically motivated by fame or mischief, but today's attacks are organized attacks designed to steal data and resources from the computers of victims for profit. The scale of their global criminal operations is so extensive that computer security company Sophos (sophos.*com*) discovers a new infected Web page every 14 seconds—24 hours a day, 365 days a year.

Virus. A universal attack method is the **virus,** which is computer code (program). It receives its name from the program's ability to attach itself to and infect other computer programs, without the owner of the program being aware of the infection, as shown in Figure 5.5. When the infected software is used, the virus spreads, causing damage to that program and possibly to others.

Worm. Unlike a virus, a **worm** spreads without any human intervention, such as checking e-mail or transmitting files. Worms use networks to propagate and infect anything attached to them—including computers, handheld devices, Web sites, and servers. Worms can spread via instant or text messages. Worms' ability to self-propagate through a network can clog and degrade a network's performance, including the Internet.

Trojan horse or RAT. Trojans horses are referred to as backdoors because they give the attacker illegal access to a network or account through a **network port.** A network port is a physical interface for communication between a computer and other

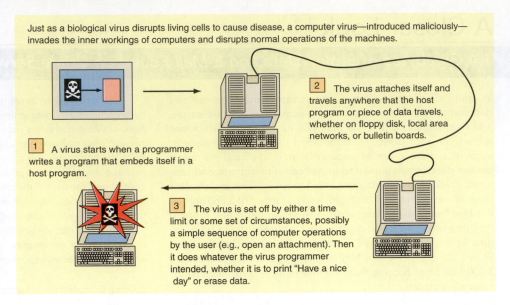

Just as a biological virus disrupts living cells to cause disease, a computer virus—introduced maliciously—invades the inner workings of computers and disrupts normal operations of the machines.

1. A virus starts when a programmer writes a program that embeds itself in a host program.

2. The virus attaches itself and travels anywhere that the host program or piece of data travels, whether on floppy disk, local area networks, or bulletin boards.

3. The virus is set off by either a time limit or some set of circumstances, possibly a simple sequence of computer operations by the user (e.g., open an attachment). Then it does whatever the virus programmer intended, whether it is to print "Have a nice day" or erase data.

Figure 5.5 How a computer virus can spread.

devices on a network. **Remote administration Trojans (RATs)** are a class of backdoors that enable remote control over the compromised (infected) machine. The crime server discussed in *A Closer Look 5.5* involved RAT-infected computers for stealth data collection. RATs open a network port on a victim computer giving the attacker control over it. Infected PCs are also called *zombies* or *bots*.

A Trojan horse attaches itself to a zombie's operating system and always has two files, the client file and the server file. The server, as its name implies, is installed in the infected machine while the client is used by the intruder to control the compromised system. Trojan horse functions include managing files on the zombied PC, managing processes, remotely activating commands, intercepting keystrokes, watching screen images, and restarting and closing down infected hosts. Common Trojans are NetBus, Back Orifice (BO) 2000, SubSeven, and Hack'a'tack.

BOTNETS

A botnet is a collection of bots (computers infected by software robots). Those infected computers, called zombies, can be controlled and organized into a network of zombies on the command of a remote botmaster (also called bot herder). Storm worm, which is spread via spam, is the most prevalent botnet agent and is embedded inside up to 25 million computers. Storm's combined power has been compared to the processing might of a supercomputer, and Storm-organized attacks are reputed to be capable of crippling any Web site.

Botnets expose infected computers, as well as other network computers, to the following threats (Edwards, 2008):

- **Spyware:** Zombies can be commanded to monitor and steal personal or financial data.
- **Adware:** Zombies can be ordered to download and display advertisements. Some zombies even force an infected system's browser to visit a specific Web site.
- **Spam:** Most junk email is sent by zombies. Owners of infected computers are usually blissfully unaware that their machines are being used to commit a crime.
- **Phishing:** Zombies can seek out weak servers that are suitable for hosting a phishing Web site, which looks like a legitimate Web site, to trick the users into inputting confidential data.
- **DoS Attacks:** Perhaps the most ominous botnet threat, and the one that's toughest to counter, is one in which infected computers are rounded up and commanded to overload and cripple a targeted Web site.

The combined power of botnets can scan for and compromise other computers, and then be used for every type of crime and attack against computers, servers, and networks.

MALWARE DEFENSES

Since malware and botnets use many attack methods and strategies, multiple tools are needed to detect them and/or neutralize their effects. Three essential defenses are the following:

1. **Anti-Malware Technology:** Anti-malware tools are designed to detect malicious codes and prevent users from downloading them. They can also scan systems for the presence of worms, Trojan horses, and other types of threats. This technology does not provide complete protection because it cannot defend against *zero-day exploits*. Zero-day refers to the day the exploits hit the Internet. Anti-malware may not be able to detect a previously unknown exploit.

2. **Intrusion Detection Systems (IDS):** As the name implies, an IDS scans for unusual or suspicious traffic. An IDS can identify the start of a DoS attack by the traffic pattern, alerting the network administrator to take defensive action, such as switching to another IP address and diverting critical servers from the path of the attack.

3. **Intrusion Prevention Systems (IPS):** An IPS is designed to take immediate action—such as blocking specific IP addresses—whenever a traffic-flow anomaly is detected. ASIC (application-specific integrated circuit)-based IPS have the power and analysis capabilities to detect and block DoS attacks, functioning somewhat like an automated circuit breaker.

Lavasoft offers free software, called Ad-Aware, to identify and remove Trojans and other infections at *lavasoft.com*. Their Web site also provides news about current malware threats.

In the next section, we discuss crime—specifically fraud, which is also known as white-collar crime, and computer crime. Companies suffer tremendous loss from occupational fraud. It is a widespread problem that affects every company, regardless of size, location, or industry. The FBI has labeled fraud one of the fastest growing crimes.

Review Questions

1. Define and give three examples of an unintentional threat.
2. Define and give three examples of an intentional threat.
3. What is social engineering? Give an example.
4. What is a crime server?
5. What are the risks from data tampering?
6. List and define three types of malware.
7. Define botnet and explain its risk.
8. Explain the difference between an IDS and an IPS.

5.3 Fraud and Computer-Mediated Crimes

Crime can be divided into two categories: violent crime and nonviolent crime. Fraud is nonviolent crime. Instead of a gun or knife, fraudsters use deception, confidence, and trickery. Fraudsters carry out their crime by abusing the power of their position or taking advantage of the trust of others. While statistics show that violent crime is down, fraud is at an all-time high and shows no signs of diminishing.

Computer crimes appear frequently and with novel names that quickly become part of our everyday vocabulary. For example, spyware researchers at Webroot Software had uncovered a stash of tens of thousands of stolen identities from 125 countries that they believe were collected by a new variant of a Trojan program the company named Trojan-Phisher-Rebery. Rebery is an example of a banking Trojan, which is programmed to come to life when users visit one of a number of online banking or e-commerce sites. Without strong defenses—including AUP and secure procedures—e-commerce can lose a lot of customers. Next, we discuss the most common and devastating types of fraud and computer crimes.

FRAUD

When a person uses his or her occupation for personal gain through deliberate misuse of the organization's resources or assets, it is called **occupational fraud.** Examples of occupational fraud are listed in Table 5.3.

Internal audits and internal controls (covered later in the chapter) are critical to the prevention and detection of occupation frauds. High-profile examples of occupational fraud committed by senior executives during the early 2000s that led to increased government and SEC regulation, such as SOX, include the following:

- **Adelphia.** A year after the public learned of the $600 million Enron scandal, several chief executive officers of Adelphia, including John Rigas and Tim Rigas, made Enron's fraud look small. The SEC uncovered the misappropriation and theft of tens of billions of dollars by some of Adelphia's chief executives. In addition to the $2.3 billion that was stolen from the company, the fraud caused losses to investors of more than $60 billion.

- **Global Crossing.** Corporate insiders knowingly sold more than $1.5 billion of artificially inflated company stock. In April 2005, the SEC filed a settled action for civil penalties against Global Crossing's former CEO, CFO, and VP of Finance for aiding and abetting the fraud. Each executive agreed to pay a $100,000 civil penalty.

- **Tyco.** In 2003, the SEC charged former CEO Dennis Kozlowski, CFO Swartz, and Chief Corporate Counsel Mark Belnick with many counts of fraud. Kozlowski and Swartz had swindled over $170 million in corporate loans and pocketed $430 million by manipulating the company's stock price. Belnick was indicted for falsifying business records to hide $17 million in loans given to him by Tyco.

INTERNAL FRAUD PREVENTION AND DETECTION

IT has a key role to play in demonstrating good corporate governance and fraud prevention. Regulators look favorably on companies that can demonstrate good corporate governance and best practice operational risk management. Management and

TABLE 5.3	Types of Organizational Fraud	
Type of fraud	**Financial statement fraud?**	**Typical characteristics**
Operating management corruption	No	Occurs *off the books*. Median loss due to corruption: over 6 times greater than median loss due to misappropriation ($530,000 vs. $80,000)
Conflict of interest	No	A breach of confidentiality, such as revealing competitors' bids; often occurs with bribery
Bribery	No	Uses positional power or money to influence others
Embezzlement or "misappropriation"	No	Employee theft: employees' access to company property creates the opportunity for embezzlement
Senior management financial reporting fraud	Yes	Involves a massive breach of trust and leveraging of positional power
Accounting cycle fraud	Yes	"Earnings management" in violation of GAAP (Generally Accepted Accounting Principles); see *aicpa.org*

staff of such companies will then spend less time worrying about regulations and more time adding value to their brand and business.

Internal fraud prevention measures are based on the same controls used to prevent external intrusions—perimeter defense technologies, such as firewalls, e-mail scanners, and biometric access. They are also based on human resource (HR) procedures, such as recruitment screening and training.

Much of this detection activity can be handled by intelligent analysis engines using advanced data warehousing and analytics techniques. These systems take in audit trails from key systems and personnel records from the human resources and finance departments. The data are stored in a data warehouse where they are analyzed to detect anomalous patterns, such as excessive hours worked, deviations in patterns of behavior, copying huge amounts of data, attempts to override controls, unusual transactions, and inadequate documentation about a transaction. Information from investigations is fed back into the detection system so that it learns. Since insiders might work in collusion with organized criminals, insider profiling is important to find wider patterns of criminal networks.

ETHICS

An enterprisewide approach that combines risk, security, compliance, and IT specialists greatly increases the prevention and detection of fraud. Prevention is the most cost-effective approach, since detection and prosecution costs are enormous in addition to the direct cost of the loss. It starts with corporate governance culture and ethics at the top levels of the organization.

| **IDENTITY THEFT**

One of the worst and most prevalent crimes is identity theft. Such thefts where individuals' Social Security and credit card numbers are stolen and used by thieves are not new. Criminals have always obtained information about other people—by stealing wallets or dumpster digging. But widespread electronic sharing and databases have made the crime worse. Because financial institutions, data processing firms, and retail businesses are reluctant to reveal incidents in which their customers' personal financial information may have been stolen, lost, or compromised, laws continue to be passed that force those notifications. Examples in Table 5.4 illustrate different ways in which identity crimes have occurred.

Furthermore, computer criminals do not need IT skills to steal a laptop (recall the VA employee's home robbery), cell, or PDA, or find one that was left behind. Therefore, unencrypted sensitive data on laptops or handheld devices that leave the office increase the risk.

TABLE 5.4	Examples of Identity Crimes Requiring Notification	
How it happened	**Number of individuals notified**	**Description**
Stolen desktop	3,623	Desktop computer was stolen from regional sales office containing data that was password protected, but not encrypted. Thieves stole SSNs and other information from TransUnion LLC, which maintains personal credit histories.
Online, by an ex-employee	465,000	Former employee downloaded information about participants in Georgia State Health Benefits Plan.
Computer tapes lost in transit	3.9 million	CitiFinancial, the consumer finance division of Citigroup Inc., lost tapes containing information about both active and closed accounts while they were being shipped to a credit bureau.
Online "malicious user" used legitimate user's login information	33,000	The U.S. Air Force suffered a security breach in the online system containing information on officers and enlisted airmen, and personal information.
Missing backup	200,000 tape	A timeshare unit of Marriott International Inc. lost a backup tape containing SSNs and other confidential data of employees and timeshare owners and customers.

**TOP CYBER SECURITY
MENACES**

The SANS (SysAdmin, Audit, Networking, and Security) Institute publishes a yearly list of the top 10 cybersecurity threats. The list for 2008 includes new exploitations of browser vulnerabilities; worms with advanced P2P (peer-to-peer) technologies; and insider attacks by rogue employees, consultants or contractors. Twelve cyber security experts worked together to compile the following list of the attacks most likely to cause substantial damage during 2008 (see *sans.org/ 2008menaces*).

1. Increasingly Sophisticated Web Site Attacks that Exploit Browser Vulnerabilities—Especially on Trusted Web Sites. Web site attacks on browsers are targeting components, such as Flash and QuickTime, that are not automatically patched when the browser is patched. Also, Web site attacks are more sophisticated attacks that can disguise their destructive payloads (the malicious part of the malware). Attackers are putting exploit code on popular, trusted Web sites that visitors believe are secure. Putting hidden attack tools on trusted sites gives attackers a huge advantage.

2. Increasing Sophistication and Effectiveness in Botnets. Storm worm, which was not a worm, began spreading in January 2007 with an e-mail saying, "230 dead as storm batters Europe," and was followed by subsequent variants. Within a week, it accounted for one out of every twelve infections on the Internet, installing **rootkits** (sets of network administration tools to take control of the network) and making each infected system a member of a new type of botnet. Previous botnets used centralized command and control; the Storm worm used peer-to-peer (P2P) networks to launch (control) the attack, so there is no central controller to take down to stop it. New variants and increasing sophistication will keep Storm worm and other even more sophisticated worms as serious threats.

3. Cyber Espionage Efforts by Well-Resourced Organizations Looking to Extract Large Amounts of Data, and Phishing. One of the biggest security stories of 2007 was disclosure of massive penetration of federal agencies and defense contractors and theft of terabytes of data. Economic espionage will increase as nations steal data to gain economic advantage in multinational deals. The attack involves targeted phishing with attachments, using social engineering methods so the victim trusts the attachment.

4. Mobile Phone Threats, Especially against iPhones and VoIP. Mobile phones are general purpose computers so they are targeted by malware. A mobile platform is also a platform for unforeseen security risks. The developer toolkits provide easy access for hackers. Vulnerabilities of VoIP phones and attack tools that exploit those vulnerabilities have been published on the Internet.

5. Insider Attacks. Insiders have a significant head start in attacks that they can launch. Insider-related risk as well as outsider risk has skyrocketed. Organizations need to put into place substantial defenses against this kind of risk, one of the most basic of which is limiting access according to what users need to do their jobs.

6. Advanced Identity Theft from Persistent Bots. A new generation of identity theft is being powered by bots that stay on machines for three to five months collecting passwords, bank account information, surfing history, frequently used email addresses, and more. They will gather enough data for advanced identify theft until criminals have enough data to pass basic security checks.

7. Increasingly Malicious Spyware. Criminals and nations continue to improve the capabilities of their malware. Additionally, some of Storm variants are able to detect investigators' activity and respond with a DoS attack against the investigators, making investigation more difficult. Advanced tools will resist anti-virus, anti-spyware, and anti-rootkit tools to help preserve the attacker's control of a victim machine. In short, malware will become stickier on target machines and more difficult to shut down.

8. Web Application Security Exploits. Large percentages of Web sites have vulnerabilities resulting from programming errors. Adding to the risk exposure are Web 2.0 applications that are vulnerable because user-supplied data (which could have been supplied by hackers or others with malicious intent) cannot be trusted. In 2008, web attacks will increase because of the exposure created by Web 2.0 vulnerabilities and programming errors.

9. Increasingly Sophisticated Social Engineering Including Blending Phishing with VoIP and Event Phishing. Blended approaches will increase the impact of common attacks. For example, the success of phishing is increased by first stealing users' IDs. A second area of blended phishing combines e-mail and VoIP. An inbound e-mail, disguised to look as though it was by a legitimate credit card company, asks recipients to re-authorize their credit cards by calling a 1-800 number. The number leads them via VoIP to an automated system in a foreign country that asks that they key in their credit card information.

10. Supply Chain Attacks Infecting Devices (e.g., thumb drives and GPS) Distributed by Trusted Organizations. Retailers are becoming unwitting distributors of malware. Devices with USB connections and CDs packaged with them sometimes contain malware that infect victims' computers and connect them into botnets. Even more targeted attacks using the same technique are starting to hit conference attendees who are given USB thumb drives and CDs that supposedly contain just the conference papers, but also contain malicious software.

There is a growing tendency for workers to blur their personal and professional lives. For example, they are surfing social networking sites or IMing with friends while at work. And they are accessing corporate networks from hot spots while on vacation. These are very dangerous trends.

Review Questions

> 1. Define fraud and occupational fraud. Give two examples of each.
> 2. Explain why data on laptops and computers should be encrypted.
> 3. What is a rootkit? Explain why hackers use them.
> 4. Why are Web 2.0 applications vulnerable?
> 5. Why is spyware expected to grow more malicious?

5.4 IT Security Management Practices

The objective of IT security management practices is to defend all of the components of an information system, specifically data, software applications, hardware, and networks. Before they make any decisions concerning defenses, people responsible for security must understand the requirements and operations of the business, which form the basis for a customized defense strategy. In the next section, we describe the major defense strategies.

DEFENSE STRATEGY

The defense strategy and controls that should be used depend on what needs to be protected and the cost-benefit analysis. That is, companies should neither underinvest nor overinvest. The SEC and FTC impose huge fines for data breaches to deter companies from underinvesting in data protection. The following are the major objectives of defense strategies:

1. Prevention and deterrence. Properly designed controls may prevent errors from occurring, deter criminals from attacking the system, and, better yet, deny access to unauthorized people. These are the most desirable controls.

2. Detection. Like a fire, the earlier an attack is detected, the easier it is to combat, and the less damage is done. Detection can be performed in many cases by using special diagnostic software, at a minimal cost.

3. Containment (contain the damage). This objective is to minimize or limit losses once a malfunction has occurred. It is also called damage control. This can be accomplished, for example, by including a *fault-tolerant system* that permits operation in a degraded mode until full recovery is made. If a fault-tolerant system does not exist,

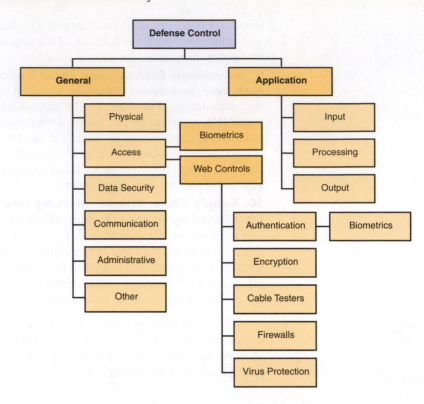

Figure 5.6 Major defense controls.

a quick (and possibly expensive) recovery must take place. Users want their systems back in operation as fast as possible.

4. Recovery. A recovery plan explains how to fix a damaged information system as quickly as possible. Replacing rather than repairing components is one route to fast recovery.

5. Correction. Correcting the causes of damaged systems can prevent the problem from occurring again.

6. Awareness and compliance. All organization members must be educated about the hazards and must comply with the security rules and regulations.

A defense strategy is also going to require several controls, as shown in Figure 5.6. **General controls** are established to protect the system regardless of the specific application. For example, protecting hardware and controlling access to the data center are independent of the specific application. **Application controls** are safeguards that are intended to protect specific applications. In the next two sections, we discuss the major types of these two groups of information systems controls.

GENERAL CONTROLS

The major categories of general controls are physical controls, access controls, data security controls, communication network controls, and administrative controls.

Physical Controls. Physical security refers to the protection of computer facilities and resources. This includes protecting physical property such as computers, data centers, software, manuals, and networks. It provides protection against most natural hazards as well as against some human hazards. Appropriate physical security may include several controls such as the following:

- Appropriate design of the data center (for example, the site should be noncombustible and waterproof)
- Shielding against electromagnetic fields
- Good fire prevention, detection, and extinguishing systems, including sprinkler system, water pumps, and adequate drainage facilities

- Emergency power shutoff and backup batteries, which must be maintained in operational condition
- Properly designed, maintained, and operated air-conditioning systems
- Motion detector alarms that detect physical intrusion

Access Control. Access control is the management of who is and is not authorized to use a company's hardware and software. Access control methods, such as firewalls and access control lists, restrict access to a network, database, file, or data. It is the major defense line against unauthorized insiders as well as outsiders. Access control involves authorization (having the right to access) and authentication, which is also called user identification (proving that the user is who he claims to be). Authentication methods include

- Something only the user *knows*, such as a password
- Something only the user *has*, for example, a smart card or a token
- Something only the user *is*, such as a signature, voice, fingerprint, or retinal (eye) scan; implemented via *biometric controls*, which can be physical or behavioral

Biometric Controls. A **biometric control** is an automated method of verifying the identity of a person, based on physical or behavioral characteristics. Most biometric systems match some personal characteristic against a prestored profile. The most common biometrics are:

- **Thumbprint or fingerprint.** Each time a user wants access, a thumb- or fingerprint (finger scan) is matched against a template containing the authorized person's fingerprint to identify him or her.
- **Retinal scan.** A match is attempted between the pattern of the blood vessels in the back-of-the-eye retina that is being scanned and a prestored picture of the retina.
- **Voice scan.** A match is attempted between the user's voice and the voice pattern stored on templates.
- **Signature.** Signatures are matched against the prestored authentic signature. This method can supplement a photo-card ID system.

Biometric controls are now integrated into many e-business hardware and software products. Biometric controls do have some limitations: they are not accurate in certain cases, and some people see them as an invasion of privacy.

Administrative Controls. While the previously discussed general controls are technical in nature, administrative controls deal with issuing guidelines and monitoring compliance with the guidelines. Examples of such controls are shown in Table 5.5.

TABLE 5.5	Representative Administrative Controls

- Appropriately selecting, training, and supervising employees, especially in accounting and information systems
- Fostering company loyalty
- Immediately revoking access privileges of dismissed, resigned, or transferred employees
- Requiring periodic modification of access controls (such as passwords)
- Developing programming and documentation standards (to make auditing easier and to use the standards as guides for employees)
- Insisting on security bonds or malfeasance insurance for key employees
- Instituting separation of duties, namely, dividing sensitive computer duties among as many employees as economically feasible in order to decrease the chance of intentional or unintentional damage
- Holding periodic random audits of the system

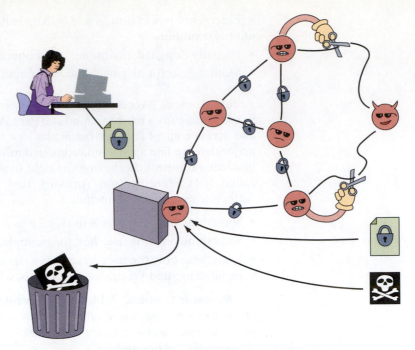

Figure 5.7 Intelligent agents.
(Source: Courtesy of Sandia National Laboratories.)

Agents in collective communicate over secured links on the Internet or an intranet. Malicious agents (with horns) are detected and cut off from the collective. Properly authenticated data is allowed into the collective, but bad information is rejected.

APPLICATION CONTROLS

Sophisticated attacks are aimed at the application level, and many applications were not designed to withstand such attacks. For better survivability, information-processing methodologies are being replaced with agent technology. **Intelligent agents,** also referred to as softbots or knowbots, are highly intelligent applications. The term generally means applications that have some degree of reactivity, autonomy, and adaptability—as is needed in unpredictable attack situations. An agent is able to adapt itself based on changes occurring in its environment, as shown in Figure 5.7.

In the next section, the focus is on the company's digital perimeter—the network. We discuss the security of wireline and wireless networks and their inherent vulnerabilities.

Review Questions

1. What are the major objectives of a defense strategy?
2. What are general controls? What are application controls?
3. Define access control.
4. What are biometric controls? Give four examples.
5. What is the general meaning of intelligent agents?

5.5 Network Security

As a defense, companies need to implement network access control (NAC) products. NAC tools are different from traditional security technologies and practices that focus on file access. While file-level security is useful for protecting data, it does not keep unauthorized users out of the network in the first place. NAC technology, on the other hand, helps businesses lock down their networks against criminals.

Network security measures involve three layers: *perimeter security* (access), *authentication,* and *authorization.* Details of these layers are shown in Figure 5.8. Some commercial products include security measures for all three levels—all in one product, e.g., WebShield from McAfee. Many security methods and products are available to protect the Web. We briefly describe the major ones in the following sections.

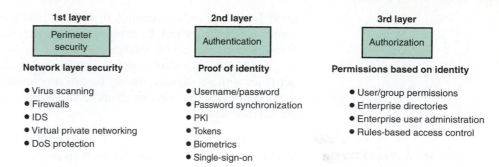

Figure 5.8 Three layers of network security measures.

PERIMETER SECURITY AND FIREWALLS

The major objective of perimeter security is access control, as seen in Figure 5.8. The technologies used to protect against malware (e.g., IDS and IDP) also protect the perimeter. Another technology is firewalls. A firewall is a system, or group of systems, that enforces an access-control policy between two networks. It is commonly used as a barrier between a secure corporate intranet or other internal networks and the Internet, which is unsecured. The firewall follows strict guidelines that either permit or block traffic; therefore, a successful firewall is designed with clear and specific rules about what can pass through. Several firewalls may exist in one information system. Useful as they are, firewalls do not stop viruses that may be lurking in networks. Viruses can pass through the firewalls, especially if they are hidden in an e-mail attachment.

All Internet traffic (i.e., packets) needs to pass through a firewall, but that is rarely the case for IM and wireless traffic, which, as a result, "carry" malware into the network and applications on host computers. Firewalls do not control anything that happens after a legitimate user (who may be a disgruntled employee or whose username and password have been compromised) has been authenticated and granted authority to access applications on the network. For these reasons, firewalls are a necessary, but insufficient defense.

NETWORK AUTHENTICATION AND AUTHORIZATION

As applied to the Internet, an authentication system guards against unauthorized access attempts. The major objective of authentication is the proof of identity (see Figure 5.8). The attempt here is to identify the legitimate user and determine the action he or she is allowed to perform.

Because phishing and identity theft prey on weak authentication, and usernames and passwords do not offer strong authentication, other methods are needed. There are **two-factor authentication** (also called multifactor authentication) and two-tier authentication. With two-factor authentication, other information is used to verify the user's identity, such as biometrics.

There are three key questions to ask when setting up an authentication system:

1. Who are you? Is this person an employee, a partner, or a customer? Different levels of authentication would be set up for different types of people.

2. Where are you? For example, an employee who has already used a badge to access the building is less of a risk than an employee or partner logging on remotely. Someone logging on from a known IP address is less of a risk than someone logging on from Nigeria or Kazakhstan.

3. What do you want? Is this person accessing sensitive or proprietary information or simply gaining access to benign data?

When dealing with consumer-facing applications, such as online banking and e-commerce, strong authentication must be balanced with convenience. If authentication makes it too difficult to bank or shop online, users will go back to the brick and mortars. There is a trade-off between increased protection and turning customers away from your online channel. In addition, authentication of a Web site to the customer is equally critical. E-commerce customers need to be able to identify if it is a fraudulent site set up by phishers.

Authorization refers to permission issued to individuals or groups to do certain activities with a computer, usually based on verified identity. The security system, once it authenticates the user, must make sure that the user operates within his or her authorized activities.

SECURING WIRELESS NETWORKS

Wireless networks are more difficult to protect than wireline ones. All of the vulnerabilities that exist in a conventional wireline network apply to wireless technologies. Wireless access points (APs or WAPs) behind a firewall and other security protections can be a backdoor into a network. Sensitive data that are not encrypted or that are encrypted with a weak cryptographic technique used for wireless, such as **wired equivalent privacy (WEP),** and that are transmitted between two wireless devices may be intercepted and disclosed. Wireless devices are susceptible to DoS attacks because intruders may be able to gain connectivity to network management controls and then disable or disrupt operations. Wireless packet analyzers, such as AirSnort and WEPcrack, are readily available tools putting wireless networks at great risk.

Unauthorized wireless APs could be deployed by malicious users—tricking legitimate users to connect to those rogue access points. Malicious users then gain access to sensitive information stored on client machines, including logins, passwords, customer information, and intellectual property.

Through war driving, malicious users can connect to an unsecured wireless AP and gain access to the network. See *A Closer Look 5.6* for details on war driving. Data can be extracted without detection from improperly configured devices. *Online Brief 5.3* also describes wireless and VoIP security. A schematic view of all major defense mechanisms, which protect against attackers of all types, is shown in Figure 5.9.

With an understanding of the vulnerabilities, risk exposure, and types of crimes committed with or against IT resources, we examine issues of great importance to executive management and the entire enterprise—internal control and compliance management.

Review Questions

1. What are network access control (NAC) products?
2. Define authentication, and give three examples of authentication methods.
3. Define authorization.
4. What is a firewall? What can it *not* protect against?
5. Define war driving and a resulting risk.

A Closer Look 5.6

War Driving

A number of people have also made a hobby or sport out of war driving. **War driving** is the act of locating wireless local area networks while driving around a city or elsewhere (see *wardriving.com*). To war drive, you need a vehicle, a computer or PDA, a wireless card, and some kind of an antenna that can be mounted on top of or positioned inside the car.

Because a WLAN (wireless local area network) may have a range that extends beyond the building in which it is located, an outside user may be able to intrude into the network, obtain a free Internet connection, and possibly gain access to important data and other resources.

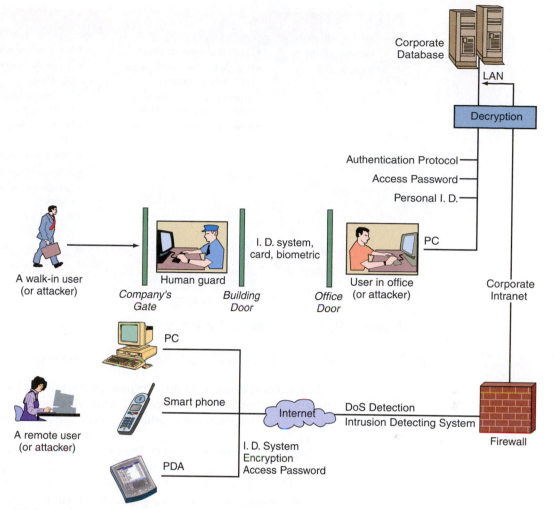

Figure 5.9 Where the defense mechanisms are located.

5.6 Internal Control and Compliance Management

The **internal control environment** is the work atmosphere that a company sets for its employees. *Internal control (IC)* is a process designed to achieve: (1) reliability of financial reporting, (2) operational efficiency, (3) compliance with laws, (4) regulations and policies, and (5) safeguarding of assets. Figure 5.10 illustrates how the role of IT in internal control has changed.

INTERNAL CONTROLS REQUIRED TO BE SOX COMPLIANT

SOX is an antifraud law. It forces better business reporting and disclosure of GAAP (generally accepted accounting principles) violations, thus making it necessary to find and root out fraud.

Section 302 deters corporate and executive fraud by requiring that the CEO and CFO verify that they have reviewed the financial report, and, to the best of their knowledge, the report does not contain an untrue statement or omit any material fact. To motivate honesty, executive management faces criminal penalties including long jail terms for false reports. Table 5.6 lists the symptoms, or red flags, of fraud that internal controls can be designed to detect.

Section 805 mandates a review of the Sentencing Guidelines to ensure that "the guidelines that apply to organizations . . . are sufficient to deter and punish organizational criminal conduct." The Guidelines also focus on the establishment of

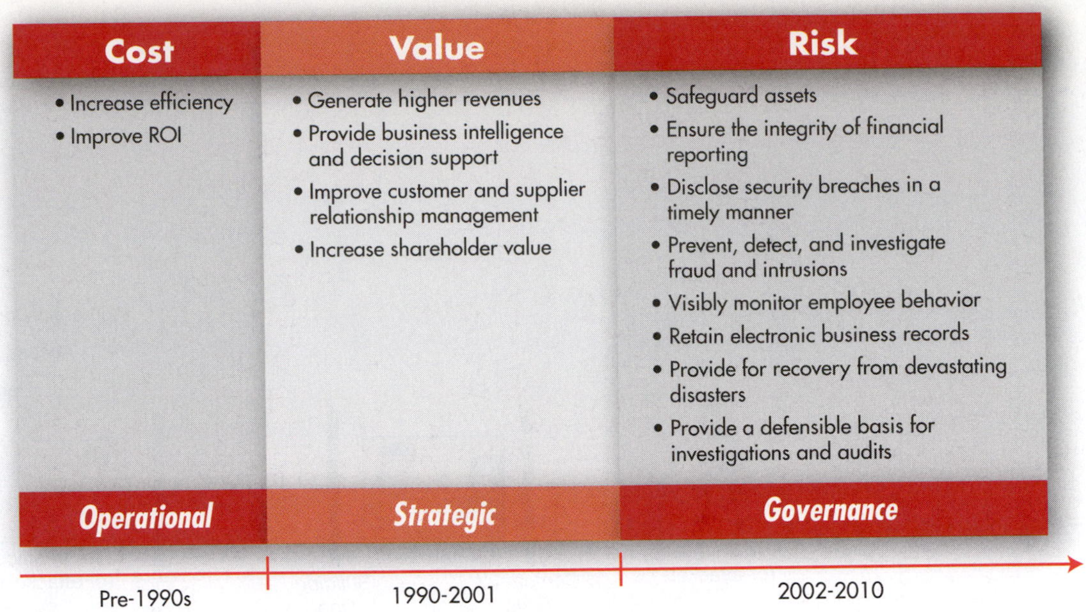

Cost	Value	Risk
• Increase efficiency • Improve ROI	• Generate higher revenues • Provide business intelligence and decision support • Improve customer and supplier relationship management • Increase shareholder value	• Safeguard assets • Ensure the integrity of financial reporting • Disclose security breaches in a timely manner • Prevent, detect, and investigate fraud and intrusions • Visibly monitor employee behavior • Retain electronic business records • Provide for recovery from devastating disasters • Provide a defensible basis for investigations and audits
Operational	*Strategic*	*Governance*
Pre-1990s	1990-2001	2002-2010

Figure 5.10 Increasing role of IT in internal control.

"effective compliance and ethics" programs. As indicated in the Guidelines, a precondition to an effective compliance and ethics program is promotion of "an organizational culture that encourages ethical conduct and a commitment to compliance with the law."

Among other measures, SOX requires companies to set up comprehensive internal controls. There is no question that SOX, and the complex and costly provisions it requires public companies to follow, has had a major impact on corporate financial accounting. For starters, companies have had to set up comprehensive internal controls over financial reporting to prevent fraud and catch it when it occurs. Since the collapse of Arthur Andersen, following the accounting firm's conviction on criminal charges related to the Enron case, outside accounting firms have gotten tougher with clients they are auditing, particularly regarding their internal controls.

SOX and the SEC are making it clear that if controls can be ignored, there is no control. Therefore, fraud prevention and detection require an effective monitoring system. If the company shows its employees that the company can find out everything that every employee does and use that evidence to prosecute that person to the fullest extent, then the feeling that "I can get away with it" drops drastically.

TABLE 5.6	Symptoms of Fraud That Can Be Detected by Internal Controls
Missing documents
Delayed bank deposits
Holes in accounting records
Numerous outstanding checks or bills
Disparity between accounts payable and receivable
Employees who do not take vacations or go out of their way to work overtime
A large drop in profits
A major increase in business with one particular customer
Customers complaining about double billing
Repeated duplicate payments
Employees with the same address or telephone number as a vendor

Approximately 85 percent of occupational fraud could have been prevented if proper IT-based internal controls had been designed, implemented, and followed.

SOX requires an enterprisewide approach to compliance, internal control, and risk management because they cannot be dealt with from a departmental or business-unit perspective. However, fraud also requires a worldwide approach, as many incidents have indicated, such as the crime server in Malaysia.

WORLDWIDE ANTI-FRAUD REGULATORS

Well-executed internal fraud or money-laundering operations can damage the financial sector, capital (money) markets, and, as a result, a nation's economy. A capital market is any market where a government or a company can raise money to finance operations and long-term investment. Examples are the stock and bond markets.

Preventing internal fraud is high on the political agenda, with the Financial Services Authority (FSA) in the United Kingdom and the SEC in the United States both requiring companies to deal with the issue. In May 2007, the FSA fined French investment bank BNP Paribas £350,000 for systems and control failures at its London-based private banking unit that allowed a senior manager to steal £1.4 million from client accounts (Reuters UK, 2007). It was the first time a private bank has been fined for weaknesses in antifraud systems by the FSA, which warned that it is "raising its game" against firms with lax controls.

There is also the Basel II Accord (named after Basel, Switzerland; also called the *Basel II Capital Accord*) that imposes rigorous antifraud requirements for banks. This Accord aims to promote enhanced risk-management practices among large, international banking organizations. For current issues on Basel II, see The Federal Reserve Bank at *federalreserve.gov/GeneralInfo/basel2/*. The Basel II Capital Accord provides guidance for managing operational risk and internal fraud. It recommends that any internal risk measurement system be consistent with the following seven types of potential losses:

1. Internal fraud
2. External fraud
3. Employment practices and workplace safety
4. Clients, products, and business practices
5. Damage to physical assets
6. Business disruption and systems failures
7. Execution, delivery, and process management

Managing risk has become the single most important issue for the regulators and financial institutions. Over the years, these institutions have suffered high costs for ignoring their exposure to risk. However, growing research and improvements in IT have improved the measurement and management of risk.

Review Questions

1. Define internal control.
2. What is the role of IT in internal control? (see Figure 5.10)
3. How does SOX Section 302 deter fraud?
4. List three symptoms or red flags of fraud that can be detected by internal controls.
5. What does the Basel II Accord recommend?

5.7 Business Continuity and Disaster Recovery Planning

Disasters may occur without warning. The best defense is to be prepared. Therefore, an important element in any security system is the **business continuity plan,** also known as the disaster recovery plan. Such a plan outlines the process by which businesses should recover from a major disaster. Destruction of all (or most) of the computing facilities can cause significant damage. Therefore, it is difficult for many organizations to obtain insurance for their computers and information systems

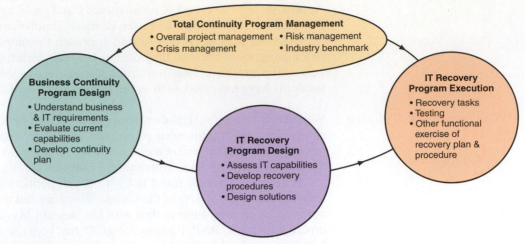

Figure 5.11 Business continuity services managed by IBM. *(Courtesy of IBM)*

without showing a satisfactory disaster prevention and recovery plan. The comprehensiveness of a business recovery plan is shown in Figure 5.11.

BUSINESS CONTINUITY PLANNING

Disaster recovery is the chain of events linking the business continuity plan to protection and to recovery. The following are some key thoughts about the process:

• The purpose of a business continuity plan is to keep the business running after a disaster occurs. Each function in the business should have a valid recovery capability plan.

• Recovery planning is part of *asset protection*. Every organization should assign responsibility to management to identify and protect assets within their spheres of functional control.

• Planning should focus first on recovery from a total loss of all capabilities.

• Proof of capability usually involves some kind of what-if analysis that shows that the recovery plan is current.

• All critical applications must be identified and their recovery procedures addressed in the plan.

• The plan should be written so that it will be effective in case of disaster, not just in order to satisfy the auditors.

• The plan should be kept in a safe place; copies should be given to all key managers, or it should be available on the intranet. The plan should be audited periodically.

Disaster recovery planning can be very complex, and it may take several months to complete. Using special software, the planning job can be expedited. See *IT at Work 5.2* for a discussion of the importance of business continuity and the ability to recover from a disaster.

Disaster Avoidance. **Disaster avoidance** is an approach oriented toward *prevention*. The idea is to minimize the chance of avoidable disasters (such as fire or other human-caused threats). For example, many companies use a device called *uninterrupted power supply* (UPS), which provides power in case of a power outage.

Review Questions

1. Why do organizations need a business continuity plan?
2. List three issues a business continuity plan should cover.
3. Identify two factors that influence a company's ability to recover from a disaster.
4. What types of devices are needed for disaster avoidance?
5. Explain why business continuity/disaster recovery (BC/DR) is not simply an IT security issue.

IT at Work 5.2

Business Continuity and Disaster Recovery

Ninety-three percent of companies that suffer a significant data loss die within five years, according to Freeman Mendel, the chair of the FBI's 2006 Infragard National Conference. Even though business continuity/disaster recovery (BC/DR) is a business survival issue, many managers have dangerously viewed BC/DR as an IT security issue.

Disasters teach the best lessons for both IT managers and corporate executives who have not implemented BC/DR processes. The success or failure of those processes depends on IT, as the following case indicates.

The city of Houston, Texas, and Harris County swung into action by turning Reliant Park and the Houston Astrodome into a "temporary city" with a medical facility, pharmacy, post office, and town square to house more than 250,000 hurricane Katrina evacuees. Coast Guard Lt. Commander Joseph J. Leonard headed up the operation, drawing on his knowledge of the National Incident Command System. As Leonard explained, ineffective communication between the command staff and those in New Orleans, who could have informed Houston authorities about the number and special needs of the evacuees, caused a serious problem. In addition, agencies and organizations with poor on-scene decision-making authority hampered and slowed efforts to get things done.

Now businesses in hurricane alleys, earthquake corridors, and major cities are deploying BC/DR plans supported with software tools that allow them to replicate, or back up, their mission-critical applications to sites away from their primary data centers. In case of a disaster, companies can transmit vital accounting, project management, or transactional systems and records to their disaster recovery facilities, limiting downtime and data loss despite an outage at the primary location.

Globally, regulators are increasingly paying closer attention to business continuity and recovery times, which are now measured in hours rather than days. The Australian Prudential Regulation Authority (APRA) released its prudential standard on business continuity in April 2005. APRA gave Australian firms only 12 months to fix their compliance gaps.

Sources: Compiled from Fagg (2006), *Fiber Optics Weekly* (2006), and the Infragard (*infragardconferences.com*).

For Further Exploration: Why might a company that had a significant data loss not be able to recover? Why are regulators requiring that companies implement BC/DR plans?

5.8 Auditing and Risk Management

Implementing controls in an organization can be a very complicated task, particularly in large, decentralized companies where administrative controls may be difficult to enforce. Of the many issues involved in implementing controls, three are described here: auditing information systems, risk analysis, and IT security trends, including use of advanced intelligent systems.

Controls are established to ensure that information systems work properly. Controls can be installed in the original system, or they can be added once a system is in operation. Installing controls is necessary but not sufficient. It is also necessary to answer questions such as the following: Are controls installed as intended? Are they effective? Are they working reliably? Did any breach of security occur? If so, what actions are required to prevent recurrence? These questions need to be answered by independent and unbiased observers. Such observers perform the information system *auditing* task.

AUDITING INFORMATION SYSTEMS

An **audit** is an important part of any control system. Auditing can be viewed as an additional layer of controls or safeguards. It is considered as a deterrent to criminal actions, especially for insiders. Auditors attempt to answer questions such as these:

- Are there sufficient controls in the system? Which areas are not covered by controls?
- Which controls are not necessary?
- Are the controls implemented properly?
- Are the controls effective? That is, do they check the output of the system?
- Is there a clear separation of duties of employees?
- Are there procedures to ensure compliance with the controls?
- Are there procedures to ensure reporting and corrective actions in case of violations of controls?

Auditing a Web site is a good preventive measure to manage the legal risk. Legal risk is important in any IT system, but in Web systems it is even more important due to the content of the site, which may offend people or be in violation of copyright laws or other regulations (e.g., privacy protection). Auditing EC is also more complex since, in addition to the Web site, one needs to audit order taking, order fulfillment, and all support systems.

RISK-MANAGEMENT AND COST-BENEFIT ANALYSIS

It is usually not economical to prepare protection against every possible threat. Therefore, an IT security program must provide a process for assessing threats and deciding which ones to prepare for and which ones to ignore or provide reduced protection against.

Risk-Management Analysis. Risk-management analysis can be enhanced by the use of DSS software packages. A simplified computation is shown here:

$$\text{Expected loss} = P_1 \times P_2 \times L$$

where:

P_1 = probability of attack (estimate, based on judgment)
P_2 = probability of attack being successful (estimate, based on judgment)
L = loss occurring if attack is successful

Example:

$$P_1 = .02, P_2 = .10, L = \$1,000,000$$

Then, expected loss from this particular attack is

$$P_1 \times P_2 \times L = 0.02 \times 0.1 \times \$1,000,000 = \$2,000$$

The amount of loss may depend on the duration of a system being out of operation. Therefore, some add duration to the analysis.

Ethical Issues. Implementing security programs raises many ethical issues. First, some people are against any monitoring of individual activities. Imposing certain controls is seen by some as a violation of freedom of speech or other civil rights. A Gartner Group study showed that even after the terrorist attacks of 9/11/2001, only 26 percent of Americans approved a national ID database. Using biometrics is considered by many a violation of privacy.

Handling the privacy versus security dilemma is tough. There are other ethical and legal obligations that may require companies to "invade the privacy" of employees and monitor their actions. In particular, IT security measures are needed to protect against loss, liability, and litigation. Losses are not just financial, but also include the loss of information, customers, trading partners, brand image, and ability to conduct business, due to the actions of hackers, malware, or employees. Liability stems from two legal doctrines: *respondeat superior* and duty of care. *Respondeat superior* holds employers liable for the misconduct of their employees that occurs within the scope of their employment. With wireless technologies and a mobile workforce, the scope of employment has expanded beyond the perimeters of the company. Under the doctrine of duty of care, senior managers and directors have a fiduciary obligation to use reasonable care to protect the company's business operations. Litigation, or lawsuits, stems from failure to meet the company's legal and regulatory duties. According to a *Workplace E-Mail and Instant Messaging Survey* of 840 U.S. companies from American Management Association and the ePolicy Institute (*epolicyinstitute.com*), more than one in five employers (21 percent) have had employee e-mail and IM subpoenaed in the course of a lawsuit or regulatory investigation (see *epolicyinstitute.com*).

5.9 Managerial Issues

1. What is the business value of IT security and internal control? IT security risks are business risks. IT security is so integral to business objectives that it cannot be treated as a stand-alone function. Information security has evolved into a core business issue with legal obligations.

2. Why are there legal obligations? The legal issues surrounding information security are rooted in the fact that virtually all of a company's daily transactions and confidential records are created, used, communicated, and stored in electronic form and must be protected.

3. How important is IT security to management? Management's obligation to insure data security has increased significantly. The financial damages and disruption caused by hackers, phishers, spammers, identity thieves, malware, and terrorists worldwide are tremendous.

4. IT security and internal control must be implemented top-down. Effective enterprisewide IT security begins with senior management commitment and support. The power of senior managers is needed to enforce secure and ethical security and privacy practices.

5. Acceptable use policies (AUPs) and security awareness training are important for any organization. The number one threat to IT security since 2002 has been human error. IT security depends on people as well as processes and technology.

6. Digital assets are relied upon for competitive advantage. At a strategic level, the totality of a company's data resources is nearly irreplaceable. BI, ERP, CRM, and e-commerce business operations depend on the integrity, availability, and authorized use of IT resources.

7. What does risk management involve? Risk management includes securing corporate systems, networks, and data; ensuring availability of systems and services; planning for disaster recovery and business continuity; complying with government regulations and license agreements; and protecting the organization against malware, spyware, and profit-motivated hacking.

8. What are the impacts of IT security breaches? Privacy breaches and security incidents lead to fines and customer attrition. IT security failures have a direct impact on business performance because they can no longer be hidden.

9. Federal and state regulations. Stringent federal and state regulations are having a major impact on data security practices. Record-setting fines are being used to compel management to invest in all reasonable security defenses.

10. Internal control. If internal controls can be ignored, there is no control. If the company shows its employees that the company can find out everything that every employee does and use that evidence to prosecute that person to the fullest extent, then the feeling that "I can get away with it" drops drastically.

How *IT* Benefits You

Pressure to meet compliance, security, and risk management responsibilities is felt by every business department. Defenses against formidable external and internal threats, business continuity, and quick recovery from control and policy failures are demanded by customers, trading partners, investors, regulators, professional ethics boards, and various laws.

For the Accounting Major

The information security requirements for public companies, their accountants, and auditors have changed significantly. Accountants are being held professionally responsible for reducing risk, assuring compliance, eliminating fraud, and increasing the transparency of transactions according to GAAP (Generally Accepted Accounting Principles). The SEC and PCAOB (Public Company Accounting Oversight Board), among other regulatory agencies, demand information security, fraud prevention and detection, and internal controls over financial reporting. One of the hottest accounting careers is forensic accounting.

For the Finance Major

As IT security becomes ever more critical to the success of any organization, it is no longer just the concern of the CTO or CIO. With global regulatory requirements and Sarbanes-Oxley §302, responsibility for information security lies with the CEO and CFO. As a result, all aspects of the audit, including security of information and IT systems, are a key concern for the finance function.

At the same time, CFOs and treasurers are increasingly involved in IT investment decision making. They are realizing that a security breach of any kind can have catastrophic financial effects on a company. Just as it is important to have a good insurance policy in place to protect against unforeseen business circumstances, so, too, is it important to have good security protocols in effect to protect against unforeseen attacks.

For the Human Resources Management Major

The HR function is responsible for two key legal obligations: (1) the duty to provide reasonable security for their corporate data and information systems, and (2) the duty to disclose security breaches to those who may be affected adversely by them. HR departments have clear obligations to secure confidential employee data and provide a nonhostile work environment. Getting explicit consent from all employees verifying that they understand the acceptable use policy is a critical defense against charges of harassment, discrimination, and wrongful termination.

For the IS Major

All application development, network deployment, and introduction of new IT have to be guided by IT security considerations. Some of the technologies the IS department must understand are spam filtering, VoIP, WEP, server access controls, intrusion detection, encryption, password management, authentication, and biometrics. The IS department must customize the risk exposure security model to help the company identify security risks and prepare responses to incidents or disasters.

Senior executives look to the ISD for help in meeting its SOX mandates, particularly in detecting "significant deficiencies" or "material weaknesses" in internal controls and remediating them. Other departments look to the ISD to help them meet their security responsibilities.

For the Marketing Major

Customers expect their data to be safe. Profit-motivated hackers want those data. Marketers need to weigh the risk exposure of their operations. Failure to protect corporate and customer data is likely to bring on significant public relations problems and enrage customers. CRM operations and tracking customers' online buying habits can expose data to misuse (if not encrypted) or result in privacy violations. Marketers need to insure customer data security and privacy, which can be used to attract and retain customers.

For the Production/Operations Management Major

Every process in a company's operations—inventory purchasing, receiving, quality control, production, and shipping—can be disrupted by an IT security failure or the failure of a trading partner. Basically, any weak link in supply chain management or enterprise resource management systems puts everyone at risk. Companies are held liable for IT security failures that impact other companies.

Key Terms

Chapter Highlights

(Numbers Refer to Learning Objectives)

❶ Businesses that neglect to consider and implement privacy requirements are subject to enforcement actions, huge lawsuits, penalties, and fines that significantly increase expenses.

❶ A company's top line (revenue) suffers when customers discover that their private information has been compromised.

❶ Criminals invest considerable effort planning and preparing tactics to bypass company security measures.

❷ Responsibility for internal control and compliance rests directly on the shoulders of senior management and the board of directors. SOX and other antifraud regulations force better business reporting and disclosure of GAAP violations, thus making it necessary and easier to find and root out fraud.

❷ The chief privacy officer (CPO) and chief security officer (CSO) are corporate-level positions demonstrating the importance and changing role of IT security in organizations.

❸ Data, software, hardware, and networks can be threatened by internal and external hazards.

❸ One of the biggest mistakes managers make is they underestimate vulnerabilities and threats.

❸ Computer criminals are increasingly profit-driven.

❹ The risk exposure model for digital assets has five factors: the asset's value to the company, attractiveness to criminals, legal liability attached to its loss or theft, impact on business performance, and likelihood of a successful attack.

❹ The consequences of wireless attacks include data theft, legal and recovery expenses, tarnished image, lost customers, and disrupted operations due to loss of network service.

❺ With two-factor authentication, two types of information are used to verify the user's identity, such as passwords and biometrics.

❺ Biometric controls are used to identify users by checking physical characteristics such as a fingerprint or voice-print.

❺ Encryption is extremely important for confidential data that are sent or stored.

❻ The Committee of Sponsoring Organizations of the Treadway Commission (COSO) defines internal control as a process designed to provide reasonable assurance of effective operations and reliable financial reporting.

❻ There is no such thing as small fraud, only large fraud that was detected and stopped early.

❼ Disaster recovery planning is an integral part of effective internal control and security management.

❼ Business continuity planning includes data backup and a plan for what to do when disaster strikes.

❽ Protecting critical infrastructures, including energy, IT, telecommunications, and transportation sectors, is a key part of national security.

❽ A large range of IT security tools, including intelligent agents and antifraud measures, help defend against counterterrorist activities.

Virtual Company Assignment

Managing Information Resources and Security at The Wireless Café

Go to The Wireless Café's link on the Student Web Site. There you will be asked to analyze security vulnerabilities of the restaurant's information resources.

Instructions for accessing The Wireless Café Web Site on the Student Web Site:

1. Go to wiley.com/college/turban.
2. Select *Turban/Volonino's Information Technology for Management*, Seventh Edition.
3. Click on Student Resources site, in the toolbar on the left.
4. Click on the link for Virtual Company Web Site.
5. Click on Wireless Café.

Questions for Discussion

1. Many firms concentrate on the wrong questions and end up throwing a great deal of money and time at minimal security risks while ignoring major vulnerabilities. Why?

2. How can the risk of occupational fraud be decreased?

3. Why should information control and security be of prime concern to management?

4. Compare the computer security situation with that of insuring a house.

5. Explain what firewalls protect and what they do not protect. Why?

6. Describe how IS auditing works and how it is related to traditional accounting and financial auditing.

7. Why are authentication and authorization important in e-commerce?

8. Some insurance companies will not insure a business unless the firm has a computer disaster recovery plan. Explain why.

9. Explain why risk management should involve the following elements: threats, exposure associated with each threat, risk of each threat occurring, cost of controls, and assessment of their effectiveness.

10. Some people have recently suggested using viruses and similar programs in wars between countries. What is the logic of such a proposal? How could it be implemented?

11. Why is cybercrime expanding rapidly? Discuss some possible solutions.

12. Discuss why the Sarbanes-Oxley Act focuses on internal control. How does that focus influence infosec?

13. Discuss the shift in motivation of criminals.

Exercises and Projects

1. A critical problem is assessing how far a company is legally obligated to go. Since there is no such thing as perfect security (i.e., there is always more that you can do), resolving these questions can significantly affect cost.
   a. When are security measures that a company implements sufficient to comply with its obligations? For example, does installing a firewall and using virus detection software satisfy a company's legal obligations?
   b. Is it necessary for an organization to encrypt all of its electronic records?

2. The SANS Institute publishes the Top 20 Internet Security Vulnerabilities (*sans.org/top20*).
   a. Which of those vulnerabilities are most dangerous to financial institutions?
   b. Which of those vulnerabilities are most dangerous to marketing firms?
   c. Explain any differences.

3. Read the "Fact Sheet 24(e): Is Your Financial Information Safe?" (at *privacyrights.org/fs/fs24e-FinInfo.htm*) provided by the Privacy Rights Clearinghouse.
   a. Describe the federal Gramm-Leach-Bliley Act (GLB). What does it require of financial institutions?
   b. What must companies do to protect financial information?

4. Access the Anti-Phishing Working Group Web site (*antiphishing.org*) and download the most recent Phishing Activity Trends Report.
   a. Describe the recent trends in phishing attacks.
   b. Explain the reasons for these trends.

5. Assume that the daily probability of a major earthquake in Los Angeles is .07 percent. The chance of your computer center being damaged during such a quake is 5 percent. If the center is damaged, the average estimated damage will be $1.6 million.
   a. Calculate the expected loss (in dollars).
   b. An insurance agent is willing to insure your facility for an annual fee of $15,000. Analyze the offer, and discuss whether to accept it.

6. The theft of laptop computers at conventions, hotels, and airports is becoming a major problem. These categories of protection exist: physical devices (e.g., *targus.com*), encryption (e.g., *networkassociates.com*), and security policies (e.g., at *ebay.com*). Find more information on the problem and on the solutions. Summarize the advantages and limitations of each method.

7. Should an employer notify employees that their usage of computers is being monitored? Why or why not?

8. Twenty-five thousand messages arrive at an organization each year. Currently there are no firewalls. On the average there are 1.2 successful hackings each year. Each successful hacking results in loss to the company of about $130,000. A major firewall is proposed at a cost of $66,000 and a maintenance cost of $5,000. The estimated useful life is 3 years. The chance that an intruder will break through the firewall is 0.0002. In such a case, the damage will be $100,000 (30%), or $200,000 (50%), or no damage. There is an annual maintenance cost of $20,000 for the firewall.
   a. Should management buy the firewall?
   b. An improved firewall that is 99.9988 percent effective and that costs $84,000, with a life of 3 years and annual maintenance cost of $16,000, is available. Should this one be purchased instead of the first one?

Group Assignments and Projects

1. Each group is to be divided into two parts. One part will interview students and businesspeople and record the experiences they have had with computer security problems. The other part of each group will visit a computer store (and/or read the literature or use the Internet) to find out what software is available to fight different computer security problems. Then, each group will prepare a presentation in which they describe the problems and identify which of the problems could have been prevented with the use of commercially available software.

2. Create groups to investigate the latest development in IT and e-commerce security. Check journals such as *cio.com* (available free online), vendors, and search engines such as *techdata.com,* and *google.com.*

3. Research a botnet attack. Explain how the botnet works and what damage it causes. What preventive methods are offered by security vendors?

4. Read *In the Matter of BJ's Wholesale Club, Inc.,* Agreement containing Consent Order, FTC File No. 042 3160, June 16, 2005 at *ftc.gov/opa/2005/06/bjswholesale.htm.* Describe the security breach at BJ's Wholesale Club. What was the reason for this agreement? Using the enterprisewide IT security and internal control model in Figure 5.4, identify some of the causes of the security breach and how BJ's can better defend itself against hackers and legal liability.

Internet Exercises

1. Visit *cert.org* (a center of Internet security expertise). Read one of the recent Security Alerts or CERT Spotlights and write a report.

2. Visit *cert.org/csirts/services.html.* Discover the security services a CSIRT can provide in handling vulnerability. Write a summary of those services.

3. Visit *dhs.gov/dhspublic* (Department of Homeland Security). Search for an article on E-Verify. Write a report on the benefits of this verification program and who can benefit from it.

4. Visit *first.org* (a global leader in incident response). Find a current article under "Global Security News" and write a summary.

5. Visit *issa.org* (Information Systems Security Association) and choose a Webcast to listen to—one concerned with systems security. Write a short opinion essay.

6. Visit *wi-fi.org* (Wi-Fi Alliance) and discover what their mission is and report on what you think about their relevance in the overall wireless security industry.

7. Visit *securitytracker.com* and select one of the vulnerabilities. Describe the vulnerability, its impacts, its cause, and the affected operating system.

8. Visit *cio.com* and search for a recent article on security, privacy, or compliance. Write a brief summary of the article.

9. Enter *scambusters.org.* Find out what the organization does. Learn about e-mail and Web site scams. Report your findings.

10. Enter *epic.org/privacy/tools.html,* and examine one of following groups of tools: snoop proof e-mail, encryption, or firewalls. Discuss the security benefits.

11. Access the Web sites of any three major antivirus vendors (e.g., *symantec.com, mcafee.com,* and *antivirus.com*). Find out what the vendors' research centers are doing. Also download VirusScan from McAfee and scan your hard drive with it.

12. You have installed a DSL line in your home and you need a firewall. Enter *securitydogs.com, macafee.com,* or *symantec.com.* Find three possible products. Which one do you like best? Why?

13. Access a good search engine (e.g., *google.com* or *findarticles.com*). Find recent articles on disaster planning. Prepare a short report on recent developments in disaster recovery planning.

14. The use of smart cards for electronic storage of user identification, user authentication, changing passwords, and so forth is on the rise. Surf the Internet and report on recent developments.

15. Research vendors of biometrics. Select one vendor and discuss three of its biometric devices or technologies. Prepare a list of major capabilities. What are the advantages and disadvantages of its biometrics?

Minicase

NEC's Weak Internal Controls Contribute to Nasdaq Delisting

In September 2007, the Japan-based electronics company NEC announced that it could not complete the financial analysis it was required to file with the SEC (Securities and Exchange Commission). SEC filings are mandatory for every company listed on any U.S. stock exchange. The key reason NEC could not properly prepare its financial statements stemmed from at least two frauds that had been committed by NEC employees from 1999 through 2005. Weak internal controls allowed the frauds to continue for years.

Weak Internal Control Enables Uncontrolled Fraud

Fraud #1: In 2006, NEC had to restate its earnings for five prior years after discovering that a 50-year-old manager/engineer had been fabricating business deals. His bogus deals inflated sales by 36.3 billion yen ($311 million). The false transactions enabled him to embezzle tens of millions of yen, which he spent on entertainment. NEC discovered that he had made a series of false transactions from March 2002 until December 2005 in the semiconductor production department at NEC Engineering (NECE) Ltd., a wholly owned subsidiary. The fraudulent transactions amounted to nearly 10 percent of NECE's sales between 2001 and 2004.

The NECE manager, who in March 2002 anticipated poor performance in his department, convinced a client-company to make up bogus transactions. He went on to make up about 200 orders and payments by forging order and estimation forms. He allowed firms that pretended to have received deliveries to make payments to NECE for items that were never delivered.

NEC filed criminal actions against the manager, reviewed its internal control system, and strengthened the administration of those controls. The company had not been able to detect the fraud because the manager involved had been in a position to prepare all of the necessary documents to make the fictitious trades look real. There was no separation of duties, oversight, surprise audits, or forced vacation times, which might have caught the fraud. For more information on preventing and detecting fraud, see *ACFE.com* and *AICPA.org*. Despite an internal investigation, it did not become clear how the manager was able to falsify all of the data and payments.

"NEC deeply regrets the occurrence of these fraudulent transactions at a time when strengthening of corporate compliance and the improvement of internal controls is being strongly sought after, and sincerely apologizes for any inconvenience caused," the company said in the filing. A NEC spokesperson stated "We don't expect a big impact," from the accounting fraud. They were wrong. Another fraud was discovered soon afterwards.

Fraud #2: NEC discovered fraud carried out by ten employees during the seven-year period ending March 31, 2006. The fraudulent transactions amounted to roughly $18 million. The 10 NEC employees convinced contractors to inflate or create fictitious orders to their subcontractors, such as orders for software, maintenance, and installation. This resulted in the fraudulent outflow of NEC's money through these contractors. The 10 employees received approximately 500 million yen ($4.1 million) in kickbacks from the subcontractors, and used it for their own personal purposes, such as on entertainment.

Internal Controls Implemented

The company explained that fraud was not discovered for a prolonged time because the information systems enabled validation of the orders and confirmation by the same employees who made the orders. In response to its internal control deficiencies, NEC established an internal control system by which confirmation is carried out by a third-party administrative division. Other internal controls have been implemented to meet SOX compliance mandates.

Outcome

The frauds have had a very real and long-lasting effect on NEC's standing with the regulatory authorities. NEC released the following cautionary note in their April 21, 2006, financial forecast:

> As announced on March 22, 2006, NEC had to restate its earnings in its financial statements for past fiscal years as a result of the fraud and other revisions based on U.S. generally accepted accounting principles (U.S. GAAP).

In May 2007, NEC disclosed that it was at risk of losing its listing on the Nasdaq stock market because of its long overdue SEC filings. By September 2007, after requesting multiple extensions for financial filing from Nasdaq, NEC finally admitted defeat. With sincere apologies to investors everywhere, NEC said its financial statements from 2000 to 2006 were now unreliable, and that it would accept delisting in New York.

Sources: Compiled from NEC (2006), Nakamoto (2006), Taylor (2007a, 2007b), and Yomiuri (2006).

Questions for Minicase

1. What might have been some of the indicators that the NECE manager/engineer was committing fraud? What type of information systems could have helped to detect the fraud?

2. Use an Internet browser to do a search on the term "restatement of earnings." Explain the results.

3. Create a table consisting of five columns. In the columns list (1) the company names, (2) the period over which the restatement was made, (3) the incident or regulatory agency that prompted or required the restatement, (4) the impact of earnings, and (5) the stock price at the start of the period of restatement and the stock price soon after the announcement of the restatement.

4. From your Internet search, select four companies that had announced within the past three years that they were restating their earnings, and fill in the first four columns.

5. Use a financial Web site, such as *finance.yahoo.com*, to find the stock prices for the fifth column.

6. What impact did the restatement have on each of the four companies?

7. What internal controls might have prevented or detected the fraud?

Problem-Solving Activity

Estimating Investment in Anti-Spam Protection

It is difficult for companies to assess the costs of not implementing infosec defenses. Most companies do not do a proper postmortem, or if they do, they have no idea what to include in the analysis. Cost estimates may include the soft costs (i.e., *hard to quantify* costs) of diverting the IT department from a strategic project, lost sales, and customer attrition, or take a minimalist approach that only includes recovery costs. Rather than a single point estimate, several estimates can be made using a DSS to support the decision regarding infosec investments.

Using the model for estimating the cost of spam, shown in Figure 5.12, design a DSS using Excel or other spreadsheet software. Enter the formulas as shown in the Figure. Then enter data to calculate three scenarios—optimistic, realistic, and pessimistic. This is your cost analysis using a range of estimates.

Write a report that includes your DSS model (spreadsheet) showing the results. Estimate how much the company should invest in anti-spamware. Explain your answer.

Model for Estimating the Cost of Spam (Optimistic, Pessimistic, and Realistic Estimates)

	Labor Costs	Optimistic	Pessimistic	Realistic
A	Number of employees	5	10	8
B	Average employee annual salary	$ 50,000	$ 70,000	$ 60,000
C	Average number of working days/year	245	250	248
D	Average number of emails per day per employee	25	50	38
E	Percentage of emails that are spam	20%	40%	30%
F	Average time to process each one (seconds)	5	10	8
	Technical Costs			
G	Cost of bandwidth per year per site			–
H	Number of sites			–
I	Annual cost of bandwidth (G*H)			–
J	Percentage of bandwidth used by email			–
K	Total annual cost of bandwidth used by spam (I*J)			–
L	Cost of email storage per GB			
M	Size of average spam, in KB			
N	Total annual cost of storing spam (A*C*E*M*0.000008) (storage cost/KB)			–
O	Support costs per user per year			–
P	Percentage attributable to spam			–
Q	Total support cost of spam (O*P*A)			–
R	Number of email servers			–
S	Hardware cost (R*$5,000 per server)			–
T	% of email server capacity used by spam			–
U	Spam cost in hardware (S*T)			
V	Average annual cost of time lost per employee ((E*F)/60*C)*(B/((C*8)*60))			
W	Total productivity cost of spam (A*V)			–
	Anti-Spam Costs			
X	Annual cost of anti-spam software & tuning			–
Y	Percentage of spam stopped by filters			
Z	Total cost of spam (K+N+Q+U+W)			
	Totals			
AA	Total cost after filtering (Z*(1-Y)+X)			–
BB	Total savings (Z-AA)			–
CC	Total percentage cost savings (BB/Z)			–

Figure 5.12 Model for estimating cost of spam.

Online Resources

More resources and study tools are located on the Student Web Site and on WileyPLUS. You will find additional chapter materials and useful Web links. In addition, self-quizzes that provide individualized feedback are available for each chapter.

Online Briefs for Chapter 5 are available at wiley.com/college/turban:

5.1 *Managing Internet Security*

5.2 *Spyware: A Financial Assault Weapon*

5.3 *Wireless and VoIP Secrity*

Online Minicases for Chapter 5 are available at wiley.com/college/turban:

5.1 *UBS PaineWebber Debilitated by Malicious Code*

5.2 *Computer Network Intrusion Affects Millions of Hannaford Shoppers*

References

Altman, H., "Jihad Web Snares Online Shops, Buyers," *Tampa Tribune*, February 20, 2006.

CompTIA, *comptia.org* (accessed June 2008).

Computer Economics, *computereconomics.com* (accessed June 2008).

Committee of Sponsoring Organizations of the Treadway Commission (COSO), *coso.org/key.htm* (accessed June 2008).

Edwards, J., "The Rise of Botnet Infections," *Network Security Journal*, Feb. 13, 2008, *networksecurityjournal.com/features/botnets-rising-021308* (accessed June 2008).

ePolicy Institute, *epolicyinstitute.com* (accessed June 2008).

Fagg, S., "Continuity for the People," *Risk Management Magazine*, March 2006.

Fiber Optics Weekly Update, "Telstra Uses NetEx Gear," January 13, 2006.

Gross, G., "ChoicePoint's Error Sparks Talk of ID Theft Law," *IDG News Service*, February 23, 2005, *pcworld.com/news/article/0,aid, 119790,00.asp* (accessed 2008).

Higgins, K. J., Crime Server Discovered Containing 1.4 Gigabytes of Stolen Data," *Dark Reading*, May 6, 2008, *darkreading.com/document.asp?doc_id=153058* (accessed June 2008).

Information Security Forum, *securityforum.org* (accessed June 2008).

ISACA, *isaca.org* (accessed June 2008).

IT Governance Institute, *itgi.org* (accessed June 2008).

Kaplan, D., "ChoicePoint Settles Lawsuit over 2005 Breach," *SC Magazine*, Jan. 28, 2008, *scmagazineus.com/ChoicePoint-settles-lawsuit-over-2005-breach/article/104649/* (accessed June 2008).

McGlasson, L., "'Crime Server' Found with Thousands of Bank Customer Records: FBI Investigating Breach Affecting 40 Global Institutions," *Bank Info Security*, May 7, 2008, *bankinfosecurity.com/articles.php?art_id=846* (accessed June 2008).

Mimoso, M. S., "Cleaning Up After a Data Attack: CardSystems' Joe Christensen," *Information Security*, April 14, 2006, *searchsecurity. techtarget.com/originalContent/0,289142,sid14_gci1180411,00.html* (accessed June 2008).

Nakamoto, M., "NEC to Restate Earnings After Fraud," *Financial Times*, March 23, 2006.

NEC, "Revision of NEC Corporation's Financial Forecast for Fiscal Year Ended March 31, 2006, *nec.co.jp/press/en/0604/2101.html* (accessed June 2008).

Reuters UK, "BNP Paribas Fined for UK Anti-Fraud Failings," May 10, 2007, *uk.reuters.com/article/UK_SMALLCAPSRPT/idUKWLA850120070510* (accessed June 2008).

SANS, Top Ten Cyber Security Menaces for 2008, *sans.org/2008menaces* (accessed June 2008).

Scalet, S. D., "The Five Most Shocking Things About the ChoicePoint Debacle," *CSO*, May 1, 2005.

Sophos, *sophos.com* (accessed June 2008).

Spangler, T., "What You Can Learn from the VA's Snafu," *Baseline*, May 24, 2006, *baselinemag.com/article2/0,1540,1966952,00.asp* (accessed June 2008).

Symantec, *symantec.com* (accessed June 2008).

Taylor, C., "NEC Employees Behind $18M Fraud Scheme," *EDN*, May, 29, 2007a, *dn.com/article/CA6447014.html* (accessed June 2008).

Taylor, C., "NEC Stock Faces Nasdaq Delisting," *EDN*, September 21, 2007b, *edn.com/index.asp?layout=article&articleid=CA6480624* (accessed June 2008).

U.S. Department of State, *state.gov* (accessed June 2008).

Venator, J., "The State of Information Security," *IT Security Journal*, November 27, 2007, *itsecurityjournal.com/index.php/Latest/The-State-of-Information-Security.html* (accessed June 2008).

Westervelt, R., "Employee Error Fuels Data Security Breaches, Survey Finds," *Searchfinancialsecurity.com*, September 24, 2007, *searchfinancialsecurity.techtarget.com/news/article/0,289142,sid185_gci1294559,00.html* (accessed June 2008).

Wolfe, D., "Security Watch," *American Banker*, June 2, 2006.

Yomiuri, "NEC Eyes Charges Over Fake Deals," *The Daily Yomiuri*, March 23, 2006.

Cisco Systems in the Business of Helping Customers Transform Their Businesses

Cisco Systems, Inc. (*cisco.com*) (Nasdaq: CSCO) is a Fortune 500 company, ranking 71 in 2008, that routes data packets and routs its competitors with equal efficiency. Its 2007 net profits were $7.33 billion, with worldwide sales revenues from all product lines totaling almost $35 billion, as shown in Table PII.1. Cisco's Internet protocol (IP) systems remain the backbone of networks used in businesses, home communication, education, and government—that is, anything connected to the Internet. Its IP products are found in most businesses worldwide.

Cisco maintains its market dominance by its skill at identifying business needs far in advance, and then following through by implementing forward-looking business solutions. The company positions itself through numerous acquisitions and collaboration (even with rival Microsoft) to help its customers transform their businesses with Cisco's products and services.

Cisco also helps companies reduce their environmental footprint because consumers and investors are looking more closely at how companies respond to environmental issues. Their keyword phrase is corporate social responsibility (CSR), a term that covers how companies act charitably and responsibly toward employees, the environment, and the developing world. Increasingly, companies are issuing CSR reports along with their annual reports to demonstrate their social commitments. General Electric, British Telecom, Accenture, Exxon, Cisco, and others all do this on a regular basis.

Cisco's Target Customers

Cisco dominates the market for IP-based networking equipment with routers and switches used to direct data, voice, and video traffic. Other products include remote access servers, IP telephony equipment, optical networking components, Internet conferencing systems, set-top boxes, and network

service and security systems. Cisco offers products designed for large enterprises and telecommunications service providers, as well as products for small and medium businesses (SMBs). Company growth and expansion of its product lines have been achieved via acquisition of other companies and their products. Acquisitions during 2007 and 2008 are listed in Table PII.2. Comparable numbers of acquisitions had occurred in prior years, too. Cisco also markets products designed for small businesses and consumers through its Linksys division.

The global company, which has regional headquarters in San Jose, Singapore, and Amsterdam, is named after the city of San Francisco.

Company History

Cisco Systems was founded by Stanford University computer science engineers, Len Bosack and Sandra Lerner, and three colleagues in 1984. While working at Stanford, Len, Sandra, and others made major design enhancements to one of the essential Internet technologies, the router. Their multi-protocol router enabled two networks to communicate and share data. These *blue boxes*, as the routers were called, eventually would connect innumerable computers to the Internet. Cisco sold its first network router in 1986. The owners applied for venture capital to start a business marketing the blue boxes, which would become part of infrastructure of data networks and the Internet. But in 1986, that Internet concept had not been proven, making it difficult for them to raise venture capital. After 77 unsuccessful proposals (rejections) to venture capitalists, the group finally raised $2.5 million in venture capital from Sequoia Capital in 1987. The owners continued to develop, and then later to acquire, innovative technologies to support networking.

TABLE PII.1	Cisco Systems, Inc. 2007 Sales by Region and Product Line		
		2007 Sales	
Regions	**Sales Revenues (in billions)**		**Percent of Total Sales**
U.S. and Canada	$ 19.29		55%
Europe	$ 7.33		21%
Asia/Pacific Japan	$ 1.29		4%
Other countries	$ 3.55		10%
Emerging markets	$ 3.44		10%
Total	**$ 34.92**		**100%**
Products	**Sales Revenues (in billions)**		**Percent of Total Sales**
Switches	$ 12.47		36%
Advanced technologies	$ 8.07		23%
Routers	$ 6.92		20%
Other	$ 1.99		6%
Services	$ 5.46		15%
Total	**$ 34.92**		**100%**

TABLE PII.2	Cisco Systems' Acquisitions in 2007 and 2008
Acquired Company (and acquisition date)	**Products and Capabilities Acquired**
DiviTech (June 2008)	digital video networking software
Nuova Systems (April 2008)	data center switches
Securent (November 2007)	security software
Navini Networks (December 2007)	WiMax equipment
Latigent (October 2007)	Web-based business intelligence software for call centers
Cognio (October 2007)	wireless spectrum analysis
BroadWare Technologies (June 2007)	video networking and storage systems
IronPort Systems (June 2007)	Web messaging and email security software
WebEx Communications (May 2007)	Web conferencing systems
Spans Logic (April 2007)	networking semiconductor design
NeoPath Networks (April 2007)	file storage management systems
Utah Street Networks (March 2007)	social networking communities
Reactivity (March 2007)	XML gateways
Five Across (March 2007)	social networking software
Tivella (January 2007)	digital signage software and systems

Also in 1987, Cisco developed the Interior Gateway Routing Protocol, which revolutionized communications between computers by allowing for routing within an autonomous system. By 1989, the company's sales revenues hit $27 million with only three products on the market and 100 employees. With the rise of the World Wide Web, Cisco's web communication products were in very high demand. The company went public on the Nasdaq in 1990, and due to management clashes, owners Len and Sandra sold their stock for about $200 million, giving most to favorite causes, including animal charities and a Harvard professor looking for extraterrestrials. In 1995, John Chambers became chairman and CEO of Cisco Systems, Inc., and remains so as of 2008.

In 1998, Cisco made headlines by becoming the first company in history to reach a market capitalization of $100 billion in only 14 years. But soon afterward, the economic downturn and slump in the telecommunications and technology market were a big hit to Cisco. Its sales revenue dropped for the first time in its history, forcing the company to write off $2.5 billion worth of inventory.

Cisco's Market Breadth Growth Strategy

Cisco has used acquisitions—more than 120 of them since 1993—to broaden its product lines and secure engineering talent in the highly competitive networking sector. Cisco remains committed to investments that insure the dominance of its core lines of switches and routers, which account for 60% of sales, while at the same time moving into new markets through acquisitions. (The diversity of Cisco's acquisitions during 2007 and 2008 are evident in Table PII.2.)

A significant acquisition was WebEx Communications, a leading provider of Internet conferencing systems, for $3.2 billion in 2007. The 2006 acquisition of cable set-top box leader Scientific Atlanta for $6.9 billion was the second largest purchase in its history. Cisco had paid $7 billion for optical networking equipment maker Cerent in 1999. Cisco based its strategy on what it foresaw as the critical importance of technology convergence for data, voice, and television networks. Its acquisition of Scientific Atlanta made it one of the leading providers of the set-top boxes that cable service providers use to deliver advanced features, for example, movies-on-demand. It also put Cisco into a fierce competitive battle with Motorola in the set-top box market.

Key Competitors

Market expansion put Cisco into competition with other megacorporations as well as smart, well-financed upstarts across all of its market segments. Its three top competitors are:

1. **Alcatel–Lucent.** France's Alcatel acquired U.S. rival Lucent Technologies for $11.6 billion in late 2006, forming the new Alcatel–Lucent. The company, with 2007 sales revenues of $26.2 billion, is a leading global supplier of high-tech equipment for telecommunications networks. Specifically, it provides network switching and transmission systems for wireline and wireless networks primarily for telecom carriers, other businesses, and government agencies. Alcatel–Lucent is made up of five business units: wireline, wireless, convergence, enterprise, and services. Alcatel–Lucent's key customers include Verizon, AT&T, BellSouth, and China Telecom.

2. **Juniper Networks.** Juniper Networks has managed to grow in a market dominated by Cisco, with 2007 sales revenues of $2.83 billion. The company designs and sells network infrastructure for private and public access networks. Customers use its products to securely deploy

and manage services and applications across IP networks. The company's product portfolio includes routers, network traffic management software, virtual private network (VPN) and firewall devices, data center and wide area network (WAN) acceleration tools, intrusion detection and prevention (IDP) systems, and support services. Juniper sells directly and through resellers to network service providers, enterprises, government agencies, and schools. Juniper has traditionally catered to Internet and telecommunications service providers, but the company continues to expand its offerings for the enterprise market.

3. **Nortel Networks Corp**. One of the top global makers of telecom equipment in North America, Toronto-based Nortel makes core network switching, enterprise network equipment, wireless, and optical systems for customers worldwide. Despite its 2007 sales revenues of Cdn$10.87 billion, it had a negative net income of almost a billion dollars. In early 2005, Nortel belatedly released its 2003 financial statements following a massive accounting investigation that uncovered billions in fraudulently overstated revenues for the years 1999 and 2000. In early 2006, Nortel agreed to pay $2.5 billion to settle class-action lawsuits that alleged securities laws violations.

Clearly, these are three fierce competitors that Cisco needs to outperform on a daily basis through market intelligence and smart acquisitions. Cisco needs to make strategic decisions so that they are ready when the demand for new products and services arises. For example, the company expanded from a product line limited to hardware by making software investments in 2007, including the acquisition of network and e-mail security applications developer IronPort Systems for $830 million, and wireless spectrum analysis specialist Cognio.

In another competitive move, Cisco entered the social networking sector by acquiring software platform developer Five Across, and assets of Utah Street Networks, the operator of the *Tribe.net* online communities. Cisco acquired WiMax equipment maker Navini Networks for about $330 million in 2007.

Cisco has invested heavily to build its international presence. From 2005 through 2008, the company spent more than $1 billion to expand its operations in India. Late in 2007, it unveiled a $16 billion expansion plan for China, including investments in manufacturing, education programs, and venture capital.

Selling Business Solutions—Not Point Solutions

Much of Cisco's recent success is due to its focus on selling business solutions instead of point products. Businesses are increasingly interested in innovative products that they can count on to integrate and work with other network and IT products. Plus, customers want one company to call upon for help when those devices do not work as promised.

Cisco is focused on developing (or acquiring) its ability to deliver advanced multimedia solutions, applications, and managed services—all of which are based on the network infrastructure. The following strategic initiatives illustrate Cisco's responsiveness and adaptability to the changing markets of its business customers. Those customers want better data management solutions (Chapter 3) and secure high-speed networks that support collaboration and presence and business continuity (Chapters 4 and 5).

Managed Services 3.0—The Market Opportunity Solution Providers Cannot Ignore

In 2008, Cisco launched a massive new Managed Services 3.0 initiative, dubbed *Services 3.0*. Services 3.0 are managed services that vendors (Cisco's customers) can sell to their own customers. Services 3.0 helps vendors, such as telecom carriers, value-added resellers (VARs), and system integrators, to improve their network availability, performance, and data center processes. Managed Services 3.0 give all types of service providers (Internet service providers or application service providers, referred to collectively as xSPs) the ability to take over the management of their customers' IT networks. The benefits to xSPs are the competitive advantages from being able to provide managed services and stronger strategic relationships with customers.

Rather than only supplying bandwidth, xSPs can support their customers' business technology alignment needs, and thereby gain a competitive advantage. Services 3.0 enable vendors to respond to their customers' growing IT and network utilization patterns and future requirements.

Cisco Collaborates with Microsoft to Provide Interoperability

In August 2007, the CEOs of Microsoft and Cisco, Steve Ballmer and John Chambers, together presented a press conference to show the collaborative efforts between the two companies. The discussions were largely focused on informing potential customers and investors of their new collaborative strategy, which is to support the transition to voice, video, and data over the Internet. The companies are designing and building next-generation networks to deliver communications and services over the Internet and to support the transition to Web 2.0 using equipment and software from multiple vendors. This move is significant because Cisco and Microsoft are recognizing that customers need multi-vendor solutions with guaranteed interoperability.

The phrase "Web 2.0" represents the change from the Internet as a "network of networks" with hardwired applications at the end points (e.g., Web sites stored on servers and viewed through browsers, or stand-alone applications on users' computers) to one where networked applications can flexibly use data transported over the Internet in standardized formats.

The network is a platform that connects applications, devices, and ultimately the people using those applications to enable simple manipulation of services, content creation, and input from users. This, together with the move toward delivering triple-play services of voice, video, and data, defines the objectives of closer collaboration between Cisco, a major infrastructure vendor, and Microsoft, the software giant. The two companies have worked together from 1998 to 2008, but have increasingly found that customer requirements have dictated a closer working relationship as next-generation networks are deployed to handle voice, video, and data over a single IP architecture.

While they will collaborate to ensure interoperability and maximize their revenue opportunities, Microsoft and Cisco remain fierce competitors in other markets.

There are seven areas (which were discussed in Chapters 3 through 5) of collaboration between the two companies that are viewed as key areas of development:

1. **IT Architecture:** The companies are optimizing how Windows Vista uses the IP network to maximize bandwidth use and maintain quality of service.
2. **Security:** Security needs to exist throughout the network, from the routers to the computer, as part of Defense in Depth, "an integrated, multi-tiered security strategy." Information also needs to be shared across networks, and Cisco, Microsoft, and a third infrastructure vendor specializing in storage solutions—EMC—have been key players in producing off-the-shelf solutions using the secure information-sharing architecture (SISA) being used to share information between government departments in the United States.
3. **Management:** Network and system management becomes increasingly difficult as disparate systems are used—vendors now also act as system integrators to ensure a cohesive network is built.
4. **Wireless and Mobility:** While Cisco has a range of wireless VoIP products (e.g., the iPhone from subsidiary Linksys), Cisco does not have a presence in the cellular/mobile market. Cisco and Microsoft are working to extend the Unified Communications Manager to Windows Mobile devices.
5. **Unified Communications:** Microsoft takes a software-oriented approach to communications while Cisco views the network as "the hub of all communications," but the two companies will work together in some areas and compete to deliver unified communications solutions, ensuring

interoperability, such as integrating MS Exchange server or MS Office Communications Server and Cisco Unified Communications Manager.
6. **Connected Entertainment:** Microsoft Media Centre provides the central PC facility while Cisco (under the Linksys and Scientific Atlanta customer premises equipment brands) produces "media extenders" that connect the PC to the TV and stereo, allowing the distribution of content around the home.
7. **Small and Medium Businesses:** Packaged solutions using combined solutions from both companies will be jointly marketed.

"Tell Us Your Business Challenge" Connects to Entrepreneurs

Each week, *Business Solutions,* sponsored by Cisco, answers a problem common to many entrepreneurs. They state: "If your business is facing a challenge, please send it, along with contact information, to *solutions@nationalpost.com.* You and your business could be featured in a future Business Solutions." In addition, Cisco offers helpful business tools at *financialpost.com/solutions.* For example, one challenge was: How do you manage and secure data in a cost-effective manner? Responses are posted as learning experiences for all. Another support for entrepreneurs is Cisco networking solutions, which helps them improve their small business with technology they can trust (see *cisco.com/ca/smb*).

Conclusion: Cisco's Strategy Is Serving Customers' Needs

Organizations of all sizes, in every industry, and throughout the world rely on networking technology to improve and protect business performance. Basic ways to improve or protect performance include a combination of the following:

- Increasing productivity of workers
- Reducing labor costs, product costs, service costs, or maintenance costs
- Collaborating with supply chain partners to reduce costs or delivery times
- Reducing time-to-market of new products or services
- Creating new revenue sources
- Responding to customers' needs or actions in real-time or near real-time
- Correcting operational problems quickly

- Responding quickly to competitive opportunities and threats
- Complying with regulators' requirements, such as protecting the confidential data of customers, employees, and business partners
- Providing secure, real-time visibility of the status of CRM, ERP, and supply chain systems

Cisco is leading the transition to intelligent network environments. Its success has resulted from continuously planning three to five years ahead of important market transitions. As Chambers said, "Historically, the transitions we've been a part of have been technological; they've been relatively orderly and predictable. Now, however, we're seeing a wider-reaching, more dramatic transition. So our ability to predict successfully where the market will go is even more critical and offers much greater potential import for the company."

References

"Alliances Keeps Network Management Specialist Moving up the Application Stack," *Manufacturing Business Technology*, 25(7), July 2007.

Dilger, K., "NetFlow-Infused Systems Watch for Trending, Traffic Patterns, Network Abnormalities," *Manufacturing Business Technology*, 26(5), May 2008.

Duffy, J., "Q&A: Cisco's CTO Talks First Impressions," *Network World*, 25(26), June 30, 2008.

Hoover's Company Records—In-depth Records, July 8, 2008.

Hoover's Company Records—Basic Record, July 22, 2008.

Silver, S., "In the Battle with Cisco, Tiny Nortel Plays Energy Card," *The Globe and Mail* (Canada), June 16, 2008.

White, B., "Brocade to Buy Foundry for Almost $3 Billion," *The Wall Street Journal*, July 22, 2008.

Questions

1. How does Cisco maintain its market dominance?
2. Identify three ways in which Cisco helps its business customers improve their business performance? (Chapters 3 and 4).
3. What products or services are provided by Cisco to support each of the following: business continuity, security, knowledge sharing, and collaboration? (Chapters 3, 4, and 5).
4. Review Table PII.2 showing Cisco's acquisitions during 2007 and 2008. Map the capabilities acquired to the categories in Table 4.5 in Chapter 4. How many of the acquired technologies are considered most likely to provide business value? What percent is that of the total number of acquired technologies?
5. Explain this statement: Competing companies, Cisco and Microsoft, are collaborating because of convergence. (Chapter 4).
6. What value does Cisco offer to entrepreneurs? To SMBs?
7. What security support does Cisco provide? (Chapter 5).
8. How does Cisco help its customers improve their performance?
9. How important was prediction to Cisco's former success? How important is prediction to Cisco's current and future success? Explain the difference.
10. Extra credit: Cisco has been a remarkably successful networking company. How would you categorize the company today? That is, is Cisco still primarily a networking company? Visit *cisco.com* for a current view of the company. Explain your answer.

Chapter 6

E-Business and E-Commerce

Learning Objectives

After studying this chapter, you will be able to:

❶ Describe electronic commerce, its scope, benefits, limitations, and types.

❷ Explain how online auctions and bartering work.

❸ Understand the major applications of business-to-consumer commerce, including service industries and the major issues faced by e-tailers.

❹ Describe business-to-business applications.

❺ Explain why intrabusiness and B2E are considered e-commerce.

❻ Describe e-government activities and consumer-to-consumer e-commerce.

❼ Identify the e-commerce support services, specifically payments and logistics.

❽ Understand the importance and activities of online advertising.

❾ Identify and describe ethical and legal issues relating to e-commerce.

Integrating IT

 ACC   **FIN**   **MKT**   **OM**   **HRM**   **IS**

IT-PERFORMANCE MODEL

In this chapter we show how e-business and e-commerce help organizations to sell, buy, collaborate, and communicate in order to increase productivity and competitive advantage. E-commerce is using a diversity of business models some of which are illustrated in the Dell's opening case.

Where Do We Want to Go? Mission, Goals, Objectives
- Become e-business
- E-commerce as marketing channel
- Digital supply chain
- Go for enterprise social networking

- Private marketplace
- Auction infrastructure
- Order taking and fulfillment
- Wireless infrastructure
- EC support mechanism

Information Technology (IT)

How Can We Improve Performance? Solutions, Critical Responses
- Advertise in social networks
- New collaborative methods
- E-procurement
- Innovative EC models

How Shall We Get There? Strategy, Plans
- Strategy or social networking
- E-commerce strategy
- EC/IT strategy alignment
- How to go global

How Well Are We Doing? Monitoring, Performance, Comparing
- Cost/benefit of EC application
- Comparing EC performance

The business performance management cycle and IT model.

DELL IS USING E-COMMERCE FOR SUCCESS

MKT

The Business Problem/Opportunity

Founded in 1984 by Michael Dell, Dell Computer Corp. (now known as Dell) was the first company to offer personal computers (PCs) via mail order. Dell designed its own PC system and allowed customers to configure their own customized systems using the build-to-order model. It then shipped the PCs to them by direct mail. These concepts were, and are, Dell's cornerstone *business models*. By 1993, Dell had become one of the top five computer makers worldwide, threatening Compaq, which started a price war causing Dell to start losing money. At that time, Dell was taking orders by fax and snail mail. Losses exceeded $100 million by 1994. The company was in trouble.

The Solution: Direct Marketing Online

The commercialization of the Internet in the early 1990s and the introduction of the Web in 1993 provided Dell with an *opportunity* to expand rapidly by selling online. Dell implemented aggressive online order-taking and opened subsidiaries in Europe and Asia. Dell also started to offer all products on its Web site (e.g., printers, servers). This enabled Dell to batter Compaq, and in 1999 Dell became number one in worldwide PC shipments. By 2008 Dell (dell.com) was selling about $62 billion a year in computer-related products online, from network switches to printers, employing over 65,000 people. It is the leading systems provider in the United States and the second-leading provider worldwide.

Dell sells to individuals for their homes and home offices, small businesses (up to 200 employees), medium and large businesses (over 200 employees), and government, education, and healthcare organizations.

Sales to the first group are classified as *business-to-consumer* (B2C). Sales to the other three groups are classified as *business-to-business* (B2B). Consumers shop at *dell.com* using online electronic catalogs. The sales are completed using mechanisms described later in this chapter.

In addition, Dell sells refurbished Dell computers and other products in electronic auctions at *dellauction.com*.

Here are Dell's major EC initiatives:

Business-to-Business (B2B)

Most of Dell's sales are to businesses. These sales are facilitated by standard shopping aids (e.g., catalogs, shopping carts, comparison engine, and credit card payments). B2B customers obtain additional help from Dell. Dell provides each of its nearly 100,000 business customers with Premier Dell service.

For example, British Airways (BA) considers Dell to be a strategic supplier. Dell provides notebook and desktop computers to 25,000 BA users. Dell offers two e-procurement (electronic purchasing) services to BA purchasing agents. The more basic service, Premier Dell, allows BA (and other businesses) to browse, buy, and track orders on a Dell Web site customized for the user's requirements. The site enables authorized users to select preconfigured PCs for their business unit or department. This provides automatic requisition and order fulfillment once an authorized user has chosen to buy a PC from Dell. BA has placed the e-procurement tools on its E-Working intranet. This allows authorized staff to purchase PCs through a portal that connects directly into Dell's systems.

Business-to-Consumer (B2C)

Dell sells direct to individuals from its private marketplace (store). Using fairly standard mechanisms such as electronic catalog, shopping carts, and payment gateway and shipping, any customer can configure and price a desktop, laptop, or other product sold by Dell. Payment must be arranged in advance. Customers can also participate in auctions of refurbished computers, which are periodically conducted online.

In addition to supporting its business customers with *e-procurement* tools, such as in the case of BA, Dell is using EC in its own procurement. Actually, Dell developed an e-procurement model that it shares with its business partners, such as BA. One aspect of this model is the use of electronic tendering (bidding online for jobs). Dell uses electronic tendering when it buys the components for its products.

E-Collaboration

Dell has many business partners with whom communication and collaboration are necessary. For example, Dell uses shippers such as UPS and FedEx to deliver its computers to individuals. It also uses third-party logistics companies to collect, maintain, and deliver components from its suppliers, and it has many other partners. Dell is using leading-edge technologies such as Web Services to facilitate communication and reduce inventories. Web Services facilitate B2B integration that links customers' existing ERP or procurement systems directly with Dell and other trading partners.

Finally, Dell has a superb communication system with its over 15,000 service providers around the globe.

E-Customer Service

Dell uses a number of different tools to provide superb customer service around the clock. To leverage customer relationship management (CRM), a customer service approach that is customer centered is implemented for lasting relationships. Dell provides a virtual help desk for self-diagnosis and service as well as direct access to technical support data. In addition, a phone-based help desk is open 24/7. Product support includes troubleshooting, user guides, upgrades, downloads, news and press releases, FAQs, order status information, a "my account" page, a community forum (to exchange online ideas, information, and experiences), bulletin boards and other customer-to-customer interaction features, training books (at a discount), and much more. Dell keeps a large database of its customers. Using data mining tools, it learns a great deal about its customers and attempts to make them happy. The database is used to improve marketing as well.

Intrabusiness EC

To support its build-to-order capabilities, significantly improve its demand-planning and factory-execution accuracy, reduce order-to-delivery time, and enhance customer service, Dell partnered with Accenture to create a high-performance supply chain management solution. Now in place in Dell's plants around the world, the program, which paid for itself five times during the first 12 months of operation, enables Dell to adapt more quickly to rapidly changing technologies and the business environment and maintain its position as a high-performance business.

Dell also has automated its factory scheduling, demand-planning capabilities, and inventory management using information technology and e-supply chain models.

Dell is using many other EC initiatives. For example, you can join Dell's *affiliate program* by placing Dell's banner and logo on your Web site. If a customer comes to your site and clicks on Dell's banner and then purchases an item at Dell, you get 1–4 percent commission for the referral. Another example is EducateU at *learndell.com*, which allows online self-learning about Dell products as well as about many IT and management topics. Finally, using an intranet (*inside.dell.com*), Dell serves its own employees with information they need to do their job better, providing them with customer data, financial reports, product information, training, and much more.

The Results

Dell has been one of *Fortune's* top five "Most Admired" companies since 1999, and it continuously advances in the rankings of the Fortune 500 and the Fortune Global 500. Dell has over 100 country-oriented Web sites in many languages, and profits are nearing $4 billion a year. If you had invested $10,000 in Dell's initial public offering (IPO) in 1987, you would be a millionaire just from that investment. Dell actively supports EC research at the University of Texas in Austin (Dell's headquarters are in Austin).

Dell is expanding its business not only in the computer industry, but also in consumer electronics (camera, TVs, GPS).

Sources: Compiled from *dell.co* and *dellauction.com* (accessed May 2008), and from Kraemer and Dedrick (2001) and Rappa (2006).

Lessons Learned from This Case

Dell exemplifies the major EC business models. First, it pioneered the *direct-marketing model* for PCs, and then it moved online. Furthermore, Dell supplemented its direct marketing with the build-to-order or custom-built model on a large scale (mass customization). In doing so, Dell benefited from the elimination of intermediation by selling direct, from extremely low inventories, and from superb cash flow by getting paid in advance. To meet the large demand for its quality products, Dell is using other EC models, notably e-procurement for improving the purchasing of components, collaborative commerce with its partners, and intra-business EC for improving its internal operations. Finally,

Dell uses e-CRM (CRM done online; see Chapter 10 for details) with its customers. Dell believes that the most efficient path to customers is through a direct relationship that minimizes confusion and cost. By successfully using e-commerce models, Dell became a world-class company, winning over all of its competitors. Dell's EC business models have become classic examples of best practices, and they are followed today by many other manufacturers, notably car makers.

This chapter defines EC and lists the types of transactions that are executed in it. Various EC models and the benefits and limitations of EC are also examined.

6.1 Overview of E-Business and E-Commerce

The field of EC is wide and diversified, but it is united by the following definitions and concepts. The diversity is due to the many types and models used as shown in this section.

DEFINITIONS AND CONCEPTS

Electronic commerce (EC or e-commerce) describes the process of buying, selling, transferring, serving, or exchanging products, services, or information via computer networks, including the Internet. Some people view the term *commerce* as describing only *transactions* conducted between business partners. When this definition is used, some people find the term *electronic commerce* to be fairly narrow. Thus, many use the term *e-business* instead. *E-business* refers to a broader definition of EC, not just the buying and selling of goods and services, but also servicing customers, collaborating with business partners, conducting e-learning, and conducting electronic transactions within an organization. Others view e-business as the "other than buying and selling" activities on the Internet, such as collaboration and intrabusiness activities. The two terms *will be used interchangeably* throughout the chapter and the remainder of the text.

In this book we use the broadest meaning of electronic commerce, which is basically equivalent to e-business.

Note that the broad view includes the narrow one. Thus, buying and selling online constitute the major portion of EC dollar value, and it is covered mostly in Sections 6.2–6.4. Other aspects are covered in Sections 6.5–6.7.

Pure versus Partial EC. EC can take several forms, depending on the *degree of digitization*—the transformation from physical to digital—involved. The degree of digitization can relate to: (1) the product (service) sold, (2) the process, or (3) the delivery agent (or intermediary). Choi et al. (1997) created a framework that explains the possible configurations of these three dimensions. A product can be physical or digital, the process can be physical or digital, and the delivery agent can be physical or digital. In traditional commerce all three dimensions are physical. Purely physical organizations are referred to as **brick-and-mortar organizations.** In *pure EC* all dimensions are digital. All other combinations that include a mix of digital and physical dimensions are considered EC (but not pure EC).

If there is at least one digital dimension, we consider the situation *partial EC.* For example, buying a shirt at Wal-Mart Online or a book from Amazon.com is partial EC, because the merchandise is physically delivered by a shipper. However, buying an e-book from Amazon.com or a software product from Buy.com is *pure EC*, because the product, its delivery, payment, and transfer agent are all done online. In this book we use the term EC to denote either pure or partial EC.

Note that some pure EC companies add some physical facilities. For example, Expedia.com opened sales offices, and Amazon.com has physical warehouses and allows customers to pick up merchandise at physical locations.

EC Organizations. Companies that are engaged only in EC are considered **virtual** (or pure-play) **organizations. Click-and-mortar** (or click-and-brick) **organizations** are those that conduct some e-commerce activities, yet their primary business is done in the physical world, such as Godiva (see Online Minicase 6.1). Gradually, many brick-and-mortar companies are expanding to click-and-mortar ones (e.g., Wal-Mart Online). So, many people expect traditional companies to offer some form of e-commerce, as your bank, airline, or Godiva and Wal-Mart do.

THE EC LANDSCAPE

To better understand how EC works, let's look at Figure 6.1. As can be seen in the figure, a company such as Dell (labeled "our company") provides products and/or services to customers (individuals or organizations), shown on the right side. To do so, our company buys inputs such as material, parts, and/or services from suppliers and other business partners in a procurement process. Processing the inputs is done in its production/operations department. Other departments (e.g., finance, marketing) support the conversion of inputs to outputs and the sale to customers.

The basic idea of EC is to *automate* as many business processes as possible. A process can be order initiation, order fulfillment, procurement of material, manufacturing parts (production), delivery, or providing CRM.

EC activities support selling, buying, and providing relationships, as well as the internal and external transactions involved. This is done by EC mechanisms such as e-markets, e-procurement, and e-CRM as shown in Figure 6.1. Note that the processes in the figure involve several types of transactions.

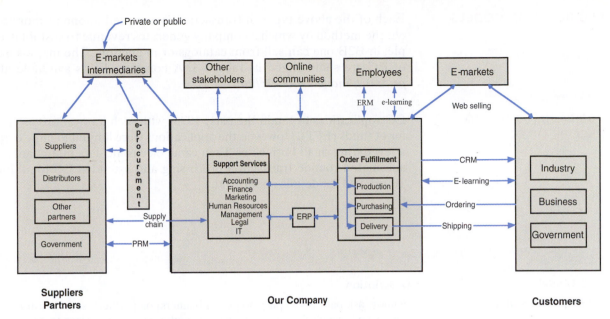

Figure 6.1 E-commerce in our company. *(Source: Drawn by E. Turban.)*

TYPES OF E-COMMERCE TRANSACTIONS

E-commerce transactions can be done between various parties. The common types of e-commerce transactions are described below, some of which were described in the Dell opening case.

- **Business-to-business (B2B).** In B2B transactions, both the sellers and the buyers are business organizations. The vast majority of EC volume is of this type.
- **Collaborative commerce (c-commerce).** In c-commerce, business partners collaborate (rather than buy or sell) electronically. Such collaboration frequently occurs between and among business partners along the supply chain (see Chapter 10).
- **Business-to-consumers (B2C).** In B2C, the sellers are organizations, and the buyers are individuals. B2C is also known as *e-tailing*. **Electronic retailing** (e-tailing) is the direct sale of the products and services through electronic storefronts or electronic malls, usually designed around an electronic catalog format and/or auctions. For the difference between retailing and e-retailing, see Lee and Brandyberry (2003).
- **Consumer-to-consumer (C2C).** In C2C, an individual sells products or services to other individuals. You also will see the term C2C used as "customer-to-customer." The terms are interchangeable, and both will be used in this book.
- **Business-to-business-to-consumers (B2B2C).** In this case, a business sells to a business but delivers the product or service to an individual consumer, such as in Godiva's case (Online Minicase 6.1).
- **Consumers-to-businesses (C2B).** In C2B, consumers make known a particular need for a product or service, and suppliers compete to provide the product or service to consumers. An example is Priceline.com, where the customer names a product or service and the desired price, and Priceline tries to find a supplier to fulfill the stated need.
- **Intrabusiness (intraorganizational) commerce.** In this case, an organization uses EC internally to improve its operations. A special case of this is known as **business-to-employees (B2E) EC,** in which an organization delivers products or services to its employees.
- **Government-to-citizens (G2C) and others.** In this case, a government entity (unit) provides services to its citizens via EC technologies. Government units can engage in EC with other government units—**government-to-government (G2G)** or with businesses—**government-to-business (G2B).**

EC BUSINESS MODELS

Each of the above types of transaction is executed in one or more *business models,* the method by which a company generates revenue to sustain itself. For example, in B2B one can sell from catalogs or in auctions. The major business models of EC are summarized in Table 6.1. A complete list is available at *digitalenterprise.org/models/models.html.*

BRIEF HISTORY AND SCOPE OF EC

EC applications began in the early 1970s with such innovations as electronic transfer of funds (EFT). However, the applications were limited to large corporations and a few daring small businesses. Then came electronic data interchange (EDI), which automated routine transaction processing and extended EC to all industries. (See Tutorial #3 for details about EDI.)

TABLE 6.1	E-Commerce Business Models
EC Model	**Description**
Affiliate marketing	Vendors ask partners to place logos (or banners) on partner's site. If customers click on logo, go to vendor's site, and buy; then vendor pays commissions to partners. (See *performics.com.*)
Bartering online	Intermediary administers online exchange of surplus products and/or company receives "points" for its contribution, and the points can be used to purchase other needed items.
Deep discounters	Company (e.g., *Half.com*) offers deep price discounts. Appeals to customers who consider only price in their purchasing decisions.
E-Classifieds	Presentation of items for sale at fixed prices. Popular sites are *craigslist.com* and *classifieds2000.com.*
Electronic marketplaces and exchanges	Transactions are conducted efficiently (more information to buyers and sellers, less transaction cost) in virtual marketplaces (private or public).
Electronic tendering system	Businesses conduct online tendering, requesting quotes from suppliers. Used in B2B with a *reverse auction* mechanism (see Section 6.2).
Find-the-best-price	Customers specify a need; an intermediary (e.g., *Hotwire.com*) compares providers and shows the lowest price. Customers must accept the offer in a short time or may lose the deal.
Group purchasing (e-co-ops)	Small buyers aggregate several demands to get a large volume; then the buying group conducts tendering or negotiates a low price (see *njnonprofits.org/groupbuy.html*).
Information brokers and matching services	Brokers provide services related to EC information, such as trust, content, matching buyers and sellers, evaluating vendors and products.
Membership	Only members can use the services provided, including access to certain information, conducting trades, etc. (e.g., *Egreetings.com*).
Name-your-own-price	Customers decide how much they are willing to pay. An intermediary (e.g., *Priceline.com*) tries to match a provider.
Online auctions	Companies or individuals run auctions of various types on the Internet. Fast and inexpensive way to sell or liquidate items.
Online direct marketing	Manufacturers or retailers sell directly online to customers. Very efficient for digital products and services. Can allow for product or service customization.
Product customization	Customers use the Internet to self-configure products or services. Sellers then price them and fulfill them quickly (*build-to-order*).
Supply-chain improvers	Organizations restructure supply chains to hubs or other configurations. Increases collaboration, reduces delays, and smoothes supply chain flows.
Value-chain integrators	Integrators aggregate information and package it for customers, vendors, or others in the supply chain.
Value-chain service providers	Service provider offers specialized services in supply chain operations such as providing logistics or payment services.
Viral marketing	Receivers of e-mails send the received or related information about your product to their friends (word-of-mouth). (Be on the watch for viruses.)

A Closer Look 6.1

Interesting Student-Targeted Web Sites

Including high schools and universities, there are millions of students in the United States, and every year new students join schools while others join the workforce. No wonder that many Web sites were developed for such a large population. Note that college students spend more than $200 billion a year (*harrisinteractive.com*), making students' sites attractive to online advertisers and marketers. Here are a few examples:

- **Facebook** is a popular place for students to socialize (available to nonstudents as of summer 2006).

- **Swook** is one of several sites that enables students to exchange textbooks.

- **Collegerecruiting.com** matches students with universities for best admission and helps you write your resume.

- **RateMyProfessor.com** provides a free message board where students can post opinions about college professors. The site attracts 2 million new visitors each month.

- **Finaid.com** is a comprehensive site about getting financial aid with all related information, dozens of calculators, and information about college admissions and jobs.

- **Powerstudents.com** combines information from over 20 leading student-oriented Web sites from searchable scholarships to file sharing.

- **Collegerecruiter.com** helps you find an internship or a job once you have graduated.

In the early 1990s, EC applications expanded rapidly, following the commercialization of the Internet and the introduction of the Web. A major shakeout in EC activities began in 2000 and lasted about three years; hundreds of dot-com companies went out of business. Since 2003, EC has continued to show steady progress. Today, most organizations are practicing some type of EC transaction.

Over the last 15 years, EC has continuously added products and services. According to Forrester (April 2008), EC retail sales in the United States grew from about $75 billion in 2002 to over $204 billion in 2008 and will hit $335 billion in 2012 (Schuman, 2008). In the same period, high-speed Internet connections in the United States grew from 5 million to over 80 million. Also, in addition to buying and selling on the Internet, new services ranging from arranging weddings online to scheduling your medical appointments and collaborating with your suppliers overseas are growing rapidly.

EC Newcomers: Social Network Sites. As described in Chapters 1 and 2, social network sites are growing in popularity and providing for EC opportunities.

Many of these sites target certain groups such as teenagers, senior citizens, women, or students (see *A Closer Look 6.1*). Because many of these Web sites offer many services, they need a sponsor to pay their expenses. For example, MySpace is owned by News Corporation, YouTube by Google, and eBay owns 25 percent of Craigslist.org.

CarnivalConnections is an example of how a socially oriented site is sponsored by a company.

Example: CarnivalConnections in Action. Carnival Cruise Line is sponsoring a social networking site (*carnivalconnections.com*) that attracts cruise fans to the site to exchange opinions, get organized in groups for a trip, and much more. It cost the company $300,000 to set up the site, but the company anticipates covering the cost through increased business. For details, see Fass (2006).

Social Commerce. In the era of Web 2.0 (see Chapter 8), setting up a shop (physical or online) and waiting for customers to arrive may no longer be enough. Instead, companies must be proactive by finding ways to engage customers, build relationships, and create communities. The creation of a trend, known as social commerce on the Internet today, is brought about by the merging of Web 2.0 technologies, e-business opportunities, and online communities. What differentiates social commerce from an ordinary e-business site is the social elements involved. Social

A Closer Look 6.2

Blogger.com: Web 2.0 Social Commerce of Google

Google embodies many of the concepts of Web 2.0. One of the most basic uses of Web 2.0 technologies is collaborative interfacing with others. Collaborative editing technologies, such as Wiki, and collaborative content technologies, such as social networking sites, share a common heritage of belief in the power of teamwork and individual contribution.

One of Google's earliest ventures into social networking is the social networking and blogging site Blogger.com, acquired by the company in 2002. Blogger.com was one of the earliest social networking sites, having been established in 1999 as a small social network site. Blogger.com's corporate policies remain adherent to the ideals of openness and availability of content that is often expressed in Web 2.0 definitions. Limitations on content are restricted only to the legally required minimum, and copyrights are explicitly assigned to the writer in order to encourage content creation and sharing.

It is not only Blogger.com's publishing and collaborative content creation capabilities that are in line with Web 2.0 philosophies, but also its technological capabilities. Blogger.com provides its own Application Programming Interface (API) and Web services for developers, allowing for extension and creation of entirely new applications within the bounds of its site. The site also offers a wide range of other APIs that allow users to customize the application experience within their site, including Atom format standard APIs and Google APIs. Perhaps more commonly used than its APIs, however, is the ability to modify the layout and appearance of its pages using customizable CSS and HTML tools. The tools available for Blogger.com allow the user to modify not only the appearance of his or her personal blog, but also the functionality of it. The outcome of these modifications can be as different as the Blogger Buzz development blog (available at *buzz.blogger.com*) and the Poem of the Week Blog (available at *poem-of-the-week.blogspot.com*). While it is clear that these two blogs share a common heritage of the base code, the look and feel, function, and operation of the site has been modified such that they no longer are standardized in any way. This is one of the most powerful aspects of Web 2.0 technology, and one of the most enthusiastically adopted by content providers. Blogger.com provides a powerful content creation and collaboration tool that is used by many individuals in many ways, and customized in ways varying from superficial changes in appearance to profound changes in the underlying application base.

Driven by their allowance of 20 percent time for private projects within their programming teams, Google's tools are constantly evolving in order to stay abreast of new technologies and paradigms. There is no way to predict what turns will come in their minor tools as the political and technological focus of the company evolves. However, Google's adoption of the Blogger.com platform, as well as its further experiments in social networking through tools such as Orkut and Google Blogs, demonstrates a dedication to social networking and the Web 2.0 paradigm. Further improvements in tools that are not nominally social networking sites will continue to occur as the collaborative decision support concept spreads and increased information input becomes more important to the average user of these tools. The modern world demands an increasingly high amount of information, while offering less and less; Google's embracing of collaborative decision support and social networking offers one way to circumvent this tendency and restore the availability of information.

Sources: Compiled from Google (2008) and *google.com* (accessed May 2008).

---

commerce is concerned with the creation of places where people can collaborate online, solicit advice from trusted individuals, and avail themselves of goods and services. Thus, the research and purchasing cycle are shrunk by the establishment of a single destination powered by the power of many (Rubel, 2005). Blogging is one of the successful Web 2.0 technologies (see *A Closer Look 6.2*).

The Minicase at the end of this chapter illustrates how a relatively small company, Stormhoek Vineyards, is using blogs and other Web 2.0 tools to advertise and increase sales.

The Scope of EC. Figure 6.2 describes the broad field of e-commerce. As can be seen in the figure, there are many *EC applications* (top of the figure); most of these are shown throughout the book. Figure 6.2 shows that the EC applications are supported by an *infrastructure* (bottom part), which includes hardware, software, and networks, ranging from browsers to multimedia, and also by the following five support areas (shown as pillars in the middle):

1. **People.** They are the sellers, buyers, intermediaries, information systems specialists, and other employees, and any external participants.

2. **Public policy.** There are legal and other policy and regulating issues, such as privacy protection and taxation, that are determined by the government and by international agreements.

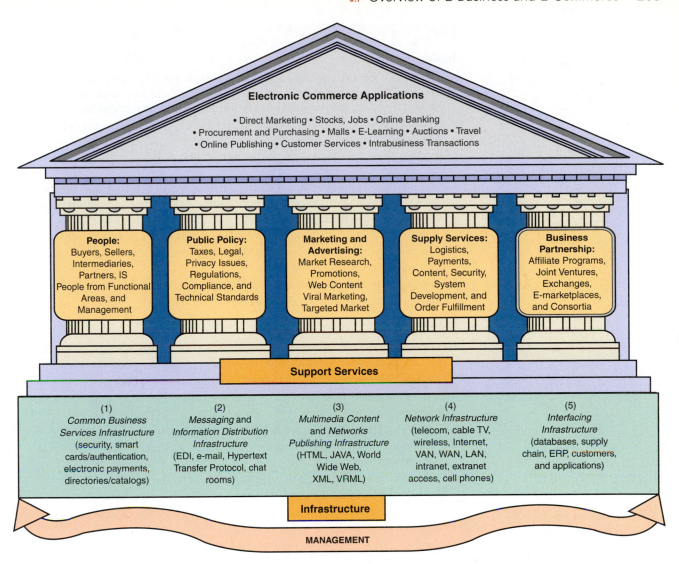

Figure 6.2 A framework for E-commerce. *(Source: Drawn by E. Turban.)*

3. Marketing and advertising. EC usually requires the support of marketing and advertising, like any other business. This is especially important in online transactions where the buyers and sellers usually do not know each other.

4. Support services. Many services, ranging from payments to order fulfillment and content creation, are needed to support EC.

5. Business partnerships. Joint ventures, e-marketplaces, and business partnerships are common in EC. These occur especially throughout the supply chain (i.e., the collaboration between a company and its suppliers, customers, and other partners).

All of these EC components require good coordination and *management practices* to unify the applications, infrastructure, and support. This means that companies need to plan, coordinate, organize, motivate, devise strategy, and restructure processes as needed, that is, to manage the EC.

BENEFITS AND LIMITATIONS OF E-COMMERCE

Few innovations in human history encompass as many benefits to organizations, individuals, and society as does e-commerce. These benefits will increase significantly as EC expands. The major benefits are listed in Table 6.2.

TABLE 6.2	Benefits of E-Commerce

To Organizations

- Expands a company's selling and buying opportunities to national and international markets. With minimal capital outlay, a company can quickly locate more customers, the best suppliers, and the most suitable business partners worldwide.
- Enables companies to procure material and services from other countries rapidly and at less cost.
- Shortens or even eliminates marketing distribution channels, making products cheaper and vendors' profits higher.
- Decreases (by as much as 90 percent) the cost of creating, processing, distributing, storing, and retrieving digitizable products and services (e.g., music, software).
- Allows lower inventories by facilitating "pull"-type supply chain management (see Online Appendix 2A). This allows product customization and reduces inventory costs.
- Lowers telecommunications costs because the Internet is much cheaper than value-added networks (VANs).
- Helps some small businesses compete against large companies.
- Enables a very specialized niche market (e.g., *cattoys.com*).

To Customers

- Frequently provides less expensive products and services by allowing consumers to conduct quick online searches and comparisons (e.g., *Froogle.com*).
- Gives consumers more choices in selecting products and vendors.
- Enables customers to shop or make other transactions 24 hours a day, from almost any location.
- Retrieves relevant and detailed information in seconds.
- Enables consumers to get customized products or services, from PCs to cars, at competitive prices.
- Makes it possible for people to work and study at home.
- Makes possible electronic auctions that benefit buyers and sellers.
- Allows consumers to interact in electronic communities and to exchange ideas and compare experiences.

To Society

- Enables individuals to work at home and to do less traveling, resulting in less road traffic, less energy use, and less air pollution.
- Allows some merchandise to be sold at lower prices, thereby increasing people's standard of living.
- Enables people in developing countries and rural areas to enjoy products and services that otherwise are not available. This includes opportunities to learn professions and even earn college degrees, or to receive better medical care.
- Facilitates delivery of public services, such as government entitlements, reducing the cost of distribution and chance of fraud, and increasing the quality of social services, police work, healthcare, and education.

Counterbalancing its many benefits, EC has some limitations, both technological and nontechnological, which have slowed its growth and acceptance. The major limitations are listed in Table 6.3. As time passes, the limitations, especially the technological ones, will lessen or be overcome. In addition, appropriate planning can minimize the negative impact of some of them.

Despite its limitations, e-commerce has made very rapid progress. Also, various B2B activities, e-auctions, e-government, e-learning, and some B2C activities are ballooning. As experience accumulates and technology improves, the ratio of EC benefits to cost will increase, resulting in an even greater rate of EC adoption.

TABLE 6.3	**Limitations of E-Commerce**

Technological Limitations

- Lack of universally accepted standards for quality, security, and reliability.
- Insufficient telecommunications bandwidth.
- Still-evolving software development tools.
- Difficulties in integrating the Internet and EC applications and software with some existing (especially legacy) applications and databases.
- Need for special Web servers in addition to the network servers.
- Expensive and/or inconvenient Internet accessibility for many would-be users.

Nontechnological Limitations

- Some unresolved legal issues (see Section 6.7).
- Lack of national and international government regulations and industry standards.
- Lack of mature methodologies for measuring benefits of and justifying EC.
- Many sellers and buyers waiting for EC to stabilize before they take part.
- Customer resistance to changing from a real to a virtual store. Many people do not yet sufficiently trust paperless, faceless transactions.
- Perception that EC is expensive and unsecured.
- An insufficient number (critical mass) of sellers and buyers exists for many EC products and services.

Review Questions

1. Define e-commerce and pure vs. partial ones.
2. List the major types of EC transaction.
3. Distinguish between business-to-consumer, business-to-business, and intrabusiness EC.
4. Define social commerce and distinguish it from e-commerce.
5. Define a business model and list five EC business models.
6. Relate EC to blogging and wikis.
7. Describe the scope of EC and list its major participants.

6.2 Major EC Mechanisms

The major mechanisms for buying and selling on the Internet are electronic markets, electronic catalogs, electronic auctions, and online bartering. These are the topics of this section. Other mechanisms—e-storefronts, e-malls, and exchanges—are described in Sections 6.3 and 6.4.

ELECTRONIC MARKETS

The major place for conducting EC transactions is the electronic market or marketplace (e-market). An **e-market** is a virtual marketplace in which sellers and buyers meet and conduct different types of transactions. The functions of e-market are the same as those of a physical marketplace; however, computerized systems tend to make markets much more efficient by providing more updated information to buyers and sellers. The functions of e-markets are provided in Online Brief 6.1. The major types of e-markets are described in Section 6.4.

ELECTRONIC CATALOGS AND CLASSIFIEDS

Catalogs have been printed on paper for generations. Electronic catalogs on CD-ROM and the Internet have gained popularity. Electronic catalogs consist of a product database, directory and search capabilities, and a presentation function. They are the backbone of most e-commerce sites. For merchants, the objective of electronic catalogs is to advertise and promote products and services. For the customer, the purpose of such catalogs is to provide a source of information on products and services.

ELECTRONIC AUCTIONS (E-AUCTIONS)

An **auction** is a competitive process in which either a seller solicits bids from buyers or a buyer solicits bids from sellers. The primary characteristic of auctions, whether offline or online, is that prices are determined dynamically by competitive bidding. Auctions have been an established method of commerce for generations, and they are well-suited to deal with products and services for which conventional marketing channels are ineffective or inefficient. Electronic auctions generally increase revenues for sellers by broadening the customer base and shortening the cycle time of the auction. Buyers generally benefit from e-auctions by the opportunity to bargain for lower prices and the convenience of not having to travel to an auction site to "attend" the auction. They can also find rare and collector's items online. Additional benefits of electronic auctions are shown in Online Brief 6.2.

The Internet provides an efficient infrastructure for executing auctions at lower administrative cost and with many more involved sellers and buyers. Individual consumers and corporations can participate in this growing form of e-commerce. There are several types of electronic auctions, each with its motives and procedures. Auctions are divided here into two major types: *forward* auctions and *reverse* auctions.

Forward Auctions. **Forward auctions** are auctions that *sellers* use as a selling channel to many potential buyers. Usually, items are placed at a special site for auction, and buyers will bid continuously for the items. The highest bidder wins the items. Sellers and buyers can be individuals or businesses. The popular auction site eBay.com conducts mostly forward auctions. There are two types of forward e-auctions. One is to *liquidate* existing inventory; the other one is to *increase marketing outreach and efficiency*. Customers in the first type seek the lowest price on widely available goods or services; customers in the second type seek access to unique products or services.

Reverse Auctions. In **reverse auctions,** there is one buyer, usually an organization, that wants to buy a product or a service. Here, a company that wants to buy items places a *request for quote* (RFQ) on its Web site or in a third-party bidding marketplace. Once RFQs are posted, sellers (usually preapproved suppliers) submit bids electronically. Such auctions attract large pools of willing sellers, who can be manufacturers, distributors, or retailers. The bids are routed via the buyer's intranet to the engineering and finance departments for evaluation. Clarifications are made via e-mail, and the winner is notified electronically. Suppliers are invited to submit bids. Online bidding is much faster than conventional bidding, and it usually attracts many more bidders. The reverse auction is the most common auction model for large purchases, in terms of either quantities or price. Everything else being equal, the lowest-price bidder wins the auction. Governments and large corporations frequently mandate this approach for procurements (known as request for quotes), which may provide considerable savings.

Auctions are used in B2C, B2B, C2B, e-government, and C2C commerce, and they are becoming popular in many countries. The Internet opens many opportunities for e-auctions. Auctions can be conducted from the seller's site, the buyer's site, or from a third party's site. For example, as described in *IT at Work 6.1*, eBay, the best-known third-party site, offers hundreds of thousands of different items in several types of auctions. Over 300 other major companies, including *amazon.com* and *dellauction.com*, offer online auctions as well.

BARTERING AND NEGOTIATIONS

Related to auctions is **electronic bartering,** the electronically supported exchange of goods or services *without a monetary transaction*. Electronic bartering is done through means of individual-to-individual bartering ads that appear in some newsgroups, bulletin boards, and chat rooms. There also are several intermediaries that arrange for corporate e-bartering (e.g., *barterbrokers.com*). These intermediaries try to match online partners to a barter transaction. Online negotiation can be done via sites such as *ioffer.com*.

IT at Work 6.1

EBay—World's Largest Auction Site

EBay (*ebay.com*) is the world's largest auction site, and one of the most profitable e-businesses. The successful online auction house has its roots in a 50-year-old novelty item—Pez candy dispensers. Pamela Kerr, an avid collector of Pez dispensers, came up with the idea of trading them over the Internet. When she shared this idea with her boyfriend (now her husband), Pierre Omidyar, he was instantly struck with the soon-to-be-famous e-business auction concept. In 1995, the Omidyars started the company, later renamed eBay, that has since become the premier online auction house. The business model of eBay was to provide an electronic infrastructure for conducting mostly C2C auctions, although it caters to businesses (sellers and buyers) as well. Technology replaces the traditional auctioneer as the intermediary between buyers and sellers.

On eBay, people can buy and sell just about anything. It has millions of unique auctions in progress and over 500,000 new items are added each day. The company collects a submission fee upfront, plus a commission as a percentage of the sale amount. The submission fee is based on the amount of exposure you want your item to receive. For example, a higher fee is required if you would like to be among the "featured auctions" in your specific product category, and an even higher fee if you want your item to be listed on the eBay home page under Featured Items.

The seller must specify a minimum opening bid. Sellers might set the opening bid lower than the *reserve price*, a minimum acceptable bid price, in order to generate bidding activity. If a successful bid is made, the seller and the buyer negotiate the payment method, shipping details, warranty, and other particulars. EBay serves as a liaison between the parties; it is the interface through which sellers and buyers can conduct business.

After a few years of successful operations and tens of millions of loyal users, eBay started to do B2C (e-tailing), mostly in fixed prices (known as classifieds). By 2003, eBay operated several specialty sites, such as eBay Motors. eBay also operates a *business exchange* in which small- and medium-sized enterprises can buy and sell new and used merchandise, in B2B or B2C modes. In addition, *half.com*, the famous discount e-tailer, is now part of eBay and so is *paypal.com*, the person-to-person payment company. EBay has become so popular that it has led to academic recognition with the creation of a new course at the University of Birmingham (UK). The course, "Buying and Selling on eBay.co.uk," offers a step-by-step guide to trading online (Lyons, 2004).

A special feature is eBay Stores. These stores are rented to individuals and companies. The renting companies can use these stores to sell from catalogs or conduct auctions. In 2002, eBay introduced the Business Marketplace, located at *ebay.com/businessmarketplace*. This site brings together all business-related listings on eBay to one destination, making it easier for small businesses to find the equipment and supplies they need.

Many individuals are using eBay Stores and Marketplace to make a living. Some of them are very successful. Holden (2006) describes how 10 different entrepreneurs tapped into the power of eBay and are making millions.

EBay operates *globally*, permitting international trades to take place. Country-specific sites are located in over 25 countries. Buyers from more than 160 other countries also participate. Finally, eBay operates locally: it has over 60 local sites in the United States that enable users to easily find items located near them, to browse through items of local interest, and to meet face-to-face to conclude transactions. The domain *ebay.com* attracted at least 902 million visitors annually by May 2008. According to company financial statements, eBay reported $58 billion in sales in 2007, and it anticipated net revenue of $9 billion in 2008.

For more on eBay, see *digitalenterprise.org/cases/ebay.html*.

Sources: Compiled from press releases and descriptions at *ebay.com* (2002–2008); Staff (2005) and Schonfield (2005), and from Holden (2006).

For Further Exploration: Does eBay's 2003 change of business model, from pure auctions to adding classifieds and e-tailing, make sense? Why are wireless auctions promoted?

Until recently, e-bartering matched only two individuals at a time who basically exchanged products or services (e.g., see Peerflix, Bookins, and La La). Another company, Swaptree (*swaptree.com*), developed a mechanism that allows up to four traders to exchange products/services in one transaction (initially CDs, videogames, books, and DVDs). Each trade lists what they have to give and what they need. Swaptree does the matching, assuming all items have the same value. Swaptree.com provides the service for free and plans to make money from advertising. For details, see Copeland (2006).

Review Questions

1. Describe electronic markets.
2. Define forward and reverse auctions.
3. How are forward auctions used as a selling channel?
4. Describe the process of using reverse auctions for purchasing.
5. Define electronic bartering.

6.3 Business-to-Consumer Applications

Selling and buying in EC is divided into two major categories: Businesses selling to individual customers (B2C) which we cover in this section, and businesses selling to businesses (B2B) which we cover in Section 6.4.

B2C E-commerce began when companies such as Amazon.com and Godiva.com (Online Minicase 6.1) started selling directly to consumers using the Internet. Here we will look at some of the major categories of B2C applications, which are expected to exceed $2 trillion by 2009.

ELECTRONIC RETAILING MECHANISMS: STOREFRONTS AND MALLS

For generations home shopping from catalogs has flourished, and television shopping channels have been attracting millions of shoppers for more than two decades. Shopping online offers an alternative to catalog and television shopping.

Like any mail-order shopping experience, e-commerce enables you to buy from anywhere, and to do so 24 hours a day, 7 days a week. However, EC offers a wider variety of products and services, including the most unique items, often at lower prices. Furthermore, within seconds, shoppers can get very detailed supplementary information on products and can easily search for and compare competitors' products and prices. Finally, using the Internet, buyers can find hundreds of thousands of products and sellers.

Both goods and services are sold online. Goods that are bought most often online are computers and computer-related items, office supplies, books and magazines, CDs, cassettes, movies and videos, office supplies, clothing and shoes, and toys. Services that are bought most often online include entertainment, travel services, stocks and bonds trading, electronic banking, insurance, and job matching. (Services will be presented as a separate topic later in this section.) Directories and hyperlinks from other Web sites and intelligent search agents help buyers find the best stores and products to match their needs.

Two popular B2C shopping mechanisms online are electronic storefronts and electronic malls.

Electronic Storefronts. Hundreds of thousands of solo storefronts can be found on the Internet, each with its own Internet address (URL), at which orders can be placed. Called **electronic storefronts,** they may be an *extension* of physical stores such as Home Depot, The Sharper Image, Godiva.com, or Wal-Mart. Or they may be new businesses started by entrepreneurs who saw a niche on the Web, such as *cdnow.com, uvine.com, restaurant.com,* and *alloy.com.* Besides being used by retailers (e.g., Officedepot.com), storefronts also are used by manufacturers (e.g., *dell.com*). Retailers' and manufacturers' storefronts may sell to individuals (B2C) and/or to organizations (B2B).

Electronic Malls. An **electronic mall,** also known as a cybermall or e-mall, is a collection of individual shops under one Internet address. The basic idea of an electronic mall is the same as that of a regular shopping mall—to provide a one-stop shopping place that offers many products and services. Each cybermall may include thousands of vendors. For example, *shopping.msn.com* includes tens of thousands of products from thousands of vendors. A special mall that provides discounts and cash back is *cashbackstores.net.*

Two types of malls exist. First, there are *referral malls* (e.g., *hawaii.com*). You cannot buy in such a mall, but instead you are automatically transferred from the mall to a participating storefront. In the second type of mall (e.g., *shopping.yahoo.com*), you can actually make a purchase. At this type of mall, you might shop from several stores but you make only one purchase transaction at the end; an *electronic shopping cart* enables you to gather items from various vendors and pay for them all together in one transaction. (The mall organizer, such as Yahoo, takes a commission from the sellers for this service.)

As is true for vendors that locate in a physical shopping mall, a vendor that locates in an e-mall gives up a certain amount of independence. Its success depends on the popularity of the mall, as well as on its own marketing efforts. On the other hand, malls generate streams of prospective customers who otherwise might never have stopped by the individual store. For interesting malls, see *shopping-headquarters.com* and *choicemall.com*.

E-TAILING: THE ESSENTIALS

The concept of *retailing* implies sales of goods and/or services from many manufacturers to many individual customers. When it is done online, it is referred to as e-tailing. One of the most interesting properties of e-tailing is the ability to offer *customized* products and services to individual customers at a reasonable price and fairly fast (as done by Dell Computer). Many sites (e.g., *nike.com* and *lego.com*) offer product *self-configuration* from their B2C portals. The most well-known B2C site is Amazon.com, whose story is presented in *IT at Work 6.2*. A potential major competitor is Wal-Mart.com (see Online Minicase 6.2).

ONLINE SERVICE INDUSTRIES

Selling books, toys, computers, and most other products on the Internet may reduce vendors' selling costs by 20 to 40 percent. Further reduction is difficult to achieve because the products must be delivered physically. Only a few products (such as software or music) can be digitized to be delivered online for additional savings. On the other hand, delivery of *services*, such as buying an airline ticket or buying stocks or insurance online, can be done 100 percent electronically, with considerable cost reduction potential. This is why the airlines are pushing self-service e-tickets and your stock broker wants you to get your confirmations electronically. Therefore, online delivery of services is growing very rapidly.

IT at Work 6.2

MKT   GLOBAL

Amazon.Com: The King of E-Tailing

Entrepreneur and e-tailing pioneer Jeff Bezos, envisioning the huge potential for retail sales over the Internet, selected books as the most logical product for e-tailing. In July 1995, Bezos started Amazon.com, offering books via an electronic catalog from its Web site. Key features offered by the Amazon.com "superstore" were broad selection, low prices, easy searching and ordering, useful product information and personalization, secure payment systems, and efficient order fulfillment. Early on, recognizing the importance of order fulfillment, Amazon.com invested hundreds of millions of dollars in building physical warehouses designed for shipping small packages to hundreds of thousands of customers.

Over the years since its founding, Amazon.com has continually enhanced its business model by improving the customer's experience. For example, customers can personalize their Amazon accounts and manage orders online with the patented "One-Click" order feature. This personalized service includes an electronic wallet, which enables shoppers to place an order in a secure manner without the need to enter their address, credit card number, and so forth, each time they shop. One-Click also allows customers to view their order status and make changes on orders that have not yet entered the shipping process.

In addition, Amazon has been adding services and alliances to attract customers to make more purchases. For example, the company now offers specialty stores, such as its professional and technical store. It also is expanding its offerings beyond books.

For example, in June 2002 it became an authorized dealer of Sony Corp. for selling Sony products online. Today you can find almost any product that sells well on the Internet, ranging from beauty aids to sporting goods to cars.

Amazon has more than 500,000 affiliate partners that refer customers to Amazon.com. Amazon pays a 3 to 5 percent commission on any resulting sale. In yet another extension of its services, in September 2001 Amazon signed an agreement with Borders Group Inc., providing Amazon's users with the option of picking up books, CDs, and so on at Borders' physical bookstores. Amazon.com also is becoming a Web-fulfillment contractor for national chains such as Target and Circuit City.

In January 2002, Amazon.com declared its first-ever profit—for the 2001 fourth quarter; 2003 was the first year it cleared a profit in each quarter. The company employed 17,000 full-time staff by the end of 31 December 2007. In addition, net sales increased from $5 billion in 2003 to $15 billion in 2007. For more on Amazon, see *digitalenterprise.org/cases/amazon.html*.

Sources: Compiled from *amazon.com* (accessed May 2008), Bayers (2002), and Daisey (2002).

For Further Exploration: What are the critical success factors for Amazon.com? What advantages does it have over other e-tailers (e.g., *walmart.com* or see *barnesandnoble.com*)? What is the purpose of the alliances Amazon.com has made?

We will take a quick look here at the leading online service industries: banking, trading of securities (stocks, bonds), job matching, travel services, and real estate.

Cyberbanking. Electronic banking, also known as **cyberbanking,** includes various banking activities conducted from home, a business, or on the road instead of at a physical bank location. Electronic banking has capabilities ranging from paying bills to applying for a loan. It saves time and is convenient for customers. For banks, it offers an inexpensive alternative to branch banking (for example, about 2 cents' cost per transaction versus $1.07 at a physical branch) and a chance to enlist remote customers. Many conventional banks now offer online banking, and some use EC as a major competitive strategy. In addition to regular banks with added online services, we are seeing the emergence of *virtual banks*, dedicated solely to Internet transactions, such as the E*Trade Bank (*bankus.etrade.com*).

International and Multiple-Currency Banking. International banking and the ability to handle trading in multiple currencies are critical for international trade. Transfers of electronic funds and electronic letters of credit are important services in international banking. An example of support for EC global trade is provided by TradeCard (*tradecard.com*) in conjunction with MasterCard. Banks and companies such as Oanda also provide currency conversion of over 160 currencies. Although some international retail purchasing can be done by giving a credit card number, other transactions may require cross-border banking support. For example, Hong Kong and Shanghai Bank (*hsbc.com.hk*) has developed a special system (called Hexagon or HSBCnet) to provide electronic banking in 60 countries. Using this system, the bank has leveraged its reputation and infrastructure in the developing economies of Asia to rapidly become a major international bank without developing an extensive new branch network.

Online Securities Trading. In Korea, more than half of stock traders are using the Internet for their trades. Why? Because it makes a lot of dollars and "sense": An online trade typically costs the trader between $5 and $15, compared to an average fee of $100 from a full-service broker and $25 from a discount broker. Orders can be placed from anywhere, any time, even from your cell phone, and there is no waiting on busy telephone lines. Furthermore, the chance of making mistakes is small because online trading does away with oral communication of orders. Investors can find on the Web a considerable amount of information regarding specific companies or mutual funds in which to invest (e.g., *money.cnn.com,* *bloomberg.com*).

FIN

Example. Let's say that you have an account with Charles Schwab. You access Schwab's Web site (*schwab.com*) from your PC or your Internet-enabled mobile device, enter your account number and password to access your personalized Web page, and then click on "stock trading." Using a menu, you enter the details of your order (buy or sell, margin or cash, price limit, market order, etc.). The computer tells you the current "ask" and "bid" prices, much as a broker would do on the telephone, and you can approve or reject the transaction. Some well-known companies that offer only online trading are E*Trade, and Ameritrade.

However, both online banking and securities trading require tight security. Otherwise, your money could be at risk. Most online banks and stock traders protect you with ID numbers and passwords. Yet even this may not be secure enough. See Section 6.6 for more information on how to improve online security.

The Online Job Market. The Internet offers a promising environment for job seekers and for companies searching for hard-to-find employees. Thousands of companies and government agencies advertise available positions, accept résumés, and take applications via the Internet. The online job market is especially effective and active for technology-oriented jobs (e.g., *dice.com*). The online job market is used by job seekers to reply online to employment ads, to place résumés on various sites, and to use recruiting firms (e.g., *monster.com, jobdirect.com, jobcentral.com*). Companies that have jobs to offer advertise openings on their Web sites or search the bulletin boards of recruiting firms. In many countries, governments must advertise job openings on the Internet. In addition, hundreds of job-placement brokers and related services are active on the Web. (You can get help from *jobweb.com* or *brassring.com* to write your résumé.)

Travel Services. The Internet is an ideal place to plan, explore, and economically arrange almost any trip. Online travel services allow you to purchase airline tickets, reserve hotel rooms, and rent cars. Most sites also offer a fare-tracker feature that sends you e-mail messages about low-cost flights to your favorite destinations or from your home city. Examples of comprehensive online travel services are Expedia.com, Travelocity.com, and Orbitz.com. Services are also provided online by all major airline vacation services, large conventional travel agencies, car rental agencies, hotels (e.g., *hotels.com*), and tour companies. Priceline.com allows you to set a price you are willing to pay for an airline ticket or hotel accommodations and then attempts to find a vendor that will match your price. A similar service offered by Hotwire.com tries to find the lowest available price for you.

Real Estate. Real estate transactions are ideal for e-commerce. You can view many properties on the screen, and sort and organize properties according to your preferences and decision criteria. In some locations, brokers allow the use of real estate databases only from inside their offices, but considerable information is now available on the Internet. For example, Realtor.com allows you to search a database of over 2.5 million homes across the United States. The database is composed of local "multiple listings" of all available properties, in hundreds of locations. Those who are looking for an apartment can try Apartments.com or Rents.com. Housevalues.com offers many services at several URLs (see Internet Exercise #9).

CUSTOMER SERVICE

Whether an organization is selling to organizations or to individuals, in many cases a competitive edge is gained by providing superb customer service, which is part of CRM (Chapter 10). In e-commerce, customer service becomes even more critical, since customers and merchants do not meet face-to-face.

Phases in the Customer Service Life Cycle. Customer service should be approached as a business life cycle process, with the following four phases:

Phase 1. Requirements. Assist the customer to determine needs by providing photographs of a product, video presentations, textual descriptions, articles or reviews, sound bites on a CD, or downloadable demonstration files. Also use intelligent agents to make requirements suggestions and help in comparing other product/vendor attributes (e.g., see *google.com/products*).

Phase 2. Acquisition. Help the customer acquire a product or service (online order entry, negotiations, closing of sale, and delivery).

Phase 3. Ownership. Support the customer on an ongoing basis (interactive online user groups, online technical support, FAQs (frequently asked questions) and answers, resource libraries, newsletters, and online renewal of subscriptions).

Phase 4. Retirement. Help the client dispose of a service or product (online resale, classified ads).

Many activities can be conducted in each of these phases. For example, when an airline offers information such as flight schedules and fare quotes on its Web site, it is supporting phases 1 and 2. Similarly, when computer vendors provide electronic help desks for their customers, they are supporting phase 3. Dell will help you to auction your obsolete computer, and Amazon.com will help you to sell used books. These are activities that support phase 4.

FIN

Example: Fidelity Investments provides investors with "the right tools to make their own best investment decisions." The site (*fidelity.com*) has several sections, which include daily updates of financial news, information about Fidelity's mutual funds, material for interactive investment and retirement planning, and brokerage services. This is an example of support given to phase 1 in the online selling of services. The site also helps customers buy Fidelity's products (phase 2), handle their accounts (phase 3), and sell their securities (phase 4).

E-Entertainment. During the last few years we have witnessed an explosion of e-entertainment on the Web. Some is free and some for fee. Some of the entertainment is pure EC and some enhances a click-and-mortar business such as that of Netflix (*IT at Work 6.3*).

Customization and Personalization. A major benefit of EC is its ability to offer product and service customization or personalization at an affordable cost. Using the build-to-order concept, a manufacturer can offer you a product of your choice, as Dell is doing. Of course, the product/service is made of standard components in most cases. This is why it can be offered at a low price.

For example, Motorola gathers customer needs for a pager or a cellular phone, transmits the customer's specifications electronically to the manufacturing plant where the device is manufactured, and then sends the finished product to the customer within a day. General Motors and other car manufacturers use the same approach in building their products. Customers can use the Web to design or configure products for themselves. For example, customers can use the Web to design T-shirts, furniture, cars, jewelry, and even a Swatch watch. With the use of mass-customization methods, the cost of customized products is at or slightly above the comparable retail price of standard products.

According to *Business 2.0*, Timberland Boot Studio gets three times as many hits on its customized boots (allowing different leathers and colors), and Lands' End is enjoying more repeat customers and higher sales on their customized product online (reported by Esfahani, 2005).

ISSUES IN E-TAILING

Despite e-tailing's ongoing growth, many e-tailers continue to face some major issues related to e-tailing. If not solved, they can slow the growth of an organization's e-tailing efforts. Major representative issues are described below.

1. Resolving channel conflict. If a seller is a click-and-mortar company, such as Levi's or GM, it may face a conflict with its regular distributors when it sells directly online. It is one of possible **channel conflicts** between an online selling channel and the physical selling channels. It may be internal (e.g., regarding pricing or advertising policies), or between a company that wants to sell direct to customers, and its existing distributors (such as in this case). Channel conflict has forced some companies to limit their B2C efforts; others (e.g., some automotive companies) have decided not to sell direct online. An alternative approach is to try to collaborate in some way with the existing distributors whose services may be restructured. For example, an auto company could allow customers to configure a car online, but require that the car be picked up from a dealer, where customers could also arrange financing, warranties, and service.

2. Resolving conflicts within click-and-mortar organizations. When an established company decides to sell direct online on a large scale, it may create a conflict within its offline operations. Conflicts may arise in areas such as pricing of products and services, allocation of resources (e.g., advertising budget), and logistics services provided by the offline activities to the online activities (e.g., handling of returns of items bought online). As a result of these conflicts, some companies have completely separated the "clicks" (the online portion of the organization) from the "mortar" or "bricks" (the traditional, offline brick-and-mortar part of the organization). Such separation may increase expenses and reduce the synergy between the two organizational parts.

IT at Work 6.3

Netflix Increases Sales Using Movie Recommendations

SVR   MKT

Netflix (netflix.com) is the world's largest online movie rental subscription company. The company has more than 1,500 employees and over 7 million subscribers. It offers more than 90,000 titles in over 200 categories and more than 55 million DVDs as well as over 5,000 full-length movies and television episodes that are available for instant watching on PCs. A typical neighborhood movie store generally has fewer than 3,000 titles and has multiple copies of only a fraction of them. Netflix distributes one million DVDs each day.

The Problem. Because of the large number of titles available on DVD, customers often had difficulty determining which ones they would like to rent. In most cases, they picked up the most popular recent titles, which meant that Netflix had to maintain more and more copies of the same title. In addition, some unpopular titles were not renting well, even though they matched certain customers' preferences. For Netflix, matching titles with customers and maintaining the right level of inventory is critical.

A second major problem facing Netflix is the competitive nature of the movie rental business. Netflix competes against Blockbuster and other rental companies, as well as against companies offering downloads of movies and videos.

The Solution. Netflix reacted successfully to the first problem by offering a recommendation intelligent agent (Chapter 12) called CineMatch. This software agent uses data mining tools to sift through a database of over one billion film ratings (which is growing rapidly), as well as through customers' rental histories. Using proprietary formulas, CineMatch recommends rentals to individuals. It is a personalized service, similar to the one offered by Amazon.com that recommends books to customers. The recommendation is accomplished by comparing an individual's likes, dislikes, and preferences against people with similar tastes using a variant of collaborative filtering (described later in this chapter). (Both Blockbuster and Walmart.com are emulating Netflix's model.) With the recommendation system, Netflix tells subscribers which DVDs/CDs they will probably like. CineMatch is like the clerk at a small movie store who sets aside titles he knows you will like.

Netflix subscribers can also invite one another to become "friends" and make movie recommendations to each other, peek at one another's rental lists, and see how other subscribers have rated other movies using a social network called FriendsSM. All these personalized functions make the online rental store very customer-friendly. It is an example of a social network.

To improve CineMatch's accuracy, in October 2006 Netflix began a contest offering $1 million to the first person or team to write a program that would increase the prediction accuracy of CineMatch by 10 percent. The company understands that this will take quite some time; therefore, it is offering a $50,000 Progress Prize each year the contest runs. This prize goes to the team whose solution shows the most improvement over the previous year's accuracy bar (see *netflixprize.com*).

Starting September 13, 2006, Netflix launched a 5-week trivia sweepstakes program with *USA Weekend* magazine. Trivia questions were published each week in USA Weekend, directing its 50 million readers to *netflix.com/usaweekend* to enter the sweep-

stakes and qualify to win weekly prizes. Prizes ranged from $250 to $4,000, costing the company over $140 million.

The Results. As a result of implementing its CineMatch system, Netflix has seen very fast growth in sales and membership. The benefits of CineMatch include the following:

- **Effective recommendations.** According to Netflix (2006), members select 70 percent of their movies based on CineMatch's recommendations.

- **Increased customer satisfaction and loyalty.** The movies recommended generate more satisfaction than the ones customers choose from the new releases page. As a result, between 70 and 80 percent of Netflix rentals come from the company's back catalog of 38,000 films rather than recent releases. It increases customer loyalty to the site and satisfaction for over 90 percent of the customers.

- **Broadened title coverage.** Renters expand their taste. Seventy percent of the movies Netflix customers rent are recommended to them on the site; 80 percent of rental activity comes from 2,000 titles. This decreases demand for popular new releases, which is good for Netflix, whose revenue-sharing agreements require larger payouts for newly released films. One example is Control Room, a documentary film about Arab television outlet Al Jazeera. Netflix has a 12 percent share of the total movie rental market, and you would expect its share of the rentals for Control Room to be in the same range. But Netflix accounted for 34 percent of the title's rental activity in the United States the week it was released on DVD. The difference is primarily due to Netflix's recommendation tools.

- **Better understanding of customer preference.** Netflix's recommendation system collects more than 2 million ratings forms from subscribers daily to add to its huge database of users' likes and dislikes.

- **Fast membership growth.** Netflix found that the most reliable prediction for how much a customer will like a movie is what the customer thought of other movies. The company credits the system's ability to make automated, yet accurate, recommendations as a major factor in its growth from 600,000 subscribers in 2002 to nearly 7 million by the end of 2007.

CineMatch has become the company's core competence. Netflix's future relies heavily on CineMatch's making accurate recommendations and subscribers' accepting them, which is why the company strives to increase its accuracy.

Sources: Compiled from Flynn (2006); Null (2003); and from *netflix.com* (accessed May 2008).

For Further Exploration: Do you like a Web site to make recommendations for when you visit a physical video store such as Blockbuster, or do you prefer to listen to a person? How about recommendations from online rental stores such as Netflix? Why do you like or dislike them? What about downloading the movies from Movielink and CinemaNow? You pay much more, but you download the movie in an hour and it is yours to keep!

3. Organizing order fulfillment and logistics. E-tailers face a difficult problem of how to ship very small quantities to a large number of buyers. This can be a difficult undertaking, especially when returned items need to be handled.

4. Determining viability and risk of online e-tailers. Many purely online e-tailers folded in 2000–2002, the result of problems with cash flow, customer acquisition, order fulfillment, and demand forecasting. Online competition, especially in commodity-type products such as CDs, toys, books, or groceries, became very fierce due to the ease of entry to the marketplace. So a problem most young e-tailers face is to determine how long to operate while you are still losing money and how to finance the losses.

5. Identifying appropriate revenue models. One early dot-com model was to generate enough revenue from advertising to keep the business afloat until the customer base reached critical mass. This model did not work. Too many dot-coms were competing for too few advertising dollars, which went mainly to a small number of well-known sites such as AOL, MSN, Google, and Yahoo!. Advertising is the primary source of income of such portals (Luo and Najdawi, 2004). In addition, there was a "chicken-and-egg" problem: sites could not get advertisers to come if they did not have enough visitors. To succeed in EC, it is necessary to identify appropriate revenue models. (For further discussion of EC revenue models, see Turban et al., 2008).

To successfully implement e-tailing and solve the five issues just discussed (and others), it is frequently necessary to conduct *market research*. Market research is needed for product design, marketing, and advertising decisions, pricing, and strategy. For a discussion of market research in e-commerce, see Online Brief 6.3.

Review Questions

1. Describe electronic storefronts and malls.
2. What are some general features (critical success factors) that make the delivery of online services (e.g., cyberbanking, securities trading, job hunting, travel services) successful for both sellers and buyers?
3. Describe how customer service is provided online and list its four phases.
4. List the major issues relating to e-tailing.

6.4 Business-to-Business Applications

In *business-to-business (B2B) applications,* the buyers, sellers, and transactions involve only organizations. Business-to-business comprises about 85 percent of EC dollar volume. It covers applications that enable an enterprise to form electronic relationships with its distributors, resellers, suppliers, customers, and other partners. By using B2B, organizations can restructure their supply chains and partner relationships.

There are several business models for B2B applications. The major ones are sell-side marketplaces, buy-side marketplaces, and electronic exchanges. Other B2B systems are described in Chapter 11.

SELL-SIDE CORPORATE MARKETPLACES

In the **sell-side marketplace** model, organizations attempt to sell their products or services to other organizations electronically from their own private e-marketplace and/or from a third-party site. This model is similar to the B2C model in which the buyer is expected to come to the seller's site, view catalogs, and place an order. In the B2B sell-side marketplace, however, the buyer is an organization.

The key mechanisms in the sell-side model are (1) electronic catalogs that can be customized for each large buyer, and (2) forward auctions. Sellers such as Dell Computer (*dellauction.com*) use auctions extensively. In addition to auctions from their own Web sites, organizations can use third-party auction sites, such as eBay, to liquidate items. Companies such as Overstock.com (see *liquidation.com*) are helping organizations to auction obsolete and old assets and inventories.

The sell-side model is used by hundreds of thousands of companies and is especially powerful for companies with superb reputations. The seller can be either a manufacturer (e.g., Dell, IBM), a distributor (e.g., *avnet.com* is an example of a large distributor in IT), or a retailer (e.g., *Walmart.com*). The seller uses EC to increase sales, reduce selling and advertising expenditures, increase delivery speed, and reduce administrative costs. The sell-side model is especially suitable to customization. For example, organizational customers can configure their orders online at *cisco.com*, and others. Self-configuration of orders results in fewer misunderstandings about what customers want and much faster order fulfillment.

BUY-SIDE CORPORATE MARKETPLACES

The **buy-side marketplace** is a model in which organizations attempt to buy needed products or services from other organizations electronically. A major method of buying goods and services in the buy-side model is a *reverse auction*, which was described in Section 6.2.

The buy-side model uses EC technology to streamline the purchasing process in order to reduce the cost of items purchased, the administrative cost of procurement, and the purchasing cycle time. Procurements using a third-party buy-side marketplace model are especially popular for medium and small organizations.

E-Procurement. Purchasing by using electronic support is referred to as **e-procurement.** E-procurement uses reverse auctions as well as two other popular mechanisms: group purchasing and desktop purchasing.

Group Purchasing. In **group purchasing,** the orders of many buyers are aggregated so that they total to a large volume, in order to merit more seller attention and discounts. The aggregated order can then be placed on a reverse auction, and a volume discount can be negotiated. Typically, the orders of small buyers are aggregated by a third-party (independent, not the seller, nor the buyer) vendor, such as United Sourcing Alliance (*usa-llc.com*). Group purchasing is especially popular in the healthcare industry (see *all-health.com*), and in education (*tepo.org*).

Desktop Purchasing. In a special case of e-procurement known as **desktop purchasing,** suppliers' catalogs are aggregated into an internal master catalog on the buyer's server, so that the company's purchasing agents (or even end users) can shop more conveniently. Desktop purchasing is most suitable for *indirect maintenance, replacement, and operations (MRO) items,* such as office supplies. The term *indirect* refers to the fact that these items are not inputs to manufacturing. In the desktop purchasing model, a company has many suppliers, but the quantities it purchases from each one are relatively small. This model is most appropriate for government entities and large companies. Online Minicase 6.3 examines how the U.K. Government Department for Environment, Food, and Rural Affairs (Defra) utilizes desktop purchasing.

PUBLIC EXCHANGES

E-marketplaces in which there are many sellers and many buyers (usually both businesses) and where entry is open to all are called **public exchanges** (in short, **exchanges**). They frequently are owned and operated by a third party. According to Kaplan and Sawhney (2000), there are four basic types of exchanges: (1) vertical exchanges for direct materials, (2) vertical exchanges for indirect materials, (3) horizontal exchanges, and (4) functional exchanges. *Vertical exchanges* serve one industry (e.g., automotive, chemical), and along the entire supply chain. *Horizontal exchanges* serve many industries that use the same products or services (e.g., office supplies, cleaning materials).

Types of public exchanges. Three major types of exchanges are

1. Vertical exchanges for direct materials. These are B2B marketplaces where *direct materials*—materials that are inputs to manufacturing—are traded, usually in *large quantities* in an environment of long-term relationship known as *systematic sourcing.* Examples are Plasticsnet.com and Papersite.com. Plastics are used in the furniture industries, while paper is used in the publishing industry.

2. Vertical exchanges for indirect materials. Here indirect materials in *one industry* are purchased usually on an as-needed basis (called *spot sourcing*). Buyers and sellers may not even know each other. ChemConnect.com and Isteelasia.com are examples. In such vertical exchanges, prices are continually changing, based on the matching of supply and demand. Auctions are typically used in this kind of B2B marketplace, sometimes done in private trading rooms, which are available in exchanges like ChemConnect.com (see *IT at Work 6.4*). Companies may trade the same commodity or parts in both types of markets (usually large quantity in type 1, direct materials; smaller or emergencies, in type 2, indirect material).

3. Horizontal exchanges. These are many-to-many e-marketplaces for indirect (MRO) materials, such as office supplies, light bulbs, and cleaning materials used by *any industry*. The quantities traded are usually not very large. Prices are fixed or negotiated in this systematic sourcing-type exchange. Examples are EcEurope.com, Globalsources.com, and Alibaba.com.

4. Functional exchanges. Here, needed services such as temporary help or extra space are traded on an as-needed basis (spot sourcing). For example, Employease.com can find temporary labor using employers in its Employease Network. Prices are dynamic, and vary depending on supply and demand.

All four types of exchanges offer support services, ranging from payments to logistics. Vertical exchanges are frequently owned and managed by a group of big players in an industry, referred to as a *consortium*. For example, Marriott and Hyatt own a procurement consortium for the hotel industry, and ChevronTexaco owns an energy e-marketplace. The vertical e-marketplaces offer services particularly suited to the community they serve.

Since B2B activities involve many companies, specialized network infrastructure is needed. Such infrastructure works either as an Internet/EDI or as extranets (see Tutorial #6).

IT at Work 6.4

Chemical Companies "Bond" at ChemConnect

Buyers and sellers of chemicals and plastics today can meet electronically in a large vertical commodity exchange called ChemConnect (*chemconnect.com*). Using this exchange, global chemical-industry leaders such as British Petroleum, Dow Chemical, BASF, and Sumitomo can reduce trading cycle time and cost and can find new markets and trading partners around the globe.

ChemConnect provides a public trading marketplace and an information portal to more than 9,000 members in 150 countries. In 2003, over 60,000 products were traded in this public, third-party-managed e-marketplace. ChemConnect provides three marketplaces: a commodity markets platform, a marketplace for sellers, and a marketplace for buyers, as described below. At the *commodity markets platform*, prequalified producers, customers, and distributors come together in real time to sell and buy chemical-related commodities such as natural-gas liquids, oxygenates, olefins, and polymers. They can even simultaneously execute multiple deals. Transactions are done through regional trading hubs.

The *marketplace for sellers* has many tools, ranging from electronic catalogs to forward auctions. It enables companies to find buyers all over the world. ChemConnect provides all of the necessary tools to expedite selling and achieving the best prices. It also allows for negotiations. The *marketplace for buyers* is a place where thousands of buyers shop for chemical-related indirect materials (and a few direct materials). The market provides for automated request for quote (RFQ) tools as well as a complete online reverse auction. The sellers' market

is connected to the buyers' market, so that sellers can connect to the RFQs posted on the marketplace for buyers.

In the three marketplaces, ChemConnect provides logistics and payment options. In all of its trading mechanisms, up-to-the-minute market information is available and can be translated into 30 different languages. Members pay transaction fees only for successfully completed transactions. Business partners provide several support services, such as financial services for the market members. The marketplaces work with certain rules and guidelines that ensure an unbiased approach to the trades. There is full disclosure of all legal requirements, payments, trading rules, and so on. (Click on "Legal info and privacy issues" at the ChemConnect Web site.) ChemConnect is growing rapidly, adding members and trading volume.

In 2006, ChemConnect expanded its offerings in the petroleum coke marketplace, enabling better price visibility, more efficient inventory management, broader sales channels, more efficient procurement, and effective risk management. Also, the exchange offers real-time dynamic auctions, real-time market intelligence, trade in real time, and detailed reporting and analytics.

Sources: Compiled from *chemconnect.com* (accessed May 2008), and Case Study: ChemConnect (2008).

For Further Exploration: What are the advantages of the ChemConnect exchange? Why are there three trading places? Why does the exchange provide information portal services?

Review Questions

1. Briefly differentiate between the sell-side marketplace and the buy-side market-place.
2. Explain how forward and reverse auctions are used in B2B commerce.
3. List and compare the various methods of e-procurement.
4. What is the role of exchanges in B2B?
5. Describe intrabusiness EC and list its major types.

6.5 Major Models of E-Business: From E-Government to C2C

As indicated earlier, the broad definition of EC includes other EC activities in addition to buying and selling. The major activities described in this section are EC intrabusiness (within organizations), collaborative commerce (within and among organizations), e-government, and consumer-to-consumer EC.

BUSINESS-TO-EMPLOYEES (B2E) COMMERCE

Companies are finding many ways to do business electronically with their own employees. They disseminate information to employees over the company intranet, for example, as part of their employee relationship management (see Chapter 10). Employees can manage their benefit packages and take training classes electronically. In addition, employees can use the corporate intranet to purchase discounted corporate products and services, insurance, travel packages, and tickets to events. They can also electronically order supplies and material needed for their work. In addition to the intranet, companies also disseminate information via wikis and blogs.

E-COMMERCE BETWEEN AND AMONG CORPORATE EMPLOYEES

Many large organizations allow employees to post classified ads on the company intranet, through which employees can buy and sell products and services from and to each other. This service is especially popular in universities, where it was conducted even before the commercialization of the Internet.

E-COMMERCE BETWEEN AND AMONG UNITS WITHIN THE BUSINESS

Large corporations frequently consist of independent units, or *strategic business units* (SBUs), which "sell" or "buy" materials, products, and services to or from each other (intranet transactions). Transactions of this type can be easily automated and performed over the intranet. An SBU can be either a seller or a buyer. An example is company-owned dealerships, which buy goods from the main company. This type of EC helps improve the internal supply chain operations.

COLLABORATIVE COMMERCE

Collaborative commerce (c-commerce) refers to the use of digital technologies that enable companies to collaboratively plan, design, develop, manage, and research products, services, and innovative EC applications. It is also referred to as e-collaborative, as shown in the Dell case. These activities differ from selling and buying. An example would be a company that is collaborating electronically with a vendor that designs a product or a part for the company. C-commerce implies communication, information sharing, and collaborative planning done electronically using tools such as groupware and specially designed EC collaboration tools.

Numerous studies suggest that collaborative relationships may result in significant improvement in organizations' performance. Major benefits cited are cost reduction, increased revenues, and better customer retention. These benefits are the results of fewer stockouts, less exception processing, reduced inventory throughout the supply chain, lower materials costs, increased sales volume, and increased competitive advantage. For examples, see Brook (2004).

C-commerce activities usually are conducted between and among supply chain partners, as shown in Online Minicase 6.4.

There are several varieties of c-commerce, ranging from joint design efforts to forecasting. Collaboration can be done both between and within organizations. Lately, collaboration is being facilitated by wikis, as will be illustrated in Chapter 8.

E-GOVERNMENT

As e-commerce tools and applications improve, greater attention is being given to their use to improve the business of public institutions and governments (country, state, county, city, etc.). **E-government** is the use of Internet technology and e-commerce to deliver information and public services to citizens, business partners and suppliers of government entities, and people who work in the public sector.

E-government offers a number of benefits: It improves the efficiency and effectiveness of the functions of government, including the delivery of public services. It enables governments to be more transparent to citizens and businesses by giving access to more of the information generated by government. E-government also offers greater opportunities for citizens to provide feedback to government agencies and to participate in democratic institutions and processes. As a result, e-government may facilitate fundamental changes in the relationships between citizens and governments. Online Minicase 6.5 demonstrates the changing role of a government when electronic commerce initiatives mature and are fully utilized at the Hong Kong SAR of China.

E-government transactions as described earlier can be divided into three major categories: G2C, G2B, and G2G. In the G2C category, government agencies increasingly are using the Internet to provide services to citizens. An example is *electronic benefits transfer* (EBT), in which governments (usually state or national) transfer benefits, such as Social Security and pension payments, directly to recipients' bank accounts or to smart cards. In G2B, governments use the Internet to sell to or buy from businesses. For example, *electronic tendering systems* using reverse auctions are becoming mandatory, to ensure the best price for government procurement of goods and services. G2G includes intragovernment EC (transactions between different governments) as well as services among different governmental agencies. For an overview, see *whitehouse.gov/omb/egov*.

CONSUMER-TO-CONSUMER E-COMMERCE

Consumer-to-consumer (C2C) e-commerce refers to e-commerce in which both the buyer and the seller are individuals (not businesses). C2C is conducted in several ways on the Internet, where the best-known C2C activities are auctions.

C2C Auctions. In dozens of countries, C2C selling and buying on auction sites is exploding. Most auctions are conducted by intermediaries, such as eBay.com. Consumers can select general sites, such as *auctionanything.com;* they also can use specialized sites, such as *bid2bid.com*. In addition, many individuals are conducting their own auctions. For example, *greatshop.com* provides software to create online C2C reverse auction communities.

Classified Ads. People sell to other people every day through classified ads in newspapers and magazines. Internet-based classified ads have one big advantage over these more traditional types of classified ads: they offer a national, rather than a local, audience (e.g., see *craigslist.org* or *traderonline.com*). This wider audience greatly increases the supply of goods and services available and the number of potential buyers. Internet-based classifieds often can be edited or changed easily, and in many cases they display photos of the product offered for sale. The major categories of online classified ads are similar to those found in the newspaper: vehicles, real estate, employment, pets, tickets, and travel. Classified ads are available through most Internet service providers (AOL, MSN, etc.), at some portals (Yahoo!, etc.), and from Internet directories, online newspapers, and more. To help narrow the search for a particular item on several sites, shoppers can use search engines. Once users find an ad and get the details, they can e-mail or call the other party for additional information or to make a purchase. Classified sites generate revenue from affiliate sites.

Personal Services. Numerous personal services (lawyers, handy helpers, tax preparers, investment advisors, dating services) are available on the Internet. Some are in the classified ads, but others are listed in specialized Web sites and directories. Some are for free, some for a fee. *Be very careful before you purchase any personal services online.* Fraud or crime could be involved. For example, an online lawyer may not be an expert in the area he or she professes, or may not deliver the service at all.

Support Services to C2C. When individuals buy products or services from individuals, they usually buy from strangers. The issues of ensuring quality, receiving payments, and preventing fraud are critical to the success of C2C. One service that helps C2C is payments by companies such as PayPal.com (see Section 6.6). Another one is *escrow services*, intermediaries that take the buyer's money and the purchased goods, and only after making sure that the seller delivers what was agreed upon, deliver the goods to the buyer and the money to the seller (for a fee).

Review Questions

1. What EC is done in B2E?
2. Describe the activities done in e-commerce.
3. Define e-government and its various transaction types.
4. What are typical G2B activities?
5. Define C2C EC and list some types of C2C activities.

6.6 E-Commerce Support Services: Payment and Order Fulfillment

The implementation of EC may require several support services. B2B and B2C applications require payments and order fulfillment; portals require content. Figure 6.3 portrays the collection of the major EC services. They include e-infrastructure (mostly technology consultants, system developers and integrators, hosting, security, wireless, and networks), e-process (mainly payments and logistics), e-markets (mostly marketing and

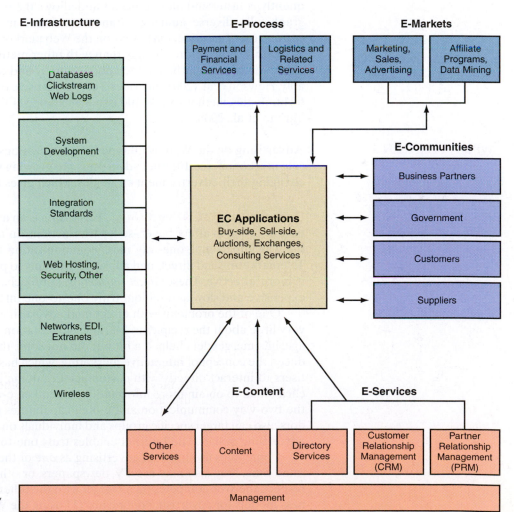

Figure 6.3 E-commerce support services. *(Source: Drawn by E. Turban. Based on S. Y. Choi et al., 1997, p. 18.)*

advertising), e-communities (different audiences and business partners), e-services (CRM, PRM, and directory services), and e-content (supplied by content providers). All of these services support the EC applications in the center of the figure, and all of the services need to be managed.

Here we will focus on three of the above topics—market research and advertisement, payments, and order fulfillment. For details on the other services, see Turban et al. (2008).

MARKET RESEARCH FOR EC

The goal of market research is to find information and knowledge that describe the relationships among consumers, products, marketing methods, and marketers. Its aim is to discover marketing opportunities and issues, to establish marketing plans, to better understand the purchasing process, and to evaluate marketing performance. On the Web, the objective is to turn browsers into buyers. Market research includes gathering information about topics such as the economy, industry, firms, products, pricing, distribution, competition, promotion, and consumer purchasing behavior.

Business, educational institutions, and governments use various tools to conduct consumer market research both *offline* and *online*. The major ones that are used in e-commerce are described by Zimmerman (2007). For further details, see Online Brief 6.3.

Methods for Conducting Market Research Online. EC market research can be conducted through conventional methods, or it can be done with the assistance of the Internet. Although telephone or shopping mall surveys will continue, interest in Internet research methods is on the rise. Market research that uses the Internet frequently is faster and more efficient and allows the researcher to access a more geographically diverse audience than those found in offline surveys (see FAQs at *casro.org and accutips.com*). Also, on the Web market researchers can conduct a very large study much more cheaply than with other methods. An online survey will cost a fraction of a similarly sized telephone survey and can expedite research considerably. Hewson et al. (2003) provides a comprehensive review of online market research technologies, methods, tools, and issues, including ethical ones. For further details, see Turban et al., 2008.

WEB ADVERTISING

Advertising on the Web by all types of organizations plays an extremely important role in e-commerce. Internet advertisers are growing very rapidly and companies are changing their advertisement strategies, which gives them a competitive edge.

Overview of Web Advertising. *Advertising* is an attempt to disseminate information in order to affect buyer–seller transactions. In *traditional* marketing, advertising was impersonal, one-way mass communication that was paid for by sponsors. Telemarketing and direct mail ads were attempts to personalize advertising to make it more effective. These *direct marketing* approaches worked fairly well but were expensive and slow and seldom truly one-to-one interactive.

One of the problems with direct mail advertising was that the advertisers knew very little about the recipients. Market segmentation by various characteristics (e.g., age, income, gender) helped a bit but did not solve the problem. The Internet introduced the concept of **interactive marketing,** which has enabled marketers and advertisers to interact directly with customers. In interactive marketing, a consumer can click an ad to obtain more information or send an e-mail to ask a question. Besides the two-way communication and e-mail capabilities provided by the Internet, vendors also can target specific groups and individuals on which they want to spend their advertising dollars. The Internet enables truly one-to-one advertising.

Companies use Internet advertising as *one* of their advertising channels. At the same time, they also may use TV, newspapers, or other traditional channels. In this respect, the Web competes on a budget with the other channels. The two major business models for advertising online are (1) using the Web as a channel to advertise a firm's own products and services, and (2) making a firm's site a public portal site and using captive audiences to advertise products offered by other firms. For example, the audience might come to a P&G Web site to learn about Tide, but they might also receive additional ads for products made by companies other than P&G.

REPRESENTATIVE ADVERTISING STRATEGIES ONLINE

Several advertising strategies can be used over the Internet. In this section, we will present the major strategies used.

Affiliate Marketing and Advertising. **Affiliate marketing** is the revenue model by which an organization refers consumers to the selling company's Web site. Affiliate marketing is used mainly as a revenue source for the referring organization and as a marketing tool for sellers. However, the fact that the selling company's logo is placed on many other Web sites is free advertising as well. Consider Amazon.com, whose logo can be seen on about 1 million affiliate sites!

Search Engine Advertisement. Most search engines allow companies to submit their Internet addresses, called universal resource locators (URLs), for free so that people can search them electronically. Search engine intelligent software programs (known as spider) crawl through each site, indexing its content and links. The site is then included in future searches. Because there are several thousand search engines, advertisers who use this method should register URLs with as many search engines as possible. In some cases, URLs may be searched even if they are not submitted. For details, see Chase (2006).

The major advantage of using URLs as an advertising tool is that it is *free*. Anyone can submit a URL to a search engine and be listed. By using URLs, it is likely that searchers for a company's products will receive a list of sites that mention the products, including the company's own site. Search engine advertisement has become the most popular online advertising method, mainly thanks to Google (see Online Minicase 6.6).

Ads as a Commodity. With the *ads-as-a-commodity* approach, people are paid for time spent viewing an ad. This approach is used at *mypoints.com*, *clickrewards.com*, and others. At Mypoints.com, interested consumers read ads in exchange for payment from the advertisers. Consumers fill out data on personal interests, and then they receive targeted banners based on their personal profiles. Each banner is labeled with the amount of payment that will be paid if the consumer reads the ad. If interested, the consumer clicks the banner to read it, and after passing some tests as to its content, is paid for the effort.

Viral Marketing. **Viral marketing** or advertising refers to *word-of-mouth* marketing in which customers promote a product or service by telling others about it. This can be done by e-mails, in conversations facilitated in chat rooms, by posting messages in newsgroups, in wikis and blogs (see the Stormhoek Vineyards Minicase at end of this chapter), and in electronic consumer forums. Having people forward messages to friends, asking them, for example, to "check out this product," is an example of viral marketing. This marketing approach has been used for generations, but now its speed and reach are multiplied by the Internet. This ad model can be used to build brand awareness at a minimal cost (*MoreBusiness.com*, 2007), because the people who pass on the messages are paid very little or nothing for their efforts.

Customizing Ads. The Internet has too much information for customers to view. Filtering irrelevant information by providing consumers with customized ads can reduce this information overload. BroadVision (*broadvision.com*) provides a customized ad service platform called BroadVision eMarketing. The heart of eMarketing is a customer database, which includes registration data and information gleaned from site visits. The companies that advertise via one-to-one advertising use the database to send customized ads to consumers. Using this feature, a marketing manager can customize display ads based on users' profiles. The product also provides market segmentation.

Online Events, Promotions, and Attractions. Today, promotions are regular events on thousands of Web sites. Contests, quizzes, coupons (see *coolsavings.com*), and giveaways designed to attract visitors are as much a part of online marketing as they are of offline commerce. Some innovative ideas used to encourage people to pay attention to online advertising are provided in Turban et al. (2008).

Live Web Events. Live Web events (concerts, shows, interviews, debates, sport matches, videos), if properly done, can generate tremendous public excitement and bring huge crowds to a Web site. These can be specially prepared for web showing, or general events that are broadcasted on tv and/or the web. According to Akamai Technologies, Inc. (2000), the best practices for successful live Web events are:

• Carefully planning content, audience, interactivity level, preproduction, and schedule
• Executing the production with rich media, if possible
• Conducting appropriate promotion via e-mails, affinity sites, and streaming media directories, as well as conducting proper offline and online advertisement
• Preparing for quality delivery
• Capturing data and analyzing audience response so that improvements can be made

Advertising in Newsletters. Free newsletters are abundant; in e-commerce there are many. An example is *Ecommerce Times*. This informative newsletter (*ecommercetimes.com*) solicits ads from companies (see "How to Advertise"). Ads are usually short, and they have a link to details. They are properly marked as "Advertisement."

Posting Press Releases Online. Millions of people visit popular portals such as Yahoo!, MSN, AOL, and Google every day looking for news. Thus, it makes sense to try to reach an audience through such sites. Indeed, Southwest Airlines was successful in selling $1.5 million in tickets by posting four press releases online.

Advergaming. **Advergaming** is the practice of using games, particularly computer games, to advertise or promote a product, an organization, or a viewpoint. Advergaming normally falls into one of three categories:

• A company provides interactive games on its Web site in the hope that potential customers will be drawn to the game and spend more time on the Web site or simply become more product (or brand) aware. The games themselves usually feature the company's products prominently. Examples are *intel.co.uk/itgame* and *clearahill.com*.
• Games are published in the usual way, but they require players to investigate further. The subjects may be commercial, political, or educational. Examples include *America's Army* (*americasarmy.com/downloads*), intended to boost recruitment for the United States Army, and *pepsiman.com*.
• With some games, advertising appears within the actual game. This is similar to subtle advertising in films, whereby the advertising content is within the "world" of the movie or game. An example is *cashsprint.com*, which puts advertising logos directly on the player's racing vehicle and around the racetrack.

For further discussion, see *en.wikipedia.org/wiki/Advergaming*, *adverblog.com*, and Gurau (2006).

ELECTRONIC PAYMENTS   Payments are an integral part of doing business, whether in the traditional way or online. Unfortunately, in several cases traditional payment systems are not effective for EC, especially for B2B. Cash cannot be used because there is no face-to-face contact. Not everyone accepts credit cards or checks, and some buyers do not have credit cards or checking accounts. Finally, contrary to what many people believe, it may be

TABLE 6.4	Electronic Payments Methods
Method	**Description**
Electronic funds transfer	Popular for paying bills online. Money is transferred electronically from payer's account to the recipient's.
Electronic checks	Digitally signed e-check is encrypted and moved from the buying customer to the merchant.
Electronic credit cards	Paying with regular credit cards (encrypted numbers); example: *eCharge.com*.
Purchasing e-cards	Corporate credit cards, with limits, work like regular credit cards, but must be paid quicker (e.g., in one week).
e-Cash—stored-value money cards	Prepaid card can be used for transportation, making copies in the library, parking (in some cities), telephone calls, etc.
e-Cash—smart cards	Cards that contain considerable information can be manipulated as needed and used for several purposes, including transfer of money.
e-Cash—person-to-person	Special online account from which funds can be sent to others is created. PayPal is the best-known company (an eBay company). You can pay businesses as well. Another example is Yahoo Pay Direct.
Electronic bill presentment and payments	Bills are presented for payer's approval. Payment is made online (e.g., funds transfer). Examples: *CheckFree.com*, Yahoo Bill Pay.
Pay at ATMs	ATM allows you to pay monthly bills (e.g., to utility companies) by transferring money from your account to the biller.
Micropayments	Payments are too small to be paid with credit cards. Can be paid with stored-value money cards, or with special payment methods, including payments from cell phones.
B2B special methods	Enterprise invoice presentment and payment, wire transfer, and electronic letter of credit are popular methods.

less secure for the buyer to use the telephone or mail to arrange or send payment, especially from another country, than to complete a secured transaction on a computer. For all of these reasons, a better way is needed to pay for goods and services in cyberspace. This better way is *electronic payment systems*.

Electronic Payment Systems. There exist several alternatives for paying for goods and services on the Internet. The major ones are summarized in Table 6.4. The details of these are provided in Turban et al. (2008).

The most common methods, paying with credit cards and electronic bill payments, are discussed briefly here.

Electronic Credit Cards. *Electronic credit cards* make it possible to charge online payments to one's credit card account. For security, only encrypted credit cards should be used. Credit card details can be encrypted by using the SSL protocol in the buyer's computer (available in standard browsers).

Here is how electronic credit cards work: When you buy a book from Amazon, your credit card information and purchase amount are encrypted in your browser, so the information is safe while "traveling" on the Internet. Furthermore, when this information arrives at Amazon, it is not opened but is transferred automatically (in encrypted form) to a clearing house, where the information is decrypted for verification and authorization. The complete process of how e-credit cards work is shown in Figure 6.4. Electronic credit cards are used mainly in B2C and in shopping by SMEs (small-to-medium enterprises).

Electronic Bill Payments. There are three major ways to pay bills over the Internet:

1. Online banking. The consumer signs up for a bank's online bill-pay service and makes all of his or her payments from a single Web site. Some banks offer the service for free with a checking account, or if the account holder maintains a minimum balance.

2. Biller direct. The consumer makes payments at each biller's Web site either with a credit card or by giving the biller enough information to complete an electronic withdrawal directly from the consumer's bank account. The biller makes the billing information available to the customer (presentment) on its Web site or the site of a

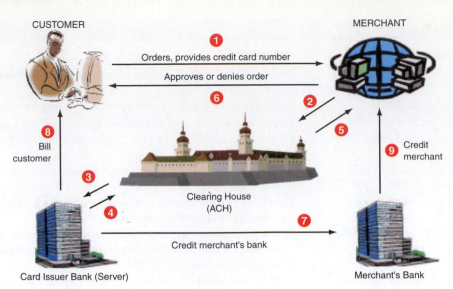

Figure 6.4 How e-credit cards work. (The numbers 1–9 indicate the sequence of activities.) *(Source: Drawn by E. Turban.)*

billing hosting service. Once the customer views the bill, he or she authorizes and initiates payment at the site. The payment can be made with a credit/debit card or by using the Automated Clearing House (ACH) transfer system. The biller then initiates a payment transaction that moves funds through the payment system, crediting the biller and debiting the customer. This method is known as electronic bill presentment and payments (EBPP).

3. Bill consolidator. The customer enrolls to receive and pay bills for multiple billers with a third-party bill consolidator. The customer's enrollment information is forwarded to every biller that the customer wishes to activate (service initiation). For each billing cycle, the biller sends a bill summary or bill detail directly to the consolidator. The bill summary, which links to the bill detail stored with the biller or the consolidator, is made available to the customer (presentment). The customer views the bill and initiates payment instructions. The consolidator initiates a credit payment transaction that moves funds through the payment system to the biller.

Security in Electronic Payments. Two main issues need to be considered under the topic of payment security: what is required in order to make EC payments safe, and the methods that can be used to do so.

Security Requirements. Security requirements for conducting EC are the following:

• **Authentication.** The buyer, the seller, and the paying institutions must be assured of the identity of the parties with whom they are dealing.

• **Integrity.** It is necessary to ensure that data and information transmitted in EC, such as orders, replies to queries, and payment authorizations, are not accidentally or maliciously altered or destroyed during transmission.

• **Nonrepudiation.** Merchants need protection against the customer's unjustified denial of placing an order. On the other hand, customers need protection against merchants' unjustified denial of payments made. (Such denials, of both types, are called *repudiation*.)

• **Privacy.** Many customers want their identity to be secured. They want to make sure others do not know what they buy. Some prefer complete anonymity, as is possible with cash payments.

• **Safety.** Customers want to be sure that it is safe to provide a credit card number on the Internet. They also want protection against fraud by sellers or by criminals posing as sellers.

Security Protection. Several methods and mechanisms can be used to fulfill the above requirements. One of the primary mechanisms is *encryption* (Chapter 5), which is often part of the most useful security schemes. For more detailed

Figure 6.5 The use of a mobile phone as an e-wallet. *(Source: Koichi Kamoshida/Getty Images.)*

explanation of encryption, see Chapter 5. Other representative methods are discussed below.

E-Wallets. **E-wallets** (or **digital wallets**) are software mechanisms that provide security measures and convenience to EC purchasing. The wallet stores the financial information of the buyer, such as credit card number, shipping information, and more. Thus, sensitive information does not need to be reentered for each purchase. If the wallet is stored at the vendor's site, it does not have to travel on the Net for each purchase, making the information more secure.

The problem is that you need an e-wallet with each merchant. One solution is to have a wallet installed on your computer (e.g., MasterCard Wallet or AOL Wallet). In that case, though, you cannot use the e-wallet to make a purchase from another computer, nor is it a totally secured system. The latest development of e-wallet is to integrate RFID (radio frequency identification) technology into mobile phones (Figure 6.5). Commuters in Japan now can pay their train fares at station gates and carry out other purchases with specially equipped cellphones. (See *A Closer Look 6.3*).

Virtual Credit Cards. A **virtual credit card** allows you to shop with an ID number and a password instead of with a credit card number. Such cards are used primarily by people who do not trust browser encryption sufficiently to use their credit card numbers on the Internet. The virtual credit card gives an extra layer of security. The bank that supports your traditional credit card, for example, can provide you with a transaction number valid for online use for a short period. For example, if you want to make a $200 purchase, you would contact your credit card company to charge that amount to your regular credit card account. You would be given a transaction number that is good for charges up to $200. This transaction number is encrypted for security, but even in the worst possible case (that some unauthorized entity obtained the transaction number), your loss would be limited, in this case to $200.

Payment Using Fingerprints. An increasing number of supermarkets allow their regular customers to pay by merely using their fingerprint for identification. A computer template of your fingerprint is kept in the store's computer system. Each time you shop, your fingerprint is matched with the template at the payment counter. You approve the amount, which is then charged either to your credit card or bank account.

A Closer Look **6.3**

E-Money: The Future Currency

You walk through the crowded train station in central Tokyo, heading straight for the entry barriers, and you can ignore the people in queue at the ticket machines. You take out your mobile phone and wave it at a card reader. A beep is heard and you can pass through, ready for your train.

The growing e-money lifestyle in Japan is making life more convenient for consumers by allowing a number of transactions to be conducted via mobile phone, instead of the traditional paper bills and coins given at the cash register. The system is called Mobile Suica and it debuted publicly in January 2006, as an offering by NTT DoCoMo, which is the leading Japanese mobile phone provider, and East Japan Railway. Mobile Suica is a cellphone-based smartcard that can be used for buying rail tickets or for accessing buildings. It is based on RFID.

Europe is updated, making money obsolete in places such as France, where Societe Generale, in partnership with Visa Europe and Gemalto, introduced a Visa Premier "contactless" bank card in July 2007 for consumers to make small purchases with. In England, *The Evening Standard*, a popular newspaper, is sold at special kiosks where the only contact made is between card and scanner.

The Bank of Japan has not released any figure for e-money, but analysts say e-money represents about 20% of the ¥300 trillion (US$2.8 trillion) in Japanese consumer spending. Experts say the new technology will promote the growth of e-money. "With contactless Mobile Suica on your mobile phone, you can check your balance, and upload more money into your account at anytime, from anywhere," said an expert (see attached photo).

There are causes for concern, however, especially for security. "Losing my phone would be like losing my money," said a consumer. To address these, some mobile phone providers have already introduced biometric security measures that include fingerprint, facial, and voice recognition needed to activate phones.

Sources: Compiled from *International Herald Tribune* (2008), *nttdocomo.com* (accessed May 2008) and *slashphone.com* (accessed May 2008).

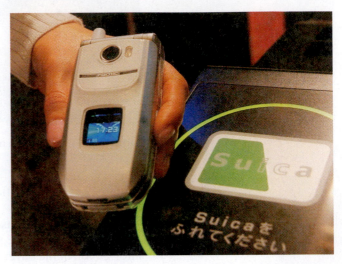

(Source: Kyodo/Landov)

ORDER FULFILLMENT

We now turn our attention to another important EC support service—*order fulfillment*. Any time a company sells direct to customers a product delivered physically, it is involved in various order fulfillment activities. It must perform the following activities: quickly find the products to be shipped; pack them; arrange for the packages to be delivered speedily to the customer's door; collect the money from every customer, either in advance, by COD, or by individual bill; and handle the return of unwanted or defective products.

It is very difficult to accomplish these activities both effectively and efficiently in B2C, since a company may need to ship small packages to many customers, and do it quickly. For this reason, both online companies and click-and-mortar companies often have difficulties in their B2C supply chain, and they outsource deliveries and sometimes packaging (see the FedEx case at the end of Part II). Here, we provide a brief overview of order fulfillment. For a more detailed discussion, see Bayles (2001), Croxton (2003), and Turban et al. (2008).

Order fulfillment includes not only providing customers with what they ordered and doing it on time, but also providing all related customer service. For example, the customer must receive assembly and operation instructions to a new appliance. (A nice example is available at *livemanuals.com*.) In addition, if the customer is not happy with a product, an exchange or return must be arranged. (See *fedex.com* for how returns are handled via FedEx.) Order fulfillment is basically a part of what are called a company's *back-office operations* (activities such as inventory control, shipment, and billing).

The EC Order Fulfillment Process. A typical EC fulfillment process is shown in Figure 6.6. The process starts on the left, when an order is received and after verification that it is a real order. Several activities take place, some of which can be done

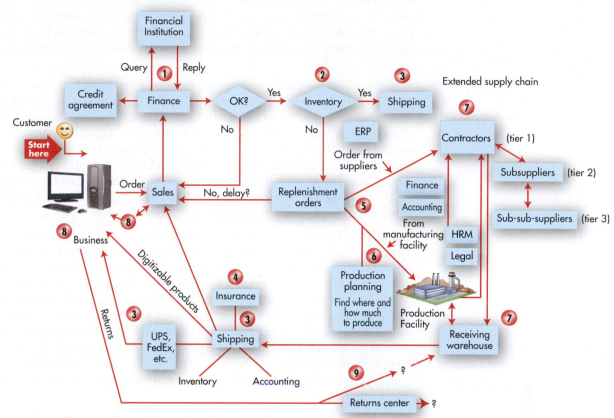

Figure 6.6 Order fulfillment and the logistics system. (*Source: Turban et al., Electronic Commerce: A Managerial Perspective 2008, Exhibit 13.2, p. 591.*)

simultaneously; others must be done in sequence. These activities include the following steps:

- **Activity 1:** Assurance of customer payment. Depending on the payment method and prior arrangements, the validity of each payment must be determined. In B2B, the company's finance department or financial institution (i.e., a bank or a credit card issuer, such as Visa) may do this. Any holdup may cause a shipment to be delayed, resulting in a loss of goodwill or a customer. In B2C, the customers usually prepay, frequently by credit card.

- **Activity 2:** Check of in-stock availability. Regardless of whether the seller is a manufacturer or a retailer, as soon as an order is received, an inquiry needs to be made regarding stock availability. Several scenarios are possible here that may involve the material management and production departments, as well as outside suppliers and warehouse facilities. In this step, the order information needs to be connected to the information about in-stock inventory availability.

- **Activity 3:** Shipment arrangement. If the product is available, it can be shipped to the customer right away (otherwise, go to step 5). Products can be digital or physical. If the item is physical and it is readily available, packaging and shipment arrangements need to be made. It may involve both the packaging or shipping department and internal shippers or outside transporters. Digital items are usually available because their "inventory" is not depleted. However, a digital product, such as software, may be under revision, and unavailable for delivery at certain times. In either case, information needs to flow among several partners.

- **Activity 4:** Insurance. Sometimes the contents of a shipment need to be insured. This could involve both the finance department and an insurance company, and again, information needs to flow, not only inside the company, but also to and from the customer and insurance agent.

• **Activity 5:** Replenishment. Customized orders will always trigger a need for some manufacturing or assembly operation. Similarly, if standard items are out of stock, they need to be produced or procured. Production can be done in-house or by contractors. The suppliers involved may have their own suppliers (subsuppliers or tier-2 suppliers).

• **Activity 6:** In-house production. In-house production needs to be planned. Production planning involves people, materials, components, machines, financial resources, and possibly suppliers and subcontractors. In the case of assembly, manufacturing, or both, several plant services may be needed, including possible collaboration with business partners. Services may include scheduling of people and equipment, shifting other products' plans, working with engineering on modifications, getting equipment, and preparing content. The actual production facilities may be in a different country than the company's headquarters or retailers. This may further complicate the flow of information and communication.

• **Activity 7:** Contractor use. A manufacturer may opt to buy products or subassemblies from contractors. Similarly, if the seller is a retailer, such as in the case of Amazon.com or *walmart.com*, the retailer must purchase products from its manufacturers. Several scenarios are possible. Warehouses can stock purchased items, which is what Amazon.com does with its best-selling books, toys, and other commodity items. However, Amazon.com does not stock books for which it receives only a few orders. In such cases, the publishers or intermediaries must make the special deliveries. In either case, appropriate receiving and quality assurance of incoming materials and products must take place. Once production (step 6) or purchasing from suppliers (step 7) is completed, shipments to the customers (step 3) are arranged.

• **Activity 8:** Contacts with customers. Sales representatives need to keep in constant contact with customers, especially in B2B, starting with notification of orders received and ending with notification of a shipment or a change in delivery date. These contacts are usually done via e-mail and are frequently generated automatically.

• **Activity 9:** Returns. In some cases, customers want to exchange or return items. Such returns can be a major problem, as more than $100 billion in North American goods are returned each year (Kuzeljevich, 2004).

Order fulfillment processes may vary, depending on the product and the vendor. The order fulfillment process also differs between B2B and B2C activities, between the delivery of goods and of services, and between small and large products. Furthermore, certain circumstances, such as in the case of perishable materials or foods, require additional steps.

Warehousing and Inventory Management Improvements. A popular EC inventory management solution is a **warehouse management system (WMS).** WMS refers to a software system that helps in managing warehouses. It has several components. For example, in the case of Amazon.com, the system supports item pickers as well as packaging. Amazon.com's B2C WMS can handle hundreds of millions of packages. Online Minicase 6.7 Schurman Fine Paper has utilized its WMS to improve demand forecasting and inventory management.

Review Questions

1. What are the various electronic payment mechanisms? Which of these are most often used for B2B payments?
2. List the security requirements for EC.
3. Describe the issues in EC order fulfillment.
4. List the nine steps of the order fulfillment process
5. What is the meaning of Internet market research?
6. Identify the drivers of Internet advertisement.
7. What are some of the online advertisement strategies?

6.7 Ethical and Legal Issues in E-Business

Ethical standards and laws frequently lag behind technological innovation. E-commerce is taking new forms and enabling new business practices that may bring numerous risks—particularly for individual consumers—along with their advantages. We begin by considering ethical issues relating to e-business. We then examine the legal environment in which e-commerce operates.

ETHICAL AND IMPLEMENTATION ISSUES

Many of the ethical and implementation issues related to IT in general apply also to e-business. The ethical issues are discussed in the Tutorial #3 at our Web site. In this section we touch on some ethical and implementation issues particularly related to e-commerce.

Privacy. Most electronic payment systems know who the buyers are; therefore, it may be necessary to protect the buyers' identities. A privacy issue related to employees also involves tracking: many companies monitor employees' e-mail and have installed software that performs in-house monitoring of Web activities to discover employees who extensively use company time for non-business-related activities, including harassing other employees. Many employees don't like being watched, but companies may be obligated to monitor.

Web Tracking. Log files are the principal resources from which e-businesses draw information about how visitors use a site. Applying analytics to log files means either turning log data over to an application service provider (ASP) or installing software that can pluck relevant information from files in-house. By using tracking software, companies can track individuals' movements on the Internet. Programs such as cookies raise privacy concerns. The tracking history is stored on your PC's hard drive, and any time you revisit a certain Web site, the computer knows it (see NetTracker at *sane.com*). In response, some users install programs such as Cookie Cutter, CookieCrusher, and Spam Butcher, which are designed to allow users to have some control over cookies. Or they delete their cookie files.

However, the battle between computer end users and Web trackers has just begun. There are more and more "pesticides" for killing these "parasites." For example, Privacy Guardian, MyPrivacy, and Tracks Eraser Pro are examples of software that can protect users' online privacy by erasing a browser's cache, surfing histories, and cookies. Programs such as Ad-Aware are specially designed to detect and remove spyware and data miners such as SahAgent, an application that collects and combines users' Internet browsing behavior and sends it to ShopAtHomeSelect servers. (For more information about anti-spy software, see Chapter 5.)

Loss of Jobs. The use of EC may result in the elimination of some company employees as well as brokers and agents. The manner in which these unneeded workers are treated may raise ethical issues, such as how to handle the displacement and whether to offer retraining programs.

Disintermediation and Reintermediation. One of the most interesting EC issues relating to loss of jobs is that of *intermediation*. Intermediaries provide two types of services: (1) matching and providing information, and (2) value-added services such as consulting. The first type of services (matching and providing information) can be fully automated, and therefore these services are likely to be assumed by e-marketplaces and portals that provide free services. The second type of services (value-added services) requires expertise, and these can be only partially automated. Intermediaries who provide only (or mainly) the first type of service may be eliminated, a phenomenon called **disintermediation** (elimination of the intermediaries). For example, airlines sell tickets directly to customers, eliminating some travel agents. Direct sales from manufacturer to customers may eliminate retailers. On the other hand, brokers who provide the second type of service or who manage electronic intermediation, also known as *infomediation*, are not only surviving, but may actually prosper. This phenomenon is called **reintermediation.** In reintermediation of travel agents, for example, new activities may include organizing groups that go to exotic places (see Gilden, 2004). Intermediaries therefore may fight manufacturers in fear that the traditional sales channel will be negatively affected by online channels. For instance, Wal-Mart and Home Depot warned Black & Decker that they would take its products off their shelves if Black & Decker began to sell its products directly through the Internet. Also, confronted with dealer complaints, Ford executives recently agreed to discontinue plans for future direct online car sales.

LEGAL ISSUES SPECIFIC TO E-COMMERCE

Many legal issues are related to e-commerce. When buyers and sellers do not know each other and cannot even see each other (they may even be in different countries), there is a chance of fraud and other crimes over the Internet. During the first few years of EC, the public witnessed many of these, ranging from the creation of a virtual bank that disappeared along with the investors' deposits, to manipulation of stock prices on the Internet. Unfortunately, fraud on the Internet is increasing. Representative examples of legal issues specific to e-commerce are discussed below and in Online Brief 6.4.

PROTECTION OF EC BUYERS AND SELLERS

There are several ways buyers can be better protected against fraud in e-commerce. Representative methods are described next.

Buyer Protection. Some tips for safe electronic shopping are shown in Table 6.5. In short, do not forget that you have shopper's rights. Consult your local or state consumer protection agency for general information on your consumer rights.

Seller Protection. Online sellers, too, need protection. They must be protected against consumers who refuse to pay or who pay with bad checks and from buyers' claims that the merchandise did not arrive. They also have the right to protect against the use of their name by others as well as to protect the use of their unique words and phrases, slogans, and Web address (trademark protection). Security features such as authentication, nonrepudiation, and escrow services provide some needed protections. Another seller protection applies particularly to electronic media: Sellers have legal recourse against customers who download without permission copyrighted software and/or knowledge and use it or sell it to others, as the music industry has proved.

Review Questions

1. List some ethical issues in EC.
2. List the major legal issues of EC.
3. Describe buyer protection in EC.
4. Describe seller protection in EC.

TABLE 6.5	**Tips for Safe Electronic Shopping**

- Look for reliable brand names at sites such as Wal-Mart Online, Disney Online, and *Amazon.com*. Before purchasing, make sure that the site is authentic by entering the site directly and not from an unverified link.
- Search any unfamiliar selling site for the company's address and phone and fax numbers. Call up and quiz the employees about the seller.
- Check out the vendor with the local Chamber of Commerce or Better Business Bureau (*bbbonline.org*). Look for seals of authenticity such as TRUSTe.
- Investigate how secure the seller's site is by examining the security procedures and by reading the posted privacy policy.
- Examine the money-back guarantees, warranties, and service agreements.
- Compare prices to those in regular stores. Too-low prices could prove too good to be true, and some "catch" is probably involved.
- Ask friends what they know. Find testimonials and endorsements in community sites and well-known bulletin boards.
- Find out what your rights are in case of a dispute. Consult consumer protection agencies and the National Fraud Information Center (*fraud.org*).
- Check *consumerworld.org* for a listing of useful resources.
- Check *cfenet.com* and *isaca.org*.

6.8 Managerial Issues

1. E-commerce failures. Failures of EC initiatives are fairly common. Furthermore, during 2000–2002, large numbers of dot-com companies failed. Pioneering organizations saw the potential for e-commerce, but expertise and EC business models were just developing. Failures of EC projects started as early as 1996. However, the major wave of Internet-based EC failures started in 2000, as second-round funding (funding subsequent to a firm's original funding but before it goes to the stock market with a stock offering) began to dry up.

According to Useem (2000), the major reasons for EC failure are incorrect revenue model, lack of strategy and contingency planning, inability to attract enough customers, lack of funding, too much online competition in standard (commodity) products (e.g., CDs, toys), poor order-fulfillment infrastructure, and lack of qualified management. Also, channel conflicts (see issue #2) may cause EC to fail. To learn more about EC failures, visit *whytheyfailed.com* and *techdirt.com*.

2. Failed EC initiatives within organizations. Whereas failed companies, especially publicly listed ones, are well advertised, failed EC initiatives within companies, especially within private companies, are less known. However, news about some failed EC initiatives has been publicized. For example, Levi Strauss stopped online direct sales of its apparel (jeans and its popular Levi's and Dockers brands) on its Web site (*levis-trauss.com*) after its major distributors and retailers put pressure on the company not to compete with their brick-and-mortar outlets (channel conflict). Another EC initiative that failed was a joint venture between Intel and SAP, two world-class companies, which was designed to develop low-cost solutions for SMEs. It collapsed in August 2000 due to low demand and too few customers. Large companies such as Citicorp, Disney, and Merrill Lynch also closed EC initiatives after losing millions of dollars in them.

3. Success stories and lessons learned. Offsetting the failures are hundreds of EC success stories, primarily in specialty and niche markets. Some of the reasons for EC success and some suggestions from EC experts on how to succeed are provided in Online Brief 6.5.

4. Managing resistance to change. Electronic commerce can result in a fundamental change in how business is done, and resistance to change from employees, vendors, and customers may develop. Education, training, and publicity over an extended time period offer possible solutions to the problem.

5. Integration of e-commerce into the business environment. E-commerce needs to be integrated with the rest of the business. Integration issues involve planning, competition for corporate resources with other projects, and interfacing EC with databases, existing IT applications, and infrastructure.

6. Lack of qualified personnel and outsourcing. Very few people have expertise in e-commerce. There are many implementation issues that require expertise, such as when to offer special promotions on the Internet, how to integrate an e-market with the information systems of buyers and sellers, and what kind of customer incentives are appropriate under what circumstances. For this reason, it may be worthwhile to outsource some e-commerce activities. Yet, as shown in Chapter 13, outsourcing decisions are not simple.

7. Managing the impacts and the implementation. The impacts of e-commerce on organizational structure, people, marketing procedures, and profitability may be dramatic. Therefore, establishing a committee or organizational unit to develop strategy and to manage e-commerce is necessary. An implementation plan may be useful. Because of the complexity and multifaceted nature of EC, it makes sense to prepare an implementation plan. Such a plan should include goals, budgets, timetables, and contingency plans. It should address the many legal, financial, technological, organizational, and ethical issues that can surface during implementation.

8. Alliances. It is not a bad idea to join an alliance or consortium of companies to explore e-commerce. Alliances can be created at any time. Some EC companies (e.g.,

Amazon.com) have thousands of alliances. The problem is which alliance to join, or what kind of alliance to form and with whom.

9. Choosing the company's strategy toward e-commerce. Generally speaking, there are three major options: (1) *Lead:* Conduct large-scale innovative e-commerce activities. (2) *Watch and wait:* Do nothing, but carefully watch what is going on in the field in order to determine when EC is mature enough to enter it. (3) *Experiment:* Start some e-commerce experimental projects (learn by doing). Each of these options has its advantages and risks.

10. Justifying e-commerce by conducting a cost-benefit analysis is very difficult. Many intangible benefits and lack of experience may produce grossly inaccurate estimates of costs and benefits. Nevertheless, a feasibility study must be done, and estimates of costs and benefits must be made.

How *IT* Benefits You

Accounting Major

Accounting personnel are involved in several IT/EC activities. For example, designing an e-ordering system and its relationship with inventory management requires accounting attention. Billing and payments are also accounting activities, as are determining cost and profit allocation. Replacing paper documents by electronic means will affect many of the accountant's tasks, especially the auditing of EC activities and systems. Taxing online transactions requires accountants' attention as do some compliance and security issues. Finally, building a cost-benefit and cost-justification system of which products/services to take online, and creating a chargeback system, are critical to the success of EC.

Finance Major

The worlds of banking, securities and commodities markets, and other financial services are being reengineered due to EC. Online securities trading and its supporting infrastructure are growing more rapidly than any other EC activity. Many innovations already in place are changing the rules of economic and financial incentives for financial analysts and managers. Online banking, for example, does not recognize state boundaries, and it may create a new framework for financing global trades. Public financial information is now accessible in seconds. Compliance with regulations, and especially with SOX, can be facilitated by EC software as can pricing optimization and investment decisions.

Human Resources Management Major

HR majors need to understand both the new labor markets and the impacts of EC on old labor markets. Also, the HRM department may use EC tools for such functions as procuring office supplies. Becoming knowledgeable about new government online initiatives and online training is critical. Finally, HR personnel must be familiar with the major legal issues related to EC and employment.

IS Major

The information systems department (ISD) is responsible for providing the IT infrastructure necessary for EC to function. In particular, this infrastructure includes the company's networks, intranets, extranets, EC portals, and EC mechanisms. The ISD is also responsible for training in the use of EC initiatives, in deploying applications, in collaborating with EC vendors and users, and in ensuring that EC transactions are secure.

Marketing Major

EC changed marketing and sales with online direct sales, CRM, one-on-one advertising and sales, and customized and interactive marketing. Also, marketing channels are being combined, eliminated, or recreated. The EC revolution is creating more new products and markets and significantly altering others. The direct producer-to-consumer channel is expanding rapidly and is fundamentally changing the nature of customer service. As the battle for customers intensifies, marketing and sales personnel are becoming the most critical success factor in many organizations. The major changes may introduce conflicts internally and with distributors, and must be clearly understood. Finally, many opportunities for sales and marketing, including going global, are being created by EC. Special attentions are drawn to the power of viral marketing created by Web 2.0 social networking sites.

Operations Management Major

EC is changing the manufacturing system from product-push mass production to order-pull mass customization. This change requires a robust supply chain, information support, and redesign of internal and external business processes. Using extranets, suppliers can monitor and replenish inventories without the need for manual reorders. In addition, EC initiatives help reduce cycle times and increase quality. Many production/operations problems that have persisted for years, such as complex scheduling and excess inventories, are being solved with the use of Web technologies. Also, the Web is enabling e-procurement by helping companies conduct electronic bids for parts and subassemblies, thus reducing cost.

Key Terms

Advergaming *224*

Affiliate marketing *223*

Auction *208*

Brick-and-mortar organizations *200*

Business-to-employees
(B2E) *201*

Business-to-business
(B2B) *201*

Business-to-business-
to-consumers
(B2B2C) *201*

Business-to-consumers (B2C) *201*

Buy-side marketplace *217*

Channel conflicts *214*

Click-and-mortar organizations *200*

Collaborative commerce
(c-commerce) *201, 219*

Consumer-to-consumer
(C2C) *201, 220*

Consumers-to-businesses
(C2B) *201*

Cyberbanking *212*

Desktop purchasing *217*

Disintermediation *231*

E-government *220*

E-market *207*

E-procurement *217*

E-wallets *227*

Electronic bartering *208*

Electronic commerce *199*

Electronic mall *210*

Electronic retailing *201*

Electronic storefronts *210*

Forward auctions *208*

Government-to-business (G2B) *201*

Government-to-citizens (G2C) *201*

Government-to-government
(G2G) *201*

Group purchasing *217*

Interactive marketing *222*

Intrabusiness (intraorganizational)
commerce *201*

Public exchanges *217*

Reverse auctions *208*

Reintermediation *231*

Sell-side marketplace *216*

Viral marketing *223*

Virtual credit card *227*

Virtual organizations *200*

Warehouse management system
(WMS) *229*

Chapter Highlights

(Numbers Refer to Learning Objectives)

❶ E-commerce can be conducted on the Web and on other networks. It is divided into the following major types: business-to-business, collaborative commerce, business-to-consumers, consumer-to-consumer, business-to-business-to-consumer, consumers-to-business, intrabusiness, e-government, and mobile commerce. In each type you can find several business models.

❶ Social Commerce is a new trend created by the merging of Web 2.0 technologies (such as wikis and blogs), e-business opportunities, and online communities. What differentiates social commerce from an ordinary e-business site is the social elements involved.

❶ E-commerce offers many benefits to organizations, consumers, and society, but it also has limitations (technological and nontechnological). The current technological limitations are expected to lessen with time.

❷ The major mechanism of EC is the use of electronic markets, which frequently includes online catalogs.

❷ Another mechanism of EC is auctions. The Internet provides an infrastructure for executing auctions at lower cost, and with many more involved sellers and buyers, including both individual consumers and corporations. Two major types of auctions exist: forward auctions and reverse auctions. Forward auctions are used in the traditional process of *selling* to the highest bidder. Reverse auctions are used for *buying*, using a tendering system to buy at the lowest bid.

❷ A minor mechanism is online bartering, in which companies or individuals arrange for *exchange* of physical items and/or services.

❸ B2C e-tailing can be pure (such as Amazon.com), or part of a click-and-mortar organization (such as Wal-Mart). Direct marketing is done via solo storefronts or in malls. It can be done via electronic catalogs or by using electronic auctions. The leading online B2C service industries are banking, securities trading, job markets, travel, and real estate.

❸ The major issues faced by e-tailers are channel conflict, conflict within click-and-mortar organizations, order fulfillment, determining viability and risk, and identifying appropriate revenue models.

❹ The major B2B applications are selling from catalogs and by forward auctions (the sell-side marketplace), buying in reverse auctions and in group and desktop purchasing (the buy-side marketplace), and trading in electronic exchanges.

❺ EC activities can be conducted inside organizations. Three types are recognized: between a business and its employees, between units of the business, and among employees of the same organization.

❻ E-government commerce can take place between government and citizens, between businesses and governments, or among government units. It makes government operations more effective and efficient.

❻ EC also can be done between consumers (C2C), but should be undertaken with caution. Auctions are the most popular C2C mechanism. C2C also can be done by use of online classified ads.

❼ New electronic payment systems are needed to complete transactions on the Internet. Electronic payments can be made by e-checks, e-credit cards, purchasing cards, e-cash, stored-value money cards, smart cards, person-to-person payments via services such as PayPal, electronic bill presentment and payment, and e-wallets.

❼ Order fulfillment is especially difficult and expensive in B2C, because of the need to ship relatively small orders to many customers. Several activities take place, some of which can be done simultaneously; others must be done in sequence. These activities that take place in order fulfillment include (1) making sure the customer will pay, (2) checking for in-stock availability, (3) arranging shipments, (4) insurance, (5) replenishment, (6) in-house production, (7) use contractors, (8) contacts with customers, and (9) returns (if applicable).

8 EC truly requires market research and advertising, both of which are conducted online.

9 There are increasing fraud and unethical behavior on the Internet, including invasion of privacy by sellers and misuse of domain names.

9 Protection of customers, sellers, and intellectual property is also important.

Virtual Company Assignment

E-Commerce at The Wireless Café

Go to The Wireless Café's link on the Student Web Site. There you will find a description of the e-commerce activities that have been taking place at the restaurant. You will be asked to identify ways to use both B2C and B2B e-commerce at The Wireless Café.

Instructions for accessing The Wireless Café on the Student Web Site:

1. Go to *wiley.com/college/turban*.
2. Select Turban/Leidner/McLean/Wetherbe's *Information Technology for Management*, Seventh Edition.
3. Click on Student Resources site, in the toolbar on the left.
4. Click on the link for Virtual Company Web Site.
5. Click on Wireless Café.

Questions for Discussion

1. Discuss the major limitations of e-commerce. Which of them are likely to disappear? Why?
2. Discuss the reasons for having multiple EC business models in one company.
3. Distinguish between business-to-business forward auctions and buyers' bids for RFQs.
4. Discuss the benefits to sellers and buyers of a B2B exchange.
5. What are the major benefits of e-government?
6. Discuss the various ways to pay online in B2C. Which one(s) would you prefer and why?

7. Why is order fulfillment in B2C considered difficult?
8. Discuss the reasons for EC failures.
9. Discuss the role of recommendation agents in EC.
10. What are Amazon.com's critical success factors? Is its decision not to limit its sales to books, music, and movies, but to offer a much broader selection of items, a good marketing strategy? With the broader selection, do you think the company will dilute its brand or extend the value proposition to its customers?

Exercises and Projects

1. Assume you're interested in buying a car. You can find information about cars at *autos.msn.com*. Go to *autoweb.com* or *autobytel.com* for information about financing and insurance. Decide what car you want to buy. Configure your car by going to the car manufacturer's Web site. Finally, try to find the car from *autoby-*

tel.com. What information is most supportive of your decision-making process? Write a report about your experience.

2. Visit *amazon.com* and identify at least three specific elements of its personalization and customization features. Browse specific books on one particular subject, leave

the site, and then go back and revisit the site. What do you see? Are these features likely to encourage you to purchase more books in the future from Amazon.com? Check the 1-Click feature and other shopping aids provided. List the features and discuss how they may lead to increased sales.

3. In August 2006, Google and MySpace signed a deal in which MySpace users can conduct a search on Google without leaving the MySpace site. Find information about the deal (try GoogleNews) and summarize the benefits to both companies.

4. Compare the various electronic payment methods. Specifically, collect information from the vendors cited in the chapter and find more with *google.com*. Pay attention to security level, speed, cost, and convenience.

5. Go to *nacha.org*. What is the National Automated Clearing House Association (NACHA)? What is its role? What is the ACH? Who are the key participants in an ACH e-payment? Describe the "pilot" projects currently underway at ACH.

6. Enter *espn.com*. Identify at least five different ways it makes revenue.

Group Assignments and Projects

1. Have each team study a major bank with extensive EC offerings. For example, Wells Fargo Bank is well on its way to being a cyberbank. Hundreds of brick-and-mortar branch offices are being closed. In Spring 2003, the bank served more than 1.2 million cyberaccounts (see *wellsfargo.com*). Other banks to look at are Citicorp, Netbank, and HSBC (Hong Kong). Each team should attempt to convince the class that its e-bank activities are the best.

2. Assign each team to one industry. Each team will find five real-world applications of the major business-to-business models listed in the chapter. (Try success stories of vendors and EC-related magazines.) Examine the problems the applications solve or the opportunities they exploit.

3. Have teams investigate how B2B payments are made in global trade. Consider instruments such as electronic letters of credit and e-checks. Visit *tradecard.com* and examine their services to SMEs. Also, investigate what Visa and MasterCard are offering. Finally, check Citicorp and some German and Japanese banks.

4. Conduct a study on selling diamonds and gems online. Each group member investigates one company such as *bluenile.com, diamond.com, thaigem.com, tiffany.com,* or *jewelryexchange.com*.
   a. What features are used in these sites to educate buyers about gemstones?
   b. How do the sites attract buyers?
   c. How do the sites increase trust for online purchasing?
   d. What customer service features are provided?
   e. Would you buy a $5,000 diamond ring online? Why, or why not?

5. Enter *dell.com*, read Rappa (2006), and find information on the EC direct model, affiliate programs, and Enterprise Command Center (*dell.com/ecc*). Write a report.

6. Conduct a study on social networking sites. Each group will check a specific type. For example, one group can check company-sponsored sites, such as *mycoke.com, carnivalconnections.com,* or *nissanclub.com*. Each group prepares a report on the objectives of the sites, on their members, content, and mode of operation. Find how they are sponsored or generate ad revenue.

Internet Exercises

1. Use the Internet to plan a trip to Paris. Visit *lonelyplanet.com, yahoo.com,* and *expedia.com*.
   a. Find the lowest airfare.
   b. Examine a few hotels by class.
   c. Get suggestions of what to see.
   d. Find out about local currency, and convert $1,000 to that currency with an online currency converter.
   e. Compile travel tips.
   f. Prepare a report.

2. Access *realtor.com*. Prepare a list of services available on this site. Then prepare a list of advantages derived by the users and advantages to realtors. Are there any disadvantages? To whom?

3. Enter *alibaba.com*. Identify the site's capabilities. Look at the site's private trading room. Write a report. How can such a site help a person who is making a purchase?

4. Enter *campusfood.com*. Explore the site. Why is the site so successful? Could you start a competing one? Why or why not?

5. Enter *dell.com*, go to "desktops," and configure a system. Register to "my cart" (no obligation). What calculators are used there? What are the advantages of this process as compared to buying a computer in a physical store? What are the disadvantages?

6. Enter *checkfree.com* and *lmlpayment.com* and find their services. Prepare a comparison.

7. Enter *resumix.yahoo.com* and summarize the services they provide.

8. Read the Amazon.com case (*IT at Work 6.2*) and WalMart.com (Online Minicase 6.2). Visit both sites and search for the same products. Compare the sites' functionalities and ease of use. Prepare a report.

9. Enter *housevalues.com* and find the various services it provides under several URLs. What is its revenue model?

10. Enter *queendom.com* and examine its offerings. Try some. What type of EC is this? How does the site make money?

11. Enter *ediets.com*. Prepare a list of all services the company provides. Identify its revenue model. Check the company's stock (NASDAQ: DIET).

12. Enter *tradecard.com*. Run the procure-to-pay demo. Summarize the processes and benefits of the service to a small exporter.

13. Enter *cybersource.com*. Identify the services available for B2B payments. Write a report.

14. Enter *knot.com* and identify its revenue sources.

Minicase

Stormhoek Vineyards Excels with Web 2.0 Tools

Stormhoek Vineyards is a small winery in South Africa (*stormhoek.com*). Annual sales in 2005 were only $3 million, but with Web 2.0 technologies, sales grew to $10 million in 2007 and are projected to reach $30 million in 2010. The company devised a marketing campaign called "100 Geek Dinners in 100 Days." Each dinner was to be hosted by one person and used for wine tasting by several dozen guests in the United Kingdom and the United States. How can you get 100 people to host a wine tasting and how do you find 40 to 60 guests for each event? The answer: Web 2.0 technologies. Here is what the company did:

- **Blogging.** The CEO of Orbital Wines, Stormhoek's parent company, in collaboration with a well-know blogger, Mr. Macleod, wrote dozens of blog entries about the events, soliciting volunteer hosts, including bloggers and wine enthusiasts. (See *stormhoek.com/blog*.)

- **Wiki.** Each volunteer was provided with contact and location information on a wiki. The wiki technology was mainly used for customer relations management (CRM). The wiki included wine-related cartoons and other entertainment and advertising.

- **Podcasts.** Web-content feed (enabled by an RSS) was used to push information to participants' in-boxes. Information included wine news, wine analyses, and descriptions of the 100 parties.

- **Video and Photo Links.** The corporate blog supported video links. Bloggers could cut and paste embedded links to YouTube videos directly into an entry. The company also posted videos in YouTube (*youtube.com/stormhoekwines*), and pictures at *flickr.com flickr.com/search/?w=all&q= stormhoek&m=text*.

- **Shopping.** The blog site acted as a portal to Stormhoek and included support for order placement and shopping carts for promotional "swag," such as posters and T-shirts.

- **Mashups.** An interactive map was integrated into the wiki using mashup software. This allowed dinner hosts to display a map of the location of the event. Also, guests could click an event on the map to make a reservation, get a reserva-

tion confirmation, send a query to the host, and receive photos of the house and the hosts. The company's wiki also had a link to host-blogger's home page. (For more details about mashups, see *en.wikipedia.org/wiki/mashup*.)

- **Social Networks.** The company has a page at Facebook with news, discussion group, information, photos, videos, and a dedicated group. See *facebook.com/group.php? gid=2388408693*.

The parties were attended by over 4,500 people, and the publicity enabled the vineyard to triple sales in 2 years (mainly in the United Kingdom). The only problem was a profusion of blog spam—random comments that were automatically posted by marketers for promotions. This required a daily purging and cleaning of the blog from unwanted postings.

The blogging resulted in word-of-mouth publicity. The blogging was done by a professional blogger (Hugh Macleod at *gapingvoid.com*). The blog offered a free bottle of wine. Macleod also organized the 100 dinners described earlier. RSS pioneer Dave Winer attended one of the dinners. A final word: Stormhoek wine is really good! Viral marketing cannot sell bad wine.

Sources: Compiled from Bennett (2007), McNichol (2007), *stormhoek.com* (accessed May 2008), and *New Communications Review* (2006).

Questions

1. What was the corporate blog used for?

2. What were the hosts' blogs used for?

3. What capabilities were introduced by the mashups?

4. How did the wiki help in communication and collaboration?

5. Why do you think the Web 2.0 technologies were successful in increasing sales?

6. What is blog spam and why is it a problem?

Problem-Solving Activity

Inventory Control Problem at Hi-Life Corporation

Hi-Life Corporation owns and operates 720 convenience retail stores in Taiwan, where the company sells over 3,000 different products. A major problem is keeping a proper level of inventory of each product in each store. Overstocking is expensive due to storage costs and tying up space and money to buy and maintain the inventory. Understocking reduces potential sales and could result in unhappy customers who may go to a competitor.

To calculate the appropriate level of inventory, it is necessary to know exactly how many units of each product are in stock at specific times. This is done by what is known as stock count. Periodic stock count is needed since the actual amount in stock frequently differs from the computed one (inventory = previous inventory − sales + new arrivals). The difference is due to "shrinkage" (e.g., theft, misplaced items, spoilage, etc.). Until 2007, stock counts at Hi-Life were done manually. Employees counted the quantity of each product and recorded it on data collection sheets on which the products' names were preprinted. Then the data were painstakingly keyed into each store's PC. The process took over 21 person-hours in each store, each time a count was needed, sometimes once a week. This process was expensive and frequently was delayed, causing problems along the entire supply chain due to delays in count and mismatches of computed and actual inventories.

Exercises to Do

You are a final year undergraduate student and have just finished taking a course on IT for management. The Hi-Life Corporation has asked for your help. You understand (from Tutorial #1) that Hi-Life's inventory control problems are typical, experienced in both offline and online commerce. You decided to derive a solution for the problem.

Here is what you need to do (your action plan):

1. Identify the business processes that may have caused the inventory control problem.

2. Read Chapter 4 and understand more about wireless and mobile computing.

3. Visit the website of Hewlett-Packard (*hp.com*) and look for an appropriate Pocket PC (a handheld device) that enables employees of Hi-Life to enter the inventory tallies directly into electronic forms, using Chinese characters for additional notes. The inventory information should be relayed instantly to Hi-Life's headquarters once the Pocket PC is placed in its synchronized cradle.

4. Search for a compact barcode scanner that can be added on in the Pocket PC's expansion slot. Employees of Hi-Life can scan the products' barcodes and then enter the quantity found on the shelf. It is expected that this new feature will expedite data entry and minimize errors in product identification. The up-to-the-second information will enable Hi-Life headquarters to compute appropriate inventory levels in minutes, to better schedule shipments, and to plan purchasing strategies using decision-support system formulas.

5. Use the Internet (with a secured feature known as VPN; see Technology Guide 5) to upload data to the intranet at headquarters.

Consider your action plan and write a report titled "Better Inventory Control at Hi-Life Corporation." In your report you should include the following:

a. Suggest how the corporate decision making process can be improved.

b. Summarize the benefits to the customers, suppliers, store management, and employees.

c. Comment on the proposal that the data collected at the handheld devices be uploaded to a PC and transmitted to the corporate intranet via a wireless system.

Sources: Compiled from *hp.com/jornada*, *microsoft.com/asia/mobile*, and *hilife.com* (all accessed May 2008).

Online Resources

More resources and study tools are located on the Student Web Site and on WileyPLUS. You'll find additional chapter materials and useful Web links. In addition, self-quizzes that provide individualized feedback are available for each chapter.

Online Briefs for Chapter 6 are available at wiley.com/college/turban:

6.1 *The Functions of an e-Market*
6.2 *Benefits of Electronic Auctions*
6.3 *Online Market Research*
6.4 *Legal Issues in EC*
6.4 *Success Stories in EC*

Online Minicases for Chapter 6 are available at wiley.com/college/turban:

References

Akamai Technologies, Inc., "Best Practices for Successful Live Web Event," Akamai Technologies, Inc., report, 2000.

Bayers, C., "The Last Laugh (of Amazon's CEO)," *Business 2.0*, September 2002.

Bayles, D. L., *E-Commerce Logistics and Fulfillment*. Upper Saddle River, NJ: Prentice Hall, 2001.

Bennett, E., "Winery Blogs to Turn Browsers into Buyers," *Baseline*, June 2007.

Brook, O., "Auto-Tech Display Shows Promise for Future of Collaborative Commerce," *MSI*, 22(11), 2004.

"Case Study: ChemConnect," *digitalenterprise.org/cases/chemconnect.html* (accessed May 2008).

Chase, L., "Top Ten Success of Secrets of Email Marketing," 2006, *rightnow.com/resource/RN_EmailSuccess.html?look=p* (accessed May 2008).

Choi, S. Y., et al., *The Economics of Electronic Commerce*. Indianapolis: Macmillan Technical Publications, 1997.

Copeland, M. V., "The eBay of Swap," *Business 2.0*, May 2006.

Croxton, K. L., "The Order Fulfillment Process," *International Journal of Logistics Management*, 14(1), 2003, pp. 19–32.

Daisey, M., *21 Dog Years: Doing Time @amazon.com*. New York: Free Press, 2002.

Esfahani, E., "Why 'Buy' Buttons Are Booming," *CNNMoney.com*, July 1, 2005, *money.cnn.com/magazines/business2/business2_archive/2005/07/01/8265513/index.htm* (accessed May 2006).

Fass, A., "TheirSpace.com," *Forbes*, May 8, 2006.

Flynn, L. J., "Like This? You'll Hate That. (Not All Web Recommendations Are Welcome)," *New York Times*, January 23, 2006.

Gilden, J., "Popularity of Web Forces Travel Agents to Adjust," *Chicago Tribune*, March 14, 2004.

Google, "Google Company Overview," 2008, *google.com/corporate/index.html* (accessed May 2008).

Gurau, C., "Managing Advergames," in Khosrow-Pour (2006).

Hewson, C., et al. *Internet Research Methods*. London: Sage, 2003.

Holden, G., "Fast Forward," *Entrepreneur*, May 2006.

International Herald Tribune, "Cellphones in Japan Make Wallets Obsolete," February 25, 2008.

Kaplan, S., and M. Sawhney, "E-Hubs: The New B2B Marketplaces," *Harvard Business Review*, May 1, 2000.

Khosrow-Pour, M. (ed.)., *Encyclopedia of E-Commerce, E-Government, and Mobile Commerce*. Hershey, PA: Idea Group Reference, 2006.

Kraemer, K., and J. Dedrick, "*Dell Computer: Using E-Commerce to Support a Virtual Company*," special report, June 2001. Available in Rappa (2008).

Kuzeljevich, J., "Targeting Reverse Logistics," *Canadian Transportation Logistics*, 107, (9), 2004.

Lee, S. C., and A. A. Brandyberry, "The E-Tailer's Dilemma," *Data Base*, Spring 2003.

Luo, W., and M. Najdawi, "Trust-Building Measures: A Review of Consumer Health Portals," *Communications of the ACM*, 47(1), 2004, pp. 108–113.

Lyons, R., "eBay Course for Beginners at University," *Birmingham Post*, Birmingham, UK, April 23, 2004, p. 4.

McNichol, T., "How a Small Winery Found Internet Fame," *Business 2.0*, August 8, 2007.

MoreBusiness.com, "Viral Marketing and Brand Awareness," March 5, 2007, *morebusiness.com/running_your_business/marketing/viral-marketing.brc* (accessed July 2008).

Netflix, "Netflix and USA Weekend Partner on 'Netflix Movie Picks' Promotion," September 13, 2006, *netflix.com/MediaCenter?id=5363* (accessed July 2008).

New Communications Review, "Award of Excellence - Business Category: Stormhoek Winery," October 31, 2006, *newcommreview.com/?p=578* (accessed May 2008).

Null, C., "How Netflix Is Fixing Hollywood by Finding a Market for Niche Titles," *CNNMoney.com*, July 1, 2003.

Rappa, M., "Case Study: Dell Computer," *digitalenterprise.org/cases/dell.html* (accessed May 2008).

Rubel, S., "Steve Rubel on Social Commerce," *Technosailor*, December 29, 2005, *technosailor.com/2005/12/29/1226-steve-rubel-on-social-commerce* (accessed July 2008).

Schonfield, E., "The World According to eBay," *Business 2.0*, January 19, 2005.

Schuman, E., "Forrester: E-Commerce Dollars Growing but Cannibalization a Big Factor," *Storefront Backtalk*, April 10, 2008, *storefrontbacktalk.com/story/041008ecommerce* (accessed July 2008).

Smith, S., "Sharing the Wealth" (contextual advertising), *EContent*, April 2004.

Staff, "The Complete Guide to Using eBay," Reference Series, *Smart Computing*, 9(2), 2005.

Turban, E., et. al., *Electronic Commerce: A Managerial Perspective 2008*. Upper Saddle River, NJ: Prentice Hall, 2008.

Useem, J., "Dot-Coms: What Have We Learned?" *Fortune*, October 2000.

Zimmerman, J., *Web Marketing For Dummies*. Hoboken, NJ: Wiley Publishing, 2007.

Chapter

7

Mobile Commerce

Learning Objectives

After studying this chapter, you will be able to:

❶ Discuss the characteristics, attributes, and drivers of mobile computing and m-commerce.

❷ Understand the technologies that support mobile computing.

❸ Discuss m-commerce applications in financial and other services, advertising, marketing, and providing of content.

❹ Describe the applications of m-commerce within organizations (mobile enterprise, intrabusiness).

❺ Understand B2B and supply chain applications (interorganizational) of m-commerce.

❻ Describe consumer and personal applications of m-commerce.

❼ Describe location-based commerce (l-commerce).

❽ Discuss the key characteristics and current uses of pervasive computing.

❾ Describe the major inhibitors and barriers of mobile computing and m-commerce.

Integrating *IT*

ACC   **FIN**   **MKT**   **OM**   **HRM**   **IS**

IT-PERFORMANCE MODEL

In this chapter we describe how IT support is provided to mobile employees mainly by wireless technology to improve their performance and productivity, and how mobile commerce is conducted to improve sales, customer services, and organizational performance.

The business performance management cycle and IT model.

Where Do We Want to Go?
Mission, Goals, Objectives
• Widespread wireless systems
• Pervasive computing applications
• M-commerce, L-commerce

• Wide area infrastructure
• Wi-Fi
• Wi-Max
• Wearable devices

Information Technology (IT)

How Shall We Get There?
Strategy, Plans
• How to use wireless systems?
• Expanding EC to M-commerce
• Where to use RFID?
• How to manage wireless?

How Well Are We Doing?
Monitoring, Performance, Comparing
• Cost/benefit of applications
• Monitoring performance

How Can We Improve Performance?
Solutions, Critical Responses
• Innovative applications
• Location-based advertisement
• Mobile social networking
• GPS/GIS applications

FOOD LION EXCELS WITH WIRELESS INNOVATIONS

The Problem

Food Lion grocer is a supermarket chain (1,300 stores) that decided to distinguish itself from the competition, which is extremely fierce among grocers. (A major competitor is Wal-Mart.) The company created *Bloom*, an upscale brand of grocery store that provides a sensible, uncomplicated, hassle-free shopping experience that leaves shoppers feeling smart, relaxed, and confident. The problem was to find the appropriate technology to support Bloom.

The Solution

The company decided to use wireless technology. Here are some of the projects:

• **Mobile checkstand.** This is a mobile check-out POS terminal equipped with wheels that can be moved to any location in the store or outside (e.g., front for special sales). This brings flexibility and ability to expedite checkout time. These devices can be added whenever checkout lines are getting long.

• **Personal scanner.** This is a handheld device that is a POS terminal emulating the IBM checkout system. The device is given to the customers. When a shopper picks up an item off the shelf, he or she scans that item before putting it into the cart. The device shows the price of the item and the running $ subtotal of all items bagged. The Personal Scanner [from Symbol Technology (Motorola)] also enables sending messages to the customers while shopping, including special marketing offers. The final bill is downloaded to the cash register.

• **Employee handheld devices.** These devices enable employees to execute inventory counts, enter orders for low or out-of-stock items, do shelf-tag printing, and conduct price management, anywhere in the store.

- **Cart-mounted tablet PC.** This device, which is mounted on the shopping cart (see attached photo), enables customers to check prices and get product location and information while pushing their carts. Currently, this is done on an experimental basis due to the high cost.
- **Marketing opportunities.** Handheld devices that are given to customers while shopping can provide product information, price comparisons, recommendations for complementary products, and more.
- **Tablet PCs for employees.** The device is docked in the office and carried around wherever the manager goes while maintaining a wireless connection to the store system. The managers may prefer it over PDAs and smart cell phones due to the large screen (but it is heavy, so not all managers like it).
- **Mobile manager.** This is a cell-phone-sized portable device used to improve communication and supervision.
- **Wi-Fi access.** This is an in-store wireless local area network (WLAN) that supports the above devices.

To deter cheating in the self-scanning during checkout, a random audit is done, but this may alienate a customer, especially if the customer is in a hurry. In the future, the company will install an RFID system that will improve the existing system and reduce the possibility of cheating.

The Results

Speedier checkout is the main benefit since all the customer has to do is to pay. Also, in the future, the purchase amount calculated by the personal scanner is debited directly to the customers' bank account to make checkout even faster. The customers are also happy since they can compare the running total against their budget while shopping. The use of the personal scanner enables the company to reduce prices and increase revenue. Other devices help to increase employee productivity and satisfaction.

METRO shopping cart with display screen. *(Source: Courtesy of METRO AG.)*

Note: Food Lion is a Delhaige Group Company. Separate financial results are not available. The Bloom concept is still under experimentation in several stores. If successful, it will be installed in many stores.

Sources: Compiled from Clark (2005), McGuire (2004), and *foodlion.com/AboutFoodLion/FastFacts.asp* (accessed May 2008).

Note: Food Lion is not the only retailer experimenting with wireless devices. Metro Group in Germany (2,400 stores) is experimenting with future stores with all of the devices cited earlier plus some others. For example, a Tablet PC helps shoppers navigate their way to any product, using a store map (see photo). For details, see Heinrich (2005).

Lessons Learned from This Case

The opening case illustrates several applications of different wireless devices. We can see that the technology improved the operation of the business in what is known as *mobile enterprise*. Benefits are observed for the customers, employees, and management. Using wireless technologies, one can create applications that are not available or which have fewer functionalities than with wireline systems. However, some wireless systems may be expensive (e.g., the cart-mounted tablet PCs). This case's applications are based on a local area infrastructure, called Wi-Fi.

This opening case is an example of mobile commerce. In addition, some EC services can be provided to customers located at specific places at the time they need such services.

This capability, which is not available in regular EC, may change many things in our lives. Mobile computing is also a computing paradigm designed for workers who travel outside the boundaries of their organizations or for people on the move.

Mobile computing and commerce are spreading rapidly, replacing or supplementing wired computing. Mobile computing involves mostly wireless infrastructure. Mobile computing may reshape the entire IT field (see Taniar, 2007, and Longino, 2006). The technologies, applications, and limitations of mobile computing and mobile commerce are the main focus of this chapter. Later in the chapter, we will look briefly at futuristic applications of *pervasive computing*.

7.1 Overview of Mobile Computing and Commerce

Mobile computing and commerce is growing rapidly with the explosive growth of mobile devices and networks. This section provides an overview of this field. Specifically we cover the content (landscape) of the field, its terminology, attributes, drivers, and benefits. We also describe some of the supporting technologies and provide an overview of mobile commerce.

THE MOBILE COMPUTING LANDSCAPE

In the traditional computing environment it was necessary to come to the computer to do some work on it. All computers were connected to each other, to networks, servers, and so on via *wires*. This situation limited the use of computers and created hardship for people and workers on the move. In particular, salespeople, repair people, service employees, students, law enforcement agents, and utility workers can be more effective if they can use information technology while at their jobs in the field or in transit. There are also mobile vacationers, people on holiday who wish to be connected with the Internet from any place at any time.

The first solution was to make computers small enough that they can be easily carried around. First, the laptop computer was invented, and later on smaller and smaller computers, such as the PDAs and other handhelds, appeared. These *mobile devices* have become lighter and more powerful as far as processing speed and storage. At the end of the day, mobile workers were able to download (or upload) information from (or to) a regular desktop computer in a process known as *synchronization*. To speed up the "sync," special connecting cradles (docking stations) were created (see Online Minicase 7.1 in this chapter (Washington Township) and the Maybelline Online Minicase in Chapter 2).

The second solution to the need for mobile computing was to replace wires with *wireless communication media*. Wireless systems have been in use in radio, TV, and telephones for a long time, so it was natural to adapt them to the computing environment.

The third solution was a combination of the first two, namely, to use mobile devices in a wireless environment. Referred to as **wireless mobile computing,** this combination enables a real-time connection between a mobile device and other computing environments, such as the Internet or an intranet. This innovation changed the way people use computers. It is used in education, healthcare, entertainment, security, and much more. This computing model is basically leading to *ubiquity*—meaning that computing is available anywhere at any time. (*Note:* Since many mobile applications now go wireless, the term *mobile computing* today is often used generally to describe *wireless* mobile computing; (see Taylor, 2007, and Taniar, 2007.)

Using wireline portable computers, salespeople can make proposals at customers' offices, or while traveling, a traveler could read and answer all of the day's e-mails at the hotel room as long as there is wireless or wireline Internet access.

For example, National Distributing Company (NDC), one of the three top alcoholic beverage distributors in the United States, needed a point-of-service (POS) tool for its 1,000-person sales team to perform order entry and CRM applications while at the customer location. The company chose Fujitsu's pen Tablet PCs (Stylistic 3500) and a cellular phone. NDC's sales representatives now dial up the company's mainframe computer directly and access its CRM applications and Web-enabled order entry. The pen Tablet PCs provide NDC's sales representatives with real-time data on order status, product availability, customer account status, and other information, while they meet face-to-face with the customer. It has a wireless option, too (Fujitsu Computer Systems, 2008).

OM

Due to some current technical limitations, we cannot (yet) do with mobile computing all of the things that we do with regular computing. On the other hand, we can do things in mobile computing that we cannot do in the regular computing environment. We explore the advantages of mobile computing later in the chapter.

TABLE 7.1	Mobile Computing Basic Terminology

Bluetooth. A chip technology wireless standard designed for temporary, short-range connection (data and voice) among mobile devices and/or other devices (see *bluetooth.org*).

Enhanced messaging service (EMS). An extension of SMS that is capable of simple animation, tiny pictures, and short melodies.

Global positioning system (GPS). A satellite-based tracking system that enables the determination of a GPS device's location. (See Section 7.7 for more on GPS.)

Multimedia messaging service (MMS). The next generation of wireless messaging, this technology will be able to deliver rich media.

Personal digital assistant (PDA). A small portable computer, such as Palm handhelds and the Pocket PC devices from companies like H-P.

Short messaging service (SMS). A technology for sending short text messages (up to 160 characters in 2006) on cell phones. SMS messages can be sent or received concurrently, even during a voice or data call. Used by hundreds of millions of users, SMS is known as "the e-mail of m-commerce." Some companies offer multilanguage text creation.

Smart phones. Internet-enabled cell phones that can support mobile applications. These "phones with a brain" are becoming standard devices. They include WAP microprocessors for Internet access and the capabilities of PDAs as well (see Malykhina, 2007, and Null, 2007).

WiMax. A wireless technology based on the IEEE 802.16-2004 standard, designed to provide Internet access across metro areas to fixed (not moving) users. It is considered wireless broadband technology. For details, see Chapter 4 and Technology Guide 4.

Wireless application protocol (WAP). A technology that offers Internet browsing from wireless devices.

Wireless local area network (WLAN). A broad term for all 802.11 standards. Basically, it is a wireless version of the Ethernet networking standard. (For discussion of the Ethernet standard, see Technology Guide 4.)

For an extensive list of other terms, see *mobileinfo.com/Hot_Topics/index.htm* and *mobileinfo.com/Glossary/index.htm*.

Mobile Computing Basic Terminology. Now that we have a sense of how mobile computing works, we need to learn the basic technology. Table 7.1 lists and defines some common mobile computing terms. Please study this table carefully because we will be referring to these terms throughout the chapter. Note that some of these terms are covered in Chapter 4 and in Technology Guide 4.

With these terms in mind, we can now look more deeply at the attributes and drivers of mobile computing.

ATTRIBUTES AND DRIVERS OF MOBILE COMPUTING

Generally speaking, many of the EC applications described in Chapter 6 can be done in m-commerce. For example, c-shopping, e-banking, and e-stock trading are gaining popularity in wireless B2C. Auctioning is just beginning to take place on cell phones, and wireless collaborative commerce in B2B is emerging. However, there are several *new* applications that are possible *only* in the mobile environment. To understand why this is so, first let's examine the major attributes of mobile computing and m-commerce.

Specific Attributes of Mobile Computing and M-Commerce. Mobile computing has two major characteristics that differentiate it from other forms of computing: *mobility* and *broad reach*.

Mobility. Mobile computing and m-commerce are based on the fact that users carry a mobile device anywhere they go. Mobility implies portability. Therefore, users can initiate a *real-time* contact with other systems from wherever they happen to be if they can connect to a wireless network.

Broad Reach. In mobile computing, people can be reached at any time. Of course, users can block certain hours or certain messages, but when users carry an open mobile device, they can be reached instantly.

These two characteristics break the barriers of geography and time. They create the following five value-added attributes that drive the development of m-commerce: ubiquity, convenience, instant connectivity, personalization, and localization of products and services.

Ubiquity. *Ubiquity* refers to the attribute of being available at *any location* at *any given time.* A smart phone or a PDA offers ubiquity—that is, it can fulfill the need both for real-time information and for communication, independent of the user's location.

Convenience. It is very convenient for users to operate in the wireless environment. All they need is an Internet-enabled mobile device such as a smart phone. By using *GPRS* (General Packet Radio Service, a cell phone standard), it is easier and faster to access the Web without booting up a PC or placing a call via a modem. Also, more and more places are equipped with Wi-Fi connections ("hot spots"), enabling users to get online from portable laptops any time (as was shown in the Dartmouth College case in Chapter 1). You can even watch an entire movie on a PDA (see *pock-etpcfilms.com*).

Instant Connectivity. Mobile devices enable users to connect easily and quickly to the Internet, intranets, other mobile devices, and databases. Thus, wireless devices could become the preferred way to access information.

Personalization. *Personalization* refers to the preparation of customized information for individual consumers. For example, a user who is identified as someone who likes to travel might be sent travel-related information and advertising. Product personalization is still limited on mobile devices. However, the need for conducting transactions electronically, availability of personalized information, and transaction feasibility via mobile portals will move personalization to new levels, leading ultimately to the mobile device becoming a major EC tool.

Localization of Products and Services. Knowing where the user is physically located at any particular moment is key to offering relevant products and services. E-commerce applications based on localization for the customers are known as **location-based e-commerce** or **l-commerce**. Precise location information is known when a GPS is attached to a user's wireless device. For example, you might use your mobile device to find the nearest ATM or FedEx drop box. In addition, the GPS can tell others where you are. Localization can be general, such as to anyone in a certain location (e.g., all shoppers at a shopping mall). Or, even better, it can be targeted so that users get messages that depend both on where they are and what *their preferences* are, thus combining localization and personalization. For instance, if it is known that you like Italian food and you are strolling in a mall that has an Italian restaurant, you might receive an SMS that tells you that restaurant's "special of the day" and gives you a 10 percent discount. GPS is becoming a standard feature in many mobile devices as of 2008.

Drivers of Mobile Computing and M-Commerce. In addition to the value-added attributes just discussed, the development of mobile computing and m-commerce is driven by the following factors.

Widespread Availability of Mobile Devices. According to *Romow.com* (2008), 50 percent of the world population will use mobile phones in 2008. It is estimated that within a few years, about 70 percent of cell phones will have Internet access ("smart-phones"). Thus, a potential mass market is available for conducting discovery, communication, collaboration, (e.g., see "Global Mobile," a special report, *ComputerWorld*, May 14, 2007), and m-commerce. Cell phones are spreading quickly even in developing countries.

No Need for a PC. Today's PDAs and some cell phones have as much processing power as personal computers did just a few years ago, and possess the range of software available to PC users. This suggests that the smart phone—not the PC—may soon become the foremost tool that connects people to the Internet.

The Handset Culture. Another driver of m-commerce is the widespread use of cell phones, which is a social phenomenon, especially among the 15-to-25-year-old age group. These users will constitute a major force of online buyers once they begin to make and spend larger amounts of money. The use of SMS has been spreading like wildfire in several European and Asian countries. In the Philippines, for example, SMS is a national phenomenon, especially in the youth market. As another example, Japanese send many more messages through mobile phones than do Americans, who prefer the desktop or laptop for e-mail.

Declining Prices and Increased Functionalities. The price of wireless devices is declining, and the per-minute pricing of mobile services declined by 50 percent in recent years. At the same time, functionalities are increasing. Also, a flat fee (e.g., monthly) encourages more use of mobile devices.

Improvement of Bandwidth. To properly conduct m-commerce, it is necessary to have sufficient bandwidth for transmitting text; however, bandwidth is also required for voice, video, and multimedia. The 3G (third-generation) and 3.5G technologies (described in Chapter 4) provide the necessary bandwidth.

The Centrino Chip. A major boost to mobile computing was provided in 2003 by Intel with its Centrino chip. This chip, which became a standard feature in most laptops by 2005, includes three important capabilities: (1) a connection device to a wireless local area network; (2) low usage of electricity, enabling users to do more work on a single battery charge; and (3) a high level of security. The Centrino (Centrino 2 in 2008) is making mobile computing the common computing environment.

Availability of Internet Access in Automobiles. The number of cars equipped with high-speed Internet access (e.g., see *autonetmobile.com* and *nvtl.com*) has increased and will continue to grow.

Networks. A driving development of mobile computing is the introduction of the third- and fourth-generation wireless environments known as 3G and 4G, and the adoption of Wi-Fi as a wireless local area network (LAN), WiMax, and wide area networks. They were described in Chapter 4.

MOBILE COMMERCE

While the impact of mobile computing on our lives will be very significant, a similar impact is already occurring in the way we conduct business. This impact is described as **mobile commerce** (also known as *m-commerce*), which is basically any e-commerce or e-business done in a wireless environment, especially via the Internet. Like regular EC applications, m-commerce can be done via the Internet, private communication lines, smart cards, or other infrastructures (e.g., see Golding, 2008, *en.wikipedia.org/wiki/Mobile_commerce*, and Taniar, 2007).

Mobile devices create an opportunity to deliver new services to existing customers and to attract new ones. Varshney and Vetter (2002) classified the applications of m-commerce into the following 12 categories:

1. Mobile financial applications (B2C, B2B)
2. Mobile advertising (B2C)
3. Mobile inventory management (B2C, B2B)
4. Proactive service management (B2C, B2B)
5. Product locating and shopping (B2C, B2B)
6. Wireless reengineering (B2C, B2B)
7. Mobile auction or reverse auction (B2C)
8. Mobile entertainment services (B2C)
9. Mobile office (B2C)
10. Mobile distance education (B2C)
11. Wireless data center (B2C, B2B)
12. Mobile music/music-on-demand (B2C)

For details, see *mobiforum.org*.

Many of these applications, as well as some additional ones, will be discussed in this chapter. For an overview, see Golding (2008).

M-Commerce Value Chain, Revenue Models, and Justification. Like EC, m-commerce may be a complex process involving a number of operations and a number of players (customers, merchants, mobile operators, service providers, and the like). Several types of vendors provide value-added services to m-commerce. These include mobile portals, advertisers, software vendors, content providers, mobile portal, mobile network operators, and more (see *en.wikipedia.org/wiki/mobile_commerce*).

The revenue models of m-commerce are the following: access fees, subscription fees, pay-per-use, advertising, transaction fees, hosting, payment clearing, and point-of-traffic.

The capabilities and attributes of mobile computing presented earlier provide for many applications, as shown in Figure 7.1. These attributes are supported by infra-structure. According to Nokia's advertising, mobility moves from productivity improvement to a strategic part of the enterprise's IT portfolio.

Justifying M-Commerce. Justifying m-commerce may not be easy due to its intangible benefits. *CIO Insight* (2007), for example, reports that mobile banking is slow to adopt due to the difficulty to justify it. According to MobileInfo (2008), developing a business case for mobile computing or commerce projects is a serious and complex exercise. It requires analysis of both costs and benefits from undertaking such a project. First of all, there are a number of ways in which you can evaluate IT investment. While some of the methods are qualitative, most financial officers want quantitative analysis. MobileInfo provides a few methods. Others are provided in Chapter 17.

Microsoft developed a special calculator for wireless justification. (See the problem-solving activity at the end of this chapter.)

Impact on Enterprises. Mobile technologies not only provide convenience and efficiency benefits, but can lead in both core competencies and competitive advantage and impact entire strategies and business models. Google activities in the area are good examples.

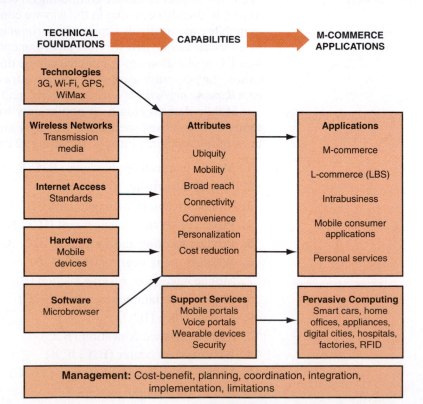

Figure 7.1 The landscape of mobile computing and com-merce. (*Source: Drawn by E. Turban.*)

WIRELESS LOCAL AREA NETWORKS AND WI-FI

As you have read in Chapter 4, wireless local area networks have been making their way to the wireless forefront. A *wireless LAN (WLAN)* is like a wired LAN without the cables. WLANs transmit and receive data over the airwaves from a short distance in what is known as Wi-Fi (Wireless Fidelity). Wi-Fi is described in Table 7.1 and in Chapter 4.

The Wi-Fi Revolution. In a typical configuration, a transmitter with an antenna, called a *wireless access point* (WAP) connects to a wired LAN from a fixed location or to satellite dishes that provide an Internet connection. A WAP provides service to a number of users within a couple hundred feet, known as a "hotspot zone," or *hotspot*. Several WAPs are needed to support larger numbers of users across a larger geographical area. End users can access a WLAN with their laptops, desktops, or PDAs by adding a wireless network card. Figure 7.2 shows how Wi-Fi works. Mitchell (2008) provides a step-by-step guide for building Wi-Fi at home or in small-business settings.

WLANs provide fast and easy Internet or intranet broadband access from public hotspots such as airports, hotels, Internet cafes, and conference centers. WLANs are also being used in universities, offices, and homes in place of the traditional wired LANs (see *weca.net*).

Figure 7.2 How Wi-Fi works.

1 Radio-equipped access point connected to the Internet (or via a router). It generates and receives radio waves (up to 400 feet).

2 Several client devices, equipped with PC cards, generate and receive radio waves.

3 Router is connected to the Internet via a cable or DSL modem, or is connected via a satellite.

TABLE 7.2	Examples of Wi-Fi Applications

- Like other airports in the United States, the Minneapolis–St. Paul International airport is served by Wi-Fi. The fee is $7.95 for unlimited daily access. Northwest Airlines has 570 hotspots in the United States (*jiwire.com*, accessed May 2006).

- Lufthansa offers in-flight Wi-Fi service on its long-haul fleet. The hotspots on the planes are connected to the Internet via satellites. American Airlines, Alaska Airlines, JetBlue, and Virgin America offer connection to the Web to fliers as of 2008. Many other airlines plan or already offer similar service.

- Since 2002, T-Mobile has installed Wi-Fi networks in several thousand Starbucks stores in the United States. T-Mobile is also installing Wi-Fi in hundreds of Borders Books & Music stores. T-Mobile charges annually, monthly, daily, or pay as you go (see *hotspot.tmobile.com/services_plans.htm*).

- McDonald's now offers Wi-Fi hotspots in more than 30,000 restaurants around the world, and the number is increasing daily. Local service providers provide high-quality wireless service through online credit card payment, subscriptions, prepaid cards, and sometimes promotional coupons (see *mcdonalds.com/wireless.html*).

- Using a wireless ticketing system, Universal Studios in Hollywood is shortening the waiting lines for tickets at its front gate. The ticket sellers, armed with Wi-Fi–enabled devices and belt-mounted printers, not only sell tickets but also provide information. For details, see Scanlon (2003).

- CVS Corp., the largest retail pharmacy in the United States, uses Wi-Fi–based devices throughout its 6,200 stores. The handheld computers support a variety of in-store applications, including direct store delivery, price management, inventory control, and receiving. Benefits include faster transfer rates, increasing productivity and performance, reduced cost, and improved customer service. For details, see *Symbol.com* (1998, 2003).

- Several mining companies in Europe installed hundreds of Wi-Fi hotspots in their coal mines. Information from drills and trucks, such as their positions and the weight of their loads, is transmitted wirelessly to the control center. It increases both productivity and safety.

The major benefits of Wi-Fi are its lower cost and its ability to provide simple Internet access. As a matter of fact, Wi-Fi is the greatest facilitator of the *wireless Internet*.

Illustrative Applications of Wi-Fi. The years 2004 through 2008 were a breakthrough era for wireless networking in offices, airports, hotels, and campuses around the world. Since then, each month brings new examples of businesses that have added Wi-Fi, RFID, or other wireless services for their employees, business partners, or customers. Several examples are presented in Table 7.2. Many more examples of Wi-Fi are included in this chapter and throughout the book.

Despite all of the development, progress is still slow, as shown next.

Barriers to Commercial Wi-Fi Growth. Two factors are standing in the way of Wi-Fi market growth: cost and security. First, some analysts question why anyone would pay $30 a month, $7.95 a day, or any other fee for Wi-Fi access when it is readily available in many locations for free (e.g., in certain cities, airports, and shopping malls such as in Manila, Philippines). Because it's relatively inexpensive to set up a wireless access point that is connected to the Internet, a number of businesses offer their customers Wi-Fi access without charging them for the service. In fact, there is an organization, *freenetworks.org*, aimed at supporting the creation of free community wireless network projects around the globe. In areas such as San Francisco, where there is a solid core of high-tech professionals, many "gear heads" have set up their own wireless hotspots that give passersby free Internet connections. This is a part of a new culture known as *war chalking* and *war driving* (see *en.wikipedia.org/wiki/Warchalking*).

In Sections 7.2 through 7.6 of this chapter, we will study m-commerce applications in a number of diverse categories. A summary of the applications is provided at *en.wikipedia.org/wiki/Mobile_Commerce*.

Review Questions

1. Describe the mobile computing field.
2. List five major attributes of mobile computing.
3. List five drivers of mobile computing and commerce.
4. Define mobile commerce and list its revenue models.
5. Describe the Wi-Fi revolution and applications.

7.2 Mobile Applications in Financial Services

Mobile financial applications include banking, wireless payments and micropayments, wireless wallets, bill payment services, brokerage services, and money transfers. While many of these services are simply a subset of their wireline counterparts, they have the potential to turn a mobile device into a business tool, replacing bank branches, ATMs, and credit cards by letting a user conduct financial transactions with a mobile device any time and from anywhere. For example, in Japan cell phones have a built-in smart card that is used for micropayments. In this section we will look at some of the most popular mobile applications in banking and in financial services.

MOBILE BANKING AND STOCK TRADING

Mobile banking is generally defined as carrying out banking transactions and other related activities via mobile devices. The services offered include bill payments and money transfers, access administration and check book requests, balance inquiries and statements of account, interest and exchange rates, and so on, and the sale/purchase of stocks.

Throughout Europe, the United States, and Asia, an increasing percentage of banks offer mobile access to financial and account information. For instance, Merita Bank in Sweden pioneered many services, and Citibank and Wachovia in the United States has a diversified mobile banking service. Consumers in such banks can use their mobile handsets to access account balances, pay bills, and transfer funds using SMS. The Royal Bank of Scotland, for example, uses a mobile payment service, and Banamex, one of Mexico's largest banks, is a strong provider of wireless services to customers. Many banks in Japan allow for all banking transactions to be done via cell phone. For a demo, go to *Wachovia.com*, find mobile banking, and click on "go mobile today."

According to *CIO Insight* (2007), Wells Fargo provides an increasing number of banking services to wireless customers. The major objective is to increase customer loyalty. Basic wireless services are being offered by most major banks worldwide. Among services are mobile alerts (e.g., when your balance is low). Also, mobile browsing, downloading, and text messaging are becoming popular.

As the wireless technology and transmission speeds improve, the rate of mobile financial service increases. The same picture holds true for other mobile financial applications such as mobile brokering, insurance, and stock market trades.

WIRELESS ELECTRONIC PAYMENT SYSTEMS

Wireless payment systems transform mobile phones into secure, self-contained purchasing tools capable of instantly authorizing payments over the cellular network. The city of Montreal, Canada, installed smart parking payment terminals that process *Pay & Go mode* wireless secure e-payments powered by solar panels. The parking terminals also provide information on parking space utilization to a central system (*8d.com*, 2006). In many countries wireless purchase of tickets to movies and other events is popular.

Micropayments. If you were in Frankfurt, Germany, or Tokyo, Japan, for example, and took a taxi ride, you could pay the taxi driver using your cell phone. As discussed in Chapter 6, electronic payments for small-purchase amounts (generally $3 or less) are called *micropayments*. The demand for wireless micropayments systems is fairly high. Edgar, Dunn & Company's 2006 *Mobile Payments Study* found that:

• Survey respondents believe that mobile payments will reach a critical mass of consumers and become as important as other types of payments, such as credit and debit cards, but it may take 10 years.
• The most significant barriers to the adoption of online mobile payments are the transaction costs charged by mobile carriers and the limited availability of micropayments alternatives.

Payments by cell phones are becoming popular in Japan, where customers can pay train fares, vending machines, etc., using their cell phones (see Foster, 2008).

An Israeli firm, TeleVend, Inc. (*televend.com*), has pioneered a secure platform that allows subscribers to make payments using mobile phones of any type on any cellular infrastructure. A customer places a mobile phone call to a number stipulated by the merchant, to authorize a vending device to dispense the service. Connecting to a TeleVend server, the user selects the appropriate transaction option to authorize payment. Billing can be made to the customer's bank or credit card account or to the mobile phone bill. Micropayment technology has a wide range of applications, such as making payments to parking garages, restaurants, grocery stores, and public transportation.

SVR

Mobile (Wireless) Wallets. An *e-wallet* (see Chapter 6) is a piece of software that stores an online shopper's credit card numbers and other personal information so that the shopper does not have to reenter that information for every online purchase. In the recent past, companies such as Motorola offered **m-wallet** (*mobile wallet*, also known as *wireless wallet*) technologies that enabled cardholders to make purchases with a single click from their mobile devices. While most of these companies are now defunct, some cell phone providers have incorporated m-wallets in their offerings. Since 2004, NTT DoCoMo Japan has been selling phones with chips in them that can be scanned by a short-range wireless reader at tens of thousands of stores. Similar capabilities using Near Field Communications (NFC) started to grow in the United States beginning in 2007 and are forecasted to reach more than half of all handsets sold by 2010 (Smith, 2006).

A handset-based service allowing consumers to send money to individuals both in and outside the United States through Western Union locations incorporates mobile wallets. That development allows, for example, users of Trumpet Mobile, a reseller of prepaid wireless service for Sprint Nextel Corp., to send money to other persons directly, without the need for prepaid cards. It also allows users to make point-of-sale transactions with their phones, relying either on contactless technology or PIN code capability. In 2008, Affinity Mobile initiated a nationwide person-to-person money-transfer service involving Western Union and Radio Shack Corp., whose electronics stores sell Trumpet's phones and service.

Motorola m-wallet solutions available as of 2008 include: New Merchant/Bank Service—transaction fees, merchant handsets; Value-Added Services—person-to-person, money orders, ticketing and coupons, bill payments; and Co-Branding and Cross-Selling with banks and merchants (Motorola, 2008).

Wireless Bill Payments. In addition to paying bills through wireline banking or from ATMs, a number of companies are now providing their customers with the option of paying their bills directly from a cell phone. HDFC Bank of India (*hdfcbank.com*), for example, allows customers to pay their utility bills using SMS.

FIN

Review Questions

1. Describe wireless banking.
2. How are micropayments done wirelessly?
3. Describe a mobile e-wallet.

7.3 Mobile Shopping, Advertising, and Content-Providing

M-commerce B2C applications are concentrated in three major areas —retail shopping (for products and services), advertising, and providing digitized content (e.g., music, news, videos, movies, or games) for a fee via portals. Let's examine these areas.

SHOPPING FROM WIRELESS DEVICES

An increasing number of online vendors allow customers to shop from wireless devices. For example, customers who use Internet-ready cell phones can shop at certain sites such as *mobile.yahoo.com* or *amazon.com*. Shopping from wireless devices enables customers to perform quick searches, compare prices, use a shopping cart, order, pay, and view the status of their order using their cell phones or wireless PDAs. Wireless shoppers are supported by services similar to those available for wireline shoppers.

MKT

An example of food shopping from wireless devices is that of a joint venture between Motorola and Food.com. The companies offer restaurant chains an infrastructure that enables consumers to place an order for pickup or delivery virtually any time, anywhere. Donatos Pizzeria was the first chain to implement the system in 2002.

Cell phone users can also participate in online auctions. For example, eBay offers "anywhere wireless" services. Vendio and gNumber partnered to provide mobile eBay applications and PayPal introduced its pay-by-phone service. The ShopWiki Mobile Search engine is accessible from a PDA or cell phone browser. It allows you to compare prices of online stores and then buy from any physical location. ShopWiki serves 60 million products from more than 180,000 stores (Comiskey, 2006).

M-commerce in Japan is growing exponentially and now represents the largest amount of m-commerce sales in the world. Over 60 million Japanese are buying over their cell phones even while riding the trains, buying, for example, their train tickets. Wireless shopping is popular with busy single parents, executives, and teenagers (who are doing over 80 percent of their EC shopping from cell phones). Cell phones allow direct communication with consumers.

Traditional retailers in Japan, such as 7-Eleven and I Holding Company, have been losing millions of customers to Web shopping companies such as Rakuten Inc. A group of convenience stores and 7-Eleven Japan Co. have set up *7dream.com*, offering online services for music, travel, tickets, gifts, and other goods to its 8,000 7-Eleven stores in Japan. Meanwhile, pure m-commerce operators such as Xavel Inc. (*xavel.com*) are growing rapidly, forcing traditional retailers such as Marui department stores to expand their e-commerce to include m-commerce.

According to the Daiwa Institute of Research (reported by *Textually.org*, 2006), impulse shopping accounts for most of the purchases that are done on mobile phones, but only if the users are on flat-fee-based service.

An example of purchasing movie tickets by wireless device is illustrated in Figure 7.3. Notice that the reservation is made directly with the merchant. Then money is transferred from the customer's account to the merchant's account.

TARGETED ADVERTISING

Knowing the current location of mobile users (e.g., when a GPS is attached to the cell phone) and their preferences or surfing habits, marketers can send user-specific advertising messages to wireless devices. Advertising can also be location-sensitive, informing about shops, malls, and restaurants close to a potential buyer. SMS messages and short paging messages can be used to deliver this type of advertising to cell phones and pagers, respectively. Many companies are capitalizing on targeted advertising, as shown in *A Closer Look 7.1*.

As more wireless bandwidth becomes available, content-rich advertising involving audio, pictures, and video clips will be generated for individual users with specific needs, interests, and inclinations.

Getting Paid to Listen to Advertising. Would you be willing to listen to a 10-second ad when you dial your cell phone if you were paid 2 minutes of free long-distance time? As in the wireline world, some consumers are willing to be paid for exposure

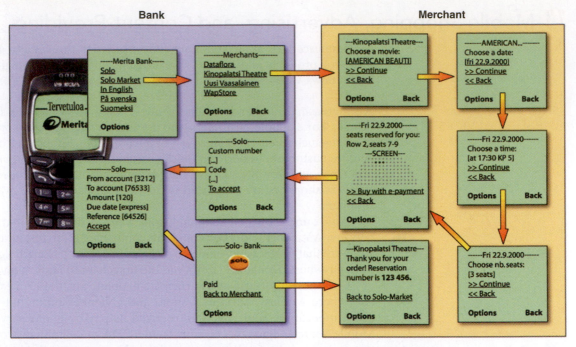

Figure 7.3 Purchasing movie tickets with WAP Solo. *(Source: Sadeh, 2002, Fig. 1.5.)*

MKT

to advertising. It depends on which country you are in. In most places where it was offered in the United States, this service was a flop and was discontinued.

In Singapore, though, getting paid to listen to advertising works very well. Within a few months of offering the ad service, more than 100,000 people subscribed to the free minutes in exchange for listening to the ads offered by SingTel Mobile (Eklund, 2002). Subscribers to SingTel's service fill out a personal questionnaire when they sign up. This

A Closer Look 7.1

Wireless Advertising in Action

The following are a few examples of wireless advertising in action.

Vindigo.com (*vindigo.com*) is a distributor of mobile applications and it has a large database of customers (over a million in May 2004) willing to accept promotional materials on their wireless devices. This is known as *permission marketing*. The users download special software on their PDAs that allows Vindigo.com to deliver timely, accurate information about places to go and things to do in their area. Along with every listing, the company can deliver a customized message to the users at a time and place where it is of most interest to them and they are most likely to act on it.

Vindigo targets ads by city (New York, San Francisco, Los Angeles, etc.) and channel (Eat, Shop, or Play). Vindigo.com tracks which ads a user sees and selects, and even allows a user to request information from an advertiser via e-mail. Vindigo.com determines a user's location through GPS or by asking which neighborhoods they want to be matched with. For example, if you own an Italian restaurant chain, you can use Vindigo.com to send a message to anyone looking for Italian food within a few blocks of one of your locations. You can give them directions to that restaurant and even offer them the list of specials on the menu and discounts.

MyAvantGo.Com (*avantgo.com*) has 250 major marketing brands targeting over 7 million registered users (*avantgo.com*, accessed April 2008). The content is delivered to PDAs and handsets running Palm or PocketPC operating systems. MyAvantGo offers an m-business channel and direct promotions to deliver advertising from some of the world's top brands, including American Airlines, Chevy Trucks, the Golf Channel, CNN, the *New York Times*, and Yahoo!. (See *myavantgo.com*.)

Hoping to become the king of location-based Web domains, Go2Online (*go2online.com*) helps mobile travelers find everything from lodging (choose *go2hotels*) to Jiffy Lube stations. Partnering with Sprint, Nextel, Verizon, and Boost, Go2 makes its services available on every Web-enabled phone, Palm i705, and BlackBerry RIM pager in America. Entering "JiffyLube" or any of hundreds of other brand names into the Go2 system will bring up the nearest location where one can find that product or service.

Sources: Compiled from the Web sites of Vindigo.com, AvantGo.com, and Go2Online.com (accessed April 2008).

information is fed into the Spotcast database (*spotcastnetwork.com*) and encrypted to shield subscribers' identities—Spotcast cannot match phone numbers to names, for example. To collect their free minutes—one minute per call, up to 100 minutes a month—subscribers dial a four-digit code, then the phone number of the person they want to talk to. The code prompts SingTel to forward the call to Spotcast and, in an instant, Spotcast's software finds the best ad to send to the subscriber based on the subscriber's profile.

MOBILE PORTALS

A **mobile portal** is a customer channel, optimized for mobility, that aggregates and provides content and services for mobile users. These portals offer services similar to those of desktop portals such as AOL, Yahoo!, and MSN. (See *en.wikipedia.org/wiki/Mobile_portal* for additional discussion of portals.) An example of the best "pure" mobile portal (whose only business is to be a mobile portal) is *zed.com* from Sonera in Finland. The world's best-known mobile portal, with over 52 million members, mostly in Japan, is i-mode from DoCoMo.

The services provided by mobile portals include news, sports, e-mail, entertainment, and travel information; restaurants and event information; leisure-related services (e.g., games, TV and movie listings); community services; and stock trading. A sizeable percentage of the portals also provide downloads and messaging, music-related services, and health, dating, and job information. Mobile portals frequently charge for their services. For example, you may be asked to pay 50 cents to get a weather report over your mobile phone. Alternatively, you may pay a monthly fee for the portal service and get the report free any time you want it. In Japan, for example, i-mode generates revenue mainly from subscription fees. A special service for travelers is offered at Avantgo (from iAnywhere).

Example. AvantGo (described earlier) is the world's largest mobile Internet service that delivers rich, personalized content and applications to PDA, wireless PDA, and smartphone users. Today, hundreds of major media brands and marketers deliver their online content through the AvantGo mobile Internet service portal.

In addition, over 250 major marketing brands use AvantGo mobile advertising to target and reach a valuable trendsetter audience of over 7 million unique users. For more details, see *avantgo.com/biz/aboutus/index.html*.

Increasingly, the field of mobile portals is being dominated by a few big companies. The big players in Europe, for instance, are companies such as Vodafone, Orange, O2, and T-Mobile; in the United States the big players are Cingular, Verizon, AT&T, and Sprint PCS. Also, mobile-device manufacturers offer their own portals (e.g., Club Nokia portal, My Palm portal). And, finally, the traditional portals (such as Yahoo!, AOL, and MSN) have mobile portals as well. For example, Google Mobile provides news, e-mail, and more to cell phones.

Sina Corporation, a major portal network in China (*sina.com*), in its Sina Mobile, offers mobile value-added services including news and information, community services such as dating and friendship, and multimedia downloads of ring tones, pictures, and screensavers. Users can order these services through the Sina Web site or through their mobile phones on either a monthly subscription or a per-message basis.

VOICE PORTALS

A **voice portal** is a Web site that can be accessed by voice. Voice portals are not really Web sites in the normal sense because they are not accessed through a browser.

In addition to retrieving information, some sites provide true interaction. *iPing.com* is a reminder and notification service that allows users to enter information via the Web and receive reminder calls. In addition, iPing.com can call a group of people to notify them of a meeting or conference call.

Voice portals are used extensively by airlines, for example, enabling you to make reservations, find flight status, and more. Many other organizations use voice portals to replace or supplement help desks. The advantage to the company is cost reduction.

Users can save time, since they do not have to wait for help. ("All lines are busy . . . an operator will be with you as soon as possible . . .")

A benefit for Internet marketers is that voice portals can help businesses find new customers. Several of these sites are supported by ads; thus, the customer profile data they have available helps them deliver targeted advertising. For instance, a department-store chain with an existing brand image can use short audio commercials on these sites to deliver a message related to the topic of the call.

Review Questions

1. Describe mobile shopping.
2. How is targeted advertising done wirelessly?
3. Describe a *mobile portal*.
4. Define and describe a *voice portal*.

7.4 Mobile Enterprise and Interbusiness Applications

Although B2C m-commerce is getting considerable publicity, many of today's applications are used within organizations. This section looks at how mobile devices and technologies can be used *within, outside*, and *between* organizations.

MOBILE ENTERPRISE APPLICATIONS

Many companies offer innovative mobile and wireless applications in the enterprise. Examples of three applications are provided in Online Brief 7.1. Wireless applications fall into the following categories:

• Supporting salespeople while they are waiting on customers (see Online Brief 7.1 for examples)

• Supporting field employees doing repairs or maintenance on corporate premises or for clients

• Supporting traveling (or off-corporate-site) executives, managers, or other employees

• Supporting employees while they do work inside the enterprise, but where there is no easy access to desktop computers (e.g., in a warehouse, outdoor facilities, or, as in the case of Food Lion, when employees check inventory in the store)

• Employees driving trucks, while they are on the road

The basic objective is to provide employees with communication and collaboration tools, and access to data, information, and people inside the organization.

Two types of devices are the following:

1. Portable devices are connected to wireline networks such as via a docking station. In this category, we can include tablet PCs, PDAs, laptop computers, etc. These are portable, but not necessarily wireless.

2. Wireless devices that enable real-time connection to corporate data or the Internet. There are many types of wireless devices ranging from smart phones to handheld companions carried by mobile workers. All of the above provide the infrastructure for many applications.

MOBILE ENTERPRISE APPLICATIONS: EXAMPLES

In this section we will provide illustrative examples of popular applications ranging from wearable devices for field/service employees to sales force automation.

In Retailing. The Food Lion example is only one of many enterprise applications. Symbol Technology (*symbol.com*) from Motorola provides small, rugged handheld computers that enable data capture applications, collaboration, and price markdowns. The Symbol MC series, for example, can facilitate inventory taking and management. Warehouse management systems are greatly improved with software that is combined with the device (e.g., from M-Netics). Several supermarkets' employees use handheld computers to reorder supplies. When an employee scans the barcode of a product, the handheld recommends if, when, and how much to order.

Sales Force Automation (SFA). Sales representatives need to check on stock items' availability, special pricing, order status, and so on, all during their visits with customers. For example, a customer may want to know how soon the order will arrive. Devices such as Palm OS and BlackBerry products offer such capabilities. (For details, check *eweek.com/c/s/Mobile-and-Wireless*.) For SFA cases, see *symbol.com* and *sybase.com*.

The use of Tablet PCs by salespeople is widespread. For example, most MarketSource employees work outside their company. They need to capture sales information, competitive data, and inventories, and they need to report sales. According to Microsoft, 650 corporate and remote workers use the device successfully. (See *download.microsoft.com/documents/customerevidence/6364_MarketSource_XP_FINAL.doc*.)

Hospitals. Many hospitals introduce wireless applications ranging from wearable push-button communication devices (badge clips from Vocera Communications) to wireless laptops for bedside registration. According to Vocera Communications (2008), the T1000 phone (a 2008 product) has many support capabilities for mobile employees.

In Operations. Many devices can facilitate different tasks of mobile employees. For example, Driscoll Strawberry Associates uses wireless data collection devices, mobile printers, and handheld devices to accelerate transactions, increase accuracy, and enable real-time receiving and inventory management. The company arranges the delivery of berries to market. The company achieved a 25 percent reduction in transaction processing time, 30 percent reduction in account reconciliation errors, and improved employee feedback due to ease of use. For details, see the Driscoll's Berries case study at *symbol.com* (accessed April 2008).

Home Depot equipped close to 14,000 service agents with the EnfoTrust system (Wi-Fi based). The system can take photos as well. See *enfotrust.com/Our_Customers/Case_Studies.aspx* for details.

Tracking Employees. Using PDAs, Todd Pacific Shipyards accurately tracks their employees, including the hours and projects they've worked on, and assesses daily staffing needs. This knowledge is a key to improved profitability (see Schuman, 2004). This is accomplished with wireless devices.

Wearable Devices. Employees who work on buildings, electrical poles, or other difficult-to-climb places may be equipped with a special form of mobile wireless computing devices called **wearable devices**. People wear these devices on their arms, clothes, or helmets. Examples of wearable devices include:

• **Screen.** A computer screen is mounted on a safety hat, in front of the wearer's eyes, displaying information to the worker.
• **Camera.** A camera is mounted on a safety hat. Workers can take digital photos and videos and transmit them instantly to a portable computer nearby. (Photo transmission is made possible via Bluetooth technology.)
• **Touch-panel display.** In addition to the wrist-mounted keyboard, mobile employees can use a flat-panel screen, attached to the hand, which responds to the tap of a finger or stylus.
• **Keyboard.** A wrist-mounted keyboard enables typing by the other hand. (Wearable keyboards are an alternative to voice recognition systems, which are also wireless.)
• **Speech translator.** For those mobile employees who do not have their hands free to use a keyboard, a wearable speech translator is handy.

- **Watch-like device.** Such a device is carried on the arm like a watch and can display information or be used as a cell phone. Swatch and Microsoft offer such watches. You can get news, weather, and so forth from Microsoft's MSN broadcasts.

For examples of wearable devices used to support mobile employees, see *IT at Work 7.1, xybernaut.com, essworld.net*, and *en.wikipedia.org/wiki/wearable_computing*.

Job Dispatch. Mobile devices are becoming an integral part of groupware and workflow applications. For example, nonvoice mobile services can be used to assist in dispatch functions—to assign jobs to mobile employees, along with detailed information about the tasks. The target areas for mobile delivery and dispatch services include the following: transportation (delivery of food, oil, newspapers, cargo, courier services, tow trucks, and taxis); utilities (gas, electricity, phone, water); field service (computer, office equipment, home repair); healthcare (visiting nurses, doctors, social services); and security (patrols, alarm installation).

A dispatching application for wireless devices allows improved response with reduced resources, real-time tracking of work orders, increased dispatcher efficiency, and a reduction in administrative work. For example, Michigan CAT (*michigancat.com*), a

IT at Work 7.1

Wearable Devices for Bell Canada Workers

 GLOBAL **OM**

For years mobile employees, especially those who had to climb trees, electric poles, or tall buildings, were unable to enjoy the computerized technologies designed to make employees work or feel better. Thus, their productivity and comfort were inferior. That is all beginning to change.

On a cold, damp November day in Toronto, Chris Holm-Laursen, a field technician with Bell Canada (*bell.ca*), is out and about as usual, but this time with a difference: A small but powerful computer sits in a pocket of his vest, a keyboard is attached to the vest's upper-left side, and a flat-panel display screen hangs by his waist. A video camera attached to his safety hat enables him to take pictures without using his hands and send them immediately to the office. A cell phone is attached as well, connected to the computer. A battery pack to keep everything going sits against his back. (See nearby photo.)

Holm-Laursen and 18 other technicians on this pilot project were equipped like this for 10 weeks during fall 2000. By summer 2003 an increasing number of Bell Canada's employees had been equipped with similar devices. The wearable devices enabled the workers to access work orders and repair manuals wherever they were. These workers are not typical of the group usually most wired up, that is, white-collar workers. The hands-free aspect and the ability to communicate any time, from anywhere, represent major steps forward for these utility workers. A wide variety of employees—technicians, medical practitioners, aircraft mechanics, and contractors—are using or testing such devices. By 2006, many more employees were equipped with wearable devices.

So far, only a few companies make and sell wearables for mobile workers. Bell Canada's system was developed by Xybernaut, a U.S. company that in 2002 had more than a thousand of its units in use around the world, some in operation and others in pilot programs.

Of course, a practical problem of wearable devices in many countries is the weather. What happens when the temperature is

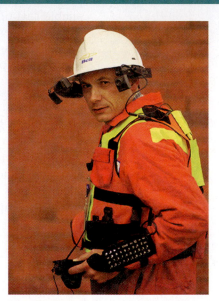

Wearable devices. *(Source: Brian Willer Photography.)*

minus 50 degrees or the humidity is 99 percent? Other potential problems also exist. If you are wearing thick gloves, how can you use a keyboard? If it is pouring rain, will the battery short circuit? Various solutions are being developed, such as voice input, tapping on a screen instead of typing, and rainproof electrical systems.

Sources: Compiled from Guernsey (2000), and xybernaut.com (accessed April 2008).

For Further Exploration: What are some other industrial applications of similar wearable devices? How do you think wearable devices could be used in entertainment?

large vendor of used heavy machinery equipment, offers an interesting solution. Michigan CAT's system uses Cloudberry from Air-Trak (*airtraksoftware.com*) which supports both cellular and satellite networks. It entails a hybrid approach to the use of a GPS tracking and messaging system that enables information and forms generated by Caterpillar's database (DBS) and Service Technician Workbench (STW) software to be transmitted wirelessly between the field operations staff and service vehicles equipped with laptop. Data gathered from the field can be easily integrated into a back-end system. A simple extraction program was created to move data, service reports, and time sheets from one program to the other, eliminating duplicate keying of the same information into separate systems. Other dispatchers can access the information to add comments or notes. The system's benefits include increased productivity, reduced staff time, timely parts ordering, faster invoicing, and secure, precise service information with seamless integration between the company's systems (DeMuro, 2005).

OM

Supporting Other Types of Work. Wireless devices may support a wide variety of other mobile workers and work. The applications will surely grow as the technology matures and as workers think up new ways to apply the functions of wireless devices to their jobs. Here are some examples.

1. Tractors equipped with sensors, onboard computers, and a GPS help farmers save time, effort, and money. GPS determines the precise location of the tractor and can direct its automatic steering. Because the rows of planting resulting from GPS-guiding are more exact, the farmers save both on seeds and on fertilizers, due to minimized overlapping and spillage. Farmers can also work longer hours with the satellite-controlled steering, taking advantage of good weather, for example. Another saving is due to instant notification to the maintenance department about any machine that breaks down.

OM

2. Like e-mail, SMS can be used to bolster collaboration. According to Kontzer (2003), the following are 10 applications of SMS for mobile workers:
- Alerting mobile technicians to system errors
- Alerting mobile employees and managers to urgent voice messages
- Confirming with mobile sales personnel that a faxed order was received
- Informing travelers of delays and changes
- Enabling contract workers to receive and accept project offers
- Keeping stock traders up to date on urgent stock activity
- Reminding data services subscribers about daily updates
- Alerting doctors to urgent patient situations
- Enabling mobile sales teams to input daily sales figures into corporate database
- Sending mobile sales reps reminders of appointments and other schedule details

OM

3. To increase national security and safeguard national borders, countries are using facial-recognition and iris-scanning *biometrics* (Chapter 5), both of which are supported by wireless systems.

GOV

WIRELESS INTRABUSINESS APPLICATIONS

Wireless intrabusiness applications in the non-Internet environment have been around since the early 1990s. Examples include such applications as wireless networking used to pick items out of storage in warehouses via PCs mounted on forklifts, delivery-status updates entered on PCs inside distribution trucks, and collection of data such as competitors' inventories in stores and customer orders using a handheld (but not networked) device, from which data were transferred to company headquarters each evening.

Since then, a large number of Internet-based wireless applications have been implemented inside enterprises. Some examples follow.

Example 1. Kemper Insurance Company is using an application that lets property adjusters report from the scene of an accident. Kemper attached a wireless digital imaging system to a camera that enables the adjusters to take pictures in the field and transmit them to a processing center. The cameras are linked to Motorola's

OM

Private Data File data-enabled cellular phone service, which sends the information to a database. These applications eliminate the delays in obtaining information and in film processing that exist with conventional methods.

MKT

Example 2. A medical care organization developed a mobile enterprise application that allows its sales representatives to check order status and inventory levels during their visits with physicians, and instantly report what they can deliver to the physician's office and when.

As these last two examples indicate, a variety of intrabusiness workflow applications are possible. Some of these can be delivered on a wireless intranet; some are offered over the Internet. (For details on intrabusiness applications, see MDSI-Advantex at *mobileinfo.com/ProductCatalog/MDSI-Advantex.htm* and *symbol.com*. The advantages offered by intrabusiness wireless solutions can be seen through an examination of workflow applications from MDSI-Advantex via *mobileinfo.com*. However, not all applications are successful. An example is the US Census Bureau's mobile snafu. For the 2010 census the government allocated $3 billion for handheld devices to improve the interviewer's performance in the field. Unfortunately, due to poor program management, poor contract estimate and hardware and software delays, the program had to be delayed to the 2020 census. The cost of manual data taking and programming increased the cost of the project by $2.2–3 billion. For details see Thilmany (2008). Thilmany also contrasts this failure with successes of many companies.

Finally, RFID is gaining popularity in both intrabusiness and interbusiness applications. Mobile intrabusiness applications are very popular and are typically easier to implement than nonmobile interbusiness applications.

CUSTOMER SUPPORT AND MOBILE CRM

Mobile access extends the reach of customer relationship management (CRM)—both inside and outside the company—to both employees and business partners on a 24/7 basis, to any place where recipients are located. A 2006 Visiongain (a U.K. market research and analysis company) study predicts that mobile CRM will grow from 10 percent of total CRM revenues in 2006 to 20 percent by 2010 (Lyman, 2006).

In the large software suites such as Siebel's CRM (an Oracle company), the two CRM functions that have attracted the most interest are *sales force automation* and *field service.* For instance, a salesperson might be on a sales call and need to know recent billing history for a particular customer. Or, a field service representative on a service call might need to know current availability of various parts in order to fix a piece of machinery. It is these sorts of situations where real-time mobile access to customer and partner data is invaluable. Two of the more recent offerings in this arena are Salesforce.com's App Exchange Mobile and CRMondemand's Alerts (*oracle.com/crmondemand/index.html*).

MKT

Voice portal technology can also be used to provide enhanced customer service or to improve access to data for employees. For example, repair people who are away from the office could use a vendor's voice portal to check on the status of deliveries to a job site. Salespeople could check on inventory status during a meeting to help close a sale.

Now let's examine some B2B and supply chain applications.

MOBILE B2B AND SUPPLY CHAIN APPLICATIONS

Mobile computing solutions are also being applied to B2B and supply chain relationships. Such solutions enable organizations to respond faster to supply chain disruptions by proactively adjusting plans or by shifting resources related to critical supply chain events as they occur. Furthermore, mobile computing may have strategic implications regarding supply chains by enabling to smooth them, shorten time, reducing delays, and improving supplier and customer relationship. With the increased interest in collaborative commerce comes the opportunity to use wireless communication to collaborate along the supply chain. For this to take place, interorganizational information systems integration is needed.

One example of an integrated messaging system is wireless *telemetry*, which combines wireless communications, vehicle monitoring systems, and vehicle location devices. (Telemetry is described further in Section 7.6.) Mobile intrabusiness technology makes possible large-scale automation of data capture, improved billing timeliness and accuracy, less overhead than with the manual alternative, and increased customer satisfaction through service responsiveness. For example, vending machines can be kept replenished and in reliable operation by wirelessly polling inventory and service status continually in real time to avert costly machine downtime.

Mobile devices can also facilitate collaboration among members of the supply chain. There is no longer any need to call a partner company and ask someone to find certain employees who work with your company. Instead, you can contact these employees directly on their mobile devices.

By enabling sales force employees to type orders or queries directly into an ERP (Chapter 10) while at a client's site, companies can reduce clerical mistakes and improve supply chain operations. By allowing salespeople to check production schedules and inventory levels, and to access product configuration and availability as well as capacity available for production, the sales people can obtain quantities and real-time delivery dates. Thus, companies empower their sales force to make more competitive and realistic offers to customers. Today's ERP systems tie into broader supply chain management solutions that extend visibility across multiple tiers (subsuppliers, their suppliers, etc.) in the supply chain. Mobile supply chain management (SCM, Chapter 10) empowers the workforce to leverage these broader systems through inventory management and ATP/CTP functionality that extend across multiple supply chain partners and take into account logistics considerations.

Example. Sales teams at Adidas America (athletic footwear, clothing, and related products) use Blackberry's Enterprise Solution and PDAs to check inventory levels from anywhere in real time. This enables better customer service and increases sales productivity. For details, see *blackberry.com* (search for Adidas America case study).

Review Questions

1. Describe mobile applications inside organizations.
2. Describe wireless salesforce applications.
3. What are wearable devices? Provide examples.
4. Describe mobile CRM.
5. Describe intrabusiness applications.
6. Describe supply chain applications.

7.5 Mobile Consumer Services and Entertainment

A large number of applications exist that support consumers and provide personal services. As an example, consider the situation of a person going to an international airport. Tasks such as finding the right check-in desk, checking for delayed flights, waiting for lost luggage, and even finding a place to eat or the nearest washroom can be assisted by mobile devices.

Other consumer and personal service areas in which wireless devices can be used are described next. (See also *att.com/wireless.*)

MOBILE ENTERTAINMENT

Mobile entertainment is expanding on wireless devices. Notable are music, movies, videos, games, adult entertainment, sports, gambling, and more. For more details, see Online Brief 7.2. As an illustration, we provided several examples of what is offered in sports in *A Closer Look 7.2* (p. 262).

Following are some other areas of entertainment.

MOBILE GAMES

In the handheld segment of the gaming market, Nintendo has been the longtime leader. In contrast, Nintendo has shown minimal interest in online or mobile games.

A Closer Look 7.2

Mobile Applications in Sports—Related Applications

MKT

- In May 2006, Nike and Apple introduced an iPod shoe called Nano that can provide real-time feedback on distance, time, and calories burned during a workout. A sensor and receiver embedded in the shoe provide a wireless connection to the iPod, with workout information stored on the device and displayed on the screen. Runners can get audible feedback through the headphones, and data stored on the Nano can be downloaded to a Mac or PC after a run. In addition to these functions, the Nike+iPod system delivers music and commentary to help joggers make it through their workouts. Nike is offering workout-related podcasts that include advice from marathon runner Alberto Salazar and inspiration from bicycling champion Lance Armstrong. In fall 2006, Nike delivered six additional footwear styles designed to hold the iPod sensor. The company also is planning to unveil a collection of jackets, tops, shorts, and armbands designed for the Nike+iPod Sport Kit. A similar service is offered by BonesinMotion.com together with Sprint. It uses a GPS to turn mobile phones into exercise-tracking devices.

- In winter 2006, Levi Strauss introduced a new line of jeans specifically geared toward iPod users. The $200 trousers come complete with headphones, a joystick, and even a docking cradle.

- ESPN's Sport Center with Sanyo offers a cell phone dedicated to sports. You can get quick access to news and your favorite teams. Video clips of up to 30 seconds are available and so is a built-in camera. To alleviate waiting time, sports trivia are offered. Alerts are sent by request. The service is relatively expensive.

- The Slipstream/Chipotle bike team uses BlackBerry Pearl wireless devices to let the manager schedule drug tests with just a few hours' notice. The team also tracks its riders' biological profiles for sharp changes that might indicate doping. This makes it virtually impossible to cheat since the riders are connected to the managers via the BlackBerry 24/7 (see Martin, 2007).

- *Invisible* is a term that characterizes a device manufactured and sold by Fitsense Technology (*fitsense.com*), a Massachusetts developer of Internet sports and fitness monitors. With this one-ounce device that is clipped to a shoelace, runners are able to capture their speed and the distance they have run. The device transmits the data via a radio signal to a wrist device that can capture and transmit the data wirelessly to a desktop computer for analysis. Along the same lines, Champion Chip (*championchip.com*), headquartered in the Netherlands, has developed a system that keeps track of the tens of thousands of participants in very popular long-distance races. The tracking system includes miniature transponders attached to the runners' shoelaces or ankle bracelets and antenna mats at the finish line that use radio frequencies to capture start times, splits, and finish times as the runners cross them.

SVR

By 2005, Sonic the Hedgehog (from Sega) and his friends were among the most familiar icons in video games. Since 1991, he has appeared in over 30 games that have sold more than 38 million units of software and is consistently a top-selling franchise (*Business Wire*, 2005). In Japan, where millions of commuters "kill time" during long train rides, cell phone games have become a cultural phenomenon. Now mobile games are very popular in many countries.

With the widespread use of cell phones, the potential audience for mobile games is substantially larger than the market for other platforms, PlayStation and Gameboy included. Because of the market potential, Nokia has decided to enter the mobile gaming world, producing not only the phone/console but also the games that will be delivered on memory cards. It also develops and markets near-distance multiplayer gaming (over Bluetooth) and wide-area gaming using cellular networks. For details, see *en.wikipedia.org/wiki/mobile_gaming*.

In July 2001, Ericsson, Motorola, Nokia, and Siemens established the Mobile Games Interoperability Forum (MGIF) (*openmobilealliance.org*) to define a range of technical standards that will make it possible to deploy mobile games across multi-game servers and wireless networks, and over different mobile devices. Microsoft is active in this field as well. For an overview on mobile gaming, platforms used, and more, see Soh and Tan (2008).

A topic related to games is *mobile gambling* which is legal and extremely popular in some countries (e.g., horse racing in Hong Kong and racing and other events in Australia). (For more on mobile gambling, see *sportodds.com*.)

HOTEL SERVICES AND TRAVEL GO WIRELESS

A number of hotels now offer their guests in-room, wireless or wireline high-speed Internet connection. Some of these same hotels offer Wi-Fi Internet access in pub-

SVR

lic areas (e.g., the lobby) and meeting rooms. One of these is Marriott, which manages about 3,000 hotels worldwide. Marriott has partnered with STSN (stsn.com), an Internet service provider specializing in hotels, to provide Wi-Fi services in many Marriott hotels. Most other large hotel chains (e.g., Best Western), as well as small hotels, offer Internet connections.

While Wi-Fi provides guests with Internet access, to date it has had minimal impact on other sorts of hotel services (e.g., check-in). However, a small number of hotels are testing use of the Bluetooth technology. Guests are provided with Bluetooth-enabled phones that can communicate with access points located throughout the hotel. This technology can be used for check-in and checkout, for making purchases from hotel vending machines and stores, for tracking loyalty points (see *tesalocks.com*), and for opening room doors in place of keys.

OTHER MOBILE-COMPUTING SERVICES FOR CONSUMERS

Many other mobile computer services exist for consumers, in a variety of service categories. Examples include services providing news, city events, weather, and sports reports; online language translations; information about tourist attractions (hours, prices); and emergency services. Many applications are in the area of telemedicine (see Online Brief 7.3 for more details). Many other services are available to cell phones with Internet access. For example, Skype offers its voice, text, and video free service. For more examples, see the case studies at *mobileinfo.com*.

Mobile Social Networks. **Mobile social networking** is social networking where one or more individuals of similar interests or commonalities, conversing and connecting with one another, use mobile devices (usually cell phones). Much like Web-based social networking, mobile social networking occurs in virtual communities. A current trend for Internet social networking Web sites such as MySpace and Facebook is to add wireless capabilities. There are two basic types of mobile social networks. The first is companies that partner with wireless phone carriers to reach their communities via the default start pages on mobile phone browsers; examples are those operated by Jumbuck and AirG (e.g., MySpace and Cingular, per Kharif, 2006b). The second type is companies that do not have such carrier relationships (also known as "off deck") and rely on other methods to attract users; examples are MocoSpace and Bluepulse. Advances in software technology have facilitated the existence of mobile virtual social networks. Industry wireless network technologies include SMS, WAP, Java, BREW, and i-Mode.

With the current available software, interactions within mobile social networks are not limited to exchanging simple text messages on a 1-to-1 basis (SMS), but are constantly evolving toward the sophisticated interactions of virtual communities (Chapter 8).

According to Gonsalves (2008), U.S. smartphone users spend almost 5 hours per month in social networks (in Britain less than 2 hours). These figures more than doubled between 2006 and 2007. According to Shannon (2008), over 50 million people are using cell phones for social networking.

Popular dedicated wireless services are Brightkite, Zyb, Groovr, Gypsii, and Fon11. They capitalize on location information, for example, that will show you where your friends are in real time.

M-Government. **Mobile government**, or **m-government**, is the wireless implementation of e-government applications (see *en.wikipedia.org/wiki/M-government*), mostly to citizens (e.g., Government of Canada Wireless Portal), but also to businesses. M-government is a value-added service because it enables government to reach a larger number of citizens and is more cost effective than other IT applications (per Trimi and Sheng, 2008). In addition, governments employ large numbers of mobile workers who can be supported by wireless devices.

Future Applications. Of the many forthcoming applications, we like to cite the pre-emptive applications of RFID, such as collecting data, as users are using a product and suggesting to the manufacturer what type of customer support is needed. For example, tracking the mileage in a car and suggesting when it is time to change tires. Also, sending information to insurance companies about the distance the customer has driven and even potential accidents that may happen.

NON-INTERNET MOBILE-COMPUTING APPLICATIONS FOR CONSUMERS

Non-Internet mobile applications for consumers, mainly those using smart cards, have existed since the early 1990s. Active use of the cards is reported in transportation, where millions of "contactless" cards (also called *proximity cards*) are used to pay bus and subway fares and road tolls. Amplified remote-sensing cards that have an RF (radio frequency) of up to 30 meters are used in several countries for toll collection. *IT at Work 7.2* describes one use of proximity cards for toll collection. Other non-Internet applications are embedded in cell phones, especially payments.

Review Questions

1. List types of mobile entertainment.
2. Describe mobile games.
3. How does wireless work in hotels?
4. How is wireless used in public transportation?

IT at Work 7.2

The Highway 91 Project

SVR

Route 91 is a major eight-lane, east-west highway near Los Angeles. Traffic is especially heavy during rush hours. California Private Transportation Company (CPT) built six express toll lanes along a 10-mile stretch in the median of the existing Highway 91. The express lane system has only one entrance and one exit, and it is totally operated with EC technologies. The system works as follows.

Only prepaid subscribers can drive on the road. Subscribers receive an automatic vehicle identification (AVI) device that is placed on the rearview mirror of the car. The device, which uses RFID technology, about the size of a thick credit card, includes a microchip, an antenna, and a battery. A large sign over the tollway tells drivers the current fee for cruising the express lanes. In a recent year it varied from $0.50 in slow traffic hours to $3.25 during rush hours.

Sensors in the pavement let the tollway computer know that a car has entered; the car does not need to slow or stop. The AVI makes radio contact with a transceiver installed above the lane. The transceiver relays the car's identity through fiber-optic lines to the control center, where a computer calculates the fee for that day's trip. The system accesses the driver's account and the fare is automatically deducted from the driver's prepaid account. A monthly statement is sent to the subscriber's home.

Surveillance cameras record the license numbers of cars without AVIs. These cars can be stopped by police at the exit or fined by mail. Video cameras along the tollway also enable managers to keep tabs on traffic, for example, sending a tow truck to help a stranded car. Also, through knowledge of the traffic volume, pricing decisions can be made. Raising the price as traffic increases ensures that the tollway will not be jammed. In similar systems, nonsubscribers are allowed to enter via special gates where they pay cash.

The system saves commuters between 40 and 90 minutes each day, so it is in high demand. An interesting extension of the system

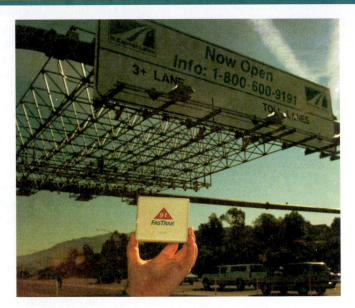

(Source: UPI Photo/Newscom.)

is the use of the same AVIs for other purposes. For example, they can be used in paid parking lots. Someday you may even be recognized when you enter the drive-through lane of McDonald's and a voice asks you, "Mr. Smart, do you want your usual meal today?"

Sources: 91expresslanes.com (accessed May 2008) and *en.wikipedia/ org/wiki/91_Expresslanes* (accessed May 2008).

For Further Exploration: What is the role of the wireless component of this system? What are the advantages of the system to commuters? (Take the virtual "test drive.")

7.6 Location-Based Services and Commerce

Location-based commerce (l-commerce) refers to the delivery of advertisements, products, or services to customers whose locations are known at a given time [also known as location-based services (LBSs)]. Location-based services are beneficial to both consumers and businesses alike. From a consumer's viewpoint, l-commerce offers safety (you can connect to an emergency service with a mobile device and have the service pinpoint your exact location), convenience (you can locate what is near you without having to consult a directory, pay phone, or map), and productivity (you can optimize your travel and time by determining points of interest within close proximity). From a business supplier's point of view, l-commerce offers an opportunity to sell more. For an overview, see Junglas and Watson (2008).

The basic l-commerce services revolve around five key concepts:

1. **Location:** determining the basic position of a person or a thing (e.g., bus, car, or boat), at any given time
2. **Navigation:** plotting a route from one location to another
3. **Tracking:** monitoring the movement of a person or a thing (e.g., a vehicle or package) along the route
4. **Mapping:** creating digital maps of specific geographical locations
5. **Timing:** determining the precise time at a specific location

L-COMMERCE TECHNOLOGIES

Providing location-based services requires the following location-based and network technologies (shown in Figure 7.4).

- **Position Determining Equipment (PDE).** This equipment identifies the location of the mobile device (either through GPS or by locating the nearest base station). The position information is sent to the mobile positioning center.
- **Mobile Positioning Center (MPC).** The MPC is a server that manages the location information sent from the PDE.

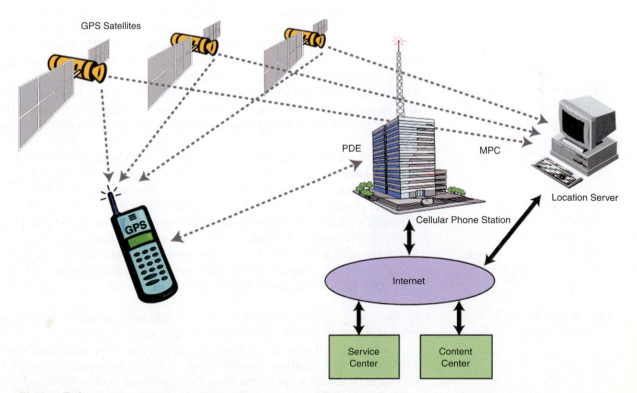

Figure 7.4 A smart phone with GPS system in l-commerce.

- **Location-based technology.** This technology consists of groups of servers that combine the position information with geographic- and location-specific content to provide an l-commerce service. For instance, location-based technology could present a list of addresses of nearby restaurants based on the position of the caller, local street maps, and a directory of businesses. It is provided via the content center via the Internet.
- **Geographic content.** Geographic content consists of digitized streets, road maps, addresses, routes, landmarks, land usage, Zip codes, and the like. This information must be delivered in compressed form for fast distribution over wireless networks (e.g., as digital maps). It is provided via content center.
- **Location-specific content.** Location-specific content is used in conjunction with the geographic content to provide the location of particular services. Yellow-pages directories showing the location of specific business and services exemplify this type of content. It is provided from the content center.

Figure 7.4 also shows how these technologies are used in conjunction with one another to deliver location-based services that are managed via the service center. Underlying these technologies are global positioning and geographical information systems.

Global Positioning System (GPS). A **global positioning system (GPS)** is a wireless system that uses satellites to enable users to determine where the GPS device is located (its position) anywhere on the earth. GPS equipment has been used extensively for navigation by commercial airlines and ships and for locating trucks and buses.

GPS is supported by 24 U.S. government satellites that are shared worldwide. Each satellite orbits the earth once every 12 hours on a precise path, at an altitude of 10,900 miles. At any point in time, the exact position of each satellite is known, because the satellite broadcasts its position and a time signal from its onboard atomic clock, which is accurate to one-billionth of a second. Receivers also have accurate clocks that are synchronized with those of the satellites.

GPS handsets can be stand-alone units or can be plugged into or embedded in a mobile device (for cell phones with GPS, see O'Reilly, 2007). They calculate the position (location) of the handsets (or send the information to be calculated centrally). Knowing the speed of the satellite signals (186,272 miles per second), engineers can find the location of any receiving station (latitude and longitude) to within 50 feet by *triangulation*, using the distance from a GPS to *three* satellites to make the computation. GPS software then computes the latitude and longitude of the receiver (this process is referred to as *geocoding*). For an online tutorial on GPS, see *trimble.com/gps*. For more information, see *en.wikipedia/org/wiki/GPS*.

Geographical Information System (GIS). The location provided by GPS is expressed in terms of latitude and longitude. To make that information useful to businesses and consumers it is necessary in many cases to relate those measures to a certain place or address. This is done by inserting the latitude and longitude onto a digital map, which is known as a **geographical information system (GIS)**. The GIS data visualization technology integrates GPS data onto digitized map displays. (See the description in Chapter 12.) Companies such as *mapinfo.com* provide the GIS core spatial technology, maps, and other data content needed in order to power location-based GIS/GPS services (see Figure 7.5).

LOCATION-BASED APPLICATIONS

An increasing number of applications is evidenced in several industries, particularly in transportation. These applications mainly relate to customer service, advertising/marketing, and operations. One example of customer information about public transportation is Nextbus. NextBus.com provides information about bus/shuttle arrivals to particular stops in real time. The system is based on GPS, and it is described in *IT at Work 7.3*.

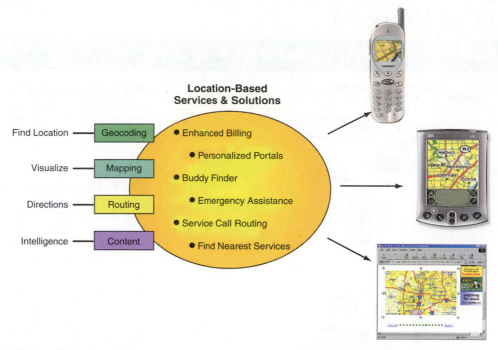

Figure 7.5 Location-based services involving maps. *(Source: Mapinfo.com, 2001.)*

An interesting application of GPS/GIS is now available from most car manufacturers or can easily be added to any car. (e.g., Hertz; see Minicase). Many cars have a navigation system that indicates how far away the driver is from gas stations, restaurants, and other locations of interest. The GPS can map the route for the driver to a particular destination (usually combined with voice for each turn on the road). However, be careful!

Car Navigation Systems May Be Hazardous for Your Health. According to *Ananova News* (October 14, 2003), a U.S. tourist's trip through Germany ended with an unexpected visit to a supermarket when his car's navigation system led him straight through the store's doors. The car only came to a stop when the driver crashed into a row of shelves. The driver, who has not been named, but was celebrating his birthday the same day, told police that he had relied entirely on the automatic navigation system as he did not know the area. He added that he did not notice the doors of the supermarket looming before him until he had crashed through them. The driver, luckily, was unhurt, but he has been told he will have to foot the bill for the damage caused.

VERT intelligent displays: Advertising used atop taxi cabs. *(Source: Courtesy of Vert Incorporated.)*

Location-Based Advertising. Imagine that you are walking near a Starbucks store, but you do not even know that one is there. Suddenly your cell phone beeps with a message: "Come inside for a latte." The location of your wireless device was detected, and similar to the pop-up ads on your PC, advertising was directed your way. You can use permission marketing to shield yourself from location-based advertising, you can block all ads, or you can be selective. For example, if the system knows that you do not drink coffee, you would not be sent a message from Starbucks.

IT at Work 7.3

NextBus: A Superb Customer Service

SVR

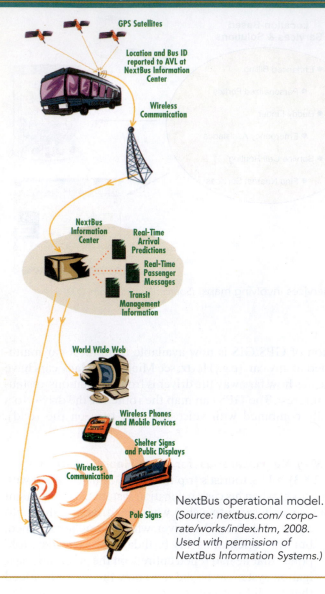

NextBus operational model. *(Source: nextbus.com/ corporate/works/index.htm, 2008. Used with permission of NextBus Information Systems.)*

The Problem. Buses in certain parts of San Francisco have difficulty keeping up with the posted schedule, especially in rush hours. Generally, buses are scheduled to arrive every 20 minutes, but at times, passengers may have to wait 30 to 40 minutes. The schedules become meaningless, and passengers are unhappy because they waste time.

The Solution. San Francisco bus riders carrying an Internet-enabled wireless device, such as a cell phone or PDA, can quickly find out when a bus is likely to arrive at a particular bus stop. The system tracks public transportation buses in *real time*. Knowing where each bus is and factoring in traffic patterns and weather reports, NextBus (*nextbus.com*) dynamically calculates the estimated arrival time of the bus to each bus stop on the route. The arrival times are also displayed on the Internet and on a public screen at each bus stop.

The NextBus system has been used successfully in several other cities around the United States (e.g., Fairfax, Virginia), in Finland, and in several other countries. The figure shows how the NextBus system works. The core of the NextBus system is a GPS satellite that can tell the NextBus information center where a bus is at any given time. Based on a bus's location, the scheduled arrival time at each stop can be calculated in real time. Users can access the information from their cell phones or PCs any time, anywhere. NextBus schedules are also posted in real time on passengers' shelters at bus stops and public displays.

Currently, NextBus is an ad-free customer service, but in the near future advertising may be added. As the system knows exactly where you are when you request information and how much time you have until your next bus, it could send you to the nearest Starbucks for a cup of coffee, giving you an electronic discount coupon for a cup of coffee as you wait.

Sources: Compiled from *en.wikipedia/org/wiki/NextBus* (accessed May 2008), and *nextbus.com* (accessed June 2008).

For Further Exploration: Can NextBus make money? How? Who should sponsor the service? How can marketing/advertising work?

Another (experimental) use of wireless devices for advertising is described by Raskin (2003). In this case, a dynamic billboard ad could be personalized specifically for you when your car approaches a certain billboard and the system knows what your likes and preferences are. Your car will be tracked by a GPS every 20 seconds to determine its location in the areas in which billboards are visible to you, and by cross-referencing information about your location and your likes, a *personalized ad* could be placed on the billboard so you would see it as you pass.

Yet another method of location-based advertising involves putting ads on the top of taxicabs. The ad is changed based on the taxi location (by Vert Inc.). For example, a taxi cruising in the theater district in New York City might show an ad for a play or a restaurant in that area; when the cab goes to another neighborhood, the ad might be for a restaurant or a business in that area of the city. (See *vert.net*.)

APPLICATIONS OF LOCATION-BASED SERVICES (LBSS)

New and innovative applications appear almost daily. Here are some examples:

- The Luxor casino in Las Vegas preregisters guests when they land at the airport and turn on their cell phones. Also, the hotel can determine when guests leave the hotel, luring them back with mobile incentives and pitches.

- GlobalPetFinder (*globalpetfinder.com*) is an under-5-ounce, $290 (on sale) device that snaps onto your pet's collar. If Fido wanders outside the "virtual fence" you set up, you'll receive a text alert and the pet's whereabouts on your phone. Monthly monitoring fees start at $17, plus there's a one-time $35 activation charge.

- KnowledgeWhere Mobile service (*knowledgewhere.com*), Kamida's Socialight (*socialight.com*), and Proxpro (*proxpro.com*) are applying LBSs to social networking. Socialight, now in beta, lets people publish pictures, words, sound, and video tagged to specific locales; you might offer your take on a tourist spot.

- Wal-Mart sends text messages about weather alerts ("bad weather is coming") to customers who own GPS-equipped Sprint mobile devices.

- Papa John's customers with GPS-enabled cell phones can track their pizza delivery status on a street-by-street basis (TrackMyPizza.com).

For further discussion and examples, see Kolbasuk-McGee (2008), and Junglas and Watson (2008).

E-911 EMERGENCY CELL PHONE CALLS AND INCREASED SAFETY

If someone dials 911 from a regular wired phone, it is easy for the emergency 911 service to pinpoint the location of the phone. But, what happens if someone places a 911 call from a mobile phone? How can the emergency service locate the caller? A few years ago, the U.S. Federal Communications Commission (FCC) issued a directive to wireless carriers, requiring that they establish services to handle **wireless 911 (e-911)** calls. To give you an idea of the magnitude of this requirement, more than 50 million wireless 911 calls were made every day in 2007 in the United States (Reuters, 2008).

The e-911 directive is to take effect in two phases, although the specifics of the phases vary from one wireless carrier (e.g., Verizon, T-Mobile, Cingular, Sprint, etc.) to another. Phase I requires carriers, upon appropriate request by a local *Public Safety Answering Point* (PSAP), to report the telephone number of a wireless 911 caller and the location of the cellular antenna that received the call. Phase II, which was rolled out over a four-year period from October 2002 to December 2005, requires wireless carriers to provide information that will enable the PSAP to locate a caller within 50 meters 67 percent of the time and within 150 meters 95 percent of the time. By the end of Phase II, 100 percent of the new cell phones and 95 percent of all cell phones will have these location capabilities. It is expected that many other countries will follow the example of the United States in providing e-911 service.

Some expect that, in the future, cars will have a device for **automatic crash notification (ACN)**. This still-experimental device will automatically notify the police of an accident involving an ACN-equipped car and its location. Also, U.S. states mandate satellite tracking in all school buses. Another up-coming device is GPS-based from Motorola. Cars equipped with this device will be able to avoid accidents at intersections (see Dizikes, 2006, and collision avoidance in Section 7.7).

TELEMATICS AND TELEMETRY APPLICATIONS

Telematics refers to the integration of computers and wireless communications in order to improve information flow (see *en.wikipedia.org/wiki/Telematics*). It uses the principles of *telemetry,* the science that measures physical remoteness by means of wireless transmission from a remote source (such as a vehicle) to a receiving station.

Using *mobile telemetry*, technicians can diagnose from a distance maintenance problems in equipment. Car manufacturers use the technology for remote vehicle diagnosis and preventive maintenance. Finally, doctors can monitor patients and control medical equipment from a distance.

Telematics services become less about responding to an event (e.g., a crash, a stolen vehicle, a disabled vehicle, a lost driver) and more about an always-on experience wherever you are mobile. It will be less about technology and more about personalization of services and strict protection of vehicle owners' personal information and preferences, delivering to them a unique ownership experience compatible with the OEMs brand values (*ATX*, 2008).

General Motors Corporation popularized automotive telematics with its OnStar (*onstar.com*) system. Nokia has set up a business unit, called Smart Traffic Products, that is focusing solely on telematics. Nokia believes that every vehicle will be equipped with at least one Internet Protocol (IP) address by the year 2010. Smart cars and traffic products are discussed in more detail in Section 7.7.

SVR

BARRIERS TO L-COMMERCE

What is holding back the widespread use of location-based commerce? Several factors come into play:

- **Accuracy.** Some of the location-finding devices are not as accurate as people expect them to be. However, a good GPS provides a location that is accurate up to 15 meters. Less expensive, but less accurate, technologies can be used instead to find an approximate location (within about 500 meters).

- **The cost-benefit justification.** For many potential users, the benefits of l-commerce do not justify the cost of the hardware or the inconvenience and time required to utilize the service. After all, users seem to feel that they can just as easily obtain information the old-fashioned way.

- **The bandwidth of GSM networks.** GSM bandwidth is currently limited; it is improving as 3G technology spreads. As bandwidth improves, applications will improve, which will attract more customers.

- **Invasion of privacy.** When "always-on" cell phones are a reality, many people will be hesitant to have their whereabouts and movements tracked throughout the day, even if they have nothing to hide. This issue will be heightened when our cars, homes, appliances, and all sorts of other consumer goods will be connected to the Internet, as discussed in the next section.

Review Questions

1. Define location-based services.
2. How does location-based EC work? Provide an example.
3. Define GPS. What is it used for?
4. Describe GIS and its advantages.
5. Describe location-based applications and particularly advertising.
6. Describe how e-911 works.
7. Define telematics. How does it relate to mobile and wireless computing?
8. Relate l-commerce to its cost assessment and justification.

7.7 Pervasive Computing, Content Awareness, and RFID

Steven Spielberg's sci-fi thriller *Minority Report* depicts the world of 2054. Based on a 1956 short story by Philip K. Dick, the film immerses the viewer in a consumer-driven world of pervasive computing by 2054. Spielberg put together a three-day think tank, headed by Peter Schwartz, president of Global Business Network (*gbn.com*), to produce a realistic view of the future (Mathieson, 2002). The think tank projected out from today's marketing and media technologies—Web cookies, GPS, Bluetooth, personal video recorders, RFID scanners, and the like—to create a society where billboards beckon you by name, newspapers are delivered instantly over broadband wireless networks, holographic hosts greet you at retail stores, and cereal boxes broadcast live commercials. While the technologies in the film were beyond the leading edge, none was beyond the realm of the plausible.

A world in which virtually every object has processing power with wireless or wired connections to a global network is the world of **pervasive computing.** (The term *pervasive computing* also goes by the names *ubiquitous computing, embedded computing, ambient computing,* or *augmented computing.*) The idea of pervasive computing has been around for years. However, the current version was articulated by Mark Weiser in 1988 at the computer science lab of Xerox PARC. From Weiser's perspective, pervasive computing was the opposite of virtual reality. In virtual reality, the user is immersed in a computer-generated environment. In contrast, pervasive computing is invisible "everywhere computing" that is embedded in the objects around us—the floor, the lights, our cars, the washing machine, our cell phones, our clothes, and so on (Weiser, 1991, 2002).

INVISIBLE COMPUTING EVERYWHERE

By "invisible," Weiser did not mean to imply that pervasive computing devices would not be seen. He meant, rather, that unlike a desktop computer, these embedded computers would not intrude on our consciousness. Think of a pair of eyeglasses. The wearer does not have to think about using them. He or she simply puts them on and they augment the wearer's ability to see. This is Weiser's vision for pervasive computing. The user does not have to think about how to use the processing power in the object; rather, the processing power automatically helps the user perform a task.

Example. *Active badges* can be worn as ID cards by employees who wish to stay in touch at all times while moving around the corporate premises. The clip-on badge contains a microprocessor that transmits its (and its wearer's) location to the building's sensors, which send it to a computer. When someone wants to contact the badge wearer, the phone closest to the person is identified automatically. When badge wearers enter their offices, their badge identifies them and logs them on to their personal computers.

Similarly, *memory buttons* are nickel-sized devices that store a small database relating to whatever it is attached to. These devices are analogous to a barcode, but with far greater informational content and a content that is subject to change. For example, the U.S. Postal Service is placing memory buttons in some mailboxes to track and improve collection and delivery schedules.

A major area in pervasive computing is contextual computing.

CONTEXTUAL COMPUTING AND CONTEXT AWARENESS

Location can be a significant differentiator when it comes to advertising services. However, knowing that the user is at the corner of the street will not tell you what he or she is looking for. For this, we might need to know the time of day, the user's planned schedule, or other relevant *contextual attributes.* **Context awareness** refers to capturing a broad range of contextual attributes to better understand what the consumer needs, and what products or services he or she might possibly be interested in.

Context awareness is part of **contextual computing**, which refers to the enhancement of a user's interactions by understanding the user, the context, and the applications and information being used, typically across a wide set of user goals. Contextual computing is about actively adapting the computational environment for each user, at each point of computing. It can be, together with ubiquitous computing, a major innovation that will lead to new applications that will change the way many processes are done, which in turn will increase competitive advantage and customer service (see Kanaracus, 2008 and *en.wikipedia.org/wiki/Contextual_design*).

Contextual computing and context awareness are viewed by many as a major potential cornerstone of m-commerce. They feel that contextual computing ultimately offers the prospect of applications that could anticipate our every wish and provide us with the exact information and services we are looking for—and also help us filter all those annoying promotional messages that we really do not care for. Such applications are futuristic at the present time, but as shown in *IT at Work 7.4,* they already exist in a research university.

IT at Work 7.4

Context-Aware Environment at Carnegie Mellon University

SVR

Carnegie Mellon University (CMU) is known for its advanced science projects including robotics and artificial intelligence. Students participate in a context-awareness experiment in the following manner: each participating student is equipped with a PDA from which he or she can access Internet services via the campus Wi-Fi network. The students operate in a context-aware environment whose architecture is shown in the attached figure.

A user's context (left of figure) includes his or her:

- Calendar information
- Current location (position), which is regularly updated using location-tracking technology (GPS)
- Weather information, indicating whether it is sunny, raining, or snowing, and the current outside temperature (environment)
- Social context information, including the student's friends and his or her teachers, classmates, and so forth

The preferences of each student are solicited and entered into the system, to create a personal profile, shown as "Preferences and Permissions" in the figure. All of the above information helps the system to arrange for certain services automatically. For example, it filters incoming messages, and determines what to show to the students, and when. That is, certain messages will be shown only if the student is in a certain place and/or time; others will not be shown at all.

A user's context information can be accessed by a collection of *personal agents*, each in charge of assisting with different tasks, while locating and invoking relevant Internet services identified through services registries (see the figure). An example of a simple agent is a restaurant concierge that gives suggestions to students about places to have lunch, depending on their food preferences, the time they have available before their next class, their location on campus, and the weather. For example, when it is raining, the agent attempts to find a place that does not require going outside of the building where the student is located. The recommendation (usually several choices) appears on the student's PDA, with an overall rating and a "click for details" possibility. The right side of the figure below shows the various technologies that support the process.

Sources: Compiled from Sadeh (2002) and Gandon and Sadeh (2004).

For Further Exploration: Does the usefulness of such a service justify the need to disclose private preferences? Can such a system be developed for consumers who are not members of a defined community such as a university?

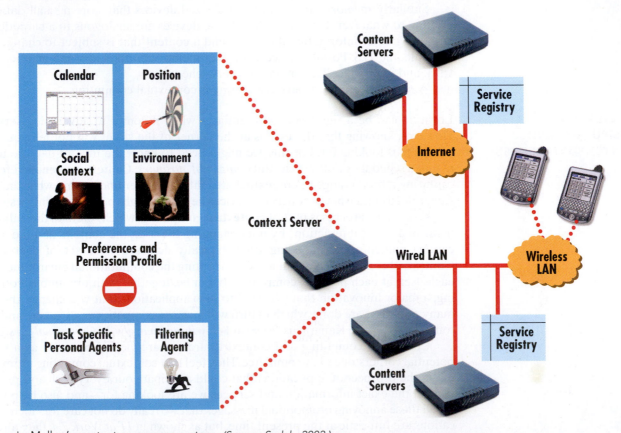

Carnegie Mellon's context-awareness system. *(Source: Sadeh, 2002.)*

Context awareness is only one aspect of pervasive computing, and it is mostly futuristic. Several other applications are already in use.

APPLICATIONS OF PERVASIVE COMPUTING

According to Estrin et al. (2000), 98 percent of all processors on the planet are not in traditional desktop computer systems, nor even in laptops. They are in household appliances, vehicles, and machines. Some of these applications are described in the remainder of this section. Here we will look at smart homes and smart cars. More details about smart appliances and other smart items can be found in Online Brief 7.4.

SMART HOMES

In a *smart home*, your home computer, television, lighting and heating controls, home security system, and many appliances within the home can "talk" to each other via the Internet or a home intranet. These linked systems can be controlled through various devices.

In the United States, tens of thousands of homes are already equipped with home-automation devices, and there are signs that Europe—which has much lower home Internet penetration levels—is also warming to the idea. For instance, a study by the United Kingdom's Consumers' Association found that almost half those surveyed were interested in having the functions a "smart home" could offer, if they were affordable (Bertolucci, 2006).

Some of the tasks supported today by home automation systems are:

- **Lighting.** You can program your lights to go on, off, or dim to match your moods and needs for comfort and security.

- **Energy management.** A home's HVAC (heat, ventilation, and air conditioning) system can be programmed for maximum energy efficiency, controlled with a touch panel, and accessed via your telephone or PDA.

- **Water control.** Watercop (*watercop.com*) is a device that relies on a series of strategically placed moisture-detection sensors. When the moisture level rises in one of these sensors, it sends a wireless signal to the Watercop control unit, which turns off the main water supply.

- **Home security and communications.** Window blinds, garage doors, front door, smoke detectors, and home security systems can all be automated from a network control panel. These can all be programmed to respond to scheduled events (e.g., when you go on vacation).

- **Home theater.** You can create a multisource audio and video center around your house that you can control with a touch pad or remote. For example, if you have a DVD player in your bedroom but want to see the same movie in your child's room, you can just click a remote to switch rooms.

Do-it-yourself components of a smart home are available at Home Depot, Lowe's, and online at *smarthome.com* and *bestbuy.com*. Look for ZigBee and Z-Wave products. For entertainment in the smart home, see Malik (2004).

Analysts generally agree that the market opportunities for smart homes will take shape by 2010–2015. These opportunities are being driven by the increasing adoption of broadband services and the proliferation of wireless local area networks (Wi-Fi) within the home and by the trend to integrate currently independent devices. Online Brief 7.5 shows a wireless connected house.

SMART CARS

Every car today has at least one computer on board to operate the engine, regulate fuel consumption, and control exhaust emissions. The average automobile on the road today has actually 20 or more microprocessors, which are truly invisible. They are under the hood, behind the dash, in the door panels, and on the undercarriage.

In 1998, the U.S. Department of Transportation (DOT) identified eight areas where microprocessors and intelligent systems could improve or impact auto safety (*its.dot.gov/ivbss*). The list included four kinds of collision avoidance (see *en.wikipedia.org/wiki/collision_avoidance*), computer "vision" for cars, vehicle stability, and two kinds of driver monitoring. The automotive industry is in the process of testing a variety of experimental systems addressing the areas identified by the

SVR

DOT. For example, GM in partnership with Delphi Automotive Systems has developed an Automotive Collision Avoidance System that employs radar, video cameras, special sensors, and GPS to monitor traffic and driver actions in an effort to reduce collisions with other vehicles and pedestrians (Sharke, 2003).

To increase safety, drivers can use voice-activated controls, and even to access the Web. GM's OnStar system (*onstar.com*) already supports many of these services (see Online Brief 7.6 for more details).

OnStar is the forerunner of smart cars of the future. The next generation of smart cars is likely to provide even more automated services, especially in emergency situations. For instance, while OnStar will automatically signal the service center when the air bags are deployed and will immediately contact emergency services if the driver and passengers are incapacitated, it cannot provide detailed information about a crash. Newer systems can automatically determine the speed upon impact, whether the car has rolled over, and whether the driver and passengers were wearing seat belts. Information of this sort might be used by emergency personnel to determine the severity of the accident and what types of emergency medical services will be needed.

Ideally, smart cars eventually will be able to drive themselves. Known as *autonomous land vehicles* (ALVs), these cars follow GIS maps and use sensors in a wireless environment to identify obstacles. These vehicles are already on the roads in California, Pennsylvania, and Germany (on an experimental basis, of course). For more, see *en.wikipedia.org/wiki/driverless_car*.

RFID: A POTENTIAL REVOLUTION—BUT CONSIDER THE RISKS

RFID technology was introduced in several earlier chapters to illustrate its potential benefits. Here we redefine it and present the concept and some applications in more detail. **Radio frequency identification (RFID)** is a technology that uses radio waves to identify items. An RFID system consists of (1) an RFID tag (also known as a transponder) that includes an antenna and a chip with information about the item, and (2) an RFID reader that contains a radio transmitter and receiver. An RFID tag remains inactive until radio frequency energy from the radio transmitter hits its antenna, giving the chip enough power to emit a string of information that is read by the radio receiver. This is several times the amount of information a barcode can hold, and the tag can be read through cardboard, wood, and plastic at a range of up to 30 feet. The reader passes this information to a computer for processing, either wirelessly or through a wireline. Incidentally, RFID tags attached to clothes can be washed, ironed, and pressed (news item, *itworld.com*, May 2006).

Figure 7.6 shows the RFID tag attached to a product (razor blade). The RFID reader collects the information from the tag, wirelessly transporting it to the corporate network. For details on how RFID works, see Heinrich (2005). Other advantages of RFID over a barcode are that it is much faster and the margin of error of barcode usage is higher.

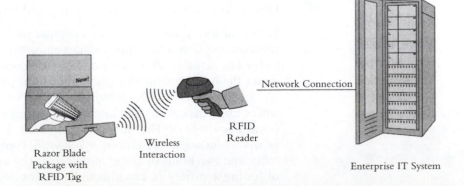

Figure 7.6 How RFID works.
(*Source: C. Heinrich, RFID and Beyond, Indianapolis, Wiley Publishing, 2005, Figure 3.5, p. 65.*)

Potential Applications. There are hundreds of potential applications of RFID (e.g., see *en.wikipedia.org/wiki/RFID*, and *rfidjournal.com*) with many potential benefits. (See the list of benefits in Online Brief 7.7.) We provide a sampler in *IT at Work 7.5*, and an example of how RFID is used by 7-Eleven to track inventory in Online Minicase 7.2.

IT at Work 7.5

Illustrative Examples of RFID Use

MKT   GOV   SVR   OM

- **Circuit City stores are embedding RFID into loyalty cards.** When customers enter the store, their card is scanned by a reader. A coupon dispenser at the door then dispenses specific coupons based on their past buying habits. The store automatically knows that the specific customer was on the Circuit City Web site recently evaluating plasma TVs. For example, when the customer's card is read in the plasma TV section, Circuit City could offer the customer a $500 coupon right on the spot. For further details see Schuman (2005).

- **Medical equipment in hospitals.** Hundreds of pieces of portable equipment are moved through hospitals and are sometimes difficult to detect. But RFID tags make it easy and quick to find such items. General Electric and Centrak developed this technology.

- **RFID in Federal Government/U.S. Department of Defense (DoD).** Inventory tracking is a logistical challenge throughout the armed services and federal agencies. At the same time, there is an urgent need to ensure the safety of military personnel and improve security worldwide. The end result is that RFID-based applications in the federal government and defense sectors are growing exponentially. RFID technology offers a viable solution with reliable, secure identification and tracking that integrates into existing enterprise mobility systems. For example, the U.S. Marine Corps uses RFID to improve flows in their supply chains (Ferguson, 2004). See Chapters 10 and 11 on the use of RFID in supply chains.

- **Tracking moving vehicles.** The E-Z Pass prepay toll system uses RFID, as does Singapore's Electronic Road Pricing system, which charges different prices to drive on different roads at different times. *IT at Work 7.2* (p. 264) provides an example of the use of RFID technology for toll collection.

- **Tracking people.** In some Japanese schools, tags in backpacks or clothes track students' entry and departure from school buildings. In Denmark, the Legoland amusement park offers parents a child-tracking system that combines RFID and Wi-Fi. Beginning in 2006, all new U.S. passports contain an RFID tag, scanned upon entry and departure from the United States (see attached photo).

- **Tracking animals.** The United States Department of Agriculture (USDA) is launching a nationwide animal identification system that is intended to track outbreaks of animal diseases. The program has been resisted by farmers and ranchers, so it is slow to gain acceptance (Bartholomew, 2008). Yet, its function is to track diseases—whether as a result of natural causes or bioterrorism. Somark. innovations.com patented a RFID-like (chipless) tattoo for identification of cows, pets, and other animals. It can reduce

U.S. passport with RFID chip. *(Source: "U.S. Issues First RFID Passports," Engadget.com, March 13, 2006, engadget.com/ 2006/03/13/us-issues-first-rfid-passports, accessed April 2008.)*

the losses from cases of mad cow disease by properly identifying the cows.

- **Tracking golf balls.** RadarGolf Co. is selling balls with RFID tags. Wayward balls can be detected up to 100 feet away.

- **Protecting secure areas.** FedEx uses RFID-tagged wristbands to give drivers access to their vehicles, reducing theft and speeding delivery time. The New York Police Department uses RFID tags embedded in ID tags to track visitors.

- **Improving supply chains.** This is probably one of the most promising uses of RFID, as will be illustrated in Chapters 10 and 11.

Other Uses

- An RFID chip with patient information (called SurgiChip, approved by the FDA) goes with the patient into surgery to help prevent errors (about what surgery is needed and when it is scheduled to take place). RFIDs are also used for patient identification in hospitals.

- RFID embedded in cell phones started to replace credit cards, cash, train passes, keys to your car and home, business cards, and more (see Kharif, 2006a). DoCoMo of Japan introduced such a cell phone in 2004 and its use is growing rapidly.

- RFID can be used in "Sensor Networks" (see discussion later in this chapter).

Implementing RFID. Several factors will determine the speed with which RFID will take off. The first of these is how many companies will mandate that business partners use RFID. So far, Wal-Mart and the U.S. Department of Defense and a small number of other companies have required such use. The second factor is the success of attempted legislation to limit the amount of information on the tag due to privacy protection concerns, or to force removal of the tags when customers pay for the items. Finally, the cost of the tags and the needed information system support is still high and is likely to remain so at least in the short-run. For an overview of the implementation issues and attempted solutions, see Brown (2006). The potential risks of RFID are summarized in *A Closer Look 7.3*.

In 2007 alone, 22 states in the United States have introduced legislation regarding RFID (see Zappone, 2007). Major issues are privacy protection and security. The industry opposes the legislation.

LARGE-SCALE PERVASIVE SYSTEMS

Smart appliances, cars, and barcodes can certainly make our lives more comfortable, but pervasive computing can make an even larger contribution when large numbers of computing devices are put together, creating massive intelligent systems. These systems include factories, airports, schools, and even entire cities. At the moment such applications are experimental in many places. Let's look at some examples.

Smart Schools. The University of California at Los Angeles is experimenting with a smart kindergarten. Exploring communication between students, teachers, and the environment, the project aims to create a smart learning environment.

Intelligent Elder Care. The increased age of the population in many countries brings a problem of caring for more elderly for longer times. Long-term care facilities, where different patients require different levels of care, bring the problem of how to provide such care efficiently and effectively. The experimental project titled Elite Care has demonstrated the benefits of using pervasive computing in such facilities, as described in Chapter 2.

A Closer Look 7.3

RFID and Privacy and Other Risks

ETHICS

Since its introduction in the late 1990s, several advocacy groups raised objections to the use of RFID, citing privacy concerns. Several states started legislation that aims to protect privacy.

Privacy concerns are frequently addressed by controlling access to the database that links the tag to individual information, and more narrowly restricting the uses of RFID to those areas of concern.

A major privacy concern is that when individual items are tagged, and they are taken by customers out of stores, it might be possible to track the movements of the customer (remote surveillance). Therefore, some recommend that the tags be removed before a sale is recorded. This increases the cost to the store. Tracking customers is currently very difficult since the readers have a very limited range from which they can be read. In contrast, if a person carries a GPS device, he or she can be tracked anywhere.

Neumann and Weinstein (2006) review certain concerns regarding data integrity, personal well-being, and privacy. They claim, for example, that tags may be counterfeited, duplicated, swapped, damaged, intentionally disabled, or otherwise misused. The encryption protocols may be weak. In addition to the tags themselves, their supporting databases can be misused, provid-

ing an opportunity for identity theft, fraud, harassment, and blackmail. All of these must be considered prior to implementation.

Other risks are the following: metals and fluids may possibly interfere with the radio signals, tag quality may be uneven, the cost of attaching the tags can be too high, and the cost of the tags is too high.

RFID vendors already include a number of security features designed to address privacy issues by protecting consumer information. For example:

- In most applications, RFID safety tags placed on cargo pallets or ID cards contain nothing more than a unique identifying number, much like a license plate on a car. Sensitive information is maintained in a separate database and protected by firewalls and other security features.

- To guard against unauthorized access, transmissions between RFID readers and safety tags can be protected by encryption and authentication protocols. Generally, transmissions between an RFID reader and a back-end database also are encrypted to protect confidential and personal information.

Sources: Compiled from Neumann and Weinstein (2006) and Reda (2004).

Smart Offices. The original work of Weiser (1991) centered around an intelligent office. And indeed, several projects are experimenting with such an environment, which can interact with users through voice, gesture, or movements and can anticipate their activities. By monitoring office employees, the SmartOffice (*Indiatimes*, 2006) even anticipates user intentions and augments the environment to communicate useful information to the users.

Smart Factories. Several large companies already offer intelligent factories. For example, Siemens AG (*siemens.com*) offers a blending of virtual and physical worlds. All of the participants work together in the virtual world. Their collaboration includes the entire lifecycle of a product along all steps of the value chain, even before a single screw has been tightened in the real world. This makes it possible to optimize products and their manufacturing processes from the very beginning, including studying their effects on the environment.

Digital Cities. The concept of *digital cities* is to build an area in which people in regional communities can interact and share knowledge, experiences, and mutual interests. Digital cities integrate urban information (both real-time and stored) and create public spaces for people living in or visiting the cities. Digital cities are being developed all over the world (see *Wireless Internet Institute*, 2008). In the United States alone there are over 300 city projects.

GLOBAL

In the city of Kyoto, Japan, for example, the digital city complements and corresponds to the physical city (Kyoto City Government, 2007). Three layers are constructed: The first is an information layer, where Web archives and real-time sensory data are integrated to provide information anywhere, any time. The second layer is 2-D and 3-D interfaces, which provide views of cars, buses, and pictures that illustrate city services (for attractive and natural presentation). Finally, there is an interactive layer. Extensive use of GIS supports the project. One area of emphasis is a digital tour guide for visitors. Also, the system uses avatars (animated computer characters) that appear on a handheld device and "walk" with visitors around the city in real time.

Another digital-city experiment is the city of Lancaster (UK), where wireless devices are being used to improve services to both visitors and residents (see *city_visitor.com/lancoster/television.html*). The experimental Lancaster City Guide is based on a network of Wi-Fi context-sensitive and location-aware applications. One area that was developed first is services to tourists. By knowing where the tourist is (using a GPS) and his or her preferences, the system can recommend tourist sites in the same general area. (This application is similar to the Carnegie Mellon application described earlier in *IT at Work 7.4*, page 272.)

GOV

For other digital-city experiments, see *Digital Communities* (2007). For information on pervasive computing projects for hospitals, see Bardram and Christensen (2007).

WIRELESS SENSOR NETWORKS (WSNs)

Wireless sensor networks (WSNs) are networks of interconnected, battery-powered, wireless sensors called *motes* (analogous to nodes) that are placed into specific physical environments. Each mote collects data and contains processing, storage, and radio frequency sensors and antennas. The motes provide information that enables a central computer to integrate reports of the same activity from different angles within the network. Therefore, the network can determine information such as the direction a person is moving, the weight of a vehicle, or the amount of rainfall over a field of crops with great accuracy.

A new type of wireless sensor network is mesh networking. A **mesh network** is composed of motes, where each mote "wakes up" or activates for a fraction of a second when it has data to transmit and then relays those data to its nearest neighbor. So, instead of every mote transmitting its information to a remote computer at a base station, an "electronic bucket brigade" moves the data mote by mote until a central computer is reached where the data can be stored and analyzed.

An advantage of a mesh network is that, if one mote fails, another one can pick up the data. This process makes a mesh network very efficient and reliable. Also, if more bandwidth is needed, it is easy to boost performance by placing new motes when and where they are required. There are many diverse uses for WSNs as the following example indicates.

WSN Enhances Homeland Security. Science Applications International Corporation (*saic.com*) is using motes from Dust Networks (*dustnetworks.com*) to help secure border crossings and other sensitive areas. This application combines the networked motes, which can detect people, vehicles, voices, and motion, with a tiny camera for capturing images. SAIC is also working on applications to use motes on ships or in shipping containers to detect radiation from a nuclear weapon emitted during transit. See *saic.com*, and *dustnetworks.com* (accessed April 2008).

Review Questions

1. Define pervasive computing and describe its major characteristics.
2. What is contextual computing and awareness?
3. Describe smart homes and cars.
4. Define RFID and describe its potential benefits.
5. What are the concerns regarding RFID?
6. What is a digital city?
7. Describe wireless sensor networks.

7.8 Managerial Issues

1. Inhibitors and barriers of mobile computing. Several limitations either are slowing down the spread of mobile computing or are leaving many m-commerce customers disappointed or dissatisfied (e.g., see Islam and Fayad, 2003). Representative inhibitors and barriers of mobile computing are covered in Online Brief 7.8.

2. The future of WiMax. The success of many wireless applications depends on the success of WiMax. By 2008 it was not clear if the technology is really successful. Major players are Sprint, Nextel, Clearwire, Ericsson, and even Google.

3. Ethical and legal issues. Several ethical and legal issues are unique to mobile computing. For example, fashion retailer Benetton Group SpA was considering attaching RFID "smart tags" to its Sisley line of clothing to help track shipping, inventory, and sales in the company's 5,000 stores worldwide. (Also, the tags could help prevent shoplifting.) The idea was to integrate the RFID tag into the clothing labels. Using the tags, the store would know where each piece of clothing is at any given time. However, privacy groups expressed concern that the tags could also be used to track buyers, and some groups even urged that the company's clothing be boycotted. As a result, Benetton backed away from the plan, at least until an impact study is done (Rosencrance, 2003).

ETHICS

Numerous states have pending legislation regarding privacy issues about RFID tags in retail goods. Most legislation is "RFID right to know," requiring disclosure of the use of RFID devices and personal information that is gathered; labeling of retail products or packages containing an RFID tag; point-of-sale removal of RFID tags; restricting of aggregation and disclosure of personal information; and provision for enforcement by a legal agency (RFID Public Information Center, 2006).

According to Hunter (2002), privacy is in great danger in the world of ubiquitous computing because of the proliferation of networked devices used by individuals, businesses, and government. The Elite Care project described in Online

Minicase 2.3 (Chapter 2), for example, raised the issue of protecting information collected by sensors. Also, privacy is difficult to control in other types of context-aware systems. As indicated earlier, security is especially difficult in Wi-Fi systems.

4. Failures in mobile computing and m-commerce. As with any other technology, especially a new one, there have been many failures of applications as well as entire companies in mobile computing and m-commerce. It is important to anticipate and plan for possible failures as well as to learn from them.

SVR

The case of Northeast Utilities provides some important insights. According to Hamblen (2001), Northeast Utilities (located in Berlin, Connecticut), which supplies energy products and services to 1.2 million customers from Maine to Maryland, embarked on a wireless project in 1995 in which its field inspectors used wireless devices to track spills of hazardous material and report them to headquarters in real time. After spending a year and a half and $1 million, the project failed. The reasons for the failure can be seen in the following lessons learned:

- Do not start without appropriate infrastructure.
- Do not start a full-scale implementation; use a small pilot for experimentation.
- Pick up an appropriate architecture. Some users don't need to be persistently connected, for example.
- Talk with a range of users, some experienced and some not, about usability issues.
- Users must be involved; hold biweekly meetings if possible.
- Employ wireless experts if you are not one.
- Wireless is a different medium from other forms of communication. Remember that people are not used to the wireless paradigm.

Having learned from the above "lessons" and correcting the deficiencies, Northeast made its next wireless endeavor a success. Today, all field inspectors carry rugged wireless laptops that are connected to the enterprise intranet and databases. The wireless laptops are used to conduct measurements related to electricity transformers, for example. Then the laptops transmit the results, in real time, to chemists and people who prepare government reports about hazardous materials spills. In addition, time is saved because all of the information is entered directly into proper fields of electronic forms without having to be transcribed. The new system is so successful that it has given IT workers the confidence to launch other applications such as sending power-outage reports to managers via smart phones and wireless information to crews repairing street lights.

5. Implementation issues. Representative implementation issues which were not discussed earlier in the text are:

a. Timetable. Although there has been much hype about m-commerce in the last few years, only a small number of large-scale mobile computing applications have been deployed to date. The most numerous applications are in e-banking, entertainment, stock trading, emergency services, and some B2B tasks. Companies must carefully craft an m-commerce strategy. This will reduce the number of failed initiatives and bankrupted companies. For calculating the total cost of wireless computing ownership and how to justify it, see Intel (2002) and the Problem-Solving Activity at the end of this chapter.

b. Setting applications priorities. Finding and prioritizing applications is a part of an organization's e-strategy. One attractive area may be location-based advertising; unfortunately its effectiveness may not be known for several years. Therefore, companies should be very careful in committing resources to m-commerce. For the near term, applications that enhance the efficiency and effectiveness of mobile workers are likely to have the highest payoff.

c. Choosing a system. The multiplicity of standards, devices, and supporting hardware and software can confuse a company planning to implement mobile computing. An unbiased consultant can be of great help. Checking the vendors and products carefully, as well as who is using them, is also critical. This issue is related to the issue of whether to use an application service provider (ASP) for m-commerce.

According to Taylor (2007), the following are mobile enterprise management issues: asset management, security management, network and connectivity management, and trouble tickets and remote management. Nokia provides suggestions of what to do as well as best practices for enterprise mobile device management.

6. **Mobile device management plan.** Companies that have hundreds or thousands of mobile devices need to treat them as an important issue and have a strategy of planning, maintenance, purchasing, security, replacement, etc. According to *InformationWeek* (May 10, 2008) there is proliferation of devices in most companies and no management plan (see Taylor, 2007).

How *IT* Benefits You

Accounting Major

Wireless applications help with inventory counting and auditing. They also assist in expediting the flow of information for cost control. Price management (recall the Food Lion case), inventory control, and other accounting-related activities can be improved by use of wireless technologies. Finally, reporting (such as inventory taking) can be greatly improved.

Finance Major

Wireless services can provide banks and other financial institutions with a competitive advantage. For example, wireless electronic payments, including micropayments, are more convenient (any place, any time) than traditional means of payments, and they are also less expensive. Electronic bill payment via mobile devices is becoming more popular, increasing security and accuracy, expediting cycle time, and reducing processing costs.

Human Resources Management Major

Mobile computing can improve HR training and extend it to any place at any time. Payroll notices can be delivered as SMSs. Self-service selection of benefits and updating of personal data can be extended to wireless devices, making these functions even more convenient for employees to handle their own benefits management. Note that workforce readiness can be improved, contributing to competitive advantage.

IS Major

IS personnel provide the wireless infrastructure that enables employees to compute and communicate any time, anywhere. This convenience provides exciting, creative new applications for organizations to cut costs and improve the efficiency and effectiveness of operations (for example, to gain transparency in supply chains). Unfortunately, as we discussed earlier, wireless applications might not be secure. Lack of security is a serious problem for which IS personnel are responsible.

Marketing Major

Imagine a whole new world of marketing, advertising, and selling with the potential to increase sales dramatically. This is the promise of mobile computing. Of special interest for marketing are location-based advertising as well as the new opportunities resulting from pervasive computing and RFIDs. Finally, wireless technology also provides new opportunities in sales force automation (SFA), enabling faster and better communications with both customers (CRM) and corporate partners.

Operations Management Major

Wireless technologies offer many opportunities to support mobile employees of all kinds. Wearable computers enable repair personnel working in the field and off-site employees to service customers faster, better, and at lower cost. Wireless devices can also increase productivity within factories by enhancing communication and collaboration as well as managerial planning and control. In addition, mobile computing technologies can increase safety by providing quicker warning signs and instant messaging to isolated employees.

Key Terms

Automatic crash notification
(ACN) *269*
Context awareness *271*
Contextual computing *271*
Geographical information system
(GIS) *266*
Global positioning system
(GPS) *266*
Location-based e-commerce *246*
Mesh network *277*

Mobile commerce *247*
Mobile portal *255*
Mobile Positioning Center
(MPC) *265*
m-wallet *252*
Pervasive computing *271*
Position Determining Equipment
(PDE) *265*
Radio frequency identification
(RFID) *274*

Telematics *269*
Voice portal *255*
Wearable devices *257*
Wireless 911 (e-911) *269*
Wireless mobile computing *244*
Wireless sensor networks
(WSNs) *277*

Chapter Highlights   (Numbers Refer to Learning Objectives)

1 Mobile computing is based on mobility and reach. These characteristics provide ubiquity, convenience, instant connectivity, personalization, and product and service localization.

2 The major drivers of mobile computing are large numbers of users of mobile devices, especially cell phones; no need for a PC; a developing "cell phone culture" in some areas; vendor marketing; declining prices; increasing bandwidth; and the explosion of EC in general.

3 Mobile computing and m-commerce require mobile devices (e.g., PDAs, cell phones) and other hardware, software, and wireless network technologies. Commercial services and applications are still emerging. These technologies allow users to access the Internet any time, anywhere.

3 For l-commerce, a GPS receiver is also needed.

4 Many EC applications in the service industries (e.g., banking, travel, and stocks) can be conducted with wireless devices. Also, shopping can be done from mobile devices.

4 Location-based advertising and advertising via SMSs on a very large scale is expected.

4 Mobile portals provide content (e.g., news) to millions.

5 Large numbers of intrabusiness applications, including inventory management, sales force automation, wireless voice, job dispatching, wireless office, and more are already evident inside organizations.

6 Emerging mobile B2B applications are being integrated with the supply chain and are facilitating cooperation between business partners.

7 M-commerce is being used to provide applications in travel, gaming, entertainment, and delivery of medical services. Many other applications for individual consumers are available or planned for, especially targeted advertising.

8 Most non-Internet applications involve various types of smart cards. They are used mainly in transportation, security, and shopping from vending machines and gas pumps.

9 Location-based commerce, or l-commerce, is emerging in applications such as calculating arrival time of buses (using GPS) and emergency services (wireless 911). In the future, it will be used to target advertising to individuals based on their location. Other innovative applications also are expected.

10 In the world of invisible computing, virtually every object has an embedded microprocessor that is connected in a wired and/or wireless fashion to the Internet. This Internet of things—homes, appliances, cars, and any manufactured items—will provide a number of life-enhancing, consumer-centric, and B2B applications.

10 In context-aware computing, the computer captures the contextual variables of the user and the environment and then provides, in real time, various services to users.

10 The major limitations of mobile computing are small screens on mobile devices, limited bandwidth, high cost, lack of (or small) keyboards, transmission interferences, unproven security, and possible health hazards. Many of these limitations are expected to diminish over time. The primary legal/ethical limitations of m-commerce relate to privacy issues.

Virtual Company Assignment

Mobile Computing at The Wireless Café

Go to The Wireless Café's link on the Student Web Site. You will be asked to consider mobile and wireless applications that can be implemented at the restaurant.

Instructions for accessing The Wireless Café on the Student Web site:

1. Go to *wiley.com/college/turban.*
2. Select Turban/Volonino's *Information Technology for Management*, 7th Edition.
3. Click on Student Resources site, in the toolbar on the left.
4. Click on the link for Virtual Company Web site.
5. Click on Wireless Café.

Questions for Discussion

1. Discuss how mobile computing can solve some of the problems of the *digital divide* (the gap within a country or between countries with respect to people's ability to access the Internet). (See International Telecommunications Union, 1999, and Chapter 15).
2. Compare mobile portals to voice portals.
3. Discuss how m-commerce can expand the reach of e-business.
4. Discuss the impact of wireless computing on emergency medical services in cases of accidents.
5. How are GIS and GPS related?
6. How can you use a GPS to help you find a stolen car, a parking place, or the closest gas station?
7. Some people see location-based tools as an invasion of privacy. Discuss the pros and cons of location-based tools.
8. Discuss how wireless devices can help people with disabilities.
9. Discuss the benefits of telemetry-based systems.
10. Discuss the ways in which Wi-Fi is being used to support mobile computing and m-commerce. Describe the ways in which Wi-Fi is affecting the use of cellular phones for m-commerce.
11. Which of the applications of pervasive computing—smart cars, homes, appliances, and things—do you think are likely to gain the greatest market acceptance in the next few years? Why?
12. Which of the current mobile computing and m-commerce limitations do you think will be minimized within 5 years? Which ones will not?
13. Describe some m-commerce B2B applications along the supply chain.
14. Discuss how RFID can increase the control of checkout systems in stores.

Exercises and Projects

1. Wireless transmission of video and voice is an essential success factor for wireless applications. Find the issues and some of the solutions (best practices). Start with *mobileinfo.com* and *flukenetworks.com.*
2. Investigate commercial applications of voice portals as they relate to wireless access. Visit several vendors (e.g., *tellme.com, bevocal.com,* etc.). What capabilities and applications are offered by the various vendors?
3. Using a search engine, try to determine whether there are any free or for-fee Wi-Fi hotspots in your area. (*Hint:* Access *wifinder.com* or *technewsworld.com/hotspot-locator.*) Enter *wardriving.com.* Based on information provided at this site, what sorts of equipment and procedures could you use to locate hotspots in your area?
4. Examine how new data capture devices such as RFID tags help organizations to accurately identify and segment their customers for activities such as targeted marketing. Browse the literature and the Web, and develop five potential new applications of RFID technology (not listed in this text). What issues could arise if a country's laws required such devices to be embedded in everyone's body as a national identification system?
5. Conduct a study on wearable computers. Find five vendors. Start with *nexttag.com, mobileinfo.com, xybernaut.com,* and *eg3.com,* and look for others as well.
   a. Identify 5 to 10 consumer-oriented wearable devices. What are the capabilities of these products? What advantages do they offer users?
   b. Identify 5 to 10 industry-oriented wearable devices. What are the capabilities of these products? What advantages do they offer users?
   c. See if you can find "What's cooking" in the research labs. For example, visit MIT's wearable computing lab.
6. Investigate commercial uses of GPS. Start with *gpshome.ssc.nasa.gov;* then go to *gpsstore.com.* Also, check the combination of GPS and voice technologies. Can some of the consumer-oriented products be used in industry? Prepare a report on your finding.
7. Enter *google.com* and find all of their mobile activities (e.g., Google Mobile). Prepare a summary.
8. Using a search engine, try to determine whether there are any commercial Wi-Fi hotspots in your area. Enter *wardriving.com.* Based on information provided at this site, what sorts of equipment and procedures could you use to locate hotspots in your area?

9. Enter *onstar.com*. What types of *fleet* services does OnStar provide? Are these any different from the services OnStar provides to individual car owners? Look for the demo and video.

10. Enter *sap.com/USA/solutions/rfid/index.epx* and identify all contributions for supply chain improvements, asset management, and adaptive manufacturing using RFID technologies.

Group Assignments and Projects

1. Each team should examine a major vendor of mobile devices (Nokia, Kyocera, Motorola, Symbol Technology, Palm, BlackBerry, etc.). Each team will research the capabilities for *enterprise solutions*, and prices of the devices offered by each company and then make a class presentation, the objective of which is to convince the rest of the class why one should buy that company's products.

2. Each team should explore new commercial applications of m-commerce in one of the following areas: financial services, including banking, stocks, and insurance; marketing and advertising; manufacturing; travel and transportation; human resources management; public services; and healthcare. Each team will present a report to the class based on their findings. (Start at *mobiforum.org*.)

3. One group studies *blackberry.com/go/fieldforce*, also including enterprise solutions from the company. Make a list of all the services offered. A second group studies the services offered by Sony Ericsson for mobile workers. A third group investigates Nokia's Enterprise Solutions. Finally, a group checks Symbol Technology Inc.'s (a Motorola company) offerings. Prepare a list of capabilities and present them to the class.

4. Each team should take one of the following areas—homes, cars, appliances, or other consumer goods such as clothing—and investigate how embedded microprocessors are currently being used and will be used in the future to support consumer-centric services. Each team will present a report to the class based on its findings.

5. Assign teams to vendors of mobile enterprise devices (e.g., Symbol and Sybase). Find their major products and list their capabilities.

Internet Exercises

1. Learn about PDAs by visiting vendors' sites such as Palm, Sony, Research in Motion, Hewlett-Packard, IBM, Philips, NEC, Hitachi, Casio, Brother, Texas Instruments, and others. List some m-commerce devices manufactured by these companies.

2. Research the status of 3G and the future of 4G by visiting *itu.int*, and *3gnewsroom.com*. Prepare a report on the status of 3G and 4G based on your findings.

3. Explore *nokia.com*. Prepare a summary of the types of mobile services and applications Nokia currently supports and plans to support in the future.

4. Enter *ibm.com*. Search for *wireless e-business*. Research the resulting stories to determine the types of wireless capabilities and applications IBM's software and hardware supports. Describe some of the ways these applications have helped specific businesses and industries.

5. Enter *mapinfo.com* and look for the location-based services demos. Try all of the demos. Find all of the wireless services. Summarize your findings.

6. Enter *pocketvideo.com* and *microsoft.com/mobile/pocketpc*. Examine their demos and products and list their capabilities.

7. Enter *internethomealliance.com* and review their whitepapers. Based on these papers, what are the major appliances that are currently in most U.S. homes? Which of these appliances would most homeowners be likely to connect to a centrally controlled network?

8. Enter *java.sun.com/developer/technicalArticles/ Ecommerce/rfid*. Read about the Internet of Things. What is it? What types of technologies are needed to support it? Why is it important?

9. Review the wireless products for the enterprise with MDSI-Advantex at *mobileinfo.com/ProductCatalog/ MDSI-Advantex.htm*. Summarize the advantages of the different products.

10. Enter *wirelesscar.com*. Examine all of the services provided and relate them to telemetry.

11. Enter the site of a wireless e-mail provider (BlackBerry, T-mobile, Handspring); collect information about the capabilities of the products and compare them.

12. Enter *media.mit.edu/wearables* and prepare a report about new developments (most recent 12 months).

13. Enter *med-i-nets.com* and find information about Pharm-i-net. Trace the supply chain and the support of wireless. Make a diagram of the supply chain.

14. Enter *rfgonline.com* and find information about RFID benefits and risks. Write a summary.

Minicase

Hertz Goes Wireless

The car rental industry is very competitive, and Hertz (*hertz.com*), the world's largest car rental company, competes against hundreds of companies in thousands of locations. The competition focuses on customer acquisition and loyalty. In the last few years, competition has intensified, and profits in the industry have been drifting downward. Hertz has been a "first mover" to information technologies since the 1970s, so it has pioneered some mobile commerce applications:

- **Quick rentals.** Upon arrival at the airport, Hertz's curbside attendant greets you, confirms your reservations, and transmits your name wirelessly to the renting booth. The renting-booth employee advises the curbside attendant about the location of your car. All you need to do is go to the slot where the car is parked and drive away. This system is now part of a national wireless network that can check credit cards, examine your rental history, determine which airline to credit your loyalty mileage to, and more.

- **Instant returns.** A handheld device connected to a database via a wireless system expedites the car return transaction. Right in the parking lot, the lot attendant uses a handheld device that automatically calculates the cost of the rental and prints a receipt for the renter. You check out in less than a minute, and you do not have to enter the renting booth at all.

- **In-car cellular phones.** Starting in 1988, Hertz began renting cell phones with its cars. Today, of course, this is not as big a deal as it was in 1988, when it was a major innovation.

- **NeverLost Onboard.** Some Hertz cars come equipped with an onboard GPS system, which provides route guidance in the form of turn-by-turn directions to many destinations. The information is displayed on a screen with computer-generated voice prompts. An electronic mapping system (GIS) is combined with the GPS, enabling you to see on the map where you are and where you are going. Also, consumer information about the locations of the nearest hospitals, gas stations, restaurants, and tourist areas is provided.

- **Additional customer services.** Hertz's customers can download city guides, Hertz's location guide, emergency telephone numbers, city maps, shopping guides, and even reviews of restaurants, hotels, and entertainment into their PDAs and other wireless devices. Of course, driving directions are provided.

- **Car locations.** Hertz is experimenting with a GPS-based car-locating system. This will enable the company to know where a rental car is at any given time, and even how fast it is being driven. Although the company promises to provide discounts based on your usage pattern, this capability is seen by many as an invasion of *privacy*. On the other hand, some may feel safer knowing that Hertz knows where they are at all times.

- **Wi-Fi connection.** High-speed Internet access is available in Hertz's rental areas in all major airports served by Hertz in the United States.

Sources: Compiled from *hertz.com* (accessed April 2008) and Martin (2003).

Questions for Minicase

1. Which of these applications are intrabusiness in nature?
2. Identify any finance- and marketing-oriented applications.
3. What are the benefits to Hertz of knowing exactly where each of its cars is? As a renter, how do you feel about this capability?
4. What competitive edge can Hertz get from the system?

Problem-Solving Activity

Should You Give Mobile Workers Wireless Tools?

Along with the proliferation of wireless devices and the services they provide and their increased capabilities comes the issue of what and how many devices to provide the mobile employees with.

You are a consultant to a company that considers equipping its maintenance employees at its several outdoor yards and large warehouses with wireless devices so they can instantly view data, diagrams, charts, manuals, etc., which are stored in the corporate headquarters. It is clear that this would help the employees do their jobs more efficiently. But, can you really save money?

In this exercise, you are asked to calculate the saving, considering the following information.

Assume that there are 250 employees sharing 125 rugged laptops, and assume that all employees can save 10% of their time when equipped with the devices.

Employees work 37.5 hours per week and their salary including fringe benefits is $35.00 per hour. IT employees cost $40.00 per hour.

Start up costs. Management wants to buy 125 mobile devices such as rugged laptops at $4,000.00 each. The system is to be developed on existing infrastructure by two IT people during 20 weeks. Finally, a training of all 250 employees will take four hours each. (Hint: consider lost productivity due to employee training at their hourly cost.)

Operating cost. (Calculate per year) Monthly fee for wireless devices is $75.00 per computer.

Technical support of IT employees, per user per year, is estimated at 3 hours.

Shared overhead cost equals 10% of operating cost.

Improvements. In addition to 10% in productivity improvement of all 250 employees, management figures that there will be a 7% reduction in inventory level (average inventory level is estimated at $1.5 million/average with an annual carrying cost of 15 percent. Also, the money saved on inventory reduction can be invested in 6% bonds. Another benefit is the reduction of downtime of machines due to faster communication and collaboration. Downtime reduction is esti-

mated at 4%. Each percentage of downtime is calculated at $200.00 per month.

Management would like to know the first year ROI, in percentage, and the payback period of the entire investment (in months).

Note: Use a spreadsheet for this activity. Also, you may utilize Microsoft's calculator (*Microsoft.com/windowsmobile/business/calculator/default.mspx*).

Online Resources

More resources and study tools are located on the Student Web Site and on WileyPLUS. You'll find additional chapter materials and useful Web links. In addition, self-quizzes that provide individualized feedback are available for each chapter.

Online Briefs for Chapter 7 are available at wiley.com/college/turban:

7.1   *Intrabusiness Applications of Mobile Computing*
7.2   *Mobile Entertainment: Music, Pictures, and Video*
7.3   *Wireless Telemedicine*
7.4   *Smart "Things"*
7.5   *The Wireless Connected House*
7.6   *The Capabilities of OnStar*
7.7   *Benefits of RFID*
7.8   *Inhibitors and Barriers of Mobile Computing*

Online Minicases for Chapter 7 are available at wiley.com/college/turban:

7.1   *Washington Township (OH)*
7.2   *7-Eleven Tracks Inventory Wirelessly*

References

8d.com, "Cale Uses 8D Technologies' 8D ECO to Deliver World-Leading Parking System that Features Wireless, Secure Online Payment—From Solar-Powered Terminals—and Advanced Management Functions, to Large North American City," *8d.com,* 2006, *8d.com/content.php?section=products&subsection=eco&subsubsection=eco_case&id=1* (accessed April 2008).

91expresslanes.com (accessed April 2008).

ATX, "Telematics 2008: A Global Snapshot," 2008, *atxg.stationhq.com/node/87* (accessed April 2008).

Bardram, J. E., and H. B. Christensen, "Pervasive Computing Support for Hospitals: An Overview of the Activity-Based Computing Project," *IEEE Pervasive Computing,* 6(1), January–March 2007, pp. 44–51.

Bartholomew, D., "Bovine Intervention (RFID)," *Baseline,* May 2008.

Bertolucci, J., "Make Your Home a Smart Home," *Kiplinger's,* May 2006.

Brown, D., *RFID Implementation.* New York: McGraw-Hill, 2006.

Business Wire, "SEGA Reinvents Sonic the Hedgehog Experience for Next-Generation Video Game Platforms; Gaming Icon to Celebrate 15th Year on PS3 and Xbox 360," *BusinessWire.com,* September 9, 2005, *findarticles.com/p/articles/mi_m0EIN/is_2005_Sept_9/ai_n15377444* (accessed April 2008).

Clark, K., "Food Lion's High Wireless Act," *Retail Technology Quarterly,* July 2005.

CIOInsight, "Will Mobile Banking Take Off?" editorial, *CIO Insight,* May 16, 2007, *cioinsight.com/index2.php?option=content&task=view&id=881357&pop=1&* . . . (accessed May 2008).

Comiskey, D., "ShopWiki Launches Mobile Shopping Search Engine," *Ecommerce-guide.com,* May 17, 2006, *ecommerce-guide.com/news/article.php/3606926* (accessed April 2008).

DeMuro, M., "Michigan CAT Case Study," *Directions Magazine,* April 7, 2005, *directionsmag.com/article.php?article_id=823&trv=1* (accessed June 2008).

Digital Communities, "Chicago Suburb Deploys Mesh Municipal Network as Cornerstone of 'Digital City' Project," May 24, 2007, *govtech.com/dc/122871* (accessed April 2008).

Dizikes, P., "Wireless Highway," *Technology Review,* March—April 2006.

Edgar, Dunn & Company, "2006 Mobile Payments Study," 2006, *digitaldebateblogs.typepad.com/digital_money/files/edgardunnreport.pdf* (accessed April 2008).

Eklund, R., "Mobile CRM Comes of Age," *CRM,* July 15, 2002, *destinationcrm.com/articles/default.asp?ArticleID=2352* (accessed April 2008).

Estrin, D., R. Govindan, J. S. Heidemann., "Embedding the Internet," *Communications of the ACM,* 43(5), May 2000, pp. 38–42.

Ferguson, R. B., "Marines Deploy RFID," *eWeek,* November 15, 2004, *eweek.com/article2/0,1759,1723353,00.asp* (accessed April 2008).

foodlion.com/AboutFoodlion/FastFacts.asp (accessed May 2008).

Foster, M., "Cell Phones in Japan Make Wallets Obsolete," *International Herald Tribune,* February 25, 2008.

Fujitsu Computer Systems, "Fujitsu Computer Systems National Distributing Company Case Study," *fujitsupc.com/www/about.shtml?aboutus/casestudies/ndc* (accessed April 2008).

Gandon, F., and N. Sadeh, "Semantic Web Technologies to Reconcile Privacy and Context Awareness," *Web Semantics Journal,* 1(3), 2004.

Golding, P., *Next Generation Wireless Applications: Creating Mobile Applications in a Web 2.0 and Mobile 2.0 World,* 2nd ed. Hoboken, NJ: John Wiley & Sons, 2008.

Gonsalves, A., "Social Networking, E-Commerce Driving Smartphone Users to the Web," *InformationWeek,* May 21, 2008.

Guernsey, L., "Wearable Computers for the Working Class, *New York Times,* December 14, 2000.

Hamblen, M., "Get Payback on Wireless," *Computer World,* January 1, 2001, *computerworld.com/printthis/2001/0,4814,54798,00.html* (no longer available online).

Heinrich, C., *RFID and Beyond.* Indianapolis: Wiley Publishing, 2005. *hertz.com* (accessed April 2008).

Hunter, R., *World Without Secrets: Business, Crime, and Privacy in the Age of Ubiquitous Computing.* New York: Wiley, 2002.

Indiatimes, "Offices, They Are A-Changing," *Indiatimes.com,* May 12, 2006, *infotech.indiatimes.com/articleshow/1527370.cms* (accessed April 2008).

InformationWeek, "Trouble Ahead: Most Companies Don't Have a Mobile Device Management Plan," May 10, 2008.

Intel, "Building the Foundation for Anytime Anywhere Computing," White Paper 25 1290–002, Intel Corporation, June 13, 2002.

International Telecommunications Union, "Challenges to the Network: Internet for Development," October 1999, *itu.int/ITU-D/ict/publications/inet/1999/ExeSum.html* (accessed April 2008).

Islam, N., and M. Fayad, "Toward Ubiquitous Acceptance of Ubiquitous Computing," *Communications of the ACM,* February 2003.

Junglas, I. A., and R. T. Watson, "Location-Based Services," *Communications of the ACM,* March 2008.

Kanaracus, C., "Multicore, Clouds, Social Nets Top Disruptive List," *InfoWorld,* April 8, 2008, infoworld.com/article/08/04/08/Multicore-clouds-social-nets-top-disruptive-list_1.html (accessed April 2008).

Kharif, O., "What's Lurking in That RFID Tag?" *BusinessWeekOnline,* March 16, 2006a, *businessweek.com/technology/content/mar2006/tc20060316_117677.htm* (accessed April 2008).

Kharif, O., "Social Networking Goes Mobile," BusinessWeek.com, May 31, 2006b. *businessweek.com/technology/content/may2006/tc20060530_170086.htm* (accessed June 2008).

Kolbasuk-McGee, M., "Track This," *Information Week,* February 11, 2008.

Kontzer, T., "Top Ten Uses for SMS," *Information Week,* June 11, 2003, *informationweek.com/story/showArticle.jhtml;jsessionid=1M2IE0XVSIDMMQSNDBCSKHSCJUMEIJVN?articleID=10300804* (accessed April 2008).

Kyoto City Government, "Master Concept of Kyoto City," *Computerworld Honors Program,* 2007, *cwhonors.org/viewCaseStudy.asp?NominationID=143* (accessed April 2008).

Longino, C., "Your Wireless Future," *Business 2.0,* May 2006.

Lyman, J., "Will Mobile CRM Finally Break Through in 2006?" *CRMBuyer.com,* January 3, 2006, *crmbuyer.com/story/48054.html* (accessed April 2008).

Malik, O., "Home Entertainment to Go," *Business 2.0,* December 2004.

Martin, J. A., "Mobile Computing: Hertz In-Car GPS," *PC World,* March 13, 2003.

Martin, R., "Saving Pro Cycling, One BlackBerry at a Time," *InformationWeek,* November 16, 2007, *informationweek.com/news/mobility/showArticle.jhtml;jsessionid=VUDACUWNEMGN2QSNDLPCKH0CJUNN2JVN?articleID=203101658&_requestid=504931* (accessed April 2008).

Mathieson, R., "The Future According to Spielberg: Minority Report and the World of Ubiquitous Computing," *MPulse,* August 2002, *rickmathieson.com/articles/0802-minorityreport.html* (accessed April 2008).

McGuire, C., "Food Lion Checking Out with Wi-Fi," *Wi-Fi Plant News,* May 27, 2004, *internetnews.com/wireless/article.php/3360601* (accessed April 2008).

Mitchell, B., "How to Build a Wireless Home Network—Tutorial," About.com, 2008, *compnetworking.about.com/cs/wirelessproducts/a/howtobuildwlan.htm* (accessed April 2008).

MobileInfo, "Mobile Computing Business Case," *mobileinfo.com/business_cases.htm* (accessed May 3, 2008).

Motorola, "Motorola M-Wallet Solutions," 2008, *motorola.com/networkoperators/pdfs/M-Wallet-Brochure.pdf* (accessed April 2008).

Neumann, P. G., and L. Weinstein, "Risks of RFID," *Communications of the ACM,* May 2006. *NextBus.com* (accessed April 2008).

Null, C., "Smart Phones Get Smarter," *PC World,* February 2007.

O'Reilly, D., "Cell Phones that Tell You Where to Go," *PC World,* July 2007.

Raskin, A., "Your Ad Could Be Here! (And Now We Can Tell You Who Will See It)," *Business 2.0,* May 2003, *money.cnn.com/magazines/business2/business2_archive/2003/05/01/341929/index.htm* (accessed April 2008).

Reda, S., "Prada's Pratfall," *Stores,* June 2004.

RFID Public Information Center, "RFID and Privacy," 2006, *rfidprivacy.mit.edu/access/happening_legislation.html* (no longer available online).

Reuters, "GSI Labs Leading Wireless 911 Monitoring Company in 2007," *Reuters*.com, February 14, 2008, *reuters.com/article/pressRelease/idUS225736+14-Feb-2008+BW20080214* (accessed April 2008).

Romow.com, "Mobile Phone Use Reaches 50% Worldwide," February 21, 2008, *romow.com/shopping-blog/mobile-phone-use-reaches-50-worldwide* (accessed April 2008).

Rosencrance, L., "Update: Benetton Backs Away from 'Smart Tags' in Clothing Line," *Computer World,* April 4, 2003.

Sadeh, N., *M-Commerce.* New York: Wiley, 2002.

Schuman, E., "Circuit City's New Approach to Customer Service," *eWeek,* January 17, 2005.

Schuman, E., "A Tight Ship," *Baseline,* March 2004.

Shannon, V., "Mobile War Over Social Networking," *International Herald Tribune,* March 6, 2008.

Sharke, P., "Smart Cars," *MEmagazine.org,* May 2003, *memagazine.org/contents/current/features/smartcar/smartcar.html* (accessed April 2008).

Smith, B., "Goodbye Wallet, Hello Phone," *Wireless Week,* April 1, 2006, *wirelessweek.com/article.aspx?id=81050* (accessed April 2008).

Soh, J. O. B., and B. C. Y. Tan, "Mobile Gaming," *Communications of the ACM,* March 2008.

Stanford, V., "Pervasive Computing Goes to Work: Interfacing to the Enterprise," *Pervasive Computing,* 1(3), July–September 2002.

Taniar, D. (ed.), *Encyclopedia of Mobile Computing and Commerce.* Hershey, Pa: IGI Global, 2007.

Taylor, D., "Mobile and Enterprise Management Issues, Mobile Management Part II," *SearchMobileComputing.com,* June 11, 2007, *searchmobilecomputing.techtarget.com/tip/0,289483,sid40_gci1260285,00.html* (accessed April 2008).

Textually.org, "Mobile Commerce Seen as Future for Japan Retailers, September 10, 2006, *textually.org/textually/archives/cat_mobile_success_explained_japan_europe_usa_china.htm* (accessed July 2008).

Trimi, S., and H. Sheng, "Emerging Trends in M-Government," *Communications of the ACM,* May 2008.

Thilmany J., "Behind the Census Bureau's Mobile Snafu," *CIO Insight,* May 20, 2008.

Varshney, U., and R. Vetter, "Mobile Commerce and Applications: Frameworks, Applications, and Networking Support," J*ournal on Mobile Networks and Applications,* June 2002.

Vocera Communications, "T1000 Vocera Phone," 2008, *vocera.com/downloads/T1000_overview_0208.pdf* (accessed April 2008).

Weiser, M., "The Computer for the Twenty-First Century," *Scientific American,* September 1991. Reprinted in *Pervasive Computing,* January–March 2002.

Wireless Internet Institute, "Digital Cities Convention," *w2i,* 2007, *w2i.com/events/schedule/event_overview/p/eventId_37/id_126* (accessed June 2008).

Zappone, C., "Backlash against RFID Is Growing," *CNNMoney.com,* news item May 21, 2007, *money.cnn.com/2007/05/21/technology/rfid* (accessed June 2008).

Chapter

Social Networks in the Web 2.0 Environment

Learning Objectives

Upon completion of this chapter, you will be able to:

❶ Understand the Web 2.0 revolution, social and business networks, and industry and market disruptors.

❷ Understand the concept, structure, types, and issues of virtual communities and worlds.

❸ Understand social networking and social networking sites.

❹ Describe enterprise social networks.

❺ Understand the Web 2.0, social networking, and e-commerce relationship.

❻ Describe the Web 3.0 concept.

Integrating *IT*

 ACC   **FIN**   **MKT**   **OM**   **HRM**   **IS**

IT-PERFORMANCE MODEL

The focus of this chapter is on social networking and the use of Web 2.0 tools to improve organizational performance, mostly via information sharing, collaboration, and aggregation of the wisdom of individuals. Social networking can be used in most steps of our business performance management model, starting with joint goal setting and ending with improved problem solving.

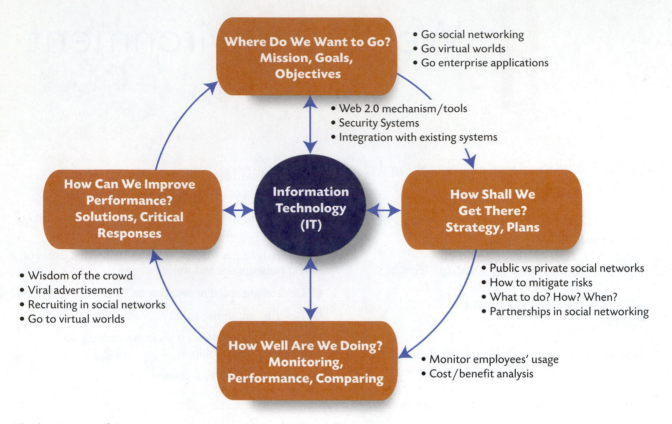

The business performance management cycle and IT model.

WIKIPEDIA AND ITS PROBLEMS OF CONTENT QUALITY AND PRIVACY PROTECTION

The Problem

Wikipedia is a free online pop culture collaborative encyclopedia that Web 2.0 communities have created. In 2008, it had over 7 million articles in over 250 languages, and it generated some 80 million hits per day. By comparison, Wikipedia is 42 times bigger than the *Encyclopedia Britannica*, which contains only 120,000 articles (reported by McNichol, 2007a, and Wikipedia, 2008). However, Wikipedia's greatest strength is also its biggest weakness. Its contents are user created; therefore, sometimes people with no special expertise on their chosen topics or people with malicious agendas post so-called "facts." For instance, there was once a contributor to a Pope Benedict article who substituted the Pontiff's photo with that of Emperor Palpatine from the *Star Wars* films. Another example was an accusation made by a contributor against distinguished journalist and long-time civil rights advocate John Seigenthaler that alleged Seigenthaler was involved in the assassinations of President John Kennedy and his brother Bobby Kennedy. The contributor practically fabricated the entire article. Seigenthaler pursued legal action against the anonymous Wikipedia contributor through a lawsuit using the poster's IP address and charged the unidentified accuser with defamation. For Seigenthaler, Wikipedia is "populated by volunteer vandals with poison-pen intellects," and should not be permitted to exist in its current form. According to Farrell (2007), Microsoft paid experts to write information about the company. This information was found to be inaccurate. (For more about the inaccuracy issue, see McNichol, 2007a.)

Another problem is invasion of privacy. Even if information about a certain individual or company is correct (i.e., no defamation), the individuals may not care for the information to become public. Because most contributors do not ask permission from those they are writing about, an invasion of privacy occurs.

Solution

In order to avoid false or misleading entries, the Wikimedia Foundation, which operates Wikipedia along with several other wiki initiatives (such as Wikibooks), is evaluating alternatives to improve the quality. The first step was the creation of a more formal advisory board. The second step was to empower system administrators to block access to the site to certain users who repeatedly vandalized entries. Next, the process of handling complaints has also been improved.

Ultimately, the owners plan to change the site to Wikipedia 2.0 and are considering the following three options:

1. The editing of mediocre Wikipedia articles by experts in the specific field; especially the use of quality art editors to improve Wikipedia's humanities coverage.
2. The creation of original articles from the ground up. According to Larry Sanger, one of the owners and creators, this could provide a more distinctive culture that will provide more pride in the articles. In this case, the name of the site would change to *citizendium*.
3. Making the users' policy more interactive. Wikipedia is asking readers to notify the company whenever they read inaccurate or incomplete content.

The Results

The Seigenthaler's issue was debated in Fall 2005, early quality measures were instituted, and the site founder, Jimmy Wales, appeared on CNN with Seigenthaler in December 2005, the traffic to Wikipedia nearly tripled (Martens, 2006), mostly due to the publicity of the CNN presentation and the subsequent publicity in newspapers and TV. Yet the problems still persist, with complaints against both content and privacy invasion online. And, after years of enormous growth, the rate of editing articles, new account registration, user block, article protection and deletion, and uploads all declined (Riley, 2007).

Sources: Compiled from Martens (2006), Cone (2007a), Flynn (2006), and McNichol (2007a).

Lessons Learned from This Case

The Wikipedia case illustrates a *wiki implementation*, a collaborative online encyclopedia that volunteers primarily write. Murray-Buechner (2006) lists it as one of the 25 sites "we cannot live without" and labeled it as a "real Web wonder." It is a typical Web 2.0 application done for people by people. Also, it illustrates the phenomenon of the "wisdom of the crowd," namely, having many people contributing their knowledge to create better knowledge and to solve problems. Now many companies are using a similar concept internally; for example, Pfizerpedia.com uses a wiki network, organized like an encyclopedia, to accumulate knowledge internal to Pfizer drug company. Many other companies use the wisdom of the crowd to create corporate knowledge directories. It also illustrates the potential of invasion of privacy, potential of litigation against the site, and the need for financial viability, especially when money is needed to check what people contribute for the online publishing.

In this chapter, we present several of the Web 2.0 applications, mostly virtual communities, virtual worlds, and social networks and their impact on the way we live and do business, relating it to the experience of Wikipedia and other companies. We also present specific companies, such as Second Life, Facebook, Cyworld, Craigslist, YouTube, and Flickr, that have already changed the work and/or lives of millions of people.

8.1 The Web 2.0 Revolution, Social Media, and Industry Disruptors

This new chapter of the text deals with the newest areas of IT—social networks and other Web 2.0 applications. Let's see what it is all about.

THE WEB 2.0 REVOLUTION

Time Magazine 2006 Person of the Year was "You," reflecting the Web's digital democracy (Grossman, 2006/2007). Yes, ordinary and regular people such as you and I now control, use, and are immersed in the information age. What makes this possible is the phenomenon known as Web 2.0. It has become the framework for bringing together the contributions of millions of people, no matter how small and inconsequential or huge and significant the systems are—and Web 2.0 applications to make everyone's work, thoughts, opinions, and essentially their identity, matter (see *rheingold.com*). If Web 1.0 was organized around pages, software, technology, and corporations, Web 2.0 is organized around ordinary people and services. According to *The Economist* (2007), Tim Berners-Lee, the creator of the Web, regards Web 2.0 as a movement that encompasses a range of technologies such as blogs, wikis, and podcasts—representing the Web adolescence. It has all the hallmarks of youthful rebellion against the conventional social order and is making many traditional media companies tremble. By 2008, no one had more power to influence society than Web 2.0 communities. For a description, see Gillin (2007). Yet, does this influence truly benefit us, or will we suffer because of it?

You can view Web 2.0 as a large-scale and global social experiment, and like any other experiment that is worth undertaking, it needs to be evaluated in the future, and it may fail. Why? As seen in the Wikipedia case, there are serious concerns regarding the quality and integrity of user-created content on the Web, as well as security and other problems.

As of 2007 there is an increasing recognition of the business opportunities of social networks (e.g., see Weber, 2007; Terdiman, 2008; and Zimmerman, 2007).

WHAT IS IN WEB 2.0?

Web 2.0 is the popular term for advanced Internet technology and applications including blogs, wikis, RSS, and social networks (see preview in Chapter 1). One of the most significant differences between Web 2.0 and the traditional Web is greater collaboration among Internet users and other users, content providers, and enterprises. As an umbrella term for an emerging core of technologies, trends, and principles, Web 2.0 is not only changing what's on the Web but also how it works. Many believe that companies that understand these new applications and technologies—and apply the benefits early on—stand to greatly improve internal business processes and marketing. Among the biggest advantages is better collaboration with customers, partners, and suppliers, as well as among internal users (see the minicase about Eastern Mountain Sport at the end of this chapter; McAfee, 2006; and Libert et al., 2008).

Here are some key Web 2.0 blogging statistics as of April 2007 that illustrate the magnitude of just the blogging aspect (Sifrey, 2007):

- Over 75 million blogs exist online and about 120,000 new blogs are being added each day, or 1.4 new blogs every second.
- From 3000 to 7000 new splogs (fake or spam blogs) are created every day.
- At least 1.5 million comments are posted in blogs every day, or 17 posts per second.
- Growing from 35 to 75 million blogs took only 320 days.
- Japanese is the #1 blogging language at 37 percent, English second at 33 percent, and Chinese third at 8 percent.

REPRESENTATIVE CHARACTERISTICS OF WEB 2.0

The following are representative characteristics:

- The ability to tap into the collective intelligence of users. The more users contribute, the more popular and valuable a Web 2.0 site becomes.
- Making data available in new or never-intended ways. Web 2.0 data can be remixed or "mashed up," often through Web-service interfaces, much the way a dance-club DJ mixes music.

- Web 2.0 uses user-generated and controlled content and data.
- The presence of lightweight programming techniques and tools that lets nearly anyone act as a developer.
- The virtual elimination of software-upgrade cycles makes everything a *perpetual beta* or work in progress and allows rapid prototyping using the Web as a platform for developing applications.
- Networks as platforms, delivering and allowing users to use applications entirely through a browser.
- An architecture of participation and *digital democracy* encourages users to add value to the application as they use it.
- New business models are rapidly and continuously being created (Chesbrough, 2006).
- A major emphasis is on social networks.
- A rich interactive, user-friendly interface based on Ajax or similar frameworks is often used. Ajax, (Asynchronous JavaScript and XML), is a Web development technique for creating interactive Web applications. The intent is to make Web pages feel more responsive by exchanging small amounts of data with the server behind the scenes so that the entire Web page does not have to be reloaded each time the user makes a change. This is meant to increase the Web page's interactivity, speed, and usability.

Web 2.0 Companies. Schonfeld (2006a) believes that a major characteristic of Web 2.0 is the global spreading of innovative Web sites. As soon as a successful idea is deployed as a Web site in one country, other sites appear around the globe. He presents 23 Web 2.0 type sites in 10 countries. This section presents some of these sites. Others appear in different sections of this chapter. Another excellent source for material on Web 2.0 is Search CIO's *Executive Guide: Web 2.0* (see *searchcio.techtarget.com/general/0,295582,sid19_gci1244339,00.html#glossary*).

O'Reilly (2005) listed some representative companies such as Flickr. Later on, dozens of companies emerged as providers of infrastructure and services to social networks. In addition, many companies provide the technology for Web 2.0 activities (see list in Chapter 4). A large number of startups appeared in 2005–2008. Here are some examples: Sloan (2007) provides a guide to the 25 hottest Web 2.0 companies and the powerful trends that are driving them. (Others are described in Gillin, 2007.) The 25 include:

- In social media: StumbleUpon (*stumbleupon.com*), Slide (*slide.com*), Bebo (*bebo.com*), Meebo (*meebo.com*), and Wikia (*wikia.com*).
- In video: Joost (*joost.com*), Metacafe (*metacafe.com*), Dabble (*dabble.com*), Revision3 (*revision3.com*), and Blip TV (*blip.tv*).
- In the mobile area: Mobio (*mobio.com*), Soonr (*soonr.com*), TinyPicture (*tinypicture.com*), Fon (*fon.com*), and Loopt (*loopt.com*). (For 20 companies in this area, see Longino, 2006.)
- In advertising: Adify (*adify.com*), Admob (*admob.com*), Turn (*turn.com*), Spotrunner (*spotrunner.com*), and Vitrue (*vitrue.com*).
- In enterprise: SuccessFactors (*successfactors.com*), Janrain (*janrain.com*), Logowork (*logowork.com*), Simulscribe (*simulscribe.com*), and ReardenCommerce (*reardencommerce.com*).

Several of these companies are described in this chapter.

SOCIAL MEDIA

One of the major phenomena of Web 2.0 is the emergence and rise of mass social media. **Social media** refers to the online platforms and tools that people use to share opinions and experiences including photos, videos, music, insights, and perceptions with each other. Social media can take many different forms including text, images, audio, or video clips. The key is that people, rather than the organizations, *control* and use them.

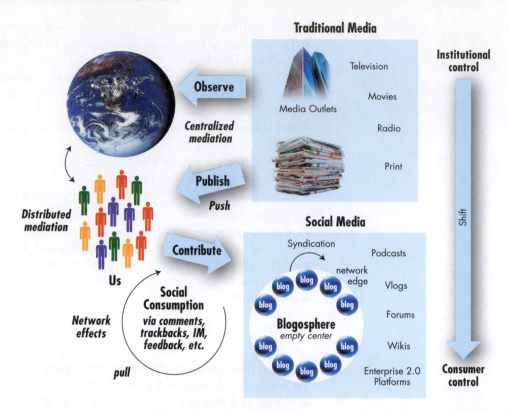

Figure 8.1 The emergence and rise of mass social media. (*Source:* Hinchcliffe, D., Web 2.0 Blog, *web2.wsj2.com.*)

Furthermore, people can use these media with ease at little or no cost. It is a powerful democratization force; the network structure enables communication and collaboration on a massive scale. For details, see Hinchcliffe (2006). Figure 8.1 shows the emergence and rise of mass social media. The figure compares traditional and social media and illustrates the new tools of social media (e.g., blogs, video blogs (vlogs), and so forth) as being in the consumer's control. Content is produced and consumed by people (us) in the social media, rather than pushed to or observed by people in the traditional media.

Notice that traditional media content goes from the technology to the people, whereas in social media, people create and control the content.

INDUSTRY AND MARKET DISRUPTORS

Several companies have introduced Web 2.0-based innovations that could disrupt and reorder markets or even entire industries. They introduce a major change in the way companies do business (see Schonfeld and Borzo, 2006). An example is Blue Nile (*bluenile.com*), which displaced hundreds of jewelers and is changing the jewelry retail industry. Some refer to such companies as **disruptors.** Disruptors are companies, such as ZOPA, that facilitate person-to-person lending; thus, they may change the lending business (Online Minicase 8.1).

Business 2.0 created The Disruption Group with its blog (e.g., see Urlocker (2006) and Schonfeld (2006b). This Disruption Group developed a checklist of questions to help identify disruptors (see the Disruption Scorecard at *ondisruption.com*). The top four questions are:

1. Is the service or product simpler, cheaper, or more accessible?
2. Does the disruptor change the basis of competition with the current suppliers?
3. Does the disruptor have a different business model?
4. Does the product or service fit with what customers value and pay for?

Figure 8.2 illustrates how consumer-generated content is disrupting traditional media. Specifically, a large number of blogs and videos is posted everyday and then viewed by millions around the world. Content is created continuously by millions of people as well. The result is people being both publishers of content (Web-based) and consumers of content, all of which may disrupt the traditional media.

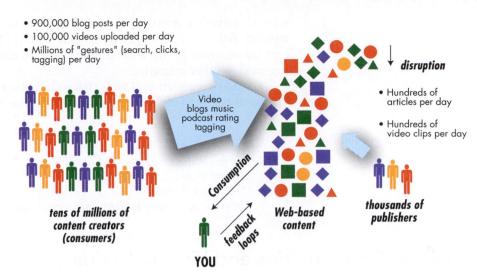

- 900,000 blog posts per day
- 100,000 videos uploaded per day
- Millions of "gestures" (search, clicks, tagging) per day

Video blogs music podcast rating tagging

↓ disruption

- Hundreds of articles per day
- Hundreds of video clips per day

Consumption

feedback loops

tens of millions of content creators (consumers)

YOU

Web-based content

thousands of publishers

Figure 8.2 The *You* era: Consumer-generated content swamping, disrupting traditional media. (*Source:* Hinchcliffe, D., Web 2.0 Blog, *web2.wsj2.com*.)

Example #1: Will Online Wedding Services Disrupt the Traditional Industry?

Wedding services is a big industry. However, more online competition is coming because people use technology to disintermediate traditional vendors, such as live bands, DJs, and invitation printers (see *A Closer Look 8.1*).

Example #2: Disruptors of the Real Estate Industry.

Disruption in the real estate brokerage industry is made by companies such as Zillow (*zillow.com*) and Homegain (*homegain.com*), which provide more services and information than Web 1.0 companies such as *realtor.com*, *realtytrack.com*, and similar sites provide. According to O'Brien (2007), you can enter *zillow.com* and go to estimate to get an approximation of your home's market value and a map of your neighborhood. Then you add all the extra features of your house. This triggers a comparison of the new estimate that can be made with your neighbors' homes (see Team Exercise #1 at the end of this chapter). Users can list their homes for free after calculating the actual selling price in the neighborhood. The service is good not only for sellers. Buyers can use Zillow to buy a house that is not even on the market—without open houses, bidding

A Closer Look 8.1

Weddings Are Going W2.0 High Tech

Technology in the United States and some other countries has shaken up the traditional wedding business. Today, many couples create their own wedding sites to keep their guests informed about the wedding plans. Many couples use the Internet for bridal registries. Guests can buy the most preferred gifts online from major department stores. Wedding Webcasts are becoming popular, too: couples can broadcast the wedding ceremony on the Web for people who are not able to attend, as well as post wedding videos on YouTube and pictures on Flickr. Friends can start a blog or a wiki, too.

Next is the use of digital music. Couples create their own playlists on their iPods and use them for both wedding ceremony and reception music, especially for small, intimate weddings. This is noninteractive, but it is original and less costly. Couples also save money by using the Internet to compare items they need to buy (e.g., see *theknot.com*). Finally,

couples can design and buy their wedding rings online (e.g., see *bluenile.com*). All in all, there is more competition among vendors to serve 2.4 million weddings annually in the United States.

The Internet lets you be very innovative. For example, Bernie Peng reprogrammed Tammy Li's favorite video game, "Bejeweled," so that a ring and a marriage proposal would show up on the screen when she reached a certain score. (In this popular game, players score points by swapping gems to form vertical and horizontal chains.) The reprogramming was a tricky task and took him a month. Tammy reached the needed score—and said yes. The couple plan to marry over Labor Day weekend (2008), and PopCap, the Seattle company that makes "Bejeweled," will fly the couple to Seattle as part of their honeymoon. The company is also supplying copies of "Bejeweled" to hand out as favors to the wedding guests (*CNN.com*, 2008).

wars, or buyer's remorse—and get it cheaper by passing over the 6 percent commission. Will real estate agents be made extinct? Some will. More likely the 6 percent commission in the United States will be closer to the 1 percent commission common in other countries.

The major application of Web 2.0 is social networks such as MySpace and Facebook. These are based on the concept of *virtual communities*, the topic we present next.

Review Questions

1. Define *Web 2.0.*
2. List the major characteristics of Web 2.0.
3. List the Web 2.0 technologies.
4. Define *social media.*
5. Define *industry and market disruptors.* Provide an example.

8.2 Virtual Communities and Virtual Worlds

A *community* is a group of people with common interests who interact with one another. A **virtual (Internet) community** is one in which the interaction takes place by using a computer network, mainly the Internet. Virtual communities parallel typical physical communities, such as neighborhoods, clubs, or associations, but people do not meet face-to-face. Instead, they meet online. Virtual communities offer several ways for members to interact, collaborate, and trade (see Table 8.1). Similar to the EC click-and-mortar model, many *physical communities* have a Web site for Internet-related activities that supplement the physical activities.

CHARACTERISTICS OF TRADITIONAL ONLINE COMMUNITIES AND THEIR CLASSIFICATION

Pure-play Internet communities may have thousands or even millions of members. This is one major difference with purely physical communities, which usually are smaller. Another difference is that offline communities frequently are confined to one geographic location, whereas only a few online communities are geographically confined. For further information, see *en.wikipedia.org/wiki/Virtual_community*.

TABLE 8.1	Elements of Interaction in a Virtual Community
Category	**Element**
Communication	Bulletin boards (discussion groups)
	Chat rooms/threaded discussions (string Q&A)
	E-mail and instant messaging and wireless messages
	Private mailboxes
	Newsletters, "netzines" (electronic magazines)
	Blogging, wikis, and mush ups
	Web postings
	Voting
Information	Directories and yellow pages
	Search engines
	Member-generated content
	Links to information sources
	Expert advice
EC Element	Electronic catalogs and shopping carts
	Advertisements
	Auctions of all types
	Classified ads
	Bartering online

A Closer Look 8.2

Examples of Communities

The following are examples of online communities.

- **Associations.** Many associations have a Web presence. These range from Parent–Teacher Associations (PTAs) to professional associations. An example of this type of community is the Australian Record Industry Association (*aria.com.au*).

- **Ethnic communities.** Many communities are country or language specific. An example of such a site is *elsitio.com*, which provides content for the Spanish- and Portuguese-speaking audiences mainly in Latin America and the United States. A number of sites, including *china.com, hongkong.com, sina.com,* and *sohu.com*, cater to the world's large Chinese-speaking community.

- **Gender communities.** *Women.com* and *ivillage.com*, the two largest female-oriented community sites, merged in 2001 in an effort to cut losses and become profitable.

- **Affinity portals.** These are communities organized by interest, such as hobbies, vocations, political parties, unions (e.g., *workingfamilies.com*), and many more. Many communities are organized around a technical topic (e.g., a database) or a product (e.g., Lotus Notes). A major subcategory here is medical- and health-related. According to Johnson and Ambrose (2006), almost 30 percent of the 90 million members who participated in communities in 2005 were in this category.

- **Catering to young people (teens and people in their early twenties).** Many companies see unusual opportunities here. Three community sites of particular interest are *alloy.com,* *bolt.com,* and *blueskyfrog.com.* Alloy.com is based in the United Kingdom and claims to have over 10 million members and reaches more than 17 million through *teen.com*, which the company launched in December 2007. Bolt.com claims to have 12 million members and operates from the United States. Blueskyfrog.com operates from Australia, concentrating on cell phone users, and claims to have more than 7 million devoted members.

- **Megacommunities.** Megacommunities combine numerous smaller communities under one "umbrella" (under one name). GeoCities is one example of a megacommunity with many sub-communities. Owned by Yahoo!, it is by far the largest online community.

- **B2B online communities.** Chapter 6 introduced many-to-many B2B exchanges. These are referred to as communities. B2B exchanges support community programs such as technical discussion forums, blogs, interactive Webcasts, user-created product reviews, virtual conferences and meetings, experts' seminars, and user-managed profile pages. Classified ads can help members to find jobs or employers to find employees. Many also include industry news, directories, links to government and professional associations, and more.

- **Social networks sites.** These are megacommunities, such as MySpace, Facebook, LinkedIn, and Bebo, in which millions of unrelated members can express themselves, find friends, find jobs, exchange photos, view video tapes, and more (Sections 8.3 and 8.4).

Many thousands of communities exist on the Internet. Communities are growing rapidly. MySpace (see *IT at Work 1.4* in Chapter 1) grew to 100 million members in about a year. *A Closer Look 8.2* presents common types of online communities. Sections 8.3 through 8.6 present social networking types of communities.

Virtual communities can be classified in several other ways. One possibility is to classify the members as *traders, players, just friends, enthusiasts,* or *friends in need.* A more common classification is the one proposed by Hagel and Armstrong (1997). This classification (modified) recognizes the six types of Internet communities shown in Table 8.2. For issues of participation and design of communities, see *en.wikipedia.org/wiki/Virtual_community.* For a complete classification, see the classification proposed by Schubert and Ginsburg (2000).

Cashel (2001) proposed another classification of communities, identifying 10 specific niches within the online community space that are bucking the trend and demonstrating strong revenues. These 10 important trends include: (1) search communities, (2) trading communities, (3) education communities, (4) scheduled events communities, (5) subscriber-based communities, (6) community consulting firms, (7) e-mail-based communities, (8) advocacy communities, (9) CRM communities, and (10) mergers and acquisitions activities. See Cashel (2001) for details. One of the major types of virtual communities is the virtual world.

Example. In 2008 Sony Corporation launched a virtual community service for its PlayStation 3 (PS3) videogame network with 8 million members. The 3D service called Home allows users to create avatars, decorate homes, and interact and socialize with other users in a virtual world. Sony considers this an important part of the

TABLE 8.2	Types of Virtual Communities
Community Type	**Description**
Transaction and other business	Facilitates buying and selling (e.g., *ausfish.com.au*). Combines information portal with infrastructure for trading. Members are buyers, sellers, intermediaries, etc., focused on a specific commercial area (e.g., fishing).
Purpose or interest	No trading, just exchange of information on a topic of mutual interest. Examples: Investors consult The Motley Fool (*fool.com*) for investment advice; rugby fans congregate at the Fans Room at *nrl.com.au*; music lovers go to *mp3.com*; *geocities.yahoo.com* is a collection of several areas of interest in one place.
Relations or practices	Members are organized around certain life experiences. Examples: *ivillage.com* caters to women, *seniornet.com* to senior citizens. Professional communities also belong to this category. Examples: *isworld.org* for information systems faculty, students, and professionals.
Fantasy	Members share imaginary environments. Examples: sport fantasy teams at *espn.com*; GeoCities members can pretend to be medieval barons at *dir.yahoo.com/Recreation/games/role_playing_games/titles*. See *games.yahoo.com* for many more fantasy communities.
Social networks	Members communicate, collaborate, create, share, form smaller groups, entertain, and more. *MySpace.com* is the leader.
Virtual worlds	Members use avatars to represent them in a simulated 3D environment where they can play, conduct business, socialize, and fantasize.

game-playing experience. The avatars can interact with each other, and users can play games with friends at a virtual arcade. The community is regional due to language and cultural considerations. As an extension, the service allows downloading of content and movies to PS3.

VIRTUAL WORLDS

One of the most interesting Web 2.0 applications is the *virtual world*. A **virtual world** is a user-defined 3D world in which people can interact, play, and do business with the help of avatars (see White, 2008). Virtual worlds are computer-based simulated environments intended for its users to inhabit and interact via avatars. The world presents perceptual stimuli to the user, who in turn can manipulate elements of the modeled world. The model world may simulate rules based on the real world or some hybrid fantasy world. Example rules are gravity, topography, locomotion, real-time actions, and communication. Communication between users has ranged from text, graphical icons, visual gesture, sound, and, rarely, forms using touch and balance senses. Virtual worlds emerged from several concepts, primarily as an evolutionary process of virtual reality (*en.wikipedia.org/wiki/Virtual_worlds*) and massively multiplayer games (*en.wikipedia.org/wiki/Massively_multiplayer_online_game*). For example, one of the most popular online games, *World of Warcraft,* hosts millions of players connected on hundreds of servers worldwide. Its scenarios often encourage *team play* and the formation of "guilds" or groups of gamers who play and chat together. Virtual worlds, especially WebKinz and Club Penguin, are popular with children.

But virtual worlds are much more than just games. As a matter of fact, hosting companies such as Second Life function more as platforms than as supporters of games. Second Life users are given a framework (virtual real estate and construction tools) to create whatever they please from building houses to activities with parameters defined only by the user's imagination and fantasies (see Mansfield, 2008, and Rymaszewski, 2008). However, virtual worlds are much more than entertainment. They are used for education, art, socialization, and business as well (see examples in Second Life in *IT at Work 8.1*).

Virtual worlds in general and Second Life in particular have been receiving lots of attention lately as the educational, business, and entertainment uses in them are spreading (e.g., see Kaye, 2008; Robbins and Bell, 2008).

IT at Work 8.1

Second Life

In 2003, a 3-dimensional virtual world called Second Life was opened to the public. The world is entirely built and owned by its residents. In 2003, the virtual world consisted of 64 acres and by 2007 had grown to 65,000 acres and is inhabited by millions of residents from around the planet (*SecondLife.com*, 2008). The virtual world consists of a huge digital continent, people, entertainment, experiences, and opportunities.

Thousands of new residents join each day and *create their own avatars* through which they travel around the Second Life world meeting people, communicating, having fun, and buying virtual land and other virtual properties where they can open a business or build a personal space limited only by their imaginations and their ability to use the virtual 3-D applications (see Terdiman, 2008). Avatars have unique names and are moved around in imaginative vehicles including helicopters, submarines, and hot-air balloons.

Second Life is dedicated to creativity, and everything in Second Life is resident-created. Residents retain the rights to their digital creations and can buy, sell, and trade with other residents and are able to sell them at Second Life marketplaces. Residents can also socialize and participate in group activities. Businesses succeed by the ingenuity, artistic ability, entrepreneurial acumen, and the owners' reputation.

Residents get some free virtual land (and they can buy more) where they build houses or businesses. They can then sell the virtual properties or the virtual products or services they create. Residents can also sell real world products or services. For example, Copland and Kelleher (2007) report that more than 25,000 aspiring entrepreneurs trade virtual products or services at Second Life. Stevan Lieberman is one of these. He uses his expertise in intellectual property and the site to solicit work mainly from programmers who are looking to patent their codes.

Second Life is managed by Linden Labs, which provides Linden dollars that can be converted to U.S. dollars. Second Life uses several Web 2.0 tools such as blogs, wikis, RSS, and tags (from *del.icio.us*). These tools are described in Chapter 2.

Many organizations use Second Life for 3D presentations of their products. Even governments open virtual embassies on "Diplomacy Island," located on the site. Over 100 universities offer educational courses and seminars in virtual classrooms (see "EduIslands" on the site) and educators have forums to discuss how to use Second Life for teaching.

Roush (2007) describes how to combine Second Life with Google Earth. Such combinations enable investigation of phenomena that would otherwise be difficult to visualize or understand.

Real-world businesses use the virtual world, too. For example, IBM uses it as a location for meetings, training, and recruitment (Reuters, 2006). American Apparel is the first major retailer to set up shop in Second Life. Starwood Hotels uses Second Life as a relatively low-cost market research experiment in which avatars visit Starwood virtual Aloft hotel. While the endeavor has created publicity for the company, feedback on the design of the hotel is solicited from visiting avatars and will be reflected in brick and mortar when the first real-world Aloft hotels open in 2008 (Carr, 2007). The Mexican Tourism Board and Morocco Tourism are examples of 3D presentations of major tourist attractions. Many companies use Second Life as a hot place to go to try new business ideas (see Rosedale, 2007). For example, you can test drive a Toyota Scion, or examine toymakers prototype toys, and anyone can become a virtual architect.

Sources: Copeland and Kelleher (2007), Reuters (2006), Rosedale (2007), Roush (2007), and *secondlife.com* (accessed May 2008).

For Further Exploration: Enter the Second Life site (*secondlife.com*) and identify EC activities there. (You need to register for free and create an avatar.) Which types of transactions are observable at the site? Which business models are observable at the site? How can a university utilize the site? If you were a travel agent, how would you utilize the site? Have your avatar communicate with five others. Write a report on your experience.

Business Aspects of Virtual Worlds.   As seen in the Second Life case, there is an increased interest in the business opportunities in virtual worlds. Hof (2008) and Terdiman (2008) discuss the various opportunities of conducting business in Second Life. Specifically, Hof introduces seven residents who are already making a substantial amount of money. These include the Anshe Chung avatar which is known as the "Rockefeller of Second Life," who buys virtual land from Second Life, "develops" it, and sells or rents it globally. Her business has grown so rapidly that she employs 20 people who design and program the development projects.

According to Alter (2008), the research firm Gartner Media estimates that, by 2011, 80 percent of all Internet users worldwide will have avatars, making animated online persons as common as e-mail and screen names today. This means that there will be a need for many jobs to provide support for virtual worlds.

An interesting business activity is for the students to make money in virtual worlds, especially if they cannot get summer (or other) jobs, as described in *A Closer Look 8.3*.

A Closer Look 8.3

Summer Jobs in Virtual Worlds

Can't find a summer job in the real world? Try the *virtual world* one. With summer jobs in short supply, more young people are pursuing money-making opportunities in virtual worlds. According to Alter (2008), a new breed of young entrepreneurs is honing their computer skills to capitalize on the growing demand for virtual goods and services.

Alter provides examples of six young and successful entrepreneurs:

1. Mike Mikula, 17. His avatar Mike Denneny in Teen Second Life helps him earn $4,000 per month as a builder and renovator of sites at Second Life, using graphic design tools. He acts as an architect of virtual buildings.

2. Ariella Furman, 21. She earns $2,000 to $4,000 per month using her avatar Ariella Languish in Second Life. She sticks to business suits to dress her avatars, and wants to capture how people live and socialize in Second Life. She specializes in assisting video and film making.

3. John Eikenberry, 25. His avatar Lordfly Digeridoo in Second Life earns $2,000 to $4,000 per month. He builds entire Second Life neighborhoods that spread malls, coffee shops, and even an auditorium over 16 landscaped acres called regions.

4. Kristina Koch, 17. Kristina is a character designer. Her avatar Silver Bu in Teen Second Life earns $600 to $800 per month. Using the Second Life tools, she adds such effects as shadows to avatars. She and her boyfriend design and sell virtual fairy wings and wizard's robes to dress avatars.

5. Mike Everest, 18. Mike is a virtual hunter and trader, selling the skins of what he hunts. His avatar Ogulak Da Basher in the virtual world of Entropia Universe earns $200 to $1,000 per month. He's the family's money maker and was able to finance his brother's college education. He learned to transform virtual ore into virtual weapons that he sells.

6. Andy and Michael Ortman, 19. These twin brothers are inventors. Their avatars Alpha Zaius and Ming Chen in Teen Second Life earn about $2,500 per month each. Both are engineering majors, working for Deep Think Labs, a virtual world development company based in Australia. They program Open Simulator, which allows companies and individuals to hold private meetings and training sessions in virtual environments similar to Second Life.

Sources: Compiled from Alter (2008) and Hof (2008).

For more on the business aspects of virtual worlds, see Hof (2008) and Robbins and Bell (2007). A major category of virtual communities is social networking and social networking sites, which we present next.

Review Questions

1. Define *virtual (Internet) communities* and describe their characteristics.
2. List the major categories of virtual communities.
3. Define a virtual world.
4. Describe Second Life.
5. How is business done in a virtual world?

8.3 Online Social Networking: Basics and Examples

CONCEPTS AND DEFINITIONS

As you may recall, we defined a **social network** as a place where people create their own space, or home page, on which they write blogs (web logs); post pictures, videos, or music; share ideas; and link to other Web locations they find interesting. Social networkers tag the content they post with keywords they choose themselves, which makes their content searchable. In effect, they create online communities of people with similar interests. The mass adoption of social networking Web sites points to an evolution in human social interaction (Weaver and Morrison, 2008).

A *social network* is basically a social structure made of nodes that are usually individuals or small groups. It indicates the ways in which individuals are connected through various social familiarities ranging from casual acquaintance to close familial bonds.

Social Network Theory. Social network theory views social relationships in terms of *nodes* and *ties*. Nodes are the individual actors within the networks, and ties are the relationships between the actors. There can be many kinds of ties between the nodes. In its simplest form, a social network is a map of all of the relevant ties between the nodes being studied. The network can also determine the social assets of individuals. Often, a social network diagram displays these concepts, where nodes are the points and ties are the lines.

Social Networking Services. To participate in social networking, people must join a company that provides the services described earlier. Such a company is called **social network service** or *social network site* (abbreviated as SNS). Examples of SNSs are Facebook, MySpace, and Bebo. They are frequently referred to as just *social networks*.

Social network analysis (SNA) is the mapping and measuring of relationships and flows between people, groups, organizations, computers, or other information or knowledge processing entities. The nodes in the network are the people and the groups, whereas the links show relationships or flows between the nodes. SNA provides both a visual and a mathematical analysis of relationships.

Social Networking Tools. There are many tools that are used in social networks; the most advertised are blogs and wikis. Other tools are presented in Chapter 4. For more details on these tools, see Online Brief 8.1.

REPRESENTATIVE SOCIAL NETWORK SERVICES

There are thousands of social networks services with many added each week. (For a list of the major sites including user count, see *en.wikipedia.org/wiki/List_of_social_networking_websites.*)

Here, we provide a small list of representative Web sites with minimal details (details are changing frequently). The Wikipedia Web site (*wikipedia.org*), where content is constantly updated, describes all of these companies. Further information is available at the social networking Web sites and in books such as the "For Dummies" series. Finally, we present six SNSs in more detail in Section 8.4.

Representative Social Networking Web Sites. Today there are thousands of social network services around the globe. Here are some popular sites.

Classmates Online. Classmates Online (*classmates.com*) helps members find, connect, and keep in touch with friends and acquaintances from throughout their lives—including kindergarten, primary school, high school, college, work, and the U.S. military. Classmates Online has more than 40 million active members in the United States and Canada.

It is free for people to register as a Basic member of Classmates Online in order to list themselves to be found and to search the entire database for friends. Members may also post photographs, announcements, biographies, read community message boards, and be informed of upcoming reunions. Gold members, who pay a fee, can also initiate sending e-mail to any member, use Web site tools for planning reunions and events, and form private groups and use My Network to communicate with friends. Owned by United Online, the company itself owns social networking companies in Germany and Sweden. The site is profitable.

Friendster. Friendster (*friendster.com*) is based on the Circle of Friends technique for networking individuals in virtual communities and demonstrates the small-world phenomenon.

Friendster was considered the top online social network service until around April 2004, when it was overtaken by MySpace. Friendster has also received competition from all-in-one sites (sites that offer a diversity of services), such as Windows Live Spaces and Facebook. Generally speaking, the members of Friendster's service are young adults in Europe, North America, and Asia about 21 to 30 years old. (For more details on Friendster, see Online Minicase 8.2.)

Xanga. Xanga (*xanga.com*) is a Web site that hosts Weblogs, photoblogs, and social networking profiles. It is operated by Xanga.com, Inc. Users of Xanga are referred to as "Xangans." Xanga's origins can be traced back to 1998, when it began as a site for sharing book and music reviews. It has since then evolved into one of the most popular blogging and networking services on the Web, with an estimated 27 million users worldwide (see *en.wikipedia.org/wiki/Xanga*).

A blogring connects a circle of Weblogs with a common focus or theme. All Xanga users are given the ability to create a new blogring or join an existing one. Blogrings are searchable by topic. A list of blogrings that the user is associated with appears in a module typically on the left side of the Web site. Each user is allowed a maximum of eight blogrings.

Digg. Digg (*digg.com*) is a community-based popularity Web site with an emphasis on technology and science articles; see *en.wikipedia.org/wiki/Digg*. The site has recently expanded to provide a variety of other categories such as politics and videos. It combines social bookmarking, blogging, and syndication with a form of nonhierarchical, democratic editorial control. Users submit news stories and Web sites, and then a user-controlled ranking system promotes these stories and sites to the front page. This differs from the hierarchical editorial system that many other news sites employ. When you read many news items, you can see an option "digg it" or "digg that."

Readers can view all of the stories that fellow users have submitted in the "digg/All/ Upcoming" section of the site. Once a story has received enough "diggs," it appears on Digg's front page. Should the story not receive enough diggs, or if enough users report a problem with the submission, the story will remain in the "digg all" area, where it may eventually be removed. For further details, see *en.wikipedia.org/wiki/Digg* and Heilemann (2006).

Some Other Social Network Sites. The following sites are interesting:

Piczo.com—popular in Canada and the United Kingdom; it is a teen-friendly site designed to deter perverts.

His.com—most popular in Mexico and Spain; it is a major competitor of MySpace.

Reunion.com—connects alumni of schools and organizes reunions; it owns several related Web sites.

Hi5.com—a very diversified global, multilanguage social network popular in Asia, Europe, Africa, and South America.

Friendsreunited.co.uk—similar to Reunion.com; it is the U.K. version where users can also find dating and job-search sites.

Iwiw.net—a Hungarian social network with a multilingual interface.

Migente.com—focuses on the America Latino community.

Blackplanet.com—focuses on African American issues and people.

Grono.net—a Poland-based social network.

Ning.com—provides a platform for users to create their own social networks.

Xing.com—a network where millions of business professionals (over 17,000 groups in July 2008) meet, converse in 16 languages, and generate and find contacts.

One of the most popular social networks is YouTube, which is described in detail in Online Minicase 8.3 and is changing the media and advertising industries. Related to this are the activities in the area of entertainment that are described in Online Brief 8.2. Several representative SNSs are described in the next section.

Review Questions

1. Define social network.
2. Define social network analysis and services.
3. Describe Digg.

8.4 Major Social Network Services: From Facebook to Flickr

Now that you are familiar with social network services, let's look at some of them, detailing each one's distinctive characteristics.

FACEBOOK: THE NETWORK EFFECT

Facebook is the second largest social networkin the world, with more than 70 million active users (Spring 2008). Facebook was launched in 2004 by a former Harvard student, Mark Zuckerberg. Photos, groups, events, marketplace, posted items, and notes are the basic applications already installed in Facebook. Apart from these basic applications, users can develop their own applications or add any of the millions of Facebook-available applications that have been developed by other users. In addition, Facebook owns two special features called "news feed" and "mini-feed" that allow users to track the movement of friends in their social circles. For example, when a person changes his profile, the updates are broadcast to others who subscribe to the feed. Facebook also launched an application called "People You May Know" that helps new users connect with their old friends (Vander Veer, 2008).

When Zuckerberg first created Facebook, he had very strong social ambitions and aimed at helping people connect to others on the Web. Facebook was initially an online social space for college and high school students. It started by automatically connecting students to all others at the same school. In 2006, Facebook opened its doors to anyone 13 or older with a valid e-mail address. The lack of privacy controls (e.g., tools that restrict who sees your profile) has been the biggest reason why many business people resisted joining Facebook. In 2008, Facebook introduced new controls that allow users to set different levels of access to information about themselves for each of their groups (e.g., family, friends from school, friends from work, non-friends who placed you into "friending" that they created at Facebook and attracted friends to join). For example, close friends might see your mobile phone number, music favorites, e-mail address, and so forth, while other friends might see only the basics of your resume (Abram and Pearlman, 2008).

Facebook is also expanding to the rest of the world. Two-thirds of its 90 million members from outside the United States Facebook adopted a wiki-like approach to translate itself into other languages: Engineers first collected thousands of English words and phrases throughout the site and invited members to translate those bits of text into another language. Members then rate translations until a consensus is reached. The Spanish version was done by about 1,500 volunteers in less than a month. The German version was done by 2,000 volunteers in less than two weeks. In early March 2008, Facebook invited French members to help out. They did the translations in a few days. The team is continuing to build the translation for other languages, even relatively small ones (Kirkpatrick, 2008).

A primary reason that Facebook expands is the network effect: that is, more users mean more value. The more users involved in the social space, the more they can connect to other people. Facebook realized that by only focusing on college and university users, they could keep them for only four years. However, such expansion means a direct competition with MySpace, and losing its original concentration in high schools and colleges.

Facebook is encouraging organizations to open pages where they can couduct advertisements and promotions (see the Scion case, Chapter 1). Also, the site is open to developers who create applications both for entertainment and business.

BEBO

Bebo (*bebo.com*), an acronym for the phrase "blog early, blog often," was launched in January 2005 and skyrocketed to one of the foremost social networking platforms online today. Based out of San Francisco, Bebo boasts a usership of over 40 million, making billions of page views per month.

Bebo was acquired by AOL for $850 million in March 2008. This places the site alongside MySpace and YouTube, other Web sites that were acquired by media conglomerates for enormous sums of money despite possessing mostly intangible property. Similar to Facebook and MySpace, Bebo provides a canvas for users to display personal profiles using such media as photos, diaries, music, embedded video, commercial applications, quizzes, and so forth. It allows its users to add other users as friends who can view their profiles and post messages. Bebo adopts a private setting whenever a new friend is added. This limits the friend's access to information on the user's profile unless special authorization by the owner is granted. This tactic ensures more privacy for its users, which has been an early issue among social networking sites.

As the evolution of social networking sites progresses, Bebo has certainly kept pace while maintaining standards of quality and security. Growth areas include the network medium, corporate partners, available applications, and geographic distribution.

During 2007 and 2008 wireless became the big trend in social networking sites. For example, MySpace has signed as partners with ten wireless providers in the United States, Facebook is available on seven wireless carriers in both the United States and Canada, and Bebo has joined forces with O2 Wireless in the United Kingdom and Ireland. This phenomenon is just the next step in the race to establish access to social networking sites across multiple media. Some argue that these deals do more to sell mobile phones than to promote the Web site; however, the social networks are more than happy to collect the residual attention.

Growth has also been seen in the media applications available on Bebo profiles. The applications have grown to include audio track and embedded video and flash games. Obviously, the more popular and exclusive the applications, the better it is for the total usership. Bebo's corporate partners play a major role in developing optional applications for users to include on their profiles in order to fulfill their own interests, making Bebo's job easier.

A key challenge currently facing Bebo is penetrating the North American market where MySpace and Facebook are both deeply entrenched. The concept of social networking sites is so new and has so many more directions in which to grow, that the notion of this market becoming mature seems odd. However, the torrid pace by which these sites grow could make it necessary for Bebo to jostle its way into other geographical markets in order to maintain its phenomenal growth rate. This would eventually mean direct competition with sites popular in North America or other foreign markets such as Europe, Asia, and Latin America. Just recently, Bebo has pursued this agenda by launching a Polish version, with plans for both French and German versions in the near future.

In order to facilitate such competition, Bebo strategists would need to pay close attention to the switching behavior of users of social networks and the key motivations for joining in the first place.

CRAIGSLIST: A TRADING FLOOR OF THE CYBER REVOLUTION

A young, former software engineer based in San Francisco quickly turns a small online start-up into a multi-million dollar Web phenomenon. Haven't we heard this story somewhere before? Of course we did. The unconventional business opportunities that the Web creates have resulted in this unlikely narrative coming to pass strikingly often. Such is the case for Craigslist founder, Craig Newmark.

Newmark began Craigslist (*craigslist.org*) in 1995 merely as a weekend activity. It was meant to be used only as a corner on the Web where friends and colleagues from the Bay area could post items for sale or barter, but like many Internet phenomenon, once enough users got their hooks into it, it grew far beyond anything Newmark had initially anticipated.

Within less than a decade, Craigslist became the most authoritative e-classifieds service. Classified listings include housing, jobs, personals, erotic services, for sale/wanted, and local activities, all of which are easily searchable by urban location. More than 450 cities in 50 countries are available. New urban areas are being added every week. Finally, 30 million new ads are added per month; that number is sure to be out of date by the time this book goes to print. The site is free to use, as is posting ads, except for a small number of job ads and rental availability in a few select areas.

Craigslist has revolutionized traditional commerce by facilitating direct buyer–seller interaction for free in an online context. The free posting, immediacy of the Internet, and sheer scope of buyers and sellers allows for goods and services to be found, bought, and/or exchanged far more quickly than any physical market could allow. This levels the playing field for small businesses looking for a fast and cheap way to promote their business.

Fans and advocates of Craigslist applaud its altruistic and noncommercial nature. The unobtrusive moderation of ads and user movement is a welcome respite from an online environment where one seemingly can't go two page-views without being bombarded by online ads. The deadpan gray color of the homepage and its basic ".org" domain contribute to its grassroots appeal. Establishing a noncorporate culture is a value for Newmark, who now acts merely as a customer service rep for the site; however, some say the site is missing out on millions of dollars of potential revenue by not going the way of Facebook and selling ad space or consumer information. Newmark so far has resisted an onslaught of advertising offers and multi-million dollar buy-outs. An exception is eBay, which has a 25 percent stake in the company.

Official financial revenue for Craigslist is unknown, but best estimates place it at a modest $150 million in 2007. That's a mere fraction of the $1.6 billion that the founders of YouTube were paid by Google.

Further questions regarding the future of Craigslist have to do with the very hands-off mentality that made Craigslist famous. The issue is of users posting illegitimate and possibly illegal ads and the inability of Craigslist staff to fully police such matters. Some users have complained over questionable ads being posted, especially in the "jobs" section. This would include pyramid schemes and beneath-the-counter work. Craigslist is also a stomping ground for criminals seeking to commit fraud by way of misleading gullible traders into accepting false checks. Some con artists knowingly overpay for items via checks and then arrange to have the overpaid amount wired back to them by the seller, just before it is discovered that the check was never good to begin with. The seller would now be without the money "refunded" as well as the item sold. The anonymity of Craigslist users and the lack of ratings systems create an environment where deceitful users could not be held accountable for their actions.

Another serious cause of concern is the use of Craigslist for the promotion and solicitation of underage prostitution. Erotic services make up a significant portion of the total traffic on the site, and it has been feared that a number of the encounters facilitated using Craigslist have been with underage girls. With the sheer volume of users and ads posted per day, such policing is not possible, given the modest workforce of only 22 that the site employs.

In addition, many supporters contend that attempts to control Craigslist may simply cause users to relocate to a different, less-regulated site. Surely the design of Craigslist shouldn't be too difficult to duplicate. However, its brand is extremely strong.

ORKUT: EXPLORING THE VERY NATURE OF SOCIAL NETWORKING SITES

Orkut.com was the brainchild of a Turkish Google programmer of the same name. Orkut was to be Google's homegrown answer to MySpace and Facebook. Orkut follows a format similar to that of other major social networking sites: a homepage where users can display every facet of their personal life they desire, using various multimedia applications including embedded videos, detailed personal information, flash games, and diary applications.

A major highlight of Orkut is the individual power afforded to those who create their own groups and forums called "communities" on the site, The autonomy over who can join and how posts are edited and controlled lies solely in the hands of the creator of that community. Moderating an Orkut community is comparable to moderating ones' own site, given all of the authority the creator possesses as to design and control of content. This phenomenon gives users substantial experience with Web 2.0 tools, creating an enormous wave of online proficiency which is sure to contribute to the development of the online environment.

Initially aiming to reach an audience primarily in the United States, Orkut has in fact flourished in more unlikely parts of the world. Orkut is the most visited Web site in Brazil, where 67.5 percent of its traffic comes from, and is the second most visited Web site in India, where it gets 15.4 percent of its traffic. Orkut has had a strong following even in the Middle East (de Mel, 2008). Orkut has found its primary following in these regions an unexpected home, however. Google is no doubt pleased with its unintentional success.

This situation has brought its fair share of issues. A number of cultural objections to social networking sites have created controversy for Orkut in various parts of the world. With these cultural controversies, Orkut is being forced to make moral decisions about what the rights and responsibilities of a social networking site are, both legally and morally.

The nature of the Web allows for freedom of expression; however, this is not the most cherished value of a handful of foreign governments and cultures. Freedom of expression can convey negative comments and blasphemy as well. This has caused a number of incidents in India where local governments have called for the banning of social networking sites, specifically Orkut, where hate groups exist and are difficult to control due to freedom of speech. The government of Iran has banned the use of Orkut, citing national security worries and the dangers of online match-making. Proxy Orkut sites have popped up in the Middle East in response to the state censorship, proving that the will of the users ultimately determines how and where online networking takes place. That is the power of the Web.

Orkut recognizes that it is the users who dictate the actions of their chosen social networking site. Given this, Orkut has adapted in a number of ways. It has plans to add to its offered languages, expanding with Hindi, Bengali, Marathi, Tamil, and Telugu sites. The site habitually greets its users on national holidays with fun features. For example, it wished Indian users a Happy Diwali (*en.wikipedia.org/wiki/Diwali*) by providing a feature that allowed users to redesign their personal site with Diwali-themed colors and decorations.

Orkut is especially popular in Brazil where about 30 million members participate in Portuguese (Brazil's official language); the magnitude of this many members created a legal problem. In 2006, a Brazilian judge ordered Google to release the user information of more than 20 Brazilians who were suspected of distributing drugs or child pornography, or having links to hate speech. The judge ordered that Google be fined $23,000 for every day that the information was not divulged. However, as Google servers are in the United States and not Brazil, the low court in Brazil agreed that Google is not subject to Brazilian law. (The issue had not been resolved by the time this book was written in July 2008.) One can imagine that had Google divulged the information, it would have set a precedent and created many questions as to what would constitute means for release of information.

FLICKR TICKS OFF SOME OF ITS USERS

Flickr was created by a small Vancouver-based company called Ludicorp. Users of the photo-networking site Flickr are accustomed to adding new friends to their online profiles. The site, which allows for the storage and organization of photos, was launched in 2004 and drew fans who were seeking a place to manage and share their photos. Users require an individual account in order to add friends to their network and share their photos. One of the first Web 2.0 applications ever, Flickr today (May 2008) hosts more than two billion images.

When Yahoo! acquired Flickr in 2005, users were initially not required to obtain a Yahoo account in order to login to their Flickr profile; however, two years later Yahoo! required Flickr's users to register with Yahoo! This stipulation ruffled many feathers with existing users who would prefer to have the content of their Flickr account separate from their Yahoo! account. The nature of one's photos, due to matters of privacy or for commercial protection, is the cause for more concern over security. Some users felt that having the accounts separate would create a safer and more comfortable environment. It would also mean that Flickr users would not be susceptible to Yahoo's terms and conditions, nor accessible to Yahoo's group of advertisers. The switch is claimed to be a strategy to simply limit the costs of maintaining an independent means of authentication; however, existing users suspect corporate interests are to be credited for the restriction.

Controversy arises over the fact that the original users of Flickr were the very reason Flickr had become valuable enough to sell. Had these original users not chosen Flickr, there would not have been any talk of Yahoo! purchasing the site at all. Why now are these grassroots members being treated as common customers?

The organized displeasure over the continuing association between Flickr and media giant Yahoo! is a testament to the communal nature of Flickr users. A petition site was created called Flickoff in response to the stipulation, where original users showed solidarity in denouncing Yahoo's intentions.

Despite some displeasure with corporate ownership and everything that comes with it, Flickr users now enjoy far more applications than could have been provided had the site still been run by Ludicorp. The upload restrictions of 2GB have been removed for users with paid ProAccounts, and users with free accounts can now add up to 100 MB instead of 20 MB. As of April 2008, users can add video clips up to 90 seconds long as well as photos.

Review Questions

1. Apart from the privacy control, what other factors inhibit adults to join Facebook?
2. Much of Facebook's early success was due to the close affiliation of its members' networks. How does Facebook expand into new markets without losing what originally made the site popular and alienating their existing users?
3. What strategies should Bebo pursue in order to compete head-on with other social networking sites?
4. Picture yourself as a Bebo strategist. How would you go about further expanding the site?
5. If Craigslist were to pursue more commercial activity and revenue streams such as tracking user information and selling targeted ad space, what effect would it have upon usership? Would any increased revenue offset any potential disadvantages?
6. Is it possible for Web sites to "go corporate" while retaining their grassroots credibility?
7. Can Craigslist be responsible for the content of the ads posted on its site? If yes, what should the extent of that responsibility include?
8. What steps could Craigslist take to better inform users as to the integrity of ads posted?
9. What makes Orkut different from other social networks?
10. How should Orkut respond to demands of local governments that culturally disapprove of some ideas and practices of social networking sites?
11. Who ultimately deserves the credit for the success of Flickr as a social networking site: the founding developers, initial users, corporate backers, or others?
12. How might Flickr garner the favor of its original members rather than their criticism regarding the Yahoo deal?
13. Most SNSs now offer the services of Flickr. Will this cause the demise of Flickr?

8.5 Business (Enterprise) Social Networks

In Chapter 1 we introduced a business-oriented network named Xing.com. Here, we describe some other similar networks.

BUSINESS-ORIENTED SOCIAL NETWORKS

A **business network** is defined as a group of people that have some kind of commercial or business relationship—for example, the relationships between sellers and buyers, buyers among themselves, buyers and suppliers, and colleagues and other colleagues. They are also referred to as business social networks or enterprise social networks. Business networking functions best when individuals offer to help others to find connections rather than "cold-calling" on prospects themselves (see *en.wikipedia.org/wiki/Business_network*). Business networking can take place outside of traditional business physical environments. For example, public places such as airports or golf courses provide opportunities to make new business contacts if an individual has good social skills. Similarly, the Internet is also proving to be a good place to network.

Example: LinkedIn. The main purpose of LinkedIn is to allow registered users to maintain a list of contact details of people they know and trust in business (see *en.wikipedia.org/wiki/LinkedIn*). The people in the list are called *connections*. Users can invite anyone, whether he or she is a LinkedIn user or not, to become a connection. Barak Obama is a connection there.

Here is how the site works:

• A contact network is built up consisting of users' direct connections, each of their connections' connections (called second-degree connections), and also the connections of second-degree connections (called third-degree connections). This can be used, for example, to gain an introduction to someone you wish to know through a mutual, trusted contact. LinkedIn's officials are members and have hundreds of connections each (see Copeland, 2006, and *linkdin.com*).

• LinkedIn can then be used to find jobs, people, and business opportunities recommended by anyone in your contact network. It can be used also to list job seekers' resumes.

• Employers can list jobs and search for potential candidates.

• Job seekers can review the profiles of hiring managers and discover which of their existing contacts can introduce them to a specific hiring manager.

The "gated-access approach," where contact with any professional requires either a preexisting relationship or the intervention of a mutual contact, is intended to build trust among the service's users. LinkedIn participates in the EU Safe Harbor Privacy Framework.

As of January 2007, LinkedIn featured "LinkedIn Answers." As the name suggests, the service is similar to Answers.com or Yahoo! Answers. The service allows LinkedIn users to ask questions for the community to answer. "LinkedIn Answers" is free, and the questions are usually business-oriented.

For more on LinkedIn and its capabilities and success, see Elad, 2008. One class of business networks deals with entrepreneurship.

Entrepreneurial Networks. In business, *entrepreneurial networks* are social organizations offering different types of resources to start or improve entrepreneurial projects. Combined with leadership, the entrepreneurial network is an indispensable kind of social network not only necessary to properly run the business or project but also to differentiate the business from similar ones.

The goal of most entrepreneurial networks is to bring together a broad selection of professionals and resources that complement each others' endeavors (see *en.wikipedia.org/wiki/Entrepreneurial_network*). Initially, a key priority is to aid successful business launches. Subsequently, the networks provide motivation, direction, and increased access to opportunities and other skill sets. Promotion of each member's talents and services both within the network and out in the broader market increases opportunities for all participants.

One of the key needs of any start-up is capital, and often entrepreneurial networks focus on help in obtaining financial resources particularly tailored to their membership demographic. Entrepreneurial networks may be involved in endorsing reforms, legislation, or other municipal drives that accommodate their organization's goals.

Examples of entrepreneurial networks are the following:

• Ecademy.com (*ecademy.com*) is a global social network for business people. There you can build trust with business professionals; share contacts, knowledge, and support; find jobs, prospects and clients; attend networking events; and trade across the globe.

• European young professionals (*eyplondon.org*) promotes links between European business professionals.

CHARACTERISTICS AND ACTIVITIES OF ENTERPRISE SOCIAL NETWORKS

An increasing number of companies create their own social networks for their employees, former employees, and/or customers. There are several formats for creating such entities, depending on their purpose, the industry, the country, and so forth.

Example. Wachovia (*wachovia.com*) is a large financial banking holding company. Wachovia introduced its social networking service to its 110,000 employees in early 2008. Like the popular Facebook service, the network allows users to upload photos of themselves—not just corporate ID mug-shots either—and personal information. Community-building across the vast company is one of the goals.

The purpose of this network is all business. Think of it as a nervous system for the enterprise, one that gets more valuable the more it's used. Wachovia envisions a sophisticated knowledge-management platform integrated with multiple applications to let workers locate information—and the people who use it—simply and intuitively. In July 2008, participation of employees was voluntary. Look up co-workers, and you can see their relationships to other employees and departments, and determine their availability at any given moment as well. Search for the best practices on topics, and review blogs and wikis written by informed employees, along with an in-house encyclopedia (similar to Pfizerpedia.com described earlier) of all things; all are available at Wachovia. People use the social network in many imaginative ways.

Interfacing with Social Networking. Enterprises can interface with social networking in several ways. Such interfaces create **enterprise social networks,** meaning that companies are conducting enterpreneurial social networking activities in one or more ways. One way is participating in business-oriented networks, such as LinkedIn or entrepreneurial networks (both types described earlier). There are several other ways in which companies can interface with social networking. The major ones are shown in Figure 8.3 and are described briefly next.

The major interfaces include the following:

• Utilize existing public social networks, such as Facebook, MySpace, or virtual worlds such as Second Life. Companies can create pages and micro communities (subgroups), and advertise products or services there, post a request for advice, announce job openings, and so forth. (For many examples, see Weber, 2007, and Demopoulos, 2007.)

• Create an in-house private social network and then use it for communication and collaboration among employees and retirees, or with outsiders (e.g., customers, suppliers, designers). Employees create virtual rooms in their company's social networks

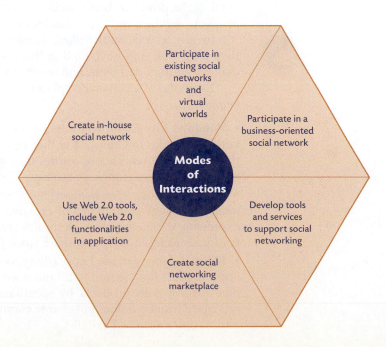

Figure 8.3 Typical modes of interaction with social networks.

where they can use applications to share information (e.g., see *wiki.oracle.com*).

- Conduct several business activities in a social network where the primary objective is business-oriented (such as LinkedIn, Spoke, or Xing), or sponsor such a site.
- Create services for social networks such as developing software, providing security devices, consulting services, and more (e.g., Oracle, IBM, Microsoft).
- Use Web 2.0 tools, mostly blogs, wikis, workspaces, and team rooms; create innovative applications for them for both internal and external users (see the minicase at the end of this chapter).
- Create and/or participate in a social marketplace (such as *fotila.com*).

Many large corporation including IBM, Coca Cola, Sony, Cisco, and Deloitte Touche have developed innovative in-house social networks. Others create groups within MySpace or other social networks (see Weber, 2007; Demopoulos, 2007; and Cone, 2007b, for many examples). For a more detailed description of one innovative application used for recruiting, see Online Brief 8.3.

Some corporate-based social networks do not fly. They simply do not attract enough members and/or visitors. An example is Wal-Mart (see Section 8.6).

Enterprise 2.0. Enterprise social networking, including the various ways that companies interact with Web 2.0 tools and social networks, resulted in an IT strategy that moved companies to be not only digital enterprises, but *enterprises 2.0*. **Enterprise 2.0** refers to Web 2.0-style collaboration via blogs and wikis. Hoover (2007) provides the following examples of Enterprise 2.0: Motorola uses 3,900 blogs; Procter & Gamble uses Microsoft SharePoint and Office Communications for the company's 140,000 employees, many of whom use blogs; Wells Fargo uses blogs throughout the enterprise, as do thousands of other corporations. According to an InformationWeek survey (see Hoover, 2007), the most useful Web 2.0 tools in Enterprise 2.0 are instant messaging (69 percent), collaborative tools (61 percent), integrated search tools (56 percent), unified communication (49 percent), wikis (47 percent), and mashups (43 percent). Ajax, RSS, blogs, and presence awareness are 30 to 40 percent each. The major concerns in Enterprise 2.0 are security (64 percent), lack of expertise (56 percent), integration with existing IT systems (52 percent), and difficulty in proving ROI (51 percent). For more on Enterprise 2.0, see McAfee (2006).

SOCIAL MARKETPLACES

The term **social marketplace** is derived from the combination of social networking and marketplaces, such that a social marketplace acts like an online community harnessing the power of one's social networks for introducing, buying, and selling of products, services, and resources, including people's own creations.

Ideally, a social marketplace should enable members' own creations as much as they blog, link, and post. Online Brief 8.2 describes a market for musicians, filmmakers, authors, designers, and other creative individuals.

Examples of social marketplaces include (per *en.wikipedia.org/wiki/Social_marketplace*):

- **Windows Live Expo.** Windows Live Expo (*expo.live.com*) is an online social marketplace similar to Craigslist in that it provides online classifieds. A major focus of the site is that users choose listings they want to search sorted either by friends and contacts or by geographic proximity.
- **Fotolia.** Fotolia (*fotolia.com*) is a social marketplace for royalty-free stock images—a huge community of creative people who enjoy sharing, learning, and expressing themselves through forums and blogs, allowing other individuals and professionals to legally buy and share stock images and illustrations.
- **Flipsy.** Anyone can use Flipsy (*flipsy.com*) to list, buy, and sell books, music, movies, and games. It was created to fill the need for a free and trustworthy media marketplace. Flipsy sells products by identification using bar codes. In order to foster increased trading, it does not charge commissions. Payment processing is handled by a third party, such as PayPal.

Review Questions

1. Define a business network.
2. Describe LinkedIn and its capabilities.
3. Define entrepreneurial network.
4. Describe enterprise-based social networks.
5. List six ways organizations can interface with Web 2.0 tools and social networks.
6. Define a social marketplace.

8.6 Commercial Aspects of Web 2.0 Applications and Social Networks

Web 2.0 sites, especially social networks and similar communities, attract a large number of visitors. Therefore they provide an opportunity for vendors to advertise and sell to community members.

WHY IS THERE AN INTEREST?

Web 2.0 applications and especially social networks attract a huge number of visitors. Furthermore, they are spreading rapidly, and many of them cater to a specific *segment* of the population (e.g., music lovers, travelers, game lovers, cars fans, etc.). Finally, a large proportion of the visitors is young—but in the future will grow up and will have more money to spend (see Regan, 2006, for a discussion). For these reasons, many believe that social networks, blogging, and other Web 2.0 activities will play a major role in the future of e-commerce. In the following sections, we will cover a few areas where success is already evidenced.

Retailers stand to benefit from online communities in several important ways:

- Consumers can be a source of feedback (similar to a focus group) on existing product features, new product design, and features on marketing and advertising campaigns, and how well customer service and support are performing, which can lead to innovation for a retailer.
- Brand awareness, such as at Toyota's Scion case (chapter 1), is a major objective, of many companies. This way the social aspects are maintained and the commercial objectives are not evidenced.
- Word-of-mouth (i.e., *viral marketing*) is free advertising that increases the visibility of niche retailers and products.
- Increased Web site traffic, a common effect of viral marketing, inevitably brings with it more ad dollars.
- Increased sales can come from harnessing techniques based on personal preferences such as collaborative filtering; at a more advanced level, retailers strive for a higher degree of relevance in matching the knowledge of one person to someone of like interests who has a need to know (the "twinsumer" concept).

All of the above may result in revenue and profit. *IT at Work 8.2* illustrates some of the potential revenue sources of EC social networks.

ADVERTISING

A large number of advertisers are already placing ads on MySpace and YouTube or are using Google AdSense with user searches in social networking sites. The following areas are developing.

Viral (Word-of-Mouth) Marketing. Young adults are especially good at viral marketing. What they like can spread very quickly, sometimes to millions of people at a minimal cost to companies (e.g., see Weber, 2007). One example is YouTube. The company conducted almost no advertising in the first months of its inception, but millions joined. Similarly, if members like a certain product or service, word-of-mouth advertising works rapidly. Note that SpiralFrog.com (*spiralfrog.com*) provides free downloads of songs; instead of paying money for Apple's iTunes, you need to watch ads to obtain the free songs. The company aims at mobile phones only.

IT at Work 8.2

Revenue Sources at YouTube

Some people think that Google paid too much for YouTube, especially in light of their copyright-related legal problems (see Online Minicase 8.3). The opposite may be true. Consider these examples:

1. **Two minute YouTube clips were just the start.** As television comes to the Internet, dozens of companies are gunning to become the networks of tomorrow. Where the ants go, advertisers are expected to follow. YouTube's ad-revenue potential in 2007 alone has been pegged at $200 million by Citigroup. And wherever there's video programming, viewers will be seeing more video ads. One forecast from research firm eMarketer calls for overall video advertising on the Web (including video ads replacing banners on regular Web pages) to hit $2.9 billion in 2010, a sevenfold leap from the 2006 tally of $410 million (Schonfeld, 2007).

2. **Brand-created entertainment content.** In 2005, Nike produced a pseudo home digital video of soccer star Ronaldinho, practicing while wearing his new Nike Gold shoes. The clip was downloaded 3.5 million times on YouTube in one week worldwide and provided Nike with tremendous exposure to its core mostly young male audience. As the young generation moves away from traditional TV, it dedicates its time to watching the likes of YouTube. Videos about the U.S. 2008 presidential candidates were downloaded by millions, and so were videos of the Beijing 2008 Olympics.

3. **User-driven product advertising.** User-generated videos could be leveraged in a fashion similar to product placement on TV. Although not intentional, the use of Logitech's Webcam features on a short clip by a 17-year-old girl talking about the breakup with her boyfriend was viewed by YouTube users and greatly contributed to the awareness of Logitech's offering. The product placement trend is also expanding across the blogosphere, with Nokia, for example, promoting its N90 phone through the 50 most influential bloggers in Belgium and establishing a blogger relationship blog.

4. **Multichannel word-of-mouth campaign.** When Chevrolet decided to combine its *Apprentice* Tahoe Campaign with an online consumer-generated media (CGM) campaign, it did not anticipate the additional viral impact of YouTube. On the Chevrolet site, users could create their own customized video commercial, complete with text and background music. Environmentalists took the opportunity to produce spoof videos and published them on YouTube. However, the word-of-mouth advertising Chevrolet got on YouTube was ultimately beneficial to Chevrolet and contributed to the 4 million page views, 400,000 unique visitors, and 22,000 ad submissions on their site. This has been one of the most creative and successful promotions.

Note: YouTube announced that they will share revenue with the users who helped generate the revenue.

Sources: Compiled from Sahlin and Botello (2007) and Schonfeld (2007).

For Further Exploration: List the different advertising models on YouTube. List the success factors from these cases. What are the benefits for the advertisers?

An example of viral marketing on social networks is provided by McNichol (2007b), who describes the story of Stormhoek Vineyards (see the minicase at the end of Chapter 6). The company first offered a free bottle of wine to bloggers. About 100 of these bloggers posted voluntary comments about the winery on their own blogs within six months. Most had positive results.

Example. The MyPickList.com (*mypicklist.com*) viral marketing program seems to utilize the usual loyalty program mechanisms without the worries of discounting perception or loyalty erosion. Here is how it is done: MyPickList.com helps consumers make purchase decisions by creating a social commerce network Web site that drives word-of-mouth commerce by leveraging the community aspects of a social network. The effort integrates a user profile and favorite product recommendations (hence, the name "pick list") into a networked community. Once a user creates a pick list, the user can share it with family, friends, or the public at large. When creating a pick list, a user goes through the following steps:

1. Pick a product category. Categories include books, movies, music, electronics, computers, photo and imaging, games and toys, women's apparel, men's apparel, shoes, sports and outdoor items, jewelry and accessories, and gifts.

2. Choose a preferred merchant for product sale direct from the pick list.

3. Add the product and merchant to the pick list.

4. Write a short product review.

5. Tag the "pick."

Any product from a retailer or the Internet can be added to the pick list, but only products that are sold through a retailer in their network are eligible for a commission when someone purchases an item off a member's pick list. The members can request payment of their commission once they have accumulated $25 or more in their account. All payments are made via PayPal; therefore, members must have a PayPal account set up. Once a user creates the pick list, there are several primary ways to get a pick list viewed or distributed. For details, see *Revenue News* (2006).

According to Megna (2007), many retailers are capitalizing on the word-of-mouth marketing of bloggers. This brings up an interesting question: can Bloggers be bought? According to Wagner (2006), companies pay bloggers to endorse products via an intermediary such as PayPerPost.

Example. PayPerPost (*payperpost.com*) runs a marketplace where advertisers can find bloggers, video bloggers, online photographers, and podcasters willing to endorse the advertisers' products.

This is how it works: A company with a product or service to advertise registers with PayPerPost and describes what it wants. A sneaker company, for example, might post a request for people willing to write a 50-word blog entry about their sneakers or upload a video of them playing basketball in the sneakers. The company also says what it is willing to pay for the posting.

Bloggers and other content creators sign up with PayPerPost and shop for opportunities they like. They create the blog post (or whatever content is requested), and inform PayPerPost, which checks to see that the content matches what the advertiser asked for, and PayPerPost arranges payment. The criticism is that bloggers are not required to disclose that they're being paid for the endorsements (see Wagner, 2006). When viral marketing is done by bloggers, it is referred to as **viral blogging.** For details, see Demopoulos (2007).

Classified Ads and Job Listing. MySpace has provided classifieds and job listings since fall 2005, competing with Craigslist and CareerBuilder. According to O'Malley (2006), MySpace is already a force in e-commerce: it sends more traffic to shopping and classifieds sites than MSN, and it is fast closing on Yahoo!.

Google partnered in 2006 with eBay to roll out "click-to-call" advertising across Google and eBay sites—a deal that is expanding to MySpace's giant network.

Mobile Advertising. Mobile advertising is a rapidly developing area (Sharma, 2007). It refers to advertisement on cell phones and other mobile devices. The competition for ad revenue is intensifying, especially with the increasing use of the cell phones with access to the Internet. Internet advertising will also swell. Recently, watching video clips has become popular on cell phones. Advertisers are starting to attach ads to these video clips.

SHOPPING

Shopping is a natural area for social networks to be active in. Although by 2007 it was only beginning to grow, it has enormous potential. Here are some examples:

• According to Kafka (2007), many of MySpace's most popular pages came from e-tailers who stock the site with low-cost come-on cosmetics, coupons, other Web site ads, and the like. The value is $140 million or more per year.

• MySpace lets brand owners create profile pages such as the Burger King mascot, "The King." This has been a tremendous success.

• MySpace is starting its own behavioral targeting, which is similar to collaborative filtering (Chapter 6). Based on the members' voluntary information on what they like and what they don't, MySpace will serve up its users to relevant advertisers with the users' permission. For example, DaimlerChrysler's Jeep has a successful MySpace page. In the future, it can conduct sales campaigns to targeted individuals.

• MySpace's music-download service allows the site's independent and signed musicians to sell their work directly from their profile pages. Snocap, a copyright-services company cofounded by Napster creator Shawn Fanning, supports the project. MySpace and Snocap get a cut of every track sold. By allowing users to self-publish, MySpace has become a launching pad for about 3 million musicians, from garage bands to big names.

• In 2006, Google signed an agreement to pay more than $900 million over five years in ad revenue to MySpace for the right to serve searches inside MySpace. The deal includes exposure of Google's checkout payment service (enabling customers to pay once for several vendors) to MySpace.

FEEDBACK FROM CUSTOMERS

Companies are starting to utilize Web 2.0 tools to get feedback from customers.

Conversational Marketing. In Online Brief 6.3, we described customer feedback via questionnaires, focus groups, and other methods. However, Web 2.0 brings in feedback via blogs, wikis, online forums, chat rooms, and social networking sites. Companies are finding these "conversational marketing" outlets not only generate faster and cheaper results than traditional focus groups, but also foster closer relationships with customers. For example, Macy's quickly removed a metal toothbrush holder from its product line after receiving several complaints about it online (see Gogoi, 2007). Companies such as Dell are also learning that conversational marketing is less expensive and yields quicker results than from focus groups. The computer maker operates a feedback site called IdeaStorm, where it allows customers to suggest and vote on improvements in its offerings. Cookshack created an online forum (*forum.cookshack.com/groupee*) that invites customers to ask and answer questions about barbecue sauces, smokers, barbecue ovens, and cooking techniques. The community helps save money by freeing up customer-service personnel. The community also fosters cohesive and loyal customers.

Using an approach known also as *enterprise feedback management*, companies are interested not only in collecting information but also in interaction between customers and company employees, and in properly distributing customer feedback throughout the organization.

According to Gogoi (2007), retailers know that customers, especially the younger and more Net-savvy, want to be heard, and they also want to hear what others like them say. So, increasingly, retailers are opening up their Web sites to customers, letting them post product reviews, ratings, and in some cases photos and videos. The result is that *customer reviews* are emerging as a prime place to visit for online shoppers.

Marketing companies have longed for years to have a window on how consumers use their products in order to develop product innovations and improve marketing. Customer reviews have long been part of cutting-edge sites such as Amazon.com and Netflix, but by the end of 2006, 43 percent of EC sites offered customer reviews and ratings. As much as 50 percent of customers 18 to 34 years old have posted a comment or review on products they bought or used. A large part of the reason for this achievement is the confluence of social computing and the success of sites such as MySpace, Facebook, and YouTube.

Example. PETCO operates 800 pet supply stores in the United States. The site launched customer reviews in October 2005 and within a week noticed that customers who clicked on the highest customer-rated products were 49 percent more likely to buy something.

PETCO also noticed that top customer-rated pet toys and other items draw more customers, even if the new customers weren't necessarily planning on buying the products; people trust someone else's opinion that is independent of the manufacturer or retailer.

PETCO's experience is not unique. According to an eVoc Insights study, 47 percent of consumers consult reviews before making an online purchase, and 63 percent of shoppers are more likely to purchase from a site if it has ratings and reviews. Negative reviews not only help the retailer address a defect or poorly manufactured item, and consequently they also help decrease the number of returns. In addition, people are less likely to return an item due to personal expectation because reviews give realistic views of a product and its characteristics. (See Gorgoi, 2007, for details.)

RISKS TO ENTERPRISES WHEN INTERFACING WITH SOCIAL NETWORKS

There are some risks involved in opening up your marketing and advertising to the less controlled social networks. For example, according to Regan (2006), aligning a product or company with such sites where *content* is user-generated and often not edited or filtered has its downsides. A company needs to be willing to have negative reviews and feedback. If your company has really positive customer relationships and strong feedback, and you are willing to have customers share the good, the bad, and the ugly, you are a good candidate. If you worry about what your customers would say if they were alone in a room with your prospects, your product or business might not be ready to use Web 2.0.

Another key consideration is the 20–80 rule, which posits that a minority of individuals contributes most of the content material in some blogs, wikis, and similar tools. For example, about 1,000 of the millions of contributors write most of the Wikipedia. According to *Business 2.0* Staff (2007), in an analysis of thousands of submissions over a three-week period on audience voting sites such as Digg and Reddit, the *Wall Street Journal* reported that one-third of the stories that made it to Digg's home page were submitted by 30 users (out of 900,000 registered), and that one single person on Netscape, who goes by the online handle "Stoner," was responsible for 13 percent of the top posts on that site.

Any social media site that relies on the contributions of its users will find a similar distribution curve, with a relatively small number of top contributors representing the bulk of submissions. For instance, user-submitted stock photography site iStockphoto has more than 35,000 contributing photographers, but only about 100 have sold more than 100,000 images (at about $1 to $5 a pop). The difference is that with iStockphoto, users submit work in hopes of getting paid. Companies such as BuzzMetrics offer several services that tell companies what these companys' customers are saying on the Internet and what it means to their brands and markets.

Finally, according to *Innovations* (2006), 74 percent of all CIOs surveyed said that Web 2.0 applications will significantly increase their security risk over the next three years. For more on security and other Web 2.0 implementation issues, see D'Agostino (2006).

Failure of Enterprise Social Networking Initiatives. It may not always be rosy, even for a world class company like Wal-Mart. Failures of enterprise initiatives do occur.

Example: Why and How the In-House Social Network of Wal-Mart Is Not Working. For the largest retailer in the world, creating its own social network seemed to be natural and simple—but it was not. Some retailers such as Nike, Coca Cola, and Sony were successful in creating an in-house SNS. Wal-Mart created such a network in 2007 in order to bolster its image among youngsters. The company hired professional actresses and actors to pose as teens. But this was not convincing. Also, in an attempt to avoid future lawsuits, Wal-Mart allowed parents to control page content. The young viewers were turned off. As the number of visitors was small, Wal-Mart pulled down the Web page after a short period.

OTHER REVENUE-GENERATION STRATEGIES IN SOCIAL NETWORKS

The following are some other interesting ways social networks generate revenues: offer premium service for a monthly or per service fee; partner organizations with the social networks, paying them a monthly service fee; provide local physical venues where members can meet (e.g., *meetup.com*). These venues, such as coffee shops, may choose to pay a fee to be affiliated with the social network.

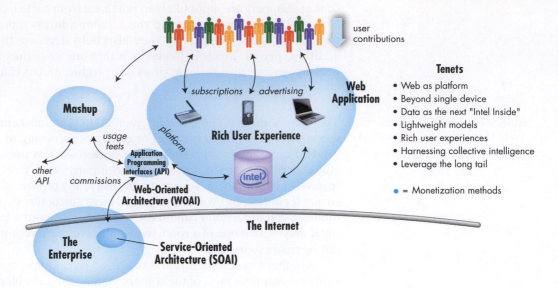

Tenets
- Web as platform
- Beyond single device
- Data as the next "Intel Inside"
- Lightweight models
- Rich user experiences
- Harnessing collective intelligence
- Leverage the long tail

● = Monetization methods

Figure 8.4 Generating revenue from Web 2.0 applications.
(*Source:* Hinchcliffe, D., Web 2.0 Blog, *web2.wsj2.com.*)

According to Millard (2004), Tickle Inc. implemented an integrated advertising campaign with Fox TV studio's program *North Shore*. The site created social networking profiles for some of the key characters on the show and promoted them on the site as "featured members." To learn how a blog can bring in big money, see Wright (2006).

Figure 8.4 illustrates revenue generation from Web 2.0 applications. It shows users' contributions and the relationship among people, advertising, and Web 2.0 tools such as mashups. The Web applications may generate revenue, for example, via subscription fees and advertising. In addition, the following strategies enable companies to make maximum use of Web 2.0 applications (Hinchcliffe, 2006):

1. There are three direct ways to monetize Web 2.0: advertising, subscriptions, and commissions.

2. Some indirect ways that lead to *revenue growth, user growth,* and *increased resistance to competition*, which in turn lead to increased subscriptions, advertising, and commission revenue, are:

• **Strategic acquisition.** Identifying and acquiring Web 2.0 companies that are on the exponential growth curve before the rest of the market realizes what they're worth.

• **Maintaining control of hard to recreate data sources.** Let users access everything, but do not let them keep it, such as Google's providing access to their search index only over the Web.

• **Building attention trust.** By being fair with customer data and leveraging users' loyalty, you can get them to share more information about themselves, which in turn leads to much better products and services tailored to them.

• **Turning applications into platforms.** One single use of an application is simply a waste of software. Online platforms are actually easy to monetize, *but having compelling content or services first* is a prerequisite.

• **Fully automated online customer self-service.** Let users get what they want, when they want it, without help.

WEB 2.0 COMMERCIAL ACTIVITIES INSIDE THE ENTERPRISE

Whereas many companies use Web 2.0 technology for supporting B2C and B2B e-commerce by building up their brand online, advertising, selling, and collaborating (see Online Brief 8.4), other companies use Web 2.0 technologies inside the enterprise. McGillicuddy (2006) describes the following guidelines:

• Allow employees to collaborate and communicate in an employee-driven system (e.g., see the Minicase at the end of this chapter).

- Promote the use of enterprise wikis via demonstrations.
- Set up internal blogs and incorporate them into internal directories so users can see who has a blog.
- Set up enterprise social bookmarking systems so users can see what sort of content their colleagues are tagging.
- CIOs should be involved from the beginning to make sure the right infrastructure and tools are in place.

For an example of how T. Rowe Price Group Inc. is using internal Web 2.0 technology, see McGillicuddy (2006). For tutorials, see Hinchcliffe (2006) and *web2. 0central.com*.

Review Questions

> 1. Why is there so much interest in EC via social communities?
> 2. How can a social network facilitate viral marketing?
> 3. How can social networks support shopping?
> 4. How is customer feedback solicited in social networks?
> 5. List some risks in enterprise social networking.
> 6. What types of revenues can be generated in social networks?

8.7 The Future: Web 3.0

Web 2.0 is here. What's next? This unknown entity is referred to as Web 3.0, the future wave of Internet applications. Some of its characteristics are already in the making. Based on nontechnological success factors and technological factors and trends, there is general optimism about the future of the Web and EC. For a discussion, see Stafford (2006).

WEB 3.0: WHAT'S NEXT?

Web 3.0 will not be just about shopping, entertainment, and search. **Web 3.0** will deliver a new generation of business applications that will see business and social computing converge on the same fundamentals as on-demand architecture is converging with consumer applications. So this is not something that's of merely passing interest to those who work in enterprise IT. The Web 3.0 era will radically change individuals' career paths as well as the organizations where they work (see Rouch, 2006).

According to Stafford (2006) and *en.wikipedia.org/wiki/Web_3,* the next-generation Internet won't just be more portable and personal, it will also harness the power of people, making it even easier to zero in on precisely what you're looking for. To do it, we already see or will see very soon:

- Faster, far-flung connectivity; richer ways of interacting
- New Web Services that work entirely within a browser window
- More powerful search engines
- More clout for everyday people and more user-friendly application creation capabilities
- New possibilities of artificial intelligence applications
- 10 MB of bandwidth (instead of 1 MB in Web 2.0 on the average)
- More uses of 3D and virtual worlds
- Larger utilization of wireless

Web 3.0 Structure. The topology of Web 3.0 can be divided into four distinct layers: API services, aggregation services, application services, and serviced clients.

Application Program Interface (API) Services. API services are the hosted services that have powered Web 2.0 and will become the engines of Web 3.0. Google's search and AdWord's APIs, Amazon.com's affiliate APIs, a large number of RSS feeds, a multitude of functional services, such as those included in the StrikeIron Web Services Marketplace (*strikeiron.com*) (Wainewright, 2005), are just some examples. One of the most significant characteristics of this foundation layer is that it is a commodity layer. As Web 3.0 matures, an almost perfect market will emerge and squeeze out virtually all of the profit margin from the highest-volume services.

Aggregation Services. These services are the intermediaries that take some of the hassle out of locating all of those raw API services by bundling them together in useful ways. Representative examples are the various RSS aggregators and emerging Web services marketplaces such as the StrikeIron service.

Application Services. This layer is where the biggest, most durable profits should be found. These services will not be like the established enterprise application categories, such as CRM or ERP, but a new class of composite applications that bring together functionality from multiple services to help users achieve their objectives in a flexible, intuitive way. An example of an area that is expected to grow is **voice commerce (v-commerce)**, which is an umbrella term for the use of speech recognition to allow voice-activated services including Internet browsing and e-mail retrieval. It includes novel ways of building applications.

Serviced Clients. There is a role for client-side logic in the Web 3.0 landscape, but users will expect it to be maintained and managed for them.

From the billions of documents that form the Web and the links that weave them together, computer scientists and a growing number of start-up companies are finding new ways to mine human intelligence. Their goal is to add a layer of meaning on top of the existing Web that will make it less of a catalog and more of a guide—and even provide the foundation for systems that can reason in a human fashion. That level of artificial intelligence, with machines doing the thinking instead of simply following commands, has eluded researchers for more than half a century. One of the major Web 3.0 technologies is the Semantic Web.

Web 3.0 and the Semantic Web. One potential area for Web 3.0 is the increased use of the Semantic Web (see *en.wikipedia.org/wiki/Semantic_Web*). According to *The Economist* (2007), a Semantic-Web browser will be available soon in which people will be able to display the data, draw graphs, and so on. An example would be "friend-of-a-friend" networks, where individuals in online communities provide data in the form of links between themselves and friends. The Semantic Web could help to visualize such complex networks and organize them to allow deeper understanding of the communities' structures.

The **Semantic Web** is an evolving extension of the Web in which Web content can be expressed not only in natural language but also in a form that can be understood, interpreted, and used by intelligent computer software agents, permitting them to find, share, and integrate information more easily. The technology is derived from W3C director Tim Berners-Lee's vision of the Web as a universal medium for data, information, and knowledge exchange. At its core, the Semantic Web comprises a philosophy, a set of design principles, collaborative working groups, and a variety of enabling technologies.

A similar view about the role of the Semantic Web is expressed by Borland (2007), according to which the role of it in Web 3.0 is certain, and coming soon. Borland believes that the Web 3.0 new tools (some of which are already helping developers "stitch" together complex applications) improve and automate database searches, help people choose vacation destinations, and sort through complicated financial data more efficiently. For more on Web 3.0 and the Semantic Web, see Markoff (2006) and *en.wikipedia.org/wiki/Web_3*.

Web 3.0 also will be characterized by an explosion of mobile social networks.

Mobile Social Networks. An explosive growth of mobile social networks is predicted by ABI Research (see Mello, 2006), tripling the 50 million members in 2006 to 174 million in 2011. The explosion of wireless Web 2.0 services and companies enables many social communities to be based on the mobile phone and other portable wireless devices. This extends the reach of social interaction to millions of people who don't have regular or easy access to computers. For example, MySpace can be accessed via Cingular's mobile system. At minimum, existing members who use PCs will supplement their activities with wireless devices. Thus, wireless would be the environment of choice for the Web 3.0 users.

Future Threats. According to Stafford (2006), the following four trends may slow EC and Web 3.0 and even cripple the Internet:

- **Security concern.** Both shoppers and users of e-banking and other services worry about online security. The Web needs to be made safer.
- **Lack of Net neutrality.** If the big telecom companies are allowed to charge companies for a guarantee of faster access, critics fear that small innovative Web companies could be crowded out by the Microsofts and Googles that can afford to pay more.
- **Copyright complaints.** The legal problems of YouTube, Wikipedia, and others may result in a loss of vital outlets of public opinion, creativity, and discourse.
- **Choppy connectivity.** Upstream bandwidths are still constricted, making uploading of video files a time-consuming task. Usable mobile bandwidth still costs a lot, and some carriers impose limitations on how Web access can be employed.

Review Questions

1. What is Web 3.0, and how will it differ from Web 2.0?
2. Describe the future of mobile social networks.
3. List the major potential inhibitors of e-commerce and Web 3.0.

8.8 Managerial Issues

1. The impacts on business that social networking is expected to make. The impacts of social networking and the Internet can be so strong that the entire manner in which companies do business will be changed, with significant impacts on procedures, people, organizational structure, management, and business processes.

2. The impacts of the Web 2.0 boom. With the push toward Web 2.0 technologies, *Time Magazine* (Grossman, 2006/2007) named "you" as the person of the year for 2006. In the new information age, no one has more power to influence society than Web 2.0 communities. Yet, does this influence truly benefit us, or will we suffer because of it?

3. Should we explore Web 2.0 collaboration? Consider whether your corporate culture is ready to experiment with public collaboration (Web 2.0) tools. Work with your corporate-learning or organization-development department to find areas likely for experimentation.

4. How shall we start using Web 2.0 tools? Start small: determine whether a collaborative tool would benefit a team or group working on a specific project. Marketing groups are often good first targets for information sharing with others because they're usually the ones tasked with sharing corporate information. Try establishing a wiki for a team's collaborative project. Some wikis are hosted on an internal server while others are available as open source or via a hosted service.

5. Do we need to sponsor a social network? Although sponsoring a social network may sound like a good idea, it may not be simple to execute. Community members need services, which cost money to provide. The most difficult task is to find an existing community that matches your business.

6. How should we deal with Web 2.0 risks? There are several possible risks depending on the applications. Consult your internal security experts and get some outside legal advice. Use a consultant for large projects to examine the risks.

7. Should we have an in-house social network? This is a debatable strategy. While most companies should probably opt to go into a successful SNS, there are cases where an in-house service can be much more beneficial.

How *IT* Benefits You

Accounting Major

Evaluating and analyzing social networking sites, especially in virtual worlds, create a challenge for accountants. Next, cost-benefit and justification for starting a social network may not be simple due to the many intangible benefits. The accountant may be also involved in risk assessment and in auditing of social networks. Also, several accounting societies have supplemented their activities with virtual community activities. Due to the shortage of accountants, recruiting in social networks and virtual worlds is becoming popular.

Finance Major

Several social networking innovations, such as person-to-person money lending and real estate matching, should be of interest to finance majors. The revenue models of social networking require the attention of the finance people as do payment schemes for advertising. Setting up payment mechanisms especially for trading virtual properties requires both innovative approaches and legal financial considerations. Payments for bloggers require attention of the finance people as well as payments to social networks services. Finally, assessing the viability of in-house social networks could be a complex financial-oriented project.

Human Resources Management Major

Recruiting is extensively done both in social networks and in virtual worlds. Special social-oriented innovations were developed for the recruitment of difficult-to-find talents. Experimenting with the "wisdom of the crowds" for the purpose of peer evaluation and promotions should be carefully examined by the HRM department. Using social networking, especially virtual worlds, for training is becoming popular and is enriched with interactive simulation and gaming.

IS Major

The IS department will play a critical role in supporting the interfaces of enterprises with social networking. It is not only the knowledge of new Web 2.0 tools and virtual worlds, but also their integration with existing information systems that matters. Furthermore, building useful and innovative applications in social networks sites could be rewarding for your company. Understanding the social computing environment is therefore critical. It is also possible that some IS employees will need training in the new tools, while others may resist change. All of these may change the role of the IS department in the future—be aware.

Marketing Major

The major interface of enterprises and social networking is in the areas of advertising and sales. The opportunities are amazing and success stories are abundant; however, failures do occur. Alliances between enterprises and social network sites usually are structured around advertising. In addition, advertising and sales in virtual worlds are growing rapidly, but so are some implementation difficulties. Social networking probably provides the best opportunity for viral marketing. Innovative advertising methods (e.g., see Weber, 2007, and Zimmerman, 2007) must be learned by any progressive marketer. All in all, social networking brings an important additional marketing channel that cannot be ignored.

Operations Management Major

Managing the supply chains of services and projects related to transactions conducted in social networks presents a challenge due to the special nature of activities that take place in these networks. Managing the huge number of members could also be a challenge, as well as supporting transactions with business partners. Remember that supply chains include the movement of information and money, both of which can be complex in social networking. Finally, order fulfillment related to transactions with social networks can be intriguing. All of these should be reasons for you to know more about this emerging technology.

Key Terms

Chapter Highlights

(Numbers Refer to Learning Objectives)

❶ Web 2.0, social media, and disruptors. Web 2.0 is about innovative application of existing technologies. Web 2.0 has brought together the contributions of millions of people and made their work, opinions, and identity matter. The consequences of the rapid growth of person-to-person computing such as blogging are currently hard to understand and difficult to estimate. User-created content is a major characteristic of Web 2.0, as is the emergence of social networking. One impact of Web 2.0 is the creation of industry disruptors.

❷ The structure and role of virtual communities and worlds. Virtual communities create new types of business opportunities—people with similar interests that congregate at one Web site are a natural target for advertisers and marketers. Using chat rooms, members can exchange opinions about certain products and services. Of special interest are communities of transactions, whose interest is the promotion of commercial buying and selling. Virtual communities can foster customer loyalty—increase sales of related vendors that sponsor communities and facilitate customer feedback for improved service and business.

❷ Virtual worlds. Virtual worlds are special sites that use rich media (3D, virtual reality) to create virtual properties and scenarios using avatars, where people can play, transact, communicate, collaborate, advertise, and learn. The most well-known virtual world is Second Life where you get virtual land (and can buy more) to use for building hotels, houses, factories, roads, and even complete cities, if you so desire.

❸ Online social networks. These are very large Internet communities that allow the sharing of content, including videos, photos, and virtual socialization and interaction. Hundreds of networks are popping up around the world, some of which are global, competing for advertising money.

❸ Representative social networking sites. In addition to MySpace (Chapter 1), we acknowledge Facebook, Bebo, Orkut, Flickr, Craigslist, and Cyworld.

❹ Enterprise social networks. These are communities concentrating on business issues both in one country and around the world (e.g., recruiting, finding business partners). Social marketplaces meld social networks and some aspects of business. Notable are LinkedIn and Xing. Also, some companies own private social networks while others conduct business in SNSs such as Facebook.

❺ Social networks and e-commerce. The major areas of interface are online shopping, online advertising, online market research, and innovative revenue models. The major attraction is the volume of social networks and the hope that the young people in the communities will be online buyers in the future.

❻ Web 3.0. Web 3.0, the next generation of the Web, will combine social and business computing. It will be more portable and personal, with powerful search engines, clout to the people, and more connectivity in the wireless environment and on-demand applications. The Semantic Web will play a major role in Web 3.0 applications.

Questions for Discussion

1. Discuss the differences between Web 2.0 and the traditional Web.
2. Discuss the major characteristics of Web 2.0. What are some of their advantages?
3. Discuss the relationship between virtual communities and doing business on the Internet.
4. Discuss why Cyworld may take over members from other social networks.
5. Discuss why a social marketplace is considered to be a Web 2.0 instrument.
6. Discuss the benefits of social networks to viral marketing.
7. Discuss the commercial opportunities of virtual worlds.
8. Distinguish between a virtual community and a virtual world.
9. What are the benefits of conversational marketing?
10. Discuss the nature of industry disrupters.

Exercises and Projects

1. Access Hof's "My Virtual Life" (2008) at *businessweek.com/print/magazine/content/06_18/b3982001.htm?chang=g1* and meet the seven residents in the slide show. Prepare a table that shows the manner in which they make money, the required skills, and the reason they do it in Second Life.

2. Identify two virtual worlds (other than Second Life). Explore what is going on there. Join as a member and write a report.

3. Enter *cyworld.com* and compare its content and possible activities to that of *myspace.com*. Write a report.

4. Enter *craigslist.org*. From what you know about the design of Web sites and from comparisons with *monster.com*, what suggestions would you make to improve the site?

5. Enter secondlife.com and find the commercial activities of the following avatars: Fizik Baskerville, Craig Altman, Shaun Altman, FlipperPA Peregrine, and Anshe Chung. Describe these activities.

Group Assignments and Projects

1. Each group member selects a single family house where he(she) lives, or where a friend lives. Next, enter *zillow.com* and find the value of a house in the neighborhood. Then, add all improvements and reprice the house. Find out how to list the house for sale on Zillow and other sites (e.g., *craigslist.org*). Write a summary. Compare each member's experiences.

2. Assign each team member a different type of community, per Exhibit 8.4. Identify the services offered by that type of community. Have each team compare the services offered by each type of community. Prepare a report.

3. The group signs into *secondlife.com* and creates its own avatar(s). Each member is assigned to a certain area (e.g., virtual real estate, educational activities, diplomatic island) to explore what is going on in the specific area. Make sure the avatar interacts with other people's avatars. Write a report.

4. Enter *facebook.com* and find out how 10 well-known corporations use the site to conduct commercial activities (as per Section 8.6).

Internet Exercises

1. Enter the Web site of a social network service (e.g., *myspace.com* or *facebook.com*). Build a home page free of charge. Add a chat room and a message board to your site using the free tools provided. Describe the other capabilities available. Make at least five new friends.

2. Investigate the community services provided by Yahoo! to its members (*groups.yahoo.com*). List all of the services available and assess their potential commercial benefits to Yahoo!.

3. Enter *calastrology.com*. What kind of community is this? Check the revenue model. Then enter *astrocenter.com*. What kind of site is this? Compare and comment on the two sites.

4. Enter *ediscovery.com* and describe its functionalities. (See also Carr, 2006.) Write a report.

5. Enter *classmates.com*, *myspace.com*, and *linkedin.com* and find their sources of revenue.

6. Enter *xing.com* and *linkedin.com* and compare their functionalities. Write a report.

7. Enter *flip.com* and compare its rich media with that of *myspace.com* and *cyworld.com*. Prepare a report.

8. Enter *clickstar.com*. Why is it an online entertainment service? What are the benefits to viewers? Compare this site to *starz.com*.

9. Enter *gnomz.com*. What does this site help you accomplish?

10. Enter *advertising.com*. Find what innovative/scientific methods they use. Relate Web 2.0 to online search methods.

11. Enter the *paulgillin.com* blog and find information related to enterprise applications of Web 2.0 technologies. Write a report.

12. Enter *pandora.com*. Check how you can create and share music with friends. Why is this a Web 2.0 application?

13. Enter *webkinz.com* and compare its activities to that of *facebook.com*. Enter *netratings.com* and find the average stay time in both social network sites.

14. Enter *smartmobs.com*. Go to blogroll. Find three blogs related to Web 2.0 and summarize their major points.

15. Enter *mashable.com* and review the latest news regarding social networks and network strategy. Briefly summarize three of each.

16. Enter *entropiauniverse.com* and find out how they handle payments. Write a report.

Minicase

Web 2.0 Applications at Eastern Mountain Sports

Eastern Mountain Sports (EMS) (*ems.com*) is a medium-sized specialty retailer (annual sales $200 million) selling via over 80 physical stores, a mail order catalog, and online. Operating in a very competitive environment, the company uses leading-edge IT technologies and lately has introduced a complementary set of Web 2.0 tools in order to increase collaboration, information sharing, and communication among stores and their employees, suppliers, and customers. Let's see how this works.

The Business Intelligence Strategy and System

During the last few years, the company implemented a business intelligence (BI) system that includes business performance management and dashboards. A BI system collects raw data from multiple sources, processes them into a data mart, and conducts analyses that include comparing performance to operational metrics in order to assess the health of the business (see details in Chapter 12).

The attached figure illustrates how the system works. Point-of-sale (POS) information and other relevant data, which are available on an IBM computer, are loaded into Microsoft's SQL Server and then into a data mart. The data are then analyzed with Information Builders' business and analytics tool (BI analytics). The results are presented via a series of dashboards that users can view via their Web browsers; they are invited to make comments via blogs. This way users can access a unified, high-level view of key performance indicators (KPI) such

as sales, inventory, and margin levels, and drill down to granular details that analyze specific transactions. Communication and collaboration is done mainly via blogs, wikis, and other Web 2.0 tools that are described next with the process.

The Web 2.0 Collaboration, Sharing, and Communication System

The company created a multifunction employee workbench called E-Basecamp. It contains all of the information relevant to corporate goals, integrated with productivity tools (e.g., Excel) and role-based content, customized to each individual user. Then, it added a set of Web 2.0 tools (see the attached figure). The system facilitates collaboration among internal and external stakeholders. EMS is using 20 operation metrics (e.g., inventory levels and turns). These also include e-tailing where e-commerce managers monitor hour-by-hour Web traffic and conversion rates (Chapter 6). The dashboard shows deviations from targets with a color code. It uses the following Web 2.0 tools:

- **RSS feeds.** These are embedded into the dashboards to drive more focused inquiries. These feeds are the base for information sharing and online conversations. For example, by showing which items are selling better than others, users can collectively analyze the transaction characteristics and selling behaviors that produce the high sales. The knowledge acquired then cascades throughout the organization. For instance, one manager observed an upward spike in

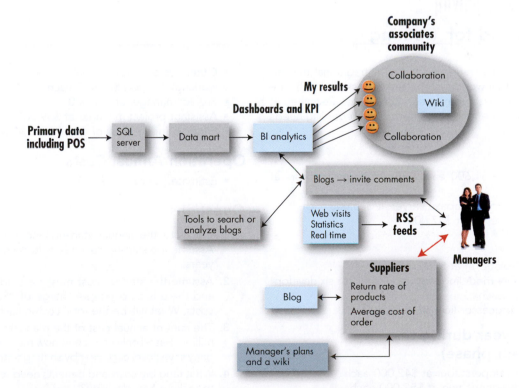

Figure 8U.1

footwear sales at store X. Investigating "why" revealed that store X employees had perfected a multistep sales technique that included recommending (both online and in stores) special socks designed for specific uses along with an inner sole. The information was disseminated using the RSS feed. As a result, sales of footwear increased 57 percent in a year.

- **Wikis.** The wikis are used to encourage collaborative interaction throughout the company. Dashboard users are encouraged to post a hypothesis or requests for help, and invite commentary and suggestions, almost like a notepad alongside the dashboard.
- **Blogs.** Blogs were created around specific data or a key metric. The blogs are used to post information and invite comments. Then tools are used to archive, search, and categorize blogs for easy reference. For example, store managers post an inquiry or explanation regarding sale deviations. Keeping comments on blogs lets readers observe patterns they might have overlooked using data analysis alone.

Going to Business Partners Externally

In the next phase, suppliers have been added. For example, suppliers can monitor the return rate of their product on the dashboard and invite store managers to provide explanations and suggestions using wikis or blogs. Assuming proper security of data is installed, suppliers can get almost real-time data about how well their products sell so they can prepare a better production plan.

The objectives are to build a tighter bond with the business partners. For example, by having store managers attach blogs to the suppliers' dashboards, the suppliers view current sale information and post comments to the blogs. Product managers use a wiki to post challenges for the next season, such as a proposed percentage increase in sales, and then ask vendors to suggest innovative ways to achieve these goals. Several of the customers and other business partners subscribe to RSS feed.

Called Extreme Deals (big discounts for a limited time), blogs are also embedded into the EMS product management lifecycle (PLM) tool (Chapter 9). This allows vendors to have virtual conversations with the product development managers.

The major impact of the Web 2.0 collaboration tools is that instead of having conversations occur in the hallway (where you need to be in the right place at the right time), conversations take place on blogs and wikis where all interested parties can participate.

Sources: Compiled from Nerille (2007) and from *ems.com* (accessed May 2008).

Questions

1. Why not just have regular meetings and send e-mails rather than use blogs, wikis, and RSS feeds?
2. What are the benefits to EMS of combining its BI system and Web 2.0 tools?
3. In what ways is corporate performance bolstered?
4. What kind of community is this? Who are the members?
5. Can the company use any other Web 2.0 technologies? What, and how?
6. What information on *ems.com* is typical for what you find in social network sites?

Problem-Solving Activity

Virtual World for Training

Management is considering replacing a traditional training system with a virtual-world system (see Gronstedt, 2008). The company has one classroom where 45 students are trained at a time. You know the following information regarding needs at the start-up cost:

Hardware

- 45 laptops at $1,600 each with 45 larger monitors at $200 each
- Web server and database server at $25,000 each
- Application server at $47,000

Software

- Virtual 3D platform at $260,000
- Virtual reality modeling language tools for six developers at $800 each
- Database processor license at $42,000

Salary (per year during the development phase)

- System developers: four at $42,000 each
- Graphic designers: two at $52,000 each

- Other system professionals (integration, security, networking): three at $45,000 each
- Project manager at $67,000
- Assistant project manager at $39,000
- Fringe benefits to all of the above: 24%

Operation Annual Costs

- Estimated to be $375,000

Questions

1. Calculate the annual start-up and total annual cost. Assume the start-up cost needs to be recouped in four years.
2. Assume the start-up cost must be paid in three years and there is an overhead charge of 12% of all annual costs. What will be the total cost in such a case?
3. The current annual cost of the manual training is $1.15 million. Based only on money, how much would the company save (lose) each year by shifting to the new system?
4. What tangible costs and benefits need to be considered to make a final decision?

Online Resources

More resources and study tools are located on the Student Web Site and on WileyPLUS. You'll find additional chapter materials and useful Web links. In addition, self-quizzes that provide individualized feedback are available for each chapter.

Online Briefs for Chapter 8 are available at wiley.com/college/turban:

8.1 Social Networking Software Tools
8.2 Entertainment Web 2.0 Style: From Communities to Entertainment Marketplaces
8.3 Using Intelligent Software and Social Networking to Improve Recruiting Processes
8.4 Successful Commercial Efforts

Online Minicases for Chapter 8 are available at wiley.com/college/turban:

8.1 ZOPA and Prosper
8.2 Friendster
8.3 YouTube

References

Abram, C., and L. Pearlman, *Facebook For Dummies*. Hoboken, NJ: John Wiley & Sons, 2008.

Alter, A., "My Virtual Summer Job," *The Wall Street Journal*, May 16, 2008.

Borland, J., "A Smarter Web," *Technology Review*, March/April 2007.

Business 2.0 Staff, "The Next Net 25," (Web 2.0 Companies) *Business 2.0*, February 22, 2007.

Carr, D. F., "E-Discovery," *Baseline*, November 2006.

Carr, D. F., "Tapping into Virtual Markets," *Baseline Magazine*, March 1, 2007.

Cashel, J., "Top Ten Trends for Online Communities," *ProvidersEdge.com*, July 2001, *providersedge.com/docs/km_articles/Top_Ten_Trends_for_Online_Communities.pd* (accessed May 2008).

Chesbrough, H. W., *Open Business Models*. Boston, MA: Harvard Business School Press, 2006.

CNN.com, "Love-Struck Hacker Proposed Using 'Bejeweled,'" April 15, 2008, *cnn.com/2008/TECH/04/15/bejeweled.proposal.ap* (accessed May 2008).

Cone, E., "Comment: Put a Fork in the Plan to Fork," *Blog.eweek.com*, January 22, 2007a.

Cone, E., "Social Networks at Work Promise Bottom-Line Results," *CIO Insight*, October 8, 2007b.

Copeland, V. M., and K. Kelleher, "The New New Careers," *Business 2.0*, May 2007.

D'Agostino, D., "Security in the World of Web 2.0," *Innovations*, Winter 2006.

de Mel, E., "Google's Orkut Goes Mobile in Stealth Mode," Mobileopen.com, April 18, 2008, *mobilopen.org/index.php/2008/04/18/101-google-s-orkut-goes-mobile-in-stealth-mode* (accessed May 2008).

Demopoulos, T., *Blogging and Podcasting*. Chicago, IL: Kaplan Publishing, 2007.

The Economist, "Watching the Web Grow Up," March 10, 2007.

Elad J., *LinkedIn for Dummies*, Indianapolis, Ind.: Wiley Pub. Co., 2008.

Farrell, N., "Microsoft Rumbled over Wikipedia Edits," *The Inquirer*, January 24, 2007. *theinquirer.net/gb/inquirer/news/2007/01/24/microsoft-rumbled-over-wikipedia-edits* (accessed May 2008).

Flynn, N., *Blog Rules: A Business Guide to Managing Policy, Public Relations, and Legal Issues*. Saranac Lake, NY: AMACOM, 2006.

Gillin, P., *The New Influencers*. Sanger, CA: Quill Driver Books, March 2007.

Gogoi, P., "Retailers Take a Tip from MySpace," *Business Week Online*, February 13, 2007, *businessweek.mobi/detail.jsp?key=6158&rc=sb&p=4&pv=1* (accessed May 2008).

Gronstedt, A., *Training in Virtual Worlds*. New York: ASTD Press, 2008.

Grossman, L., "Time Person of the Year: YOU," and "Power to People," *Time*, December 25, 2006–January 1, 2007.

Hagel, J., and A. Armstrong, *Net Gain*. Boston: Harvard Business School Press, 1997.

Heilemann, J., "Digging Up News," *Business 2.0*, April 2006.

Hinchcliffe, D., "Profitably Running an Online Business in the Web 2.0 Era," *SOA Web Services Journal,* November 29, 2006, *web2.wsj2.com* (accessed May 2008).

Hof, R. D., "My Virtual Life," *BusinessWeek*, May 1, 2008.

Hoover, J. N., "Enterprise 2.0," *InformationWeek*, February 26, 2007.

Innovations, "Going Beyond Networking," Winter 2006.

Johnson, G. J., and P. J. Ambrose, "Neo-Tribes: The Power and Potential of Online Communities in Health Care," *Communications of the ACM*, January 2006.

Kafka, P., "Blue Sky," *Forbes*, February 12, 2007.

Kaye, E., *Virtual Worlds: The Next Big Thing*. Dallas, TX: The Wave Group, 2008.

Kirkpatrick, M., "Facebook Censoring User Messaging: Spam Prevention or Unaccountable Control of Conversation," ReadWriteWeb, May 21, 2008, *readwriteweb.com/archives/facebook_censoring_user_messages.php* (accessed July 2008).

Libert, B., and thousands of contributors, *WE are smarter than ME*. Upper Saddle River, NJ: Pearson Education Inc., 2008.

Longino, C., "Your Wireless Future," *Business 2.0*, May 2006.

Mansfield, R., *How to Do Everything with Second Life*. New York: McGraw-Hill, 2008.

Markoff, J., "Entrepreneurs See a Web Guided by Common Sense," *The New York Times*, November 12, 2006.

Martens, C., "Wikipedia to Strive for Higher Quality Content," *PC World*, August 4, 2006.

McAfee, A. P., "Enterprise 2.0: The Dawn of Emergent Collaboration," *MIT Sloan Management Review*, Spring 2006.

McGillicuddy, S., "IT Executives Eager to Exploit 2.0 Wave," *SMB News*, October 24, 2006, *searchcio.techtarget.com/originalContent/0,289142,sid182_gci1226050,00.htm* (accessed May 2008).

McNichol, T., "Building a Wiki World," (Wikia vs. Wikipedia), *Business 2.0*, March 2007a.

McNichol, T., "Vin Du Blogger," *Business 2.0*, August 2007b.

Megna, M., "Bust or Boon? Calculate Blog ROI," *E-Commerce Guide*, February 8, 2007, *ecommerce-guide.com/solutions/article.php/3658776* (accessed May 2008).

Mello, J. P., "Explosive Growth Predicted for Mobile Social Networks," *E-Commerce Times*, December 12, 2006.

Millard, E., "Online Social Networks and the Profit Motive," *E-Commerce Times*, June 12, 2004, *ecommercetimes.com/story/34422.html* (accessed May 2008).

Murray-Buechner, M., "25 Sites We Can't Live Without," *Time*, August 3, 2006.

Nerille, J., "X-treme Web 2.0," *Optimize Magazine*, January 2007.

O'Brien, J. M., "What's Your House Really Worth?" *Fortune*, February 29, 2007.

O'Malley, G., "MySpace vs. eBay? Site Leaps into E-Commerce," *Advertising Age*, September 11, 2006.

O'Reilly, T., "What is Web 2.0?" *OReillynet.com*, September 30, 2005, *oreillynet.com/pub/a/oreilly/tim/news/2005/09/30/what-is-web-20.html* (accessed May 2008).

Regan, K., "Plugging In: Can E-Commerce Leverage Social Networks?" *E-Commerce Times*, November 2, 2006.

Reuters, A., "IBM Eyes Move into Second Life 'V-Business,' " *Second Life News Center*, October 24, 2006, *secondlife.reuters.com/stories/2006/10/24/ibm-eyes-move-into-second-life-v-business* (accessed May 2008).

Revenue News, "MyPickList Tackles Social Networking and Word-of-Mouth Advertising," May 25, 2006.

Riley, D., "Wikipedia Hits Mid Life Slow Down," *TechCrunch*, October 11, 2007, *techcrunch.com/2007/10/11/wikipedia-hits-mid-life-slow-down* (accessed May 2008).

Robbins, S., and M. Bell, *Second Life For Dummies*. Hoboken, NJ: Wiley Publishing, Inc., 2008.

Rosedale, P., "Alter Egos," *Forbes*, May 7, 2007.

Rouch, W., "Social Networking 3.0," *Technology Review from MIT's Emerging Technologies Conference*, September 27–29, 2006, *technologyreview.com/read_article.aspx'id=15908&ch=infotech* (accessed May 2008).

Roush, W., "Second Earth," *Technology Review*, July/August 2007.

Rymaszewski, M., et al., Second Life: The Official Guide. Hoboken, NJ: Sebex Publishers/Wiley Publications, 2008.

Sahlin, D., and C. Botello, *YouTube For Dummies*. Hoboken, NJ: Wiley Publishing, Inc., 2007.

Schonfeld, E., "Cyworld Attacks!" *Business 2.0*, August 2006a.

Schonfeld, E., "The Disruptors Get Rowdy," *The.Next.Net*, October 27, 2006b, *emedia.blogspot.com/2006/10/next-net-27102006-disruptors-get-rowdy.html* (accessed May 2008).

Schonfeld, E., "Make Way for Must Stream TV," *Business 2.0*, March 2007.

Schonfeld, E., and J. Borzo, "The Next Disruptors," *Business 2.0*, October 2006.

Schubert, P., and M. Ginsburg, "Virtual Communities of Transaction: The Role of Personalization in E-Commerce," *Electronic Markets*, 10 (1), 2000.

SecondLife.com, "What is Second Life?" *secondlife.com/whatis* (accessed May 2008).

Sharma, A., "Banner Year: Companies Compete for Ad Revenue on Mobile Internet," *Wall Street Journal*, January 18, 2007.

Sifrey, D., "The State of the Live Web, April 2007," *Sifrey.com*, April 05, 2007, *sifry.com/stateoftheliveweb* (accessed May 2008).

Sloan, P., "The Next Net 25 (Web 2.0 Companies)," *Business 2.0*, March 2007.

Stafford, A., "The Future of the Web," *PC World*, November 2006.

Terdiman, D., *The Entrepreneur's Guide to Second Life: Making Money in the Metaverse*, Indianapolis, IN: Wiley Pub. Inc., 2008.

Urlocker, M., "Urlocker on Disruption," *The Disruption Group*, September 20, 2006, *ondisruption.com/my_weblog/2006/09/business_20_top.html* (accessed May 2008).

Vander Veer, E., *Facebook: The Missing Manual*. Cambridge, MA: Pogue Press, 2008.

Wagner, M., "Can Bloggers Be Bought?" *InformationWeek*, October 16, 2006.

Wainewright, P., "What to Expect from Web 3.0," *ZDNet.com*, November 29, 2005, *blogs.zdnet.com/SAAS/?p=68* (accessed May 2008).

Weaver, A. C., and B. B. Morrison, "Social Networking," *Computer*, February 2008.

Weber, S., *Plug Your Business*. Falls Church, VA: Weber Books, 2007.

White, B. A., *Second Life: A Guide to Your Virtual World*. Indianapolis, IN: Que Publishers (A Pearson Publishing Company), 2008.

Wikipedia, "About Wikipedia," 2008, *en.wikipedia.org/wiki/Wikipedia:About* (accessed May 2008).

Wright, J., *Blog Marketing*. New York: McGraw Hill, 2006.

Zimmerman, J., *Web Marketing For Dummies*, Hoboken, NJ: Wiley Pub. Inc., 2007.

Google Is Changing Everything

Introduction

Of all the companies associated with EC, probably no other company has impacted our work and life as much as Google has. More than that, according to Carr (2006), Google's unconventional IT and EC management strategy is both effective and efficient, and it offers a glimpse into how organizations might deploy technology in the future. Google runs on close to 500,000 servers. Google has grown more quickly than any other EC company, and it started to generate profit faster than most start-ups. By 2006, its revenue had reached $9.3 billion (estimates for 2008 are $20 billion), about the same as IBM and more than Ford and General Motors combined (Goldberg, 2006).

Google is known primarily for its search engine and its related targeted-advertising tools (AdWords and Adsense, see Online Minicase 6.6. in Chapter 6). In Chapter 6, we will explain Google's ad-matching strategy. Google delivers its advertisers far more revenue per click in search results than its competitors (mainly Microsoft and Yahoo!) do. However, Google is doing many other things.

Let's examine some of Google's many EC activities.
Google's goal is to deliver technologies to organize the world's information and make it universally accessible and useful. For example, Google is trying to reinvent the spreadsheet as a Web-based application that makes it simple for users to input and share data. Google Spreadsheet is a free Web-based application that can be shared with up to 10 users simultaneously, overcoming a key limitation of Microsoft's Excel.

How Does Google Compete? What Products Does It Offer? Google is meeting the competitive challenges it faces head on. Google offers an expanding repertoire of tools in line with its core competency in search technology. It also offers several other value-added tools. The major tools are the following:

- Google Product Search (*google.com/products*) is a product-comparison search engine for online shopping. A similar search tool is Google Catalogs (*catalogs.google.com*), which searches a database of mail-order catalogs.
- Google News (*news.google.com*) searches news-oriented Web sites and displays stories according to a computer algorithm that rates stories based on how many news sites are publishing the stories, how recently the articles were published, and, for searches, keyword occurrence.
- Google Earth (*earth.google.com*) is a collection of zoomable aerial and satellite 3D photos of the earth that enables you to find information linked to geographic location. It is one of Google's most notable desktop applications.
- Google Maps (*maps.google.com*) and Google Maps for Mobile (*google.com/gmm*) present countless maps of cities and streets around the globe. It enables you to get driving instructions from one location to another.

- Google Scholar (*scholar.google.com*) searches the scholarly literature, including peer-reviewed papers, theses, books, preprints, abstracts, and technical reports. Many hits are abstracts or citations, not full articles, and some are "cloaked" behind subscription-only journal subscriptions.
- Google also has introduced Google Wireless (*google.com/mobile*) where you get Search Maps, Gmail, SMS, GOOG411 (find local businesses), YouTube, and Google Groups (*groups.google.com*), the latter where you can discuss issues online via e-mail, create custom pages with rich formats, and customize your page with your own graphics.

Strategically, Google is leveraging its widely recognized brand name and search technology expertise into areas beyond Web searching. Sometimes these projects bring Google into direct competition with Microsoft and other IT giants mentioned earlier.

- Google Print (*books.google.com*) is similar to Amazon.com's "search inside the book" feature. Users can search by keyword (e.g., "books about Nelson Mandela") and then search for keywords or phrases within the books.
- Gmail (*gmail.google.com*) is Google's offering in the huge Web-based e-mail market that is currently dominated by Microsoft's Hotmail and Yahoo! Mail. Gmail offers new services such as grouping related messages together and keyword searching through e-mail messages.
- Google Mini (*google.com/mini*) is a cost-effective appliance business used to deploy corporate searches that mimic the main Google Web search engine.
- Google Desktop (*desktop.google.com*) searches the contents of computer files, e-mail messages, books, and even recently viewed Web pages. This is a dramatic improvement on the Windows "Find" feature, which searches only computer files and then mostly by file name. Google Desktop preempts technology that Microsoft is intending to put into Longhorn, and it is part of its enterprise search.
- Google Labs is a collection of incomplete applications that are still being tested for use by the company and the general public.
- Orkut (*orkut.com*) is a social-networking service that competes in one of the fastest-growing Internet markets—Web sites that connect people through networks of friends or business contacts to find new friends or contacts. In order to sign in at Orkut, you must have a Google account.

In 2006, Google expanded into the software business, offering Google Office (initially free, to compete with Microsoft). Also, Google offers a set of Web programs (e.g., for e-mail, communications, and scheduling).

Other Google Products. Google offers many other products. For example, it offers *Google Video*, which not only allows users to search and view freely available videos, but also offers users and media publishers the ability to publish their contents, including television shows on CBS, NBA basketball games, and music videos. In August 2007, Google announced that it would shut down its accompanying video rental and sales program and offer refunds and *Google Checkout* credits to consumers who had purchased videos to own.

In 2007, some reports surfaced that Google was planning the release of its own mobile phone, possibly a competitor to Apple's iPhone. The project, called Android provides a standard development kit that will allow any "Android" phone to run software developed for the *Android SDK*, no matter the phone manufacturer. By June 2008, the Android Development Challenge was in its second round. In October 2007, *Google SMS Service (google.com/sms)* was launched in India, allowing users to get business listings, movie show times, and information by sending an SMS.

Google Product Search entry at Wikipedia.org contains a revolving list of all of Google's products. Products Related to Social Networking and Web 2.0. Google is very active in these areas. In addition to Orkut (discussed earlier) and Blogger.com (Chapter 6), Google launched the *Google Sites wiki* as a *Google Apps components* in 2008.

In an attempt to compete with Wikipedia, Google launched its *Google Knol* in 2007. This endeavor is still in testing.

Google Product Search is an example of the use of the concept of *collective wisdom*, which is used in Google Knol. It uses Google's collaborative ranking paradigm, which applies Google PageRank in order to determine a best-match for a given product entry. PageRank, Google's proprietary ranking algorithm, returns sorted results depending on the outcome of a "crawl" by a Web bot that determines the degree to which a given site is linked.

For more on Google products, visit *google.com/options*. The strategic moves Google is making are all in line with its mission statement: "To organize the world's information and make it universally useful and accessible."

Disruptors of Googel, Will They Succeed?

Many companies want to displace or to become as successful Google. Here are two examples:

Intelligent Search Engine—Will It Work? The various search engine models are based on keywords, which may result in poor or incorrect answers. So people can improve a search by adding one or two keywords (which many people do not like to do) for an advanced search. Powerset.com, a new start-up company, wants to use natural language queries (by typing your question in normal conversational syntax) instead of keywords as a model. So Powerset cut a deal with Xerox's PARC labs, a top research company on natural language understanding. Major unknowns are the quality of the natural language processing, and whether searchers will be willing to key in the long natural language queries instead of simple short keywords. However, if successful, this concept may disrupt the search engine industry and intensify the industry wars.

According to Sloan (2007), Web advertisers are moving beyond search by using powerful science to figure out what people want—sometimes before the searchers even know. By amassing data on the individual's online activities, advertiser can match ads to people using behavioral targeting.

Wikia.com and Collaborative Innovation. Wikia.com is a for-profit Web site related to Wikipedia Foundation (which is a not-for-profit organization). Wikia is growing very rapidly; 30,000 contributors created 500,000 Wikia articles in 45 languages in a 2–year period (see McNichol, 2007). One of its projects uses the people's community brain to build a better search engine than Google. The idea is to tap into the enthusiasm of users (see McNichol, 2007, for details).

Other potential competitors are *clusty.com, mooter.com,* and *snap.com.*

Enterprise Search

Enterprise searches can be integrated with other applications to improve performance. An enterprise search identifies and enables specific content across the enterprise to be indexed, searched, and displayed to authorized users. Google has partnered with BearingPoint, an IT consulting firm, to supply enterprise search capabilities. BearingPoint has experience in extending Google to provide search services to specific industries. A crucial enterprise search issue is programming search engines to crawl through all of the various data sources at a company and index their contents.

Example. Kaiser Permanente (*kaiserpermanente.org*), America's largest nonprofit health maintenance organization (HMO), has almost 9 million members. The amount of available medical knowledge doubles about every 7 years, so keeping up with new knowledge is an important aspect of good care giving by HMOs.

When Kaiser Permanente developed a clinical knowledge corporate portal for its 50,000 doctors, nurses, and other caregivers, enterprise search was a part of the plan. The Permanente Knowledge Connection, available from anywhere in the Kaiser wide area network, gives medical staff access to diagnostic information, best practices, publications, educational material, and other clinical resources. The portal's resources are distributed across the entire United States. Putting the right information quickly and easily into caregivers' hands is essential to the clinical portal's success.

Kaiser turned to the Google Search Appliance, which enabled the HMO to index 150,000 documents across the Kaiser network. Clinicians now search the site in situations that range from leisurely research to urgent care, from the exam room to the emergency room. Doctors and nurses use the search engine to help them reach diagnoses and specify treatments, check the side effects of new medications, and consult clinical research studies and other medical publications. Google's spell-checking capability is especially useful in the medical profession: Doctors' handwriting can be problematic, and pharmaceutical product names are difficult for small businesses.

Sources: Compiled from Carr (2006), Brown (2008), and Hicks (2004).

Questions

1. Use Google to conduct a search. What advertisements appear next to the search results?
2. What is Google trying to do with spreadsheets?
3. What is an enterprise search?
4. Identify potential revenue models in Google's activities described here and on Google's Web site.
5. How do Google's services benefit a company such as Kaiser?
6. Why is Google considered a Web 2.0 company? How is it related to social networking?
7. Enter *google.com* and identify all wireless activites.

8. Google derives most of its income from advertisement. Yet, it provides many other services for free. Speculate on the reasons.
9. Identify Google's activities related to e-commerce.

References

"Brown, M. C., "Hacking Google Maps: A Conceptual Approach," *ExtremeTech.com*, August 31, 2006, extremetech.com/article2/0,1558,2011239,00.asp (accessed June 2008).

Carr, D. F.,"How Google Works," *Baseline*, July 2006.

Goldberg, M.,"Market Wrap Up," *Financial Sense Online*, December 13, 2006, financialsense.com/Market/goldberg/2006/1214.html (accessed June 2008).

Hicks, M.,"Google's Next Step: Banner Ads," *SmartDeviceCentral.com*, May 13, 2004, *smartdevicecentral.com/article/Googles+Next+Step+Banner+Ads/127143_1.aspx* (accessed June 2008).

McNichol, T.,"Building a Wiki World (Wikia vs. Wikipedia)," *Business 2.0*, March 2007.

Sloan, P. "The Quest for the Perfect Online Ad," *Business 2.0*, March 2007.

Chapter

9

Transaction Processing, Functional Applications, and Integration

Learning Objectives

After studying this chapter, you will be able to:

❶ Relate functional areas and business processes to the value chain model.

❷ Define a functional management information system, and list its characteristics.

❸ Understand the transaction processing system and demonstrate how it is supported by IT.

❹ Analyze the support provided by IT and the Web to production/operations management, including logistics.

❺ Describe the support provided by IT and the Web to marketing and sales.

❻ Understand the support provided by IT and the Web to accounting and finance.

❼ Analyze the support provided by IT and the Web to human resources management.

❽ Describe the benefits and issues of integrating functional information systems.

Integrating *IT*

 ACC
 FIN
 MKT
 OM
 HRM
 IS

IT-PERFORMANCE MODEL

The focus of this chapter is the classification of information systems into several categories both inside organizations and among and between organizations. In each class we present the supporting role of IS via discussion and examples. The major objectives of these systems are to monitor performance, assess it, compare it to established targets, and, ultimately, improve it. In these ways the systems contribute to all steps in the performance management cycle.

The business performance management cycle and IT model.

WIRELESS INVENTORY MANAGEMENT SYSTEM AT DARTMOUTH-HITCHCOCK MEDICAL CENTER

SVR

OM

The Problem

Dartmouth–Hitchcock Medical Center (DHMC) is a large medical complex in New Hampshire, with hospitals, a medical school, and over 600 practicing physicians in its many clinics. DHMC was growing rapidly and was encountering a major problem in the distribution of medical supplies. These supplies used to be ordered by nurses. But nurses are usually in short supply, so having nurses spending valuable time ordering supplies left them less time for their core competency—patient care. Furthermore, having nurses handling supply

orders led to inventory management problems: Busy nurses tended to overorder in an effort to spend less time in managing inventory. On the other hand, they frequently waited until the last minute to order supplies, which led to costly rush orders.

One solution would have been to transfer the task of inventory ordering and management to other staff, but doing so would have required hiring additional personnel, and the DHMC was short on budget. Also, the coordination with the nurses to find what was needed and when, as well as maintaining the stock, would have been cumbersome.

What the medical center needed was a solution that would reduce the burden on the nurses, but also reduce the inventory levels and the last-minute, expensive ordering. Given the size of the medical center, and the fact that there are over 30,000 different inventory items, this was not a simple task.

The Solution

DHMC realized that its problem was related to the supply chain, and so it looked to IT for solutions. The idea that DHMC chose was to connect wireless handheld devices with a purchasing and inventory management information system. Here is how the new system works (as of the summer of 2002): The medical center has a wireless LAN (Wi-Fi) into which handhelds are connected. Information about supplies then can be uploaded and downloaded from the devices to the network from anywhere within the range of the Wi-Fi. In remote clinics without Wi-Fi, the handhelds are docked into wireline network PCs.

For each item in stock, a "par level" (the level at which supplies must be reordered) was established, based on actual usage reports and in collaboration between the nurses and the materials management staff. Now nurses simply scan an item each time it is consumed, and the software automatically adjusts the recorded inventory level. When a par level is reached for any inventory item, an order to the supplier is generated automatically. Similarly, when the inventory level at each nursing station dips below the station's par level, a shipment is arranged from the central supply room to that nursing station. The system also allows for nurses to make restocking requests, which can be triggered by scanning an item. The system works for the supplies of all non-nursing departments as well (e.g., human resources or accounting).

The system is integrated with other applications from the same vendor (PeopleSoft Inc., now an Oracle company). One such application is Express PO, which enables purchasing managers to review and act on standing purchase orders, e-procurement, and contract management.

The Results

Inventory levels were reduced by 50 percent, paying for the system in just a few months. Materials purchasing and management now are consistent across the enterprise; the last-minute, sometimes expensive ordering has been eliminated; the time spent by nurses on ordering and tracking materials has been drastically reduced; and access to current information has been improved. All of this contributed to reduced costs and improved patient care.

Sources: Compiled from Grimes (2003), Supply Chain Management and Logistics (2004), *peoplesoft.com* (now at *oracle.com;* material no longer available online), and *dhmc.org* (accessed May 2008).

Lessons Learned from This Case

The DHMC case provides some interesting observations about implementing IT: First, IT can support the routine processes of inventory management, enabling greater efficiency, more focus on core competencies, and greater satisfaction for employees and management. The new system also helped to modernize and redesign some of the center's business processes (e.g., distribution, procurement), and was able to support several business processes (e.g., operations, finance, and accounting), not just one. Although the system's major application is in inventory management, the same software vendor provided ready-made modules, which were *integrated* with the inventory module and with each other (for example, with purchasing and contract management). The integration also included connection to suppliers, using the Internet. This IT solution has proven useful for an organization whose business processes cross the traditional functional departmental lines. (In this case nursing is considered operations/production, and so is inventory control; purchasing and contract management are in the finance/accounting area.)

Functional information systems get much of their data from the systems that process routine transactions (*transaction processing systems, TPSs*). Also, many applications in business intelligence, e-commerce, CRM, and other areas use data and information from two or more functional information systems. Therefore, there is a need to integrate the functional systems applications among themselves, with the TPS, and with other applications. These relationships are shown in Figure 9.1, which provides a pictorial view of the topics discussed in this chapter. (Not shown in the figure are related applications discussed in other chapters, such as e-commerce and knowledge management.)

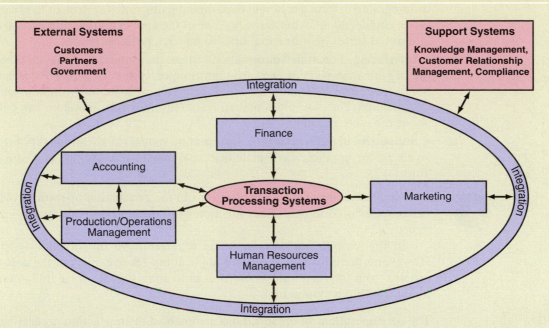

Figure 9.1 The functional areas, TPS, and integration connection. Note the flow of information from the TPS to the functional systems. Flow of information between and among functional systems is done via the integration component.

9.1 Functional Information Systems and Transaction Processing Systems

Traditionally, information systems were designed within each functional area to support the area by increasing its internal effectiveness and efficiency. However, the traditional functional structure may not be the best structure for some organizations, because certain business processes involve activities that are performed in several functional areas. Suppose, for example, a customer wants to buy a particular product. When the customer's order arrives at the marketing department, the customer's credit needs to be approved by Finance. Someone (usually in the production/operations area) checks to find if the product is in the warehouse. If it is there, then someone needs to pack the product and forward it to Shipping, which arranges for delivery. Accounting prepares a bill for the customer, and Finance may arrange for shipping insurance. The flow of work and information between the different departments may not work well, and coordination may be difficult, creating delays or poor customer service.

One possible remedy is an *integrated approach* that keeps the functional departments as they are, but creates an integrated supportive information system to facilitate communication, coordination, and control. The integrated approach is discussed in Section 9.6 and Chapter 10.

A frequent type of integrated functional area is the TPS, which is also discussed in this section.

MAJOR CHARACTERISTICS OF FUNCTIONAL INFORMATION SYSTEMS

Before we demonstrate how IT facilitates the work of the functional areas, and makes possible their integration, we need to look at the characteristics of the functional areas. Functional information systems share the following characteristics:

• **Composed of smaller systems.** A functional information system consists of several smaller information systems that support specific activities performed in the functional area (e.g., recruiting and promotions in HRM).

331

- **Integrated or independent.** The specific IS applications in any functional area can be integrated to form a coherent departmental functional system, or they can be completely independent. Alternatively, some of the applications within each area can be integrated across departmental lines to match a business process.

- **Interfacing.** Functional information systems may interface with each other to form the organization-wide or *enterprise* information system such as ERP (Chapter 10). Some functional information systems interface with the environment outside the organization. For example, a human resources information system can collect data about the labor market.

- **Supportive of different levels.** Information systems applications support the three levels of an organization's activities: *operational, managerial*, and *strategic* (see Tutorial 2).

An illustration of the IS applications in the production/operations area is provided in Online Brief 9.1. Other functional information systems have a similar basic structure.

In this chapter we describe some representative functional IT applications. However, since information systems applications receive much of the data that they process from the corporate *transaction processing system* or are integrated with it, we deal with this system first.

TRANSACTION PROCESSING INFORMATION SYSTEMS

The core operations of organizations are enabled by transaction processing systems.

In every organization there are business transactions that provide its mission-critical activities. Such transactions occur when a company produces a product or provides a service. For example, to produce toys, a manufacturer needs to order materials and parts, pay for labor and electricity, create a shipment order, and bill customers. A bank that maintains the toy company's checking account must keep the account balance up-to-date, disperse funds to back up the checks written, accept deposits, and mail a monthly statement.

Every transaction may generate additional transactions. For example, purchasing materials will change the inventory level, and paying an employee reduces the corporate cash on hand. Because the computations involved in most transactions are simple and the transaction volume is large and repetitive, such transactions are fairly easy to computerize.

The *transaction processing system* (TPS) monitors, collects, stores, processes, and disseminates information for all routine core business transactions. These data are input to functional information systems applications, as well as to data warehouse, customer relationship management (CRM), and other systems. The TPS also provides critical data to e-commerce, especially data on customers and their purchasing history.

Transaction processing occurs in all functional areas. Some TPSs occur within one area; others cross several areas (such as payroll). Online Brief 9.2 provides a list of TPS activities by the major functional areas. The information systems that automate transaction processing can be part of the departmental systems, and/or part of the enterprisewide information systems. For a comprehensive coverage of TPSs, see *en.wikipedia.org/wiki/Transaction_processing* and Bernstein and Newcomer (2006).

OBJECTIVES AND EXAMPLES OF TPSs

The primary goal of a TPS is to provide all of the information needed by law and/or by organizational policies to keep the business running properly and efficiently. Specifically, a TPS has to efficiently handle high volume, avoid errors, be able to handle large variations in volume (e.g., during peak times), avoid downtime, never lose results, and maintain privacy and security. To meet these goals, a TPS is usually automated and is constructed with the major characteristics listed in Table 9.1.

Examples of Computerized TPSs. Some examples of TPSs are

- Payroll preparation
- Traffic control at airports
- Registration at Facebook

TABLE 9.1	The Major Characteristics of a TPS

- Typically, *large amounts of data* are processed.
- The *sources of data are mostly internal,* and the output is intended mainly for an *internal audience.* This characteristic is changing somewhat, since trading partners may contribute data and may be permitted to use TPS output directly.
- The TPS processes information on a *regular basis:* daily, weekly, biweekly, and so on.
- *High processing speed* is needed due to the high volume.
- The TPS basically *monitors and collects current or past data.*
- Input and output *data are structured.* Since the processed data are fairly stable, they are formatted in a standard fashion.
- A *high level of detail* (raw data, not summarized) is usually observable, especially in input data but often in output as well.
- *Low computation complexity* (simple mathematical and statistical operations) is usually evident in a TPS.
- A high level of *accuracy, data integrity, and security* is needed. Sensitive issues such as privacy of personal data are strongly related to TPSs.
- *High reliability* is required. The TPS can be viewed as the lifeblood of the organization. Interruptions in the flow of TPS data can be fatal to the organization.
- *Inquiry processing* capacity is a must. The TPS enables users to query files and databases (sometimes in real time).

American Airlines (AA) and American Express partnered to offer passengers the convenience of in-flight card payments. A pilot program in 2005 led to AA customers' use of their credit and charge cards to purchase sandwiches, drinks, or headsets. Wireless, handheld devices process the transactions. The new system, which accepts most major credit and debit cards, became available across the entire fleet in June 2006 (*Cheapflights.com,* 2006). Other airlines use a similar device. These systems are so successful that cash is not accepted any more.

To process companies' tax returns faster and with fewer errors, the U.S. government and other governments mandate electronic filing. Furthermore, a fraud analysis by smart programs identifies potential cheaters.

As can be seen in some of the above examples, a TPS can be solely with a company (e.g., payroll preparation) or it may involve also customers and/or suppliers. The latter type of system is further discussed in Chapter 10 (supply chain–type systems) and Chapter 11 (interorganizational and global systems).

ACTIVITIES AND METHODS OF TPS

Regardless of the specific data processed by a TPS, a fairly standard process occurs, whether in a manufacturer, in a service firm, or in a government organization. First, raw data are collected by people or sensors (or data are already in files), and then the data are entered into the computer via any input device. Generally speaking, organizations try to automate the TPS data entry as much as possible because of the large volume involved.

Next, the system processes data in one of two basic ways: *batch* or *online processing.* In **batch processing,** the firm collects data from transactions as they occur, and stores them. The system then prepares and processes the collected data periodically (say, once every night). Batch processing is particularly useful for operations that require processing for an extended period of time. Once a batch job begins, it continues until it is completed. An example is a weekly payroll preparation, or a monthly budget utilization report. Your grade sheet is prepared at the end of the semester. In **online processing,** data are processed as soon as a transaction occurs, possibly even in *real time* (instantly).

Examples. In some companies, as soon as a spare part is used, an order for a new one is placed. When you place an order online, your credit card authorization is done instantly (e.g., ordering a book from Amazon.com).

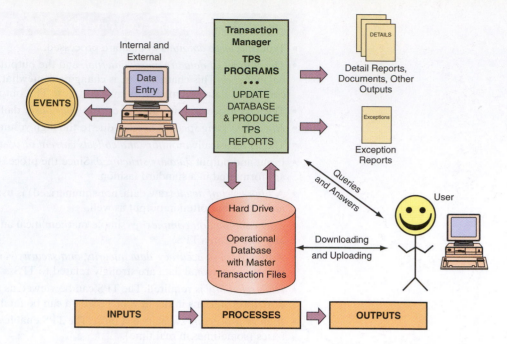

Figure 9.2 The flow of information in transaction processing.

To implement online transaction processing, *master transaction files* containing key information about important business entities are placed on hard drives as an operational database (see Figure 9.2) where they are directly accessible. The *transaction files* containing information about business activities, such as orders placed by customers, are also held in online files until they are no longer needed for everyday transaction processing activity. This ensures that the transaction data are available to all applications, and that all data are kept up-to-the-minute. These data can also be processed and stored in a data warehouse. The entire process is managed by a *transaction manager* (see the center of Figure 9.2 and *en.wikipedia.org/wiki/Transaction_processing* for details).

The flow of information in a typical TPS is shown in Figure 9.2. An event, such as a customer purchase, is recorded by the TPS program (e.g., by a barcode reader at the supermarket check out). The processed information (output) can be either a report or an activity in the database. In addition to a scheduled report, users can query the TPS for nonscheduled information (such as, "What was the sales volume of item B during the first five days, by day,"). The system will provide the appropriate answer by accessing a database containing transaction data (see bidirectional arrows in Figure 9.2).

WEB-BASED AND ONLINE TRANSACTION PROCESSING SYSTEMS

Transaction processing systems may be fairly complex, involving customers, vendors, telecommunications, and different types of hardware and software. Traditional TPSs are centralized and run on a mainframe. In **online transaction processing (OLTP),** transactions are processed as soon as they occur. For example, when you pay for an item at a POS at a store, the system records the effects of the sale by instantly reducing the inventory on hand by a unit, increasing the store's cash position by the amount you paid, and increasing sales figures for the item by one unit. For more on OLTP, see Chapter 12.

With OLTP and Web technologies such as a portal and an extranet, suppliers can look at the firm's inventory level or production schedule in *real time*. The suppliers themselves, in partnership with their customers, can then assume responsibility for inventory management and ordering in what is known as **vendor-managed inventory (VMI);** see Chapter 10. Customers, too, can enter data into the TPS to track orders and even query it directly. Other Web-based applications are described in *IT at Work 9.1.*

IT at Work 9.1

Modernizing the TPS Cuts Delivery Time and Saves Money

Here are some examples of how modernizing transaction processing systems has saved time and/or money:

Domino's Pizza. Domino's uses Microsoft's Tellme service to route the thousands of callers to its nearest outlet. The system is experimenting with automatic order taking. When you call and say "delivery," the system checks to see if the customer has called before and reads back the address where the delivery is to be made. Voice technologies are popular in other customer service applications, including wireless ones.

Kinko's (a FedEx company). Each time you make a copy at Kinko's, both a copying transaction and a payment transaction occur. In the past you received a device (a card, the size of a credit card) and inserted it into a control device attached to the copy machine, and it recorded the number of copies that you made. Then you stood in line to pay: The cashier placed the device in a reader to see how many copies were made. Your bill was computed, with tax added. Kinko's cost was high in this system, and some customers were unhappy about standing in line to pay for only a few copies. Today, using Kinko's new system, you insert your credit card (or a stored-value card purchased from a machine) into a control device, make the copies, print a receipt, and go home. You no longer need to see a Kinko's employee to complete your purchase.

Carnival Line. Carnival Line, the operator of cruise ships, needs to rapidly process sometimes over 2,500 people leaving the ship at the ports of call, and later returning to the ship. The company used printed name lists with space for manual checkmarks. Today,

passengers place a smart card into a reader. This way the company knows who left the ship and when, and who has returned. Each smart-card reader can process over 1,000 people in 30 minutes. In the past it was necessary to use 10–15 employees to process the people leaving and returning to the ship, and it took almost an hour. Today, one person supervises two card readers.

California Department of Motor Vehicles (DMV). The California DMV processes 15 million vehicle registration fees each year. To smooth the process, the DMV is using a rule-based expert system that calculates the fees (see *blazesoft.com* for details).

UPS Store. Seconds after you enter an address and a Zip code into a terminal at UPS delivery outlets at a UPS Store, a shipping label and a receipt are generated. Your shipping record stays in the database, so if you send another package to the same person, you do not need to repeat the address again.

Sprint Inc. Using an object-oriented approach, Sprint Inc. has improved its order processing for new telephones. In the past it took a few days for a customer to get a new telephone line; with its new system, Sprint can process an order in only a few hours. The order application itself takes less than 10 minutes, experiences fewer errors, and can be executed on electronic forms on a salesperson's desktop or laptop computer.

For Further Exploration: Could Kinko's operate completely without employees at their outlets? What effect does Carnival's smart-card reader have on security? Whose time is being saved at UPS and Sprint?

TYPICAL TASKS IN TRANSACTION PROCESSING

Transaction processing exists in all functional areas. Here we describe in some detail one application that crosses several functional areas—order processing.

Order Processing. Orders for goods and/or services may flow from customers to a company by phone, on paper, or electronically. Fast and effective order processing is recognized as a key to customer satisfaction. Orders can also be internal—from one department to another. Once orders arrive, an order processing system needs to receive, document, route, summarize, and store the orders. A computerized system can also track sales by product, by zone, by customer, or by salesperson, providing sales or marketing information that may be useful to the organization. As described in Chapter 6, more and more companies are providing systems for their salespeople that enable them to enter orders from a business customer's site using wireless notebook computers, PDAs, or Internet-enabled smart phones. Some companies spend millions of dollars reengineering their order processing as part of their transformation to e-business. IBM, for example, restructured its procurement system so its own purchasing orders are generated quickly and inexpensively in its e-procurement system.

Orders can be for services as well as for products. Otis Elevator Company, for example, tracks orders for elevator repair. The processing of repair orders is done via wireless devices that allow effective communication between repair crews and

IT at Work 9.2

Automatic Vehicle Location and Dispatch System in Singapore

SVR OM GLOBAL

Taxis in Singapore are tracked by a *global positioning system* (GPS), which is based on the 24 satellites originally set up by the U.S. government. The system allows the taxi dispatcher to get an instant fix on the geographical position of each taxi equipped with GPS (see attached figure).

Here's how the system works: Customer orders are usually received via cell phone, regular telephone, fax, or e-mail. Customers can also dispatch taxis from special kiosks (called CabLink) located in shopping centers and hotels. Other booking options include portable taxi-order terminals placed in exhibition halls. Frequent users enter orders from their offices or homes by keying in a PIN over the telephone. That number identifies the user automatically, together with his or her pickup point. Infrequent customers use an operator-assisted system.

Once an order has been received, the system finds (via the GPS) a vacant cab nearest the customer, and a display panel in the taxi alerts the driver to the pickup address. The driver has 10 seconds to push a button to accept the order. If he does not, the system automatically searches out the next-nearest taxi for the job.

The system completely reengineered taxi order processing. First, the transaction time for processing an order for a frequent user is much shorter, even during peak demand, since the user is immediately identified. Second, taxi drivers are not able to pick and choose which trips they want to take, since the system will not provide the commuter's destination. This reduces the customer's average waiting time significantly, while minimizing the travel distance of empty taxis. The system increases the capacity for taking incoming calls by 1,000 percent, providing a competitive edge to those cab companies that use the system. It also reduces misunderstanding between drivers and dispatchers, and driver productivity increased since drivers utilize their time more efficiently. Finally, customers who use terminals do not have to wait a long time just to get a telephone operator (a situation that exists during rush hours, rain, or any other time of high demand for taxis). Three major taxi companies with about 50,000 taxis are connected to the system.

Sources: Compiled from Liao (2003) and *Entersingapore.com* (2008).

For Further Exploration: What TPS tasks do computers execute in this order processing system? What kinds of priorities can be offered to frequent taxi customers?

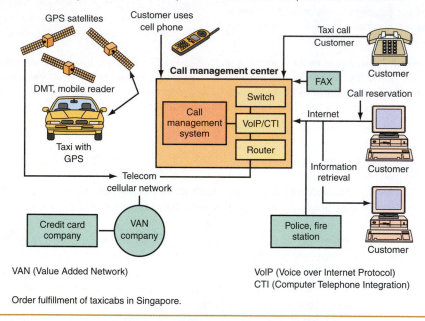

Order fulfillment of taxicabs in Singapore.

Otis physical facilities. Orders also can be processed by using innovative IT technologies such as global positioning systems; see *IT at Work 9.2.*

Web Analytics. Transaction processing can also be done on the Web in what is known as Web analytics. **Web analytics** is the analysis of data to understand visitor behavior on a Web site. Web analytics begins by identifying data that can assess the effectiveness of the site's goals and objectives (e.g., too frequent visits to a site map may indicate site navigation problems). Next, analytics data are collected, such as where site visitors are coming from, what pages they look at and for how long while visiting the site, and how they interact with the site's information. For example, the data can reveal the impact of an online advertising campaign, the effectiveness of Web site design and navigation, and, most important, visitor buying behavior. Because

TABLE 9.2	Typical TPS Activities
Activities	**Description**
The ledger	The entire group of an organization's financial accounts. Contains all of the assets, liabilities, and owner's (stockholders') equity accounts.
Accounts payable and receivable	Records of all accounts to be paid and those owed by customers. Automated system can send reminder notes about overdue accounts.
Receiving and shipping records	Transaction records of all items sent or received, including returns.
Inventory-on-hand records	Records of inventory levels as required for inventory control and taxation. Use of barcodes improves ability to count inventory periodically.
Fixed-assets management	Records of the value of an organization's fixed assets (e.g., buildings, cars, machines), including depreciation rate and major improvements made in assets, for taxation purposes.
Payroll	All raw and summary payroll records.
Personnel files and skills inventory	Files of employees' history, evaluations, and record of training and performance.
Reports to government	Reports on compliance with government regulations, taxes, etc.
Other periodic reports and statements	Financial, tax, production, sales, and other routine reports.

the goal of most EC sites is to sell product, the most valuable Web analytics are those related to step-by-step conversion of a visitor to a customer.

Web analytics is becoming a popular topic in management (e.g., see Sostre and LeClaire, 2007). It is used in all areas of business, helping to improve performance management. It employs a variety of tools and it can revolutionize e-business. For further details see *en.wikipedia.org/wiki/web_analytics*.

Information about Web analytics is also available from *emetrics.org*, and *jimnovo.com*. Two of many Web analytics tools include Web trends (*webtrends.com*) and ClickTracks (*clicktracks.com*).

Other TPS Activities. Other typical TPS activities are summarized in Table 9.2. Most of these routine tasks are computerized.

WHAT IF A TPS FAILS?

TPSs deal with the core activities of the organization. Their failure can cause a disaster. Several years ago, the U.S. Social Security Administration had some major TPS failures, as did insurance companies, hospitals, and banks. One might think that a large financial institution should be immune from IT failure, but this was not the case with TIAA-CREF, as illustrated in *IT at Work 9.3*.

TRANSACTION PROCESSING SOFTWARE

There are dozens of commercial TPS software products on the market. Many are designed to support Internet transactions.

The problem, then, is how to evaluate so many software packages. In Online Chapter 16, there is a discussion on software selection that applies to TPSs as well. But the selection of a TPS software product has some unique features. Therefore, one organization, the Transaction Processing Performance Council (*tpc.org*), has been trying to assist in this task. This organization is conducting *benchmarking* for a TPS. It checks hardware vendors, database vendors, middleware vendors, and so forth. Recently it started to evaluate e-commerce transactions (*tpc.org/tpcw*; there, see "transactional Web e-commerce benchmark"). Also, the organization has several decision support benchmarks (e.g., TPC-App, TPC-H, and TPC-R).

Review Questions

1. Define a functional information system.
2. List the major characteristics of functional information systems.
3. Define a TPS and list its major characteristics.
4. Describe the components and process of a TPS.
5. How is a TPS done on the Web?
6. List five typical TPS activities.
7. Describe the importance of Web analytics and show some of its applications.

IT at Work 9.3

The TIAA-CREF Computerized Reporting Failed

TIAA-CREF is a huge company serving the retirement, insurance, investment, and other needs of teachers and professors. It is one of the largest financial institutions of its kind.

In September 2005, thousands of TIAA-CREF members were unable to withdraw funds from their pensions. The company assured clients that this was just a small delay due to the IT platform upgrade. However, the problems lingered for months and expanded to inflow of money as well (Boucher-Ferguson, 2006a). The problem resulted from an attempt to introduce a powerful new platform, called Open Plan Solutions, whose objectives were to bring together fixed annuities, variable annuities, mutual funds, and homegrown platforms onto a single, connected platform with:

- **Flexible**, state-of-the-art record keeping
- **Streamlined** enrollment process
- **Comprehensive** remittance services
- **Improved** Web-based institutional reporting on accumulations, transactions, and salary reduction agreements

- **New** and improved participant quarterly statements

The problems included synchronization issues between the company's Web-access software and the record-keeping system during the batch transaction processing. In other words, the new system was not in sync with the old one. By April 2006, the problem became a disaster (Boucher-Ferguson, 2006b) because of the inability to solve all of the IT integration problems fast enough. At that time, the company set up a new cross-functional team to catch issues before they escalated.

Sources: Compiled from Boucher-Ferguson (2006a, 2006b) and from TIAA-CREF (2007).

For Further Exploration: If such a giant finance company had such problems, what about small companies? Could proper IT planning (Chapter 13) have prevented the problem? What are the damages to TIAA-CREF?

9.2 Managing Production/Operations and Logistics

The production and operations management (POM) function in an organization is responsible for the processes that transform inputs into useful outputs (see Figure 9.3). In comparison to the other functional areas, the POM area is very diversified, as are its supporting information systems. It also differs considerably among organizations. For example, manufacturing companies use completely different processes than do service organizations, and a hospital operates much differently from a university.

Figure 9.3 The production/operations management functions transform inputs into useful outputs. *(Source: J. R. Meredith and S. M. Shafer,* Operations Management. *New York: Wiley, 2002. Reprinted by permission of John Wiley & Sons, Inc.)*

Environment
- Customers
- Government regulations
- Competitors
- Technology
- Suppliers
- Economy

Inputs
- Capital
- Materials
- Equipment
- Facilities
- Supplies
- Labor
- Knowledge
- Time
- Energy

Transformation Process
- Alterations
- Transportation
- Storage
- Inspection

Outputs
- Facilitating goods
- Services

Action   Data   Action   Data   Data

Monitoring and control

Because of the breadth and variety of POM functions, here we present only three IT-supported POM topics: in-house logistics and materials management, planning production/operations, and computer-integrated manufacturing (CIM).

IN-HOUSE LOGISTICS AND MATERIALS MANAGEMENT

Logistics management deals with ordering, purchasing, inbound logistics (receiving), and outbound logistics (shipping) activities. In-house logistics activities are a good example of processes that cross several functional departments. Both conventional purchasing and e-procurement result in incoming materials and parts. The materials received are inspected for quality and then stored. While the materials are in storage, they need to be maintained until distributed to those who need them. Some materials are disposed of when they become obsolete or their quality becomes unacceptable (e.g., perishable or spoiled foods).

All of these activities can be supported by information systems. For example, many companies today are moving to some type of e-procurement (see Online Minicase 9.1 about Regent Inns). Scanners, RFID, and voice technologies, including wireless ones, can support inspection, and robots can perform distribution and materials handling. Large warehouses use robots to bring materials and parts from storage, whenever needed. The parts are stored in bins, and the bins are stacked one above the other (similar to the way safe deposit boxes are organized in banks). Whenever a part is needed, the storekeeper keys in the part number. The mobile robot travels to the part's "address," takes the bin out of its location (e.g., using magnetic force), and brings the bin to the storekeeper. Once a part is taken out of the bin, the robot is instructed to return the bin to its permanent location. In intelligent buildings in Japan, robots bring files to employees and return them for storage. In some hospitals, robots even dispense medicines. An example of a parts-tracking system is provided by Carr (2005).

Inventory Management. *Inventory management* determines how much inventory to keep. Both overstocking and keeping insufficient inventory can be expensive. Three types of costs play important roles in inventory decisions: the cost of maintaining inventories, the cost of ordering (a fixed cost per order), and the cost of not having inventory when needed (the shortage or opportunity cost). The objective is to minimize the total of these costs.

Two basic decisions are made by operations: when to order, and how much to order. Inventory models, such as the economic order quantity (EOQ) model, support these decisions. Dozens of models exist, because inventory scenarios can be diverse and complex. A large number of commercial inventory software packages to automate the application of these models are available at low cost. More and more companies are improving their inventory management and replenishment, better meeting customers' demands.

Many large companies (such as Wal-Mart) allow their suppliers to monitor the inventory level and ship when needed, eliminating the need for sending purchasing orders (a VMI strategy). The monitoring can be done by using mobile software agents over the Internet. It also can be done by using Web Services, as Dell Computer is doing. An emerging solution is the use of RFIDs. Reducing inventories and managing them properly is a major objective of supply chain management.

Quality Control. Manufacturing quality-control systems can be stand-alone systems or can be part of an enterprisewide total quality management (TQM) effort. They provide information about the quality of incoming materials and parts, as well as the quality of in-process semifinished and finished products. Such systems record the results of all inspections. They also compare actual results to metrics. One such matrix is the Six Sigma (*en.wikipedia.org/wiki/Six_Sigma*).

Quality-control data may be collected by Web-based sensors and interpreted in real time, or they can be stored in a database for future analysis. Also, RFIDs can be used to collect data. Periodic reports are generated (such as percentage of defects, percentage of rework needed), and management can compare performance among departments on a regular basis or as needed (recall our BPM model).

Web-based quality control information systems are available from several vendors (e.g., HP and IBM) for executing standard computations such as preparing quality control charts. First, manufacturing data are collected for quality-control purposes by sensors and other instruments. After the data have been recorded, it is possible to use Web-based expert systems to make interpretations and recommend actions (e.g., when to replace equipment).

Example. KIA Motors introduced an intelligent quality control system to analyze customer complaints for fast investigation and correction. The analysis was done with data mining tools.

PLANNING PRODUCTION/ OPERATIONS

The POM planning in many firms is supported by IT. Some major areas of planning and their computerized support are described here. An automatic defect-reporting system is described by Duvall (2005).

Just-in-Time Systems. In mass customization and build-to-order production (Tutorial #1), the *just-in-time* concept is frequently used. **Just-in-time (JIT)** is an inventory strategy that attempts to minimize inventories and to continuously improve processes and systems (see *en.wikipedia.org/wiki/just_in-time*). For example, if materials and parts arrive at a workstation *exactly when needed*, there is no need for inventory, there are no delays in production, and there are no idle production facilities or underutilized workers. Many JIT systems are supported by software from vendors such as HP, IBM, CA, and Cincom Systems. For how IT works with JIT, see Gillium et al. (2005).

As of 2001, car manufacturers adopted a make-to-order process. To deliver customized cars quickly and with cost efficiency, manufacturers need a JIT system. Oracle, Siemens, and other vendors offer a demand-driven *lean manufacturing*, which is a derivative of JIT (see Gillium et al., 2005), which means manufacturing with removal of waste of any kind. (e.g., labor, material space, energy). Like any other system, JIT needs to be justified with a cost/benefit analysis.

Project Management. A *project* is usually a one-time effort composed of many interrelated activities, costing a substantial amount of money, and lasting for weeks or years. The management of a project is complicated by the following characteristics.

- Most projects are unique undertakings, and participants may have little prior experience in the area.

- Uncertainty of cost and timing exists due to the generally long completion times.

- There can be significant participation of outsiders, which is difficult to control.

- Extensive interaction may be needed among participants.

- The many interrelated activities make changes in planning and scheduling difficult.

- Projects often involve high risks of delays, failures, and costly changes, but also high profit potential.

The management of projects is enhanced by computerized project management tools such as the *program evaluation and review technique* (PERT) and the *critical path method* (CPM). For example, developing Web applications is a major project, and several IT tools are available to support and help manage these activities (see Project Net from *citadon.com*). Merrill–Lynch uses such computerized tools to plan and manage its main projects, significantly improving resource allocation and decision making. Project management can be streamlined through online solutions, as demonstrated by Perkins–Munn and Chen (2004). Microsoft offers several project management tools (e.g., Project and Enterprise Project Management).

Other Areas. Many other areas of planning production and operations are improved by IT. For example, a Web-based production planning optimization tool, product routing, tracking systems, order management, factory layout planning and design, and other tasks have improved due to IT tools.

Examples. A Web-based system at Office Depot matches employee scheduling with store traffic patterns to increase customer satisfaction and reduce costs. Schurman Fine Papers (a retailer and manufacturer of greeting cards and specialty products) uses special *warehouse management* software to improve demand forecasting and inventory processes. Its two warehouses efficiently distribute products to over 30,000 retail stores.

Intelligent Factories for Mass Customization. Producing customized goods at competitive prices is done at the product development stage when manufacturers plan and simulate their production steps. Then, individual manufacturing processes can be optimized and coordinated with each other in a simulated factory. There all processes are rapidly fine tuned. All this can be done at a reasonable cost. Similarly, entire factories are planned and designed long before they are built. Using Virtual 3-D models with thousands of parameters, optimal processes are calculated. For how this is done, see *usa.siemens.com/answers/en/us/industry.htm?stc=219.*

COMPUTER-INTEGRATED MANUFACTURING

Computer-Integrated Manufacturing (CIM) is a concept or philosophy that promotes the integration of various computerized factory systems. CIM has three basic goals: (1) the *simplification* of all manufacturing technologies and techniques, (2) *automation* of as many of the manufacturing processes as possible, and (3) *integration and coordination* of all aspects of design, manufacturing, and related functions via computer hardware and software. Typical technologies to be integrated are flexible-manufacturing systems (FMSs), JIT, MRP, CAD, CAE, and group technology (GT).

The major advantages of CIM are its comprehensiveness and flexibility. These are especially important in business processes that are being completely restructured or eliminated. Without CIM, it may be necessary to invest large amounts of money to change existing information systems to fit the new processes. For an example of how a furniture company uses CIM, see *kimball.com* (click on Kimball Electronics Group). For more information, see *en.wikipedia.org/wiki/Computer_Integrated_Manufacturing.*

Review Questions

1. What is the function of POM in an organization? How can it be enhanced with IT?
2. What are logistics and materials management tasks?
3. List some POM planning activities and the IT support for those activities.
4. What is CIM?

9.3 Managing Marketing and Sales Systems

In Chapters 1 through 8 we emphasized the increasing importance of a customer-focused approach and the trend toward customization and personalization. How can IT help? First we need to understand how products reach customers, which takes place through a series of marketing entities known as *channels.*

Channel systems (in marketing) are all of the systems involved in the process of getting a product or service to customers and dealing with all customers' needs. The complexity of channel systems can be observed in Figure 9.4, where several major marketing systems are interrelated.

Channel systems can link and transform marketing, sales, procurement, logistics and delivery, and other activities. Added market power comes from the integration of channel systems with the corporate functional areas. The problem is that a change in any of the channels may affect the other channels. Therefore, the supporting information systems must be coordinated or even integrated.

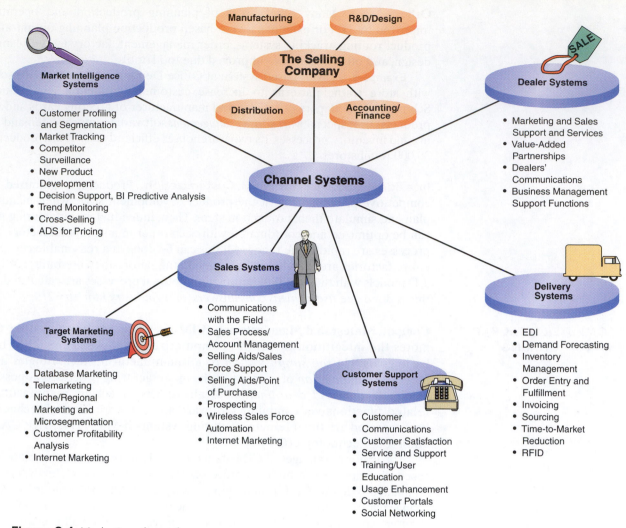

Figure 9.4 Marketing channel systems.

Channel-driven advantages are (1) transaction speed (real-time response) because of the interactive nature of the process, (2) global reach, (3) reduced costs, (4) add multimedia content, add strategic elements, and (5) reliability.

We describe only a few of the many channel-system activities here, organizing them into three groups: customer relations, distribution channels and in-store innovations, and marketing management. A fourth topic, telemarketing and online shopping, is presented in Online Brief 9.3.

"THE CUSTOMER IS KING/QUEEN"

It is essential for companies today to know who their customers are and to treat them like royalty. New and innovative products and services, successful promotions, customization, and world-class customer service are becoming a necessity for many organizations. In this section we will briefly describe a few activities related to *customer-centric* organizations. More are described in Chapter 10, where customer relationship management (CRM) is presented.

Customer Profiles and Preference Analysis. Information about existing and potential customers is critical for success. Sophisticated information systems have been developed to collect data on customers, their demographics (age, gender, income level), and their preferences. For example, shoppers' in-store activities can be monitored and then analyzed to better arrange the layouts and employees' scheduling. Analysis of shopping habits can help in organizing layouts of stores (see Nishi, 2005).

Prospective Customer Lists and Marketing Databases. All firms need to know who their customers are, and IT can help create customer databases of both existing and potential customers. It is possible today to purchase computerized lists from several sources and then merge them electronically. These prospective-customer lists then can be analyzed and sorted by any desired classification for direct mailing, e-mailing, or telemarketing. Customer data can be stored in a corporate database or in special marketing databases for future analysis and use. For example, Staples, Inc., uses software to identify its profitable customers as well as those who try to get refunds for shoplifted items or other kinds of refund fraud.

Mass Customization. Increasingly, today's customers want customized products. Some manufacturers offer different product configurations, and in some products dozens of options are available. The result is *mass customization*, as practiced successfully by Dell Computer and many other companies (see Tutorial #1). It is achieved by using easy-to-change computerized manufacturing systems. Thus, one can produce large quantities of customized products at a low cost, which usually is achieved only in production of large noncustomized items (called mass production). Customization is possible both in manufactured goods and in services.

As shown throughout this book, the changes introduced by mass customization are being supported by IT. For example, the Web can be used to expedite the ordering and fulfillment of customized products, as demonstrated in *IT at Work 9.4*, about building a Jaguar.

Mass customization is not for everyone, and it does have several limitations. The major limitations are that it requires a highly flexible production technology, an elaborate system for eliciting customers' wants and needs, and a strong direct-to-customer logistics system. Another limitation is cost: Some people are unable or unwilling to pay even the slightly higher prices that customization often entails. Butcher (2006) provides some guidelines for how to overcome these limitations.

IT at Work 9.4

MKT   GLOBAL

Build Your Jaguar Online

Prospective Jaguar car buyers can build, see, and price the car of their dreams online. As of October 2000, you can configure the car at *jaguar.com* in real time. Cars have been configured online since 1997, but Jaguar was the industry's first to offer comprehensive services, delivered in many languages.

Using a virtual car, users can view more than 1,250 possible exterior combinations, rotating the car through 360 degrees, by moving directional arrows. As you select the model, color, trim, wheels, and accessories, both image and price information automatically update. The design choices are limited to current models. Up to 10 personalized car selections per customer can be stored in a "virtual garage." Customers can "test" virtual cars and conduct comparisons of different models. Once the buyer makes a decision, the order is forwarded to a dealer of his or her choice.

Like most other car manufacturers, Jaguar will not let you consummate the purchase online. To negotiate price, customers can go to a Jaguar dealer or use Auto By Tel (*autobytel.com*), which connects nearby dealers to the customer. However, Jaguar's system helps get customers to the point of purchase. It helps them *research* the purchase and explore, price, and visualize options.

Customers thus familiarize themselves with the Jaguar before even visiting a showroom. The ability to see a 3-D photo of the car is an extremely important customer service. Finally, the order for the customer-configured car can be transmitted electronically to the production floor, reducing the time-to-delivery cycle.

The IT support for this innovation includes a powerful configuration database integrated with Jaguar's production system (developed by Ford Motor Company and Trilogy Corp.) and the "virtual car" (developed by Global Beach Corp.).

As of mid-2000, most car manufacturers had introduced Web-based make-to-order systems. In order to avoid channel conflicts, these systems typically involve the dealers in the actual purchase. All major car manufacturers are attempting to move some part of car ordering to the Web.

Sources: Compiled from *jaguar.com* press releases (October–November 2000), *ford.com* (accessed May 2008) (go to Services), and *autobytel.com* (accessed May 2008).

For Further Exploration: Why would manufacturers be interested in the Web if the actual purchase is done at the dealers' site?

Personalization. Using cameras, retailers can find what people are doing while they visit physical stores. Similarly, tracking software can find what people are doing in a virtual store. This technology provides information for real-time marketing and is also used in m-commerce. Personalized product offers then are made, based on where the customer spent the most time and on what he or she purchased. A similar approach is used in Web-based *cross-selling* (or *up-selling*) efforts, in which advertising of related products is provided. For example, if you are buying a car, car insurance is automatically offered.

Advertising and Promotions. The Internet opens the door to online advertising, mainly via e-mail and targeted banners, and it is growing rapidly. Innovative methods such as affiliate marketing are possible only on the Internet. Wireless and pervasive computing applications also are changing the face of advertising. For example, in order to measure attention to advertising, a mobile-computing device from Arbitron (see Portable People Meter at *arbitron.com*) is carried by customers. Whoever is wearing the device automatically logs advertising seen or heard any time, anywhere in his or her daily movements.

DISTRIBUTION CHANNELS AND IN-STORE INNOVATIONS

Organizations can distribute their products and services through several delivery channels. For instance, a company may use its own outlets or distributors. Digitizable products can be distributed online, or can be delivered on CD-ROMs. Other products can be delivered by trucks or trains, with the movement of goods monitored by IT applications. The Web is revolutionizing distribution channels. Here we look at some representative topics relating to distribution channels.

Improving Shopping and Checkout at Retail Stores. The modern shopper is often pressed for time, and most are unhappy about waiting in long lines. Using information technology, it is possible to reengineer the shopping and the checkout process, as illustrated in Chapter 1. Additional examples are the following:

- An information kiosk enables customers to view catalogs in stores, conduct product searches, and even compare prices with those of competitors. Kiosks at some stores (e.g., 7-Eleven stores in some countries) can be used to place orders on the Internet. In Macy's you can check the current price on computerized screens with barcode readers.

- Some stores that have many customers who pay by check (e.g., large grocery stores, Costco, Wal-Mart stores) have installed check-writers. All you have to do is submit the blank check to the cashier, who runs it through a machine attached to the cash register. The machine prints the name of the store as the payee and the amount, you sign the check, and in seconds the check is validated, your bank account is debited, and you are out of the store with your merchandise.

- The Exxon Mobil Speedpass allows customers to fill their tanks by waving a token, embedded with an RFID device, at a gas-pump sensor. Then the RFID starts an authorization process, and the purchase is charged to your debit or credit card. Customers no longer need to carry their Mobil corporation credit cards. (See *speedpass.com/forms/frmSpHome.aspx*.)

- An increasing number of retailers are installing self-checkout machines. For example, Home Depot has self-checkouts in their stores. Not only does the retailer save the cost of employees' salaries, but cus-

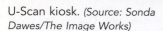

U-Scan kiosk. *(Source: Sonda Dawes/The Image Works)*

tomers are happier for saving time. (And some enjoy "playing cashier" briefly.) A major vendor is U-Scan, which is used in many supermarkets (see photo). Soon, RFIDs will improve the process even further.

MARKETING MANAGEMENT

Many marketing management decision applications are supported by computerized information systems. Here are some representative examples of how marketing management is being done.

Pricing of Products or Services. Sales volumes are largely determined by the prices of products or services. Price is also a major determinant of profit. Pricing is a difficult decision, and prices may need to be changed frequently. For example, in response to price changes made by competitors, a company may need to adjust its prices quickly or take other actions. Checking competitors' prices is commonly done by retailers. But instead of carrying paper and pen, one can use wireless price checkers (e.g., PriceMaster Plus, from SoftwarePlus). These devices make data collection easy.

Pricing decisions are supported by a number of computerized systems. Many companies are using business analytical processing to support pricing and other marketing decisions (see Chapter 12). Web-based comparison engines enable customers to select a vendor at the price they want, and they also enable vendors to see how their prices compare with others. For an example of price optimization, see Chapter 12. For more on price optimization, see *en.wikipedia.org/wiki/Demand_optimization*.

Salesperson Productivity. Salespeople differ from each other; some excel in selling certain products while others excel in selling to a certain type of customer or in a certain geographical zone. This information, which is usually collected in the sales and marketing TPS, can be analyzed using a comparative performance system in which sales data by salesperson, product, region, and even the time of day are evaluated. Actual current sales can be compared to historical data and to standards. Multidimensional spreadsheet software facilitates this type of analysis. Assignment of salespeople to regions and/or products and the calculation of bonuses can also be supported by this system. Wireless systems are used extensively by salespeople (see the Musco Food example in Online Minicase 9.2).

In addition, sales productivity can be boosted by Web-based systems. For example, in a Web-based call center, when a customer calls a sales rep, the rep can look at the customer's history of purchases, demographics, services available where the customer lives, and more. This information enables reps to work faster, while providing better customer service.

Productivity Software. **Sales automation software** is especially helpful to small businesses, enabling them to rapidly increase sales and growth. Such Web-based software (e.g., from *salesforce.com*) can manage the flow of messages and assist in writing contracts, scheduling, and making appointments. Of course, it also provides word processing and e-mail, and it helps with mailings and follow-up letters. Electronic stamps (e.g., *stamps.com*) can assist with mass mailings.

Profitability Analysis. In deciding on advertising and other marketing efforts, managers often need to know the profit contribution of certain products and services. Profitability information for products and services can be derived from the cost-accounting system. For example, profit performance analysis software available from IBM, Oracle, SAS, and Microstrategy, Inc., is designed to help managers assess and improve the profit performance of their line of business, products, distribution channels, sales regions, and other dimensions critical to managing the enterprise. Several airlines, for example, use automated decision systems to set prices based on profitability.

New Products, Services, and Market Planning. The introduction of new or improved products and services can be expensive and risky. An important question to ask about a new product or service is, "Will it sell?" An appropriate answer calls for careful analysis, planning, and forecasting. These can best be executed with the aid of IT because of the large number of determining factors and the uncertainties that may be involved (e.g., using predictive analysis, Chapter 12). Market research also can be conducted on the Internet. A related issue is the speed with which products are brought to market. An example of how Procter & Gamble expedites the time-to-market by using the Internet is provided in *IT at Work 9.5*.

Web-Based Systems in Marketing. Web (or Internet) marketing refers to marketing done over the Internet. It is basically a new marketing channel that is growing rapidly, and it is a major part of e-commerce. While Web marketing shares many

IT at Work 9.5

Internet Market Research Expedites Time-to-Market at Procter & Gamble

For decades, Procter & Gamble (P&G) and Colgate–Palmolive have been competitors in the market for personal care products. Developing a major new product, from concept to market launch, used to take over 5 years. First, a concept test was done; the companies sent product photos and descriptions to potential customers, asking whether they might buy it. If the feedback was negative, they tried to improve the product concept and then repeated the concept testing. Once positive response was achieved, sample products were mailed out, and customers were asked to fill out detailed questionnaires. When customers' responses met the companies' expectation regarding success of the new product, the company would start with mass advertising on television and in magazines.

However, thanks to the Internet, it took P&G only three and a half years to get Whitestrips, the teeth-brightening product, onto the market and to a sales level of $200 million a year—considerably quicker than other oral care products. In September 2000, P&G threw out the old marketing test model and instead introduced Whitestrips on the Internet, offering the product for sale on P&G's Web site. The company spent several months studying who was coming to the site and buying the product; it collected responses to online questionnaires, which was much faster than the old mail-outs.

The online research, which was facilitated by data mining conducted on P&G's huge historical data (stored in a data ware-

house) and the new Internet data, revealed the most enthusiastic groups. These included teenage girls, brides-to-be, and young Hispanic Americans. Immediately, the company started to target these segments with appropriate advertising. The Internet created a product awareness of 35 percent, even before any shipments were made to stores. (*Note:* This percentage of people who are aware about a new product is extremely high here in comparison to previous similar situations.) This "buzz" created a huge demand for the product by the time it hit the shelves.

From this experience, P&G learned important lessons about flexible and creative ways to approach product innovation and marketing. The whole process of studying the product concept, segmenting the market, and expediting product development has been revolutionized. Lately, P&G is experimenting with market research done in social networks such as MySpace and Facebook (see Chapter 8).

Sources: Compiled from Buckley (2002), and from *pg.com* (accessed May 2008).

For Further Exploration: How did the Internet decrease time-to-market in this situation? What is the role of data mining? Why is so much testing needed? And what other business applications can this concept fit?

things with traditional marketing, it uses new techniques that can significantly increase sales. As described throughout the book, Web marketing enables innovative advertising, market research, and sales opportunities. While it is a supplemental channel in most companies, it is extremely important in some. For a comprehensive coverage of the methods opportunities, integration with the traditional market, implementation, and success factors, see Zimmerman (2007).

Other Applications. Many other applications exist. For example, IT systems including RFID are utilized to reduce theft in stores.

Marketing activities conclude the *primary* activities of the value chain. Next we look at the functional systems that are *secondary* (support) activities in the value chain: accounting/finance and human resources management.

Review Questions

1. Define channel systems.
2. What is product/customer profitability?
3. Explain how the Web enables mass customization.
4. How does IT support marketing and sales?
5. What marketing strategies can be enhanced by the Web?

9.4 Managing Accounting and Finance Systems

A primary mission of the accounting/finance functional area is to manage money flows into, within, and out of organizations. This is a very broad mission since money is involved in all functions of an organization. Some repetitive accounting/financing activities such as payroll, billing, and cash management were computerized as early

ACC **FIN**

as the 1950s. Today, accounting/finance information systems are very diverse and comprehensive. Note that, while in universities, accounting and finance are separate departments, in industry they are frequently united in one department.

The general structure of an accounting/finance system is presented in Online Brief 9.4. It is divided into three levels: strategic, tactical, and operational. Information technology can support almost all of the activities listed, as well as the communication and collaboration of accounting/finance with internal and external environments. We describe selected activities in the rest of this section.

FINANCIAL PLANNING AND BUDGETING

Appropriate management of financial assets is a major task in financial planning and budgeting. Managers must plan for both the acquisition of financial resources and their use. Financial planning, like any other functional planning, is tied to the overall organizational planning and to other functional areas. It is divided into short-, medium-, and long-term horizons, much like activities planning. Financial analysts use Web resources and computerized analytics (Chapter 12) to accomplish the organization's financial planning and budgeting activities.

Financial and Economic Forecasting and Budgeting. Knowledge about the availability and cost of money is a key ingredient for successful financial planning. Especially important is the projection of cash flow, which tells organizations what funds they need and when, and how they will acquire them. This function is important for all firms, but is especially so for small companies, which tend to have little financial cushion. Inaccurate cash flow projection is the number-one reason why many small businesses go bankrupt. Availability and cost of money depend on corporate financial health and the willingness of lenders and investors to infuse money into the company.

Financial and economic analysis can be facilitated by intelligent systems such as data mining. For example, many software packages are available for conducting economic and financial forecasting, which are frequently available over the Internet for free or a fee.

Budgeting. The best-known part of financial planning is the annual budget, which allocates the financial resources of an organization among participants and activities. The budget is the financial expression of the organization's plans. It allows management to allocate resources in the way that best supports the organization's mission and goals. IT enables the introduction of financial logic and efficiency into the budgeting process.

Software Support. Several software packages, many of which are Web-based, are available to support budget preparation and control (e.g., Prophix Express from PROPHIX Software, and budgeting modules from Oracle and Capterra.com) and to facilitate communication among all participants in the budget preparation.

Example: Software support for budgeting is available from PROPHIX. The key benefits of the package are a familiar Windows Explorer interface, customizable flexibility that supports a variety of budgeting templates, a controlled database that secures data and allows for multiple user accessibility, and various data manipulation tools for complicated budgeting.

Since budget preparation may involve both top-down and bottom-up processes, modeling capabilities in some packages allow the budget coordinator to take the top-down numbers, compare them with the bottom-up data from the users, and reconcile the two.

The major benefits of using budgeting software are that it can reduce the time and effort involved in the budget process, explore and analyze the implications of organizational and environmental changes, facilitate the integration of the corporate strategic objectives with operational plans, make planning an ongoing continuous process, and automatically monitor exceptions for patterns and trends.

Capital Budgeting. *Capital budgeting* is the financing of asset acquisitions, including the disposal of major organizational assets. It usually includes a comparison of alternatives such as keep the asset, replace it with an identical new asset, replace it with a different one, or discard it. The capital budgeting process also evaluates buy-versus-lease options.

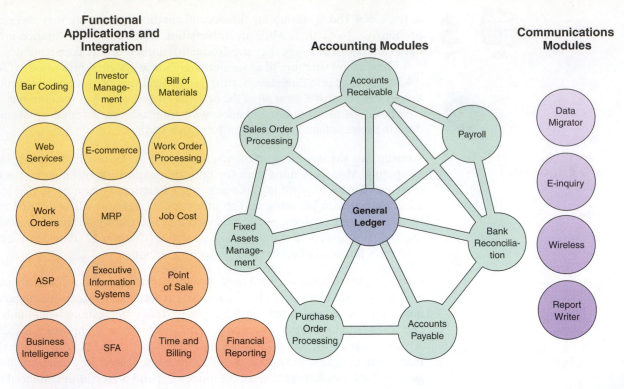

Figure 9.5 Integrated accounting/business software.

Capital budgeting analysis uses standard financial models, such as net present value (NPV), internal rate of return (IRR), and payback period (all presented in Online Chapter 17), to evaluate alternative investment decisions. Most spreadsheet packages include built-in functions of these models.

MANAGING FINANCIAL TRANSACTIONS

An accounting/finance information system is also responsible for gathering the raw data necessary for the accounting/finance TPS, transforming the data into information, and making the information available to users, whether aggregate information about payroll, the organization's internal reports, or external reports to stockholders or government agencies.

Many packages exist to execute routine accounting transaction processing activities. Several are available free on the Internet (try *tucows.com*). Many software packages are integrated. In these integrated systems, the accounting/finance activities are combined with other TPSs such as those of marketing and production and operations management. The data collected and managed for the accounting/finance transaction processing system are also inputs for the various functional information systems.

One such integrated system is MAS 90 ERP, MAS 200 ERP, and Sage MAS 500 ERP (from *sagemas.com*). It is a collection of standard accounting modules, as shown in Figure 9.5 (the "wheel" in the diagram). Communication and inquiry modules (right side) support the accounting modules. The user can integrate as many of the modules as needed for the business. On the left side is a list of other business processes and functional applications that can interface with accounting applications. Note that the software includes an e-commerce module, which provides dynamic Web access to MAS 90. This module includes account and order inquiry capabilities as well as a shopping cart for order entry. The 2008 version of MAS 90 and 200 includes modules for business intelligence, distribution, manufacturing, CRM, and financial reporting.

Another integrated accounting software package is *peachtree.com*, which offers a sales ledger, purchase ledger, cash book, sales order processing, invoicing, stock control, job casting, fixed-assets register, and more. Other accounting packages can be found at *2020software.com* and *findaccountingsoftware.com*.

The accounting/finance TPS also provides a complete, reliable audit trail of all routine transactions transmitted through the network. This feature is vital to accountants and auditors. (For more, see the "Control and Auditing" section on the next page..)

XBRL: Extensible Business Reporting Language. **XBRL** is a programming language and an international standard for electronic transmission of business and financial information. As of September 2005, it can be used to file financial reports electronically with the SEC and FDIC. With XBRL, all of the company's financial data are collected, consolidated, published, and consumed without the need to use Excel spreadsheets. Figure 9.6 illustrates how XBRL works (also see Pinsker and Li, 2008). Such submission allows government analysts to validate information submitted in hours instead of two to three weeks. For other benefits, see *en.wikipedia. org/wiki/XBRL*.

The U.S. government agencies plan to mandate the use of XBRL. According to Malykhina (2006), the Federal Financial Institutions Examination Council found that XBRL helps financial institutes:

• Generate cleaner data, including written explanations and supporting notes.
• Produce more accurate data with fewer errors that require follow-up by regulators (better quality).
• Transmit data faster to regulators and meet deadlines.
• Increase the number of cases and amount of information that staffers can handle.

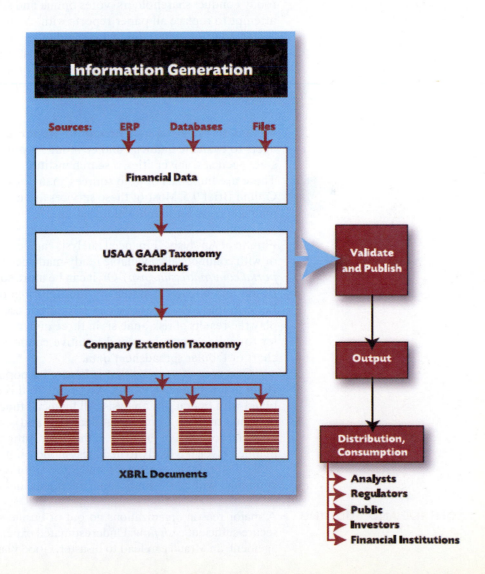

Figure 9.6 How XBRL works.

- Make information available faster to regulators and the public.
- Address issues and concerns in their filings rather than after the fact.
- Reduce report cycle time.
- Lead to more efficient capital market.

Detailed benefits to the various stakeholders (management, regulatory agencies, bankers, vendors, etc.) are provided at *ey.com/global/content.nsf/International/XBRL-How_Does_It_Work*.

INVESTMENT MANAGEMENT

Effective investment management is a difficult task, both for individuals and for corporations. For one thing, there are thousands of investment alternatives. On the New York Stock Exchange alone, there are more than 2,000 stocks, and millions of possible combinations for creating portfolios. Investment decisions are based on economic and financial forecasts and on various multiple and conflicting objectives (such as high yield, safety, and liquidity). The investment environment also includes opportunities in other countries. Another factor that contributes to the complexity of investment management is that investments made by many organizations are subject to complex regulations and tax laws. Finally, investment decisions need to be made quickly and frequently. Decision makers can be in different locations, and they need to cooperate and collaborate. Therefore, computerization is especially popular in financial institutions that are involved in investments. Many other banks and financial institutions have similar systems, especially for portfolio management. Companies today conduct shareholders' votes online and send reports to shareholders. Brokers attempt to replace all paper reports with electronic ones.

In addition, data-mining tools and other analytical tools are used by many institutional investment managers to analyze historical databases, so they can make better predictions and investment decisions. For a data-mining tool, see *wizsoft.com*.

The following are the major areas of support that IT can provide to investment management.

Access to Financial and Economic Reports.

Investment decisions require managers to evaluate financial and economic reports and news provided by federal and state agencies, universities, research institutions, financial services, and corporations. There are hundreds of Web sources, many of which are free; a sampling is listed in Online Brief 9.5. Most of these services are useful both for professional investment managers and for individual investors.

Financial Analysis.

Financial analysis can be executed with a spreadsheet program, or with commercially available ready-made decision support software (e.g., see *tradeportal.com/matrixsuite.asp*). Or, it can be more sophisticated, involving complex algorithms and intelligent systems. Other information technologies can be used as well. For example, Morgan Stanley and Company uses virtual reality on its intranet to display the results of risk analysis in three dimensions. Seeing data in 3-D makes it easier to make comparisons and intuitive connections than would a two-dimensional chart or tabular spreadsheet data.

One area of analysis that is becoming popular is referred to as **financial value chain management (FVCM).** According to this approach, financial analysis is combined with operations analysis. All financial functions are analyzed (including international trades). Combining financial and operations analysis provides better financial control. For example, if the organization runs its operations at a lower-than-planned level, it is likely to need less money; if it exceeds the operational plan, it may well be all right to exceed the budgeted amounts for that plan. FVCM is frequently combined with performance managements and facilitated by IT.

CONTROL AND AUDITING

A major reason organizations go out of business is their inability to forecast and/or secure sufficient *cash flow*. Underestimated expenses, overspending, financial mismanagement, and fraud can lead to disaster. Good planning is necessary, but not sufficient, and must be supplemented by skillful control. Control activities in organizations take many forms, including control and auditing of the information systems themselves. Information systems play an extremely important role in supporting organizational control, as we show throughout the text. Specific forms of financial control are presented next.

Risk Analysis. Companies need to analyze the risk of doing business with partners or in other countries. Giving credit to customers can be risky, so one can use products such as FICO (from *fairisaac.com*) for calculating risk. Also see @ RISK for Excel from *palisade.com*. Risk management is related to compliance (see *ca.com/gre*).

Budgetary Control. Once the annual budget has been decided upon, it is divided into monthly allocations. Managers at various levels then monitor departmental expenditures and compare them against the budget and operational progress of the corporate plans. Simple reporting systems summarize the expenditures and provide *exception reports* by flagging any expenditure that exceeds the budget by a certain percent or that falls significantly below the budget. More sophisticated software attempts to tie expenditures to program accomplishment. Numerous software programs can be used to support budgetary control; most of them are combined with budget preparation packages from vendors such as *claritysystems.com* and *capterra.com*.

Auditing. The major purpose of auditing is to ensure the accuracy and condition of the financial health of an organization. Internal auditing is done by the organization's accounting/finance personnel, who also prepare for external auditing by CPA companies.

IT can facilitate auditing. For example, intelligent systems can uncover fraud by finding financial transactions that significantly deviate from previous payment profiles. Also, IT provides real-time data whenever needed.

Financial Ratio Analysis. A major task of the accounting/finance department is to watch the financial health of the company by monitoring and assessing a set of financial ratios. These ratios are mostly the same as those used by external parties when they are deciding whether to invest in an organization, loan money to it, or buy it. But internal parties have access to much more detailed data for use in calculating financial ratios.

The collection of data for ratio analysis is done by the transaction processing system, and computation of the ratios is done by financial analysis models. The *interpretation* of the ratios, and especially the prediction of their future behavior, requires expertise and is sometimes supported by intelligent systems.

Profitability Analysis and Cost Control. Many companies are concerned with the profitability of individual products or services as well as with the financial health of the entire organization. Profitability analysis DSS software allows accurate computation of profitability and allocation of overhead costs. One way to control cost is by properly estimating it. This is done by using special software.

Profitability Management from Hyperion (an Oracle Company) provides potent multidimensional and predictive analysis, and proven query, reporting, and dashboard functionality with ease-of-use and deployment. The solution delivers powerful, insightful activity-based cost analysis and what-if modeling capabilities to help create and test new business strategies. Sophisticated business rules are stored in one place, enabling analyses and strategies to be shared easily across an entire enterprise (*SAS.com*, 2007).

Expense Management Automation. **Expense management automation (EMA)** refers to systems that automate data entry and processing of travel and entertainment expenses. These expenses can account for 20 percent of the operating expenses of large corporations (Degnan, 2003). EMA systems [by companies such as Captura, Concur, Extensity (now part of Infor), and Necho (now part of Cybershift)] are Web-based applications

A Closer Look 9.1

ACC   FIN

Expense and Spend Management Automation

Companies are interested in controlling all types of expenses, not just for travel. For these purposes there are several specialized IT programs. Most notable are those from Ariba.com. Ariba Spend Management software provides tools to analyze spending, buy products and services from suppliers via the Web, host online auctions (to reduce purchasing prices), and manage the bid process for prospective suppliers. Ariba even provides software tools to save money on SOX compliance as well as allocating resources for online sourcing.

Example. Diebold Inc., a global provider of security and integrated self-service delivery systems, saves over $100 million a year by using Ariba's *spend management* (the way in which companies control and optimize the money they spend) system. For

details, see customer case study of Diebold at *ariba.com/pdf/CaseStudy_Diebold.pdf.*

Another company that provides tools for **spend management** and analysis is Ketera Technologies (*ketera.com*). They also provide procurement and sourcing services (e.g., automating interactions with suppliers). Finally, they provide a repository for contracts and manage approval workflow.

SAP E-Sourcing (*sap.com*) provides software to analyze spending transactions to see whether purchases are being made with suppliers that have negotiated contracts (SRM Explorer). Online auctions and RFP are managed by Enterprise Sourcing.

About a dozen other companies provide tools for expense and spend management. Some relate it to compliance software.

---

that replace the paper forms and rudimentary spreadsheet. These systems let companies quickly and consistently collect expense information, enforce company policies and contracts, and reduce unplanned purchases of airline and hotel services. The software forces travelers to be organized before a trip starts. Not only does this result in benefits to the companies, but employees also benefit from quick reimbursement (since expense approvals are not held up by sloppy or incomplete documentation). For more on expense and spend management automation, see *A Closer Look 9.1.*

Several more applications in the financial/accounting area are described in Online Brief 9.6. Many more can be found in Reed et al. (2001).

Review Questions

1. How is financial planning and budgeting facilitated by IT?
2. Relate budgeting to planning and to IT support.
3. Define XBRL. Why is it so important?
4. How can IT better enable investment management?
5. List the major controls supported by IT.
6. How does IT enable spend and expense management?

9.5 Managing Human Resources Systems

Developments in Web-based systems increased the popularity of human resources information systems (HRISs) as of the late 1990s. Initial HRIS applications were mainly related to transaction processing systems. (For examples, see *en.wikipedia.org/wiki/Human_Resource_Management_Systems.*) In recent years, as systems generally have been moved to intranets and the Web, so have HRIS applications, many of which can be delivered via an HR portal and Intranets. Many organizations use their Web portals to advertise job openings and conduct online hiring and training. Gomez-Mejia et al. (2007) describe the impact of the Internet on acquiring, rewarding, developing, protecting, and retaining human resources. Their findings are summarized in Online Brief 9.7. Perhaps the biggest benefit to companies of human relations IT services is the release of HR staff from intermediary roles (e.g., by self-services, such as self-entry of an address change), so they can focus on strategic planning and human resources organization and development. In the following sections we describe in more detail how IT facilitates the management of human resources (HRM).

HRM

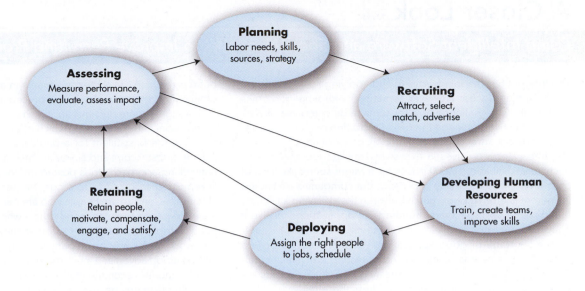

Figure 9.7 HRM activities.

To better understand how IT facilitates the work of the HRM department, let us look at Figure 9.7. The figure summarizes the role HRM plays in acquiring and keeping people in organizations. Note that the activities are cyclical in nature. The major activities are recruitment; human resources development, maintenance and assessment; and human resources planning and management. Details follow.

RECRUITMENT

Recruitment is finding employees, testing them, and deciding which ones to hire. Some companies are flooded with viable applicants, while others have difficulty finding the right people. Information systems can be helpful in both cases. Here we present some examples.

Using the Web for Recruitment. With millions of resumes available online, it is not surprising that companies are trying to find appropriate candidates on the Web, usually with the help of specialized search engines. Also, hundreds of thousands of jobs are advertised on the Web. Many matching services exist (see Internet Exercise #3). Online recruiting is able to "cast a wide net" to reach more candidates faster (Field, 2006), which may bring in better applicants. In addition, the costs of online recruitment are lower.

Recruitment online is beneficial for candidates as well. They are exposed to a larger number of job offerings, can get details of the positions quickly, and can begin to evaluate the prospective employer. To check the competitiveness of salary offerings, or to see how much one can make elsewhere in several countries, job candidates can go to *monster.com*.

As more companies expand operations overseas, global recruiting is becoming a vexing problem. Companies simply have problems finding qualified people, especially engineers and salespeople. Using the Internet to recruit from other countries is becoming popular, yet it requires expertise (see Shah, 2008).

Example: The Finish Line Corp. had to process more than 330,000 candidates that applied for employment with the company in a 12-month period; more than 75 percent of them applied online. Using screening software (by Unicru), 112,154 candidates were eliminated immediately. More than 60,000 hours of store managers' time were saved because of the reduction in the number of interviews conducted (see Field, 2006).

Using Social Networks and Intelligent Software. Recruitment at virtual worlds and social networking sites is very popular. It is done at most major sites (e.g., LinkedIn, MySpace, Facebook, Craigslist, and Second Life). Recruitment online is

A Closer Look 9.2

Using Intelligent Software and Social Networks to Improve Recruiting Processes

The Internet has made advertising and applying for jobs online a much simpler process. However, sometimes with simplicity comes complexity. The challenge now for some large companies is how to cost-effectively manage the online recruiting process, because online ads are attracting large numbers of applicants. For example, Infosys now receives in excess of 1 million job applications each year to fill about 9,000 positions. It might sound like a good problem to have too many applicants, but companies are finding that there is often a poor match between the skills and attributes they require and the many hundreds of applications received. Thus, despite attracting a lot of applicants, they often still suffer from a shortage of good applications. Furthermore, how can a company be sure it is accessing and attracting the very best talent in a particular field? Some interesting new developments are changing the way companies may address these issues.

Trovix offers a service to companies based on its award-winning HR software, which uses embedded intelligence to help manage the entire recruitment process. Trovix argues that its tools Trovix Recruit and Trovix Intelligent Search can emulate human decision makers and assess a candidate's amount, depth, relevance and recency of work experience, education, and the like. The software presents in rank order the best candidates to fit an advertised position. Other features enable tracking of applicants, reporting, and communications. A number of institutions are using this service, including Stanford University, which needs to fill thousands of positions each year. Trend Micro adopted Trovix and was able to screen 700 applicants and list the top 10 in about 20 minutes. The accuracy is probably no better than manual processing,

but the software can screen applicants in a much shorter period of time. For other companies and procedures see Balch (2008).

A slightly more personal approach is available through some of the social networking sites, which offer support for companies to locate the best talent for a particular position. Sites such as Jobster (*jobster.com*) and LinkedIn (*linkedin.com*) rely more on a networking approach. Jobs posted on Jobster, for example, are linked to other job sites, to blogs, to user groups, to university alumni sites, and so on. People who are part of the social network are encouraged to recommend others who might be suited to a particular job, irrespective of whether they are actively seeking new work. In this way, a company looking to recruit the best talent has its job advertised much more widely and may benefit from word-of-mouth recommendations and referrals. For example, LinkedIn offers prospective employers a network of more than 8 million people across 130 industries, meaning much larger exposure for job vacancies and a much larger talent pool to seek referrals from. Sites such as Jobster can also track where applicants come from, helping companies adopt better recruitment strategies and thus achieve better returns from their investments in seeking the best staff.

Another application of intelligent software is pre-employment screening. Tests, research background, and more can save time and increase accuracy (see Taylor-Arnold 2008).

Sources: Compiled from McKay (2004), Totty (2006), *Ere.net* (2006), *trovix.com* (accessed June 2008), *jobster.com* (accessed June 2008), and *LinkedIn.com* (2006).

---

frequently supported by intelligent software agents. For a complete analysis of and guidelines for e-recruitment, see Field (2006). For an example of how this is done, see *A Closer Look 9.2*.

HRM Portals and Salary Surveys. One advantage of the Web is the large amount of information related to job matching. There are also many private and public HR-related portals. For example, several large companies (e.g., IBM, Xerox, GE) created jointly with 120 companies a career portal called DirectEmployer.com (now available at *jobcentral.com*). Commercial, public online recruiters, such as Monster.com, help corporate recruiters find candidates for difficult-to-fill positions.

Another area for HR portals is salary surveys. Salary surveys help companies determine how much to pay their employees. Companies used to pay consultants up to $10,000 for a one-time survey. Now they can conduct such surveys themselves by utilizing free data from vendors such as Salary.com (check "What you are worth"). Salary Wizard Pro covers pay scales in small businesses.

Employee Selection. The human resources department is responsible for screening job applicants, evaluating, testing, and selecting them in compliance with state and federal regulations. The process of employee selection can be very complex since it may involve many external and internal candidates and multiple criteria. To expedite the testing and evaluation process and ensure consistency in selection, companies use information technologies such as Web-based intelligent systems.

HUMAN RESOURCES MAINTENANCE AND DEVELOPMENT

Once recruited, employees become part of the corporate human resources pool, which needs to be maintained and developed. Some activities supported by IT are the following.

Performance Evaluation. Most employees are periodically evaluated by their immediate supervisors. Peers or subordinates may also evaluate others. Evaluations are usually recorded on paper or electronic forms. Using such information manually is a tedious and error-prone job. Once digitized, evaluations can be used to support many decisions, ranging from rewards to transfers to layoffs. For example, Cisco Systems is known for developing an IT-based human capital strategy. Many universities evaluate professors online. The evaluation form appears on the screen, and the students fill it in. Results can be tabulated in minutes. Corporate managers can analyze employees' performances with the help of intelligent systems, which provide systematic interpretation of performance over time. Several companies provide software for performance evaluation (e.g., *people_trak.com, talco.com*).

Wage review is related to performance evaluation. For example, Hewlett-Packard's Atlanta-based U.S. Field Services Operations (USFO) Group has developed a paperless wage review (PWR) system. The Web-based system uses intelligent agents to deal with quarterly reviews of HP's 15,000 employees. (A similar system is used by most other groups, covering a total of 150,000 employees.) The agent software lets USFO managers and personnel access employee data from both the personnel and functional databases. The PWR system tracks employee review dates and automatically initiates the wage review process. It sends wage review forms to first-level managers by e-mail every quarter.

Training and Human Resources Development. Employee training and retraining is an important activity of the human resources department. Major issues are planning of classes and tailoring specific training programs to meet the needs of the organization and employees. Sophisticated human resources departments build a career development plan for each employee. IT can support the planning, monitoring, and control of these activities by using workflow applications.

IT also plays an important role in training. Some of the most innovative developments are in the areas of *intelligent computer-aided instruction* (ICAI) and application of multimedia support for instructional activities. Training salespeople is an expensive and lengthy proposition. To save money on training costs, companies are providing sales-skills training over the Internet or intranet. Online Brief 9.8 provides an example of the variety of employee training available on the Internet and intranets. Interesting implementations of computer-based training at Sheetz convenience stores is reported by Korolishin (2004b).

Training can be improved using Web-based video clips. For example, using a digital video-editing system, Dairy Queen's in-house video production department produced a higher-quality training video at half the cost than by outsourcing it. The affordability of the videos encourages more Dairy Queen franchises to participate in the training program. This improves customer service as well as employee skill. For tools for online training, see *flextraining.com* and Camtasia from *techsmith.com*.

Mobile devices are increasingly being used for training as well as for performance improvement (Gayeski, 2004). Training can be enhanced by virtual reality. Intel, Motorola, Samsung Electronic, and IBM are using virtual reality and *virtual worlds* to simulate different scenarios and configurations. The training is especially effective in complex environments where mistakes can be very costly. For more on training with virtual worlds, see Gronstedt (2008).

Most promising Web-based training tools are those that are based on interactive simulation and virtual environments where the user learns by operating or playing in a simulated environment (e.g., in games like SIM City and in Second Life). The aircraft industry has been using flight simulators for decades for training pilots. Second Life has a special forum on traing and learning using virtual worlds. An

A Closer Look 9.3

Using Interactive Simulation in Training

HRM

An effective technology for e-training and e-learning is *visual interactive simulation* (VIS), which uses computer graphic displays to present the impact of decisions. It differs from regular graphics in that the user can adjust the decision-making process and see the results of the intervention. Some learners respond better to graphical displays, and this type of interaction can help students and managers learn about decision-making situations. For example, VIS was applied to examining the operations of a physician clinic environment within a physician network to provide high-quality, cost effective healthcare in a family practice. The simulation system identified the most important input factors that significantly affected performance. These inputs, when properly managed, led to lower costs and higher service levels.

VIS can represent a static or a dynamic system. Static models display a visual image of the result of one decision alternative at a time. Dynamic models display systems that evolve over time, and the evolution can be represented by animation.

The learner can interact with the simulated model, watch the results develop over time, and try different decision strategies online. Enhanced learning, both about the problem and the impact of the alternatives tested, can and does occur.

The major potential benefits of such systems are

- Shortening the trainee's learning time
- Easing the learning of operating complex equipment
- Enabling self-learning, any place, any time
- Achieving better memorization
- Lowering the overall cost of training
- Recording the learning progress of individuals and improving it

Several companies provide the necessary software and learning procedure. One product is SimMAGIC, from Hannastar Technology Co., Ltd., in Taiwan. The attached photos show application in a pharmaceutical company (on the left), and trainee progress charts (on the right).

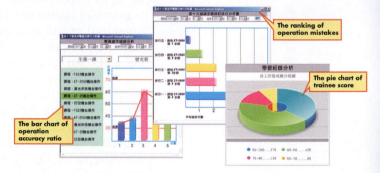

SimMagic training application in the pharmaceutical industry. *(Courtesy of HamStar Technology Ltd.)*

SimMagic presenting data of the training process. *(Courtesy of HamStar Technology Ltd.)*

example of how interactive simulation is utilized in training for the use of complex equipment is provided in *A Closer Look 9.3*.

HUMAN RESOURCES PLANNING AND MANAGEMENT

Managing human resources in large organizations requires extensive planning and detailed strategy (Gomez-Mejia, 2007). In some industries, labor negotiation is a particularly important aspect of human resources planning and it may be facilitated by IT. For most companies, administering employee benefits is also a significant part of the human resources function. Here are some examples of how IT can help.

Personnel Planning and HR Strategies. The human resources department forecasts requirements for people and skills. In some geographical areas and for overseas assignments it may be difficult to find particular types of employees. In such cases the HR department plans how to find (or develop from within) sufficient human resources. Also, compliance with regulations regarding safety and privacy is facilitated by IT.

Large companies develop qualitative and quantitative workforce planning models. Such models can be enhanced if IT is used to collect, update, and process the information. Radio Shack uses special software to develop HR strategies (for details, see Reda, 2004).

Benefits Administration. Employees' contributions to their organizations are rewarded by salary/wage, bonuses, and other benefits. Benefits include those for health and dental care as well as contributions for pensions. Managing the benefits system can be a complex task, due to its many components and the tendency of organizations to allow employees to choose and trade off benefits ("cafeteria style"). In large companies, using computers for self-benefits selection can save a tremendous amount of labor and time for HR staff (see *iemployee.com*).

Providing flexibility in selecting benefits is viewed as a competitive advantage in large organizations. It can be successfully implemented when supported by computers. Some companies have automated benefits enrollments. Employees can self-register for specific benefits using the corporate portal or voice technology. Employees self-select desired benefits from a menu. Payroll pay cards are now in use in numerous companies, such as Payless Shoes, which has 30,000 employees in 5,000 stores. The system specifies the value of each benefit and the available benefits balance of each employee (see Korolishin, 2004a). Some companies use intelligent agents to assist the employees and monitor their actions. Expert systems can answer employees' questions and offer advice online. Simpler systems allow for self-updating of personal information such as changes in address, family status, and so on. Self-entry saves money for the company and is usually more accurate.

Employee Relationship Management. In their effort to better manage employees, companies are developing *human capital management* (HCM), facilitated by the Web, to streamline the HR process. These Web applications are more commonly referred to as **employee relationship management (ERM).** For example, self-services such as tracking personal information and online training are very popular in ERM. Improved relationships with employees results in better retention and higher productivity. ERM technologies and applications are very similar to those of customer relationship management (CRM), which we discuss in Chapter 10. For an example of ERM, see Online Minicase 9.3.

Note: The acronym ERM also stands for *Employee Resource Management.* This type of software is usually an integrated suite that includes many of the systems described in Section 9.5. Furthermore, ERM software can be a part of ERP. An example can be seen in products by Oracle and NetSuite. Such offerings demonstrate *integrated systems* which are discussed next.

Review Questions

1. List IT-supported recruitment activities.
2. How can training be done online?
3. Explain human resources information systems.
4. Describe IT support for employee selection, promotion, and development.

9.6 Integrating Functional Information Systems

Functional information systems can be built in-house, they can be purchased from large vendors (such as Computer Associates, Best Software Inc., Microsoft, Oracle, or IBM), and dozens of small software vendors, or they can be leased from application service providers (ASPs). In any of these cases, there is a need for their integration with other information systems, including databases.

REASONS FOR INTEGRATION

For many years most IT applications were developed in the functional areas, independent of each other. This created potential problems with information sharing, especially when the business processes were done in several departments, such as order fulfillment or preparing a payroll. For example, *Baseline* reported in its May 2006 issue on problems in the payroll and personnel system of the U.S. Army. Many companies developed their own customized systems, referred to as home-grown systems, which dealt with standard procedures to execute transaction processing/operational activities. These procedures are fairly similar, regardless of what company is performing them. Therefore, the trend today is to buy commercial, off-the-shelf functional applications or to lease them from ASPs. The smaller the organization, the more attractive such options are. Indeed, several hundred commercial products are available to support each of the major functional areas.

Development tools are also available to build custom-made applications in a specific functional area. For example, there are software packages for building financial applications, a hospital pharmacy management system, and a university student registration system. Some software vendors specialize in one or a few areas. For example, Lawson Software concentrates on retailing for companies such as Dollar General (see the minicase at the end of this chapter).

However, to build information systems along business processes (which cross functional lines) requires a different approach. Matching business processes with a combination of several functional off-the-shelf packages may be a solution in some areas. For example, it may be possible to integrate manufacturing, sales, and accounting software if they all come from the same software vendor (as shown in the opening case). However, combining existing packages from several vendors may not be practical or effective. To build applications that will easily cross functional lines and reach separate databases often requires new approaches, such as Web Services, and integrated suites, such as those offered by Oracle.com.

Information systems integration tears down barriers between and among departments and corporate headquarters and reduces duplication of effort.

One of the key factors for integration, especially with business partners, is agreement on appropriate standards (see *openapplications.org*). Integration can be done by computer software, known as middleware, that connects other software programs (see the Oracle Fusion Project at *searchoracle.techtarget.com/generic/0,295582,sid41_gci1218686,00.html#latestnews* and Technology Guide 2) and by Web Services (Technology Guide 5).

Integrated information systems can be built easily in a small company. In large organizations, and even in multinational corporations, integration may require more effort, as shown in *IT at Work 9.6*.

Another approach to integration of information systems is to use existing ERP software. However, ERP requires a company to fit its business processes to the software. As an alternative to ERP, companies can choose the *best-of-breed systems* (best systems for specific use available from different vendors) on the market and integrate them, or use some of their own home-grown systems and integrate them. The latter approach may not be simple, but it may be more effective.

By whatever method it is accomplished, integrating information systems helps to reduce cost, increase employees' productivity, and facilitate information sharing and collaboration, which are necessary for improving customer service.

INTEGRATION OF FRONT-OFFICE WITH BACK-OFFICE OPERATIONS

A frequent cross-departmental integration is the one that involves front-office with back-office operations. Front-office refers to customer facing systems, mostly marketing, advertising, and order taking. Back-office refers to activities related to order fulfillment, accounting, finance, production, and shipments. This is a difficult task. It is easier to integrate the front-office operations among themselves and the back-office operations among themselves (which is basically what systems such as MAS 90 are doing).

USING ENTERPRISE 2.0 AND VIRTUAL WORLDS

Integrating functional areas can be facilitated by Web 2.0 tools (e.g., blogging, wikis) to enhance interdepartmental collaboration. Companies can open pages on social networks that may involve several departments. There is an increasing presence in social networks (e.g., recruiting and marketing at LinkedIn, as well as a presence in Second Life (see Exercises and Projects #6).

Review Questions

1. Why is application integration necessary?
2. List some approaches to integration.

IT at Work 9.6

Software Helps Cirque du Soleil

MKT OM

Cirque du Soleil is a Canada-based traveling circus. Using IT, the circus is able to entertain more people each year than the Red Sox and Yankees combined (over ten million in 2007, in four continents). How do they do it? First, this is no ordinary circus. It features astonishing acrobatics and Broadway-caliber music and dance in 18 different shows (in addition to traditional circus and opera). All this is done by 20,000 performers and 4,000 management employees, who are constantly on the move using 250 tractor-trailers. Twenty thousand performers are scheduled and transported with all of the stage equipment and costumes that are constantly changing. The company grew very rapidly between 2000 and 2008, and several problems were created as a result of the rapid growth.

The logistics of people, transportation, accommodations, food, supplies, and so on, in hundreds of different cities each year, for several traveling groups is fairly difficult. And there are 200 different applications in all functional areas, from finance to POM, accounting, marketing, and human resources management. These applications were unable to share data, threatening the productivity of people and causing delays, problems, and unnecessary expenses. For example, if an employee gets sick, how quickly can a replacement be found? What is done if equipment is lost, or a tractor-trailer is delayed?

The problem was compounded by the rapid growth of the business to include five permanent shows in Las Vegas and the frequent changes in programs and plans.

Because of the unique nature of the business, most of the applications were done in-house. For example, special software was needed to make or buy costumes and to assign artists to the "make" job. In addition, the company installed ERP, for human resources management, production scheduling, logistics, and finance. Even the medical records of the performers were tracked. To enable the various applications to communicate with each other, the company implemented IBM WebSphere Business Integration software to connect all of its disparate systems and applications. The integrated system replaced the manual work of the production managers, who do an inventory whenever a group arrives at a destination. If something was missing, several people were engaged in finding a replacement. Now, due to data sharing, there are very few cases of missing items. Furthermore, IBM WebSphere helped cut the development time for new applications, as well as the modification time of existing applications, by about 25 percent. Also, time to connect new business software to the intranet has been reduced by 20 percent. All of this helped increase productivity. In 2001, there were 65 tickets sold per employee, but by 2005 the total was about 200.

Sources: Compiled from Barrett (2005), IBM (2005), and *cirquedusoleil.com* (accessed May 2008).

For Further Exploration: Why was it necessary to integrate the functional applications? Could the company grow so rapidly otherwise? How?

9.7 Managerial Issues

1. Integration of functional information systems. Integration of existing stand-alone functional information systems is a major problem for many organizations. Although client/server architecture is more amenable to integration than legacy systems, there are still problems of integrating different types of data and procedures used by functional areas. Also, there is an issue of willingness to share information, which may challenge existing practices and cultures.

2. Priority of transaction processing Transaction processing may not be an exotic application, but it deals with the core processes of organizations. It must receive top priority in resource allocation, balanced against innovative applications needed to sustain competitive advantage and profitability, because the TPS collects the information needed for most other applications.

3. Finding innovative applications. Tools such as Lotus Notes, corporate portals, and Web-based business intelligence enable the construction of many applications that can increase productivity and quality. Finding opportunities for such applications can be best accomplished cooperatively by end users and the IS department.

4. Using the Web. Web-based systems should be considered in all functional areas. They are effective, cost relatively little, and are user friendly. In addition to new applications, companies should consider conversion of existing applications to Web-based ones.

5. Systems integration. Although functional systems are necessary, they may not be sufficient if they work independently. It is difficult to integrate functional information systems, but there are several approaches to doing so. In the future, Web Services could solve many integration problems, including connecting to a legacy system.

ETHICS

6. Ethical issues. Many ethical issues are associated with the various topics of this chapter. Professional organizations, relating to the functional areas (e.g., marketing associations), have their own codes of ethics. These codes should be taken into account in developing functional systems. Likewise, organizations must consider privacy policies. Several organizations provide comparisons of privacy policies and other ethics-related topics. For an example, see *socap.org*.

HRM applications are especially prone to ethical and legal considerations. For example, training activities that are part of HRM may involve ethical issues in recruiting and selecting employees and in evaluating performance. Likewise, TPS data processing and storage deal with private information about people, their performance, and so forth. Care should be taken to protect this information and the privacy of employees and customers.

For more on business ethics as it applies to topics in this chapter, see *ethics.ubc.ca/resources/business*.

How *IT* Benefits You

Accounting Major

Executing TPSs effectively is a major concern of any accountant. It is also necessary to understand the various activities of all functional areas and how they are interconnected and supported by IT. Also, many supply chain management issues, ranging from inventory management to risk analysis, fall within the realm of accounting.

Other accounting tasks are taxation, auditing, and government reports. They all can be improved with appropriate accounting software. Appropriate controls and auditing can eliminate fraud and are executed with software.

Finance Major

IT helps financial analysts and managers perform their tasks better. Of particular importance is analyzing cash flows and securing the financing required for smooth operations. In addition, financial applications can support such activities as risk analysis, investment management, and global transactions involving different currencies and fiscal regulations.

A major area of concern for the finance department is compliance with SOX. Many innovative software packages can help here. Also, financial performance, budgeting and its analysis, and many more finance activities can be facilitated with IT.

Human Resources Management Major

Human resources managers can increase their efficiency and effectiveness by using IT for some of their routine functions. Using the Web for recruiting, for example, has revolutionized the HRM area. Human resources personnel need to understand how information flows between the HR department and the other functional areas.

Preparing and training employees to work with business partners (frequently in foreign countries) requires knowledge about how IT collaboration software operates. Finally, compliance with government safety regulations and other human resources-related requirements can be facilitated by IT software.

IS Major

The IS function is responsible for the shared enterprise information systems infrastructure, and the transaction processing systems. TPSs provide the data for the databases. In turn, all other information systems use these data. IS personnel develop applications that support all levels of the organization (from clerical to executive) and in all functional areas (or they work with vendors that develop them). The applications also enable the firm to work better with its partners.

Marketing Major

Due to increased competition, marketing decisions about advertising, promotions, and pricing become critical, and in many cases require software support. E-CRM is frequently a critical success factor. In addition, marketing and sales expenses are usually targets in a cost-reduction program. Also, sales force automation not only improves salespeople's productivity (and thus reduces costs), but also improves customer service.

Another area is the supply chain and its improvements by IT as well as its relationships to marketing channels.

As competition intensifies globally, finding new global markets and global partners becomes critical. Use of electronic directories, for example, provides an opportunity to improve marketing and sales. Understanding the capabilities of marketing and sales support technologies and their implementation issues will enable the marketing department to excel.

Operations Management Major

Managing production tasks, materials handling, and inventories in short time intervals, at a low cost, and with high quality is critical for competitiveness. These activities can be achieved only if they are properly supported by IT. Because they are in charge of procurement, production/operations managers must understand how their supporting information systems interface with those of their business partners. In addition, collaboration in design, manufacturing, and logistics requires knowledge of how modern information systems can be connected. Finally, on-demand manufacturing must be done at a competitive cost. Optimization with appropriate computerized analysis is very helpful.

Key Terms

Batch processing *333*

Computer-integrated manufacturing (CIM) *341*

Channel systems *341*

Expense management automation (EMA) *351*

Employee relationship management (ERM) *357*

Financial value chain management (FVCM) *350*

Just-in-time (JIT) *340*

Online processing *333*

Online transaction processing (OLTP) *334*

Sales automation software *345*

Spend management *352*

Vendor-managed inventory (VMI) *334*

Web analytics *336*

XBRL *349*

Chapter Highlights

(Numbers Refer to Learning Objectives)

① Information systems applications can support many functional activities. Considerable software is readily available on the market for much of this support (for lease or to buy).

② The major business functional areas are production/operations management, marketing, accounting/finance, and human resources management.

③ The backbone of most information systems applications is the transaction processing system (TPS), which keeps track of the routine, mission-central operations of the organization.

④ The major area of IT support to production/operations management is in logistics and inventory management: JIT, mass customization, and CIM.

⑤ Marketing and sales information systems deal with all activities related to customer orders, sales, advertising and promotion, market research, customer service, and product and service pricing. Using IT can increase sales, customers' satisfaction, and profitability.

⑥ Financial information systems deal with topics such as investment management, financing operations, raising capital, risk analysis, and credit approval.

⑥ Accounting information systems also cover many non-TPS applications in areas such as cost control, taxation, and auditing.

⑦ Most tasks related to human resources development can be supported by human resources information systems. These tasks include employee recruitment and selection, hiring, performance evaluation, salary and benefits administration, training and development, labor negotiations, and work planning.

⑦ Web-based HR systems are extremely useful for recruiting and training.

⑧ Integrated functional information systems are necessary to ensure effective and efficient execution of activities that cross functional lines or that require functional cooperation.

⑧ Integrating applications is difficult; it can be done in different ways, such as buying off-the-shelf applications from one vendor or using special connecting software known as middleware. A promising new approach is that of Web Services.

Virtual Company Assignment

Transaction Processing at The Wireless Café

Go to The Wireless Café's link on the Student Web Site. There you will be asked to think about the business activities and transactions, other than cooking, that the restaurant engages in. You will be asked to consider types of transaction processing applications that could be implemented at The Wireless Café.

Instructions for accessing The Wireless Café on the Student Web Site:

1. Go to *wiley.com/college/turban*.
2. Select Turban/Volonino's *Information Technology for Management*, Seventh Edition.
3. Click on Student Resources site, in the toolbar on the left.
4. Click on the link for Virtual Company Web site.
5. Click on Wireless Café.

Questions for Discussion

1. Why is it logical to organize IT applications by functional areas?

2. Describe the role of a TPS in a service organization.

3. Why are transaction processing systems a major target for restructuring?

4. Which functional areas are related to payroll, and how does the relevant information flow?

5. Discuss the benefits of Web-based TPS and Web analytics.

6. The Japanese implemented JIT for many years without computers. Discuss some elements of JIT, and comment on the potential benefits of their computerization (consult Wikipedia.org).

7. Explain how Web applications can make the customer king/queen.

8. Why are information systems critical to sales-order processing?

9. Describe how IT can enhance mass customization. (Hint: Check how SiemensAG,Siemens.com does it.)

10. Describe how XBRL can help financial institutions.

11. Discuss how IT facilitates the budgeting process.

12. Why is risk management important, and how can it be enhanced by IT?

13. How can the Internet support investment decisions?

14. Describe the benefits of an accounting integrated software such as MAS 90; compare it to MAS 200.

15. Discuss the role IT plays in support of auditing.

16. Investigate the role of the Web in human resources management.

17. Geographical information systems are playing an important role in supporting marketing and sales. Provide some examples not discussed in the text (Chapters 7, 12).

18. Discuss the need for application integration and the difficulty of doing it.

19. Discuss the approaches and reasons for integrating front-office with back-office operations.

20. Discuss why some of the services provided by *iemployee.com* are considered support to on-demand workforce management solutions.

Exercises and Projects

1. Review the Dartmouth-Hitchcock Medical Center case. Assume that RFID tags cost 5 cents each. How might use of RFID tags change the supply chain management? Would the new system at the medical center still be needed? Write a report on your conclusions.

2. The chart shown in Figure 9.3 portrays the flow of routine activities in a typical manufacturing organization. Explain in what areas IT can be most valuable.

3. Enter Teradata Student Network and find the podcast titled Best-Practice Enterprise Risk Management (by R. M. Mark). View the presentation and write a report on how IT can help a company with their risk management.

4. Enter Teradata Student Network and find the assignment regarding Advent Technology. Use the MicroStrategy Sales Force Analysis Module and answer the questions about sales at Advent.

5. Enter *geac.com*. Take the demo. Prepare a list of all the capabilities of your chosen product.

6. Enter *secondlife.com* and find an island of your interest. For the accountants we suggest to look for the "CPA Island." Make a list of 10 major activities conducted on the site. (You need to register; it is free).

Group Assignments and Projects

1. Each group should visit (or investigate) a large company in a different industry and identify its channel systems. Prepare a diagram that shows the components shown in Online Brief 9.4. Then find how IT supports each of those components. Finally, suggest improvements in the existing channel system that can be supported by IT technologies and that are not in use by the company today. Each group presents its findings.

2. The class is divided into groups of four. Each group member represents a major functional area: production/operations management, sales/marketing, accounting/finance, and human resources. Find and describe several examples of processes that require the integration of functional information systems in a company of your choice. Each group will also show the interfaces to the other functional areas. For example, accounting students can visit *accountantsworld.com* just

to be surprised at what is there, and *1040.com* can be useful to both the accounting and finance areas.

3. Each group investigates an HRM software vendor (Oracle, SAP, Lawson Software). The group prepares a list of all HRM functionalities supported by the software. Then the groups make a presentation to convince the class that its vendor is the best.

4. Enter *searchcio-midmarket.techtarget.com*, *google.com*, and other sites and look for "business software." Then categorize the software by functional areas. Prepare a list of current packages available (about 15–20 in each area). Concentrate on software for small business (see Cassavoy, 2006).

5. Analyze the financial crisis of 2008. In your opinion, what roles did IT play to accelerate the crisis? Also, how did IT help to rectify some of the problems? Be specific.

Internet Exercises

1. Surf the Net and find free accounting software (try *shareware.com, rkom.com, tucows.com, passtheshareware.com,* and *freeware-guide.com*). Download the software and try it. Write a report on your findings.

2. Enter the site of Federal Express (*fedex.com*) and learn how to ship a package, track the status of a package, and calculate its cost. Comment on your experience.

3. Finding a job on the Internet is challenging; there are almost too many places to look. Visit the following sites: *careerbuilder.com, craigslist.org, LinkedIn.com, careermag.com, hotjobs.yahoo.com, jobcentral.com,* and *monster.com.* What do these sites provide you as a job seeker?

4. Enter the Web site *tpssys.com* and *hp.com* (look for NonStop software) and find information about software products available from those sites. Identify the software that allows Internet transaction processing. Prepare a report about the benefits of the products identified.

5. Enter *sas.com* and access revenue optimization there. Explain how the software helps in optimizing prices.

6. Enter *sas.com/solutions/profitmgmt/brief.pdf*, and download the brochure on profitability management. Prepare a summary.

7. Enter *iemployee.com* and find the support it provides to human resources management activities by IT. View the

demos and read the white paper by Shah (2008). Prepare a report.

8. Enter *techsmith.com/camtasia/features.asp* and take the product tour. Do you think it is a valuable tool?

9. Enter *halogensoftware.com* and *successfactors.com*. Examine their software products and make a comparison.

10. Examine the capabilities of the following financial software packages: TekPortal (from *teknowledge.com*), Financial Analyzer (from *oracle.com*), and Financial Management (from *sas.com*). Prepare a report comparing the capabilities of the software packages.

11. Surf the Internet and find information from three vendors on sales force automation (try *captera.com* first). Prepare a report on the state of the art.

12. Enter *eleap.com* and review the product that helps with online training (training systems). What are the most attractive features of this product?

13. Enter *microsoft.com/dynamics/sl/product/demos.mspx*. View three of the demos in different functional areas of your choice. Prepare a report on the capabilities.

14. Find Simply Accounting Basic from Sage Software (*simplyaccounting.com/products/basic*). Why is this product recommended for small businesses?

Minicase

Dollar General Uses Integrated Software

Dollar General (*dollargeneral.com*) operates more than 8,000 general stores in 35 states, with sales exceeding $9.5 billion in 2007, fiercely competing with Wal-Mart, Target, and thousands of other stores in the sale of food, apparel, home-cleaning products, health and beauty aids, and more. The chain doubled in size between 1996 and 2002 and has had some problems due to its rapid expansion. For example, moving into new states means different sales taxes, and these need to be closely monitored for changes. Personnel management also became more difficult with the organization's growth. An increased number of purchasing orders exacerbated problems in the accounts payable department, which was using manual matching of purchasing orders, invoices, and what was actually received in the "receiving" department before bills were paid.

The IT department was flooded with requests to generate long reports on topics ranging from asset management to general ledgers. It became clear that a better information system was needed. Dollar General started by evaluating information requirements that would be able to solve the above and other problems that cut into the company's profit.

A major factor in deciding which software to buy was the integration requirement among the existing information systems of the various functional areas, especially the financial applications. This led to the selection of the Financials suite (from Lawson Software). The company started to implement

applications one at a time. Before 1998, the company installed the suite's asset management, payroll, and some HR applications which allow the tens of thousands of employees to monitor and self-update their benefits, 401k contributions, and personal data (resulting in big savings to the HR department). After 1998, the accounts payable and general ledger modules of Lawson Software were activated. The accounting modules allow employees to route, extract, and analyze data in the accounting/finance area with little reliance on IT personnel. During 2001–2003, Dollar General moved into the sales and procurement areas, thus adding the marketing and operation activities to the integrated system.

Here are a few examples of how various parts of the new system work: All sales data from the point-of-sale scanners of some 6,000 stores are pulled each night, together with financial data, discounts, etc., into the business intelligence application for financial and marketing analysis. Employee payroll data, from each store, are pulled once a week. This provides synergy with the sales audit system (from STS Software). All sales data are processed nightly by the STS System, broken into hourly journal entries, processed and summarized, and then entered into the Lawson's general ledger module.

The original infrastructure was mainframe based (IBM AS 400). By 2002, the 800 largest suppliers of Dollar General were submitting their bills on the EDI (see Tutorial #6). This allowed instantaneous processing in the accounts payable module. By 2003, service providers, such as utilities, were added to the system. To do all of this, the system was migrated in 2001 from the old legacy system to the Unix operating system, and then to a Web-based infrastructure, mainly in order to add Web-based functionalities and tools.

A development tool embedded in Lawson's Financials allowed users to customize applications without touching the computer programming code. This included applications that are not contained in the Lawson system. For example, an employee-bonus application was not available at Lawson, but was added to Financial's payroll module to accommodate Dollar General's bonus system. A customized application that allowed additions and changes in dozens of geographical areas also solved the organization's state sales-tax collection and reporting problem.

The system is very scalable, so there is no problem in adding stores, vendors, applications, or functionalities. In 2003, the system was completely converted to Web-based, enabling authorized vendors, for example, to log onto the Internet and view the status of their invoices by themselves. Also, the Internet/EDI (see Tutorial #6) enables small vendors to use the system. (An EDI is too expensive for small vendors,

but the EDI/Internet is affordable.) Also, the employees can update personal data from any Web-enabled desktop in the store or at home. Future plans call for adding an e-purchasing (procurement) module using a desktop purchasing model (see Chapter 5).

Sources: Compiled from Amato-McCoy (2002), *lawson.com* (accessed May 2008), and *dollargeneral.com* (accessed May 2008).

Questions for Minicase

1. Explain why the old, nonintegrated functional system created problems for the company. Be specific.
2. The new system cost several million dollars. Why, in your opinion, was it necessary to install it?
3. Lawson Software Smart Notification Software (*lawson.com*) is being considered by Dollar General. Find information about the software and write an opinion for adoption or rejection.
4. Another new product of Lawson is Services Automation. Would you recommend it to Dollar General? Why or why not?

Problem-Solving Activity

Argot International Improves Productivity and Profitability

Argot International (a fictitious name) is a medium-sized company in Peoria, Illinois, with about 2,000 employees. The company manufactures special machines for farms and food processing plants, buying materials and components from about 150 vendors in six different countries. It also buys special machines and tools from Japan. Products are sold either to wholesalers (about 70) or directly to clients (from a mailing list of about 2,000). The business is very competitive.

The company has the following information systems in place: financial/accounting, marketing (primarily information about sales), engineering, research and development, and inventory management. These systems are independent of each other, although they are all connected to the corporate intranet.

Argot is having profitability problems. Cash is in high demand and short supply, due to strong business competition from Germany and Japan. The company wants to investigate the possibility of using information technology to improve the situation. However, the vice president of finance objects to the idea, claiming that most of the tangible benefits of information technology are already being realized.

You are hired as a consultant to the president. Respond to the following:

a. Prepare a list of 10 potential applications of functional information technologies that you think could help the company to increase profitability.
b. From the description of the case, would you recommend any portals? Be very specific. Remember, the company is in financial trouble.
c. Go to Oracle.com and find 10 specific products that can be used to improve productivity.
d. Argot is using a large sales force that visits farms and customers. What wireless systems can be used and for what purposes?
e. What information technologies can be used in the company's operation area (assume it does some manufacturing and assembly?
f. Consider the use of RFID for the internal operations.

Online Resources

More resources and study tools are located on the Student Web Site and on WileyPLUS. You'll find additional chapter materials and useful Web links. In addition, self-quizzes that provide individualized feedback are available for each chapter.

Online Briefs for Chapter 9 are available at wiley.com/college/turban:

9.1 Information Systems in POM

9.2 Transaction Processing in Different Functional Areas

References

Amato-McCoy, D. M., "Dollar General Rings up Back-Office Efficiencies with Financial Suite," *Stores,* October 2002.

autobytel.com (accessed May 2008).

Barrett, L., "Juggling Act," *Baseline,* June 2005.

Bernstein, P., and E. Newcomer, *Principles of Transaction Processing.* St. Louis, MO: Elsevier Science & Technology Books, 2006.

Bolch M., "Nice Work," *HR Magazine,* Feb. 2008.

Boucher-Ferguson, R., "Playing Tough with TIAA-CREF," *eWeek,* January 2006a.

Boucher-Ferguson, R., "TIAA-CREF Dissects the Disaster," *eWeek,* April 2006b.

Buckley, N., "E-Route to Whiter Smile," *Financial Times,* August 26, 2002.

Butcher, D. R., "Mass Customization: A Leading Paradigm in Future Manufacturing," *ThomasNet Industrial Newsroom,* February 14, 2006.

Carr, D. F., "Leaner Machine," *Baseline,* June 2005.

Cassavoy, L., "The NEXT Generation," *Entrepreneur,* May 2006.

Cheapflights.com, "Plastic Purchases Onboard American Airlines," May 4, 2006, *news.cheapflights.com/airlines/2006/05/plastic_purchas.html#more* (accessed May 2008).

cirquedusoleil.com (accessed May 2008).

Degnan, C., "Best Practices in Expense Management Automation," Special Report. Aberdeen Group, Boston, January 2003, *ofm.wa.gov/roadmap/modeling/expense/Aberdeen_BestPractices_Spend_Management.pdf* (accessed May 2008).

dhmc.org (accessed June 2008).

dollargeneral.com (accessed May 2008).

Duvall, M., "Lemon Aid," *Baseline,* June 2005.

Entersingapore.com, "Public Transport," *entersingapore.info/sginfo/public-transport.php* (accessed May 2008).

Ere.net, "Trovix Makes Good at Stanford University: Premier Educational Institution Turns to Intelligent Search Provider for Recruiting Top Talent," March 8, 2006, *ere.net/newswire/announcement.asp?LISTINGID=%7B66B8732B-C61D-4906-B35F-490AD939DE23%7D* (no longer available online).

Field, K., "High Speed Hiring," *Chain Store Age,* June 2006.

ford.com (accessed May 2008).

Gayeski, D., "Going Mobile," *TD,* November 2004.

Gillium, D., et al., *The Quantum Leap: Next Generation—The Manufacturing Strategy for Business.* Fort Lauderdale, FL: J. Ross Publishers, 2005.

Gomez-Mejia, L., et al., *Managing Human Resources,* 5th ed. Upper Saddle River, NJ: Prentice Hall, 2007.

Grimes, S., "Declaration Support: The B.P.M. Drumbeat," *Intelligent Enterprise,* April 23, 2003.

Gronstedt, A., *Training in Virtual Worlds.* New York: ASTD Press, 2008.

IBM, "Increasing Cirque du Soleil's Agility," *IBM.com,* July 1, 2005, *www-1.ibm.com/businesscenter/smb/us/en/contenttemplate/gcl_xmlid/33893/nav_id/resources* (accessed May 2008).

jaguar.com (accessed May 2008).

jobster.com (accessed June 2008).

Korolishin, J., "Payroll Pay Cards Pay Off at Payless," *Stores,* February 2004a.

Korolishin, J., "Sheetz Keeps Tab on Training Compliance via Web Portal," *Stores,* February 2004b.

lawson.com (accessed May 2008).

Liao, Z., "Real Time Tax: Dispatching Using GPS," *Communications of the ACM,* May 2003.

LinkedIn.com, "LinkedIn's Simple Philosophy: Relationships Matter," 2006, *linkedin.com/static?key=company_info* (accessed June 2008).

Malykhina, E., "XBRL: More Than a Must-Do," *Information Week,* May 29, 2006.

McKay, J. "Where Did Jobs Go? Look in Bangalore." March 21, 2004, *post-gazette.com/pg/04081/288539.stm* (accessed June 2009).

Meredith, J. R., and S. M. Shafer, *Operations Management.* New York: Wiley, 2002.

Nishi, D., "Market-Basket Mystery," *Retail Technology Quarterly,* May 2005.

Perkins–Munn, T. S., and Y. T. Chen, "Streamlining Project Management Through Online Solutions," *Journal of Business Strategy,* January 2004.

peoplesoft.com (now at *oracle.com*) (no longer available on line).

pg.com (accessed May 2008).

Pinsker, R., and S. Li, "Costs and Benefits of XBRL Adoption: Early Evidence," *Communication of the ACM,* March 2008.

Reda, S., "Evelyn Follit Fuses Technology, Business, and HR Strategies," *Stores,* March 2004.

Reed, C., et al., *eCFO: Sustaining Value in New Corporations.* Chichester, UK: Wiley, 2001.

SAS.com, "SAS Profitability Management," 2007, *sas.com/solutions/profitmgmt/brief.pdf* (accessed May 2008).

Shah, S., *The Five Foundations of Next Generation HRO Technology,* a white paper from *iemployee.com/products/whitepapers/index.asp* (downloaded May 2008).

Sostre, P., and J. Le Claire, *Web Analytics for Dummies.* Hoboken, NJ: Wiley Publishing Company, 2007.

Supply Chain Management and Logistics, "Health Care/Pharmaceuticals: Safety and Security in the Spotlight," June 1, 2004, *66.195.41.11/index.php?option=com_content&task=view&id=90&Itemid=87* (accessed May 2008).

Taylor-Arnold J., "Getting Facts Fast", *HR Magazine,* Feb. 2008.

TIAA-CREF, Annual Report 2006, July 2007. Available for download at *tiaa-cref.org/about/governance/corporate/topics/annual_reports.html* (accessed May 2008).

Totty, M., "Career Journal: Recruiters Try New Tools to Find the Best Candidates—Services Analyze, Rank Online Resumes, Saving Valuable Time," *The Wall Street Journal Asia,* October 24, 2006, *awsj.com.hk/factiva-ns* (no longer available online).

trovix.com (accessed June 2008).

Zimmerman, J., *Web Marketing for Dummies.* Hoboken, NJ: Wiley Publishing Company, 2007.

10

Enterprise Systems: Supply Chains, ERP, CRM, and KM

Learning Objectives

After studying this chapter, you will be able to:

❶ Understand the essentials of enterprise systems and computerized supply chain management.

❷ Describe some major problems of implementing supply chains and some innovative solutions.

❸ Describe the need for integrated software and how ERP does it.

❹ Describe CRM and its support by IT.

❺ Describe KM and its relationship to IT.

Integrating *IT*

 ACC   **FIN**   **MKT**   **OM**   **HRM**   **IS**

IT-PERFORMANCE MODEL

The focus of this chapter is on the support IT provides to business processes that are being conducted by two or more functional departments, mostly along the *supply chain*, via three types of IT: ERP, CRM, and KM. These systems enable organizations to improve performance and increase competitiveness.

The business performance management cycle and IT model.

CHEVRONTEXACO MODERNIZED ITS SUPPLY CHAIN WITH IT

The Problem

ChevronTexaco, the largest U.S. oil company, is multinational in nature. Its main business is drilling, refining, transporting, and selling gasoline (oil). In this competitive business, a saving of even a quarter of a penny per gallon totals up to millions of dollars. Two problems have plagued the oil industry: running out of gasoline at individual pumps, and a delivery that is aborted because a tank at the gas station is too full (called "retain"). Run-outs and retains, known as the industry's "twin evils," have been a target for improvements for years, with little success.

The causes of the twin evils have to do with the supply chain: Gasoline flows in the supply chain start with oil hunting, drilling, and extraction. After the oil is taken from the ground, it is delivered to and then processed in refineries, and finally it goes to storage and eventually to the retail pump and to the customer. The time frame for the entire supply chains may take several months to years depending on locations, means of transportation, and more. Due to the above reasons, it is difficult matching the three parts of the supply chain: oil acquisition, processing, and distribution.

ChevronTexaco owns oil fields and refineries, but it also buys both crude and refined oil to meet peak demand. Purchases are of two types: those that are made through long-term contracts and those that are purchased "as needed," in what is called the *spot market*, at prevailing prices (usually higher than contract purchases).

In the past, ChevronTexaco acted like a mass production manufacturing company, just trying to make lots of oil products and then sell them (a supply-driven strategy). The problem with this strategy is that each time you make too much, you are introducing extra inventory or storage costs. If you make too little, you lose sales.

The Solution

The company decided to change its business model from *supply driven* to *demand driven*. Namely, instead of focusing on how much oil it would process and "push" to customers, the company started thinking about how much oil its customers wanted and then about how to get it. This change necessitated a major transformation in the business and extensive support by information technologies.

To implement the IT support, the company installed in each tank in each gas station an electronic monitor. The monitor transmits real-time information about the oil level, through a cable, to the station's IT-based management system. That system then transmits the information via a satellite to the main inventory system at the company's main office. There, an advanced DSS-based planning system processes the data to help refining, marketing, and logistics decisions. This DSS also includes information collected at trucking and airline companies, which are major customers. Using an enterprise resource planning (ERP) and business planning system (BPS), ChevronTexaco determines how much to refine, how much to buy in spot markets, and when and how much to ship to each retail station.

To combine all of these data, it is necessary to integrate the supply and demand information systems, and this is where the ERP software is useful. These data are used by planners at various points across the supply chain (e.g., refinery, terminal management, station management, transportation, and production) who process and share data constantly. This data processing and data sharing are provided by the various information systems.

Recent IT projects support the supply chain and extend it to a global reach. These projects include the NetReady initiative that enables the operations of 150 e-business projects, the Global Information Link (GIL2) that enables connectivity throughout the company, the e-Guest project that enables sharing of information with business partners, and a global human resources information system. In 2006, Chevron began to implement a program that would provide a visual dashboard system to enable refinery executives to quickly, easily, and clearly access supply chain and production information that could help them make decisions and meet operating goals (*SCDigest*, 2006).

The Results

The integrated system that allows data to be shared across the company has improved decision making at every point in the customer-facing and processing parts of the supply chain. It resulted in an increase in the company's profit of more than $300 million in its first year and more than an additional $100 million each year after.

According to Worthen (2002), studies indicate that companies in the top 20 percent of the oil industry operate their supply chains twice as efficiently as the average oil companies. These successful companies also carry half as much inventory, can respond to a significant rise in demand (20% or higher) twice as fast, and know how to minimize the number of deliveries to the gas stations. ChevronTexaco is in this category.

Sources: Compiled from Worthen (2002); *SCDigest* (2006); and from *chevrontexaco.com*, see "Human Energy Stories" (accessed May 2008).

Lessons Learned from This Case

The ChevronTexaco case illustrates the need to drastically improve the management of the supply chain. All decision makers along the supply chain need to share information and collaborate. Doing so is not a simple task, as will be seen in this chapter, but IT solutions enable even a large multinational company to manage its supply chain.

ChevronTexaco successfully implemented the concepts of *supply chain management* and *enterprise resource planning*. Such a system is considered an enterprise system. Enterprise systems such as supply chain management (SCM), ERP, CRM, and KM are the subjects of this chapter.

10.1 Essentials of Enterprise Systems and Supply Chains

Enterprise systems (also called **enterprisewide systems**) are systems or processes that involve the entire enterprise or two or more departments of it. This is in contrast to functional systems, which are confined to one department each.

Several enterprise systems can be found in organizations. Typical examples are

- Enterprise resource planning (ERP), which usually supports the internal supply chain.
- Extended ERP, which supports business partners as well. Most ERP systems today are extended.
- Customer relationship management (CRM), which provides customer care.
- Knowledge management (KM) systems, whose objective is to support knowledge creation, storage, maintenance, and distribution throughout the enterprise.
- Partner relationship management (PRM), which is designed to provide care to business partners.
- Business process management (BPM), which involves the understanding and realignment of processes in the organization, including reengineering and managing the flow of activities and tasks.
- Supply chain management systems, such as materials requirement planning (MRP).
- Product life cycle management (PLM), which involves conceptualization, design, building, and support of products and services. The management of PLM seeks to reduce cycle times, streamline production costs, and get more products to market.
- Decision support systems (DSSs), whose purpose is to support decision making throughout the enterprise, frequently with the help of a data warehouse. This category includes executive information systems.
- Intelligent systems, which include a knowledge component, such as an expert system or neural network.
- Business intelligence (BI), which is computer-based decision analysis usually done online by managers and staff. It includes forecasting, analyzing alternatives, and evaluating risk and performance.

These and other enterprise systems and their potential integration are shown in Figure 10.1.

The first three systems are described in this chapter; PLM is described in Online Brief 10.1, PRM is described in Chapter 11, and business intelligence, decision support, and intelligent systems are presented in Chapter 12.

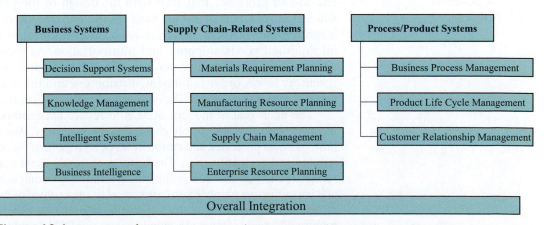

Figure 10.1 Overview of enterprise system. (*Source:* Prepared by E. Turban and D. Amoroso.)

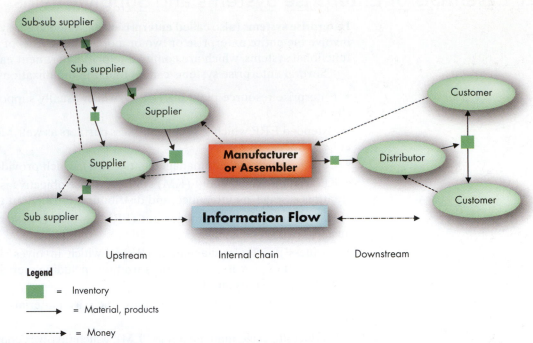

Figure 10.2 The structure of a typical supply chain. (*Source:* Drawn by E. Turban.)

WHAT IS A SUPPLY CHAIN?

A *supply chain* is defined as a set of relationships among suppliers, manufacturers, distributors, and retailers that facilitate the transformation of raw materials into final products. The supply chain includes all of the interactions between suppliers, manufacturers, distributors, warehouses, and customers. Supply chains involve the flow of materials, information, money, and services from raw materials suppliers, through factories and warehouses, to the end consumers. Although the supply chain is comprised of several businesses, the chain itself is viewed as a single entity. The essentials of supply chains are provided in Tutorial #1.

The supply chain also includes the organization processes for developing and delivering products, information, and services to end customers. The structure of a simple supply chain is illustrated in Figure 10.2. Notice that in Figure 10.2, materials move from sub-suppliers to suppliers until they reach the manufacturer. Materials are then processed into final products which are then transported via distributors and other marketing channels to the end customers. Market research data, scheduling information, design data, and order and cash flow data move in the opposite direction from the customers to the suppliers.

SUPPLY CHAIN MANAGEMENT CONCEPTS

Supply chain management (SCM) is the efficient management of the supply chain end-to-end processes that start with the design of the product or service and end when it is sold, consumed, or used by the end consumer. Some activities include inventory management, materials acquisition, and transformation of raw materials into finished goods, shipping, and transportation. As shown in Figure 10.2, supply chain management involves vendors, financial accounting transfers, warehousing and inventory levels, order fulfillment, distributors, and the information needed to manage it. For details, see *en.wikipedia.org/wiki/Supply_chain_management*.

The main goal of modern SCM is to reduce uncertainty, variability, and risks, and increase control in the supply chain, thereby positively affecting inventory levels, cycle time, business processes, and customer service. These benefits contribute to increased profitability and competitiveness. The benefits of supply chain management have long been recognized in business and in the military. In today's competitive business environment, efficient, effective supply chains are critical to the survival of most organizations, and they are greatly dependent upon the supporting information systems. Different product types require different features of a supply chain, and SCM should aim to ensure that the supply chain matches the requirements of an organization's products and services.

Effective management of the supply chain provides a major opportunity for an organization to reduce costs while increasing operating efficiencies. Thus, SCM may provide a significant competitive advantage. Organizations need to know how much, and in what sequence, they will be investing in various supply chain efforts to leverage the benefits of the technology. SCM models need to focus on more than one variable. The optimal strategy will look at multiple variables including inventory, forecasting, lead time, capacity, and price.

Information technology must support the basic infrastructure and coordination needed for the supply chain to function. Implementation issues include the following:

- Procurement and supplier decisions
- Production decisions
- Distribution decisions
- Information support decisions
- Material flow decisions
- Cash flow decisions

Supply Chain Management Software. **SCM software** refers to software needed to support specific segments of the supply chain, such as in manufacturing, inventory control, scheduling, and transportation. This software concentrates on improving decision making, optimization, and analysis.

E-Supply Chain. When a supply chain is managed electronically, usually with Web-based software, it is referred to as a **digital supply chain** or an **e-supply chain.** A digital supply chain can take many shapes. An example is provided in Figure 10.3. Notice that communication and collaboration are illustrated with broken lines signifying communications to a hub. Another element of digitization is collaborative networks. Also shown in the figure are RFID, global data synchronization, and visibility in the network. For further details on digital supply chains, see Intel (2005).

As will be shown in this chapter, improvements in supply chains frequently involve attempts to convert a traditional supply chain to an e-supply chain, namely,

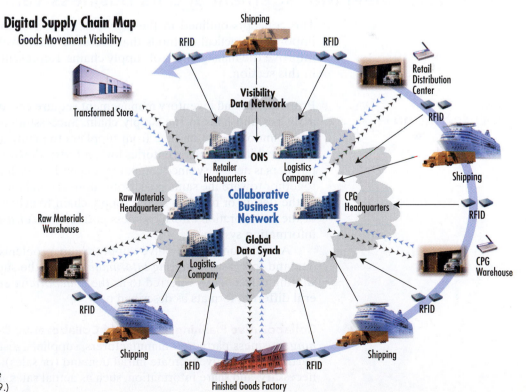

Figure 10.3 Digital supply chains. (*Source:* Intel, "Building the Digital Supply Chain: An Intel Perspective," *Intel Solutions* White Paper, January 2005, Figure 5, p. 9.)

to automate the information flow in the chain. Thus, supply chains, as shown in Tutorial #1, Chapter 2, and Figure 10.2, are composed of three major components:

- **Upstream:** The flows and activities conducted between a company (e.g., manufacturer, assembler) and its suppliers and their sub-suppliers, all the way to the origin of the materials.
- **Internal:** The flows and activities conducted within a company among its own departments. It includes the processing of the materials.
- **Downstream:** The flow of materials, products, and activities from the manufacturing company to its distributors, marketing channels, and so forth, all the way to the end consumer.

INTEGRATING ENTERPRISE SYSTEMS

Enterprise systems that used to be stand-alone are being integrated at an accelerated rate. Oracle is probably the best example of a software vendor that buys software vendors with specialized enterprise systems and integrates the systems together. A most common integration is that of ERP (which is already an integrated system) and CRM. For this reason, Oracle, which is known as an ERP leader, purchased Siebel, which was a major CRM vendor. Here is an example of integration.

Example. In 2006 and 2007, Green Mountain Coffee Roasters (GMCR) deployed an integrated enterprise system that was structured around its supply chain, financial management, ERP, and CRM. In addition, it includes tools for salesforce automation and campaign management tools to sharpen marketing intelligence. For details, see Miley (2006).

Review Questions

> 1. Define enterprise system.
> 2. List the major enterprise systems.
> 3. Define a supply chain.
> 4. Describe SCM.

10.2 Supply Chain Management and Its Business Value

The concepts outlined in the previous section enable us to understand several important practical methods that are used extensively in industry in attempts to improve the management of supply chains. Representative practices are described in this section.

MANAGING COLLABORATION

Proper SCM and inventory management require coordination of all of the different activities and links in the supply chain. Successful coordination enables goods to move smoothly and on time from suppliers to manufacturers to distributors to customers while keeping inventories low and costs down. Collaboration of supply chain partners is necessary since companies depend on each other, but do not always work together toward the same goal. Both suppliers and buyers must participate together in the design or redesign of the supply chain to achieve their shared goals. As part of the collaboration effort, business partners must *trust* each other and each other's information systems.

A common way to solve supply chain problems, and especially to improve demand forecasts, is *sharing information* along the supply chain. Such information sharing is frequently referred to as the *collaborative supply chain*. It may take several different formats as described next.

Collaborative Planning, CPFR, and Collaborative Design. In *collaborative planning*, business partners—manufacturers, suppliers, distribution partners, and other partners—collectively create initial demand (or sales) forecasts, provide changes as necessary, and share information, such as actual sales, and their own forecasts. Thus,

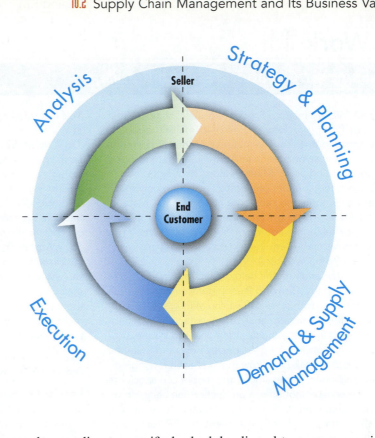

Figure 10.4 CPFR model.
(*Source:* VICS.org, "Collaborative Planning, Forecasting, and Replenishment (CPFR): An Overview," May 18, 2004, Figure 1, p. 6.)

all parties work according to a unified schedule aligned to a common view, and all have access to order and forecast performance that is globally visible through electronic links. Schedule, order, or product changes trigger immediate adjustments to all parties' schedules.

Collaborative planning, forecasting, and replenishment (CPFR) is a business practice in which suppliers and retailers collaborate in planning and demand forecasting in order to ensure that members of the supply chain will have the right amount of raw materials and finished goods when they need them. The goal of CPFR is to streamline product flow from manufacturing plants all the way to customers' homes. Large manufacturers of consumer goods, such as Warner–Lambert (WL), have superb supply chains resulting from their use of CPFR.

As part of a pilot project, WL shared strategic plans, performance data, and market insight with Wal-Mart. The company realized that it could benefit from Wal-Mart's market knowledge, just as Wal-Mart could benefit from WL's product knowledge. In CPFR, trading partners collaborate on making *demand forecasts* (see *IT at Work 10.1* for details).

Collaborative planning is designed to synchronize production and distribution plans and product flows, optimize resource utilization over an expanded capacity base, increase customer responsiveness, and reduce inventories. For an example of how it is done at West Marine Corp., see Online Minicase 10.1. Collaborative planning is a necessity in e-SCM (see *vics.org/committees/cpfr*). The planning process is difficult because it involves multiple parties and activities, as shown in Figure 10.4.

The figure shows the model of the CPFR concept. It is divided into four major areas: (1) strategy and planning for collaboration on supply and inventory levels, which leads to (2) joint demand forecasting and managing supplies and inventories accordingly; (3) then the above plans are executed and the results are analyzed, leading to (4) adjustment in strategy if needed. These activities are centered along the supply chain from a seller to a buyer to end customer.

The various aspects of collaborative planning and collaborative design are presented in Online Brief 10.2.

IT at Work 10.1

Warner-Lambert Collaborates with Retailers

Warner-Lambert (WL) is a major U.S. pharmaceutical company that is now owned by Pfizer (*pfizer.com*). One of its major products is Listerine antiseptic mouthwash. The materials for making Listerine come mainly from eucalyptus trees in Australia and are shipped to the WL manufacturing plant in New Jersey. The major problem there is to *forecast* the *overall demand* to determine how much Listerine to produce; then one can figure how much raw material is needed and when. A wrong forecast will result either in high inventories of raw materials and/or of finished products, or in shortages. Inventories are expensive to keep; shortages may result in loss of business (to competitors).

WL forecasts demand with the help of Manugistics Inc.'s (now a JDA Software company) Demand Planning Information System (an SCM product). Used with other software in Manugistics' Supply Chain Planning suite, the system analyzes manufacturing, distribution, and sales data against expected demand and business climate information. Its goal is to help WL decide how much Listerine (and other products) to make and how much of each raw ingredient is needed, and when. For example, the model can anticipate the impact of seasonal promotion or a production line being down.

WL's supply chain excellence stems from the collaborative planning, forecasting, and replenishment (CPFR) program.

This is a retailing industry project for which piloting was done at WL.

Overall, WL can determine the right quantity of raw materials to buy from its suppliers with its demand planning system. The system analyzes manufacturing, distribution, and sales data against expected demand and business climate information to help WL decide how much product to make and distribute. Because WL can smooth seasonality forecasts, it has dramatically cut costs in the manufacturing and raw materials inventory areas.

With its supply chain systems and ERP modules, WL increased its products' shelf-fill rate—the extent to which a store's shelves are fully stocked—from 87 percent to 98 percent, earning the company about $8 million a year in additional sales. This was the equivalent of a new product launch, but for much less investment. WL is now using the Internet to expand the CPFR program to all of its major suppliers and retail partners.

Sources: Compiled from *en.wikipedia.org/wiki/CPFR*; *VICS.org (2004)*; Fedotov (1995); and Bresnahan (1998).

For Further Exploration: Why would Listerine have been a target for the pilot CPFR collaboration? For what industries, besides retailing, would such collaboration be beneficial?

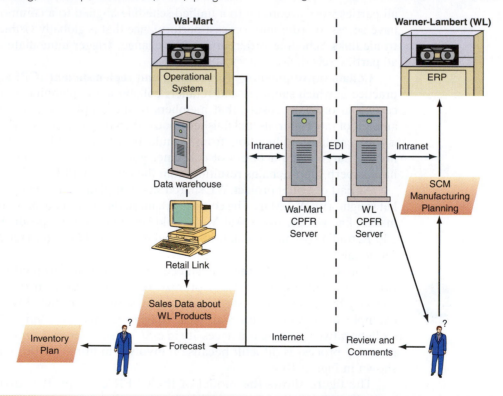

Vendor-Managed Inventory. Information sharing between Wal-Mart and Procter & Gamble (P&G) is done automatically. It is part of a *vendor-managed inventory* (VMI) strategy. **Vendor-managed inventory (VMI)** indicates that the vendor, usually a distributor, manages the inventories for the manufacturer or buyer. This reduces warehousing costs for suppliers. This is how it is done:

Example. Wal-Mart provides P&G with access to daily sales information from every store for every item P&G makes for Wal-Mart. Then P&G is able to manage the *inventory replenishment* for Wal-Mart stores. By monitoring inventory levels, P&G knows when inventories fall below the reorder threshold for each product at any Wal-Mart store. These data trigger an immediate shipment to Wal-Mart.

P&G has similar agreements with other major retailers. The benefit for P&G is accurate and timely demand information. Thus, P&G can plan production more accurately, minimizing the bullwhip effect (described in Tutorial #1). To do so, P&G deployed a Web-based "Ultimate-Supply System," which replaced 4,000 different EDI links to suppliers and retailers in a more cost-effective way, and is reaping huge cost savings as of 2006.

E-BUSINESS SYSTEMS AND THE SUPPLY CHAIN

The increase in e-commerce has resulted in new opportunities to improve the performance of the supply chain. Primary advantages of Internet utilization in SCM are

- Better cost performance from improved productivity and lower costs
- Enhanced customer service from improved quality of service
- Improved process capabilities from online business quality consistency
- Higher productivity and dependability from increased control of material flows along the supply chain
- Shortened cycle times due to fewer delays and higher speed
- Greater flexibility in planning and replanning
- Shortened supply chain
- Smoother related production processes

The following are examples of e-business activities that can improve supply chain management:

- *Collaborative fulfillment networks (CFNs)* enable coordination among multiple participating firms at different stages of the supply chain. Collaborative fulfillment networks can help alleviate concerns related to coordination, shorten delays, expedite shipments, and so forth. For example, it has been found that if organizations use a coordinated inventory approach with a replenishment policy that does order smoothing to reduce order size variability, then overall system costs will be reduced (both inventory and transportation costs).
- *Electronic marketplaces* (using business-to-business Internet-based technologies) allow organizations, even competitors in the supply chain, to identify upstream suppliers. Electronic marketplaces provide for more efficient resource allocation within the organization and between organizations, better information flow and dissemination on products and services in the supply chain, and the ability to better manage risk in the organization.
- *Electronic data interchange* (EDI) is a communication standard that enables the electronic transfer of routine documents, such as purchase orders, between business partners. It formats these documents according to agreed-upon standards. EDI has been around for about 30 years in the non-Internet environment (usually VANs). EDI often serves as a catalyst and a stimulus to improve the standard of information that flows between organizations.

The specific benefits of this process are that data entry errors are minimized (only one entry, and an automatic check by the computer), the length of the message can be shorter, the messages are secured, and EDI fosters collaborative relationships and strategic partnerships. Other benefits are reduced cycle time, better inventory management, increased productivity, enhanced customer service, minimized paper usage and storage, and increased cash flow (per *1edisource.com*).
- *Electronic ordering and funds transfer* (EOFT) is an important component in e-business transactions. EOFT uses tools such as XML, extranets, Web Services, and EDI (see Tutorial #6). A *supply chain integration hub* allows for the electronic

connection of trading partners with the organization's e-business systems. It transmits information while simultaneously populating the customer's systems on demand. One option is to change a linear supply chain into a hub. In linear supply chains, information is processed in a sequence, which slows down its flow. Section 11.4 in Chapter 11 illustrates how this is done.

Electronic Data Interchange (EDI). Transactions between organizations often use **electronic data interchange (EDI),** which is a standardized data-transmittal format for electronic transactions. An expanded version of EDI is called *advanced shipping notice* (ASN), which is a shipping notice delivered directly from the vendor to the purchaser.

MANAGING INVENTORY

The most common solution used by companies to solve supply chain problems is *building inventories* as "insurance" against supply chain uncertainties. The main problem with this approach is that it is very difficult to correctly determine inventory levels for each product and part. If inventory levels are set too high, the cost of keeping the inventory will be very large. (And, as we have seen, high inventories at multiple points in the supply chain can result in the bullwhip effect.) If the inventory is too low, there is no insurance against high demand or slow delivery times, and revenues (and customers) may be lost. In either event, the total cost—including the cost of holding inventories, the cost of lost sales opportunities, and bad reputation—can be very high. Thus, companies make major attempts to optimize and control inventories. Managing inventories can be done in different ways . Several methods are illustrated in this chapter. An emerging method is the use of RFID, which is described in Chapter 11 and in Part III Case: Wal-Mart.

MANAGING E-PROCUREMENT

E-procurement is the use of Internet technologies to purchase or provide goods and services. As described in Chapter 5, E-procurement systems require the use of integrated database systems, WAN communication systems, Web-based systems, inventory systems, and interaction with accounting systems (see *en.wikipedia.org/wiki/ E-procurement*).

Cost efficiencies in the purchasing process have been a major catalyst for the adoption of e-procurement. E-procurement reduces purchase prices through greater transparency of market pricing and lower search costs. E-procurement allows, for example, organizations that purchase similar products to form a cooperative in the supply chain to get significantly lower pricing through volume discounts (group purchasing). Organizations can also use e-procurement systems to standardize purchasing processes within the organization, thereby improving internal purchasing processes as well as employee satisfaction. Procurement auctions give buyers access to raw materials at very reduced costs. In e-procurement, requesters directly search for and select products in electronic catalogs. Part of this strategy is a shift from managing transactions to managing suppliers.

MANAGING OTHER IT-ASSISTED SOLUTIONS

Companies employ multiple other methods to achieve supply chain superiority. Wal-Mart, for example, is well-known for its ability to collaborate with companies across its supply chain. It is able to combine information from its suppliers with demand and inventory data from its stores to minimize operating costs and reduce prices. Large companies such as Nestlé USA created a vice-president-level position exclusively to manage business with Wal-Mart. Several other mechanisms, such as supply chain teams and virtual factories, heavily utilize IT to generate information and share it with their suppliers. We introduce these two methods next.

Supply Chain Teams. A **supply chain team** is a group of tightly coordinated employees who work together to serve the customer. Each task is done by a member of the team who is best positioned, trained, and capable of doing that specific task, regardless of which department or even company the member works for. For example, in a supply chain team, the team member who deals with the delivery will handle a delivery problem, even if he or she works for the delivery company rather than for the retailer whose product is being delivered. This way, redundancies can be minimized. The delivery company will deal with the customer directly so that the customer does not need to pass the problem along to the retailer, who would end up having to contact the delivery company.

Virtual Factories. A **virtual factory** is a collaborative enterprise application that provides a computerized model of a factory. In the virtual factory, proposed designs can be tested, relationships with suppliers can be simulated, and manufacturing processes and how they are connected can be modeled. If potential problems in these areas are spotted in the digital model of the factory, simulated solutions can be worked out in the virtual model before they are implemented in the real-world factory. Usually, the virtual factory application would connect suppliers to the B2B system and clearly present the needed demand to suppliers. This "demand visibility" can help the company focus on two important key performance indicators, lead times and transaction cost. Uniting the entire supply chain and creating visibility between suppliers and buyers can help the companies forecast and plan demand more effectively. Virtual factories also enable all companies involved to work together collaboratively using common tools, and they provide greater flexibility and responsiveness by getting information and goods flowing much more quickly. For an example, see *Danfoss.com* (2006).

MOBILITY AND WIRELESS SOLUTIONS

In the last few years we have seen an increased number of wireless solutions to supply chain problems. In addition to RFID (see Chapter 11), one can use mobile devices, as illustrated in *IT at Work 10.2*.

The Leaning of the Supply Chain. Mobility eliminates wasted time hidden in your business processes—time that slows your entire chain of operations. Without mobility, processes are tied to an application that can be accessed only on a desktop computer, leaving businesses dependent upon paper to disseminate information (such as work orders) to employees as well as to collect needed information throughout business processes. But paper-driven processes require time to handwrite data and time to enter that information into the computer—a process that requires the data to be handled twice. And this "double touch" of business data leads to an inefficient use of time, high labor costs, and a larger opportunity for error.

Through mobility, computing power is moved from a stationary desktop computer to a mobile computer—the tools workers need to automate business processes are always in hand. Workers can now access and capture data in real time—right at the point of work. Manual processes are replaced with real-time computing. Instead of paper work orders being issued to employees, an electronic work order can be issued instantly and automatically by your business systems. Instead of collecting data on paper-based forms that must then be entered into the computer at a later time, workers can enter the information directly into your business systems.

For a comprehensive review, see Motorola (2007) and *motorola.com/supplychainmobility*.

BUSINESS VALUE OF SCM

The flows of goods, services, information, and financial resources are usually designed to effectively transform raw items to finished products and services, and to do so *efficiently*. The goals of SCM are to reduce uncertainty and risks along the supply chain, and to improve collaboration, thereby decreasing inventory levels and cycle time, and improving business processes and customer service. All of these benefits contribute to increased profitability and competitiveness, as demonstrated in the opening case, and therefore SCM has a significant strategic value. The benefits of SCM have long been recognized both in business and in the military, as illustrated in the following examples:

Example. Coca-Cola Enterprises (CCE) is saving millions in distribution costs by implementing new technologies to manage the supply chain network in 2007/2008. SAP-based direct-store-delivery systems allow CCE to react to rivals' sales and promotions as soon as delivery representatives send competitive data back from the retail stores.

IT at Work 10.2

Peacocks Retails Uses Wireless to Smooth Its Supply Chain

OM   GLOBAL

Peacocks Retails (*peacocks.co.uk*) of Wales operates about 490 retail stores, selling clothes and home furniture in Wales and the south of England. The company had a problem in its internal supply chain: its paper-based system of managing the distribution of products was prone to problems, such as incorrectly completed pick-lists, wrongly picked items, transcription errors, delays in generating and receiving data, and much more. These problems interfered with the company's growth strategy and reduced its profit.

In 1997, Peacocks Retails consolidated its six warehouses to a single distribution center (100,000 square feet). Stores were ordering more than 4,000 SKUs (stock-keeping units) each day. These needed to be picked and shipped to stores effectively and efficiently. Using one warehouse instead of six solved some problems, but the paper-based communication system was as bad as before. With a paper-based pick system, it is easy to run out of product in a specific location. Then the picker has to either wait for more units to arrive or move to another location. There is frequently a built-in delay, and the company has no idea about possible stock problems until they happen.

In 1998, Peacocks Retails started to replace the paper-based system with a wireless system (from Symbol.com). Specifically, the fully automated distribution center is equipped with a hands-free and real-time put-away and picking system. It is based on a combination of 28 wearable computers and 6 truck-mounted terminals supported by wireless LAN.

The wireless system provides real-time control. Whether an item is moved by hand or by truck, Peacocks knows precisely where it is located. If at any point in the process someone is at the wrong location, handling the wrong product, or trying to send it to the wrong place, the system simply sends out an alert and prevents a wrong action. When Peacocks receives a delivery from a manufacturer, the consignment is checked, and the individual cartons from each delivery are given an identifying barcode label and scanned to report receipt. In this way, every item can be tracked through the distribution center from the minute it arrives. Immediately, the system will know if there is a requirement at a pick location. Once individual cartons are labeled, Peacocks uses the automated conveyor system to send cartons to the desired locations, as directed by the wireless warehouse management system.

Each member of the picking team wears a wrist-mounted terminal that receives picking instructions via the wireless LAN from Peacocks' host system. As an empty trolley arrives in the pick area, a picker scans its barcode, and the terminal's LCD screen tells the picker which aisle to go to, which location to pick from, and which items to pick. When a picker arrives at the pick face, she first scans the barcode mounted at the end of the aisle. This verifies that she is in the correct aisle. She then scans another barcode at the product location to verify she is at the correct place. Finally, she scans each item as it is picked into her trolley. Once each pick is complete, the conveyor system takes each trolley to the dispatch area to be loaded into a crate for delivery to a specific Peacocks store.

Because data are sent to the host in real time, as the picking operation proceeds, the system knows when pick "face stocks" are approaching the replenishment level set by Peacocks. Once this happens, the system sends an alert to a truck-mounted terminal in the pallet store. As with the wrist-mounted terminals, an LCD screen on the truck terminal directs the driver to a precise location in the pallet racking. On arrival at the location, the driver uses a handheld scanner to scan the location barcode. This confirms that he is at the right location and selecting the right product.

Some other benefits: The hands-free arrangement saves time; it is not necessary to keep putting down the terminals when hands are needed. Also, wearable computers are not dropped, so they are not damaged. The system is user-friendly, so training is minimal. Another benefit is the positive impact on team morale. Everyone likes the wearables because they are comfortable to wear and easy to use, making the job easier and leading to efficiency improvements.

Sources: Compiled from Peacocks Case Study (2004); *peacocks.co.uk* (accessed June 2008); and *gmb.org.uk* (2005).

For Further Exploration: Identify all segments of the supply chain that are improved by the system and describe the improvement. Also, investigate how RFID may impact this system.

Example. Sears, Roebuck and Co. and Kmart Holding Company merged in 2004; they had to integrate 40 different supply chain systems between the two organizations operating 3,500 stores. There has been a large IT integration effort to manage supply chain operations. Sears Holding, the combined company, had to determine how to merge two different businesses and consolidate supply chain operations.

Example. Corning Inc., a glass manufacturer headquartered in upstate New York, developed solutions to enable the optimization of its global supply chain network. The supply chain technology strategy group and the process owners in the organization conducted a wide-ranging analysis of each business unit. Because of planned improvements in the supply chain process, Corning was able to integrate the relevant activities of manufacturers, suppliers, customer service organizations, sales organizations, and technology innovators.

Example. Oracle rolled out new enterprise applications to enable manufacturers to have better control over their supply chain, especially partners and suppliers. The Oracle business suite upgrade includes RFID support for SCM processes.

SUPPLY CHAINS AND INFORMATION INTEGRATION

Twentieth-century computer technology was *functionally* oriented. Functional systems may not let different departments communicate with each other in the same language. Worse yet, crucial sales, inventory, and production data often have to be painstakingly entered manually into separate computer systems every time a person who is not a member of a specific department needs ad-hoc information related to the specific department. In many cases, employees using functionally oriented technology simply do not get the information they need, or they get it too late (e.g., see the Northern Digital Minicase). Thus, managing the twenty-first-century enterprise cannot be done effectively with old technology.

Internal versus External Integration. There are two basic types of systems integration—internal and external. *Internal integration* refers to integration within a company between (or among) applications, and/or between applications and databases. For example, an organization may integrate inventory control with an ordering system, or a CRM suite with the database of customers. Large companies that have hundreds of applications may find it extremely difficult to integrate the newer Web-based applications with the older legacy systems.

External integration refers to integration of applications and/or databases among business partners—for example, the suppliers' catalogs with the buyers' e-procurement system. Another example of external supply chain integration is product-development systems that allow suppliers to dial into a client's intranet, pull product specifications, and view illustrations and videos of a manufacturing process. External integration is especially needed for B2B and for partner relationship management (PRM) systems, as will be discussed in Chapter 11. For more on integration, see Online Minicase 10.2, the case of Cybex International.

ETHICAL ISSUES RELATED TO SUPPLY CHAIN SOLUTIONS

Conducting an SCM project may result in the need to lay off, retrain, or transfer employees. Should management notify the employees in advance regarding such possibilities? And what about older employees who may have been loyal employees? Other ethical issues may involve sharing of personal information, which may be required for a collaborative organizational culture, but which some employees may resist. Finally, individuals may have to share computer programs that they designed for their personal use on the job. Such programs may be considered the intellectual property of the individuals. (Should the employees be compensated for the programs' use by others?) To provide the solutions discussed in this section, IT utilizes a number of software packages. These are described in the next two sections.

Review Questions

1. Define collaborative supply chain.
2. Describe how vendor-managed inventory works.
3. How can e-business improve the supply chain?
4. Describe how e-procurement improves the supply chain.
5. How is collaboration for the supply chain managed?
6. Define CPFR and describe how it works.
7. Define virtual factory; compare and contrast virtual and regular factories.
8. What is the business value of SCM?

10.3 Enterprise Resource Planning (ERP) Systems

One of the most successful tools for managing supply chains, especially internal ones, and related internal activities, is enterprise resource planning (ERP).

WHAT IS ERP?

With the advance of enterprisewide client/server computing comes a new challenge: how to control all major business processes in *real time* with a single software architecture. The most common *integrated software* solution of this kind is known as **enterprise resource planning (ERP).** This software integrates the planning, management, and use of all of the resources in the entire enterprise. It is comprised of *sets of* *applications* that automate *routine* back-end operations (such as financial, inventory management, and scheduling) to help enterprises handle jobs that are done in several departments such as order fulfillment. For example, there is a module for cost control, for accounts payable and receivable, and for fixed assets and treasury management. ERP promises benefits ranging from increased efficiency to improved quality, productivity, and profitability. (See *en.wikipedia.org/wiki/Enterprise_resource_planning* for details.)

The Purpose and Advantages of ERP. ERP's major objective is to *integrate all departments and functional information flows across a company* onto a single computer system that can serve all of the enterprise's needs. This overcomes the difficulty of working together with information systems that do not "speak" with each other. For example, improved order entry allows immediate access to inventory (thus improving inventory management), product data, customer credit history, and prior order information. Such availability of information helps to optimize production schedules, raises productivity, and increases customer satisfaction, resulting in a competitive advantage. Furthermore, errors are being reduced, so money is saved. An example of how ERP smoothes over the supply chain is provided in *IT at Work 10.3*. ERP systems are in use in thousands of large and medium companies worldwide, and some ERP systems are producing dramatic results (see *erp.ittoolbox.com* and customers' success stories at *sap.com* and *oracle.com*). ERP integrates all routine transactions within a company, including those of internal suppliers and customers (e.g., when departments serve each other). Later it was expanded, in what is known as *extended ERP software,* to incorporate external suppliers and customers. The advantages of ERP stem from its capabilities.

Capabilities of ERP. ERP projects are focused on specific business process areas, such as:

- Combining *less than truckloads* (LTLs) shipments in order to fill trucks, reduce pickup/delivery times, and eliminate unneeded storage facilities
- Dynamically sourcing products from different manufacturing and distribution facilities based on inventory and capacity
- Showing a single face to global customers across business lines
- Consolidating country-based sales, marketing, and distribution operations in geographic areas, such as Europe, that have lower barriers to trade
- Coordinating procurement and logistics of key commodities across business units and geographies
- Creating supplier portals that consolidate the needs of each business unit and provide a way of deepening the relationship and partnership with the suppliers

The success of ERP depends on successful implementation and on the ability to overcome some of its limitations.

ERP IMPLEMENTATION

Implementing ERP is composed of multiple activities that depend on where, when, who, and what is involved. First, let us look at some successful cases of implementation.

Examples of Successful ERP Implementation. The following are a few examples of successful ERP implementation:

Example: Rolls-Royce. The implementation of ERP enables Rolls-Royce not only to lower its IT costs but also to deliver customized cars to the customer on time. Timely delivery increases customer satisfaction and confidence in the company and, it is hoped, future orders as well (Yusuf et al., 2004).

IT at Work 10.3

Colgate-Palmolive Uses ERP to Smooth Its Supply Chain

OM   **GLOBAL**

Colgate-Palmolive is the world leader in oral-care products (toothpaste, toothbrushes, and mouthwashes) and a major supplier of personal-care products (baby care, deodorants, shampoos, and soaps). In addition, the company's Hill's Health Science Diet is a leading pet-food brand worldwide. International sales account for about 70 percent of Colgate's total revenues.

To stay competitive, Colgate continuously seeks to streamline its supply chain, through which thousands of suppliers and customers interact with the company. At the same time, Colgate faces the challenges of accelerating new-product development, which has been a factor in driving faster sales growth and improved market share. Also, Colgate is devising ways to offer consumers a greater choice of better products at a lower cost to the company. To better manage the complexities of its manufacturing and the supply chains, Colgate embarked on an ERP implementation. The new system allows the company to access more timely and accurate data and reduce costs. The structure of the ERP is shown in the attached figure.

In 2005, Colgate started to see return on investment with the successful implementation of the Advanced Planning and Optimization module, a SAP R/3 module that includes demand and production planning for the integration of raw materials in regional procurement decisions. More than 100 business processes were standardized worldwide to enable SAP process definitions to be widely accepted.

An important factor for Colgate was whether it could use the ERP software across the entire spectrum of the business. Colgate needed to coordinate globally and act locally. Colgate's U.S. division installed SAP R/3 for this purpose. The new initiative for 2008 is the full integration of the business warehouse, supply chain, and CRM systems into the core functionality of SAP R/3 functions.

Sources: Compiled from Sullivan (2005), and Kalakota and Robinson (2001).

For Further Exploration: What is the role of the ERP for Colgate-Palmolive? Who are the major beneficiaries of the new system? How is the SCM being improved?

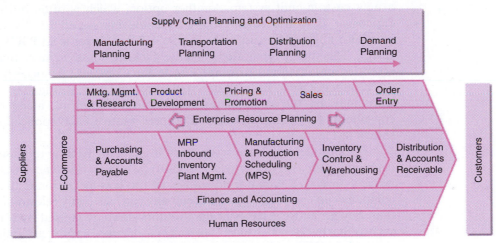

Colgate-Palmolive ERP implementation. (*Source:* R. Kalakota and M. Robinson, *E-Business 2.0*, Boston, MA, Addison Wesley, 2001.)

Example: Comark Corp. Using ERP, Comark Corp. (*comarkcorp.com*) reduced inventories of its precision measurement products and eliminated voluminous reports. ERP is also used to track information more accurately.

Example: Consolidation Applications via ERP. Exxon Mobil consolidated 300 different information systems by implementing SAP R/3 (see below) in its U.S. petrochemical operations alone.

Specific Implementation Issues and Potential Limitations of Use. Some major implementation issues are presented in Online Brief 10.3. They include ERP vendor and product selection, matching commercial software with organizational processes, installing ERP commercial software, complexity of the software, reasons for either successful or failed implementations, value generated from ERP systems, and integrations issues.

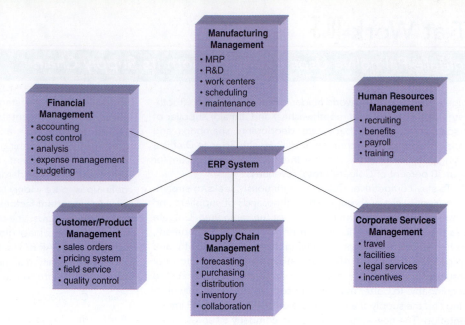

Figure 10.5 ERR application modules. (*Source:* Prepared by D. Amoroso.)

For businesses that want to use ERP, one option is to self-develop an integrated system, either by linking together existing functional packages or by programming a new, custom-built system. Another option, which is often quicker and/or less expensive, is to use commercially available integrated ERP software (see the Northern Digital Minicase). The leading ERP software is **SAP R/3** (from SAP AG Corp.). This highly integrated software package contains more than 115 business activities modules (and growing). Oracle and Computer Associates also make similar products. Due to its large size, some maintain (e.g., Rettig, 2007) that ERP software may be too complex to be effective. Therefore, many companies use consultants for its implementation. Representative ERP application modules are shown in Figure 10.5.

Yet another way for a business to implement ERP is to lease ERP systems from *application service providers* (ASPs) (see *en.wikipedia.org/wiki/Application_service_provider*). A major advantage of the leasing option is that even a small company can enjoy ERP: a small company can lease only relevant modules, rather than buy an entire ERP package. Another strategy is used by some companies, such as Starbucks, which have chosen a *best-of-breed* approach—building their own customized ERP with ready-made components leased or purchased from several vendors, using the best modules of the different vendors.

Because it is much less expensive for businesses to lease ERP systems from application service providers (ASPs) than it is to develop their own, more and more mid-sized companies are now using ERP. Overall, ERP investments are much more affordable for smaller enterprises today than they were 10 years ago.

ERP also can be used to manage resources, including employees. MySAP ERP Human Capital Management is one example of an ERP module that optimizes HR activities by aligning employees' skills, activities, and incentives with business objectives and strategies. The module provides tools for managing, measuring, and rewarding individual contributions. Human capital management modules are fully integrated with payroll functions, regulatory requirements for hiring, employee development, and best practices across the world.

Corporate services is another module within an ERP system that gives functionality for travel management; managing real estate and facilities; environment, legal, health, and safety concerns; and an incentive and commission management. In an ERP system, financial management and accounting are managed and integrated into the supply chain and internal control processes. Financial modules provide transaction accounting, management of internal controls, budgeting, and financial analysis.

In addition to integrating ERP with SCM systems, ERP can be integrated with other enterprise systems, most notably with e-commerce and CRM. Online Minicase 10.2 describes the integration of ERP and EC at Cybex International. Other typical integrations are done with KM and business process management. Oracle is an example of a vendor that provides the infrastructure and architecture for such integrations. ERP, like other software tools, is ever evolving (e.g., see Beatty and Williams, 2006).

Review Questions

1. Define ERP and describe its objectives.
2. List and briefly describe the options for acquiring ERP.
3. Describe the logic of integrating ERP and SCM software.
4. List the capabilities of ERP systems.
5. Describe retailer–supplier integrated supply chains.

10.4 Customer Relationship Management (CRM)

WHAT IS CUSTOMER RELATIONSHIP MANAGEMENT?

Customer relationship management (CRM) is an enterprisewide effort to acquire and retain profitable customers. CRM focuses on building long-term and sustainable customer relationships that add value for both the customer and the company. (See *crm-forum.com, en.wikipedia.org/wiki/Customer_relationship_management,* and *crmassist.com.*) There are many definitions of CRM. The reason is that CRM is new and still evolving. Also, it is an interdisciplinary field, so each discipline (e.g., marketing, management) defines CRM differently.

In general, CRM is an approach that recognizes that customers are the core of the business and that the company's success depends on effectively managing relationships with them (see Figure 10.6). In other words, CRM is a business strategy to select and manage customers to optimize long-term value. CRM requires a

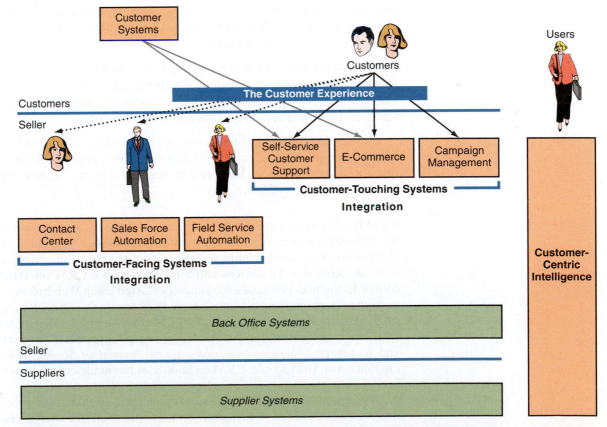

Figure 10.6 CRM applications. (*Source:* Patricia Seybold Group, *An Executive's Guide to CRM*, March 21, 2002.)

customer-centric business philosophy and culture to support effective marketing, sales, and services processes. CRM overlaps somewhat with the concept of *relationship marketing,* but not everything that could be called relationship marketing is in fact CRM (see Peppers and Rogers, 2004).

CRM is basically a simple idea: *Treat different customers differently,* because their needs differ and their value to the company may be different. CRM involves much more than just sales and marketing because a firm must be able to change how its products are configured or its service is delivered, based on the needs of individual customers. Smart companies have always encouraged the active participation of customers in the development of products, services, and solutions.

One reason so many firms are beginning to focus on CRM is that this kind of service can create high customer loyalty and, additionally, help the firm's profitability. Involvement of almost all other departments, and especially engineering (design), accounting, and operations, is critical in CRM.

CLASSIFICATION OF CRM APPLICATIONS

Another way of looking at CRM is to focus on the tools used by the CRM applications. The Patricia Seybold Group (2002) distinguishes among *customer-facing, customer-touching,* and *customer-centric intelligence* CRM applications. These three categories of applications are described below and are shown in Figure 10.6. The figure also shows how customers interact with these applications.

1. **Customer-facing applications.** These include all of the areas where customers interact with the company: call centers, including help desks; sales force automation; and field service automation. Such CRM applications basically automate the information flow or support employees in these areas.

2. **Customer-touching applications.** In this category, customers interact directly with the applications. Notable are self-service, campaign management (for promotions and advertisements), and general-purpose e-commerce applications.

3. **Customer-centric intelligence applications.** These are applications that are intended to analyze the results of operational processing and use the results of the analysis to improve CRM applications. Data reporting and warehousing and data mining are the prime topics here.

To this classification of CRM applications we add a fourth category:

4. **Online networking applications.** Online networking refers to methods that provide the opportunity to build personal relationships with a wide range of people in business. These include chat rooms and discussion lists.

Notice that the above categories of applications are supported by back-office systems at the sellers' sites and by different supplier systems. (Further details on the first three categories can be found at *psgroup.com,* in the free download of *An Executive's Guide to CRM.*)

E-CRM

CRM has been practiced manually by corporations for generations. However, since the mid-1990s, various types of information technologies have enhanced CRM. CRM technology is an evolutionary response to changes in the business environment, making use of new IT devices and tools. The term **e-CRM (electronic CRM)** was coined in the mid-1990s, when businesses started using Web browsers, the Internet, and other electronic touchpoints (e-mail, POS terminals, call centers, and direct sales) to manage customer relationships. E-CRM covers a broad range of topics, tools, and methods, ranging from the proper design of digital products and services to pricing and to loyalty programs (e.g., see *e-sj.org, Journal of Service Research,* and *ecrmguide.com*). The use of e-CRM technologies has made customer service, as well as service to partners, much more effective and efficient.

Through Internet technologies, data generated about customers can be easily fed into marketing, sales, and customer service applications for analysis. Electronic CRM also includes online applications that lead to segmentation and personalization. The success of these efforts can be measured and modified in real time, further elevating customer expectations. In a world connected by the Internet, e-CRM has become a requirement for survival, not just a competitive advantage. In this section we will discuss several issues related to E-CRM and its implementation.

The Levels and Types of e-CRM. We can differentiate three levels of e-CRM:

1. Foundational service. This includes the *minimum necessary* services such as Web site responsiveness (e.g., how quickly and accurately the service is provided), site effectiveness, and order fulfillment.

2. Customer-centered services. These services include order tracking, product configuration and customization, and security/trust. These are the services that *matter the most* to customers.

3. Value-added services. These are *extra services,* such as online auctions and online training and education. One such service is loyalty programs.

Loyalty Programs. An important activity in e-CRM is a loyalty program.

Loyalty programs are programs that recognize customers who repeatedly use the services (products) offered by a company. A well-known example is the airlines' *frequent flyers* program. Casinos use their players' clubs to reward their frequent players. Many supermarkets use some kind of program to reward frequent shoppers, as do many other companies. These programs include some kind of database (or data warehouse) to manage the accounting of the points collected and the rewards. Analytical tools such as data mining are then used to explore the data and learn about customer behavior.

A special loyalty program is offered by 1-800-FLOWERS.COM, as shown in *IT at Work 10.4.*

In addition to the three levels of e-CRM, we distinguish three major types of CRM *activities*: operational, analytical, and collaborative. *Operational CRM* is related to typical business functions involving customer services, order management, invoice/billing, and sales/marketing automation and management. *Analytical CRM* involves activities that capture, store, extract, process, interpret, and report customer data to a corporate user, who then analyzes these data as needed. *Collaborative CRM* deals with all necessary communication, coordination, and collaboration between vendors and customers.

Customer Service on the Web. A primary activity of e-CRM is customer service on the Web, which can take many forms. We describe some of these different kinds of Web-based customer service below. (For fuller details, see Greenberg, 2006.)

Search and Comparison Capabilities. With the hundreds of thousands of online stores, it is difficult for customers to find what they want, even inside a single Internet mall (see Chapter 6). Search and comparison capabilities are provided internally in large malls (e.g., *smartmall.biz*) or by independent comparison sites (*mysimon.com*).

Free Products and Services. One approach companies use to differentiate themselves is to give away some product or service. For example, Compubank.com once offered free bill payments and ATM services. Companies can offer free samples over the Internet, as well as free entertainment, customer education, and more.

Technical and Other Information and Services. Interactive experiences can be personalized to induce the consumer to commit to a purchase or to remain a loyal customer. For example, General Electric's Web site provides detailed technical and maintenance information and sells replacement parts for discontinued models for those who need to fix outdated home appliances. Such information and parts are quite difficult to find offline. Another example is Goodyear, which provides

IT at Work 10.4

1-800-FLOWERS.COM Uses Data Mining to Foster Customer Relationship Management

1-800-FLOWERS.COM (1-800-flowers.com) is a true Internet pioneer. It had an Internet presence in 1992 and full-fledged e-store capabilities in 1995. Online sales are a major marketing channel (in addition to telephone and fax orders). Competition is very strong in this industry. The company's success was based on operational efficiency, convenience (24/7 accessibility), and reliability. However, all major competitors provide the same features today. To maintain its competitive advantage, the company transformed itself into a customer-intimate organization, caring for more than 15 million customers. The challenge was to make 1-800-FLOWERS.COM the only retailer that customers really trust when shopping for gifts online or by phone.

The company decided to cultivate brand loyalty through customer relationships, which is based on intimate knowledge of customers. How is this accomplished? SAS software spans the entire decision-support process for managing customer relationships. Collecting data at all customer contact points, the company turns those data into knowledge for understanding and anticipating customer behavior, meeting customer needs, building more profitable customer relationships, and gaining a holistic view of a customer's lifetime value. Using SAS Enterprise Miner, 1-800-FLOWERS.COM sifts through data (such as historical purchases) to discover trends, explain outcomes, and predict results so that the company can increase response rates and identify profitable customers. The rationale for the customer-intimate effort is to build loyalty. In addition to selling and campaign management, the ultimate goal is to make sure that when a customer wants to buy, he or she continues to buy from 1-800-FLOWERS.COM and cannot be captured by a competitor's marketing. To build that kind of loyalty, it is necessary to know your customers and build a solid relationship with each one of them.

Identifying Each Customer. At 1-800-FLOWERS.COM, the objective is not just about getting customers to buy more. It is about making sure that when they decide to purchase a gift online or by phone, they do not think of going to the competition. Loyalty is earned through the quality of the relationship offered. The difficulty is that not every customer wants the same relationship. Some want you to be more involved with them than others; some will give you different levels of permission on how to contact them. At the end of the day, the data mining software helps the company identify the many different types of customers and how each would like to be treated.

The company plans its ad campaigns based on the results of the data mining done on a one-to-one basis. For example, some customers like to be notified about sales; others do not. Some prefer notification via e-mail. The customers' purchasing history and other data needed for the analysis are stored in a data center (Chapter 3).

Many factors have contributed to the company's recent revenue growth—customer relationship management among them. The data mining analysis provides rapid access to better customer information and reduces the amount of time the company needs to spend on the phone with customers, which makes better use of everybody's time. The net result is that customer retention has increased by over 15 percent.

Sources: Compiled from Anonymous (2006), Reda (2006), and *1800flowers.com* (accessed July 2008).

For Further Exploration: Why is being number one in operation efficiency not enough to keep 1-800-FLOWERS.COM at the top of its industry? What is the role of data mining? How is the one-to-one relationship achieved in such systems?

---

information about tires and their use at *goodyear.com*. The ability to download manuals and problem solutions at any time is another innovation of electronic customer service.

Customized Products and Services. Dell Computer revolutionized the purchasing of computers by letting customers configure their own systems. This mass customization process is now used extensively by online vendors. Consumers are shown prepackaged "specials" and are given the option to "custom-build" products using online product configurators.

Other companies have found ways that are unique to their industries to offer customized products and services online. Web sites such as *gap.com* allow you to "mix and match" your entire wardrobe. Web sites such as *hitsquad.com, musicalgreeting. com*, or *surprise.com* allow consumers to handpick individual music titles from a library and customize a CD, a feature that is not offered in traditional music stores. Instant delivery of any digitized entertainment is a major advantage of EC. Salesforce.com offers comprehensive customization capabilities for the users of their products.

Account or Order Status Tracking. Customers can view their account balances or check merchandise shipping status at any time from their computers or cell phones. If you ordered books from Amazon, for example, you can find the anticipated arrival date. Many companies follow this model and provide similar services.

All of these examples of customer service on the Web demonstrate an important aspect of CRM: a focus on the individual customer.

Other Tools for Customer Service. There are many innovative Web-related tools to enhance customer service and CRM. Here are the major ones.

Personalized Web Pages. Many companies allow customers to create their own individual Web pages. These pages can be used to record purchases and preferences, as well as problems and requests. For example, using intelligent agent techniques, American Airlines generates personalized Web pages for each of about 800,000 registered travel-planning customers.

Also, customized information (such as product and warranty information) can be efficiently delivered when the customer logs on to the vendor's Web site. Not only can the customer pull information as needed, but the vendor also can push information to the customer. Transaction information stored in the vendor's database can be used to support the marketing of more products, for example.

FAQs. Frequently asked questions (FAQs) are the simplest and least expensive tool for dealing with repetitive customer questions. Customers use this tool by themselves, which makes the delivery cost minimal. However, any nonstandard question requires an e-mail message.

E-Mail and Automated Response. The most popular tool of customer service is e-mail. Inexpensive and fast, e-mail is used mostly to answer inquiries from customers but also to disseminate information (e.g., confirmations), to send alerts, to send product information, and to conduct correspondence regarding any topic.

Chat Rooms. Another tool that provides customer service, attracts new customers, and increases customers' loyalty is a chat room. For example, retailer QVC offers a chat room where customers can discuss their QVC shopping experiences (see Online Minicase 10.3).

Live Chat. Live chat allows customers to connect to a company representative and conduct an instant messaging talk. The advantage over a phone conversation is the ability to show documents and sometimes photos. For a demo and details, see *livechatinc.com* and *websitealive.com*. Some companies conduct a chat with a computer rather than a real person using natural language processing.

Call Centers. One of the most important tools of customer service is the *call center*. Call centers are typically the "face" of the organization to its customers. For example, investment company Charles Schwab's call center effectively handles over 1 million calls from investment customers every day.

New technologies are extending the functionality of the conventional call center to e-mail and to Web interaction. For example, *epicor.com* combines Web channels, such as automated e-mail reply, Web knowledge bases, and portal-like self-service, with call center agents or field service personnel. Such centers are sometimes called *telewebs*.

Troubleshooting Tools. Large amounts of time can be saved by customers if they can solve problems by themselves. Many vendors provide Web-based troubleshooting software to assist customers in this task. The vendors dramatically reduce their expenses for customer support when customers are able to solve problems without further intervention of customer service specialists.

Wireless (Mobile) CRM. Many CRM tools and applications are going wireless. As shown in Chapter 7, mobile salesforce automation is becoming popular. In addition, use of wireless devices by mobile service employees is enabling these employees to provide better service while they are at the customer's site. Also, using SMS and e-mail from handheld devices is becoming popular as a means of improving CRM. Overall, we will see many CRM services going wireless fairly soon. The advantages of mobile CRM are shown in Figure 10.7.

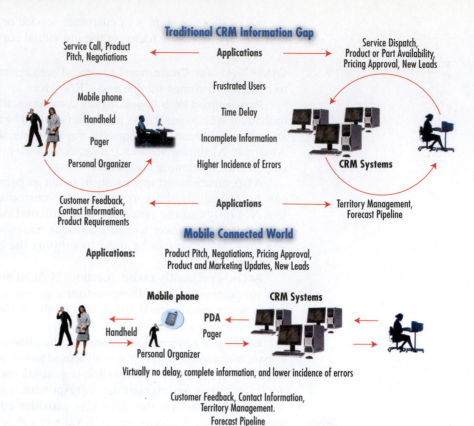

Figure 10.7 Traditional vs. mobile CRM.

CRM SUCCESSES AND FAILURES

A large number of companies reported successful deployment and use of e-CRM. *IT at Work 10.5* provides several examples.

As with many IT innovations, there have been initially a large number of CRM failures, which have been reported in the media. Numerous failures have been reported by *thinkanalytics.com*, *cio.com*, *CRM-forum.com*, and many more. However, according to *itgreycells.com*, CRM failures are declining, from a failure rate of up to 80 percent in 1998 to about 40 percent and even lower after 2003.

Some of the major issues relating to CRM failures are the following:

• Difficulty in measuring and valuing intangible benefits. There are only a few tangible benefits to CRM (see Chapter 17).

• Failure to identify and focus on specific business problems that the CRM can solve.

• Lack of active senior management (non-IT) sponsorship.

• Poor user acceptance. This issue can occur for a variety of reasons, such as unclear benefits (i.e., CRM is a tool for management, but it may not help a rep sell more effectively) and usability problems.

• Trying to automate a poorly defined business process in the CRM implementation.

Example of a failure: Citizen National Bank's experience is an example of a failure, changing the CRM vendors, and then a success. The lessons learned, at a cost of $500,000, were

• Be absolutely clear on how the CRM application will add value to the sales process.

• Determine if and why sales people are avoiding CRM.

• Provide incentives for the sales team to adopt CRM.

• Find ways to simplify the use of the CRM application.

• Adjust the CRM system as business needs change.

For details of this example, see Bartholomew (2007).

IT at Work 10.5

How Companies Use e-CRM

Almost all large companies have a formal CRM program (Agarwal et al., 2004). However, CRM programs may be implemented in a variety of different ways, due to the large number of programs, applications, and tools available. Here are a few examples of how companies have implemented CRM:

- Continental Airlines monitors telephone calls to its data center, using intelligent software from Witness Systems (*witness.com*) to analyze recorded conversations. The analysis tells Continental Airlines what customers really want. It also helps the company craft marketing plans and business strategy. Results serve customers better and resolve problems immediately, saving the company $1 million annually. To increase efficiency, Continental Airlines uses a program that automatically transcribes conversations into digitized text.

- Micrel Inc., a leading manufacturer of integrated circuit solutions for enterprise, consumer, industrial, mobile, telecommunications, automotive, and computer markets, has become known for being "fast on its feet" in responding to customer needs. To improve response time and relevancy of information delivered to customers online, the company uses a sophisticated self-service search and navigation engine that directs customers to the right information at the right time to help them reach buying decisions. As a result, Web site traffic grew by 300 percent, retention rate for new site visitors increased by 25 percent, saved $40,000 a year, and customer satisfaction increased significantly (see IBM, 2006, for details).

- Employees at more than 200 Sheraton Hotels owned by Starwood Hotels and Resorts are using an e-CRM system to coordinate fast responses to guests' complaints and unmet needs. When an employee does not respond to a request or complaint within a time frame predetermined by hotel management, the color of a computerized notice changes from green to yellow, and possibly to red. Red triggers management to quickly intervene and perhaps include special compensation for the guest. Starwood has reported significantly better operating results since it implemented the system. For details, see Babcock (2004).

- The Kassel region in Germany uses a CRM-based social networking platform to attract businesses, tourists, and potential residents. The site won the Most Innovative CRM Deployment Award at the *CRM Expo*, Europe's largest CRM show (see Boucher-Ferguson, 2008).

- The U.S. Department of Agriculture is using Microsoft Dynamics CRM 4.0 as a platform to build an application for tracking its conservation management efforts (see Boucher-Ferguson, 2008).

- Boots the Chemists, a UK retailer of over 1,400 health and beauty stores, uses e-CRM analytics to learn about customers in its e-loyalty programs. The retailer uses data mining to acquire insights into customer behavior. Customer service agents can analyze, predict, and maximize the value of each customer relationship. This enables better one-to-one marketing efforts and reduces customer dissatisfaction.

- Harrah's Entertainment Inc. treats its customers differently: the more a customer spends in a casino, the more rewards the customer gets. The company assigns a value to each customer by using data mining.

- FedEx's CRM system enables the company to provide superb service to millions of customers using 56 call centers. Each of its 4,000 call center employees has instant access to a customer's profile. The profile tells the employee how valuable the customer is and the details of the current transaction. The more an agent knows about the customer, the better the service provided. Customers use one phone number regardless of where the company is or the destination of the package. The CRM reduced calls for help, increased customer satisfaction, and enabled better advertising and marketing strategy. For details, see Guzman (2004).

For Further Exploration: What are the common elements of CRM in these examples? CRM systems provide managerial benefits. What are they? Why is data mining becoming so important in CRM?

Strategies to deal with these and other problems are offered by many. (For example, see *cio.com* for CRM implementation. Also see Mochal and Pace (2006) for "10 steps for CRM success.") Finally, the use of metrics to compare results is highly recommended.

CRM failures can create substantial problems. Some companies are falling behind in their ability to handle the volume of site visitors and the volume of buyers. Managerial guidelines for implementing CRM and avoiding CRM failure are provided in Table 10.1.

BUSINESS VALUE OF CRM

Many organizations are adopting CRM systems, with software to help acquire, manage, and retain loyal customers. DePaul University manages students and information using the CRM module of PeopleSoft Enterprise (an Oracle company) technology. Bell Canada, one of North America's largest communications providers, has adopted the CRM package from SSA that focuses on inbound marketing. There are three areas of CRM that should be given priority to realize the total business value of CRM: (1) marketing, (2) sales, and (3) service. The rise of Internet technologies has made obsolete many

TABLE 10.1	**How to Implement CRM to Avoid Its Failure**

- Conduct a survey to determine how the organization responds to customers.
- Carefully consider the four components of CRM: sales, service, marketing, and channel/partner management.
- CRM includes the analytical aspects of understanding your customers, their buying habits, and the reasons they make the decisions they do. Survey how CRM accomplishments are measured; use defined metrics. Make sure quality, not just quantity, is addressed.
- Consider how CRM software can help vis-à-vis the organization's objectives.
- Decide on a strategy: refining existing CRM processes, or reengineering the CRM.
- Evaluate all levels in the organization but particularly frontline agents, field service, and salespeople. Strong executive sponsor support is necessary for getting people to change how they do their jobs and to adopt a CRM culture.
- Prioritize the organization's requirements as one of the following: *must, desired*, or *not so important*.
- Select appropriate CRM software. There are more than 60 vendors. Some (like Salesforce.com, Microsoft) provide comprehensive packages; others provide only certain functions. Decide whether to use the best-of-breed approach or to go with one vendor. ERP vendors (e.g., Oracle and SAP) also offer CRM products.

Source: Compiled from DeFazio (2002) and Mochal and Pace (2006).

traditional concepts of CRM. Today, many of the benefits are realized in conjunction with Internet-based applications. The State of Florida Department of Revenue implemented a CRM initiative that provided the customer service where Florida residents can access account information online. First Union lagged at customer service, but using Wachovia's CRM system they were able to provide a higher level of service to customers. Boston Medical Center is a 547-bed hospital using CRM to attract physicians with special expertise and give access to information to enhance customer satisfaction (Chen, 2005).

Justifying e-CRM. One of the biggest problems in CRM implementation is the difficulty of defining and measuring success. Additionally, many companies say that when it comes to determining value, intangible benefits (Chapter 17) are more significant than tangible cost savings. Yet companies often fail to establish quantitative or even qualitative measures in order to judge these intangible benefits.

A formal business plan must be in place before the e-CRM project begins—one that quantifies the expected costs, tangible financial benefits, and intangible strategic benefits, as well as the risks. The plan should include an assessment of the following:

- **Tangible net benefits.** The plan must include a clear and precise cost-benefit analysis that lists all of the planned project costs and tangible benefits. This portion of the plan should also contain a strategy for assessing key financial metrics, such as ROI, NPV, or other justification methods (see Chapters 13 and 17).
- **Intangible benefits.** The plan should detail the expected intangible benefits, and it should list the measured successes and shortfalls. Often, an improvement in customer satisfaction is the primary goal of the e-CRM solution, but in many cases this key value is not measured.
- **Risk assessment.** The risk assessment is a list of all of the potential pitfalls related to the people, processes, and technology that are involved in the e-CRM project.

Having such a list helps to lessen the probability that problems will occur. And, if they do occur, a company may find that, by having listed and considered the problems in advance, the problems are more manageable than they would have been otherwise.

While a special approach is recommended for all enterprise systems, the CRM approach is most challenging, as you will find in the Problem-Solving Activity at the end of this chapter.

Tangible and intangible benefits. Benefits typically include increases in staff productivity (e.g., close more deals), cost avoidance, revenues, and margin increases, as well as reductions in inventory costs (e.g., due to the elimination of errors). Other benefits include increased customer satisfaction, loyalty, and retention.

Potential Pitfalls and Risks of e-CRM.

• *Taking on more than can be delivered.* The e-CRM solution should target specific sales or service business functions or specific groups of users. Additionally, it is essential to manage the project's scope, goals, and objectives throughout the project-development phase and deployment.

• *Getting over budget and behind schedule.*

• *Poor user adoption.* Ease of use and adequate training are essential.

• *Expensive maintenance and support.*

• *Isolation.* The effectiveness of a project may suffer if the CRM data are not used throughout the company.

• *Garbage in–garbage out.* Because e-CRM systems require so much data entry, users often put in placeholders, misguided estimates, or inaccurate information, which leads to poor analytical results and decision-making errors.

• *Failure to measure success.* Measurement of pre-project status and post-project achievements is essential for a company to show success.

On-Demand CRM.
Like several other enterprise systems, CRM can be delivered in two ways: *on-premise* and *on-demand.* The traditional way to deliver such systems was on-premise—meaning users purchased the system and installed it on site. This was very expensive, with a large upfront payment. Many SMEs could not justify it, especially because most CRM benefits are intangible.

The solution to the situation, which appears in several similar variations and names, is to lease the software. Initially, this was done by ASPs for SMEs. Later, Salesforce.com pioneered the concept for its several CRM products (including supporting salespeople), under the name of *On-Demand CRM*, offering the software over the Internet. The concept of on-demand is known also as *utility computing* or *software as a service* (Chapters 2 and 13). **On-demand CRM** is basically CRM hosted by an ASP or other vendor on the vendor's premise, in contrast to the traditional practice of buying the software and using it on site.

However, according to Overby (2006), the hype surrounding hosted, on-demand CRM must be weighed against the following implementation problems:

• ASPs can go out of business, leaving customers without service.
• It is difficult, or even impossible, to modify hosted software.
• Upgrading could become a problem.
• Relinquishing strategic data to a hosting vendor can be risky.
• Integration with existing software may be difficult.

The benefits are

• Improved cash flow due to savings in front-up purchase
• No need for corporate software experts
• Ease of use with minimal training
• Fast time-to-market (can use it quickly)
• Vendors' expertise available

These issues determine the IT strategy in general, as will be shown in Chapter 13.

CRM is also related to knowledge management, the topic of Section 10.5. The software for these two enterprise systems is frequently integrated.

1. Define CRM.
2. List the major types of CRM.
3. What is e-CRM?
4. List some customer-facing, customer-touching, and customer-intelligent CRM tools.
5. What is on-demand CRM?

10.5 Knowledge Management and IT

CONCEPTS AND DEFINITIONS

With roots in expert systems, organizational learning, and innovation, the idea of knowledge management is itself not new. Successful managers have always used intellectual assets and recognized their value. But these efforts were not systematic, nor did they ensure that knowledge gained was shared and dispersed appropriately for maximum organizational benefit. Moreover, sources such as Forrester Research, IBM, and Merrill Lynch estimate that 85 percent of a company's knowledge assets are not housed in relational databases, but are dispersed in e-mail, Word documents, spreadsheets, and presentations on individual computers. The application of information technology tools to facilitate the creation, storage, transfer, and application of previously uncodifiable organizational knowledge is a new and major initiative in organizations.

Knowledge management (KM) is a process that helps organizations identify, select, organize, disseminate, and transfer important information and expertise that are part of the organization's memory and that typically reside within the organization in an unstructured manner. Such treatment of knowledge enables effective and efficient problem solving, expedited learning, strategic planning, and decision making. Knowledge management initiatives focus on identifying knowledge, explicating it in such a way that it can be shared in a formal manner, and leveraging its value through reuse. For an overview and benefits, see Tutorial #5, *brint.com/KM*, *en.wikipedia.org/wiki/knowledge_management*, and *cio.com/research/knowledge/edit/kmabcs.html*.

Through a supportive organizational climate and modern information technology, an organization can bring its entire organizational memory and knowledge to bear upon any problem anywhere in the world and at any time. For organizational success, *knowledge, as a form of capital, must be exchangeable among persons, and it must be able to grow.* Knowledge about how problems are solved can be captured, so that knowledge management can promote organizational learning, leading to further knowledge creation. See Schwartz (2006).

Knowledge. In the information technology context, knowledge is very distinct from data and information (see Figure 10.8). Whereas *data* are a collection of facts, measurements, and statistics, *information* is organized or processed data that are timely (i.e., inferences from the data are drawn within the time frame of applicability) and accurate (i.e., with regard to the original data) (Holsapple, 2003). **Knowledge** is information that is *contextual, relevant,* and *actionable.*

For example, a map giving detailed driving directions from one location to another could be considered data. An up-to-the-minute traffic bulletin along the freeway that indicates a traffic slowdown due to construction could be considered information. Awareness of an alternative, back-roads route could be considered knowledge. In this

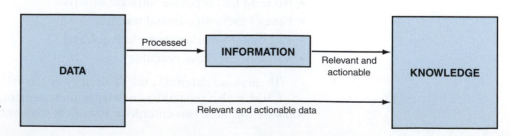

Figure 10.8 Data, information, and knowledge.

case, the map is considered data because it does not contain current relevant information that affects the driving time and conditions from one location to the other. However, having the current conditions as information is useful only if the individual has knowledge that will enable him or her to avoid the construction zone. Having knowledge implies that it can be used to solve a problem, whereas having information does not carry the same connotation.

Knowledge has the following characteristics that differentiate it from an organization's other assets (Holsapple, 2003):

- **Extraordinary leverage and increasing returns.** Knowledge is usually not subject to diminishing returns. When it is used, it is not consumed. Its consumers can add to it, thus increasing its value.
- **Fragmentation, leakage, and the need to refresh.** As knowledge grows, it branches and fragments. Knowledge is dynamic; it is information in action. Thus, an organization must continually refresh its knowledge base to maintain it as a source of competitive advantage.
- **Uncertain value.** It is difficult to estimate the impact of an investment in knowledge. There are too many intangible aspects.
- **Uncertain value of sharing.** Similarly, it is difficult to estimate the value of sharing the knowledge, or even who will benefit most.
- **Rooted in time.** The utility and validity of knowledge may vary with time; hence, the immediacy, age, perishability, and volatility of knowledge are important attributes.

Intellectual capital (or **intellectual assets**) is another term often used for knowledge, and it implies that there is a financial value to knowledge. Though intellectual capital is difficult to measure, some industries have tried. For example, the value of the intellectual capital of the property-casualty insurance industry has been estimated to be between $270 billion to $330 billion (Mooney, 2000). The Organization for Economic Co-operation and Development (OECD) has scored its 30 member nations according to their investments in intellectual capital, such as R&D, education, and patents. According to OECD, those countries with the most intellectual capital activities will be the winners of future wealth. A simple method to assess intellectual capital or "know how" is shown in *A Closer Look 10.1.*

Knowledge evolves over time with experience, which puts connections among new situations and events in context. Given the breadth of the types and applications of knowledge, we adopt the simple and elegant definition that knowledge is information in action.

A Closer Look 10.1

How Much Is the Knowledge in Your Company Worth?

Paul Strassmann, an IT consultant and writer (*strassmann.com*), devised several ways to measure KM (visit his Web site as well as *baselinemag.com*). One of his measures postulates that in the case of public companies, it is possible to assess the know-how of employees by following this simple calculation:

1. Find the market capitalization of a company. This is done by multiplying the number of shares by the price of each share on any given date (capitalization is also provided by *money.cnn.com*, *bloomberg.com*, and others).
2. Take the shareholder equity from the balance sheet for the same date (also available at the above URLs).
3. Subtract item 2 from item 1. If it is negative, stop—there is no value to your KM.

4. The difference is the knowledge value.
5. Divide the knowledge value by the shareholder equity. You get a percentage. The higher the percentage, the higher the value of the KM.
6. Find the number of employees (use the same sources).
7. Divide the total knowledge value (item 5) by the number of employees. This will give you the knowledge value per employee.

Now you can compare companies for their KM value. See Exercise #6.

Sources: Compiled from Strassmann (2005a and 2005b).

Explicit and Tacit Knowledge. **Explicit knowledge** deals with more objective, rational, and technical knowledge (data, policies, procedures, software, documents, etc.). **Tacit knowledge** is usually in the domain of subjective, cognitive, and experiential learning; it is highly personal and difficult to formalize (Nonaka and Takeuchi, 1995). For details, see Tutorial #5.

THE NEED FOR KNOW-LEDGE MANAGEMENT SYSTEMS

The goal of knowledge management is for an organization to be aware of individual and collective knowledge so that it may make the most effective use of the knowledge it has. Historically, MIS has focused on capturing, storing, managing, and reporting explicit knowledge. Organizations now recognize the need to integrate both explicit and tacit knowledge in formal information systems. **Knowledge management systems (KMSs)** refers to the use of modern information technologies (e.g., the Internet, intranets, extranets, LotusNotes, software filters, agents, data warehouses) to systematize, enhance, and expedite intra- and inter-firm knowledge management (Ahlawat and Ahlawat, 2006). KMSs are intended to help an organization cope with turnover, rapid change, and downsizing by making the expertise of the organization's human capital widely accessible. They are being built in part from increased pressure to maintain a well-informed, productive workforce. Moreover, they are built to help large organizations provide a consistent level of customer service. They also help organizations retain the knowledge of departing employees, as described in Online Minicase 10.4 (Northrop Grumman). Many organizations have been building KM systems in order to capitalize on the knowledge and experience of employees worldwide. For an example, see the case of Infosys in *IT at Work 10.6*. Siemens's experience with knowledge management is described in Online Minicase 10.5. Online Minicase 10.6 describes how Frito-Lay uses knowledge management to support its dispersed sales team. For additional successful implementation cases, see McCormick (2007).

KNOWLEDGE MANAGE-MENT SYSTEM CYCLE

A functioning knowledge management system follows six steps in a cycle (see Figure 10.9). The reason the system is cyclical is that knowledge is dynamically refined over time. The knowledge in a good KM system is never complete because, over time, the environment changes, and the knowledge must be updated to reflect the changes. The cycle works as follows:

1. Create knowledge. Knowledge is created as people determine new ways of doing things or develop know-how. Sometimes external knowledge is brought in.

2. Capture knowledge. New knowledge must be identified as valuable and be represented in a reasonable way.

3. Refine knowledge. New knowledge must be placed in context so that it is actionable. This is where human insights (tacit qualities) must be captured along with explicit facts.

4. Store knowledge. Useful knowledge must then be stored in a reasonable format in a knowledge repository so that others in the organization can access it.

5. Manage knowledge. Like a library, the knowledge must be kept current. It must be reviewed to verify that it is relevant and accurate.

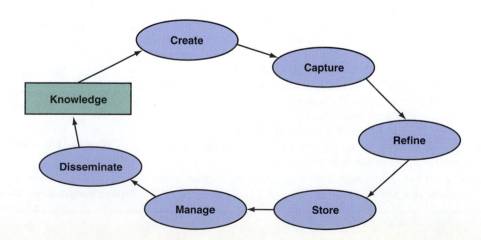

Figure 10.9 The knowledge management system cycle.

IT at Work 10.6

Knowledge Management at Infosys Technologies

IS   GLOBAL

The Problem. A global software services company based in India, Infosys Technologies is a worldwide leader in outsourcing. With over 23,000 employees and globally distributed operations, Infosys develops IT solutions for some of the largest corporations in the world. During the past 10 years, Infosys has experienced 30 percent annual growth rates. Infosys faced a challenge of keeping its large employee base up-to-date and ahead of both its competitors and clients, and ensuring that the lessons learned in one part of the organization were available to other parts. Said a member of the knowledge management (KM) group: "An IT company like ours cannot survive if we don't have mechanisms to reuse the knowledge that we create. . . . 'Learn once, use anywhere' is our motto." The vision is that every instance of learning within Infosys should be available to every employee. But how does an organization turn such a vision into a reality?

The Solution. Infosys Technologies' effort to convert each employee's knowledge into an organizational resource began in the early 1990s and extended well into the first decade of 2000. In the early 1990s, Infosys launched its *bodies of knowledge (BOK)* initiative. This involved encouraging employees to provide written accounts of their experiences across various topics, such as technologies, software development, and living abroad. These were shared in hard-copy form with all other employees. This early effort ballooned into a full-fledged KM effort supported by e-mail, bulletin boards, and various knowledge repositories. In 1996, a corporate intranet was developed to make BOKs, in HTML format, easily accessible to all, and in 1999, Infosys began an organizationwide program to integrate the various knowledge initiatives. A central knowledge portal was created, called KShop, and while the KM group developed the technology infrastructure, local groups were encouraged to maintain their own content on KShop.

The content of KShop consisted of different content types—BOKs, case studies, reusable artifacts, and downloadable software—each with its own homepage. Content was carefully categorized by the KM group to ensure that as the amount of content increased, it would still be possible for people to quickly find what they needed.

In early 2000, Infosys appeared to have a very functional KM system, and yet patronage by employees remained low. The KM group therefore initiated a reward scheme to increase participation. The scheme gave employees who contributed to KShop knowledge currency units (KCUs) that could be accumulated and exchanged for monetary rewards or prizes.

This case illustrates that knowledge management initiatives are much more than the implementation of technology tools to allow employees to post knowledge. Such initiatives involve processes to organize knowledge, to categorize knowledge, and to rate knowledge usefulness, as well as processes to encourage knowledge sharing and reuse.

The Results. Within a year of the introduction of the KCU scheme, 2,400 new knowledge assets had been contributed to KShop by some 20 percent of Infosys' employees. However, as the volume of content increased, so, too, did problems relating to finding useful information. Moreover, the heavy growth in contributions taxed the limited number of volunteer reviewers, who served an important quality control function. The KM group therefore modified the KCU incentive scheme. It developed a new KCU scheme that rated the usefulness of knowledge from the perspective of the users of the knowledge, rather than the reviewers. And, to increase accountability, the KM group requested tangible proof to justify any high ratings. Finally, the KM group raised the bar for cashing in KCU points for monetary awards.

Sources: Compiled from *infosys.com* (accessed June 2008), and from Garud and Kumaraswamy (2005).

For Further Exploration: Why are consulting types of organizations so interested in KM? How can organizations deal with the knowledge overload? Is a reward system the best approach to participation?

---

6. Disseminate knowledge. Knowledge must be made available in a useful format to anyone in the organization who needs it, anywhere and any time.

Details of the activities in these steps are provided in Tutorial #5 (Section T5.2).

As knowledge is disseminated, individuals develop, create, and identify new knowledge or update old knowledge, with which they replenish the system. Knowledge is a resource that is not consumed when used, though it can age or become obsolete. (For example, driving a car in 1900 was different from driving one now, but many of the basic principles still apply.) Knowledge must be updated. Thus, the amount of knowledge usually grows over time.

COMPONENTS OF KNOWLEDGE MANAGEMENT SYSTEMS

Knowledge management systems are developed using the following sets of technologies: *communication* and *collaboration*, and *storage* and *retrieval*.

Communication and collaboration technologies allow users to access needed knowledge, and to communicate with each other and with experts. Communication and collaboration also allow for knowledge solicitation from experts.

Storage and retrieval technologies originally meant using a database management system to store and manage knowledge. This worked reasonably well in the early days for storing and managing most explicit knowledge, and even explicit knowledge about tacit knowledge. However, capturing, storing, and managing tacit knowledge usually requires a different set of tools. Electronic document management systems and specialized storage systems that are part of collaborative computing systems fill this void. *Desktop search* is a major tool in knowledge retrieval.

**KNOWLEDGE
MANAGEMENT
SYSTEM IMPLEMENTATION**

In the early 2000s, KMS technology has evolved to integrate collaborative computing, databases, and network technology (previously independent of each other) into a single KMS package. Today, these include enterprise knowledge portals and knowledge management suites. These are sold with other enterprise systems packages, especially CRM, and are available on an *on-demand* basis, so even SMEs can use them (see Chan and Chao, 2008). In addition, there were some innovative specific applications, such as expert locating systems.

Finding Experts Electronically and Using Expert Location Systems. Companies know that information technology can be used to find experts. People who need help may post their problem on the corporate intranet (e.g., on wikis and blogs) and ask for help. Similarly, companies may ask for advice on how to exploit an opportunity. IBM frequently uses this method. Sometimes it obtains hundreds of useful ideas within a few days. It is a kind of brainstorming. The problem with this approach is that it may take days to get an answer, if an answer is even provided, and the answer may not be from the top experts. Therefore, companies employ expert location systems. **Expert (or expertise) location systems (ELSs)** are interactive computerized systems that help employees find and connect with colleagues who possess the *expertise* (i.e., experts) required for specific problems—whether they are across the country or across the room—in order to solve specific, critical business problems in seconds (see Totty, 2006, for details and examples). ELS software is made by companies such as AskMe (*askmecorp.com*). Such software works similarly, exploring knowledge bases either for an answer to the problem (if it exists there) or locating qualified experts. The process includes the following steps (see Figure 10.10):

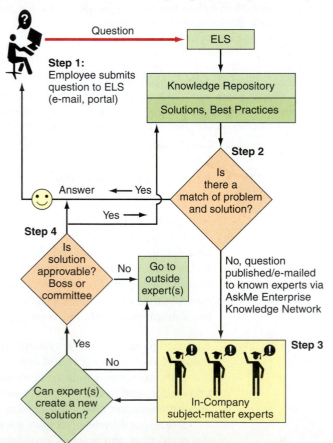

Figure 10.10 Expert location system of AskMe Corp. (*Source:* Drawn by E. Turban.)

IT at Work 10.7

How the U.S. Department of Commerce Uses an Expert Location System

The U.S. Commercial Service Division at the Department of Commerce (DOC) conducts approximately 200,000 counseling sessions a year involving close to $40 billion in trade. The division employs specialists who frequently need to do research or call on experts to answer a question posed by a U.S. corporation.

For example, in May 2004, a United States-based software company called Brad Anderson, a DOC specialist, for advice. The software company wanted to close a deal with a customer in Poland, but the buyer wanted to charge the U.S. company a 20 percent withholding tax, a tax it attributed to Poland's recent admission into the European Union (EU). Was the tax legitimate?

To find out, Anderson turned to the DOC Insider, an ELS from AskMe. After typing in his question, Anderson first found some documents that were related to his query, but they did not explain the EU tax code completely. Anderson next asked the system to search the 1,700-expert-strong Commercial Service for a live expert, and within seconds he was given a list of 80 people in the DOC who might be able to help him. Of those, he chose the 6 people he felt were most qualified and then forwarded his query.

Before the DOC Insider was in place, Anderson says, it would have taken him about three days to get the answer to the question. "You have to make many phone calls and deal with time zones," he says. Thanks to the ELS, however, he had three responses within minutes, a complete answer within an hour, and the sale went through the following morning. Anderson estimates that he now uses the system for roughly 40 percent of the work he does.

The DOC Insider is an invaluable tool. Anderson thinks the tool is vital enough to provide it to other units at the agency. In the first nine months the system has been in place, it has saved more than 1,000 hours of work. For more applications at DOC, see Totty (2006).

Sources: Compiled from D'Agostino (2004) and Fox (2004).

For Further Exploration: What are the benefits of such a system? Will the system impact privacy? Can it be integrated with wireless devices? If so, then for what purposes?

Step 1: An employee submits a question into the ELS.

Step 2: The software searches its database to see if an answer to the question already exists. If it does, the information (research reports, spreadsheets, etc.) is returned to the employee. If not, the software searches documents and archived communications for an "expert."

Step 3: Once a qualified candidate is located, the system asks if he is able to answer a question from a colleague. If so, he submits a response. If the candidate is unable to respond (perhaps he is in a meeting or otherwise indisposed), he can elect to pass on the question. The question is then routed to the next appropriate candidate until one responds.

Step 4: After the response is sent, it is reviewed for accuracy and sent back to the querist. At the same time, it is added to the knowledge database. This way, if the question comes up again, it will not be necessary to seek real-time assistance.

IT at Work 10.7 demonstrates how such a system works for the U.S. government.

Enterprise Knowledge Portals. *Enterprise knowledge portals* (EKPs) are the doorways into many knowledge management systems. EKPs have evolved from the concepts underlying executive information systems, group support systems, Web browsers, and database management systems. According to a 2007 KMWorld/IDC report, individuals may spend as much as 25 percent of their time looking for information (Feldman, 2008). An enterprise knowledge portal presents a single access point for a vast body of explicit information, such as project plans, functional requirements, technical specifications, white papers, training materials, and customer feedback survey data.

Enterprise knowledge portals are a means of organizing the many sources of unstructured information in an organization. (See the example in Online Minicase 10.7 about Xerox Corp.) Most EKPs combine data integration, reporting mechanisms, and collaboration, while a server handles document and knowledge management. The portal aggregates each user's total information needs: data and documents, e-mail, Web links and queries, dynamic feeds from the network, and shared calendars and task lists.

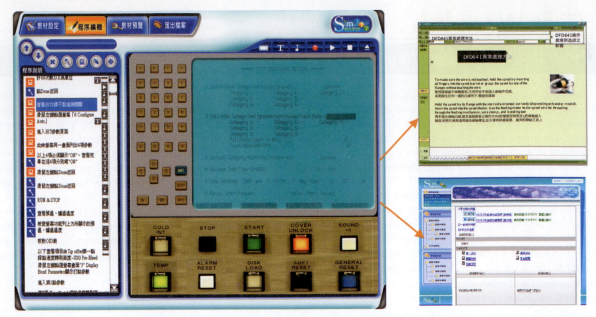

Figure 10.11 KM and e-learning (SimMAGIC). (*Source:* Courtesy of HamStar Technology Ltd.)

One highly successful EKP is Cisco's Employee Connection. The portal provides any time, anywhere access to the company's intranet; it has been credited with helping save the company $551 million each year, thanks primarily to improved self-service. The intent of the system is to connect as many systems and applications as possible so that the user has a single entree into all of Cisco's information systems.

Using KM in Training and Learning. Accumulated knowledge in organizations can be used for training new employees and retraining existing ones. Expert systems, for example, can be used to facilitate training (e.g., see *exsys.com*). Several companies provide methodologies that contain knowledge bases and KM for training.

Example: SimMAGIC is a product of HamStar of Taiwan (*hamastar.com.tw*). The company combines KM and e-learning. It uses the knowledge stored in corporate knowledge bases to create learning modules that are shown in Figure 10.11.

INTEGRATION OF KM SYSTEMS WITH OTHER BUSINESS INFORMATION SYSTEMS

Since a knowledge management system is an enterprise system, it is usually integrated with enterprise and other information systems in an organization. Obviously, when a KMS is designed and developed, it cannot be perceived as an add-on application. It must be truly integrated into other systems. Through the help of the organizational culture, a knowledge management system and its activities can be directly integrated into a firm's business processes. For example, a group involved in customer support can capture its knowledge to provide help on customers' difficult problems. In this case, help-desk software would be one type of package to integrate into a KMS, especially into the knowledge repository. A major challenge is to integrate data that reside in a variety of systems, locations, and formats.

In Tutorial #5 we look at how KM systems can be integrated with other types of business information systems.

Review Questions

1. Define KM and relate it to knowledge and intellectual capital. What are the major benefits of KM to a company?
2. Distinguish knowledge from data and information.
3. Draw the KM life cycle and explain the major steps.
4. Describe the major components of a KM system.
5. Describe an expert location system.
6. Define a knowledge portal. What is it used for?
7. Relate KM to training.

10.6 Managerial Issues

ETHICS

1. Ethical issues. Conducting a supply chain management project may result in the need to lay off, retrain, or transfer employees. Should management notify the employees in advance regarding such possibilities? And what about those employees who are difficult to retrain? Other ethical issues may involve sharing of personal information, which may be required for a collaborative organizational culture.

2. How much to integrate? While companies should consider extreme integration projects, including ERP, CRM, and KM, they should recognize that integrating along long or complex supply chain segments may result in failure. Therefore, many times companies tightly integrate the upstream, inside-company, and downstream activities, each part by itself, and loosely connect the three.

3. Role of IT. Almost all major enterprise system projects use IT. However, it is important to remember that in most cases the technology plays a supportive role, and the primary role is organizational and managerial in nature. On the other hand, without IT, most enterprise efforts do not succeed.

4. Organizational adaptability. To adopt ERP, organization processes must, unfortunately in many cases, conform to the software, not the other way around. When the software is changed, in a later version, for example, the organizational processes must change also. Some organizations are able and willing to do so; others are not.

GLOBAL

5. Going global. EC provides an opportunity to expand markets globally. However, it may create long and complex supply chains. Therefore, it is necessary to first check the logistics along the supply chain as well as regulations and payment issues.

6. The customer is king/queen. In implementing IT applications, management must remember the importance of the customer/end user, whether external or internal. Some innovative applications intended to increase customers' satisfaction are difficult to justify in a traditional cost-benefit analysis. Empowering customers to enter into a corporate database can make customers happy since they can conduct self-service activities such as configuration and tracking and get quick answers to their queries. Self-services can save money for a company as well, but they may raise security and privacy concerns. Corporate culture is important here, too. Everyone in the organization must be concerned about customers. Management should consider installing a formal CRM program for this purpose.

7. Set CRM policies with care. In practicing CRM, companies may give priority to more valuable customers (e.g., frequent buyers). This practice may lead to perceived discrimination. For example, in one case, when a male catalog customer found that Victoria's Secret charged him more than it did female buyers, he sued. In court it was shown that he was buying less frequently than the specific female he cited; the company was found not guilty of discrimination. Companies need to be very careful with CRM policies.

8. The lasting importance of knowledge management. Knowledge management is extremely important. It is not another management fad. If it is correctly done, it can have massive impact by leveraging know-how throughout the organization. If it is not done or is not correctly done, the company will not be able to effectively compete against another major player in the industry that does KM correctly. However, organizations need to identify ways to measure the value of intellectual assets and the value of providing them to the organization in order to justify a KM program.

9. Implementation in the face of quickly changing technology. Technology has to be carefully examined, and experiments done, to determine what makes sense. By starting now, an organization can get past the managerial and behavioral issues, which have greater impact on the eventual success (or not) of a KMS. As better and cheaper technology is developed, the KMS can be migrated over to it, just as legacy systems have migrated to the PC.

How *IT* Benefits You

Accounting Major

Accounting systems are totally dependent on enterprise resource planning systems, and many modules are available for organizations to implement, including accounts payable, accounts receivable, inventory control, and general ledger. Accounting personnel need to be trained in the use of these complex organizational systems. Major CPA and management service companies (e.g., Accenture) pioneered KM applications and the creation of organizational knowledge bases. This way they can provide better consultation to their customers and continuously improve their best practices.

Finance Major

Financial systems are critical in the enterprise resource planning modules as they are needed to generate payment of invoices and supplies. Automated payment systems are standard in e-business for customers ordering products and services from the organization and are also important for suppliers. Also, valuation and justification of investment in enterprise systems are critical for their success.

Human Resources Management Major

Human resources managers use enterprise systems to enable employees to be more effective in their work. Supply chain systems enable staff to more closely align with suppliers and build key relationships. Training in the use of CRM, KM, and ERP systems is vital as most areas of the organization are using these systems for their work. Motivation (and perhaps compensation) of employees who contribute and document their expertise is done by HRM. Also, job descriptions and requirements for those working with the new systems must be rewritten.

IS Major

There are a lot of components in enterprise systems that may need to be assembled. Information systems personnel play a critical role there. For example, in customizing ERP packages, IS personnel may have to provide the interfaces between several organizations as well as get current modules upgraded and running within the organization. Enterprise systems are constantly evolving, interfacing, and integrating among other IT systems (e.g., portals, collaboration, e-training, intelligent systems), and therefore they may require IS skills. Also, working with vendors and their products is a critical necessity.

Marketing Major

The entire supply chain is crucial when marketing and selling online products to consumers. For the consumer to know that a product or service usually ships within 24 hours, the e-commerce systems have to check the inventory levels of all suppliers via the enterprise resource planning systems. An integral part of KMSs is their interface with customer service and CRM. Understanding the potential benefits to customers and how these are accomplished is clearly important. Furthermore, KMSs can help employees in call centers and assist salespeople in the field by providing them with real-time knowledge of how to handle different situations and scenarios.

Operations Management Major

Enterprise resource planning systems are crucial for organizations that are managing their supply chains. ERP systems require the production person to understand logistics, shipping, and product distribution, and even tailor product design to meet customer needs in reverse supply chain systems.

POM systems are complex and require expertise and knowledge for their implementation (e.g., production scheduling and sequencing, multi-item inventory systems, logistics, maintenance, and new technology purchasing). The accumulation, updating, and use of knowledge can assist many POM people in their strategies, tactics, and operations.

Key Terms

Chapter Highlights

1 Enterprise systems are information systems that support several departments and/or the entire enterprise. The most notable are ERP, which supports supply chains, and CRM.

1 Supply chains connect suppliers to a manufacturing company, departments inside a company to one another, and a company to its customers. The supply chain must be completely managed, from the raw materials to the end customers. Typical supply chains involve three segments: upstream, internal, and downstream. Most supply chains are supported by a variety of IT application programs.

2 It is difficult to manage the supply chain due to the uncertainties in demand and supply and the need to coordinate several (sometimes many) business partners' activities. One of the major problems is known as the bullwhip effect, in which lack of coordination and/or communication results in large, unnecessary inventories.

2 A number of solutions to supply chain problems are supported by IT, such as appropriate inventory management, vertical integration, information sharing, VMI, supply chain hubs, supply chain collaboration, RFID, supply chain teams, virtual factories, and wireless solutions.

3 The next step in SCM was to integrate routine transactions, including internal suppliers/customers and external suppliers/customers, in ERP and extended ERP software. The latest step in the evolution of integrated supply chain software is the addition of business intelligence and CRM applications.

4 CRM is an enterprisewide activity through which an organization takes care of its customers and their needs. It is based on the idea of one-to-one relationships with customers. CRM is done by providing many communication and collaboration services, most of which are IT-supported and many of which are delivered on the Web.

5 Knowledge management is a process that helps organizations identify, select, organize, disseminate, and transfer important information and expertise that typically reside within the organization in an unstructured way. The knowledge management model involves the following cyclical steps: create, capture, refine, store, manage, and disseminate knowledge.

5 A variety of technologies can make up a knowledge management system: the Internet, intranets, data warehousing, decision-support tools, groupware, and so on. Intranets are the primary means of displaying and distributing knowledge within organizations.

5 KM has many potential benefits resulting from reuse of expertise. The problem is how to collect, store, update, and properly reuse the knowledge. It is difficult to measure the success of a KMS. Traditional methods of financial measurement fall short, as they do not consider intellectual capital an asset. Nonfinancial metrics are typically used to measure the success of a KM, yet some firms have been able to determine financial payoffs.

Virtual Company Assignment

Transaction Processing at The Wireless Café

Go to The Wireless Café's link on the Student Web Site. There you will be asked to apply some ERP principles to The Wireless Café and to propose some enterprisewide applications that could benefit the restaurant's operations.

Instructions for accessing The Wireless Café on the Student Web Site:

1. Go to *wiley.com/college/turban*.
2. Select Turban/Volonino's *Information Technology for Management,* Seventh Edition.
3. Click on Student Resources site, in the toolbar on the left.
4. Click on the link for Virtual Company Web site.
5. Click on Wireless Café.

Questions for Discussion

1. Distinguish between ERP and SCM software. In what ways do they complement each other? Why should they be integrated?
2. Discuss the benefits of e-procurement.
3. Find examples of how two of the following organizations improve their supply chains: manufacturing, hospitals, retailing, education, construction, agribusiness, and shipping. Discuss the benefits to the organizations.
4. It is said that supply chains are essentially "a series of linked suppliers and customers; every customer is in turn a supplier to the next downstream organization, until the ultimate end-user." Explain. Use of a diagram is recommended.

5. Discuss why it is difficult to justify CRM and how metrics can help.

6. A supply chain is much more powerful in the Internet marketplace. Discuss how Internet technologies can be used to manage the supply chain.

7. Explain how vendor-managed inventory can save costs in the supply chain.

8. State the business value of enterprise systems and how they can be used to make management of the supply chain more effective.

9. Discuss each of the steps in the ERP selection process.

10. What are the problems in implementing ERP systems? State solutions that make implementations more successful.

11. How is a linear supply chain changed into a hub? What are the advantages?

12. Describe and relate the different characteristics of knowledge.

13. Explain why it is important to capture and manage knowledge.

14. Compare and contrast tacit knowledge and explicit knowledge.

15. How can employees be motivated to contribute to and use knowledge management systems?

16. What is the role of a knowledge repository in knowledge management?

17. Explain how the Internet and its related technologies (Web browsers, intranets, and so on) enable knowledge management.

18. Describe an enterprise knowledge portal and explain its significance.

19. Discuss the need for expert locating systems.

Exercises and Projects

1. Identify the supply chain(s) and the flow of information described in the opening case. Draw it. Also, answer the following.
   a. "The company's business is not to make the product, but to sell the product." Explain this statement.
   b. Why was it necessary to use IT to support the change?
   c. Identify all of the segments of the supply chain.
   d. Identify all supporting information systems in this case.

2. Enter Teradata Student Network and find the podcasts that deal with CRM (by Claudia Imhoff) and supply chains (by Jill Dyche). Identify the benefits cited in the podcasts.

3. Go to a bank and find out the process and steps of obtaining a mortgage for a house. Draw the supply chain. Now assume that some of the needed information, such as the value of the house and the financial status of the applicant, is found in a publicly available database (such a database exists in Hong Kong, for example). Draw the supply chain in this case. Explain how such a database can shorten the loan approval time.

4. Enter Teradata Student Network and find the Web seminar on Data Integration (by Colin White, 2005). Relate these tools to the integration issues discussed in this chapter.

5. Based on your own experience or on the vendor's information, list the major capabilities of a particular knowledge management product, and explain how it can be used in practice.

6. Using the calculations in *A Closer Look 10.1,* compare the knowledge value per employees in Wal-Mart, Google, GM, and Microsoft.

7. Enter *askmecorp.com* and review its AskMe Enterprise and Employee Knowledge Networks concepts and products. Prepare a report.

8. Enter SAP.com and identify all modules that are related to financial management and all those related to HRM.

9. Enter SAP.com/usa and Sap.com/usa/solutions/enterprise-performance-management/index.epx and identify this ERP connection to the business performance management model of this book. Write a report organized by the steps of our model.

Group Assignments and Projects

1. Each group in the class will be assigned to a major ERP/SCM vendor such as SAP, Oracle, Microsoft, and so forth. Members of the groups will investigate topics such as: (a) Web connections, (b) use of business intelligence tools, (c) relationship to CRM and to KM, (d) major capabilities, and (e) availability of ASP services by the specific vendor.

   Each group will prepare a presentation for the class, trying to convince the class why the group's software is best for a local company known to the students (e.g., a supermarket chain).

2. Create groups to investigate the major CRM software vendors, their products, and the capabilities of those products in the following categories. (Each group represents a topical area of several companies.)
   - Sales force automation (Oracle, Onyx, Salesforce, Saleslogix, Pivotal)
   - Call centers [Clarify, LivePerson, NetEffect, Inference, Marketing automation (Annuncio, MarketFirst)]
   - Customer service [Brightware (from Oracle), Broadvision]
   - Sales configuration (Selectica, Cincom)

   Start with searchcrm.com and crmguru.com (to ask questions about CRM solutions). Each group must present arguments to the class to convince class members to use the product(s) the group investigated.

3. Search the Internet for knowledge management products and systems and create categories for them. Assign one vendor to each team. Describe the categories you created and justify them. Examine Tolisma Knowledgebase (see *knowledgebase.net*) and Intactix Knowledge base (from JDA Software, *jda.com*). What did the vendors' knowledge bases accomplish?

4. Enter expertise-providing sites such as *answers.com, knowledgebase. net, askmehelpdesk.com,* and *rightan-* *swers.com.* Each team member presents the capabilities of one vendor's site.

5. Enter Teradata Student Network and find the First American Corporation Case (by Watson, Wixon, and Goodhue), regarding CRM implementation. Make a class presentation of the case and answer the questions.

Internet Exercises

1. Enter *ups.com.* Examine some of the IT-supported customer services and tools provided by the company. Write a report on how UPS contributes to supply chain improvements.

2. Enter *supply-chain.org, cio.com, findarticles.com,* and *google.com* and search for recent information on supply chain management integration.

3. Enter *mySap.com.* Identify its major components. Also review the Advanced Planning and Optimization tool. How can each benefit the management of a supply chain?

4. Enter *i2.com* and review its SCM products that go beyond ERP. Examine the OCN Network and Rhythm. Write a report.

5. Enter *searchcio.techtarget.com* and go to "Executive Guides." Find the ERP guide. Identify the ERP-CRM connection.

6. Enter *anntaylor.com* and identify the customer service activities offered there.

7. Enter *oracle.com.* Find the ERP modules offered by Oracle (Siebel) and identify their connection to CRM and customer services.

8. Enter *salesforce.com* and take the tour. What enterprisewide system does the company support? How?

9. Enter *2020software.com.* Find information about the top 10 ERP solutions. View the demo; write a report on your findings.

10. How does knowledge management support decision making? Identify products or systems on the Web that help organizations accomplish knowledge management. Start with *brint.com, decisionsupport.net,* and *knowledge-management.ittoolbox.com.* Try one out and report your findings to the class.

11. Try the KPMG Knowledge Management Framework Assessment Exercise at *kmsurvey.londonweb.net* and assess how well your organization (company or university) is doing with knowledge management. Are the results accurate? Why or why not?

12. Identify three real-world knowledge management success stories by searching vendor Web sites (use at least three different vendors). Describe them. How did knowledge management systems and methods contribute to their success? What features do they share? What different features do individual successes have?

13. Enter *askmecorp.com.* View the three demos and examine their products. Write a report about their capabilities.

14. Enter *internetdashboard.com.* View their products and relate them to the different enterprise systems described in this chapter.

15. Enter *livechatinc.com* and *websitealive.com* and see their demos. Write a report on how live chat works. Make sure to discuss all of the available features.

Minicase

OM GLOBAL

ERP Helps Productivity at Northern Digital Inc.

Northern Digital Inc. (ndigital.com) in Ontario, Canada, is a supplier of electronic measurement products. The relatively small company employs 90 people and generates over $20 million in annual revenue.

The Problem

Northern Digital Inc. (NDI) faced a challenge when rapid growth and aging technology threatened to stand in the way of company goals. Instead of enabling operational improvements, NDI's existing systems were impeding progress. Existing technology was causing missed deliveries and creating a high number of back orders. Inventory control was poor, and the planning was inaccurate. With some customers expecting shipment in as long as nine months and others expecting shipment in as little as nine days or even less, more sophisticated and accurate planning was critical. Customer satisfaction was at risk, and internal morale was slipping. With almost 20 years in business, NDI's well-established reputation for high-quality, high-performance products was at risk.

The Solution

NDI selected an ERP system (from Intuitive Manufacturing Systems) based on factors that directly supported corporate objectives. Intuitive's ERP provided a level of system functionality that could immediately improve inventory management and the expandability and flexibility to support NDI's growth. The software includes a complete planning system, automated inventory management, and enhanced technology infrastructure. Equally important was the system's level of ease of implementation and ease of use.

The Results

After implementing Intuitive ERP, Northern Digital experienced continued success in improving inventory management and increasing revenue. Prior to implementation, the company struggled to achieve even two inventory "turns" (turnovers) per year. Inventory turns have now more than doubled, and expectations are that the company will better that in the near future. Since implementation, Northern Digital's revenue has increased from $10 million to over $20 million with little increase in inventory value. In addition, the company has reduced order cycle time for its flagship product from 4 months to 4 weeks, an improvement of almost 80 percent. This was a result of improved planning capabilities due to the ERP.

Improvements in production control and inventory management have had a direct impact on customer delivery. The material requirements planning and forecasting capabilities of Intuitive ERP have allowed Northern Digital to better service its customers. The addition of better planning capabilities had

an immediate positive impact on labor and materials. "We were able to better understand what was in stock, what we were buying, and what was needed," said Tom Kane, production manager. "Improved planning has made a huge difference in improving delivery."

Ease of use and system scalability have been important in utilizing Intuitive ERP to improve operations. When the system was first implemented, NDI needed only five user seats (user licenses). As NDI grew, that number increased to 25. Significantly increasing the number of users, and doing so without a lot of training (due to the ease of use), allowed the company to expand without worrying about putting constraints on its business infrastructure, supporting the growth strategy.

For Northern Digital, improving operations is more than just a way to reduce expenses. With the implementation of Intuitive ERP, the NDI has found a way to increase the value it provides to customers while also improving financial performance.

Sources: Compiled from *managingautomation.com* (accessed June 2008), and from *ndigital.com* (accessed June 2008).

Questions for Minicase

1. For a small company such as NDI, why is an ERP better than SCM applications?
2. Identify the supply chain segments that the ERP supports; be specific.
3. Relate this case to Porter's value chain and to its competitive model (Tutorial #2). Show the ERP's contribution.
4. Enter intuitivemfg.com and report on the capabilities of the company's ERP product.
5. Relate this case to business planning and strategy.

Problem-Solving Activity

Assessing E-CRM

A large food processing company would like to find the cost/benefit of installing an e-CRM application. They list both tangible and intangible costs and benefits of the project.
   Your assignment is:

1. Calculate the tangible costs and benefits.
2. List the intangible costs (and risks).
3. List the intangible benefits.
   The data you need to consider (per 1 year) are:

- E-CRM software licensing: Cost per user $1,200; number of users 86 (including 50 direct sales employees).
- Technical support and maintenance: $20,000.

- Training of 86 users for 5 days: Productivity loss $120/day.
- Training of 4 supervisors: Productivity loss $200/day.
- Fees to trainers: $8,000.
- Additional hardware, networks and so forth: $27,000.
- Annual operating cost: 2 IT employees at $72,000 each; other costs $18,000.
- Average *monthly* sales per direct sales employee: $50,000; gross profit from sales = 8%.
- Productivity increase per CRM employee using the new system = 12%.
- Overhead cost is computed at 10%.

Online Resources

More resources and study tools are located on the Student Web Site and on WileyPLUS. You'll find additional chapter materials and useful Web links. In addition, self-quizzes that provide individualized feedback are available for each chapter.

Online Briefs for Chapter 10 are available at wiley.com/college/turban:

10.1 *The Essentials of PLM*

10.2 *CPFR Implementation*

10.3 *ERP Implementation Issues*

Online Minicases for Chapter 10 are available at wiley.com/college/turban:

10.1 *West Marine Corp.*

10.2 *Cybex International*

10.3 *QVC*

10.4 *Northrop Grumman*

10.5 *Siemens*

10.6 *Frito Lay*

10.7 *Xerox Corp.*

References

Agarwal, A., D. P. Harding, and J. R. Schumacher, "Organizing for CRM," *McKinsey Quarterly,* member edition, August 2004.

Ahlawat, S. S., and S. Ahlawat, "Competing in the Global Knowledge Economy: Implications for Business Education," *Journal of American Academy of Business,* 8(1), March 2006.

Anonymous, "In Ultimate Relationships in Bloom," 1-800-FLOWERS.com, *SAS.com,* 2006, *sas.com/success/1800flowers.html* (accessed July 2008).

Babcock, C., "Five-Star Application Service," *Information Week,* March 22, 2004, *informationweek.com/story/showarticle.jhtml'articleid=18400885* (no longer available online).

Bartholomew, D., "A Banker's $500,000 Lesson in CRM," *Baseline,* February 2007.

Beatty, R. C., and C. D. Williams, "EFP II: Best Practices for Successfully Implementing an ERP Upgrade," *Comunications of the ACM,* March 2006.

Boucher–Ferguson, R., "10 Cool CRM Developments," *eWeek.com,* March 24, 2008, *eweek.com/c/a/CRM/10-Cool-CRM-Developments* (accessed July 2008).

Bresnahan, J., "The Incredible Journey," *CIO.com,* August 15, 1998, *cio.com/archive/enterprise/081598_jour.html* (accessed June 2003).

Chan, I., and C. K. Chao, "Knowledge Management in Small and Medium-sized Enterprises," *Communications of the ACM,* April 2008.

Chen, A., "CRM Pays Off," *eWeek,* May 23, 2005.

D'Agostino, D., "Expertise Management: Who Knows about This?" *CIO Insight,* July 1, 2004.

Danfoss.com, "Virtual Factory Improving Efficiency for a Chiller OEM," *Envisioneering.Danfoss.com,* 5(1), 2006, *ra.danfoss.com/TechnicalInfo/Approvals/Files/RAPIDFiles/RA/Article/VirtualFactory/VirtualFactory.pdf* (accessed June 2008).

Fedotov, I., "Collaborative Planning, Forecasting, and Replenishment: Explanation of CPFR," *12Manage.com,* 1995, *12manage.com/methods_cpfr.html* (accessed July 2008).

Feldman, S., "What Are People Searching for, and Where Are They Looking?" *KMWorld,* February 29, 2008, *kmworld.com/Articles/Editorial/Feature/What-are-people-searching-for-and-where-are-they-looking-41012.aspx* (accessed June 2008).

Fox, P., "Using IT to Tap Experts? Know-How," *Computerworld,* March 15, 2004.

Garud, R., and A. Kumaraswamy, "Vicious and Virtuous Circles in the Management of Knowledge: The Case of Infosys Technologies," *MIS Quarterly,* 29(1), March 2005.

gmb.org.uk, "Regional Distribution Centres," June 3, 2005, *gmb.org.uk/.../uploadedfiles/95420EED-6333-4746-9BC0-432145FDD379_RegionalDistributionCentres.doc* (accessed October 2006).

Greenberg, P., *CRM at the Speed of Light: Capturing and Keeping Customers in Internal Real Time,* 4th ed. New York: McGraw-Hill, 2006.

Guzman, Y., "FedEx Delivers CRM," *SearchCRM.com,* April 14, 2004, *searchcrm.techtarget.com/originalcontent/0,289142,sid11_gci958859,00.hm* (no longer available online).

Holsapple, C. W., and K. D. Joshi, "A Knowledge Management Ontology," in *Handbook on Knowledge Management,* Volume 1k, C. W. Holsapple (ed.). New York: Springer-Verlag, 2003.

IBM, "Micrel Triples Web Site Traffic with IBM Self-Service Module for OmniFind Discovery Edition," June 9, 2006 (no longer available online).

Intel, "Building the Digital Supply Chain: An Intel Perspective," White Paper, Intel Corp., Santa Clara, CA, January 2005.

Kalakota, R., and M. Robinson, *E-Business 2.2 Roadmap for Success.* Boston, MA: Addison Wesley, 2001.

McCormick, J., "5 Big Companies that Got Knowledge Management Right," *CIO Insight,* October 5, 2007.

Miley, M., "Brewing Good Business," *Oracle Magazine,* July/August 2006.

Mochal, T., and S. Pace, "10 Steps to CRM Success," *TechRepublic,* November 28, 2006, *zdnet.com.au/insight/software/soa/Ten-steps-to-CRM-success/0,139023769,339272393,00.htm* (accessed June 2008).

Mooney, S. F., "P-C 'Knowledge Capital' Can Be Measured," *National Underwriter*, 104(51–52), December 25, 2000.

Motorola, "Synchronizing the Distribution Supply Chain with Mobility," White Paper, Motorola Corp., December 2007, *spiritdatacapture.co.uk/PDF/Downloads%20Guides/Motorola_Supply_Chain_White_Paper.pdf* (accessed July 2008).

Nonaka, I., and H. Takeuchi, *The Knowledge-Creating Company: How Japanese Companies Create the Dynamics of Innovation*. New York: Oxford University Press, 1995.

Overby, S., "The Truth about On-Demand CRM," *CIO Magazine*, January 15, 2006.

Patricia Seybold Group, *An Executive's Guide to CRM*. Boston, MA: Patricia Seybold Group, 2002, *e-learning.dmst.aueb.gr/mis/Cases/Chemconnect/Case/Training_Files/An_Executive's_Guide_To_CRM.pdf* (accessed June 2008).

Peacocks Case Study, *symbol.com/uk/solutions/case_study_peacocks.html*, 2004 (no longer available online).

Peppers, D., and M. Rogers, *Managing Customer Relationships: A Strategic Framework*. New York: Wiley, 2004.

Reda, S., "1-800-FLOWERS.COM and AT&T Cultivate Relationship Rooted in Common Business Objectives," *Stores*, October 2006.

Rettig, C., "The Trouble with enterprise software," *MIT Sloan Managements Review*, Fall, 2007.

SCDigest, "Supply Chain Best Practices Tip: Building Real-Time Supply Chain Dashboards That Provide Value Is Harder Than You Think," Supply Chain Digest, October 26, 2006, *scdigest.com/assets/newsViews/06-10-26-3.cfm'cid=764&ctype=content* (accessed June 2008).

Schwartz, D. G. (ed.), *Encyclopedia of Knowledge Management*. Hershey, PA: Idea Group Reference, 2006.

Strassmann, P., "How Much Is Know-How Worth?" *Baseline,* November 8, 2005a.

Strassmann, P., "Putting a Price on Brainpower," *Baseline*, November 8, 2005b.

Sullivan, L., "Global Smarts: Colgate-Palmolive Finesses Procurement," *InformationWeek*, July 11, 2005.

Totty, M., "A New Way to Keep Track of Talent," *Wall Street Journal*, May 15, 2006.

VICS.org, "Collaborative Planning, Forecasting, and Replenishment (CPFR): An Overview," May 18, 2004. *vics.org/Committees/cpfr/CPFR_Overview_US-A4.pdf* (accessed July 2008).

Worthen, B., "Drilling for Every Drop of Value," *CIO Management*, June 1, 2002.

Yusuf, Y., A. Gunasekaran, and M. Abthorpe, "Enterprise Information Systems Project Implementation: A Case Study of ERP in Rolls-Royce," *International Journal of Production Economics*, 87(3), February 2004.

Chapter 11

Interorganizational, Large-Scale, and Global Information Systems

Boeing's Global Supply Chain for The Dreamliner 787

11.1 Interorganizational Activities and Order Fulfillment

11.2 Interorganizational Information Systems and Large-Scale Information Systems

11.3 Global Information Systems

11.4 Facilitating IOS and Global Systems: From Demand-Driven Networks to RFID

11.5 Interorganizational Information Integration and Connectivity

11.6 Partner Relationship Management and Collaborative Commerce

11.7 Managerial Issues

Minicase: *How Volkswagen Runs Its Supply Chain in Brazil*

Problem-Solving Activity: *Assisting in Managing the Supply Chain of Music Distributors*

Online Minicases:

Learning Objectives

After studying this chapter, you will be able to:

1 Describe interorganizational activities, particularly order fulfillment.

2 Define and classify interorganizational information systems.

3 Define and classify global information systems.

4 Identify the major issues surrounding global information systems.

5 Present demand-driven networks and RFID as supply chain facilitators.

6 Explain B2B exchanges, hubs, and directories.

7 Describe interorganizational integration issues and solutions.

8 Understand Partner Relationship management and its relationship to collaborative commerce.

Integrating *IT*

 ACC
 FIN
 MKT
 OM
 HRM
 IS

IT-PERFORMANCE MODEL

The focus of this chapter is on large information systems that connect different organizations, including organizations located in different countries. Such systems bolster productivity, effectiveness, and competitive advantage.

The business performance management cycle and IT model.

BOEING'S GLOBAL SUPPLY CHAIN FOR THE DREAMLINER 787

 IS   **OM**

The Problem

Your company is losing market share to its major competitor. Your industry is in a bit of a slump, thanks in part to rising oil prices and global terrorism concerns. The next product, which may well be critical to the company's future success, will cost millions and take years to develop and produce. You can't afford to fail. This sounds like a high-pressure, risky undertaking. Essentially, this was the situation facing Boeing, a company with a proud tradition as leader of the civilian aircraft industry, when it announced the development of a super-efficient, midsized aircraft—the 787 Dreamliner.

Designing and manufacturing an aircraft is an immensely complex undertaking. In fact, the current Dreamliner project is said to be one of the largest, most complex, and challenging engineering projects being undertaken recently in the world. The supply chain involved in the design and production of this aircraft involves millions of different parts and component materials and thousands of different suppliers, partners, contractors, and outsourcing vendors scattered across 24 countries working from 135 different sites. Absolute precision and meticulous attention to detail is required, and safety and quality are paramount. In addition to designing and producing a new aircraft, new production processes had to be designed, tested, and implemented. Close collaboration and communication among thousands of employees, information and knowledge workers, and management were critical, and sound management of this complex global supply chain was essential to the project's success.

The Solution

Boeing had been increasingly relying on sophisticated information technology (IT) to support its operations for some time and had been a user of CAD/CAM technologies (Chapter 9) since the early 1980s. The Dreamliner, however, was to be a "paperless airline," with IT being employed to support many critical activities. Boeing teamed with Dassault Systemes to create a Global Collaboration Environment (GCE), a product management lifecycle solution, to support the virtual rollout of the new aircraft. The GCE enabled Boeing to digitally monitor the design, production, and testing of every aspect of the aircraft and its production processes before the actual production started.

The GCE included the following components:

- **CATIA.** A collaborative 3D-design platform that enabled engineers worldwide to collaborate on the design of each and every part of the 787.
- **ENOVIA.** A system that supported the accessing, sharing, and managing of all information related to the 787 design in a secure environment.
- **DELMIA.** An environment for defining, simulating, and validating manufacturing and maintenance processes and establishing and managing workflows before actually building tools and production facilities.
- **SMARTEAM.** A Web-based system to facilitate collaboration, which included predefined and auditable processes and procedures, project templates, and best-practice methodologies, all geared toward ensuring compliance with corporate and industry standards.

In addition, Boeing also decided to integrate all databases associated with the Dreamliner, teaming up with IBM to employ a DB2 Universal Database for this purpose and ensuring partners access to the Dassault's suite of systems.

As the Dreamliner moved toward physical production using the new manufacturing processes, excellent supply chain management was required to carefully coordinate the movement of components and systems across multiple tier partners around the world. Boeing teamed with Exostar to provide software to support its supply chain coordination challenges. The Exostar supply chain management solution enables all suppliers access to real-time demand, supply, and logistics information so that crucial components and systems arrive at Boeing's production facilities just in time for assembly over a 3-day period. The Exostar solution includes the following functionalities: planning and scheduling, order placement and tracking purchase order changes, exchanging shipping information, managing inventory consumption across suppliers, managing returns, and providing a consolidated view of all activities in the manufacturing process. Business process exceptions can also be monitored across partners, allowing for informed evaluation of the impacts of these exceptions to take place across affected parties.

RFID technologies were deployed in the aircraft to support maintenance activities. By tagging component parts, Boeing expects to reduce maintenance and inventory costs.

The Results

The goal of the Dreamliner project was to produce a fuel-efficient (and less polluting, hence environmentally responsible), cost-effective, quiet, and comfortable mid-size aircraft that could travel long distances without stopping. It is a critical innovation for Boeing, which has in recent years struggled in the face of rising competition from Airbus. IT has played a critical role in supporting collaboration throughout this massive project, reducing the need for physical prototyping and testing, and making substantial improvement in the supply chain. IT has enabled faster decision making, better management of critical information and knowledge assets, increased sharing and exchange of product-related information and processes, reduced time-to-market, less rework, and reduced costs of manufacturing by reducing the assembly time for an aircraft from 13 to 17 days to just 3 days.

In just the first two years, Boeing received orders for hundreds of planes and commitments in excess of $55 billion. Dreamliner may be the most successful commercial airplane launch in history.

Sources: Kumar and Gupta (2006), Kidman (2006), *Supply and Demand Chain Executive* (2006), *RFID Gazette* (2006), and *CompMechLab* (2006).

Lessons Learned from This Case

In increasingly global industries, effective communication and collaboration are essential to an organization's success. Modern IT and Web-based systems have made collaboration, both internally and externally with key players along an industry supply chain, simpler and cheaper than ever before. Boeing recognized this, and implemented a range of technologies to facilitate the access, sharing, and storage of critical information related to the Dreamliner project. The company also introduced IT to expedite design and reduce problems along the supply and value chains of the design process, thus reducing cost, cycle time, and assembly time dramatically. This case demonstrates several applications of IT and a range of Web-enabled technologies, including collaborative commerce and streamlining complex global supply chains. Unfortunately, the projects also had problems which signify issues in collaborative design backed by IT and information sharing. There were delays due to incorrect pieces, non-fitting materials and more. This illustrates the challenges of global information systems sharing. While the information is there, it's not shared properly and made available in the right form (e.g., messages to the US were written in Italian; this show the importance of properly designing the global information systems). These issues are the topics of this chapter. We also describe interorganizational information systems, large-scale information systems, global systems, and IT support to all of the above. In addition, we explore the integration and connectivity issue with business partners as well as partner relationship management.

11.1 Interorganizational Activities and Order Fulfillment

ON-DEMAND ENTERPRISE AND REAL-TIME OPERATIONS

The new business environment described in Chapters 1 and 2 contains the elements of an *on-demand enterprise* and *real-time* operations. These two concepts have a great impact on the topics discussed in this chapter. So, before we start our presentation, we review them:

- **On-demand enterprise.** The concept of on-demand enterprise is based on the premise that manufacturing (or service fulfillment) will start its operation only after an order is received. We referred to this as build-to-order and mass customization as well. As time passes, more and more enterprises are converting to this concept (or adding it to the traditional "produce-to-stock" manufacturing).

- **On-demand and real-time.** An on-demand process implies that no production step would be ahead or behind because the entire fulfillment cycle would be primed to respond to real-time conditions. There will be no backorders, safety stock, lag time, or excess inventory.

These two concepts have revolutionized the supply chain. For achieving on-demand and real-time processes, companies must reengineer their supply chain. This is referred to as demand-driven supply networks, which is discussed in Section 11.4.

INTERORGANIZATIONAL ACTIVITIES

Before we delve into the topic of information systems that support activities conducted among two or more organizations (referred to as interorganizational activities), let's briefly describe some of the common activities conducted between and among business partners. They are:

Joint Ventures. Business partners conduct large numbers of joint ventures, sometimes as virtual corporations (see Section 11.2). Such activities require collaboration.

Collaboration. This topic was presented in Chapters 4 and 10. Later in this chapter, we will discuss the topic of collaborative commerce. For an interesting example, see Cone (2006) for the Boeing case.

Buying and Selling. Probably the most common activity that is going on between organizations is buying and selling. This activity includes finding a partner, viewing catalogs, negotiating, order taking, order fulfillment, billing, payments, after-sale service, and more. To show why IT support is needed, we use order fulfillment as an example (see the overview of the order fulfillment section below).

Other Activities. Several other activities can take place between companies. For example, they may work jointly on standards, conduct research, appeal to the government, and refer business they cannot do.

In all of the above, communication, collaboration, and search using the support of IT are involved.

The major objective of this chapter is to show how to improve interorganizational activities using IT, most of which are related to the supply chain. We begin by presenting the major activity of the order fulfillment process.

OVERVIEW OF ORDER FULFILLMENT

Order fulfillment refers to providing customers with what they have ordered and doing so on time, and to providing all related customer services. For example, a customer must receive assembly and operation instructions with a new appliance. This can be done by including a paper document with the product or by providing the instructions on the Web. (A nice example of this is available at *livemanuals.com*.) In addition, if the customer is not happy with a product, an exchange or return must be arranged.

Order fulfillment is basically a part of **back-end (or back-office) operations**, which are the activities that support the fulfillment of orders, such as accounting, inventory management, and shipping (see Chapter 10). It also is strongly related to **front-office operations** or *customer-facing activities*, which are activities such as sales and advertising that are visible to customers (recall the discussion in Chapter 9).

Overview of Logistics. **Logistics** is defined by the Council of Logistics Management as "the process of planning, implementing, and controlling the efficient and effective flow and storage of goods, services, and related information from point of origin to point of consumption for the purpose of conforming to customer requirements" (*Logisticsworld.com,* 2008). Note that this definition includes inbound, outbound, internal, and external movement and the return of materials and goods. It also includes *order fulfillment.* However, the distinction between logistics and order fulfillment is not always clear, and the terms are sometimes used interchangeably. Other times logistics is viewed as part of order fulfillment. The key aspects of order fulfillment are delivery of materials or products at the right time, to the right place, and at the right cost.

The Order Fulfillment Process. To understand why there are problems in order fulfillment, it is beneficial to look at a typical order fulfillment process, as shown in Figure 11.1. The process starts on the left, when an order is received (by e-mail, fax, phone, etc.). Several activities take place, some of which can be done simultaneously; others must be done in sequence. These activities include the following steps:

Step 1. Make sure the customer will pay. Depending on the payment method and prior arrangements, the validity of each payment must be determined. This activity may be done by the company's finance department or financial institution (i.e., a bank or a credit card issuer such as Visa). Any holdup may cause a shipment to be delayed, resulting in a loss of goodwill or a customer. In B2C, the customers usually prepay by credit card.

Step 2. Check for in-stock availability. Regardless of whether the vendor is a manufacturer or a retailer, as soon as an order is received, an inquiry needs to be made regarding stock availability. Several scenarios are possible here that may involve the material management and production departments, as well as outside suppliers and warehouse facilities. For small orders, an automatic search by an intelligent software

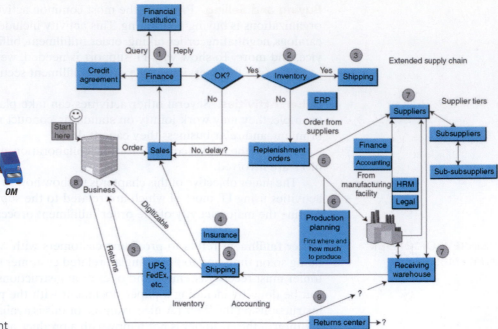

Figure 11.1 Order fulfillment and the logistics system.

Note: Demand forecasts and accounting are conducted at various points throughout the process.

agent may be done. In this step, the order information needs to be connected to the information about in-stock inventory availability. Sometimes buyers can check availability of small quantities by themselves using the Web.

Step 3. Arrange shipments. If the product is available, it can be shipped to the customer (otherwise, go to step 5). Products can be digital or physical. If the item is physical and it is readily available, packaging and shipment arrangements need to be made. Both the packaging/shipping department and internal shippers or outside transporters may be involved. Digital items are usually available because their "inventory" is not depleted. However, a digital product, such as software, may be under revision, and thus unavailable for delivery at certain times. In either case, information needs to flow among several partners.

Step 4. Insurance. Sometimes the contents of a shipment need to be insured. Both the finance department and an insurance company could be involved, and again, information needs to flow, not only inside the company, but also to and from the customer and the insurance agent.

Step 5. Replenishment. Customized (build-to-order) orders will always trigger a need for some manufacturing or assembly operation. Similarly, if standard items are out of stock, they need to be produced or procured. Production can be done in-house or by contractors. The suppliers involved may have their own suppliers.

Step 6. In-house production. In-house production needs to be planned. Production planning involves people, materials, components, machines, financial resources, and possibly suppliers and subcontractors. In the case of assembly and/or manufacturing, several plant services may be needed, including possible collaboration with business partners. The actual production facilities may be in a different country than the company's headquarters or retailers. This may further complicate the flow of information and communication.

Step 7. Use suppliers. A manufacturer may opt to buy products or subassemblies from suppliers. Similarly, if the seller is a retailer, such as in the case of *Amazon.com* or *Walmart.com*, the retailer must purchase products from its manufacturers. In this case, appropriate receiving and quality assurance of incoming materials and products must take place.

Once production (step 6) or purchasing from suppliers (step 7) is completed, shipments to the customers (step 3) are arranged.

Step 8. Contacts with customers. Sales representatives need to keep in constant contact with customers, especially in B2B, starting with notification of orders received and ending with notification of a shipment or a change in delivery date. These contacts are usually done via e-mail and are frequently generated automatically.

Step 9. Returns. In some cases, customers want to exchange or return items. The movement of returns from customers back to vendors is called **reverse logistics.** Overall, between $50 and $100 billion in U. S. goods are returned each year (ThomasNet, 2006). Such returns can be a major problem, especially when they occur in such large volumes. Many United States retailers allow 30 days for no questions asked returns. Consumers take advantage and sometimes buy two or more items in order to decide at home which one to keep, with input from family and friends.

Typical problems are shipment, packaging, and return cost. It is necessary to study why items are returned and look for patterns.

Order fulfillment processes may vary, depending on the product and the vendor. The order fulfillment process also differs between B2B and B2C activities, between the delivery of goods and of services, and between small and large products. Furthermore, additional steps may be required in certain circumstances, such as in the case of perishable materials or foods. Finally, there are differences in fulfilling regular orders with a long lead time or on-demand orders that must be fulfilled quickly.

Order Fulfillment and the Supply Chain. The nine-step order fulfillment process just described, as well as order taking, are integral parts of the *supply chain*. The flows of orders, payments, information, materials, and parts need to be coordinated among all of the company's internal participants, as well as with and among external partners.

Problems and Solutions: An Overview. The process presented in Figure 11.1 can be lengthy. Since it involves material, information, money, and possibly many people located in different places (even different countries), it is very likely that one or more of the following will occur:

- Delays in transportation/shipments
- Human errors in information sending
- Misunderstanding of orders
- Over- or understocked inventories
- Shipments of wrong quantities or to wrong places.
- Late or wrong reporting on delivery
- Slow or incorrect billing
- Difficult product/part configuration
- Inability of IT systems of two organizations to "talk" to each other
- High cost of expedited shipments

If a foreign country is involved, additional problems may develop (see Section 11.3).

While many solutions have been developed over the years in an attempt to solve these problems, some of which were very successful, the most successful and promising approach is to *automate* as many of the activities as possible. ERP, for example, has been extended to include suppliers and customers. Automation is done by using IT, and due to the capabilities of IT, it is possible to increase speed, reduce (or eliminate) errors, reduce cost of administering the process, minimize delays, reduce inventories, and so forth.

We will describe in Sections 11.4 through 11.6 how IT helps. But first, let's look at interorganizational and global systems in more detail.

Review Questions

1. Define order fulfillment and logistics.
2. List the nine steps of the order fulfillment process.
3. Compare logistics with reverse logistics.
4. List five problems of order fulfillment.

11.2 Interorganizational Information Systems and Large-Scale Information Systems

An **interorganizational information system (IOS)** involves information flow among two or more organizations. Its major objectives are efficient processing of transactions, such as transmitting orders, bills, and payments, and the support of collaboration and communication. As we will show in this chapter, an IOS can be local or global, dedicated to only one activity (e.g., transfer of funds), or intended to support several activities (e.g., to facilitate trade, research, communication, and collaboration).

Interorganizational information systems have developed in direct response to two business pressures: the desire to reduce costs, and the need to improve the effectiveness and timeliness of business processes. More specifically, by connecting the information systems of business partners, IOSs enable both partners to reduce the costs of routine business transactions, improve the quality of the information flow by reducing or eliminating errors, compress cycle time in the fulfillment of business transactions, eliminate paper processing and its associated inefficiencies and costs, and make the transfer and processing of information easy for users.

A major characteristic of an IOS is that the customer–supplier relationship frequently is determined in advance with the expectation that it will be ongoing. Advance arrangements result in agreements between organizations on the nature and format of the business documents and payments that will be exchanged. Interorganizational systems may be built around privately or publicly accessible networks. When IOSs use telecommunications companies for communication, they may employ *value-added networks* (VANs). These are *private*, third-party networks that can be tailored to specific business needs. However, use of *publicly accessible* networks (Internet, extranet) is growing with the increased use of the Web.

One category of IOS is virtual corporations (see Online Brief 11.1).

TYPES OF INTERORGANIZATIONAL INFORMATION SYSTEMS

Interorganizational information systems include a variety of business activities, from data interchange to messaging services to funds transfers. The most prominent types of interorganizational systems are the following.

- **B2B trading systems.** These systems are designed to facilitate trading between (among) business partners. The partners can be in the same or in different countries. B2B trading systems were covered in Chapter 6.

- **B2B support systems.** These are nontrading systems such as shipment hubs, directories, and other services.

- **Global systems.** Global information systems connect two or more companies in two or more countries. The airline reservations system SABRE is an example of a huge global system. The SAP-based Netafim company described in the book's online case is another example.

- **Electronic funds transfer (EFT).** In EFT, telecommunications networks transfer money among financial institutions.

- **Groupware.** Groupware technologies facilitate communication and collaboration between and among organizations. These include a transmission system that can be used to deliver electronic mail and fax documents between organizations.

- **Shared databases.** Trading partners sometimes share databases and other information in order to reduce time in communicating information between parties and to arrange cooperative activities.

LARGE-SCALE INFORMATION SYSTEMS

In Chapters 9 and 10 we described information systems within organizations. When the organizations deal with business partners in other countries, we talk about global systems. Both global systems and internal enterprise systems can be very large, result-

ing in complex technologies and procedures. Here are some examples of large-scale systems:

- Government systems (e-government), including national, state, countries, and city systems
- Military systems
- Large corporations' systems
- State University systems; other educational systems
- Large not-for-profit organizations (e.g., churches)
- Health care systems
- Airline reservation systems
- Global (multi-country) systems
- Financial institutions and banking systems
- Search engine-based systems (e.g., Google)
- Special systems such as the 2008 Beijing Olympic system

The 2008 Beijing Olympic Information System. It was one of the most complex and expensive information systems ever built (cost over $3 billion), but it existed only during two weeks. It covered 7 cities in China and it did what it was designed to do: support the summer Olympics, and do it in real time.

The system served more than 300,000 athletes, trainers and referees, security people, and others from over 200 countries who spoke several dozen different languages. There were more than 10 times more videos, many in real time, than in the previous (2004) Olympics. The times of the competitions, which were measured in the 1932 Olympics with 30 stopwatches, were measured by 420 tons of equipment, including dozens of photo-finish cameras, 110 miles of cables, thousands of PCs, and hundreds of GPSs (320 of which were attached to the Marathon runners).

Special attention was given to digital videos delivered on a special Cisco network. Viewers were able to watch in real time on large public screens in hundreds of locations, wireless devices globally, and of course on TV and PCs. Twelve million tickets were secured against counterfeit with RFID tags. And all major social networks covered the events, created discussion forums, and enabled exchanges of photos and videos. Olympic-network.net and many other sites provided videos, news, and more. YouTube broadcast the entire Olympics (but not in the United States). NBOlympic.com streamed millions of videos.

In summary, the Beijing Olympic Information System earned a gold medal for top performance.

IOS INFRASTRUCTURE TECHNOLOGIES

Four major IOS infrastructure technologies are described in Tutorial #6:

1. Electronic data interchange (EDI). The electronic movement of business documents between business partners. EDI runs on VAN(s), but it can be Internet-based, in which case it is known as EDI/Internet. EDI is frequently supplements on ERP, such in the Netafim online case.

2. Extranets. Internet-based, secure systems that link business partners via their intranets.

3. XML. An emerging B2B standard, promoted as a companion or even a replacement for EDI systems.

4. Web Services. The emerging technology for integrating B2B and intrabusiness applications.

5. Enterprise Application Integration. To facilitate IOS it is necessary sometimes to integrate systems internally before they are connected to business partners, as can be seen in the Limited Brands case, Online Minicase 11.1. Oracle Inc. provides such a connection in its fusion system.

6. Extended ERP. ERP systems (e.g., from SAP and Oracle) are extended to suppliers, customers, and other business partners. This enables both smooth integration of the systems of different companies as well as effective and secure communication. An example of such a case is provided in the Netafim online case.

In addition, there are specialized support technologies such as XBRL in finance (Chapter 9).

Review Questions

1. Define IOS and describe its major characteristics.
2. List the major types of IOSs.
3. List the major infrastructure for IOSs.

11.3 Global Information Systems

GLOBAL

Interorganizational systems that connect companies (or parts of one company) located in two or more countries are referred to as **global information systems.** Multinational companies, international companies, and virtual global companies typically need global information for their B2B operations. Companies that have global B2C operations usually use the Internet.

Multinational companies are those that operate in several countries. Their headquarters are in the home country while manufacturing, sales, and sometimes research activities take place in other countries. Examples are Coca-Cola, McDonald's, IBM, and Siemens AG (a German company). Multinational organizations may have sales offices and/or production facilities in several countries (e.g., see the Minicase at the end of this chapter). They may conduct operations in locations where factory workers are plentiful and inexpensive, or where highly skilled employees are available at low salaries, or where there is a need to be close to the market. SAP/AG, for example, has a large research and development division in Silicon Valley, California, and distribution and sales offices in dozens of countries. Microsoft has a research center in China.

International companies are those that do business with other companies in different countries. For example, Boeing Corporation solicits bids from and does contract work with manufacturers in over 40 countries.

Virtual global companies are joint ventures whose business partners are located in different countries. The partners form a company for the specific purpose of producing a product or service. Such companies can be temporary, with a one-time mission (such as building an oil pipeline), or they can be permanent.

All of the above companies use some global information systems. Examples include airline reservation systems such as SABRE (*sabre.com*), police and immigration systems, electronic funds transfer (EFT) systems (including networks of ATMs), and many commercial and educational systems for international organizations such as the United Nations.

BENEFITS OF GLOBAL INFORMATION SYSTEMS

Regardless of its structure, a company with global operations relies heavily on IT. The major benefits of global information systems for such organizations, made possible by IT, are:

- **Effective communication at a reasonable cost.** The partners are far from each other, yet they are able to work together, make decisions, monitor transactions, and provide controls. Business partners communicate through e-mail, EDI, Web Services, and extranets. Communication is even more critical if the partners speak different languages. Intelligent IT systems can provide automatic language and Web page translation (to be described later).

- **Standardize procedures and common languages.** By using SAP or Oracle extended ERP, companies can standardize their routine information world wide as done by Netafim (online book's case).

• **Effective collaboration to overcome differences in distance, time, language, and culture.** Collaboration can be enhanced with groupware software (Chapter 4), group decision support systems (see Chapter 12), extranets, and teleconferencing devices (Chapter 4). For an interesting case, see the Boeing 787 case at the opening of this chapter. Collaboration/communication can also be improved with ERP software.

• **Access to databases of business partners and ability to work on the same projects while their members are in different locations.** Information technologies such as video teleconferencing and screen sharing are useful for this purpose.

ISSUES IN GLOBAL IS DESIGN AND IMPLEMENTATION

The task of designing any effective interorganizational information system is complicated. It is even more complex when the IOS is a *global system* because of differences in cultures, regulations, economics, and politics among parties in different countries.

Although the potential for a global economy certainly exists, some countries are erecting artificial borders through local language preference, local regulation, and access limitations. In addition, barriers of various sorts must be dealt with before global information systems can achieve their potential. Some issues to consider in designing global IOSs are cultural differences, localization, economic and political differences, and legal and ethical issues (see Porter, 2006).

Cultural Differences. *Culture* consists of the objects, values, and other characteristics of a particular society. It includes many different aspects ranging from tradition to legal and ethical issues, to what information is considered offensive. When companies plan to do business in countries other than their own, they must consider the cultural environment. A well-known example is GM's car Nova. *No va* means "no go" in Spanish. GM did not pay attention to this issue, and the model's sales in Spanish-speaking countries suffered as a result. For details, see Burgess and Hunter (2005).

Localization. Many companies use different names, colors, sizes, and packaging for their overseas products and services. This practice is referred to as *localization*. In order to maximize the benefits of global information systems, the localization approach should also be used in the design and operation of the supporting information system. For example, many Web sites offer different language and/or currency options, as well as special content. Europcar (*europcar.com*), for example, offers portals in 118 countries, each with an option for one of 10 languages. For more on localization, see *A Closer Look 11.1.*

Economic and Political Differences. Countries also differ considerably in their economic and political environments. One result of such variations is that the information infrastructures may differ from country to country. For example, many countries own the telephone services; others control communications very tightly. France, for example, insisted for years that French should be the sole language on French Web sites. Additional languages are now allowed, but French must also appear in every site with a URL address ending with .fr as the upper domain name. China controls the content of the Internet, blocking some Web sites from being viewed in China.

Legal Issues. Legal systems differ considerably among countries. Examples are copyrights, patents, computer crimes, file sharing, privacy, and data transfer. All of these issues have the potential to affect what is transmitted via global information systems, and so they must be considered. The impact of legal, economic, and political differences on the design and use of global information systems can be clearly seen in the issue of cross-border data transfer.

Transfer of Data Across International Borders. Several countries, such as Canada and Brazil, impose strict laws to control **cross-border data transfer,** the flow of corporate data across nations' borders. These countries usually justify their laws as

A Closer Look 11.1

What Is Involved in Localization?

When companies bring their products and services to foreign markets, they may need to move away from standardization. The problem is how to do it in an efficient way. Rigby and Vishwanath (2006) provide a list of items that demand attention. Details are available in the original article.

Variables Considered in Localization

- Branding (names, language)
- Store formats (size, layout)
- Merchandise spaces and assortment (size, color, style, flavor, package design)
- Pricing (range, changes, financing)
- Promotions (types, duration, discount level)
- Vendor policies

- Management programs
- Store service levels
- Vendor services
- Operating policies

Location Variables

- Consumer characteristics
- Special demand drivers
- Competitor characteristics
- Company's own stores' characteristics versus others

Sources: Compiled from Rigby and Vishwanath (2006) and SDL International (2005).

protecting the privacy of their citizens, since corporate data frequently contain personal data. Other justifications are intellectual property protection and keeping jobs within the country by requiring that data processing be done there.

The transfer of information in and out of a nation raises an interesting legal issue: Whose laws have jurisdiction when records are in a different country for reprocessing or retransmission purposes? For example, if data are transmitted by a Polish company through a United States satellite to a British corporation, whose laws control the data, and when? In order to solve some of these issues, governments are developing laws and standards to cope with the rapid increase of information technology, and international efforts to standardize these laws and standards are underway (e.g., see *oecd.org*). Some issues of cross-border data transfer are shown in Online Brief 11.2. Legal issues can be complicated when regulations and compliance are involved. They are similar to the compliance issues described in Chapters 5 and 15.

Designing Web Sites for a Global Audience. Designing Web sites for a global audience is important. Web sites need to address cultural, legal, language, and other factors. These factors are summarized by Kyrinin (2008). Seventy percent of all Internet users are non-English–speaking; thus, doing business on the Internet must include *localization*, which includes translating languages, adapting content to meet cultural standards, and more. Customizing Web sites and evaluating the power of machine translation (only 60 percent accurate) is crucial to a successful global site (ICANN, 2008).

Globalization and Offshoring of Software and Other IT Activities. One of the key issues related to IT and globalization is that of offshore outsourcing. Initially, there was only outsourcing of programming. However, since 2000 many other IT activities have been outsourced, ranging from call centers to software research and development. A comprehensive report on the topic was published by *Communications of the ACM*, as it related to the migration of jobs worldwide (see details in Aspray et al., 2006). We return to this topic in Chapter 13 where we explore the issue in greater detail.

Globalization and Personnel Issues. A major issue in globalization is the orientation and, if needed, training of personnel. Companies may need to send their employees to other countries and also hire local personnel. IT programs can help in finding people and hiring them, and in training. For details, see the HRM section in Chapter 9. Large organizations may have a major undertaking in this area, as the case of Hewlett-Packard (HP) demonstrates.

HRM

Example: HP Consulting. HP has over 6,000 consultants who live and work across the globe, speak scores of different languages, and operate in a multitude of business cultures. HP created a special Global People Development unit whose mission is to make sure the consultants stay on top of technical issues from e-intelligence to IT infrastructure, and then help them tailor their consulting and client-relationship skills to their particular business environment.

To organize and plan the training session, HP is using a special software from Mindjet Corp. (*mindjet.com*). The company uses the MindManager tool that allows them to map the activities involved in various tasks of the planning. The maps enable the HR managers to convey complex ideas in a very simple, visually appealing format. The presentation is not an outline that uses line after line of text, or a slide-based presentation that asks viewers to remember previous screens. MindManager maps use a system of text, graphics, and icons to present complex ideas on a one-page map. Some, but not all, software vendors provide assistance for dealing with globalization issues.

CHARACTERISTICS AND PROBLEMS ALONG GLOBAL SUPPLY CHAINS

A special issue for global companies and their global information systems is how to optimize their supply chains. Supply chains that involve suppliers and/or customers in other countries are referred to as *global supply chains*. E-commerce has made it much easier to find suppliers in other countries (e.g., by using e-directories and electronic bidding) as well as to find customers in other countries (see Turban et al., 2008).

Global supply chains are usually longer than domestic ones, and they may be complex. Therefore, interruptions and uncertainties are likely. Some of the issues that may create difficulties in global supply chains are legal issues, customs fees and taxes, language and cultural differences, fast changes in currency exchange rates, and political instabilities. An example of difficulties in a global supply chain can be seen in *IT at Work 11.1*.

According to Prahalad and Krishnan (2008) global supply chains if properly managed with IT, can overthrow aging business models, contributing to competitiveness and superb performance. Information technologies have proven to be extremely useful in supporting global supply chains, but one needs to carefully design global information systems. For example, TradeNet in Singapore connects sellers, buyers, and government agencies via electronic data interchange (EDI). A critical element is appropriate sharing of knowledge among business partners. On how to do it and how it is facilitated by IT, see Myers and Cheung (2008).

IT provides not only EDI and other communication infrastructure options, but also online expertise in sometimes difficult and fast-changing regulations. IT also can be instrumental in helping businesses find trading partners (via electronic directories and search engines, as in the case of *alibaba.com*). In addition, IT can help solve language problems through use of automatic Web page translation.

Machine Translation of Languages. A major application of natural language processing (NLP; Chapter12) is *automatic translation* of documents from one language to another (see *A Closer Look 11.2*). Such translation is important for creating Web pages for a multinational audience, understanding large volumes of documents in foreign languages (e.g., for security reasons), learning foreign languages, collaboration in teams whose members speak different languages (see the Volkswagen Minicase), and conducting global e-business. Chung (2008) presents a study on how to best support non-English web searching. Let's see how automatic translation works.

Translation of Content to Other Languages. In the global marketplace, content created in one language often needs to be translated to another to reach collaborative business partners in other countries. This is true for both paper and electronic documents. For example, in some cases, an effective Web site may need to be specifically designed and targeted to the market that it is trying to reach. Language translation is especially important in countries such as China, Japan, and Korea, where relatively few people understand English well enough to use it

IT at Work 11.1

LEGO Struggles with Global Issues

MKT   GLOBAL

Lego Company of Denmark (*lego.com*) is a major producer of toys, including electronic ones. It is the world's best-known toy manufacturer (voted as "the toy of the 20th century") and has thousands of Web sites and blogs created by fans all over the world.

In 1999 the company decided to market its LEGO Mindstorms on the Internet (now MindStorm NXT; see Turner, 2006). This product is a unique innovation. Its users can build a Lego robot using more than 700 traditional LEGO elements, program it on a PC, and transfer the program to the robot. Lego sells its products in many countries using several regional distribution centers.

When the decision to do global electronic commerce was made, the company had the following concerns. (Note that although this is a B2C example, many of the concerns are common to B2B as well.)

- It did not make sense to go online to all countries, since sales are very low in some countries, and some countries offer no logistical support services. In which countries should LEGO sell the product?
- A supportive distribution and service system would be needed for e-commerce sales, including returns and software support.
- There was an issue of merging the offline and online operations versus creating a new centralized unit, which seemed to be a complex undertaking.
- Existing warehouses were optimized to handle distribution to commercial buyers (retailers), not to individual customers. E-commerce sales to individual customers would need to be accommodated.
- It would be necessary to handle returns around the globe.
- LEGO products were selling in different countries in different currencies and at different prices. Should the product be sold on the Net at a single price? In which currency? How would this price be related to the offline prices?
- How should the company handle the direct mail and track individual shipments?

- Invoicing must comply with the regulations of many countries.
- Should Lego create a separate Web site for Mindstorms? What languages should be used there?
- Some countries have strict regulations regarding advertising and sales to children. Also laws on consumer protection vary among countries. Lego needed to understand and deal with these differences.
- How should the company handle restrictions on electronic transfer of individuals' personal data?
- How should the company handle the tax and import duty payments in different countries?

In the rush to get its innovative product to the online market, LEGO did not address these issues before it introduced the direct Internet marketing. This resulted in delays, extra cost of expanding shipments, slow response time, poor customer service, losses due to currency conversion, and pricing conflicts. The resulting problems forced LEGO to close the Web site for business in 1998. It took about a year to solve all global trade-related issues and eventually reopen the site. By 2001 LEGO was selling online many of its products, priced in United States dollars, but the online service was available in only 19 countries (2008).

As of 2003, *lego.com* has been operating as an independent unit, allowing online design of many products (e.g., see "Make and Create"). Lego also offers electronic games at *club.lego.com/eng/games/default.asp?bhcp=1*. The site offers many Web-only deals, and it is visited by over 5 million unique visitors each day.

Sources: Compiled from lego.com (accessed June 2008) and Damsgaard and Horluck (2000).

For Further Exploration: Is the Web the proper way to go global? Why does it make sense to sell the Lego products on the Internet? Some companies sell certain products only online. Does it make sense for Lego to do this, too?

---

online. The language barrier between countries and regions presents an interesting and complicated challenge (see *worldlingo.com* for translation and localization in 141 languages).

For example, travelers may not be able to read signs in other countries, or they prefer information to be in their native, or a selected, language. A device called InfoScope (from IBM) can read signs, restaurant menus, and other text written in one language and translate them into several other languages. Currently, these translators are available only for short messages.

The primary problems with language translation, especially for the Web sites, are cost and speed. It currently takes a human translator about a week to translate a medium-size Web site into just one language. For larger sites, the cost ranges from $30,000 to $500,000, depending on the complexity of the site and the languages of translation.

Multilingual Text Messages. People who speak different languages and do not share one of them can now send text messages (SMS) in their own languages to their business partners. The messages are translated automatically by special software (from Geneva Software Technology of Bangalore, India). The initial product was to translate English text messages automatically to languages such as Malay, Tamil,

A Closer Look 11.2

Automatic Translation of Web Pages

SVR GLOBAL

Here are some major vendors and their automatic translations products:

- WorldPoint (*worldpoint.com*) offers a WorldPoint Passport multilingual software tool that allows Web developers to create a Web site in one language and deploy it in several other languages.
- Yahoo! offers the free Babel Fish Translation (*babelfish.yahoo. com*) that translates Web pages, e-mail, and text. Babel Fish supports 19 language pairs. It is linked to *Newstran.com*, which translates online newspapers to English.
- The U. S. Air Force Research Lab (*rl.af.mil/div/IFB/techtrans/ datasheets/ASLT.html*) developed an automatic spoken language translation. The project has been expanded so that it now includes Web translation as well.
- *Google.com/language-tools* offers a service called Language Tools that translates automatically to English the content of Web pages published in French, German, Italian, Spanish,

Portuguese, and more. All you have to do is click on the "Translate This Page" button that appears after a title in a foreign language.

- *Trados.com* offers software that does multilingual translation for companies that want to provide translated Web pages from their URLs. Product documentation, Web sites, marketing materials, and software interfaces can be localized in many languages quickly and cost-effectively. The company's site, *Translationzone.com*, also is a portal for translation professionals worldwide and offers resources to help translators expand their customer bases. Professional translators can purchase the latest releases of Trados software (*trados.com*) as well as create online professional profiles, through which they can market themselves to potential clients.
- *Rikai.com* is an online character translator that allows users to translate Japanese Web pages.

Bahasa, and Sinhala regarding tsunami situations, and deliver them to cell phones. This is an example of how IT could make a big difference in disaster warnings.

Existing text-messaging technology requires that both sender and receiver have devices that use Unicode, the standard international system for representing characters on a digital screen. But in rural areas of developing countries, few people can afford Unicode-compliant handsets.

The system Geneva devised can display characters from 14 Indian languages and 57 others used around the world without the need for common standards. Instead, language characters are transmitted as pictures encoded in simple binary format, which almost any phone can provide on-screen. Messages can be targeted to specific regions using the cellular networks' databases of phone subscribers' preferred languages.

The multilingual messaging software is compact enough to be stored on a subscriber identity module (SIM) card.

Like all computer-rendered translations, Geneva's translations vary in accuracy, depending in part on the languages translated and on the content of the messages. But the company has been working with the Indian Meteorological Department to create standard templates that should minimize this problem in disaster alerts.

According to Sullivan (2001), the best way to assess machine translation is to use the following criteria: (1) intelligibility (i.e., how well can a reader get the gist of a translated document?), (2) accuracy (i.e., how many errors occur during a translation?), and (3) speed (i.e., how many words per second are translated?).

For more on automatic language translation for Web pages see Online Minicase 11.2, the case of the City of Denver.

In order to overcome logistics problems along the supply chain, especially global ones, companies are outsourcing logistics services to logistics vendors. Global information systems help enable tight communication and collaboration among supply chain members, as shown in *IT at Work 11.2* (page 422).

As IT technologies advance and global trade expands, more organizations will find the need to implement global information systems.

Financial Global Supply Chains. As explained in Chapter 10, supply chains involve flows of money as well as products. This may be a problem in some companies or countries.

IT at Work 11.2

How BikeWorld Uses Global Information Systems to Fulfill Orders

OM   GLOBAL

BikeWorld (San Antonio, Texas) is a small company (16 employees) known for its high-quality bicycles and components, expert advice, and personalized service. The company opened its Web site (*bikeworld.com*) in February 1996, using it as a way to expand its reach to customers outside of Texas, including other countries.

BikeWorld encountered two of Internet retailing's biggest problems: fulfillment and after-sale customer service. Sales of its high-value bike accessories over the Internet steadily increased, including global markets. But the time BikeWorld spent processing orders manually, shipping packages, and responding to customers' order status inquiries was overwhelming for the company.

In order to focus on its core competency (making bicycles and their components), BikeWorld decided to outsource its order fulfillment. FedEx offered reasonably priced, quality express delivery, exceeding customer expectations while automating the fulfillment process. Whit Snell, BikeWorld's founder, knew that his company needed the help that FedEx's global systems could provide: "To go from a complete unknown to a reputable worldwide retailer was going to require more than a fair price. We set out to absolutely amaze our customers with unprecedented customer service. FedEx gave us the blinding speed we needed," Snell said. The shipping is free for a normal delivery. You pay extra for expedited delivery on some items.

The nearby figure shows the five steps in the fulfillment process. (Explanations are provided in the figure.) Notice that the logistics vendor (FedEx), with its sophisticated information system, provides services to the customers (such as order tracking).

Four years after BikeWorld ventured online, the company had become consistently profitable, and its sales volume had more than quadrupled. Thanks to its outsourcing of order fulfillment, and to FedEx's world-class information systems, BikeWorld has a fully automated and scalable fulfillment system; has access to real-time order status data, which enhances customer service and leads to greater customer retention; and has the capacity to service global customers. The site offers free topographical maps (take the tour), order tracking, customer support, employment opportunities, and more.

Sources: Compiled from FedEx (2000), and from *bikeworld.com* (accessed June 2008).

For Further Exploration: Identify the necessary IOSs between FedEx and the customers, and between BikeWorld and FedEx. Visit *fedex.com* and find out how FedEx can help any company in global trade.

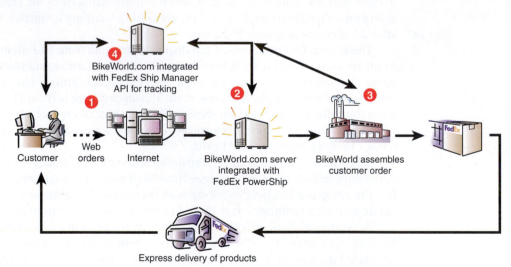

BikeWorld's order fulfillment process. (*Source:* FedEx, 2000.)

The flow of money in global trade is usually facilitated by IT systems starting with an electronic letter of credit and ending with solutions provided by companies such as TradeCard. A major topic is how to pay suppliers in other countries. For how it is done by RITE Aid, see Robbins–Gentry (2006). Electronic funds transfer (EFT), which has been in place for decades, is more sophisticated, so payments can be transferred faster.

One crucial issue is dynamic currency conversion. Some currencies fluctuate very fast, so an exact exchange rate must be known to sellers and buyers all the time. Currency conversion sites may provide inaccurate information such as the closing exchange rate the previous day. Currency conversion may be subject to government regulations and restrictions. These regulations may be important to trade partners.

With increased emphasis on real-time demand and fast order fulfillment, e-payments have become a critical element in financial global supply chains.

Several organizations and individuals have developed guides for properly managing IT in a global organization. One such organization is UNICEF (Online Minicase 11.3). A summary of principles for managing IT in global organizations proposed by Spatz is available in Online Brief 11.3.

Review Questions

1. Define global information systems.
2. List the major benefits of global information systems.
3. Describe the major issues related to global information systems.
4. Describe global supply chain issues.
5. Describe the relationship between IT and language translation.

11.4 Facilitating IOS and Global Systems: From Demand-Driven Networks to RFID

A large number of IT solutions are available to facilitate information flow and processing in IOS and global systems. Some of these solutions are presented next.

DEMAND-DRIVEN SUPPLY NETWORKS

Traditionally, the supply chain has been driven by producers and manufacturers "driving products to market." The dominant action in a traditional supply chain was to (1) forecast demand, (2) make-to-stock, and (3) push products downstream toward end customers. In this environment, demand could often be erratic and therefore hard to predict. Items could go from a situation of understock to overstock in a very short time, resulting in large safety overstocks, a situation known as the bullwhip effect (see Chapter 10 and Tutorial #1), and businesses across the supply chain did not have timely and accurate information to balance the turbulence.

In contrast to the traditional supply chain that was driven by suppliers and producers, **demand-driven supply networks (DDSNs)** are driven by customer demand. Instead of products being pushed to market, they are pulled to market by customers. Is the once-dominant force of pushing merely being replaced by a dominant force of pulling? Not entirely. DDSN does not remove the ability of a company to push product to market. Rather, it merely indicates that companies in a supply chain will work more closely to shape market demand *sharing* information and *collaborating*. In doing so, they will have a greater and more timely view of demand. The aim of this collaboration is to better position everyone in the supply chain with the ability to more closely follow market demand and produce, in tandem, what the market wants. The idea behind DDSN is to bring the supply chain ecosystem into balance.

The benefits of DDSN are:

- More accurate and detailed demand forecasting (often to SKU-level detail or location/store-level detail).
- Lower supply chain costs (with reduced inventories, expediting, and write-offs).
- Improved perfect-order performance (an order that is delivered complete, accurate, on time, and in perfect condition).
- Reduced days of inventory (average days of inventory on hand, including raw materials, components, work in process, and finished goods).
- Improved cash-to-cash performance (the length of time between when a company spends cash to buy raw materials and the time the cash flows back into the company from its customers).
- It provides a customer-centric approach, as opposed to a factory-centric approach.

- All participants in the supply chain are able to take part in shaping demand, minimizing the bullwhip effect.
- Probabilistic optimization is used to better deal with uncertainties (e.g., simulation and "what-if"; see Chapter 12).

DDSN capabilities provide for agility, adaptability, and alignment, which are defined as follows:

Agility—the ability to respond quickly to short-term changes in the demand and supply equation and to manage external disruptions more effectively

Adaptability—the ability to modify supply network strategies, products, and technologies, and to adjust the design of the supply chain to meet structural shifts in markets

Alignment—the ability to create shared incentives that align the interests of businesses across the supply chain

Demand-driven supply network software is available from Oracle, Teradata, IBM, SAP, Syspro, Microsoft, and many other vendors. For details, see *amrresearch. com/content/* (click on resource center).

One component of DDSN is real-time demand-driven manufacturing.

Real-Time Demand-Driven Manufacturing. Successful manufacturing organizations must respond quickly and efficiently to demand. Strategies and techniques of the past no longer work, and it's a challenge to transform from the traditional, inventory-centric model to a more profitable and flexible demand-driven enterprise. *Demand-driven manufacturing* (DDM) provides customers with exactly what they want, when and where they want it. Effective communication between the supply chain and the factory floor is needed to make it happen. Partnerships must be focused on reducing costs through shared quality goals, shared design responsibility, on-time deliveries, and continuous performance reviews. The DDM process is illustrated in Figure 11.2. An explanation of the headings in the figure is provided in Online Brief 11.4.

Figure 11.2 Real-time demand-driven manufacturing. (*Source:* PeopleTalk, "Real Time Demand Driven Manufacturing," 15(3), July–Sept. 2004, pp. 14–15. XXPLANATIONS© by XPLANE©, 2005, XXPLANE.com, courtesy of Oracle.)

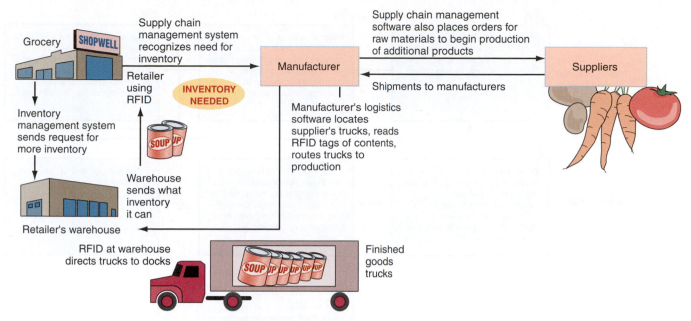

Figure 11.3 How radio frequency ID tags smooth supply chains.

USING RFID TO IMPROVE SUPPLY CHAINS

One of the newest (and possibly most revolutionary) solutions to supply chain problems is RFID. See a comprehensive presentation in Niederman et al. (2007). We introduced the concept of RFID in Chapters 2, 7, and 10. We said that large companies and governments require that their largest suppliers attach RFID tags to every pallet or box they ship to them. Eventually, RFIDs will be attached to every item. This can be done due to their potentially tiny size (a grain of sand) and the low cost (less than one cent per tag).

How might RFIDs improve the supply chain? Look at Figure 11.3, which shows the supply chain relationships among a retailer, a manufacturer, and suppliers, all of whom use RFID tags. Because the RFIDs are used by all companies in the figure, automatic alerts can be sent within each company and between companies. There is no longer a need to count inventories, and visibility of inventories is provided to all business partners. These benefits can go several tiers down the supply chain. Additional applications, such as rapid checkout in a retail store, eliminating the need to scan each item, will be available in the future.

Other applications of RFID are shown in Figure 11.4. The upper part of the figure shows how the tags are used when merchandise travels from the supplier to the retailer. Note that the RFID transmits real-time information about the location of the merchandise. The lower part of the figure shows the use of the RFID at the retailer, mainly to locate merchandise, control inventory, prevent theft, and expedite processing of relevant information.

More about RFID. The RFID tag is about the size of a pinhead or grain of sand. The tag includes an antenna and a chip that contains an *electronic product code* (EPC). The EPC stores much more information than a regular barcode (e.g., when and where the product was made, where the components come from, and when they might expire).

Unlike barcodes, which need line-of-sight contact to be read, RFID tags also act as passive tracking devices, signaling their presence over a radio frequency when they pass within yards of a special scanner. The tags have long been used in high-cost applications such as automated tolling systems and security-ID badges. Recent innovations have caused the price of the tags to plummet and their performance to improve, enabling them to be used more widely.

RFID has become a very important device in global transportation, both in land and sea logistics. Many companies are now tagging cases, containers, pallets

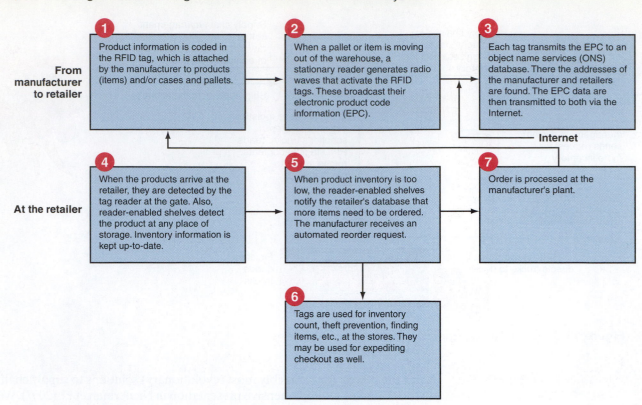

Figure 11.4 How RFID works in a manufacturer–retailer supply chain. (*Source:* Drawn by E. Turban.)

etc., not only to improve the supply chains but also as a measure to facilitate anti-terrorism. Notable is the global Smart and Secure Tradelanes initiative aimed at making international companies more secure by RFID scales that signal in real time if tampering commences.

The prospect of affordable RFID tags has retailers drooling. If every item in a shop were tagged, RFID technology could be used to locate mislaid products, to deter theft, and even to offer customers personalized sales pitches through displays mounted in dressing rooms. Ultimately, tags and readers could replace barcodes and checkout labor altogether. For more about RFID, see *en.wikipedia.org/wiki/RFID*.

Limitations of RFID. For small companies, the cost of an RFID system may be too high (at least for the foreseeable future). Also, there may be atmospheric interference (expected to be minimized in the future), as well as limited range (only 30–50 feet at this time). The fear of violating customers' privacy is another issue. Agreeing on universal standards, as well as connecting the RFIDs with existing IT systems, are technical issues to be solved. For other limitations, see Organisation for Economic Co-operation and Development (2008).

Where Does RFID Go? In Chapter 7, we presented the benefits and limitations of RFID and pointed to its potential use in supply chains. Here we provide an illustration of how RFID can work. Given the potential benefits and limitations of RFID, the question is: Where does RFID go?

By 2006, several large retailers (e.g., Sears, Target) were using the technology at least on containers and trucks (e.g., Scheraga, 2006). Placing tags on individual items has proven to be expensive, and was resisted by privacy advocates (e.g., at Levi Strauss Inc.). Applications started to spread to nonretailing, such as in airports to improve baggage handling and security (e.g., the Hong Kong airport; see Robinson, 2005). The military is using RFID extensively in its global supply chain (Boucher-

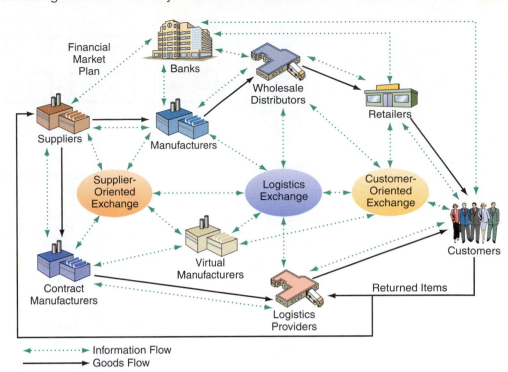

Figure 11.5 Web-based supply chain involving public exchanges.

Ferguson, 2006). Philip Morris is using tags to track the flow of illegal movement of cigarettes (Barrett and Carr, 2005). Pharmaceutical companies use RFID tags to track their products, and the list of applications is increasing rapidly. More detailed information is available in Chapters 7 and 10.

Despite the limitations and privacy advocates' objections to the use of RFID, it seems that the benefits, especially in the supply chain area, have the upper hand over the negatives. Tags and system cost are still a major issue (*Baseline* provides a calculator; and see Nolan, 2005).

B2B EXCHANGES

Considerable support to B2B supply chains can be provided by electronic exchanges. Communications and transactions are done on IOSs. The IOS in a private exchange is usually controlled by the sole seller or buyer; it usually uses an extranet or EDI (see Tutorial #6).

A system of several interconnected public exchanges is shown in Figure 11.5. Notice that in this example there are three interconnected exchanges (designated by the ovals in the center of the figure). In other cases there may be only one exchange for an entire industry.

B2B public exchanges are sometimes the initial point for contacts between business partners. Once such contact is made, the partners may move to a private exchange or to the private trading rooms provided by many public exchanges to do their subsequent trading activities. Also, partners may continue to work directly with each other, avoiding the public exchange.

ELECTRONIC HUBS

B2B exchanges are used mainly to facilitate trading among companies. In contrast, a *hub* is used to facilitate communication and coordination among business partners, frequently *along the supply chain*. Hubs are structured in such a way that each partner can access a Web site, usually a portal, which is used for an exchange of information. Furthermore, each partner can deposit new information, make changes, and receive or leave messages. In some hubs it is possible to conduct trade as well. A structure of an electronic hub is shown in Figure 11.6. An example of a company that provides an electronic hub as well as some public exchange capabilities is Asite, as described in *IT at Work 11.3* (page 429).

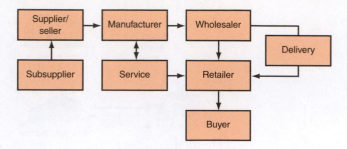

Traditional Intermediaries

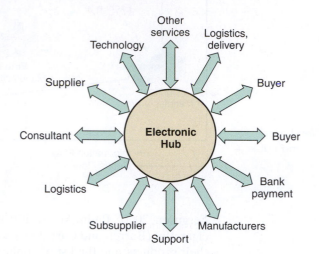

Figure 11.6 Electronic hub (bottom) compared to traditional intermediaries (top). (*Source:* Drawn by J. Lee and E. Turban.)

Electronic Hub

A variation of a hub is *supplier networks*, which can be used for purposes such as ordering and even for training (Dyer and Hatch, 2004).

B2B hubs are popular in global trading. Hubs are related to or even combined with B2B directories, which can be very large and require good KM and search engine support.

Review Questions

> 1. Define demand-driven supply networks.
> 2. List the major benefits of DDSN.
> 3. Describe DDMs.
> 4. How can RFID help supply chain management?
> 5. Define electronic hubs.

11.5 Interorganizational Information Integration and Connectivity

Only a few organizations have an open source infrastructure and applications. In many cases, companies' technologies are proprietary. Therefore, there are difficulties in connecting information systems of different organizations and transferring data in IOSs and global information systems. Furthermore, integrating new technologies such as RFID with existing ones, internally and with business partners, becomes a challenge to organizations. In this section, we'll cover a few representative issues that are related to IOS and global systems' integration and connectivity.

INTEGRATING THE INFORMATION SYSTEMS OF MERGING COMPANIES

When Sears and Kmart united in 2005, their comprehensive and complex systems had to be integrated as well. Many other companies—for example, Verizon and MCI, Wells Fargo and First Interstate—faced a similar scenario. According to Chabrow (2006),

IT at Work 11.3

Asite's B2B Exchange and E-Hub for the Construction Industry

Asite Network (*asite.com*) is a B2B marketplace and exchange for the construction industry in the United Kingdom. The construction industry is typified by a high degree of physical separation and fragmentation; communication among the members of the supply chain (e.g., contractors, subcontractors, architects, engineers, supply stores, and building inspectors) has long been a primary problem. Founded in February 2000 by leading players in the construction industry, Asite understands two of the major advantages of the Internet: the ability it provides to communicate more effectively, and the increase in processing power that Internet technologies make possible. Taking advantage of the functions of an online portal as information broker, Asite developed a comprehensive portal for the construction industry. The company's goal is to be the leading information and transaction hub in the European construction and related industries.

Within its portal, Asite set up several interconnected marketplaces (e.g., logistics, insurance, etc.; see the oval area in the figure). These marketplaces serve the needs of the participants in the construction and related industry (i.e., from design through procurement to materials delivery). Participating firms need nothing more sophisticated than a browser to connect to Asite's portal. This ease of access makes it particularly well suited to an industry such as construction, which is distinguished by a high proportion of small, and even single-person, firms.

Through its portal Asite also delivers complete and flexible solutions for every point in the supply chain, enabling the whole enterprise to work together more closely. The product portfolio includes tools for collaboration, trading, and sourcing:

- **Collaboration** (workspace, project work flow, and collaboration platform)
- **Trading** (buy, supply, exchange, invoicing, and catalog management; details on these are available at *asite.com*)
- **Sourcing** (directory, prequalifing, and tendering/bidding)

The Asite Buy and Supply solutions can be either hosted and accessed by logging securely onto the Asite platform, or integrated with existing back-office systems of the users, utilizing Asite technology.

The Asite Buy solution enables buyers to manage their entire purchasing cycle from requisition to payment, including internal approval processes. By automating and streamlining the purchasing process, companies can make significant gains in efficiency, reducing transactional costs.

Asite Supply allows suppliers to receive order requests and generate key documentation, such as advanced shipping notices and invoices, for immediate transmission to buyers. Both the Buy and Supply sides are integrated into the *Asite Exchange*.

Asite Exchange gives trading partners the flexibility to use the Asite Buy and Asite Supply solutions integrated directly into their back-office systems and to achieve automation of the purchasing process (see attached figure). Alternatively, Asite can integrate back-office systems directly with an organization's supply chain. This solution is built on state-of-the-art mapping and messaging technologies to receive an electronic data map, translate it as necessary, and route it on to its destination.

The Asite Exchange affords scalability to handle other trading documents and multiple trading partners. The flexibility of this approach allows Asite to integrate data between numerous marketplaces and organizations.

Asite's partnerships allow it to seamlessly interact with other e-marketplaces. The open standards adopted by vendors in these e-marketplaces enable Asite's technology to be easily incorporated with participating firms' back-end technologies. Such linkages allow full visibility of the supply and demand chains.

Sources: Compiled from Aberdeen Group (2001) and Asite (2008).

For Further Exploration: What type of IOS is this? What are the advantages to the participating companies? Why is the exchange connected to different marketplaces?

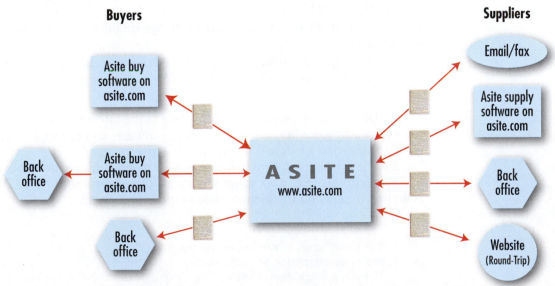

Asite Exchange. (*Source:* Asite, "Asite Buy, Asite Supply, and Asite Exchange," p. 4.)

the ability to integrate an acquired company's IT systems can determine whether a merger is successful. Chabrow provides three examples with lessons learned. Brown et al. (2003) provide an analysis of the successful IT integration of USA Group into Sallie Mae. Among the lessons learned are the following:

- Establish an IT leadership team to direct the integration.
- For customer-facing applications, select the option with the lowest business integration risks.
- Ensure that customer-facing applications have priority over back-office applications.
- Offer generous retention packages for top-talent IT personnel to ensure they do not leave.
- Maintain high morale among IT personnel.
- Increase the company's normal level of project risk to achieve aggressive business integration goals.
- Use rich communication media to read emotions and recognize successes, because a merger is an emotional event.

According to Duvall (2004), Bank of America spent tens of millions of dollars to convert the 1,500 branches of FleetBoston after its acquisition. Duvall also looks at the many difficulties other companies have had in similar cases.

FACILITATING INTEGRATION

The first step in conducting a large-scale integration is to check the business processes, understand them, and make improvements if necessary (e.g., Limited Brands case, Online Minicase 11.1). Here IT plays a major role.

The necessary IT infrastructure needs to be planned for, once processes are improved. The two activities can be done at the same time.

INTEGRATING IT TECHNOLOGIES

Several IT technologies assist in IOS and global integration (as well as in internal integration). Note that several types of integration exist. Most applicable to our chapter are *data integration* and *application integration*. The common technologies include the following:

- The extranet provides a less expensive and more flexible option than VANs (Tutorial #6).
- XML and similar standards and the related Web Services provide for an open-source environment that facilitates integration (Tutorial #6 and Chapter 16).
- Portals can piece together services from multiple applications where data sharing is supported by SOAs (Chapter 16).
- Converters that have the capability to change traditional EDI to an XML-based one are useful.
- Enterprise application integration (EAI) platforms include tools for transporting messages. For further details see Umar (2005).

EDI. EDI is a major technology for assisting in the integration of information systems of two or more business partners (e.g., a retailer and its suppliers, a manufacturer and its contractors that do product design).

ERP is a major software tool that is used to assist integration of two or more business partners (e.g., a company with its suppliers). In contrast with EDI, its use is limited to standard transactions such as order processing.

Review Questions

1. List some issues of systems integration.
2. How can integration be facilitated?
3. List some integrations tools and their capabilities.

11.6 Partner Relationship Management and Collaborative Commerce

Due to their complexity and the involvement of two or more organizations, IOSs and global systems face issues relating to partner relationship management and collaborative commerce.

PARTNER RELATIONSHIP MANAGEMENT

Every company that has business partners has to manage the relationships with them. Partners need to be identified, recruited, and maintained. Communication needs to flow between the organizations. Information needs to be updated and shared. **Partner relationship management (PRM)** is a business strategy and practice that recognizes the need to develop long-term relationships with business partners by providing each partner with the services that are most beneficial to that partner. This strategy is similar to that of CRM, and it is supported by similar IT tools.

Before the spread of Internet technology, there were few automated processes to electronically support business partnerships. Organizations were limited to manual methods of phone, fax, and mail. EDI was used by large corporations, but usually only with their largest partners. Also, there was no systematic way of conducting PRM. Internet technology changed the situation by offering a way to connect different organizations easily, quickly, and affordably.

What PRM Does. PRM solutions connect companies with their business partners (suppliers, customers, services) using Web technology to securely distribute and manage information. At its core, a PRM application facilitates partner relationships. Specific functions include partner profiles, partner communications, management of customer leads, targeted information distribution, connecting the extended enterprise, partner planning, centralized forecasting, group planning, e-mail and Web-based alerts, messaging, price lists, and community bulletin boards. Many large companies offer supplier or partner portals for improved communication and collaboration. (For more on PRM, see *blueroads.com*, and *bitpipe.com/tlist/PRM.html*.)

OM

 Example: Supporting PRM at SkyMall. *SkyMall.com* (now a subsidiary of Gem-Star TV Guide International) is a retailer that sells from catalogs on board airplanes, over the Internet, and by mail order. It relies on its catalog partners to fill the orders. For small vendors that do not handle their own shipments and for international shipments, SkyMall contracts with distribution centers owned by fulfillment outsourcer Sykes Enterprise.

To coordinate the logistics of sending orders to thousands of customers, SkyMall uses integrated EC order-management software called Order Trust. SkyMall leases this software and pays transaction fees for its use. As orders come in, SkyMall conveys the data to Order Trust, which disseminates the information to the appropriate partners (either a vendor or a Sykes distribution center). A report about the shipment is then sent to SkyMall, and SkyMall pays Order Trust the transaction fees. This arrangement has allowed SkyMall to increase its online business by more than 3 percent annually without worrying about order fulfillment. The partners (the makers of the products) also benefit by receiving the electronically transmitted orders quickly.

Companies are interested in finding ways to use PRM extensively, as shown in *IT at Work 11.4* (page 432).

Supplier Relationship Management. One of the major categories of PRM is **supplier relationship management (SRM)**, where the partners are the suppliers. For many companies (e.g., retailers and manufacturers), the ability to work properly with suppliers is a major critical success factor.

 PeopleSoft's (now an Oracle company) SRM Model. PeopleSoft's (*oracle.com/applications/peoplesoft/srm/ent/index.html*) SRM model is generic and could be

IT at Work 11.4

CRM/PRM Initiatives at New Piper Aircraft

MKT   OM

Today, New Piper Aircraft is the only general-aviation manufacturer offering a complete line of business and pleasure aircraft (from trainers and high-performance aircraft for personal and business use to turbine-powered business aircraft). In 1992, the company (then Piper Aircraft) was making fewer than 50 planes per year and had $15 million in bank debt and only $1,000 in cash. However, by 2001, the company delivered 441 planes and took in $243 million in revenue. How was this possible?

The fundamental reason for the company's success was its new ownership and management that realized that its ability to provide assistance to customers and partners needed to be completely overhauled. The company purchased Siebel Systems' MidMarket, a CRM software tool, and customized it for PRM. The result was the PULSE Center. PULSE stands for Piper Unlimited Liaison via Standards of Excellence. The system tracks all contacts and communications between New Piper and its dealers and customers. It also helps meet the growing needs of its partner- and customer-care programs.

In less than one year after implementation, the Web-based call center's productivity had increased by 50 percent, the number of lost sales leads was reduced by 25 percent, and sales representatives handled 45 percent more sales. Before the system was instituted, an 11-person call center used spiral notebooks crammed into numerous cabinets to store the data and contacts; it took 30 minutes to locate a contact. Today, the call center tracks 70,000 customers among 17 dealers, and contact information is available in less than a minute.

Development of the PULSE Center took place in stages. The first three phases had been completed by October 2002: Phase 1—loading data regarding current aircraft owners, dealers, fleet customers' aircraft, and new customer service employees into the system to develop the organization infrastructure; Phase 2—enabling the Customer Service Center to process activities; and Phase 3—enabling dealers to access sales opportunities pertinent to their territory.

The company currently is in Phases 4 and 5 and is planning Phases 6–8. Phase 4 is the opening of the Dealer Web Portal, which allows partners (aircraft dealers) access to particular areas of PULSE and provides the technology to make online service requests. Phase 5 streamlines entry of warranty claims. Phase 6, the Partner Web Portal, will allow key suppliers access to areas of the PULSE system and assist in communication with those suppliers. Phase 7 will provide for ordering parts online. Finally, Phase 8 is the Customer Web Portal, which will provide customers with access to open service requests, online logbooks, and product and survey information.

Piper's Vice President for Customers, Dan Snell, says, "New Piper's goal is to lead the industry with respect to quality, excellence, and customer care. It is a challenging mission, but certainly not daunting, and will be achieved through initiatives such as PULSE."

Sources: Compiled from Galante (2002); and *New Piper* news releases (2002, 2004).

For Further Exploration: Describe the major features of the CRM/PRM program. Why does the company need such an elaborate program? How would you justify it?

---

considered by any large company. It includes 12 steps, illustrated in Figure 11.7. The details of the steps are shown in Online Brief 11.5. The core idea of this model is that an e-supply chain is based on integration and collaboration. The supply chain processes are connected, decisions are made collectively, performance metrics are based on common understanding, information flows in real time (whenever possible), and the only thing a new partner needs in order to join the SRM system is a Web browser.

COLLABORATIVE COMMERCE

Collaborative commerce (c-commerce) refers to non–selling/buying electronic transactions within, between, and among organizations. An example would be a company collaborating electronically with a vendor that is designing a product or part for this company. C-commerce implies communication, information sharing, and collaboration done electronically by means of tools such as groupware, wikis, and specially designed collaboration tools, meaning that IOSs and c-commerce coexist. Use of c-commerce requires some IOS technology, such as an extranet, EDI, or groupware. Let's look at some areas of collaboration using IOSs.

Retailer-Suppliers. As discussed in Chapter 10, large retailers such as Wal-Mart collaborate with their major suppliers to conduct production and inventory planning and forecasting of demand. Such forms of collaboration enable the suppliers to improve their production planning as well.

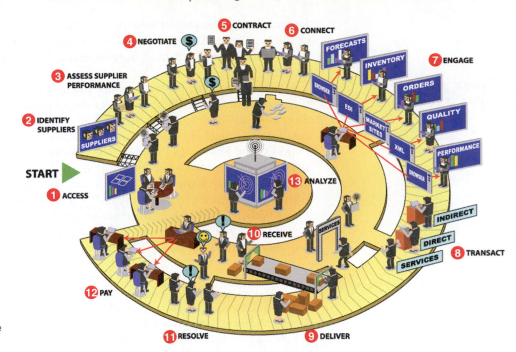

Figure 11.7 Supplier relationship management (SRM). (*Source:* B. Schecterle, "Managing and Extending Supplier Relationships," *People Talk*, April–June 2003, courtesy of Oracle Corp.)

Product Design. All of the parties that are involved in a specific product design may use software tools that enable them to share data and collaborate in product design. One such tool is *screen sharing* (see *en.wikipedia.org/wiki/screen_sharing*), in which several people can work on the same document on a computer screen while in different locations. Changes made in one place are visible to others instantly. Documents that can be processed through a collaborative product design IOS include blueprints, bills of material, accounting and billing documents, and joint reports and statements.

Collaboration along a Global Supply Chain. In a global supply chain we usually see several partners in two or more countries, including government agencies. In such cases IT can automate processes, smoothing the supply chain, as can be seen in the following FedEx example.

OM   *IS*

    Example: FedEx. Fresh fish for the finest restaurants in the United States must move from the "hook to the kitchen" in less than 36 hours. Tobago Wild (Tobago and Trinidad in the Caribbean) uses FedEx not only to deliver the fish but also to manage all of the administration of the transport. FedEx is using IT to coordinate all parties involved in the global supply chain. For every shipment, these include clearances from government offices in Tobago and Trinidad and clearances from the custom brokerage in the United States as well as the FDA clearance. Electronic manifests are pre-cleared by customs before the flights land in the United States. Using this service, Tobago Wild tripled its export volume in its first 16 months with FedEx. For details, see FedEx (2008).

IS

Service Desk. The use of service desk is popular in c-commerce applications service companies such as DHL.

    Example: DHL Uses IT to Help Its Partners in Its Service Desk. DHL is a German overnight shipping company that competes with FedEx and UPS. Its serves 220 countries and over 170,000 users, and is growing rapidly. Its service desk is critical to its success, but it was not working effectively with its legacy-based technology. In collaboration with HP, DHL created a comprehensive IT support system. To do so, it was necessary to align the individual country IT strategies with the global IT strategy. This included the establishment of a common service desk platform (Global

Service Desk). The project won the IT Service Management Forum (ITSMF) "Project of the Year" award for 2004. ITSMF is an international organization dedicated to best practices and standards in IT Service Management (HP, 2005).

OTHER IOS INFRASTRUCTURES

Information systems of two or more organizations can be connected in less structured ways than by EDI or extranets. As a matter of fact, most large software vendors, such as Microsoft, Oracle, SAP, and IBM, offer several solutions that can be customized to include existing systems, such as ERPs. An example can be seen in Six Flags Online Minicase 11.4, where the construction of a global system connecting 40 sites in eight countries is demonstrated. In Europe, Pierre Lang Corp. of Austria, a large jewelry company, gained control over 60 million customers throughout Western European countries by using mySAP ERP (see SAP AG, 2004). Oracle 9i is used extensively to provide infrastructure support to IOSs. Finally, one should remember that VANs, while more expensive, provide more functionalities to IOSs and are used not only for EDI but also for other types of systems (e.g., EFT).

Review Questions

1. Define partner relationship management (PRM).
2. List some of the benefits of PRM.
3. Define collaborative commerce.
4. List the major types of c-commerce.

11.7 Managerial Issues

GLOBAL

1. Facilitating global trade. As countries' borders begin to disappear in global trading, language translation is becoming very important. This topic is very important in e-commerce, where appropriate translation of Web pages is a critical success factor. The use of intelligent systems in automatic language translation has been progressing rapidly since the mid-1990s.

Many other systems and applications are used to facilitate international trade. For example, authorities employ intelligent systems to fight money laundering across international borders, and to expedite transactions via automatic and fast checks, and multinational companies utilize hybrid intelligent systems to develop global marketing strategies. As international trade is expanding, mainly due to the Internet and trading blocks such as the European Union and NAFTA, expertise will be needed in many areas, ranging from legal issues to export and import licenses. Such expertise can be provided to a global audience online. Also, expert systems can provide to users in developing countries the advice of top experts in the fields of medicine, safety, agriculture, and crime fighting. These various systems and applications work with different types of IOSs and technologies.

2. Selecting a system. Companies have an option to select an IOS infrastructure from several types and vendors. Selection could follow the guidelines suggested in Chapter 16.

3. Partners' collaboration. An IOS has at least two participating organizations, so collaboration is critical. Many failures of EDI adoption, for example, result from lack of partners' cooperation. If you are Wal-Mart, you may be able to mandate that your partner cooperate (or be excluded from doing business with you). But most other companies need to *persuade* partners, showing them mutual benefits, or provide them with incentives.

4. New infrastructures. XML, Web Services, and other tools are gaining converts but are not universally accepted. Companies such as Dell can lead in using such new infrastructures, but smaller companies might be better off to wait and see. However, management must assess the risk of waiting while competitors are moving.

GLOBAL

5. Globalization. The issue of going global or not, or to what extent, depends on what information systems are needed for supporting the globalization. Issues such as multiple languages, different currencies, tax requirements, legal aspects, and cultural considerations need to be reflected in the supporting IT. Globalization may not be simple or inexpensive. Finally, remember that managing a workforce goes beyond using software. It requires collaboration, communication, and teamwork.

6. Using exchanges, hubs, and other services. These are viable options since the service providers provide the IOS infrastructure. Also, frequently the Internet can be used. Using third-party providers can be cheaper, but you may lose some control over the system. Again, selecting the appropriate system(s) is critical.

7. Partner and supplier relationship management. Modern business is increasingly using partners, as we have seen in several examples throughout the book. The trend for outsourcing, for example, means more partners. (Even Microsoft has used a partner to implement its business solutions.) Cultivating PRM and especially SRM is not a simple task and needs to be planned for and organized properly (look again at Figure 11.7).

8. Implementing global information systems. It is a good practice to conduct a detailed process analysis and business process management (Chapter 14) and to educate and train both top management and end users (see Biehl, 2007).

9. Using ERP. Extended ERP systems are popular in large companies when dealing with their foreign subsidiaries, suppliers, and customers. One issue is that some ERP modules are inflexible, and companies need to change their procedures and business processes to fit the software. This issue has been solved by Netafim (online case) where all subsidiaries were placed on SAP's software, giving away their home grown procedures and processes.

How *IT* Benefits You

Accounting Major

Organizations may have different accounting systems, especially if they are in different countries. These need to be considered when IT applications are planned. Also, integration and flow of information to and from organizations may impact the accountant's work, especially in auditing.

Finance Major

Financial supply chains and global flows of information are of utmost importance for the finance staff, as are currency conversion, electronic letters of credit, and other IT-support payment mechanisms. Also, standards such as EDI and XBRL play an increasing role in financial transactions.

Human Resources Management Major

E-training for preparing personnel for foreign countries is just one reason why HRM should be interested in this chapter. Recruitment for a global mission using the Internet is another one. Also, overcoming resistance to change during integration can be critical.

IS Major

Interorganizational and global systems have several characteristics that must be considered during IT design and implementation. Understanding the issues and the impacting factors is of high importance as well. Finally, working with the IT vendors that usually build these systems is of paramount importance.

Marketing Major

An effective supply chain starts and ends with customers. Salespeople and marketing must, therefore, understand supply chain problems, impacting factors, and solutions. Furthermore, localization is key for selling in certain markets, especially foreign ones. Also, integration issues with customers' systems are vital. Finally, relating advertising campaigns to logistics and synchronizing interorganizational processes impact the marketer's success.

Operations Management Major

Manufacturers are usually in the middle of the supply chain and must interact with both customers and suppliers. Inventory problems in IOS, such as the bullwhip effect, need to be understood and addressed.

Key Terms

Back-end (or back-office)
  operations *411*
Cross-border data transfer *417*
Demand-driven supply networks
  (DDSNs) *423*
Front-office operations *411*

Global information systems *416*
Interorganizational information
  system (IOS) *414*
Logistics *411*
Order fulfillment *411*

Partner relationship management
  (PRM) *431*
Reverse logistics *413*
Supplier relationship management
  (SRM) *431*

Chapter Highlights

(Numbers Refer to Learning Objectives)

❶ The major interorganizational activities are buying and selling, collaborating with business partners, conducting joint ventures, and communicating. IT enables smoother interaction between organizations, usually at a reasonable cost.

❶ A major IOS activity is order taking and fulfillment. This is a process that requires a considerable amount of interaction among business partners. There are many potential problems in this process ranging from fulfilling wrong orders to late deliveries and the inability to deliver on time (backlogging).

❷ Information systems that involve two or more organizations are referred to as interorganizational information systems (IOSs). They can be local or global, dedicated to only one activity (e.g., transfer funds), or intended to support several activities (e.g., to facilitate trade, communication, or collaboration).

❷ IOSs are classified into the following types: B2B trading and support, global systems, EFT, groupware, and shared databases. Technologies that support IOSs are EDI, extranets, groupware, XML, Web Services, enterprise application integration, and extended ERP.

❸ Global information systems exist when at least two parties of an information system are in different countries.

❸ Three types of companies use global information systems: multinational (one company operates in two or more countries), international (at least one business partner is in a different country), and virtual global (partners in at least two countries form one company jointly).

❹ Some of the major issues that affect global information systems are cultural issues, political and economic issues (including currency conversion), legal issues such as cross-border data transfer, different languages, and logistics. Global supply chains are usually longer, requiring complex supporting information systems.

❺ Demand-driven supply networks support on-demand systems where the cycle starts with customer orders. Their major

mission is to provide the agility and flexibility needed to be successful. Such networks may work in real time and frequently are connected to enterprise systems such as ERP.

❺ RFID may create a revolution in supply chains by allowing much quicker and easier identification of tagged items. It may replace a barcode in many cases. While today's companies use it mainly for identifying merchandise in containers and pallets, it may one day be on every single item if the cost of tags continues to decrease.

❺ RFID can be beneficial for suppliers, buyers, logistics companies, and manufacturers for a number of interesting applications.

❻ Communication and collaboration among companies can be done via IOSs that are organized as either public or private B2B exchanges (usually designed for trading) or hubs (designed to improve the supply chain). Directories provide listings of B2B products, vendors, and services.

❼ Integrating IOS and global systems' components is necessary to assure frictionless flows of goods, material, and money along the supply chain. Some of the solutions are EDI, extranets, XML, and Web Services.

❼ Some representative IOS implementation issues are appropriate partner relationship management, c-commerce, and the use of automatic language translation and other methods to facilitate global trade.

❽ PRM covers the one-to-one relationships among business partners and the IT systems that support them. Large numbers of activities are included in PRM (Figure 11.7) including collaborative commerce.

❽ Collaborative commerce refers to e-commerce activities between business partners such as joint design of parts, provision of service desk, collaboration in planning, and information sharing.

Virtual Company Assignment

Interorganizational Systems at The Wireless Café
Go to The Wireless Café's link on the Student Web Site. There you will be asked to propose some interorganizational systems that could benefit the restaurant's operations.

Instructions for accessing The Wireless Café on the Student Web site:

1. Go to *wiley.com/college/turban.*
2. Select Turban/Volonino's *Information Technology for Management,* Seventh Edition.
3. Click on Student Resources site, in the toolbar on the left.
4. Click on the link for Virtual Company Web site.
5. Click on Wireless Café.

Questions for Discussion

1. Discuss some reasons for the complexity of global trade and the potential assistance of IT.

2. In what way is a B2B exchange related to a global supply chain? To a global information system?

3. Discuss why RFID may completely revolutionize the management of supply chains. Can it solve the bullwhip problem? If so, how? (*Hint:* see Tutorial #1.)

4. Discuss the relationships between RFID and DDSN.

5. Discuss the relationships between the global supply chain and the global financial supply chain.

6. Discuss the differences between DDSN and driving products to markets.

7. Compare PRM and SRM.

Exercises and Projects

1. Enter *oracle.com* and find material on the different IOSs discussed in this chapter. Prepare a report.

2. Examine the Lego case and *lego.com.* Design the conceptual architecture of the relevant IOSs you think LEGO needs. Concentrate on the marketing portion of the supply chain, but point out some of the suppliers of plastic, paper, electronics, and wood that LEGO uses, as well as the payment flow and inventory management.

3. Enter *bluenile.com, bluenile.ca,* and *bluenile.co.uk.* Identify all of the features of localization. Does the company really need three Web sites?

4. MySpace is available in dozens of countries and in many languages. Prepare a report on the extent of this diversification.

5. Enter SAP.com/USA and check all its modules. Prepare a list of all those related to global and multi-language operations.

6. Enter SAP.com/USA/solutions/business-suite/SRM/index.epx and identify all IT support to supplier relationship management. Write a report.

Group Assignments and Projects

1. Have each team locate several organizations that use IOSs, including one with a global reach. Students should contact the companies to find what IOS technology support they use (e.g., an EDI, extranet, etc.). Then find out what issues they faced in implementation. Prepare a report. (*Hint:* Use customer success stories of EDI vendors.)

2. Have each team prepare the following regarding globalization:
   a. List of potential issues
   b. Advantages of going global
   c. Limitations and disadvantage

Internet Exercises

1. Enter *i2.com* and review the products presented there. Explain how some of the products facilitate collaboration.

2. Enter *collaborate.com* and read about recent issues related to collaboration. Prepare a report.

3. Enter *smarterwork.com.* Find out how collaboration is done. Summarize the benefits of this site to the participants. Then enter *vignette.com*; look at the products listed under Collaboration. Compare the two sites.

4. Enter *1edisource.com* and see the demo of WebSource. What are the benefits of this product?

5. Visit *wordlingo.com* and identify issues of localization and solutions. Write a report.

6. Enter *amrresearch.com* and find its resource center. Find information about DDSN. Determine where the ERP backbone fits into the networks. Write a report.

Minicase

How Volkswagen Runs Its Supply Chain in Brazil

OM GLOBAL

The Problem

Like many other companies, Volkswagen (VW) works with many vendors in its assembly plants. However, there were problems in coordination and communication with some global vendors. Vendors' materials were shipped to VW factories, where VW employees assembled trucks. But the supply chain was long, and problems with materials often developed. Each time there was a problem, VW had to wait for a partner to come to the plant to solve the problem. Also, materials arrived late, and so VW maintained large inventories to deal with problems such as a delayed shipment. Finally, quality was frequently compromised. There was a need for a computer-based collaborative system.

The Solution

In its Brazilian truck plant 100 miles northwest of Rio de Janeiro, Volkswagen (VW) radically altered its supply chain. The Rio plant is relatively small: Its 1,000 workers are scheduled to produce 100 trucks per day. Only 200 of the 1,000 workers are Volkswagen employees; they are responsible for overall quality, marketing, research, and design. The other 800 workers, who are employees of suppliers such as Rockwell International and Cummins Engines, do the specific assembly work. The objective of the lean supply chain was to reduce the number of defective parts, cut labor costs, and improve efficiency.

Volkswagen's major suppliers are assigned space in the VW plant, but they supply and manage their own components, supplies, and workers. Workers from various suppliers

build the truck as it moves down the assembly line. The system is illustrated in the nearby figure. At the first stop in the assembly process, workers from Iochepe-Maxion mount the gas tank, transmission lines, and steering blocks. As the chassis moves down the line, employees from Rockwell mount axles and brakes. Then workers from Remon put on wheels and adjust tire pressure. The MWM/Cummins team installs the engine and transmission. Truck cabs, produced by the Brazilian firm Delga Automotivea, are painted by Eisenmann, and then finished and upholstered by VDO, both of Germany. Volkswagen employees do an evaluation of the final truck. The various national groups still need to communicate with their headquarters, but only infrequently (mostly by e-mail). The system is heavily supported by collaborative tools. To overcome the different language problems, all employees are required to know English. However, machine translation is being considered. IT tools help in scheduling and coordinating work as well as dealing with changes.

The Results

Volkswagen's innovative supply chain has already improved quality and driven down costs, as a result of each supplier having accepted responsibility for its units and workers' compensation. Encouraged by these results, VW is trying a similar approach in plants in Buenos Aires, Argentina, and with Skoda, in the Czech Republic. Volkswagen's new level of integration in supply chain management may be the wave of the future.

Sources: Compiled from Heizer and Render (2006), and from *vw.com* (accessed June 2008).

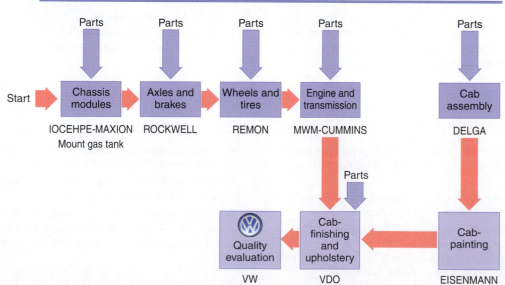

Truck Assembly Plant in Brazil
800 assembly-line workers of other companies
200 VW employees research design, quality, markets

Questions for Minicase

1. Draw the supply chain of VW's manufacturing plant.
2. What IOSs might be necessary to support such an arrangement? Distinguish between upstream, internal, and downstream supply chain activities. (See Chapter 10 for review of these terms.)
3. Identify the PRM activities needed in this case.
4. Which of the following is most appropriate for the old process: extranet, EDI, or EDI/Internet (consult tutorial #6). Why?
5. What additional IT support may be used in the new arrangement?

Problem-Solving Activity

Assisting in Managing the Supply Chain of Music Distributors

Music is a universal commodity. It is created by many thousands of artists; then, record companies such as Warner Music Group and Universal Music Group publish the music, selling it via different marketing channels (e.g., CDs, Internet, mobile devices) to millions of consumers around the globe. The record companies not only create products, such as CDs, DVDs, and videos, and sell them, they also must redistribute royalties to artists, unions of artists, and other recipients. The various artists, consumers, royalty processors, banks, and other partners of the record companies are located in different countries.

Information Flows:

- From artists and other recipients of royalties to the record companies (as music, contracts, etc.)
- From the record companies to sales channels and from there to the consumer (as music, bills)
- From the sellers to the record companies and to royalty processors (e.g., sales records)
- From the royalty processor to accountants and other support services (contracts, royalty sharing, taxation)

Money Flows:

- From consumers to sales channels to banks
- From banks to royalty processors and other payors, then to recipients and to other business partners

Assignment:

Design a global information system to accommodate the above flows. Specifically:

a. Specify the networks to be used (Intranets, extranet, EDI, etc.), for each segment of the information flows.

b. Prepare a diagram of the flows and the networks.

c. What security and privacy measures do you suggest to deploy and where (relate the flows)?

d. Which of the following will you use and for which flows: ERP, CRM, KM, functional (departmental) information systems, and TPS?

e. Which special global-related computerized applications will you suggest (consult Section 11.3)? Be specific.

f. Enter *ifpi.org*. Find material related to this activity (e.g., legal issues).

Online Resources

More resources and study tools are located on the Student Web Site and on WileyPLUS. You'll find additional chapter materials and useful Web links. In addition, self-quizzes that provide individualized feedback are available for each chapter.

Online Briefs for Chapter 11 are available at wiley.com/college/turban:

11.1 Virtual Corporations and IT Support
11.2 Issues of Data Transfer Across International Borders
11.3 Principles for Managing IT in Global Organizations
11.4 Real-Time Demand-Driven Manufacturing (DDM) Activities
11.5 Details of PeopleSoft's SRM Model

Online Minicases for Chapter 11 are available at wiley.com/college/turban:

11.1 Limited Brands
11.2 City of Denver
11.3 UNICEF
11.4 Six Flags

References

Aberdeen Group Inc., "Asite Builds E-Marketplace Using Combined Strength of Commerce One, Microsoft, and Attenda," *Aberdeen Group Profile*, 2001.

Asite, "Asite Buy, Asite Supply, and Asite Exchange," *Asite.com*, 2008, *asite.com/docs/Asite_trading.pdf* (accessed July 2008).

Aspray, W., et al., *Globalization and Offshoring of Software*, Special Report #001-0782/06/0200. New York: Association for Computing Machinery, 2006.

Barrett, L., and D. F. Carr, "Smoke Screen," *Baseline*, February 2005.

Biehl, M., "Success Factor for Implementing Global Information Systems," *Communication of the ACM*, January 2007.

Boucher-Ferguson, R., "RFID: Locked and Loaded," *eWeek.com*, February 20, 2006.

Brown, C. V., G. Clancy, and R. Scholer, "A Post Merger IT Integration Success Story: Sallie Mae," *MIS Quarterly Executive*, March 2003.

Burgess, S., and M. G. Hunter, "Studies in IT and Small Business Involving International and/or Cross Cultural Aspects," *Journal of Global Information Systems*, July–Sept. 2005.

Chabrow, E., "No One Size Fits All," *Information Week*, June 20, 2006.

Chung, W., "Web Searching in a Multilingual World," *Communications of the ACM*, May 2008.

CompMechLab, "Boeing 787 Dreamliner Program Uses DELMIA, CATIA and ENOVIA," December 13, 2006, *eng.fea.ru/FEA_news_370.html* (accessed July 2008).

Cone, E., "Flyin' in Formation," *CIO Insight*, March 2006.

Damsgaard, L., and J. Horluck, "Designing *www.LEGO.com/shop:* Business Issues and Concerns," case 500-0061, *European Clearing House*, 2000.

Duvall, M., "Aiming Higher," *Baseline*, November 2004.

Dyer, J. H., and N. W. Hatch, "Using Supplier Networks to Learn Faster," *MIT Sloan Management Review*, Spring 2004.

FedEx, "BikeWorld Goes Global Using FedEx Technologies and Shipping," *FedEx.com*, 2000, *fedex.com/us/ebusiness/ecommerce/bikeworld.pdf?link=4* (accessed June 2008).

FedEx, "Case Study: FedEx Takes Family Fish Business to Global Markets, Fast," *news.van.fedex.com/node/5641* (accessed July 2008).

Galante, D., "Case Studies: Digital Do-Overs," *Forbes*, October 7, 2002,

Heizer, L., and B. Render, *Principles of Operations Management*, 6th ed. Upper Saddle River, NJ: Prentice Hall, 2006.

HP, "ITSMF 2004 Awards: HP and HP customer DHL win Project of the Year Award, HP honoured with Innovation of the Year Award," January 10, 2005, *h41131.www4.hp.com/uk/en/press/ITSMF_2004_Awards_HP_and_HP_customer_DHL_win_Project_of_the_Year_Award_HP_honoured_with_Innovation_of_the_Year_Award.html* (accessed July 2008).

ICANN, "Translation Programme Put Out for Community Review," February 13, 2008, *icann.org/announcements/announcement-13feb08.htm* (accessed June 2008).

Kidman, A., "Dreamliner Sets SOA in Flight for Boeing." *Zdnet News*, July 12, 2006, *zdnet.com.au/news/software/soa/Dreamliner_sets_SOA_in_flight_for_Boeing/0,130061733,139263107,00.htm* (accessed July 2008).

Kumar, M. V., and V. Gupta, "The Making of Boeing's 787 'Dreamliner,'" *ICFAI Center for Management Research*, Hyderabad, India, 2006, OPER/053.

Kyrinin, J., "Writing Web Sites for a Global Audience," *About.com*, 2008, *webdesign.about.com/od/writing/a/aa080800a.htm* (accessed June 2008).

Logisticsworld.com, "What Is Logistics?" 2008, *logisticsworld.com/logistics.htm* (accessed June 2008).

Myers M., and M. S. Cheung, "Sharing Global Supply Chain Knowledge," *MIT Sloan Management Review*, summer 2008.

New Piper, "New Piper Rolls Out Further Customer Relations Initiatives," news release, *newpiper.com*, 2002, 2004.

Niederman, F., R. G. Mathieu, R. Morley, and I-W Kwon, "Examining RFID Applications in Supply Chain Management," *Communications of the ACM*, July 2007.

Nolan, S., "Planner: Calculating the Cost of Tracking Individual Items with RFID," *Baseline*, February 20, 2005.

Organisation for Economic Co-operation and Development, "Radio Frequency Identification (RFID): A Focus on Information Security and Privacy," OECD.org, January 14, 2008, *olis.oecd.org/olis/2007doc.nsf/LinkTo/NT00005A7A/$FILE/JT03238682.PDF* (accessed June 2008).

Porter, K., "Globalization: What Is It?" *About.com*, 2006, *usforeignpolicy.about.com/od/trade/a/whatisgz.htm* (accessed June 2008).

Prahalad C. K., and M. S. Krishnan, *The New Age of Innovation*, New York: McGraw-Hill, 2008.

RFID Gazette, "RFID Used on Boeing's 787 Dreamliner," April 4, 2006, *rfidgazette.org/2006/04/rfid_used_on_bo.html* (accessed July 2008).

Rigby, D. K., and V. Vishwanath, "Localization: The Revolution in Consumer Markets," *Harvard Business Review*, April 2006.

Robbins–Gentry, C., "Moving Money," *Chain Store Age*, February 2006.

Robinson, B., "Hong Kong Airport Tunes," FCWCOM, August 29, 2005.

SAP AG, Customer Success Story #50868084, *SAP.com*, March 2004.

Scheraga, D., "Wal-Smart: The World's Largest Retailer is Building a Better Supply Chain and RFID Is Only Part of It," *Retail Technology Quarterly*, January 2006.

SDL International, "Creating, Managing, and Maintaining a Global Web Site," *SDL.com*, March 2005, *sdl.com/files/pdfs/white-paper-creating-managing-maintaining-global-website.pdf* (accessed July 2006).

Sullivan, D., "Machine Translation: It Can't Match the Human Touch," *E-Business Advisor*, June 2001.

Supply and Demand Chain Executive, "Exostar Marks One Year Enabling Boeing's 787 Supply Chain," December 19, 2006, *sdcexec.com/online/article.jsp?id=9020&siteSection=29* (accessed July 2008).

ThomasNet, "Software Automates Returns Management Process," October 11, 2006, *news.thomasnet.com/fullstory/801179* (accessed June 2008).

Turban, E., et al., *Electronic Commerce 2008*. Upper Saddle River, NJ: Prentice Hall, 2008.

Turner, D., "LEGO MindStorm NXT: A Hack," *Technology Review*, July/August 2006, *technologyreview.com/Infotech/17093/?a=f* (accessed July 2008).

Umar, A., "IT Infrastructure to Enable Next Generation Enterprise," *Information Systems Frontiers*, 7(3), 2005.

How Wal-Mart Is Driven by IT

Introduction

Wal-Mart Stores, Inc., that runs a chain of large, discount department stores, is the world's largest public corporation by revenue and the largest private employer in the world (about 2,100,000 employees in 2008), and is also the largest grocery retailer and toy seller in the United States. In 2008, the company operated about 4,000 stores in the United States (discount, super centers, neighborhood markets, and Sam's clubs) and over 2,200 stores in other countries, mostly in Mexico, Canada, Brazil, and the United Kingdom. In 2008, its revenue exceeded $400 billion with a net income of about $15 billion. For further details, see *en.wikipedia.org/wiki/Walmart*, and *walmartfacts.com*. A major determinant of the success of Wal-Mart is its IT-driven supply chain.

Wal-Mart's Supply Chain

Wal-Mart pioneered the world most efficient IT-driven supply chain. Let's look at some of its components.

Wal-Mart invited its major suppliers to codevelop profitable supply chain partnerships. These partnerships are intended to amplify product flow efficiency and, in turn, Wal-Mart's profitability. A case in point is Wal-Mart's supplier relationship with P&G. This relationship enables interoperation between the companies' systems at transactional, operational, and strategic levels. Since 1988, the relationship evolved to yield tremendous value to both companies, and their mutual business grew manifold. Examples of intercompany innovations are vendor-managed inventory, CPFR, and RFID (Chapter 10). Let's look closer at a few of these areas.

Inventory Management

Inventory management is done at the corporate and individual store levels. In both cases, computerized systems facilitate proper inventory levels and reorder of goods. Stores manage their inventories and order goods as needed instead of the company doing a centralized control. By networking with suppliers, a quick replenishment order could be placed via Wal-Mart's own satellite communication system. This way suppliers can quickly deliver the goods directly to the store concerned or to the nearest distribution center. The suppliers are able to reduce costs and prices due to better coordination. In 1991, Wal-Mart invested $4 billion in a *retail link* collaboration system. About 20,000 suppliers use the retail link system to monitor the sales of their goods at individual stores and accordingly replenish inventory. The system has been upgraded with Internet-enabled technologies. Wal-Mart also uses advanced IT-based communication and processing systems, and it has extensive disaster recovery plans, enabling the company to track goods and inventory levels when disaster strikes. This ensures uninterrupted service to Wal-Mart customers, suppliers, and partners.

Managing Distribution Centers

Wal-Mart uses hundreds of distribution centers worldwide. Goods are transported to these centers from suppliers and then stored. When needed, goods are reorganized in trucks and delivered to the stores. Wal-Mart uses a computerized warehouse management system (WMS) to track and manage the flow of goods through its distribution centers. This system manages not only the forklifts within the distribution center, but also Wal-Mart's fleet of trucks.

Wireless Industrial Vehicle Management System.

Forklifts and other industrial vehicles are the workhorses of material handling within the distribution centers, and thus they are critical factors in facility productivity. Wal-Mart installs in each center a comprehensive wireless vehicle management system (VMS). The major capabilities of this system (from I. D. Systems, Inc.) are listed below and organized by productivity and safety features:

Productivity Features

- A two-way text messaging system that enables management to divert material handling resources effectively and quickly to the point of activity where they are needed the most.
- The software displays a graphical facility map, which enables not only near real-time visibility of vehicle/operator location and status, but also the ability to play back the trail of a vehicle movement over any slice of time. The system helps to locate vehicles in real time.
- Unique metrics on operators' activities identify opportunities for productivity improvement and help optimize labor allocation across periods of varying activity levels. It also helps in scheduling periodic preventive maintenance.
- Unique data on peak vehicle utilization that enables optimal fleet "right sizing." It also helps work assignments and communication, especially in response to unexpected changes and needs.

Safety Features

- Electronic safety checklist system for identifying and responding to vehicles' problems.
- Access authorization to drive certain vehicles by trained drivers only.
- Impact sensing that provides a broad choice of automated management responses, from alerting a supervisor with visual or audible alarms, to generating a warning icon on a graphical software display of the facility, to sending an email or text page to management.
- Automatic reporting and prioritization of emergency repair issues that are identified on electronic safety checklists, where operator responses are flagged by severity of the vehicle condition.

- Wireless, remote lock-out of vehicles that are unsafe or in need of repair.

For further details, see the Wal-Mart case at id-systems.com.

Warehouse Management System. A warehouse management system (WMS) is a key part of the supply chain that primarily aims to control the movement and storage of material within a warehouse and process the associated transactions including receiving, shipping, and in-warehouse picking. The systems also optimizes stock levels based on real-time information about the usage of parts and materials.

Warehouse management systems often utilize information technologies, such as barcode scanners, mobile computers, Wi-Fi, and RFID, to efficiently monitor the flow of products. Once data have been collected, there is either a batch synchronization with, or real-time wireless transmission to, a central database. The database can then provide useful reports about the status of goods in the warehouse.

Warehouse management systems can be stand-alone systems, or modules in an ERP system (e.g., at SAP and Oracle) or in a supply chain management suite. The role and capabilities of WMS's are ever expanding. Many vendors provide WMS software (e.g., see qssi-wms.com, inventoryops.com, supplychain.ittoolbox.com). For a comprehensive coverage of WMS, see Piasecki (2008).

Fleet and Transportation Management. Several thousands of company-owned trucks move goods from the distribution centers to stores. Wal-Mart uses several IT tools for managing the trucks. These include a decision support system (DSS) for optimal scheduling, dispatching, and matching of drivers with vehicles; a computerized system for efficient purchasing and use of gasoline; a computerized preventive maintenance management system for efficient maintenance and repairs procedures; and a system that helps maximize the size of truck necessary for any given shipment. The company is studying the possibility of using a wireless GPS/GIS system for finding the trucks' locations at any given time.

Decisions about *cross docking* are computerized. Cross docking involves the elimination of the distribution center and instead uses direct delivery to the customer after picking and sorting the goods from the suppliers. This is possible only if the suppliers ensure delivery within a specified time frame.

Wal-Mart and RFID Adoption

One of Wal-Mart's major initiatives in the supply chain area is pioneering the use of RFID. In the first week of April 2004, Wal-Mart launched its first live test of RFID tracking technology. Using one distribution center and seven stores, 21 products from participating vendors were used in the pilot test.

In the pilot application, passive RFID chips with small antennae were attached to cases and pallets. When passed near an RFID "reader," the chip was activated and its unique product identifier code transmitted back to an inventory control system. Cases and pallets containing the 21 products featuring RFID tags were delivered to the distribution center in Sanger, Texas, where RFID readers installed at the dock doors notified both shippers and Wal-Mart what products had entered the Wal-Mart distribution center and where the products were stored. RFID readers were also installed in other places, such as conveyor belts, so that each marked case could be tracked. The readers used by Wal-Mart have an average range of 15 feet. A schematic view of the system is shown in Figure IV.1.

Wal-Mart set a January 2005 target for its top 100 suppliers to place RFID tags on cases and pallets destined for Wal-Mart stores. The system is expected to improve flows along the supply chain, reduce theft, increase sales, reduce inventory costs (by eliminating overstocking), and provide visibility and accuracy throughout Wal-Mart's supply chain.

Although some of Wal-Mart's suppliers have been late in implementing the system, to encourage suppliers to cooperate, in January 2008 Wal-Mart started to charge them $2 per case or pallet not tagged (see Hayes-Weier, 2008). It is clear that if the pilot is successful (and so far it is), RFID will become an industry standard. After all, nearly $70 billion is lost in the retail sector alone in the United States every year due to products getting lost in the supply chain or being stored in wrong places.

In addition to requiring RFID tags from its suppliers, Wal-Mart is installing the technology internally. According to Scherago (2006), more than 2,000 Wal-Mart stores were RFID-enabled with gate readers and handhelds at loading docks, facility entrances, stockrooms, and sales floors by the end of 2006. According to Songini (2007), the emphasis now is on the use of RFID in stores rather than in distribution hubs.

The next step in Wal-Mart's pilot is to mark each individual item of large goods with a tag. This plan raises a possible privacy issue: What if the tags are not removed from the products? People fear that they will be tracked after leaving the store. Wal-Mart can also use RFID for many other applications. For example, it could attach tags to shoppers' children, so when they are lost in the megastore they could be tracked in seconds.

Retailers such as Wal-Mart believe that the widespread implementation of RFID technology marks a revolutionary change in supply chain management, much as the introduction of barcodes was seen revolutionary over two decades ago.

The RFID initiative is an integral part of improving the company's supply chain (Scherago, 2006). RFID along with a new EDI improves collaboration with the suppliers and helps reduce inventories. Companies that conformed early to Wal-Mart's RFID mandate enjoy benefits, too. For example, Daisy Brand, the manufacturer of sour cream and cottage cheese, started shipping RFID-tagged cases and pallets to Wal-Mart in the fall of 2004. Daisy says its investment in RFID has been a boon, helping it better manage the flow of its perishable products through Wal-Mart stores and ensuring that marketing promotions proceed as planned (Hayes-Weier, 2008).

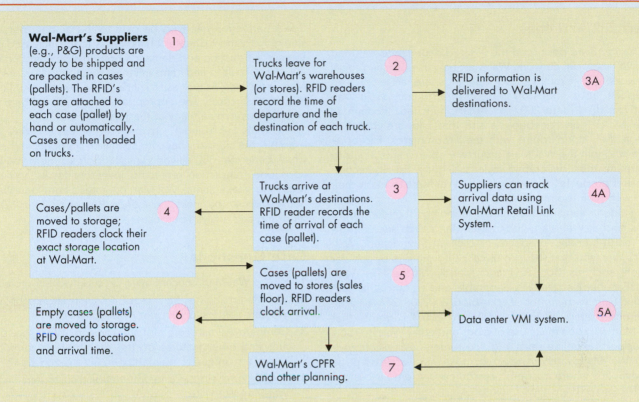

Figure IV.1 RFID at Wal-Mart and its suppliers: the seven steps process. (*Source:* Drawn by E. Turban.)

Wal-Mart Online

Wal-Mart has had an online presence since 1996. However, one problem with its strategy for growing online sales has been the demographics of its primary customer base. Wal-Mart's target demographic is the household with an average of $25,000 in annual income, whereas the median income of online consumers is perhaps $60,000. Therefore, Wal-Mart has to market online to new customers with higher incomes (see Wailgum, 2007). Despite these demographics differences, online sales (primarily in music, travel, and electronics) through *walmart.com* have grown steadily. However, Wal-Mart needs to develop new marketing strategies for its online business (Wailgum, 2007).

Wal-Mart's alliance with AOL is designed to provide cobranded low-cost Internet access to dwellers in both very rural and very urban areas, where there are no Wal-Mart stores nearby. Wal-Mart also provides free Wi-Fi access in some of its upscale stores. The intent is to lure new market segments and thus cancel the effect of cannibalization. Wal-Mart also has concerns about cannibalizing its in-store sales. Ultimately, a hybrid e-tailer that can offer a combination of huge selection with the click-and-mortar advantages of nearby stores (for merchandise pickup or returns) may prove to be the 800-pound gorilla of online consumer sales.

As of 2002, Walmart.com matured, offering shopping cart, order status and tracking, a help desk, a clear return policy and returns mechanisms, a store locator, and information on spe-cial sales and liquidations. Also, community services, such as photo sharing, 1-hour photos, and gift registry, are provided.

Wal-Mart offers only some of its merchandise online, but the selection is increasing. In 2008, it offered over 1,000,000 items including some not available in all stores (e.g., spas, mattresses). In 2004, Wal-Mart started selling songs online for 88 cents each, competing with Apple's iTunes. Inexpensive items (e.g., those that sell for less than $5) are not available online. Also in 2004, during a 4-day Thanksgiving special, Wal-Mart began to court more affluent shoppers with new and more expensive items available only online. Products ranged from cashmere sweaters to shiatsu massage chairs.

Wal-Mart added many new products to its online catalog. Using the "Site to Store" program, shoppers order products on the Web and pick them up at a local Wal-Mart store. International customers can buy Wal-Mart products directly from Wal-Mart, if shipping is available, or from affiliate sites. For example, see ASDA (*asda.co.uk*), a Wal-Mart owned U.K. company.

According to Nielsen/NetRatings, in 2006 Wal-Mart recorded the second-largest increase in Web traffic among the top 10 online shopping and travel sites. For example, site vis-its to Walmart.com in July 2006 were 19.5 million, up 27 per-cent over July 2005. For July 2008, Walmart.com was ranked the third top site by Nielsen/NetRatings in terms of the num-ber of visits, following the top sites of eBay, and Amazon.com (*Internetretailer.com*, 2008). WalMart.com is a subsidiary of Wal-Mart stores.

Web 2.0 Activities

In Chapter 8 we described the ill-fated experience Wal-Mart had with its social network. Wal-Mart now uses existing social networks. For example, job openings are advertised on MySpace jobs (*jobs.myspace.com/a/ms-jobs/list/q-Wal-Mart,+north*). In late 2007, Wal-Mart launched "Roommate Style Match" on Facebook, a site that allows students to design their dorm rooms with their roommates. Facebook users who join the Wal-Mart group are able to take a quiz to determine their decorating style and get a list of "recommended products" they can buy at Wal-Mart to mesh their style with their roommate's.

Students can also download a shopping list of dorm room items sold at Wal-Mart, link to Wal-Mart's Web site promoting "earth-friendly" products, or click on Soundcheck, Wal-Mart's Web site that shows musical performances by popular singers such as Bon Jovi and Mandy Moore. The Wal-Mart/Facebook strategy is debatable and so far not so successful (see *web-strategist.com/blog/2007/08/24/walmarts-facebook-strategy-sinking/*). Wailgum (2007) suggests that Wal-Mart will soon make use of blogs and other Web 2.0 tools to support its online sales (e.g., customers reviews of products). Wal-Mart watch (*myspace.com/walmartwatch*) is a page on MySpace where frustrated customers and employees get a chance to express their feelings.

Going Green

Wal-Mart is known for its efforts in implementing environmental measures to increase energy efficiency, mostly supported by an IT system.

The primary goals include spending $500 million a year to increase fuel efficiency in Wal-Mart's truck fleet by 25 percent over three years and double it within ten; reduce greenhouse gas emissions by 20 percent in seven years; reduce energy use at stores by 30 percent; and cut solid waste from United States stores and Sam's Clubs by 25 percent in three years. Wal-Mart's goal is ultimately to use only renewable energy sources and produce zero waste. The company also designed three new experimental stores with wind turbines, photovoltaic solar panels, biofuel-capable boilers, water-cooled refrigerators, and xeriscape gardens (using plants appropriate to the site and sustainable with little or no supplemental water). Wal-Mart is also the biggest seller of organic milk and the biggest buyer of organic cotton products in the world. For example, by eliminating excess packaging on their toy line *Kid Connection*, Wal-Mart saves $2.4 million per year in shipping costs, 3,800 trees, and a million barrels of oil.

Conclusion

Wal-Mart's competitiveness and its future success depend upon IT's ability to deliver applications and systems that are agile and easy to adopt to changing market conditions.

Special attention needs to be paid to the global operation (see globalization, Chapter 11) as well as to the increased customer's satisfaction and demands both in stores and online. It is still difficult to find items in stores due to the lack of Wal-Mart associates, as well as to check prices due to poor labeling in some cases. The appropriate use of IT can help the company overcome many of these problems.

Wal-Mart is using IT in many other applications. For example, the company has over 30 million shoppers each day, which generates 800 million transactions (each item you buy adds one transaction regarding inventory levels and one regarding sales volume). Wal-Mart operates a huge data warehouse and uses business intelligence (BI) (see Chapter 12) for reporting and analysis purposes.

Case Questions

1. Why is Wal-Mart concentrating on supply chain projects?
2. Wal-Mart mandates RFID tags from all its large suppliers. Why are some suppliers not in compliance?
3. Compare *walmart.com* with *amazon.com*. What shopping aids and other features do the sites have in common? Which are unique to *walmart.com*? To *amazon.com*?
4. Investigate the options for international customers on the Wal-Mart Web site.
5. Compare *walmart.com* with *target.com*, *costco.com*, *kmart.com*, and other direct competitors. Write a report.
6. Review the technologies discussed in Chapters 9 through 11. Which ones can be useful but are not used by Wal-Mart? Why?
7. Envision how TPSs are used in Wal-Mart stores. Go to Wal-Mart and pay with a check. How has IT improved the old way of paying with checks?

References and Bibliography

Duvall, M., "Radio Interference," *Baseline*, October 2007.

en.wikipedia.org/wiki/walmart (accessed July 2008).

Hayes–Weier, M., "Sam's Club Suppliers Required to Use Tags or Face $2 Fee," *Information Week*, January 21, 2008.

InternetRetailer.com, "eBay Tops in Online Ad Volume, but Amazon Leads in Online Buzz, Study Says," April 28, 2008, *internetretailer.com/dailynews.asp?id=26196* (accessed July 2008).

Niederman, F., R. G. Mathieu, R. Morley, and I-W. Kwon, "Examining RFID Applications in Supply Chain Management," *Communication of the ACM*, July 2007.

Piasecki, D., "Warehouse Management Systems (WMS)," *InventoryOps.com*, *inventoryops.com/warehouse_management_systems.htm* (accessed July 2008).

Scherago, D., "Wal-Smart," *Retail Technology Quarterly*, January 2006.

Songini, M. L., "Wal-Mart Shifts RFID Plans," *Computerworld*, February 26, 2007.

Walmart.com, "An Introduction to Walmart.com," *walmart.com/catalog/catalog.gsp?cat=542413* (accessed July 2008).

Wailgum, T., "How Wal-Mart Lost Its Technology Edge," *CIO Insight*, October 4, 2007.

Chapter

12

Business Intelligence and Decision Support Systems

Learning Objectives

After studying this chapter, you will be able to:

1 Identify factors influencing adoption of business intelligence (BI) and business performance management (BPM).

2 Describe data mining, predictive analytics, digital dashboards, scorecards, and multidimensional data analysis.

3 Identify key considerations for IT support of managerial decision making.

4 Understand managerial decision making processes, the decision process, and types of decisions.

5 Describe decision support systems (DSSs), benefits, and structure.

6 Recognize the importance of real-time BI and decision support for various levels of information workers.

7 Be familiar with automated decision support, its advantages, and areas of application.

Integrating *IT*

ACC

FIN

MKT

OM

HRM

IS

IT-PERFORMANCE MODEL

Business intelligence, decision support systems, data visualization tools, and data mining are ITs that support enterprise performance. Together they collect enterprise data from disparate (unlinked) information systems (e.g., CRM, ERP, and POS databases), integrate these data into meaningful information, and present this information in easy-to-understand reports or Web pages. These tools keep managers up-to-date on key performance indicators (KPIs) that alert managers and decision support systems (DSS), when faced with adverse market or economic conditions, such as mature (no growth) markets, brutal global competition, recession, inflation, and soaring energy costs, to learn about and respond to changes in demand. Companies that can respond quickly to opportunities and threats significantly outperform those that cannot. From the perspective of management profitability, responsiveness maximizes revenue, and efficiency minimizes costs. In this chapter, we cover BI, DSS, and related technologies that give greater visibility into all corners of the enterprise.

The business performance management cycle and IT model.

MKT   LESSONS FROM FAILURES   OM   GLOBAL

BudNet: ANHEUSER-BUSCH'S INTELLIGENCE TOOL

Anheuser-Busch Companies wants to be the life of every party with its beers and theme parks. The Fortune 500 company is one of the world's largest brewers best known for its Budweiser, Bud Light, and Michelob labels. Heineken, Molson, Coors, and SABMiller are its fiercest competitors. Anheuser-Busch's 2007 worldwide beer volume was 161.6 million barrels, with roughly 104 million barrels sold in the United States. They had 48 percent market share in the United States in 2008, which is impressive in any business, but a decline from 49 percent in 2006 and 50 percent in 2005. Each 1 percent represents 1.4 million barrels of beer.

Anheuser-Busch's business strategy can be summed up in one word—*responsiveness*. The ability to respond quickly to opportunities and threats relies on IT applications that support the analysis and interpretation of company, market, and economic data. For example, by monitoring and analyzing sales data as precisely as its ITs allow, the company was first to identify the shift in customer purchasing preferences toward more healthy beverages. Armed with this intelligence, the company responded with and captured the low-carb beer market.

The Problem

The beer market had reached saturation by 2005 in much of the developed world. The domestic beer market was particularly mature with flat U.S. consumption levels for three reasons: greater awareness of problems associated with alcohol, slow population growth, and an aging population. Young adults are the largest beer-drinking segment. There were few options for growth other than winning over customers from their rivals or focusing on emerging markets. Stealing from competitors is extremely risky because it triggers hostile retaliation, leading to unprofitable price and advertising wars. Entering emerging markets was the strategy of many brewers.

There were also price constraints and pressures. The industry-wide decline in beer consumption prevented Anheuser-Busch from raising its prices, a strategy that had added to profits in prior years. Both SABMiller and Coors were discounting their brands, and Anheuser-Busch had to follow along or risk losing sales or consumers who might never return to Bud or its other labels.

Faced with adverse and uncontrollable conditions, Anheuser-Busch sought to streamline and better manage its business processes to ensure that they met consumer demand.

The Solution

Anheuser-Busch implemented BudNet, a network-based, real-time data warehousing solution capable of collecting data on dozens of its KPIs. BudNet provided the network and data infrastructure for BI and DSS capabilities. As new technologies emerged and became affordable, they were added to BudNet. For example, BudNet was enhanced with wireless network capabilities and data capture via handheld devices. Wireless capabilities and mobile technology provided two-way communication. Company-owned and independent distributors updated sales and inventory data in real-time. In the United States, distributors reported critical facts about competitors' shelf space, displays, and pricing, as well as its own inventory levels and shelf situation, using PDAs. And the company sent instruc-

tions to the sales reps before they left the store as to how to move displays and tailor promotions to influence market share.

Wireless capabilities provide managers with data that are analyzed immediately to get better insight into the beer distribution chain and to provide actionable feedback to maximize sales. BudNet reduces uncertainty. Managers are informed of relevant details, such as whether a six-pack of Bud Light was warm or cold when it was bought, and what it cost at neighboring stores.

The Results

With the BudNet system, data from invoices are transmitted to the network every time a shipment enters a store. Sales data from wholesalers are received promptly; for example, Monday sales data are reported to Anheuser-Busch by Tuesday at 4 PM, but many report earlier. The brewer can then correlate the sales data with data on the gender, age, and other characteristics of shoppers in a given area received from third parties on a weekly basis. Anheuser-Busch also integrates data from its distributors' ISs with other key data, such as U.S. census data on the ethnic and economic makeup of neighborhoods, to design local promotions that effectively match their markets. Business decisions are data-driven and fact-based.

Anheuser-Busch uses sophisticated data analytics to gain a decisive edge and outsmart its rivals in a competitive mature industry. Businesses have plenty of data and data crunchers, but not all companies have invested in the IT infrastructure and BI capabilities to turn them into strategic weapons.

Anheuser-Busch's ability to collect, analyze, and act on data is the essence of their competitive advantage and the source of their superior performance. Company financials, listed in Table 12.1, show the increases in net profit, sales growth of 6.2 percent, and income growth of 7.6 percent in 2007. Management has made a science out of monitoring the metrics that allow it to understand when, where, and why consumers buy beer. Insights have allowed the company to post double-digit profit gains for 20 straight quarters.

Source: Compiled from Garretson (2007) and Schachter (2007).

TABLE 12.1	Anheuser-Busch Financials		
	2007	**2006**	**2005**
Revenue*	$16,685.7	$15,717.1	$15,035.7
Net Income*	$2,115.3	$1,965.2	$1,839.2
Net Profit	12.7%	12.5%	12.2%
Employees	30,849	30,183	31,485
• One-Year Sales Growth: 6.2%			
• One-Year Income Growth: 7.6%			
*Millions of U.S. dollars.			

The opening case illustrates the value of BI, data analytics, and DSS for day-to-day operational decision making and competitive advantage. These systems help decision makers collect, compile, and analyze raw data using business models to respond and make decisions. BI tools enhance employee productivity and enable a high degree of self-sufficiency.

This chapter describes BI, business performance management, DSS, and data visualization. From a business perspective, the term *business intelligence* refers to an enterprise's ability to make informed, data-driven decisions at the time they are needed. We explain how enterprise systems provide insight into key indicators of business and operational performance. We discuss how BI integrates disparate data sources into a single coherent framework for real-time reporting and detailed analysis by anyone—customers, partners, employees, power users, and analysts.

Note that BI is both a management process and a collection of software applications and underlying technology that enable organizations to make better business decisions by exposing key metrics that drive the organization.

12.1 The Need for Business Intelligence (BI)

Before the introduction of BI in the 1980s, a common complaint of managers was that they could not get the information they needed for decision making, planning, or to assess performance. For most organizations, IT investments had not translated into more sales. When it came to understanding customers and their buying decisions, there were many more data than real answers. When attempting to develop a complete view of each customer across all product lines, companies hit a brick wall. For many companies, years of data were, in effect, *locked up* in transactional **data silos.** Data silos, nonstandardized data, and disparate information systems (ISs) made getting a unified view of individual customers impossible.

SVR

For example, in 1990, AT&T wanted its customer service representatives (CSR) to up-sell (e.g., offer the customer a higher-level of service, such as upgrading the call plan) or cross-sell (e.g., offer the customer a complementary service, such as adding text messaging to a cell plan) each customer who called in. But up- or cross-selling cannot be done unless the CSR sees what services and plans the customer already has to identify what to up- and cross-sell. Customers are not going to listen to the CSR read off a long list of extras to buy. Typically, the CSR had the opportunity to make one offer, so it had to be on target for the customer. Therefore, before implementing the CRM initiative, AT&T had to invest in **ETL (Extract, Transform, and Load) tools** to create a data store that held a complete record of all of the AT&T services and accessories of each customer. In AT&T's situation, ETL tools were needed to extract relevant customer data from the various data silos maintained by each of its local, long distance, and cellular divisions; transform the data into standardized formats; and then load and integrate the data into an operational data store or system.

Operational systems are designed to store data required by an organization (e.g., sales orders, customer deposits) and are optimized to capture and handle large volumes of transactions. For comparison, a data warehouse is a database system optimized for reporting. A common standardization process would be to collect raw sales data for all transactions from the operational data store together with sales dates, and then convert the raw sales data into a *daily sales* format in a single currency (dollars, euros, etc.) and denomination (thousands, millions, etc.). Operational data stores and ETL are components for real-time BI, which will be discussed in this chapter.

You will also learn in this chapter that BI is no longer reserved for business analysts and mathematicians at large corporations to identify trends or anomalies in prior periods. BI has emerged as a critical IT that provides measurable business value to smaller companies as costs decline and vendors design products for small and medium

TABLE 12.2	Strategic, Tactical, and Operational BI: Business Focus and Users		
	Strategic BI	**Tactical BI**	**Operational BI**
Primary Business Focus	To achieve long-term enterprise goals and objectives	To analyze data; deliver alerts and reports regarding the achievement of enterprise goals	To manage day-to-day operations
Primary Users	Executives, analysts	Executives, analysts, line-of-business managers	Line-of-business managers, operations
Measures	Measures are a feedback mechanism to track and understand how the strategy is progressing, and what adjustments need to be made to the plan.	Measures are a feedback mechanism to track and understand how the strategy is progressing, and what adjustments need to be made to the plan.	Individualized so each line manager gets insight into performance of his or her business processes.
Time Frame	Monthly, quarterly, yearly	Daily, weekly, monthly	Immediately, intra-day
Data Types or Uses	Historical, predictive	Historical, predictive modeling	Real time or near–real time

Sources: Adapted from Oracle (2007) and Imhoff (2006).

companies. In addition, BI technology has progressed to the point where companies are implementing BI for various types of primary users, as shown in Table 12.2, arming their business users with BI capabilities. Increased pervasiveness of BI throughout the organization and its use as a feedback mechanism are growing trends.

As early as 2006, according to a Gartner survey, many CIOs (chief information officers) had made BI their top IT priority—over security technologies, mobile workforce enablement applications, and other IT plans (Oracle, 2007).

RESOLVING PROBLEMS CAUSED BY DISPARATE DATA STORES

With constantly changing business environments, companies want to be responsive to competitors' actions, regulatory requirements, mergers and acquisitions, and the introduction of new channels for the business. As you have read, responsiveness requires intelligence, which in turn requires having trusted data and reporting systems. Like many companies, global securities firm Bear Stearns (acquired by J.P. Morgan Chase in 2008) had suffered from a patchwork of reporting systems that could not be easily integrated because of their lack of standardization. The acquisition will also create integration nightmares. When data are not integrated into a single reporting system, there is no trusted real-time view of what is going on across the enterprise. Quarterly financial reports, required by the SEC, are not valuable for managing profitability.

The product data for international retailers in particular is a problem. Countries use different bar codes, but they need to be linked so that retailers can optimize products availability and revenues.

A trusted view is not achievable because ISs are much better at collecting data than they are at helping people understand these data. Other deficiencies that have frustrated decision makers because of disparate ISs are the following:

• Getting information too late
• Getting data at the wrong level of detail—either too detailed or too summarized
• Getting too many directionless data
• Not being able to coordinate with other departments across the enterprise
• Not being able to share data in a timely manner

Faced with those deficiencies, decision makers had to rely on the IT department to extract data to create a report, which usually took too long. Or they extracted data and created their own decision support spreadsheets, which were subject to data errors and calculation mistakes. Making matters worse, if spreadsheets were not

TABLE 12.3	BI Functions and Features		
Reporting and Analysis	**Analytics**	**Data Integration**
Enterprise reporting and analysis	Predictive analytics	ETL (extract, transformation, load)
Enterprise search	Data, text, and Web mining	EII (enterprise information integration)
Scorecards	OLAP (online analytic processing)	
Dashboards		
Visualization tools		

shared or updated, then decisions were being made based on old or incomplete data. The solution to many of these data problems was BI.

BI concepts can seem confusing at first because *business intelligence* is an umbrella term that includes architectures, tools, databases, and applications that have been implemented over several decades under different names by various researchers and vendors. Moreover, new technologies are added frequently to the existing set of BI tools. For examples, see *spotfire.tibco.com/*. However, there are core BI functions and features, which are listed in Table 12.3 and discussed throughout this chapter.

There are many examples of BI resolving data problems at large companies that could afford the high investment and maintenance costs. As the cost of BI has decreased and it becomes more downward scalable or modular, BI solutions are being implemented at smaller firms.

Let's explore how BI began and why it is such a successful technology. We will first present BI as a set of technologies, and then look at how those technologies are deployed as business solutions. To **deploy** means to install, test, and implement an IS or application.

BUSINESS INTELLIGENCE TECHNOLOGIES

In the 1990s, BI was associated with back-office operations and employees, primarily accounting, finance, and human resources. Data from these operations were collected and loaded into a data repository (operational database, data mart, or warehouse) each night and then formatted into a standardized format so they could be analyzed. The analyzed data ultimately were inserted into predefined reports that were delivered or made available to decision makers.

Back-office workers remained the primary users of BI until the early 2000s. Eventually, others, including managers and executives, began wanting better insights from what became known as *enterprise data*. Vendors responded to (and also helped to create) demands for BI with advanced analytics, decision support, easy-to-use interfaces, improved data visualization tools, and Web-based delivery features. The growing importance and potential of BI is evident by the size of the vendors and mergers in the BI vendor market.

BI VENDORS

BI vendors include major software companies, such as Business Objects, Cognos, IBM, Oracle, SAP, SAS, MicroStrategy, Microsoft, Information Builders, and Hyperion. Until 2007, the BI market was dominated by Cognos and Business Objects. In 2008, three multi-billon-dollar acquisitions helped consolidate the BI vendor market and intensified competition among the mega-vendors. SAP acquired Business Objects for $7 billion, IBM acquired Cognos for $4.9 billion, and Oracle acquired Hyperion for $3.3 billion. These acquisitions highlighted two important trends in modern business: (1) BI has evolved into one of the hottest segments in the software market, and (2) major software corporations plan to integrate BI capabilities into their product mix.

POWER OF PREDICTIVE ANALYTICS, ALERTS, AND DECISION SUPPORT

BI technnology evolved beyond being primarily a reporting system when the following features were added: sophisticated predictive analytics, event-driven (real-time) alerts, and operational decision support. Using a BI system for reporting alone was like driving a car looking through the rear-view mirror. The view was always of

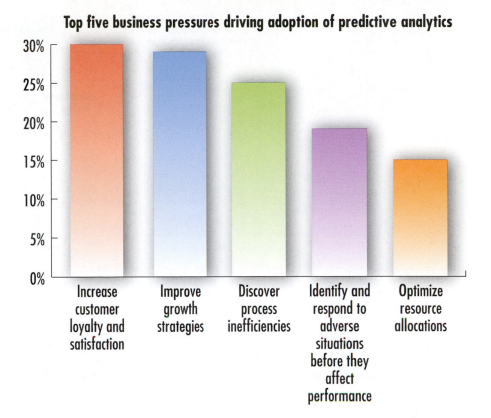

Top five business pressures driving adoption of predictive analytics

Figure 12.1 Top five business pressure driving the adoption of predictive analytics. (Data from Aberdeen Group.)

the past. The greatest strength of a company's predictive analytical technology is that it allows a company to react to things as they happen and to be proactive with respect to their future. Companies investing in BI expected do so because they need these capabilities, which tend to be stated as the need for

- Improved data quality
- Shared, common vision of business activity that benefits key management across the enterprise
- Full visibility and real-time access to company data
- Simple-to-review KPIs
- Easy-to-create accurate, up-to-the-minute reports
- Informed, fast decision making
- Complete audit trails and comprehensive reports for compliance audits.

For a discussion of how BI facilitates SOX compliance, see *Online Brief 12.1*.

Predictive Analytics. **Predictive analytics** is the branch of data mining that focuses on forecasting trends (e.g., regression analysis) and estimating probabilities of future events. The top five business pressures driving the adoption of predictive analytics are shown in Figure 12.1. Business analytics, as it is also called, provides the models, which are formulas or algorithms, and procedures to BI. (An **algorithm** is a set of rules or instructions for solving a problem in a finite number of steps. Algorithms can be represented with a flow chart, as in Figure 12.2.) There are predictive analytic tools designed for hands-on use by managers who want to do their own forecasting and predicting. Demand for this capability to predict grew out of frustration with BI that helped only managers understand *what had happened*. Recall from Chapter 3 that managers want to *learn and earn* from their data.

While there were many query, reporting, and analysis tools to view what had happened, managers wanted tools to predict what would happen and where their

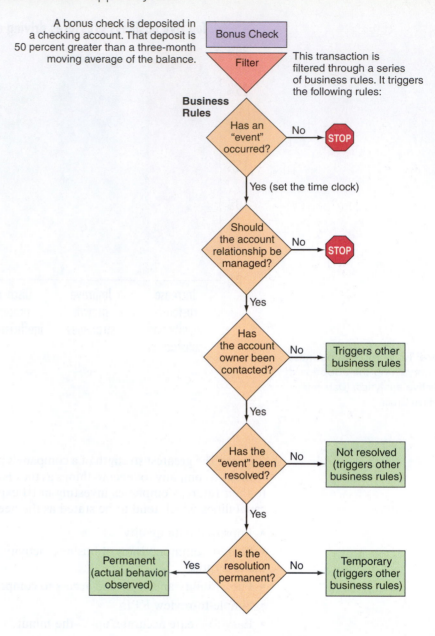

Figure 12.2 Real-time alerts triggered by customer-driven events.

A bonus check is deposited in a checking account. That deposit is 50 percent greater than a three-month moving average of the balance.

Bonus Check

Filter

This transaction is filtered through a series of business rules. It triggers the following rules:

Business Rules

Has an "event" occurred? — No → **STOP**

Yes (set the time clock)

Should the account relationship be managed? — No → **STOP**

Yes

Has the account owner been contacted? — No → Triggers other business rules

Yes

Has the "event" been resolved? — No → Not resolved (triggers other business rules)

Yes

Is the resolution permanent? — Yes → Permanent (actual behavior observed) — No → Temporary (triggers other business rules)

businesses were going. The value of predictive analytics at eHarmony is discussed in *IT at Work 12.1.*

Building predictive analytic capabilities requires computer software and human modeling experts. Experts in advanced mathematical modeling build and verify the integrity of the models and interpret the results. This work is done is two phases. The first phase involves identifying and understanding the business metrics that the enterprise wants to predict, such as compatibility matches, customer churn, or best cross-sell or up-sell marketing opportunities by customer segment. While a Ph.D. degree is not needed to identify metrics, Ph.D.-level expertise is necessary for the second phase—defining the predictors (variables) and analytical models to accurately predict future performance.

Event-Driven Alerts. As the name implies, event-driven alerts are real-time alerts or warnings that are broadcast when a predefined event, or unusual event, occurs. See Figure 12.2 for a representation of the processing that occurs when a predefined event—in this case, an unusually large deposit—occurs. Since events need to be quantified, an unusually large deposit is considered a deposit that is 50 percent greater

IT at Work 12.1

eHarmony Uses Predictive Analytics for Compatibility Matching

Founded in 2000, eHarmony is the first relationship Web service to use a scientific approach to match compatible singles. eHarmony markets itself based on its ability to predict compatibility between two people. In 2006, with 11 million registered members, eHarmony turned to more advanced analytics and proprietary algorithms to improve its matchmaking capabilities.

The company purchased predictive analytics software from SPSS (*spss.com*) to build models that would more accurately measure compatibility variables. In addition to model building, the software supports scientific research, brand development, and customer satisfaction and retention. One research objective was to start tracking couples from the time before they were married

to monitor relationships that lasted and those that did not, and to use those data to develop models to predict successful outcomes. eHarmony states that its analytic approach is successful as measured by their claim that they are responsible for over 90 members marrying each day.

Sources: Compiled from Hatch (2008), *spss.com* (2008), and *aberdeen.com* (2008).

For Further Exploration: Explain the purpose and value of predictive analytics at eHarmony. What are the data sources for model building? Is eHarmony's proprietary algorithm a competitive advantage? Explain your answer.

---

than a three-month moving average of the balance. Notice that the event (deposit) triggers an analysis of the event (using business rules) to determine what type of action would improve profitability.

Alerts require real-time monitoring to know when the event of interest has occurred, and business rules to know what to monitor. In Figure 12.2, the business rules are in the diamonds. In this scenario, when a deposit is made that is more than double the amount of the average deposit over the past three months, it triggers a series of business rules. The bank may contact the customer with offers for a one-year CD, investment plan, insurance product, etc. Based on the answers to the business rules, further processing may stop or other rules leading to an alert to take action may be triggered.

For a credit card company, a customer's sudden payoff of the entire balance might trigger a business rule that leads to an alert because the payoff could be a signal that the customer is planning to cancel the card. There may be intervention, such as a special low interest rate offering, to reduce the risk of losing the customer.

Event-driven alerts can also be built into a business process or application. For example, the process could be programmed to predict the impact of events such as sales, orders, trades, shipments, and out-of-stock items on the company's performance. Typically, the results would be presented through a portal or Web-based dashboard. Figure 12.3 shows a sample performance dashboard, which includes KPIs. Note that the dashboard is configurable by using the drop-list controls to select period and product, and by using the tabs across the top of the dashboard. (Dashboards are discussed in the *User Interface* section of this chapter.) The software can be configured to alert staff to unusual events and to automatically trigger defined corrective actions.

Event-driven alerts are an alternative to more traditional (non-real-time) BI systems that extract data from applications, load it into databases or data warehouses, and then run analytics against the data stores. While demand for near real-time information always existed in customer-facing departments (e.g., marketing), the costs and complexity of loading data in traditional BI systems several times per day kept data out of their reach. Those technological BI limitations have been resolved to a large extent.

Operational Decision Support. The BudNet opening case discussed the use of BI for operational decisions as well as other decision types, such as those shown previously in Table 12.2. It is easier to understand operational decision support by looking at examples of the types of business decisions within their different time horizons:

1. Operational decisions ensure that day-to-day operations are running correctly and efficiently. For example: Is there enough inventory to fulfull all outstanding orders for lightweight 22-inch carry-on luggage?

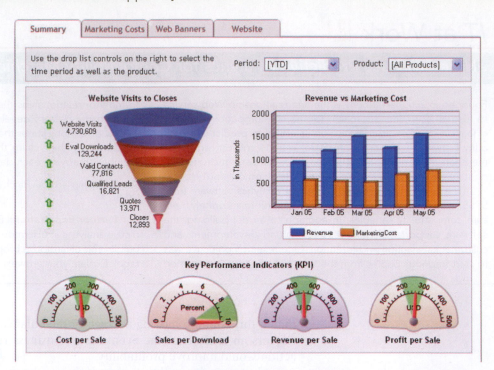

Figure 12.3 Sample performance dashboard.

2. Tactical decisions ensure that existing operations and processes are in alignment with business objectives and strategies. For example: What are the monthly inventory and sales trends for all sizes of lightweight luggage?

3. Strategic decisions create a road map for sustained success and business growth. For example: What other products could be complementary to the existing lightweight carry-on luggage product mix? What developments may cause an overall increase or decrease in demand for luggage? Or for lightweight luggage?

From these types of decisions, you can see that the time frame for receiving data and feedback ranges from real-time operational decisions to less time-sensitve strategic (quarterly or yearly) decisions. Operational decision support depends on ISs that have the ability to process and deliver operational data in real time or near–real time, as with event-driven alerts. Figure 12.4 illustrates basic BI components that support operational decisions in real-time and tactical and strategic decisions. Operational raw data are commonly kept in corporate or operational databases.

Figure 12.4 Basic BI components.

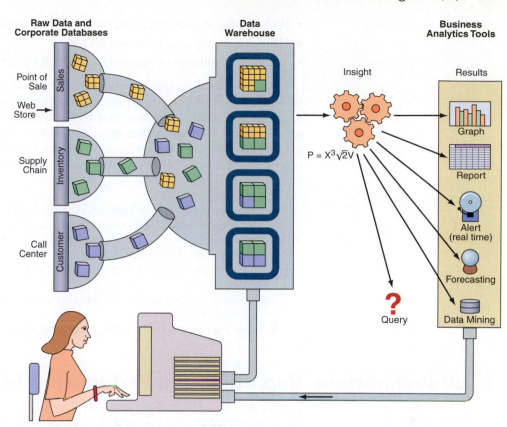

Figure 12.5 How a BI system works.

To understand how a BI system works (see Figure 12.5), consider a national retail chain that sells everything from grills and patio furniture to paper products. This company stores data about inventory, customers, past promotions, and sales numbers in various databases. Even though all these data are scattered across multiple systems—and may seem unrelated—ETL tools can bring the data together to the data warehouse (DW). In the DW, tables can be linked, and *data cubes* (another term for multidimensional databases) are formed. For instance, inventory data are linked to sales numbers and customer databases, allowing for extensive analysis of information. Some DWs have a dynamic link to the databases; others are static. Operational decision support can also be automated, as will be discussed in Section 12.6.

From an IT perspective, BI is a collection of software and tools, as we have just described. Next, we discuss BI in terms of business solutions from a business perspective.

BUSINESS INTELLIGENCE SOLUTIONS

BI solutions designed to improve decision making and data delivery must be able to access multiple enterprise data sources, including

- Transaction processing systems (TPS)
- E-business and e-commerce processes
- Operational platforms
- Databases

In competitive and challenging environments, companies need to continually assess and adjust their actions to stay on top of the markets they choose to serve. In order to make the needed changes, managers need answers to questions such as

- Which of our customers are most profitable and least profitable?
- Which products or services can be cross-sold and up-sold to which customers most profitably?
- Which sales and distribution channels are most effective and least effective for which products?

- What are the response rates and profit contributions of current marketing campaigns?
- How can we improve customer loyalty?
- What is the full cost of retaining a satisfied customer?

Answers to important questions such as these require BI systems and analysts to define how to measure customer profitability, costs to retain a customer, and so forth. It is helpful to recognize that BI concepts are not new, but have been implemented under different names by many vendors who created tools and methodologies over two decades. BI integrates or incorporates many different ISs that you have read about in other chapters, as we discuss in the next sections.

Review Questions

1. What are three reasons companies invest in BI?
2. What three conditions made getting a unified view of individual customers impossible?
3. What is meant by a "trusted view" of the data? Why wouldn't data be trusted?
4. What are three data deficiencies that frustrate decision makers because of disparate data?
5. Explain predictive analytics. What are two business pressures driving adoption of predictive analytics?
6. What are operational, tactical, and strategic decisions?

12.2 BI Architecture, Reporting, and Performance Management

One of the biggest challenges facing IT directors in every industry is how to deal with the growing volume of data that they accumulate. Some retailers have been at the forefront of using BI and managing data effectively. Leading international retailers such as Wal-Mart, for example, understand the need to know as much about their customers and products as possible. The downside is managing the volume of stored data to improve performance.

To implement BI, an extensive and complex architecture is needed to be able to monitor and manage the performance of the enterprise as a whole. Of course, the complexity of the architecture depends on the number and type of disparate ISs, volume of data, and the need for real-time support. In this section, we discuss three components of BI architecture: data extraction and integration, enterprise reporting systems, and data mining, query, and analysis tools. We then discuss business performance management.

DATA EXTRACTION AND INTEGRATION

To begin, tools extract data of interest from various sources such as OLAP, ERP, CRM, SCM, other applications, legacy and local data stores, and the Web. The extracted data will lack standardization and consistency because different systems use different data terminology or field names. Nonstandardization makes it impossible to integrate data until the data have been transformed into a uniform format. The three data integration processes, ETL, move data from multiple sources, reformat it, and load it into a central repository, such as another database, a data mart, or a data warehouse, for analysis or to another operational system to support a business process. The central data repository together with data security and administrative tools form the **information infrastructure.** Now the data can be used for reporting, analysis, and so on.

ENTERPRISE REPORTING SYSTEMS

Enterprise reporting systems provide standard, ad hoc, or custom reports that are populated with data from a single trusted source to get a *single version of the truth*. Leading companies, including at least 95 percent of the Fortune 500, rely on BI for self-service information delivery giving all user-levels—managers and power analysts—access to the information and reports they need. Users can create their own reports if they have easy access to necessary data. This approach reduces costs, improves control, and reduces **data latency.** Technically, the speed with which data is captured is referred to as data latency. It is a measure of data "freshness," specifically, data that are less than 24 hours old. Overall, self-service reporting decreases the time users must spend collecting the data and, instead, increases their time spent on analyzing the data to make business-critical decisions.

Routine Reporting. Routine operational reports are generated automatically and distributed periodically to internal and external subscribers on mailing or distribution lists. Examples are weekly sales figures, units produced each day and each week, and monthly hours worked. Here is an example of how a report is used in BI: A store manager receives store performance reports generated weekly by the BI software. After a review of one weekly report on store sales, the manager notices that sales for computer peripherals have dropped off significantly from previous weeks. She clicks on her report and immediately drills down to another enterprise report for details, which shows her that the three best-selling hard drives are surprisingly underselling. Now the manager needs to investigate why. Further drill-down by individual day may reveal that bad weather caused the drop in sales.

User Interfaces: Dashboards and Scorecards. Dashboards and scorecards are interactive user interfaces as well as reporting tools. Dashboards (like the dashboard of a car) provide easy-to-use access to enterprise data and help companies track business performance and optimize decision making. Dashboard users are typically supervisors and specialists, whereas scorecard users are executives, managers, and staff. For examples, see *businessobjects.com.* Information is presented in graphs, charts, and tables that show actual performance vs. desired metrics for at-a-glance views of the health of the organization. Table 12.4 lists the valuable capabilities of digital dashboards.

Advanced dashboard technology presents KPIs, trends, and exceptions using Adobe Flash animation. *MicroStrategy Dynamic Enterprise Dashboards* allows dashboard designers to integrate data from a variety of sources to provide multidimensional performance feedback and optimize decision making in an interactive Flash mode.

Dashboards can be designed to support marketing or other functions. For example, marketing dashboards may report on traditional metrics, such as customer acquisition costs, customer retention, sales volume, channel margins, and the ROI of marketing campaigns. Given rising demands from customers, employees, shareholders, and policymakers mandating environmentally friendly business practices, companies are also using dashboards for tracking progress toward green marketing improvement.

The **balanced scorecard methodology** is a framework for defining, implementing, and managing an enterprise's business strategy by linking objectives with factual measures. In other words, it is a way to link top-level metrics, such as the financial information created by the chief financial officer (CFO), with actual performance all the way down the corporate pecking order.

TABLE 12.4	Digital Dashboards Capabilities
Capability	**Description**
Drill-down	Ability to go to details at several levels; can be done by a series of menus or by query.
Critical success factors (CSFs)	The factors most critical for the success of business. These factors can be organizational, industry, departmental, etc.
Key performance indicators (KPIs)	The specific measures of CSFs.
Status access	The latest data available on KPI or some other metric, ideally in real time.
Trend analysis	Short-, medium-, and long-term trend of KPIs or metrics, which are projected using forecasting methods.
Ad-hoc analysis	Analyses made any time, upon demands and with any desired factors and relationships.
Exception reporting	Reports that highlight deviations larger than certain thresholds. Reports may include only deviations.

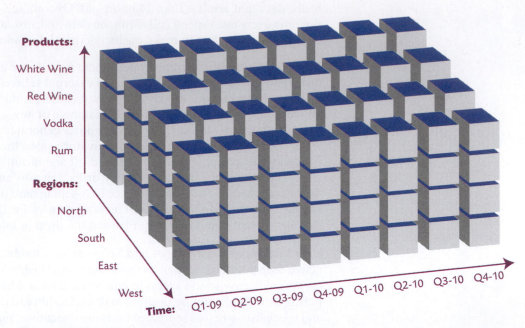

Figure 12.6 Multidimensional view of sales revenue data.

DATA MINING, QUERY, AND ANALYSIS

Data mining, ad hoc and planned queries, and analysis tools provide the means to investigate and understand the forces driving the enterprise and to feed the results back to decision makers. (To avoid confusion, here is the general difference between analysis and analytics: analysis is a more general term referring to a process; analytics is a method that uses data to learn something. Analytics always involves historical or current data.) The trend in BI is toward self-sufficiency. BI prepares and provides the data for real-time reporting, decision support, and detailed analysis by end users. Users are able to explore the data to learn from it themselves.

There are many software tools for users to create queries and analyze data. These tools give users fast, simple, and controllable access to data to perform ad hoc analysis in multiple dimensions. An example of a multidimensional business query is: *For each of the four sales regions, what was the percent change in sales revenue for the top four products per quarter year compared to the same quarters for the three past years?*

This business question (query) identifies the data—*sales revenues*—that the user wants to examine. Those data can be viewed in three dimensions: *sales regions, products*, and *time* in quarters. The results of this query would be shaped like the multi-dimensional cube shown in Figure 12.6.

Any query that cannot be determined prior to the moment the query is issued is considered an ad hoc query. The user may decide to place such a query after he or she gets a report that triggers a concern or interest. Ad hoc queries allow users to request information that is not available in periodic reports, as well as to generate new queries or modify old ones with significant flexibility over content, layout, and calculations. These answers expedite decision making. The system must be intelligent enough to understand what the user wants. Simple ad hoc query systems are often based on menus. Data mining is further discussed in Section 12.3.

BUSINESS PERFORMANCE MANAGEMENT

Business performance management (BPM) requires that managers have methods to quickly and easily determine how well the organization is achieving its goals and objectives, and whether or not all of the organization is aligned with the strategic direction. BPM relies on BI analysis reporting, queries, dashboards, and scorecards. The relationship between BPM and other components can be seen in Figure 12.7.

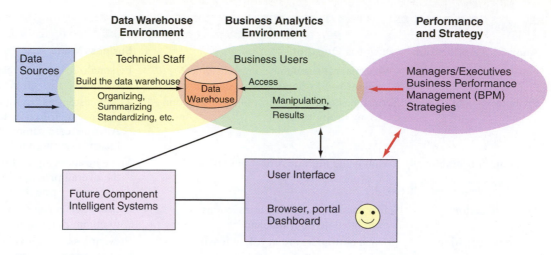

Figure 12.7 Business performance management (BPM) for monitoring and assessing performance.

The objective of BPM is strategic—to optimize the overall performance of an enterprise. By linking performance to corporate goals, decision makers can use the day-to-day data generated throughout their organization to monitor KPIs and make decisions that make a difference. The details of BPM are presented in Section 12.6.

BI PAYOFFS AND APPLICATIONS

BI has paid big dividends for companies in competitive marketplace environments, as illustrated in *IT at Work 12.2* at the retailer, Bank, in the United Kingdom.

IT at Work 12.2

U.K. Fashion Chain Uses BI and DSS to Predict and Replenish Intelligently

The fashion chain Bank, headquartered in Macclesfield, was identified as one of the 100 fastest growing businesses in the United Kingdom in 2006. Bank had doubled its store portfolio from 22 outlets in 2005 to 44 outlets as of mid-2007. The retailer partly attributes its success to the BI and DSS tools in the Futura Retail Management Solution software that it uses. The BI software has allowed better stock availability, faster replenishment, more accurate forecasting, and minimized merchandising and buying costs. The *what if* functionality enables managers to see the effects of buying one range of clothes over another. Real-time visibility of current stock levels has improved product performance and profitability.

Intelligent Product Ordering. A key reason cited by Bank for its expansion is its ability to consistently have the right customer sizes in stock. Bank's buyers have used BI tools to analyze which trends are taking off and to take full advantage of this knowledge to make sure the goods are in stock.

Using historical data, the system forecasts future buying patterns, enabling buyers to model the effects of purchasing one range over another. For instance, when Bank analyzed its customers' size profiles, it found it was buying too many large sizes. The retailer altered its size ratios for appropriate styles, and estimates this has increased sell-through by 5 percent.

Buyers and managers can quickly see current stock levels, product performance, and profitability in real time on the system and, importantly, what customers are not buying. By comparing sales with previous years' figures, buyers can establish when sales

patterns are different to determine price elasticity, so stock items can be priced correctly and mid-season promotions can be changed overnight when necessary.

Intelligent Replenishment. Merchandisers' target minimum stock levels are predefined for each store, so when the new stock arrives in the warehouse, it is sorted quickly and dispatched in a very smooth operation. This method of allocations and replenishment has created massive efficiencies. Seven merchandising and buying staff have managed the extra volume of work as store numbers have doubled, and the retailer predicts that only one extra person will be needed for the next 25 percent growth. Warehousing staff levels have also been reduced by 15 percent in the past year, even with the opening of 15 stores.

General administration has also been reduced. Bank's management uses Futura's performance management and analytical tools to model future sales, costs, cash, and inventories, and then to define the top-level budget. Computerizing this exercise has cut down on data entry and manpower, as well as improved the accuracy of the information delivered.

Sources: Compiled from *Futurauk.com* (2008), Goulden (2006), and Perry (2007).

For Further Exploration: What is the impact of "increased visibility" on managers' performance at Bank? What efficiencies have BI and DSS capabilities provided Bank? How do these efficiencies create a competitive advantage? Why was Bank able to increase the number of stores and reduce the number of employees?

TABLE 12.5	Business Value of BI Analytical Applications	
Analytical Application	**Business Questions**	**Business Value**
Customer segmentation	What market segments do my customers fall into and what are their characteristics?	Personalize customer relationships for higher customer satisfaction and retention.
Propensity to buy	Which customers are most likely to respond to my promotion?	Target customers based on their need to increase their loyalty to your product line. Also, increase campaign profitability by focusing on those most likely to buy.
Customer profitability	What is the lifetime profitability of my customers?	Make business interaction decisions based on the overall profitability of customers or customer segments.
Fraud detection	How can I detect which transactions are likely to be fraudulent?	Quickly detect fraud and take immediate action to minimize cost.
Customer attrition	Which customers are at risk of leaving?	Prevent loss of high-value customers and let go of lower-value customers.
Channel optimization	What is the best channel to reach my customers in each segment?	Interact with customers based on their preference and your need to manage cost.

Source: Ziama and Kasher (2004). Courtesy of Teradata, division of NCR Corp.

BI had ranked near the top of many companies' IT purchase plans in 2008 and 2009. An underlying reason for this interest is that companies cannot afford mistakes or waste. At a time when inflation and energy prices are cutting into net profit margins (net profit margin = net profit ÷ total revenue) and consumers' disposable income, managers need to make smarter, more informed decisions. Net profit margin indicates how well the business has managed its operating expenses. Exxon/Mobil and Cigna Insurance credit their profitability and explosive growth to implementing BI with balanced scorecards that enabled them to precisely gauge their market opportunities and position their companies to become financial and performance leaders in their market niches. Examples of common BI applications are listed in Table 12.5.

Because BI needs vary among business sectors, many BI tools are highly industry-specific. Using business analytics software, the user can make queries, request ad hoc reports, or conduct analyses. For example, because all of the databases are linked, you can search for which products are overstocked in a particular store. You can then determine which of these products commonly sell with popular items, based on previous sales. After planning a promotion to move the excess stock along with the popular products (e.g., bundling them together), you can dig deeper into the data to see where this promotion would be most popular (and most profitable). The results of your request can be reports, predictions, alerts, and/or graphical presentations. These can be disseminated to decision makers. For an example of an application at Ben & Jerry's, see *IT at Work 12.3*.

Review Questions

1. Define data extraction and data integration, and explain why they are needed.
2. What is data latency? How does giving users the ability to create their own reports reduce data latency? What is the age of fresh data?
3. Explain the capabilities of dashboards and scorecards. Why are they important BI tools?
4. What is the benefit to end users of having ad hoc query capabilities?
5. What is a multidimensional view of data? Sketch such a view in 3D and label the multiple dimensions for a service company.
6. Define business performance management (BPM). What is the objective of BPM?

IT at Work 12.3

Ben & Jerry's Keeps Track of Its Pints

BI allows Ben & Jerry's (*benjerry.com*), the U.S. ice cream maker, to track, understand, and manage information on the thousands of consumer responses it receives on its products and promotional activities. Through daily customer feedback analysis, Ben & Jerry's is able to identify trends and modify its marketing campaigns and its products to suit consumer demand.

At its factory in Waterbury, Vermont, huge pipes pump out more than 200,000 pints of ice cream each day. Throughout the day, refrigerated tractor-trailers pull up, pick up the pints, and deliver them to depots. From there, the ice cream is shipped to about 60,000 grocery stores in the United States and 14 other countries. At the company's headquarters, the life of each pint of ice cream—from ingredients to sale—is tracked. Once the pint is stamped and sent out, Ben & Jerry's stores its tracking number in an Oracle data warehouse and later analyzes the data. Using business analytics software, the sales team can check to see if Chocolate Chip Cookie Dough is gaining ground on Cherry Garcia for the coveted Number 1 sales position.

The marketing department checks the effectiveness of promotions and advertising by tracking changes in sales. The finance people use the tracking number in their analyses to show profit generated from each type of ice cream. Since the company started using the software, the accounting department has sharply reduced the amount of time it takes to reconcile and close the books at the end of each month. And equally important to a company focused on customer loyalty, the consumer affairs staff matches up each pint with the 225 calls and e-mails received each week, checking to see if there were any complaints.

Sources: Compiled from *BusinessObjects.com* (2007), Schlosser (2003), and *essaypage.com* (2006).

For Further Exploration: What other analyses can Ben & Jerry's do with its business intelligence software? What competitive advantage does BI offer the company?

12.3 Data, Text, and Web Mining and BI Search

Data are not the only type of content that can be mined for insights, although they certainly are the easiest. Textual information (or simply, *text*) from documents, electronic communications, and e-commerce activities can be mined. Content that is mined include unstructured data from documents, unstructured text from e-mail messages, and log data from Internet browsing histories. Organizations are now recognizing that a major source of competitive advantage is the firm's unstructured knowledge. All of this textual information needs to be codified with XML (eXtensible Markup Language) and extracted so that predictive data mining tools can be used to generate real value. Given that perhaps 80 percent of all information we collect and store is in text (at least *nonnumeric* data) format and the size of e-commerce, it is natural that text mining and Web mining are major growth areas. Web mining (or *Web-content mining*) is used to understand customer behavior, evaluate a Web site's effectiveness, and quantify the success of a marketing campaign. Text mining is not the same thing as a search engine on the Web. In a search, we are trying to find what others have prepared. With text mining, we want to discover new patterns that may not be obvious or known.

Documents containing unstructured data can contribute to the decision making of BI, but they cannot be used directly in data-driven reports and analyses unless facts discovered in unstructured data are extracted and transformed into structured data that are conducive to reporting and analysis. Tools to accomplish this are **text analytics.** Text analytics transforms unstructured text into structured "text data." Those text data can then be searched, mined, or discovered. Text search, mining, and discovery address two of today's most pressing data management problems: customer and product data management.

All indications are that text analytics, as a means to parse and index unstructured or semistructured data, is growing in importance, as are other BI search technologies. BI search and text analytics are being added to the BI infrastructure to accommodate unstructured data—via text analytics—and related techniques such as search.

CHARACTERISTICS AND BENEFITS OF DATA MINING

Data mining describes knowledge discovery in databases. Data mining is a process that uses statistical, mathematical, artificial intelligence, and machine-learning techniques to extract and identify useful information and subsequent knowledge from large databases, including data warehouses. This information includes patterns usually extracted from large sets of data. These patterns can be rules, affinities, correlations, trends, or prediction models. The following are the major characteristics and objectives of data mining:

- Data are often buried deep within very large databases, which sometimes contain data from several years. In many cases, the data are cleaned and consolidated in a data warehouse.
- Sophisticated new tools, including advanced visualization tools, help to remove the information buried in corporate files or archival public records. Finding it involves massaging and synchronizing these data to get the right results. Cutting-edge data miners are also exploring the usefulness of soft data (unstructured text stored in such places as Lotus Notes databases, text files on the Internet, or an enterprisewide intranet).
- The miner is often an end user, empowered by data drills and other power query tools to ask ad hoc questions and obtain answers quickly with little or no programming skill.
- Striking it rich often involves finding an unexpected result and requires end users to think creatively.
- Data mining tools are readily combined with spreadsheets and other software development tools. Thus, the mined data can be analyzed and processed quickly and easily.
- Because of the large amounts of data and massive search efforts, it is sometimes necessary to use parallel processing or supercomputers to execute data mining.
- The data mining environment is usually a client/server architecture or a Web-based architecture.

POWER USERS OF DATA MINING TOOLS

Business sections that most extensively use data mining are finance, retail, and healthcare. For example, in the financial sector, data mining is used in various tasks by banks, investment funds, hedge funds, and insurance companies as well as sophisticated private investors and traders. Financial data are structured and are often in time series, e.g., stock market prices, commodity prices, utility prices, or currency exchange rates observed over time. Data mining techniques are well-suited to analyze financial time series data to find patterns, detect anomalies and outliers, recognize situations of chance and risk, and predict future demand, prices, and rates.

That's why data mining can support analysts, investors, and traders in their decisions when trading stocks, options, commodities, utilities, or currencies. Data mining is also important in detecting fraudulent behavior, especially in insurance claims and credit card use; to identify buying patterns of customers; to reclaim profitable customers; to identify trading rules from historical data; and to aid in market basket analysis.

ADVANTAGES AND DISADVANTAGES OF DATA MINING TOOLS

Data mining tools are interactive, visual, and understandable, and work directly on the data warehouse of the organization. The simpler tools could be used by frontline workers for immediate and long-term business benefits.

However, some techniques deployed by data mining tools may be far beyond the understanding of the average business analyst or knowledge worker. These tools are designed for expert statisticians involved in the science of predictive modeling. If this advanced level of analysis is reserved for the few, instead of for the masses, the full value of data mining in the organization cannot be realized. For those with average analytical capabilities, data mining is not nearly as effective as it could be.

CAPABILITIES OF DATA MINING

Data mining discovers intelligence from data warehouses that queries and reports cannot discover. For example, convenience stores discovered that beer and baby diapers were very often bought at the same time—and moved those products nearby. Data mining can speed analysis by focusing attention on the most important variables. Dramatic drops in the cost/performance ratio of computer systems have made data mining techniques affordable for most companies.

DATA MINING APPLICATIONS

The following are typical application examples whose intent is to identify a business opportunity in order to create a sustainable competitive advantage.

- **Retailing and sales.** Predicting sales, determining correct inventory levels and distribution schedules among outlets, and loss prevention.
- **Banking.** Forecasting levels of bad loans and fraudulent credit card use, credit card spending by new customers, and which kinds of customers will best respond to and qualify for new loan offers.
- **Manufacturing and production.** Predicting machinery failures; finding key factors that control optimization of manufacturing capacity.
- **Healthcare.** Correlating demographics of patients with critical illnesses; developing better insights on symptoms and their causes and how to provide proper treatments.
- **Broadcasting.** Predicting which programs are best to air during prime time, and how to maximize returns by interjecting advertisements.
- **Marketing.** Classifying customer demographics that can be used to predict which customers will respond to a mailing or Internet banners, or buy a particular product, as well as to predict other consumer behavior.

TEXT MINING AND WEB MINING AND ANALYSIS

Text Mining. Documents are rarely structured, except for forms (e.g., invoices) or templates. Text mining helps organizations to do the following:

1. Find the "hidden" content of documents, including additional useful relationships;
2. Relate documents across previously unnoticed divisions; for example, discover that customers in two different product divisions have the same characteristics;
3. Group documents by common themes; for example, find all of the customers of an insurance company who have similar complaints.

In biomedical research, text analytics and mining have the potential for reducing the time it takes researchers to find relevant documents and to find specific factual content within documents that can help researchers interpret experimental data, clinical record information, and BI data contained in patents. *A Closer Look 12.1* shows how text mining can form the basis for text-based knowledge management and discovery.

Web Mining with Predictive Analysis. Each visitor to a Web site, each search on a search engine, each click on a link, and each transaction on an e-commerce site creates data. Analysis of these data can help us make better use of Web sites, and provide a better relationship and value to visitors of our own Web sites. **Web mining** is the application of data mining techniques to discover actionable and meaningful patterns, profiles, and trends from Web resources. The term Web mining is used to refer to both Web-content mining and Web-usage mining. *Web-content mining* is the process of mining Web sites for information. *Web-usage mining* involves analyzing Web access logs and other information connected to user browsing and access patterns on one or more Web localities.

Web mining is used in the following areas: information filtering (e-mails, magazines, and newspapers); surveillance (of competitors, patents, technological development); mining of Web-access logs for analyzing usage (clickstream analysis); assisted browsing; and services that fight crime on the Internet.

A Closer Look 12.1

Text-based Knowledge Management and Discovery

A variety of technologies are available to support text-based knowledge management and discovery. The functions the technologies perform range from accessing and managing documents (unstructured information) from various sources to delivering analysis results to end user applications.

Managing unstructured text information begins with accessing text information using crawling or federated search methods. Once text is accessed, it needs to be filtered or converted from a variety of coded formats, such as PDF (portable document format), HTML (HyperText Markup Language), or XML (a form of tagging text to give it structure), into a standard form for further processing. The latter includes document parsing to extract text content and meta-data (properties of the document), and storing this information in local data warehouses within an organization as an XML file that can be presented to an end user as a dynamic interactive HTML Web page. Collected text information is typically stored in diverse and heterogeneous data stores, including public and corporate Web sites and internal corporate databases. These basic functions are available in IBM's DB2 Information Integrator or other vendor products in the domain of content and document management.

In e-commerce, Web-content mining is critical. For example, when you search for a certain book on Amazon.com, the site uses mining tools to also provide you with a list of books purchased by the customers who have bought the specific book you searched for—which is an example of cross-selling. Amazon.com has been extremely successful at cross-selling because it knows what to suggest to its customers at the critical point of purchase.

Predictive analytics is a component of Web mining that sifts through data to identify patterns of behavior that suggest, for example, what offers customers might respond to in the future, or which customers you may be in danger of losing. For instance, when sifting through a bank's data warehouse, predictive analytics might *recognize* that customers who cancel an automatic bill payment or automatic deposit and are of a certain age often are relocating and will be moving to another bank within a certain period of time. Predictive analysis appears in many different formats, as illustrated in the following example and in *IT at Work 12.4*.

Example: Recognizing What Customers Want Even Before They Enter a Restaurant. HyperActive Technologies (*HyperActiveTechnologies.com*) developed a system in which cameras mounted on the roof of a fast-food restaurant track vehicles pulling into the parking lot or drive-through. Other cameras track the progress of customers moving through the ordering queue. Using predictive analysis, the system predicts what arriving customers might order (based on queueing theory). A database includes historical car-ordering data, such as "20 percent of cars entering the lot will usually order at least one cheeseburger at lunch time." Based on the camera's real-time input and the database, the system predicts what customers will order 1.5–5 minutes before they actually order. This gives the cooks a chance to prepare the food, so customers' waiting time is minimized. Also, the food does not have a chance to get cold (reheating takes time, expense, and kills the taste of the food).

The *core element* of predictive analytics is the *predictor*, a variable that can be measured for an individual or entity to predict future behavior. For example, a credit card company could consider age, income, credit history, and other demographics as predictors determining an applicant's risk factor.

Review Questions

1. What is text mining? Give three examples of text that would be mined for intelligence purposes.
2. How does text mining differ from search?
3. What is Web mining? Give three examples of Web content that would be mined for intelligence purposes.
4. Describe one advantage and one disadvantage of data mining tools.
5. List three data mining applications for identifying business opportunities.

IT at Work 12.4

Predictive Analysis Helps Save Gas and Protect Green

Traffic congestion across the United States increased nearly 2 percent in 2007 over 2006 and continued to grow throughout 2008, although higher fuel prices and the economy are affecting the rate of growth. The fallout from heavy traffic congestion hits Americans hard on several different levels. With many drivers paying more than $4 a gallon at the pump, and roads clogged with traffic congestion averaging 60 hours a week across the nation's 100 worst bottlenecks, traffic continues to have a major impact on personal lives, businesses, and the economy. Predictive analysis and numerous technologies discussed in this chapter are being deployed by INRIX (*inrix.com*) to help save gas, frustration, and time. INRIX is the leading provider of traffic information.

The *INRIX National Traffic Scorecard* measures U.S. traffic congestion problem by evaluating real-time traffic on almost every major metropolitan roadway. INRIX's Smart Dust Network collects data from one million anonymous, GPS-equipped commercial vehicles that report their speed and location continually. INRIX then processes and blends other relevant traffic-related data such as road sensors, toll tags, traffic incident data, and other resources to provide the most comprehensive and accurate traffic information available.

INRIX takes traffic information to a new level, helping drivers make better decisions through real-time, historical, and predictive traffic data generated from a wide range of sources. INRIX's exclusive modeling and prediction technologies offer the highest accuracy and broadest coverage on the market today. Services can give customers the guidance they want for impor-

tant practical driving questions such as:

- When will traffic start to back up at the I-5/I-90 interchange?
- What will traffic be like at 6:00 tonight? How long will it take me to get home?
- How long will it take for the congestion on the bridge to clear up?
- What time should I leave for work in the morning to avoid rush-hour traffic?
- How long will it take me to get to the airport tomorrow morning?
- When I fly into JFK airport in two weeks, how long will it take me to get to my hotel in Manhattan?

As of July 2008, drivers along the I-95 corridor on the east coast began benefitting from such information. In partnership with the sixteen states representing the *I-95 Corridor Coalition* along the eastern seaboard, INRIX identifies where traffic is at its worst, enabling drivers to have access to real-time information on traffic flows, crashes, and travel times to help them anticipate and avoid delays. The systems' architecture is shown in the attached figure.

Sources: Compiled from INRIX.com (2008) and PRNewswire (2008).

For Further Exploration: What factors have increased demand for this information service? Which individuals may use this service? What are the immediate and long-term benefits to transportation (trucking) companies and emergency services? What are the green benefits? What are three personal benefits to drivers?

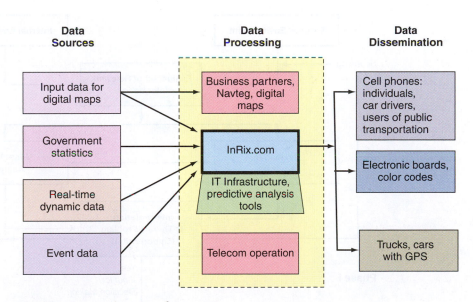

INRIX system architecture for one city.

12.4 Managers and Decision-Making Processes

To appreciate how and why ISs were designed to support managers, you need to understand what managers do. We can divide managers' roles into three categories that are still relevant today (Mintzberg, 1973):

1. *Interpersonal roles*: leader, figurehead, liaison. Today, the role of coach would be added here.

2. *Informational role*: monitor, disseminator, spokesperson.

3. *Decisional role*: entrepreneur, problem solver, resource allocator, and negotiator.

Early ISs mainly supported informational roles, in part, because that was the easiest role to support. With the introduction of ISs in organizations, managers would receive an avalanche of data about issues and problems, which led to information overload. Managers lacked ISs that could adequately support doing something about those issues and problems. The situation created was what we call the *in-box problem*, which is a metaphor for a growing in-box of problems that managers find out about, but that remained in the in-box because they lacked tools for dealing with the problems and communicating results. Many new ITs emerge or are enhanced to solve problems of existing ones. You can see that trend in BI as new features are added.

ISs have grown to support all managerial roles. In this section, we are mainly interested in IT that supports decisional roles. We divide the manager's work, as it relates to decisional roles, into two phases. Phase I is the identification of problems and/or opportunities. Phase II is the decision of what to do about them. Figure 12.8 provides a flowchart of this process and the flow of information in it.

Decision Making and Problem Solving. A *decision* refers to a choice made between two or more alternatives. Two broad decision categories are *problem solving* and *opportunity exploiting*. Some managers try to avoid making decisions for fear of making a mistake.

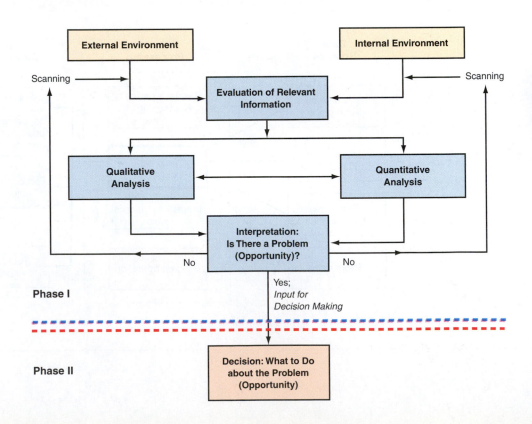

Figure 12.8 Manager's decision role.

In a study conducted by the Boston-based Harbridge House, about 6,500 managers from 100 companies, including many large, blue-chip corporations, were asked to rate the importance of 10 practices performed by managers. They also were asked to estimate how well managers performed these practices. The survey ranked "making clear-cut decisions when needed" as the most important, followed by "getting to the heart of the problems rather than dealing with less important issues." Most of the remaining eight practices were related directly or indirectly to decision making. Going further, only 10 percent thought management performed "very well" on any given practice. The primary reason the managers offered for this response was the difficult decision-making environment. The trial-and-error method, or guessing (also called intution) method, which might have been an acceptable approach in the past, is too expensive and risky today.

Therefore, managers need to learn how to use IT tools and techniques, many of which involve quantitative analysis or models. IT decision supports are described in the rest of this chapter.

DECISION SUPPORT TOOLS

Our discussion of IT decision support deals with three basic questions: (1) Why do managers need IT support in making decisions? (2) To what extent can a manager's job be automated? (3) What IT tools are available to support managers?

Why Managers Need IT Support. Smart decisions require valid and relevant information. Information is needed for each phase and activity in the decision-making process.

Making decisions while processing information manually is growing increasingly difficult due to the following trends:

- There are too many alternatives, scenarios, and risks to consider.
- Many decisions must be made under time pressure.
- Due to increased fluctuations and uncertainty in the decision environment, it is frequently necessary to conduct a sophisticated analysis.
- Decision makers can be in different locations as can the information. Bringing them all together quickly and inexpensively may be a difficult task.
- Decision making frequently requires an organization to conduct a forecast of prices, market share, and so on. Reliable forecasting requires analytical and statistical tools.

A DSS can (1) examine numerous alternatives very quickly, (2) support forecasting, (3) provide a systematic risk analysis, (4) be integrated with communication systems and databases, and (5) support group work. *How* all this is accomplished will be shown later.

Can the Manager's Job Be Fully Automated? The generic decision-making process involves specific tasks (such as forecasting consequences and evaluating alternatives). This process can be fairly lengthy, which is bothersome for a busy manager. Automation of certain tasks can save time, increase consistency, and enable better decisions to be made. Thus, the more tasks we can automate in the process, the better. A logical question that follows is this: Is it possible to completely automate the manager's job?

In general, it has been found that the job of middle managers is the most likely job to be automated. Mid-level managers make fairly routine decisions, and these can be fully automated. Managers at lower levels do not spend much time on decision making. Instead, they supervise, train, and motivate nonmanagers. Some of their routine decisions, such as scheduling, can be automated; other decisions that involve behavioral aspects cannot. But, even if we completely automate their decisional role, we cannot automate their jobs. *Note*: The Web also provides an opportunity to automate certain tasks done by *frontline* employees. The job of top managers is the least routine and therefore the most difficult to automate.

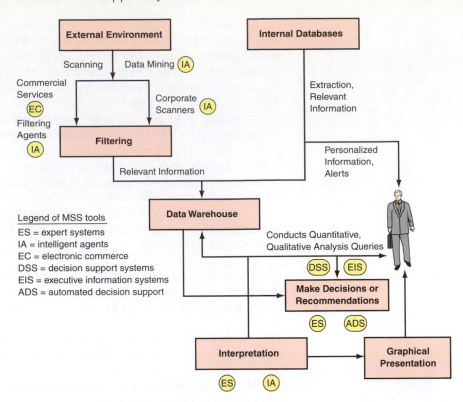

Figure 12.9 IT support for decision making.

What ITs Are Available to Support Managers? In addition to discovery, communication, and collaboration tools that provide *indirect support* to decision making, several other ITs have been successfully used to support managers. The Web can facilitate them all. The first of these technologies is *decision support systems*, which have been in use since the mid-1970s. DSSs provide support primarily to analytical, quantitative types of decisions. Second, *executive (enterprise) support systems* represent a technology developed initially in the mid-1980s, mainly to support the informational roles of executives. This technology is the predecessor of BI. A third technology, *group decision support systems (GDSS)*, supports managers and staff working in groups remotely or closely. (We discuss GDSS in detail in Section 12.5.) A fourth technology is *intelligent systems*. These four technologies and their variants can be used independently, or they can be combined, with each one providing a different capability. They are frequently related to data warehousing.

A simplified model of management support systems (MSS) is shown in Figure 12.9. As the figure shows, managers need to find, filter, and interpret information to identify potential problems or opportunities and then decide what to do about them. The model shows the support of the various MSS tools (in yellow circles) as well as the role of a data warehouse.

Several other personal productivity tools support managers and have become indispensable. Common examples are PDAs, Blackberrys, and smart phones with Internet connectivity and e-mail capabilities.

THE PROCESS OF IT-SUPPORTED DECISION MAKING

Decision makers go through four fairly systematic phases: *intelligence, design, choice*, and *implementation*, as diagrammed in Figure 12.10. Note that there is a continuous flow of information from intelligence to design to choice (bold lines), but at any time there may be a return to a prior phase (broken lines).

The decision-making process starts with the *intelligence phase*, in which managers examine a situation, then identify and define the problem. In the *design phase*, decision makers construct a model that represents and simplifies the problem or opportunity. This is done by making assumptions and expressing the relationships among all variables. The model is then validated, and decision makers set criteria

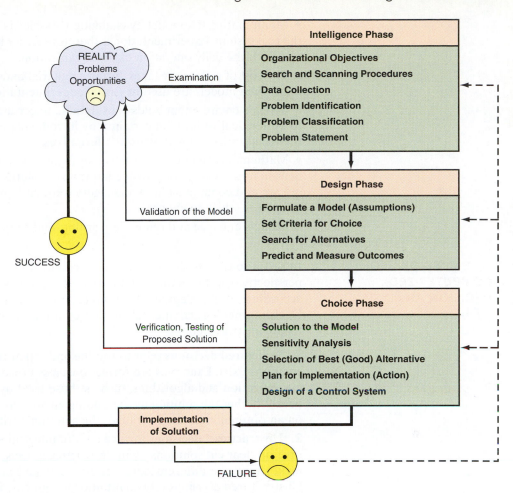

Figure 12.10 Phases in the decision-making process.

for the evaluation of alternative potential solutions that are identified. The process is repeated for each subdecision in complex situations. The output of each subdecision is an input for the main decision. The *choice phase* involves selecting a solution, which is tested "on paper." Once this proposed solution seems to be feasible, we are ready for the last phase—implementation. Successful *implementation* results in resolving the original problem or opportunity. Failure leads to a return to the previous phases. A DSS attempts to automate several tasks in this process, in which modeling is the core.

Decision Modeling and Models. A **decision model** is a *simplified representation*, or abstraction of reality. Simplicity is helpful because a lot of complexity may be irrelevant to a specific problem. One simplification method is making assumptions, such as assuming that growth in customer demand in the next quarters will be the same as the current quarter. The risk when using assumptions is when they are wrong, then the entire foundation for the analysis is flawed. For example, in July 2008, General Motors' (GM) sales of SUVs, minivans, and trucks had plunged due to very high gas prices that consumers knew were not going to drop. Since GM selects its models three years in advance, in 2005, GM's managers had assumed that the demand for large vehicles would remain at 2005 levels. That highly inaccurate assumption had a devastating influence on the company's sales and profits.

With modeling, one can perform virtual experiments and an analysis on a model of reality, rather than on reality itself. The benefits of modeling in decision making are as follows:

• The cost of virtual experimentation is much lower than the cost of experimentation conducted with a real system.

• Models allow for the simulated compression of time. Years of operation can be simulated in seconds of computer time.

• Manipulating the model by changing variables is much easier than manipulating the real system. Experimentation is therefore easier to conduct, and it does not interfere with the daily operation of the organization.

• The cost of making mistakes during a real trial-and-error experiment is much lower than when models are used in virtual experimentation.

• Today's environment holds considerable uncertainty. Modeling allows a manager to better deal with the uncertainty by introducing many "what-ifs" and calculating the risks associated with various alternatives.

• Mathematical models allow the analysis and comparison of a very large, sometimes near-infinite number of possible alternative solutions. With today's advanced technology and communications, managers frequently have a large number of alternatives from which to choose.

• Models enhance and reinforce learning, and support training.

A FRAMEWORK FOR COMPUTERIZED DECISION ANALYSIS

In order to discuss the decision support and what DSS tools can do, we provide a perspective on the nature of the decision process. Decisions can be categorized according to the degree of structure involved in the decision-making activity. Decision-making activities fall along a continuum ranging from highly structured to highly unstructured.

1. Structured decisions refer to routine and repetitive problems for which standard solutions exist. Examples are formal business procedures, cost minimization, profit maximization and algorithms, such as those used by eHarmony to match its members. Whether the solution means finding an appropriate inventory level or deciding on an optimal investment strategy, the solution's criteria are clearly defined.

2. Unstructured decisions involve a lot of uncertainty for which there are no definitive or clear-cut solutions. With unstructured decisions, for example, each decision maker may use different data, assumptions, and processes to reach a conclusion. Unstructured decisions rely on intuition, judgment, and experience. Typical unstructured problems include planning new services to be offered, hiring an executive, predicting markets, or choosing a set of research and development projects for next year.

3. Semistructured decisions fall between the polar positions. Most of what are considered to be true decision support systems are focused on semistructured decisions. Semistructured problems, in which only some of the phases are structured, require a combination of standard solution procedures and individual judgment. Examples of semistructured problems are trading bonds, setting marketing budgets for consumer products, and performing capital acquisition analysis. Here, a DSS is most suitable. It can improve the quality of the information on which the decision is based, and consequently the quality of the decision, by providing not only a single solution but also a range of what-if scenarios.

IT Support for Structured Decisions. Structured and some semistructured decisions, especially of the operational and managerial control type, have been supported by computers since the 1950s. Decisions of this type are made in all functional areas, especially in finance, marketing, and operations management.

Problems that are encountered fairly often have a high level of structure. It is therefore possible to abstract, analyze, and classify them into standard classes. For example, a "make-or-buy" decision belongs to this category. Other examples are capital budgeting (e.g., replacement of equipment), allocation of resources, distribution of merchandise, and some inventory control decisions. For each standard class, a prescribed solution was developed through the use of mathematical formulas. This approach is called *management science* or *operations research*, and it is also executed with the aid of computers.

Management Science. The *management science* approach takes the view that managers can follow a fairly systematic process for solving problems. Therefore, it is possible to use a scientific approach to managerial decision making. Management science frequently attempts to find the best possible solution, an approach known as **optimization.**

12.5 Decision Support Systems

DSS CONCEPTS

A **decision support system (DSS)** combines models and data to solve semistructured and some unstructured problems with intensive user involvement. But the term DSS, like the terms MIS and MSS, means different things to different people. DSSs can be viewed as an *approach* or a *philosophy* rather than a precise methodology. However, a DSS does have certain recognized characteristics, which we will present later. First, let us look at a classic case of a successfully implemented DSS, which though it occurred long ago is a typical scenario, as shown in *IT at Work 12.5*.

The case demonstrates some of the major characteristics of a DSS. The risk analysis performed first was based on the decision maker's initial definition of the situation, using a management science approach. Then, the executive vice president, using his experience, judgment, and intuition, felt that the model should be modified. The initial model, although mathematically correct, was incomplete. With a regular simulation system, a modification of the computer program would have taken a long time, but the DSS provided a very quick analysis. Furthermore, the DSS was flexible and responsive enough to allow managerial intuition and judgment to be incorporated into the analysis.

Many companies are turning to DSSs to improve decision making. Reasons cited by managers for DSS use include the following:

IT at Work 12.5

Using a DSS to Determine Risk

FIN

An oil and minerals corporation in Houston, Texas, was evaluating a proposed joint venture with a petrochemical company to develop a chemical plant. Houston's executive vice president (EVP) responsible for the decision wanted analysis of the risks involved in areas of supplies, demand, and prices. Bob Sampson, manager of planning and administration, and his staff built a model-based DSS in a few days using specialized planning language. The results strongly suggested that the project should be accepted.

Then came the confidence test. Although the EVP accepted the validity and value of the results, he was worried about the potential downside risk of the project, the chance of a catastrophic outcome. The EVP said something like this to Sampson: "I realize the amount of work you have already done, and I am 99 percent confident of it. But I would like to see this in a different light.

I know we are short of time and we have to get back to our partners with our yes or no decision."

Sampson replied that the EVP could have the risk analysis in less than one hour. As Sampson explained, "Within 20 minutes, there in the executive boardroom, we were reviewing the results of his *what-if* questions that focused on catastrophic conditions. Those results led to the eventual dismissal of the project, which otherwise would probably have been accepted."

Source: Information provided to author by Comshare Corporation (now a subsidiary of Geac Computer Corp., a Goldengate Capital Company).

For Further Exploration: What were the benefits of the DSS? Why was the initial decision reversed? What assumption was factored into the later decision?

- New and accurate information was needed.
- Information was needed fast.
- Tracking the company's numerous business operations was increasingly difficult.
- The company was operating in an unstable economy.
- The company faced increasing foreign and domestic competition.
- The company's existing computer system did not properly support the objectives of increasing efficiency, profitability, and entry into profitable markets.
- The IS department was unable to address the diversity of the company's needs or management's ad hoc inquiries.

Another reason for the development of DSS was the *end user computing movement*. With the exception of large-scale DSSs, end users can build systems themselves using DSS software such as Excel. Before DSS software was developed, they had to be developed using programming languages.

CHARACTERISTICS AND CAPABILITIES OF DSSs

Most DSSs have at least some of the attributes shown in Table 12.6. DSSs also employ mathematical models and have a related, special capability, known as sensitivity analysis.

Sensitivity Analysis: *What-If* and Goal Seeking. **Sensitivity analysis** is the study of the impact that changes in one or more parts of a model have on other parts or the outcome. Usually, we check the impact that changes in input (or independent) variables have on dependent variables or outcomes. For example, *quantity demanded* is a dependent variable, whereas *price, advertising, disposable income*, and *competitor's price* are four examples of the independent variables in the classic economic model. The dependent variable changes in response to changes in the independent variables. (An easy way to view the relationship between dependent and independent variables is: the number of umbrellas sold [dependent variable] is affected by the amount of rainfall. Of course, the reverse is not true.) Each of the independent variables would be adjusted in various ways and combinations to determine the sensitivity of *quantity demanded* to those adjustments.

Sensitivity analysis is extremely valuable in DSSs because it makes the system flexible and adaptable to changing conditions and to the varying requirements of different decision-making situations. It allows users to enter their own data, including the pessimistic data (worst-case scenario), and to view how systems will behave under varying circumstances. It provides better understanding of the model and the prob-

TABLE 12.6	Capabilities of a DSS

A DSS provides support for decision makers at all management levels, whether individuals or groups, mainly in semistructured and unstructured situations, by bringing together human judgment and objective information.

A DSS supports several interdependent and/or sequential decisions.

A DSS supports all phases of the decision-making process—intelligence, design, choice, and implementation—as well as a variety of decision-making processes and styles.

A DSS is adaptable by the user over time to deal with changing conditions.

A DSS is easy to construct and use in many cases.

A DSS promotes learning, which leads to new demands and refinement of the current application, which leads to additional learning, and so forth.

A DSS usually utilizes quantitative models (standard and/or custom made).

Advanced DSSs are equipped with a knowledge management component that allows the efficient and effective solution of very complex problems.

A DSS can be disseminated for use via the Web.

A DSS allows the easy execution of *sensitivity analyses*.

lem it purports to describe. It may increase the users' confidence in the model, especially when the model is not very sensitive to changes. A *sensitive model* means that small changes in conditions (variables) suggest a different solution. In a *nonsensitive model*, changes in conditions do not significantly change the recommended solution. Two popular types of sensitivity analyses are *what-if* and *goal seeking,* as described in *Online Brief 12.2.*

STRUCTURE AND COMPONENTS OF DSS

Basic components of a DSS are a database, model base, user interface, and the users. An additional component is a knowledge base.

Database. A DSS database system, like any database, contains data from multiple sources. Some DSSs do not have a separate database; data are entered into the DSS model as needed (e.g., as soon as they are collected by sensors).

Model Base. A model base contains completed models and sets of rules, which are the building blocks necessary to develop DSS applications. Types of models include financial, statistical, management science, or economic. Model-building software, such as Excel, has built-in mathematical and statistical functions. These models provide the system's analytical capabilities.

User Interface. The *user interface* covers all aspects of the communications between a user and the DSS. A well-designed user interface can greatly improve the productivity of the user and reduce errors.

Users. A DSS is a tool for the user, the decision maker. The user is considered to be a part of the highly interactive DSS system. A DSS has two broad classes of users: managers and staff specialists (such as financial analysts, production planners, and market researchers).

Knowledge Base. Many unstructured and semistructured problems are so complex that they require expertise for their solutions. Such expertise can be provided by a knowledge-based system, such as an expert system. Therefore, the more advanced DSSs are equipped with a component called a *knowledge base.* A knowledge base provides the expertise to solve some part of the problem. For example, a knowledge base can estimate the cost of a massive construction job based on dimensions, materials, labor costs, weather delays, and numerous other cost factors. It is a complex process that requires models, a database, and judgment. Knowledge-based subsystems are the key component in automated decision support (ADS), covered in Section 12.6.

HOW A DSS WORKS

The DSS components (see Figure 12.11) are all software, they run on standard hardware, and they can be facilitated by additional software (such as multimedia). Tools such as Excel include some of the components and therefore can be used for DSS construction by end users.

The figure also illustrates how the DSS works. DSS users get their data from the data store. When a user has a problem, it is evaluated by the processes described in Figures 12.9 and 12.10. A DSS system is then constructed. Data are entered from the sources on the left side and the models from the right side in Figure 12.11. Knowledge can be also tapped from the corporate knowledge base. As more problems are solved, more knowledge is accumulated in the organizational knowledge base.

DSS APPLICATIONS

A large number of DSS applications can be found in almost any industry, including manufacturing and services, as shown in the following examples.

Example 1: Wells Fargo Targets Customers. Wells Fargo (*wellsfargo.com*) has become so good at predicting consumer behavior that it practically knows what customers want before they do. The bank developed a DSS in-house that collects data on every transaction—phone, ATM, bank branch, and online—and combines those

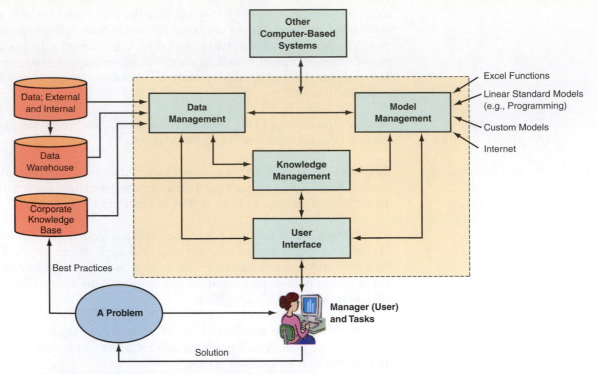

Figure 12.11 Conceptual model of DSS and its components.

FIN

data with personal data from the customer. The Wells Fargo DSS program then analyzes the data and models the customer's behavior to automatically come up with prospective offers, such as a home equity loan, just at the right time for the customer.

FIN

Example 2: Schwab Targets the Rich. Back in 2000, Charles Schwab (*schwab.com*) changed its advertising strategy to target high net worth investors. The new strategy meant transforming itself from a discount brokerage into a full-service investment firm. To avoid the $20-million-per-year cost of hiring analysts, it made a $20 million investment in a DSS. Schwab Equity Ratings, an online intelligent DSS, offers recommendations for buying and selling thousands of stocks. It automatically sends e-mail alerts to customers and analysts. Schwab says the system picks stocks as efficiently as its human counterparts. In addition, the system does away with potential employee conflicts of interest.

Example 3: Lowering Costs in HealthCare. For Owens & Minor (*owens-minor.com*), one of the largest suppliers for the healthcare industry, success means driving down the price of thousands of hospital supplies. The company uses its DSS to help customers hunt for bargains among hundreds of competing medical suppliers. The DSS pinpoints lower pricing on similar items, helping customers take advantage of discounts already negotiated. Hospitals keep better tabs on their bills and cut costs an average of 2 to 3 percent. For Owens & Minor, the DSS attracts new customers, and when existing customers find lower prices, they order more.

SVR   **ACC**

These examples exhibit the diversity of decisions that DSSs can support. In addition, many examples can be found at *sas.com* or *microtrategy.com*, where hundreds of applications and success stories are listed by industry.

The DSS methodology just described was designed initially to support individual decision makers. However, most important organizational decisions are made by groups, such as an executive committee. Next we see how IT can support such situations.

SPECIAL TOOLS FOR DECISION SUPPORT

Over the last four decades, several specialized tools were developed for decision support. One of the most popular tools is *simulation*, which is described in *Online Brief 12.3*. Also, it is possible to improve decision support results (such as those generated by spreadsheets) by using visualization.

**GROUP DECISION
SUPPORT SYSTEMS**

Decision making is frequently a shared process. For example, meetings among groups of managers from different areas are an essential element for reaching consensus. The group may be involved in making a decision or in a decision-related task, such as creating a short list of acceptable alternatives or deciding on criteria for accepting an alternative. When a decision-making group is supported electronically, the support is referred to as *group decision support*. Two types of groups are considered: a same-room group whose members are in one place (e.g., a decision room), and a virtual group (or team), whose members are in different locations.

A **group decision support system (GDSS)** is an interactive computer-based system that facilitates the solution of semistructured and unstructured problems when made by a group of decision makers by concentrating on the *process* and procedures during meetings. The objective of a GDSS is to support the decision *process*. Important characteristics of a GDSS are shown in *Online Brief 12.4*. These characteristics can negate some of the dysfunctions of group processes described in Chapter 4, Table 4.7. The first generation of GDSSs was designed to support face-to-face meetings in a decision room.

**SOME APPLICATIONS
OF GDSSs**

An increasing number of companies are using GDSSs, especially when virtual groups are involved. One example is the Internal Revenue Service, which used a decision room to implement its quality-improvement programs based on the participation of a number of its quality teams. The GDSS was helpful in identifying problems, generating and evaluating ideas, and developing and implementing solutions. Another example is the European automobile industry, which used a decision room to examine the competitive automotive business environment and make ten-year forecasts, needed for strategic planning.

12.6 Automated Decision Support (ADS)

Automated decision support (ADS) systems are rule-based systems that automatically provide solutions to repetitive managerial problems. ADSs are closely related to BI and business analytics in the following ways:

- Business analytic models may be used to create and/or operate the business rules.
- Business rules can be used to trigger the automatic decisions in BI applications. This is true in performance monitoring and analysis systems in which the results of what is monitored are analyzed and some action is triggered by the ADS.

Before we examine how ADSs are implemented, let's look at the concept of *business rules*.

BUSINESS RULES

Automating the decision-making process is usually achieved by capturing a manager's expertise in a set of *business rules* that are embedded in a rule-driven workflow (or other action-oriented) engine (business rules had been shown in Figure 2.2). These business rules can be part of expert systems or other intelligent systems. As an analysis is called for (e.g., by a performance monitoring system), a signal is passed to the rule engine for evaluation against the associated business rules. These rules determine what action needs to be taken, based on the results of the evaluation. An example is provided in *Online Minicase 12.1: Cigna Uses Business Rules to Support Treatment Request Approval*.

**CHARACTERISTICS AND
BENEFITS OF ADSs**

ADSs are most suitable for repetitive decisions that are made frequently, or responses that are needed rapidly using online information. Automated support requires that the decision criteria and business rules be well-defined or so structured that the problem's solution is well understood. Analysis of a loan application and approval of the amount of the loan and interest rate are an example of a well-defined problem with a structured solution.

Using an ADS system adds skill and precision to decision making because of the following capabilities:

- Rapidly builds business rules to automate or guide decision makers, and deploys them into almost any operating environment (as was shown in *Online Minicase 12.1*)
- Injects predictive analytics into rule-based applications, increasing their power and value
- Combines business rules, predictive models, and optimization strategies flexibly into enterprise applications

ADS APPLICATIONS

Examples of successful ADSs in a variety of industries are:

- **Product or service customization.** Purchasers can customize a product or service such as a PC or cell phone plan. The ADS then *configures* the most appropriate final product (service) and its cost (considering profitability to the manufacturer). Dell Computer is using this approach.
- **Yield or price optimization.** Airlines use automated decision-making applications to set prices based on seat availability and hour or day of purchase, also known as *revenue management* or *yield management*. A method called *price optimization* is used to maximize profitability in real estate rentals.
- **Routing or segmentation decisions.** Companies that use automated filters for sorting cases and transactions have improved productivity. For example, the insurance industry uses filtering for handling claims and prioritizing them. Hospitals use routing to manage the variety and volume of emergency room patients.
- **Corporate and regulatory compliance and fraud detection.** Routine policy decisions are time-consuming, technical, and structured. For example, in the home mortgage industry, lenders must categorize and process loans that conform to government regulations and requirements of the lenders. Automated screening is used to identify symptoms of fraud or identity theft.
- **Dynamic forecasting and SCM.** With automated demand forecasting, manufacturers schedule production levels to meet forecasted customer demand. Simulation and optimization of supply chain flows reduce excess inventory and stockouts.
- **Operational control.** Some automated decision systems are programmed to sense changes in the physical environment and respond based on rules or algorithms (e.g., temperatures affecting power supply needs; controlling traffic lights at intersections, based on real-time traffic volume recorded by cameras).
- **Customer selection, loyalty, and service.** Identify customers with the greatest profit potential; increase likelihood that they will want the product or service offered; retain their loyalty. (Examples: Harrah's, Capital One, Barclays.)
- **Human capital.** Select the best employees for particular tasks or jobs, at particular compensation levels. (Examples: major league sports.)

ADS FOR FRONTLINE EMPLOYEES

Decisions at all levels in the organization contribute to the success of a business. But decisions that maximize a sales opportunity or minimize the cost of customer service requests are made on the frontlines—that is, by those who interact with customers and other business partners on a daily basis. When there is an order exception, an up-selling opportunity, resolving a customer complaint, or a contract that hangs on a decision, workers on the frontline must be able to make smart decisions on the spot while interacting with customers, but according to company policy.

Review Questions

1. Describe an automated decision support (ADS) system.
2. What are business rules? What role do they play in automating the decision-making process?
3. What types of decisions are best suited for ADSs? Why?
4. Explain two examples of ADS applications.

12.7 Managerial Issues

1. **Why BI projects fail.** Organizations must understand and address many critical challenges for achieving BI success. Several reasons why BI projects fail are:

   a. Failure to recognize BI projects as enterprise-wide business initiatives, and that they differ from typical standalone solutions

   b. Lack of business sponsors with the ability to insure funding

   c. Lack of cooperation by business representatives from the functional areas

   d. Lack of qualified and available staff

   e. No appreciation of the negative impact of "dirty data" on business profitability

   f. Too much reliance on vendors

2. **System development and the need for integration.** Developing an effective BI application is complex. For this reason, most BI vendors offer highly integrated collections of applications, including connection to ERP and CRM. Notable are Oracle, BusinessObjects, MircroStrategy, IBM, and Microsoft. Most BI vendors provide for application integration, usually Web-enabled (see *businessobjects.com*).

3. **Cost–benefit issues and justification.** Some BI solutions discussed in this chapter are very expensive and are justifiable only in large corporations. Smaller organizations can make the solutions cost effective if they leverage existing databases rather than create new ones. A careful cost–benefit analysis must be undertaken before any commitment to BI is made.

4. **Legal issues and privacy.** Data mining may suggest that a company send electronic or printed catalogs or promotions to only one age group or one gender. A man sued Victoria's Secret Corp. because his female neighbor received a mail order catalog with deeply discounted items and he received only the regular catalog (the discount was actually given for volume purchasing). Settling discrimination charges can be very expensive. Conducting data mining may result in the invasion of individual privacy. What will companies do to protect individuals? What can individuals do to protect their privacy?

5. **BI and BPM today and tomorrow.** The quality and timeliness of business information for an organization is not the choice between profit and loss—it may be a question of survival. No enterprise can deny the inevitable benefits of BI and BPM. Recent industry analyst reports show that in the coming years, millions of people will use BPM dashboards and BI analytics every day. Enterprises are getting more value from BI by extending information to many types of employees, maximizing the use of existing data assets. Visualization tools including dashboards are used by producers, retailers, government, and special agencies. Industry-specific analytical tools will flood the market to support analysis and informed decision making from top level to user level. BI takes advantage of existing IT technologies to help companies leverage their IT investments and use their legacy and real-time data.

6. **Cost justification; intangible benefits.** While enterprise systems provide tangible benefits, it is difficult to quantify their intangible benefits. In a down-turned economy with high energy costs, mortgage crises, and political unrest, IT investments must be economically justified.

7. **Documenting and securing support systems.** Many employees develop their own DSSs to increase their productivity and the quality of their work. It is advisable to have an inventory of these DSSs and make certain that appropriate documentation and security measures exist, so that if the employee is away or leaves the organization, the productivity tool remains. Taking appropriate security measures is a must. End users who build a DSS are not professional systems builders. For this reason, there could be problems with data integrity and the security of the systems developed.

8. Specialized ready-made decision support. Initially, DSSs were custom-built either by the end user using Excel, or by IT staff and/or vendors with special tools. Single-user DSSs are still built by the actual user. Vendors offer customizable DSSs in specialized areas such as financial services, banking, hospitals, or profitability measurements.

9. Ethical issues. BI and predictive analytics can lead to serious ethical issues such as privacy and accountability. In addition, mistakes can cause harm to others as well as the company. For example, a company developed a DSS to help people compute the financial implications of early retirement. However, the DSS developer did not include the tax implications, which resulted in incorrect retirement decisions.

ETHICS

Another important ethical issue is human judgment, which is frequently used in DSSs. Human judgment is subjective or corrupt, and therefore, it may lead to unethical decision making. Companies should provide an ethical code for DSS builders. Also, the possibility of automating managers' jobs may lead to massive layoffs.

There are ethical issues related to the implementation of expert systems and other intelligent systems. The actions performed by an expert system can be unethical, or even illegal. For example, the expert system may advise you to do something that will hurt someone or will invade the privacy of certain individuals. An example is the behavior of robots, and the possibility that the robots will not behave the way that they were programmed to. There have been many industrial accidents caused by robots that resulted in injuries and even deaths. The issue is, Should an organization employ productivity-saving devices that are not 100 percent safe?

Another ethical issue is the use of knowledge extracted from people. The issue here is, Should a company compensate an employee when knowledge that he or she contributed is used by others? This issue is related to the motivation issue. It is also related to privacy. Should people be informed as to who contributed certain knowledge?

A final ethical issue that needs to be addressed is that of dehumanization and the feeling that a machine can be "smarter" than some people. People may have different attitudes toward smart machines, which may be reflected in the manner in which they will work together.

10. DSS failures. There have been many cases of failures of all types of decision support systems. There are multiple reasons for such failures, ranging from human factors to software glitches. Here are two examples:

a. The ill-fated Challenger Shuttle mission failure was partially attributed to a flawed GDSS (see *cs.toronto.edu/~sme/papers/1993/csrp227.pdf*). NASA used a mismanaged GDSS session in which anonymity was not allowed and other procedures were violated.

b. In an international congress on airports, failures in Denver, Hong Kong, and Malaysia airports were analyzed. Several DSS applications did not work as intended for reasons such as poor planning and inappropriate models.

How *IT* Benefits You

For the Accounting Major

The accounting function is concerned with keeping track of the transactions and internal controls. Data warehouses and data mining enable accountants to perform their jobs more effectively and detect material weaknesses in violation of Sarbanes-Oxley and other government regulations. Intelligent systems are used extensively in auditing to uncover fraud and irregularities. Accounting personnel also use intelligent agents for several mundane tasks such as managing accounts and monitoring employees' Internet use.

For the Finance Major

Financial managers make extensive use of computerized databases that are external to the organization, such as CompuStat of Dow Jones, to obtain financial data on organizations in their industry. They can use these data in BPM to determine if their organization meets industry benchmarks in return on investment, cash management, and other financial ratios. A prime finance task is to determine pricing strategies with marketing. Data mining techniques are effective in finance, particularly for the automated discovery of relationships in investment and portfolio management. Innovative DSS applications exist for activities such as investment decisions, refinancing bonds, assessing debt risks, analyzing financial health, predicting business failures, forecasting financial trends, and investing in global markets.

For the Human Resources Management Major

Enterprises keep extensive data on employees, including gender, age, race, current and past job descriptions, and performance evaluations. Human resources (HR) personnel access these data to provide reports to government agencies regarding compliance with federal equal opportunity guidelines. HR managers also use these data to evaluate hiring practices, evaluate salary structures, and manage any discrimination grievances or lawsuits brought against the firm. HR people need to analyze vast amounts of data for building employee relationship management. Expert systems are used in evaluating candidates (tests, interviews). Intelligent systems are used to facilitate training and support self-service of fringe benefits.

For the IS Major

Installing BI systems is usually done by vendors collaborating with the IS department, which operates the data warehouse. IS personnel—and users as well—can now generate ad-hoc reports with query tools much more quickly than was possible using old mainframe systems. The IS function provides the data and models that managers use in their DSSs. Knowledge engineers are often IS employees, and they have the difficult task of interacting with subject-area experts to develop expert systems.

For the Marketing Major

Marketing personnel need to access data about customers and the organization's marketing transactions. Analytical models have been used in many marketing and sales applications, ranging from allocating advertising budgets to evaluating alternative routings of salespeople. New marketing approaches such as targeted marketing and database marketing are heavily dependent on IT analytical support in general and on intelligent systems in particular. Intelligent systems are particularly useful in mining customer databases and predicting customer behavior. ADSs and business rules deal with many marketing decisions ranging from appropriate pricing to sales force optimization.

For the Production/Operations Management Major

The POM people are responsible for fulfilling orders generated by marketing effectively and efficiently. They need access to enterprise data to determine optimum inventory levels for raw materials and parts in a production process. Firms also keep quality data that inform them not only about the quality of finished products but also about quality issues with incoming raw materials, production irregularities, shopping, and logistics, and after-sale use and maintenance of the product. POM controls many segments of the supply chain, and BI reports, queries, and analyses are essential for managing the supply chain.

POM decisions of scheduling, production planning, inventory control, and routing have been supported by computerized decision models for over 50 years. Also, intelligent systems and ADSs are being used more as their price declines and functionality increases. For example, intelligent systems were developed in the POM field for tasks ranging from diagnosis of machine failures and prescription of repairs to complex production scheduling and inventory control.

Key Terms

Chapter Highlights

❶ Business intelligence is driven by the need to get accurate and timely information in an easy way, and to analyze it, sometimes in minutes, possibly by the end users.

❶ BPM is an umbrella term covering methodologies, metrics, processes, and systems used to drive performance of the enterprise. It encompasses a closed-loop set of processes such as strategize, plan, monitor, analyze, and act (adjust).

❷ The major components of BI are data warehouse and/or marts, predictive analytics, data mining, data visualization software, and a business performance management system.

❷ Predictive analysis uses different algorithms to forecast results and relationships among variables as well as to identify data patterns. Data mining is one of the tools.

❷ Scorecards and dashboards are a common component of most, if not all, performance management systems, performance measurement systems, and BPM suites.

❷ The fundamental challenge of dashboard design is to display all of the required information on a single screen, clearly and without distraction, in a manner that can be assimilated quickly.

❸ Managerial decision making is synonymous with management.

❸ Decision making involves four major phases: intelligence, design, choice, and implementation; they can be modeled as such.

❹ Models allow fast and inexpensive virtual experimentations with new or modified systems. Models can be iconic, analog, or mathematical.

❺ A DSS is an approach that can improve the effectiveness of decision making, decrease the need for training, improve management control, facilitate communication, reduce costs, and allow for more objective decision making. DSSs deal mostly with unstructured problems. Structured decisions are solved with management science models.

❺ The major components of a DSS are a database and its management, the model base and its management, and the user friendly interface. An intelligent (knowledge) component can be added.

❺ Computer support to groups is designed to improve the process of making decisions in groups, which can meet face-to-face or online. The support increases the effectiveness of decisions and reduces the wasted time and other negative effects of face-to-face meetings.

❻ BI can be designed to support the real-time enterprise environment.

❼ Automated decision support systems are routine, repetitive decisions for situations where business rules can be applied (e.g., approve consumer loans).

Virtual Company Assignment

Management Decision Support at The Wireless Café

Go to The Wireless Café's link on the Student Web Site. There you will be asked to think about how automated tools could support better decision making at the restaurant.

Instructions for accessing The Wireless Café on the Student Web Site:

1. Go to *wiley.com/college/turban*.
2. Select Turban/Volonino's *Information Technology for Management*, Seventh Edition.
3. Click on Student Resources site, in the toolbar on the left.
4. Click on the link for Virtual Company Web Site.
5. Click on Wireless Café.

Questions for Discussion

1. Discuss the strategic benefits of business analytics.
2. Will BI replace the business analyst? Discuss.
3. Differentiate predictive analysis from data mining. What do they have in common?
4. Describe the concepts underlying Web mining and Web analytics.
5. Relate competitive analysis to BI.
6. Why is real-time BI becoming critical?
7. Discuss the need for real-time computer support.
8. What could be the biggest advantages of a mathematical model that supports a major investment decision?
9. Your company is considering opening a branch in China. List several typical activities in each phase of the decision (intelligence, design, choice, and implementation).
10. How is the term *model* used in this chapter? What are the strengths and weaknesses of modeling?
11. American Can Company announced that it was interested in acquiring a company in the health maintenance organization (HMO) field. Two decisions were involved in this act: (1) the decision to acquire an HMO, and (2) the decision of which one to acquire. How can a DSS, ES, or ESS be used in such a situation?

12. Discuss how GDSSs can negate the dysfunctions of face-to-face meetings (Chapter 4).
13. Read the CIGNA case (*Online Minicase 1*) and answer the following questions:

    a. Describe the motivation for developing the eCare system.

    b. Explain the role of the intelligent systems and their potential benefits in the case.

c. What are the major difficulties you can anticipate in the process of developing and using the system?

d. How are these systems different from traditional analytical systems described earlier in the chapter?

14. Explain why even an intelligent system can fail.

Exercises and Projects

[For exercises that involve the Teradata Student Network (TSN), see the directions for registering with TSN in the *Problem-Solving Activity*.]

1. Enter *teradatastudentnetwork.com* (TSN) and find the paper titled "Data Warehousing Supports Corporate Strategy at First American Corporation" (by Watson, Wixom, and Goodhue). Read the paper and answer the following questions:

   a. What were the drivers for the DW/BI project in the company?

   b. What strategic advantages were realized?

   c. What operational and tactical advantages were achieved?

   d. What were the CSFs for the implementation?

2. Enter TSN and find the Web seminar titled: "Enterprise Business Intelligence: Strategies and Technologies for Deploying BI on Large Scale" (by Eckerson and Howson). View the Web seminar and answer the following:

   a. What are the benefits of deploying BI to the many?

   b. Who are the potential users of BI? What does each type of user attempt to achieve?

   c. What implementation lessons did you learn from the seminar?

3. Enter TSN and find the Harrah's case (by Watson and Volonino). Also read the opening case in Chapter 3. Answer the following:

   a. What were the objectives of the project?

   b. What was the role of the DW?

   c. What kinds of analyses were used?

   d. What strategic advantages does the BI provide?

   e. What is the role and importance of an executive innovator?

4. Visit *teradatastudentnetwork.com*. Search recent developments in the field of BI.

   a. Find the Web seminar on information visualization. View it and answer the following questions.

      i. What are the capabilities of Tableau Software's products?

      ii. Compare the two presentations and cite similarities and differences between them.

   b. Find the assignment "AdVent Technology" and use MicroStrategy's "Sales Analytical Model." Answer the three questions. Ask your instructor for directions.

5. Sofmic (fictitious name) is a large software vendor. About twice a year, Sofmic acquires a small specialized software company. Recently, a decision was made to look for a software company in the area of data mining. Currently, there are about 15 companies that would gladly cooperate as candidates for such acquisitions.

   Bill Gomez, the corporate CEO, asked that a recommendation for a candidate for acquisition be submitted to him within one week. "Make sure to use some computerized support for justification," he said. As a manager responsible for submitting the recommendation to Gomez, you need to select a computerized tool for the analysis. Respond to the following points:

   a. Prepare a list of the three tools that you would consider.

   b. Prepare a list of the major advantages and disadvantages of each tool as it relates to this specific case.

   c. Select a computerized tool.

   d. Mr. Gomez does not assign grades to your work. You make a poor recommendation and you are out. Therefore, carefully justify your recommendation.

6. Consider this perspective on BI and BPM. Conceptually, BI is simple: data produced by an organization's transactional processing and operational IT systems can be collected and summarized into totals and reports that give managers an immediate view of how they are doing. Business performance management (BPM) is about people and culture and should involve every knowledge worker within an organization, but there are some behavioral hurdles that still need to be overcome.

   Respond to the following points:

   a. Prepare a table that lists the BI technologies involved in each step of the process, from data production through to reports that give managers an immediate view of how they are doing. List the process (e.g., extraction from TPS) in the first column, and the BI technology in the second column.

   b. Using the table produced in (a), search for two vendors that provide a BI tool for each process. Put the results of your research in the third column. Include the brand name of the BI tool, the vendor's name, and the URL to the BI tool.

   c. Find one vendor, white paper, or article that addresses potential behavioral problems associated with BI or BPM. How do they respond to or address such obstacles? (*intelligententerprise.com/* may be a good place to research.) Report what you learn.

7. Read *Online Minicase 2* and answer these questions:

   a. Why do airlines need optimization systems for crew scheduling?

   b. What role can experts' knowledge play in this case?

    c. What are the similarities between the systems in Singapore and Malaysia?

8. Search and enter a blog dedicated to BI or predictive analytics. Verify that the blog has current content.

    a. What are the BI-related topics discussed in five of the posts?

    b. Using Table 2.2, identify what types of decisions and decison makers these issues relate to.

    c. Write a one-page report to management that identifies four current issues and explain their significance to the competitive edge of an enterprise.

Group Assignments and Projects

1. Data visualization is offered by all major BI vendors, as well as by other companies. Students are assigned one to each vendor to find the products and their capabilities. For a list of vendors, see *tdwi.org* and *dmreview.com*. Each group summarizes the products and their capabilities.

2. Prepare a report regarding DSSs and the Web. As a start, go to *dssresources.com*. Take the DSS tour. Each group represents one vendor, such as *microstrategy.com*, *sas.com*, and *cai.com*. Each group should prepare a report that aims to convince a company why its DSS Web tools are the best.

3. Enter *dmreview.com/resources/demos.cfm*. Go over the list of demos and identify software with analytical capa-

bilities. Each group prepares a report on at least five companies.

4. Enter *sas.com* and look for success stories related to BI. Find five that include an SAS video and prepare a summary of each in a class presentation.

5. Search for vendors in Web analytics and prepare a report on their products and capabilities. Each group presents the capabilities of two companies.

6. Each group member composes a list of mundane tasks he or she would like an intelligent system to prepare. The group will then meet and compare and draw some conclusions.

Internet Exercises

1. Enter the site of *microstrategy.com* and identify its major analytics products. Find success stories of customers using these products.

2. Enter *groupsystems.com* and select two customer success stories. Write a summary of each.

3. Find five case studies about DSSs. (Try *microstrategy.com*, *sas.com*, and *google.com*.) Analyze for DSS characteristics.

4. Enter *solver.com*, *ncr.com*, *hyperion.com*, and *ptc.com*. Identify their frontline system initiatives.

5. Visit *spss.com*, *informatica.com*, or *accure.com* and identify their Internet analytical solutions. Compare and comment. Relate your findings to business performance measurement.

6. Enter *fairisaac.com* and find how credit risk scores are calculated. Also find how fraud is treated.

7. Access the Web and online journals in your library to find at least three articles or white papers on the use of predictive analytics. Identify the vendor or enterprise, the predictive analytic software product, and the benefits gained from its use.

8. America Online, stock brokerages, and many portals (e.g., *money.cnn.com*, *bloomberg.com*) provide a free personalized service that shows the status of investors' desired or actual list of stocks, including profits (losses) and prices (with a 15-minute delay or even in real time). How is such individualized information retrieved so quickly? Why must such data be updated so quickly?

9. Find three recent cases of successful business analytics applications. Try BI vendors and look for cases or success stories (e.g., *sap.com*, *businessobjects.com*, *microstrategy.com*). What do you find in common among the various success stories? How do they differ?

Minicase

Lexmark International Improves Operations with BI

Lexmark International (*lexmark.com*) is a global manufacturer of printing products and solutions with about 12,000 employees and over 50 sales offices worldwide. Thousands of retail partners sell Lexmark's products in over 160 countries.

The Problem

Being in an extremely competitive business, Lexmark needs detailed, accurate, and timely information for decision support

and strategy implementation. This is especially important when it comes to data flow between Lexmark and its retail partners. The most important information is detailed by item, sales volumes, and inventory levels. The old system was slow, inefficient, and error-ridden. Problems occurred both with flows from the partners and with data delivery. In delivering the data, results were often copied from spreadsheets and pasted into reports, typically taking four days or longer to produce answers to common business questions. Sales representatives out in the field had to dial into the intranet. Once a connection was established, analysts and sales representatives had to write SQL queries and navigate the mainframe to generate reports for management, some of which were based on inaccurate, week-old data.

The Solution

Lexmark implemented a BI solution from MicroStrategy. The application is a BI adaptation for retailing, known as Retail BI System. The system enables buyers, financial analysts, marketing analysts, regional managers, merchandisers, and field sales representatives to analyze sales and inventory data from their desktop or mobile devices. The system, which is fed by IBM's data warehouse, provides users with the ability to track sales performance and inventory levels of every Lexmark product at each of the thousands of retail stores worldwide. A large number of reporting and analysis tools are available in the software, including extensive reports, statistical models (over 50), and visualization techniques. Using the system, Lexmark's user community can answer queries such as these instantly and easily:

- "What are my weekly sales and inventory levels in each of a specific customer's stores throughout the country"?
- "Who were my top retailers for a given product last week, last month, or this weekend versus last weekend"?
- "Looking at a given store that reports electronic data interchange (EDI) sales and inventory data to Lexmark, what are the inventory levels of a certain top-selling product"?

The Results

Lexmark reported that decision makers now receive timely, accurate, and detailed information. It helped to identify sales opportunities, increased partner loyalty, eliminated inventory

problems, and increased profitability. For example, the company identifies that a specific retail location is about to sell out of a certain printer. An automatic *alert* is then sent to the store manager and, within hours, a replenishment order is placed, avoiding a stockout. Overall, $100,000 of potentially lost sales were recovered. The retail stores appreciate Lexmark for this service, making Lexmark a preferred vendor.

Almost all Lexmark employees are using the systems. Novice workers are able to use the information to improve how they do their job. Management can better understand business trends and make appropriate strategic decisions. They have a better understanding of consumer demand by country and store, so they can better decide, for example, on pricing and promotions. Also, customer and partner services have been greatly improved.

Sources: Compiled from *Microstrategy.com* (2008) and Valentine (2004).

Questions for Minicase

1. Identify the challenges faced by Lexmark regarding information flows.
2. How were information flows provided before and after implementation of the BI system?
3. Identify decisions supported by the new system.
4. How can the system improve customer service?
5. Go to MicroStrategy's Web site (*microstrategy.com*) and examine the capabilities of Retail BI System. Prepare a list.
6. Go to the SAS Web site (*sas.com*) and find their Retail Intelligence product (take the interactive tour). Compare it with MircoStrategy's product. Also, compare it with Oracle Retail (*oracle.com/retek*).

Problem-Solving Activity

Dashboards at Eden, Inc.

This activity involves the use of multimedia content from the *Teradata Student Network*. There are two sets of directions. The first set explains how to register with the Teradata Student Network. The second set explains how to access the Eden Case pdf and flash video, which is the problem-solving activity that you are to study and then complete.

The Teradata Student Network is a unique academic resource. It is a source of real-world information and insight about data warehousing, DSS/BI, and database technology for both professors and students alike.

Directions to register with the Teradata Student Network.

1. You need to obtain the general password for the Teradata Student Network from your professor. For prevent copyright violations, the Teradata Student Network's password is changed at the beginning of each year. This is the *general password* to access this site.

2. Access *TeradataStudentNetwork.com* using the password provided to you.
3. Click Register in the upper-left corner of the screen. Complete the registration, which requires that you enter your e-mail address and select a personal password between 4 and 10 characters long. You use your *personal (private) password* to access your account on the Teradata Student Network.
4. After completing the registration process, you have access to this valuable BI/DSS resource.

Directions for the problem-solving assignment.

1. Click **Case Studies** on the left-side of the menu bar.
2. Click **Dashboards at Eden Case Study** to access the pdf entitled "Dashboards at Eden, Inc," Case Study, 2005. This case describes the situation at a fictitious company, the

Eden Corporation. The case is tied to the business performance management demonstration module on "Eden, Inc." Read the case.

3. From the Teradata Student Network home page, click SOFTWARE, then DEMONSTRATION, then select the **Eden Corporation-Flash Demo**. This professionally developed 15-minute flash demo highlights various role-based dashboards used by executives at the Eden Corporation, an electronics company.

4. Give an informed response to the questions found at the bottom of page 3, that relate to Strong's review of the nature of Eden's dashboards. Those questions are: Did he do the right thing? Did they take accountability too far? Isn't accountability a good thing? Would you redesign the dashboards? If so, how? If not, what would be your expectation of COO Edward's future behaviors?

5. Answer the questions at the end of the case on page 6. Those questions are: What technical approaches might be suggested for this? What would the steps be to begin talking with the suppliers about this prospect? Would this be a standards effort, or a simple file transfer type of approach, or are there other ways this could be handled?

Online Resources

More resources and study tools are located on the Student Web site and on WileyPLUS. You'll find additional chapter materials and useful Web links. In addition, self-quizzes that provide individualized feedback are available for each chapter.

Online Briefs for Chapter 12 are available at wiley.com/college/turban:

12.1 How BI Facilitates SOX Compliance

12.2 Sensitivity Analysis

12.3 Simulation for Decision Making

Online Minicases for Chapter 12 are available at wiley.com/college/turban:

12.1 Cigna Uses Business Rules to Support Treatment Request Approval

12.2 KLM, Singapore, and Malaysia Airlines Opt for Intelligent Crew Management Systems

References

aberdeen.com (accessed June 2008).

Agres, A. B., et al., "A Tale of Two Cities Case Studies of Group Support Systems Transition," *Group Decision and Negotiation*, July 2005.

dmreview.com, 2008 (accessed June 2008).

Garretson, R., "IT Still Matters," *CIO Insight*, May 7, 2007.

Goulden, B., "Fashion Chain Store on the Way," *Coventry*, July 14, 2006.

Haley Case Brief, "CIGNA Creates eCare Treatment Request Approval System with Haley Systems' Technology," February 2006.

Hatch, D., "Predictive Analytics: The BI Crystal Ball," Aberdeen Group, May 2008, *aberdeen.com/summary/report/benchmark/4875-RA-predictive-analytics-bi.asp* (accessed June 2008).

Imhoff, C., "Enterprise Business Intelligence," *Intelligent Solutions, Inc.*, May 2006.

InfoWorld.com, "China Everbright Bank Selects ILOG JRules to Streamline Its Loan and Credit Decisioning Processes," June 20, 2006, *infoworld.com/ILOG_JRules/product_48127.html?view = 8 &curNodeId = 7&prId = SFTU09020062006-1* (accessed July 2008).

INRIX.com (accessed July 2008).

Microstrategy.com (2008).

Mintzberg, H., *The Nature of the Managerial Work*. New York: Harper & Row, 1973.

Oracle, "Business Interest in Business Intelligence Solutions for JD Edwards EnterpriseOne," an Oracle White Paper, April 2007.

Oracle Retail, *oracle.com/retek* (accessed July 2008).

Perry, J., "All the Right Answers," *Retail Week*, June 1, 2007.

PRNewswire, "INRIX and WSI Partner to Make Commutes Easier with Traffic Forecasts for Broadcast and Cable Television Stations Across North America," *BNet*, April 14, 2008.

Schachter, H., "Making Data Make the Difference," *The Globe and Mail*, August 8, 2007.

Schlosser (2003), pp. 12–27.

Schlosser, J., "Looking for Intelligence in Ice Cream," *Fortune*, May 17, 2003.

Turban, E., et al., *Decision Support Systems and Intelligent Systems*, 8th ed. Upper Saddle River, NJ: Prentice Hall, 2007.

Valentine, L., "Lexmark CIO Croswell P. Chambers: Supporting a Changing Business Environment," *CIO Today*, July 21, 2004, *cio-today.com/story.xhtml?story_id=25966* (accessed July 2008).

Wright, R., "Mining for Love in Myriad Places, *InformationWeek*, May 29, 2006, *informationweek.com/news/management/showArticle.jhtml?articleID=188500521* (accessed June 2008).

Chapter 13

IT Strategy and Planning

Learning Objectives

After studying this chapter, you will be able to:

❶ Explain the importance of aligning the business strategy and IT strategy and how this alignment is achieved.

❷ Recognize the challenges in IT–business alignment and how to address them.

❸ Recognize why IT plays a critical strategic role within organizations.

❹ Explain how IT is providing value to businesses.

❺ Describe IT strategic planning within organizations.

❻ Understand the major reasons for outsourcing.

❼ Understand how to manage outsourcing and offshoring opportunities.

Integrating IT

ACC   **FIN**   **MKT**   **OM**   **HRM**   **IS**

IT-PERFORMANCE MODEL

In today's highly competitive business environment, productivity is the key to success. Companies must produce more, with fewer resources, at a lower cost, and in less time than ever before. IT investments are often made to align IT with business goals. Decisions are also based on estimated improvements including high returns on investment. In this chapter, we focus on how IT can support the strategic direction of the business and how companies can optimize IT investments to achieve long-term, measurable cost savings.

The business performance management cycle and IT model.

IT STRATEGIC ALIGNMENT AT KIMBERLY-CLARK: THE INNOVATION DESIGN STUDIO

ETHICS   FIN   GOV   ACC

Kimberly-Clark (K-C) Corporation (*kimberly-clark.com*), a multinational consumer products manufacturing company headquartered in Dallas, Texas, is committed to using innovation to become an indispensable business partner. As a leading global health and hygiene company, Kimberly-Clark's brands, such as Kleenex and Huggies, are sold in more than 150 countries, achieving sales of $16.7 billion in 2006. K-C has operations in 37 countries and employs more than 55,000 people worldwide.

The Strategic Plan

K-C's Global Business Plan includes the objective of building on the key capabilities of customer development, innovation, and marketing to sustain growth. Customer development is directed toward the core strategy of the customer, shopper, user focus, which is at the heart of K-C's execution of its Global Business Plan. To transform this enterprisewide strategic commitment into action, K-C is partnering with its retail customers, such as Kroger, Safeway, Target, and Wal-Mart, to implement changes for positive benefit on long-term success. K-C promotes mutually beneficial relationships with its retail customers, involving shared information and best practices as well as collaboration with retail customers on new product concepts and innovations. Strengthening relationships with key retail customers is essential to the company's growth plans.

HRM

IS

OM

Aligning Information Technology with the Strategic Plan

The Chief Information Officer (CIO), Ramon Baez, recognizes that the primary way to build the key capabilities of customer development, innovation, and marketing is through relationships with business functions or units, such as research and development (R&D) and marketing. Information technology (IT) business partners, who are senior-level IT staffers, serve as de facto CIOs to business functions or units. IT business partners work in the functional areas, but report directly to the CIO and recommend IT investment opportunities from their knowledge of business needs. Baez employs a portfolio approach to evaluate opportunities and secure support for worthy investments from the chief executive officer (CEO).

IT has become more strategically aligned as a result of four features:

1. R&D is an especially important functional area within which IT interaction and involvement is critical for ongoing innovation.
2. The organizational structure of embedding senior level IT staffers within functional areas connects and engages IT in the creation of business ideas. Directly reporting to the CIO integrates IT within business idea generation.
3. The embedded IT staffers are at the senior level within the organization. Such status provides them with a de facto CIO role in interacting with executives within the functional areas, while reporting directly to the CIO who manages a portfolio of opportunities.
4. The portfolio approach, managed by the CIO, allows cross-functional opportunities to be evaluated, with worthwhile ideas moved forward to the CEO for funding approval.

K-C recognizes that IT offers opportunities to improve relationships with retailers by assisting them to more effectively market and sell products. Specifically, IT can improve efficiency, effectiveness, and data collection and analysis. Delivering good information to decision makers more quickly drives new ideas to improve the shopping experience and develop new product concepts and innovations. Innovative approaches to assess consumer shopping behavior bring insights to improve in-store designs and merchandising to encourage purchases.

The Innovation Design Studio

In May 2007, Kimberly-Clark opened its *Innovation Design Studio* in Neenah, Wisconsin, which includes a life-sized 3-D virtual reality system. Those who visit, including store managers and consumers, are surrounded with full-length rear-projection screens, creating a virtual store powered by applications running on eight Hewlett-Packard PCs. In this simulated shopping experience, a virtual store takes on the look and feel of a specific retail store. For example, the simulated Target, a discount retail chain, has the same red bulls-eye logo, floor tile, reddish lighting, wide aisles, and drop ceilings of an actual Target store.

Consumers "walk through the aisles" and "shop" via a touch screen panel. As consumers react to different shopping environments or product packaging, sensors embedded in the floors, walls, and ceiling, along with eye-tracking technology, measure the level of engagement to assess influencing factors on purchase decisions. K-C and its customers thereby test and explore various in-store design and merchandising concepts without incurring the time and cost of physically constructing alternative layouts, displays, and shelving mock-ups. K-C is also using the new simulation tools to elicit immediate customer feedback on new product initiatives.

The Impact

The Innovation Design Studio helps K-C develop new product initiatives based on immediate customer feedback, decreasing the time-to-market for introducing new products by 50 percent. Retail customers are able to create the most effective display designs that will sell more K-C products faster. For example, Safeway, a leading grocery retailer, teamed with K-C to design a new baby care aisle based on consumer feedback from the virtual store environment. Test stores incorporating the newly designed baby aisle realized increased sales for diapers, training pants, baby wipes, and toiletries. K-C in turn benefited as well. The introduction of a new line of K-C sun care products, Huggies® Little Swimmers®, was prompted by feedback to make the baby aisle a one-stop shop for moms.

This virtual reality technology, however, is delivering even more by providing retailers with ideas on how to better sell other merchandise not offered by K-C, such as clothing. The benefit to K-C is in image-building as a technology innovator, fostering more open collaboration for a variety of initiatives. Based on the image of technology innovator, retailers will likely look to K-C in undertaking technology-intensive initiatives, such as the use of radio frequency identification (RFID) for logistics. Kroger, a retail supermarket chain, sought better ideas for shelving, which led them to team with K-C to explore using RFID to improve the process of getting products from delivery trucks to store shelves.

K-C's plan of commitment to marketing, innovation, and customer development is working. The Innovation Design Studio is not only driving innovation, but also helping K-C become a better partner to consumers and to retailers. The customer, shopper, user focus is driving top-line growth and bottom-line results.

Sources: Compiled from Jusko (2007), McGee (2007), Wailgum (2008), and *kimberly-clark*.com (accessed June 2008).

The opening case about Kimberly-Clark illustrates that improved business partnering, essential to the company's growth plans, is achieved by innovatively strengthening relationships with key retail customers and consumers. The Innovation Design Studio is driving innovation. New consumer product development initiatives, based on immediate consumer feedback from "shopping" in a virtual store, decreased the time-to-market for introducing new products by 50 percent. Retail customers are able to test alternative display designs, without incurring the time and cost of physically constructing alternative layouts, displays, and shelving mock-ups, to create the most effective display designs that will sell more K-C products faster.

In this chapter, we demonstrate the importance of aligning business and IT strategies. We present some tools and methodologies to facilitate IT strategic planning. We discuss how IT strategy is initiated and provide an overview of the IT strategic planning process. We discuss the strategic approaches to managing IT, including outsourcing, offshoring, and the supporting role of IT in organizations.

13.1 Alignment of Business and IT Strategies

A survey of business leaders, by Diamond Management & Technology Consultants, found that 87 percent indicated they believe that IT is critical to their companies' strategic success (Worthen, 2007). Yet, few businesses work with IT to achieve strategic success. In developing their business strategy, only 33 percent of business leaders polled reported that the IT division is very involved. Further, only 30 percent reported that the business executive responsible for strategy works closely with the IT division. According to the Diamond study, no alignment between the business and IT strategies can result in the abandonment of IT projects. A reported 76 percent abandoned at least one IT project and 29 percent abandoned more than 10 percent of IT projects.

For companies that align business strategy and IT strategy, however, more revenue may be gained. For example, at Travelers Companies, Inc., a property and casualty insurance company based in St. Paul, MN, a 75 percent increase in new customer sales was realized with the use of a new system for independent agents. The successful software deployment was attributed to the chief information officer's (CIO) extensive involvement in strategy development and the close working relationship between the IT division and the responsible business unit.

Business strategy sets the overall direction for the business. The **information systems (IS) strategy** defines *what* information, information systems, and IT architecture are required to support the business. Based on a prioritization of needs, the **information technology (IT) strategy** indicates *how* the infrastructure and services are to be delivered. Figure 13.1 illustrates the relationship among business, IS, and IT strategy.

Information technology (IT)–business alignment refers to the degree to which the information technology (IT) division understands the priorities of the business and expends its resources, pursues projects, and provides information consistent with these priorities. IT–business alignment includes two facets. One facet is aligning the IT function's strategy, structure, technology, and processes with those of the business units so that IT and business units are working toward the same goals. This facet is referred to as *IT alignment* (Chan, 2002). Another type of alignment, referred to as *IT strategic alignment,* involves aligning IT strategy with organizational strategy. The goal of IT strategic alignment is to ensure that IS priorities, decisions, and projects are consistent with the needs of the entire business. Failure to properly align IT with the organizational strategy may result in large investments in systems that have a low payoff, or in failure to invest in systems that might potentially have a high payoff.

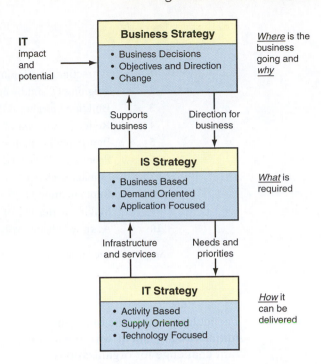

IT
impact
and
potential

Business Strategy
- Business Decisions
- Objectives and Direction
- Change

Where is the business going and *why*

Supports business

Direction for business

IS Strategy
- Business Based
- Demand Oriented
- Application Focused

What is required

Infrastructure and services

Needs and priorities

IT Strategy
- Activity Based
- Supply Oriented
- Technology Focused

How it can be delivered

Figure 13.1 The relationship among business, IS, and IT–strategies. (*Source:* Ward and Peppard, 2002.)

The business strategy and IT strategy must be aligned with shared ownership and shared governance of IT among all members of the senior executive team (Shpilberg et al., 2007). To achieve IT alignment, the entire IT organization must align with the strategic objectives of the overall business, with a governance structure in place that crosses organizational lines and makes business executives responsible for the success of key IT initiatives (Shpilberg et al., 2007).

GOVERNANCE STRUCTURE FOR IT–BUSINESS ALIGNMENT

The governance structure within an organization should be designed to facilitate IT–business alignment. The CIO oversees the IT division and is responsible for the company's technology direction. The CIO is a member of the C-suite of "chief officers" in the company who share authority in their respective areas of responsibility, such as chief executive officer (CEO), chief financial officer (CFO), chief marketing officer (CMO), or chief compliance officer (CCO). To whom the CIO reports is telling of how IT is perceived within the company. For example, if IT is perceived as a strategic weapon to grow revenues and increase operational effectiveness, then the CIO likely reports to the CEO.

If IT is perceived as a cost-cutting center, the CIO likely reports to the CFO. Interestingly, a survey of CEOs undertaken by Forrester Research revealed that while 79 percent indicated the CIO is included on the executive team, only 63 percent keep the CIO as a direct report to the CEO (Orlov, 2007). Even fewer, 52 percent, hired the CIO. The CEO–CIO relationship is just one point in alignment; the CIO must have a relationship with each member of the executive team (Hoffman, 2007). The CIO's role has become so important that within some organizations it can serve as a steppingstone to the position of CEO (Basu and Jarnagin, 2008).

ACHIEVING IT–BUSINESS ALIGNMENT

The most recent study of CIOs (Luftman, 2007), sponsored by the Society for Information Management (*simnet.org*), found IT and business alignment to be the second most important issue facing CIOs, from their own perspective. Table 13.1 shows the top 10 issues facing CIOs.

Strategic alignment has long been an issue of importance both in information systems research and to IS practitioners, and continues in importance today. Alignment remains an important issue for CIOs in part because failure to align IT to business strategy is believed to result in the failure of many IS initiatives.

TABLE 13.1	Top Issues Facing CIOs
Rank	**Issue**
1	Attracting, developing, and retaining IT professionals
2	Aligning IT and business
3	Building business skills in
4	Reducing the cost of doing business
5	Improving IT quality
6	Promoting IT security and privacy
7	Managing change
8	Implementing IT strategic planning
9	Making better use of information
10	Acknowledging evolving CIO leadership role

Source: Adapted from Luftman (2007).

Particularly in the case of organizationwide (or enterprisewide) information systems initiatives, alignment with the strategic objectives of the organization is an important challenge for organizations.

IT–business alignment can be fostered within an organization by focusing on activities central to alignment (Scott, 2005):

1. Understanding IT and Corporate Planning. A prerequisite for effective IT–business alignment is a deep understanding of business planning on the part of the CIO. Similarly, the CEO and business planners need to possess solid knowledge of their company's IT planning.

2. CIO is a Member of Senior Management. Full participation within the C-suite in company business activities instills in the CIO an intimate knowledge of the direction in which the company is moving, its position in the industry, industry dynamics, and the expected and potential role of IT in supporting the company.

3. Shared Culture and Good Communications. The CIO must understand and buy into the corporate culture. Communication between the line and IS executives and an interconnected planning process is necessary so that IS planning does not occur in isolation. Frequent, open, and effective communication is essential to ensure a shared culture and keep all apprised of planning activities and business dynamics.

4. Deep Commitment to IT Planning by Senior Management. Senior managers must maintain a deep commitment to IT planning to assure company success. Important in this commitment is communicating the strategic business plans to IT managers, including company policies and expected IT support.

5. Shared Plan Goals. An explicit effort should be made to jointly and simultaneously develop and evaluate goals shared by the business plan and the IT plan to ensure that these shared goals are in concert.

6. Deep End User Involvement. The IT–business alignment should extend to deep involvement of the end users with both IT planners and business planners for the purpose of establishing what projects need to be developed to support business tactics and operations.

7. Joint Architecture/Portfolio Selection. Overall corporate information needs and the necessary IT architecture should be jointly addressed in IT strategic planning to link the IT architecture plans and the development projects to the strategic business plans.

8. Identity of Plan Factors. A linkage between the business and IT plans should be made at the strategic, tactical, and operational levels.

CHALLENGES IN ACHIEVING IT-BUSINESS ALIGNMENT

Despite the importance of IT alignment, organizations continue to demonstrate limited actual alignment. IT alignment remains a dominant organizational challenge for CIOs (Weiss et al., 2006). Alignment is a complex management activity, and its complexity increases with the increasing complexity of organizations as the pace of global competition and technological change increases.

The key to achieving IT-business alignment is for the CIO to attain strategic influence. Rather than being narrow technologists, CIOs must be both business and technology savvy. CIOs who have a more strategic role are more successful in (Center for CIO Leadership, 2007):

- Promoting collaboration between IT and organizational business units
- Persuading senior management about the importance of IT to the business
- Contributing to strategic planning and business growth initiatives
- Identifying opportunities for business process automation and improvement
- Improving internal and external user experience and satisfaction

CIOs found to be stronger in the above strategic CIO activities were also found to exhibit a collection of effective skills in interacting and collaborating with different constituents, including:

- *Political savvy.* Effectively understand other workers and use such understanding to influence others to act to enhance personal and/or organizational objectives.
- *Influence, leadership, and power.* Inspire, and promote a vision. Persuade and motivate others. Skillful at influencing superiors. Delegate work effectively.
- *Relationship management.* Build and maintain working relationships with coworkers and those external to the organization. Negotiate problem solutions without alienating those impacted. Understand others and get their cooperation in nonauthority relationships.
- *Resourcefulness.* Think strategically and make good decisions under pressure. Can set up complex work systems and engage in flexible problem resolution. Work effectively with senior management to deal with complexities of the management job.
- *Strategic planning.* Capable in developing long-term objectives and strategies and can translate vision into realistic business strategies.
- *Doing what it takes.* Persevere and focus in the face of obstacles. Take charge and stand alone, yet be open to learning from others.
- *Leading employees.* Delegate to employees effectively. Broaden employee opportunities. Interact fairly with direct reports, and hire talented employees.

In Table 13.2, these core strategic CIO activities, central to strategic and innovative success, are mapped along with the underlying skills associated with attaining success with each of these activities. As shown in the table, the three strategic activities that require the CIO to exhibit CIO skills are promoting collaboration between IT and the business units, persuading executive leadership of the importance of IT to the organization, and contributing to strategic planning and growth initiatives. Businesses striving to attain IT–business alignment may hire or develop CIOs who are capable in these important strategic activities.

Successful alignment also requires the development of a partnership between the IT division and business management. In a survey of over 175 CIOs from leading companies, undertaken by the Center for CIO Leadership in collaboration with Harvard Business School and MIT Sloan Center for Information Systems Research, 80 percent responded that they are valued members of the senior leadership team (Center for CIO Leadership, 2007). In some cases, however, there is a "glass wall" between the IT division and the rest of the company, according to a *Wall Street Journal* article focusing on the value of IT to organizations (Basu and Jarnagin, 2008). This wall prevents the CIO and senior IT staff from close interaction with the CEO and senior executive business leaders. This may result in a failure to recognize the

TABLE 13.2	Important CIO Activities and Skills					
	Core Strategic CIO Activities					
Underlying CIO Skills	Promoting Collaboration between IT and Business Units	Persuading Leadership of Importance of IT	Delivering High–Profile Projects	Contributing to Strategic Planning and Growth Initiative	Identifying Opportunities for Process Enhancement	Developing IT Staff
Political savvy	X	X		X		
Influence, leadership, and power	X	X		X		
Relationship management	X					
Resourcefulness	X	X	X	X	X	
Strategic planning	X	X		X		
Doing what it takes	X					
Leading employees						X

Source: Center for CIO Leadership (2007).

value of IT to the business strategy. The wall can be removed or prevented through effective communication. Further, the wall may be dispelled by creating a partnership between the IT division and business management.

Another challenge to successful alignment is clearly defining IT's role in an organization. CIOs need to ensure that the IT department is focused on building those systems that help the organization achieve its major objectives and help business units succeed in achieving their major goals. An ongoing issue is that the technology infrastructures built to support one strategy often outlast the strategy that they were intended to support (Beal, 2004).

A Closer Look 13.1 discusses how Hewlett-Packard addresses alignment.

A Closer Look 13.1

Hewlett-Packard Aligns Business and IT Strategies

MKT

Hewlett-Packard (HP, *hp.com*) developed a planning methodology in which business process strategies and technologies are defined and aligned concurrently. This methodology was designed to allow the company to make process changes regardless of the limitations of the existing technology, and it gives visibility to the impacts that new technologies and processes have on each other.

In the past, HP had used a sequential process. First, it defined the business strategy and the operations and supporting strategies, including technologies. Then, all of these functions were aligned and replanned, taking into consideration the technologies available. In the new methodology, the planning is performed for all areas *concurrently*. Furthermore, the entire approach is complemented by a strong focus on teamwork, specialized and objective-driven functional areas and business units, and a commitment to quality and customer satisfaction. The approach links strategy and action. The business alignment framework takes into account the necessary process changes resulting from changes in the business environment, as well as potential technological developments. But, because major changes may result in a change in value systems as well as culture and team structures of the organization, HP includes these factors within the planning methodology.

Target processes, technologies, and standards drive the selection of potential solutions. The participative management approach ensures effective implementation. According to the framework, business processes and information requirements are defined in parallel with technology enablers and models, which are then linked throughout the alignment process.

HP's focus on strategic alignment is evident not only in its planning for internal technology solutions, but also in its quest for technological innovation through a centralized R&D function with an annual budget of $4 billion. The R&D function actively participates in the strategy development process, which helps the R&D department better understand what is driving customers while simultaneously offering a strong technology perspective that influences the business as a whole.

Sources: Compiled from Beal (2004), Collins (2004), and *hp.com* (accessed June 2008).

For Further Exploration: Why is concurrent planning superior? What communication and collaboration support is needed?

Review Questions

> 1. What is IT–business alignment? What are the two facets of IT–business alignment?
> 2. Explain what is necessary within the organizational governance structure to facilitate IT–business alignment.
> 3. Discuss the importance of IT–business alignment to CIOs.
> 4. Why does IT–business alignment continue to be a dominant organizational challenge for CIOs?
> 5. What is the main challenge to achieving IT–business alignment?
> 6. CIOs who have a more strategic role are more successful in what core strategic activities?

13.2 IT Strategy Initiation

It is important to set a clear direction for the organization prior to initiating the IT strategic planning process. Once the corporation's strategic direction has been devised, the first step in initiating the IT strategy is to understand the critical strategic role of IT within that business plan.

THE CRITICAL STRATEGIC ROLE OF INFORMATION TECHNOLOGY

The global economy is defined by innovative use of IT (Center for CIO Leadership, 2007). For example, as the automobile industry becomes increasingly global and the competitive business pressures intensify, IT becomes increasingly important, according to the Director of IT Governance at the Americas Region of Volkswagen AG, the fourth largest auto maker in the world (Licker, 2006). The ability to keep pace and respond to market opportunities worldwide by delivering appropriate products requires a global IT perspective and architecture to match the emerging global nature of business.

Companies must determine the use, value, and impact of IT to identify opportunities and create value that supports the organization's strategic vision. This requires that the CIO, and other senior IT staff, closely interact with the CEO and the most senior officers in functional areas and business units. As technology becomes increasingly central to business, the CIO becomes a key mover in the ranks of upper management.

For example, at Toyota Motor Sales USA, headquartered in Torrance, CA, the new CIO, Barbra Cooper, arrived to find that six enterprisewide IT projects so overwhelmed the workload of the IS group that there was little time for communication with the business units (Wailgum, 2005). IS was viewed as an "order taker" rather than as a partner with whom to build solutions. CIO Cooper radically changed the structure of Toyota's IS department in six months to build close communication with business operations. In just over a year later, IS and the business units now work closely together when planning and implementing IT projects. In some cases, this partnership extends to become a fusion, wherein the CIO is responsible for some core business functions, in addition to IT (Hoffman and Stedman, 2008). The CIO must be in a position to influence how IT can assume a strategic role in the firm, by leveraging the value added and gaining a competitive advantage through innovative applications of IT.

The Value Added by IT to the Business. IT can add value to a company in one of two general ways—either *directly* or *indirectly*. IT can add value *directly* by *reducing the costs* associated with a given activity or subset of activities. Cost reduction usually occurs when IT enables the same activity or set of activities to be performed more efficiently. Hence, the firm may reduce its workforce while not reducing its production level. Cost reduction is also possible when IT enables an activity to be redesigned such that it is performed more efficiently. In this case, personnel may also be reduced.

IT can add value *indirectly* by *increasing revenues*. The increase in revenues occurs when IT enables a firm to be more effective. This may occur when a firm is able to either produce more or service more without having to hire more employees. In other words, IT enables the firm to grow in terms of service and revenue without having to grow significantly more in terms of personnel. For example, IT can be used to enable self-service on the part of clients, such as supermarket self checkout or airline self check-in. This enables a firm to both decrease costs and increase revenues.

There is another means by which IT can play a strategic role in a firm, and that is through enabling a temporary or sustained competitive advantage. Both a firm's IT and a firm's deployment of IT may provide a source of competitive advantage.

Competitive Advantage through Information Technology. **Competitive advantage** is gained by a company by providing real or perceived value to customers. To determine how IT can provide a competitive advantage, the firm must know its products and services, its customers, its competitors, its industry, related industries, and environmental forces—and have insight about how IT can enhance value for each of these areas. To understand the relationship of IT in providing a competitive advantage, we next consider the potential of a firm's IT resources to add value to a company.

Three characteristics of resources give firms the potential to create a competitive advantage: value, rarity, and "appropriability." Firm resources can be a source of competitive advantage only when they are *valuable*. A resource has value to the extent that it enables a firm to implement strategies that improve efficiency and effectiveness. But even if valuable, resources that are equitably distributed across organizations are commodities. Resources also must be *rare* in order to confer competitive advantages. Finally, to provide competitive advantage, a resource must be appropriable. *Appropriability* refers to the ability of the firm to create earnings through the resource.

Even if a resource is rare and valuable, if the firm expends more effort to obtain the resource than it generates through the resource, then the resource will not create a competitive advantage. Wade and Hulland (2004) give the example of firms attempting to hire ERP-knowledgeable personnel during the 1999–2000 time period, only to discover that they were unable to realize a return on their investment because of the higher compensation demanded by these high-in-demand (and hence, rare) and valuable knowledge resources. Table 13.3 lists the three characteristics necessary to achieve competitive advantage and three additional factors needed to sustain it.

The three characteristics described above are used to characterize resources that can create an initial competitive advantage. In order for the competitive advantage to be sustained, however, the resources must be inimitable, imperfectly mobile, and have low substitutability. *Imitability* is the facility with which a rival firm can copy the resource. Factors that contribute to low imitability include firm history, causal

TABLE 13.3	Key Resource Attributes That Create Competitive Advantage
Resource Attributes	**Description**
Value	The degree to which a resource can help a firm improve efficiency or effectiveness
Rarity	The degree to which a resource is nonheterogeneously distributed across firms in an industry
Appropriability	The degree to which a firm can make use of a resource without incurring an expense that exceeds the value of the resource
Imitability	The degree to which a resource can be readily emulated
Mobility	The degree to which a resource is easy to transport
Substitutability	The degree to which another resource can be used in lieu of the original resource to achieve value

TABLE 13.4	IS Resources and Capabilities	
IS Resource/Capability	**Description**	**Relationship to Resource Attributes**
Technology resources	Includes infrastructure, proprietary technology, hardware, and software.	Not necessarily rare or valuable, but difficult to appropriate and imitate. Low mobility but a fair degree of substitutability.
IT skills	Includes technical knowledge, development knowledge, and operational skills.	Highly mobile, but less imitable or substitutable. Not necessarily rare but highly valuable.
Managerial IT resources	Includes vendor and outsourcer relationship skills, market responsiveness, IS–business partnerships, IS planning, and management skills.	Somewhat more rare than the technology and IT skill resources. Also of higher value. High mobility given the short tenure of CIOs. Nonsubstitutable.

ambiguity, and social complexity (Wade and Hulland, 2004). *Mobility* (or *tradability*) refers to the degree to which a firm may easily acquire the resource necessary to imitate a rival's competitive advantage. Some resources, such as hardware and software, are easy to acquire and are thus highly mobile and unlikely to generate sustained competitive advantage. Even if a resource is rare, if it is possible to either purchase the resource (or in the case of a rare expertise, hire the resource), then the resource is mobile and incapable of contributing to a sustained advantage. Finally, *substitutability* refers to the ability of competing firms to utilize an alternative resource in lieu of the resources deployed by the first-moving firm in achieving an advantage.

Information systems can contribute three types of resources to a firm: technology resources, technical capabilities, and IT managerial resources.

Technology resources include the IS infrastructure, proprietary technology, hardware, and software. The IS infrastructure is the foundation of IT capability delivered as reliable services shared throughout the firm. The creation of a successful infrastructure may take several years to achieve and is somewhat different for each organization. Thus, even while competitors might readily purchase the same hardware and software, the combination of these resources to develop a flexible infrastructure is a complex task. It may take firms many years to catch up with the infrastructure capabilities of rivals.

Technical capabilities (skills) include IS technical knowledge (programming languages), IS development knowledge (experience with new technologies and experience with different development platforms), and IS operations (cost-effective operations and support). Technical IT skills include the expertise needed to build and use IT applications. IT skills may form the basis of competitive advantage to a firm in an industry where staying abreast of technology is a critical aspect of being competitive.

Managerial resources include both those related to IS and those related to IT. IS managerial resources include vendor relationships, outsourcer relationship management, market responsiveness, IS-business partnerships, and IS planning and change management.

Table 13.4 provides definitions for IS resources and capabilities, and suggests the degree to which they embody the attributes described in the table.

THE VALUE OF IT TO THE BUSINESS

The CIO must clearly communicate the value of IT to the business so that the potential and role of IT are understood. IT has the capability to contribute to improvements in many domains of business activity, as presented in the opportunity matrix of business improvement with IT shown in Table 13.5.

In order that business and IT executives have a common understanding of the potential business improvements attainable through the use of IT, each of these benefits should be evaluated in terms of the value to be provided to the business. One

TABLE 13.5	Opportunity Matrix of Business Improvement with IT				
Business Improvement with IT	High Impact Value	Low Impact Value	No Value	Description of the Business Value of the Improvement	
1. Improve process efficiencies					
2. Increase market share and global reach					
3. Reach new markets, audiences, and channels					
4. Improve external partnering capabilities					
5. Enable internal collaboration					
6. Launch innovative product and service offerings					
7. Improve time to market					
8. Enhance customer service experience					
9. Improve information access and effectiveness in decision-making processes					
10. Bring about new business models					
11. Enable a business to gain, or simply maintain, a competitive advantage					
12. Other					

Sources: Compiled from Kesner (2003) and Center for CIO Leadership (2007).

or more improvements may be attained through IT. For example, if customer service, number 8 in Table 13.5 is expected to be improved through the use of IT in a package delivery service, such an improvement may be regarded as providing high impact value. The description of the business value of enhancing the customer service experience would state:

> *The currently high volume of customer complaints about late delivery of packages will be addressed with an automatically generated personalized email message, to each customer experiencing late delivery, to provide notification of the revised delivery date. This email communication also provides an opportunity for each customer to express any remaining concerns. The external focus on improving customer service will contribute to a positive image of the company.*

This process change to improve customer service may also improve process efficiencies, number 1 in the table, providing low impact value to the business. The description of the business value of this process improvement would state:

> *Customer service agents will be freed from personally attending to all customer complaints, allowing them to focus on resolving the most serious complaints. This improved use of customer service agents' time is expected to improve operational efficiencies and costs.*

Being able to explain how IT is providing value to the business is a critical skill that can be facilitated with this matrix. To provide a common understanding, this matrix serves as a tool to discuss and clarify expectations concerning the potential impact of the improvement(s) to the business. Clear, frequent, and effective communication should underscore this potential.

A PARTNERSHIP BETWEEN THE IT DIVISION AND BUSINESS MANAGEMENT

Inclusion of the CIO on the CEO's senior management team promotes a partnership between the CIO and the CEO. For example, at Walgreen Company, a leading drugstore chain based in Deerfield, IL, the CIO has been on the top management team since the late 1990s (Worthen, 2007). This arrangement facilitated the delivery of a single system to connect all Walgreen pharmacies, with continual improvements based on feedback and suggestions from both employees and customers. The CEO recognizes that inclusion of the CIO in strategy meetings encourages teamwork to meet the expectations of stakeholders such as customers, business partners, and stockholders. Thus, critical goal congruence between the CIO and CEO is created. To maintain this mutually beneficial relationship, the CIO must continually educate and update the other executives in the C-suite (chief executive) team about technological advances and capabilities relevant to the business needs. The focus should be on the use, value, and impact of technology as well as the technology itself (Center for CIO Leadership, 2007).

The partnership between the IT division and business management can extend to fuse with the business. Such a fusion could be achieved with a new organizational structure, wherein the CIO becomes responsible for managing some core business functions. For example, the CIO at Hess Corporation, a leading energy company based in New York City, is part of a new organizational structure (Hoffman and Stedman, 2008). The CIO will begin managing some core business functions. Additionally, Hess Corporation is creating a joint IT and business group to develop new operating processes and advanced technologies. Comprised of IT workers with geologists, scientists, and other employees, this unit will report to the senior vice president of oil exploration and production.

Alternatively, the CIO could work directly with other top executives to influence strategic directions, suggest changes in internal business processes, and lead a diversity of initiatives that encompass more than just technology projects. For example, the Vice President of IT at PHH Mortgage, in Mount Laurel, NJ, works alongside the sales managers (Hoffman and Stedman, 2008). This working relationship has fostered a rapport between the CIO and sales executives, building the necessary trust for the CIO to drive the IT function and deliver business innovation. In discussions with the sales team about potential changes in some of the mortgage application processes, the CIO is able to take the lead on business improvement opportunities by communicating his understanding of concerns and offering insightful recommendations.

A Closer Look 13.2

ACC   FIN

The Emerging Role of the Strategic CIO

It is not typical for a traditional CIO to routinely work with business leaders to work on their strategy and translate it into action, and then be asked by the CEO to manage business strategy worldwide. Nor is it typical that the CEO ask a traditional CIO to run a line of business, in addition to the IT function. A traditional CIO would not be expected to manage the process of opening 10,000 seasonal tax preparation locations and hiring 100,000 seasonal tax preparers, but that's what happened at H&R Block, a tax and financial services company. The emergence of these responsibilities for the CIO are, however, typical for the strategic CIO.

The strategic CIO is a business leader who uses IT as a core tool to leverage IT to add value and gain a competitive advantage. The strategist's focus is on how a company creates shareholder value and serves its customers. Rather than being directed primarily toward internal operations, the strategic CIO looks at the company from the outside-in by asking how the company is perceived by customers and how competitors apply IT to compete. The role of strategic CIO is much more focused on business strategy and innovation. This broader, more business-oriented, and strategic focus is expected to be the future direction for the CIO role, which in time will become the norm for most CIOs.

Marc West, the senior VP and CIO at H&R Block, began as a traditional CIO, focusing 95 percent of his efforts on the technology foundation. In preparing for tax season, CIO West was engaged in delivering tax preparation software for its seasonal storefront locations. This activity helped him to acquire insight into the core business, operations, and how customers are served. This further led him to compare what H&R was doing against the competition, gaining a big picture perspective of the industry. He shared his strategic insights with the CEO and management team. Encouraged by the CEO, CIO West continued his "outside-inside" strategic assessment, gaining an industrywide, business-oriented strategic mindset. The CEO then asked CIO West to lead a new line of business, driving growth in the commercial markets.

IT is more and more pervasive in businesses. Businesses must respond by forming a strong relationship between business goals and the technology that will help achieve those goals. The new role of leading strategist for the CIO requires an understanding of strategy and business goals, and work to identify opportunities and integrate IT for business advantage.

Sources: Compiled from Ehrlich and West (2007) and *hrblock.com* (accessed June 2008).

For Further Exploration: How does the traditional CIO differ from the strategic CIO? What is the focus of the strategic CIO? Why is the role of strategic CIO emerging?

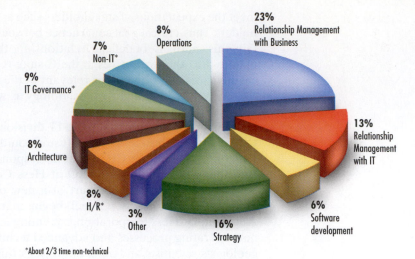

Figure 13.2 How CIOs spend their time. (*Source:* Luftman, 2007.)

*About 2/3 time non-technical

The CIO's focus on managing business activities is revealed by looking at how CIOs spend their time. As shown in Figure 13.2, about two-thirds of a CIO's time is spent on nontechnical duties, including relationship management with the business, strategy-related activities, non-IT activities, and other. The largest percentage among nontechnical duties (23%) is spent on managing relationships with business functional areas and business units (Luftman, 2007).

To realize the greatest potential from IT, the business strategy must include the IT strategy and the use of IT must support the business strategy. The next largest slice of the CIO's time (16%) is spent on business and IT strategy. Critical in addressing strategy is the alignment of business and IT strategies. To achieve this alignment, a firm must carefully plan its IT investments. We therefore now turn to the topic of IT planning.

Review Questions

1. Why does IT play a critical strategic role in organizations?
2. Explain what is meant by the "glass wall" between the IT division and the rest of the company. What can be done to remove or prevent this wall?
3. In what two ways can IT add value to a company?
4. What are three characteristics of resources that give firms the potential to create a competitive advantage?
5. Describe the three types of resources that information systems can contribute to a firm.
6. Describe the relationship among business strategy, IS strategy, and IT strategy.
7. Why is it important for the CIO to be included as a member of the CEO's senior management team?

13.3 IT Strategic Planning

CIOs typically undertake IT strategic planning on a yearly, quarterly, or monthly basis. In the recent survey of the key issues facing CIOs, strategic IT planning was ranked eighth among the top ten issues (see Table 13.1). A good IT planning process can help ensure that IT aligns, and stays aligned, within an organization. Because organizational goals change over time, it is not sufficient to develop a long-term IT strategy and not reexamine the strategy on a regular basis. For this reason, IT planning is a continual process, not a one-shot process.

The IT planning process may result in a formal IT strategy or may result in a reevaluation each year (or each quarter) of the existing portfolio of IT resources to be developed.

IT strategic planning is the organized planning of IT resources done at various levels of the organization. The topic of IT strategic planning is very important for both planners and end users: End users often do IT planning for their own units, and they also frequently participate in the corporate IT planning. Therefore, end users must understand the planning process. Corporate IT planning determines how the IT infrastructure will look. This in turn determines what applications end users can deploy. Thus, the future of every unit in the organization could be impacted by the IT infrastructure.

THE IT STRATEGIC PLANNING PROCESS

The focus of IT strategy is on how IT creates business value. Typically, annual planning cycles are established to identify potentially beneficial IT services, to perform cost–benefit analyses, and to subject the list of potential projects to resource-allocation analysis. Often the entire process is conducted by an IT *steering committee*. See *A Closer Look 13.3* for the duties of an IT steering committee.

Figure 13.3 presents the IT strategic planning process. The entire planning process begins with the creation of a strategic business plan. The *long-range IT plan*, sometimes referred to as the *strategic IT plan*, is then based on the strategic business plan. The IT strategic plan starts with the IT vision and strategy, which defines the future concept of what IT should do to achieve the goals, objectives, and strategic position of the firm and how this will be achieved. The overall direction, requirements, and **sourcing** (i.e., outsourcing or insourcing) of resources, such as infrastructure, application services, data services, security services, IT governance, and management architecture; budget; activities; and timeframes are set for three to five years into the future. The planning process continues by addressing lower-level activities with a shorter time frame.

The next level down is a *medium-term IT plan*, which identifies general project plans in terms of the specific requirements and sourcing of resources as well as the **project portfolio.** The project portfolio lists major resource projects, including infrastructure, application services, data services, and security services, that are consistent with the long-range plan. Some companies may define their portfolio in terms of applications. The **applications portfolio** is a list of major, approved IS projects that are also consistent with the long-range plan. Expectations for sourcing of resources in the project or applications portfolio should be driven by the business strategy. Since some of these projects will take more than a year to complete, and others will not start in the current year, this plan extends over several years. For more detailed information on application portfolios, see *Online Brief 13.1*.

A Closer Look 13.3

IT Steering Committees

The corporate *steering committee* is a group of managers and staff representing various organizational units that is set up to establish IT priorities and to ensure that the IS department is meeting the needs of the enterprise. The committee's major tasks are:

- **Direction setting.** In linking the corporate strategy with the IT strategy, planning is the key activity.
- **Rationing.** The committee approves the allocation of resources for and within the information systems organization. This includes outsourcing policy.
- **Structuring.** The committee deals with how the IS department is positioned in the organization. The issue of centralization–decentralization of IT resources is resolved by the committee.

- **Staffing.** Key IT personnel decisions involve a consultation-and-approval process made by the committee, including outsourcing decisions.
- **Communication.** Information regarding IT activities should flow freely.
- **Evaluating.** The committee should establish performance measures for the IS department and see that they are met. This includes the initiation of *service-level agreements* (SLAs).

The success of steering committees largely depends on the establishment of *IT governance*, formally established statements that direct the policies regarding IT alignment with organizational goals and allocation of resources.

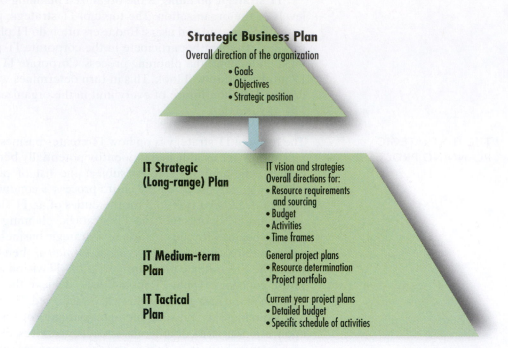

Figure 13.3 IT strategic planning process. (*Source:* Drawn by J. Sipior.)

The third level is a *tactical plan*, which details budgets and schedules for current-year projects and activities. In reality, because of the rapid pace of change in technology and the environment, short-term plans may include major items not anticipated in the other plans.

The planning process just described is currently practiced by many organizations. Specifics of the IT planning process, of course, vary among organizations. For example, not all organizations have a high-level IT steering committee. Project priorities may be determined by the IT director, by his or her superior, by company politics, or even on a first-come, first-served basis.

The output from the IT planning process should include the following: an evaluation of the strategic goals and directions of the organization and how IT is aligned; a new or revised IT vision and assessment of the state of the IT division; a statement of the strategies, objectives, and policies for the IT division; and the overall direction, requirements, and sourcing of resources.

TOOLS AND METHODOLOGIES OF IT STRATEGIC PLANNING

Several tools and methodologies exist to facilitate IT strategic planning. These methods are used to help organizations align their business IT/IS strategies with the organizational strategies, to identify opportunities to add value with IT or utilize IT for competitive advantage, and to analyze internal processes. Most of these methodologies start with some investigation of strategy that checks the industry, competition, and competitiveness, and relates them to technology (*alignment*). Others help create and justify new uses of IT (*impact*). In the next section, we look briefly at some of these methodologies.

Business Service Management. Business service management is an approach for linking key performance indicators (KPIs) of IT to business goals to determine the impact on the business. KPIs are metrics that measure the actual performance of critical aspects of IT, such as essential projects and applications, servers, the network, and so forth, against predefined business goals, such as growing revenue, lowering costs, and reducing risk. For a critical project, for example, performance metrics include the status of the project, the ability to track milestones to budget, and a view of how the IT staff spends its time (Biddick, 2008).

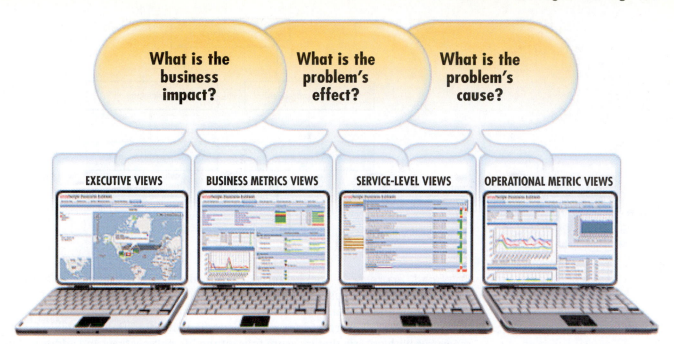

Figure 13.4 Business service management (from FireScope). (*Source: firescope.com/solutions/businessservicemanagement/*. FireScope delivers a single view into the business impact of IT operations by aggregating all IT technology and business metrics into realtime dashboards, customizable for the needs of each member of IT. Used with permission.)

KPIs can be classified into two types. The first type includes those that measure *real-time performance or predict future results*. These KPIs assist in proactive, rather than reactive, responses to potential user and customer problems. For example, 80 percent of IT staff may be needed to work on active projects. An evaluation of KPIs may predict that the following month a projected slowdown of project activity will reduce the utilization rate to 70 percent, allowing time to adjust staffing or add more projects. The second type of KPI measures *results of past activity*. For example, an IT organization may have committed to an application availability rate of 99 percent for certain applications, such as a Web-based customer order entry system (Biddick, 2008). A KPI can be set to measure the availability rate of these applications. Tracking other "non-key" metrics may also be helpful in remaining focused on issues that affect the organization.

As shown in Figure 13.4, business service management software tools provide real-time dashboard views for tracking KPIs at the executive, functional business areas, services, and operations levels. These views enable an understanding and the capability to predict both how technology impacts the business and how business impacts the IT architecture. As changes in technology and the environment continue to increase in complexity and scope, the need to track IT performance information as it evolves is essential to generate a global view of IT operations and influence positive business outcomes.

The Business Systems Planning Model. The **business systems planning (BSP) model** was developed by IBM, and has influenced other planning efforts such as Accenture's *method/1*. BSP is a top-down approach that starts with business strategies. It deals with two main building blocks—*business processes* and *data classes*—which become the basis of an information architecture. From this architecture, planners can define organizational databases and identify applications that support business strategies, as illustrated in Figure 13.5.

BSP relies heavily on the use of metrics in the analysis of processes and data, with the ultimate goal of developing the information architecture.

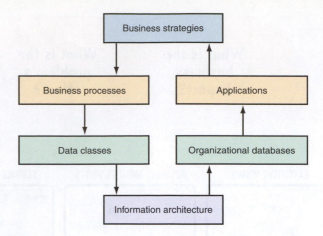

Figure 13.5 Business systems planning (BSP) approach.

Balanced Scorecard. The **balanced scorecard** is a performance measurement approach that links business goals to performance metrics (Kaplan and Norton, 2008). Goals and measures are derived from the vision and strategy of an organization. The balanced scorecard framework supplements traditional tangible financial measures with criteria that measure four intangible perspectives and address important questions including (Kaplan and Norton, 2005):

1. How do customers see the company?
2. At what must the company excel?
3. Can the company continue to improve and create value?
4. How does the company appear to shareholders?

The balanced scorecard, however, can be adapted to the specific assessment needs of a company. This framework may be applied to link KPIs of IT to business goals to determine the impact on the business. The focus for the assessment could be, for example, the project portfolio or the applications portfolio. As shown in Table 13.6, the balanced scorecard is used to assess the IT project portfolio of a retail department store chain. Projects are listed along the vertical dimension, and specific measures, critical to what the organization needs to track, are presented horizontally. The Data Services project, for example, has been allocated a high project budget to focus on improving data management. By using business intelligence software with internal proprietary data, the retailer is able to learn about customer product preferences by identifying trends in customer purchases. This may lead to the addition of new product offerings, displays, and promotions. This project contributes to the strategic focus on innovation. Knowledge about future changes in business processes to support new products, displays, and promotions is evolving. The degree of change needed in the project is high because customer preferences continually change, requiring new approaches to further discover, understand, and react to these changes. The balanced scorecard helps managers to clarify and update strategy; align IT strategy with business strategy; link strategic objectives to long-term goals and annual budgets; identify and align strategic initiatives; and conduct periodic performance reviews to improve strategy (Kaplan and Norton, 2007).

Critical Success Factors. **Critical success factors (CSFs)** are the essential things that must go right in order to ensure the organization's survival and success. The *CSF approach* to IT planning was developed to help identify the information needs of managers. The fundamental assumption is that in every organization there are three to six key factors that, if done well, will result in the organization's success. Therefore, organizations should continuously measure performance in these areas, taking corrective action whenever necessary. CSFs also exist in business units, departments, and other organizational units.

TABLE 13.6	IT Project Balanced Scorecard					
IT Project	**Project's Role in Strategic Business Plan**	**Project's Evolving versus Stable Knowledge**	**Degree of Change Needed in the Project**	**Where the Project Gets Sourced**	**Data's Public or Proprietary Nature**	**Project Budget**
Infrastructure	Efficiency	Stable	Low	Outsourced	Proprietary	Small
Application Services	Customer focus	Evolving	High	ERP software	Proprietary	High
Data Services	Innovation	Evolving	High	Business intelligence software	Proprietary	High
Security Services	Compliance requirement	Evolving	Low	Outsourced	Proprietary	Small

Source: Based loosely on Prahalad and Krishnan (2002).

Critical success factors vary by broad industry categories—manufacturing, service, or government—and by specific industries within these categories. For organizations in the same industry, CSFs will vary depending on whether the firms are market leaders or weaker competitors, where they are located, and what competitive strategies they follow. Environmental issues, such as the degree of regulation or amount of technology used, influence CSFs. In addition, CSFs change over time, based on temporary conditions, such as high interest rates or long-term trends.

IT planners identify CSFs by interviewing managers in an initial session, and then refine CSFs in one or two additional sessions. Sample questions asked in the CSF approach are

- What objectives are central to your organization?
- What are the critical factors that are essential to meeting these objectives?
- What decisions or actions are key to these critical factors?
- What variables underlie these decisions, and how are they measured?
- What information systems can supply these measures?

The first step following the interviews is to determine the organizational objectives for which the manager is responsible, and then the factors that are critical to attaining these objectives. The second step is to select a small number of CSFs. Then, determine the information requirements for those CSFs and measure to see whether the CSFs are met. If they are not met, it is necessary to build appropriate applications (see Figure 13.6).

The critical success factors approach encourages managers to identify what is most important to their performance and then develop good indicators of performance in these areas.

Scenario Planning. **Scenario planning** is a methodology in which planners first create several scenarios; then a team compiles as many future events as possible that may influence the outcome of each scenario. This approach is used in planning situations that involve much uncertainty, like that of IT in general and e-commerce in particular. With the rapid changes of technologies and business environment, Stauffer (2002) emphasized the need for scenario planning. Five reasons to do scenario planning are

1. To ensure that you are not focusing on catastrophe to the exclusion of opportunity
2. To help you allocate resources more prudently
3. To preserve your options

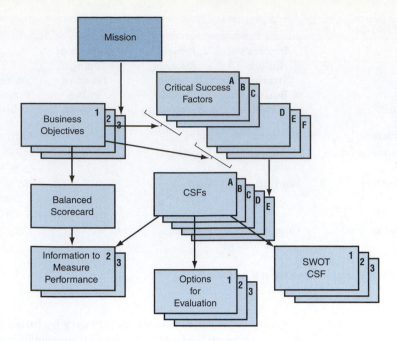

Figure 13.6 Critical success factors—basic processes.

4. To ensure that you are not still "fighting the last war"

5. To give you the opportunity to rehearse testing and training of people to go through the process.

Scenario planning follows a rigorous process; the essential steps are summarized in Table 13.7.

Scenario planning has been widely used by major corporations to facilitate IT planning (e.g., *ncri.com* and *gbn.com*). It also has been particularly important to e-commerce planning. For instance, creating customer scenarios helps the company better fit the products and services into the real lives of the customers, resulting in sales expansion and customer loyalty. National Semiconductor, Tesco, and Buzzsaw.com, for example, have used customer scenarios to strengthen customer relationships, to guide business strategy, and to deliver business value.

A major aspect of IT planning is allocating an organization's IT resources to the right set of projects. Organizations simply cannot afford to develop or purchase each application or undertake each application enhancement that business units and end

TABLE 13.7	Essential Steps of Scenario Planning

- Determine the scope and time frame of the scenario you are flashing out.
- Identify the current assumptions and mental models of individuals who influence these decisions.
- Create a manageable number of divergent, yet plausible, scenarios. Spell out the underlying assumptions of how each of these imagined futures might evolve.
- Test the impact of key variables in each scenario.
- Develop action plans based on either (a) the solutions that play most robustly across scenarios, or (b) the most desirable outcome toward which a company can direct its efforts.
- Monitor events as they unfold to test the corporate direction; be prepared to modify it as required.

The educational experience that results from this process includes

- Stretching your mind beyond the groupthink that can slowly and imperceptibly produce a sameness of minds among top team members in any organization.
- Learning the ways in which seemingly remote potential developments may have repercussions that hit close to home.
- Learning how you and your colleagues might respond under both adverse and favorable circumstances.

Source: Compiled from Stauffer (2002).

users might like. The IT steering committee therefore has an important responsibility in deciding how IT resources will be allocated. An example of identifying high-payoff projects is provided in *A Closer Look 13.4.*

A Closer Look 13.4

Identifying High-Payoff Projects

Wing Fat Foods (WFF) is a wholesaler, delivering perishable and nonperishable foodstuffs, as well as hardware, kitchenware, and household goods, to restaurants, groceries, and similar businesses along the Atlantic Coast of the United States. WFF is famous for its quality and service, which is accomplished with a relatively low level of IT investment. WFF hopes that its additional IT investment will help it to sustain its edge over competitors.

In response to the need for identifying potential new IT projects, researchers Peffers and Gengler (2003) proposed to WFF a new method, the *critical success chain (CSC) method*, for IT planning. The CSC method includes four steps:

Step 1. *Pre-study preparation: Determine scope and participants and collect project idea stimuli.* The analyst invited 25 IT users (6 senior managers, 11 middle managers, 5 journeyman employees, and 3 WFF customers) to participate in an in-depth interview. At the same time, she collected project ideas to serve as stimuli. For example, she asked each participant to describe the functionality of a system that would benefit WFF.

Step 2. *Participant interviews: Elicit personal constructs from organization members.* The analyst then conducted 25–50-minute interviews with each participant, showing the participant three system descriptions and asking him or her to rank the system attributes and explain their importance to the organization. A line of questions was asked until the participant suggested a concrete feature or attribute that would become part of the project idea. This line of questions was designed to produce specific ideas for features of the system, expected performance, and related organizational values or objectives. In this study, the analyst collected about eight chains of suggestions per participant.

Step 3. *Analysis: Aggregate personal constructs into CSC models.* The analyst first clustered the interview statements into constructs and mapped the constructs into a matrix. She then clustered the chains using the Ward and Peppard strategic planning framework. (For more detailed information on the Ward and Peppard strategic planning framework, see *Online Brief 13.2.*) Mapping each cluster into a CSC map, she represented the constructs as nodes and the links in the chains as lines connecting the nodes. The figure depicts an organization-specific CSC model consisting of, from left to right, descriptions of desired system attributes, resulting expected performance outcomes (CSFs), and associated organizational goals.

Step 4. *Idea workshops: Elicit feasible strategic IT from technical and business experts and customers.* The CSC maps were used by both IT professionals from within WFF and non-IT customers as a starting point for developing a portfolio of IT proposals. Providing the technical and business experts at WFF with the CSC maps, the workshop finally yielded 14 project ideas, including a decision support system for scheduling, routing, and loading trucks for delivery, as well as the support activities for existing systems, including training and updated equipment and maintenance support.

Source: Peffers and Gengler (2003).

For Further Exploration: Why is the method called the CS chain? Why is such a lengthy process, with so many participants, needed?

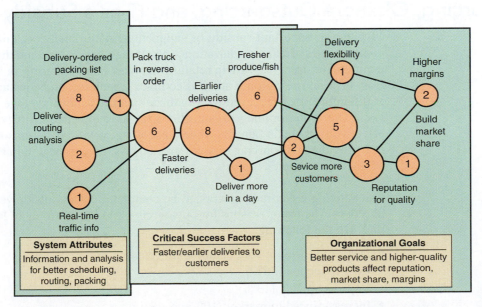

Critical success chain network map. (Sources: Peffers and Gengler, 2000, 2003.)

RESOURCE ALLOCATION

Resource allocation consists of developing the plans for hardware, software, data communications and networks, facilities, personnel, and financial resources needed to execute the master development plan, as defined in the requirements analysis. Resource allocation is a contentious process in most organizations because opportunities and requests for spending far exceed the available funds. This can lead to intense, highly political competition among organizational units, which makes it difficult to objectively identify the most desirable investments.

Requests for funding approval from the steering committee fall into two categories. The first category consists of projects and infrastructure that are critical for the organization to stay in business. For example, it may be imperative to purchase or upgrade hardware if the network, or disk drives, or the processor on the main computer are approaching capacity limits. Obtaining approval for this type of spending is largely a matter of communicating the gravity of the problems to decision makers.

The second category includes less-critical items, such as new projects, maintenance or upgrades of existing systems, and infrastructure to support these systems and future needs. Approval for projects in this category may become more difficult to obtain because the IS department is already receiving funding for the critical projects. Generally speaking, organizations set aside funds for the first category of projects and then use the remainder of the IT budget for the second category.

Review Questions

1. What is the typical timing for undertaking IT strategic planning? Why must IT strategic planning be revisited on a regular basis?
2. Describe the committee that usually conducts the IT strategic planning process? Who is included on this committee? What are the major tasks of this committee? On what is this committee's success dependent?
3. What is the focus of IT strategy?
4. Describe the IT strategic planning process.
5. Describe the project portfolio. Describe the applications portfolio. When are these portfolios developed?
6. What tools and methodologies are available to assist in the IT strategic planning process? How are these methods used to help organizations?
7. What is resource allocation? What are the two types of funding requests?

13.4 Outsourcing, Offshore Outsourcing, and IT as a Subsidy

IT plays an important subsidy, or supporting, role in many organizations. The core competencies of many organizations—the things they do best and that represent their competitive strengths—are in retailing, services, manufacturing, or some other function. IT is an *enabler* only, and it is complex, expensive, and constantly changing. IT is difficult to manage, even for organizations with above-average IT management skills. Therefore, for many organizations, the most effective strategy for managing IT effectively, to obtain benefits while controlling costs, may be **outsourcing.** The vendor providing outsourcing services may be offshore, or located in a country outside of the organization's country.

OUTSOURCING

Outsourcing is contracting work to be completed by an outside vendor (Aspray et al., 2006). The major reasons for outsourcing, cited by a survey of large U.S. companies, are the following:

- Desire to focus on core competency (36%)
- Cost reduction (36%)
- Improve quality (13%)
- Increase speed to market (10%)
- Faster innovation (4%) (Corbett, 2001)

CIOs are now focusing more on outsourcing to deliver business value, beyond the traditional areas of cost savings and operational efficiencies, in response to an increasingly dynamic environment (IBM, 2008). New technologies continue to emerge, and firms are transformed by global expansion, mergers and acquisition, and other new disruptive business models. Further, CIOs are taking on a more strategic role. The requirements of outsourcing have been driven by these changes. Over 45% of the firms that expect to be involved in outsourcing reported applications development is likely to lead all other IT functions outsourced, followed by applications maintenance (35%), telecommunications/LAN (33%), and PC maintenance (33%), according to a survey (Fish and Seydel, 2006).

Since the late 1980s, many organizations have outsourced the *majority of their IT functions*, rather than just incidental parts. The trend became classic in 1989 when Eastman Kodak transferred its data centers to IBM under a 10-year, $500 million contract. This example, at a prominent multibillion-dollar company, gave a clear signal that outsourcing was a legitimate approach to managing IT. Since then, many mega outsourcing deals were announced, some for several billion dollars. The trend, however, has turned away from the mega-deal in favor of the *multi-vendor approach,* incorporating the services of several best-of-breed vendors to meet IT demands (Overby, 2007).

Outsourcing Advantages and Disadvantages. According to a survey by Forrester Research, about 57 percent of client companies are somewhat satisfied with their primary outsourcer and 22 percent are very satisfied (Overby, 2007). Some outsourcing arrangements are more advantageous than others, according to a recent study by CIO magazine and MIT's Center for Information Systems Research. *Transactional outsourcing agreements*, in which a company outsources discrete processes that have well-defined business rules, have a success rate of 90 percent. *Co-sourcing alliances*, in which the client company and outsourcer vendor jointly manage projects, such as application development or maintenance work, have a success rate of 63 percent. Finally, *strategic partnerships*, in which a single outsourcer takes responsibility for the majority of a client company's IT services, has a success rate of about 50 percent. The potential benefits of outsourcing are presented in Table 13.8.

In contrast, as companies find their business strategy is increasingly tied to IT solutions, the concerns about outsourcing increase. A key finding of a 2005 study, undertaken by Deloitte Consulting LLP, is that outsourcing generates new risks and renders compliance regulation complex (Marquis, 2006). Of 25 organizations in this study, spending a combined $50 billion annually on outsourcing, 70 percent reported having negative experiences with outsourcing. As a result, this study revealed that 64 percent of those companies brought at least some IT functions back in-house due to the negative experiences. In general, risks increase as the boundaries between the client company and outsourcing vendor responsibilities blur and the scope of responsibilities expands (Overby, 2007). The failure rate of outsourcing relationships remains high, with estimates ranging from 40 to 70 percent. Clemons (2000) identifies the following risks associated with outsourcing:

• *Shirking* occurs when a vendor deliberately underperforms while claiming full payment (e.g., billing for more hours than were worked, providing excellent staff at first and later replacing them with less qualified ones).

• *Poaching* occurs when a vendor develops a strategic application for a client and then uses it for other clients (e.g., vendor redevelops similar systems for other clients at much lower cost, or vendor enters into client's business, competing against it).

• *Opportunistic repricing ("holdup")* occurs when a client enters into a long-term contract with a vendor and the vendor changes financial terms at some point or overcharges for unanticipated enhancements and contract extensions.

TABLE 13.8	Potential Outsourcing Benefits

Financial

- Avoidance of heavy capital investment, thereby releasing funds for other uses.
- Improved cash flow and cost accountability.
- Improved cost benefits from economies of scale and from sharing computer housing, hardware, software, and personnel.
- Less need for expensive office space.
- Reduction and control of operating costs.

Technical

- Access to new information technologies.
- Greater freedom to choose software due to a wider range of hardware.
- Ability to achieve technological improvements more easily.
- Greater access to technical skills not available internally.
- Faster application development and placement of IT applications into service.

Management

- Concentration on developing and running core business activity. Improved company focus.
- Delegation of IT development (design, production, and acquisition) and operational responsibility to suppliers.
- Elimination of need to recruit and retain competent IT staff.
- Reduced risk of bad software.

Human Resources

- Opportunity to draw on specialist skills available from a pool of expertise, when needed.
- Enriched career development and opportunities for remaining staff.

Quality

- Clearly defined *service levels* (see Chapter 13).
- Improved performance accountability.
- Improved quality accreditation.

Flexibility

- Quick response to business demands (agility).
- Ability to handle IT peaks and valleys more effectively (flexibility).

Other risks are: irreversibility of the outsourcing decision, possible breach of contract by the vendor or its inability to deliver, loss of control over IT decisions, loss of critical IT skills, vendor lock-in, loss of control over data, loss of employee morale and productivity, and uncontrollable contract growth. Another possible risk of outsourcing is failure to consider all of the costs.

Some costs are hidden. Among the most significant additional expenses associated with outsourcing are: (1) benchmarking and analysis to determine if outsourcing is the right choice, (2) investigating and contracting with a vendor, (3) transitioning work and knowledge to the outsourcer, (4) ongoing staffing and management of the outsourcing relationship, and (5) transitioning back to in-house IT after outsourcing (Barthelemy, 2001, and Overby, 2007). These hidden costs should be considered when making a business case for outsourcing. Depending on what is outsourced and to whom, an organization might end up spending 10 percent above the budgeted amount to set up the relationship and manage it over time. The budgeted amount may increase anywhere from 15 to 65 percent, however, when outsourcing is sent offshore and the costs of travel and cultural differences are added.

The use of IT outsourcing is still very controversial (Marquis, 2006). One reason for the contradicting opinions about outsourcing is that many of the benefits of outsourcing are intangible or have long-term payoffs. Despite concerns, the use of IT outsourcing continues to increase.

Strategies for Outsourcing. Rather than enter into a traditional client–provider relationship, companies may prefer the establishment of a strategic partnership to extend opportunities for growth. When the risks and rewards are shared between the company and its outsourcer, both also share business values and objectives. A secure strategic relationship with outsourcers increases collaborative opportunities for innovation and business transformation. This focus on value creation for both the company and its outsourcer represents a significant shift in the outsourcing relationship.

In making a decision to outsource, executives should consider five major risk areas: (1) higher developmental or operational costs than anticipated, (2) inability to provide the expected service levels at implementation, (3) exceeding the time anticipated for development or transition, (4) allowing the current technical failure(s) to continue, and (5) neglecting to navigate the internal politics of the outsourcing company (Rubin, 2004). Therefore, organizations should consider the following strategies in managing the risks associated with outsourcing contracts (Fish and Seydel, 2006).

1. **Understand the project.** Clients must have a high degree of understanding of the project, including its requirements, the method of its implementation, and the source of expected economic benefits. A common characteristic of successful outsourcing contracts is that the client was generally capable of developing the application but chose to outsource simply because of constraints on time or staff availability.

2. **Divide and conquer.** Dividing a large project into smaller and more manageable pieces will greatly reduce outsourcing risk and provides clients with an exit strategy if any part of the project fails.

3. **Align incentives.** Designing contractual incentives based on activities that can be measured accurately can result in achieving desired performance.

4. **Write short-period contracts.** Outsourcing contracts may be written for five- to ten-year terms. Because IT and the competitive environment change so rapidly, it is very possible that some of the terms will not be in the customer's best interests after five years. If a long-term contract is used, adequate mechanisms for negotiating revisions should be included.

5. **Control subcontracting.** Vendors may subcontract some of the services to other vendors. The contract should give the customer some control over the circumstances, including choice of subcontractors, and any subcontract arrangements.

6. **Do selective outsourcing.** This is a strategy used by many corporations who prefer not to outsource the majority of their IT, but rather to outsource certain areas (such as system integration or network security). Cramm (2001) suggests that an organization *insource* important work, such as strategic applications, investments, and HRM.

The general consensus of the various sources of anecdotal information is that the cost savings of outsourcing are not large (perhaps around 10 percent) and that not all organizations experience savings. This still leaves the question of whether outsourcing IT can improve organizational performance by making it possible to focus more intensely on core competencies. Further research is necessary to answer this question. One area that can provide cost savings is offshore outsourcing.

THE OFFSHORE AND GLOBAL OUTSOURCING DEBATE

Offshore outsourcing of software development, or offshoring, has become a common practice in recent years. Offshore outsourcing is outsourcing with a vendor located in a country other than the one in which the client company is based. This trend is primarily due to global markets, lower costs, and increased access to skilled labor. About one-third of Fortune 500 companies outsource software development to software companies in India.

Worldwide, regional divisions of labor are emerging. India tends to serve the United States, while Eastern Europe and Russia tend to serve Western Europe, and China tends to serve the Asia Pacific area, particularly Japan (Aspray, 2006).

Outsourcing can be done in many countries with various outsourcers. About one-third of Fortune 500 companies outsource software development to software companies in India. It is not only the cost and the technical capabilities that matter. Several factors should be considered, including the business and political environments in the selected country, the quality of the infrastructure, and risks such as IT competency, human capital, the economy, the legal environment, and cultural differences.

Offshore outsourcing can reduce IT expenditures by 15 to 25 percent within the first year, and in the long term, outsourcing can help reduce cost and improve the quality of IT services delivered (Davison, 2004). However, organizations must balance the risks and *uncertainties* involved in offshore outsourcing, including

- Cost-reduction expectations
- Data/security and protection
- Process discipline, which is the use of the same process repeatedly without innovation
- Loss of business knowledge
- Vendor failure to deliver
- Scope creep, which is the request for additional services not included in the outsourcing agreement.
- Government oversight/regulation
- Differences in culture
- Turnover of key personnel
- Knowledge transfer

Based on case studies, the types of work that are not readily offshore outsourced include the following:

- Work that has not been routinized
- Work that if offshored would result in the client company losing too much control over critical operations
- Situations in which offshoring would place the client company at too great a risk to its data security, data privacy, or intellectual property and proprietary information
- Business activities that rely on an uncommon combination of specific application-domain knowledge and IT knowledge in order to do the work properly

EVALUATING OUTSOURCING

Outsourcing relationships are now being assessed on how well business value is delivered, not just on improvements in operational efficiencies and reduced cost. The key drivers of this less tangible goal of business value include the desire to be agile in an increasingly dynamic environment, to continually innovate, and to align with business requirements. In a survey of senior IT managers in the United States and Europe, undertaken by IDG Research Services, the majority rated their ability to measure the business value of outsourcing relationships as "fair" or "poor" (Manter, 2007). They had difficulty in measuring key business benefits, including innovation and thought leadership, risk mitigation, and linking IT value to business value.

A tool useful in measuring the business value of outsourcing relationships is the balanced scorecard. As described in Section 13.3 and presented in Table 13.6, the balanced scorecard framework can be adapted according to an organization's needs. For outsourcing, the balanced scorecard can be applied to assess value creation in the outsourcing relationship. Objectives, divided into value creating processes and outcomes, can be listed along the vertical dimension and specific measures important to the outsourcing relationship can be presented horizontally. Software applications for measurement, such as dashboards for tracking specific measures, can provide metrics. The balanced scorecard can also be used to provide periodic feedback of the value of the outsourcing agreement.

A Closer Look 13.5

JP Morgan Chase Moves from Outsourcing to Insourcing

IS   FIN

JP Morgan Chase, the second-largest bank in the United States, is one of the world's largest financial institutions, with more than $1.2 trillion in assets. In September 2004 Chase scrapped a seven-year, $5 billion IT outsourcing contract with IBM after its $58 billion acquisition of Bank One. The merger automatically voided the outsourcing contract. As a result, the company carefully evaluated its sourcing options over two to three months and decided to bring IT back in-house, a strategy known as **insourcing.** The acquisition created massive economies of scale, and such a large organization is able to attract and retain talented IT professionals. Furthermore, CIO Austin Adams achieved early career success by building on his ability to integrate bank mergers quickly and make the merged entity more competitive through its use of technology.

People who oppose outsourcing, especially offshoring, declared the "end of outsourcing." As a matter of fact, Adams, who pushed for the scrapping, said that his move was greatly misunderstood by the media who pegged him as a patriot trying to keep IT jobs in the United States. "I am clearly an advocate of offshoring." While in the case of such a large bank there was a reason for insourcing, mainly to get a better competitive advantage from IT, Adams believes that in smaller organizations, large-scale outsourcing is logical. Further, Adams presides over 3,000 offshore employees in India, who work in the bank's call center and also do basic operations and accounting functions. This offshoring is expected to grow rapidly.

Adams was key in the decision to insource IT at JP Morgan Chase and offers his observations:

- The cancellation was driven mainly by the merger with Bank One, which made the combined bank very large.
- Outsourcing of major parts of mission-critical technologies is not a best solution for a large firm. Technology development should be in-house; support services can be outsourced.
- Four criteria were used to determine what and how much to outsource: (1) the size of the company (should be large enough to attract good IS employees), (2) cost of outsourcing vs. cost of insourcing, (3) the interest level of top management to have and properly manage IT assets, and (4) financial arrangements of the outsourcing.
- It may be difficult to align business and technology objectives when large-scale outsourcing exists.
- The insourcing includes data centers, help desks, data processing networks, and systems development.
- Buying technology directly from vendors saved the bank a considerable amount of money (10 to 15 percent).

Sources: Compiled from Adams (2006) and Barrett (2006).

For Further Exploration: How can one determine when a company is large enough for insourcing? How important is the financial consideration? How accurate is it?

For the *multi-vendor approach,* wherein the services of several outsourcing vendors are contracted, measures should be applied to each. A company may choose to institute a project management office to track all outsourcing agreements. A dedicated staff, with financial as well as technical skills, would be assigned to oversee each vendor relationship and establish regular reviews of vendor performance. A balanced scorecard, which applies metrics from measurement software applications such as dashboards, could be used to assess the performance of each of the various vendors. *A Closer Look 13.5* illustrates circumstances under which insourcing becomes preferable to outsourcing.

Review Questions

1. What is outsourcing?
2. What are some of the major reasons for outsourcing?
3. What IT functions are outsourced?
4. Distinguish between mega outsourcing and the multi-vendor approach to outsourcing.
5. What are the benefits of outsourcing? What are the risks of outsourcing?
6. Discuss the strategies organizations should consider in managing the risks associated with outsourcing contracts.
7. Distinguish between outsourcing and offshore outsourcing.
8. What types of work are not readily outsourced offshore?
9. Describe a tool useful in measuring the business value of outsourcing relationships.

13.5 Managerial Issues

1. **Aligning IT strategy and business strategy.** Alignment remains an important issue for CIOs, in part because failure to align IT to business strategy is believed to result in the failure of many IS initiatives. For IT planners to achieve the desired linkage between the business strategy and IT strategy, they should possess a deep understanding of their company's business planning. Similarly, business managers must possess solid knowledge of their company's IT planning.

2. **Organizing for effective planning.** Many issues are involved in planning: What should be the role of the CIO and the IT division within the organization and the planning process? What is the strategic direction of the organization? With this business direction, what strategies and objectives should IT pursue?

3. **Initiating IT strategy.** Corporations must initiate the formulation of IT strategy, once the corporation's overall strategic plan has been devised. Important in addressing IT strategy is an understanding of the critical strategic role of IT to the business. How does IT assume a strategic role in the firm?—by leveraging the value added and gaining a competitive advantage through innovative applications of IT.

4. **Undertaking the IT strategic planning process.** A good IT planning process can help ensure that IT aligns, and stays aligned, within an organization. The focus of IT strategy is on how IT creates business value. An IT *steering committee* formulates the *long-range IT plan*, sometimes referred to as the *strategic IT plan*, based on the strategic business plan. Included is the IT vision and strategy to define the future concept of what IT should do to achieve the goals, objectives, and strategic position of the firm and how this will be achieved. The overall direction, requirements, and sourcing of resources are set for five to ten years into the future.

5. **Dealing with outsourcing and offshoring.** As opportunities for outsourcing become cheaper, available, and viable, the concept becomes more attractive. How much to outsource, whether to outsource offshore, and how to evaluate how well business value is delivered are major managerial issues.

How *IT* Benefits You

For the Accounting Major

For the IT strategic plan, huge up-front investments may be required. Accountants need to assess the direct impact of the costs associated with the IT strategic plan on a firm's bottom line. Accountants are involved in the processes of business planning, controlling, cost behavior, cost allocation, budgeting, and performance measurement of IT investments. Accountants must understand and be able to balance the need for cost control and containment with the need to invest in IT innovations to remain competitive. Cost allocation methods and budgeting may be complex. Costs may be difficult to justify using purely quantitative methods; the balanced scorecard approach may be a useful tool.

For the Finance Major

With IT budgets and staff trimmed down to the essentials, finance managers need to work closely with IT managers to jointly set priorities for capital investments, negotiate service levels, keep one another up-to-date about how IT is impacting day-to-day business performance, and calculate returns on IT investments. The profitability of the firm depends on the finance function's ability to correctly determine which IT project plans to approve and which to deny.

That determination requires understanding the sustainability of competitive advantages provided by various IT architectures and their alignment with the business strategy.

For the Human Resources Management Major

Not only must new information systems be planned to support strategic objectives, their impacts on personnel must be planned for and controlled. When a company designs new information systems, it redesigns the organization. Outsourcing IT activities relates to personnel levels and required skills. Human resources managers need to understand the potential impacts of IT plans on workers to minimize negative consequences on employees and the system itself. Not all employees are comfortable working remotely, in a virtual world, or with different cultures, should offshore outsourcing be contracted. Employee training and other preparations may make the difference between the success and failure of new IT investments.

For the IS Major

Information systems managers and professionals must have a business understanding in addition to technical skills. The information systems department must focus on the integration of internal operations with each other and with the environment, the evaluation of business risk and strategy alternatives, and the development of long-range IT plans and programs. Understanding the strategic potential of information systems is crucial to obtaining significant value from information system investments. Generating value from information systems continues to be one of the most significant challenges facing IS personnel—and of considerable interest to senior executives in other functional areas.

For the Marketing Major

Without the ability to deliver quality products and services at competitive prices and at the time they are needed (or wanted), the ability to attract new customers and retain existing ones is at risk. Marketers need to be involved in IT planning because they bring to the table the customer's perspective as well as knowledge of what competitors are doing. One of the most strategic IT initiatives is customer relationship management (CRM). Marketers are responsible for ensuring that the requirements for successful customer-facing strategic applications are understood by the IT department as well as those in accounting and finance.

For the Production/Operations Management Major

Flexible production systems and integrated supply chain systems are complex undertakings that require the active involvement of production and operations managers. Suppliers or customers expect, and may even demand, that their business partners provide flexible, integrated systems to be part of their supply chain. Strategic information systems can quickly become necessary for survival. Information systems are needed that alert production managers of delivery delays, production disruptions, product defects, order cancellations, and so on.

Key Terms

Applications portfolio   *499*

Balanced scorecard   *502*

Business strategy   *488*

Business systems planning (BSP) model   *501*

Competitive advantage   *494*

Critical success factors (CSFs)   *502*

Information systems (IS) strategy   *488*

Information technology (IT) strategy   *488*

Information technology (IT)–business alignment   *488*

Insourcing   *511*

IT strategic planning   *499*

Offshore outsourcing   *509*

Outsourcing   *506*

Project portfolio   *499*

Resource allocation   *506*

Scenario planning   *503*

Sourcing   *499*

Chapter Highlights

(Numbers Refer to Learning Objectives)

1 IT strategic alignment ensures that IS priorities, decisions, and projects are consistent with the needs of the entire business.

1 The business strategy and IT strategy must be aligned with shared ownership and shared governance of IT among all members of the senior executive team.

1 IT–business alignment can be fostered within an organization by focusing on activities central to alignment.

2 The main challenge to achieving IT–business alignment is for the CIO to attain strategic influence.

3 The global economy is defined by innovative use of IT.

4 IT can add value to a company in one of two general ways—either *directly* by *reducing costs* or *indirectly* by *increasing revenues.*

4 IT can enable a temporary or sustained competitive advantage through both a firm's IT and its deployment of IT.

4 Information systems can contribute three types of resources to a firm: technology resources, technical capabilities, and IT managerial resources.

5 The focus of IT strategy is on how IT creates business value.

5 The entire planning process begins with the creation of a strategic business plan. The *long-range IT plan,* or *strategic IT plan,* is then based on the strategic business plan. The IT strategic plan starts with the IT vision and strategy.

5 The planning process also addresses lower-level activities with a shorter timeframe. A *medium-term IT plan* identifies general project plans in terms of the specific requirements and sourcing of resources as well as the project portfolio. Some companies may also define their application portfolio.

5 Several tools and methodologies facilitate IT strategic planning, including business service management, the business systems planning (BSP) model, the balanced scorecard, critical success factors (CSFs), and scenario planning.

6 The major reasons for outsourcing include a desire to focus on core competency, cost reduction, improve quality, increase speed to market, and faster innovation.

7 Outsourcing may reduce IT costs and can make it possible for organizations to concentrate on their core competencies. However, outsourcing may reduce the company's flexibility to find the best IT fit for the business, and it may also pose a security risk.

7 In making a decision to outsource, executives should consider major risk areas.

Virtual Company Assignment

IT Strategic Planning at The Wireless Café

Go to The Wireless Café's link on the Student Web Site. There you will be asked to identify how IT is providing value, either *directly* by *reducing costs* or *indirectly* by *increasing revenues*, to the restaurant.

Instructions for accessing The Wireless Café on the Student Web Site:

1. Go to *wiley.com/college/turban*.
2. Select Turban/Volonino's *Information Technology for Management*, Seventh Edition.
3. Click on Student Resources site, in the toolbar on the left.
4. Click on the link for Virtual Company Web site.
5. Click on Wireless Café.

Questions for Discussion

1. What does failure to properly align IT with the organizational strategy result in?
2. How can the governance structure within an organization be designed to facilitate IT–business alignment?
3. Why does IT–business alignment continue to be an important issue for CIOs?
4. What does successful IT–business alignment require?
5. Discuss how a CIO might interact with executive management as technology becomes increasingly central to a business.
6. Three characteristics of resources give firms the potential to create a competitive advantage. Discuss the potential of a firm's IT resources to add value to a company.
7. What is an opportunity matrix of business improvement with IT and how could a CIO employ this matrix?
8. Discuss how the partnership between the IT division and business management can extend to fuse with the business.
9. Describe the IT strategic planning process.
10. What tools facilitate IT strategic planning?
11. Discuss resource allocation to execute IT development plans.
12. A company may choose to outsource or offshore outsource. Compare and discuss these options.
13. Describe strategies for outsourcing.
14. Describe how a company might assess the business value delivered by an outsourcing relationship.

Exercises and Projects

1. Read "IT Strategic Alignment at Kimberly-Clark: The Innovation Design Studio" at the beginning of the chapter. Identify critical success factors (CSFs) for Kimberly-Clark.
2. Read "IT Strategic Alignment at Kimberly-Clark: The Innovation Design Studio" at the beginning of the chapter. Refer to Table 13.5 to prepare an opportunity matrix of business process improvement with IT for Kimberly-Clark.
3. Read "IT Strategic Alignment at Kimberly-Clark: The Innovation Design Studio" at the beginning of the chapter. Apply the balanced scorecard to address the four important questions within the balanced scorecard framework.
4. Visit the Web site of Amazon.com. Click on "Careers at Amazon" and read "About Amazon." Begin applying the business systems planning (BSP) approach by identifying
Amazon's business strategies and what applications support these strategies.
5. Consider the airline industry. Identify how IT adds business value within this industry. Be sure to address value added both directly and indirectly by IT.
6. Visit *teradatastudentnetwork.com*. Read and answer the questions to the case: "Data Warehousing Supports Corporate Strategy at First American Corporation." Describe the customer relationship-oriented strategy of First American Corporation and how it is supported by IT. Contrast this strategy with that of other financial service companies.
7. Select two companies with which you are familiar. Find their mission statement and current goals (plans). Explain how IT adds value in achieving each of these goals.
8. Identify reasons why the alignment of business strategy and IT strategy might not be achieved.

Group Assignments and Projects

1. Innovative use of IT has become increasingly important in the global economy. Choose multiple industries and provide an example company for each industry in which IT plays a strategic role by adding value and providing a competitive advantage through innovative application of IT. Now identify competitive counterpart companies for which IT does not play a strategic role. Report on the successes/failures of each pair of companies.

2. A strategic CIO focuses on the use of IT as a core business tool with which to add value and provide a competitive advantage. Identify a CIO, such as Marc West, the

senior VP and CIO at H&R Block, introduced in *A Closer Look 13.2* "The Emerging Role of the Strategic CIO." Research the CIO you identified. Report on his/her background, education, experience, management style, and, most importantly, why you believe this CIO is a strategic CIO.

3. Considerable discussions and disagreements occur among IT professionals regarding outsourcing. Divide the group into two parts: One will defend the strategy of large-scale outsourcing. One will oppose it. Start by collecting recent material at *google.com* and *cio.com*. Consider the issue of offshore outsourcing.

Internet Exercises

1. Visit *cio.com* to find articles addressing the changing role of the CIO. Read these articles and write a report highlighting the changes.

2. Visit the IBM CIO Interaction Channel at *http://www-935.ibm.com/services/ie/cio*. This site showcases insights and perspectives on the issues that matter most to CIOs, including the most important one of all—aligning IT with overall business goals. Select a topic that interests you, read a report on that topic, and summarize the main points of the report.

3. Visit the Web site of Amazon.com. Discuss how IT adds value to the customer's purchase experience at Amazon.com.

4. Enter the Web site for Cognos at *cognos.com* and search on balanced scorecard software. Identify and describe their balanced scorecard software product.

5. Visit FireScope at *firescope.com*. Discuss how business service management software tools provide real-time

dashboard views for tracking key performance indicators at the executive, functional business areas, services, and operations levels.

6. Visit *accenture.com* and search on outsourcing. Prepare a report that overviews the IT outsourcing services offered by Accenture. Do the same for the four largest international accountancy and professional services firms: Deloitte Touche Tohmatsu at *deloitte.com*, Ernst & Young at *ey.com*, KPMG at *kpmg.com*, and PricewaterhouseCoopers at *pwc.com*.

7. Enter the Web site for the Association for Computing Machinery to access their report on "Globalization and Offshoring of Software" at *acm.org/globalizationreport*. Select two of the case studies presented in Section 4.2 on pages 136–152. Write a report contrasting the two companies.

Minicase

The Second Life Strategy of American Apparel

American Apparel (*americanapparel.net*) is a vertically integrated manufacturer, distributor, and retailer of branded apparel, based in Los Angeles, California. Recognized as a "unique and exciting retail brand in the global market" (Anonymous, 2008), American Apparel operates 190 retail stores in 15 countries, employing over 7,000 people. The company's progressive business strategy and provocative advertising campaigns have set the company apart in the fashion world. One first-mover strategy to set them apart was to enter Second Life.

Second Life

Launched on June 23, 2003, Second Life is an Internet-based 3-D virtual world of elaborate landscapes and cityscapes. Developed by Linden Research, Inc. (a.k.a. Linden Labs),

Second Life (*secondlife.com*) received international attention via mainstream news media in late 2006 and early 2007, emerging as a social network of real promise. Interaction, collaboration, and commerce are brought to a new level. The number of registered users skyrocketed from 100,000 at the beginning of 2005 to more than 1.5 million.

In this simulated world, populated by animated cartoon avatars fashioned by their human alter egos, "residents" use Linden dollars to buy and sell things that exist only "in world." About 280 Linden dollars are equivalent to one U.S. dollar. As much as $6.6 million in user transactions changed hands in one month. Avatars pay real money to buy land and buildings from Linden and to shop in virtual stores for virtual clothing and music. In addition to shopping, users role-play, chat, hold jobs, build homes, open restaurants, travel, attend concerts or parties, and push politics. What distinguishes Second Life from some of the other virtual worlds is that players have access to 3-D modeling tools and scripting technology, freeing them to create and sell clothes, homes, and other products, rather than being confined to an established environment designed by a game company's programmers.

The Commercial Promise of Second Life

Three-dimensional virtual worlds such as Second Life are becoming a very real component of people's lives. The ability to engage consumers has great appeal. Some firms are using virtual worlds as marketing tools to reach consumers. The demographics are appealing for marketers. According to Linden Lab, the average user is 32 years of age, 57% are male, and 40% live outside the United States. That's an audience increasingly hard to reach through traditional media such as TV.

Online synthetic worlds are expected to play an increasingly vital role in business-to-consumer relationships, building customer loyalty through time and commitment. Such virtual environments may even come to dominate and drive brand building for major companies.

American Apparel Ventures into a New Strategy

Recognizing the demographic of Second Life as a prized market segment, American Apparel saw a unique opportunity for marketing, sales, and building customer relationships. Marketing to a youth audience—a broad youth audience, ages 18–30—is more challenging than ever because it is fragmented. Marketers cannot put all of their money into one thing or another, such as television or print. Instead of targeting passive viewers of such advertising, marketers will have to try new channels. American Apparel sees the Second Life world as a platform to actively interact with and sell to engaged users, thereby developing a relationship with them.

Raz Schionning, director of Web services, became convinced that the online role-playing game is the market of tomorrow. These emerging social computing networks of online communities sharing interests and activities hold the potential to redefine customer relationship management. Schionning recalls, "I pitched the idea to the creative team here—the people who handle our print and traditional marketing." American Apparel set out on a bold boundary-pushing experiment to reach a young, tech-savvy audience and to explore what the future of the Internet might mean for business. Schionning commented, "When we think about Web marketing, it makes sense to not just put your money in banner panels." American Apparel took an experimental approach, focusing on long-term added value, "not a profit-making venture."

American Apparel's Virtual Store

American Apparel was the first major real-world company to formally enter Second Life by opening a virtual store on June 21, 2006. Among waterfalls and lights on an idyllic island, American Apparel launched the grand opening of its first virtual mega-store. The gala event included music, virtual tacos, virtual goody bags, and virtual beer. Free virtual T-shirts were handed out to avatar shoppers.

American Apparel hired virtual sales clerks from among Second Life's residents. Additional clothing merchandise items were added to the 20 styles offered at the time of opening. Two months before being introduced in physical stores, American Apparel test-marketed its first line of jeans. And, in an effort to drive traffic to both the virtual and the physical stores, anyone purchasing clothes in Second Life after the grand opening party received a coupon for a 15% discount on merchandise bought in real-world stores.

Not surprisingly, clothing became one of the hottest items to purchase in Second Life. A few short months later, in August 2006, the 20 best-selling Second Life fashion designers generated a combined $140,466 in sales, according to Linden Labs. The American Apparel store realized sales of 4,000 items. If the retailer can attract and maintain the attention of its online and physical customers, it just might attain the increased sales revenue it is seeking.

American Apparel is not alone in establishing a presence in Second Life. For example, Pontiac, Nissan, and Toyota are selling virtual cars. Adidas and Reebok sell sneakers, but forming customer relationships, not sales, is the primary goal. Starwood started testing a virtual version of its new Aloft hotel chain. Coca-Cola and Sears have set up virtual stores to market products and test prototypes. Ad agency Leo Burnett built an "Ideas Hub" where its global staff can meet and interact. Sun Microsystems hosted a "virtual news conference" to tout its new gaming strategy. INSEAD, an international business school based in Fontainebleau near Paris, built a virtual campus and classrooms to supplement in-class learning.

American Apparel's Business Outcome

Schionning admits to some initial ambivalence about the Second Life store and notes, "We know there is a lot to be learned in this arena." In summer 2007, American Apparel chained shut its virtual store in Second Life and posted the following:

Sorry, We're Closed

Last summer [2006] we opened up our Second Life American Apparel store with a grand opening party with tacos, a few cases of beer, and a piñata. We didn't know what to expect or if anybody would even show up.

Needless to say, it's been quite a year. We've had thousands of visitors from all over the world and made a ton of new friends, seen some interesting things from furry folks to virtual terrorism, caused a bit of a clamor, and sold some virtual t-shirts and it's been great. But we feel like our time is up here. So we're closing our doors on Lerappa Island for now. This doesn't mean we're finished with the virtual world. Stay tuned to see what we do next.

What American Apparel did next was move to the younger, hipper MTV's Virtual Lower East Side (*vles.com*), which opened to the public in January 2008. A new online social network that revolves around New York City's Lower East Side, vLES, encourages new visitors to stop by the American Apparel store to "get actual, literal clothes that you can put on your actual, literal body. Then you can get virtual clothes for your avatar too, which is pretty awesome."

Lessons Learned from This Case

Numerous companies have explored synthetic worlds, though many eventually abandoned them. Reebok, Adidas, and Starwood Hotels also closed their Second Life stores because they were not making a profit. New cutting edge technologies require a willingness to experiment. American Apparel has accepted this inevitability within their IT strategy. Virtual worlds may indeed play a significant role in the future of the Internet, but it is yet to be determined what value this new and evolving IT platform holds for American Apparel in particular and business in general.

Sources: Compiled from *americanapparel.net* (accessed June 2008), American Apparel, Inc. (2008), Lardi-Nadarajan (2008), Lavallee (2006), and Ohrstrom (2008).

Questions for Minicase

1. Did American Apparel fail at its business strategy by closing the virtual store in Second Life? In your opinion, does a presence in an Internet-based 3-D virtual world provide value to a company?

2. How does the opening of store in Second Life support American Apparel's business strategy?

3. What are the benefits to American Apparel opening a store in Second Life?

4. Visit the Web site for YouTube and view the "American Apparel" video at *youtube.com/watch?v=ksjnNmL1bGw*. What is your reaction to the video?

5. Do you believe the Second Life experience in the American Apparel store is an effective form of advertising?

6. In your opinion, do the Second Life user experiences develop a relationship between American Apparel and customers that results in increased customer loyalty?

7. Visit MTV's Virtual Lower East Side at *vles.com* and explore the site. Will American Apparel's presence on this online social network support American Apparel's business strategy better than the virtual store in Second Life? Explain why or why not.

Problem-Solving Activity

Assessing IT Strategic Planning at Sleepwell Hotels

Sleepwell Hotels is a national chain of low-budget hotels, with more than 325 locations nationwide that serve 700,000 customers annually. The company's net income is $310 million, and its assets total $8.1 million. Sleepwell Hotels has been known as a leader in economy lodging because of its dedication to guest satisfaction. The recently hired CEO, Paul Carlson, is developing a new customer-focused business strategy. According to Susie Siesta, CIO and executive VP of national distribution services, Sleepwell Hotels does not have a current formally documented IT strategic plan.

CIO Siesta explains that a documented IT strategic plan is not really necessary yet, because:

- The CEO is new and has not yet finished his new business strategy.

- She attends meetings with executive management regularly, at least once a month if not more frequently. Information technology is a regular topic in these meetings, and she feels she has executive management's support in the current direction of the IT division.

- The IT division is managing two very large development projects currently under way:
  1. Upgrading to a new version of the Fidelio front-office (FO) management system, which provides a complete array of hotel management modules, including reservations, front desk, cashiering, housekeeping, night audit, leisure management, rates and availability, groups and blocks, guest history, reporting, and security
  2. A Business Intelligence system to analyze customer purchases at a macro level, as opposed to gathering data only from individual customer transactions

- A data warehouse is not yet implemented.

- The Marketing department has contracted with an outside consultation firm to install a new Customer Relationship Management system.

- There is a hardware acquisition plan based on a capacity planning study first done two years ago with the help of the hardware vendor and updated every six months. The plan covers the next three years and takes into account the computing equipment for the hotel's headquarters and all hotel locations.

Your Mission

Prepare a report for CIO Siesta that addresses the following:

1. Convince CIO Siesta to undertake a formal IT strategic plan. What is the rationale and what arguments would you make to convince her?

2. If you succeeded in convincing her, what overall approach to the IT strategic plan would you recommend to her? Who should be included?

3. What specific issues confronting Sleepwell Hotels and the IT division should be addressed in the IT strategic plan and why? Be sure to discuss the relationship between the business strategy and IT strategy.

4. What tools and methodologies for IT strategic planning do you recommend and why?

5. How should resource allocation be undertaken?

Online Resources

More resources and study tools are located on the Student Web Site and on WileyPlus. You'll find additional chapter materials and useful Web links. In addition, self-quizzes that provide individualized feedback are available for each chapter.

Online Briefs for Chapter 13 are available at wiley.com/college/turban:

13.1 Applications Portfolios
13.2 Ward and Peppard's Strategic Planning Framework

Online Minicases for Chapter 13 are available at wiley.com/college/turban:

13.1 GM's Globally Positioned Outsourcing Strategy
13.2 The Grid Utility Computing Strategy for the STAR Experiment

References

Adams, A., "Mistaken Identity," *CIO Insight,* March 2006.

American Apparel, Inc., "Dov Charney of American Apparel Named Retailer of the Year," *Science Letter,* May 27, 2008.

Aspray, W., F. Mayadas, and M. Y. Vardi (eds.), *Globalization and Offshoring of Software,* A Report of the ACM Job Migration Task Force. New York City, NY: ACM, 2006.

Barrett, L., "A Return Home," *Baseline,* January 2006.

Barthelemy, J., "The Hidden Costs of IT Outsourcing," *MIT Sloan Management Review,* Spring 2001.

Basu, A., and C. Jarnagin, "How to Tap IT's Hidden Potential," *Wall Street Journal,* March 14, 2008.

Beal, B., "IT–business Alignment Elusive for Some," *searchCIO.com,* March 24, 2004.

Biddick, M., "Hunting the Elusive CIO Dashboard," *InformationWeek,* March 3, 2008, Issue 1175.

Carmel, E., and R. Agarwal, "The Maturity of Offshore Sourcing of IT Work," *MISQ Executive,* 1(2), June 2002.

Center for CIO Leadership, "The CIO Profession: Driving Innovation and Competitive Advantage," October 2007.

Chan, Y. E., "Why Haven't We Mastered Alignment? The Importance of the IT Informal Organization Structure," *MIS Quarterly Executive,* June 2002.

Clemons, E. K., "The Build/Buy Battle," *CIO,* December 1, 2000.

Collins, L., "Efficient and Effective," *IEE Review,* 50(1), January 2004.

Corbett, M. F., "Taking the Pulse of Outsourcing," *Firmbuilder.com* (data and analysis from the 2001 Outsourcing World Summit), December 6, 2001.

Cramm, S. H., "The Dark Side of Outsourcing," *CIO,* November 15, 2001.

Davison, D., "Top 10 Risks of Offshore Outsourcing," Meta Group Inc., 2004, *www2.cio.com/analyst/report2224.html* (accessed June 2008).

Ehrlich, L., and M. West, "The Strategic CIO: Using Leadership Skills and IT to Create Competitive Advantage," *CIO.com,* May 1, 2007, *cio.com/article/107058* (accessed June 2008).

Farrell, D., "Smarter Offshoring," *Harvard Business Review,* June 2006.

Fish, K. E., and J. Seydel, "Where IT Outsourcing Is and Where It Is Going: A Study Across Functions and Department Sizes," *The Journal of Computer Information Systems,* 46(3), Spring 2006, p. 96.

Hewlett-Packard Company, "IT Consolidation: Journey to an Adaptive Enterprise—An Overview," *hp.com,* February 1, 2004, *wp.bitpipe.com/resource/org_1000733242_857/IT_Consolidation_Journey_WP4_In_Net ork.pdf?site_cd=gtech* (accessed June 2008).

Hoffman, T., and C. Stedman, "Forget IT-Business Alignment—It's All about Fusion Now, CIOs Say," *Computerworld,* March 12, 2008, *computerworld.com/action/article.do?command=viewArticleBasic&articleId=9068178* (accessed June 2008).

Hoffman, T., "Change Agents," *Computerworld,* April 23, 2007.

IBM, "The Outsourcing Decision for a Globally Integrated Enterprise: From Commodity Outsourcing to Value Creation," January 2008.

"Open-Source Adopters Prove a Mixed Bag," *IT Week,* London, March 10, 2008.

Jakovljevic, P. J., "Get on the Grid: Utility Computing," *Technology Evaluation Centers,* March 31, 2005.

Jusko, J., "Kimberly–Clark Embraces Virtual Reality," December 1, 2007, *industryweek.com/ReadArticle.aspx?ArticleID=15349* (accessed June 2008).

Kaplan, R. S., and D. P. Norton, "Mastering the Management System," *Harvard Business Review,* 86(1), January 2008.

Kaplan, R. S., and D. P. Norton, "Using the Balanced Scorecard as a Strategic Management System," *Harvard Business Review,* 85(7, 8), July/August 2007.

Kaplan, R. S., and D. P. Norton, "The Balanced Scorecard: Measures That Drive Performance," *Harvard Business Review,* 83(7, 8), July/August 2005.

Kesner, R. M., "Running Information Services as a Business," *IS Management Handbook,* 8th ed., Carol V. Brown and Heikki Topi (eds.). Boca Raton, FL: CRC Press, 2003.

Lardi-Nadarajan, K., "Doing Business in Virtual Worlds," *CIO Insight,* March 3, 2008, *cioinsight.com/c/a/Trends/Doing-Business-in-Virtual-Worlds/1* (accessed June 2008).

Lavallee, A., "Now, Virtual Fashion: Second Life Designers Make Real Money Creating Clothes for Simulation Game's Players," *Wall Street Journal,* September 22, 2006.

Licker, P. S., "An Interview with Warren Ritchie, Director of IT Governance Americas Regions," *Journal of Global Information Technology Management,* 9(4), 2006.

Luftman, J., "SIM 2007 Survey Findings SIM 2007 Survey Findings," *SIMposium 07,* October 7–12, 2007, *simposium.simnet.org.*

Marquis, H. A., "Finishing Off IT," *MIT Sloan Management Review,* 47(4), Summer 2006.

Manter, T., "Smarter Sourcing: Measuring and Communicating the Success of Sourcing Relationships," *CXO Media Inc.,* 2007, *noa.co.uk/UserFiles/File/ClientBriefs_CXO_SmarterSourcing.pdf* (accessed June 2008).

McGee, M. K., "Kimberly–Clark—Virtual Product Center Yields Real Ideas," *InformationWeek,* September 17, 2007.

Minevich, M., and F. J. Richter, "The Global Outsourcing Report," *CIO Insight,* special whiteboard report, 2005.

Ohrstrom, L., "American Apparel Opens Virtual Lower East Side Store," *The New York Observer,* January 10, 2008, *observer.com/2008/american-apparel-opens-new-branch-virtual-lower-east-side* (accessed June 2008).

Orlov, L. M., "Closing the CEO–CIO Gap," *Business Executives and IT series,* Forrester Research, Inc., February 2007.

Overby, S., "ABC: An Introduction to Outsourcing," *CIO.com,* March 9, 2007, *cio.com/article/40380* (accessed June 2008).

Patterson, D. A., "Offshoring: Finally Facts vs. Folklore," *Communications of the ACM,* 49(2), February 2006.

Peffers, K., and C. E. Gengler, "Understanding Internal IS Customer Models of Firm Performance to Identify Potential High-Impact Projects," *Proceedings of the 33rd Annual Hawaiian International Conference on Systems Sciences,* January 4–7, 2000, Maui, Hawaii.

Peffers, K., and C. E. Gengler, "How to Identify New High-Payoff Information Systems for the Organization," *Communications of the ACM,* 46(1), January 2003.

Prahalad, C. K., and M. S. Krishnan, "The Dynamic Synchronization of Strategy and Information Technology," *Sloan Management Review,* 43(4), Summer 2002.

Rubin, R., "Outsourcing Imperative: Do or Die," *Optimize,* January 2004.

Scott, G. M., "Still Not Solved: The Persistent Problem of IT Strategic Planning," *Communications of the AIS,* 16, 2005.

Serva, M. A., S. A. Sherer, and J. C. Sipior, "'When Do You ASP?' The Software Life Cycle Control Model," *Information Systems Frontiers,* 5(2), January 2003.

Seybold, P. B., "Get Inside the Lives of Your Customers," *Harvard Business Review,* May 2001.

Shpilberg, D., S. Berez, R. Puryear, and S. Shah, "Avoiding the Alignment Trap in Information Technology," *MIT Sloan Management Review,* 49(1), Fall 2007.

Stauffer, D., "Five Reasons Why You Still Need Scenario Planning," *Harvard Business Review,* June 2002.

Wade, M., and J. Hulland, "The Resource-based View and Information Systems Research: Review, Extension, and Suggestions for Future Research," *MIS Quarterly,* March 2004.

Wailgum, T., "How to Stay Close to the Business," January 10, 2008, *cio.com/article/171150/How_to_Stay_Close_to_the_Business* (accessed June 2008).

Ward, J., and J. Peppard, *Strategic Planning for Information Systems,* 3rd ed. New York: Wiley, 2002.

Weiss, J. W., A. Thorogood, and K. D. Clark, "Three IT–Business Alignment Profiles: Technical Resource, Business Enabler, and Strategic Weapon," *Communications of the Association for Information Systems,* 18, 2006.

Worthen, B., "Business Technology: The IT Factor: Tech Staff's Bigger Role; Increased Input Helps Products Debut Faster, Deals Become Successful," *Wall Street Journal,* December 4, 2007.

Learning Objectives

After studying this chapter, you will be able to:

1 Understand the concept of the technology adoption lifecycle.

2 Describe the five stages of the adoption lifecycle.

3 Understand the impact of technology, task, individual, organizational, and environmental characteristics on the adoption of new technologies.

4 Describe Rogers' five adopter categories.

5 Understand typical causes for IT implementation failures.

6 Discuss challenges associated with implementing IT projects.

7 Understand the concept of business process management (BPM) and how it can be used to enhance effectiveness in an organization.

8 List and describe the steps in creating an effective BPM strategy.

9 Describe the role of change management in systems implementation.

Integrating *IT*

ACC

FIN

MKT

OM

HRM

IS

IT-PERFORMANCE MODEL

As we have discussed in previous chapters, IT expenditures have unquestionably transformed organizations. In fact, these technologies have become an integral aspect of almost every business process. The business and technology presses publish many "success stories" about major benefits from information technology projects at individual organizations or even industries (e.g., electronic airline ticketing). It seems self-evident that these investments must have increased productivity, not just in individual organizations, but throughout the economy. In this chapter, we consider the management of IT projects, processes, and the organizational changes that result from IT implementations. We discuss the increases in ROI and profitability that result when all three dimensions—projects, processes, and people—are managed correctly.

The business performance management cycle and IT model.

CON-WAY, INC. IMPLEMENTS INNOVATIVE TECHNOLOGY AND WINS NATIONAL RECOGNITION

Named *Fortune* magazine's "Most Admired Company" in transportation and logistics for 2007, Con-way, Inc. is a $4.7 billion freight transportation and logistics services company headquartered in San Mateo, California. Con-way delivers industry-leading services through its primary operating companies of Con-way Freight, CFI and Con-way Truckload, and Menlo Worldwide Logistics.

Con-way, Inc. and its subsidiaries operate from 460 operating locations across North America and in 17 countries across five continents. Con-way capabilities include:

- Global operations in 17 countries across five continents
- A network of 460 operating locations across North America
- More than 27,000 highly trained personnel
- Con-way Freight: Local, regional, and transcontinental LTL (less than truckload) transportation services
- Menlo Worldwide Logistics: Designs, implements, and manages supply chain solutions, including logistics and transportation management, warehousing and distribution
- Con-way Truckload and CFI: A network of full truckload services across the United States and Canada

The Problem

Over the years, Con-way had moved from using basic technology to handle its complex logistics problems to the deployment of leading-edge information technologies, including asset management software, a service-oriented architecture (SOA), business intelligence tools, and virtualization technology. These ITs improve internal processes, offer innovative new services to its customers, and reduce costs of hardware and service administration.

For example, in 2006, Con-way was experiencing inefficiencies in its dock operations and needed to reduce its planning time and forklift traffic and increase the pounds of freight handled per labor-hour. To accomplish these tasks, Con-way developed a Web-based, interaction Step Saver tool to automate the planning process enabling dock coordinators to achieve optimal loads. Step Saver has been implemented at 26 facilities and has achieved a 5.2 percent improvement in pounds handled per labor-hour, a 35 percent reduction in planning time, and a 21 percent decrease in forklift travel.

In 2007, the company began testing Wi-Fi systems and RFID technology to track shipments across its North American network of service centers.

One of Con-way's biggest challenges, however, was not related to tracking shipments, but instead centered around recording and transmitting driver payroll data at Con-way Freight. Con-way Freight is the premier provider of regional, inter-regional, and nationwide LTL service to customers across an integrated North American network of LTL operating locations. These operating units provide high-performance, LTL, full truckload, and intermodal freight transportation; logistics, warehousing, and supply chain management services; and trailer manufacturing. From its facility located in the San Francisco Bay area, Con-way sends out 46 short-haul pickup and delivery drivers and 16 line-haul truckers, who cover longer-distance overnight and two-day trips, every day. In any 24-hour period, more than 700 shipments are received and dispatched at the Hayward operation that acts as a staging point for local Bay Area shipments and as a freight assembly center for overnight loads. Hayward is just one of 440 Con-way service centers scattered across North America with a total of 15,000 drivers.

Despite deployment of innovative technology to handle shipping activities, payroll sheets—known as Form 265s—were still being handwritten by its 15,000 drivers. The forms were then collected at individual service centers across the country and sent by courier to Con-way's Portland operations center for manual entry by data clerks. It is ironic that Con-way, a major freight-shipping company, was relying on an outside provider to transport its Form 265s each week and paying nearly $500

thousand annually for this service. The problem was that forms were being lost, misplaced, or delivered late, and employee satisfaction and morale was suffering. It was evident that this would not be an easy fix—the Form 265s was complex and difficult to read. Con-way truckers are paid based on time spent on loading and unloading and mileage to and from the destination. They are also paid on filling out paperwork, so a number of different items need to be captured on the payroll sheets. Then the forms have to be put together and shipped to the Portland operations center for entry. Form 265s were due every Tuesday consistent with the weekly schedule for paying the truck drivers. Forms were entered all day and the volume often caused the data entry clerks to have to stay late into the night to complete the task. The drivers' handwriting didn't help either, making the information difficult to read. This added to the clerks' frustration and negatively affected morale.

The Solution

The task of "fixing" the broken payroll system was handed to IT manager John Reich. After he studied the complex Form 265s and reviewed various software and hardware solutions, he knew that an off-the-shelf software/scanner combination wouldn't serve the purpose. While some of Con-way's managers felt that the optical character recognition (OCR) scanning systems were up to the task, CIO Jacquelyn Barretta was concerned that the technology was not mature enough to handle the volume and complexity of Form 265s. Con-way CFO, Kevin Schick, also had reservations: "If it was a 50% solution and we were still having people paw through these forms and determine the drivers' work, it wasn't going to do us any good." (Informationweek.com 2008).

To address their concerns, Reich arranged for three vendors to develop a simple application to demonstrate that their products could accommodate the complexities of the Form 265s. Of these only one succeeded. Reich recalls, "One of the vendors did it, another tried and gave up, and the third decided not to participate."

The main sticking point was not the content of the forms, but the drivers' illegible handwriting.

The vendor who was able to meet Con-way's requirements was Pegasus Imaging. It demonstrated its SmartScan Xpress character-recognition software that runs on Panasonic KV-S3065CL and KV-S2026C scanners. At the beginning of implementation, the system achieved an 80% success rate, but this soon increased to 99.9% after business rules were incorporated to visually highlight fields where missing or incorrect data were likely to occur. The total system cost just a little more than Con-way spent in one year for courier service.

The Results

Since September 2007 the Form 265s have been assembled and scanned at 38 different locations across North America and forwarded to the Portland service center. Focusing on the highlighted fields, the forms can be validiated quickly and easily. As a result of the adoption and implementation of the new system, Con-way truckers are paid on time, and morale among the data entry clerks has improved significantly. As a result of the foresight of Stotlar, Schick, and Barretta, Con-way rose to top rank in the 2007 InformationWeek 500—an annual ranking of the most innovative companies employing information technology in their businesses—and on June 2, 2008, *CIO* magazine announced Con-way, Inc. as the recipient of the 2008 CIO 100 award for its use of innovative technologies to generate business value. As Abbie Lundberg, editor-in-chief of *CIO*, remarked, "Unlike other top lists, it's not just about who's biggest—it's about who's doing the most interesting and relevant things." Clearly Con-way is doing just that and they aren't finished yet. Barretta and Reich are currently exploring the possibility of using OCR technology to process bills of lading and delivery receipts.

Sources: Compiled from *Con-way.com* (2008), *CIO* magazine (2008), and *informationweek.com* (2007).

Lessons Learned from This Case

This opening case about Con-way, Inc. illustrates the importance of adopting and implementing IT that closely aligns with all business goals, not just those focused on core competencies. It shows that although Con-way Freight was in the business of moving LTL shipments, its IT needed to address not only trucking but also the broader business goal of maintaining an acceptable level of employee morale.

Although the company was adopting leading edge technologies to improve operational efficiencies that improved their bottom line, the morale of its data entry clerks and truckers was plummeting because of its antiquated payroll form processes. In addition, the payroll process was incurring huge *shipping* costs for the payroll forms to be delivered from the various service centers to the Portland operations center.

Clearly, non-core business functions are not the only areas in which IT can be applied to achieve huge gains by an organization.

The case also demonstrates the need to carefully fit the technology to its purpose. In this case it was to address problems with a complex business form—and to carefully consider the alternative methods of acquiring a system and evaluating vendors.

In this chapter, we will explore the different issues associated with adopting and implementing IT projects and the management issues associated with improving business processes. We will also focus on the organizational transformation that follows from the introduction of new and innovative technology.

14.1 Adopting IT Projects

Worldwide end user spending on IT in 2006 was reported at $1.16 trillion and is expected to grow at a compound annual growth rate (CAGR) of 6.3 percent to $1.48 trillion in 2010 (IDC, 2007). Estimates of hardware, software, and IT service spending by 2010 are projected at $327 billion, $562 billion, and $587 billion, respectively.

The question then is how can organizations best adopt and implement information systems to maximize return on their investment? And, looking at the bigger picture, how do organizations address issues of change management and business process management that arise from the adoption and implementation of new technology?

This chapter attempts to answer these questions to assist organizations in achieving the best outcomes from their investments in IT. Information systems are typically adopted to create value by enabling or improving one or more business processes or to contribute positively to faster and more effective decision making. Consequently, as discussed in Chapter 13, their planning must be aligned with the organization's overall business strategy and specific processes involved.

A FRAMEWORK FOR ADOPTING IT PROJECTS

The **technology adoption lifecycle** was originally developed in 1957 at Iowa State College (Beal, Rogers, and Bohlen, 1957). Its purpose was to track the purchase patterns of hybrid seed corn by farmers. Six years later, social scientist Everett Rogers broadened the use of this model in his book, *Diffusion of Innovations* (now in its 5th edition), to include the adoption of emerging technologies. He introduced the innovation diffusion process that has become widely used in assessing technology adoption and diffusion. Rogers proposes there are four elements of adoption of any technology: (1) the technology itself, (2) the communication channels through which information is exchanged between potential adopters (e.g., mass media and interpersonal), (3) the speed at which the emerging technology is being adopted, and (4) the social system into which the innovation is introduced that can be influenced by internal opinon leaders and external change agents.

ADOPTION STAGES

As shown in Figure 14.1, the **adoption process** occurs over time and passes through five stages: (1) acquire knowledge, (2) persuade, (3) decide, (4) implement, and (5) confirm. During the knowledge and persuasion stages, the potential adopter becomes aware of the technology and forms an attitude toward it, culminating in the decision stage that leads to adoption or rejection of the innovation. Accordingly, the innovation diffusion process is the process through which an individual or other decision-making unit passes (Rogers, 2003, p. 161):

1. Knowing of an innovation
2. Forming an attitude toward the innovation
3. Making a decision to adopt or reject
4. Implementation and initial use of the new technology
5. Confirming the decision through continued use or disconfirming it through discontinuance

The adoption process isn't linear, but cyclical in nature. For example, if the adopter has an unfavorable attitude toward the technology under consideration, he or she can seek new information and return to the knowledge stage to acquire further information, or if the adopter realizes that he or she has acquired insufficient knowledge when moving into the persuasion stage, he or she can return to the knowledge stage.

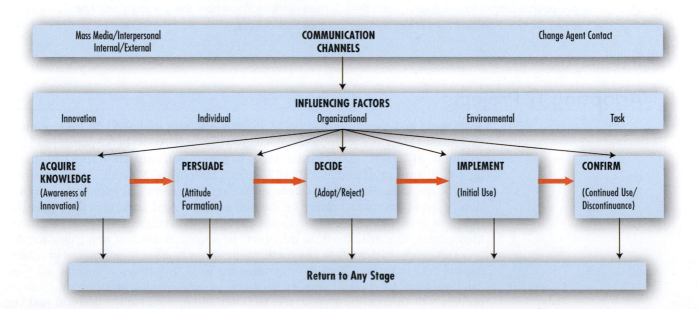

Figure 14.1 IT adoption process. (*Source:* Drawn by C. Pollard.)

While the adoption process is relatively predictable, we can't assume that the process will be the same for the introduction of all types of technology introduced into different types of organizations, or even the same technology introduced into a different organization, or vice versa. By nature, *technology, tasks, individuals, organizations,* and *environments* will differ depending on their characteristics, and have the potential to significantly affect the adoption process. In this section we examine the differences in these five elements, beginning with differences in technology.

TECHNOLOGY DIFFERENCES

Every innovation has four basic characteristics: compatibility, complexity, reliability, and relative advantage. All new systems are measured along these characteristics when they are being considered for adoption (Rogers, 2003).

Compatibility is the degree to which the new system is perceived to fit with the existing values, past experiences, and needs of potential adopters. Organizations are either looking for a minor improvement to a current business process or looking for fundamental changes in technology or a business process.

Complexity is the degree to which the new system is perceived to be difficult to understand and use. Complexity is measured on a continuum from easy to difficult. The more difficult the new system is to understand or use, the more difficult it will be to get users to accept it. Complexity must be measured relative to the skill set of adopters to obtain an accurate assessment. What is difficult to some users will be easy to others.

Reliability is the extent to which the new system is robust and dependable. If systems are not operating, companies can virtually be *out of business* for the period of time that the system is not functioning.

Relative Advantage is the degree to which the new system is perceived as better than the system it replaces. It is often expressed in the economic or social status terms that will result from its adoption. For example, relative advantage may be measured in terms of cost or time savings and by its added functionality. It is important to assess both the business value added and the consequences of not adopting the system.

Measuring the new system along these characteristics is useful in assessing the suitability of a new system early in the adoption process and projecting how easy it will be to get users to accept it after implementation.

TASK DIFFERENCES

Task-technology dependency is the ability of a technology to efficiently and effectively execute a task. It is an interesting and important feature to consider when assessing the adoption of different types of technology. For example, have you ever used a Microsoft Word document to create a list of customers or calculate customer discounts based on product prices and date of payment? You can make it work, but it isn't very efficient, and its functionality is very limited. Using Microsoft Access would be far preferable for maintaining a list of customers, and Microsoft Excel would be much easier to use for calculating customer discounts. The message here is that it is important to assess the purpose of the new system: What do you want the system to do? What type of business process is it designed to enhance? Given those answers, the chosen technology must have the characteristics that lend themselves best to the task at hand.

INDIVIDUAL DIFFERENCES

Rogers introduced another important concept—that of the differing characteristics of the adopters. According to Rogers, people fall into five different adopter categories—innovators, early adopters, early majority, late majority, and laggards. The characteristics of each of the adopter categories are summarized in Table 14.1. Rogers suggested that innovations, such as the personal computer, would spread through a social system (such as an organization), as the early adopters select the technology first, followed by the majority, until the technology is commonly accepted.

Attitude toward a new technology is a key element of IT adoption and diffusion. Those who have a more positive attitude toward change are more likely to adopt

TABLE 14.1	Characteristics of Adopter Categories
Adopter Category	**General Discerning Characteristics**
Innovator	younger than average
	well educated
	risk seeker
	high financial status
	respected for being successful, but sometimes ridiculed by their more conservative peers
Early Adopter	younger than average
	well educated
	opinion leader
	financially well off
	respected by other members of social group
Early Majority	slightly above average in age
	above average in education
	risk-averse; need to be sure an idea will work before they adopt it
	moderate financial status
	respected as informal leaders
Late Majority	older than average
	less educated
	adopt new ideas just after average member of a system
Laggard	oldest of all categories
	least educated
	risk-averse
	pay little attention to the opinions of others

earlier and adapt to the new system more easily than those who prefer to stay with the status quo.

Understanding adopter categories helps IT managers, consultants, and vendors understand that not all clients rush to adopt new technology. Many people are not innovators or early adopters, as you can see when the frequency of adopter categories is plotted on a bell curve (see Figure 14.2). We can expect roughly 50 percent of people to be late majority or laggard adopters. That means that one-half of the general population is slow to adopt new technology!

What exactly do these adopter categories mean? They tell us that people are social creatures. They like to fit in. A lot of people like to follow the lead of others. People learn and emulate the behavior of those they trust and respect. However, inherent in each individual are certain characteristics that make up who they are. For example, one person might like to skydive. This is a person who seeks out risky endeavors. Another person might be very traditional, and focused on *the way things have always been done*. This person is likely to be risk-averse and skeptical of new things. It is this combination of social comparison and individual characteristics that determine where a person fits on the adoption/innovation curve. Once an organization understands the *social system* in which it is operating, it needs to assess how new or established technologies are already being used. To do this, organizations *scan the environment* by reading reviews in trade publications, vendor websites, and the efforts of early adopting organizations.

Age, gender, and education are also important individual differences affecting when certain individuals will adopt new technology and how easily they will accept the associated changes (Wei, 2006). These differences require little explanation. Suffice to say that earlier adopters tend to be younger and have more years of for-

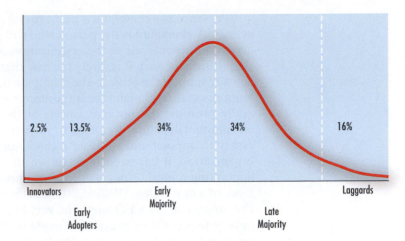

Figure 14.2 Adopter category distribution.

mal education. These characteristics presumably enable early adopters to cope with higher levels of uncertainty and suggest that it is important to consider them in planning for IT adoption.

ORGANIZATIONAL DIFFERENCES

Since no new system can exist without some interaction with its corporate surroundings, it isn't surprising that organizational differences influence IT adoption. Not all organizations are capable of providing the same level of support to assist in the introduction of new technology. Larger organizations are usually best equipped to obtain up-to-date information and have highly skilled technology specialists who can facilitate the technology change. Small organizations are often more agile and can move faster to adopt technology. Regardless, however, of the size of the organization, there are other factors that influence the adoption of a new system when planning for one. Planning needs to occur at each stage of the adoption process; all stakeholders must be considered and informed, and the plan adjusted as needed throughout the adoption process. Planning for the changes that will be introduced into an organization by the adoption of a new system includes a number of factors. These are a supportive IT infractructure, management support, and the presence of a champion.

A supportive IT infrastructure refers to physical equipment and personnel to fulfill all of the roles necessary to ensure successful adoption of a new system. Hardware, software, and staff members with IT skills to support various aspects of the adoption of the new system are necessary. Some need to be familiar with the technical operation of the system to assist with implementation, others will be equipped to assist in integrating the new system into existing business processes and getting users *onboard*, while still others will be skilled at training users in-house. Finally, staff will be needed to maintain the new system.

Management support is critical to the successful introduction of a new system because of the potentially extensive business changes that will be associated with its introduction (Camara, Sanchez, and Ortiz, 2004). Although it isn't necessary to have support from the highest level within the organization, it is important to gain support from middle to upper levels of management. Resources typically flow from upper management. Without their strong support, adoption and implementation can be delayed because of lack of funds, difficulty in accessing necessary personnel, and unavailable facilities or equipment. Identifying the appropriate source of management support will usually be dependent on the type of new system being adopted. For example, if a new accounting system is being introduced, it would make sense to obtain the support of the chief financial officer (CFO) or an upper-level manager in the accounting department. This brings us to the next organizational factor that can impact the success or failure of IT adoption.

Presence of a champion is also a strong predictor of successful adoption of a new system. A **champion** is the person who will promote the benefits of the new system across different levels of the organization on an ongoing basis. While management support is necessary, it is rarely the case that top executives have the time needed to actively support the project. The champion is available to answer questions, find information, create and maintain enthusiasm for change, maintain momentum, and generally promote the positive aspects of the adoption of the new system. Often, a champion will naturally emerge to sponsor a new system; other times, it will be necessary to appoint and cultivate a champion to fight for the new system. In a large organization, it has even been shown that the greatest benefits are gained from appointing a local or departmental champion to facilitate the adoption and acceptance of a new system (Pollard, 2003). In the example given in the section above, while the support of the CFO would be very beneficial, it is likely that the success of the new system could be greatly increased by the appointment of a mid-level accounting manager to act as a champion for the new system throughout its adoption and implementation.

ENVIRONMENTAL DIFFERENCES

Finally, the environment into which the system will be introduced can differ. For example, *vendor support and training* will differ, and *customer skill levels* with technology and *accessibility to online services* may be very different. Coupling environmental differences with organizational differences, it has been found that fostering and maintaining close *vendor-champion alliances* is a very beneficial tactic to take in adopting new technology (Pollard, 2003).

The successful adoption and implementation of an information system depends on the proper assessment of numerous individual, technology, task, organizational, and environmental factors. The most important differences that influence the adoption of a new system are summarized in Table 14.2.

IDENTIFYING TECHNOLOGY FOR ADOPTION

The first step in adopting a new IT-based system is to identify technologies that may be useful in improving or enabling business processes and assess how well they fit the organizational culture. Some useful tools for identifying IT-based systems are available for this purpose and will be discussed next.

TABLE 14.2	Factors That Influence IT Adoption
Category	**Influencing Factors**
Technology	Compatibility
	Relative advantage
	Complexity
	Reliability
Task	Compatibility
Individual	Attitude to change
	Age
	Education
	Gender
Organization	Supportive IT infrastructure
	Management support
	Training
	Champion(s)
Environment	Vendor support
	Customer technology skill levels
	Access to online services
	Vendor-champion alliances

A Closer Look 14.1

Adoption of Web Services Get Swedish Banking Applications Talking to Each Other

Centrala Studie Stodsnamnden (CSN) is the Swedish government's banking authority responsible for providing student loans and grants to Swedes who are pursuing higher education. Each year, CSN loans out 2.5 billion Swedish Krona to a half-million people and delivers a host of financial services to thousands more. In January 2002, at the start of the new school semester, when online traffic to the organization is typically four to five times greater than in other months, CSN's Web site went down. Students were forced to phone CSN representatives directly to receive help with new loan and grant applications and payback information. The voice-response system, which was designed to meet a much lower demand, had proved inadequate.

A group of technicians led by the production team worked hard to stabilize the Web site and ease the burden caused by overuse of the voice-response system. "We found the load problem and tried to tame it by adding servers, but the solution was like patchwork—and in the following weeks we could see the same pattern with instability occur," says Orjan Carlsson, Chief Architect of CSN's information technology department (Plummer and McCoy 2006). Consistently poor Web site performance coupled with long waits on the telephone was enough to cause a public outcry.

Given CSN's heterogeneous enterprise environment—comprised of IBM mainframes, UNIX-based applications, and systems running Microsoft Windows NT—a solution that could support cross-platform communication was a necessity. Only a flexible, scalable, open-standards-based integration architecture could supply the level of interoperability for the high volume during the start of a semester.

A locally based IBM team worked closely with CSN to investigate solution possibilities. Together, the technical teams decided that the best way to realize cross-platform, program-to-program communication was through Web Services built on IBM WebSphere. This architecture allows CSN's disparate applications to exchange information with each other without human intervention. The team implemented a system that also eliminated the organization's reliance on an outsourced application service provider for its voice-response system. The system leverages Web Services to enable the Windows NT–based voice-response system to execute transactions that are easily recognized by CSN's back-end (back-office) operations.

The new Web Services-enabled system allows CSN to deliver student account status and transaction information to phones (voice response) and to CSN's portal at a significantly reduced cost. "Web Services are essential for us today and in the future," says Carlsson. According to Carlsson, Web Services enable a loosely coupled architecture, resulting in a highly integrated solution.

Reuse of code also gives CSN an advantage. One interface can serve several business systems using different channels, making it easy to modify existing channels or add new ones, a feature that significantly reduces total cost of ownership. CSN dramatically saves on developer costs as well as gets new functionality to market faster. The result is a flexible and scalable Web services–enabled architecture that is essentially transparent to end users, giving CSN the cross-platform communication system it needs to operate efficiently, serve its customers, and lower costs.

Sources: Compiled from Plummer and McCoy (2006) and IBM (2002).

For Further Exploration: How did this application arise? What does the solution provide? What role does the business partner play?

The Hype Cycle. The *hype cycle* is a useful tool used widely by organizations to identify and assess emerging technologies and decide when to adopt. The hype cycle was developed by Gartner, Inc., an international research and advisory firm, operating in 75 countries. By 2006, Gartner, Inc. was producing 70 different hype cycles that evaluated more than 1,500 information technologies and trends across 75 industries. These annual hype cycles (see Figure 14.3) provide a snapshot of the relative maturity of different categories of technologies, IT methodologies, and management disciplines. They highlight overhyped areas vs. those technologies that are high impact, and provide estimates of how long technologies and trends will take to reach maturity.

Each hype cycle has five stages that reflect the basic adoption path any technology follows, starting with a trigger point, through overblown hype and then enduring disillusionment, before finally becoming more mainstream and accepted.

Technology Trigger. A breakthrough, public demonstration, product launch, or other event that generates significant media and industry interest.

Peak of Inflated Expectations. A phase of overenthusiasm and unrealistic projections during which a flurry of publicized activity by technology leaders results in some successes but more failures as the technology is pushed to its limits. The only enterprises making money at this stage are conference organizers and magazine publishers.

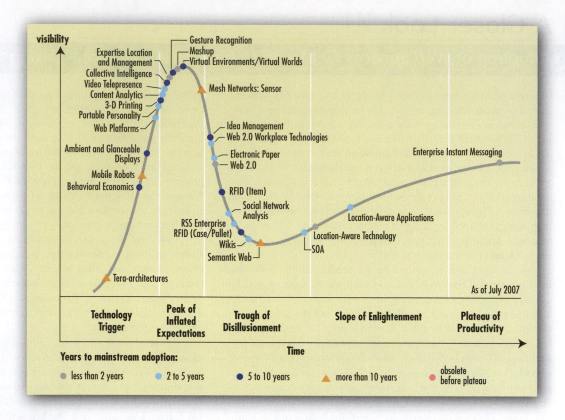

Figure 14.3 Gartner 2007 emerging technologies hype cycle. (*Source:* Gartner Inc.)

Trough of disillusionment. The point at which the technology becomes unfashionable and the media abandons the topic, because the technology did not live up to its inflated expectations.

Slope of enlightenment. Focused experimentation and solid hard work by an increasingly diverse range of organizations lead to a true understanding of the technology's applicability, risks, and benefits. Commercial off-the-shelf methodologies and tools become available to ease the development process.

Plateau of productivity. The real-world benefits of the technology are demonstrated and accepted. Tools and methodologies are increasingly stable as they enter their second and third generation. The final height of the plateau varies according to whether the technology is broadly applicable or benefits only a niche market.

Priority Matrix. The benefit of a particular technology can vary significantly across industries, so planners must determine which opportunities relate closely to their organizational objectives. To make this easier, a new feature in Gartner's 2006 hype cycle was the addition of a **priority matrix** (Figure 14.4). The priority matrix is a simple diagramming technique that assesses a technology's potential impact—from transformational to low—against the number of years it will take before it reaches mainstream adoption.

The vertical axis of the priority matrix measures the impact of the technology on a particular organization, and the horizontal axis measures the number of years it will take for the technology to realize widespread adoption. Technologies that rate high on impact and low in number of years reflect adoption priorities.

The pairing of each hype cycle with a priority matrix is recommended to help organizations better determine the importance and timing of investments based on benefits beyond the *hype*. When an organization is satisfied that a technology fits its requirements and that the timing is right for adoption, the organization decides to

Potential Impact	Years to mainstream adoption			
	< 2 yrs.	2-5 years	5-10 years	> 10 years
Transformational	• Web 2.0	• SOA	• 3-D Printing • Collective Intelligence • RFID • Virtual Worlds	• Mobile Robots
High	• Enterprise Instant Messaging • Location-Aware Technology • Mashups	• Location-Aware Applications • Portable Personality • Social Network Analysis	• Behavioral Economics	• Mesh Networks • Semantic Web • Tera-Architectures
Moderate		• Content Analytics • RSS Enterprise	• Idea Mgmt.	
Low			• Gesture Recognition	

Figure 14.4 Sample priority matrix based on 2007 hype cycle data.

adopt (or not) and explores ways to "acquire" the technology, or returns to *scan the environment* for other more suitable technologies and goes through the adoption process again (see Figure 14.1).

The Forrester Wave. Another respected research firm, Forrester, offers the Forrester Wave™, a series of annual reports that classify technologies into categories—leaders, strong performers, contenders, and risky bets. In addition, it allows organizations to customize the criteria to match their needs. Forrester also hosts an IT Forum annually to inform and educate IT professionals about newly emerging technologies and IT methodologies.

The diffusion process, hype cycle, priority matrix, and Forrester Wave™ reports are among the most widely used tools in identifying potential technologies for new IT-based systems and can be accessed at their Web sites (www.gartner.com and www.forrester.com).

Research Reports. In addition to these "tools," research organizations also produce numerous reports that are useful in assessing suitable technologies for IT-based systems. A sampling of research reports from Gartner, Inc. and Forrester is shown in Table 14.3. In addition, IT publications and Web sites (e.g., InformationWeek, CIO, BusinessEdge, SaaStream, ITToolbox, Computerworld, and many others) provide informative articles in print and online that assess the current status and value of many different technologies.

Whereas Gartner, Inc. and Forrester subscriptions are very expensive and generally are subscribed to only by larger organizations, many of the other publication outlets are available free of charge. Interestingly, though, despite the fact that

TABLE 14.3	A Sampling of Informative Research Reports
Source	**Report**
Forrester	The Art of the EA Deal
	Building a World-Class Security Operations Function
	2008 CISO Priorities: The Right Objectives but the Wrong Focus
	Managing IT When Times Get Tough
	Best Practices: Centers of Excellence for BPM
	Five Green IT Trends That Will Impact the IT Infrastructure and Operations Professional
	US IT Market Outlook: Q1 2008
	2008 Trends in Backup and Data Protection
	Measuring and Aligning Business Performance
	Building the Business Case for Disaster Recovery Spending
Gartner, Inc.	The Skills Gap Will Limit Success with Corporate Performance Management
	The Role of SaaS in IT Modernization
	Findings: IT Management Must Not Wait for a Business Strategy to Be Delivered
	When Servers Go Virtual: The Impact on Configuration Management
	2008 Update: What Organizations Are Spending on IT Security
	Cool Vendors in IT Support, 2008
	How to Understand and Select Business Continuity Management Software
	Making Do with Less: Tactics for Managing the Impact of Security Budget Cuts
	Open Source in Database Management Systems, 2008
	The State of Open Source, 2008
	The Business Impact of Service-Oriented Architecture
	Gartner's Top 12 Actions for the Healthcare CIO, 2008
	Key Issues for the Risk and Security Roles, 2008

acquiring knowledge and identification of technologies is a critical first step in adoption, very few organizations have a formal process in place to guide them through the masses of information available to them.

Once appropriate information technology has been identified, the next step is to acquire it. In Chapter 16, a detailed explanation is given of the five-step acquisition approach, together with acquisition options and suggestions for vendor and product selection. In Chapter 13, the pros and cons of insourcing vs. outsourcing are discussed. When an acquisition approach has been chosen and the IT project has been developed, attention turns to the issues of implementing the system. These concerns are discussed in the next section.

Review Questions

1. Name the five different categories of adopters.
2. Consider the five different categories of adopters. How would you approach each of the different types to encourage adoption of a new system?
3. List the stages of innovation adoption.
4. What do you think are the most important considerations you would need to assess in adopting a new system in a small organization with little IT experience?
5. What are the main characteristics of technology that must be considered when adopting technology?

14.2 Implementing IT Projects

It is important to first understand what the term *implementation* means. Broadly speaking, *systems implementation* is the delivery of a system into day-to-day operation. For our purposes, we define **implementation** as *all organizational activities* *involved in the introduction, management, and acceptance of technology to support one or more organizational processes.*

CREATING AN IMPLEMENTATION ROADMAP

In general, organizations implement two broad categories of information systems: applications with very specific objectives that are implemented over a relatively short time period (i.e., 12 to 24 months), and infrastructure needs that are generally implemented over longer periods of time.

IT infrastructure provides the foundations for IT applications in the enterprise. Examples are a data center, networks, data warehouse, and a corporate knowledge base. Infrastructure exists and is shared by many applications throughout the enterprise.

IT applications are specific systems and programs for achieving certain objectives—for example, providing a payroll or taking a customer order. The number of IT applications is large, and they can be in one functional department or shared by several departments.

Implementation of a new system typically involves a change in the way business is conducted. As a result, the systems analyst must plan for and execute a smooth transition from the old system to the new one. This transition often involves helping users cope with normal start-up problems. The process of implementation can be very complex, when large numbers of people in different departments or locations are affected. The way in which a system is implemented is critical to its acceptance. Consequently, it's easy to understand how important it is to have an implementation roadmap before proceeding.

THE FOUR P'S OF SYSTEM IMPLEMENTATION

The first step in establishing an implementation plan is determining *how* to put the new system in place. There are four approaches used to implement an IT-based system. We refer to them here as **the four P's of implementation:** plunge, parallel, phased, and pilot (see Figure 14.5). The approach(es) used can significantly affect the way that work is performed. Each of the four major approaches can be used independently or in combination with other approaches to create a larger variety of approaches depending on the system's size and complexity.

In the **plunge approach,** the old system is turned off at end of business on Day 0 and the new system is put into operation at the beginning of Day 1. The implementation date is often chosen to coincide with the beginning or ending of the fiscal year or quarter. Although transition costs for the plunge approach are low, it is a high-risk approach. For example, major problems may arise if errors in the system were not identified during testing. This approach, however, may be the best choice if an organization is under time pressure to comply with a new government regulation or a new business policy comes into effect with little prior notice. This technique is also referred to as the "big bang" or "abrupt cut-over" approach.

Using the **parallel approach,** both new and old systems operate concurrently for a designated period of time. During this time period, major problems can be identified and solved before the old system is abandoned. Final cutover is typically abrupt, but can be combined with the phased approach (described later) as various key modules undergo final testing and acceptance. Risk is lower in this approach. However, running two systems is resource-intensive and naturally results in higher costs than operating only one system. This cost may be incurred in the form of added labor costs or the use of an unreasonable amount of computer resources.

The **pilot approach** is used when a system is intended for adoption and implementation in more than one business unit or geographic location. The system can be *pilot tested* at one site first using either the plunge or parallel approach. This first site is referred to as the *beta* site. When the first site has resolved all major problems and approved the system, it can be rolled out to other sites using the plunge approach. When using the pilot approach, it is considered *best practice* to implement the system in a relatively easy but typical unit first and then roll out

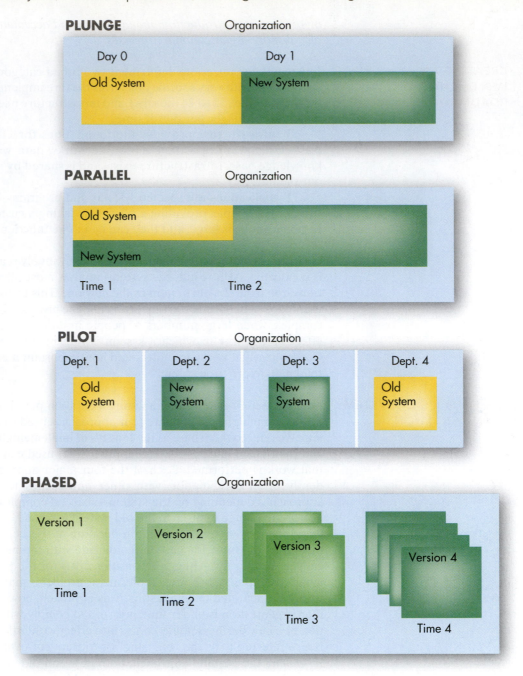

Figure 14.5 The four P's of implementation.

the implementation to other more complex or atypical units. One benefit of this approach is that subsequent sites are able to learn from the experiences of the beta sites, thus promoting a higher level of user confidence and a lower level of user resistance over time. Again, cost and risk may vary depending on the extent to which the new system is *pilot tested*.

The **phased approach** is based on the module or version concept. Each module or version of the system is implemented as it is developed and tested. This approach can be used with the plunge or parallel approaches. A useful strategy is to implement the key modules first using the plunge approach (sales, purchasing, materials planning, etc.) and then the peripheral modules, such as human resources, document management, maintenance, and financials, later using the phased approach. Risk and cost vary depending on the way in which the phased approach is used.

Regardless of implementation approach, there are no guarantees of success. In the next section, we will discuss the many reasons for success and failure of IT implementation.

SUCCESS AND FAILURE OF IT IMPLEMENTATIONS

Not all IT-based projects succeed. Estimates of failed projects range from 30 to 70 percent. Those implementations that are enterprisewide, such as ERP and CRM, are particularly prone to failure because they affect major changes across the organization (McNurlin and Sprague, 2006). Choice of implementation approach is an important first step, but there are other considerations to be made when putting a new system in place. The systems analyst may restructure processes that can significantly impact job tasks and interactions between individuals and groups/departments.

For example, skill set requirements may change, locus of data or information moves from one individual or group to another, and stakeholders (sponsors, users, etc.) can become disenfranchised and feel as though their power base is being eroded. To lessen the potential negative effects of these changes, the systems analyst must establish clear and open lines of communication to keep stakeholders fully informed. He or she must also act as mediator for conflicts that may arise between competing groups.

Despite improved methodologies in systems development—which we discuss in Chapter 17—and a careful selection of implementation approaches, a large percentage of IT projects still fail to meet the expectations of the users. If a new system doesn't solve the problems for which it was intended, it will not be accepted and used. If the organization does not have personnel with the IT skill set required, it will be difficult or impossible to successfully implement a new system. This situation often occurs because of a lack of communication or understanding between the system analysts/designers and the business *client* or a failure to establish partnerships with external technology providers.

FACTORS THAT IMPACT IMPLEMENTATION SUCCESS

Implementation success and failure have been influenced by a number of important factors. Some of the major factors are listed below.

- Top management support
- Level of risk
- Training of users
- User acceptance of the IT project
- Management of the implementation process

Top Management Support. Top management support is as important in IT implementation as it is in IT adoption. There are several reasons to seek support of top management for the design, development, and implementation of a new system. First, the necessary resources (money, people, time) will be easier to obtain. Second, the system is more likely to be perceived positively by both business and IT personnel who may align themselves with the attitudes of top management for political reasons. In those cases where top management is not the system sponsor or owner, the most successful IT projects slowly gain management support through gradual involvement over time. In this way, managers have time to adjust to escalating levels of responsibility instead of being faced with them all at once.

Level of Risk. Risk associated with IT projects vary greatly depending on three variables: project size, project structure, and complexity of the implementation effort.

The larger the project, in terms of dollars spent, number of staff involved, time needed for implementation, and number of business units involved, the greater the risk. The more structured a project, the lower the uncertainty, which lowers the risk.

Directly associated with project size and structure is the issue of complexity. Some projects are relatively simple, such as when a single business unit upgrades to a new version of an existing software package. Others are extremely complex. One

A Closer Look 14.2

Maslo Partners with a Technology Provider

Maslo is an independent, full-service brokerage, trading secondary fibers or "recovered paper" within the paper-recycling segment of the pulp and paper industry. The company operates from offices in Malvern, PA, and Charlotte, NC. In 2007, Maslo sold over 250,000 tons of scrap paper. Although much of that paper never crosses Maslo's threshold, paper lots still need to be tracked and recorded while the product is in transit.

To stay competitive, Maslo needed to manage the mountain of paperwork to efficiently process its large number of incoming shipments and outgoing orders. Without a real-time picture of accounts payable and receivable, Maslo executives had a problem.

Seeing the need for a computer system where data would be entered only once and reports could be generated in minutes rather than days, the Maslo executives began to look for a suitable technology to assist them. Like so many small and medium-sized businesses, Maslo didn't have a full-time computer person, and none of Maslo's current employees had the technology knowledge or skills to implement the much-needed computer system.

Maslo's first attempt to find technical expertise failed. They hired a retired IT specialist as a consultant to set up a network and inventory system, but his knowledge was dated and he didn't have the necessary technical skills. Then, one of the executives remembered Ben Spalding, who had consulted to Maslo in the past. Ben had moved on to found Computerized Inventory Systems Specialists, Ltd. (CISS, Ltd.), a major provider of standard inventory management software packages. CISS analyzes a current working environment, assesses future needs, and provides the most cost-effective solution for organizations. Based in Allentown, PA, the company developed Inventory Pro, an inventory management software package designed to provide companies of all sizes with a flexible, scalable, easy to use, and easy to afford inventory management tool.

Maslo decided that the solution to their implementation problems was to hire CISS, Ltd., which would be responsible for setting up a reliable computer network, installing business software, and creating a customized database that would allow instant access to crucial vendor, buyer, and business information.

Prior to hiring CISS, day-to day operation was largely paper-based. This was frustrating, and restrictive to growth. The basic computer infrastructure was severely out of date and unreliable: inventory was tracked via a program that was little more than a spreadsheet, payables and receivables were handled using a stand-alone computer program, and the server was known mainly for its crashes. All personnel involved were overworked and frustrated by vendor and customer requests for more information. Perhaps the most frustrating of all—no one knew the state of the business at the end of the day. The company was operating in what vice president and general office manager Rob Loose Jr., summed up as "the crudest sense."

Ben Spalding immediately assessed Maslo's needs and set about turning the "technologically challenged" office into a "technologically sophisticated" business. Through a series of steps, Spalding created a computer environment that enabled Maslo to increase its volume of business, increase profits, and actually expand to a second office several states away.

Sources: Compiled from *cisltd.com/cas study.asp* and *maslocompany.com* (accessed May 2008).

For Further Exploration: What techniques might Maslo have used to look for suitable technology assistance? Consider why Maslo chose to look for a technology partner rather than create the needed technology themselves.

---

of the most complex projects is that of implementing an ERP system. By its very nature, the successful implementation of a large project is highly dependent on the company environment and its culture.

Systems analysts must recognize the subtle differences that exist between the business units that create the corporate culture and develop an implementation plan that works around, or avoids, bottlenecks or pitfalls. Some questions to be asked of each business unit involved might include

- What is the attitude toward teamwork vs. individual effort?
- What is the management philosophy?
- What types of conflict management strategies are in place?
- Is the company project focused?
- Is there adequate resource commitment?
- Will top management support remain steadfast despite project problems?

Training of Users. Training is another issue that must be addressed in the planning phase. How should you handle people's fear of not understanding or being able to work with the new system? Many companies make the serious mistake of not insisting on a comprehensive training program to maximize employees' knowledge and confidence levels in adapting to and using the new systems. Many view training as an unnecessary expense. It is not. Insufficient training can lead to errors or other expenses. The increases in hidden cost can far exceed cost cutting savings. Training is an item that should receive the most serious attention during implementation. Once training scope and budget are determined, they should be adjusted only if the project scope changes.

To provide a basis for training efforts, systems developers need to provide comprehensive system documentation to IT personnel and easy-to-read and understand user documentation (online and hardcopy) for the users to guide them. Training can be provided using a number of different *methods* to different groups of users. A well-accepted axiom for delivery of training is the "See it, hear it, do it" concept. Good training is participative and interactive. You see how a task is done, you hear an explanation of how to do it, and then you do it.

Timing of training is also important. The greatest benefits are obtained from *just in time* delivery of training, that is, users are trained as close to the time of implementation of the new system as possible. In this way, the hands-on portion of the training is essentially carried over into initial and continued use of the system and the training concepts are reinforced *on the job*. Typically users cannot retain information that is offered to them in short, intense sessions. If it is necessary to spend 10 days delivering training at a pace at which users can comfortably digest and retain the information, it is essential that management be prepared to authorize a 10-day training course. Unfortunately, in some instances, trainers have been coerced into delivering the same training in a 5-day format that they know will not deliver long-term benefits.

Finally, the *quality of training* is just as important as the methods of delivery and length of time devoted to it. An important criterion is *reputation*. All training providers are assessed on quality of materials, subject matter expertise of trainers, level of instructor support, training skills of trainers, track record, quality and accessibility of facilities, and cost. While cost is a major issue in IT training, in many instances it is a deciding factor. Effective training can impact the next important factor to consider in implementation—user acceptance.

User Acceptance of the IT Project. **User Acceptance** is the extent to which a new system is perceived as being useful and easy to use by the system users. Acceptance of a system will be higher if users are involved in systems design. When they are offered the opportunity to provide input into the design and development, users are more inclined to *buy into* the system. The more people feel they have had a say in setting priorities and selecting a system, the more they feel compelled to stay involved, even during difficult phases of system development and implementation. One of the biggest challenges is sustaining enthusiasm and commitment throughout the entire project. Employee involvement secured early and maintained consistently can mean the difference between success and failure. For example, if software selection is viewed as being done by a chosen few, other users may feel justified in remaining detached and uncooperative.

Sometimes incentives need to be offered to gain a higher degree of acceptance. For example, if managers' end-of-year bonuses are dependent on specific project and financial goals, their buy in will increase.

MANAGING THE IMPLEMENTATION PROJECT

Management support, project risk, training, and user acceptance need to be managed. Typical consequences of bad project management include

- Cost overruns
- Failure to meet deadlines
- System performance that fails to meet user expectations
- Missing functionality

Any one of these will result in a failed implementation. For example, if costs are not controlled, there may not be funds available for training, and implementation success will be jeopardized. Similarly, if time is not controlled, functionality and system performance may be adversely affected, with only a partial system being delivered into production within the timeframe allotted. A worst case, time-related scenario would be that a system is not implemented on time to comply with a government regulation, such as Sarbanes-Oxley.

While it is impossible to control or plan for every aspect of the implementation process, it is possible, through experience and the use of project management tools and methodologies, to anticipate potential problems and put in place effective strategies to increase system success.

Project managers need to have strong technical and business knowledge and the ability to put the right people on the team. Any essential technical skills not available internally should be secured from sources outside the organization. If it is necessary to use the services of an external technology provider, the provider's credentials should be closely assessed.

An important thing to remember in managing the implementation process is that the system belongs to and has been designed for the user, not the IT staff. At this point, it bears repeating that a critical challenge of managing the implementation process is meeting user needs head-on and addressing them in a satisfactory manner through planning, training, understanding, and obtaining "buy-in" to the implementation effort. If you pay attention to these needs and address them in your implementation roadmap, you will be more likely to achieve success. People's resistance to change severely influences the success of implementing a new system, regardless of the size and structure of the project or the level of IT experience of the various project participants, and must be carefully managed.

An important step in wrapping up management of any implementation process is taking the time to capture **lessons learned** from the current project to help guide the next project. Capturing lessons learned requires a retrospective examination of the implementation project to document successes and failures in each systems development phase as well as the project as a whole. Documenting what worked, what didn't work, and how things could have been done better provides invaluable insight. Project plans, training materials, meeting agenda and minutes, and other materials should also be archived with the lessons learned. These materials then become a helpful resource for future implementation teams.

Review Questions

1. Name the four P's of implementation and describe the differences between them.
2. Give examples of situations when it would be best to use each implementation approach listed in answer to review question 1.
3. Physical requirements of a system are an important consideration when implementing a system, but how do the *social* aspects of a system impact IT implementation success?
4. What are some important factors to consider in ensuring a new system is successfully implemented by an organization?

14.3 Business Process Management

A 2006 survey of IT executives conducted by CIO Insight and Equation Research, LLC, reported that 66 percent of IT executives ranked business process improvement as their No. 1 priority and more than 90 percent of the respondents said they were conducting more process-improvement projects than they did in 2004. However, problems with vendors, ill-defined processes, and a lack of interdepartmental cooperation hinder organization's progress.

There are many reasons why an organization might need to document its processes. Companies that have merged need to examine processes across their

Figure 14.6 Business process management circle.

lines of business to discover which one is the most efficient and effective. Other organizations might want to improve their existing processes or automate manual processes. In some countries, organizations have to comply with government regulations that require organizations to accurately document their business processes, such as the Sarbanes-Oxley Act in the United States and the ASX Principles in Australia.

THE CONCEPT OF BUSINESS PROCESS MANAGEMENT

A **business process** is a collection of related activities that produce something of value to the organization, its stakeholders, or its customers. A process has inputs and outputs, with activities and tasks that can be measured. Many processes cut across functional areas. For example, a product development process cuts across several departments including marketing, development, and production. Complex processes often need to be broken into a number of sub-processes for easier management. Improving processes can greatly improve the efficiency and effectiveness of an organization regardless of its industry sector, size, or geographic location.

Business process management (BPM) is a popular management technique that includes methods and tools to support the design, analysis, implementation, management, and optimization of operational business processes (Kettinger, Teng, and Guha, 1997). BPM can be viewed as an extension of **workflow management (WFM),** where documents, information, and activities flow between participants according to existing process models and rules. The activities of business process management consist of designing, analyzing, implementing, managing, and optimizing a process for both effectiveness and efficiency, as shown in Figure 14.6.

In the short term, BPM helps companies improve profitability by decreasing costs and increasing revenues. In the long run, BPM helps create competitive advantage by improving organizational agility. BPM can provide cost benefits for most companies, increase customer satisfaction, enable business differentiation, and reduce errors.

The BPM approach has its roots in **business process reengineering.** Business process reengineering is the radical redesign of an organization's business. Reengineering takes a current process and simplifies it to increase its efficiency and create new processes. In the 1990s most organizations failed to achieve fundamental process improvement because they looked at processes in isolation and failed to focus on larger, enterprisewide objectives. Despite decades of reengineering, organizations still have problems with their business operations. They duplicate processes. They perform hundreds of non-core tasks that should be outsourced, and they spend vast amounts on proprietary process-management software that's difficult to update. To address these issues, BPM has evolved as a technique that ties people, processes, and technology to strategic performance improvement goals, as shown in Figure 14.7.

To properly address process improvement, organizations must develop a carefully crafted BPM strategy.

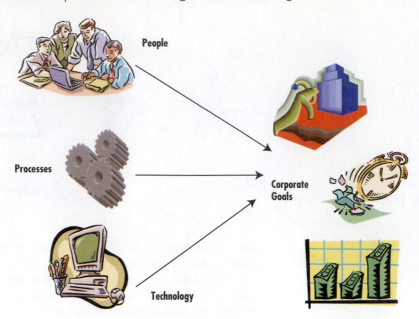

Figure 14.7 BPM focus.

Specifically, a well-implemented BPM strategy enables an organization to

- Gain greater visibility into processes
- Identify root causes of bottlenecks within processes
- Pinpoint hand-offs in processes

The result is that BPM helps an organization cut costs, improve service, achieve growth, or comply with regulations.

CREATING A BPM STRATEGY

The Business Project Management Institute (IDS Scheer AG, 2005) reports on the benefits of an effective BPM strategy:

- Reduces product design time by 50 percent
- Achieves faster time-to-market of competitive products
- Reduces order fulfillment time by 80 percent
- Improves customer satisfaction with the ordering process
- Helps organizations achieve efficiency gains of 60 percent in call centers

Most organizations want to bring their customer-focused, financial, and operational goals in line with the expectations of shareholders or owners. With this in mind, it is important to conduct a thorough assessment of core strategic and operational processes to identify those processes that need to be improved. In core strategic processes, such as customer acquisition, bookings, invoicing, backlogs, and order-to-cash, the focus is typically on improving throughput. In the case of operational processes, such as manufacturing, order fulfillment, and field service, companies typically fall into the trap of measuring efficiency alone. The point of the assessment is to identify strategic and operational processes and link them with organizational strategic objectives.

For example, a manufacturer with a strategic goal of improving product quality and reliability must look at its operational manufacturing processes and see how they link to this business objective. If organizations focus exclusively on automation and cost savings, they might achieve significant operational efficiencies but lose their competitive edge and fall short of their performance targets, as British Telecom (BT) and United Airlines did when they failed to link strategic goals with their process improvement initiatives.

TABLE 14.4	Steps to Creating a BPM Strategy
Activities	**Description**
1	Align customer-focused, financial, and operational goals with expectations of shareholders or owners
2	Conduct assessment of core strategic and operational processes
3	Link strategic and operational processes with organizational objectives
4	Develop a process performance plan
5	Prioritize processes based on potential impact on strategic objectives

Once the assessment is complete, it is necessary to develop a process performance plan that documents the ways in which the identified operational processes contribute to strategic goals. If a strategic goal is customer satisfaction, for example, appropriate process benchmarks should be established to accurately and consistently analyze progress of your BPM initiative. In improving an order-to-fulfillment process, although order throughput and on-time delivery are important, other measures might have a direct impact on customer satisfaction, such as fulfillment accuracy.

Finally, processes must be prioritized with highest priority being given to those processes that are determined to have the greatest potential impact on strategic objectives.

To put an effective BPM strategy into place, Merrifield, Calhoun, and Stevens (2008) stress the need to focus strongly on desired outcomes—not on the people who carry out the operations or how they carry out the operations—activities and capabilities. For example, instead of creating a long list of items such as "accounts payable sends a customer an invoice" (who does it) or "check all orders against invoices payable" (how they do it), a more concise statement of desired outcomes should be

A Closer Look 14.3

Harvard Pilgrim Health Care Benefits from an Effective BPM Strategy SVR OM HRM

When *U.S. News and World Report's* 2007 health plan rankings assessed the best of the hundreds of commercial, Medicare, and Medicaid managed-care plans across the United States, Harvard Pilgrim Health Care Systems came out on top. Plans were scored from 0 to 100 based on data collected and analyzed by the National Committee for Quality Assurance (managed care's major accrediting and standards-setting body). Scores reflected results of consumer surveys and success in preventing and treating illness compared with the average plan. Prevention and treatment were measured across 50 individual items. Harvard Pilgrim Health Care ranked No. 1 with a score of 91.7 out of 100.

Almost bankrupt in 2000, Harvard Pilgrim, a full-service health benefits company serving members throughout Massachusetts, New Hampshire, Maine, and beyond, is now solidly in the black, and in 2006 reported just under 1,000,000 members. Harvard Pilgrim has repeatedly received top awards and rankings for its service quality and customer satisfaction, including receiving the highest numerical score in the J.D. Power and Associates 2007 National Health Insurance Plan Satisfaction Study of large commercial health plans in the northeastern United States. Harvard Pilgrim achieved these distinctions by employing a carefully developed BPM strategy that combines insourcing and outsourcing to align process improvement with its organizational objectives.

Harvard Pilgrim identified its healthcare critical activities, including identifying subscribers at high risk or in the early stages of developing chronic illnesses such as diabetes and heart disease. Early recognition of these people enabled the company to enroll them in preventive care or disease management programs before their conditions grew serious. They realized that sophisticated data mining and analysis technology would be needed to sift through claims and other information to identify those at risk. Recognizing that it lacked this technology and expertise, Harvard Pilgrim entrusted those activities to a reputable outside provider.

Harvard Pilgrim also outsourced non-core activities, such as pharmacy benefits management. This enterprisewide strategy enabled Harvard Pilgrim to focus its internal resources on improving high priority activities that afforded it a strategic advantage in the healthcare marketplace, such as creating new offerings and selling to large groups, and thus achieving its goal of being the No. 1 commercial, Medicare, and Medicaid managed-care plan in the nation.

Source: Compiled from Harvard Pilgrim Health Care Annual Report 2006 (*harvardpilgrim.org/pls/portal/docs/PAGE/MEMBERS/ABOUT/2006_ANNUAL_REPORT.PDF*), U.S. News and World Report (*usnews.com/listings/health-plans/commercial/harvard_pilgrim_health_care*), and *jdpower.com* (accessed June 2008).

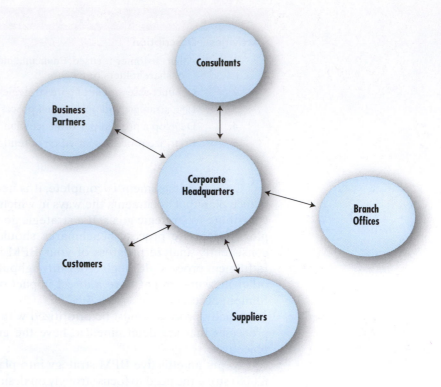

Figure 14.8 BPM without boundaries.

developed, such as "Collect customer payment." Following from this, they suggest a few basic rules to follow in creating a BPM strategy:

1. Describe operations in terms of desired outcomes.
2. Identify activities that support the desired outcomes.
3. Identify capabilities needed to support each of these activities.
4. Identify activities most critical to organizational success.
5. Design a more efficient way of operating.

Most successful BPM solutions incorporate the following components:

- Business process mapping: modeling the core processes and interdependencies
- Business rules engine: encapsulating procedural rules and decisions
- Workflow automation: routing information to the right people at the right time
- Application integration: middleware that enables data exchange between software
- Knowledge base: data repository that stores business rules and other information
- Business activity monitoring: system that monitors all activities in a process

An important point to keep in mind when setting a BPM strategy is that managing business processes is an activity that is not limited to the organization itself, but instead extends beyond the internal and external walls of the enterprise to include partners, suppliers, customers, and consultants, as shown in Figure 14.8.

BUSINESS PROCESSING MODELING

Business process modeling, sometimes referred to as business process mapping, includes techniques and activities used as part of the larger business process management discipline. The purpose of modeling business processes is to create a blueprint of how the company works, much like the blueprint created by an architect prior to building a house. The set of business process models are blueprints for how the process will work after it is created or improved.

A process model is similar to an income statement in accounting in that it looks at the entire organization over a long period of time (e.g., a year). It is not a "snapshot" of specific time periods. Therefore, time is not a fundamental driver in creating business process models. We might find that we get a very similar set of high-level processes for many organizations, regardless of their size or industry. For example, a set of processes for a local pet store, a large international furniture manufacturer, or an online video store at the highest level might be:

- Sell products to customers.
- Manage finances.
- Order and supply products.
- Manage employees.
- Maintain facilities.

MEASURING PROCESSES

Before BPM initiatives can proceed and designers can identify those processes that are effective and those which are inefficient, they must be measured. Six Sigma, total quality management (TQM), and ISO 9000 are quality techniques to measure and improve an organization's processes and are often used in conjunction with BPM initiatives.

Six Sigma is a methodology to manage process variations that cause defects, defined as unacceptable deviation from the mean or target, and to systematically work toward managing variation to prevent those defects. Six Sigma has five phases:

1. Define. Formally define the goals of the design that are consistent with customer demands and enterprise strategy.

2. Measure. Identify product capabilities, production process capability, risk assessment, and so forth.

3. Analyze. Develop and design alternatives, create high-level design, and evaluate design capability to select the best design.

4. Design. Develop detailed design specifications, optimize design, and plan for design verification. This phase may require simulations.

5. Verify. Check designs, set up pilot runs, implement production process, and hand over to process owners.

Total quality management (TQM) is a management strategy aimed at embedding awareness of quality in all organizational processes. One major aim of TQM is to reduce variation from every process so that greater consistency of effort is obtained (Royse et al., 2006). TQM utilizes multifunctional teams comprised of professional staff and workers from all departments involved to solve problems.

In the mid-1980s, W. Edwards Deming, a U.S. statistician, university professor, author, and consultant, developed the Plan, Do, Check, Act (PDCA) cycle to achieve continuous improvement. The PDCA cycle is widely used in organizations that are seeking to improve processes for achieving efficiency and effectiveness (Deming, 1986). The PDCA cycle achieves continuous improvement by repeating the basic cycle of:

PLAN	Establish the objectives and processes necessary to deliver results to achieve with organizational objectives.
DO	Implement the processes.
CHECK	Monitor and evaluate the processes and results against objectives and report the outcome.
ACT	Take action needed for improvement. Review all steps (Plan, Do, Check, Act) and modify the process to continue to improve it before its next implementation.

ISO 9000 was developed as a standard for business quality systems by the International Organization for Standardization (ISO). To be certified, businesses must document their quality system and verify compliance through reviews and audits. A key element of ISO 9000 is the identification of nonconforming processes and the development of a plan to prevent nonconforming processes from being repeated. Specific quality improvement steps are not prescribed within ISO 9000.

During measurement of a process, diagramming techniques, such as flow charts and process maps, are used to graphically illustrate the process and visualize the flow of product or documents through a series of process steps. The predominant goal of **process improvement teams** is to eliminate the non-value-adding steps and to resolve quality problems by adding new processes or deleting, splitting, combining, expanding, or reducing existing processes.

SOFTWARE TO SUPPORT BPM

BPM software helps organizations automate workflows and processes such as marketing and supply chain, accounts payable, and placing orders. The shift from "data-centric" information systems in the 1980s to "process-centric" information systems in the 1990s and, more recently, "object-oriented" information systems has led to enterprisewide information systems that support end-to-end business processes. BPM software tools have evolved over time from tools that simply document processes (text-based word processors) to those that graphically depict processes (drawing tools, such as flowcharts, data flow diagrams, integrated case tools, etc.); automate, integrate, and optimize individual processes; deliver integrated process and knowledge through the integration of people, technology, and content (BPMS); and, most recently, analytics functionality through BPMS bundled with business intelligence (BI), as shown in Figure 14.9.

Word Processors. One of the simplest ways to document a process is to use a text-based document processor. Text documents have been used for many years to capture business processes. Their advantage is that virtually every organization has a word processor.

Drawing Tools. Managers have used flowcharts and other graphics for years for one simple reason: something that would take many pages in a document can be

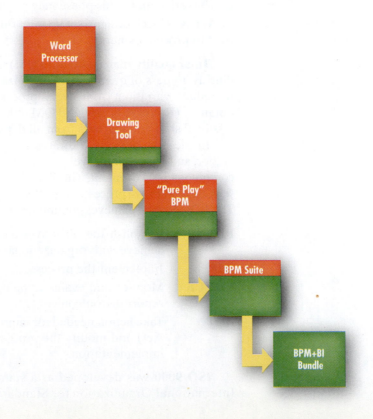

Figure 14.9 Evolution of BPM software tools.

expressed quickly and simply in a graphic such as a diagram or a chart. A flowchart or data flow diagram is good at showing the big picture, instead of bogging you down in the details like a text document can. However, drawing tools alone can't express a business process. To capture the details, a text-based tool and a drawing tool need to be used together and synchronized. Together they work better than either one does alone, but they still fall short of being an optimal BPM solution.

"Pure Play" BPM Tools. The need for greater synchronicity and flexibility led to the development of basic "pure play" BPM software tools that combine text and graphics and offer more advanced features such as a repository that allows reuse of resources and simulations. The process can be captured in greater detail, with a higher degree of accuracy. Simulation enables process redesign, and useful artifacts can be generated for later use by IT developers.

Business Process Management Suites. In *Business Process Management — The Third Wave*, Smith and Fingar (2002) foretold of a new type of BPM software — the BPM suites (BPMS), in which a business analyst could graphically *compose* a process model, *optimize* it through simulation and analysis, and *execute* it on a built-in process engine. By 2008, BPMS had become a reality. Current BPMS include a collection of critical software technologies that enable the control and management of business processes. Unlike other model-oriented development tools, a BPMS emphasizes user involvement in the process improvement lifecycle, from design through implementation, deployment, monitoring, and ongoing optimization. Rather than reducing reliance on people through automation, a BPMS emphasizes the value of coordinating people, information, and systems as central resources. Using a BPMS, the modified process can then be merged into the current business process environment.

BPMS are most appropriate for processes that need to balance people, systems, and information, and where management of the interactions and interdependencies among all three aspects is critical to work outcomes (Hill, Cantara, and Kerremans, 2007). The classic use scenario of a BPMS is most valuable for extended processes that change frequently, cross multiple physical boundaries (organizational, departmental, system, information), and need a high degree of coordination of human activities, information, business transactions, and business rules. For example, a multinational company administers and tracks the bank accounts of its various subsidiaries worldwide and has to comply with country-specific rules and regulations.

As the concept of BPM matures, vendors are responding to the piecemeal process improvement methods and techniques. The majority of BPMS vendors have evolved from pure-play BPM tool providers, and these vendors continue to lead the BPMS market, although many large middleware and software infrastructure vendors are strengthening their BPMS products. Gartner classified 22 vendors who are the leading contenders for long-term global success in the BPM arena. A list of those vendors is provided in Table 14.5.

Among the leading BPMS offerings, Fujitsu's Interstage BPM 8.1 allows for Web modeling of business processes with process rules updates and management tools, and starts at $60,000 per workstation. TIBCO Software Inc. (*tibco.com*) has released its Business Studio 2.0 software that spans BPM, workflow, and enterprise application integration (EAI) areas. Meanwhile, IBM has introduced WebSphere Business Modeler and Business Monitor that are intuitive for business users and analysts, and facilitate involvement in the design, monitoring, and analysis phases of process improvement life cycles.

By the end of 2006, the BPMS market had reached nearly $1.7 billion in total software revenue and had begun to establish itself with proven technology, stable vendors, vendor consolidation, and rapid user adoption. In their 2007 report on software revenue in the portal, process, and middleware software market, Cantara, Biscotti, Correia, and Raina (2007) estimated that the BPMS market will increase more than 24% from 2006 to 2011, compared with a five-year compound annual

TABLE 14.5	Leading Contenders in the BPMS Market	
Vendor	Class	Product
Adobe	Challenger	LifeCycle Enterprise Suite
Appian	Leader	Appian Enterprise 5.6
		Appian Analytics Everywhere
Ascentn	Visionary	Ascentn AgilePoint
AuraPortal	Visionary	AuraPortal
BEA Systems	Leader	AquaLogic BPM Suite 6.0
Captaris	Niche	Captaris Workflow
EMC	Challenger	Documentum Process Suite
Fujitsu	Challenger	Fujitsu's Interstage Business Process Manager 8.1
Global 360	Leader	Global 360
IBM	Leader	WebSphere Business Modeler Websphere Business Monitor
Intalio	Visionary	Intalio BPMS Enterprise Edition 5.0
Lombardi	Leader	Blueprint
		Lombardi Teamworks 6
Metastorm	Leader	Metastorm
Microgen	Niche	Aptitude BPM Suite
Oracle	Challenger	Oracle BPA Suite
		BPEL Process Manager
		Oracle BAM
Pegasystems	Leader	SmartBPM Suite
Savvion	Leader	BusinessManager 7.0
Singularity	Visionary	Process Platform
Software AG	Leader	WebMethods BPMS 7.1
SunGard	Visionary	Carnot
Tibco Software	Leader	Business Studio 2.0
Ultimus	Visionary	Ultimus BPM Suite 8.0

growth rate of 9.9% in total revenue across offerings in that software market sector. In 2007, the BPMS market was the second fastest growing middleware software segment.

BPMS-BI Bundle. Some of the more sophisticated BPMS products are including business analytics to enhance the features of their offerings. For example, BPM vendors Lombardi Software and Ultimus bundle Business Object's reporting software with their BPMS. Additionally, business intelligence (BI) software vendors such as Cognos are providing links between their BI software and several BPM vendor tools.

Whatever the level of BPM software tools, when dealing with BPM vendors, it is critical to identify products that are closely aligned with current organizational operations, technologies, and underlying business events and activities.

BUSINESS VALUE OF BPM

The value of BPM can be seen in a number of organizations that are using IT tools to manage their business processes. For example, Hasbro Inc. deployed TeamWorks software to streamline the toy maker's ordering process (Chen, 2004). Hasbro improved not only the toy order process, but also the inquiry process. Great Clips, a chain of 2,600 hair salons, uses Metastorm BPM software that includes BI function-

A Closer Look 14.4

Chubb Links Strategic Innovation with BPM

In May 2006, Chubb, a multi-billion-dollar global property and casualty insurance firm based in Warren, NJ, went live with its new Commercial Underwriting Workstation Inventory Management System (CUW). With the help of Metastorm's BPM Suite, Chubb Commercial Insurance (CCI), the largest operational division of Chubb Group, was able to transform multiple local rate-book-issue (RBI) processes corresponding to its 40 field branches into one standardized process and condense its formerly disparate service force into three service centers.

Todd Ellis, Senior VP of Chubb & Son and CIO of Chubb Commercial Insurance (CCI), credits the significant efficiency gains to BPM. Ellis claims that the BPM initiative "provides greater cost transparency, quality, and throughput CCI is able to track down bottlenecks in the processing life cycle," and, "in the long run, reduce overall delivery costs, and improve overall efficiency" (O'Donnell, 2007). Chubb's success had taken nearly four years to come to fruition.

In 2002, Chubb wanted to create a process model to geographically separate their branch underwriting employees and rate-book-issue (RBI) customer service representatives. Their objective was to centralize their RBI representatives in lower-cost locations and establish a higher degree of standardization among their branches. First, they organized a business process study team of home-office experts and field personnel who concluded that an underlying BPM/workflow tool was essential to their efforts. Late in 2003, the team set out to find a BPM tool that could integrate with their existing portal for underwriters and their assistants. Following a formal RFP process that took approximately one year, the team identified Metastorm BPM as the best tool.

Chubb worked closely with Metastorm on a proof of concept that involved use-case scenarios and workflow maps that would be needed to implement the tool. This process gave Chubb the opportunity to see firsthand how the tool could be used and to evaluate its ease of maintenance. To feed Web services from the CUW to the Metastorm BPM suite, CCI built a middle layer using an open-source business-rules engine to prioritize work orders before they reached the workflow engine. CCI used an iterative testing strategy to make sure the application could withstand nationwide deployment. The greatest challenge was to prepare the underwriting staff to work separately, in a geographic sense, from the customer-service representatives. Chubb achieved this by implementing a work-request documentation process supported by a Microsoft Word template that would ready them for an automated work request provided by Metastorm's BPM suite. Filling out these word processor templates and emailing them was painful and tedious for the employees, so much so that when Metastorm was rolled out, there was easy acceptance of the new automated process. In 2005, the new process was phased into a limited number of branches on the West Coast where the first of the three service centers would be located. CCI completed the rollout in 2006 when the two remaining centers located in the Midwest and on the East Cost were successfully deployed. The BPM initiative is expected to achieve its ROI by the end of 2009.

One of the lessons Chubb learned from the BPM initiative is the need for a close alignment between BPM and business rules. CCI's successful initiative highlights the value of defining business models and business architecture, and encourages future BPM efforts.

Sources: Compiled from *insurancetech.com* and O'Donnell (2007).

For Further Exploration: What led Chubb to realize there was a need for a closer alignment between BPM and business rules? What other challenges might have Chubb had to face in this case if things had been handled differently?

ality to manage the recruitment process for its 200 new franchisees each year. This software enabled Great Clips to identify internal inefficiencies associated with developing its new stores and improve the way it manages external processes including the acquisition of construction permits (Whiting 2006).

Park University in Missouri used BP tools to change University processes, manage documents, and create a nearly paperless environment. Automotive firms are using BPM to change processes that create scheduling stability and manage production in transit batch sizes.

Just gaining a better understanding of the current state of organizational processes is valuable in itself. However, eliminating non-valued-added processes or outsourcing non-core processes can have major positive effects on performance.

Review Questions

1. Define business process management (BPM).
2. List and discuss the benefits of developing a business process management (BPM) strategy.
3. List the benefits of utilizing BPM within an organization.
4. Describe the steps to creating a successful BPM strategy.

14.4 Change Management and Organizational Transformation

It is impossible to consider making changes in information technology without considering the costs of changes to the organization that occur when a new system is introduced or an existing system is modified. The ability to successfully introduce change to individuals and organizational units is critical to successfully implementing a new system.

The purpose of this section is to discuss ways to manage the human factor as well as the technical issues that arise in IT systems adoption and implementation.

THE CONCEPT OF CHANGE MANAGEMENT

Change management is a structured approach to transition individuals, teams, and organizations from a current state to a desired future state. In the case of IT systems, it includes managing change as part of systems development to avoid user resistance to business and system changes. Change management issues arise when organizations and their suppliers or new business partners—in the case of a merger or acquisition—follow very different work practices. Addressing these differences and creating an environment that supports the development and implementation of common technical platforms, appropriate levels of data sharing, and acceptable ways of interacting on a personal level is a challenging proposition. Changes and compromise are always difficult to achieve, and change is often resisted regardless of the advantages that new processes and systems have to offer.

When changes in a system cause people to relate to others and work in ways that conflict with their basic values (corporate, cultural, and personal), a project's success can be put at risk, despite the absence of any substantial technical issues. Indeed, in the vast majority of cases (approximately 90–95%), the problem in introducing new systems is not in the technology. Cravens (2005) contends that while some of the problems come from either misapplication or malfunction of hardware or software, most change management issues arise because people and the work they do are impacted by the introduction of new or modified IT systems. Problems with hardware and software can usually be fixed by redesign, integration, or upgrade. The problems with people are more difficult to address. Disgruntled or disenfranchised people can be constant threats to the success of any project. Dhillon (2004) reinforces the proposition originally offered by Markus (1984) that the origins for resistance to system implementation can often be attributed to the distribution of power implied by the new system compared to the existing power base. Faced with potential shifts in power, key stakeholders may consciously or unconsciously resist by delaying, sabotaging, or insisting on the modification of system development. These tactics may include

- Withholding resources (money, people, time) needed for the project
- Purposely identifying the wrong people to work on the project
- Raising continual objections to project requirements
- Changing project requirements
- Expanding the size and complexity of the project

At the corporate level, it is important to keep in mind that no two organizations are exactly alike. Organizations are highly specialized entities and can be classified along many different dimensions, such as industry sector (manufacturing, retail, services, etc.), profit orientation (for-profit, nonprofit), sector (public vs. private), regulatory status (regulated, not regulated), locale (domestic vs. multinational, or foreign), holding status (sole ownership, partnership, corporation, LLC, LLP), form (mechanistic vs. organic), and structure (hierarchical, matrix, projectized).

For these reasons, it is important to fit the change management plan and the process used to facilitate change management to the individual organization under review.

A Closer Look 14.5

FIN   SVR

Lincoln Financial Uses IT to Change Customer Interaction with Partner Web Sites

Lincoln Financial is a $5 billion provider of life insurance, retirement products, and wealth management services. It distributes offerings through financial advisors, banks, and independent brokers. In most of the insurance industry, if consumers want to access their accounts or download a form from a broker site, they click on a link that takes them to the insurance provider's site, where they input a separate password or user ID. To become a "partner of choice" on such sites, Lincoln Financial wanted tighter integration with brokers' Web sites. Lincoln wanted to go a step further, providing content and account access within its partners' Web sites, as well as single sign-on for consumers.

This was not a simple undertaking. Outlining the Lincoln content in an HTML frame would not provide the partner's look and feel. A pure Web services approach was also out, because most of Lincoln's clients could not support that kind of system, since the partner then had to process the XML/SOAP messages. For a short time, Lincoln maintained subsites for its partners who wanted them, and those sites linked to requested content. However, maintenance of the subsites was burdensome.

The ultimate answer was Service Broker. It took three developers four months to build the pilot of Service Broker, which is a Web Services–based application with a front end that the company calls a servlet. When the servlet is installed on a partner's server, it provides a way to accept Lincoln's content and applications and still maintain the partner's look and feel. The servlet manages authentication, digital signature, passwords, and page rendering. When the partner wants to include Lincoln content or an application, it needs to add just one line of code.

In 2004, Lincoln was the only insurer that did not require customers to leave a partner's Web site to access information. This capability provided Lincoln with competitive advantage and changed the way in which customers interact with partner Web sites.

Source: Compiled from Brandel (2004) and *lfg.com* (accessed June 2008).

For Further Exploration: What changes occurred when systems were connected between the business partners? Why was it important to maintain the look and feel of a partner's Web site?

CHANGE PROCESS MODELS

The **change process** is a structured technique to effectively transition groups or organizations through change. When combined with an understanding of individual change management, these techniques provide a framework for managing the people side of change. A number of process models have been proposed to facilitate organizational change at an individual and corporate level.

Most process models are based on the simple three-stage model that was originally theorized by Kurt Lewin (1951), a German-born psychologist and one of the modern pioneers of social, organizational, and applied psychology. **Lewin's three-stage change process** consists of three stages of change (Figure 14.10). These stages are unfreezing, change, and (re)freezing.

Unfreezing—in this first stage, people have a tendency to seek out a situation in which they feel relatively safe and have a sense of control. They want to remain in a comfortable state. Alternative situations are not appealing, even if they appear to

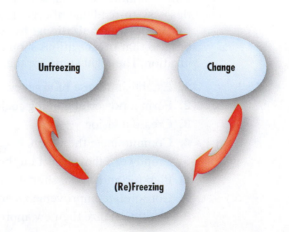

Figure 14.10 Lewin's three-stage change process.

be preferable to the current state. Talking about the benefits of moving to *what could be* is seldom enough to move them from this *frozen* state, and significant efforts are often necessary to *unfreeze* people. Some people accept change easily, whereas others are reluctant to move out of their comfortable situation. It is the task of the manager to determine the level and location of resistance and address it to move people toward the next stage.

Change—sometimes referred to as *transition*—is a key part of Lewin's model. It encompasses the notion that change is a journey rather than a simple step. This stage often requires people to go through several stages of apprehension before they are prepared to move forward. The *change* stage requires time—the amount of time is often closely related to the extent of the change that is required. It is important to ensure that leaders don't focus solely on their own personal journey during the period of time that it takes to move to the next stage. If they ignore the needs of everyone else and expect them to *cross the chasm* between the current state and the desired state in a single step, it is likely that their efforts will be unsuccessful. Often the most difficult part of *change* is taking the first step. As a result, good leadership is important in this stage, and includes providing coaching, counseling, or other psychological support for those undergoing change.

Refreezing—The third and final stage in the change process involves the process of moving to a new place of stability. Refreezing may be a slow process because the *change* stage seldom ends cleanly, particularly when large numbers of people are being subjected to the change. At any given point in time, not everyone will be at the same point of transition from the old way of doing things to the new.

Change can occur unexpectedly and involve an individual, department, or the entire organization. Change can also be used to correct a problem, or to develop a new opportunity. Any of these types of change can be incremental, or they can be radical.

ORGANIZATIONAL TRANSFORMATION

A major change in the way that an organization does business is typically referred to as **organizational transformation.** John Kotter, a Harvard Business School professor, is one of the foremost authorities on leadership and radical change. In his recent book, entitled *Our Iceberg is Melting* (2006), Kotter teamed up with Holger Rathgeber to present a simple story of radical change and the issues associated with managing such a change. Using the allegory of an emperor penguin colony in Antarctica, Kotter and Rathgeber explain, in layperson's terms, how radical change can be effectively addressed. They integrate actual innovative and creative solutions they have seen applied to organizational change problems, into the fanciful story of Fred, the concerned penguin. When Fred notices that a small part of the iceberg which his colony of penguins inhabit has disappeared, he goes about trying to manage this potentially devastating change to his environment. The eight-step process originally proposed by Kotter in his original book, *Leading Change* (1996), and used successfully in hundred of organizations during the past decade, provides the foundation for this easy-to-read tale of organizational change.

Kotter's organizational transformation model consists of an eight-step change process that organizations should follow in order to successfully transform an organization. The eight steps are the following:

1. Establish a sense of urgency.
2. Form a powerful guiding coalition.
3. Create a vision.
4. Communicate the vision.
5. Empower others to act on the vision.
6. Plan for and create short-term wins.
7. Consolidate improvements and produce more change.
8. Institutionalize the new approaches.

Kotter's model applies to organizational transformation in general, but its utility can be seen in two highly successful data warehousing initiatives at First American Corporation (AMC) and Harrah's Entertainment. In both companies there was a sense of urgency. First American Corporation (a bank) was losing money and operating under letters of agreement from regulators. It was likely to be closed unless a new business strategy could be successfully implemented. Harrah's Entertainment (gaming) was not in financial trouble but changes in the gaming laws allowed gambling on Indian reservations and riverboats, which created a tremendous opportunity for growth.

In both companies, senior management agreed on a business strategy and a vision for how it would be implemented. First American Corporation implemented a customer-centric business strategy that was supported by a data warehouse that stored the customer data necessary to support the business strategy. Harrah's Entertainment grew through the acquisition and opening of new properties, and the promotion of cross-casino play through an innovative rewards program. A data warehouse that stored casino, hotel, and special events data was the enabler for their new business strategy.

Regardless of the nature or extent of the change, it is advisable to take a structured approach to affecting any type of organizational change. Jones, Aguirre, and Calderone (2004) of Booz, Allen, Hamilton, a global strategy and technology consulting company, headquartered in McLean, VA, offer a set of useful principles to assist in guiding successful change management. These 10 principles are:

10 PRINCIPLES OF CHANGE MANAGEMENT

1. **Address the "human side" of change systematically:** Develop a formal approach for managing change and adapt it often as circumstances change within the organization.

2. **Start at the top:** Top managers, including the CEO and CIO, must show full support for the change in order to challenge and motivate the rest of the organization. They must act as role models and present a unified front on all matters related to the change initiative.

3. **Involve every layer:** Change occurs at all levels of the organization. In addition to securing top-level support, it is important to cultivate leaders at various levels to support the change so that the change *cascades* down. These leaders must be given the resources they need to execute their job and kept motivated to achieve the needed change.

4. **Make the formal case:** The need for change is always challenged. A formal written statement of the envisioned change helps create and solidify alignment between change leaders and the change team.

5. **Create ownership:** Top management leaders need to work with the design teams to fully understand the changes that will result from the introduction or modification of technology. Leaders must be willing to accept responsibility for achieving change and offer incentives for participation in problem identification and solution generation.

6. **Communicate the message:** Issues related to change must be clearly communicated. Employees must be repeatedly provided with the right information at the right time through multiple channels to ensure they understand the consequences of the change initiative.

7. **Assess the cultural landscape:** As change cascades down through organizational levels, the culture and behaviors of employees must be addressed up front. Cultural assessments are often made too late or not at all. Core cultural values, behaviors, and perceptions must be addressed in regard to readiness for change; conflict areas must be identified and factors that can impact resistance must be defined.

8. Address Culture Explicitly: Once understood, the culture must be addressed head on. In the case of new departments, a new culture is created; in merger/acquisitions, existing cultures are combined, and in well-established companies culture will be reinforced. A baseline measurement of current vs. the desired culture must be developed along with a detailed plan for moving from current state to desired state.

9. Prepare for the Unexpected: No matter how well a plan is executed, there are always surprises along the way. The impact of change must be continually re-examined to measure the source and level of resistance, and necessary adjustments made to maintain momentum and achieve objectives.

10. Speak to the Individual: All organizational change involves change at the individual level; for the company to change, the individual and the way he or she works must change also. Employees must be involved in the change process, and individual rewards, in the form of monetary incentives, personal recognition, and promotions, must be offered to reinforce the organization's commitment to the change process.

Technology adoption and implementation is a major cause of business process change and organizational transformation. Given that technology is advancing exponentially, it is difficult, if not impossible, to stay current with all of the new developments in available and emerging technology. The IT sector as a whole is also in a constant state of change.

Whether an organization is introducing a new materials handling system, a new robotics installation, or undergoing basic business systems integration, it is making continuous improvements to do things better, faster, and cheaper. Change is central to the concept of *automation*, and it is important to fully understand what it entails and how it can best be managed. In the next chapter, the ways in which IT changes companies will be discussed in greater detail.

Review Questions

1. Discuss change management and issues that may arise when an organization goes through change.
2. Explain the three stages of Lewin's change model.
3. Research the term "change management" and report on any other process models that you are able to find that are currently being used to effect effective change management.
4. Visit a company of your choice and discuss with a business manager and someone in the IT department a recent change that has been implemented in their organization. Compare their perceptions of the impact of the change on their daily work and the organization as a whole.

14.5 Managerial Issues

1. Global and cultural issues. Adopting and implementing systems across organizations and countries could result in problems associated with the culturally based ways in which different people interact. Change management and organizational transformation can significantly disrupt the basic values of organizational culture. Care must be taken when managing processes that will substantially change the structure and the culture of the organization.

2. Ethical and legal issues. When restructuring processes through the adoption and implementation of technology, it is important to consider the people in the system. Modifying existing or implementing new IT systems means that some employees will have to completely change the way that they perform their work and, often, the actual work that they do. Some may feel too old to do so. Others may not have the necessary skills and do not wish to acquire them. Conducting business process restructuring may result in the need to lay off, retrain, or transfer employees. Should management notify the employees in advance regarding such possibilities? What about those older employees who may be difficult to retrain?

Other ethical issues may involve sharing computing resources or personal information, which may be part of the new organizational culture. Finally, individuals may have to share computer programs that they designed for their departmental use, and may resist doing so because they consider such programs their intellectual property. Conducting interviews to find managers' needs and requirements must be done with full cooperation. Measures to protect privacy must be taken. Appropriate planning must take these and other issues into consideration.

3. User involvement. The direct and indirect users of a system are likely to be the most knowledgeable individuals concerning clarification and description of the business requirements and the most effective alternative ways of attaining them. Users are also the most affected by a new information system. IS analysts and designers, on the other hand, are likely to be the most knowledgeable individuals concerning technical and data management issues, as well as the most experienced in arriving at viable systems solutions. Functional managers must participate in the development process and should understand all of the phases. They must also participate in the make-or-buy decisions and software selection decisions. The right mixture of user involvement and information systems expertise is crucial.

4. Change management. People use information systems and get used to how existing systems work. They may react to new systems in unexpected ways, making even the best technically designed systems useless. Changes brought about by information systems need to be managed effectively. Of special interest is the issue of motivating programmers to increase their productivity by learning new tools and reusing preprogrammed modules.

Technology transfer is a transfer of knowledge rather than physical devices. It is now increasingly recognized that changes in technology and work processes are fundamentally culture changes, and preparing organizational members for such culture changes is an important undertaking that cannot be ignored.

5. Risk management. Building information systems involves risk. Systems may not be completed, completed too late, or require more resources than planned. The risk is large in enterprise systems. It is helpful to think of IT system adoption as a process of embodying technical knowledge and knowledge of customer needs into a coherent solution. Under this view, those who want to understand and manage the risks associated with IT systems adoption must first focus on the translation of customer needs into project requirements and specifications.

How *IT* Benefits You

For the Accounting Major

Accounting professionals are often required to work closely with those in information technology on the design of IT systems specifications and acquisition of enterprise systems applications such as electronic commerce and data warehouses. Accountants play important managerial, advisory, and evaluative roles in connection with the acquisition of various information technologies by organizations of all types and sizes. To maintain the accountancy profession's credibility and capability in supporting new, strategic information technology initiatives, the competence of accountants in IT resources acquisition must be preserved and enhanced.

For the Finance Major

Information systems projects require significant financial justification. The strategy to adopt IT resources today is a major managerial as well as financial decision. The choice of adopting systems is heavily determined by financial considerations, such as the total cost of ownership (TCO) and return on investment (ROI). Multiple sets of assumptions and implementation plans look into every facet of an IT project's costs and expected benefits. IT project evaluation thus requires valuable advice and input from financial professionals.

For the Human Resources Management Major

IT systems adoption and implementing does not just involve acquisition of hardware and software, but also includes changing the way people work and the jobs that they do. As a result, human resources professionals are often involved in the hiring, firing (or laying off), and retraining of staff. The importance of training on the use of a new IT-based system cannot be overemphasized. Training includes the transmission of technical expertise to fundamental change of work activities and attitudes. Thus, the role of the human resources professional in providing adequate and proper training and counseling to end users is critical in IT systems adoption and implementation.

For the IS Major

The subject of information systems grew out of computer science to fill a gap created by the failure of computer programmers to understand and solve business problems. An information system professional, by virtue of background and training, plays a key role in IT adoption and implementation. The processes of developing a new or modified system—from identification of possible technology to implementation—all require extensive skills and knowledge from IS professionals.

For the Marketing Major

An organization should leverage the power of technology and the strategic vision of marketing during the process of IT systems adoption and implementation. To improve Web traffic and increase orders and revenue, the marketing staff can redevelop the content of the Web site so that it speaks to the audience in clear, action-oriented language. Then the IT staff can explore ways to capture the traffic that comes in and organize it in ways that marketing can use. Marketing professionals should always consider what they can achieve if a particular IT infrastructure and system is acquired.

For the Production/Operations Management Major

An organization acquires IT capability not just to automate, but also to redesign its existing business processes. The implementation of enterprise systems is a technological change that leads to organizational and cultural changes. Production and operations management (POM) traditionally focuses on managing processes to produce and distribute products and services. A great deal of POM focus is on efficiency and effectiveness of processes. Therefore, the expertise and services from POM professionals are needed to acquire and implement IT infrastructure and system.

Key Terms

Chapter Highlights

1 The technology adoption lifecycle is used to explain how innovations are adopted for use in organizations.

2 The adoption process occurs over time and passes through five stages: acquire knowledge, persuade, decide, implement, and confirm. During the knowledge and persuasion stages, the potential adopter becomes aware of the technology and forms an attitude toward it, culminating in the decision stage that leads to adoption or rejection of the innovation.

2 Technology differences in a new system can be measured for compatibility, complexity, reliability, and relative advantage. This is useful to determine the suitability of a new system.

3 The ability of a technology to efficiently and effectively execute a task is important to consider when assessing the adoption of new technologies.

3 Organizational differences play a role in IT adoption, as different levels of support and interest in the new technology can influence its success or failure.

3 Environmental aspects of technology adoption must be carefully weighed and considered before and during the adoption of a new system.

4 The different characteristics of the adopters is important to observe, as people fall into five different adopter categories—innovators, early adopters, early majority, late majority, and laggards.

5 If a new system does not solve the problems for which it was intended, it will not be accepted and used. Additionally, if the organization does not have personnel with the IT skill set required, it will be difficult or impossible to successfully implement a new system.

5 The success or failure of systems implementation can be influenced by top management support, level of risk, training of users, user acceptance of the IT project, and management of the implementation process.

6 Cost overruns, failure to meet deadlines, system performance failures, and missing functionality are challenges to managing IT implementation.

7 Risk is an important aspect of IT implementation that must be managed carefully.

7 Business process management (BPM) is a strategy for creating processes, modeling processes, monitoring processes, and reengineering them.

7 BPM utilizes IT tools and quality control methods to track and improve process efficiency and effectiveness.

8 A successful BPM strategy starts with a thorough assessment of core strategic and operational processes, followed by a process performance plan. Finally, one must prioritize the processes depending on which will have the greatest potential impact on strategic objectives.

8 Before BPM initiatives can proceed and designers can identify which processes are effective and which are inefficient, they must be measured.

8 BPM software tools can range from simple word processing, to drawing tools, or can be more integrated, such as "Pure Play" BPM tools and BPMS products.

9 Change management is a structured approach to transition individuals, teams, and organizations from a current state to a desired future state.

9 It is important to fit the content of a change management plan and the process used to facilitate change management to the individual organization under review.

9 The change process is a structured technique to effectively transition groups or organizations through change.

9 Radical technology changes can transform an organization.

Virtual Company Assignment

Management Decision Support at The Wireless Café

Go to The Wireless Café's link on the Student Web Site. There you will be asked to plan and recommend how to proceed in upgrading and adding information systems for the restaurant.

Instructions for accessing The Wireless Café on the Student Web Site:

1. Go to *wiley.com/college/turban*.
2. Select Turban/Volonino's *Information Technology for Management*, Seventh Edition.
3. Click on Student Resources site, in the toolbar on the left.
4. Click on the link for Virtual Company Web site.
5. Click on Wireless Café.

Questions for Discussion

1. List and briefly discuss the five steps of the information systems adoption process.
2. Describe some implementation and management issues.
3. Consider what is involved in identifying an IT project. How is such identification done?
4. What is the basic idea of justifying a new system?
5. What strategies can be used to overcome user resistance to IT implementation?
6. What organizational considerations should be addressed when implementing a new or a modified system?
7. Create a list of problems that show that an IT implementation has failed.
8. Create a list of benefits that show that an IT implementation has been successful.
9. Describe how BPM has evolved out of the concept of business process reengineering.
10. Describe the enabling role of IT in BPM.
11. Discuss three tools used to measure and improve an organization's processes.
12. Name four software tools used to document a BPM. Discuss which one is best for integrating different aspects of a BPM.
13. Discuss why it is necessary to understand the concept of IT implementation when managing organizational change.
14. What is the difference between change management and organizational transformation?

Exercises and Projects

1. Discuss which of the "4 P's of implementation" would be best to use in each of the following examples:
   a. Small computer training company that runs classes each day for no more than 40 different users each day. There are five permanent staff members. They want to upgrade to a new operating system.
   b. Global company with 5000+ users worldwide needs to perform a software upgrade on an existing system that is used by 20 percent of the business on a daily basis.
   c. Busy airline ticketing Web site needs its software upgraded to make searches run faster.
   d. Existing software development company has new graphic design software to unveil, but wants to test it first with some of their existing customers who are willing to report performance problems and provide feedback.

   Write a short report that lists the situations and the implementation approach you chose as most appropriate for each situation. Discuss the various implementation approaches and describe how the differences in opinion were resolved.
2. Examine some business processes in your university or company. Identify two processes that need to be redesigned. Employ some of the discussed BPR drivers to plan the redesign. Be innovative.
3. Find examples of the four software tools used to document a BPM initiative. Demo each of the tools and write a report documenting which is best for integrating different aspects of BPM and explain why.

Group Assignments and Projects

1. Divide into groups, with each group visiting a local company (include your university). At each firm, study the systems acquisition process. Find out the methodology or methodologies used by each organization and the types of application to which each methodology applies. Prepare a report and present it to the class.
2. Have teams from the class visit IT acquisition efforts at local companies. Team members should interview

   members of the project team to ascertain the following information:
   a. How does the project contribute to the goals and objectives of the company?
   b. Is there any information architecture in place? If so, how does this project fit into that architecture?
   c. How was the project justified?
   d. What project planning approach, if any, was used?
   e. How is the project being managed?

Internet Exercises

1. Surf the Internet to find some recent material on the role IT plays in support of BPM. Search for products and vendors and download an available demo.
2. Identify some newsgroups that are interested in BPM. Initiate a discussion on the role of IT in BPM.
3. Enter *gensym.com* and find its modeling products. Explain how they support BPM and process restructuring.
4. Go to *ouricebergismelting.com/html/seminar_leadingchange.html* and view the 25-minute video of John Kotter explaining his 8-step change process and how it is used effectively in organizations.

Minicase

Raising Awareness and Recruiting Early Adopters for Dspace at MIT

DSpace is a groundbreaking digital library system designed to capture, store, index, preserve, and distribute scholarly research material in digital formats. DSpace was jointly developed by Massachussetts Institute of Technology (MIT) Libraries and Hewlett-Packard for use by students, faculty, and researchers worldwide. Its purpose is to:

- Store materials in an organized, secure, and searchable archive
- Preserve articles, datasets, images, course materials, and other sources of information
- Create a distribution channel for research materials
- Increase accessibility of research materials through worldwide access

By early 2008, dozens of MIT faculty, researchers, departments, labs, and centers had joined DSpace. In addition, MIT masters and Ph.D. theses dating back to the mid-1800s had grown to a whopping 15,000 stored on DSpace. Listed by academic department, they can easily be accessed by title, author name, subject area, or date. Dspace was designed to raise the research profile of MIT's students and faculty worldwide.

The idea to create a digital institutional repository at MIT developed from conversations between Ann Wolpert, Director of MIT Libraries, and MIT faculty members. She noticed a need when faculty members joked about having their research on e-mail. This initial awareness, coupled with shifting trends of electronic scholarly publishing and the requests of students and faculty's increasing for on-demand document delivery, led to a meeting with Hewlett-Packard Labs in March 2000. Finally, MIT Libraries' Associate Director MacKenzie Smith helped drive the project to completion with its November 2002 launch.

It is no surprise that, in order to succeed, a project such as DSpace had to market itself and garner the support it needed to survive. That support had to come from key members of the MIT academic community. Opinion leaders, key administrators, and respected members of the faculty had to be courted and persuaded. Their conversations about the project would create awareness and interest, and their endorsement would promote credibility. At MIT, word-of-mouth, a most infectious means of disseminating interest and excitement, proved very effective.

Though informally excitement spreads like wildfire, the fire must be lit and stoked by planned, more formal interventions. The idea of DSpace had to capture the imagination of the faculty—and the implementation had to offer the solution to problems some didn't even know existed.

How did they do this? The DSpace team used a number of communication channels to achieve their objectives, in the following ways:

- They introduced DSpace to members of the MIT community at a program level and informally.
- In addition to its individual, enthusiastic, everyday conversations, the team made presentations to small groups that elicited curiosity and created forums for discussion of what

DSpace would be and how it would help the MIT community and its various constituents.

- Ann Wolpert presented the DSpace concept to her colleagues on campus and helped solidify arrangements with early adopters.
- A free DSpace-Announce electronic mailing regularly reached subscribers, reporting on the project's news and progress.
- The Libraries' public relations office sent press releases about DSpace's milestones to the news media outside of MIT. Their pieces are collected at the DSpace News and Related Readings page (libraries.mit.edu/dspace-fed-test/news/index.html).

The word was getting out! And the DSpace team realized that gaining the support of key administrators was crucial. The project required their backing. Engaging the enthusiasm of MIT's most influential movers turned out to be contagious, as they introduced the faculty to a notion some had doubtless never contemplated.

They also knew that to recruit early adopters, it was necessary to promote the benefits of early participation. With this in mind, the DSpace team set about putting in motion a number of benefits they could promote. For example, they knew they had to stress that early DSpace adopters would benefit from the visibility that this new, exciting campus-wide technology venture offered. They decided to prominently display their names in promotional and publicity materials. They offered them the opportunity to tailor and test the software and user interfaces. They would showcase their research ahead of later entrants and reach worldwide audiences faster. They gave early adopters special and prompt attention in solving problems they encountered using the early version of DSpace.

Early adopters at MIT represented a cross section of the Institute. They included groups of different sizes, submitting varied types of research, using several formats, whose disciplinary cultures and practices also varied. They were:

- The Center for Technology, Planning and Industrial Development (CTPID)
- The Department of Ocean Engineering
- The Laboratory for Information and Decision Systems (LIDS)
- The Sloan School of Management
- The MIT Press

Librarian Margret Branschofsky, whose long experience within the MIT Libraries turned out to be invaluable, joined the DSpace team as Faculty Liaison and User Support Manager in the spring of 2000. With her help and foresight, the team's Faculty Liaison helped early adopters define their communities and their membership. They also identified policy makers and policy decisions that affected submission and accessed policies governing research materials. And a DSpace Coordinator was appointed to act as liaison to the DSpace team and work directly with the team's Faculty Liasion to manage these various activities. His job was to promote the setup and operation of the various research communities with DSpace.

In addition to assisting early adopter communities to load and submit their content, DSpace helped each community establish and name its collections and test its workflows for submission and review, and assisted with customizing individual community portal pages.

Things were going well—a critical mass of early adopters was onboard; now all DSpace had to do was gain the support of the rest of the MIT academic community!

Sources: Compiled from dspace.org/implement/case-study.pdf and Barton and Walker (2002).

Questions for Minicase

1. What tactics were used by developers of MIT's DSpace to successfully introduce the system into the organization?
2. What other tactics might have been effective?

Problem-Solving Activity

Impact of Adopter Categories on Implementing a New Information System

ABC Accounts (ABC, *a fictitious company*) is a small, family-owned and -operated business in North Carolina. It has been in existence for 32 years, and is very successful. Its owners and managers are Jon and Carol Young, a husband and wife team. The firm operates out of the home of Carol and Jon, and has done so since its inception. Customers are treated like family—they are welcome anytime and without appointment. Some clients have been with the company for over 25 years. Clients range from high profile businesses and individuals in the growing wine industry to other mom and pop businesses. Most business customers started off very small and grew considerably during their relationship with ABC.

The company mission is to provide personal service and excellent tax advice at competitive prices. Its goal is for every customer to feel like part of the family, and to be close friends. Carol and Jon have actively followed their mission in every aspect of their client interactions. They have been rewarded with life-long friendships and a referral-only business that does not advertise.

About the People

Carol and Jon have been married for twelve years. Carol is in her fifties, and Jon is in his sixties. They are both well educated in nontechnology fields. Indeed, neither Jon nor Carol are *early adopters* of technology. Through their behavior, they can be classified as *late majority adopters*.

Although Carol is not an early adopter, she likes new technology and is very interested in the *latest* tool for her work. Unfortunately, upon interviewing Jon and Carol, we find that this is a cause for marital discord (minor, of course!). Jon gets frustrated with Carol for buying the latest gadgets, and then not using them when they prove difficult or intimidating. He would rather that she learn a new technology *before* she purchases it.

Carol, on the other hand, thinks that Jon is reluctant to see new ways of doing business. She wants him to embrace the business and help her make it even more successful.

About the Technology

ABC runs a simple computer network that consists of two desktops and one laptop. The laptop is new: it has 1.33 MHz and 50 gigabytes of storage. The memory, however, is minimal—500 megabytes. One desktop is new and, according to Carol, has "more than enough" memory and speed. This is the computer she is using. Jon's computer is older, but it works quite well for the payroll he needs to generate. The company has an Internet connection, but no remote network access. The accounting and payroll applications installed on the desktops are large and require a large amount of memory and storage space. The files from those applications cannot be opened without the application present.

Considering Adopter Categories

We know from the Adopter Category Table shown earlier in the chapter that Carol and Jon will be skeptical of any new system. We know from our meeting that Jon really wants Carol to try out any software before they purchase it—he is *risk averse*. Carol, on the other hand, appears to be *risk neutral*. She has aggressively pursued creating, running, and expanding a successful business. She is going to want to have very progressive and newer technology.

Carol and Jon want to pursue a reasonably-priced IT solution that will enable them to "work anywhere." They are both mindful of Jon's age, as well as their desire to take vacations. The business they own has been very successful, and has left them much less time to travel. They would like to work "on the go." We saw that Carol and Jon are both late majority adopters.

Your Mission

Write a recommendation to ABC Accounts about the technology you would recommend to them, and what steps you would take to implement it to make the transition from existing technology to new technology as painless as possible for Jon and Carol. To prepare the recommendation report you will need to carefully research technologies that may be used to create a virtual office for ABC Accounts. In the report explain:

1. How you identified the different technologies
2. What technologies you discovered
3. Which you would recommend to ABC accounts
4. What steps you would take to implement the recommended solution

When preparing your report also make sure that you address the following issues:

1. There are two main issues when adopting new technology at ABC Accounts. What are they and how will you, as an external IT consultant, address these issues?
2. The differences between early adopters versus late adopter clients in systems adoption and implementation.
3. How understanding Jon's and Carol's adopter categories will help you to implement a better information system at ABC Accounts.

Online Resources

More resources and study tools are located on the Student Web Site and on WileyPLUS. You'll find additional chapter materials and useful Web links. In addition, self-quizzes that provide individualized feedback are available for each chapter.

Online Minicases for Chapter 14 are available at wiley.com/college/turban:

14.1 NCBJ Achieves a 500 Percent+ ROI by Rebuilding Its IT Infrastructure
14.2 BT Focuses on Value in Adoption of Social Media Tools

References

Barton, M. R., and J. H. Walker, MIT Libraries, DSpace Business Plan Project Final Report to the Andrew W. Mellon Foundation, 2002, *dspace.org/implement/mellon.pdf* (accessed June 2008).

Beal, G., E. Rogers, and J. Bohlen, "Validity of the Concept of Stages in the Adoption Process," *Rural Sociology*, 1957.

Berry, L. L., V. Shankar, J. T. Parish, S. Cadwallader, and T. Dotzel, "Creating New Markets through Service Innovation," *Sloan Management Review*, 47(2), 2006.

Brandel, M., "Lincoln Financial Syndicates Content with Web Services," *ComputerWorld*, March 15, 2004.

Camara, S. B., A. V. Sanchez, and M. J. H. Ortiz, "Organizational Determinants of IT Adoption in the Pharmaceutical Distribution Sector," *European Journal of IS*, 13(2), 2004.

Cantara, M., F. Biscotti, J. Correia, and A. Raina, Forecast: Portal, Process and Middleware Software, Worldwide, 2006–2011, Update, Gartner Inc. Report ID No. G00150223, July 13, 2007.

Chen, A., "Hasbro Plays to Win with BPM," *Eweek*, August 2, 2004.

CIO Magazine (2008), p. 14.

Cravens, J., "Introducing New Technology Successfully into an Agency and Why Your Organization Needs a Technology Plan," 2005, *coyotecommunications.com/tech/techbuy.html* (accessed June 2008).

Deming, W. E., "Out of the Crisis," MIT Center for Advanced Engineering Study, 1986,

Dhillon, G., "Dimensions of Power and IS Implementation," *Information and Management*, 41(5), May 2004.

Hill, J., M. Cantara, E. Deitert, and M. Kerremans, "Magic Quadrant" for Business Process Management Suites, 2007, Gartner Inc. Report ID No: G00152906, December 14, 2007.

Horwitt, E., "Bank Achieves over 500% ROI in 8 Months," *Techtarget Case Study*, May 3, 2006.

IBM (2002), p. 14.19.

IDC Press Release, "Worldwide Spending on Information Technology Will Reach $1.48 Billion by 2010," *idc.com/getdoc.jsp?containerId=prUS20514107, 2007* (accessed June 2008).

IDS Scheer AG, "Business Process Management," IDS White Paper, May–June 2005.

Jones, J., D. Aguirre, and M. Calderone, "10 Principles of Change Management," *Strategy+Business*, April 2004.

Kettinger, J., J. Teng, and S. Guha, "Business Process Change: A Study of Methodologies, Techniques, and Tools," *MIS Quarterly*, 21(1), 1997.

Kotter, J. P., "Leading Change: Why Transformation Efforts Fail," *Harvard Business Review*, 73(2), 1995.

Kotter, J., *Leading Change*. Boston: Harvard Business School Press, 1996.

Kotter, J., and H. Rathgeber, *Our Iceberg Is Melting*. New York: St. Martin's Press, 2006.

Lewin, K., *Field Theory in Social Science*. New York: Harper and Row, 1951.

Markus (1984), p.14.55.

McNurlin, B. C., and R. H. Sprague, *Information Systems Management in Practice*, 7th ed. Upper Saddle River, NJ; Pearson Education Inc., 2006.

Merrifield, R., J. Calhoun, and D. Stevens, "The Next Revolution in Productivity," *Harvard Business Review,* June 1, 2008.

Murphy, R. M., "Tech Doesn't Matter . . . Want to Bet?" *Fortune Small Business*, January 31, 2006.

O'Donnell, A., "BPM: Insuring Business Success," *Optimizemag.com*, April 2007.

Plummer and McCoy (2006), p. 14.19.

Pollard, C., "Exploring Continued and Discontinued Use of IT: A Case Study of OptionFinder, a Group Support System," *Group Decision and Negotiation*, 12, 2003.

Rogers, E. M., *Diffusion of Innovations*, 5th ed. New York, NY: Free Press, 2003.

Royse, D., B. Thyer, D. Padgett, and T. Logan, *Program Evaluation. An Introduction*, 4th ed. Belmont, CA: Thomson Brooks/Cole, 2006.

Smith, H., and P. Fingar, *Business Process Management: The Third Wave*. Tampa, FL: Meghan-Kiffer Press, 2002.

Straub, D., *Foundations of Net-Enhanced Organizations*. Hoboken, NJ: Wiley, 2004.

Swamy, R., "Strategic Performance Measurement in the New Millennium," *CMA Management*, May 2002.

Wei, R., "Wi-Fi Powered WLAN: When Built, Who Will Use It?" *Journal of Computer-Mediated Communication*, 12(1), 2006.

Whiting, R., "BPM Smartens Up," *Informationweek.com*, November 6, 2006.

Chapter
15

Impact of IT on Enterprises, Users, and the Environment

High-Performance Green Computing at Nanoscale Center

15.1 New and Accelerating Trends in IT

15.2 Current Perspectives on the Enterprise Web 2.0

15.3 Operating Greener Businesses and Eco-Friendly Data Centers

15.4 Impacts of Too Much Information and Connectivity

15.5 Managerial Issues

Minicase: *Wireless Mesh Networking Adds Real-time Monitoring to the Plant Floor*

Problem-Solving Activity: *The Google Generation: Lots of Access, Too Little Analytical Skills*

Online Minicases:

15.1 *Keeping an Edge on Beer and Wine Can Manufacturing with Intelligence and Dashboards*
15.2 *Do You Know Where Your Food Has Been?*

Learning Objectives

After studying this chapter, you will be able to:

❶ Recognize trends in IT that are affecting business processes, competition, and workers.

❷ Describe ways that IT can help conserve natural resources and protect the environment.

❸ Identify key uses of Web 2.0 technologies that gave rise to the concept of Enterprise 2.0.

❹ Understand green business practices and data center designs

❺ Understand the complexity of the effects of technological progress on labor markets and individual employees.

❻ Discuss the impacts of IT on the quality of life and interpersonal relationships.

❼ Recognize the physical and emotional issues related to the proliferation of IT.

Integrating *IT*

 ACC
 FIN
 MKT
 OM
 HRM
 IS

IT-PERFORMANCE MODEL

Technologies of the Internet, real-time data analysis, mobile communications, automated decision making, and powerful, yet affordable, computers have created many opportunities for change. Global competition, technological developments, more pervasive connectivity, and many other forces will continue to have an effect on enterprises, workers, lifestyles, and the condition of the environment. In this chapter, we discuss key trends driven by IT and the potential and combined impacts of these trends. In addition, we examine the greening of computing and the supply chain; that is, how companies are practicing green procurement, manufacturing, distribution, service, and recycling in an environmentally friendly manner. We conclude by considering how IT supports creativity.

The business performance management cycle and IT model.

HIGH-PERFORMANCE GREEN COMPUTING AT NANOSCALE CENTER

GOV *GLOBAL*

The U.S. Department of Energy's Argonne National Laboratory, located in Illinois, is renowned for its research centers in energy and environmental science, computation and biosciences, and national security. Argonne's Center for Nanoscale Materials (CNM) studies the behavior of nanoscale materials (*nano.anl.gov*). Nanoscale materials are slightly larger than the size of atoms and need to be studied with the CNM's nanoscope (see Figure 15.1), the world's most powerful X-ray microscope. The CNM's research mission is to find new energy technologies and to understand and mitigate the environmental impacts of energy use. Researchers study nanoscale materials and devices to learn about harvesting solar energy more efficiently, providing more efficient lighting, and enabling next-generation computing.

The Problem

To achieve its mission, the CNM needed laboratory and computing facilities that could provide or accommodate extensive processing power, which would typically take up a lot of space—in other words, have a large footprint—consume a huge amount of energy, and generate extreme heat that had to be controlled with air conditioning. The CNM had to be designed to conserve energy, space, and the environment and support future research missions.

Figure 15.1 The Center for Nanoscale Materials' *nanoscope*, the world's most powerful X-ray microscope. (*Courtesy of U. S. Department of Energy's Argonne National Laboratory.*)

Therefore, when research was just beginning at the CNM, the Department of Energy wanted to be sure that the center's infrastructure could accommodate not only current requirements, but also future needs. Its eco-friendly plan was to deliver the computer processing performance required to support world-class scientific research on nanoscale materials in such a way that it would reduce the physical footprint of hardware while minimizing power consumption, cooling costs, and real estate costs.

The Solution

The CNM team built a high-performance computer cluster with Intel processors that delivered the extreme performance required with low power consumption and a small footprint. A **computer cluster** is a group of computers linked via a LAN that work together to form the equivalent of a single computer. Using Intel software tools, CNM application developers have improved the efficiency of their research applications by 20 to 30 percent.

The Results

Built from the ground up, the new CNM facility enables scientists and engineers to conduct a wide variety of projects in a single location. The computing infrastructure delivers the computing power and data transfer rate required to capture and analyze large amounts of data in real time. Some experiments produce enormous amounts of data. Researchers are able to analyze those data in real time so they can reposition samples, adjust instruments, and fine-tune their experiments. Research performed at the facility is contributing to advances in medicine, electronics, manufacturing, and alternative energy sources.

By providing a way to achieve fast results within a single facility, the CNM can accommodate more researchers in less time. Overall, it achieved its mission of providing a powerful computing infrastructure that enables researchers to produce better science while simultaneously protecting the environment.

Sources: Compiled from Argonne National Laboratory (2008), CNM (2008), and *Intel.com* (2008).

Lessons Learned from This Case

Investments in energy-conserving data centers and other computing facilities can reduce the long-term costs of ownership and maintenance. Organizations are paying premiums to invest in green computers that are both energy efficient and environmentally responsible. Organizations that invest in green hardware find that the energy savings, extended product lifecycle, positive public image, and other benefits exceed the additional costs of that hardware.

In addition to green computing, there are key IT trends that either individually or collectively are having impacts on industries, businesses, government, the workplace, workers, and consumers, which are discussed in the next section.

15.1 New and Accelerating Trends in IT

Ray Kurzweil, inventor of and expert on artificial intelligence, wrote a forward-looking article called the "**Law of Accelerating Returns**" (2001). This law suggests that the time interval between significant events grows shorter as time passes because technological change is exponential rather than linear. For example, changes that formerly had taken decades to unfold now occur within years, changes that had taken years have shortened to months, and so on (see *kurzweilai.net*). Among Kurzweil's most intriguing forecasts are the following:

1. We will not experience only 100 years of (linear) progress during the 21st century. Rather, because of exponential technological change, during this century there will be roughly 20,000 years of progress based on today's rate.

2. The equivalent of 4,000 years of technological advancement will occur during the first two decades, from 2000 to 2020.

3. We will have a workable artificially intelligent (AI) brain that can recognize patterns much the way human brains do by 2020.

Evidence of this third forecast occurred in 2008 when AI reached a milestone with an intelligent computer system named Polaris. Polaris was launched as an AI project by computer scientist Michael Bowling at the University of Alberta in Canada. Polaris had outperformed several of the world's top Texas Hold 'em poker players at a human versus machine competition in Las Vegas. The final score was computer 3, humans 2, with 1 draw. An AI computer outperforming human experts was not new. In 1997, IBM supercomputer Deep Blue had beaten world chess champion Gary Kasparov in a six-game match by 2 wins to 1, with 3 draws. Compared to chess, poker is more intellectually complex because chess players have perfect information. That is, chess players know the location of game pieces, but poker players do not know the other players' cards. So, unlike Deep Blue, Polaris had to deal with extensive uncertainty, including deciding whether to wait or bid. An AI computer with the ability to deal with the enormous complexity of uncertainty and a changing decision situation has enormous potential.

Polaris, which ran on a laptop, played 8 billion games against itself to devise multiple strategies with slight differences. Strategies ranged from aggressive to passive. At first, Polaris could beat amateurs only. A more intelligent version of Polaris had the ability to learn—that is, to adapt to an opponent's strategy in midgame—and beat the experts. During the game, Polaris analyzed its human opponent's style of play and adjusted its strategy. For example, the system played more aggressively to get the human to give up and fold his cards. The AI poker-like computer can be useful in situations involving bidding and uncertainty, such as competing companies bidding on government contracts.

Unique developments such as Polaris, as well as fast-paced changes, make it extremely difficult to forecast what will happen to enterprises, careers, social lives, energy prices, and the condition of the environment. We can safely predict, however, that IT developments and IT management will play major roles in accelerating and/or responding to whatever changes occur, as the following trends demonstrate:

• **Robotics.** Robotics is advancing in all shapes and sizes, and robots are getting smarter. Robots will be employed or engaged in sports, war, medicine, business, entertainment, leisure, and home care, and also as pets and playmates. Autonomous nanotechnology swarms (ANTs), or nanobots, will be highly intelligent and will make smart decisions in many areas of application. Robots will increasingly substitute for human workers at home, in space, in the military, and for security, even as automation continues its relentless push into the workplace.

• The U.S. Department of Defense is working on creating robot armies, called swarms of robots, that will be able to operate autonomously.

- IBM consulting uses a software program that chooses and allocates resources for projects better and faster than humans can.
- Cisco is using software programs to replace humans in human resources, finance, customer service, and other staff areas.

An adorable but annoying robotic clock named Clocky gives a hotel guest one chance to wake up when the alarm goes off. If the guest presses the snooze button, Clocky jumps off the nightstand and rushes around the room looking for a place to hide. The next time the alarm goes off, the guest has to find the clock to turn it off. Testing may reveal negative side effects. Another IT for hotel rooms is lights that turn themselves off after sensors inform them that people have left the room.

Throughout history, progress has been marked by the substitution of new products, services, and processes for existing ones and by the substitution of machines for people. The current era is no different, but the speed and the cumulative or accelerated impact are startling.

In this section, we identify and discuss several IT trends and initiatives occurring in a cross section of industries that may have widespread impacts.

QUANTUM LEAPS DRIVEN BY IT

In the mid-1990s, two transformational ITs emerged: the *Web*, which introduced the business world to the Internet and e-commerce, and *enterprise information systems*, such as CRM, SCM, and ERP, which sought to harness the power of networks and data to improve performance (see Chapters 3 and 4). The Web and enterprise systems were not simply improvements on existing IT. They were quantum leaps forward in corporate IT, and they created a platform for the changes soon to follow—during the first decade of the 21st century. Those changes consisted of end-user-driven technologies, most notably Web 2.0 and social networking, and social media. Mashups, wikis, blogs, and software as a service (SaaS) have been shifting IT responsibilities away from centralized IT departments to business units and giving consumers an active role or voice via social marketing and feedback. Today, consumers compare prices and read reviews on product quality and value and company reputation or customer service before making their buying decisions. The Internet has become the preeminent means of communicating, conducting business, socializing, entertaining, and just living.

In this section, we examine some other major trends related to IT, including telemedicine, urban planning, outsourcing, and new delivery models. We also take a look at predictions that may not have turned out exactly as expected.

MOBILE TECHNOLOGY REVOLUTIONIZING MEDICINE

Effective telemedicine or telehealth technologies will help in increasing the number of patients treated by physicians remotely and in lowering the costs and travel times associated with treatment. Telemedicine is the use of telecommunication networks to provide medical information and services, such as consulting and remote curative medical procedures or examinations. Telehealth (see U.S. Department of Health and Human Services at *hrsa.gov/telehealth*) is a broader application of telemedicine. Telehealth is the use of electronic information and telecommunications technologies to support preventive *and* curative long-distance clinical healthcare, patient and professional health-related education, public health, and health administration. Health organizations are increasingly using telehealth technology to monitor patients remotely. Technologies used in telemedicine/health typically are videoconferencing, store-and-forward imaging (for a video of store-and-forward imaging, visit *global-media.com/capsure*), streaming media, and wired and mobile communications.

Most significant is mobile technology, which has already proven to be a cost and time saver in healthcare, and as a result, is a significant evolutionary step in medical prevention and treatment. Mobile technology allows specialists to triage (i.e., determine priorities for action in an emergency), diagnose, and monitor remote medical cases by viewing data and images conveyed wirelessly to their location. Furthermore, wireless technology allows these specialists to access medical records and reference materials related to a specific patient's case, as described in *IT at Work 15.1*.

IT at Work 15.1

Telemedicine Helps Indian Tribe Get Better Healthcare

The Alabama Coushatta Indian Tribe Reservation, located 45 miles outside of Houston, Texas, has experienced an outmigration of its people to more metropolitan areas in search of better education, jobs, and healthcare. To preserve its culture, the 300-member tribe sought ways to make living on the reservation more attractive to its young members. The partnership of Sam Houston State University (SHSU) and Rural Utilities Services, which provided $350,000 in funding, led to the creation of a network called RESNET to bridge the information and communication gaps for residents of Livingston and surrounding counties.

A fiber-optic network links the medical clinic on the reservation to the University of Texas Medical Branch in Polk County as well as to the Tyler County Hospital. Tribal members can now receive more specialized care because the network enables two-way consultations between the clinic on the reservation and the hospitals. Individuals with ailments that might require hospitalization but about which they are not sure, such as a diabetic patient with a concern about a swollen limb, can first check with the medical clinic on the reservation. The clinic can assess the patient's vital signs and share radiology images with specialists at one of the hospitals. The specialists and clinicians can then make informed decisions about whether the patient needs to travel to a hospital. These diagnostic steps improve the quality of care and save time for both patients and medical staff.

Source: USDA (2006) and shsu.edu.

For Further Exploration: What are potential legal problems associated with telemedicine? What are some trade-offs to be considered? How does the diagnosis process reduce costs and improve healthcare treatment?

Telemedicine and telehealth are rapidly becoming a significant focus in the United States' $2.0 trillion healthcare market. As of 2007, the European telemedicine market generated revenues of $118 million, and was estimated to reach $236 million by 2014 (TIE, 2008). As often happens, the technology in the telemedicine/health industry is becoming increasingly sophisticated, and the prices for computers, software, and transmission equipment are falling. However, the technology is perceived to be extremely expensive, and the lack of payer reimbursement is one of the major barriers to broader adoption.

Despite the potential benefits of telemedicine/health, issues related to information security may constrain its growth. Those issues include the cost of encryption, secure transmission, and secure storage—as well as the liability risks if personally identifiable medical information gets released or compromised. Preventing data loss is a serious issue for healthcare insurance companies, as the number of incidents and the costs to the victims continue to increase. Whether it is malicious or accidental, data loss can result in a federal investigation, reduce shareholder value, and damage the company's goodwill and reputation.

URBAN PLANNING WITH WIRELESS SENSOR NETWORKS

Traffic jams and parking problems in congested cities cause air and noise pollution, wasted fuel, stress, delays, and lost revenues. Studies of traffic congestion in New York and Los Angeles have found that cruising for parking is, in fact, a major source of gridlock. Disturbing results from studies conducted on behalf of urban planning efforts include the following:

• A study released in June 2008 by Transportation Alternatives (transalt.org), a public transit advocacy group, reported that 28 to 45 percent of traffic on some streets in New York City is generated by people circling the blocks searching for parking. Drivers searching for parking within a 15-block area on Manhattan's Upper West Side drove 366,000 miles a year. Traffic congestion costs $13 billion in lost revenue and 50,000 jobs in the city annually for workers who are late for work once too often.

• Analysis conducted in Los Angeles by Donald Shoup, an urban planning professor at UCLA, found that over the course of a year, the search for curbside parking in a 15-block business district resulted in 950,000 excess vehicle miles of travel. Those wasted miles are the equivalent to 38 trips around the earth, and they consume 47,000 gallons of gas and produce 730 tons of the greenhouse gas carbon dioxide (CO_2) (Markoff, 2008).

These adverse effects can be alleviated with the deployment of sensors and wireless networks. In late 2008, San Francisco initiated the nation's most ambitious trial of a wireless sensor network that announces which parking spaces are free at any moment. The trial involved 6,000 of its 24,000 metered parking spaces. The system will alert drivers to empty parking places either by displays on street signs or via maps on their smartphone screens. In addition, the system can be extended so that drivers may even be able to pay for parking by cell phones and add funds to their parking meters from their phones without having to return to the meter. Solving the parking crisis has special significance in San Francisco because in 2006 a 19-year-old man was stabbed to death during a fight over a parking space.

Applying IT solutions will have a series of positive effects on transportation, the economy, and the environment. About a dozen major cities are in discussions with technology companies to deploy smart parking systems.

Streetline (*streetlinenetworks.com*) is a company that provides city infrastructure technologies to improve urban operations through reliable information. Over the years, parking operations have become increasingly complex, and parking management has assumed a central role in the economic health of cities. But the quality of information to reduce their impacts has not kept up.

Streetline's product line includes *congestion management systems* that consist of parking sensors and wireless networked meters. The sensors, engineered using the same principles that make a compass operate, create a unique parking signature for each vehicle, which can determine, based on variations in parking angles and size of vehicles, when a parking space is filled, when a vehicle departs, and when a new vehicle replaces it. Wireless networked meters enable parking officials to instantly identify who has or has not paid as well as the total revenue for parking by meter and street, based on the time of day or the day of the week.

OFFSHORE OUTSOURCING

Offshore outsourcing is one of the manifestations of the trend toward globalization—blurring of geographic barriers—that is being accelerated by IT (see Chapters 7, 8, and 13). Well-educated English-speaking employees residing in countries such as India and the Philippines can perform services demanded by firms based in the United States, Great Britain, or any other country. In fact, outsourcing of white-collar services has already become mainstream, with software development and call-center operations being among the most prevalent. Furthermore, the outsourcing trends are naturally expanding into such activities as processing insurance claims, transcribing medical records, engineering and design work, financial analysis, market research, and many others.

Processing confidential data offshore creates valid concerns about identity theft and privacy issues. *Privacy standards* in the country where the data originate may be very different from the privacy laws and safeguards in the country where the data are processed. A disgruntled worker or identify theft ring can do immeasurable harm.

The remarkable communications capabilities delivered by IT promote globalization not only through offshore outsourcing of high-tech jobs, but also by enabling firms to distribute core corporate functions (e.g., marketing, accounting) around the globe. A newer type of outsourcing is business process outsourcing.

BUSINESS PROCESS OUTSOURCING (BPO)

The major business model of the 1960s was that size led to economies of scale, which was good. The creation of huge enterprises with corporate office parks was seen as a mark of success. Those enterprises would have separate warehouses just to hold their office supplies and more mid-level bureaucrats than an agency of the United States government. Was all that necessary? No, that business model hurt profitability. The latest model is business process outsourcing (BPO), which has become the cornerstone of the "lean and mean" way of doing business and staying competitive.

When the manufacturing section began outsourcing production work and processes to low-cost labor markets, unemployment rates and job displacement increased in the industrial nations. The shift by American companies toward offshoring, which is sometimes referred to as *globally integrated production*, and the consequent relocation of many operations overseas caused huge shifts in labor supply and demand. Now entire business processes are being outsourced to greater extents, similar to the way manufacturing has been outsourced for several decades. BPO is the process of hiring another company to handle business activities. BPO is distinct from IT outsourcing, which focuses on hiring a third-party company or service provider to do IT-related activities, such as application management and application development, data center operations, or testing and quality assurance.

The general purpose of outsourcing is to increase efficiency, reduce costs, and acquire innovative capabilities quickly—by buying the capabilities instead of developing them. Outsourcing can be a source of strategic advantage.

BPO often involves offshoring, or the hiring of a foreign-based company to perform the work. India is a popular location for BPO activities. A leading company offering BPO is EDS (*eds.com/services/bpo*). *IT at Work 15.2* describes how Blue Cross Blue Shield of Massachusetts outsourced its data-storage processing to EDS when its technology infrastructure could no longer effectively accommodate its rapidly growing data-storage needs.

IT DELIVERY MODELS

The common trend is the delivery of IT services that limit the amount of responsibility and risk businesses must shoulder in acquiring and maintaining technology that enables core business functions. For example, Web 2.0 applications take advantage of service-oriented architecture (SOA) to access multiple kinds of services through the Web (see Chapter 13).

IT at Work 15.2

Blue Cross Blue Shield of Massachusetts Outsources Storage Operations

HRM   SVR   ACC   IS

Blue Cross Blue Shield of Massachusetts (BCBSM) is an independent, not-for-profit healthcare company. BCBSM has most of its core applications, such as enrollment and billing, still residing on its IBM mainframe. The company provides coverage to 2.9 million members across Massachusetts and adds new members at the rate of approximately 6 percent a year as of 2007. Its need for data storage was growing faster than its membership—at an annual rate of 20 percent—due to the company's growing use of data and applications, as well as increased regulatory requirements. BCBSM needed to significantly grow its storage capacity to keep up with increasing data needs, and to increase the performance and capacity of its disaster recovery infrastructure. But it also wanted to keep storage costs flat or reduce them, to help hold down its subscriber premiums.

BCBSM was looking for a storage solution that would do the following:

- **Keep up with expanding storage needs.** The company had to find a way to keep up with its 20 percent data growth rate per year.
- **Keep costs flat or reduce them.** Blue Cross Blue Shield of Massachusetts wanted to keep its costs at a minimum, as a way to hold down subscriber premiums. It also wanted to develop an agile environment that allowed for changes as business and technology required.
- **Improve performance.** The current storage infrastructure, although sufficient to handle demands, had reached its maximum capacity and required upgrades to allow the company to take advantage of new technology features such as tiered storage.

- **Form the foundation for a more robust disaster recovery plan.** BCBSM wanted to expand its disaster recovery environment to accommodate storage growth and newer, more robust application requirements such as active Web sites and synchronized data replication.
- **Integrate storage into an intelligent data management plan.** BCBSM was looking for a storage solution that would fit into the company's overall strategy for managing data.
- **Reduce floor space.** The new storage infrastructure takes up less floor space than did the previous infrastructure, which is a significant benefit in Boston, where rent can be extremely high. The company is able to use that space for core functions.

To achieve these goals, the company turned to EDS for an outsourced solution. EDS built a high-capacity, high-performing storage area network (SAN)-based storage infrastructure that cost significantly less than the previous solution. The solution resulted in a cumulative, projected three-year net benefit of $945,000, driven by improved productivity, savings in IT maintenance and troubleshooting, and reduction in lease payments. BCBSM benefited from increased storage capacity, faster backups, a robust infrastructure for disaster recovery, and a savings in floor space due to the new solution's smaller footprint.

Sources: Compiled from *EDS.com* (accessed 2008) and Martens (2007).

For Further Exploration: What are the core competencies of Blue Cross Blue Shield and EDS? What factors led BCBSM to outsource its data storage operations? What cost savings did it achieve?

Building and maintaining enterprise systems using SOA promises speed of innovation, flexibility, and reuse of existing assets. In simple terms, an SOA is an infrastructure in which software applications are broken into modular components called services. Services are stored in an easily accessible repository and can be accessed by either users or other services. When done properly, a company can implement new business processes quickly by writing procedures that call for services to interact with one another. Like any promising IT, there are implementation challenges and even failures during the first few years. SOA projects that focus on improving business processes with customers or suppliers tend to have the longest-lasting benefits.

Anyone struggling to understand the business trend toward SOA can look to the experiences of New York City-based Coty Inc., the world's largest fragrance manufacturer. Installing an SOA helped Coty accomplish three major business goals in less than six months: (1) absorb the entire IT infrastructure of Unilever Cosmetics, a newly acquired company; (2) connect to a new IBM procurement system; and (3) implement a new SAP system in Western Europe. Coty could not have connected three major technology platforms using traditional programming methods. The initial focus was on the supply chain processes because the company had been configured to ship only two specific product lines from separate distribution centers in Germany. When they acquired Unilever, however, they added several more product lines and distribution centers. As a result, they had to figure how to split orders for shipping from the various distribution centers. They also had to ensure that customers got the right advanced shipping notices and order confirmations. After the order was delivered, all order data had to be routed back to Coty's central ERP system for proper invoicing. The success of the SOA is also important because Coty's growth strategy includes additional acquisitions. Other IT delivery models that are being deployed are

- **Storage as a Service:** Storage capacity is offered on a per-usage basis similar to SaaS.
- **Communications as a Service (CaaS):** These are multiyear communication servicers that are comprised of vendor-owned, managed, and co-located communication applications with connectivity and IT services.
- **User-owned devices:** These are devices that are owned and managed by employees responsible for providing technology to complete job-related tasks.
- **Business process utilities (BPUs):** These are outsourced business process services for standardized processes.

The trend is away from large numbers of IT staff who support internally developed applications, networks, PCs, and the infrastructures of data centers. Under new delivery models, standard or basic IT services move to a more simplistic model. Future simplification of IT will occur as in other utilities. In the past, for example, businesses used to generate their own electricity or provide their own telecommunications service. In each case, as new methods of delivery from utility companies emerged, companies were able to take advantage of the service without maintaining the costly infrastructure.

We next examine trends related to the use of Web 2.0 by enterprises, which has been dubbed Enterprise Web 2.0, or simply *Enterprise 2.0.*

Review Questions

1. What does Kurzweil's "Law of Accelerating Returns" predict about IT?
2. What are the AI capabilities of Polaris?
3. What is telemedicine? Identify one factor that is promoting telemedicine and one factor that may be limiting its growth.
4. How can wireless sensors improve urban planning efforts?
5. What is business process outsourcing (BPO)?
6. What is driving the business trend toward SOA?
7. What are two new IT services delivery methods?

15.2 Current Perspectives on the Enterprise Web 2.0

Enterprise Web 2.0 (as the term suggests) is the application of Web 2.0 technologies in the enterprise. The enterprise Web 2.0 market, which is commonly referred to as **Enterprise 2.0**, or **E 2.0**, is the deployment of blogs, wikis, RSS, and social networking within the enterprise. Major software providers such as Microsoft and IBM are doing a good job at integrating Web 2.0 tools in their collaboration platforms. Microsoft SharePoint, for instance, provides capabilities such as blogs as well as publishing and receiving RSS feeds.

FREEFORM ENTERPRISE 2.0

Enterprise 2.0 began in 2006 as a new way to collaborate using *freeform* social software platforms (e.g., blogs) within companies, or between companies and their partners or customers. Freeform software typically accepts many types of data—text, video, audio—and from anyone. It is indifferent to formal organizational structure.

Enterprise 2.0 is really about moving into a Web setting where workers can more easily conduct their day-to-day personal interactions. A company can build up its business intelligence (BI) repository by using software that integrates blogs or comment forums to supplement historical company data. Through this freeform approach, knowledge management (KM) becomes decentralized and democratic. Centralized control goes away with Enterprise 2.0.

Enterprise 2.0 stands to supplant other communication and knowledge management systems because of its ability to capture tacit knowledge, best practices, and relevant experiences throughout a company, making this information readily available to more users. The benefits are a highly productive and collaborative environment as knowledge is shared and becomes more visible.

Despite the potential benefits, as of 2008, an AIIM (*edocmanagement.com*) survey indicated that many companies had not adopted Enterprise 2.0 because they view it as just another approach to collaboration or as a marketing buzzword (Keldsen, 2008). These responses suggest that managers are not aware of what Enterprise 2.0 can do for organizations on both the business and the technical fronts.

The focus in this section is on challenging Web 2.0 issues, such as presence and privacy, reputation preservation, content infringement, and virtual worlds, as well as the unknown consequences of the Web 2.0 capabilities. We also raise important issues for you to consider. We look first at the iPhone 3G and its role in E 2.0. With iPhone 3G, users have access to the most commonly used enterprise e-mail system, Microsoft Exchange.

iPHONE 3G AND E 2.0

In July 2008, Apple launched the 3G version of iPhone, or *iPhone 3G,* which it described as the best phone for business because of features that business users need. The iPhone 3G

- can access higher speed data networks from the wireless carriers.
- supports Microsoft Exchange ActiveSync, delivering push e-mail, calendar, and contacts.
- has a virtual private network (VPN) client with authentication for improved business-grade security (see Chapter 5).

With the 3G iPhone, Apple adds enough bandwidth to enable real-time collaborative applications such as Web and video conferencing. Enterprises may look to exploit the opportunity provided by the iPhone 3G by equipping their mobile workers with the capabilities to improve productivity regardless of their location. Its E 2.0 support applications are described next.

Enterprise Applications.

- Salesforce Mobile: Provides users with critical customer information instantly through a touch screen.
- Oracle Business Indicators: This is a business intelligence (BI) application that provides real-time, secure access to business performance information on the mobile device.

Social Networking. Social networking in business will play an increasing role in our ability to connect with others and share expertise. Applications in the iTunes App Store that are geared toward social networking are

- AIM: Instant messaging to communicate or stay connected on iPhone or iPod Touch
- Whrrl: Map based on the places friends or co-workers go in the real world
- Loopt: Uses location technology to connect users to others worldwide

Search.

- Google Mobile App: Provides fast and easy search capabilities

RSS.

- NetNewsWire: This is an RSS Reader for the iPhone from Newsgator that synchronizes with their desktop readers.
- iRSS: This is a generic RSS news feed reader that supports RSS 1.0 and 2.0 standards.

Blogging and Publishing.

- TypePad: To update blogs
- Mobile Flickr: To browse and upload to Flickr
- Twitterrific: To read and publish posts on the Twitter social network
- LifeCast: To record life in text and photos. It is a blogging application for the iPhone and iPod Touch.

There is also the broader impact of the iPhone on enterprise collaboration and communication. A real impact of the iPhone is that the walls between desktop/laptop and mobile device are breaking down.

Apple revolutionized the mobile experience with the initial release of iPhone, providing a robust Web experience compared with the reduced-feature browsers available on most other mobile devices. Apple's lead has been followed by Samsung and a number of other manufacturers.

Next we discuss presence, which is the ability to see the online status of a person, for example, someone in a buddy list. If the presence of a user is known, you can immediately tell who is contactable, unlike a telephone where you have to call and wait for the person to answer.

PRESENCE, LOCATION, AND PRIVACY

Presence in the social networking world is not a reality, but it is moving in that direction. Facebook added IM to its Web site, enabling users to know when friends are online. IBM Lotus also supports presence capabilities tied into "Connections," while Microsoft offers similar capabilities for SharePoint. The *iPhone E 2.0 Impact* includes two applications, Loopt and Whrrl (listed in prior section), that enable users to see both the real-time presence and the location of others by leveraging iPhone's built-in location awareness capabilities.

What happens when LinkedIn, Facebook, or MySpace provides the ability for a GPS-enabled mobile device or iPhone to dynamically share their location status with others? Will—or how will—businesses begin to take advantage of these same capabilities to build applications to enable the tracking of field sales and support personnel by leveraging the location status capabilities already present in their mobile devices? With logs of location and presence, there will be an audit trail literally tracking people's movements. What are the privacy implications, assuming there would be any privacy remaining? Who will be held responsible or legally liable for unforeseen harm resulting from so much awareness and connectivity?

FREE SPEECH VIA WIKIS AND SOCIAL NETWORKS

Free speech and privacy rights collide in a world populated by anonymous critics and cyberbullies. But the attacks are not always from competitors or others outside the company. The nature of the Internet ensures that we, at times, may become our own

A Closer Look 15.1

A CEO's Blogging Drew the Attention of the Federal Trade Commission

The CEO of Whole Foods Market, John Mackey, was blogging on the Yahoo! Finance message boards (*messages.yahoo.com*) anonymously as *Rahodeb*. Whole Foods Market (*wholefoods-market.com*) is the world's largest retailer of natural and organic foods, with stores throughout North America and the United Kingdom. As Radodeb, the CEO told the world that "Whole Foods Is Hot, and Wild Oats is NOT." He did not disclose that he was hoping to purchase Wild Oats Market.

Whole Foods eventually completed the controversial $565 million purchase of Wild Oats, which closed in August 2007 after a six-month battle with the Federal Trade Commission (FTC). When the FTC had audited Whole Foods, they discovered the CEO's deceptive blog posts. The blogging caused significant problems for the acquisition. Manipulating or influencing financial markets is a federal crime. Therefore, blogging to influence finan-

cial markets may be deemed by the FTC or SEC as a federal crime, particularly when done by the CEO posing as someone else. The takeover also led to an investigation by the Securities and Exchange Commission (SEC) following the revelation that "Rahodeb" had been secretly promoting his company's stock and disparaging his rival's management team in postings in the Yahoo! stock message board. The investigation led to the suspension of Mackey's blogging privileges until the SEC and the Whole Foods board completed their investigations of Mackey's ill-considered blog outbursts.

While the acquisition was eventually approved, Whole Foods and the CEO suffered damage to their reputations.

The lesson learned here is that companies need to make sure that when employees do go out into the blogosphere, they know what they can and cannot say about business information.

---

worst enemies personally and professionally, based on the content or images we post on blogs, or the friends we keep on social networking pages.

Companies victimized by online gossip and rumor have legal recourse, but against whom? What if the identity of the sender or poster is not known? Who is responsible for restricting troublesome content? Furthermore, companies face legal actions if they are found to be negligent for not restricting harmful content. For negative consequences of blogging by a CEO, see *A Closer Look 15.1*.

Review Questions

1. What is Enterprise 2.0? Does it centralize or decentralize control? Explain.
2. What are three functions of iPhone 3G that provide business value? Explain what those business values are.
3. Distinguish between presence and location. Give an example of each.
4. Where and why do free speech and privacy rights collide?

15.3 Operating Greener Businesses and Eco-Friendly Data Centers

The growing power consumption of computing technology and high energy costs are having a direct negative impact on business profitability. Enterprising is trying to shrink energy costs and carbon consumption and increase the use of recyclable materials. **Green computing,** the study and practice of eco-friendly computing resources, is now a key concern of businesses in all industries—not just environmental organizations. In this section, we focus on how *going green* by adopting environmentally friendly practices is in companies' best interests financially.

At the heart of the "Next Generation Data Center" strategy is the ability to deliver and support secure IT applications through virtualization. The virtualized, dynamic data center reduces energy consumption and the number of servers needed while extending server life.

HOW TO OPERATE GREENER BUSINESSES, DATA CENTERS, AND SUPPLY CHAINS

Are eco-friendly computing and business growth compatible? Yes, they are. According to Gartner Group, 80 percent of the world's data centers are constrained by heat, space, and power requirements. In addition to the demand on processing capability to satisfy the growth of the business, there is enormous demand on power consumption and space requirements for computing platforms. Data center configurations are no longer based on one dimension (e.g., price or performance)—meaning that factors other than affordability or performance must be considered. The equation is much more complicated. Now companies must worry about their power consumption as well as the demand of physical space. All of these factors must be taken into consideration when deciding on the design of a data center.

An enterprise can cut energy costs in half, double space efficiency, and increase server utilization levels to as high as 85 percent. Gaining these efficiencies involved dealing with four separate issues and combining solutions to reach the desired results. The four areas are the desktop, data center computing power, data center power/cooling, and data center storage. Specifically enterprises need to:

• Identify those desktops to virtualize. Virtualization is a trend in enterprise data centers in which servers are consolidated (integrated) so that they can be shared. Most stand-alone servers (in a physical environment) are highly underutilized. Virtualization technology optimizes the capacity and processing power of servers so that fewer servers are needed to provide the necessary processing power. The result is savings in energy, space, and recycling. For a video on virtualization, visit either *nettalk.sun.com/bhive/c/1000/1475/index.html* or *news.zdnet.com/2422-13569_22-155248.html.*

• Identify and turn off unused computers, which is typically 8–10 percent of computers.

• Enable power management features, if available.

• Replace old servers with new energy-efficient servers.

• Replace disk technology (replace disks drives with less than 70-GB capacity with those with more than 500-GB capacity).

• Move old data to tape because tape provides 20 to 200 times more terabytes per kilowatt hour (TB/KW).

The result of Sun's consolidating and moving to more efficient data centers was a hardware reduction that provided over a 450 percent increase in computer power with about one-half the servers and over a 240 percent increase in storage capacity with about one-third the storage devices.

Green computing is a mindset that asks how we can satisfy the growing demand for network computing without putting undo stress on the environment. There is an alternative way to design a processor and a system such that they do not increase demands on the environment, but still provide an increased amount of processing capability to customers to satisfy their business needs.

Going green can start with simple adjustments. A commonsense approach to reducing household expense is to turn off the lights whenever you leave a room. This "power-management" approach can be applied to servers, workstations, and data centers, which are often left fully functional and operating 24/7/365 even though that may not be necessary. One basic solution is to introduce energy management processes that adjust to changes in the demand for computing power. For example, some companies have implemented *working-hours power management* and the less-consuming *after-hours power management.*

There are also complex changes. One such emerging trend is the *greening of the supply chain.* A green supply chain includes procurement, manufacturing, warehousing, distribution, service, and recycling in an environmentally friendly manner. Here are two examples:

• In 2008, a 147,000-square-foot warehouse was built in Tampa Bay, Florida, according to the environmentally sustainable building standards of the U.S. Green Building Council (USGBC). See *usgbc.org/.* The USGBC is a nonprofit community of leaders helping companies design and build green buildings.

• Far from a fad or feel-good initiative, green sourcing is fast emerging as a strategic business imperative. An electronics manufacturer's relationship with its suppliers (sources) is a major issue for executives, customers, and shareholders. And they are relying on procurement to proactively manage it. Sourcing and procurement have always been about more than just price. Factoring green priorities into existing processes is a natural extension of the non-price process, and an effective way to drive green goals. Companies are including green criteria in their requests for proposals (RFPs) and creating clear metrics for measuring them as part of supplier performance management.

There is a growing level of commitment among both small and midsize firms toward the adoption of applications that would support more environmentally friendly supply chain initiatives. For example, the market intelligence firm IDC questioned 250 decision makers at small and midsize enterprises involved in the manufacturing, wholesale, and distribution industries and found that even among the smallest of the supply chain companies, support for green initiatives is emerging. According to the survey, small and midsize companies will seek to use manufacturing applications that support a renewable way of producing products: mobile-enabled applications that help conserve energy and human resource applications that will help train workforces in the areas of green manufacturing (Van der Pool, 2008).

GLOBAL GREEN REGULATIONS

Global regulations also are influencing green business practices. Sustainability regulations such as RoHS (*rohs.eu* and *rohs.gov.uk*) in the European Union (EU) will increasingly impact how supply chains function regardless of location. The *RoHS Directive* stands for "the restriction of the use of certain hazardous substances in electrical and electronic equipment." For example, EU member states ensured that beginning in July 2006, new electrical and electronic equipment put on the market would not contain any of six banned substances—lead, mercury, cadmium, hexavalent chromium, polybrominated biphenyls (PBB), and polybrominated diphenyl ethers (PBDE)—in quantities exceeding maximum concentration values. Moreover, China has passed its own RoHS legislation.

Similar legislation is developing elsewhere. For example, California's Electronic Waste Recycling Act (EWRA) prohibits the sale of electronic devices banned by the EU's RoHS, including CRTs, LCDs, and other products that contain the four heavy metals restricted by RoHS. In addition, many states have enacted mercury and PBDE bans, and several are considering bills similar to EWRA. For example, Seattle has issued many regulations related to eliminating paper-based manuals and mandating recycling.

Eco-friendly practices reduce costs and improve public relations in the long run. Not surprisingly, demand for green computers is on the rise. A tool to help companies find such hardware is the Electronic Product Environmental Assessment Tool, or EPEAT.

ELECTRONIC PRODUCT ENVIRONMENTAL ASSESSMENT TOOL

Maintained by the Green Electronics Council (GEC), the **Electronic Product Environmental Assessment Tool (EPEAT)** is a searchable database of computer hardware that meets a strict set of environmental criteria. Among other criteria, products registered with EPEAT comply with the U.S. government's Energy Star 4.0 rating (see *energystar.gov*); have reduced levels of cadmium, lead, and mercury; and are easier to upgrade and recycle. Energy Star qualified products use less energy. Depending on how many criteria they meet, products receive a gold, silver, or bronze certification rating.

The EPEAT rates computers and monitors on a number of environmental criteria, including energy efficiency, materials used, product longevity, takeback programs, and packaging. Twenty-two percent of the 109 million computers shipped worldwide in 2007 were registered on EPEAT (*epeat.net*). In contrast, in 2006, only 10 percent of computers were registered. Regarding monitors, in 2008, all nine of Lenovo's ThinkVision LCD monitors were EPEAT gold certified, the highest eco-friendly ranking awarded by EPEAT. In addition, more than 280 monitors met the lower silver and bronze certifications.

THE FIELD OF GREEN TECHNOLOGY AND TELECOMMUTING

The field of green technology covers broad range of issues. Green technology focuses on reducing the harmful environmental impacts of computing and industrial processes and innovative technologies caused by the needs of the growing worldwide population. The objective is to minimize damaging the environment or depleting

TABLE 15.1	Potential Benefits of Telecommuting or Virtual Work		
Individuals	**Organizations**	**Community and Society**
• Reduces or eliminates travel-related time and expenses • Improves health by reducing stress related to compromises made between family and work responsibilities • Allows closer proximity to and involvement with family • Allows closer bonds with the family and the community • Decreases involvement in office politics • Increases productivity despite distractions	• Reduces office space needed • Increases labor pool and competitive advantage in recruitment • Provides compliance with Americans with Disabilities Act • Decreases employee turnover, absenteeism, and sick leave usage • Improves job satisfaction and productivity	• Conserves energy and lessens dependence on foreign oil • Preserves the environment by reducing traffic-related pollution and congestion • Reduces traffic accidents and resulting injuries or deaths • Reduces the incidence of disrupted families when people do not have to quit their jobs if they need to move because of a spouse's new job or family obligations • Increased employment opportunities for the homebound • Allows the movement of job opportunities to areas of high unemployment

natural resources by creating fully recyclable products, reducing pollution, and designing energy-efficient or alternative technologies.

Telecommuting or virtual work also offers many green benefits, including reducing rush-hour traffic, improving air quality, improving highway safety, and even improving healthcare. See Table 15.1 for a list of potential benefits.

Review Questions

1. What is green computing?
2. List three ways in which computing can help protect the environment or conserve resources.
3. What is a green supply chain? Give one example.
4. Is green computing or are green supply chains simply a fad or feel-good initiative that will fade away? Explain your answer.
5. What is the role of virtualization in green data centers?
6. How does RoHS in the European Union help protect the environment?
7. What is EPEAT? What are the three certification ratings?
8. How does telecommuting or virtual work conserve the environment?

15.4 Impacts of Too Much Information and Connectivity

Few people disagree that information is a valuable resource and that increased availability of information can be beneficial for individuals and organizations alike. However, IT's capability to introduce ever-growing amounts of data into our lives can exceed our capacity to keep up with the data, leading to **information overload.** Business users are not suffering from the scarcity of data, but from too much of it. Finding the information they need in massive collections of documents can be complicated, time consuming, frustrating, and expensive.

INFORMATION OVERLOAD The impact of information overload is felt not only in business circles but also in many other parts of society, including the military intelligence community. At the onset of the Information Age, intelligence professionals acquired never-before-seen data collection tools, including high-resolution satellite imagery and versatile sensors capable of penetrating natural and manmade barriers. Furthermore, IT enabled the intelligence community to establish high-speed communication links to transfer the data, build vast databases to store the data, and use powerful supercomputers with intelligent software to process the data. Clearly, these examples of IT have enabled the capture and storage of vast amounts of information and made it available to the intelligence community. The introduction of IT has also increased the speed at which data can be analyzed.

To be effective at solving the problem of information overload, information systems must differentiate between the data that can be safely summarized and the data that should be viewed in its original form. This is a difficult problem to solve.

INFORMATION QUALITY

As organizations and societies continue to generate, process, and rely on the rapidly increasing amounts of information, they begin to realize the importance of information quality. **Information quality** is a somewhat subjective measure of the utility, objectivity, and integrity of gathered information. To be valuable, both data and information must possess a number of essential characteristics, such as being complete, accurate, up-to-date, and consistent with the purpose for which they are used. The value and usability of data and information that do not satisfy these requirements are severely limited.

Information quality is mandated by several legislations. The Data Quality Act of 2001 and the Sarbanes-Oxley Act of 2002 impose strict information quality requirements on government agencies and companies. For example, one of the provisions of the Sarbanes–Oxley Act makes chief executive and financial officers personally responsible and liable for the quality of financial information that firms release to stockholders or file with the Securities and Exchange Commission (SEC). This provision emphasizes the importance of controlling and measuring data quality and information quality in BI, corporate performance management, and record management systems.

Problems with information quality are not limited to corporate data. Millions of individuals face information quality issues on a daily basis as they try to find information online, whether on publicly available Web pages or in specialized research databases, wikis, blogs, and newsfeeds.

Among the most common problems that plague online information sources is omission of materials. A number of online "full-text" periodicals databases may omit certain items that appeared in the printed versions of their publications. In addition, online sources of information leave out older documents, which are not available in digital form. Thus, one cannot be assured of having access to a complete set of relevant materials. Even materials that are available from seemingly reputable sources present information quality concerns. Information may have been incorrectly reported, whether intentionally or unintentionally, or it may have become out of date. These and other information quality issues are contributing to the frustration and anxiety that for some people have become the unfortunate side effect of the Information Age.

SPAM

Spamming, the practice of indiscriminately broadcasting unsolicited messages via e-mail and over the Internet, is one of the most widespread forms of digital noise. Spam hurts businesses by lowering the productivity of employees who have to deal with unwanted messages. In addition, it wastes computing power, making it anti-green.

Spam persists because it is not just a big nuisance; it is big, profitable business as well. Spam can originate in any country, making the anti-spam legislation of any given country largely ineffective in keeping spam out. Lost productivity and other expenses associated with spam cost U.S. businesses $17 billion in 2005, up from $10 billion in 2003, according to *The Global Economic Impact of Spam*. Not included in these figures are immeasurable items, such as the missed opportunity cost of a new customer order that is incorrectly discarded as spam. Ferris Research estimated that spam cost $140 billion worldwide in 2008, including $42 billion in the United States alone. If you compare these numbers with Ferris's 2007 estimates of $100 billion and $35 billion, then you see that the cost of spam has increased substantially.

TABLE 15.2	Impacts of IT on Structure, Authority, Power, and Job Content
Impact	**Effect of IT**
Flatter organizational hierarchies	IT increases *span of control* (more employees per supervisor), increases productivity, and reduces the need for technical experts (due to expert systems). Fewer managerial levels will result, with fewer staff and line managers. Reduction in the total number of employees, reengineering of business processes, and the ability of lower-level employees to perform higher-level jobs may result in flatter organizational hierarchies.
Change in blue-collar-to-white-collar staff ratio	The ratio of white- to blue-collar workers increases as computers replace clerical jobs, and as the need for information systems specialists increases. However, the number of professionals and specialists could *decline* in relation to the total number of employees in some organizations as intelligent and knowledge-based systems grow.
Growth in number of special units	IT makes possible technology centers, e-commerce centers, decision support systems departments, and/or intelligent systems departments. Such units may have a major impact on organizational structure, especially when they are supported by or report directly to top management.
Centralization of authority	Centralization may become more popular because of the trend toward smaller and flatter organizations and the use of expert systems. On the other hand, the Web permits greater empowerment, allowing for more decentralization. Whether use of IT results in more centralization or in decentralization may depend on top management's philosophy.
Changes in power and status	Knowledge is power, and those who control information and knowledge are likely to gain power. The struggle over who controls the information resources has become a conflict in many organizations. In some countries, the fight may be between corporations that seek to use information for competitive advantage and the government (e.g., Microsoft vs. the Justice Dept.). Elsewhere, governments may seek to hold onto the reins of power by not letting private citizens access some information (e.g., China's restriction of Internet usage).
Changes in job content and skill sets	*Job content* is interrelated with employee satisfaction, compensation, status, and productivity. Resistance to changes in job skills is common, and can lead to unpleasant confrontations between employees and management.

Internet service providers (ISPs) and software companies have tried many technological campaigns to eradicate spam. Mail-filtering software and other technologies have made it more difficult for spammers to distribute their messages. However, spammers have responded with creative new schemes to defeat the anti-spam solutions. The battle of innovations and counterinnovations between spammers and anti-spam companies continues. Some of the major anti-spam software providers include SpamAssassin, Symantec, Network Associates, McAfee, TrendMicro, GFI, SurfControl, and Sophos.

IMPACTS ON INDIVIDUALS

The IT revolution may result in many changes in structure, authority, power, and job content, as well as personnel management and human resources management. Details of these changes are shown in Table 15.2. Together, the increasing amounts of information and information technology use have potential impacts on job satisfaction, dehumanization, and information anxiety as well as impacts on health and safety. Although many jobs may become substantially more "enriched" with IT, other jobs may become more routine and less satisfying.

Dehumanization and Other Psychological Impacts. Many people feel a loss of identity, known as **dehumanization,** because of computerization. They feel like "just another number" because computers reduce or eliminate the human element that was present in the noncomputerized systems. Some people also feel this way about the Web.

On the other hand, while the major objective of technologies, such as e-commerce, is to increase productivity, they can also create *personalized*, flexible systems that allow individuals to include their opinions and knowledge in the system. These technologies attempt to be people-oriented and user-friendly (e.g., blogs and wikis).

The Internet threatens to have an even more isolating influence than has been created by television. If people are encouraged to work and shop from their living rooms, then some unfortunate psychological effects, such as depression and loneliness, could develop. Some people have become so addicted to the Web or social networks that they have dropped out of their regular social activities at school or work or home, creating societal and organizational problems.

Another possible psychological impact relates to distance learning. In some countries, it is legal to school children at home through IT. Critics contend, however, that the lack of social contacts could be damaging to the social, moral, and cognitive development of school-age children who spend long periods of time working alone on the computer. See *IT at Work 15.3* for a discussion of the shifts in responsibility brought about by the use of iPods in schools.

Impacts on Health and Safety. Computers and information systems are a part of the environment that may adversely affect individuals' health and safety. To illustrate, we will discuss the effects of *job stress* and *long-term use of the keyboard*.

Job Stress. An increase in workload and/or responsibilities can trigger job stress. Although computerization has benefited organizations by increasing productivity, it has also created an ever-increasing workload for some employees. Some workers, especially those who are not proficient with computers but must work with them, feel overwhelmed and anxious about their jobs and their job performance. These feelings of anxiety can adversely affect workers' productivity. Management's responsibility is to

IT at Work 15.3

The Dog Ate My iPod

Schools and universities are finding new ways to keep up with technology, such as the emergence of iPods on campuses. All levels of education are using this brand of portable media players, designed and marketed by Apple Computer, as a learning tool. Duke University was one of the first colleges to embrace this technology. Duke's provost, Peter Lang, said "the direct effect of iPods is they [students] learn better in the classroom." Duke was awarded a grant to give their freshmen 20-gigabyte iPods—enough storage for up to 5,000 songs.

The results have been mixed. Roughly 75 percent of students surveyed at Duke said they use their iPods for academic work. Half of the time, they use the device in ways recommended by the professors. The positive feedback is that the iPod is similar to the old recording devices used in the past, but with the ability to store, organize, and access with a click of a couple of buttons.

On the negative side, students do not have to attend the class to download the materials online or from a fellow student. Some schools are concerned that students will skip classes and rely on each other's recordings, or even use the device to cheat. According to Don McCabe, a Rutgers professor who surveyed nearly 62,000 undergraduates on 96 campuses over four years, two-thirds of the students admitted to cheating. That is a concern, especially with the compact-size, wireless earpieces, and the ability to hold podcasts—audio recordings that can be distributed over the Internet. Given the abundance of electronic gadgets, including handheld e-mail devices, classroom wireless access to the Internet, calculators that are preprogrammed with formulas, and pen-sized scanners used to copy text or exams for other students, universities have to stay ahead of the curve. Some other concerns are: How

will the lecturer's words and actions be used for unknown purposes, and when/where is copyright being infringed upon when students and faculty make their own recordings?

In spite of the worries of skipping class, personal use, and cheating, Apple Computer is supporting the use of the iPod in the education field. Six schools (Duke, Brown, Stanford, the University of Michigan, the University of Wisconsin–Madison, and the University of Missouri School of Journalism) recently participated in a pilot program called iTunes U (*apple.com/educastion/solutions/itunes_u/*). The program was so popular that Apple began to offer the program to all colleges for lectures, notes, podcasts, and information in a library for students to download.

Other schools, such as Brearley School, a private school for girls on the Upper East Side of Manhattan, use iPods predominantly in interactive exercises, such as foreign language classes. Katherine Hallissy Ayala, the head of the computer education department, says "the hope is that if students are interested in this, they'll download and explore on their own without being told to." And Jacques Houis, a French teacher at Brearley, feels that "listening to many different types of French, not just the teacher, is very important." Students have said that the iPod has enhanced their foreign language skills by giving them access to playbacks, music, and other sources besides what is taught in the classroom.

Sources: Ferguson (2005) and Moore (2005).

For Further Exploration: How does the use of iPods shift responsibility from teachers "teaching" to students "learning"? What excuses might a student use for not completing an assignment correctly or submitting it on time?

TABLE 15.3	Impacts of IT on Workers
Impact	**Effect of IT**
Shorter career ladders	In the past, many professionals developed their abilities through years of experience and a series of positions that exposed them to progressively more complex situations. The use of IT, and especially Web-based computer-aided instruction, may shorten this learning curve.
Changes in supervision	IT introduces the possibility for greater electronic supervision. In general, the supervisory process may become more formalized, with greater reliance on procedures and measurable (i.e., quantitative) outputs and less on interpersonal processes. This is especially true for knowledge workers and telecommuters.
Job mobility	The Web has the potential to increase job mobility. Sites such as *techjourney.com* can tell you how jobs pay in any place in the United States. Sites such as *monster.com* offer places to post job offerings and résumés. Using videoconferencing for interviews and intelligent agents to find jobs is likely to increase employee turnover.

help alleviate these fears by providing training, redistributing the workload among workers, and hiring more individuals. See Table 15.3 for a list of impacts of IT on workers.

Repetitive Strain (Stress) Injuries. Other potential health and safety hazards are repetitive strain injuries such as backaches and muscle tension in the wrists and fingers. *Carpal tunnel syndrome* is a painful form of repetitive strain injury that affects the wrists and hands. It has been associated with the long-term use of keyboards.

Lessening the Negative Impact on Health and Safety. Designers are aware of the potential problems associated with prolonged use of computers. Consequently, they have attempted to design a better computing environment. Research in the area of **ergonomics** (the science of adapting machines and work environments to people) provides guidance for these designers. For instance, ergonomic techniques focus on creating an environment for the worker that is safe, well lit, and comfortable. Devices such as antiglare screens have helped alleviate problems of fatigued or damaged eyesight, and chairs that contour the human body have helped decrease backaches.

Review Questions

1. What is information overload?
2. What are four causes of information overload, and what can be done to reduce this problem?
3. Why are laws generally ineffective in fighting spam? Why does spamming persist despite technology defenses?
4. What is information quality? Name one law that requires companies to ensure their information quality.
5. How might the Internet lead to isolation?
6. How can too much information or connectivity impact a person's health? Why?
7. What is ergonomics?

15.5 Managerial Issues

1. Offshore IT and business process outsourcing. The movement of computing work and business processes abroad involves economic risks and significant upfront investment and testing. Outsourcing is also the source of criticism for unemployment. Dire predictions of job losses from shifting high-technology work to low-wage nations with strong education systems, such as India and China, were exaggerated. However, managers should be aware of various legal and ethical considerations surrounding this issue as well as the impact of outsourcing on the size and morale of their workforce.

2. Managing and evaluating nonpresent workers. Telecommuting increases the number of employees working away from the office and could save billions of gallons of gasoline. According to Telework Exchange, "If white-collar employees who feel they could do their jobs from home began to telework twice a week, the United States could conserve 9.7 billion gallons of gasoline and save $38.2 billion a year." These calculations are based on 50-mile round-trips in vehicles getting 24 miles per gallon, with gasoline at $3.94/gallon. Managing teleworkers requires formal communications and secure network connections. Effective performance evaluation is different and requires a closer examination of the actual output produced by each employee.

3. Dealing with information overload. The capacity of information systems to collect, generate, and distribute information has outpaced the ability of human employees to absorb or process it. The resulting stress or confusion from information overload can negatively impact employees and their productivity. Greater investment in filtering software, decision support systems, and expert systems may help alleviate this problem.

4. Providing high-quality information. Information quality is critical to business planning and operations. It is so important that according to GartnerGroup, "more than 50 percent of data warehouse projects will suffer limited acceptance, if not outright failure, as a result of lack of attention to data quality issues" (*teradatauniversi tynetwork.com*). Furthermore, laws and regulations, such as the Sarbanes–Oxley Act, make CEOs and CFOs personally liable for the quality and accuracy of financial information disclosed to the public.

5. Displacement of employees with IT. In blue-collar, clerical, service, or white-collar jobs, intelligent machines are acquiring the capabilities to perform human tasks more effectively or efficiently. While this trend will not result in massive worldwide unemployment, it can have dramatic impacts on enterprises and employees. Thus, managers should be aware of the potentially disruptive technologies that may displace them, their colleagues, or their subordinates.

6. Use of electronic surveillance. The need to defend against computer and white-collar crime requires employers to monitor their employees, which is typically done with IT. While electronic surveillance may reduce the incidence of unlawful activities, it may also result in employee resentment and other unintended consequences. Following the tragedies of September 11, there is growing support to give law enforcement agencies more power to tap into private communications to thwart further acts of terrorism by monitoring private electronic communications. State and federal policymakers face the challenge of balancing security needs via electronic surveillance against the potential erosion of individual privacy.

7. Social and ethical issues. Today's global business environment demands an ethically conscious corporate attitude since business organizations may be taking on a greater role in solving social problems. However, the lack of a common framework for deciding what is ethical and what is not thus ultimately influences the outcome of policymaking. Globalization, the Internet, and connectivity have the power to undermine moral responsibility because it becomes relatively easy to ignore the harm that is being done to others in distant locations and the long-range consequences. Ethics is important because it has become clear that strong reliance on the law alone to safeguard the community has its limits.

How *IT* Benefits You

For the Accounting Major

Accounting and tax functions that had been carried out by entry-level accountants are increasingly being done by software—including TurboTax, Quicken, QuickBooks, and Peachtree. In addition, firms are sending tax preparation and financial reporting overseas. Outsourcing back-office finance and accounting enables accountants to focus on core business while cutting costs. But this situation can also reduce job opportunities for new accountants and, eventually, the pool of candidates to fill positions created by promotions or retirements. Offshore accounting carries the risks and problems of managing remote workers and securing data transfers. The benefits include cost savings with returns being prepared by chartered accountants in India at billable rates substantially below those of professionals in the United States. Another benefit is the ability to have returns prepared overseas during the night in one country and have them ready for review when accountants return in the morning.

Accountants must also be very concerned about the integrity and quality of information reported in financial statements because of the SEC and Sarbanes–Oxley Act. Furthermore, accountants are professionally responsible for maintaining the security and privacy of their clients.

For the Finance Major

As with other business disciplines, finance activities are being outsourced to countries with lower labor costs. For example, brokerages are hiring stock analysts in Mumbai, India and Johannesburg, South Africa.

To protect against and detect financial crimes, such as fraud or money laundering, employee monitoring is necessary. The challenge for financial professionals is to defend the company's assets without unnecessarily infringing on employees' privacy. As things become more and more complex, as technology advances, and especially where operations are extending over cultural boundaries, risk management and compliance have to address the deeper, more human issues of values, attitudes, and behaviors.

For the Human Resources Management Major

Business is not outside the realm of human relationships. Building an ethical culture is a worthwhile investment that can deliver unexpected bonuses: improved morale, high customer satisfaction, reduced turnover of staff, and reduced compliance costs. It is only logical that the human resources department should work to develop ethical training programs since such behavior can have a positive effect on employee productivity and the company's reputation.

For the IS Major

Information systems professionals—like those in accounting and finance—face competition from IT offshore outsourcing. Consulting firm A.T. Kearney found that

by 2008, financial services companies planned to offshore 500,000 information technology jobs—a total that represents 8 percent of all banking, brokerage, and insurance positions. Highly skilled computer programming work is being sent to Eastern Europe and China. Reuters recently announced it would be moving some reporting and data-collecting jobs to Bangalore, India. Deciding to outsource IT, or any area of a business, is a major commitment, and getting it right from the start is crucial due to the immense effort, hassle, and cost in management time and cash for all parties concerned.

This IT offshoring situation indicates the need for information systems professionals to provide strategic business solutions and not simply act as technologists. By offshoring programming or clearly definable tasks, the information systems department can focus its time and efforts on more value-added developments.

For the Marketing Major

Customers may be extremely sensitive to a company's social responsibility when dealing with offshore outsourced partners. The idea of outsourcing social responsibility together with outsourcing manufacturing may be "accepted" by a company, but it seldom works. For example, early in the controversy surrounding dangerous chemicals in the workplace, Allied Chemical tried to distance itself from responsibility for dangerous emissions and spills at a supplier in Hopewell, Virginia, to which it outsourced production of Kepone, a DDT-like pesticide. Public outcry, legal suits, and congressional action eventually led to a settlement, and to strict new industry regulations. Nike, too, initially distanced itself from charges of child labor and unhealthy conditions at its offshore suppliers in the late 1990s. In this case, the risk to its brand image no doubt helped lead to a change of heart. Today, Nike periodically produces an extensive corporate responsibility report that reviews working conditions at all of its suppliers. Failure to take responsibility for good governance beyond the boundaries of the firm can have a detrimental impact on sales.

For the Production/Operations Management Major

Operations is one of the most important factors in whether an organization has successful offshoring operations. A poorly governed extended enterprise—comprised of outsourced partners—not only can cost the company dearly, but also can damage the company's reputation, and customer or supplier relationships. Production managers need to understand cultural differences since these differences can impact the quality of products or services and their on-time delivery—as well as the treatment of workers in the outsourced countries. Managers also need to investigate the risks of counterfeiting, patent abuse, and other intellectual-property violations.

Key Terms

Business process utilities (BPUs) *568*

Communications as a Service (CaaS) *568*

Computer cluster *562*

Dehumanization *576*

Electronic Product Environmental Assessment Tool (EPEAT) *573*

Enterprise 2.0 *569*

Enterprise Web 2.0 *569*

Ergonomics *578*

Green computing *571*

Information overload *574*

Information quality *575*

Law of Accelerating Returns *563*

Storage as a Service *568*

User-owned devices *568*

Chapter Highlights

(Numbers Refer to Learning Objectives)

❶ Global competition, IT developments, pervasive connectivity, and workable artificially intelligent (AI) brains that can recognize patterns like human brains will continue to have an effect on enterprises, workers, lifestyles, and the condition of the environment.

❷ Organizations are paying premiums to invest in green computers that are both energy efficient and environmentally responsible. Organizations that invest in green hardware find that the energy savings, extended product lifecycle, positive public image, and other benefits exceed the additional costs of that hardware.

❸ Enterprise 2.0 is about moving into a Web setting where workers can more easily conduct their day-to-day personal interactions. A company can build up its business intelligence (BI) repository by using software that integrates blogs or comment forums to supplement historical company data. Through this freeform approach, knowledge management (KM) becomes decentralized and democratic. Centralized control goes away with Enterprise 2.0.

❹ Green computing is the study and practice of eco-friendly computing resources that is now a key concern of businesses in all industries and organizations. Now companies worry about their power consumption as well as the demand of physical space. All of these factors must be taken into consideration when deciding on the design of a data center.

❺ Globalization and telecommuting are transforming the ways in which people work and organizations operate. Now, work can

be performed at any time, in any part of the globe, which tends to make organizations more efficient. Organizational structure, job content, and the nature of management and supervision are altered significantly by this trend.

❺ Vast amounts of data and information made available via the Internet are exceeding the capacity of people to absorb and process them. Spam and other forms of electronic noise only exacerbate the problem. As the quantity of information rises, the issue of information quality takes center stage.

❺ Robotics, decision support systems, and other manifestations of information technology are improving the quality of human lives by relieving people of tedious and hazardous tasks. At the same time, increased interaction with computers replaces the conventional forms of face-to-face interaction among people. This trend may adversely impact interpersonal relationships and other aspects of the quality of life.

❻ Machines and information systems can displace humans from their jobs, both blue- and white-collar. Such changes can be extremely disruptive for an individual employee or an organization. However, on the macroeconomic level, increased efficiency of IT-enabled machines promotes lower prices and greater consumption, and ultimately results in a higher aggregate level of employment for the economy as a whole.

❼ IT significantly impacts individuals, organizations, and societies. Any given technology is likely to affect multiple entities in ways that may be both positive and negative.

Virtual Company Assignment

Management Decision Support at The Wireless Café

Go to The Wireless Café's link on the Student Web Site. There you will be asked to think about how automated tools could support better decision making at the restaurant.

Instructions for accessing The Wireless Café on the Student Web Site:

1. Go to *wiley.com/college/turban.*
2. Select Turban/Volonino's *Information Technology for Management,* Seventh Edition.
3. Click on Student Resources site, in the toolbar on the left.
4. Click on the link for Virtual Company Web Site.
5. Click on Wireless Café.

Questions for Discussion

1. IT can lead to the creation of new jobs as it eliminates existing ones. List five jobs that did not exist ten or more years ago. List five jobs that have been practically eliminated within the past ten years.

2. Which ITs make it possible to copy and distribute copyrighted material? What impact would large-scale copyright infringement have on authors and producers of intellectual property or creative works?

3. When you are hooked to your iPod or iPhone, are you plugged in or unplugged? Do personal digital devices contribute to social isolation?

4. When was the last time you sat down with your family and friends for a meal without the TV being on, or cell phones or your BlackBerry going off? How often do any of these situations occur?

5. In the aftermath of the September 11 attacks, government agencies and individuals turned to information technology to improve security. Can current security measures provide adequate security and also protect privacy? Explain.

6. Consider a typical day in your life, and list all of the instances when your activities get recorded (e.g., cell phone records, e-mail logs). What information is being collected about you that infringes on your privacy?

7. If you were an employee in a company that offered telecommuting options, would you prefer to work from home, from the office, or some combination of both? Explain your answer.

8. Clerks at 7-Eleven stores enter data regarding customers' gender, approximate age, and so on into a computer system. However, names are not keyed in. These data are then aggregated and analyzed to improve corporate decision making. Customers are not informed about this, nor are they asked for permission. What problems do you see with this practice?

9. Certain groups of people claim that globalization has predominantly positive effects, while others assert the opposite. Which of these two arguments do you find more compelling? Why?

10. Discuss whether information overload is a problem in your work or education. Based on your experience, what personal and organizational solutions can you recommend for this problem?

11. What are the risks associated with offshoring (offshore outsourcing)? What are the risks of business process outsourcing (BPO)?

Exercises and Projects

1. Read "Skype Founders Charged with Racketeering" at *techdirt.com/articles/20060327/0256249.shtml*. Why were the founders being charged with RICO violations? Are the reasons legitimate? Why or why not?

2. Read an online article on telemedicine or telehealth. What are the factors supporting telemedicine/health? What are the obstacles or challenges that still remain?

3. List five opportunities to work remotely that are available at your workplace or educational institution. If you were to take advantage of these opportunities to telework, describe what potential impacts they could have on your life.

4. List three business applications or support for business activities available on the iPhone 3G.

5. Create a log of all of your activities on a typical weekday. Calculate the amount of time you spent interacting with computers and other machines. Compute the amount of time you spent interacting with other people using telecommunications technologies (e.g., reading or writing e-mail, sending instant messages, and so on). Compare these numbers with the amount of time you spent in face-to-face interactions with other humans. Discuss how information technology impacts your social life.

Group Assignments and Projects

1. The news that the U.S. Department of Justice (DOJ) has been seeking search data from Google, Yahoo, MSN, and America Online to track activities of "people or groups of interest" has struck fear into the hearts of Web surfers. Many users are concerned, not because they've done anything wrong, but because they wonder just how much personal information can be gleaned from their online searches. With the class divided into groups, debate the issues involved.

2. In small groups, arbitrarily select an information system or information technology (e.g., e-mail, the Internet, robotics, artificial intelligence, etc.). Working individually,

each group member should consider all possible implications of this technology for people, organizations, and society. Taking the previous considerations into account, each group member should decide whether the net effect of the technology is positive or negative. Then, discuss the issue as a group, and see if the group can come to a consensus about the impact of the technology.

3. The State of California maintains a database of people who allegedly abuse children. (The database also includes names of the alleged victims.) The list is made available to dozens of public agencies, and it is considered in cases of child adoption and employment deci-

sions. Because so many people have access to the list, its content is easily disclosed to outsiders. An alleged abuser and her child, whose case was dropped but whose names had remained on the list, sued the State of California for invasion of privacy. With the class divided into groups, debate the issues involved. Specifically:

a. Who should make the decision or what criteria should guide the decision about what names should be included, and what the criteria should be?
b. What is the potential damage to the abusers (if any)?
c. Should the State of California abolish the list? Why or why not?

Internet Exercises

1. Visit the U.S. Green Building Council at *usgbc.org/*. From the menu bar, select the Quick Link for *Case for Green Building (PowerPoint)*. Download the file about LEEDS and view the slides. Identify three buildings and their eco-friendly characteristics.

2. Visit the Web site of the American Civil Liberties Union at *aclu.org*. Browse through the site, and identify five issues that are significantly influenced by the development and proliferation of IT.

3. Browse the Web sites of Wipro Technologies (*wipro.com*) and Infosys Technologies (*infosys.com*). Determine what types of offshore outsourcing services the two companies offer. Learn how these firms affect the operations of their clients.

4. Visit the *Telemedicine and Telehealth News* section of the Telemedicine Information Exchange (TIE) at *tie.telemed.org/news*. Read several of the news items that discuss legislation or marketing efforts to encourage acceptance or adoption of telemedicine/health. Identify three of those efforts.

5. Visit Microsoft Robotics at *msdn.microsoft.com/en-us/robotics/*. Review the two videos *Microsoft Robotics Tour: CCR, VPL, Simulation—Part 1 and Part II*. Identify the value or potential value of robotics discussed in the videos.

Minicase

Wireless Mesh Networking Adds Real-time Monitoring to the Plant Floor

Accent Plastics (*accentplastics.com*) is a privately owned California-based company that designs and manufactures plastic-based products for various industries. The company specializes in custom manufacturing and engineering services. Accent's competitive strategy is to provide high-quality customized products in as little as 20 working days at an affordable price.

The Problem

Maintaining a competitive edge requires minimizing any disruption in production processes and being able to monitor the status of jobs as they are running. Quite understandably, a major concern for Accent, as with all manufacturing companies, is equipment downtime, since even a small amount can be catastrophic.

The company president wanted to upgrade to a real-time system that ran on a wireless network. However, a wireless plant-floor network is risky because signals could get crossed with those from wireless networks elsewhere in the building, or even in nearby facilities. An alternative technology is wireless mesh networking because it eliminates the plant-floor signals being interrupted before reaching their intended destinations, which are the equivalent of dropped cell phone calls. Mesh networks (like the Internet itself) are a more reliable type of network because of their redundancy. That is, when one node on the mesh network fails to operate, the rest

of the nodes can still communicate with each other, directly or through one or more intermediate nodes.

Industry experts describe the manner in which a mesh network protects against interrupted signals as forming a "cloud" over the plant floor. The protective cloud makes mesh networks more reliable than other types of wireless networks.

The Solution

The wireless network selected was based on two technologies that could ultimately make plant-floor wireless networks as common as those found in office settings.

Accent has used *Enterprise IQ*, an enterprise resource planning (ERP) package for midsize companies that also contains a production monitoring component. The vendor of this system, IQMS, offers two versions of the production monitoring application: one that sends batch updates on the status of production processes, and one that transmits those data in real time. In 2007, IQMS introduced a wireless version of the real-time production monitoring application.

Accent switched from the batch system to a real-time system with wireless. Among the advantages are cost savings from not having to run wire to connect the real-time monitoring sensors to production machines. Another feature that was added to the wireless solution allows connecting a physical pole—with a light on top—to a wireless network, making it easier to monitor the status of jobs as they are running.

When a machine is set to produce a certain number of parts per minute, for example, a signal traveling from the machine will cause the light atop the pole to flash certain colors, reflecting the pace at which a job is running. A flashing green light indicates the job is running at the expected pace. Blue signals the job is running faster than expected, red says it is running slower than expected, and amber means the machine is down. The light also can be set to signal when the job is done. This last option is especially important because overrunning jobs (producing too many parts or products) is a major problem for plastics manufacturers.

The Results

The new wireless functionality is easier to use, costs less, and further supports the drive toward leaner manufacturing operations and centralized control over plant operations. The net results are improved efficiency, greater visibility, and higher levels of productivity. Wireless mesh networks will bring more applications to the plant floor, including voice-enabled systems.

Sources: Compiled from *Accentplastics.com* (2008) and Leicht (2007).

Questions for Minicase

1. Why would real-time monitoring be important to Accent's manufacturing processes? To their quality control? To their customer relationships?

2. Identify the benefits of a wireless mesh network over a non-mesh wireless network. Also identify a disadvantage of wireless mesh networks.

3. Explain why *overrunning jobs* is a major problem. That is, why would jobs get overrun instead of stopping when the necessary quantity was reached?

4. What is the value of the visual cues provided by the various colors and types of light signals from atop the poles? What is one disadvantage of this system?

5. Visit Wikipedia at *en.wikipedia.org/wiki/Image:Self-form-self-heal.gif* to view an animation of a self-forming and self-healing wireless mesh network. Explain how the network self-forms and self-heals.

Problem-Solving Activity

The *Google Generation:* Lots of Access, Too Little Analytical Skills

The Google generation is a popular term that refers to a generation of people born after 1993, who have grown up in a world dominated by the Internet. This generation has also been the subject of research. The British Library commissioned a study, which was conducted at the University College London, and whose results sparked extensive debate.

The first ever virtual longitudinal study carried out by the CIBER research team at University College London found that, although young people demonstrate an apparent ease and familiarity with computers, they rely heavily on search engines, view rather than read, and do not possess the critical and analytical skills to assess the information that they find on the Web. Other inferences and conclusions drawn from the University College London study about members of the Google Generation include:

1. They lack analytical skills necessary to assess the information they find on the Internet—which contradicts or overturns the common assumption that the Google Generation is the most Web-literate.

2. They are impatient in search and navigation, and have zero tolerance for any delay in satisfying their information needs.

3. Power browsing and viewing is the norm, instead of in-depth search. That is, they prefer easily digestible chunks of information rather than the full text.

Some educators believe that this is a real lack in education that focuses on teaching and developing critical thinking skills.

These skills are needed for analyzing the abundance of information to determine what is useful, credible, etc.

Sources: Compiled from University College London Research Study (2008) *bl.uk/news/2008/pressrelease20080116.html* (accessed July 2008).

Problem-Solving Activities and Questions

1. Download and read "Information Behaviour of the Researcher of the Future," dated January 11, 2008" (a pdf) found at *bl.uk/news/pdf/googlegen.pdf.* You may also find the article at the textbook's Web site with the filename: *OnlineBrief-15-1-Googlegen.pdf.*

2. Why does the Google Generation, in general, lack analytic skills?

3. Based on your answer to Question #2, what can be done about it? In your answer, identify three corrective actions or solutions, and explain how to implement each of them.

4. If all of the University College London research conclusions are valid, how might that affect the Google Gen's decision-making ability? Explain your answer.

5. Assume that you read about a new nonprescription drug discovery called "Ace-the-Exam." This remarkable drug, being marketed to students for $19.99 plus shipping and handling, would keep the person awake and with perfect recall of what he or she had read in the textbook in preparation for the exam. How would you verify the truth and accuracy of this drug—or any new drug treatment—before ordering it or ingesting it? Identify five sources of trusted health, medical, or drug information.

Online Resources

More resources and study tools are located on the Student Web Site and on WileyPLUS. You'll find additional chapter materials and useful Web links. In addition, self-quizzes that provide individualized feedback are available for each chapter.

Online Minicases for Chapter 15 are available at wiley.com/college/turban:

15.1 *Keeping an Edge on Beer and Wine Can Manufacturing with Intelligence and Dashboards*
15.2 *Do You Know Where Your Food Has Been?*

References

Accentplastics.com (accessed July 2008).

Center for Nanoscale Materials, *nano.anl.gov/index.html* (accessed July 2008).

EDS.com (accessed July 2008).

Ferguson, W. M., "Now Lectures Anytime, Anywhere," *New York Times*, November 6, 2005.

Gonsalves, A., "Despite the Internet, Google Generation Lacks Analytical Skills," *InformationWeek*, January 18, 2008. *informationweek.com/news/internet/search/showArticle.jhtml?articleID= 205901358* (accessed July 2008).

Intel® Multi-Core Performance Accelerates Nanoscience Research, April 9, 2008, *communities.intel.com/servlet/JiveServlet/previewBody/1489-102-1-1705/Intel_ESS_Argonne_LR.pdf* (accessed July 2008).

Keldsen, D., "Enterprise 2.0—What Is It? Does it Matter?" *AIIM E-Doc Magazine*, 22(1), Jan./Feb. 2008.

Leicht, P., "The Case for Wireless on the Plant Floor," *Manufacturing Business Technology*, January 1, 2007, *mbtmag.com/article/CA6406786.html* (accessed July 2008).

Markoff, J., "Can't Find a Parking Spot? Check Smartphone," *The New York Times*, July 12, 2008.

Martens, C., "Insurer Urges Flexible SOA Approach," *ComputerWorld*, January 12, 2007, *computerworld.com/action/article.do?command= viewArticleBasic&taxonomyName=development&articleId=9007942& taxonomyId=11&intsrc=kc_feat* (accessed July 2008).

Moore, E. A., "When iPod Goes Collegiate," *Christian Science Monitor*, April 19, 2005, *csmonitor.com/2005/0419/p11s01-legn.html* (accessed July 2008).

Samson, T., "Are Green IT Premiums Worth the Cost?" *InfoWorld*, June 19, 2008, *weblog.infoworld.com/sustainableit/archives/2008/06/prices_green_pc.html* (accessed July 2008).

Steinberg, A., "Compliance 2.0: Blogs and Wikis in the Enterprise," *IT Business Edge*, Oct. 11, 2007, *itbusinessedge.com/item/?ci=34623* (accessed July 2008).

Telemedicine Information Exchange (TIE), July 10, 2008, *http://tie.telemed.org/news/#item1679* (accessed July 2008).

University College London Research Study, 2008, *bl.uk/news/2008/pressrelease20080116.html* (accessed July 2008).

Van der Pool, L., "IDC: Small, Midsize Businesses Move Toward Green Supply Chain," *Boston Business Journal*, July 16, 2008, *bizjournals.com/boston/stories/2008/07/14/daily33.html* (accessed July 2008).

Toyota's Commitment to Innovation and Improvement Pays Off

Toyota Motor Corporation (*toyota.com*) became the world's largest automobile manufacturer in 2008, based on the 2007 annual automobile sales figures for all companies. During the first quarter of 2007, Toyota for the first time pushed out General Motors (GM) from the top global sales spot, which GM had held since 1931. Toyota sold 2.35 million vehicles worldwide in the January–March 2007 period compared to GM's 2.26 million vehicles.

In addition to competition from GM and Ford in the United States, Toyota also faces tough domestic competitors—Honda Motor, which is the third largest automobile manufacturer in Japan, and Nissan, which is the second largest.

In a fierce global industry with mega-sized enterprises, Toyota's sales achievement is remarkable. Their sales achievement is the result of the combination of intelligent long-term planning for growth (as opposed to short-term profits), innovation, strategic IT investments, and years of hard work. For many years, management has been committed to investing in IT and using innovation to become the world's largest auto manufacturer. Other success factors include investing in environment-friendly "green" vehicles, offering sharp new models, and enticing drivers with Web 2.0-centric advertising. Toyota and other Japanese carmakers have built their business slowly but steadily by aligning IT and business strategies and developing good quality cars.

Not only are Toyota's sales volumes impressive, so are its net profits. See Table V.1 for the company's financial performance. Toyota has long beaten GM in profitability, achieving record net income each year from 2000 through 2007. In 2006, for example, Toyota posted a $11.681 billion profit while GM lost $2 billion. In 2007, Toyota reported a net profit of $14 billion, which is striking, compared to GM's net loss of $38.7 billion that year. Toyota's success has a lot to do with its history and management's commitments to long-term growth.

TABLE V.1	Toyota's Financial Performance 2006–2008		
	2008*	**2007**	**2006**
Revenue (in Million U.S. Dollars)	$262,394	$202,864	$179,083
Net Income (in Million U.S. Dollars)	$17,146	$13,927	$11,681
Net Profit	6.5%	6.9%	6.5%

*Fiscal year date: March 2008.

Company's History and Commitment to Innovation and Improvement

Toyota was founded in 1937 by the Toyoda family, whose members continue to play key roles and are a symbol of emotional unity for the company and its employees. The company's innovators, such as their production executive Taiichi Ohno, are credited with:

1. Inventing *just-in-time* (JIT) production to reduce inventory costs.

2. Introducing the philosophy of worker empowerment called *kaizen*, allowing workers to keep finding ways to improve production methods.

3. Introducing the idea of stopping assembly lines in order to correct problems before continuing to achieve the highest levels of product quality.

4. Nurturing worker loyalty by offering lifetime employment. The last time Toyota resorted to massive job cuts was during difficult times in 1950.

5. Implementing a system and culture of frequent interaction between all levels (management and employees) of the enterprise.

Companies around the world, including those outside the auto industry, have adopted Toyota's methods. Universities worldwide study the *Toyota method*.

Common Characteristics of Very Large Enterprises

Regardless of industry, very large enterprises tend to have the same hierarchical corporate structure and to be publicly owned (that is, the same fiduciary structure). Within specific industries, these large enterprises also tend to eventually have similar marketing and sales models. For example, in the automobile industry, there is really not much difference between Japanese Toyota, American General Motors, and German Volkswagen in terms of their general production activities. In general, they need to purchase raw materials and subassemblies, manufacture and assemble vehicles, and then distribute them via their established distribution channels. What's different is their approach to IT.

IT and Strategies to Counteract Commonalities

Given commonalities in the auto industry, competitive advantages can be derived from how well a company aligns its IT strategy (e.g., collaboration, business intelligence, knowledge management, real-time data delivery, and software as a service) with its business strategy (see Chapter 13), the smart use of outsourcing to cut costs or acquire capabilities quickly (see Chapter 13), how well a company manages its relationships with supply chain partners and business processes (see Chapter 14), the use of innovative IT (see Chapter 14), and going green (see Chapter 15). Here are factors contributing to competitive advantage at Toyota:

- Toyota practices *continuous improvement*, which essentially consists of thousands of small collaborations. Its almost *continuous collaboration* relies on a shared pool of knowledge and the tools to easily distribute that knowledge to all those who need it. For example, quality control problems on the assembly line are announced via pagers and TV monitors to everyone. Ray Tanguay, head of Toyota Canada, gets paged whenever a flaw is found in the latest Lexus shipment on the dock in Long Beach, California, or in a service bay anywhere in North America.

- Toyota's supply chain is based on the principle that while product knowledge (e.g., a blueprint) is intellectual property, *process knowledge* is shared by all. Toyota's suppliers regularly share extensive process improvement lessons, even with their competitors. In Japan, suppliers generally are exclusive to a single original equipment manufacturer (OEM), so the collective benefit of shared information stays within the Toyota supply chain. But even in the United States, where Toyota is just one of several customers for its suppliers, the carmaker is able to share process knowledge through its Bluegrass Automotive Manufacturers Association (BAMA). BAMA is an organization consisting of suppliers to Toyota North America. It disseminates best practices to all BAMA members.

There are many other examples of Toyota's commitment to IT, as can be seen at Toyota Motor Europe and Toyota Australia. These divisions illustrate the alignment of innovative IT and business strategies and how that alignment improves performance.

Toyota Motor Europe

One of Toyota Motor Europe's key strategies is to provide a superior quality purchase experience. To do so, the company needed to integrate back-office systems and external sources of information regarding vehicle data. They deployed the Salesforce (*salesforce.com*) Software-as-a-Service (SaaS) solution and fully integrated the European sales environment in less than three month. Salesforce SaaS helps Toyota Europe target, acquire, and manage day-to-day relationships with multinational fleet customers.

Toyota Europe customized the system to meet its unique needs, which enabled the company to automate many operational or functional processes. For example, with automated sales processes, European sales territories are able to work together more efficiently, resulting in a substantial improvement in customer responsiveness.

Toyota Australia

Toyota Australia is using Oracle's BEA WebLogic Integration (*bea.com*) as part of its eBusiness Transformation Program and for Web services. BEA WebLogic Integration is a comprehensive and flexible Java-based product for rapidly integrating systems, data, and people within and across companies. The eBusiness Transformation Program is part of the company's overall strategy to implement a service-oriented architecture (SOA) to broaden the accessibility of existing applications and accelerate the rollout of new applications. The eBusiness Transformation Program is the result of an SOA strategy, with integration via standards-based Web services, instead of expensive and inflexible custom connections. Its key benefits have been:

- Successfully delivering applications using BEA software in less time than if it had not used SOA.
- Providing greater use of existing information systems and data as services across the enterprise, which reduced overhead by eliminating the need for infrastructure duplication.
- Linking sales, marketing, manufacturing, and financial applications in real time, which improved customer service by making up-to-the-minute information accessible across the value chain.

With SOA, Toyota is reducing costs and improving customer service while ensuring that neither Toyota nor its trading partners will be limited by proprietary technologies. Another beneficial method deployed was outsourcing.

U.S. Toyota Motor Sales' Outsourcing

Toyota Motor Sales (TMS), the U.S. division of Toyota Worldwide that handles marketing, sales, distribution, production, and customer service for the auto maker, decided it was time to upgrade what was now becoming an outdated IT system. The company wanted to streamline operations, improve business relationships, and ensure continued growth.

The division began an aggressive IT-update initiative that quickly became more than it could handle internally. The project involved simultaneous development of six major IT and data software initiatives. It was clear that TMS needed to outsource. The IT service provider had to incorporate changes developed by TMS's IT staff in manufacturing, management, and warehouse processing. Many of the processes they were outsourcing were proprietary. TMS outsourced to Keane, which manages software applications and IT processes for TMS's vehicle, parts, service/warranty, and enterprise systems.

Keane provides end-cycle data support for key systems (maintenance, warranty, etc.). Support staff comes from its Halifax, Nova Scotia, service center, a local project management office at TMS, and other Keane locations, assuring that TMS's systems run 24/7. This solution replaces Toyota's internal systems management core so employees can focus on developmental initiatives. Plus, outsourcing to more affordable geographic areas such as Nova Scotia has a positive impact on Toyota's bottom line. Other benefits from its outsourcing are:

- Greater efficiencies because Toyota is able to use their existing and expensive talent base more effectively.
- Twenty percent fewer negative operational events since it outsourced. When any system had gone down, TMS's costs would skyrocket due to the cascading effect on other aspects of its operations. For example, loss of one facility could cause a $150,000 loss each unproductive hour.

- Better control of fixed operational support costs. TMS is located in the Los Angeles area, which is a very expensive place to do business in the IT and software industries. Outsourcing to more affordable geographic areas has reduced costs significantly.
- 24/7 availability of TMS's online system to its dealers.
- More dedicated focus on projects that directly deliver business value.
- Continuous quality improvements that positively impact future projects.

U.S. Toyota Motor Sales' Business Process Management and Internet Portal

TMS is responsible for the sales and marketing of vehicles in the U.S., and the relationship with Toyota car dealerships. In 1998, the division began to replace the vehicle ordering and communications system for its 1,200 U.S. Toyota and Lexus dealers with an Internet portal.

Under the old system, TMS interacted with its dealers through the Toyota Dealer Network (TDN), a text-based application that ran on IBM AS/400 computers installed at each dealership. The system in turn accessed other applications running on a centralized mainframe at TMS's California headquarters. The old system had many limitations and was expensive to maintain. TDN did not integrate with any of the dealers' operational applications, such as selling, arranging financing, and processing warranty claims. In addition, whenever TDN needed to be upgraded, TMS had to create and physically mail tapes and CDs to all 1,200 dealers, who may not have rushed to install them. The upgrade process cost more than $1 million a year and there were lost opportunities from not being able to serve the customer better.

Toyota began the portal initiative by mapping out its business processes. The Dealer Daily portal initiative took four years to develop as a partnership between Toyota's IT division, Microsoft Consulting Services, Dell Computer, and Verizon. It is available to all 1,200 U.S. Lexus and Toyota dealers. The portal allows people at the dealership to enter new vehicle orders and arrange financing or warranty claims, without keying data into multiple systems. When a customer wants to finance a vehicle, dealerships submit a loan application to Toyota's financing system (which runs on an Oracle database), and often receive a response in less than a minute. Quick response helps Toyota increase its financing business. Dealer Daily also stores vehicle service information, so customers can take their cars to any dealership, where there will be a complete history of work performed.

In all, the Dealer Daily incorporates more than 120 business applications. Using business intelligence (BI) tools from Hyperion Solutions, Toyota tracks the status of the more than 35,000 vehicles that may be in transit from ports or plants to dealerships, constantly looking for the most cost-effective transportation routes based on changing circumstances. Dealer Daily saves the company and its dealers tens of millions of dollars. Users save 1.8 hours per day by using Dealer Daily instead of the older system.

References

Duvall, M., "What's Driving Toyota?" *Baseline Magazine*, September 5, 2006, *baselinemag.com/c/a/Projects-Processes/Whats-Driving-Toyota/2/* (accessed July 2008).

Evans, P., and B. Wolf, "How Toyota and Linux Keep Collaboration Simple," *Harvard Business Review*, August 1, 2005.

Hoover's Company Records, In-depth Records, July 29, 2008.

Toyota.com (accessed July 2008).

Questions

1. How did Toyota become the leading automobile manufacturer?
2. Identify two ways in which Toyota's IT strategy supports its business strategy.
3. Why is the sharing of process knowledge critical to Toyota's business strategy? How is that sharing accomplished?
4. What strategic advantages can Toyota derive from its BI system?
5. In what ways did the old vehicle ordering and communications system create problems for Toyota? For their dealers?
6. How does Dealer Daily help Toyota's dealers improve their customer service?
7. How did Toyota help its dealers expand their business and improve their performance?
8. Extra credit: Toyota has been a remarkably profitable automaker compared to GM. Research Toyota's recent IT investments or deployments. Explain the reason for that IT investment and the payback (return on investment, or ROI).

2G Second-generation mobile network standard

3G Third-generation mobile network standard

4G Fourth-generation mobile network standard

3GSM Third-generation Global System for Mobile Communications Services

Acceptable use policy (AUP) Policy that informs users of their responsibilities, acceptable and unacceptable actions, and consequences of noncompliance.

Access control Management of who is allowed access and who is not allowed access to networks, data files, applications, or other digital resources.

Adaptability The ability to adjust the design of the supply chain to meet structural shifts in markets and modify supply network strategies, products, and technologies.

Adaptive enterprise An organization that can respond properly and in a timely manner to changes in the business environment.

Administrative controls Deal with issuing guidelines and monitoring compliance with the guidelines, policies, and procedures.

Adoption process A process that occurs over time and passes through five stages, (1) acquire knowledge, (2) persuade, (3) decide, (4) implement, and (5) confirm.

Advergaming The practice of using computer games to advertise a product, an organization, or a viewpoint.

Affiliate marketing An arrangement whereby a marketing partner (a business, an organization, or even an individual) refers consumers to the selling company's Web site.

Agility An EC firm's ability to capture, report, and quickly respond to changes happening in the marketplace.

Algorithm A mathematical rule for solving a problem; a predetermined set of rules used to solve a problem in a finite number of steps.

Alignment The ability to create shared incentives that align the interests of businesses across the supply chain.

Anti-malware technology Tool that detects malicious code and prevents users from downloading them.

Application controls Safeguards that are intended to protect specific applications.

Application development 2.0. A new application development process that involves constant interaction with users and provides developers with almost immediate notification of bugs and users' desires.

Applications portfolio Major information systems applications, such as customer order processing, human resource management, or procurement, that have been or are to be developed.

Application program A set of computer instructions written in a programming language, the purpose of which is to support a specific task or business process or another application program.

Attribute Characteristic describing an entity. Also known as a *field*.

Auction A competitive process in which either a seller solicits consecutive bids from buyers or a buyer solicits bids from sellers, and prices are determined dynamically by competitive bidding.

Audit Investigation that is an important part of any control system.

Automated decision support (ADS) Rule-based systems that automatically provide solutions to repetitive managerial problems.

Automatic crash notification (ACN) Still-experimental device that would automatically notify police of the location of an ACN-equipped car involved in an accident.

Back-end (or back-office) operations The activities that support fulfillment of sales, such as accounting and logistics.

Balanced scorecard A performance measurement approach that links business goals to performance metrics.

Balanced scorecard methodology Framework for defining, implementing, and managing an enterprise's business strategy by linking objectives with factual measures.

Batch processing Processing system that processes inputs at fixed intervals as a file and operates on it all at once; contrasts with *online* (or *interactive*) processing.

Behavior-oriented chargeback Accounting system that sets IT service costs in a way that encourages usage consistent with organizational objectives, even though the charges may not correspond to actual costs.

Benchmarks Objective measures of performance, often available from industry trade associations.

Biometric control Automated method of verifying the identity of a person, based on physical or behavioral characteristics.

BitTorrent tracker Server used in the communication, usually of very large files, between peers using the BitTorrent protocol.

Bluetooth Chip technology that enables voice and data communications between many wireless devices through low power, short-range, digital two-way radio frequency.

Botnet Collection of computers infected by software robots, or bots.

Brick-and-mortar organizations Organizations in which the product, the process, and the delivery agent are all physical.

Broadband Short for broad bandwidth. A measure of a network's capacity or throughput.

Business architecture Organizational plans, visions, objectives, and problems, and the information required to support them.

Business case A written document that is used by managers to justify funding for a specific investment and also to provide the bridge between the initial plan and its execution.

Business continuity plan Plan that outlines the process by which businesses should recover from a major disaster. Also known as a *disaster recovery plan*.

Business impact analysis (BIA) A method or exercise to determine the impact of losing the support or availability of a resource.

Business intelligence (BI) Category of applications for gathering, storing, analyzing, and providing access to data to help enterprise users make better decisions.

Automatic crash notification (ACN) Still-experimental device that would automatically notify police of the location of an ACN-equipped car involved in an accident.

Business model A method by which a company generates revenue to sustain itself.

Business network A group of people who have some kind of commercial relationship. For example, the relationships between sellers and buyers, buyers among themselves, buyers and suppliers, and colleagues and other colleagues.

Business performance management (BPM) A methodology for measuring organizational performance, analyzing it through comparison to standards, and planning how to improve it.

Business process A collection of activities performed to accomplish a clearly defined goal.

Electronic Product Environmental Assessment Tool (EPEAT) A searchable database of computer hardware that meets a strict set of environmental criteria.

Electronic records Archived electronic documents that are not subject to alteration.

Electronic retailing (e-tailing) The direct sale of products and services through electronic storefronts or electronic malls, usually designed around an electronic catalog format and/or auctions.

Electronic storefront The Web site of a single company, with its own Internet address, at which orders can be placed.

E-market An online marketplace where buyers and sellers meet to exchange goods, services, money, or information.

Employee relationship management (ERM) The use of Web-based applications to streamline the human resources process and to better manage employees.

End-user development (also known as **end-user computing**) The development and use of ISs by people outside the IS department.

Enhanced messaging service (EMS) An extension of SMS capable of simple animation, tiny pictures, and short tunes.

Enterprise 2.0 Technologies and business practices that free the workforce from the constraints of legacy communication and productivity tools such as e-mail. It provides business managers with access to the right information at the right time through a web of interconnected applications, services, and devices.

Enterprise 2.0 The strategic integration of social computing tools (e.g., blogs, wikis) into enterprise business processes.

Enterprise content management (ECM) ECM is a comprehensive approach to electronic document management, Web content management, digital asset management, and electronic records management (ERM).

Enterprise data warehouse (EDW) A data repository of organizational data that is organized, analyzed, and used to enable more informed decision making and planning. See *data warehouse*.

Enterprise portal Set of software applications that consolidate, manage, analyze, and transmit information to users through a standardized Web-based interface.

Enterprise reporting systems Provide standard, ad hoc, or custom reports that are populated with data from a single trusted source to get a *single version of the truth*.

Enterprise resource planning (ERP) Software that integrates the planning, management, and use of all resources in the entire enterprise; also called *enterprise systems*.

Enterprise search Offers the potential of cutting much of the complexity accumulated in applications and intranet sites throughout an organization.

Enterprise social network A social network within an enterprise that allows employees to communicate, collaborate, and set up virtual worlds in which they can meet like-minded colleagues within the company and exchange ideas with them to improve productivity.

Enterprise (enterprisewide) system Information system that encompasses the entire enterprise, implemented on a companywide network.

Enterprise Web 2.0 (Enterprise 2.0, or E 2.0) The application of Web 2.0 technologies in the enterprise.

E-procurement Purchasing by using electronic support.

Ergonomics The science of adapting machines and work environments to people.

Ethics A branch of philosophy that deals with what is considered to be right and wrong.

ETL Extraction, transformation, and loading of data from a database into a data warehouse.

ETL tools (Extract, Transform, and Load) Tools that extract relevant customer data from the various data silos, transform the data into

standardized formats, and then load and integrate the data into an operational data store or system.

E-wallets (digital wallets) A software component in which a user stores secured personal and credit card information for one-click reuse.

Expected value (EV) A weighted average, computed by multiplying the size of a possible future benefit by the probability of its occurrence.

Expense management automation (EMA) Systems that automate data entry and processing of travel and entertainment expenses.

Expert (or expertise) location systems (ELSs) Interactive computerized systems that help employees find and connect with colleagues who have expertise required for specific problems—whether they are across the country or across the room—in order to solve specific, critical business problems in seconds.

Explicit knowledge The knowledge that deals with objective, rational, and technical knowledge (data, policies, procedures, software, documents, etc.).

Extranet Private, company-owned network that uses IP technology to securely share part of a business's information or operations with suppliers, vendors, partners, customers, or other businesses.

Field Characteristic describing an entity. Also known as an attribute.

Financial value chain management (FVCM) The combination of financial analysis with operations analysis, which analyzes all financial functions in order to provide better financial control.

Firewall System or group of systems that enforces an access-control policy between two networks.

Foreign key Field whose purpose is to link two or more tables together.

Forward auction An auction that sellers use as a selling channel to many potential buyers; the highest bidder wins the items.

Four P's of implementation Four widely accepted approaches that are usually used to implement an IT-based system; plunge, parallel, phased, and pilot.

Front-office operations The business processes, such as sales and advertising, that are visible to customers.

Functionality Entire set of capabilities of an IS or application.

Gateway An entrance point that allows users to connect from one network to another.

General controls Protects the system regardless of the specific application.

Geographical information system (GIS) Computer-based system that integrates GPS data onto digitized map displays.

Global information systems Interorganizational systems that connect companies located in two or more countries.

Global positioning systems (GPS) Wireless devices that use satellites to enable users to detect the position on earth of items (e.g., cars or people) the devices are attached to, with reasonable precision.

Government-to-business (G2B) EC E-commerce in which a government does business with other governments as well as with businesses.

Government-to-citizens (G2C) EC E-commerce in which a government provides services to its citizens via EC technologies.

Government-to-government (G2G) EC E-commerce in which government units do business with other government units.

Green computing Initiative to conserve valuable natural resources by reducing the effect computer usage has on the environment.

Green computing Study and practice of eco-friendly computing resources; now a key concern of businesses in all industries—not just environmental organizations.

Green IT The development of effective programs for IT eco-efficiency and IT eco-innovation that drive improved financial results and measurable environmental sustainable information and communications technology systems.

Green software Software products that help cut fuel bills, save energy, or help comply with EPA requirements.

Grid computing The use of networks to harness the unused processing cycles of all computers in a given network to create powerful computing capabilities.

Group decision support system (GDSS) An interactive computer-based system that facilitates the solution of semistructured and unstructured problems when made by a group of decision makers by concentrating on the *process* and procedures during meetings.

Group purchasing The aggregation of purchasing orders from many buyers so that a volume discount can be obtained.

Group work Work done together by two or more people.

Hacker Someone who gains unauthorized access to a computer system. A criminal.

HSDPA High-speed downlink (or data) packet access that allows for data speeds up to 10 Mbps (megabits per second).

Hype-cycle A useful tool developed by Gartner, Inc in 1995 that is used widely by organizations to identify and assess fruitful emerging technologies and help them decide when to adopt. It assesses the maturity, impact, and adoption speed of hundreds of technologies across a broad range of technology, application, and industry areas.

Implementation All organizational activities involved in the introduction, management, and acceptance of technology to support one or more organizational processes.

Indexed sequential access method (ISAM) File organization method that uses an index of key fields to locate individual records.

Information Data that have been organized so they have meaning and value to the recipient.

Information infrastructure The physical arrangement of hardware, software, databases, networks, and information management personnel.

Information overload The inability to cope with or process ever-growing amounts of data into our lives.

Information quality A subjective measure of the utility, objectivity, and integrity of gathered information based on its being complete, accurate, up-to-date, and fit for the purpose for which it is used.

Information system (IS) A physical process that supports an organization by collecting, processing, storing, and analyzing data, and disseminating information to achieve organizational goals.

Information systems (IS) strategy Defines *what* information, information systems, and IT architecture is required to support the business.

Information technology (IT) The technology component of an information system (a narrow definition); or the collection of the computing systems in an organization (the broad definition used in this book).

Information technology architecture High-level map or plan of the information assets in an organization; on the Web, it includes the content and architecture of the site.

Information technology (IT)-business alignment Degree to which the IT group understands the priorities of the business and expends its resources, pursues projects, and provides information consistent with these priorities.

Information technology (IT) governance Formally established statements that direct the policies regarding IT alignment with organizational goals and allocation of resources.

Information technology (IT) strategic planning Defines the IT (long-range) strategic plan, the IT medium-term plan, and the IT tactical plan.

Information technology (IT) strategy Defines the IT vision, *how* the infrastructure and services are to be delivered.

Information technology (IT) vision The longer-term direction for IT; defines the future concept of what IT should do to achieve the goals, objectives, and strategic position of the firm.

Insourcing Development and management of IT services within the organization.

Intangible benefits Benefits that are hard to place a monetary value on (e.g., greater design flexibility).

Intellectual capital (intellectual assets) The valuable knowledge of employees.

Intelligent agents Applications that have some degree of reactivity, autonomy, and adaptability to react to unpredictable attack situations. Also referred to as softbots or knowbots.

Interactive marketing Online marketing, facilitated by the Internet, by which marketers and advertisers can interact directly with customers, and consumers can interact with advertisers/vendors.

Internal control Process designed to provide reasonable assurance of effective operations and reliable financial reporting.

Internal control environment Work atmosphere that a company sets for its employees.

Internet protocol suite Standard used with almost any network service consisting of the **Internet Protocol** (IP) and **Transport Control Protocol** (TCP), or TCP/IP.

Internal threats Threats from those within the organization, such as employees, contractors, and temporary workers.

Interoperability Connectivity between devices. Refers to the ability to provide services to and accept services from other systems or devices.

Interorganizational information systems (IOSs) Communications systems that allow routine transaction processing and information flow between two or more organizations.

Intrabusiness (intraorganizational) commerce E-commerce in which an organization uses EC internally to improve its operations.

Intranet Network designed to serve the internal informational needs of a company, using Internet tools.

Intrusion Detection System (IDS) Technology tool that scans for unusual or suspicious traffic.

Intrusion Prevention Systems (IPS) Technology tool designed to take immediate action—such as blocking specific IP addresses—whenever a traffic-flow anomaly is detected.

iPhone 3G Apple's 3G version of the iPhone.

IP-based network technology Internet Protocol-based network that forms the backbone that is driving the merger of voice, data, video, and radio waves by digitizing content into packets that can be sent via digital networks.

IP telephony Voice communication over a network using the Internet Protocol. Also called VoIP.

ISO 9000 Developed as a standard for business quality systems by the International Organization for Standardization (ISO); a key element of ISO 9000 is the identification of nonconforming processes and the development of a plan to prevent nonconforming process from being repeated.

IT applications Specific systems and programs for achieving certain objectives.

IT infrastructure Provides the foundations for IT applications in the enterprise. It is shared by many applications throughout the enterprise and made to exist for a long time.

IT security Protection of information, communication networks, and traditional and e-commerce operations to assure their confidentiality, integrity, availability, and authorized use.

Just-in-time (JIT) An inventory scheduling system in which material and parts arrive at a work place when needed, minimizing inventory, waste, and interruptions.

Key performance indicators (KPIs) Metrics that measure the actual performance of critical aspects of IT, such as critical projects and applications, servers, the network, and so forth, against predefined goals and objectives.

Key performance indicators (KPI) The quantitative expression of critically important metrics.

Knowledge Data and/or information that have been organized and processed to convey understanding, experience, accumulated learning, and expertise.

Knowledge management (KM) The process that helps organizations identify, select, organize, disseminate, and transfer important information and expertise that are part of the organization's memory and that may reside in unstructured form within the organization.

Knowledge management system (KMS) A system that organizes, enhances, and expedites intra- and inter-firm knowledge management; centered around a corporate knowledge base or depository.

Knowledge workers People who create and use knowledge as a significant part of their work responsibilities.

Kotter's organizational transformation model An eight-step process that organizations should follow in order to successfully transform an organization.

Law of accelerating returns This law suggests that the time interval between significant events grows shorter as time passes because technological change is exponential, not linear.

Legacy application Application that has been used for a long period of time and that has been inherited from languages, platforms, and techniques used in earlier technologies.

Lessons learned An important step in wrapping up management of any implementation process, this step documents successes and failures in each systems development phase as well as the project as a whole.

Lewin's three-stage change model A simple change process model that consists of three stages of change; *unfreezing, change, (re)freezing*.

Local area network (LAN) Connects network devices over a relatively short distance. Capable of transmitting data at very fast rates, but operates in a limited area, such as an office building, campus, or home.

Location-based commerce (1-commerce) M-commerce transactions targeted to individuals in specific locations at specific times.

Logistics The operations involved in the efficient and effective flow and storage of goods, services, and related information from point of origin to point of consumption.

Loyalty programs Programs that recognize customers who repeatedly use the services (products) offered by a company (e.g., frequent flyers).

Malware Any unwanted software that exploits flaws in other software to gain illicit access.

Management information systems (MISs) Systems designed to provide past, present, and future routine information appropriate for planning, organizing, and controlling the operations of functional areas in an organization.

Master data management (MDM) The integration of data from various sources or enterprise applications to provide a more unified view of data.

Master reference file File that stores consolidated data from various data sources, which then feeds data back to the applications to create accurate and consistent data across the enterprise.

Mesh network A type of wireless sensor network composed of motes, where each mote "wakes up" or activates for a fraction of a second when it has data to transmit and then relays those data to its nearest neighbor. So, instead of every mote transmitting its information to a remote computer at a base station, an "electronic bucket brigade" moves the data mote by mote until it reaches a central computer where it can be stored and analyzed.

Metric A specific, measurable standard against which actual performance is compared.

Micro-blogging Sending messages up to 140 characters.

Mobile commerce (m-commerce, m-business) Any e-commerce done in a wireless environment, especially via the Internet.

Mobile commerce (m-commerce) Any e-commerce done in a wireless environment, especially via the Internet.

Mobile enterprise Enterprise that has the ability to connect and control suppliers, partners, employees, products, and customers from any location.

Mobile government (m-government) The wireless implementation of e-government applications mostly to citizens, but also to businesses.

Mobile portal A gateway to the Internet accessible from mobile devices; aggregates content and services for mobile users.

Mobile social networking Social networking where one or more individuals of similar interests or commonalities, conversing and connecting with one another, use mobile devices, usually with cell phones, and in virtual communities.

Model Simplified representation or abstraction of reality. Models are often formulas.

Multidimensional database Specialized data store that organizes facts by dimensions, such as geographical region, product line, salesperson, or time.

Multimedia messaging service (MMS) The next generation of wireless messaging, which will be able to deliver rich media.

M-wallet (mobile wallet) Technology that enables cardholders to make purchases with a single click from their mobile devices; also known as *wireless wallet*.

MySpace Social network that started as a site for fans of independent rock music in Los Angeles.

Net earnings Net income, net profit, or the "bottom line," which is calculated as revenues minus expenses.

Network port Physical interface for communication between a computer and other devices on a network.

Networked computing A corporate information infrastructure that provides the necessary networks for distributed computing. Users can easily contact each other or databases and communicate with external entities.

Occupational fraud Abuse of a person's influence in the workplace or deliberate misuse of the organization's resources or assets for personal gain.

Offshore outsourcing Contracting with a vendor, who is located outside of the organization's own country, to develop and manage IT services.

On-demand CRM CRM *hosted* by an ASP or other vendor on the vendor's premise; in contrast to the traditional practice of buying the software and using it *on-premise*.

Online analytical processing (OLAP) Systems that contain *read-only data* that can be queried and analyzed much more efficiently than OLTP application databases.

Online processing Processing system that operates on a transaction as soon as it occurs, possibly even in real time.

Online transaction processing (OLTP) A transaction processing system, where transactions are executed as soon as they occur.

Open-source software A software for which the source code (how the software was actually written) is available for anyone free of charge.

Operational data store Database for transaction processing systems that uses data warehouse concepts to provide clean data.

Operational decisions Ensure that day-to-day operations are running correctly and efficiently.

Operational risk The risk of a loss due to inadequate or failed internal processes, people, and systems or from external events.

Operational systems Systems designed to store data required by an organization (e.g., sales orders, customer deposits) and are optimized to capture and handle large volumes of transactions.

Optimization Finding the best possible solution.

Order fulfillment All of the activities needed to provide customers with ordered goods and services, including related customer services.

Organizational transformation A major change in the way that an organization does business, often enabled by the application of information technology.

Outsourcing Contracting with a vendor, who is outside of the organization, to develop and manage IT services.

Parallel approach An implementation approach where both new and old systems operate simultaneously for a designated period of time.

Partner relationship management (PRM) Business strategy that focuses on providing comprehensive quality service to business partners.

Payment Card Industry Data Security Standard (PCI DSS) Data security standard created by Visa, MasterCard, American Express, and Discover that is required for all members, merchants, or service providers who store, process, or transmit cardholder data.

Personal digital assistant (PDA) A small, handheld wireless computer.

Personal information management (PIM) A system that supports the activities performed by individuals in their work or life through the acquisition, organization, maintenance, retrieval, and sharing of information.

Pervasive computing Invisible, everywhere computing that is embedded in the objects around us.

Phased approach An implementation approach that is based on the module or version concept, where each module or version of the system is implemented as it is developed and tested.

Physical controls Protection of physical computer facilities and resources.

Pilot approach An implementation approach that is "pilot tested" at one site first, using either the plunge or the parallel approach, and later rolled out to other sites using the plunge approach.

Plunge approach An implementation system where the old system is turned off at the end of business on Day 0 and the new system is put into operation at the beginning of Day 1.

Pod or podcast Video file transferred over a network.

Podcaster Creator of pods.

Podcasting Distributing or receiving audio and video files called pods or podcasts over the Internet.

Portal Web-based gateway to files, information, and knowledge on a network.

Predictive analysis A tool that helps determine the probable future outcome for an event or the likelihood of a situation occurring. It also identifies relationships and patterns.

Predictive analytics The branch of data mining that focuses on forecasting trends (e.g., regression analysis) and estimating probabilities of future events. Business analytics, as it is also called, provides the models, which are formulas or algorithms, and procedures to BI.

Price-to-performance ratio The relative cost, usually on a per-mips (millions of instructions per second) basis, of the processing power of a computer.

Primary activities In Porter's value chain model, those activities in which materials are purchased and processed to products, which are then delivered to customers. Secondary activities, such as accounting, support the primary ones.

Primary key Field or attribute that uniquely identifies a record in a database.

Priority matrix A simple diagramming technique that assesses a technology's potential impact—from transformational to low—against the number of years it will take before it reaches mainstream adoption.

Process improvement teams Eliminates the non-value-adding steps and resolves quality problems in order to reduce the time needed to complete a process by adding new processes and/or deleting, splitting, combining, expanding, or reducing existing processes.

Productivity paradox The seeming discrepancy between extremely large IT investments in the economy and relatively low measures of productivity output.

Programming attacks Attack that involves programming techniques to modify other computer programs, such as a virus or worm.

Project portfolio IT resources, such as infrastructure, application services, data services, security services, to be developed.

Public exchange (exchange) E-marketplace in which there are many sellers and many buyers, and entry is open to all; frequently owned and operated by a third party.

"Pure Play" BPM tools Software tools that combine text and graphics and offer more advanced features such as a repository that allows reuse of resources and simulations. Using these, the process can be captured in greater detail, with a higher degree of accuracy.

Radio frequency identification (RFID) Generic term for technologies that use radio waves to automatically identify individual items.

Random file organization Records can be accessed directly regardless of their location on the storage medium. Also called direct file organization.

Reach and richness An economic impact of EC: the trade-off between the number of customers a company can reach (called *reach*) and the amount of interactions and information services it can provide to them (*richness*).

Real-time system An information system that provides real-time access to information or data.

Reintermediation Occurs where intermediaries such as brokers provide value-added services and expertise that cannot be eliminated when EC is used.

Relative advantage The degree to which the new system is perceived as being better than the system it replaces, often expressed in the economic or social status terms that will result from its adoption.

Reliability The degree to which the new system is perceived as being better than the system it replaces, often expressed in the economic or social status terms that will result from its adoption.

Remote Administration Trojan (RAT) Malicious code that is a type of backdoor used to enable remote control over a compromised (infected) machine.

Reverse auction Auction in which the buyer places an item for bid (*tender*) on a request for quote (RFQ) system, potential suppliers bid on the job, with the price reducing sequentially, and the lowest bid wins; primarily a B2B or G2B mechanism.

Reverse logistics A flow of material or finished goods back to the source; for example, the return of defective products by customers.

Rootkit Set of network administration tools to take control of the network.

RSS A standard of Web feed formats, usually Really Simple Syndication, that automate the delivery of Internet content.

Sales automation software Productivity software used to automate the work of salespeople.

SAP R/3 The leading EPR software (from SAP AG Corp.); a highly integrated package containing more than 70 business activities modules.

SCM software Applications programs specifically designed to improve decision making in segments of the supply chain.

Search engines Web sites designed to help people find information stored on other sites.

Secondary key Nonunique field that has some identifying information (e.g., country of manufacture).

Sell-side marketplace B2B model in which organizations sell to other organizations from their own private e-marketplace and/or from a third-party site.

Semantic Web An evolving extension of the Web in which Web content can be expressed not only in natural language but also in a form that can be understood, interpreted, and used by intelligent computer software agents, permitting them to find, share, and integrate information more easily.

Semistructured decisions Decisions in which only some of the phases are structured; require a combination of standard solution procedures and individual judgment.

Sensitivity analysis Study of the impact that changes in one or more parts of a model have on other parts or the outcome.

Sequential file organization Way in which data records are organized on tape requiring that they be retrieved in the same physical sequence in which they are stored.

Service-oriented architecture (SOA) An architectural concept that defines the use of services to support a variety of business needs. In SOA, existing IT assets (called services) are *reused* and *reconnected* rather than the more time consuming and costly reinvention of new systems.

Service packs Microsoft's releases to update and patch vulnerabilities in its operating systems or other software.

Session Initiation Protocol (SIP) Standardizes the signaling of calls or communications between different types of devices/end points from different vendors such as IP phones, instant messaging clients, softphones, and smartphones.

Short messaging service (SMS) Technology that allows for sending of short text messages on some cell phones.

Six sigma A methodology to manage process variations that cause defects, defined as unacceptable deviation from the mean or target, and to systematically work toward managing variation to prevent those defects.

Smart phone Internet-enabled cell phones that can support mobile applications.

Social computing An approach aimed at making the human–computer interface more natural.

Social engineering Collection of tactics used to manipulate people into performing actions or divulging confidential information.

Social marketplace The term social marketplace is derived from the combination of social networking and marketplaces, such that a social marketplace acts like an online community, harnessing the power of one's social networks for the introduction, buying, and selling of products, services, and resources, including people's own creations. A social marketplace can also be referred to as a structure that resembles a social network but has a focus on its individual members.

Social media The online platforms and tools that people use to share opinions and experiences, including photos, videos, music, insights, and perceptions, with each other.

Social network Web sites that connect people with specified interests by providing free services such as photo and video sharing, instant messaging, blogging, and wikis.

Social network analysis (SNA) The mapping and measuring of relationships and flows between people, groups, organizations, animals, computers, or other information or knowledge processing entities. The nodes in the network are the people and groups, whereas the links show relationships or flows between the nodes. SNA provides both a visual and a mathematical analysis of relationships.

Social network service (SNS) A primarily Web-based service that uses software to build online social networks for communities of people who share interests and activities or who are interested in exploring the interests and activities of others. These services provide a collection of various ways for users to interact, such as chat, messaging, email, video, voice chat, file sharing, blogging, discussion groups, and so on.

Social network services (SNSs) Web sites that allow people to build their home pages for free and provide basic communication and other support tools to conduct different activities in the social network.

Softphone Computer that functions as a telephone via VoIP.

Software-as-a Service (SaaS) Also referred to as *on-demand computing, utility computing,* or *hosted services.* Instead of buying and installing expensive packaged enterprise applications, users access applications over a network, with an Internet browser being the only absolute necessity.

Sourcing Organizational arrangement instituted for obtaining IT products and services, and the management of resources and activities required for producing these services. These arrangements include insourcing, outsourcing, and offshore outsourcing.

Spend management The way in which companies control and optimize the money they spend. It involves cutting operating and other costs associated with doing business. These costs typically show up as operating costs, but can also be found in other areas and in other members of the supply chain.

Storage as a Service Storage capacity offered on a per usage basis, similar to SaaS.

Strategic decisions Decisions for sustained enterprise success and business growth.

Strategy A broad-based formula for how a business is going to accomplish its mission, what its goals should be, and what plans and policies will be needed to carry out those goals.

Structured decisions Decisions that are routine and repetitive problems for which standard solutions exist.

Supplier relationship management (SRM) A comprehensive approach to managing an enterprise's interactions with the organizations that supply the goods and services it uses.

Supply chain management (SCM) The management of all of the activities along the supply chain, from suppliers, to internal logistics within a company, to distribution, to customers. This includes ordering, monitoring, and billing.

Supply chain team A group of tightly coordinated employees who work together to serve the customer; each task is done by the member of the team who is best capable of doing the task.

Support activities Business activities that do not add value directly to a firm's product or service under consideration but support the primary activities that do add value.

Tacit knowledge The domain of subjective, cognitive, and experimental knowledge that is highly personal and difficult to formalize.

Tactical decisions Decisions ensuring that existing operations and processes are in alignment with business objectives and strategies.

Task–technology dependency The ability of a technology to efficiently and effectively execute a task.

Technical resource strategy Defines how IT is used internally within the company to improve operational efficiencies, with associated bottom line cost savings.

Technology acceptance model (TAM) A robust, powerful, and simple model that measures an individual's intention to use technology by measuring two basic concepts: "perceived ease of use" and "perceived usefulness." The TAM is a good indicator of the success or failure of system implementation. It was originally developed by Fred Davis in 1989.

Technology adoption lifecycle A technique developed in 1957 at Iowa State College to track the purchase patterns of hybrid seed corn by farmers, and currently used to explain how innovations are adopted for use in organizations.

Telematics The integration of computers and wireless communications to improve information flow using the principles of telemetry.

Text analytics Transforms unstructured text into structured "text data" that can then be searched, mined, or discovered.

Text mining The application of data mining techniques to discover actionable and meaningful patterns, profiles, and trends from documents or other text data.

Time-to-exploitation Elapsed time between when a vulnerability is discovered and the time it is exploited.

Total benefits of ownership (TBO) An approach for calculating the payoff of an IT investment by calculating both the tangible and the intangible benefits and subtracting the costs of ownership: TBO–TCO=Payoff.

Total cost of ownership (TCO)   A formula for calculating the cost of owning and operating an IT system; includes acquisition cost, operations cost, and control cost.

Total quality management (TQM)   A management strategy aimed at embedding awareness of quality in all organizational processes.

Transaction costs   Costs that are associated with the distribution (sale) and/or exchange of products and services, including the cost of searching for buyers and sellers, gathering information, negotiating, decision making, monitoring the exchange of goods, and legal fees.

Transaction processing system (TPS)   An information system that processes an organization's basic business transactions such as purchasing, billing, and payroll.

Transport Control Protocol   (TCP) Network standard that provides a reliable, error-checking, connection-oriented delivery method.

Trojan horse   Malicious code that creates backdoors, giving an attacker illegal access to a network or account through a network port.

Tweets   Text posts to the Twitter Web site using the web, phone, or IM. Tweets are delivered immediately to those signed up to receive them via the same methods.

Two-factor authentication   System to verify a user's identity based on two pieces of information, such as a password and smart card.

Unified messaging (UM)   Bringing together all messaging media such as e-mail, voice, mobile text, SMS, and fax into a combined communications medium.

Unstructured decisions   Decisions that involve a lot of uncertainty for which there are no definitive or clear-cut solutions.

User acceptance   The extent to which a new system is perceived as being useful and easy to use by the system users. Acceptance of a system will be higher if users are involved in systems design.

User Datagram Protocol (UDP)   Network standard that does not check for errors, and as a result, has less overhead and is faster than a connection-oriented protocol such as TCP. With UDP, the quality of the transmission is sacrificed for speed.

Utility computing   Unlimited computing power and storage capacity that, like electricity, water, and telephone services, can be obtained on demand, used and reallocated for any application, and billed on a pay-per-use basis.

Value chain model   Model developed by Michael Porter that shows the primary activities that sequentially add value to the profit margin; also shows the support activities.

Vendor-managed inventory (VMI)   Strategy used by retailers of allowing suppliers to monitor the inventory levels and replenish inventory when needed, eliminating the need for purchasing orders.

Viral blogging   Viral marketing done by bloggers.

Viral marketing   Word-of-mouth marketing by which customers promote a product or service by telling others about it.

Virtual credit card   A payment mechanism that allows a buyer to shop with an ID number and a password instead of with a credit card number, yet the charges are made to the credit card.

Virtual factory   Collaborative enterprise application that provides a computerized model of a factory.

Virtual (Internet) community   A group of people with similar interests who interact with one another using the Internet.

Virtual organizations   Organizations in which the product, the process, and the delivery agent are all digital; also called *pure-play organizations*.

Virtual private network (VPN)   Connects remote sites or users together privately using "virtual" connections routed through the Internet from the company's private network to the remote site or employee.

Virtual teams   Groups of people who work interdependently with shared purpose across space, time, and organization boundaries using technology to communicate and collaborate.

Virtual world   A computer-based simulated environment intended for its users to inhabit virtual spaces and interact via avatars.

Virtual world   A user-defined 3D world in which people can interact, play, and do business with the help of avatars.

Virus   Malicious code that attaches itself and infects other computer programs, without the owner of the program being aware of the infection.

VoIP (Voice over Internet Protocol)   Voice communication over a network using the Internet Protocol. Also called IP telephony.

Voice commerce (v-commerce)   An umbrella term for the use of speech recognition to allow voice-activated services including Internet browsing and e-mail retrieval.

Voice portal   A Web site that can be accessed by voice (e.g., via cell phone), and not via a computer.

War driving   Stealth search for wireless local area networks by driving around a city or elsewhere.

Warehouse management system (WMS)   A software system that helps in managing warehouses.

Wearable devices   Mobile wireless computing devices for employees who work on buildings and other difficult-to-climb places.

Web 2.0   The second-generation of Internet-based services that let people collaborate and create information online in perceived new ways—such as social networking sites, wikis, and blogs.

Web 3.0   A term used to describe the future of the World Wide Web. It consists of the creation of high-quality content and services produced by gifted individuals using Web 2.0 technology as an enabling platform.

Web (or WWW)   Application that runs on the Internet, as does e-mail, IM, and VoIP. A system with universally accepted standards or protocols for storing, retrieving, formatting, and displaying information via client/server architecture.

Web analytics   The analysis of click-stream data to understand visitor behavior on a Web site.

Web-based system   An application delivered on the Internet or intranet using Web tools, such as a search engine.

Web mining   The application of data mining techniques to discover actionable and meaningful patterns, profiles, and trends from Web resources.

Web Services   Modular business and consumer applications, delivered over the Internet, that users can select and combine through almost any device, enabling disparate systems to share data and services. These are software systems designed to support machine-to-machine interactions over a network.

Wi-Fi   Technology that allows computers to share a network or Internet connection wirelessly without the need to connect to a commercial network.

Wiki   Software program, discovery tool, collaboration site, and social network.

WiMax   A wireless standard (IEEE 802.16) for making broadband network connections over a large area.

Wired equivalent privacy (WEP)   Weak cryptographic technique used for encryption.

Wireless 911 (e-911)   Calls from cellular phones to providers of emergency services.

Wireless application protocol (WAP)   A set of communications protocols designed to enable different kinds of wireless devices to talk to a server installed on a mobile network, so users can access the Internet.

Wireless encryption protocol (WEP)   Built-in security system in wireless devices, which encrypts communications between the device and a wireless access point.

Wireless fidelity (Wi-Fi)   The standard on which most of today's WLANs run, developed by the IEEE (Institute of Electrical and Electronic Engineers). Also known as *802.11b*.

Wireless mobile computing (mobile computing) Computing that connects a mobile device to a network or another computing device, anytime, anywhere.

Wireless sensor networks (WSNs) Networks of interconnected, battery-powered, wireless sensors called *motes* (analogous to nodes) that are placed into specific physical environments. Each mote collects data and contains processing, storage, and radio frequency sensors and antennas. The motes provide information that enables a central computer to integrate reports of the same activity from different angles within the network. Therefore, the network can determine information such as the direction a person is moving, the weight of a vehicle, or the amount of rainfall over a field of crops with great accuracy.

WLAN (Wireless Local Area Network) Type of local area network that uses high-frequency radio waves rather than wires to communicate between computers or devices such as printers, which are referred to as nodes on the network.

Wireless LAN (WLAN) LAN without the cables; used to transmit and receive data over the airwaves, but only from short distances.

Word processors A text-based document processor that is one of the simplest ways to document a process.

Workflow management (WFM) A technique where documents, information, and activities flow between participants according to existing process models and rules; refers to activities performed by businesses to optimize and adapt their processes.

Worm Malicious code that uses networks to propagate and infect anything attached to it—including computers, handheld devices, Web sites, and servers.

XBRL (eXtensible Business Reporting Language) Version of XML for capturing financial information throughout a business's information processes.

XML (eXtensible Markup Language) Meta-language for describing markup languages for documents containing structured information. XML-based systems facilitate data sharing across different systems and particularly systems connected via the Internet.